2000 SPORTS COLLECTORS Almanac

From the Editors of

Sports Collectors Digest
Voice for the Hobby

I 95
21
9-26-00

Published by

krause publications

700 E. State Street • Iola, WI 54990-0001
Telephone: 715/445-2214

Please call or write for our free catalog.
Our toll-free number to place an order or obtain a free catalog is 800-258-0929
or please use our regular business telephone 715-445-2214
for editorial comment and further information.

ISBN: 0-87341-582-5

Printed in the United States of America

TABLE OF CONTENTS

BASEBALL

BASKETBALL

FOOTBALL

HOCKEY

RACING

FIGURINES

Events that shaped the hobby in 1999

By Tom Mortenson

If 1998 will be remembered as the year of the great home run race, then 1999 will go down in history as the year of the retirement. Beginning with Michael Jordan's second — and most likely final — retirement announcement, a host of other legendary sports performers have said their goodbyes. Among the notables are Wayne Gretzky, John Elway, Barry Sanders, Reggie White, Dominik Hasek, Dino Ciccarelli, Darrell Waltrip, Steffi Graf, Wade Boggs, Ernie Irvan and Charles Barkley.

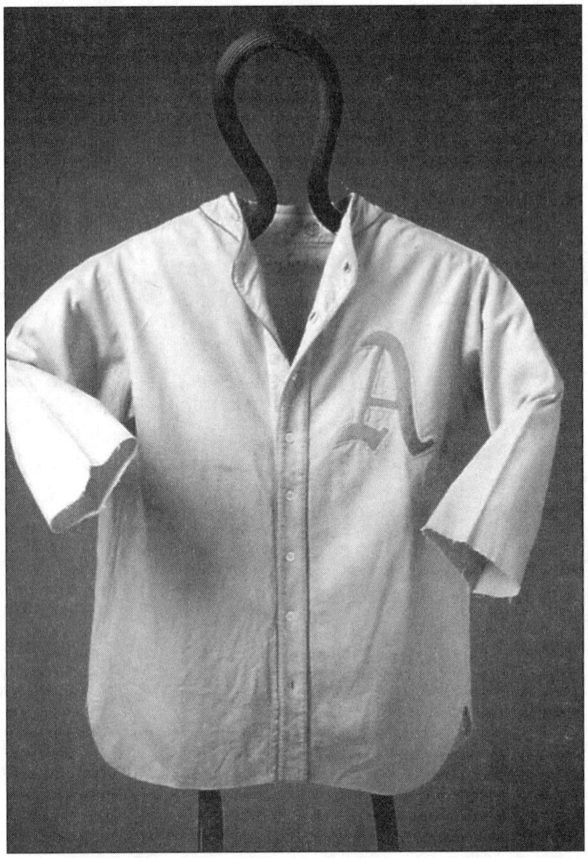

This jersey, worn by Ty Cobb in his final season (1928) with the Philadelphia Athletics, was one of the many fabulous pieces that were sold in Sotheby's auction of The Barry Halper Baseball Memorabilia Collection.

Big Mac's 70th

The year began in dramatic style. In January, the ball that Mark McGwire launched for his 70th home run of the 1998 season brought an astounding $3.005 million at Guernsey's auction at Madison Square Garden. The buyer was identified as Todd McFarlane, who made millions drawing the popular Spawn character that spawned Todd McFarlane Productions and other lucrative ventures. McFarlane also purchased McGwire home run balls Nos. 1, 63, 67, 68, 69 and Sammy Sosa balls Nos. 33, 61 and 66.

Mick's 500th

Another famous home run baseball also drew hobby headlines in 1999. In the same Guernsey's auction, the ball offered as Mickey Mantle's 500th home run ball was pulled from the sale after Merlyn Mantle, widow of the legendary Yankee slugger, called Guernsey's claiming she had the real 500th HR ball. The ball that was pulled from the auction, and owned by Oregon collector Dale Cicero, has strong provenence. It was later offered in One-Of-A-Kind's October auction in Las Vegas. It was withdrawn when it did not meet the reserve. One-Of-A-Kind also offered McGwire's 500th home run ball with the same result; it failed to meet the reserve.

Hammerin' Hank's 755th

Richard Arndt, a onetime member of the Milwaukee Brewers grounds crew who retrieved Hank Aaron's 755th, and final, home run ball in 1976 sold it for $650,000 in April. The buyer was identified as Andrew J. Knuth, owner of a Connecticut-based investment company. Arndt had kept the ball in a safety deposit box in Albuquerque, N.M., for more than 20 years after being fired from the team for failing to return team property.

Record-Setting Auctions

Just five months after setting the record for a single sports collectibles auction at $5.4 million, Mastro Fine Sports topped its own record with a $5.5 million auction in April. Paced by a PSA-8 T-206 Eddie Plank card believed to be the finest specimen known in the hobby that brought $203,992, the incredible auction averaged more than $4,700 per lot and boasted 112 lots of $10,000 or more.

A bid of $451,541 was placed for the uniform that Lou Gehrig wore in 1939 when he delivered his famous "Luckiest Man on the Face of the Earth" speech. It was offered at Leland's Heroes Auction in July. However, it was later reported that the bid was not honored by a Miami businessman.

Of course, the hobby's event of the century and the one that will be remembered for decades was Sotheby's seven-day auction of the famed Barry Halper Baseball Memorabilia Collection. At $22 million in sales, the auction featured such treasured items as Gehrig's last glove from 1939 which went for a mind-boggling $387,500 and Ty Cobb's 1928 Philadelphia Athletics jersey which brought $332,500.

The Show Circuit

Dealer sales were reported to be strong and attendance was up for SportsFest '99, held in June at the Philadelphia Convention Center. Former Phillies stars Mike Schmidt, Greg Luzinski, Steve Carlton and Tug McGraw headlined the autograph lineup along with Dan Marino, Ron Jaworski, Brooks Robinson, Johnny Unitas, Lou Brock, Bob Gibson and Whitey Ford.

In August, SportsFest made its debut at the Rosemont Convention Center near Chicago. Attendance and dealer response was reportedly strong. The autograph pavilion featured such notable guests as John Elway, Bill Russell, Reggie Jackson, Joe Namath and local Chicago favorite Dick Butkus.

Reviews of the 20th National Sports Collectors Convention held in July in Atlanta were mixed. The show featured a record number of 1,200 exhibitors. Many exhibitors felt that Atlanta had struck out as a National host city for the second time in the decade. Bill Russell, Joe Montana, Oscar Robertson and Carl Yastrzemski were among the most popular athletes in terms of autograph sales. Also attracting attention were Pamela Anderson and the celebrity formerly known as Sable.

Baseball's All-Star FanFest drew huge crowds to the Hynes Convention Center in Boston in July. John Hancock was the title sponsor in 1999, the first time it wasn't Upper Deck or Pinnacle.

Losses

The passing of Joe DiMaggio after a long illness created something of a frenzy among collectors wanting items to remember the great Yankee Clipper. Many of DiMaggio's personal collectibles have been offered on the Internet by the DiMaggio Estate.

Other men whose names are familiar with collectors and sports fans who passed away in '99 include Early Wynn, Pee Wee Reese, Catfish Hunter, Joe Adcock, Wilt Chamberlain, Walter Payton and Payne Stewart.

Well-known Pacific Coast League collector Dick Dobbins passed away in January at the age of 64. Gerry Dvorak, one of three artists to paint portraits for the 1953 Topps baseball card set, passed away in September. He was a well-known illustrator and cartoonist who drew some of America's best-loved comic characters.

Numerous cereal boxes, like this one picturing Doug Flutie, were issued in 1999.

Cereal Boxes

As it does every year, General Mills released several Wheaties cereal boxes for collectors including a 75 Years of Champions box picturing Lou Gehrig, Michael Jordan, Tiger Woods and Walter Payton. However the big winner in cereal boxes in '99 was Flutie Flakes. PLB Sports Promotions issued a second edition box picturing the Buffalo Bills quarterback. The success of Flutie Flakes set off an avalanche of other sports cereal boxes picturing such stars as Ed McCaffery, Mike Alstott, Roberto Clemente, Barry Bonds, Cal Ripken Jr., Sammy Sosa and Sergei Fedorov.

New Card Products

By far, the hottest product in trading cards was "Pokemon." The animated TV show and video game has spurred huge sales for its collectible card game made by Wizards of the Coast. In April, Topps landed a Pokemon license to produce trading cards and lollipops. Meanwhile, hobby retailers disagreed whether Pokemon cards were helping or hurting sales of sports cards. Topps also landed a license to produce trading cards based on Marvel characters.

Upper Deck's high-tech PowerDeck baseball cards were introduced in October. They were issued in three-card packs with one PowerDeck card in each pack. There are 25 video/audio, plus three interactive digital cards in the set.

The Home Front

In May, Krause Publications purchased Landmark Specialty Publications, which included *Tuff Stuff* magazine.

All this, and a whole lot more, occurred in sports collecting in the final year of the 20th Century.

Top 100 players to impact the hobby

By Tom Mortenson

With the curtain closing on the 20th Century everyone is making countdown lists of all-century this or all-century that. Not to be outdone, we've compiled a list (alphabetically) of the top 100 players that have had the biggest impact on the sports collecting hobby.

Here they are:

1. Hank Aaron (The HR King's '54 Topps rookie card is a classic. His '57 Topps card is a novelty; it's printed in reverse.)
2. Muhammad Ali (He's an international celebrity with tremendous charisma.)
3. Ernie Banks (Mr. Cub, a member of the 500 HR Club, is truly baseball's goodwill ambassador.)

Ernie Banks

4. Johnny Bench (A vital cog in the Big Red Machine, he's arguably the greatest catcher of them all.)
5. Yogi Berra (Beloved Yankee great now has his own museum. He's recognized everywhere.)
6. Wade Boggs (New member of 3,000 Hit Club. He was a big part of the rookie card craze of the early-1980s.)
7. George Brett (Popular 3,000 Hit Club member. His '75 Topps rookie is highly prized.)
8. Lou Brock (Popular and friendly Cardinals HOFer, 3,000-Hit Club member. He was the subject of the '98 All-Star FanFest Set.)
9. DeWayne Buice (Along with Wally Joyner, he was influential — to a greater degree — in the startup of The Upper Deck Co.)
10. Dick Butkus (Enjoys great popularity in Chicago where he was the spokesman at SportsFest '99.)
11. Roy Campanella (Beloved Brooklyn Dodgers star was paralyzed in an accident in 1958 that allowed him to sign autographs only with the aid of a mechanical device.)
12. Jose Canseco (The first member of the 40/40 Club. His '86 Donruss rookie was very desirable at one time.)
13. Rod Carew (A collector himself, he once took out an ad in *SCD* so his fans could get authentic items.)
14. Gary Carter (Former N.L. star is an avid baseball card collector himself.)
15. Wilt Chamberlain ("The Big Dipper" was awesome on the court and a fan favorite.)
16. Roger Clemens (The Rocket's '84 Fleer Update card is still very highly prized.)
17. Roberto Clemente (International hero and role model, 3,000 hits, Died on New Year's Day in 1973 on a mercy mission. That was before the big autograph craze began.)
18. Ty Cobb (One of his cards in the T-206 set is priced at $75,000. Memorabilia will always be in demand. Even his false teeth brought an astounding price in a recent auction.)
19. Bob Cousy (Smooth Celtics sparkplug was the subject of his own 25-card set in 1991.)
20. Eric Davis (His '85 Topps and Fleer rookie cards helped fuel the rookie card craze of the mid-'80s.)
21. Lou Dials (This former player had his own table at numerous card shows. As much as anyone, he popularized collecting autographs and memorabilia of the Negro league players.)
22. Joe DiMaggio (His mystique and style has boosted memorabilia collecting as much as anyone.)
23. Joe Doyle (One variation of his card in the 1909-11 T-206 set is extremely rare and worth about $22,500 in NM.)
24. John Elway (This two-time Super Bowl champ went out on top. His cards have helped fuel the football card market.)
25. Brett Favre (The three-time MVP was the hottest name in football cards and memorabilia in 1997 and '98.)
26. Bob Feller (The great flamethrower could very well be the leader in signing the most autographs ever.)
27. Doug Flutie (Bills star QB is pictured on his own cereal boxes.)
28. Joe Frazier (Signing sessions with Muhammad Ali have been memorable.)
29. Joe Garagiola (The popular former TV announcer and comedian is a collector of Gashouse Gang memorabilia.)
30. Kevin Garnett (Young T-Wolves superstar has helped fuel basketball card market.)
31. Lou Gehrig (The demand for his memorabilia always draws a high amount of interest at auctions.)
32. Dwight Gooden (When his 1985 cards came out, Doc was another one who influenced the rookie card craze)
33. Jeff Gordon (NASCAR star has autograph and memorabilia deal with Upper Deck Authenticated.)
34. Wayne Gretzky (The Great One's deal with UDA limits the number of autographs and memorabilia out there. He was also co-owner of the famous T-206 Honus Wagner card that was purchased for $451,000 in 1991.)
35. Ken Griffey Jr. (Junior was selected to be pictured as the No.1 card in the first Upper Deck set.)
36. Dick Groat (His Hartland Statue is the rarest of the 18 original baseball figurines.)

Wayne Gretzky

37. Tony Gwynn (This new member of the 3,000-Hit Club is collector-friendly. He's been an endorser for Pacific and Fleer.)
38. Franco Harris (He was one of the first of the big stars to become a spokesman for a card company when he went to work for Score.)
30. Grant Hill (Popular Pistons star is also a Fleer/SkyBox spokesman and endorser.)
40. Gordie Howe ("Mr. Hockey" is one of the most beloved figures in all sports. He's been called the "Babe Ruth of Hockey.")
41. Bobby and Brett Hull (The overall popularity of this father/son hockey tandem transcends generations.)
42. Raghib "Rocket" Ismail (In 1991, AW Sports created a CFL set primarily on his popularity at the time.)
43. Bo Jackson (At one time this two-sport star was a mega hobby favorite.)
44. Shoeless Joe Jackson (Autographs are especially in demand, since he was hardly able to sign his name.)
45. Reggie Jackson (A collector himself, he was associated with Upper Deck for several years. Involved in starting Mr. Octobears and the Stat Ball, he knows the hobby market better than any other celebrity.)
46. Magic Johnson (Lakers great has been a Fleer/SkyBox spokesman and goodwill ambassador for the hobby.)
47. Deacon Jones (Not only was he an intrical part of the Rams' Fearsome Foursome defense, he's also a *Tuff Stuff* hobby columnist.)
48. Michael Jordan (He's everywhere and his memorabilia will always be in demand. His contract with Upper Deck Authenticated limits the number of autographs and memorabilia.)
49. Sandy Koufax (His overall popularity never wanes. His 1955 Topps rookie is still highly prized.)
50. Tom Landry (Best known as the Dallas Cowboys coach, his early Bowman cards as a player are highly desirable.)

51. Legendary Ladies of Baseball (Dottie, Pepper, Lefty and the gals have made a lucrative second career out of bringing attention to women's pro baseball during the war years.)
52. Eric Lindros (As a teenager he became the first endorser/spokesman for Score Hockey.)
53. John Littlefield (This otherwise obscure pitcher was wrongly pictured as a lefty in the 1982 Fleer set. The rare variation was the talk of the hobby for a time.)
54. Sherry Magee (One version of his T-206 card has his name misspelled "Magie." It lists for $20,000 in NM.)
55. Peyton Manning (Top NFL draft choice helped fuel football card products in '98.)
56. Mickey Mantle (His '52 Topps card is something of a sacred shrine in the hobby. When he'd appear as an autograph guest, it was always a sellout.)
57. Dan Marino (Record-setting Dolphins QB is extremely popular. He had an exclusive signing deal with Upper Deck Authenticated for a long time.)
58. Roger Maris (The former single-season HR champ died in 1985, just before the big autograph craze began.)
59. Eddie Mathews (The '52 Topps card of this 500 HR Club member is the last one in the high-number series. He's also pictured on the cover of the first *Sports Illustrated*.)
60. Don Mattingly (More than anything else, his '84 Donruss card ignited the rookie card craze.)
61. Willie Mays (Despite his unpleasant demeanor at card shows, he's one of the greatest all-around players to ever live. You can't take that away from him.)
62. Willie McCovey (This member of the 500 HR Club was fined, along with Duke Snider, for failing to report income from card shows.)
63. Mark McGwire ("Big Mac" shattered Maris' single-season HR record in 1998. Together with Sammy Sosa, he brought a resurgence to the baseball collectibles market.)

Nolan Ryan

64. Ron Mix (This Pro Football Hall of Famer produces his own HOF art postcards.)
65. Joe Montana (One of the greatest QB's of all-time, he was associated exclusively with Upper Deck Authenticated for several years.)
66. Randy Moss (This Minnesota Vikings star with unlimited potential is still fueling the football card market.)
67. Eddie Murray (His 500th HR ball made headlines when it was sold for an astounding $500,000 to the then-owner of the Psychic Friends Network.)
68. Stan Musial (Because of contractual obligations, "The Man" didn't appear on a Topps card until 1958.)
69. Joe Namath (His 1965 rookie card is still one of the most desired football cards of all.)
70. Graig Nettles (The back of his '81 Fleer "Craig" Nettles error was the talk of the hobby at one time.)
71. Shaquille O'Neal (His early cards fueled the basketball card market.)
72. Andy Pafko (His card is the very first one numbered in the premier '52 Topps set. It's extremely tough in the high grades.)
73. Walter Payton (The all-time rushing leader, "Sweetness" was a terrific football player and a fine human being.)
74. Richard Petty (This racing icon is responsible for tons of NASCAR memorabilia.)
75. Mike Piazza (Now a big star with the Mets, His '92 Bowman is highly desired.)
76. Eddie Plank (His card in the 1909-11 T-206 tobacco card set is extremely tough to find. It's worth about $40,000 in NM.)
77. Kirby Puckett (His rookie card in the '84 Fleer Update set is one of the toughest modern day cards to find)
78. Manon Rheaume (Her brief career as a minor league goalie was highly publicized and marketed.)
79. Billy Ripken (His 1989 Fleer "obscenity" card caused a huge stir in the hobby at the time.)
80. Cal Ripken Jr. (Popular Orioles ironman inspired huge memorabilia demand in 1995.)
81. Brooks Robinson (One of the most congenial superstars on the card show circuit.)

Babe Ruth

82. Jackie Robinson (In 1997, MLB celebrated the 50th anniversary of his breaking the color barrier. Interest in his career generated interest in his cards and memorabilia.)
83. Pete Rose (His 1963 Topps rookie card with three other players was the "must-have" card of the 1980s. His appearances on TV Shop-At-Home programs and card shows keep him in the public eye.)
84. Bill Russell (At one time the Celtics' legend was a very tough autograph. Now he's signing everywhere, but the price is still relatively high.)
85. Babe Ruth (The Babe is an American icon. Although he signed many autographs, demand will always be strong. His cards and memorabilia always draw a lot of interest.)
86. Nolan Ryan (The Strikeout King and 300-Win Club member is extremely popular with collectors. His 1968 Topps rookie card is especially valuable.)
87. Barry Sanders (He abruptly retired from the Lions before setting the all-time rushing record. His 1989 Score rookie card is still highly valued.)
88. O.J. Simpson ("The Juice" signed autographs in jail and later sold his Heisman Trophy to pay off debts.)
89. Emmitt Smith (His family has operated a hobby shop in Florida selling Emmitt memorabilia.)
90. Duke Snider (Very popular Dodger, with McCovey, admitted to avoiding declaring income from card shows.)

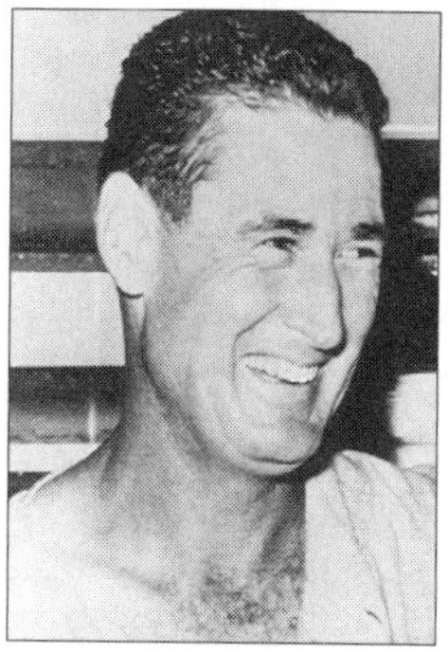

Ted Williams

91. Sammy Sosa (Extremely popular Cub. Together with McGwire, inspired the Great '98 HR Chase.)
92. Warren Spahn (Winningest lefty of all-time, often does theme-related signing sessions together with Johnny Sain of "Spahn and Sain and Pray For Rain.")
93. Darryl Strawberry (In the mid-1980s he was one of the young stars that fueled the rookie card phenomenon.)
94. Frank Thomas (The "Big Hurt" had a big presence as a Donruss/Leaf spokesman.)
95. Bobby Thomson (He and Ralph Branca are good friends and usually do autograph sessions together to benefit charity.)
96. Johnny Unitas (Baltimore Colts hero was featured on an original Hartland statue.)
97. Bill Walton (The former hoops great was a Topps spokesman for the company's 50th NBA anniversary set.)
98. Honus Wagner (The T-206 Wagner card is the most cherished and expensive card in the hobby.)
99. Ted Williams (His 1954 Bowman card is a tough one. In 1959, Fleer issued an 80-card set on his life. He's pictured on the first and last cards of the 1954 Topps set. He lent his name to the ill-fated Ted Williams Card Co.)
100. Maury Wills (He broke in with the Dodgers in 1959 but didn't appear on a Topps card until 1967.)

SCD's 100 most desirable autographs

Most coveted signatures not necessarily most expensive

By Tom Mortenson

What are the most desirable sports autographs on your want list? You know, the ones you wish you had in your collection that would impress your friends and neighbors.

Selecting the top 100 autographs of the last century is not an easy task. Certainly, not everyone will be in agreement with the following — or any other — list. But that's OK.

Some of the signatures on the following list are not necessarily all that tough to obtain. Several of them are still signing quite regularly on the card show and private signing circuits. Many are simply all-time greats in their respective sports. Others, in addition to their achievements, are desirable autographs because they are popular with the fans and/or belonged to famous teams, such as the Brooklyn Dodgers of the 1950s or the St. Louis Cardinals' "Gashouse Gang" of the 1930s.

Likewise, some signatures are coveted because the individuals are members of exclusive "clubs" or "fraternities," such as the 500-Home Run Club, the 3,000-Hit Club or the 300-Win Club.

Other autographs on the list are desirable because the individual died before the advent of mass autograph sessions and private signings.

Without further delay, here (in alphabetical order) is our list of the 100 most desirable sports autographs of the century, along with a brief description of why they are on the list:

1. **Hank Aaron** - HOF, All-Time Home Run King, 500 HR Club, 3,000 Hit Club, "The Hammer"

2. **Kareem Abdul-Jabbar** - HOF, Record-setting Lakers great. Signatures as "Lew Alcindor" are especially coveted by collectors
3. **Muhammad Ali** - HOF, Charismatic boxing legend, self-proclaimed "The Greatest," worldwide recognition and acclaim. Early signatures as "Cassius Clay" are especially desirable
4. **Walter Alston** - HOF, longtime Dodgers manager, died 10/1/84
5. **Sammy Baugh** - HOF, Native Texan became Redskins' QB immortal, popularized the forward pass, "Slingin' Sammy"
6. **Larry Bird** - HOF, Celtics and state of Indiana basketball legend

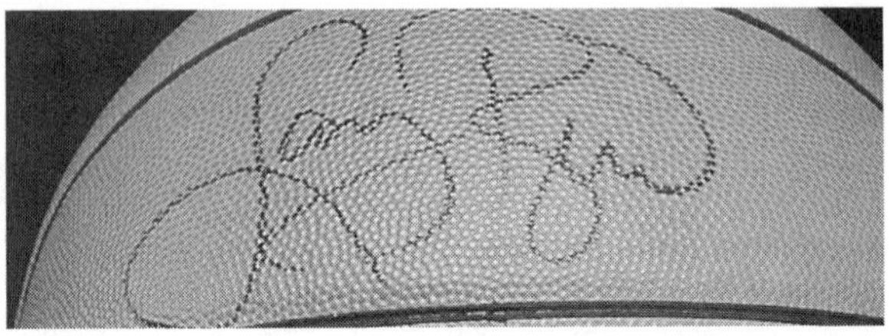

7. **Ken Boyer** - All-Star St. Louis Cardinals third baseman, Gold Glove performer, best of a baseball family, died 9/7/82
8. **Bill Bradley** - HOF, Knicks great, presidential aspirations

9. **Jim Brown** - HOF, nearly unstoppable Browns rusher of 1950s, retired in the prime of his career

10. **Paul Brown** - HOF, Legendary innovative Browns and Bengals coach, died 8/5/91
11. **Roy Campanella** - HOF, beloved Brooklyn star, accident in 1958 made it possible for "Campy" to sign only with the aid of a device, died 6/26/93
12. **Wilt Chamberlain** - HOF, "Wilt the Stilt," scored 100 points in a single NBA game. Died 10/13/99

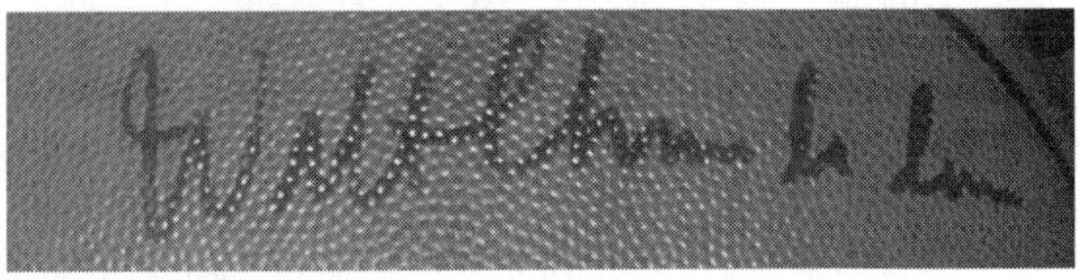

13. **Roberto Clemente** - HOF, Beloved Latino star, 3,000 Hit Club, died 12/31/72

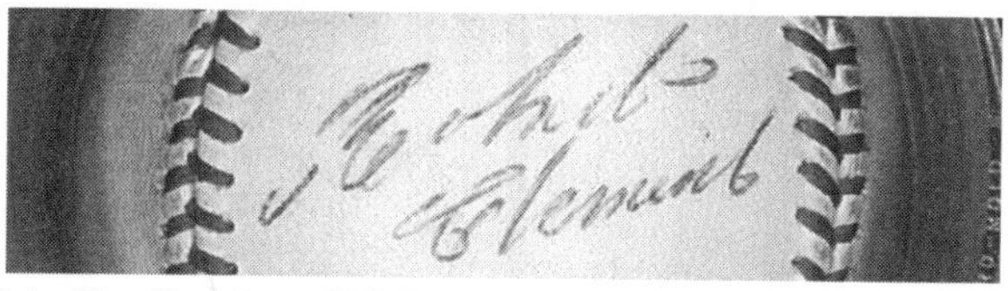

14. **Ty Cobb** - HOF, 3,000 Hit Club, ultimate competitor, "Georgia Peach," died 7/17/61
15. **Tony Conigliaro** - Very popular hometown Boston fan favorite, "Tony C." died 2/24/90
16. **Terrell Davis** - 1998 NFL MVP, Broncos star running back
17. **Dizzy Dean** - HOF, St. Louis Cardinals star, true American folk hero, died 7/17/74
19. **Jack Dempsey** - HOF, boxing legend, Heavyweight champ from 1919-1926, "The Manassa Mauler," died 5/31/83

20. **Joe DiMaggio** - HOF, graceful legend in the Bronx, "Yankee Clipper" died 3/8/99

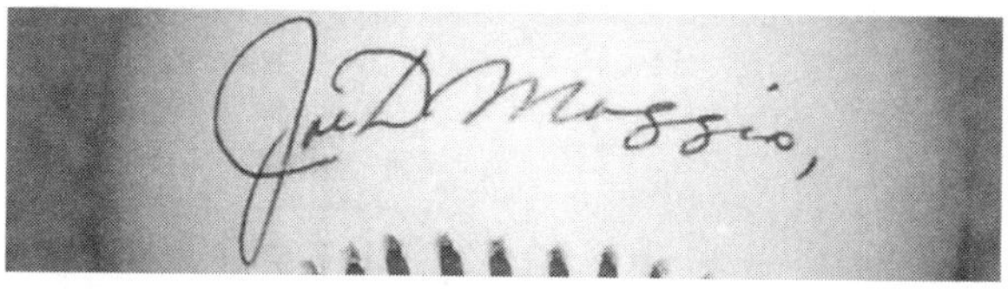

21. **Dale Earnhardt Sr.** - NASCAR fan favorite, seven Winston Cup titles

22. **John Elway** - QB great, Master of the come-from-behind victory
23. **Julius Erving** - HOF, Philadelphia great, terrific showman, "Dr. J." limits autograph show appearances

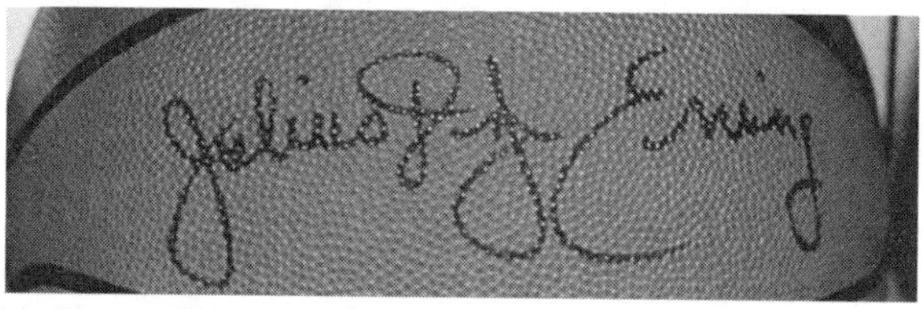

24. **Brett Favre** - Popular Packers star, three-time NFL MVP
25. **Nellie Fox** - HOF, catalyst of 1959 "Go-Go" White Sox, died 12/1/75

26. **Jimmie Foxx** - HOF, 500 HR Club, Baseball strongman, Triple Crown winner, "Double X," died 7/21/67

27. **Carl Furillo** - Brooklyn Dodgers star, died 1/21/89
28. **Nomar Garciaparra** - Popular contemporary Boston star. A hero to the youth of New England
29. **Kevin Garnett** - Talented young NBA superstar. Unlimited potential
30. **Lou Gehrig** - HOF, quiet Yankee hero, true gentleman, died 6/2/41

31. **Josh Gibson** - HOF, A legendary Negro League slugging sensation, died 1/20/47
32. **Jeff Gordon** - Popular NASCAR driver, three Winston Cup championships and 40 wins in four seasons put him in elite company. Does signings through Upper Deck Authenticated
33. **Red Grange** - HOF, Chicago Bears great, "Galloping Ghost," died 1/28/91
34. **Wayne Gretzky** - NHL's all-time biggest star, "The Great One," autographs are limited due to Upper Deck Authenticated contract

35. **Ken Griffey Jr.**- Contemporary fan favorite, fabulous natural talent

36. **George Halas** - HOF, NFL pioneer, legendary Bears coach, "Papa Bear," died 10/31/83
37. **Gil Hodges** - Dodgers great, 1969 "Miracle" Mets manager, died 4/2/72

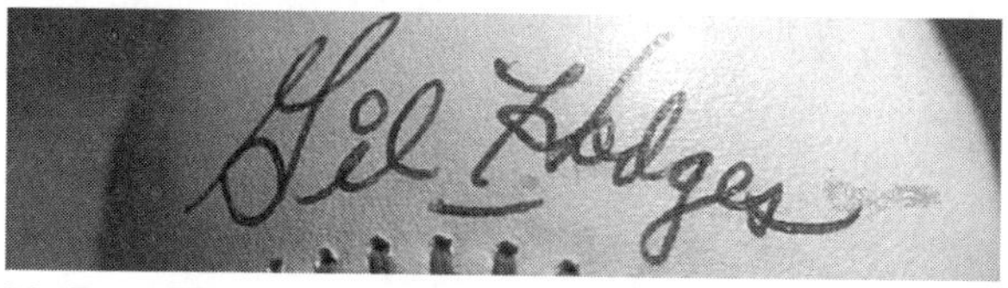

38. **Ben Hogan** - Legendary golfing figure, four-time PGA Player of the Year, died 7/25/97

39. **Rogers Hornsby** - HOF, Legendary player/manager. Died 1/5/63
40. **Elston Howard** - MVP, Yankee star of the 1960s, died 12/14/80
41. **Gordie Howe** - HOF, "Mr. Hockey," a legend in Canada and U. S.
42. **Bobby Hull** - HOF, Blackhawks great, popular and friendly on show circuit
43. **Reggie Jackson** - HOF, 500 HR Club, "Mr. October," World Series champion with A's and Yankees

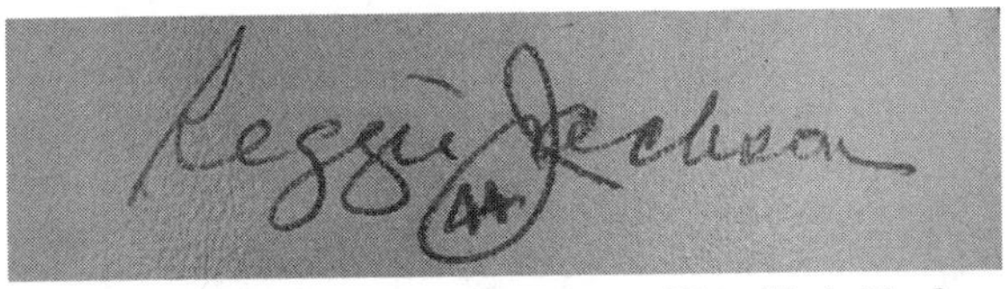

44. **Derek Jeter** - Popular young New York Yankees star
45. **Magic Johnson** - Popular basketball great, led Lakers to 5 NBA Championships
46. **Walter Johnson** - HOF, 416 lifetime wins, 110 shutouts, "The Big Train," died 12/10/46

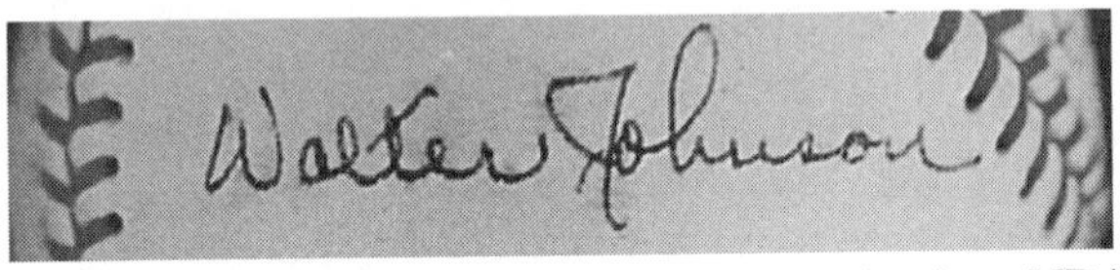

47. **Michael Jordan** - American icon, six-time NBA champion with Bulls, "Air Jordan," autographs are limited due to Upper Deck Authenticated contract
48. **Ted Kluszewski** - Popular Reds slugger, "Big Klu," died 3/29/88
49. **Bobby Layne** - HOF, exceptional field leader, clutch performer, died 12/1/86
50. **Mario Lemieux** - HOF, six-time NHL scoring leader, "Super Mario"
51. **Sugar Ray Leonard** - Flashy welterweight Olympic and pro boxing champion
52. **Vince Lombardi** HOF, led Packers to five NFL titles, first two Super Bowl crowns, died 9/3/70

53. **Joe Louis** - HOF, legendary heavyweight boxing champion, "Brown Bomber" died 4/12/81
54. **Connie Mack**- HOF, dignified Philadelphia A's manager for 50 years, "Mr. Mack," died 2/8/56
55. **Mickey Mantle** - HOF, 500 HR Club, Yankees great, Triple Crown winner, "The Mick," a national hero, Died 8/13/95

56. **Pete Maravich** - HOF, stylish showman, "Pistol Pete," died 1/5/88
57. **Rocky Marciano** - HOF, popular undefeated 1950s heavyweight boxing champ, died 8/31/69

58. **Dan Marino** - Record-setting Dolphins QB, long-time fan favorite. Autographs are limited due to his contract with Upper Deck Authenticated
59. **Roger Maris** - Yankees HR star, formed "M&M Boys" with Mickey Mantle, died 12/14/85

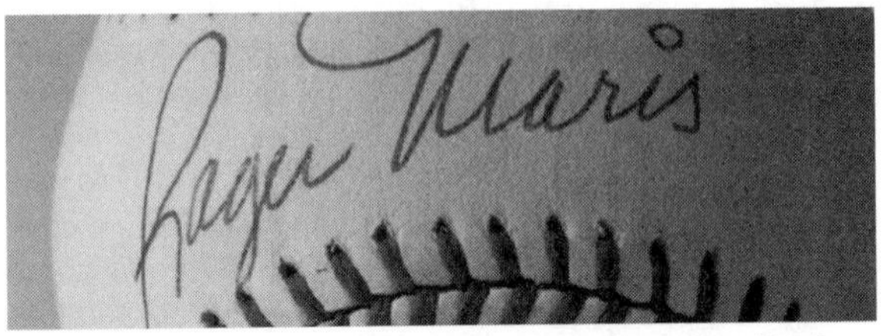

60. **Mike Marshall** - Former Los Angeles Dodgers ironman reliever, extremely tough autograph
61. **Billy Martin** - Scrappy Yankees player and manager, died 12/25/89
62. **Willie Mays** - HOF, 500 HR Club, 3,000 Hit Club, "The Say Hey Kid," New York and San Francisco great, fabulous talent

63. **George Mikan** - HOF, Legendary NBA "Big Man," Led Minneapolis Lakers to five NBA titles, does few public signings
64. **Mark McGwire** - 500 HR Club, Cardinals' single-season HR record-setting champion, contemporary role-model

65. **Joe Montana** - Popular NFL QB, Super Bowl champ with 49ers
66. **Randy Moss** - Contemporary Vikings star receiver, unlimited potential
67. **Thurman Munson** - Yankee captain and star in 1970s, died 8/2/79
68. **Eddie Murray** - 500 HR Club, 3,000 Hit Club
69. **Bronko Nagurski** - HOF, Bears blue collar fan favorite, punishing two-way performer, died 1/7/90

70. **Joe Namath** - HOF, Jets' inspirational on-field leader in Super Bowl III, "Broadway Joe"

71. **Jack Nicklaus** - Golf champion of the 1960s, "Golden Bear"
72. **Saduhara Oh** - Japanese baseball great, international HR champ with 868 HR in 22 years
73. **Hakeem Olajuwon** - Dominating Rockets big man, international appeal
74. **Shaquille O'Neal** - Los Angeles Lakers superstar, dominating force, released rap recordings, appeared in motion pictures "Kazaam" and "Blue Chips"
75. **Bobby Orr** - HOF, popular Boston Bruins star
76. **Mel Ott** - HOF, 500 HR Club, N. Y. Giants player and manager, died 11/21/58
77. **Jesse Owens** - U.S. Olympic track legend, died 3/31/80
78. **Satchel Paige** - HOF, legendary Negro League star, marvelous pitcher and showman, barnstorming performer across North and South America, died 6/8/82
79. **Arnold Palmer** - Popular golfing legend, winner of four Masters titles, leader of "Arnie's Army"
80. **Walter Payton** - HOF, All-Time NFL rushing leader, extremely popular Chicago Bears icon, "Sweetness." Died 11-1-99
81. **Brian Piccolo** - Bears star, immortalized by TV movie "Brian's Song", died 6/16/70
82. **Jacques Plante** - HOF, Hero in Canada and U.S., died 2/27/86
83. **Jerry Rice** - Considered the greatest receiver in NFL history, 49ers great

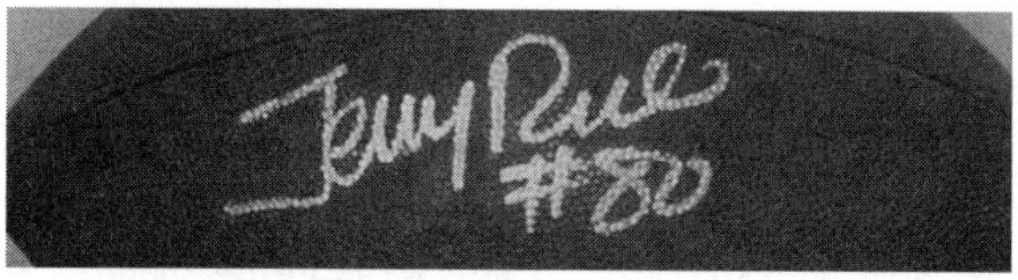

84. **Cal Ripken Jr.** - Orioles ironman, closing in on 3,000 hits, contemporary role model
85. **Alex Rodriquez** - Popular contemporary of Griffey, "A-Rod," rarely does public signings

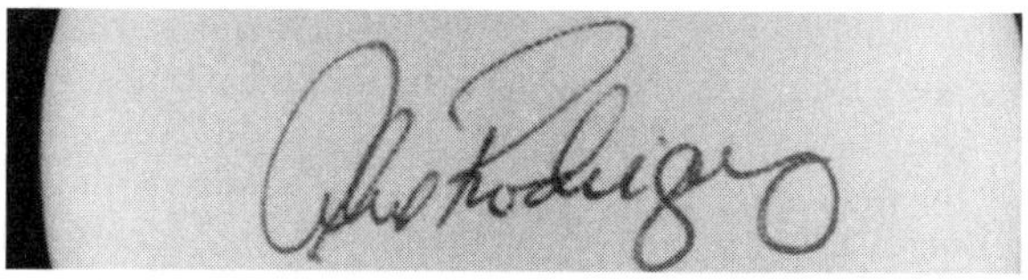

86. **Jackie Robinson** - HOF, Dodgers great, broke down racial barriers in sports, died 10/24/72

87. **Sugar Ray Robinson** - HOF, considered to be "pound-for pound" the greatest fighter of all-time, five-time middleweight champion, died 4/12/89
88. **Pete Rose** - All-Time Hit King, "Charlie Hustle," popular sparkplug of "Big Red Machine"

89. **Bill Russell** - HOF, Celtics great, champion, 5-time NBA MVP, previously very tough autograph

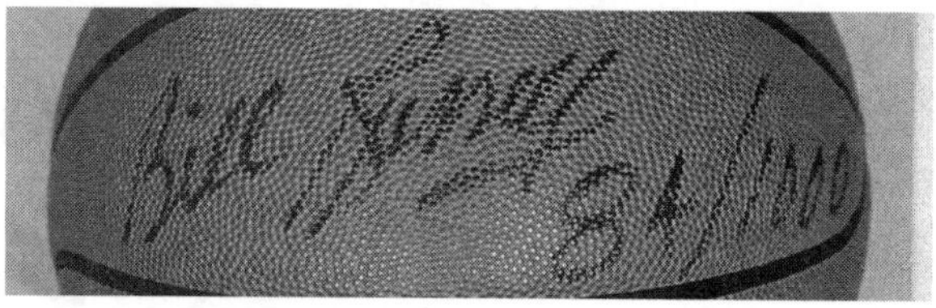

90. **Babe Ruth** - HOF, Yankees great, "The Bambino," immensely popular American icon, died 8/16/48

91. **Nolan Ryan** - HOF, 300-Win Club, Member '69 Mets, Texas great, seven no-hitters, 5,714 strikeouts
92. **Terry Sawchuk** - HOF, record-setting goaltender, 103 shutouts, played on four Stanley Cup winners, died 5/31/70
93. **Sammy Sosa** - Popular Cubs slugger, 60 HR in two consecutive years, hero in both U.S. and Caribbean

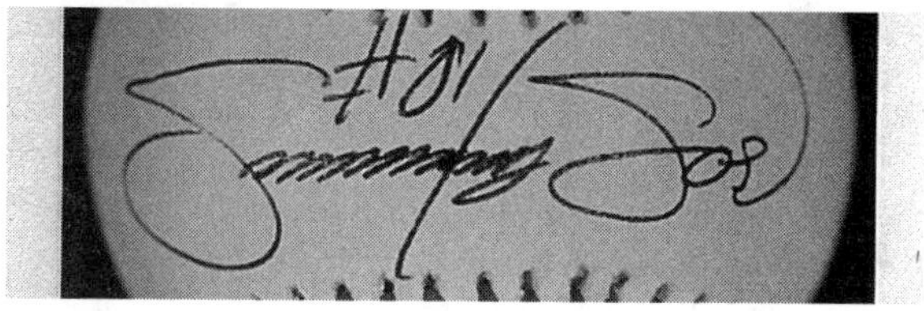

94. **Casey Stengel** - HOF, eccentric manager of great Yankee teams, manager of '62 Mets, died 9/29/75
95. **Jim Thorpe** - Native American Olympic champion, professional football and baseball player. Considered by many as the greatest athlete of the century. Died 3/28/53
96. **Norm Van Brocklin** - HOF QB for Rams and Eagles, Vikings coach died 5/2/83
97. **Honus Wagner** - HOF, 3,000 Hit Club, died 12/6/55

98. **Bob Waterfield** - HOF, NFL MVP as a rookie in 1945, died 3/25/83
99. **Tiger Woods** - Contemporary golf great, popularity and talent are extraordinary
100. **Ted Williams**- HOF, 500 HR Club, Triple Crown winner, charismatic Red Sox great, "Splendid Splinter," American legend

THE BRONX BOMBER

Derek Jeter leads Yankees to third World Championship in four years in 1999

By Robert Grayson

"If you can't have fun playing Major League Baseball every day, there's something wrong."
— Derek Jeter

It's easy to see why Derek Jeter is having so much fun playing baseball these days. During his first four big league seasons, Jeter has won three World Series rings. Who wouldn't have fun collecting free jewelry every year?

During his first big league season in 1996, Jeter was named American League Rookie of the Year, hitting .314 with 10 homers, 78 RBI and 104 runs. He also hit .361 in the postseason, leading the Yankees to a World Series title.

"I was a bit worried," said Jeter. "I thought to myself, 'It can't get much better than this.'"

But it did.

In 1998, the Yankees won the world championship again, collecting a record 125 wins and sweeping the San Diego Padres in the World Series. Jeter finished third in the 1998 American League MVP voting as he hit .324 with a career-best 19 homers, 84 RBIs and 30 stolen bases, while leading the league in runs with 127. Once again, he had to pinch himself to make sure it wasn't all a dream.

This season, the Yankees defended their title and their 25-year-old shortstop was one of the keys in their success. Jeter was among the league leaders in nine offensive categories, including batting average, hits, runs and triples.

Despite his personal success, he is quick to credit his teammates. "We have a lot of great players on

this team," Jeter said. "Every day, someone else is doing something else to help us win. I don't think it's just one person who makes a difference."

For Yankee fans, the notion of an offensive shortstop is something of an anomaly. For years, Yankee dynasties have been led by famed outfielders, all wielding powerful bats – players like Babe Ruth, Joe DiMaggio, Mickey Mantle, Roger Maris and Reggie Jackson. The Yankees also drew power in the past from catchers like Bill Dickey, Yogi Berra, Elston Howard and Thurman Munson. Even first basemen, like Lou Gehrig, Moose Skowron, Chris Chambliss and Don Mattingly, have gotten into the hard-hitting act. But a shortstop?

While the Yankees have had their share of sensational fielders at shortstop, nobody was looking for great offense from that position. Phil Rizzuto, of course, was a Yankee sparkplug. Rizzuto, who is now in the Hall of Fame, was even named American League Most Valuable Player in 1950. The '40s-era shortstop regularly got on base, made an art of bunting, started rallies and could hit for average, but the diminutive "Scooter" never put up power numbers the way Jeter does.

Last season, Jeter set the Yankee team record for most homers by a shortstop (24). He surpassed his 1998 RBI output of 84 with 102 in 1999. He finished with 219 hits and stole 30 bases in 36 tries.

Meanwhile, he covers a huge area in the field and, as he matures, he's gaining arm strength, making his throws from deep short extremely accurate. When Jeter came up to the big leagues, his fielding was a sure thing, and the Yankees thought it would be nice if he could hit a little.

To their delight, Jeter hit a home run in the first game of the '96 season and has been going strong ever since. He credits his success at the plate this year to being more selective.

"I've gone through times where I swung at a lot of bad pitches, and I'm trying not to do that this season," he said. "I'm also trying to drive the ball more and turn on it better. But I think I have a lot more work to do offensively."

Like most Yankee fans, Jeter is in awe of the team's stellar lineup. "We have a great lineup. One through nine could beat you. What impresses me most is that we have a lot of patient hitters, and I think you can see that we're capable of scoring a lot of runs."

Even though he batted .349 for the season, Jeter went through some rough games. "It's a long season. You know you're going to have rough periods. But if you have a good approach during those times when you're hot and can maintain that same approach through the games when things are going bad, you'll come out of a slump. I talk to Chris Chambliss (the Yankee batting coach) a lot about hitting, and he gives me a lot of valuable advice and insights. I find the longer you're in this game, the more you have to learn about it."

After last year's historic season, some people felt the Yankees would have trouble repeating in '99. But after a rough start – which began with manager Joe Torre being diagnosed with cancer – the Yankees again came up winners.

"Everybody wants to know if you can do it again," Jeter said. "You have to remember: Nobody had ever done what we did in '98. I think we realized in spring training this year that we couldn't be consumed with the thought that we had to do that again. We just wanted to be a better team.

"If we win 10 in a row and lose the 11th game, no one is happy with that. Our approach is we want to win every game, and if we don't, we're upset."

That kind of winning attitude is nothing new to the Yankees, whose glittering history is replete with spectacular come-from-behind wins. Many of today's Yankees, including Jeter, derive that same exuberant confidence from talking to fabled Yankees of the past.

"One of the best things about playing for the Yankees is how accessible former Yankee players are," said Jeter. "We have people working with us in spring training who are living legends, and we can talk to them about anything. And they give us a lot of time."

Most fans are enamored with Jeter's offensive accomplishments, but the young star said there's more to his game than just the bat.

"I think offense is overrated. Right now, when you turn on the sports, the first thing you see are home runs, followed by big hits. So it's obvious that's what the fans want to see. But if you're a critical observer of the game, you'll notice the defensive plays that really save a game or turn a game around. I think casual viewers of the game just know what they see on the evening sports. And that's home runs."

In other words, Jeter believes that defense wins games.

"I don't care how many home runs you hit or how many RBIs you have, if you're out in the field giving runs away, you're not helping the team," he said. "I think players focus on defense, and I think managers look for defense. I think defense is the first thing you should think about. But you do have to say that right now the fans' focus is on home runs."

A self-described "homebody," who prefers dinner and a movie at home to a night on the town, Jeter loves playing baseball in New York, not far from his birthplace across the Hudson River in Pequannock, N.J.

"New York is the greatest city in the world, the greatest place for an athlete, and I don't know why anyone wouldn't want to play here," says New York's most eligible bachelor. With a winning smile, he shrugs off all the attention focused on his marital status. "Who else are they going to pick? Most of the other guys on the team are married."

At a young age, Jeter moved with his family to Kalamazoo, Mich. But growing up, he was still an avid fan of the Yankees, never forsaking his beloved Bronx Bombers to root for a team in the Midwest. Naturally, he was thrilled when the Yankees made him their first-round pick in 1992, right out of Kalamazoo Central High School, where he hit .508 as a senior.

As a youngster, Jeter followed the career of Dave Winfield, because he believed Winfield was the best player in the game at that time. And Jeter is keenly aware of other Yankees who were the best in the game during their diamond tenures. But does he see a day when his No. 2 will be retired next to legends like Babe Ruth (No. 3) and Lou Gehrig (No. 4)?

"You have to play a long time to get to that point. I think I'm a long way off," said the heir-apparent to the Yankee captaincy.

Interestingly, though, Jeter's No. 2 is considered a fortuitous number – after all, most of the lower numbers have already been retired off the backs of other great Yankees.

"I didn't think much about it when they gave me No. 2. I figured they gave it to me because it was the smallest jersey that they had," he said.

Jeter's popularity has carried over to the card industry, where his items are among the hottest in the industry. His 1993 SP rookie card has jumped $70 this year to $90, while many of his scarce inserts are also on the rise. While Jeter understands his popularity in the hobby, he admits that he's not an active collector.

"My mom has a lot of those things," he said. "I know she bought more of them when they first came out than she does now. But I think she still gets a kick out of seeing those things and hanging on to them. Probably after my career is over, I'll take a closer look at them."

But the way he's playing right now, his career won't be over for some time to come, and could culminate with a retired jersey and a trip to Cooperstown.

Peyton's Place

Among the elite of NFL quarterbacks

By Larry Weisman

They know, but they don't really know. Quarterbacks learn and grow as they progress, from pee-wee football to Pop Warner, to junior varsity and varsity. They accept the college scholarship and the world of knowledge expands even more. They work, they get better and then, one sunny day in April, all of the effort and time invested pays off at the NFL draft.

They think they're ready. And that's when they've made their first mistake.

They're not ready. They can't just step in and play. This is no longer recreation and the only fun comes from winning. The game is so much faster, the demands more intense and other people's careers ride on their young shoulders. Pressure builds but the pace never slackens. Quarterbacks who never knew failure now stare it full in the face.

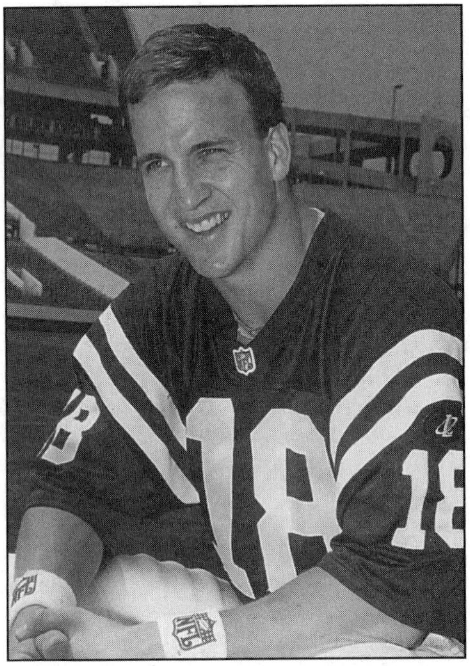

So give Peyton Manning credit. As much for what he has accomplished as the way he has set the table for future achievement. He knew. Intuitively. He didn't fail. But he understood what it would take to succeed.

Selected first overall in the NFL draft in 1998 by Indianapolis, saddled with the burden of helping the Colts rebuild a shattered franchise, Manning placed no undue expectations upon himself. Oh, it took him a while to let the game come to him, but the hardships of a rookie year with a team in the throes of rebuilding didn't take him by surprise.

"I came into last year very aware that this thing could be a struggle," he said. "I didn't think everything was going to be picture perfect and I was prepared for it."

Boy, was he right about that. The Colts finished 3-13 in 1997 and earned the right to select first in the '98 draft. They chose Manning, *The Sporting News'* College Player of the Year who finished behind Michigan's Charles Woodson for the Heisman Trophy. Manning had started four years at the University of Tennessee, deciding to stay for his senior with the Volunteers rather than opt for the NFL draft and become the top pick after his junior season.

Manning was immediately installed as the Colts' starting QB and learned the ropes of the game the hard way. Indianapolis lost its first four games as Manning threw 11 interceptions and only three TDs. But instead of giving up, Manning kept pressing forward and he had 23 TD passes and 15 INTs over the Colts' last 12 games. The on-the-job training had paid off.

Now he's beginning to reap the rewards. More confident, better equipped, smarter and savvier, Manning led the Colts to an opening-day upset of Buffalo this year and topped that with a club-record 404 yards passing in a victory over San Diego. By Week 12, the Colts had rolled to a 9-2 record behind the arm of Manning and the rushing efforts of Edgerrin James, good enough for first place in the AFC East. Oh yes, and the top-rated passer in the conference is the sophomore Manning.

"Peyton has taken on a leadership role this year," said left tackle Tarik Glenn. "He has shown us that he has a lot of confidence in himself and us. He lacked a little confidence in himself last year but expects a lot of himself and the offense this year. He has grown a lot."

When the Colts made him the foundation of their reconstruction, they didn't stop there. This off-season saw a massive retooling of the defense and the addition of James. Simply put, the whole team got better in the second year of the administration of team president Bill Polian and coach Jim Mora.

Go back to preparation. Coming in, Manning expected tough times. He knew what being the first pick in the draft meant.

"You're going to a team that has struggled. That's part of the trade-off for being a good college quarterback," he said. "You have to realize that it's not all going to happen right away."

But it's starting to happen now. His command of the offense is better, he knows his receivers and can make experience and knowledge work for him.

"He makes a lot better decisions. The game has slowed down for him," said Mora. "He recognizes what defenses are trying to do to him and makes the correct adjustment."

Take the San Diego game. On the first play, he and Marvin Harrison read the Chargers' coverage exactly right. Result: a 46-yard touchdown. Later, under pressure from San Diego's defense, Manning ran 12 yards for a touchdown.

"He just sort of took charge of the team," said Harrison, who spent 10 weeks this off-season working out with Manning. The hard work has paid off as Manning and Harrison are the most potent combination in the NFL right now.

Manning's 404-yard day broke the old team record held by some fellow named Johnny Unitas. Set in 1967. Although he has a long way to go, Manning is already drawing comparisons to the Hall of Fame quarterback who was the pride and joy of the Colts' franchise when it was in Baltimore.

"It's special because of the quarterbacks they've had here, especially Johnny Unitas," Manning said. "He's arguably the best ever."

The position had become an incredible sore spot for the Colts after their glory years and especially after the move from Baltimore to Indianapolis. After drafting and trading John Elway in 1983, the Colts started 16 different quarterbacks over the years until they installed Manning. It's an incredible list that includes another former No. 1 overall pick, Jeff George, and so many others of varied skill: Gary Hogeboom, Jack Trudeau, Paul Justin and Jim Harbaugh, among them.

The '98 draft would feature quarterbacks going first and second. The Colts sweated the choice at the time between Manning and Ryan Leaf and took Manning. The Chargers gleefully selected Leaf. Does anymore need to be said? Leaf blew up a couple of weeks into the season and wound up benched; the Chargers acquired Harbaugh from the Baltimore Ravens and signed Erik Kramer to handle the load this season. Leaf, now recovering from shoulder surgery, wonders if he'll even have a career in San Diego.

At the scouting combine in February of '98, Leaf missed his interview with the Colts in a scheduling mishap; Manning showed up with a legal pad full of questions.

"We didn't interview Peyton," said Polian. "He interviewed us."

Manning stands 6'5" and weighs 230 pounds and loves to lift weights with the linemen. He's as tough as they come, but not all of it involves the physical pounding that comes with the position. There are emotional components and intellectual ones, too.

"Football is a physical game but it's so much of a mental game," said right tackle Adam Meadows. "He's definitely on top of that."

When '98 ended – with the Colts repeating their 3-13 record from the year before – Manning thanked his offensive linemen with a little gift.

"He bought the o-line some nice boots," said Glenn. "They were sweet. He said this season we were going to kick some butt, so to speak."

"He looks like a completely different quarterback from the guy we saw at the beginning of last year," Bledsoe said. "He got through the hard times and maintained his confidence."

Manning's proud father knows a little about quarterbacking. Archie Manning played 14 seasons in the NFL, himself the second player picked in the 1971 draft. He attends half a dozen Colts games, watches the rest on satellite TV and lets others heap praise on Peyton.

"I don't stroke Peyton or go around bragging about him, but I read something Jim Mora said recently: Football is very important to Peyton. Now that doesn't sound like much, especially for guys getting a lot of money. But it is very important to Peyton – at practice, in games, during the off-season, watching film, day and night," Archie Manning said.

Only one quarterback took every snap in 1998 – Manning. And he set a bunch of rookie records: touchdown passes (26), yards (3,739), attempts (573) and completions (326). The 26 TD passes tied him for second in a single season for the Colts with Earl Morrall. Only Unitas (32) ever threw more.

But to him, the past is merely prologue.

"I don't think rookie records carry a lot of weight on your resume," he said. "The great ones are the ones who have done it year after year after year. That's why I'm in this league, to be a good quarterback for a long time. And that's my plan."

So far it's working just fine.

THE MANNING FILE

FULL NAME: Peyton Williams Manning

BORN: March 24, 1976

HEIGHT: 6'5"

WEIGHT: 230

HIGH SCHOOL: Isidore Newman (New Orleans)

COLLEGE: Tennessee

DRAFTED: Selected in first round (first pick overall) by Indianapolis in 1998 NFL draft

HONORS: Davey O'Brien Award winner (1997); Named College Player of the Year by *The Sporting News* (1997).

Peyton Manning Card Checklist

Year Set	Card No.	MT
1998 Bowman	1	$15
1998 Bowman Blue Autographs	1	140
1998 Bowman Blue Autographs Gold	1	425
1998 Bowman Blue Autographs Silver	1	275
1998 Bowman Chrome	1	55
1998 Bowman Chrome Golden Anniversary	1	200
1998 Bowman Chrome Interstate	1	50
1998 Bowman Chrome Interstate Ref.	1	200
1998 Bowman Chrome Refractor	1	150
1998 Bowman Golden Anniversary	1	225
1998 Bowman Inter-State	1	20
1998 Bowman Scout's Choice	SC1	15
1998 Bowman's Best	112	15
1998 Bowman's Best Atomic Refractors	112	125
1998 Bowman's Best Autographs	7A	150
1998 Bowman's Best Auto Atomic Ref.	7A	300
1998 Bowman's Best Autographs	7B	150
1998 Bowman's Best Auto Atomic Ref.	7B	300
1998 Bowman's Best Mirror Fusion	MI8	25
1998 B Best Mirror Image Atomic Ref.	MI8	300
1998 Bowman's Best Mirror Image Ref.	MI8	125
1998 Bowman's Best Performers	BP1	15
1998 B Best Performers Atomic Ref.	BP1	160
1998 Bowman's Best Performers Ref.	BP1	60
1998 Bowman's Best Refractor	112	60
1998 Collector's Edge Game Gear Jersey	1	200
1998 Edge First Place Rookie Markers	13	30
1998 Edge First Place Successors	16	10
1998 Edge First Place Triumph	17	10
1998 Edge First Place Triple Threat	26	15
1998 Edge First Place Rookie Ink	30	125
1998 Edge First Place	135	10
1998 Edge First Place 50-Pt	135	20
1998 Edge First Place 50-Pt Silver	135	100
1998 Edge Masters Rookie Masters	1	25
1998 Edge Masters Sentinels	8	40
1998 Edge Masters	73	25
1998 Edge Masters HoloGold	73	375
1998 Edge Masters 50-Point	73	40
1998 Edge Masters 50-Point Gold	73	75
1998 Edge Masters	183	15
1998 Edge Masters HoloGold	183	200
1998 Edge Masters 50-Point	183	25
1998 Edge Masters 50-Point Gold	183	45
1998 Edge Masters	199	7.50
1998 Edge Masters HoloGold	199	100
1998 Edge Masters 50-Point	199	10
1998 Edge Masters 50-Point Gold	199	25
1998 Edge Odyssey S.L. Edge	6	30
1998 Edge Odyssey Leading Edge	13	10
1998 Edge Odyssey	60	10
1998 Edge Odyssey Galvanized	60	15
1998 Edge Odyssey Holofoil Gold	60	100
1998 Edge Odyssey	172	14
1998 Edge Odyssey Galvanized	172	25
1998 Edge Odyssey Holofoil Gold	172	175
1998 Edge Odyssey	212	25
1998 Edge Odyssey Galvanized	212	40
1998 Edge Odyssey Holofoil Gold	212	550
1998 Edge Odyssey	239	35
1998 Edge Odyssey Galvanized	239	35
1998 Edge Odyssey Holofoil Gold	239	400
1998 Edge Supreme Pro Sign. Authentic	PM	150
1998 Edge First Place Rookie Ink Red Sigs	30	200
1998 E-X2001	54	25
1998 E-X2001 Destination Honolulu	1	175
1998 E-X2001 Essential Credentials Future	54	600
1998 E-X2001 Essential Credentials Now	54	250
1998 E-X2001 Star Date 2001	15	15
1998 Finest	121	25
1998 Finest Future's Finest	F1	40
1998 Finest Jumbos 1	2	35
1998 Finest Jumbos 1 Refractors	2	70
1998 Finest Mystery Finest 2	M2	35
1998 Finest Mystery Finest 2 Refractors	M2	50
1998 Finest Mystery Finest 2	M4	30
1998 Finest Mystery Finest 2 Refractors	M4	50
1998 Finest Mystery Finest 2	M6	25
1998 Finest Mystery Finest 2 Refractors	M6	40
1998 Finest Mystery Finest 2	M31	25
1998 Finest Mystery Finest 2 Refractors	M31	40
1998 Finest No-Protector	121	35
1998 Finest No-Protector Refractor	121	175

Year Set	Card No.	MT
1998 Finest Refractors	121	100
1998 Finest Stadium Stars Jumbos	9	25
1998 Finest Stadium Stars	S9	20
1998 Finest Undergrads	U20	50
1998 Finest Undergrads Refractors	U20	75
1998 Flair Showcase Feature Film	9	40
1998 Flair Showcase Legacy	3	175
1998 Flair Showcase Legacy Masterpiece	3	–
1998 Flair Showcase Row 0	3	120
1998 Flair Showcase Row 1	3	45
1998 Flair Showcase Row 2	3	18
1998 Flair Showcase Row 3	3	12
1998 Fleer	235	8
1998 Fleer Brilliants	120	30
1998 Fleer Brilliants Blue	120	40
1998 Fleer Brilliants Gold	120	100
1998 Fleer Brilliants Shining Stars	9	20
1998 Fleer Brilliants Shining Stars Pulsars	9	150
1998 Fleer Brilliants 24-Karat Gold	120	240
1998 Fleer Heritage	235	90
1998 Fleer Rookie Sensations	RS9	15
1998 Leaf Rookies & Stars Freshman	1	20
1998 Leaf Rookies & Stars Game Plan	2	12
1998 Leaf Rookies & Stars Masters	2	35
1998 Leaf Rookies & Stars Ticket Masters	16	15
1998 Leaf Rookies & Stars Masters Die-Cuts	16	45
1998 Leaf Rookies & Stars American Heroes	20	18
1998 Leaf Rookies & Stars Crusade	66	50
1998 Leaf Rookies & Stars Crusade Purpl.	66	75
1998 Leaf Rookies & Stars Red	66	250
1998 Leaf Rookies & Stars	233	50
1998 Leaf Rookies & Stars Longevity	233	150
1998 Leaf Rookies & Stars True Blue	233	$40
1998 Leaf Rookies & Stars	270	25
1998 Leaf Rookies & Stars Longevity	270	75
1998 Leaf Rookies & Stars True Blue	270	20
1998 Metal Universe	189	8
1998 Metal Universe Precious Gems	189	200
1998 Metal Universe Quasars	QS1	20
1998 Pacific	181	10
1998 Pacific Aurora	71	12
1998 Pacific Aurora Championship Fever	22	6
1998 Pacific Aurora Champ. Fever Copper	22	450
1998 Pacific Aurora Champ. Platinum Blues	22	150
1998 Pacific Aurora Champ. Fever Silver	22	60
1998 Pacific Aurora Cubes	9	15
1998 Pacific Aurora Face Mask Cel-Fusions	9	60
1998 Pacific Aurora Gridiron Laser-Cuts	9	10
1998 Pacific Aurora NFL Command	5	100
1998 Pacific Cramer's Choice Awards	5	$125
1998 Pacific Royale Cramer's Awds. Jumbos	5	20
1998 Pacific Crown Royale Rookie Paydirt	6	30
1998 Pacific Royale Master Performers	9	14
1998 Pacific Royale Pillars of the Game	11	6
1998 Pacific Crown Royale Pivotal Players	12	6
1998 Pacific Crown Royale	54	20
1998 Pacific Crown Royale Limited Series	54	100
1998 Pacific CRCC Awards Jumbos Blues	5	150
1998 Pacific CRCC Awards Jumbos Golds	5	450
1998 Pacific CRCC Awards Jumbos Greens	5	225
1998 Pacific CRCC Jumbos Light Blues	5	300
1998 Pacific CRCC Awards Jumbos Reds	5	275
1998 Pacific Dynagon Turf	8	12
1998 Pacific Dynagon Turf Titaniums	8	125
1998 Pacific Gold Crown Die-Cuts	14	40
1998 Pacific Omega	101	10
1998 Pacific Omega EO Portraits	10	40
1998 Pacific Omega Face To Face	1	40
1998 Pacific Omega Online	15	20
1998 Pacific Omega Prisms	9	25
1998 Pacific Omega Rising Stars	11	20
1998 Pacific Omega Rising Stars Blue	11	100
1998 Pacific Omega Rising Stars Green	11	135
1998 Pacific Omega Rising Stars Purple	11	225
1998 Pacific Omega Rising Stars Red	11	125
1998 Pacific Omega Rising Stars Gold	11	–
1998 Pacific Platinum Blue	181	200
1998 Pacific Red	181	12
1998 Pacific Revolution	58	16
1998 Pacific Revolution Prime Time	10	25
1998 Pacific Revolution Rookies and Stars	15	12
1998 Pacific Rev. Rookies/Stars Gold	15	175
1998 Pacific Revolution Showstoppers	16	15

Year Set	Card No.	MT
1998 Pacific Rev. Showstoppers Red	16	20
1998 Pacific Revolution Shadow	58	125
1998 Pacific Revolution Touchdown	10	25
1998 Pacific Team Checklists	12	20
1998 Pacific Timelines	8	100
1998 Playoff Ab Hobby Draft Die-Cut Silvers	1	20
1998 Playoff Absolute Hobby Draft Picks	1	30
1998 Playoff Ab Hobby Draft Bronze Bonus		35
1998 Playoff Ab Hobby Draft Picks Blue	1	35
1998 Playoff Absolute Hobby Checklist	12	30
1998 Playoff Ab Hobby Die-Cut Silvers P	12	20
1998 Playoff Ab Hobby Platinum Quads	18	100
1998 Playoff Absolute Hobby Shields	18	40
1998 Playoff Ab Hobby Shields Retail	18	25
1998 Playoff Absolute Hobby	165	35
1998 Playoff Absolute Hobby Silver	165	45
1998 Playoff Absolute Hobby Retail	165	15
1998 Playoff Absolute Hobby Red Retail	165	30
1998 Playoff Absolute Hobby Gold	165	350
1998 Playoff Contenders Checklist	12	15
1998 Playoff Contenders Leather	37	20
1998 Playoff Contenders Leather Gold	37	250
1998 Playoff Contenders Leather Red	37	30
1998 Playoff Contenders Pennant	42	15
1998 Playoff Contenders Pennant Red	42	20
1998 Playoff Contenders Pennant Gold	42	100
1998 Playoff Contenders Rookie/Year	4	30
1998 Playoff Contenders Rookie Stallions	6	20
1998 Playoff Contenders TD Tandems	18	15
1998 Playoff Contenders Ticket	87	150
1998 Playoff Contenders Ticket Red	87	30
1998 Playoff Contenders Ticket Gold	87	300
1998 Playoff Mom. Hobby Rookie Double	1	30
1998 Playoff Mom. Hobby EndZone Xpress	11	25
1998 Playoff Mom. Hobby Reunion Quads	16	125
1998 Playoff Mom. Hobby Headliners	16	80
1998 Playoff Hobby Reunion QuadsJumbos	16	125
1998 Playoff Mom. Hobby Team Threads	18	40
1998 Playoff Mom. Hobby Threads Away	18	75
1998 Playoff Mom. Hobby NFL Rivals	20	80
1998 Playoff Momentum Hobby	98	70
1998 Playoff Momentum Hobby Red	98	90
1998 Playoff Momentum Hobby Gold	98	350
1998 Playoff Mom. Retail Rookie Double	1	30
1998 Playoff Mom. Retail EndZone X-press	11	10
1998 Playoff Mom. Retail Reunion Tandems	16	50
1998 Playoff Momentum Retail Headliners	16	30
1998 Playoff Mom. Retail Team Jerseys	18	50
1998 Playoff Mom. Retail Jerseys Away	18	40
1998 Playoff Momentum Retail NFL Rivals	20	35
1998 Playoff Momentum Retail	146	25
1998 Playoff Momentum Retail Red	146	30
1998 Playoff Prestige	165	20
1998 Playoff Prestige Best of the NFL	23	35
1998 P Prestige Best NFL None-Die Cut	23	20
1998 Playoff Prestige Checklist	12	35
1998 Playoff Prestige Checklist Gold	12	20
1998 Playoff Prestige Draft Picks	1	30
1998 Playoff Prestige Draft Silver Jumbos	1	35
1998 Playoff Prestige Draft Picks Bronze	1	15
1998 Playoff Prestige Draft Bronze Jumbos	1	150
1998 Playoff Prestige Draft Picks Green	1	25
1998 Playoff Prestige Draft Green Jumbos	1	25
1998 P Prestige Draft Green Numbered	1	300
1998 Playoff Prestige Gold	165	400
1998 Playoff Prestige Green Retail	165	40
1998 Playoff Prestige Red	165	40
1998 Playoff Prestige Red Retail	165	40
1998 Playoff Prestige Retail	165	10
1998 Press Pass	1	3.50
1998 Press Pass Autographs	21	100
1998 Press Pass Fields of Fury	FF 1/9	30
1998 Press Pass Head Butt	HB 1/9	18
1998 Press Pass Jerseys	JC PM	200
1998 Press Pass Kick-Off	KO 1	6
1998 Press Pass Triple Threat	TT 1/9	8
1998 Press Pass Triple Threat	TT 2/9	8
1998 Press Pass Triple Threat	TT 3/9	8
1998 Press Pass Trophy Case	TC 1/12	12
1998 Score	233	8
1998 Score Rookie Preview	233	8
1998 SkyBox	231	45
1998 SkyBox Double Vision	17	16

Year Set	Card No.	MT
1998 SkyBox Intimidation Nation	10	100
1998 SkyBox Prime Time Rookies	6	40
1998 SkyBox Star Rubies	231	400
1998 SkyBox Thunder	239	10
1998 SkyBox Thunder Rave	239	125
1998 SkyBox Thunder Star Burst	SB6	20
1998 SkyBox Thunder Super Rave	239	350
1998 Stadium Club	195	15
1998 Stadium Club Co-Signers	CO1	$550
1998 Stadium Club Co-Signers	CO6	350
1998 Stadium Club Co-Signers	CO9	200
1998 Stadium Club Double Threat	1	15
1998 Stadium Club First Day	195	70
1998 Stadium Club One of a Kind	195	100
1998 Stadium Club Prime Rookies	10	15
1998 SP Authentic	14	325
1998 SP Authentic Die-Cut	14	325
1998 SP Authentic Maximum Impact	MI11	8
1998 SP Authentic Special Forces	S22	45
1998 SPx Finite	181	85
1998 SPx Finite	287	20
1998 SPx Finite	311	30
1998 SPx Finite	351	30
1998 SPx Finite Radiance	181	300
1998 SPx Finite Radiance	287	30
1998 SPx Finite Radiance	311	40
1998 SPx Finite Radiance	351	60
1998 SPx Finite Spectrum	181	–
1998 SPx Finite Spectrum	287	30
1998 SPx Finite Spectrum	311	40
1998 SPx Finite Spectrum	351	300
1998 Topps	360	12
1998 Topps Autographs	A10	120
1998 Topps Chrome	165	60
1998 Topps Chrome Refractors	165	150
1998 Topps Gold Label	20	15
1998 Topps Gold Black Label Class 1	20	40
1998 Topps Gold Black Label Class 2	20	60
1998 Topps Gold Black Label Class 3	20	100
1998 Topps Gold Class 2	20	25
1998 Topps Gold Class 3	20	30
1998 Topps Gold Red Label Class 1	20	200
1998 Topps Gold Red Label Class 2	20	300
1998 Topps Gold Red Label Class 3	20	500
1998 Topps Season Opener	1	25
1998 Topps Stars	67	15
1998 Topps Stars Bronze	67	20
1998 Topps Stars Gold	67	35
1998 Topps Stars Gold Rainbow	67	120
1998 Topps Stars Luminaries	L13	100
1998 Topps Stars Luminaries Silver	L13	120
1998 Topps Stars Luminaries Gold	L13	150
1998 Topps Stars Luminaries Gold Rain.	L13	–
1998 Topps Stars Silver	67	20
1998 Topps Stars Supernova	S5	100
1998 Topps Stars Supernova Silver	S5	125
1998 Topps Stars Supernova Gold	S5	150
1998 Topps Stars Supernova Gold Rain.	S5	–
1998 Ultra	201	40
1998 Ultra	416	20
1998 Ultra Caught in the Draft	4	20
1998 Ultra Damage Inc.	12	40
1998 Ultra Exclamation Points	5	60
1998 Ultra Gold Medallion	201	75
1998 Ultra Gold Medallion	416	40
1998 Ultra Next Century	2	40
1998 Ultra Platinum Medallion	201	250
1998 Ultra Platinum Medallion	416	125
1998 Upper Deck	1	45
1998 UD Black Diamond Rks White Onyx	ON1	30
1998 Black Diamond Rks Sheer Brilliance	B5	45
1998 Black Diamond Rookies	91	25
1998 Black Diamond Rookies Double	91	40
1998 Black Diamond Rookies Triple	91	50
1998 Black Diamond Rookies Quadruple	91	125
1998 Upper Deck Bronze	1	150
1998 Upper Deck Constant Threat	CT2	15
1998 UD Constant Threat Bronze	CT2	400
1998 UD Constant Threat Silver	CT2	30
1998 Upper Deck Encore	1	50
1998 UD Encore Constant Threat	CT2	15
1998 Upper Deck Encore F/X Gold	1	125
1998 Upper Deck Encore Milestones	1	325
1998 Upper Deck Encore Rookie Encore	RE2	20
1998 UD Encore Rookie Encore F/X Gold	RE2	65
1998 UD Encore Super Powers	S8	15
1998 UD Hobby Excl. Game Jerseys	GJ16	200
1998 Upper Deck SuperPowers	S16	6
1998 Upper Deck SuperPowers Bronze	S16	150

Year Set	Card No.	MT
1998 Upper Deck SuperPowers Silver	S16	15
1998 UD Choice	193	5
1998 UD Choice	256	6
1998 UD Choice Choice Reserve	193	20
1998 UD Choice Choice Reserve	256	20
1998 UD Choice Prime Choice Reserve	193	125
1998 UD Choice Prime Choice Reserve	256	125
1998 UD Choice Starquest Blue	SR1	3.50
1998 UD Choice Starquest Blue Green	SR1	10
1998 UD Choice Starquest Blue Red	SR1	20
1998 UD Choice Starquest Blue Gold	SR1	125
1998 UD3	1	25
1998 UD3	91	45
1998 UD3	181	10
1998 UD3 Die Cuts	1	35
1998 UD3 Die Cuts	91	50
1998 UD3 Die Cuts	181	200
1999 Collector's Edge Adv. Moments	3	12
1999 Collector's Edge Adv. Prime	4	5
1999 Collector's Edge Advantage Overture	5	12
1999 Edge Advantage Shockwaves	10	12
1999 Edge Advantage Showtime	10	15
1999 Edge Advantage	67	2
1999 Edge Advantage Gold Ingot	67	4
1999 Edge Advantage Galvanized	67	10
1999 Edge Advantage HoloGold	67	125
1999 Edge Fury Extreme Team	7	12
1999 Edge Fury X-Plosive	10	12
1999 Edge Fury Game Ball	–	40
1999 Edge Fury	89	2
1999 Edge Fury Gold Ingot	89	4
1999 Edge Fury Galvanized	89	10
1999 Edge Fury HoloGold	89	125
1999 Edge Supreme	2	.75
1999 Edge Supreme Gold Ingot	2	1.50
1999 Edge Supreme Galvanized	2	4
1999 Edge Supreme Markers	4	7
1999 Edge Supreme T3	7	15
1999 Edge Supreme Homecoming	16	10
1999 Edge Supreme	53	2.50
1999 Edge Supreme Gold Ingot	53	5
1999 Edge Supreme Galvanized	53	15
1999 Donruss Elite	118	8
1999 Donruss Elite Field of Vision	11A	$15
1999 Donruss Elite Field Die Cuts	11A	$45
1999 Donruss Elite Field of Vision	11B	15
1999 Donruss Elite Field Die Cuts	11B	60
1999 Donruss Elite Field of Vision	11C	12
1999 Donruss Elite Field Die Cuts	11C	35
1999 Donruss Elite Passing the Torch	1	15
1999 D Elite Passing the Torch Autographs	1	400
1999 Donruss Elite Passing the Torch	3	12
1999 D Elite Passing the Torch Autographs	3	175
1999 Donruss Elite Power Formulas	6	8
1999 Donruss Elite Primary Colors	35	8
1999 Donruss Elite Primary Colors Blue	35	12
1999 Donruss Elite Primary Colors Red	35	230
1999 D Elite Primary Colors Blue Die-Cut	35	150
1999 Donruss Elite Primary Red Die-Cut	35	100
1999 Elite Primary Yellow Die-Cut	35	230
1999 Fleer	2	1.50
1999 Fleer Aerial Assault	10	10
1999 Fleer Under Pressure	7	30
1999 Metal Universe	77	1.50
1999 Metal Universe Gem Masters	77	–
1999 Metal Universe Linchpins	8	60
1999 Metal Universe Planet Metal	3	15
1999 Metal Universe Precious Metal Gem	77	200
1999 Pacific	169	2.50
1999 Pacific Aurora	63C	1.50
1999 Pacific Aurora	63D	1.50
1999 Pacific Aurora Canvas Creations	5	45
1999 Pacific Aurora Championship Fever	9	3.50
1999 Pacific Aurora Complete Players	5	20
1999 Pacific Aurora Leather Bound	9	7
1999 Pacific Aurora Premiere Date	63C	75
1999 Pacific Aurora Premiere Date	63D	75
1999 Pacific Aurora Styrotechs	9	12
1999 Pacific Copper	169	125
1999 Pacific Cramer's Choice Awards	6	100
1999 Pacific Dynagon Turf	9	8
1999 Pacific Gold Crown Die-Cuts	17	20
1999 Pacific Gold	169	60
1999 Pacific Opening Day	169	200
1999 Pacific Paramount	101	1.50
1999 Pacific Para. End Zone Net-Fusions	10	30
1999 Pacific Paramount Personal Bests	16	15
1999 Pacific Paramount Team Checklists	13	8
1999 Pacific Platinum Blue	169	150

Year Set	Card No.	MT
1999 Pacific Record Breakers	11	100
1999 Pacific Revolution	74	3
1999 Pacific Revolution Chalk Talk	11	15
1999 Pacific Revolution Icons	6	35
1999 Pacific Revolution Showstoppers	19	10
1999 Pacific Revolution Thorn in the Side	11	10
1999 Pacific Team Checklists	13	10
1999 Pacific Titanium Turf	9	75
1999 Playoff Prestige SSD For the Record	3	50
1999 Playoff Prestige SSD Gridiron Heritage	5	30
1999 Playoff Prestige SSD Checklist	13	18
1999 Playoff Prestige SSD Inside Nos.	13	20
1999 Playoff Prestige SSD Checklist Auto.	13	150
1999 Playoff Prestige SSD	53	4
1999 Playoff Prestige Spectrum Blue	53	15
1999 Playoff Prestige Spectrum Gold	53	15
1999 Playoff Prestige Spectrum Green	53	15
1999 Playoff Prestige Spectrum Purple	53	15
1999 Playoff Prestige Spectrum Red	53	15
1999 Playoff Prestige SSD	152	8
1999 Playoff Prestige Spectrum Blue	152	25
1999 Playoff Prestige SSD Gold	152	.25
1999 Playoff Prestige SSD Green	152	25
1999 Playoff Prestige SSD Purple	152	25
1999 Playoff Prestige SSD Red	152	25
1999 Score	170	1.50
1999 Score	272	4
1999 Score Anniversary Artist Proof	170	300
1999 Score Anniversary Artist Proof	272	750
1999 Score Anniversary Showcase	170	10
1999 Score Anniversary Showcase	272	25
1999 Score Complete Players	15	5
1999 Score Franchise	20	10
1999 Score Future Franchise	20	12
1999 Score Numbers Game	6	6
1999 Score Scoring Core	15	5
1999 Score Settle the Score	21	6
1999 Sports Illustrated	126	12
1999 SP Signature	45	5
1999 Topps	300	1.50
1999 Topps All Matrix	19	10
1999 Topps Chrome	120	3.50
1999 Topps Chrome All Etch	19	18
1999 Topps Chrome Hall of Fame	20	18
1999 Topps Chrome Record Numbers	9	15
1999 Topps Chrome Record Numbers Ref.	9	45
1999 Topps Chrome Season's Best	10	18
1999 Topps MVP Promotion	300	100
1999 Topps Picture Perfect	4	4
1999 Topps Record Numbers	9	4
1999 Topps Record Numbers Gold	9	25
1999 Topps Season Opener Autographs	2	200
1999 Topps Season Opener	110	1.50
1999 Topps Season's Best	10	12
1999 Ultra	15	2.50
1999 Ultra As Good As It Gets	5	50
1999 Ultra Counterparts	11	15
1999 Ultra Damage Inc.	5	20
1999 Ultra Gold Medallion	15	8
1999 Ultra Platinum Medallion	15	120
1999 Upper Deck	88	2
1999 Upper Deck Game Jersey Hobby	PM	250
1999 Upper Deck Game Jersey Patch	PM	600
1999 Upper Deck Highlight Zone	15	12
1999 UD Highlight Zone Quantum Silver	15	70
1999 Upper Deck MVP	79	1.50
1999 Upper Deck MVP Dynamics	10	10
1999 UD MVP Game-Used Souvenirs	PM	125
1999 Upper Deck MVP Gold Script	79	85
1999 Upper Deck MVP Power Surge	10	4
1999 Upper Deck MVP Silver Script	79	6
1999 Upper Deck MVP Super Script	79	200
1999 Upper Deck PowerDeck I	PM-PD	60
1999 Upper Deck Quarterback Class	13	6
1999 UD QB Class Quantum Silver	13	60
1999 Upper Deck Strike Force	11	5
1999 Upper Deck UD Exclusives Silver	88	120
1999 UD Ionix	25	3
1999 UD Ionix Astronomix	5	18
1999 UD Ionix Electric Forces	11	6
1999 UD Ionix HoloGrFX	4	150
1999 UD Ionix Power F/X	1	7
1999 Victory	107	1.50
1999 Victory	294	.50
1999 Victory	320	.50
1999 Victory	344	.50

Couch is Cleveland's 'franchise QB'

By Chuck Greenwood

It's hard enough being the No. 1 pick in the National Football League's annual draft, but to be the first pick of the born-again Cleveland Browns would be enough to give many players the shakes.

Not so with the Browns' No. 1 pick, quarterback Tim Couch. While he realizes that much will be expected of him, the Hyden, Ky., native is looking forward to the challenges and comparisons.

"It is a great feeling just to be mentioned with the former No. 1 picks and all those great players," Couch said. "It's an honor in itself to have your name up there with them. I just want to go out and play up to those expectations."

Playing up to those expectations is nothing new to Couch. The most prolific quarterback in the history of high school football when he graduated from high school, he was selected as the 1995 National Player of the Year by *Parade Magazine* and Gatorade Circle of Champions. *USA Today* named him the National Offensive Player of the Year. A four-year starter at Leslie County (Ky.) High School, he was honorable mention All-State his freshman year. He was named first team All-State each of the next three years.

During his four years as the signal-caller at Leslie County, Couch set national career records for most completions (872), passing yardage (12,104), and touchdown passes (133). He was second in pass attempts (1,372).

He didn't confine his talents to the gridiron. He played on the varsity basketball team from the seventh grade on. Couch led the state of Kentucky in scoring his junior year, averaging 36 points per game. His high games were 60 and 59 points. He set numerous school scoring and three-point records.

Understandably, University of Kentucky fans were elated when Couch decided to become a Wildcat. He did little to lower their expectations as he started two games as a true freshman and played in five other games. For the season, he completed 32 of 84 passes, while only throwing one interception.

Couch broke out in 1997, when Hal Mumme moved in from Valdosta State to become the head coach in Lexington. Mumme was committed to throwing the ball, and Couch proved that he was the man for the job, completing 363 of 547 passes for 3,884 yards and 37 touchdowns. He led the nation in pass attempts, completions, yardage and completion percentage (66.4). The Wildcats quarterback was second nationally in total offense with 371.7 yards per game.

Showing no letup his junior year, the 6-5, 225-pounder threw for 4,275 yards and 36 touchdowns. He passed for at least 300 yards and one score in each game. He wrapped up his Wildcat career by piercing Penn State's defense for 336 yards and two TDs in the Outback Bowl.

As he looked back on his All-American career, Couch said, "The two games that really stick out in my mind are the LSU game from this past year, and the Alabama game my sophomore year."

Unlike some draftees who wish they had been drafted by someone else, Couch made it known that he wanted to play for the Browns.

"The main reason that I came out this year was that I knew I had a chance to go very high in the draft, possibly No. 1," Couch said. "That was the biggest thing for me."

Even though the media and the fans descended like a horde of locusts on him during the Browns' workouts, days after the draft, Couch wasn't fazed by all the attention.

"I've had a lot of publicity ever since I was in high school," Couch said. "It was the same way in college. I just try to block it out. I know the Browns organization and their fans have high expectations of me.

"The first day of minicamp was spent learning the terminology. As the weekend went on, I got used to what was going on. I started to get a feel for the offense."

As the No. 1 pick in the draft, Couch realizes that he will be besieged for autographs. Thus far, he has handled the requests with poise and dignity.

"It's a good feeling. Anytime a fan appreciates what you're doing out on the field, it makes you feel good. You feel a sense of accomplishment as a player, so it's definitely a great feeling."

To ensure his autographs are authentic for the collector, Couch has aligned himself with Total Sports Concepts.

Recently, Total Sports Concepts was profiled in *Sports Collectors Digest* along with the announcement that the company was handling authentic Sammy Sosa items.

Couch is pleased to be associated with the company.

"My marketing people brought this concept to me. They thought that Total Sports Concepts was doing the best job out there. After we talked and looked it over, we just hooked it up."

Conversely, Total Sports Concepts is ecstatic to have Couch in the fold.

"Signing a player like Tim Couch is a big boost for our company," vice president Dale Ostrander said. "We already have Sammy Sosa. Couple that with the

TIM COUCH FILE

POSITION: Quarterback
HEIGHT: 6-foot-4
WEIGHT: 225
40-YARD TIME: 4.75
COLLEGE: Kentucky
DRAFTED BY: Cleveland, Pick 1, Round 1, Overall 1

CAREER HIGHLIGHTS:
Couch was *Parade* high school Player of the Year. Regarded as the top football recruit in the country in 1996, he also was considered a top basketball prospect. He signed with Kentucky in '96 but started in just two games, completing only 32 of 84 passes for 276 yards and one touchdown with one interception. In '97, under new coach Hal Mumme and his four- and five-receiver passing game, Couch hit 363 of 547 for 3,884 yards, 37 TDs and 19 INTs. He led the nation in passes attempted, completions, yards per game and completion percentage. In '98, he was 400 of 553 passes for 4,275 yards, 36 TDs and 15 INTs. Couch was named to the All-Southeastern Conference team, made many All-American teams and finished fourth in the Heisman voting.

No. 1 pick in the NFL draft, and that really is a major boost for our company. Tim and his agent wanted to go with a company that presented a quality certified plan for authenticity.

"Both Sammy and Tim are class athletes and represent both of their sports very well," Ostrander added. "As we enter into this venture, these are the kind of guys we want to bring on board."

Total Sports Concepts will be responsible for scheduling Couch's show appearances, as well as his private signings.

Growing up in southeastern Kentucky, Couch didn't have access to players to gather their signatures.

"I never did collect autographs. I had a few football cards, but I really didn't get into it that much," Couch said. "My favorite players were Joe Montana, John Elway and Dan Marino. I was a Dallas fan growing up."

As the Browns jersey with the No. 2 on it becomes more and more popular, Couch admits that it takes him back a few years.

"It's a good feeling when you see kids with your jersey and stuff on," the young quarterback said. "I can remember when I was that age dreaming about being in the NFL and all that. It's definitely good to see the kids looking up to you."

Couch has been involved in civic causes since his high school days. He participated in the DARE program and made speaking appearances at local junior high and elementary schools, speaking on the dangers of drug abuse.

At UK, he was a celebrity guest on the 1997 Children's Miracle Network Television Show, helping raise approximately $600,000 for the UK Children's Hospital.

"I plan on getting involved with some type of charity in Cleveland," Couch said. "It's important to give something back to the community."

Couch is happy that the draft hoopla is behind him and that now he can get on with the business of being an NFL quarterback.

"I'm looking forward to having football as a job, and not having anything else to worry about, like school. I'm really convinced that I am one of the hardest-working guys on the team," Couch said.

"I am totally committed to being the best player I can be. My whole life has been geared toward this."

Couch shared some of his thoughts about trading cards and collectibles in a recent interview:

Q&A

Q: You've been on a trading card by now. What's that like to see.

A: Pretty neat. Having your own rookie card is kind of neat to see for the first time. It's a big thrill.

Q: Did you collect cards as a kid?

A: A little bit. I bought some here and there.

Q: Do you remember any favorite cards you had when you were young?

A: Jerry Rice. And I had Dan Marino.

Q: Now people will be collecting Tim Couch rookies.

A: I guess so.

Q: What kind of advice have you gotten from other quarterbacks and some of the top picks?

A: Just try not to get frustrated and try to keep working through it. There can be tough times, but just stay confident.

Q: Who did you speak to about the pressures of the NFL?

A: Peyton Manning, Brett Favre, some of those guys.

Q: What were your favorite NFL teams growing up?

A: The Cowboys were my favorite team. My favorite players were Joe Montana and John Elway.

Q: I'm sure you've been asked, going into this season, about starting or not starting. How are you approaching that?

A: I'm just going to go out and work as hard as I can and just try to improve every day and let the coaches decide.

Q: What was draft weekend like? A lot of guys were talking about the nervousness and frustration of that. How did you handle that?

A: I found out the morning of the draft that I was going No. 1. But I was still excited. It was really meaningful. It was definitely a great day.

Q: What was it like to come out and put on this uniform for the first time?

A: It's all right. It's a good feeling to put the uniform on for the first time. Hopefully, I'll be in this uniform for about 15 more years.

Q: Growing up, did you have any heroes or any role models?

A: Joe Montana.

Q: What did you like about him?

A: The way he always won and played good in the clutch situations.

Q: Was there anyone, growing up, who helped you get where you are today?

A: My brother, Greg, helped me.

Q: Have you collected or saved anything?

A: No, I think I'm off that stuff.

Q: What's the best piece of advice you've ever been given?

A: Believe in yourself.

Q: At what point in your career did it dawn on you that you could be a pro football player?

A: In high school.

Q: Where does the pressure come from now? Do you put it on yourself or do others put it on you?

A: I don't really feel any pressure. It doesn't get to me.

Changing of the guard for Yankee stars

This season's power was supplied by reliever, not sluggers

By Greg Ambrosius

When you think of past New York Yankees superstars, the first thought that comes to mind is sluggers in pinstripes.

Babe Ruth and his 714 home runs. Roger Maris and his 61-homer season. Lou Gehrig and his 493 homers and 2,130 consecutive games played. Joe DiMaggio and his 361 home runs and only 369 strikeouts. Yogi Berra and his three MVPs.

Past Yankees champions won with power and good pitching and this year's World Series champion was no different. But much of the power was supplied by a relief pitcher, not a slugger.

Reliever? As they say in New York: Get outta here.

Seriously, the most dominating Yankee on this dominating team – which has now won three of the last four World Series titles – was closer Mariano Rivera, a Panamanian who made his first baseball glove out of cardboard.

Rivera was so dominant that he didn't give up a run since July 21, a scoreless streak of more than 40 innings and 38 appearances, longest since Orel Hershiser's record 59 innings in 1988.

Rivera had two saves and a win during the four-game sweep of the Atlanta Braves to cap off his incredible season, thus earning the World Series MVP award.

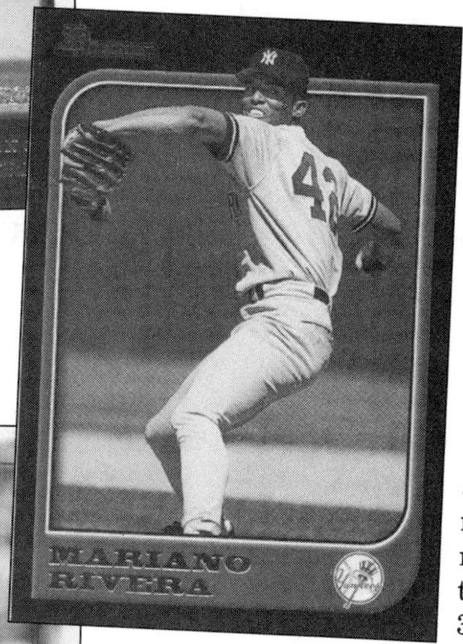

Mariano Rivera's 1997 and 1998 Bowman cards are valued at 20 and 40 cents, respectively.

Rivera's 1999 Upper Deck MVP Silver Signature

"I'll tell you what, I was surprised by that," Rivera said of the MVP honor. "I was just happy that we won the World Series and when they called me to the podium and told me I was the MVP I couldn't believe it. I was surprised."

Individual honors aren't important to Rivera, who was signed by the Yankees in 1990 as a 20-year-old out of Panama City. After a decade of being in the Yankees' system, all Rivera wants to do is win and he has three World Series rings to prove it.

"It's very enjoyable. You never get tired of winning," said Rivera. "The season was great and this team is unbelievable."

The slender 6-foot-2, 170-pounder is a big-time pitcher, as evidenced by his post-season numbers. His 0.37 career post-season earned run average stands as a major league record among those with at least 30 innings pitched.

He has allowed only two earned runs in 44 playoff innings, and he shut down the Braves in 4$\frac{2}{3}$ innings during the World Series.

"The managing stops once we get to the ninth inning with a lead," said Yankees manager Joe Torre. "The man is out there."

Rivera's post-season performance added light to his regular season accomplishments. He made good on 45 of 49 save opportunities and had a 4-3 record with a 1.80 ERA and 52 strikeouts in 69 innings.

He also held left-handers to a .143 average, surprising for a right-hander. The Braves managed just three hits off him in the World Series and he closed out the Game Four victory at raucous Yankee Stadium to get the save in relief of Roger Clemens.

"When you think of the team of the '90s, he's going

to be the guy you think of because he was on the mound for all of the big games," said Brandon Steiner, chairman of Steiner Sports, which has inked Rivera to an exclusive autograph contract.

"People identify Goose Gossage as the stopper of the '70s teams, but Mariano has done that for the last four years. He's already being talked about as one of the greatest closers the game has ever seen. Mariano doesn't say much on the mound, he just let's his pitching do the talking."

Rivera's post-season heroics has created increased attention in his cards and memorabilia.

His deal with Steiner Sports calls for Rivera to sign Yankees team items, along with single-signed baseballs (retail for $175 with a glass case) and autographed photos.

The signed memorabilia is new to Rivera, but he understands why fans want a piece of this championship team.

"I'm excited about what I'm doing with Steiner," Rivera said. "It's enjoyable and the collectors love to see these and they want to buy this stuff. It takes a few days to sign all of this, but working with Steiner has been good."

Rivera isn't a frequent signer at card shows, but he enjoys signing his name on items when asked in the proper setting.

"I'm honored when they ask for one," he added. "I just give them if I can. If I'm not running late to the ballpark I'll do it. I try to do it for a few minutes when I can."

Rivera even admits to collecting autographed items for his own personal collection. The Yankees closer asked Roger Clemens to sign a baseball when he joined the Yankees and he gave The Rocket a signed ball in return.

He's also kept his jerseys, gloves and baseballs and keeps those framed in his house.

"They're nice things to have," he said.

Rivera would like to finish his career in New York and at the age of 30 he has plenty of good years ahead of him.

Rivera talked about his future, the current team and his success in this one-on-one interview:

SCD: What is it about this New York team that makes it so successful? It seems like everyone contributes somehow each game. How does it feel to be part of this team, which is almost like a close family?

"I'm honored when they ask for one. I just give them if I can. If I'm not running late to the ballpark I'll do it. I try to do it for a few minutes when I can."

— Mariano Rivera, on signing autographs

Rivera: Oh, it really is. We play as a team first. It's like a family in there and everyone works hard. First of all, we treat everyone like a family, players, coaches, everyone. We have the best coaching staff in baseball and we're the best team ever.

SCD: How does it feel to play for Joe Torre, a manager who seems to be loved by his players?

Rivera: It's amazing. He's the best manager in baseball. Myself, I'm just so proud to have him as my manager. He's the best and I would do anything for him. He's like a father, a friend and he will always be there for you.

SCD: Do you think you'll always play for the Yankees? With free agency, it's tough to stay with one team, but do you want to stay with the Yankees?

Rivera: I want to be a Yankee forever and play in the best city for the best fans ever. I don't think I go nowhere.

SCD: Some people say that you are one of the greatest relievers of all-time. Success has come to you in a hurry, so how does it feel to hear those accolades?

Rivera: It makes me feel good. I just do my job. I'm a humble guy and I just love being in New York.

SCD: Do you think the Yankees can continue to keep winning?

Rivera: Oh yeah, if we can keep the team we have. No doubt.

SCD: What do you have for personal long-term goals?

Rivera: I would like to keep winning. The money is out of my hands. You know, George (Steinbrenner) is a businessman and it will all depend on him.

SCD: Being a closer is never easy, but you make it look so easy. Is that something you truly enjoy doing?

Mariano Rivera bio

Height: 6-foot-4; **Weight:** 168
Date of Birth: Nov. 29, 1969
Place of Birth: Panama City, Panama
Residence: La Chorrera, Panama
Acquired: Signed as free agent by Yankees in 1990
Bats: Right; **Throws:** Right
Years in Majors: 5
Position: Pitcher
Career tidbits: In 1998, he compiled a 3-0 mark, with a 1.91 ERA in 54 relief appearances and posted 36 saves in 41 chances...In 1997, racked up 43 saves and had 1.88 relief ERA (both ranked second in the A.L.)...Earned save in his first All-Star Game...Set a Yankee relief pitcher record with 130 strikeouts in 1996...Threw 26 consecutive scoreless innings, April 19 to May 21, 1996.

Rivera: I love to close. I began as a starter, but I love to be a reliever.

SCD: You finished the season without giving up an earned run over the last three months of the season. Do you realize how unhittable you were down the stretch and through the playoffs?

Rivera: I just went out and tried to do my job and get the guys out. That's my job.

SCD: Did you ever collect baseball cards when you were a youngster in Panama?

Rivera: No.

SCD: But do you understand the fascination with card collecting?

Rivera: Not really. I never got into it. It's all new to me.

Yankees team-signed jerseys, bats, baseballs a red-hot seller

By Greg Ambrosius

It was appropriate that the New York Yankees won the 1999 World Series. After all, with 25 world championships to their credit, the Team of the Century deserved to close out the century with one last title.

There's little doubt that the New York Yankees are the best franchise in baseball. With a history that boasts legendary stars such as Babe Ruth, Lou Gehrig, Joe DiMaggio, Mickey Mantle, Yogi Berra and Whitey Ford, the Yankees have won titles in every decade since 1920.

Now they've won three of the last four World Series titles and this current champion is being considered as the greatest team of all-time.

That may be debatable – especially when you begin comparing Yankee teams of the past with current teams – but there's little doubt that collectors can't get enough of this current dynasty.

Yankees memorabilia leads baseball sales and anything team-signed is quickly sold out.

Steiner Sports is a New York-based company that knows all about the Yankees' growing popularity.

Steiner gathered team members together immediately after last year's World Series sweep over San Diego and sold team-signed bats, team-signed baseballs and team-signed lithographs.

The company did the same thing with the NHL's Dallas Stars after its Stanley Cup victory and this year it grabbed the Yankees for another signing party.

The 1999 Yankees signed nearly 800 team items, ranging from 199 baseball jerseys, 199 baseballs, 199 bats to 199 photographs. According to company officials, these items are red-hot sellers.

"I don't think there's going to be enough," said chairman Brandon Steiner. "We just decided to do a lot fewer pieces this year compared to last year. A lot of guys have won three of the last four years and they just don't want to sign anymore. A person who gets an item from this team is going to get something very special. There's just not enough of it."

Prices for the Yankees team-signed items are as follows: $2,500 for a framed jersey, $2,000 for a bat, $1,500 for a baseball and $1,500 for a photograph. Putting together these signing sessions certainly isn't easy. For one thing, nobody knows who the champion will be or when the championship series will conclude.

"It's very hard to get the whole team on the same page and it's exhausting, but we have a lot of experience in these team projects."

— Brandon Steiner, Steiner Sports chairman

Then there's the problem of getting the players to sign the pieces before they leave for home, which in some cases can be back to Panama or Puerto Rico.

"It's very hard to get the whole team on the same page and it's exhausting, but we have a lot of experience in these team projects," added Steiner.

"I don't think anyone can imagine what it's like until they try to do it because everyone's agenda is different. Guys are coming and leaving, some guys don't want to sign this or that, it's crazy. You don't sleep for about a week, until it's all said and done."

But Steiner said the finished product is worth the time and effort. And right now nothing Steiner Sports has done to this point equals the interest in this year's Yankees team-signed items.

"The interest is huge," said Steiner. "The phone hasn't stopped ringing because people see there's a sequence here with each item and they know this is a tough item to get."

Cone's perfect game was third in Yankees history

Adidas recognized David Cone's perfect game with this famous photo in its ad in the 1999 Yankees postseason media guide.

By Ed Lucas and Paul Post

David Cone always puts team accomplishments ahead of personal goals making his World Series rings among the most important possessions he owns.

Still he'll always cherish what happened this past July 18 as one of the top thrills in a brilliant 12-year major league career.

When third baseman Scott Brosius grabbed a pop fly for the final out, Cone became the third player in Yankee history to pitch a perfect game.

It was the 16th in big-league history and he didn't go to a three-ball count the entire game while striking out 10 Montreal Expos hitters.

More importantly, it came on Yogi Berra Day at Yankee Stadium when none other than Don Larsen, who hurled the only perfect game in World Series history, tossed out the first pitch to Berra in pregame ceremonies.

"It just means everything," Cone said. "It was an incredible experience to go through. I just feel good about it because there were so many great plays in the game. Everyone contributed. The whole team really felt good about that game."

Indeed, the feat was a true team effort. Chuck Knoblauch, despite making 26 errors at second base this year, turned in a sparkling play up the middle to preserve Cone's perfecto while left fielder Ricky Ledee was literally blinded by the sun, but somehow managed to make a ninth-inning juggling catch to keep the gem intact.

Cone gave one of the game balls to his father, while the Hall of Fame in Cooperstown has another autographed game ball and Cone's game-worn jersey. He gave the items to Hall of Fame president Dale Petroskey in

David Cone Bio

Height: 6-foot-1; **Weight:** 190
Date of Birth: Jan. 2, 1963
Place of Birth: Kansas City, Mo.
Residence: Greenwich, Conn.
Bats: Left; **Throws:** Right
Years in Majors: 14
Career tidbits: 1990 NL strike out leader...1991 NL strike out leader...1994 AL Cy Young...Was among AL leaders in wins, winning percentage, strikeouts and ERA in 1998...His 20 wins tied a career-high, breaking the major league record for the longest stretch between 20-win seasons (was 20-3 in 1988 with the Mets).

pregame ceremonies at Yankee Stadium on Aug. 3.

"He was very cooperative, he loves the Hall of Fame," spokesman John Ralph said. "Right now these things are in the 1999 highlights exhibit. They'll stay there for the next couple of years. Later the ball will be put in our no-hitter exhibit that features every no-hitter since 1940."

Despite the demand for articles related to his achievement, Cone admits to not being a serious memorabilia collector.

"I probably should save more things, but I just save the things that mean something," he said. "Just special items, things from World Series games."

Cone grew up in Kansas City where he was a huge Royals fan and had cards of all his favorite players such as George Brett, Fred Patek and Dennis Leonard.

"I really thought he was a consummate professional and a great pitcher," he said. "I was it big Royals fan and followed them religiously.

"I certainly had baseball cards like every other kid but I never saved them. I really wish I would have."

To Cone, whose career was jeopardized by a 1996 aneurysm, just pitching in the big leagues is somewhat of a miracle let alone hurling a perfect game. It was the second serious opportunity he had at throwing a no-hitter.

On Sept. 2, 1996, Cone held the Oakland A's hitless for seven innings in his first outing since May after undergoing surgery to repair an aneurysm in his right arm. But skipper Joe Torre lifted him in that contest after 85 pitches rather than risking his long-term health.

"I was kind of doubtful whether I'd ever be in that position again," he said. "When I found myself there a second time the thought crossed my mind this might be my last chance."

His doctor had told him he'd be able to pitch again, but there were doubts in his mind because the operation was kind of precedent-setting.

Photo courtesy of New York Yankees

"I wasn't sure," Cone said. "It was a pretty rare condition. No one knew for sure, because there wasn't a lot of basis."

Surprisingly enough, he pulled off the perfect game feat despite a 33-minute rain delay.

"That was kind of key to the game that it didn't go on too long," he said. "Then I came out in the fourth inning after the delay and got a one-two-three inning, a real quick inning. I thought that was the key right there."

Plus, he had the comfort of working with an early Yankee lead.

Several little things worked in his favor that casual fans might not have noticed. For example, when catcher Joe Girardi came out in the late innings to warm up Cone between innings, he left his catcher's mask on.

"I was kind of surprised to see him warming me up with the mask on, because he rarely does that," he said. "It kind of gave me a little bit of a laugh, it broke the ice a little."

Since joining the Yankees, he's become one of the most popular players in pinstripes and has what might be considered a cult following among fans wearing trademark "Coneheads."

His 20 victories during the 1998 World Championship season solidified him as the team's top pitcher and he lived up to that billing during the postseason with triumphs over Texas and Cleveland that helped New York reach the Fall Classic.

This year he was another key reason the Yankees made it back to the World Series for the third time in four years.

"You just want to keep going," Cone said. "I certainly want to pitch more big games for the Yankees. You just never get tired of that. That never gets old. We had a good team again this year."

His one-year contract expired at season's end and he signed a new one-year extension to return to the Bronx in 2000.

Cone had many highlights from his days with the Mets, Royals and Blue Jays, but he considers being a Yankee the best part of his career.

"There's so much tradition, it's an honor to wear this uniform," he said. "I've had a chance to meet so many great former players. I've gotten to know Whitey Ford and Reggie Jackson comes around quite often. You only see that with the Yankees."

Some day, years from now, young Yankee hurlers will say the same thing about him.

Reflecting on his perfect game,

Cone couldn't help wondering about another strange twist of fate that day.

He threw 88 pitches and No. 8 was the uniform number worn by both Berra, who was honored that day, and fellow Hall of Fame Yankee catcher Bill Dickey.

"There's a lot of things that happened during the course of that game when you look at some of the numbers and some of the ironies," Cone said. "It really does give you a feeling that maybe there is something more going on here.

"It's more than ironic, it's eerie. There's no doubt about it. The odds are better winning the lottery than doing something like that. It's a day I'll never forget."

1998 Pacific Crown Collection

His teammates, particularly those who contributed most to the outcome, will cherish the memories, too.

Knoblauch recalled everything about his eighth-inning, hit-saving stab in the middle of the diamond.

"I think it was David's first two-ball count," he said. "I moved over to my left a little bit thinking the batter might try to cheat a little bit and pull the ball. He actually hit it pretty decent up the middle, two or three hard steps to my right. In that situation, with a no-hitter, you're thinking about diving and stopping any type of play you can.

"So I was really thinking about diving right away for any balls that weren't hit right at me. When he hit it I thought at first I might have to dive, but then I was fortunate enough to get over and backhand it on my feet. I was on the grass when I fielded it so I took just a little bit of time to make sure I was firmly planted. Then I turned and fired to first.

"It had rained a little that day so I really wanted to make sure I was able to make a good strong throw. It just took a split-second longer than I normally would, and everything worked out."

1999 Bowman

Brosius had the thrill of recording the game's final out. Seconds later, Cone fell to this knees in disbelief and was given a huge bear hug by Girardi as other Yankees piled on top in celebration.

"When the ball went up in the air, I was pretty excited for David most of all," Brosius said. "An opportunity like this is kind of a once-in-a-lifetime thing. A perfect game is something you're not sure you'll get to experience let alone twice in two consecutive years."

On May 17, 1998, he was manning the hot corner when David Wells recorded his flawless game for the Yankees.

Brosius said he wasn't really worried about dropping the last out.

"I wasn't nervous, I felt like the ball was going to be caught," he said. "That wasn't the problem. I just had to make sure I tempered my excitement until after I did catch the ball."

The contest involved a couple of firsts for other Yankees. Paul O'Neill became the first player in history ever to be on the winning end of three perfect games, while Joe Torre was the first skipper ever to manage two of them successfully.

In addition, the 36-year-old Cone became the second-oldest person ever to hurl a perfect game. Cy Young threw one at age 37.

Surprisingly, Cone struggled for the remainder of the regular season winning just two more games and winding up at 12-9 although his 3.44 ERA and 177 strikeouts ranked second and fourth in the American League, respectively.

He was called upon to help beat the Red Sox in the ALCS and won Game 2 at Yankee Stadium.

He's been coming up with big postseason performances throughout his career and has a 8-3 overall, including the Game 2 victory over Atlanta in this year's World Series. Cone has an outstanding career winning percentage with 180 regular-season victories against 102 defeats.

Another highlight from the 1999 season included winning New York's home opener against Detroit on April 9, holding the Tigers hitless through five innings. He also made his fifth All-Star appearance in relief of Boston Cy Young Award winner Pedro Martinez. Is Cone a candidate to reach Cooperstown's hallowed halls, too?

It's possible with a couple more solid seasons and there's little doubt he'd go in wearing a Yankee cap on his plaque.

Warner brewing up a storm in St. Louis

Rams QB has come long way since his days as a stockboy

By Tom Hultman

Kurt Warner has come a long way since his supermarket stockboy job in Cedar Falls, Iowa, in 1994.

The current St. Louis Rams phenom quarterback had just been waived by the Green Bay Packers after failing to crack their 53-man roster. Warner was stuck in the numbers game.

After all, the three quarterbacks ahead of him on the Packers' depth chart were Brett Favre, Mark Brunell and Ty Detmer. That's a tough nut to crack in anyone's book.

However, while he was making a measly $5.50 an hour at the grocery store, his dreams of playing professional football kept burning inside.

"At that point in time I wasn't happy about it (being waived)," the 28-year-old said in an exclusive phone interview. "I would have liked to have made it, but as I look back on the whole deal and see what the Lord had in store for me there was a reason that it happened the way it did."

Of course, no one at the grocery store would believe that the fellow who was stocking cans of Spaghetti-O's on shelves five years ago would lead the NFL with 41 touchdown passes and a quarterback rating of 109.2.

"The reason why I have gone the places I have gone and become the player I have become is He was just getting me ready for this time right now," said Warner, whose faith is as strong as his right arm.

Since 1995, Rams quarterback Kurt Warner has thrown for 239 touchdown passes, including a league-leading 41 in the 1999 season.

"I couldn't see that back then, but now when I look back there was definitely a reason for that happening."

Everyone seems to want to throw a party celebrating the undrafted free agent's surprise status as "the man" in St. Louis. He led the Rams – the losingest franchise of the 1990s – to a 13-3 record in 1999 and an NFC West Division title.

However, the former one-year starter at Division I-AA Northern Iowa will have nothing to do with it. The down-to-earth Warner said he's had a winning attitude throughout his career – from high school, college, the Arena League, NFL Europe and now in the NFL.

"I just think about going out and playing football and winning football games. I've done it for a long time and I didn't expect it to be any different when I got here," Warner said. "I expected to play well. I expected to lead my team and I expected to win. That's the mentality that I've had for a long time. I developed that through the Arena League and the World League and now in the NFL.

"I'm really not worried about taking it by storm or doing anything like that. I'm just concerned with winning football games."

It seems like winning is the only thing when it comes to football for Warner. In three years (1995-97), Warner paced the Arena League's expansion Iowa Barnstormers to 35 wins in 48 starts and Arena Bowl appearances in 1996 and '97.

He graduated from the Arena League to NFL Europe in 1998, where he starred for the Amsterdam Admirals and led them to a 7-3 record.

Warner credits his experience in both leagues with making him the quarterback he is

Kurt Warner Bio

Born: June 22, 1971, in Burlington, Iowa
Height: 6-foot-2
Weight: 220 pounds
College: Northern Iowa

Career TD passes at a glance

Arena League (1995-97): 183 in 40 games.
NFL Europe (1998): 15 in 10 games.
NFL (1998-99): 41 in 17 games.

Career passing yards

Arena League: 10,465 yards (completed 820 of 1,320 attempts).
NFL Europe: 2,101 yards (165 of 326).
NFL: 4,398 yards (329 of 510).

today. Looking back, if he would have made Green Bay's team in 1994, he would have been backing up Favre and never would have received the experience he gained by playing in 48 Arena and 10 NFL Europe games.

"I tell everybody that the biggest thing as a quarterback is the experience, playing football and facing a lot of different situations and being able to react to those different situations," he said.

"That's what I've been able to do by playing football. Instead of being a backup sitting on the bench, I've been out there playing and adjusting to things, seeing different things and reacting and being put in different situations and pressure. That, to me, is what a quarterback is all about is how you react to situations in a blink of an eye on the football field. There's no substitute for experience.

"You can watch as much film as you want and look at as much paper about your offense as you want, but until you get out there and run it there is no substitute for that. The number of games that I have played in over the past few years is no doubt instrumental in the success that I have had up to this point."

According to Warner, he developed his skills more in the Arena League, which allowed him to get used to the fast pace and tough situations that one finds on a 50-yard field.

"I fine tuned my skills towards the bigger field in NFL Europe," he said. "It gave me that transition period to make the adjustment from the small field to the big field and get comfortable with the skills and things I needed to do at that level before I got here."

So when multi-million dollar free-agent quarterback Trent Green ripped up his knee in an Aug. 28 pre-season game, everyone under the Rams' umbrella knew the team was in good hands with Warner, who had been the team's third-stringer in 1998.

"I told our team we could win with Kurt," St. Louis coach Dick Vermeil said in the Oct. 18 *Sports Illustrated*. "I didn't expect that he'd play well enough that we'd win because of him."

Warner came out of the chutes with guns-a-blazing, as he threw for three touchdowns in each of the first three games.

He followed that up with an exclamation point vs. San Francisco when he racked up five TD passes. From that point on, there was no denying that Warner was the real deal.

"Obviously the people around here believed in me and the skills that I have," he said. "Then again, the only thing that anybody questioned is how I would react under pressure and in a game situation because they hadn't seen me play at this level.

"They saw me in practice and they knew that I could do it in practice. They knew that I was intelligent that I could pick up the offense and I could make all the throws. They knew all that stuff and that's obviously the reason why I got the opportunity. It was just a matter of me going out and proving them right."

It also hasn't hurt Warner that Vermeil's wide-open offense features the speed-burning Isaac Bruce at wide receiver and the versatile Marshall Faulk at running back. The offense is obviously a natural fit for Warner's abilities.

"It's a great offense and it's more because I feel comfortable in it now. I feel like I can run it, like I don't have to think about anything I'm doing out there," he said. "I'm just playing football. I think any offense when you get to that point in it is a good offense for you. If you feel comfortable in it and you feel you can make all the throws

Continued on page 38

Kurt Warner appeared on this 1995 Barnstormers card (left).
Warner led the Barnstormers to the Arena Bowl in both 1996 and 1997. His 1996 and 1997 Arena League cards are pictured above (center and right).

Pacific hits paydirt with Warner rookie card in base brand set

By Tom Hultman

It's hard to believe that in today's football card hobby – where there's more than 50 football card sets to choose from – that a player can only be featured on one National Football League card.

Believe it or not, it happened to St. Louis quarterback Kurt Warner. Pegged to be Trent Green's backup with the Rams this season, no trading card company wanted to take a chance on the former Arena League player – except for Pacific Trading Cards.

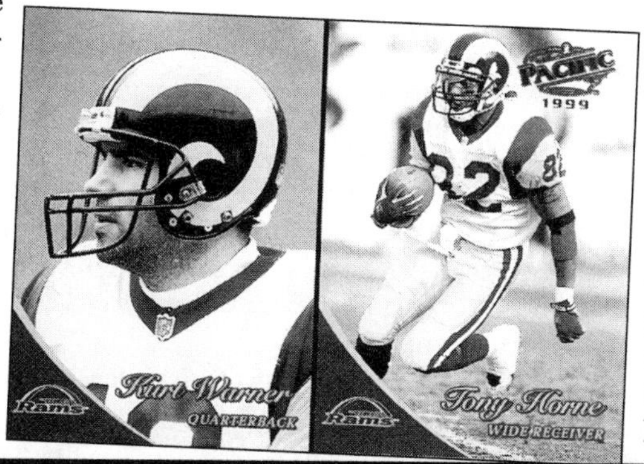

Pacific, of Lynnwood, Wash., took a flier on Warner in its 450-card base brand set, which was released May 26. Featured on card No. 343, Warner shares the card with teammate Tony Horne.

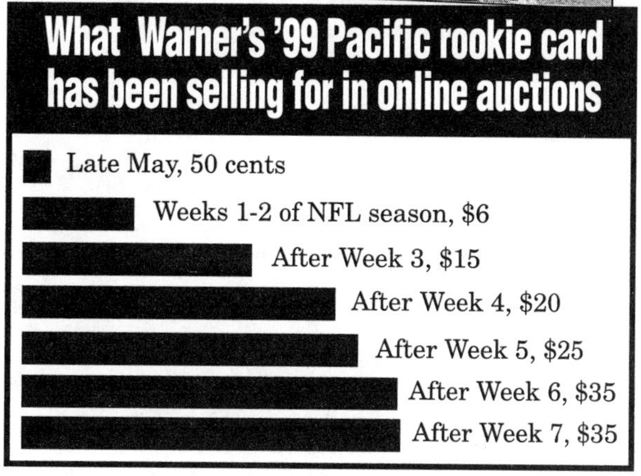

Warner's card has caught fire in the hobby recently. It debuted at 50 cents in May. At press time, the card was priced at $30 in *Sports Cards Magazine* and has sold for $35-$40 in online auctions. A PSA-10 version brought in $100 in a recent online auction.

"At the time that we put this set together, Kurt Warner wasn't the Kurt Warner we know today," Pacific spokesman Mike Monson said. "But every once in a while one of these guys breaks through, so we try to include as many different players as possible. When they pop through, they make a big impact."

When a reporter asked the very modest Warner about his thoughts on his first NFL card, he joked, "You mean my half of a card?

"I'm not surprised that there is only one card out there because up until last year nobody knew who I was. I'm assuming there will be a couple more coming out of me fairly quickly. It doesn't surprise me, it's just one of those things.

"I'm not really hung up on that and I think it is kind of funny that I only have half a card and it seems that everybody is talking about it this year. It's kind of neat at how things work out. I'm just sitting back and smiling and having a good time with it."

Actually, the time is now for hobbyists to get in on the ground floor of the Warner card bandwagon. Obviously, the Pacific card has been released, but collectors can also search for his three Arena Football League Iowa Barnstormer cards from 1995-97.

In addition, a Playoff Momentum SSD card No. 144, shipped Oct. 27.

Other Warner cards include:

Pacific: Warner appeared in Crown Royale on base card No. 116, along with chase set cards – Premium-Sized Cramer's Choice Awards No. 8, Century 21 No. 10, Card-Supials No. 17, Franchise Glory No. 19 and Premium-Sized Gold Crown Die-Cuts No. 6.

Playoff: Warner appeared in Donruss, Contenders, Leaf Rookies & Stars and Score Millennium.

Upper Deck: Warner appeared in '99 NFL Black Diamond as part of the "Diamond Skills" insert (1:29 packs) and in '99 Encore with both a regular card and an insert card.

Topps: Warner appeared in Bowman's Best as card No. 110.

Fleer/SkyBox: Warner appeared in Fleer Focus as basic card No. 40 along with the Feel The Game jersey card insert. He's also in SkyBox Molten Metal as basic card No. 93 and with an Autographics card.

Collector's Edge: Warner's first appearance was in First Place.

Warner estimated he had "a few thousand cards" in his collection as a child, but lost all of them during one of his moves.

"I ended up losing them or someone threw them out, so I

Continued on page 38

WARNER BREWING UP A STORM
Continued from page 36

and the reads, everything will just click for you.

"The offense really fits my style of play and what I like to do and what I have done in the past the way we go about things. I think that's why I have been able to flourish up to this point."

That's an understatement. The 6-foot-2, 220-pounder set an NFL record for throwing at least three touchdown passes in four consecutive games. Throwing for multiple touchdowns in games is nothing new for Warner, who racked up 183 in the AFL and 15 in NFL Europe.

Warner, however, isn't one to let all of the media attention go to his head. Through all of the records and the wins, Warner is the same old guy.

"The record was nice because it gave me a little notoriety, but the biggest thing I am worried about is winning football games," he said. "I know that if I'm throwing that many touchdown passes that we're putting the ball into the end zone and that's the main thing that I'm worried about."

With all the adversity Warner faced in his pro career, in addition to his one year as a starter at Northern Iowa, he said he never became frustrated with his situation.

He kept his dream alive even during those days as a stockboy at the supermarket. Warner said he kept his passing skills sharp during the day and stocked the shelves at night.

In fact, he stayed on an even keel when he was left unprotected by the Rams for the expansion draft after last season. However, the Browns passed on him and he returned to St. Louis.

"I was always hoping that I would get some opportunities and really get a legitimate chance, but I never got frustrated because I was enjoying playing and having a ball," he said. "I didn't know if my career would ever get to the NFL, so I wasn't going to get hung up on that and get frustrated with it. I was just going to live out the Lord's plan and follow whatever he had in store. There's obviously a reason why he wanted me there and I just waited my turn until I got this opportunity."

That Curt Warner was a running back, not a quarterback

It took a while for Kurt Warner to make a name for himself, but today nobody is mistaking the quarterback for Curt Warner the running back, who played with Seattle (1983-89) and the Los Angeles Rams in 1990.

There was, however, one person who mixed the two up last season. Last season Warner the quarterback was invited to appear on a radio show to talk about a game from his past.

"Last year I did get a request to be on a radio show and talk about the 1983 Sugar Bowl," he said. "I told him I was 12 at the time and I'd be happy to talk about it. That's the only request I ever got for the other Curt Warner.

"Actually, I did get a chance to talk to him about it the other day and we had a good laugh about it."

PACIFIC PAYDIRT
Continued from page 37

don't do that anymore," he said. "I did that as a kid because I was such a big sports fan that I liked to follow football and I had a lot of cards at that time."

He said he didn't focus on rookie cards or what cards were valued at during his childhood. Basically, he wanted to fill his collection with Dallas Cowboys cards.

"I was just trying to collect cards of guys that I liked," he said. "I was a big Cowboys fan, so I had players like 'Too Tall' Jones, Roger Staubach and Tony Dorsett and guys like that. That was what I geared my collection toward. It wasn't the rookie cards, but more trying to get the Cowboys because that was my team as a kid."

Even though Warner doesn't collect cards, he has saved many pieces of memorabilia from his career, including jerseys from every team he has played with.

"I've kept certain things like different Arena championship programs and different things of the milestones that I have reached along the way like the jerseys and helmets of this team or that team," he said. "I've collected little pieces of memorabilia that were significant throughout my career."

The hobby-friendly Warner said he enjoys signing autographs.

"The fans are really what make us go and take care of us with everything," he said. "I don't mind signing autographs, especially for kids who look up to us and use us as role models. It's nice to go out there and have people look up to you and try to be a good role model for everyone that's out there."

Unfortunately, he has been a bit slow when it comes to signing autograph requests through the mail.

As one can imagine, the requests have grown exponentially with his touchdown passes and with each Rams victory.

"It's been kind of crazy," he said "Unfortunately, I haven't really been able to respond to too many of them yet. Eventually I'll get back to all of them, but I just haven't had the opportunity as of yet.

"I have been busy with all the things going on, but eventually I'll get to them and get the requests done."

Piazza hits for power and average in New York

Decision was right to stay with the Mets

By Ed Lucas and Paul Post

Baseball's highest paid catcher certainly doesn't need memorabilia to enhance his financial portfolio.

After signing a seven-year deal worth $91 million, the New York Mets' Mike Piazza should be set for more than a few lifetimes.

But the All-Star backstop appreciates items he can collect from some of the game's other great players.

"I have a few things I try to keep around," he said. "I've got a few card sets from the 1970s when I was a kid. It's like anything. I grab a few things but I'm not really a fanatic about it."

His approach to memorabilia mirrors his personality – relaxed.

However, it's just the opposite of his approach to baseball, which he works at with single-minded intensity.

In 1999, Piazza hit .303 with 40 home runs and 124 RBI. His career batting average is .328. On top of that, during his first eight years in the big leagues he's hammered 240 home runs.

Putting things in perspective, his average is better than that of Wade Boggs, who is considered one of the premier contact hitters in recent baseball history.

But Piazza is adding power statistics

Mike Piazza hit .303 with 40 home runs and 124 RBI during the 1999 baseball season.

Mike Piazza bio

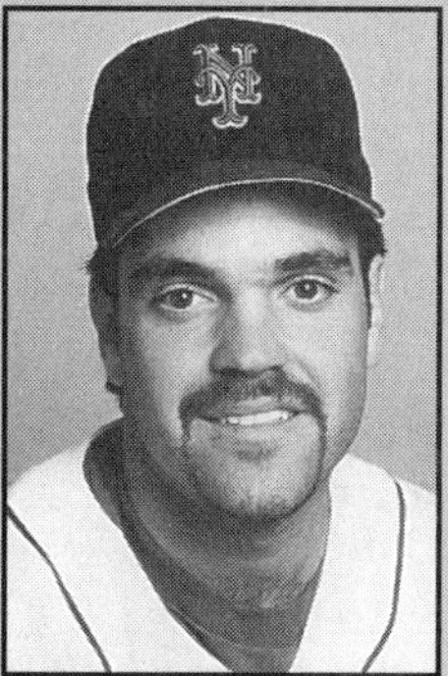

Height: 6-foot-3; **Weight:** 200
Date of Birth: Sept. 4, 1968
Place of Birth: Norristown, Pa.
Residence: Valley Forge, Pa.
Bats: Right; **Throws:** Right
Years in Majors: 8
Position: Catcher
Career tidbits: Only player in Major League Baseball history to slam at least 35 home runs in a season as a catcher on more than one occasion, Piazza has accomplished it four times....Passed Dolph Camill, Dusty Baker and Willie Davis to move into eighth place on the Dodgers' all-time career homer list.

with the best of them. New York ballclubs have had a tradition of great catchers from Ernie Lombardi to Bill Dickey, Yogi Berra, Roy Campanella and Gary Carter.

Unless his career suddenly falters, Piazza could eventually outshine them all before reaching the hallowed halls of Cooperstown.

"You've had a few great catchers. Piazza hits with the best of them," Ted Williams said recently. "(Few) catchers in history are capable of winning a batting crown. Piazza's one of them. A dangerous, dangerous hitter any way you look at him."

That's a pretty high compliment coming from someone generally considered as baseball's all-time greatest hitter.

But anyone who knows anything about baseball knows that Piazza is the real deal when it comes to hitting and handling pitchers.

It's surprising considering that he was a 62nd round draft choice of the Dodgers. In fact, the team wouldn't have signed him at all except that former manager Tommy Lasorda knew Piazza's family and pushed for it as a personal favor.

2000 Topps Power Player No. 14

The 6-foot-3, 215-pound backstop has certainly proved scouts wrong since being named National League Rookie of the Year in 1993.

He has never hit less than .303 and has hit no fewer than 32 home runs in six of his seven complete major league seasons.

His greatest year so far was in 1997 when he hit an incredible .362 with 40 home runs and 124 RBI. His average was the highest ever by a Los Angeles hitter and he became only the third catcher in National League history to reach 40 round trippers.

In 1998, even the mailman had a hard time keeping track of Piazza's whereabouts as he bounced from the Dodgers to Marlins and then to the Mets.

At first, it looked as though he might be headed elsewhere as a free agent following the season, but Shea Stadium's faithful carried huge placards and posters throughout the second half of the season urging the team's front office to keep Piazza in New York.

They obliged by signing him to the richest contract in baseball history, one that will pay him an average of $13 million per year.

1999 Fleer Mystique No. 98

He proved his value to the Mets by almost helping them reach post-season play for the first time since 1988. New York had a shot at a wild card berth until the next-to-last day of the season when Atlanta eliminated them, sending the Chicago Cubs and San Francisco into a one-game playoff.

Personal goals aside, Piazza wants nothing more than to prove his true worth by keeping a World Championship team in New York, but not the Yankees.

2000 Pacific Private Stock No. 94

Before 1999, the closest he's gotten to that ultimate baseball dream was with the 1995 and '96 Dodger teams that won the NL West.

"When we won the division in '95 it was really exciting," he said. "That was the first time I had a chance to celebrate, and have a champagne party in the big leagues. I hope one day soon I get to experience that in the World Series.

"That's the most exciting thing about what we're doing, getting to a World Series and winning it."

Piazza enjoys playing in the National League. He said his favorite stadium to play in is Montreal, while his least-favorite ballpark is Wrigley Field.

"I haven't hit that well (at Wrigley Field)," he said. "That might be hard for some people to believe, but I don't see the ball that well there.

"One of the best places I like to hit is Montreal. I've hit really well up there. I guess it's all individual. Some guys hit well some places, other guys don't hit well other places."

However, he refused to discuss the pitchers he enjoys most.

"It's kind of taboo to discuss who you like to hit off," Piazza said. "Because then they start being able to get you out. So I try to stay away from that subject. I respect all pitchers. When they have a ball in their hand they're all capable of throwing a good game on one night or another.

"There are pitchers who are really tough to hit all the time. I know after three or four pitches whether or not I'm going to like hitting off a guy. But it seems to go in cycles. Some days or some years they seem to get you out more consistently, then some years they don't."

The Norristown, Pa., native said he's not very superstitious compared to some ballplayers.

"Maybe if I'm going good I'll try to do the same things I did the previous day," he said. "Maybe I'll eat at the same place or something silly like that. But I'm not as fanatic as some guys are. Some guys are really superstitious."

2000 Ultra Diamond Mine No. 6

At age 31, Piazza has a maturity that makes him a clubhouse leader other players look up to. This is extremely important on a team such as the Mets where younger players need a winning role model to follow.

His philosophy is simple.

"Try to keep your nose clean and work hard," he said. "Moderation is the key to life. You can do things but make sure you get your work done. Try to get the most out of life. There's no secret to being happy. You have to work hard, set goals and have some resiliency and initiative.

"You have to do the best you can to get the most out of your ability no matter what it is, whether you're a ballplayer, doctor or construction worker."

Last summer, Piazza played in his sixth straight All-Star Game at Coors Field in Denver.

"I always enjoy it," he said. "It's a great honor to get there. But I don't think it should be a major deal if some guys can't make it. It's just one of those things. If a guy doesn't feel like participating, that's fine. If he wants to, that's great, too."

In some ways, his approach to handling the National League's best pitchers is almost humorous.

"I just wing it basically," Piazza said with a smile. "Being a hitter, I remember how they throw and how they pitch to me so I use that as a guideline to catch them. Most of the guys you're pretty familiar with so that's just something you enjoy."

Before coming to the Mets, one of the big question marks surrounding Piazza was how he'd get along with Todd Hundley, a former All-Star who set a major league record for most home runs in a season by a catcher. Ironically, Hundley is with the Dodgers this season. There was concern that friction between the two players could hurt the team internally. But Piazza credited Hundley for smoothing his entry to Shea Stadium last year.

"I can only say that if one day the roles were reversed I'd want to handle the situation with the class that Todd's handled it," Piazza said. "Todd and I are friends. We maintained that when I got here. It wasn't a problem. He didn't look at me with any resentment.

1999 SkyBox Premium No. 292

"One thing you have to know in this game is that there's always someone ready to take your place. No one's bigger than the game. Todd told me, 'God bless you. You earned every penny. Don't worry about me, I'm going to be fine.'

"Now all I'm going to do is go out and be the best player I can be."

He had the option of testing the free agent market but felt New York was where he wanted to spend the next seven years. "It wasn't really a hard decision to make because everything was laid out for me," Piazza said. "You just know when things are right and so the decision was not really hard to make. It wasn't a question of money, it was a question of, 'Will things work out here.' The challenges are still there, but you just know in your heart when it's meant to be."

Piazza tries to be an ambassador of baseball by signing autographs

In addition to being a star on the field, Mike Piazza also tries to be a baseball ambassador away from the ballpark by signing autographs whenever called upon.

"I try to do what I can," he said. "Of course there's times when I'm not always in the best of moods, or when we're traveling somewhere and we have to be someplace. We can't always stop, but you try to be as accommodating as you can. I sign when I can."

In addition, he's aware of the memorabilia industry's pitfalls.

"Unfortunately, there's a lot of counterfeits out there, too. That's a big problem," Piazza said. "People are buying autographed jerseys for $700 or $800. If there's a counterfeit signature, it's unfortunate that people are investing money and that it's not authentic. Unfortunately, there's no way to control it, so you're always going to have that sort of thing.

"One problem with the industry is that it's unregulated and it's nearly impossible to tell what's real and not real."

'Wally World' takes his jump shot to Minnesota

Szczerbiak hopes to become a household name on NBA scene

By Rick Firfer

Basketball fans have just called him "Wally" throughout his career. After all, when your last name is spelled with a couple of "z's" and a "c," many people would rather call you by your first name than butcher your last name.

However, there is no doubt that when the 1999-2000 National Basketball Association season is over fans across the nation will know how to pronounce — and most likely spell — "Szczerbiak."

Through 11 games this season, he ranked 19th in the NBA in field goal percentage (.508) and recorded a career high 26 points vs. Portland Nov. 24. His scoring average is 14.1 points per game

Szczerbiak, the 6-foot-8 phenom out of the University of Miami-Ohio, burst onto the scene during the last season's NCAA Tournament when he averaged 30 points per game in three contests, including 24 in an upset win over Utah and 43 points in a triumph over Washington.

As a senior, he posted 24.2 ppg and 8.5 rebounds, while shooting 52 percent from the field and 83 percent from the line.

Seeing what Szczerbiak — who *Sports Illustrated* dubbed "Wally World" in a cover story last season — could do in the tournament and during the pre-draft workouts was enough for Minnesota Timberwolves general manager Kevin McHale and coach Flip Saunders. They grabbed the shooter with the sixth pick overall.

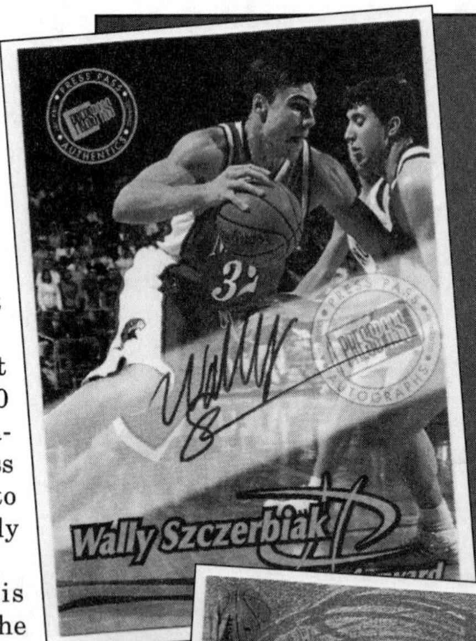

Pictured starting from top: 1999-2000 SkyBox NBA Hoops, Press Pass Autographed Authentics and Full Court Press cards.

"I think they were impressed with my defense, speed and quickness, quite honestly," he said on NBA.com. "I remember afterwards I was talking with the tape coordinator and one of the scouts and they were really impressed with how quick I defended. I matched up against Ron Artest when I worked out there and he is one of the best defenders in the country and he's really a quick guy for a guy our size.

"They were impressed with the way I moved, defended, competed and banged in the post and defended the perimeter. I think they were the one team that realized that I could be quick and athletic."

Minnesota was so impressed that the powers-that-be are hoping that playing Szczerbiak alongside Kevin Garnett will take some of the pressure off the rookie and allow him to look for his patented jump shot. There's not doubt that the T-Wolves could use his outside shooting immediately.

According to Szczerbiak, he's had a blast playing alongside Garnett in the Minnesota lineup.

"It's great. I'm having a lot of fun and adjusting well," he said. "I am enjoying playing with Kevin Garnett in particular. I really fit in with the team and everything is going real, real well.

"I am learning from the veterans, but basically I am playing hard and trying to do well night in and night out. I have to adjust to back-to-back games."

Wally followed in his father Walt's footsteps, as Walt was chosen by the Phoenix Suns with the 65th overall pick in the 1971 NBA Draft. Walt poured in 49 points in a spring scrimmage, but was later cut by the Suns. Walter later played with the ABA's Pittsburgh Condors and led Real Madrid to three European and three World Championships.

Meanwhile, Wally, who was born in Madrid, Spain, knew that one day he would make his dad proud by making a splash in the NBA.

As a youngster, Szczerbiak said his sports heroes were Larry Bird and Dave Kingman.

"I used to enjoy watching them play very much," he said.

That's how Szczerbiak learned the correct way of playing ball by watching his father play in pickup games, seeing the All-Stars play in person and leaving the athletes alone by not asking for autographs.

"I did go to a number of baseball games, but no, I was not one to chase after autographs," he said. "I just liked watching the guys play. I guess what I wanted was to be one of those guys one day, so it never occurred to me to bother them for autographs.

"My family and I went to a number of All-Star games and we used to stay in the same hotels with the players and I watched how they handled themselves, but to me they were just normal people and I saw no reason to bother them."

However, the forward said he doesn't mind signing for fans or collectors.

"I think it is an honor to sign autographs, especially for little kids," he said. "You know, it makes their day, and that is really nice. It is an honor to have those kids looking up to me.

"I am just very glad that I have been put into this position where people ask me for an autograph. I don't mind signing several items as long as the people are polite about it."

In fact, his mailbox has already been filling with fan mail.

"I have been getting fan mail, which I appreciate. But it is tough to answer it all, so I answer what I can."

— Wally Szczerbiak

"Yes, I have been getting fan mail, which I appreciate," he said. "But it is tough to answer it all, so I answer what I can and hope people understand if it takes awhile. As for multiple requests, I don't mind signing several things as long as it doesn't get out of hand.

"My experience with collectors so far has been that they are very polite and kind, so I guess if it stays that way there really is not much I can say."

Szczerbiak, who has saved a few pieces of memorabilia from his career so far, is involved in community outreach programs.

"I try to help with charitable activities as much as I can," he said. "It is important to get involved with helping others in that way."

Wally Szczerbiak Bio

Full Name: Walter (Wally) Robert Szczerbiak
Birthdate: March 5, 1977
Height: 6-foot-8;
Weight: 243 pounds
Birthplace: Madrid, Spain
High School: Cold Spring Harbor (N.Y.)
College: Miami (Ohio)
Position: Forward
Inside the numbers: Finished college career by scoring in double figures in 39 consecutive games... Unanimous selection as MAC Player of the Year as a senior...Led all NCAA Tournament scorers with 30-point average and was named to Midwest Regional all-tournament team...Miami's all-time leader in three-point FG percentage at .431...Named Second Team All-America by the Associated Press as a senior... Second on Miami's career list in scoring with 1,847 points, behind Ron Harper's 2,377 points...Second player in Miami history (joining Harper) to surpass 1,500 points, 500 rebounds and 200 assists.
Pro tidbits: Through 11 games, he ranked 19th in the NBA with a field goal percentage of .508...Hit 26 points vs. Portland Nov. 24...Made his NBA debut, scoring seven points and grabbing five rebounds in a 100-95 loss to Sacramento Nov. 5.

1999 a baseball honeymoon for Rookie of the Year Beltran

1st rookie since Lynn to drive in 100 runs

By Chuck Greenwood

Baseball is a game of numbers, which are so prominent in the history of the sport, they often make more meaning to fans than the names of the people who accomplished those numbers.

It was only fitting that rookie centerfielder Carlos Beltran was on his honeymoon when he learned that he had been selected as the American League Rookie of the Year.

After all, the past year has been a "baseball honeymoon" for the switch-hitting Kansas City Royal, who was a near-unanimous choice for the honor.

Beltran is the first rookie in 24 years to drive in at least 100 runs. Fred Lynn was the last rookie to accomplish the feat. In major league history only eight rookies have topped the century mark in both categories.

The Manati, Puerto Rico, native's numbers include a .293 batting average, 22 home runs, 108 RBI, 112 runs and 27 steals in 35 attempts.

Previous Royal winners were Lou Piniella in 1969 and Bob Hamelin in 1994. Beltran started the 1998 season at Class-A Wilmington, before being promoted to Double A Wichita in mid-season.

After hitting .352 for the Wranglers, he received a September callup to the big leagues on Sept. 14, 1998. He made his debut that night, scoring two runs and collecting his first major league hit off of Oakland's Buddy Groom.

Carlos Beltran's 1999 Bowman card is one of the Rookie of the Year that appears on many collectors' want lists.

Beltran was the Royals second-round pick in the 1995 June Free Agent Draft. Annually, he has been selected by Baseball America as one of the Royals' top prospects, highlighted by being named their top prospect last winter.

SCD: This has certainly been quite an experience for the past 1½ years.

BELTRAN: It sure has. I was in Wilmington and I got to move up last year to Double-A at the All-Star break. I finished in the big leagues as they called me up in September.

It was fun, and a great year for me. I worked very hard. I did everything right and that's the reason I am here.

SCD: What do you remember about your first game in the major leagues?

BELTRAN: My first day in the majors was amazing. I was excited that first day, and nervous too. There was a little bit of pressure.

I was trying to do good and show them that I did come to the big leagues to play. I'm glad that I have the opportunity to play every day.

I was a leadoff man in the beginning when the season started. Now they have me in the second spot, so I feel good that I have a lot of at bats.

Carlos Beltran bio

Height: 6-foot-0; **Weight:** 175
Date of Birth: April 24, 1977
Place of Birth: Manati, Puerto Rico
Residence: Manati, Puerto Rico
Bats: Switch; **Throws:** Right
Years in Majors: Two
Career tidbits: Had first major league hit off of Oakland's Buddy Groom...First rookie in 24 years to drive in at least 100 runs (Fred Lynn was the last rookie to accomplish the feat)...Was third Royals player to be named Rookie of the Year. Lou Piniella earned the award in 1969, while Bob Hamelin was selected in 1994.

SCD: How tough of an adjustment was it for you jumping from Single-A to Double-A, and then to the majors, so quickly?

BELTRAN: The biggest adjustment of being in the big leagues is that you have to be more consistent.

You have to make adjustments every time at bat. You have to be more patient at the plate. You also have to look for pitches that you can drive to the outfield and try to get good hits.

You have to work hard and I have been since last year at Wilmington, coming to the field early to work on my hitting and defense.

SCD: As a youngster growing up in Puerto Rico, who were your sports heroes?

BELTRAN: My favorite hero was Roberto Clemente. I never saw him play, but I read about him a lot. He was a great outfielder, a great player.

He was the best hero then. The other hero that I did get the chance to see play was Bernie Williams. He's a good centerfielder and that is my position.

I like to watch him play. I got my first chance in 1995 to see him play in Puerto Rico in winter ball. He was with our team. I really have learned a lot from him.

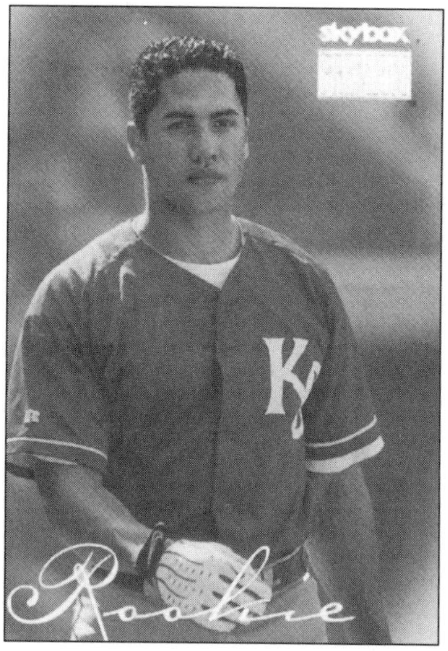

1999 SkyBox Premium

SCD: What do you do to relax when you are at home in the off-season?

BELTRAN: When I'm away from baseball, I like to go to the beach because I live in Puerto Rico. I like to fish with my dad and spend time with my family, going to see the town, going to the beaches. I also just like to relax and stay at home. I don't do much.

That's Juan Beltran pictured on Carlos' 1995 Topps Traded rookie

It's a case of a mistaken identity on Carlos Beltran's 1995 Topps Traded rookie card.

If you have that card in your collection, you're probably wondering why he doesn't look the same these days.

The American League Rookie of the Year said it is not him but Juan Beltran pictured on that card, which is currently valued at $20.

In many instances, Carlos Beltran has refused to autograph that card.

The entire '95 Topps Traded Baseball set is valued at $50.

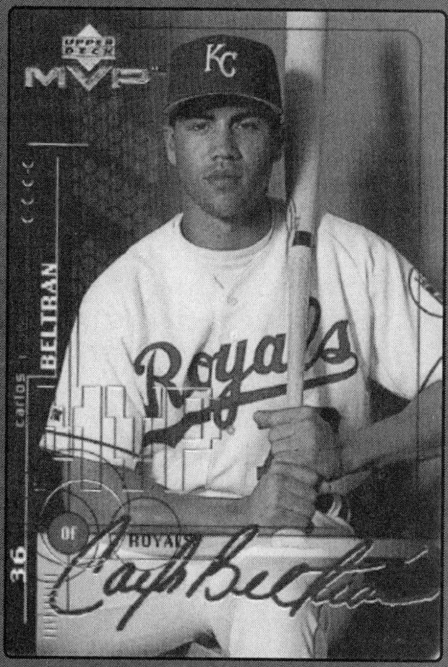

Upper Deck MVP

Signing autographs via mail, at hotel still fun for Beltran

When you're the Rookie of the Year you become a marked man for collectors.

"Yeah, I have to sign a lot of autographs," Carlos Beltran said. "Everywhere I go I have to sign an autograph. They wait for us at the hotel. People send cards and pictures. I like that because it is fun, and the fact that people recognize me and what kind of player I am."

SCD: Do you remember the first time you ever saw yourself on a baseball card?

BELTRAN: That was in 1995. I was like, "Look at me. I'm here on this baseball card!" It is fun because they can see you and they know who you are.

If they buy the cards they know who you are, and they know where you're from, and they know everything about you.

SCD: Even though you've only been in the majors for a relatively short while, have you started to collect any memorabilia?

BELTRAN: Yeah, I've got the balls from my first hit in the majors and my first home run. I've got my first bat, too, that I used in the big leagues. I've also have my glove. I've got everything at my house.

Members of 3,000-Hit Club gather for Atlantic City show

All living members of elite group attend

By Michael Stadnicki

The benchmark of hitting prowess in Major League Baseball is 3,000 hits. "The elite," remarked member George Brett who had 3,154 hits during his career in Kansas City. Tony Gwynn kept looking at the poster saying, "Look who I'm in the company of." The select "Lumber Fraternity" welcomed newcomers Gwynn and Wade Boggs to the hitters inner circle at the 3,000-Hit Show presented by Pastime Productions. The event was held Oct. 22-24 at Bally's Park Place, a Hilton Casino Resort in Atlantic City.

It may have been a coincidence but Stephen Hisler of Pastime Productions said 3,000 people attended the three-day memorabilia show and signing. "I'm very pleased," said Hisler. "It was a larger crowd than I anticipated. Saturday, we kept going from the time we opened up."

George Brett

Early Saturday there was a crowd forming as people were buying their autograph tickets. There was a buzz in the air. It was the kind of buzz you hear when collectors get excited about an event. On Sunday morning there were lines for most of the players as collectors worked to complete 3,000 hit items.

Robin Yount

Some collectors were there to add individual items to their collections. Many had tickets for Boggs and Gwynn. There were oversized flats, some 500-HR Club pieces and 3,000-Hit Club posters by Do S. Oh from a previous show.

The '99 show poster was created by well-known sports artist, Ron Lewis. The 15 living members are featured in front of a dugout, similar to the last Lewis 3,000-Hit show poster. Gwynn and Boggs are seated on the bench on opposite sides of Pete Rose. The remaining members of the club are kneeling or standing. It's another classic Lewis work.

Mike Stadnicki photos

Pete Rose, the leader of the 3,000-Hit Club, was on hand earlier than originally scheduled on Sunday so that he could make it to Atlanta to be honored for MLB's All-Century Team.

In the stands among the fans are members of the Boggs, Brett and RobinYount families.

The public purchased about 200 autograph tickets for posters. "This was a big bat show," Hisler remarked. Young Bat Co. of Brevard, N.C., made a limited-edition 3,000-Hit Club bat numbered 1-60. These bats were given to the players and sold through mail order. "The bat is two-toned with a natural wood handle and a walnut finish on the barrel," explained company spokesman Christopher T. Young. "I saw one autographed and it was beautiful."

A unique piece was a bat featuring the etched portraits of all the living club members. Young Bat Co. also makes gamers for Gwynn, Boggs, Cal Ripken, Sammy Sosa and Mark McGwire.

Gwynn was the top signer according to Hisler, as he reportedly signed 2,000 items. Boggs was

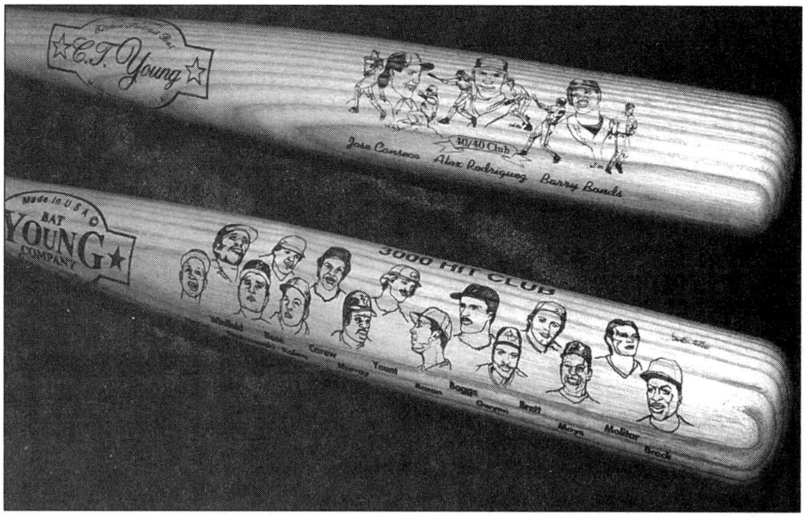

The Young Bat Co. of Brevard, N. C., produced these two commemorative bats to honor the 40/40 and the 3,000-Hit Clubs.

next autographing 1,800 pieces. These totals include mail order and the private signings completed at the event.

Autograph fees ranged from $20 for Al Kaline to $75 for Willie Mays and Brett. Most fees were in the $40 range.

Hank Aaron, Mays and Stan Musial signed on Saturday only at tables on the showroom floor. The other remaining players with the exception of Pete Rose, signed in an adjacent room. Rose signed separately on Sunday only.

Rose was originally set to sign from noon to 3 p.m., but would not have made it to Atlanta for the World Series game where he was to be honored as part of the All-Century Team. Rose signed from 10 a.m. until noon instead. He's slated to sign at the Yankee Perfect Game Pitchers show, Nov. 13-14, in Stamford, Conn., for those who missed him.

Bally's held a dinner Saturday evening for invited guests. Spencer Ross, play-by-play announcer for the New York Jets and New Jersey Nets, introduced the members of the 3,000-Hit Club. The players posed for pictures with those in attendance.

Success at the Plate

Gwynn, who has played his entire career with the San Diego Padres, collected his 3,000th hit in Montreal off Dan Smith on Aug. 6. It was a four-hit night for him. Boggs, who played for the Boston Red Sox, New York Yankees and now the Tampa Bay Devil Rays, stroked a home run off Cleveland's Chris Haney for No. 3,000 the next day, Aug. 7. Boggs expressed his joy by planting a kiss on home plate. All weekend long in Atlantic City the two were referred to as "the rookies."

Gwynn and Boggs bring the 3,000-Hit Club total to a total of 23 major leaguers. The 15 living members all attended the show. The schedule was tight as Aaron, Mays, Musial and Rose had to get to Atlanta for Game 2 of the World Series on Sunday. The four were named to the All Century team.

This "Who's Who of Hitting" can be looked at from the perspective of who isn't in the club. There is no Mickey Mantle or Joe DiMaggio. No Babe Ruth or Lou Gehrig. No Ted Williams or Rogers Hornsby. All of these baseball legends were great players but they didn't reach the 3,000-hit pinnacle.

Hitting the ball out of the park scores runs but still only counts as one hit. Aaron, Mays and Eddie Murray are the only select members of both the 500-HR and 3,000-Hit Clubs.

Longevity is a key ingredient to attaining this achievement. Brett, Lou Brock, Roberto Clemente, Gwynn, Kaline, Musial, Carl Yastrzemski and Robin Yount all played for just one team during their careers.

Cap Anson and Clemente each had an even 3,000 hits. The "Hit King" is Pete Rose with an astounding 4,256. Rose talked before he left for Atlanta, where he would step on the diamond for the first time in 10 years as a member of the All-Century Team. "This is a great honor to be named to the team," he said. "It makes all the dedication and hard work worth it — just to be mentioned in the same breath. You're with the elite. I feel bad that Tris Speaker can't be there, Babe Ruth or Lou Gehrig. It would be nice to meet the guys who paved the way," he said.

Rose said the night would mean more to his 15-year-old son and 10-year-old daughter who were too young to see him play.

Rose recalled the nine-minute ovation he received when he broke Ty Cobb's record. He hoped the reception in Atlanta would be warm and cordial. "It'll be a festive night."

Will this open the door a little more for possible reinstatement? "We'll worry about that battle when it approaches," he answered.

As a player, Rose had an insatiable drive for hitting a baseball. "I was hungry," he admitted. "You have to keep yourself hungry. If I was 3-for-3, I wanted to be 4-for-4 or 5-for-5. I tried to get a hit every time. You have to be born with that desire and determination.

"I wasn't a guess hitter. I looked for a guy's hardest pitch. You adjust to the other stuff."

His advice to young players is to work hard and practice right. "Like any other craft you have to work at it," he suggested.

Rose gave this analogy about hitting and other sports. "If Brett Favre hit three out of 10 passes and Michael Jordan made three out of 10 shots, how good are they?

If you get three hits out of 10 at bats, you're hitting .300. It's a tough game."

Murray credits his family with giving him the initiative to work hard. There was a lot of competition with four brothers in the family and three of them are older than Eddie. "We played a lot of games." he said. "It made you tough and built a lot of character."

Murray said that hitting starts in the dugout. "You watch the pitcher and try to pick up something you can use. Watch the position of his hands when he starts his windup. Where is it different? Look for the edge."

When asked what's more of an achievement for Murray, 500 homers or 3,000 hits, he answered, "I really didn't think I'd do either," he said. "It's probably, 500 home runs. It's not something I dreamed of. I dreamed of playing on TV and being in the big leagues."

He'll take that edge and the knowledge of a major league career to the Arizona Fall League where he will manage the Scottsdale Scorpions. The team is made up of prospects from the Orioles, Diamondbacks, Tigers, Marlins and Mets.

"I was talking to some of the guys here and it's tough to work with kids. I don't think they have that love for the game," Murray remarked.

What does he think about the autograph industry? "It's crazy," he said. "There's a lot of fake stuff out there. Some people aren't honest. If I stand outside the ballpark and sign there's always someone you miss. You can't sign them all."

Rod Carew said that players take a bad rap for not signing. "You see items out there being sold," Carew said. "Kids are taking them to guys in cars who will turn around and sell them. It's a business. I don't sign at the park anymore. Kids should collect for fun and to learn about the history of the game." Carew only does about two shows a year and indicated it may be less in the future.

Carew recommends that hitters focus on the pitcher. "Block out everything but the pitcher," he suggested. "Watch the windup and pick up where the ball is released. You know where the ball comes from. Set your back foot. Don't allow anything to come into your mind, just see the ball."

He played off his back foot and would open or close his stance. "Your first at bat will tell you if you're going to do well. I never worried if I was in a slump. I could always drop a few bunts for hits.

"Players today need to swing the bat more," he continued. "Too many hitters go up guessing. You need discipline for success. You have to work at it. You can't rely on ability alone."

Lou Brock played with fluidity on the bases and at the plate. He speaks about hitting like the poetry in motion he was on the field. "You have to dehumanize the pitch and take the personality out of it." said Brock. "You take the Ryan or the Koufax out of the ball and see it as a 108-seam, white sphere that weighs 4½ ounces. Hit that object, not the personality.

"Identify the pitch. Once the pitcher releases it, he can't recall it. Focus is critical to concentration. The key word is the ball. Create concentration and increase it. Dehumanize the pitch. See the ball and track it to the contact zone. Try to stay within yourself. Prepare to attack the ball.

"If you don't hit, you don't play. When the bat hits the ball there is a distinct sound. I fell in love with that sound and had a passion to hear it. As a boy I walked miles to hear that sound."

Ron Lewis' 3,000-Hit Club art illustrates members of Boggs, Brett and Yount families in the background.

Atlanta Hosts 20th National Convention

By Greg Ambrosius

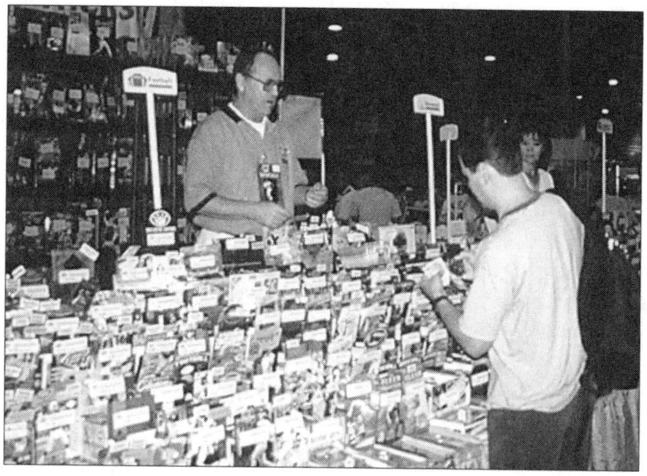

Floor traffic at the 1999 National Convention was considered to be lower than other recent Nationals.

In the 20-year history of the National Sports Collectors Convention, only five cities have hosted the National more than once. Usually, that's a sign of respect for that city, a sign of prosperity for the hobby.

The cities that have hosted the National multiple times include Anaheim, St. Louis, Chicago, Arlington and Atlanta. Anaheim and Chicago have hit grand slams the eight times they've hosted the National, while St. Louis and Arlington have hit home runs the four times they've been host sites.

But Atlanta has struck out twice, including the most recent attempt July 22-25 at the World Congress Center. This year's attendance was noticeably lower than recent Nationals in Chicago and Cleveland, and even lower than in 1992 when Atlanta hosted its first National. Sorry, two strikes and you're out when it comes to hosting the hobby's main event.

"I just don't think that the South – same thing with Texas – has enough hard-core collectors to mix with the new crowd to make a successful National to support 1,100 tables," said Alan "Mr. Mint" Rosen, a veteran of 18 Nationals. "But you know what? We have to take our show everywhere. We have to try new places, but you also have to try proven places. We tried the National Convention here twice, and it's only been so-so twice. I think we have to look elsewhere."

The Atlanta National certainly set a record in one regard: number of booths. More than 1,200 booths were spaced throughout the massive World Congress Center, taking up an additional 150,000 square feet compared to last year's Chicago National. That resulted in plenty of dealer-to-dealer activity for the record number of exhibitors.

"It's been a good show, both buying and selling," said Kevin Savage of Maumee, Ohio. "It's good for the people in the South because they get the opportunity to go to a National, but there's just fewer of them who attend here. The good thing is that at least the people who were here were active."

But many dealers were extremely disappointed by the low turnaround and disappointed that the hobby's featured event was even back in Atlanta. "This was the worst National we've ever done," said Joe Donato, a member of the National's board of directors who was attending his seventh National. "The crowds were horrible. There's no money in Atlanta."

Dealer-to-dealer activity was so strong – and walkup traffic so small at times – that Rosen said over 60 percent of his purchases were from fellow exhibitors. The veteran dealer admitted that he had his fourth best National ever, buying over $108,000 in vintage cards. Other dealers also expressed strong dealer-to-dealer sales.

"Based on the attendance here, we did okay," said Walter Hall, a veteran of every National. "But we expected more people. We all know shows are suffering all over the country and now it's affected the National. This hobby has had to make adjustments in the past and now the Internet has forced us to make another adjustment."

The Internet was just one of many variables blamed for the lower-than-expected turnout in Atlanta. The list starts at the right and deserves a hard look by the hobby to see if this is a precursor of things to come or just an aberration:

Online Auctions: eBay has become a force in the hobby over the past year as its online site had a total of 52 million auctions through the first six months of 1999. Many sports collectors and dealers now use eBay and the other auction sites – including amazon.com, bid.com, collectorsuniverse.com, to name a few – to buy and sell cards and memorabilia. The growth of these sites may have affected this year's National and could have a profound effect on all hobby shows.

"There's no question that eBay and these other online auctions have affected every show in the country. The National is no different," said Mike Gordon, a New Jersey dealer and member of the NSCC board of directors. "My son even had a portable computer here in the booth to keep track of his eBay auctions."

But not everyone in the hobby buys into that excuse, especially when it comes to the National.

"I can see it at other shows, but this is the World Series of collecting," said Rosen. "A long-time hobbyist, a die-in-the-wool collector, an advanced collector, will come no matter where it is. You could run this convention in Alaska, or Iola, Wis., and you will get 10,000 to 15,000 people to come because it's the National Convention. I don't buy the fact that just because there are people on computers, that those kind of people won't come to the convention because they're working on eBay. That I don't buy. Also, from the curiosity point and all the publicity we give our hobby, it has to draw 20,000-30,000 people just from curiosity seekers, newtime collectors, people on eBay who see the convention in their area."

Added Jeff Rosenberg of Tri-Star Promotions, promotor of the 16th National in St. Louis and the 18th National in Cleveland: "I've never subscribed to that theory. People said that home videos would kill the movie industry. That hasn't happened because the movie houses realized they had to re-invent themselves. Now you have bigger screens, better sound, bigger seats. It's an enjoyable experience to go to a movie. If the National wasn't good, then I would look more at the location and the promotion of the event. You've got the greatest dealers in the world there, so you have to look at why people weren't drawn to the show. If anything, I think the Internet is going to grow the whole industry and the people who deliver the best value for the money will survive."

Collectors look through racks of jerseys at the 1999 National Convention in Atlanta.

Location: Atlanta was chosen as the host site primarily because the Georgia World Congress Center is one of the finest facilities in the country. But the collector base can't compare to most other markets in the country, especially New York, Chicago, Los Angeles, Boston and Baltimore.

"Attendance was what we expected for Atlanta," said Janyce Mabry of Playoff, a corporate exhibitor. "It's not a collector's market, it's not Chicago."

Sites for the next three Nationals have already been chosen: Anaheim in 2000, Cleveland in 2001 and Chicago in 2002. There were reports that the National promoters were looking at Boston and Baltimore for 2003 and 2004.

"I don't think we should ever go back to Atlanta," said Bill Mastro of Mastro Fine Sports Auctions in Oak Brook, Ill. "We have to go where the population is. It's ridiculous that we've never had a National in New York City. If they have to charge more for booths and admissions, I'd rather pay twice what I pay and have the show there."

Too Many Booths: The hobby's premier event deserves the best in the business and there's no question that the National brings out the highest profile dealers and companies in the industry. But 1,200 of them? It's almost impossible for everyone to have a good show when there are that many vendors, unless a record attendance is achieved. Some dealers even suggested that National booths should be limited, although it's not a popular view.

"I hate that word limited," said Rosen. "We shouldn't tell people they can't do a convention. I have a problem with that. I have a problem in telling someone they can't do a show. It's competition. Only the strong survive and this convention is no different."

Lack Of Publicity: Although the National was advertised in hobby publications like *Sports Collectors Digest*, the lack of local publicity before the show may have played a big part in the small turnout. The local area acted like it didn't know anything about the show and the lack of ads in area newspapers may have contributed to that feeling.

"Atlanta is not the best locale when compared to some other markets the National has been to," said Rosenberg. "I also know what it takes to run a National – it's a very difficult job, and I'm not trying to criticize anyone. There just wasn't the anticipation of the event this year. There hadn't been a lot of pre-show publicity in the various hobby magazines. There used to be a lot of controversy surrounding the show, like Jim Hawkins' columns in *SCD*. People thought that was bad, but it wasn't. Those type of columns got people talking about the National."

Poor Autograph Lineup: This year's National featured many strong autograph guests, including Bill Russell, Joe Montana, Wilt Chamberlain, Magic Johnson, Steve Carlton, Carl Yastrzemski and Oscar Robertson. Actress Pamela Anderson, wrestling star Sable and The Godfather Girls were also big draws. But the fact that the Baseball Hall of Fame ceremonies were scheduled the same weekend in Cooperstown, N.Y., may have affected the autograph lineup, which lacked some of the veteran baseball stars that past Nationals had.

Lack Of Interactive Events: The National has quickly changed its look in the past three years, moving from a show that had an entire conference room devoted to interactive events in 1996 (Anaheim National) to a handful of kids activities in Atlanta. Whether this was a factor or not, there were very few kids seen at this year's show, even on Thursday when it was Kid's Free Day.

"Traffic overall was light, which was disappointing, and the interactive games that we've had in the past that has usually been the draw for kids was mostly for adults," said Mary Mancera, director of national media for Upper Deck. "We had hoped that more young collectors would have been at the show."

Despite the low turnout, those in attendance had plenty to do. Corporate participation in this year's show was strong, as every card manufacturer except for Topps had a presence at the event. This marked the third straight year that Topps has not participated in the National.

Three of the card companies – Upper Deck, Fleer/SkyBox and Pacific – had wrapper redemption giveaways at their booths. Upper Deck handed out an oversized six-card Ken Griffey Jr. set to anyone who provided five UD wrappers. Fleer/SkyBox gave away an eight-card Diamond Skills sheet that included Mark McGwire, Sammy Sosa, Kerry Wood, Derek Jeter, Alex Rodriguez, Nomar Garciaparra, Chipper Jones and Ben Grieve for five Fleer or SkyBox wrappers. Pacific gave out a 1999 Aurora Baseball sample card of Tony Gwynn that included the "20th National" logo in gold foil for five wrappers from any '99 Pacific product.

"The wrapper redemption went well and we know we drove collectors to their booths to complete the wrapper redemptions," said Mancera.

"We had a very steady flow of collectors at our booth in Atlanta, opening packs and boxes," said Mike Monson, spokesman for Pacific Trading Cards. "There were around 500 boxes of '99 Pacific product busted at our booth alone, and likely many more at dealers tables. The National was a good show for us as we were steadily busy each day at our booth."

Playoff also debuted Prestige Football at its corporate booth and it quickly became one of the best sellers at the show.

"We've been very successful," said Janyce Mabry, spokesperson for Playoff. "Prestige went live Wednesday and the show allowed us to get it into the hands of collectors."

The New ScoreBoard also debuted in Atlanta, complete with the old Score Board's huge display. The New Score Board is a division of Oxxford Express, Inc., which bought the bankrupt company's assets for $2.4 million in September 1998. The New Score Board will offer merchandise not on the market for over a year to the hobby, but will not seek a trading card license at the present time.

"Our slogan, 'It's a whole new ball game,' says it all," said Moses Cheung, president and CEO of The New Score Board. "We bring to the memorabilia and collectibles market new energy and an entire new management team. We project a bright future for the company."

Richard Fletcher, executive VP and COO for Oxxford, said, "The only thing we've kept is the Score Board name and its superior product line. The New Score Board brings back to the market the reputation for superior products, a real guarantee of authenticity, and relationships with many current star athletes."

The corporate area also featured many exhibitors devoted to the growing online auction industry. Large corporate displays included eBay, collectorsuniverse.com, ubid.com and amazon.com. Attendees could use a computer at each site to learn how to participate in online auctions and immediately sign up as a bidder or seller.

Grading services were also active members of the corporate area. The growing number of graders included PSA, SGC, Beckett Grading Services and ASA, with PSA and SGC providing on-site grading.

And as usual, the show floor contained the greatest assortment of sports cards and memorabilia – vintage and new. Everything from game-used jerseys to bobbing head dolls to tobacco cards was on display. The number of graded cards – old and new – certainly rivaled those of ungraded cards in dealers' display cases.

Other news from the National:

Fleer/SkyBox again hosted the opening night banquet for National exhibitors. VP of sales and marketing Bill Bordegon used the occasion to announce his company has spent more than $1 million to add more autographs and game-used material to its remaining 1999 card releases. The goal is to add more punch to each '99 product, which was well received by dealers.

- The opening banquet also featured guest speakers Phil Niekro and Keith Van Horn, who entertained attendees with a lively question and answer session. Each attendee then received a free autographed 8x10-inch photo from one of the stars.

"We received very positive feedback from the dealers," Drotman said of the banquet. "It's a great opportunity for us to give something back to the industry and to the dealers. It gives us a chance to tell them a little bit about ourselves and hear what's going on in their world."

- The National Auction, hosted by Beckett Publications, attracted more than 400 people and brought in a total of $111,540. Noted items included a 1933 Goudey Napoleon Lajoie PSA-5 ($22,000); Lou Gehrig signed check to The Sporting News ($10,175); Mark McGwire's 1997 Player of the Week Watch ($1,375); BGS-9 Nolan Ryan Rookie ($3,850); and a 1982 Bryan Trottier Stanley Cup Finals road jersey ($4,950). There were no bids on the Pope John Paul II signed baseball, which had a $10,000 minimum.

Windy City SportsFest

Attendance was strong and dealer response was positive as Krause Publications wrapped up the first Chicago edition of SportsFest on Aug. 22 at the Rosemont Convention Center. Traffic was particularly good on Thursday and Saturday as the Chicago market's strong veteran collector base did not disappoint.

With an autograph lineup that included John Elway, Bill Russell, Dick Butkus, Joe Namath and more than a dozen other major stars, collectors had the opportunity to get a signature from some of the game's greatest heroes and to visit the 400 dealer booths at the convention center.

Along with a first-ever Fantasy Sports Pavilion, Krause Publications continued its popular "KidStore" at Chicago, where children age 12 and under were able to buy donated product that was priced at a tiny fraction of normal retail. As was the case with earlier KidStores in Philadelphia over the past two years, proceeds from the KidStore and the charity auction held Wednesday evening one day before the show opened were given to the Special Olympics World Winter Games 2001 in Alaska and to the local Special Olympics chapters. In all, more than $75,000 was raised during the five days of SportsFest '99 in Chicago.

Krause's first-ever SportsFest in Chicago is a hit

The roster of show dealers included the biggest names in the hobby, along with a corporate presence from all of the major card companies that featured card giveaways, contests and interactive events. Several noted artists were also set up at the show: Karl Jaeger, Carlo Beninatti and James Fiorentino each worked on original art during show hours to the delight of fans and collectors.

All of which left showgoers with a wide variety of diversions during the five days of SportsFest, a nuance that was a high priority with show planners. "It's certain we offered the consumers a lot to see and do, and that's important so they have a real positive image of our industry," said Krause sports publisher Hugh McAloon. "The consumers have indicated that they'll come back, and hopefully they'll bring friends and be part of our industry for a long time. We'll be in Chicago for a long time, and this was a strong start.

"Krause Publications judges a show by how other people judge it," continued McAloon. "Early attendance figures indicate it will exceed expectations. Exhibitors seem to be in agreement that attendance was strong. It appears that most of the dealers are reporting good sales, but we won't be happy until they are all happy."

Sales were solid for most types of items, highlighted by strong activity in graded cards. New-card sales and supplies didn't fare as well, with many of those dealers speculating that youngsters were busy preparing for school, which started in the Chicago area the following Monday.

But floor traffic was good nonetheless, in large measure because of a solid local PR effort that was aided by the presence of Michael Jordan's final basketball court, displayed by Collectors Universe. It also helped that the show sponsor was the *Chicago Sun-Times*, which ran several feature articles about the show. "The local PR was very good and there was a lot of attention given to the show in the mainstream Chicago media," McAloon said.

Many of the dealers in attendance often set up at shows promoted by veteran Chicago promoter George Johnson, who said he was surprised that attendance was good considering the number of competing events that weekend, including the Air and Water Show, home Cubs and Bears games and the opening of Chicago Motor Speedway.

The disappointments included the Fantasy Sports Pavilion. Show spokesman Dick Butkus drew interest when he participated in a live football draft on Saturday, but the pavilion didn't generate much interest from collectors. Some people also thought the number of children was lower than expected. KidStore revenue was roughly half of its two Philadelphia counterparts. "The college kids are moving into the dorms, and the younger kids have spent all their money getting ready for school, and so did their parents," said one Chicago dealer. The show was run very well, but the timing wasn't right."

Premiums were a big hit with show goers.

Upper Deck buys portion of Jordan court

Upper Deck purchased more than 3,000 square feet of the court on which Jordan played his last game. The court is being sold by Collectors Universe One-Of-A-Kind Auctions. A purchase price was not announced. "What Upper Deck bought was the majority of the west side of the court," Michael Barnes of One-Of-A-Kind told *SCD* at SportsFest, where the final basket and court area were on display. "The east side is where Michael made his last shot. They bought the bulk of the west side, minus the center court and baseline."

Upper Deck didn't immediately announce plans for the court, but it will almost certainly be cut up and used for both UDA memorabilia and Upper Deck memorabilia cards. "While we don't have any definitive plans at this time as to what we'll do with the court, Jordan fans can rest assured that we'll come up with some unique collectibles," said national media manager Mary Mancera.

The rest of the basketball court will be split into six lots and appear in the One-Of-A-Kind auction on Oct. 13. Those lots are each basket, the free-throw area of the last shot, each baseline and the center-court area. "The remainder of the east side of the court will likely be sold prior to the auction, just like we sold the west side to Upper Deck," Barnes said.

Dan Bernstein of Score Radio in Chicago sank a shot from the same spot as Jordan's last shot as Collectors Universe ran a promotion at SportsFest in which it donated $10,000 to two local charities. Bernstein swished his shot, leaving no scratches on the rim or backboard as the basket heads to auction.

.....THE BUZZ

A sampling of dealer comments about the show:

Adam Martin, Dave & Adam's: "SportsFest Chicago was our single-biggest buying and selling show in our 10 years within the hobby. It was a great show."

Bill Goodwin, Goodwin & Co.: "It was more than anyone could have expected for the first time in Chicago. Attendance was far better than the National, and I thought the number of booths was just the right amount."

Floyd Parr, BC Collectibles, Danville, Ill: "It's been kind of disappointing. We do the *Sun-Times* Show all the time and we were looking to do similar to what we did at that show."

John Passero, PSA10cards.com, Long Island, N.Y.: "Sales were brisk (for graded cards), better than expected. Dealer-to-dealer sales were unbelievable."

Mitch Adelstein, vice president, Mounted Memories: "John Elway was a sellout and there were no disappointments. Chicago is a good market and autograph sales reflected that."

Alan "Mr. Mint" Rosen: "This was one of the best shows I've ever had. But more importantly, what SportsFest has meant to the business is that the big-time shows are back. This place was filled with people every day."

Putting together the Halper Collection Auction proved to be a monumental task

By T.S. O'Connell

Putting together a live auction of the largest and most significant collection in the history of the sports collecting hobby sounds like a major undertaking, but listening to veteran hobbyist Rob Lifson describe the awesome task makes it clear that it is even much more than that.

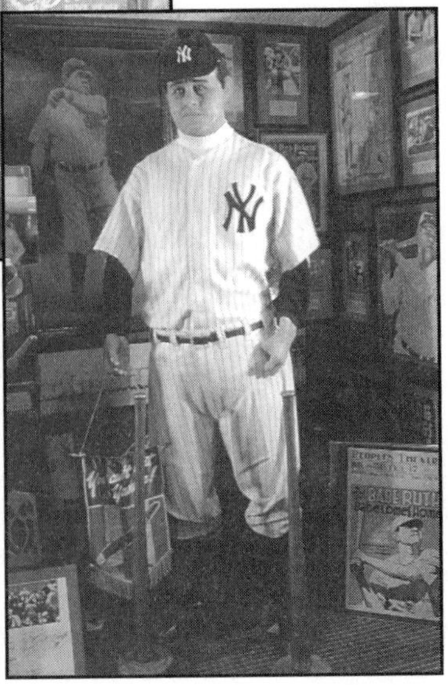

Charged with getting the incredible Barry Halper Collection ready for a seven-day, live auction by Sotheby's in New York City from Sept. 23-29 (and then for months after that on the Internet), Lifson has been working virtually round-the-clock since last fall when it was announced that the accumulation that was coveted by every collector in America was about to be dispersed. A dealer for more than two decades and one of the most prominent memorabilia experts extant, Lifson was nonetheless startled as the task unfolded.

"The collection was so large it was clearly a monumental task," recalled Lifson. "The inventory process at Halper's house took several weeks, and packing was also unusual because there were so many different kinds of pieces."

And so many pieces. Lifson said he wouldn't be surprised if there were 1 million pieces in the collection, and if you're having trouble with the math, remember that many of the lots can have hundreds or even thousands of items just within that lot. The live auction boasts 2,500 lots to be sold in 16 sessions over the seven days; once the live portion is concluded another 5,000 lots will be made available for collectors over the Internet. Plus, Major League Baseball purchased nearly 150 pieces last fall for a reported $5 million, and then promptly turned the whole batch over to the Hall of Fame in Cooperstown for permanent display at the baseball shrine.

And that's fitting, because Halper had hoped to see his collection sold intact and eventually displayed in a museum setting. After trying for several years to engineer such an arrangement, the man who almost single-handedly put memorabilia collecting on the hobby map decided that the auction was another, admittedly more complex, means of liquidating his horde.

It was Lifson who found himself wrasslin' with that, uh, complexity. "My job was to oversee and organize the entire sale," said Lifson. He likened the process to a treasure hunt, noting that even though he had visited Halper's house literally dozens of times over the years, there were still plenty of surprises.

While Halper's basement housed memorabilia crammed in every conceivable nook and cranny, there was also a pair of storage units that were filled with thousands of other pieces.

By his own admission, Lifson says his crew turned Halper's house into a Mail-boxes, Etc. Once the whole pile made it to Sotheby's in New York City, it took a couple of more months to get it all sorted and separated. "Once unpacked, it was overwhelming," said Lifson.

Sotheby's gave him free rein to assemble and organize the auction as he saw fit, a process Lifson notes involves as much art as science. He also had to decide which items should be in the live sale and which would be earmakred for the Internet. That last chore was eased a bit by the fact that there was considerable duplication in Halper's Collection, a nuance that he employed virtually from the beginning as a means of acquiring items in trade, if need be.

Thus, Lifson was confronted with the not-too-depressing prospect of deciding what to do with the Pete Rose 4,000th hit uniform, and what to do with the one Pete wore for hit No. 4,192. Now that's the kind of dilemma that auction houses don't really mind facing.

For the record, the duds for hit No. 4,000 will find a home on the Internet; the 4,192 uniform will be in the live sale. Lifson organized the live portion into 16 sessions, with headings by eras, decades and even specific groups like Murderer's Row, Hall of Famers, the Yankees from 1950-65 or art and advertising pieces. That kind of setup further accommodated the aforementioned duplication "problem," since a Ruth piece could be included in any of four or five decades and several other specific groups.

That's helpful, too, since, as most advanced collectors know, Halper accumulated more material related to Ruth than he did for any other player. "A Babe Ruth contract is an incredible item," said Lifson. "We had four or five of them." So they would be put into different sessions.

And he was quick to point out that the configuration of the sale also doesn't mean that all of the best stuff is in the live auction. The sheer enormity of the Halper Collection, and the amount of duplication and redundancy, means that the 5,000 pieces that wind up in cyberspace will hardly be anybody's castoffs.

"This (the Internet) is a way for a huge number of people to participate in the auction and get a Barry Halper item," continued Lifson, adding that there will be literally hundreds of items with pre-auction estimates in the $50 to $75 range.

That clearly offers a certain egalitarian quality to an auction that otherwise would have appeared to have been restricted to the upper crust. And he noted that the Internet proved a useful haven for last-minute additions, which were considerable, since the volume was so staggering that things would be missed along the way and suddenly surface.

Plus, Halper kept finding more and more material and he would send those pieces along. Once everything was allotted to a specific category or auction session, the experts from virtually every corner of the hobby descended upon Sotheby's for the authentication process. That must sound funny to novice collectors, but even the Barry Halper Collection must go through the process.

Noted autograph expert Mike Gutierrez was called in to spend weeks poring over the thousands of autographs in the collection. The fact that Halper got the vast majority of signatures himself made the job easier, but with a volume like that you still would wind up with some clubhouse signatures or family member signers, if only from some of the pieces Halper received in trades.

According to Lifson, that meant that occasionally a piece would be withheld from the sale even though it was probably OK. The mantra was, let's say it altogether now, "To err on the conservative side."

Over the last nine months it wasn't unusual to find anywhere from five to 10 people working full-time on the auction. And that charge was given to every expert rounded up for the process, a five-star lineup that included Grey Flannel (uniforms), Dave Bushing and Dan Knoll (bats and equipment), Barry Sloate and Don Lepore. And Lifson. Sotheby's staffers included project manager Laura Hardin, Jennifer Angerer, David Goodwillie and Sally Amon. And chipping in with the imposing job of writing up all that material for the catalog was Halper himself, Lepore (cards) and Tom D'Alonzo, who served as a consultant for the auction and was the curator of the collection for the four years leading up to the auction.

Wouldn't it be fun to know how many pieces of memorabilia and how many cards that group has examined since Nixon was in the White House, not even counting this latest undertaking?

What's in the cards?

Though the man on the street probably figures Barry Halper is first and foremost a card collector, that is not quite accurate. Though Halper started with cards just like everybody else did, he pretty quickly veered off into other areas, areas that were largely unexplored until his pioneering footsteps arrived on the scene.

"Barry hasn't considered himself a card collector for a long time, but his collection of cards still covers the scope, and he appreciated cards for what they were," said Lifson. With the veteran hobbyist Lepore examining the cards, collectors can probably be assured of the grading, which Lifson notes is again done with an eye towards the conservative.

So while many of the cards are in what old-time hobbyists used to call "collectable condition," the whole range of vintage cards is represented, along with the unique Halper touches, like the T206 Wagner proof card (estimates $50,000 to $100,000) or a 1933 Goudey Larry Lajoie *signed* card ($30,000 to $50,000). That card is one of the genuine hobby rarities; how many do you suppose there are with a signature?

And interspersed throughout the card session (Saturday, Sept. 25, at 2 p.m.) are dozens of other Halper-like

No 'Seller's Remorse' for Halper

Barry Halper

When Yogi Berra talked to his pal, **Barry Halper**, shortly before the auction, he asked whether Halper's "arrangement" with the Hall of Fame to display memorabilia from the famed collection was similar to a two-year agreement Halper has with the Hall of Fame catcher to display pieces at Yogi's museum in New Jersey.

"No, Yogi, the memorabilia (purchased by Major League Baseball) will be on display at Cooperstown in perpetuity," said Halper.

"OK, but for how many years?" said Berra.

That was probably the high point for Halper in recent weeks, but he figured to get a boost from the opening of the Barry Halper Gallery at the Hall of Fame on Sept. 1. His schedule has been virtually non-stop for several months as the opening of the live auction of the Halper Collection at Sotheby's in New York City approaches on Sept. 23, and the famed collector has done literally scores of radio, television and print interviews to promote the historic sale. And it has taken its toll.

"I'm wiped out," Halper said only days before the Hall of Fame opening. While the schedule has been taxing, he was buoyed by the prospect of the Hall of Fame festivities. With an 11,000-square-foot exhibition area on the first floor of the Hall dedicated to Halper, the collector has found that HOF's handling of his material has softened the blow from selling the rest of his holdings at auction.

"Once the HOF made the decision (to open the Halper Gallery), it was easier, because a part of my collection will forever be there," continued Halper. The HOF even had photos taken of the collection when it was still intact in the lower level of Halper's New Jersey home, and those shots have been blown up and used to complement the decor at the exhibit.

Halper chartered a bus to bring 40 family members and friends to Cooperstown for the special day. While the HOF activities cheered Halper, there have been headaches associated with the sale of his collection at auction. Due to the enormous publicity effort for the sale, a number of collectors and even family members of deceased ballplayers have surfaced and are clamoring to have memorabilia returned.

Not surprisingly, Halper has taken great care to establish the undisputed legality of any of his holdings, but he is still disheartened a bit when deals consumated decades ago are suddenly questioned because of the prospect of the massive auction. Even with that disclaimer, he's still elated about the upcoming auction and emphasizes that he's hardly struggling with "seller's remorse."

"I have my memories, pictures and good friends that I have made over the years," he concluded. When your "good friends" include some of the most famous ballplayers in history, along with countless collectors and dealers, that sounds like memories worth collecting.

additions, like seldom-seen 19th century sets and original artwork from sets like the 1935 Diamond Stars (Lefty Gomez, signed) and the coveted 1953 Topps paintings. And even though there is a condition range on some of the earlier sets, the sets from the 1950s and 1960s carry hundreds of key cards in high grades, like a 1959 Fleer Ted Williams set with a No. 68 described as mint and well centered. That makes an estimate of $1,000 to $1,500 sound fairly conservative, doesn't it?

Setting those pre-auction estimates is a fairly tricky proposition, but still one that seems in more than capable hands with Lifson. Even though he traditionally publishes minimum bids when conducting sales through his own company, Robert Edward Auctions, Lifson easily conformed to the Sotheby's high and low estimate program. And given the nature of the auction, he's absolutely confident that everything will sell.

"I set the reserves, and they are low," said Lifson. "If somebody likes an item, they don't have to worry that a reserve will be too high." The low estimates in the three-volume auction catalog total about $7 million; the high estimates top $11 million and Lifson figures the final numbers will top that. Given that the previous record auction total was about half that figure, it is more evidence (if any were needed) that this is quite clearly unchartered territory for the hobby.

Lifson said he figures probably 1,000 or more of the pieces in the auction are genuinely unique, and he added that even for those pieces where some other specimens exist in the hobby, Halper would, in turn, make it unique by having the featured players sign the items. It was his incredible access to getting autographs that contributed to his ability to separate his collection from any other known.

And even with the sale of a portion of the collection to Major League Baseball last fall, it hardly made a dent in the collection that has been the focus of countless newspaper and magazine articles, along with unprecedented television exposure. There are even videos about the famed collection, one which features Halper and former Yankee great Billy Martin touring Halper's basement.

That sale of material to MLB, which then turned over the pieces to the Hall of Fame for perpetual exhibition there, fell well short of what is known in the hobby as "cherry picking."

"You'd never know that anything was gone," said Lifson of the transfer to Cooperstown. "It was stuff that filled needs in their collection, not necessarily the best stuff that Barry had," said Lifson.

And about that catalog...

Few expressions in the hobby get abused as much as "collector's item," but I could have a lot of fun debating anybody who would suggest that the Halper Collection Catalog doesn't warrant having that particular designation.

At about 900 pages (and 2,000 photos) in three attractive volumes (with cover), the catalog nicely details thousands of pieces of the most famous collection in hobby history. That sounds like a collector's item to me.

As befitting a tome of such prominence, the print run is not announced, but Lifson said it would certainly be several tens of thousands. "It has a shelf life. People will refer to it for decades," said Lifson with no hint of exaggeration.

It is also worth noting that the auction provides a handsome bit of additional provenance for those collectors lucky (and flush) enough to come up with a winning bid. All a collector need do is point to the photo of his item in the catalog should anyone have the effrontery to question its heritage. Lifson gets the final word on that topic, too.

"Provenance has always been important in the hobby, so something from the Halper Collection will be accorded an extra degree of respect."

Nuff said.

The top-selling pieces

Lot No.		
o 2421	Lou Gehrig's last glove	$387,500
o 767	1928 Cobb Philadelphia signed jersey	332,500
o 607	Del Webb's 1947-64 Yankees WS rings	310,500
o 604	Lou Gehrig Yankees road jersey	305,000
o 1559	Circa 1960 Mantle game-worn glove	239,000
o 552	1956 Mickey Mantle Triple Crown award	211,500
o 561	1920 Sale of Ruth signed agreement	189,500
o 639	1930s Lou Gehrig Yankees cap	151,000
o 1932	1903-98 WS ticket collection of 256	140,000
o 149	Cartwright family baseball/letter	129,000
o 1549	1956 Mantle Yankees World Series ring	123,500
o 2420	Gehrig signed presentation jersey	123,500
o 88	Ruth final Stadium appearance bat	107,000

COOL STUFF

Obviously, it's not possible to list even a tolerable sample of all the incredible material in the sale, so herewith is a handful of interesting pieces:

- **A Babe Ruth personal check cashed on the morning of the same day he smacked home run No. 60**
- **George Brett's uniform (right) from the famous "Pine Tar" AL Championship Game in 1983, signed twice by the 1999 Hall of Famer**
- **A questionnaire filled out by Jackie Robinson in 1947 noting his determination "to open the door for Negroes in organized baseball."**
- **Alexander Cartwright's HOF plaque that was obtained from the family (For those not prone to swallowing the goofy Abner Doubleday myth, Cartwright serves well as the founder of the game.)**
- **The actual Oscar from the movie "Pride of the Yankees"**
- **A copy of the inaugural *Playboy Magazine* in 1953 with a Joe DiMaggio-signed Marilyn Monroe cover. This was a last-minute addition to the sale, a treasured item that Halper promised DiMaggio would never be shown to anyone as long as the Yankee Clipper was alive, a promise that Halper honored without exception.**
- **Bill Buckner's ill-fated glove and cleats (the shoes were ill-fated, too, because the ball went between his legs) from the 1986 World Series**
- **Honus Wagner T206 strip proof card, almost certainly the only one in existence (it came from his home)**
- **Yankee owner Del Webb's World Series and AL Championship rings (15) from 1947-64, purchased from Alan "Mr. Mint" Rosen and Superior Galleries**
- **Triple Crown trophies from Ted Williams (1947), Mickey Mantle (1956) and Carl Yastrzemski (1967)**
- **Phil Linz' harmonica that he played on the bus during the 1964 pennant race to the utter dismay of stressed Yankee manager Yogi Berra**
- **1903-98 World Series ticket collection (256), considered the finest accumulation of its kind**
- **Halper's famed baseball sheet music collection (257), also considered the finest known in the civilized world**
- **Nifty maple-finished, pinewood table that holds 56 Official AL balls, each signed on the sweet spot by Joe DiMaggio**

A day-by-day account of the $22 million sale

The most important auction in hobby history ended as triumphantly as it started

By T.S. O'Connell

It started simply enough. A handsome little baseball figurine was hammered down for $11,000, and what everybody anticipated would be the most incredible auction in the history of the hobby was underway. Barry Halper's unfathomable collection of baseball memorabilia was one week away from being scattered to the winds, and a year-long buildup to an historic week was over. D-Day had arrived. Or maybe, B-Day.

Seven days and $22 million later, it was over. Few things in America seem to be able to live up to their hype anymore, from Hurricane Floyd to blockbuster movies, but the auction of the famed Barry Halper Collection managed quite nicely.

Fortunately, I got to be there. Don't tell my boss, but I'd have done it for nothing. This was history, and I wanted to be there and be part of it, as, I suspect, so did a number of others. And while events this long in the unveiling often disappoint, this one didn't. Not even close.

DAY ONE➢ The first big item that got the crowd's attention was Lot No. 14, an apparently unassuming item described as 1894 National League team-signed ledgers. To the untrained eye, it might not have seemed like much of a big deal, but there weren't many untrained eyes at Sotheby's Auction House in New York City at 6 p.m. on Sept. 23. This was the deep end of the pool, as we were about to find out.

A gem with 113 signatures from major leaguers in 1894, Lot No. 14 commanded a final price of $96,000, once the buyer's premium was tacked on. It was bought by John Brigandi, a veteran hobbyist and dealer more than astute enough to realize what a prize the ledgers represented. It was a nice reminder, if anyone needed one, that the next 2,475 lots or so would be material largely unlike anything ever seen before in the hobby.

Not that the hobby hasn't seen stratospheric prices or even remarkable memorabilia specimens before, but the Halper Collection was (past tense sounds funny, doesn't it?) truly unique because he accumulated so many pieces from the players themselves, or their estates, or from the teams. Halper's ingenuity, his persistence, his foresight, his unparalleled access and certainly luck all combined to forge a collection of items that couldn't be put together again at almost any price.

Such an event would need an appropriate stage, and Halper found that at Sotheby's newly renovated digs at 72nd Street in New York City. After a week-long exhibition of the material on two floors that left literally thousands of visitors eager for the auction, the sale itself got underway in a spacious facility on the seventh floor that included seating for several hundred bidders on the main floor and skybox-type booths above the auction floor for some of the higher rollers.

Halper, of course, was comfortably situated in the luxury box, which was actually more like a suite. Food service and the like was available to all of the booths, but Halper got the Grade-A royal treatment, which seemed about right under the circumstances.

Sotheby's, certainly best known for its auction prowess in the world of antiques and fine art, did it up right for the Halper Auction. In each of the 16 sessions, a new auctioneer would turn up, with the occasional British accent sprinkled in to good effect. Somehow, it sounds cooler than the guy who auctions off the tobacco bales in North Carolina.

With each lot that came up for sale, the item itself would appear on a revolving stage, and at the same time appear on two giant screens on each side of the hall. The screens also carried an up-to-date listing of the latest bid, plus currency equivalents for about 10 other countries. The first auctioneer informed the audience that the currency numbers weren't really all that accurate, but the dollar numbers were, and nobody seemed to be waving any pesos or lira in the building anyway.

Rob Lifson, a name well-known to hobbyists through his own company, Robert Edwards Auctions, was one of the principal architects behind the auction, and he did a bang-up job of finding a coherent theme for each of the 16 sessions. The catalog, always vital at virtually any sale, was especially important here, and as we mentioned in previous articles, this one will almost certainly wind up as a collector's item and reference work.

The placement of items at a live sale is also important in sustaining a certain level of excitement, and Sotheby's accomplished that nicely, as well. Even through stretches of what might be laughably called "pedestrian" material (in this case meaning $5,000 to $15,000), Lifson would sprinkle in many of the coveted Halper uniforms and jerseys like fenceposts at reasonable intervals.

The first such fencepost appeared at Lot. No. 16, a Wilbert Robinson Orioles jersey that sold for $27,600, followed at respectable intervals by jerseys from Joe McGinnity ($31,050), Chief Bender ($27,600), Jim Thorpe ($46,000) and Babe Ruth ($48,875 for a Dodgers coach's uniform). That astute strategy would continue generally throughout the auction.

I won't use this space to recount a lot of prices: there are too many and they are listed in their entirety elsewhere in this issue. The aforementioned were included to lay some groundwork for the staggering prices paid for Lou Gehrig and Ty Cobb jerseys later on in the sale. The uniforms had always been the centerpiece of Halper's collection, so it's hardly a surprise that they held a prominent role here.

And if the uniforms were the centerpiece, then Babe Ruth was the star. That's hardly a surprise, since Halper had always stressed his affection for The Bambino and had always insisted (quite correctly, it seems) that there was no one else even close. "Ruth was the man of the 20th century," said Halper from his perch above the sales floor. I think he meant "the man of the century in the sports world," but I can't swear that he would even include that qualifier. "It's proven when you have a Ruth autographed ball that went for $46,000," continued Halper.

The ball in question, admittedly, had a really neat portrait of Babe painted on it as well, but one suspects that much of the dizzying price tag stemmed from its parentage in the Halper Collection and the fact that it was Ruth. Hobby insiders expected all along that items in the sale would carry a substantial premium just for that reason, and nothing that happened from Sept. 23-29 would cause anybody to doubt that.

Just in the first session alone, the Ruth imprint would be felt with a $40,250 handprint, a 1927 Ruth/Lou Gehrig signed photo ($29,900), a large signed photo ($43,125), a 1933 Ruth contract ($37,375), his polo cap ($24,150) and even a Ruth 1948 farewell album and letter ($57,500). And none of those even qualified as the most expensive Ruth item of the evening. That honor fell to the bat that Ruth leaned on in that 1948 farewell appearance at Yankee Stadium, which was purchased by Bill Mastro for one of his clients, at a price tag of $107,000.

As remarkable as those prices are, they probably weren't as surprising as some of the incredible sums paid for literally hundreds of other lots, from signed balls and pennants to team and panoramic photos, many of which left experienced hobbyists shaking their heads in amazement. "This is the one that sets the standard," said an elated Halper from his suite above the bidding floor at Sotheby's. "But those who know me know that this wasn't done for the money. I just couldn't collect anymore, and I'm thinking of the future and my family."

Mastro, who was the winning bidder on items totaling a couple of million dollars for a half-dozen clients, offered historical perspective. "When we did the

Copeland sale, we said it would be the biggest sale in our lifetime, but we never figured Barry would sell. This has been a barn burner. There haven't been a lot of bargains. Sotheby's obviously brought in a lot of New Yorkers who are not generally in the hobby, plus everybody in the hobby stepped up to the plate and made this a priority."

First Day Highlights: 500 Home Run Club autograph display piece with signed cards – $57,500; Ruth, Gehrig, Mantle and DiMaggio signed ball – $57,500; 1942 Oscar for "Pride of the Yankees" (purchased for $57,500 by veteran dealer Scott Goodman, who five days later would pick up Mickey Mantle's 1956 Triple Crown trophy); 1954 Norma Jean DiMaggio government ID card – $48,875; Mantle's first professional contract – $26,450; Mantle's last game-used bat – $40,250; single-signed Gehrig ball – $29,900; 1900-1930s photo and signature album – $29,900; 1920s baseball bat bench – $28,750; 1930s Moe Berg "spy" passport – $26,450; 1860 Live Oak Polka music – $25,300; and Marilyn Monroe signed baseball photo – $25,300.

DAY TWO➢ The auction got a staggering amount of major media coverage in the weeks leading up to the opening, and even as it got underway, David Letterman gave it a mention on his TV show after the first night, noting that he was wearing Babe Ruth's underwear. He was kidding, of course, but he could have purchased same the next day for a mere $1,840. As Ruth items went at this auction, that was a primo bargain.

But just as he did in their heyday 70 years ago, The Babe found himself sharing the spotlight on the second day with Gehrig. In three sessions that totaled more than $5 million, Gehrig was the guy who turned heads with a trio of items in the evening sale that totaled more than $550,000.

The big one was the 1927 Lou Gehrig Yankees road jersey that was purchased by Bill Mastro for Upper Deck for $305,000. As might be expected, that process elicited gasps from the audience, and then considerable cheering at the end when it was hammered down. Dave Bushing of Mastro Fine Sports and the eventual under bidder went back and forth at a frantic pace, causing auctioneer William Ruprecht, managing director of Sotheby's North America, to cheerfully suggest that the bidders employ "any increment that you would like to suggest."

Most of the highest ticket items that were sold were done via the telephone, with the major players from the second story booths also calling in their bids, so the identity of buyers was not immediately apparent to the crowd. Sotheby's had a bank of perhaps two dozen phones that accepted bids during the sale.

Friday's crowd of several hundred bidders was the biggest of the weekend, and the excitement from such a sale was palpable. It was announced the next day that Upper Deck had purchased the jersey and would use it for an upcoming promotion. When told who had bought the jersey, Halper commented from his booth, "I hope they don't cut it up, because I had heard those rumors." They proved to be unfounded: Upper Deck officials made it clear that the artifact would remain intact.

"We have considerable outside interest in this piece," was the frequent admonishment from the auctioneer as yet another high-profile piece was offered. "Fasten your lap strap," he added, which I assume is Brit-Speak for seat belt. Yet another gem from auctioneer David Norman to a persistent bidder from the floor who could have been hailing a taxi considering how long he had his hand in the air: "Your arm must be getting tired. Shove something else up there." Me, I was thrilled that these British-sounding guys had such a sense of humor.

Day Two included morning and afternoon sessions that offered material from the turn-of-the-century and pre-World War I, but things really heated up for the Friday evening, "Murderers' Row – The Yankees of the 1920s" session. The signed agreement that sent Babe Ruth to the Yankees from the Red Sox sold for $189,500 to a private collector, which was a dollar figure not as startling to experienced collectors as the $151,000 paid for a 1930s Lou Gehrig cap.

Just prior to that sale, Gehrig's 1927 World Series ring went for $96,000, again hardly a surprising figure for a piece of such historical significance. More jolting to the hobby elite was the $79,500 paid for an admittedly spectacular Lot No. 621, a 1927 Bustin' Babes and Larrupin' Lous barnstorming panoramic photo.

Marshall Fogel, a collector of considerable note and holder of one of the nicest accumulations of vintage photos in the hobby, was the under bidder, reluctantly throwing in the towel when the bidding reached $65,000. Heady territory indeed, but not unfamiliar to Fogel, who gained a good deal of hobby notoriety in August of 1996 when he paid a reported $121,000 for a mint 1952 Topps Mickey Mantle card.

Crestfallen but resolute in the face of the setback, Fogel made an observation that would eventually be echoed, in one form or another, by dozens of dealers and collectors over the course of the week. "My photo collection is starting to look real good," said Fogel, a reference to the hope that the Halper Auction sales figures would have an, uh, uplifting effect on high-grade, vintage hobby material.

Halper himself noted that such a price for a photo, not signed, suggested that collectors were indeed placing a premium on items from his collection. "Some of the people who have congratulated me have said, 'Only you could have accomplished this because of your reputation and the fact that people wanted a part of your collection,'" said Halper.

Earlier Friday evening, autograph dealer Kevin Keating created a bit of a stir with a winning bid of $71,250 for Cy Young's baseball glove. His client is a major league pitcher, but Keating would not name him. "I exceeded his limit," said Keating with a smile, a line that was uttered so frequently last week that it probably could have been turned into a bumper sticker.

"I know he'll be thrilled and he would have been in great pain if he had missed it," said Keating about the glove, which came directly from Cy Young's family by way of Barry Halper. "It's a $100,000 item for sure," he continued.

One of the more prominent autograph experts in the hobby, Keating purchased dozens of items at the auction, including the only two autographs of early National League president William Hulbert. Several of Keating's colleagues suggested only slightly tongue-in-check that he had cornered the market on signatures from the 1995 Hall of Fame inductee. Hulbert's a fairly tough signature: he died in 1882.

"There's a misperception out there that there's a lot of 19th century stuff around. There is – in the Halper Collection," said Keating, who was interviewed by several New York City television stations during the sale. He figures maybe half of the important 19th-century material extant is linked in some fashion to the famed New Jersey collector. "Most of this stuff has never seen the light of day," he concluded.

Another autograph dealer, Mark Jordan, figuratively stepped up to the plate Friday evening, paying $96,000 for a 1921 Babe Ruth game-worn glove, the only one known in the hobby. That too, ultimately will belong to yet another major league hurler.

"David Wells will wind up with it," said Jordan, who was the under bidder at $160,000 for the Ruth sale contract (for a different client). "David has Babe's hat, his uniform, his bat and all sorts of stuff. The glove just completes the collection."

As word spread around the hall (elapsed time about 20 seconds) that the glove had actually been won by the former Yankee, it was clear this development was a popular one for collectors. And Halper, too.

"I think it's great that Wells got the glove. I'm happy for him," said Halper, who numbers Wells among the legion of ballplayers, past and present, who visited his home when the collection was intact. "It wouldn't surprise me if he tried to use it in a game, but he's liable to get thrown out."

And while many of the most expensive pieces seemed to go to anonymous phone bidders or similarly unidentifiable select clients through the upper level booths, hundreds of lots also went to individual collectors. John Rogers, a card shop owner in Little Rock, Ark., headed back to the land of Bill Clinton on Sept. 30 with a Buick full of Babe Ruth items, including a number of really pricey pieces.

"This is great. It will never be again," said an enthused Rogers on Friday evening after winning The Bambino's equipment bag for all of $43,125. "These are pieces you're not going to see again."

He spent the week in the Big Apple with his wife, Angelica, and the Halper Auction represented the culmination of a year's worth of financial machinations. "I've been liquidating stuff for a year to put a financial package together for this," said Rogers. That effort included selling a near 30-year-old paper on ethics by a Georgetown University sophomore named Bill Clinton. I giggled, then tried to stop myself, but it turns out the Arkansas native wasn't at all defensive about such things. No doubt I wasn't the first. "That paper traded hands for more money than anything I bought here this week," said Rogers.

Hmmm. Bill Clinton for Babe Ruth. Now there's a trade for the ages.

In all, Rogers spent more than $90,000 on Ruth items, and just missed out on Babe's lounging robe, which sold for $25,300. Spotted the next day, Rogers professed no buyer's remorse. "Tell your readers (the Ruth items) will be in Little Rock if they want to stop by and see it."

Done. Plus, he's got a photocopy of that ethics paper, if you need a good laugh after a long drive.

Second Day Highlights: Alexander Cartwright family baseball and letter – $129,000 (purchased by Greg Manning Auctions); 1914-15 Ty Cobb Detroit Tigers contract – $63,000; 1861 Grand Match trophy baseball – $55,200; 1919 "Black Sox" single-signed ball collection – $52,900; Document collection relating to the sale of Ruth to the Yankees – $51,750; 1921 Lou Gehrig Yankees contract – $51,750 (Greg Manning Auctions); 1918 Babe Ruth Boston Red Sox contract – $51,750; 1859 presentation scorecard display – $51,750; and 1912 Joe Jackson signed photograph – $43,125.

DAY THREE➢ Saturday morning, the folks at Upper Deck picked right up where they left off the previous evening. With Mastro staffer Dave Bushing doing the bidding, the card company purchased what would turn out to be the second-most expensive piece in a most-expensive auction: Ty Cobb's 1928 Philadelphia Athletics signed home jersey. For $332,500, with the juice.

Though the crowd was smaller than Friday evening, there was no discernible dropoff in enthusiasm or bidding fervor. Bushing was tangling with Rick Russek of Grey Flannel for the coveted jersey, bidding for the jersey from another upper-level private booth opposite Mastro's. The excited crowd watched as auctioneer Selby Kiffer swiveled his head back and forth, sort of like watching a tennis match from well below sea level. In the end, Upper Deck (via Bushing), prevailed to the wild applause of those in attendance.

"We were buying it for our partner, Howard Rosencrantz," said Russek. "He was going to keep it for a year or two and then sell it in our auction." Disappointed, but undaunted about losing out on the Cobb jersey, Russek offered his evaluation of the proceedings. "We're here watching the hobby go nuts and hoping that this isn't lightning in a bottle and that the hobby has actually reached another level," continued Russek. "It's probably somewhere in between.

"The good news is that your collection is now worth a lot more money. The bad news is that it's going to cost more to buy the things you want."

John Brigandi was in a booth adjacent to Russek, having a good time at the sale but, just like everyone else, marveling at the stratospheric prices. "I've got to be the best under bidder in the world," said Brigandi with a wink. He bowed out of the bidding on the Lou Gehrig jersey at $200,000 and backed away at $60,000 on the Gehrig cap, which normally would be enough money to buy a Toyota-full of caps.

His luck would improve later in the week with at least one spectacular historical item (hint: think Bucky Dent/Green Monster), but he wasn't exactly empty-handed even on Saturday. Brigandi won Babe Ruth's 1948 farewell album and letter ($57,500) and a swell 1915 photograph of Babe Ruth and his father in the family tavern ($7,475), the 1932 Yankees signed photograph album ($37,775), along with the amazing 1894 ledgers from the first day.

Even as the auction wore down to its closing sessions, Brigandi figured that the giddy prices didn't abate that much because folks realized time was running out. "Some people didn't get anything and they started to get desperate. It was nuts," Brigandi said.

Another longtime dealer, Steve Verkman, was the winning bidder on a famous item that is no doubt familiar to SCD readers. The T206 Honus Wagner proof strip, which has graced the pages of both editorial and advertising sections in the magazine, sold for $85,000 Saturday afternoon, just edging the Baltimore News Babe Ruth rookie card that went for $79,500 for top laurels in the baseball card section.

But as experienced hobbyists know, Barry Halper "wasn't a card guy," as they say, having graduated from cards a long time ago. Still, his card stash grossed just over $1 million with a lineup that, while it included cards in varying grades, featured many of the toughest singles and sets in the hobby clear back to pre-1900.

A signed 1933 Goudey Nap Lajoie, almost certainly the only one of its kind in existence, sold for $28,750 to a private collector. The card was once owned by Mastro, having been traded to Halper many years ago for the very same card, in far better condition, but sans autograph.

Third Day Highlights: 1926 World Series signed photograph, including Ruth – $39,100; 1887-89 N173 Old Judge cabinet collection of 29 – $34,500; Ty Cobb signed photograph – $34,500; T206 Ty Cobb with Ty Cobb back – $28,750; Circa 1920 John McGraw Giants home jersey – $26,450; Circa 1916 BF2 Ferguson Bakery Baseball felt pennants complete set – $23,000; 1926 Lou Gehrig autographed letter – $23,000; 1909-11 T206 White Border near-complete set – $20,700; 1912 T202 Hassan Triple Folders collection of 124 (purchased by John Brigandi) – $20,700; 1933 Goudey complete set (purchased by Greg Manning Auctions) – $19,550; 1950 Bowman complete set (purchased by Steve Verkman) – $18,400: 1920s Louisville Slugger advertising display – $18,400; and 1920 Cleveland Americans panorama – $18,400.

DAY FOUR➢ Sunday was a day of rest for the Halper Auction and a game Sotheby's staff ... almost. Only one session, but still this managed to haul in $1,688,235, due in part to a number of high-ticket items.

As they had in earlier sessions, Ruth and Gehrig proved up to the task. That lineup included a Gehrig game-used bat and a 1931 Gehrig World Tour jersey that each brought $63,000, Ruth's 1932 Yankees contract that went for the same amount and a 1934 Tour of Japan album with team-signed photograph and sheet that sold for $37,375. Because Halper is such a Yankees fan in general (he is a minority owner) and a Ruth and Gehrig fan in particular, he accumulated a huge volume of material relating to the pair.

Few were in a better position to understand the scope of that passion than Barry Sloate of Sloate & Smolin, a consultant for Sotheby's for the cataloging, the live sale and the Internet sale that follows in coming months. "It's been phenomenal. Babe Ruth and Lou Gehrig pieces and the vintage Yankee material set records lot, after lot, after lot," said Sloate.

"This really helps the market. When people see these prices, they realize that the market is stronger than ever. This is very unique, a cultural event, and it's once-in-a-lifetime," continued Sloate.

Josh Evans of Leland's Auctions, agreed with that sentiment, noting that the auction included so many pieces that could be the marquee lot in an auction all by themselves. "I could take 100 pieces in this sale that could be used to build an auction around them, and that's an amazing statement," said Evans.

"This is the Halper Collection. And he didn't get the marquee items from other auctions. He got them from estates, from family members and from the countless people who contacted him over the years."

For Evans, who counts Halper as his first client when he started out nearly 20 years ago, the amazing collection may have evolved over the years, but it was no accident. "Barry is a genius – way ahead of his time – and he bought everything in sight. Barry used the same strategy as George Steinbrenner. He copied it. He would go out and get the best and pay more than anybody else."

Fourth Day Highlights: Moe Berg's "Spy" camera

from the 1934 Tour of Japan, with related letter – $63,000 (purchased by Bill Sear); Joe DiMaggio San Francisco Seals signed Pacific Coast League rookie jersey – $51,750 (purchased by Greg Manning Auctions); Rock-Ola World Series arcade game – $48,875; 1936 DiMaggio rookie year signed glove – $40,250; 1933 Chuck Klein National League All-Star uniform – $37,775; and 1932 Yankees signed photograph album – $37,775 (purchased by John Brigandi).

DAY FIVE➢ For those who thought that collectors might be running out of money by the start of the week, a $3.5 million Monday put to rest a theory that didn't merit much consideration anyway. Even if folks were starting to max out their credit cards, Barry Halper wasn't exactly running out of stuff. Not for a couple of days.

Besides, by Monday "The Mother of All Auctions" was just rolling into even more spectacular territory. While advanced collectors naturally understand and appreciate the value of rare and unique prewar material, there's also much to be said for offering items that people can readily link to their childhood. That is the underpinning of the card and memorabilia collecting hobby in the first place, so Monday's lineup of Baseball Hall of Famers, and material from the 1940s and the post-war New York Yankees dynasty had little trouble holding its own. And then some.

What Sotheby's officials described as "The Play of the Week" came Monday evening, when two phone bidders began a tug-of-war over a circa 1960 Mickey Mantle game-worn glove. The bidding quickly passed $50,000, then creeped along in $10,000 increments. The crowd began clapping as the bidding topped $200,000, then escalated to uproarious applause as the gavel fell at $239,000.

As auctioneer Jamie Niven waited to hear the paddle number, comedian Billy Crystal poked his head from the window of one of the skybox booths above the salesroom floor. Waving his bidding paddle, he asked the stunned audience, "Can I jump from here?"

It was a magical moment, almost like seeing Mickey Mantle sock a triple that rattled between the monuments in center field. "Look at me. I'm shaking. I've never done anything like this before," said the comic, who reportedly was white as a ghost at the time, but no doubt looked "maahvelous" the next day.

Crystal is one of the more well-known Mickey Mantle fans in this hemisphere, so he must have enjoyed the evening, which featured several historic Mantle items. Mantle's Triple Crown Award from 1956 was won by Joseph M. Walsh for $211,500, and will be displayed in his restaurant, The Stadium, in Garrison, N.Y. Mantle's 1956 World Series ring sold for $123,500 to Michael Fuchs, former head of HBO and Warner Music. Fuchs has counted Mantle as "his greatest hero" since childhood. "This is more than a glove or a shirt: some people complete their whole lives to get to the World Series," said Fuchs.

Lofty company, but none of the Mantle lots qualified as the most expensive of the day. That honor fell to Del Webb's 1947-64 World Series and AL Championship rings, which sold for $310,500, the third-most expensive piece in the entire sale. Those rings were purchased by another hobby name Alan "Mr. Mint" Rosen and Superior Galleries from Mrs. Webb in 1993, and later picked up by Halper in a trade/sale.

Earlier in the day, Ted Williams' 1947 Triple Crown Award sold for $97,100 and a 1939 Hall of Fame induction ceremonies signed photograph brought $63,000.

Fifth Day Highlights: Late 1940s Joe DiMaggio game-used glove – $49,450; Hall of Fame signed First Day Cover – $48,300; 1948 DiMaggio Yankees signed home jersey – $40,250; 1940 Lou Gehrig signed lawsuit release – $40,250; 1951 Joe DiMaggio Yankees World Series ring – $37,775; Circa 1894 Amos Rusie New York Giants jersey – $37,775; Babe Ruth single-signed ball – $35,650; 1945 Hank Greenberg Tigers signed road jersey – $33,350; Mike "King" Kelly signed contract – $31,625; 1956 Mickey Mantle Yankees signed road jersey – $29,900; 1946 Jackie Robinson publicity questionnaire – $28,750; DiMaggio autographed game-used bat – $25,875 (purchased by Mastro Fine Sports Auctions); Walter Johnson silver dollar – $25,875; and a 1942 Stan Musial Cardinals signed rookie home jersey – $23,000.

DAY SIX➢ For baby boomers, Tuesday was like Christmas, with opportunities to bid on everything from an original Playboy first issue signed by Joe DiMaggio to the glove and cleats that Bill Buckner wore during that fateful Game Six of the 1986 World Series. We already know where the ball is, but just as he was 13 years ago, Buckner seems a little confused about that.

Anyway, that Playboy magazine is one of the more famous pieces from the Halper stash. Halper welcomed DiMaggio into his home on dozens of occasions, and as was custom in the household, guests would sign any number of items as they moved around the shrine.

Almost timidly (which he is not), Halper handed the Yankee Clipper the inaugural issue of Playboy, which has Marilyn Monroe on the cover and in the centerfold. "What do you want me to do with this, sign it?" asked DiMaggio. Halper nodded. After some consideration, DiMaggio agreed to sign it, but only on the condition that Halper never show it to anyone as long as DiMaggio was alive. It was a request that the collector honored, without exception.

First issue Playboys have considerable collector value for all of the obvious and traditional reasons: this one apparently has a bit more than that, under the circumstances. It would be hammered down for $40,250, making it one of the priciest items of the entire day's bidding.

Josh Evans of Leland's wound up the winning bidder for the Buckner glove and cleats, which is appropriate, since Leland's also handled the ball that skipped past the glove. The final price was $51,750, about half the price that the elusive ball (bought by actor Charlie Sheen) commanded several years ago.

The most-expensive piece in the three Tuesday sessions was Halper's 1903-98 world Series Ticket Collection (256 pieces), which went to a private collector for $140,000. The third Triple Crown trophy in the auction (that's a fairly impressive statement by itself) was Carl Yastrzemski's 1967 award, and it brought $85,000 in the morning session, only minutes after a signed Sandy Koufax road jersey from 1966 was bid to $57,500.

Sixth Day Highlights: 1903 World Series program at Boston – $63,000; 1992 Roberto Alomar World Series Trophy – $37,375 (purchased by Ron Leff); 1967 Reggie Jackson Kansas City Athletics signed rookie jersey – $31,050 (purchased by Mastro Fine Sports); 1929 World Series signed photograph – $28,750; 1963 Stan Musial Cardinals signed road jersey – $27,600 (also Mastro Fine Sports); 1926 Yankees panoramic photograph – $27,600 (Mastro); Harmon Killebrew signed All-Star bat collection (12) – $26,540; 1963 Casey Stengel Mets road jersey – $25,300; Bill White's 1961 Gold Glove Award – $23,000; 1968 Pete Rose Reds signed road jersey – $19,550 (purchased by Greg Manning Auctions); 1967 Rod Carew signed rookie road jersey – $19,550; and 1965 Zoilo Versalles AL MVP Award – $19,550.

DAY SEVEN➢ In a week that never failed to live up to expectations, finding a suitable closing would seem like an imposing task, but to the surprise of few, Sotheby's and the Halper Collection managed it. With only a handful of lots to go (and more than 2,400 already gone), Lou Gehrig's final glove from the 1939 season sold for $387,500, topping all items in a week where using the term "record-breaking" sounded redundant.

Gehrig, who had a pretty good week himself, turned in a boffo final day with a presentation jersey at $123,500 and a Columbia University signed glove and ball at $68,500. Babe Ruth also got in a couple of ninth-innings licks with a 1935 Yankees jersey (not game worn – the Babe had been granted his release by then) that sold for $79,500, his last game-used bat ($74,000) and contracts from the Yankees in 1934 ($63,000) and the Braves the following season ($37,375).

Still, it was the younger generation that grabbed the spotlight on the final day, and I sure hope Nolan Ryan, Pete Rose, Hank Aaron and George Brett appreciate being thusly designated. Rose's home uniform from his 4,192nd hit game sold for $90,500; the Astros uniform that Ryan wore as he notched strikeout No. 3,509 was good for $43,125.

John Brigandi, who was busy all week at the auction both for himself and several clients, was the winning bidder on a rather nifty bit of Yankee history: Bucky Dent's playoff home run bat from 1978. The final tally at that one was $64,100, and Brigandi says he plans on keeping the piece for his collection.

Brett's "Pine Tar Game" jersey was hammered down for $31,625, Rose's silver bat for winning the NL batting crown in 1973 sold for $40,250 and a 1973 Willie Mays signed Mets road jersey went for $37,375.

One of the coolest items of the day, or the week, for that matter, came from the next-to-the-last session, a unique compilation of material from the advertising world and prominent artists. Halper's "500 Home Run Club" collection of signed paintings by Andy Jurinko once graced Mickey Mantle's Restaurant next to Central Park in Midtown Manhattan. Now it is owned by a lucky bidder who anted up $37,375 for the privilege.

Final Day Highlights: Baseball sheet music collection – $48,875; 1903-29 Yankee signature collection – $37,375; 1919 Branch Rickey Cardinals road jersey – $37,375; Hank Aaron's "Most Memorable Moment" 715th Home Run trophy – $29,900; Tom Seaver Mets signed road jersey – $24,150; and a Babe Ruth and Hank Aaron signed ball – $23,000.

And just like that, it was all over. The folks at Sotheby's tallied up all the numbers, and tell us that more than 1,500 bidders wrassled for 2,481 lots over seven days and that once the smoke had cleared, not one single lot was left unsold. They added that 85 percent of the lots sold for above the high pre-auction estimate. Not too shabby.

But of course, it's hardly over, and I am not talking now about the Internet stuff (which, believe or not, is really cool stuff, too). What I mean is that all this wonderful material is going to be floating around in our hobby for the duration of lifetimes. I am sure that lots of people who won items probably don't intend to sell, but everybody does, sooner or later.

Even Barry Halper. Talk about full circle.

We aren't losing a pioneer, we are gaining an author

Hey Barry Halper. You just sold the most amazing privately-held collection of baseball memorabila in the history of recorded civilization for $22 million. Now what are you gonna do?

Well, he's not going to Disneyland, if that's what you're thinking.

The man who used to sit atop the world's largest pile of memorabilia has made the biggest trade of his career, exchanging a pile of unparalled goodies for a similarly impressive pile of cash. One of the recurring themes that I heard from hobby veterans over the course of the seven-day auction at Sotheby's wasn't a preoccupation with all that money, but rather consternation bordering on despair that the hobby was losing one of its greatest pioneers.

The average Joe probably equates Halper's extraordinary profile with the astronomical dollar figures that all those historic pieces yielded, but hobby insiders almost to a man seemed more concerned about the man behind the memorabilia. For many, many veteran dealers and collectors, Halper was the first one to call with a question about a newly acquired piece. Over the years he graciously fielded tens of thousands of calls and was always ready to help out fellow collectors, even though we all played in a league several rungs below his.

Indeed, it was the unrelenting demands on his time that helped bring Halper to the decision to sell. He simply got too prolific as a collector, and the beast got so big that it probably got a little scary.

Now it's gone.

Perched in a plush suite overlooking the auction floor at Sotheby's during the auction, Halper seemed at peace with the decision to sell. In fact, the only one apparently battling any seller's remorse was Mrs. Halper.

"The New York Times interviewed my wife last night and she told them she was disappointed in seeing some of the items last week when they were on exhibit prior to the auction. Sharon said, 'Oh, I love that,' or, 'Maybe we should have kept that.' And I was doing the same thing when we first decided to sell," recalled Halper.

"I was pulling out this or that contract, and my son said, "Dad, if you want this to be a great sale, why hold on to 10 contracts? Then people will still want to be doing stories about you and will be trying to come over to the house. If you're going to do it, do it right and just keep the things of a personal nature.' And he was right. So I held nothing of importance back," continued Halper.

And even as he parted with treasured pieces that he had searched for over the years, he didn't seem fazed by the enomity of what was taking place. "This (the sale) was easy, because of the Hall of Fame. It will be there in perpetuity," said Halper about his earlier sale of a reported $5 million-worth of the collection to Major League Baseball, which in turn consigned the stuff to the Hall of Fame. The result was the Barry Halper Gallery, which opened with well-deserved fanfare about a week before the auction began. So Barry can visit at least some of his treasures anytime he wants.

And he doesn't figure to be bored, either. He has been offered a job by Mounted Memories to serve as an authenticating consultant, but he isn't sure whether that's the direction he wants to take right at the moment. To call the last year hectic would be something of an understatement. But he will be doing a book, a coffee table number that could even be available by next Christmas, or, barring that, Christmas 2001.

The book contract Halper signed is with John Thorn of Total Baseball, for whom Halper has high regard. "He is the man who knows more about 19-century baseball than anybody in the country ... including me," said Halper. And he wasn't kidding.

So turning into a full-fledged author should keep the hobby's favorite son occupied for some time. And the mail doesn't figure to evaporate completely. For years, Halper would get as many as 50 letters a week with questions about various items, but quite often he would get interesting stuff actually mailed directly to him

"A collector once sent me two porcelain fingers, with a note saying that they came from the family of Mordecai "Three-Finger" Brown," said Halper with a smile. "The note said, 'I know this is the missing link to your collection.'"

The same guy sent Halper a pebble that allegedly was the one that a certain ground ball struck en route to crashing into Tony Kubek's adam's apple, thus altering the outcome of the 1960 World Series.

For the record, the merry prankster doing the mailing was Marty Appel, he of considerable Yankees, Topps and freelance public relations fame.

"I still have them," said Halper, meaning the porcelain fingers, and probably not the pebble.

See, I knew the guy was holding stuff back.

— T.S. O'Connell

Oser auction nearly tops $1 million

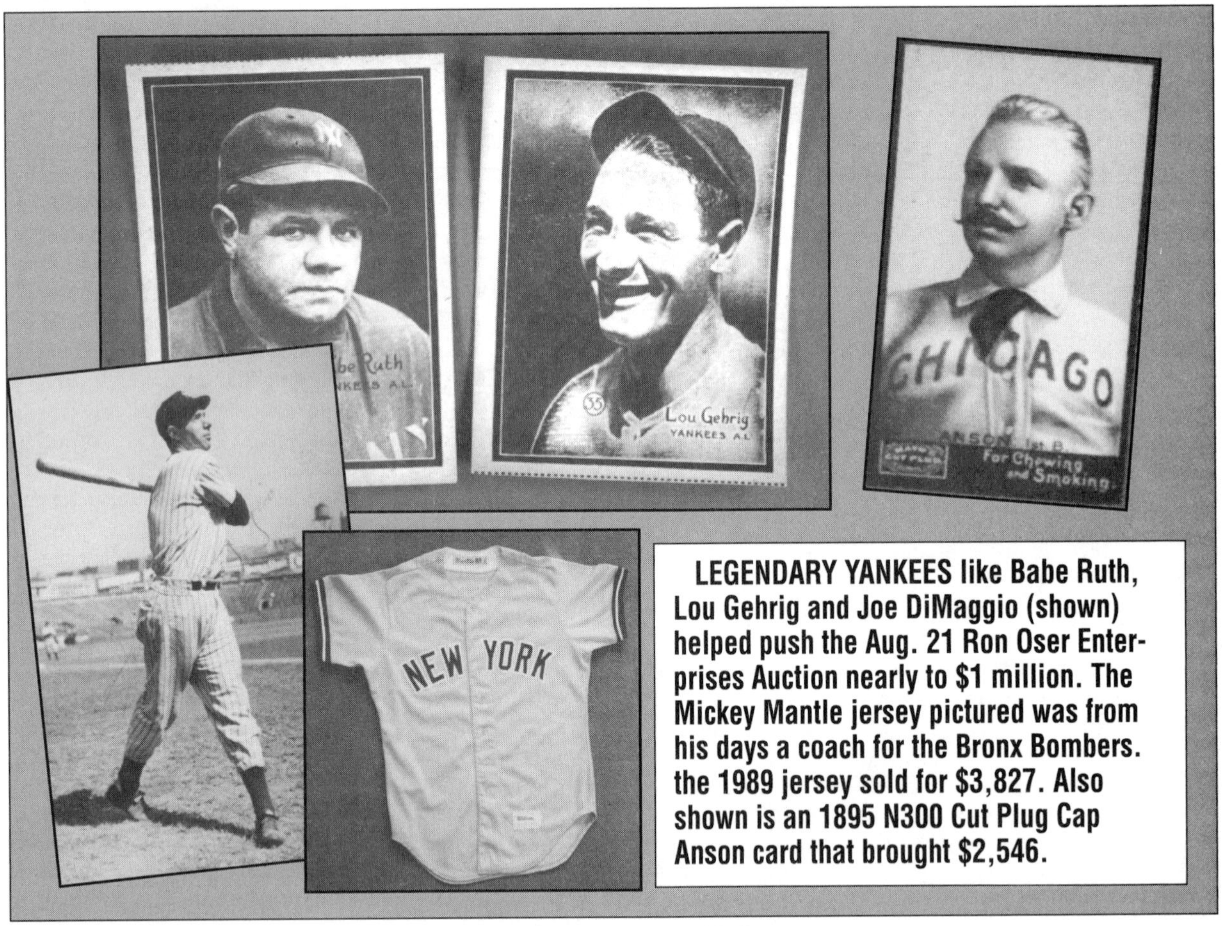

LEGENDARY YANKEES like Babe Ruth, Lou Gehrig and Joe DiMaggio (shown) helped push the Aug. 21 Ron Oser Enterprises Auction nearly to $1 million. The Mickey Mantle jersey pictured was from his days a coach for the Bronx Bombers. the 1989 jersey sold for $3,827. Also shown is an 1895 N300 Cut Plug Cap Anson card that brought $2,546.

By T. S. O'Connell

Ron Oser Enterprises' Aug. 21 auction parlayed an assortment of signed memorabilia and equipment, vintage cards and single-signed and team baseballs into a near-$1 million auction total. In all, the 1,1,62-lot sale grossed $935,000, highlighted by items like: a 1909-11 T206 Eddie Plank (vg-ex, $24,611); 1909-11 T206 Ty Cobb with Ty Cobb reverse (poor-fair, $24,611); 1909-11 T206 Sherry Magie (vg-ex, $7,143); 1933 Goudey Nap Lajoie ($8,205); 1939 Cooperstown Hall of Fame signed baseball ($14,567); 1932 New York Yankees team-signed ball ($8,243); 1937 New York Yankees team-signed ball ($6,020); Mel Ott signed baseball ($10,945); Jimmie Foxx signed baseball ($9,842); Mark McGwire signed baseball ($3,280); a pair of 1935 All-Star Game full, unused tickets ($6,197); original Pole Grounds figural double sent ($6,393); and a circa 1920s Christy Mathewson Base Ball Game ($4,076).

Other auction highlights include:

Mickey Mantle – autographed personal 1950s-1960s Yankees equipment bag ($6,734); 1989 game-worn coaches uniform ($3,827); Mantle and Maris signed, limited-edition bat ($5,604); Mantle and Maris signed baseball ($1,808); Mantle career ring ($1,531), Mantle Hartland statue in original box ($1,224); Mantle Bobbin' Head doll in original box ($1,346); 1956 "Big League Stars" unopened blister pack ($746); and 1959 Yoo-Hoo advertising display ($1,725).

Babe Ruth and Lou Gehrig autographed items – 1939 Hall of Fame Induction signed baseball with Ruth, Ty Cobb, Honus Wagner, Connie Mack, Tris Speaker, George Sisler, Walter Johnson and Eddie Collins ($14,567); Ruth-signed 9-by-11 "Tour of Japan" photo ($5,566); Ruth single-signed baseball ($4,478); Gehrig single-signed baseball ($2,982); Gehrig signed photo ($1,605); Ruth signed check ($1,682); Babe Ruth signed index card ($1,850); and Gehrig signed index card ($1,480).

Single-signed balls – Mel Ott ($10,945); Jimmie Foxx ($9,842); Wagner ($3,280); Dazzy Vance ($3,364); Gabby Hartnett ($1,183); Al Simmons ($919); Hank Greenberg ($1,482); Thurman Munson

($2,463); and Mark McGwire ($3,280).

Team-signed balls – Yankees from 1927 (partial, $2,037), 1930 ($1,897), 1931 ($1,149), 1932 ($8,243), 1933 ($1,265), 1937 ($6,020), 1953 ($1,084), 1954 ($1,112), 1956 ($1,228), 1966 ($1,348), 1977 (1,358) and 1998 ($1,020); Brooklyn Dodgers from 1947 ($2,546), 1949 ($2,530) and 1955 ($1,392); 1927 Athletics with Cobb ($1,851); 1956 Pirates with Roberto Clemente ($843); 1958 NL All-Stars ($1,547), 1960 NL All-Stars with Clemente ($1,358); and 1973 Athletics ($1,809),.

Autographed pieces – baseballs: 1958 Cardinals team ball with Cobb ($1,224); Foxx, Simmons and others ($746); Harry Heilmann and others ($1,346); Gil Hodges ($1,224); Cal Ripken Jr. "2,131" game-used ball ($1,264); and Nolan Ryan "300th Win" game-used ball ($949).

Autographed photos: Gehrig and Lefty Grove ($1,605); Home Run Baker ($1,093); Cobb ($557); Walter Johnson and Mack ($876); and Roger Maris ($839).

Checks: Ruth ($1,682); Walter Johnson ($1,011); Wagner ($923); Cobb ($903); Gil Hodges ($1,014); and Thurman Munson ($627).

Autographed baseball cards and others: 1932 US Caramel Ruth card signed "Sincerely, Babe Ruth" ($6,395); 1951 Bowman Mantle rookie card ($1,011); 1957 Topps autographed near set ($3,827); Cobb handwritten letter ($1,643); 1969 Yaz contract ($862); Alexander Cartwright signed "cut" ($690); Cy Young signed exhibit card ($928); "500 Home Run Club" signed bat No. 2/300 ($2,035); and McGwire-signed, player model bat ($1,427).

Baseball card sets – Vintage: 1931 W517 ($3,827); 1927 York Caramels partial set ($759); 1934-36 Diamond Stars ($5,566); 1937 Goudey Thum Movies ($575); 1941 Play Ball ($3795); Bowman 1951 ($7,130) and 1955 ($2,527); Topps 1951 Blue and Red Backs ($2,035); 1953 ($2,947); 1954 ($1,914); 1956 ($2,336); 1957 ($2,795); 1958 ($1,340); 1959 ($1,266); 1960 ($1,390); 1961 ($2,546); 1962 ($999); 1963 ($1,682); 1951 Berk Ross in original boxes ($2,912); 1952 Coca-Cola Playing Tips ($2,800); 1964 Topps Stand-Ups ($1,205); and 1971 Topps Greatest Moments ($1,494).

Single cards – 893 N142 Wilbert Robinson ($2,464); 1888 N162 Cap Anson, ex to ex-mt ($2,711); 1888 N321 Buckley, vg ($1,487); 1895 N300 Mayo Cap Anson, ex to ex-mt ($2,546); T3 Turkey Red Cobb, vg-ex ($2,098); T206 Cobb with Cobb reverse PSA1 ($17,250); T206 Sherry Magie, PSA4 ($7,143); T206 Cobb with bat on shoulder, PSA6 ($2,037); 1911 "Big Eater" Jack Fitzgerald, gd-vg ($1,547); 1915 Cracker Jack Huggins, PSA8 ($1,740); 1933 Goudey No. 106 Nap Lajoie, vg ($8,205); 1933 Goudey Joe Cronin, PSA9 ($3,061); 1933 Goudey Sam Rice, PSA9 ($2,602); 1939 Play Ball No. 26 Joe DiMaggio, nm ($2,239); 1955 Bowman Mantle, PSA8 ($1,392); 1955 Bowman Mantle, SGC92 ($1,494); 1968 Topps 3-D Curt Flood, nm ($1,532); and 1985 Topps McGwire collection of 30 rookie cards, all nm to nm-mt ($3,827).

Memorabilia – 1970-71 Clemente game-used jersey ($15,306); Ken Griffey Jr. game-used jersey ($2,800); George Brett game-used jersey ($1,851); Wagner pro-model bat ($1,897); 1923 Yankee Stadium opening day program ($1,978); Maris 61st HR program and ticket ($927); 1959 ($1,122) and 1964 ($927) original baseball card vending machines; 1920s "Christy Mathewson's Base Ball Game" ($4,076); original Polo Grounds figural double seats ($6,393); 1912 Cobb "'King of Clubs" sheet music, ex-mt ($1,897); and 1968 Roger Maris complete cereal box ($1,150).

Other sports – Football: 1935 National Chicle Knute Rockne, PSA5 ($834); 1957 Topps Paul Hornung rookie, PSA8 ($822); 1964 Jim Brown signed contract ($718); 1966 Chicago Bears signed team football with Brian Piccolo ($1,134); 1968 Super Bowl II program and ticket ($679); Jerry Rice game worn jersey ($1,150); **Basketball:** 1961-62 Fleer complete set, ex to nm-mt ($2,315); 1986-87 Fleer complete set, nm to nm-mt ($1,235); "NBA 50 Greatest Players" partially signed, limited-edition litho ($6,325); Bob Lanier game-worn jersey ($814); **Hockey:** 1953-54 Parkhurst complete set ($1,107); 1954-55 Topps one-cent wrapper, ex to ex-mt ($475); Mike Bossy signed, game-worn jersey ($1,265); **Golf:** Bobby Jones signed typewritten letter ($1,086); and Babe Didrickson and others signed photo ($509).

Non-sport – Complete sets: Action Gum ($1,480); Frank Buck ($1,139); G-Men and Heroes of the Law ($3,289); Horrors of War ($4,255); Sky Birds partial set ($862); True Spy Stories ($885); Freedom's War ($631); Jets, Rockets and Spacemen ($1,346); World on Wheels ($1,020); Davy Crockett Green and Orange ($919); Three Stooges Color ($616); Beverly Hillbillies ($509); Hogan's Heroes ($905); Gilligan's Island near set ($919); Brady Bunch ($839); 1941 Superman wrapper ($306); 1953 Tarzan and She Devil original artwork ($1,044); 1962 Mars Attacks wrapper ($1,601); 1973 Topps Wacky Packages Third ($3,704) and Sixth Series ($1,581) uncut sheets; **Hartland statues with original boxes:** Johnny McKay ($1,443); Sgt. Preston ($1,112); Wyatt Earp ($805); and Matt Dillon ($974).

Famous personalities – Sarah Bernhardt signed original 8-by-10 photo ($2,711); Buffalo Bill Cody collection of three original photos ($862); P.T. Barnum cabinet photo ($518); Harry Houdini cabinet photo ($1,265); Elvis Presley signed concert scarf ($885); Jimi Hendrix ($555) and The Doors ($560) original rock posters; and Princess Diana and Prince Charles signed Christmas card ($2,087).

Hunt Auctions' live sale recalls hobby's past

Hunt's "live" auction remains a bastion of hobby nostalgia amid a sea of growing electronic mayhem.

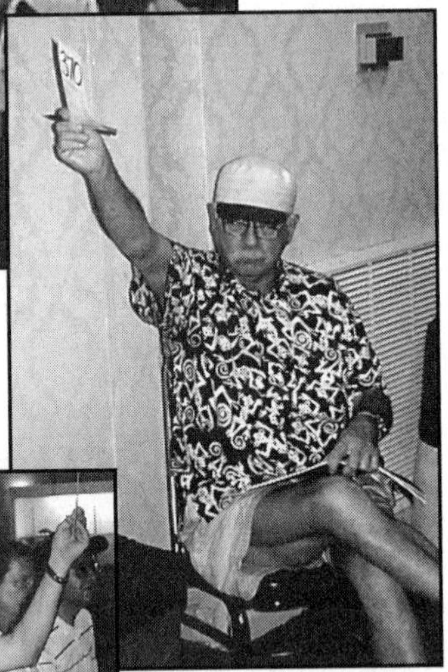

By T.S. O'Connell

The Hunt Auctions "live" sale remains a bastion of hobby nostalgia amid a sea of growing electronic mayhem. For those who think the hobby is all about dragging your mouse about in a frenzy, a visit to this particular auction is a good reminder about hobby roots.

Back in the 1970s, hobby auctions were a staple among a small group of zealous collectors who constituted what was the hobby. The auction was used as a way to move a considerable volume of product in a hobby where much of the product involved wasn't all that expensive.

Nowadays, the prevailing sentiment is something akin to, "If it isn't nailed down, auction it," or something to that effect. If there is anything NOT being auctioned, that would probably be news.

But the periodic Hunt auctions do a good job of returning the hobby to what it looked like a long time ago, putting together auction lots that offer a compilation of items (normally related) that almost defy concise description and brief encapsulation.

Which, of course, means such a lot would be just perfect for a live auction, where the potential bidders can actually look through, touch (gasp!) and otherwise sort through the material before purchasing it. What a concept!

"One of the things we're known for is trying to offer something for everyone," said David Hunt. "We try to have the $100-$200 lots and also the lots for $50,000, said Hunt about the Aug. 6-7 sale."

According to Hunt, it's that kind of mentality that differentiates the hobby from collecting antiques. "You have collectors in the sports world who will buy something for $50,000, but they still want to buy the $200 item, just because they like it."

Or a $770 item. During the Friday night bidding, somebody anted up that princely sum for a brick from Shibe Park. One brick. I don't *think* it was any of the numerous dignitaries on hand from the world's most energetic historical society (Philadelphia A's), but several were present, including the A's brain trust of Ernie Montella (general manager), Bob Warrington (VP) and Tony Risi (treasurer). I don't think you could get a treasurer to spring for $770 for one brick, at least not any treasurer that I ever met.

And as unusual as that may sound, it actually illustrates another fun aspect of the auction: spirited bidding on material with a distinct local flavor, which in this case means the Philadelphia Phillies, A's, Eagles or 76ers, probably in that order. What chance would a brick like that have on the Internet?

The attraction for hobby old-timers at a live auction is the tactile quality of the event. Which means you get to pick things up, turn them over and look at them.

I marveled at one of the Hunt staffers heroically holding up a plaque bearing Babe Ruth's name, a plaque that had been embedded into a wall of a municipal stadium adjacent to Yankee Stadium in the Bronx that bore Ruth's name. It looked heavy – maybe 50 pounds or so. At $2,300, that comes out to about $46 per pound, which would be expensive for filet mignon, but not terribly so for a sports collectible.

At a live auction you also get the ambiance of the auction itself, which is to say the fast-paced action of an auctioneer determined to sell (in this instance) about 1,200 items in about 12 hours.

Auctioneer Scott Foster, a mainstay of the Hunt auctions, was more than up to the task, and though I have no idea why I kept track of such things, he never took a break through either the Friday or Saturday auction sessions. Not a one. Clearly he has better kidneys than I have, which hardly makes him a member of an exclusive club, but no doubt enhances his credentials for his chosen calling.

Speaking of calling, the auction, while most assuredly live, also had a considerable e-mail, mail and fax component for absentee bidders beforehand, and phones during the auction for those who made arrangements beforehand.

For high ticket items, those additional elements are almost certainly a necessity, since rounding up enough folks who can pay the freight on the priciest stuff would probably be impossible.

For many of the most desirable items, absentee bids often comprised the opening salvo in a sale that clearly didn't have any of those "unannounced reserves" that are so commonplace. The two-day, Aug. 6-7 auction started from the gate with 5,000 absentee bids, a few of which carried the day where the off-premise bidder anted up enough of an opening bid to scare away anybody on hand at the sale.

Such was the case of a boffo Robin Roberts game-used road jersey from 1955, a year in which Roberts led the league in everything except restaurants visited. Even with a pre-auction high estimate of $10,000, it opened with an absentee bid of $14,500, which means our collector with a clear understanding of the term "preemptive" won the coveted flannel for a total of $15,950 with the 10 percent buyer's premium. As I mentioned earlier, items of a particularly phabulous Philadelphia phlavor, understandably, did very well, indeed.

A Shibe Park locker opened and sold immediately at $3,520, while a turnstile from the long-departed stadium opened at $2,000, then escalated just about as quickly as the auctioneer could track it from an obliging pair of phone bidders. When the smoke cleared in less than one minute, it was knocked down for a whopping $4,125, about twice the low estimate.

Like most major auctions, there were bargains available, but they frequently show up in areas that no one could have anticipated. High-end stuff often brings numbers well above the estimates, but even having said all that, you couldn't help but notice that the auction house did a remarkable job on the estimates. This is not by accident.

"We try to be accurate with our estimates," noted Hunt during one of the few moments when he could take time for the Fourth Estate. "The catalogs wind up being fairly good reference guides, along with the prices realized afterwards."

To get a feel for how much expertise is involved in a pre-auction estimate, you have to bear in mind that an old-style auction like this one includes literally hundreds of lots with stuff like: Lot of 27 early baseball paper pieces, circa. 1890-1930. Includes various color litho trade cards, advertising pieces, 1912 Baltimore schedule, die cut player, ink blotters. Range VG-NM.

Try to find that in a price guide. But that's also one of the charms of this kind of sale. You get to see a little, and in some cases a lot (pun unavoidable) of different things. Many auctions concentrate in one area, and that's cool, too, but it's hard to beat one room in a hotel where you can look at (and handle, if so inclined) baseball cards, programs, equipment, sports trophies, tickets, postcards, uniforms, pins, buttons, balls, bats, gloves and photographs. Did we mention photographs?

Live auctions are perfect for eclectic photo lots, because the bidders can sift through a lot with a dozen or more photos, most of which would be cost-prohibitive to try to comprehensively picture in an advertisement.

For high-end photos, and this auction had plenty of those, a single photo can represent a lot, but there were also dozens of lots of the multi-photo variety.

As little more than an off-the-cuff observation, this sale had the nicest accumulation of team-style photos that I have ever seen. All kinds of teams. Team photos from around the turn of the century were a genuine art form, which kind of makes you sad that the genre degenerated over the years to little more than a high school yearbook photo and eventually just about disappeared altogether.

Negro Leagues Bonanza

Too bad, because those turn of the century and 1900-20 team photos are some of the coolest items in the hobby. Even the Negro Leagues, abysmally shortchanged by the game itself and the attendant absence of things like baseball cards and related memorabilia, managed to have wonderful team pictures taken during its heyday, and several spectacular examples turned up at this sale.

One of those examples, a rare 1931 Homestead Grays photo postcard (shown), was hammered down for an imposing $6,325, about twice the high auction estimate. That nifty piece was won by noted collector/dealer Dan Knoll, who was actually buying it on behalf of another hobby legend, Bill Mastro.

Mastro may have snagged that piece, but many of the rest of the items wound up in an impressive tug of war between Negro League collectors Richard Merkin and Richard Berg. The auction included an extraordinary run of pennants, pins, tickets and photos, and while another well-known Negro League collector, Jeff Eastland, managed to win a pair of classic Jackie Robinson photos, many of the principal lots from the Negro Leagues were divvied up between Merkin and Berg, and not without a fight.

No fisticuffs, of course, but it was still a metaphorical prizefight as the pair dueled over more than a half-dozen items, with the auctioneer looking very much like a spectator at a tennis match seated precisely at the net, with his head rotating back and forth from one side of the room to the next during furious bidding. It was probably just coincidence that the two were situated at opposite sides of the room.

"There were instances where I could see (Berg) wanted something and wasn't going to stop," said Merkin, who nonetheless managed to secure nearly a dozen prized pieces. Berg, known for turning up at an auction just prior to the bidding on specific items of interest, and then promptly leaving once the last one was hammered down, stayed in form during the Saturday session. He vanished after bidding on the coveted, but so politically incorrect "Darktown Battery" mechanical baseball bank.

He anted up $5,000 or so for a half-dozen Negro League pieces, including rare photos of Rube Foster and the 1945 Cleveland Buckeyes. Merkin, not to be outdone (and he was not), ponied up almost $11,000 for nearly a dozen pieces from the group, highlighted by several of those aforementioned team pictures (1915-20 Chicago American Giants and the 1936 Puerto Rican All-Star Team in street clothes, with Buck Leonard, Ray Dandridge, Leon Day and others).

A unique Ramly piece, and 1888 Joseph Hall Cabinets

And while the mini-drama was fun to watch, the bigger numbers came from things like the Joseph Hall cabinets cards that figured to be one of the highlights of the two-day sale, along with a swell, one-of-a-kind Ramly advertising piece.

That incredible hand-painted Ramly Turkish Cigarettes piece, which featured a team picture of the 1909 Red Sox, opened at $5,000, and escalated rapidly before selling to a phone bidder for $19,800. Another hobby veteran, vintage card expert Lew Lipset, was an under bidder on that piece, going as high as $17,000 before stepping aside.

"I decided to save my money for the Joseph Hall cabinets," said Lipset, easing his disappointment over failing to snag the Ramly piece. Probably one of the handful of advanced collectors with a genuine shot at completing the rare cabinet set, Lipset was an active bidder on five of the cards, winning three, though the most elusive one got away.

Hunt officials were understandably elated about what was termed the first public offering of the complete set of 14 cabinets. The whole group sold for a total of $80,000, representing about 10 percent of the overall sales from the auction. Lipset wound up with the Baltimore, New York and Kansas City cards ($5,720, $4,840 and $4,400, respectively), and dropped out of the bidding for the Chicago cabinet just short of its final sale price of $11,000. Bryan Dec, a dealer and longtime 19th century collector, was the winning bidder on the Detroit cabinet at $7,150.

Lipset was even more tenacious with the rarest cabinet in the set, Washington, helping to push it to double the pre-auction high estimate at $16,000. Lipset passed at that figure, with the toughest card in the grouping going to another phone bidder at $17,600.

As is not uncommon at auctions, the anguish over missing a rare item can have its upside. "I'm glad I didn't get it for that," said Lipset once the Washington card was finally sold. He's been working on completing the cabinet set for nearly 20 years, long enough that he can't even remember how he acquired the initial 10 cabinets.

I could recommend some Washington team cards from the 1950s and 1960s that are a whole lot easier to find and not very expensive when you do find them, but I have a feeling he already knew that.

Business is booming at sports halls of fame as the new century arrives

With glitzy new exhibits and interactive areas, fans are flocking to the four pro sports shrines

By David Craft

If you think museums are little more than dusty old buildings filled with fading, freestanding relics, consider the halls of fame for professional hockey, football, basketball and baseball.

Those places are alive with the sights and sounds of this country's four major sports. Today's halls of fame are interactive. They offer special events. They are constantly changing their exhibits and adding new mementos in order to keep the fans interested and coming back for more.

For example, this year the National Baseball Hall of Fame and Museum in Cooperstown, N.Y., has already surpassed its all-time attendance figures for a first quarter.

But before you can say, "Thank you, Mac and Sammy," consider this: the brain trust at Cooperstown has long been aware that there is no such thing as one kind of baseball fan (even if home runs get everybody but the victimized pitchers jazzed). People who visit the Hall do so for many reasons: to study a variety of exhibits and artifacts, to see and hear videos that capture their heroes as they really were and to stand before the plaques that honor the game's greatest.

The same goes for the people who lovingly and energetically maintain the halls of fame for football, basketball and hockey. They, too, understand that change is good. Interactive exhibits, autograph signings, a constant influx of new and exciting mementos and a dedication to honor their sports in a way that both showcases the past and spotlights the present (with an eye toward the future) combine to give fans "more cool stuff" to check out than can barely, if at all, be done in one day.

HALL OF FAME officials have long been aware that there is no such thing as one kind of fan. People who visit the halls do so for many reasons: to study a variety of exhibits and artifacts, to see and hear videos that capture their heroes as they really were and to stand before the plaques that honor the game's greatest.

Spokespersons for the various halls of fame were contacted to learn what's in store for visitors who make the pilgrimage to Toronto, Canton, Springfield or Cooperstown. The following information was gleaned mostly from telephone conversations with those spokespersons. Please keep in mind that these are representative highlights and are in no way intended to encompass everything the four popular destinations offer to fans this year.

Baseball

Collectibles and mementos are an essential part of any popular sport, but baseball still seems to grab the spotlight when it comes to icons. And this year marks the unveiling of many items that most fans have only heard about.

Major League Baseball purchased between $7 million and $8 million worth of baseball memorabilia from noted collector Barry Halper and then turned night around and donated the artifacts to the National Baseball Hall of Fame and Museum. There are so many fascinating and historic gems among the donated items – nearly 200 of Halper's most significant treasures – that museum offi-

Baseball Hall of Fame

cials have the happy yet difficult task of deciding which items are displayed first and which ones will have to wait to be enjoyed by their adoring public.

In fact, the museum has a building expansion program underway in which Hall officials are developing a "changing exhibits gallery" that will be called the Barry Halper Gallery. It opened the first week of September, the first group of artifacts will remain on display for about two years before museum officials remove them and bring out other pieces for exhibition.

The contract that sold Babe Ruth from the Red Sox to the Yankees; Pete Rose's spikes, worn when he broke Ty Cobb's all-time hits mark; Ruth's 500th home run ball; Moe Berg's 1944 Army I.D. card; a Thurman Munson batting helmet; the trophy ball from an 1871 Haymakers vs. Mutuals game; a ball from the 1888 Spalding World Tour signed by such luminaries as Henry Chadwick, Cap Anson, and A.G. Spalding; jerseys once worn by Ernie Banks, Wade Boggs, Reggie Jackson; and a 1914 pennant from the Federal League are among the items the museum acquired through the generosity of Major League Baseball.

Football Hall of Fame

With the lineup of new inductees George Brett, Robin Yount, Nolan Ryan and Orlando Cepeda, attendance at the the ceremonies this year was estimated at 50,000, topping the former record from four years ago of 40,000 for the enshrinement of Richie Ashburn and Mike Schmidt.

Induction weekend festivities in Cooperstown included a New York-Penn League game at Doubleday Field; two Hall of Famer autograph sessions limited to the first 300 kids ages 7-12 who purchased a junior admission ticket; the induction ceremony on Sunday, July 25; and the Hall of Fame game between the Rangers and the Royals on Monday.

Two other noteworthy news items about the Hall: First, "The Great American Home Run Chase" is a major new exhibit that chronicles the history of the single-season home run record. Many of Sammy Sosa's and Mark McGwire's home run balls, plus their uniforms, bats, and other gear are on display, as are artifacts from the careers of Roger Maris and the Bambino.

Second, in celebration of the 25th anniversary of Hank Aaron slugging his 715th homer to set a new big-league career record, the Hall has created a special admission ticket for 1999 that features a photo collage of artifacts from Hammerin' Hank's career. The ticket will become a keepsake for any visitor to the museum. This marks the second consecutive year in which a legendary ballplayer has been honored with a commemorative admission ticket. Roberto Clemente was featured in 1998.

Football

Switching to pigskin, the Pro Football Hall of Fame is definitely going for the bomb this year.

Even if you missed the "Best of Yesterday and Today" autograph sessions in May and June, you can choose from a number of other special events, ongoing educational programs and history-rich exhibits if you visit Canton, Ohio, this year.

GameDay Stadium, the high-tech, "turntable" theater built in 1995 that combines 35mm laser discs and 10-channel surround sound, is the site of a new $1.2 million film called "Championship Chase" that NFL Films produced.

Pro football is the first, and thus far the only, sport to be projected in 35mm Cinemascope. Viewers are taken to spring training camp, where the players and coaches are miked for sound. Viewers begin watching the high-definition film at one side of the "stadium." They get a behind-the-scenes look at what goes on at camp as players and coaches prepare for the upcoming season.

A final scene from camp is shown as the turntable rotates the entire theater 180 degrees so that viewers are now looking at 40-by-20-foot screen on the other side of the stadium. When the turntable stops, viewers will see the key moments from an NFL season.

The Hall is always adding a wealth of artifacts to its display cases, walls and exhibits. Brought in from the 1998-99 season are the ball John Elway threw that surpassed the 50,000-yard career mark, the shoes and ball used in Jason Elam's record-tying field goal of 63 yards, Peyton Manning's jersey from his final game in his record-setting rookie season and items highlighting Terrell Davis' accomplishment of being only the third running back in NFL history to rush for 1,000 yards in seven or fewer games, plus Jerry Rice's record-setting mark of consecutive receptions.

Of course, the showcase event of any given year at the HOF is the induction ceremonies. This year's theme for the Pro Football Hall of Fame Festival is "Unforgettable Moments." And because the AFC-NFC Hall of Fame Game moves from its traditional Saturday time slot to the following Monday night, planners have used this opportunity to schedule extra events.

So, what was once called "Football's Greatest Weekend," because virtually all the events were packed into a Saturday and Sunday, is now an 11-day festival.

This year's festivities ranged from the Balloon Classic Invitational the weekend of July 30-Aug. 1 to the induction ceremonies on Saturday, Aug. 7, to the aforementioned Hall of Fame game on Monday, Aug. 9. That contest pitted the new Cleveland Browns against the Dallas Cowboys. Food fests, concerts, civic dinners and a fashion show were also scheduled.

The Hall offers a number of educational programs. They include field trips, a presentation (followed by a Q&A session) on careers in sports and the long-running "No Huddle" program that emphasizes the museum concept and pro football's ties to northeastern Ohio.

Contact Melissa Meadows at (330) 456-8207 for more information.

Basketball

"Heart and Soul: A Celebration of Women's Professional Basketball" continues to be a huge draw at the Pro Basketball Hall of Fame in Springfield, Mass. The show debuted in August of last year and will likely continue well into this fall.

It's a retrospective look at women in basketball from the 1890s to 1978 and the founding of the first women's professional league in the United States to other teams and other leagues in the 1980s (including women who found varying degrees of success playing hoops in Europe), to the introduction of the ABL and the WNBA in the 1990s.

Interest in women's basketball at both the amateur and professional levels is great right now. So great, in fact, that the uniforms and gear of two major stars – Rebecca Lobo and Sheryl Swoopes – are featured alongside the uniforms and gear of a dozen NBA stars in a replica NBA locker room at the museum. Plans call for additional WNBA representation in the coming years.

Basketball Hall of Fame

Women's college basketball as we know it didn't really get going until the advent of Title IX in the early 1970s. The HOF has a solid collection of memorabilia dating to that period, and it's growing more and more as new mementos are being discovered and donated.

The section on the AAU, which was a viable alternative for women cagers from the 1930s through the 1960s, is another fascinating aspect of basketball history. The Amateur Athletic Union provided spirited female athletes an opportunity to play competitive sports. In the case of basketball, women would take a job with any of a variety of companies and play for the company team.

Another forum for women with a burning desire to play basketball included, of course, the Olympics. The HOF has a considerable array of Olympic mementos from the 1976 games to the present, including the 1980 Summer Olympics, which the United States joined 61 other nations in boycotting for political reasons.

Upon their induction into the National Basketball Hall of Fame, two members of that U.S. team – Carol Blazejowski and Denise Curry – donated the uniforms they would have worn in the 1980 Summer Olympics in Moscow had they been allowed to participate.

The Hall's annual induction ceremony and its related festivities took place Thursday, Sept. 30, through Saturday, Oct. 2. The annual media awards dinner was on Thursday, the induction ceremony the next day and the Hall's annual basketball clinic was Saturday morning at Springfield College.

Last year's clinic facilitators included former player Nate Archibald and former Minneapolis Lakers coach John Kundla, both Hall of Famers.

And, like any modern museum, the National Basketball Hall of Fame is an interactive funhouse. Three conveyor belts bring the balls up to visitors, who can then shoot at a variety of baskets set at different heights and distances and

Who You Gonna Call?

***SCD* readers may either call the respective Halls of Fame or access their web sites for further information about upcoming events, special exhibits, ticket prices and hours:**

- **Hockey: (416) 360-7765, www.hhof.com**
- **Football: (330) 456-8207, www.profootballhof.com**
- **Basketball: (413) 781-6500, www.hoophall.com**
- **Baseball: (607)547-7200, www.baseballhalloffame.org**

constructed with different types of backboards and rims. One Hall official says the comment cards that visitors fill out when they leave would indicate that a sizable number of them spend much, if not most ,of their time at this shootout.

Another interactive game uses "blue screen" projection techniques to give visitors a chance to play one-on-one with Bill Walton. That, too, is a popular site at the Hall.

Visitors who immerse themselves in the game's early history flock to the exhibit that faithfully recreates the YMCA gym where Dr. James Naismith invented the game more than 100 years ago. History buffs will also learn about the barnstorming teams. And finally, they'll learn about the rowdiness factor of the early game – notably the introduction of chicken wire around the court to protect the players from over-enthusiastic fans who heaved quarters at the players while they heaped abuse on them. (The name "cagers" became synonymous with the players because the wire gave the appearance of playing inside a cage.)

One of the big news items coming out of the HOF is that a major exhibit/show – as yet unnamed – is in the works that will spotlight the integration of the game of basketball and the contributions made to the sport by African-Americans. An opening date is planned for sometime in February 2000. A prestigious committee that includes several Hall of Famers and other big names in black basketball is spearheading the project.

A key element of the project, of course, is to trace the history of African-Americans' participation in basketball at various levels. There is evidence to suggest that there was at least one black player in a professional basketball league as early as 1902. There were many blacks who played collegiately on racially mixed teams throughout the early part of this century. The integration of the college game and the pro game, the importance of the barnstorming teams such as the New York Renaissance and the Harlem Globetrotters in keeping black players in the fans' collective conscience – all of those stories and more will be part of this much-anticipated project.

Hockey

The Hockey Hall of Fame experienced a major new look in 1997 and 1998 when it opened the World of Hockey, a 3,500-square-foot exhibit that embraced the international game.

Hockey Hall of Fame

This remarkable exhibit features an impressive array of hockey artifacts that, perhaps as much as anything the Hall offers to its visitors, underscores just how much the game is embraced worldwide. There are memorabilia, histories and exhibit materials from all 53 HHOF member nations.

The World of Hockey devotes major exhibits on Olympic hockey and World championships right up through last year's games at Nagano. The European leagues, the Canada Cup, the World Cup and other global hockey events are given their due.

And with the rapid rise of women's hockey, a Women's International Hockey display continues to be a major attraction within a major attraction.

For hockey fans who like a little kick to their visit, try the Global Game Encounter sponsored by IBM. This multimedia experience is driven by its sponsor's state-of-the-art technology that is a real high-impact treat for fans of all ages (though some fans may wish to begin their visit on a mellower note and work up to this virtual-reality world). Visitors explore their favorite sport in an animated, interactive framework hosted by a computer-generated, 3-D character.

Another "hockey fan magnet" is the Blockbuster Video Dressing Room. This is a detailed replica of the Montreal Canadiens' dressing room at the Forum during the 1990s. It's unclear if this exhibit includes actual smells from the laundry piled on the floor. But visually, it's a fascinating place in which to spend some quality time.

From the name plates above the players' lockers where the uniforms hang, to the players' gear and the physiotherapy equipment, visitors are sure to gain a true feel for what it's like to be there. What's more, the exhibit includes a depiction of a dressing room from the 1920s. The contrast is amazing.

Visitors will gain further insight into hockey as it really is when they watch a video monitor that shows the Canadiens and the Buffalo Sabres preparing for a regular-season match. (So wear your hockey jersey, close your eyes and imagine yourself trading quips with your teammates.)

Then, as the two teams leave their respective dressing rooms, the doors to the Molson Theatre open and visitors get to see the start of the actual game on the big screen. This is followed by the film, "Hockey Dreams."

Dick Irvin Sr., long a respected NHL coach, is on hand in the form of an animatronic audio presentation in which he tells visitors about life in the bigs and being a "bench boss." Little kids may either be spooked by it or fascinated by it. (I'm not worried. I saw an animatronic Abe Lincoln at Disneyland years ago, so I'm okay with it.)

MILESTONES don't necessarily translate into card interest

By Dennis Thornton

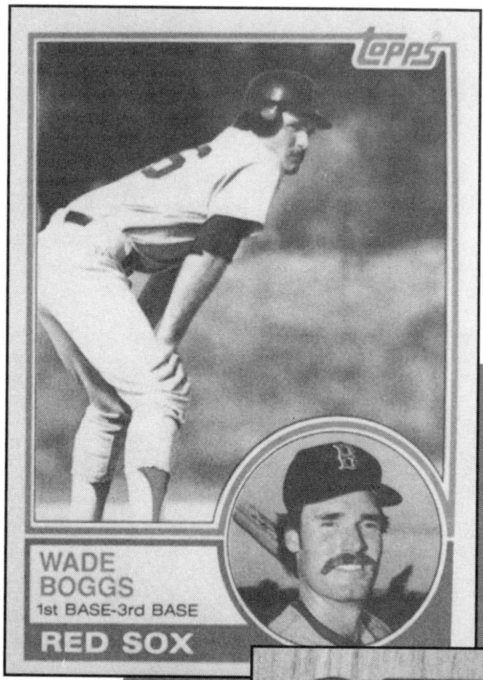

The number of hits and homers piled up rapidly in what was a huge year in baseball history.

Two veteran stars and almost certain Hall of Famers — Tony Gwynn and Wade Boggs —joined the 3,000-hit club, a mark achieved by only 21 men in baseball history.

Cal Ripken Jr., "the Iron Man of Baseball," played in just 86 games in '99 and finished nine hits short of the magical 3,000 hit milestone.

Mark McGwire followed his amazing single-season home run mark of 70, set in 1998, with entry into the select 500-home run club this season.

But those remarkable numbers did not have more than a temporary bump in the value of their rookie cards, dealers across the nation told *Sports Collectors Digest.* In fact, their cards may have already peaked in some cases.

"They're all awesome players, but they don't get much respect in the sports card market or in general," Joe Dewey of The Rookie in Des Moines, Iowa, said about Gwynn, Boggs and Ripken.

"There might be some action in their rookie cards," he said. He said a 1983 Topps Gwynn card is going for about $65, Ripken's 1982 Topps fetches about $60 and Boggs' 1983 Topps card can be bought for just $6 to $8.

"Ripken has dropped off after setting the record (for most consecutive games played, topping the legendary Lou Gehrig's record)," Dewey said.

Ripken, who spent much of his career at shortstop, should join Robin Yount and Honus Wagner as the only shortstops with 3,000 hits. Ripken has been steady and reliable throughout a long career, hitting .278. He also had 402 home runs and 1,571 RBI entering the 2000 season.

"Gwynn has inched up over the years. He's been a hitting machine," he said.

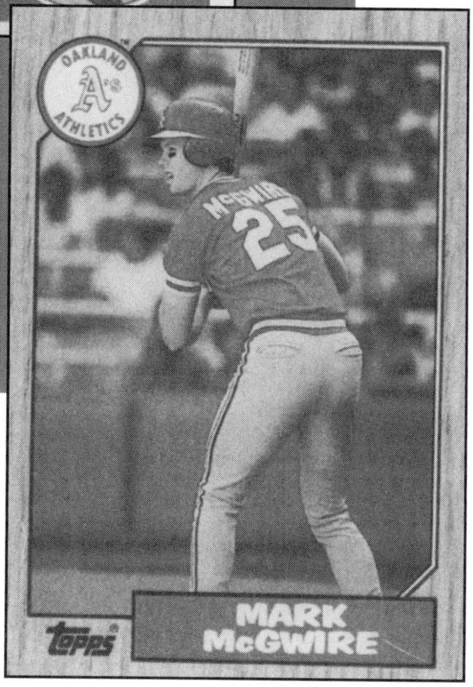

Gwynn has piled up eight National League batting titles, as well as five Gold Glove awards, in a career with just one team, the San Diego Padres.

His lifetime batting average of .338 has some experts comparing him with Ted Williams as the century's top hitter. He has flirted with the elusive .400 mark more than once, just missing with a .394 average in 1994.

Injuries slowed Gwynn in '99, including keeping him out of the All-Star Game. He played in 111 games and had 139 hits in 411 at bats.

Dewey said McGwire's 500th homer "affected him a little bit in an upward style." He said McGwire's rookie card has settled in at $200 after peaking at $250 during the '98 home run craze.

McGwire eclipsed a record of home run consistency in the '99 season originally set by Babe Ruth. He has hit 342 homers since the start of the 1995 season, bettering Ruth's record for most home runs in six consecutive seasons.

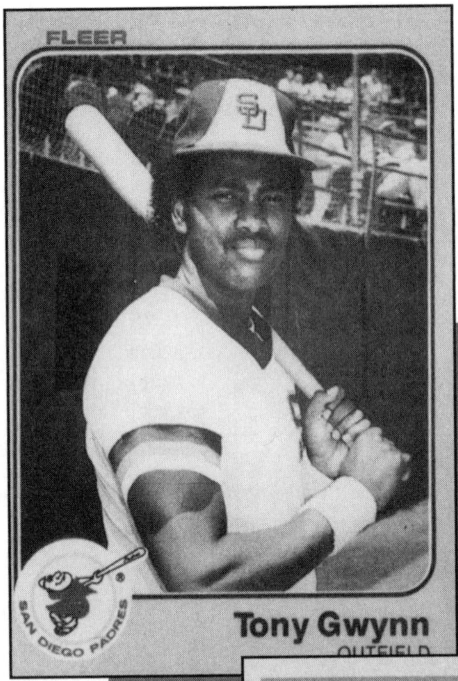

Roy Gaertner of Rock 'N Sports in Saginaw, Mich., said he's noticed more interest in the Gwynn and Ripken cards. Even Boggs, who's had little attention in the last couple of years after spectacular hitting in the '80s, is selling well. "All these Wade Boggs cards that are just 50-cent cards and $1 cards are getting scarfed right up," he said.

Boggs won five American League batting titles from 1983 to 1988 with the Red Sox and his .328 career batting average ranks 30th all-time. He announced his retirement after the season.

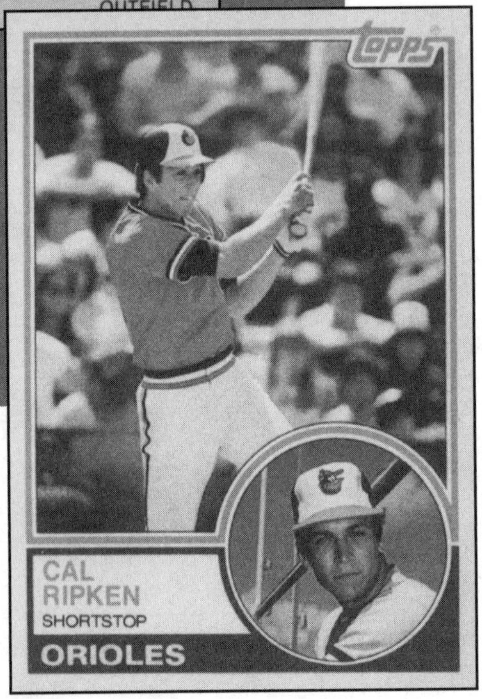

But after starring for the Red Sox from 1982-92 and having several standout seasons with the Yankees from 1993-97, he signed as a free agent with the fledgling Tampa Bay Devil Rays. He played two seasons in Tampa Bay.

"What you're going to see is we have a lot of guys who speculate on the Hall of Fame or breaking of records," he said. "They try to pick up as many of their cards as they possibly can.

"We're seeing in baseball, the emphasis is on the older stuff, the real premium stuff," Gaertner said.

"Ripken sales have increased tremendously. All of a sudden, a lot of people are picking up his cards," he added. "He's the one out of the three we do the most business on."

But Stan Dancewicz of Sportscards & Posters in Peabody, Mass., said he hasn't seen any reaction yet. "They may go up a little," he said, "but none of them are regional guys." Boggs started his career with the Boston Red Sox, but has been gone for a decade.

"We haven't sold one of his cards in a long time," Dancewicz said.

Farther south, collectors turn their attention to football and racing, said Charles Wooton of CW's Sports Cards in Hazard, Ky.

"There's no interest at all," he said. "People here aren't interested in baseball."

"It been more of a topic of conversation in the store," said Ralph Barney of Bob's Sports Collectibles in Burlingame, Calif.

"Gwynn rookies have been good sellers for a year or two, if you can find nice ones," Barney said. Part of the interest is that the many Giants fans in that area see Gwynn and his Padres frequently. Good Topps rookie cards of Gwynn bring $65-$70, he said.

There's virtually no interest in Boggs in the area. "It's been a while since he's been in the headlines," Barney said. Ripken's card peaked when he set the record, but it's "still strong," he said. "They really put Cal Ripken on a plateau."

Barney said McGwire's card is still strong, but "most of the peolple who wanted one went out and got one."

"There may be a little bit of a spike or increased volume of sales, but I don't expect either lines around the corner or prices to go crazy for any of them," Barney said.

Jon Canino of Sideline Sports in Absecon, N.J., said he's had no reaction on the 3,000 hit club and isn't expecting any. "I don't care what they do," he said.

Jordan among NBA's Top 25 Starting Lineups

'88 Malone, '92 Magic figures top the list

By Greg & Virginia Sanchez

Hobbyists always debate which cards or figurines are the tops in the hobby. Starting Lineup figurine collectors are no different.

Here is a rundown of the top 25 SLUs in the hobby compiled by basketball collectors Greg and Virginia Sanchez, who have authored multiple basketball card price guide books.

25. 1996 Kobe Bryant (Extended): We stopped getting production quotas from Kenner for SLU pieces after the 1992 issue, so it is unknown how many of these Bryants exist.

There were rumors, however, that thousands and thousands of cases were produced. True or not, if he turns out to be great in the NBA you'll wish you had his rookie SLU.

24. 1997 Tim Duncan (Extended): We do know the presses were cranked high for the extended sets, so you can expect that tons of this piece exist.

However, this is Tim Duncan, who already has an NBA title in his pocket. Also, the Upper Deck card was printed in much smaller amounts than any of the major company's regular-issue rookie cards of Duncan.

23. 1992 Larry Johnson: Not a high demand SLU on collectors want lists, so why is it in the Top 25? According to reports, only 3,000 of these were produced. It is the shortest print of all the 1992 issues, with the exception of the Magic Johnson yellow.

It is also Johnson's rookie SLU. Johnson has been a decent NBA player but collectors pretty much ignore him. This is one SLU you just don't see around much.

22. 1988 Jeff Hornacek: Limited production and his rookie year put this SLU in the Top 25. Reportedly only 4,000 pieces were produced. His card also precludes his 1989-90 NBA Hoops and Fleer rookie cards.

This means these 4,000 cards are the first-ever trading cards produced of Hornacek. This is also the top SLU in the Suns team set. Hornacek has had a fine career and couple that with the low production makes this a great SLU to own.

21. 1993 Shaquille O'Neal: His first SLU, probably with a

1989-90 One-on-One Jordan/Isiah Thomas figure

1993 Jordan

Michael Jordan placed five figurines on the Top 25 Starting Lineup list.

huge production as Kenner reversed its trend of limited production quotas that it had for the 1988-1992 issues.

With demand for more product by collectors, this Shaq piece was pretty easy to find in 1993. It will probably never be a great investment. Just the same, it is an imposing design of Shaq and worthy of the Top 25.

20. 1991 Spud Webb: We know what you're thinking – Spud Webb in the No. 20 spot? Little does anyone know that when production on this piece was happening, Webb got traded from the Hawks to the Kings and production of Spud as a Hawk was halted.

There was no switch to a Kings piece for Webb. From the mouth of the person at production, only 1,700 Spuds were produced and released. This makes it one of the rarest pieces produced. And, besides, everyone loved little Spud.

19. 1992 Larry Bird: Sure, everyone wants the 1988 Bird, but production was high. You'll find this 1992 SLU is one of his least-produced pieces.

The 1988 piece came in the all-star case and total production hovers at about 24,000. This 1992 version has a production of only 5,000 pieces. It is also Bird's final regular SLU piece.

18. 1988 Vinnie Johnson: According to sources, only 4,000 were produced. This is less than any of the other expensive 1988 Piston pieces.

The "microwave" was hot as a player and hot with his only SLU. A short print in the 1988 issue and some championship rings makes this Johnson piece worth owning.

17. 1996 Kevin Garnett: Hope you bought a few of these in 1996. Many years from now you'll wish you had. Production is unknown. We've seen the case breakdowns and read commentary that it is both in abundance and slightly tough to find.

Either way, this man will have a monster NBA career and this SLU from his rookie season will always be popular.

16. 1990 David Robinson: His rookie SLU with a moderate production of 16,000 pieces. With a ring on his finger and a great role model to all youth, this is a SLU worthy of the Top 25.

Someday those 16,000 pieces will dry up and you'll wish you had one. This is the largest produced SLU in the 1990 set. It's a marginal investment piece.

15. 1988 Mark Price: The Cavs team pieces were snapped up quickly by collectors in 1988. Production was limited on this team set. This Mark Price SLU had a very short production of 3,000 pieces, which means only 3,000 rookie cards were produced, which is a lot less than his Fleer rookie card. This has always been a tough find.

14. 1991 Dennis Rodman: The Worm's best SLU is his first one. Only 3,500 pieces were produced. This is a solid investment SLU because of the low production and the tremendous popularity of Rodman.

Forget the red hair issue, there are no tattoos or earrings on this one, but it is still the best one to own.

13. 1988 Mark Eaton: Kenner didn't even have a Jazz set in inventory in March of 1991. Production was so small for the Jazz that a lot of them were sold when collectors bought the whole 1988 set through the 800 number for $499.

The Eaton SLU was the least produced of all 1988 pieces with a meager 1,500 available.

12. 1991 Michael Jordan: All of his SLUs are pricey, this is no exception. Two versions of Jordan were made in 1991. A regular design and a jumping design. The regular design is the one you want with a production of 15,000 pieces.

The jumping or air design has 55,000 pieces, yet sells for not too much less than the regular piece. We'd say go figure out why, but we think collectors just like Jordan soaring in the air.

Any Jordan is great to own, but at 15,000 pieces this is the one you need.

11. 1988 Reggie Miller: What a great SLU to own. This SLU hits the trifecta. It has the shortest print of the 1988 Pacers team set and one of the lowest print runs of all 1988 issues at 4,000 pieces.

Fleer produced how many 1988 rookie cards of Miller? This SLU card is the one to own. Solid NBA career and solid investment with this Miller piece.

10. 1988 Scottie Pippen: Sure, it's his first SLU and he's Dream Teamer. Did you also know this SLU has a production of only 5,000 pieces and it, too, is his rookie card.

Worthy of being in the top 10,

this piece will always be considered a great investment.

9. 1989-90 One-on-One Magic Johnson vs. Larry Bird: Just typing these two names together brings back fond memories of the epic battles that took place in the 1980s between these two.

They both revolutionized the NBA. This is a terrific piece to own. Just less than 10,000 pieces were produced. This SLU is high on collector want lists. Very popular issue of two of the greatest, this is a solid investment piece.

8. 1993 Michael Jordan: The year Kenner started overproducing, we have to believe there are a lot of these Jordans out there, yet it continues to sell well because this is the final SLU Jordan ever produced. All Jordans are solid investments.

7. 1992 Dream Team Olympic team: An exceptional issue that came without trading cards. The greatest basketball team ever assembled comes in this special SLU issue.

It's a cornerstone piece for any serious SLU basketball collector. Only 25,000 of these were produced. Still fairly easy to find, make sure you have some of these tucked away.

6. 1989-90 One-on-One Michael Jordan vs. Isiah Thomas: When this one first came out, it sold for less than the Magic-Bird. Now it has a higher price tag. Does that mean that Jordan is better than Bird or Magic?

Being Laker fans, we don't want to confess anything there. Production is the same at just under 10,000 sets. This SLU is an outstanding investment.

5. 1988 John Stockton: Everything you've ever heard in the last 11 years about the 1988 Kenner SLU Jazz team issue is true – low production and they sold out in no time over the infamous Kenner 800 number.

There are only 2,800 of these Stockton pieces around. We wonder how many are still sealed?

Remember also that this is an NBA licensed product and that it contains not only the figurine but also a trading card. Forget Stockton's 1988 Fleer card, this one is real scarce at 2,800 cards produced. It's an outstanding SLU to own of the greatest assist man in NBA history.

4. 1988-89 Slam Dunk Michael Jordan: Go back to 1988. You're at the toy store and you spot a Jabbar SLU on the shelf for $4.99. It has a little coupon attached to the bubble. That coupon lead you to a free white box containing a slam dunk figure, complete with backboard and rim, of six NBA players including Jordan.

Not many went for the deal as production varied from 4,500 to 9,500 of each player. So Kenner put the Slam Dunks not given away through the coupon deal and put them in red boxes and sold them through an 800 number.

With this Jordan piece, about 8,000 went out in the white box and only 1,500 were sold in the red box, making the Slam Dunk SLU Jordan's lowest produced Kenner item.

3. 1988 Michael Jordan: We've read different production amounts on this "rookie" Jordan SLU. But back in 1988, when no one was concerned about production quotas, we got it from the horse's mouth that 30,000 pieces were produced. A large amount? Not if you realize that there are over 30,000 collectors of SLU that would want it.

2. 1992 Magic Johnson: Scarcity and the fact that it is Magic Johnson are the key to this lofty rating of No. 2. Only 750-1,000 of these yellow versions were produced before the error was corrected and the correct purple was issued.

These yellow versions were misdirected to the regular SLU issue when they were all supposed to be in the Headline issue. Some got out on the market and collectors went nuts trying to find this expensive piece.

1. 1988 Karl Malone: Call it what you want, this is the numero uno Kenner basketball SLU of all time. No other piece has or will ever dethrone it. Production was limited to 2,800 pieces.

We tried and tried and tried to find one to buy, and that was back in 1988 when they first came out. Believe it or not, we still don't have one. Collectors are enthralled with this Mona Lisa. The best of the best.

Tiger Stadium's last hurrah documented in photographs

By Robert Wimmer

Final game programs cause buying frenzy

Monday Sept. 27, 1999 was the day to say goodbye to Tiger Stadium. The Kansas City Royals were the opponents. The place was sold out even though only 43,356 fans showed up. Others kept their intact tickets for souvenirs and to sell at a later date for what they hope will be big bucks.

I arrived at Tiger Stadium about 10 a.m. to get a free parking space three blocks away. The local lots were charging $20 to $25 a pop to park. The new park will have parking controlled by the team. No more locals will benefit.

Vendors were out in force selling everything from plaques to T-shirts. But my place was going to be on Michigan and Trumbull, the "Corner" as it's known in Detroit. The crowds were starting to take over the sidewalks. The police had put up barricades in the street for extra space. Squad cars, the mounted division and hundreds of uniformed police were on hand to prevent what happened in 1984 when the Tigers won the World Series. There were even private security people all over.

This Tiger Stadium final game program is embossed and numbered.

At the corner I ran into several local dealer-collector-fan types standing around taking in the atmosphere of the final game. Then the action started. Inside the grounds a vendor came to the closed gates and started to sell final game programs which were numbered and embossed on the cover with the final game seal for $10. The way the fans reacted you would have thought they were giving the programs away. Out came 10s and 20s. Then 50s, then 100s, as fans started a buying frenzy to get these programs. Many of these people believed there were a very limited number of stamped programs available and bought on speculation.

After witnessing this frenzy, I walked to Neil Hefferman's Sportland USA store a half block away. Hefferman has been selling Tigers and sports souvenirs for years. He's seen it all, from the riots to the strikes, and now he was witnessing the Armageddon of his business and a part of Detroit history. The place was packed and people were spending.

Around 1:30 p.m., three hours before game time, they opened the doors. There was a special deal that you could get your ticket embossed with a special seal. The line hardly moved as people got their tickets embossed. It was a good thing they opened three hours before game time. I walked up Trumbull Street and found another gate with a line that wasn't embossing tickets. Moments later I was in with my camera and loads of film to record the final game. Once inside I found out that rather than scalp tickets for big bucks I should have brought extra rolls of film and sold them for big bucks. Many of these fans came to the game with only one or two rolls and were out by game time.

Then I headed off to a fenced-off area with a large group of former Tigers having a party.

I took pictures of all the former Tiger greats. Former players like Eldon Auker, Bill Freehan, Jack Morris, Mark "The Bird," Fidrych,

Willie Horton and many others. Former *SCD* columnist and current *Oakland* (Mich.) *Press* writer Jim Hawkins was there. We exchanged pleasantries and went over to his old buddy Ron LeFlore.

When I got to my seat I noticed all the ushers wore yellow T-shirts that stated FINAL GAME STAFF on the back. The Tigers will have a new group of ushers and vendors at the new park. Then I wandered around the park getting shots of the action on the field and interior shots of the concession stands, the vendors, the signs and the fans in the seats.

By the eighth inning I was back in my seat in right field. Then I recorded the final Tiger out as the Royals' Sanchez threw out Bartee at first. In the top on the ninth with two outs I got a photo of Jones with his arms in the air with the score showing 8-2 and 7:07 on the clock after he fanned Beltran for the final out ever at Tiger Stadium. After the game there were closing ceremonies as many of the former Tigers came out on the field in uniform to salute the final game. As the lights dimmed, the fans walked back to their cars to ponder the memories of the evening.

As soon as the closing ceremonies were over the Wayne County sheriff's deputies arrested LeFlore on a 1993 warrant for nonpayment of child support. The police even called a local promoter to ask how much LeFlore was paid for signing at a card show over the weekend at a Detroit area mall. The police were also monitoring the Internet after an eBay seller was offering a seat he stole during the final game, along with a program for auction. Then it was learned that autographed photos of Ty Cobb and the three DiMaggio brothers were taken from team owner Mike Ilitch's private office. Police suspect an inside job.

Tiger Stadium is now history. There was so much hoopla over the closing that everyone had all types of collectibles already. Hockey, football and basketball are starting up along with the World Series. In a short while spring will be here again and all those die-hard Tiger Stadium fans will line up for the opening game at the new stadium without a care for the old place. Life will go on.

Fans held up this banner to bid farewell to Tiger Stadium.

The final game at Tiger Stadium

Market Report

Yanks Win, Pedro Martinez Dominates and Mark McGwire Hits 65

Mark McGwire and Sammy Sosa made history in 1998 with their record-breaking home run totals. Consequently dealers expected a record-breaking season of card sales. Early '99 releases fared extremely well as they fed off the '98 season. Topps '99 Baseball Series I rode the wave with the McGwire Home Run Record subset that offered 70 different versions of card No. 220. Each one commemorates one of his 70 1998 home runs. The subset cards fueled sales, driving hobby boxes to $90 and packs to $3. McGwire's number 70 Home Run Record subset card peaked at $90 while his other singles were also in high demand.

Topps Chrome Series I also got off to a hot start with demand resting solely on the pursuit of the McGwire Home Run Record subset cards. The McGwire No. 70 Refractor peaked at an amazing $1,000, with the regular version a rapid seller for $250. Packs sold for $5 and boxes rose to $110.

Upper Deck Series I was another early release that dealers had success with. Controversy stirred with the Babe Ruth Piece of History insert that shredded a game-used bat once swung by the Bambino. It also marked the first time Upper Deck offered Game Jerseys exclusively in hobby packs, which also helped boost sales. The hobby-only game jerseys spurred Upper Deck hobby sales as hobby packs were well over SRP at $5 and boxes retailed for $110. The momentum of the early releases also carried over to Topps II and Topps Chrome II, with each product featuring the Sammy Sosa Home Run subset cards which had 66 different versions for each of Sosa's home runs.

Early season releases fared well, but late season releases struggled. The lack of impact rookies and a thriving football card market hurt late season releases, as football's rookie class overshadowed anything baseball had to offer. As a result, sales suffered.

REPEAT PERFORMANCE

McGwire held up his end of the bargain by threatening his own home run record. But this time, there wasn't the mad rush to get McGwire's and Sosa's rookie cards like the season before.

"They're chasing their own records," said Jim Roy, owner of V-J Baseball Cards in Gladstone, Mo. "Last year, they were chasing someone else's."

"There certainly hasn't been the flurry of activity like last year, as he closed in on the record," said Bob Babo, owner of Bayshore Sportscards in Hazlet, N.J.

In 1998, McGwire's 1985 Topps rookie card went from $30 to $200 after he broke the record. That's a 600 percent increase. McGwire's 65 home runs in 1999 had little effect as his rookie card remained strong at $200 throughout the season. Sosa's 1990 Leaf rookie experienced similar results as it jumped from $10 to $90 after his 66 home run performance in 1998 and actually slipped a bit during '99 to a price tag of $80.

PEDRO DOMINATES

Besides McGwire's remarkable 65 home runs in 1999, the other dominating performance in '99 was turned in by Pedro Martinez, who had one of the greatest seasons ever for a pitcher. Martinez finished with 23 wins in only 29 starts, 313 strikeouts and a 2.07 ERA and went on to unanimously win the Cy Young Award. He also would have won the AL MVP if two voters hadn't surprisingly left him off their ballots. Martinez's cards benefited from his amazing season as his 1992 Bowman doubled over the course of the season to $30. His 1991 Upper Deck Final Edition is his only true rookie card and it skyrocketed from $1.50 to $8 during the season.

NO IMPACT ROOKIES

In 1998, Kerry Wood had the baseball world on edge with his amazing achievements, including a record 20 strikeouts in one game. Wood helped spur mid and late season releases. There wasn't a dominating rookie performance in 1999. In fact, the NL Rookie of the Year was relief pitcher Scott Williamson of the Cincinnati Reds. Relief pitchers historically have had little or no impact with collectors and it's safe to say he had none.

The AL Rookie of the Year, Carlos Beltran, saw his only rookie card, 1995 Topps Traded and Rookies No. 18, catapault from $3 to $20 over the course of the season. However, his inclusion in '99 products also had no impact.

Top rookies in '99 products included Philadelphia Phillies prospect Pat Burrell. His top cards include 1999 Bowman (No. 175, $10), 1999 Bowman's Best (No. 151, $15) and 1999 Upper Deck (No. 266, $5). Alfonso Soriano is the best shortstop prospect, the problem is he's in the Yankees farm system which already has Derek Jeter. Collectors pursued Soriano's rookie cards as well, which include 1999 Bowman (No. 350, $6), 1999 Topps Gold Label (No. 30, $10) and 1999 Fleer Update (No. 5, $6).

Two late season releases: 1999 Fleer Update and 1999 Upper Deck Ultimate Victory included the most sought-after rookie card in the off-season, Rick Ankiel. They were the only products to include Ankiel's rookie and helped spur sales of both products.

YANKS WIN WORLD SERIES

For the third time in four years, the Yankees won the World Series. For the first time in his career, Roger Clemens acquired his long-awaited World Series ring. Clemens wasn't his usual dominating self. Nonetheless, he finally has a world chamionship under his belt. Despite the subpar season Clemens' cards experienced a revival. His 1985 Donruss (No. 273) and Fleer (No. 155) both jumped from $30 to $50 over the course of the season.

Jeter was the other Yankee who benefitted from a big year. He's the most popular player on baseball's best team in a high profile market so it wasn't a surprise his '93 SP rookie (No. 279) started the season priced at $30 and finished at $100. His other rookies that received a boost included 1993 Bowman (No. 511), which tripled from $10 to $30 and '93 Pinnacle (No. 457) which jumped from $5 to $12.

PLAYER OF THE YEAR

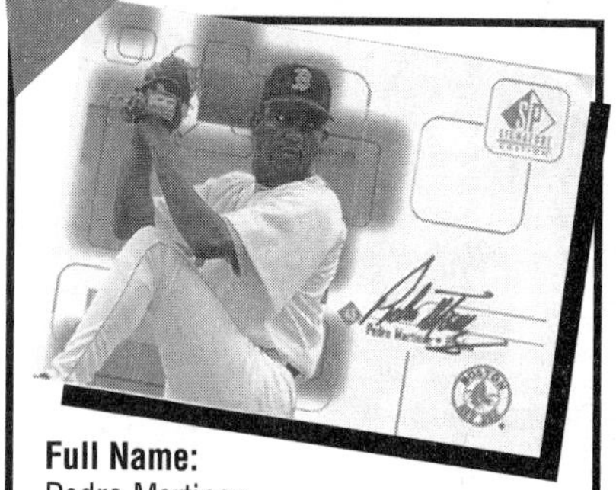

Full Name:
Pedro Martinez
Hometown:
Manoguayabo, Dominican Republic
Height: 5'11"
Weight: 170
Birthdate: 10/25/71
Drafted:
Not drafted by a MLB team.

Pedro Martinez

CARDS TO GET: Martinez has one true rookie card: 1991 Upper Deck Final Edition (#2, $8). Other top Martinez cards include 1992 Bowman (#82, $30), 1999 SP Signature Edition Autograph (#PM, $100), 2000 Ultra Feel the Game ($100), 2000 Upper Deck Game Jersey (#PM, $150) and 1996 Leaf Signature Series Autograph ($50).

TOP TENS

REGULAR-ISSUE SINGLES

1. Derek Jeter	1993 SP (#279)	$100
2. Pedro Martinez	1992 Bowman (#82)	$30
3. Alex Rodriguez	1994 SP (#15)	$100
4. Ken Griffey Jr.	1989 Upper Deck (#1)	$160
5. Mark McGwire	1999 Topps #220 (#70 Home Run)	$90
6. Mark McGwire	1985 Topps (#401)	$200
7. Shawn Green	1992 Stadium Club Dome (#67)	$15
8. Manny Ramirez	1992 Stadium Club Dome (#146)	$25
9. Carlos Beltran	1995 Topps Traded and Rookies (#18)	$20
10. Derek Jeter	1993 Bowman (#511)	$30

REGULAR-ISSUE SETS

1. 1992 Stadium Club Dome		200-card set: $40
2. 1995 Topps Traded and Rookies	$100/box	165-card set: $20
3. 1998 Leaf Rookies and Stars	$250	339-card set: $600
4. 1999 Topps I	$75	241-card set: $30
5. 1989 Upper Deck	$275	800-card set: $175
6. 1992 Bowman	$240	705-card set: $325
7. 1999 Bowman II	$80	220-card set: $130
8. 1999 Bowman Chrome II	$135	220-card set: $200
9. 1995 Bowman	$220	439-card set: $240
10. 1992 Topps Traded		132-card set: $120

BASEBALL

1998 Donruss Signature Series

The 140-card base set has a white border encasing the player photo with the logo stamped with silver foil. Card backs have a small photo and complete year-by-year statistics. Signature Proofs are a parallel to the base set utilizing holo-foil treatment and "Signature Proof" written down the left edge of the card front. Each card is numbered "1 of 150" on the card back.

		MT
Complete Set (140):		130.00
Common Player:		.25
Signature Proof Stars:		20x to 30x
Rookie Signature Proofs:		4x to 8x
1	David Justice	.40
2	Derek Jeter	2.50
3	Nomar Garciaparra	3.00
4	Ryan Klesko	.50
5	Jeff Bagwell	1.50
6	Dante Bichette	.50
7	Ivan Rodriguez	1.25
8	Albert Belle	1.25
9	Cal Ripken Jr.	4.00
10	Craig Biggio	.40
11	Barry Larkin	.40
12	Jose Guillen	.40
13	Will Clark	.50
14	J.T. Snow	.25
15	Chuck Knoblauch	.50
16	Todd Walker	.40
17	Scott Rolen	1.25
18	Rickey Henderson	.40
19	Juan Gonzalez	2.50
20	Justin Thompson	.25
21	Roger Clemens	2.00
22	Ray Lankford	.25
23	Jose Cruz Jr.	1.00
24	Ken Griffey Jr.	5.00
25	Andruw Jones	1.25
26	Darin Erstad	1.25
27	Jim Thome	.75
28	Wade Boggs	.50
29	Ken Caminiti	.40
30	Todd Hundley	.25
31	Mike Piazza	3.00
32	Sammy Sosa	4.00
33	Larry Walker	.75
34	Matt Williams	.50
35	Frank Thomas	3.00
36	Gary Sheffield	.50
37	Alex Rodriguez	3.00
38	Hideo Nomo	.50
39	Kenny Lofton	1.25
40	John Smoltz	.40
41	Mo Vaughn	1.25
42	Edgar Martinez	.25
43	Paul Molitor	1.00
44	Rafael Palmeiro	.75
45	Barry Bonds	1.25
46	Vladimir Guerrero	1.50
47	Carlos Delgado	.25
48	Bobby Higginson	.25
49	Greg Maddux	3.00
50	Jim Edmonds	.25
51	Randy Johnson	1.00
52	Mark McGwire	6.00
53	Rondell White	.40
54	Raul Mondesi	.40
55	Manny Ramirez	1.50
56	Pedro Martinez	1.00
57	Tim Salmon	.50
58	Moises Alou	.40
59	Fred McGriff	.40
60	Garret Anderson	.25
61	Sandy Alomar Jr.	.25
62	Chan Ho Park	.40
63	Mark Kotsay	.40
64	Mike Mussina	1.00
65	Tom Glavine	.50
66	Tony Clark	.75
67	Mark Grace	.50
68	Tony Gwynn	2.50
69	Tino Martinez	.75
70	Kevin Brown	.50
71	Todd Greene	.25
72	Andy Pettitte	.75
73	Livan Hernandez	.25
74	Curt Shilling	.50
75	Andres Galarraga	.75
76	Rusty Greer	.25
77	Jay Buhner	.50
78	Bobby Bonilla	.40
79	Chipper Jones	2.50
80	Eric Young	.25
81	Jason Giambi	.25
82	Javy Lopez	.40
83	Roberto Alomar	.75
84	Bernie Williams	.75
85	A.J. Hinch	.25
86	Kerry Wood	4.00
87	Juan Encarnacion	.50
88	Brad Fullmer	.25
89	Ben Grieve	1.25
90	*Magglio Ordonez*	6.00
91	Todd Helton	1.00
92	Richard Hidalgo	.25
93	Paul Konerko	.50
94	Aramis Ramirez	.50
95	Ricky Ledee	.75
96	Derrek Lee	.25
97	Travis Lee	1.00
98	*Matt Anderson*	2.00
99	Jaret Wright	1.00
100	David Ortiz	.40
101	Carl Pavano	.40
102	*Orlando Hernandez*	6.00
103	Fernando Tatis	.25
104	Miguel Tejada	.40
105	*Rolando Arrojo*	4.00
106	*Kevin Millwood*	10.00
107	Ken Griffey Jr.	2.50
108	Frank Thomas	1.50
109	Cal Ripken Jr.	2.00
110	Greg Maddux	1.50
111	John Olerud	.40
112	David Cone	.40
113	Vinny Castilla	.25
114	Jason Kendall	.40
115	Brian Jordan	.25
116	Hideki Irabu	.50
117	Bartolo Colon	.25
118	Greg Vaughn	.50
119	David Segui	.25
120	Bruce Chen	.50
121	*Julio Ramirez*	2.00
122	*Troy Glaus*	10.00
123	*Jeremy Giambi*	4.00
124	*Ryan Minor*	4.00
125	Richie Sexson	.25
126	Dermal Brown	.50
127	Adrian Beltre	1.00
128	Eric Chavez	2.00
129	*J.D. Drew*	40.00
130	*Gabe Kapler*	10.00
131	*Masato Yoshii*	1.00
132	*Mike Lowell*	2.00
133	*Jim Parque*	2.00
134	Roy Halladay	.75
135	*Carlos Lee*	4.00
136	*Jin Ho Cho*	.75
137	Michael Barrett	1.50
138	*Fernando Seguignol*	4.00
139	*Odalis Perez*	3.00
140	Mark McGwire	3.00

1998 Donruss Signature Series Autographs

Autographs were inserted one per pack and features the player photo over a silver and red foil background. The featured player's autograph appears on the bottom half portion of the card front with the logo stamped with gold foil. Autographs are un-numbered. The first 100 cards signed by each player are blue, sequentially numbered and designated as "Century Marks". The next 1,000 signed are green, sequentially numbered and designated as "Millenium Marks." Greg Maddux signed 12 regular Donruss Signature Autographs, due to scarcity it is not priced.

		MT
Complete Set (98):		
Common Player:		5.00
1	Roberto Alomar (150)	100.00
2	Sandy Alomar Jr. (700)	25.00
3	Moises Alou (900)	25.00
4	Gabe Alvarez (2,900)	5.00
5	Wilson Alvarez (1,600)	8.00
6	Jay Bell (1,500)	8.00
7	Adrian Beltre (1,900)	25.00
8	Andy Benes (2,600)	10.00
9	Aaron Boone (3,400)	5.00
10	Russell Branyan (1,650)	8.00
11	Orlando Cabrera (3,100)	5.00
12	Mike Cameron (1,150)	15.00
13	Joe Carter (400)	30.00
14	Sean Casey (2,275)	15.00
15	Bruce Chen (150)	50.00
16	Tony Clark (2,275)	15.00
17	Will Clark (1,400)	30.00
18	Matt Clement (1,400)	15.00
19	Pat Cline (400)	20.00
20	Ken Cloude (3,400)	8.00
21	Michael Coleman (2,800)	5.00
22	David Cone (25)	150.00
23	Jeff Conine (1,400)	10.00
24	Jacob Cruz (3,200)	5.00
25	Russ Davis (3,500)	5.00
26	Jason Dickson (1,400)	8.00
27	Todd Dunwoody (3,500)	5.00
28	Juan Encarnacion (3,400)	15.00
29	Darin Erstad (700)	50.00
30	Bobby Estalella (3,400)	5.00
31	Jeff Fassero (3,400)	5.00
32	John Franco (1,800)	5.00
33	Brad Fullmer (3,100)	10.00
34	Jason Giambi (3,100)	10.00
35	Derrick Gibson (1,200)	10.00
36	Todd Greene (1,400)	10.00
37	Ben Grieve (1,400)	40.00
38	Mark Grudzielanek (3,200)	8.00
39	Vladimir Guerrero (2,100)	30.00
40	Wilton Guerrero (1,900)	8.00
41	Jose Guillen (2,400)	12.00
42	Todd Helton (1,300)	30.00
43	Richard Hidalgo (3,400)	8.00
44	A.J. Hinch (2,900)	8.00
	Butch Huskey (1,900)	8.00
45	Raul Ibanez (3,300)	5.00
46	Damian Jackson (900)	5.00
47	Geoff Jenkins (3,100)	8.00
48	Eric Karros (650)	20.00
49	Ryan Klesko (400)	25.00
50	Mark Kotsay (3,600)	10.00
51	Ricky Ledee (2,200)	25.00
52	Derrek Lee (3,400)	8.00
53	Travis Lee (150)	75.00
54	Travis Lee (facsimile autograph, "SAMPLE" on back)	6.00
55	Javier Lopez (650)	20.00
56	Mike Lowell (3,500)	15.00
57	Greg Maddux (12)	
58	Eli Marrero (3,400)	5.00
59	Al Martin (1,300)	8.00
60	Rafael Medina (1,400)	5.00
61	Scott Morgan (900)	15.00
62	Abraham Nunez (3,500)	5.00
63	Paul O'Neill (1,000)	25.00
64	Luis Ordaz (2,700)	8.00
65	Magglio Ordonez (3,200)	12.00
66	Kevin Orie (1,350)	10.00
67	David Ortiz (3,400)	10.00
68	Rafael Palmeiro (1,000)	30.00
69	Carl Pavano (2,600)	8.00
70	Neifi Perez (3,300)	5.00
71	Dante Powell (3,050)	5.00
72	Aramis Ramirez (2,800)	15.00
73	Mariano Rivera (900)	20.00
74	Felix Rodriguez (1,400)	10.00
75	Henry Rodriguez (3,400)	8.00
76	Scott Rolen (1,900)	60.00
77	Brian Rose (1,400)	10.00
78	Curt Schilling (900)	25.00
79	Richie Sexson (3,500)	15.00
80	Randall Simon (3,500)	10.00
81	J.T. Snow (400)	20.00
82	Jeff Suppan (1,400)	10.00
83	Fernando Tatis (3,900)	10.00
84	Miguel Tejada (3,800)	10.00
85	Brett Tomko (3,400)	5.00
86	Bubba Trammell (3,900)	5.00
87	Ismael Valdez (1,900)	10.00
88	Robin Ventura (1,400)	20.00
89	Billy Wagner (3,900)	5.00
90	Todd Walker (1,900)	15.00
91	Daryle Ward (400)	15.00
92	Rondell White (3,400)	20.00
93	Antone Williamson (3,350)	5.00
94	Dan Wilson (2,400)	5.00
95	Enrique Wilson (3,400)	5.00
96	Preston Wilson (2,100)	10.00
97	Tony Womack (3,500)	5.00
98	Kerry Wood (3,400)	20.00

1998 Donruss Signature Series Century Marks

This 121-card set is a serially numbered, blue foil parallel of the Autographs insert set and limited to the first 100 cards signed by each featured player.

		MT
Complete Set (122):		
Common Player:		30.00
100 autos. for each player unless otherwise noted.		
1	Roberto Alomar	125.00
2	Sandy Alomar Jr.	40.00
3	Moises Alou	50.00
4	Gabe Alvarez	30.00
5	Wilson Alvarez	30.00
6	Brady Anderson	40.00
7	Jay Bell	30.00
8	Albert Belle	125.00
9	Adrian Beltre	100.00
10	Andy Benes	40.00
11	Wade Boggs	125.00
12	Barry Bonds	180.00
13	Aaron Boone	30.00
14	Russell Branyan	30.00
15	Jay Buhner	60.00
16	Ellis Burks	30.00
17	Orlando Cabrera	30.00
18	Mike Cameron	40.00
19	Ken Caminiti	60.00
20	Joe Carter	50.00
21	Sean Casey	40.00
22	Bruce Chen	40.00
23	Tony Clark	75.00
24	Will Clark	100.00
25	Roger Clemens	250.00
26	Matt Clement	40.00
27	Pat Cline	30.00
28	Ken Cloude	30.00
29	Michael Coleman	30.00
30	David Cone	50.00
31	Jeff Conine	30.00
32	Jacob Cruz	30.00
33	Jose Cruz Jr.	40.00
34	Russ Davis	30.00
35	Jason Dickson	30.00
36	Todd Dunwoody	30.00
37	Scott Elarton	30.00
38	Darin Erstad	75.00
39	Bobby Estalella	30.00
40	Jeff Fassero	30.00
41	John Franco	30.00
42	Brad Fullmer	40.00
43	Andres Galarraga	100.00
44	Nomar Garciaparra	350.00
45	Jason Giambi	40.00
46	Derrick Gibson	30.00
47	Tom Glavine	50.00
48	Juan Gonzalez	300.00
49	Todd Greene	30.00
50	Ben Grieve	125.00
51	Mark Grudzielanek	30.00
52	Vladimir Guerrero	125.00
53	Wilton Guerrero	40.00
54	Jose Guillen	40.00
55	Tony Gwynn	300.00
56	Todd Helton	90.00
57	Richard Hidalgo	40.00
58	A.J. Hinch	40.00
59	Butch Huskey	40.00
60	Raul Ibanez	30.00
61	Damian Jackson	30.00
62	Geoff Jenkins	40.00
63	Derek Jeter	300.00
64	Randy Johnson	100.00
65	Chipper Jones	300.00
66	Eric Karros (50)	50.00
67	Ryan Klesko	60.00
68	Chuck Knoblauch	100.00
69	Mark Kotsay	40.00
70	Ricky Ledee	40.00
71	Derrek Lee	30.00
72	Travis Lee	75.00
73	Javier Lopez	40.00
74	Mike Lowell	50.00
75	Greg Maddux	400.00
76	Eli Marrero	30.00
77	Al Martin	30.00
78	Rafael Medina	30.00
79	Paul Molitor	125.00
80	Scott Morgan	40.00
81	Mike Mussina	120.00
82	Abraham Nunez	30.00
83	Paul O'Neill	60.00
84	Luis Ordaz	30.00
85	Magglio Ordonez	60.00
86	Kevin Orie	30.00
87	David Ortiz	40.00
88	Rafael Palmeiro	80.00
89	Carl Pavano	40.00
90	Neifi Perez	30.00
91	Andy Pettitte	80.00
92	Aramis Ramirez	40.00
93	Cal Ripken Jr.	500.00
94	Mariano Rivera	60.00
95	Alex Rodriguez	400.00
96	Felix Rodriguez	30.00
97	Henry Rodriguez	40.00
98	Scott Rolen	160.00
99	Brian Rose	30.00
100	Curt Schilling	60.00
101	Richie Sexson	60.00
102	Randall Simon	40.00
103	J.T. Snow	30.00
104	Darryl Strawberry	60.00
105	Jeff Suppan	40.00
107	106Fernando Tatis	40.00
108	Brett Tomko	30.00
109	Bubba Trammell	30.00
110	Ismael Valdez	40.00
111	Robin Ventura	50.00
112	Billy Wagner	30.00
113	Todd Walker	60.00
114	Daryle Ward	30.00
115	Rondell White	50.00
116	116Matt Williams (80)	90.00
117	Antone Williamson	30.00

118 Dan Wilson 30.00
119 Enrique Wilson 30.00
120 Preston Wilson 40.00
121 Tony Womack 30.00
122 Kerry Wood 75.00

1998 Donruss Signature Series Millennium Marks

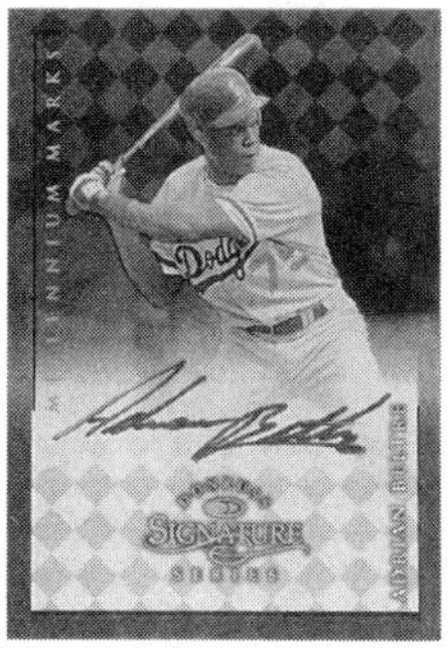

This is a green foil parallel version of the Autographs insert set and features the next 1,000 cards signed by the featured player after the initial 100. Cards are unnumbered.

	MT
Complete Set (125):	
Common Player:	12.00
1,000 autos. for each player unless noted otherwise	
1 Roberto Alomar	50.00
2 Sandy Alomar Jr.	20.00
3 Moises Alou	25.00
4 Gabe Alvarez	12.00
5 Wilson Alvarez	12.00
6 Brady Anderson (800)	20.00
7 Jay Bell	12.00
8 Albert Belle (400)	100.00
9 Adrian Beltre	40.00
10 Andy Benes	15.00
11 Wade Boggs (900)	60.00
12 Barry Bonds (400)	125.00
13 Aaron Boone	12.00
14 Russell Branyan	15.00
15 Jay Buhner (400)	35.00
16 Ellis Burks (900)	15.00
17 Orlando Cabrera	12.00
18 Mike Cameron	15.00
19 Ken Caminiti (900)	30.00
20 Joe Carter	20.00
21 Sean Casey	20.00
22 Bruce Chen	20.00
23 Tony Clark	25.00
24 Will Clark	40.00
25 Roger Clemens (400)	175.00
26 Matt Clement (900)	12.00
27 Pat Cline	12.00
28 Ken Cloude	12.00
29 Michael Coleman	12.00
30 David Cone	35.00
31 Jeff Conine	12.00
32 Jacob Cruz	12.00
33 Jose Cruz Jr. (850)	40.00
34 Russ Davis (950)	12.00
35 Jason Dickson (950)	12.00
36 Todd Dunwoody	12.00
37 Scott Elarton (900)	12.00
38 Juan Encarnacion	20.00
39 Darin Erstad	40.00
40 Bobby Estalella	12.00
41 Jeff Fassero	12.00
42 John Franco (950)	12.00
43 Brad Fullmer	20.00
44 Andres Galarraga (900)	50.00
45 Nomar Garciaparra (400)	200.00
46 Jason Giambi	15.00
47 Derrick Gibson	12.00
48 Tom Glavine (700)	40.00
49 Juan Gonzalez	120.00
50 Todd Greene	12.00
51 Ben Grieve	50.00
52 Mark Grudzielanek	12.00
53 Vladimir Guerrero	50.00
54 Wilton Guerrero	15.00
55 Jose Guillen	15.00
56 Tony Gwynn (900)	125.00
57 Todd Helton	40.00
58 Richard Hidalgo	15.00
59 A.J. Hinch	15.00
60 Butch Huskey	15.00
61 Raul Ibanez	12.00
62 Damian Jackson	12.00
63 Geoff Jenkins	15.00
64 Derek Jeter (400)	175.00
65 Randy Johnson (800)	50.00
66 Chipper Jones (900)	125.00
67 Eric Karros	15.00
68 Ryan Klesko	15.00
69 Chuck Knoblauch (900)	40.00
70 Mark Kotsay	20.00
71 Ricky Ledee	30.00
72 Derrek Lee	15.00
73 Travis Lee	40.00
74 Javier Lopez (800)	20.00
75 Mike Lowell	20.00
76 Greg Maddux (400)	275.00
77 Eli Marrero	12.00
78 Al Martin (950)	12.00
79 Rafael Medina (850)	12.00
80 Paul Molitor (900)	55.00
81 Scott Morgan	15.00
82 Mike Mussina (900)	50.00
83 Abraham Nunez	12.00
84 Paul O'Neill (900)	25.00
85 Luis Ordaz	12.00
86 Magglio Ordonez	30.00
87 Kevin Orie	15.00
88 David Ortiz	20.00
89 Rafael Palmeiro (900)	40.00
90 Carl Pavano	15.00
91 Neifi Perez	12.00
92 Andy Pettitte (900)	40.00
93 Dante Powell (950)	12.00
94 Aramis Ramirez	25.00
95 Cal Ripken Jr. (375)	300.00
96 Mariano Rivera	20.00
97 Alex Rodriguez (350)	250.00
98 Felix Rodriguez	15.00
99 Henry Rodriguez	15.00
100 Scott Rolen	80.00
101 Brian Rose	15.00
102 Curt Schilling	25.00
103 Richie Sexson	25.00
104 Randall Simon	20.00
105 J.T. Snow	12.00
106 Darryl Strawberry (900)	35.00
107 Jeff Suppan	15.00
108 Fernando Tatis	25.00
109 Miguel Tejada	20.00
110 Brett Tomko	12.00
111 Bubba Trammell	12.00
112 Ismael Valdes	15.00
113 Robin Ventura	30.00
114 Billy Wagner (900)	12.00
115 Todd Walker	25.00
116 Daryle Ward	12.00
116 Rondell White	25.00
117 Matt Williams (820)	40.00
118 Antone Williamson	12.00
119 Dan Wilson	12.00
120 Enrique Wilson	12.00
121 Preston Wilson (400)	20.00
122 Tony Womack	12.00
123 Kerry Wood	50.00

1998 Donruss Signature Series Baseball Redemptions

Redemption cards redeemable for autographed baseballs were randomly inserted in Donruss Signature Series packs. Baseballs are laser burned with a Donruss stamp to ensure authenticity. Every ball, except Ben Grieve's, are serial numbered.

	MT
Common Player:	25.00
1 Roberto Alomar (60)	60.00
2 Sandy Alomar Jr. (60)	30.00
3 Ernie Banks (12)	
4 Ken Caminiti (60)	25.00
5 Tony Clark (60)	30.00
6 Jacob Cruz (12)	
7 Russ Davis (60)	25.00
8 Juan Encarnacion (60)	40.00
9 Bobby Estalella (60)	25.00
10 Jeff Fassero (60)	25.00
11 Mark Grudzielanek (60)	25.00
12 Ben Grieve (30)	25.00
13 Jose Guillen (120)	25.00
14 Tony Gwynn (60)	125.00
15 Al Kaline (12)	
16 Paul Konerko (100)	25.00
17 Travis Lee (100)	40.00
18 Mike Lowell (60)	25.00
19 Eli Marrero (60)	25.00
20 Eddie Mathews (12)	
21 Paul Molitor (60)	75.00
22 Stan Musial (12)	
23 Abraham Nunez (12)	
24 Luis Ordaz (12)	
25 Magglio Ordonez (12)	
26 Scott Rolen (60)	100.00
27 Bubba Trammell (24)	
28 Robin Ventura (60)	40.00
29 Billy Wagner (60)	25.00
30 Rondell White (60)	30.00
31 Antone Williamson (12)	25.00
32 Tony Womack (60)	25.00

1998 Donruss Signature Series Significant Signatures

This 18-card autographed set features some of baseball's all-time great players. Each card is sequentially numbered to 2,000. The Sandy Koufax autographs weren't received in time prior to release and was redeemable by sending in the Billy Williams autograph, the collector would then receive both the Williams and Koufax back.

	MT
Complete Set (18):	800.00
Common Player:	25.00
Production 2,000 sets	
1 Ernie Banks	50.00
2 Yogi Berra	60.00
3 George Brett	80.00
4 Catfish Hunter	25.00
5 Al Kaline	40.00
6 Harmon Killebrew	40.00
7 Ralph Kiner	30.00
8 Sandy Koufax	100.00
9 Eddie Mathews	50.00
10 Don Mattingly	80.00
11 Willie McCovey	25.00
12 Stan Musial	75.00
13 Phil Rizzuto	30.00
14 Nolan Ryan	150.00
15 Ozzie Smith	60.00
16 Duke Snider	50.00
17 Don Sutton	25.00
18 Billy Williams	80.00
19 Billy Williams (redeemed)	30.00

1998 Fleer Update

Fleer produced its first Update set since 1994 with this 100-card boxed set. It arrived soon after the conclusion of the 1998 World Series and focused on rookies like J.D. Drew, Rick Croushore, Ryan Bradley, John Rocker, Mike Frank and Benj Sampson, who made their Major League debut in September and had not yet had a rookie card . The set had 70 rookies, including 15 making their Major League debut, 20 traded players and free agents. There was one subset called Season's Highlights that focused on feats like Mark McGwire's 70th home run, Sammy Sosa's single-month home run record and Kerry Wood's 20 strikeout performance.

	MT
Complete Set (100):	50.00
Common Player:	.10
U1 Mark McGwire ("Season Highlights")	3.00
U2 Sammy Sosa ("Season Highlights")	1.50
U3 Roger Clemens ("Season Highlights")	.75
U4 Barry Bonds ("Season Highlights")	.50
U5 Kerry Wood ("Season Highlights")	.75
U6 Paul Molitor ("Season Highlights")	.25
U7 Ken Griffey Jr. ("Season Highlights")	2.50
U8 Cal Ripken Jr. ("Season Highlights")	1.50
U9 David Wells ("Season Highlights")	.10
U10 Alex Rodriguez ("Season Highlights")	1.00
U11 *Angel Pena*	1.00
U12 Bruce Chen	.10
U13 Craig Wilson	.10
U14 *Orlando Hernandez*	5.00
U15 Aramis Ramirez	.25
U16 Aaron Boone	.10
U17 Bob Henley	.10
U18 Juan Guzman	.10
U19 Darryl Hamilton	.10
U20 Jay Payton	.10
U21 *Jeremy Powell*	.25
U22 Ben Davis	.10
U23 Preston Wilson	.10
U24 *Jim Parque*	1.50
U25 *Odalis Perez*	2.00
U26 Ron Belliard	.10
U27 Royce Clayton	.10
U28 George Lombard	.25
U29 Tony Phillips	.10
U30 *Fernando Seguignol*	4.00
U31 *Armando Rios*	.50
U32 *Jerry Hairston*	1.00
U33 *Justin Baughman*	.75
U34 Seth Greisinger	.10
U35 Alex Gonzalez	.10
U36 Michael Barrett	.50
U37 Carlos Beltran	.50
U38 Ellis Burks	.10
U39 Jose Jimenez	.40
U40 Carlos Guillen	.10
U41 Marlon Anderson	.10
U42 Scott Elarton	.10
U43 Glenallen Hill	.10
U44 Shane Monahan	.10
U45 Dennis Martinez	.10
U46 *Carlos Febles*	.20
U47 Carlos Perez	.10
U48 Wilton Guerrero	.10
U49 Randy Johnson	.10
U50 *Brian Simmons*	1.00
U51 Carlton Loewer	.10
U52 *Mark DeRosa*	.25
U53 *Tim Young*	.25
U54 Gary Gaetti	.10
U55 Eric Chavez	1.00
U56 Carl Pavano	.10
U57 Mike Stanley	.10
U58 Todd Stottlemyre	.10
U59 *Gabe Kapler*	6.00
U60 *Mike Jerzembeck*	.25
U61 *Mitch Meluskey*	2.00
U62 Bill Pulsipher	.10
U63 Derrick Gibson	.10
U64 *John Rocker*	1.50
U65 Calvin Pickering	.10
U66 Blake Stein	.10
U67 Fernando Tatis	.10
U68 Gabe Alvarez	.10
U69 Jeffrey Hammonds	.10
U70 Adrian Beltre	.50
U71 *Ryan Bradley*	2.00
U72 *Edgar Clemente*	.20
U73 *Rick Croushore*	.20
U74 Matt Clement	.25
U75 Dermal Brown	.10
U76 Paul Bako	.10
U77 *Placido Polanco*	.75
U78 Jay Tessmer	.10
U79 Jarrod Washburn	.10
U80 Kevin Witt	.10
U81 Mike Metcalfe	.10
U82 Daryle Ward	.10
U83 *Benj Sampson*	.20
U84 *Mike Kinkade*	.50
U85 Randy Winn	.10
U86 Jeff Shaw	.10
U87 *Troy Glaus*	6.00
U88 Hideo Nomo	.10
U89 Mark Grudzielanek	.10
U90 *Mike Frank*	1.50
U91 *Bobby Howry*	.50
U92 *Ryan Minor*	3.00
U93 *Corey Koskie*	1.00
U94 *Matt Anderson*	2.00
U95 Joe Carter	.10
U96 Paul Konerko	.10
U97 Sidney Ponson	.10
U98 *Jeremy Giambi*	4.00
U99 *Jeff Kubenka*	.20
U100 *J.D. Drew*	30.00

1998 Leaf Rookies & Stars

This 339-card set consists of three subsets: Power Tools, Lineup Card and Rookies. Card fronts feature full-bleed photos and silver foil stamping. Card backs have complete year-by-year statistics and a small photo. The base set also has short-printed base cards, which include card numbers (131-230, 301-339). Short-prints are seeded 1:2 packs. Rookies and Stars has two parallels to the base set: True Blue and Longevity. True Blues feature blue foil stamping and are each numbered "1 0f 500" on the card back. Longevitys are printed on a full-foiled card front with gold foil stamping and limited to 50 serially numbered sets.

	MT
Complete Set (339):	900.00
Common Player:	.15
Shortprints (131-230, 301-339):	
Common SPs:	.40
Inserted 1:2	
True Blues:	10x to 20x
SP True Blues:	3x to 5x
Production 500 sets	
Longevities:	60x to 100x
SP Longevities:	15x to 25x
Production 50 sets	
1 Andy Pettitte	.50
2 Roberto Alomar	.50
3 Randy Johnson	.50
4 Manny Ramirez	1.00
5 Paul Molitor	.50
6 Mike Mussina	.50
7 Jim Thome	.40
8 Tino Martinez	.30
9 Gary Sheffield	.25
10 Chuck Knoblauch	.30
11 Bernie Williams	.50
12 Tim Salmon	.25
13 Sammy Sosa	2.00
14 Wade Boggs	.25
15 Andres Galarraga	.50
16 Pedro Martinez	.50
17 David Justice	.30
18 Chan Ho Park	.30
19 Jay Buhner	.25
20 Ryan Klesko	.25
21 Barry Larkin	.25
22 Will Clark	.30
23 Raul Mondesi	.25
24 Rickey Henderson	.20
25 Jim Edmonds	.15
26 Ken Griffey Jr.	3.00
27 Frank Thomas	2.00
28 Cal Ripken Jr.	2.50
29 Alex Rodriguez	2.00
30 Mike Piazza	2.00
31 Greg Maddux	2.00
32 Chipper Jones	1.50
33 Tony Gwynn	1.50
34 Derek Jeter	1.50
35 Jeff Bagwell	.75
36 Juan Gonzalez	1.50
37 Nomar Garciaparra	2.00
38 Andruw Jones	.75
39 Hideo Nomo	.25
40 Roger Clemens	1.25
41 Mark McGwire	4.00
42 Scott Rolen	.75
43 Vladimir Guerrero	1.00
44 Barry Bonds	.75
45 Darin Erstad	.75
46 Albert Belle	.75
47 Kenny Lofton	.75
48 Mo Vaughn	.75
49 Ivan Rodriguez	.75
50 Jose Cruz Jr.	.50
51 Tony Clark	.50
52 Larry Walker	.40
53 Mark Grace	.25
54 Edgar Martinez	.15
55 Fred McGriff	.25
56 Rafael Palmeiro	.25
57 Matt Williams	.25
58 Craig Biggio	.25
59 Ken Caminiti	.20
60 Jose Canseco	.30

61	Brady Anderson	.15
62	Moises Alou	.25
63	Justin Thompson	.15
64	John Smoltz	.20
65	Carlos Delgado	.15
66	J.T. Snow	.15
67	Jason Giambi	.15
68	Garret Anderson	.15
69	Rondell White	.25
70	Eric Karros	.15
71	Javier Lopez	.25
72	Pat Hentgen	.15
73	Dante Bichette	.25
74	Charles Johnson	.15
75	Tom Glavine	.25
76	Rusty Greer	.15
77	Travis Fryman	.15
78	Todd Hundley	.15
79	Ray Lankford	.15
80	Denny Neagle	.15
81	Henry Rodriguez	.15
82	Sandy Alomar Jr.	.15
83	Robin Ventura	.15
84	John Olerud	.25
85	Omar Vizquel	.15
86	Darren Dreifort	.15
87	Kevin Brown	.25
88	Curt Schilling	.25
89	Francisco Cordova	.15
90	Brad Radke	.15
91	David Cone	.25
92	Paul O'Neill	.25
93	Vinny Castilla	.15
94	Marquis Grissom	.15
95	Brian Hunter	.15
96	Kevin Appier	.15
97	Bobby Bonilla	.15
98	Eric Young	.15
99	Jason Kendall	.25
100	Shawn Green	.15
101	Edgardo Alfonzo	.15
102	Alan Benes	.15
103	Bobby Higginson	.15
104	Todd Greene	.15
105	Jose Guillen	.25
106	Neifi Perez	.15
107	Edgar Renteria	.15
108	Chris Stynes	.15
109	Todd Walker	.25
110	Brian Jordan	.15
111	Joe Carter	.25
112	Ellis Burks	.15
113	Brett Tomko	.15
114	Mike Cameron	.15
115	Shannon Stewart	.15
116	Kevin Orie	.15
117	Brian Giles	.15
118	Hideki Irabu	.30
119	Delino DeShields	.15
120	David Segui	.15
121	Dustin Hermanson	.15
122	Kevin Young	.15
123	Jay Bell	.15
124	Doug Glanville	.15
125	*John Roskos*	.15
126	*Damon Hollins*	.15
127	Matt Stairs	.15
128	Cliff Floyd	.15
129	Derek Bell	.15
130	Darryl Strawberry	.15
131	Ken Griffey Jr. (Power Tools)	15.00
132	Tim Salmon (Power Tools)	1.50
133	Manny Ramirez (Power Tools)	5.00
134	Paul Konerko (Power Tools)	1.00
135	Frank Thomas (Power Tools)	10.00
136	Todd Helton (Power Tools)	4.00
137	Larry Walker (Power Tools)	2.00
138	Mo Vaughn (Power Tools)	4.00
139	Travis Lee (Power Tools)	3.00
140	Ivan Rodriguez (Power Tools)	4.00
141	Ben Grieve (Power Tools)	4.00
142	Brad Fullmer (Power Tools)	1.00
143	Alex Rodriguez (Power Tools)	10.00
144	Mike Piazza (Power Tools)	10.00
145	Greg Maddux (Power Tools)	10.00
146	Chipper Jones (Power Tools)	8.00
147	Kenny Lofton (Power Tools)	4.00
148	Albert Belle (Power Tools)	4.00
149	Barry Bonds (Power Tools)	4.00
150	Vladimir Guerrero (Power Tools)	5.00
151	Tony Gwynn (Power Tools)	8.00
152	Derek Jeter (Power Tools)	8.00
153	Jeff Bagwell (Power Tools)	5.00
154	Juan Gonzalez (Power Tools)	8.00
155	Nomar Garciaparra (Power Tools)	10.00
156	Andruw Jones (Power Tools)	4.00
157	Hideo Nomo (Power Tools)	1.50
158	Roger Clemens (Power Tools)	6.00
159	Mark McGwire (Power Tools)	20.00
160	Scott Rolen (Power Tools)	4.00
161	Travis Lee (Team Line-Up)	3.00
162	Ben Grieve (Team Line-Up)	4.00
163	Jose Guillen (Team Line-Up)	.60
164	John Olerud (Team Line-Up)	.60
165	Kevin Appier (Team Line-Up)	.40
166	Marquis Grissom (Team Line-Up)	.40
167	Rusty Greer (Team Line-Up)	.40
168	Ken Caminiti (Team Line-Up)	.60
169	Craig Biggio (Team Line-Up)	1.00
170	Ken Griffey Jr. (Team Line-Up)	15.00
171	Larry Walker (Team Line-Up)	2.00
172	Barry Larkin (Team Line-Up)	1.00
173	Andres Galarraga (Team Line-Up)	3.00
174	Wade Boggs (Team Line-Up)	1.00
175	Sammy Sosa (Team Line-Up)	12.00
176	Mike Piazza (Team Line-Up)	10.00
177	Jim Thome (Team Line-Up)	2.50
178	Paul Molitor (Team Line-Up)	3.00
179	Tony Clark (Team Line-Up)	2.00
180	Jose Cruz Jr. (Team Line-Up)	3.00
181	Darin Erstad (Team Line-Up)	4.00
182	Barry Bonds (Team Line-Up)	4.00
183	Vladimir Guerrero (Team Line-Up)	5.00
184	Scott Rolen (Team Line-Up)	4.00
185	Mark McGwire (Team Line-Up)	20.00
186	Nomar Garciaparra (Team Line-Up)	10.00
187	Gary Sheffield (Team Line-Up)	1.00
188	Cal Ripken Jr. (Team Line-Up)	12.00
189	Frank Thomas (Team Line-Up)	10.00
190	Andy Petitte (Team Line-Up)	2.00
191	Paul Konerko	1.00
192	Todd Helton	4.00
193	Mark Kotsay	.75
194	Brad Fullmer	.75
195	*Kevin Millwood*	30.00
196	David Ortiz	.75
197	Kerry Wood	3.00
198	Miguel Tejada	1.00
199	Fernando Tatis	.75
200	Jaret Wright	3.00
201	Ben Grieve	4.00
202	Travis Lee	3.00
203	Wes Helms	.40
204	Geoff Jenkins	.40
205	Russell Branyan	.40
206	*Esteban Yan*	.40
207	*Ben Ford*	.40
208	*Rich Butler*	4.00
209	*Ryan Jackson*	.40
210	A.J. Hinch	.40
211	*Magglio Ordonez*	60.00
212	*David Dellucci*	4.00
213	Billy McMillon	.40
214	*Mike Lowell*	6.00
215	*Todd Erdos*	.40
216	*Carlos Mendoza*	2.00
217	*Frank Catalanotto*	.40
218	*Julio Ramirez*	10.00
219	*John Halama*	.60
220	Wilson Delgado	.40
221	*Mike Judd*	4.00
222	*Rolando Arrojo*	8.00
223	Jason LaRue	4.00
224	*Manny Aybar*	.75
225	Jorge Velandia	.40
226	*Mike Kinkade*	3.00
227	*Carlos Lee*	25.00
228	Bobby Hughes	.40
229	*Ryan Christenson*	3.00
230	*Masato Yoshii*	1.00
231	Richard Hidalgo	.15
232	Rafael Medina	.15
233	Damian Jackson	.15
234	Derek Lowe	.15
235	Mario Valdez	.15
236	Eli Marrero	.15
237	Juan Encarnacion	.15
238	Livan Hernandez	.15
239	Bruce Chen	.50
240	Eric Milton	.15
241	Jason Varitek	.15
242	Scott Elarton	.15
243	*Manuel Barrios*	.30
244	Mike Caruso	.15
245	Tom Evans	.15
246	Pat Cline	.15
247	Matt Clement	.15
248	Karim Garcia	.15
249	Richie Sexson	.25
250	Sidney Ponson	.15
251	Randall Simon	.25
252	Tony Saunders	.15
253	Javier Valentin	.15
254	Danny Clyburn	.15
255	Michael Coleman	.15
256	*Hanley Frias*	.25
257	Miguel Cairo	.15
258	*Rob Stanifer*	.15
259	Lou Collier	.15
260	Abraham Nunez	.15
261	Ricky Ledee	.40
262	Carl Pavano	.15
263	Derrek Lee	.15
264	Jeff Abbott	.15
265	Bob Abreu	.15
266	Bartolo Colon	.15
267	Mike Drumright	.15
268	Daryle Ward	.15
269	Gabe Alvarez	.15
270	Josh Booty	.15
271	Damian Moss	.15
272	Brian Rose	.15
273	Jarrod Washburn	.15
274	Bobby Estalella	.15
275	Enrique Wilson	.15
276	Derrick Gibson	.15
277	Ken Cloude	.15
278	Kevin Witt	.15
279	Donnie Sadler	.15
280	Sean Casey	.25
281	Jacob Cruz	.15
282	Ron Wright	.15
283	Jeremi Gonzalez	.15
284	Desi Relaford	.15
285	Bobby Smith	.15
286	Javier Vazquez	.15
287	*Steve Woodard*	.25
288	Greg Norton	.15
289	Cliff Politte	.15
290	Felix Heredia	.15
291	Braden Looper	.15
292	Felix Martinez	.15
293	Brian Meadows	.15
294	Edwin Diaz	.15
295	Pat Watkins	.15
296	*Marc Pisciotta*	.15
297	Rick Gorecki	.15
298	DaRond Stovall	.15
299	Andy Larkin	.15
300	Felix Rodriguez	.15
301	Blake Stein	.40
302	*John Rocker*	8.00
303	*Justin Baughman*	3.00
304	*Jesus Sanchez*	4.00
305	Randy Winn	.40
306	Lou Merloni	.40
307	*Jim Parque*	6.00
308	Dennis Reyes	.40
309	*Orlando Hernandez*	15.00
310	Jason Johnson	.40
311	Torii Hunter	.40
312	Mike Piazza	15.00
313	*Mike Frank*	4.00
314	*Troy Glaus*	75.00
315	*Jin Cho*	.75
316	*Ruben Mateo*	50.00
317	*Ryan Minor*	30.00
318	Aramis Ramirez	3.00
319	Adrian Beltre	5.00
320	*Matt Anderson*	8.00
321	*Gabe Kapler*	60.00
322	*Jeremy Giambi*	15.00
323	Carlos Beltran	10.00
324	Dermal Brown	1.00
325	Ben Davis	3.00
326	Eric Chavez	15.00
327	*Bob Howry*	5.00
328	Roy Halladay	.75
329	George Lombard	5.00
330	Michael Barrett	8.00
331	*Fernando Seguignol*	15.00
332	*J.D. Drew*	100.00
333	*Odalis Perez*	15.00
334	*Alex Cora*	5.00
335	*Placido Polanco*	4.00
336	*Armando Rios*	1.00
337	Sammy Sosa (HR commemorative)	25.00
338	Mark McGwire (HR commemorative)	40.00
339	Sammy Sosa, Mark McGwire (Checklist)	30.00

1998 Leaf Rookies & Stars Cross Training

This 10-card insert set highlights players who excel at multiple aspects of the game. Card fronts are full-foiled and sequentially numbered on the card back to 1,000.

		MT
Complete Set (10):		240.00
Common Player:		8.00
Production 1,000 sets		
1	Kenny Lofton	12.00
2	Ken Griffey Jr.	60.00
3	Alex Rodriguez	40.00
4	Greg Maddux	40.00
5	Barry Bonds	15.00
6	Ivan Rodriguez	15.00
7	Chipper Jones	30.00
8	Jeff Bagwell	15.00
9	Nomar Garciaparra	40.00
10	Derek Jeter	30.00

1998 Leaf Rookies & Stars Donruss MVPs

This 20-card set is printed on a full silver foil card stock and sequentially numbered to 5,000. The first 500 of each card is treated with a "Pennant Edition" logo and unique color coating.

		MT
Complete Set (20):		150.00
Common Player:		2.00
Production 4,500 sets		
Pennant Editions:		2x to 4x
Production 500 sets		
1	Frank Thomas	12.00
2	Chuck Knoblauch	2.00
3	Cal Ripken Jr.	15.00
4	Alex Rodriguez	12.00
5	Ivan Rodriguez	5.00
6	Albert Belle	5.00
7	Ken Griffey Jr.	20.00
8	Juan Gonzalez	10.00
9	Roger Clemens	8.00
10	Mo Vaughn	5.00
11	Jeff Bagwell	5.00
12	Craig Biggio	2.00
13	Chipper Jones	10.00
14	Barry Larkin	2.00
15	Mike Piazza	12.00
16	Barry Bonds	5.00
17	Andruw Jones	5.00
18	Tony Gwynn	10.00
19	Greg Maddux	12.00
20	Mark McGwire	25.00

1998 Leaf Rookies & Stars Extreme Measures

These inserts are each printed on a full-foiled card front. Each card highlights an outstanding statistic for the featured player. Each card is sequentially numbered to 1,000.

		MT
Complete Set (10):		300.00
Common Player:		6.00
1	Ken Griffey Jr. (944)	60.00
2	Frank Thomas (653)	50.00
3	Tony Gwynn (628)	40.00
4	Mark McGwire (942)	75.00
5	Larry Walker (280)	20.00
6	Mike Piazza (960)	40.00
7	Roger Clemens (708)	30.00
8	Greg Maddux (980)	40.00
9	Jeff Bagwell (873)	20.00
10	Nomar Garciaparra (989)	40.00

1998 Leaf Rookies & Stars Extreme Measures Die-Cut

Each card highlights an outstanding statistic for each featured player, is die-cut and limited to the featured statistic.

		MT
Complete Set (10):		300.00
Common Player:		6.00
Die-Cut to featured stat		
1	Ken Griffey Jr. (56)	400.00
2	Frank Thomas (347)	70.00
3	Tony Gwynn (372)	60.00
4	Mark McGwire (58)	500.00
5	Larry Walker (720)	10.00
6	Mike Piazza (40)	275.00
7	Roger Clemens (292)	45.00
8	Greg Maddux (20)	500.00
9	Jeff Bagwell (127)	90.00
10	Nomar Garciaparra (11)	650.00

1998 Leaf Rookies & Stars Freshman Orientation

Card fronts are printed on holographic foil with silver foil stamping and features top young prospects. Card backs highlight the date of the featured player's Major League debut, have a small photo and are serially numbered to 5,000 sets.

		MT
Complete Set (20):		60.00
Common Player:		1.50
Production 5,000 sets		
1	Todd Helton	6.00
2	Ben Grieve	6.00
3	Travis Lee	5.00
4	Paul Konerko	2.50
5	Jaret Wright	4.00
6	Livan Hernandez	1.50
7	Brad Fullmer	2.50
8	Carl Pavano	1.50
9	Richard Hidalgo	1.50
10	Miguel Tejada	2.50
11	Mark Kotsay	2.00
12	David Ortiz	1.50

13	Juan Encarnacion	1.50
14	Fernando Tatis	1.50
15	Kevin Millwood	7.00
16	Kerry Wood	5.00
17	Magglio Ordonez	4.00
18	Derrek Lee	1.50
19	Jose Cruz Jr.	5.00
20	A.J. Hinch	1.50

1998 Leaf Rookies & Stars Great American Heroes

Card fronts are stamped with a holographic silver foil and done on a horizontal format. Card backs have a photo and are serially numbered to 2,500.

		MT
Complete Set (20):		250.00
Common Player:		4.00
Production 2,500 sets		
1	Frank Thomas	20.00
2	Cal Ripken Jr.	25.00
3	Ken Griffey Jr.	30.00
4	Alex Rodriguez	20.00
5	Greg Maddux	20.00
6	Mike Piazza	20.00
7	Chipper Jones	15.00
8	Tony Gwynn	15.00
9	Jeff Bagwell	8.00
10	Juan Gonzalez	15.00
11	Hideo Nomo	3.00
12	Roger Clemens	12.00
13	Mark McGwire	40.00
14	Barry Bonds	8.00
15	Kenny Lofton	8.00
16	Larry Walker	4.00
17	Paul Molitor	6.00
18	Wade Boggs	4.00
19	Barry Larkin	4.00
20	Andres Galarraga	6.00

1998 Leaf Rookies & Stars Greatest Hits

These inserts feature holographic silver foil stamping on the card front done on a horizontal format. Card backs have a photo and are serially numbered to 2,500.

		MT
Complete Set (20):		250.00
Common Player:		4.00
Production 2,500 sets		
1	Ken Griffey Jr.	30.00
2	Frank Thomas	20.00
3	Cal Ripken Jr.	25.00
4	Alex Rodriguez	20.00
5	Ben Grieve	8.00
6	Mike Piazza	20.00
7	Chipper Jones	15.00
8	Tony Gwynn	15.00
9	Derek Jeter	15.00
10	Jeff Bagwell	8.00
11	Tino Martinez	4.00
12	Juan Gonzalez	15.00
13	Nomar Garciaparra	20.00
14	Mark McGwire	40.00
15	Scott Rolen	8.00
16	David Justice	4.00
17	Darin Erstad	8.00
18	Mo Vaughn	8.00
19	Ivan Rodriguez	8.00
20	Travis Lee	6.00

1998 Leaf Rookies & Stars Home Run Derby

This 20-card set spotlights the top home run hitters on a bronze full-foiled card front. Card backs have a small photo and are serially numbered to 2,500.

		MT
Complete Set (20):		200.00
Common Player:		4.00
Production 2,500 sets		
1	Tino Martinez	4.00
2	Jim Thome	6.00
3	Larry Walker	4.00
4	Tony Clark	6.00
5	Jose Cruz Jr.	6.00
6	Barry Bonds	8.00
7	Scott Rolen	8.00
8	Paul Konerko	4.00
9	Travis Lee	6.00
10	Todd Helton	8.00
11	Mark McGwire	40.00
12	Andruw Jones	8.00
13	Nomar Garciaparra	20.00
14	Juan Gonzalez	15.00
15	Jeff Bagwell	8.00
16	Chipper Jones	15.00
17	Mike Piazza	20.00
18	Frank Thomas	20.00
19	Ken Griffey Jr.	30.00
20	Albert Belle	8.00

1998 Leaf Rookies & Stars ML Hard Drives

Card fronts are stamped with silver holographic foil. Card backs detail which field (left, center and right) the featured player hit each of his singles, doubles, triples and home runs. Each card is serially numbered to 2,500.

		MT
Complete Set (20):		220.00
Common Player:		4.00
Production 2,500 sets		
1	Jeff Bagwell	8.00
2	Juan Gonzalez	15.00
3	Nomar Garciaparra	20.00
4	Ken Griffey Jr.	30.00
5	Frank Thomas	20.00
6	Cal Ripken Jr.	25.00
7	Alex Rodriguez	20.00
8	Mike Piazza	20.00
9	Chipper Jones	15.00
10	Tony Gwynn	15.00
11	Derek Jeter	15.00
12	Mo Vaughn	8.00
13	Ben Grieve	8.00
14	Manny Ramirez	10.00
15	Vladimir Guerrero	10.00
16	Scott Rolen	8.00
17	Darin Erstad	8.00
18	Kenny Lofton	6.00
19	Brad Fullmer	4.00
20	David Justice	4.00

1998 Leaf Rookies & Stars Standing Ovation

Card fronts are stamped with silver holographic foil and card backs have a small photo of the featured player and are serially numbered to 5,000.

		MT
Complete Set (10):		90.00
Common Player:		2.00
Production 5,000 sets		
1	Barry Bonds	5.00
2	Mark McGwire	25.00
3	Ken Griffey Jr.	20.00
4	Frank Thomas	12.00
5	Tony Gwynn	10.00
6	Cal Ripken Jr.	15.00
7	Greg Maddux	12.00
8	Roger Clemens	8.00
9	Paul Molitor	4.00
10	Ivan Rodriguez	5.00

1998 Leaf Rookies & Stars Ticket Masters

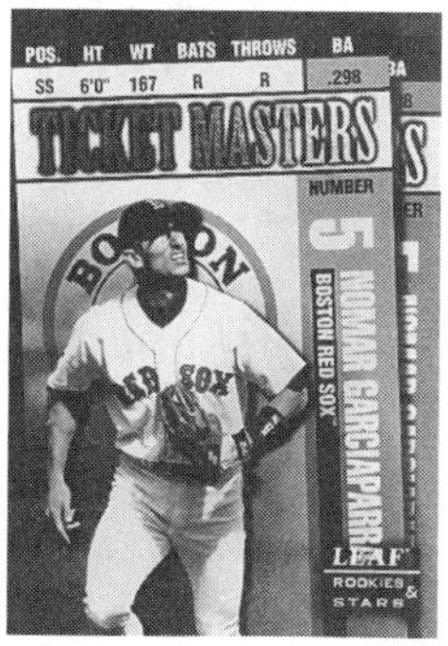

Card fronts are printed on a full-foiled card stock with silver foil stamping and have a photo of one of the two players featured from the same team. Card backs have a photo of the other featured player and are serially numbered to 2,500.

		MT
Complete Set (20):		225.00
Common Player:		4.00
Production 2,250 sets		
Die-Cuts:		2x to 3x
Production 250 sets		
1	Ken Griffey Jr., Alex Rodriguez	35.00
2	Frank Thomas, Albert Belle	20.00
3	Cal Ripken Jr., Roberto Alomar	25.00
4	Greg Maddux, Chipper Jones	20.00
5	Tony Gwynn, Ken Caminiti	15.00
6	Derek Jeter, Andy Pettitte	15.00
7	Jeff Bagwell, Craig Biggio	8.00
8	Juan Gonzalez, Ivan Rodriguez	15.00
9	Nomar Garciaparra, Mo Vaughn	20.00
10	Vladimir Guerrero, Brad Fullmer	10.00
11	Andruw Jones, Andres Galarraga	8.00
12	Tino Martinez, Chuck Knoblauch	4.00
13	Raul Mondesi, Paul Konerko	4.00
14	Roger Clemens, Jose Cruz Jr.	10.00
15	Mark McGwire, Brian Jordan	40.00
16	Kenny Lofton, Manny Ramirez	10.00
17	Larry Walker, Todd Helton	8.00
18	Darin Erstad, Tim Salmon	8.00
19	Travis Lee, Matt Williams	6.00
20	Ben Grieve, Jason Giambi	8.00

1999 Bowman

The 440-card set was issued in two 220-card series. Both series are comprised of 70 veteran cards and 150 rookie/prospect cards. Rookie/prospect cards have silver and blue foil stamping and veteran cards have silver and red foil stamping. Also on each card is the player's facsimile autograph, taken from their initial Topps contract.

		MT
Complete Set (440):		130.00
Complete Series I set (220):		60.00
Complete Series II Set (220):		70.00
Common Player:		.15
Intern. Stars:		1.5x to 2x
Intern. RCs:		1x to 1.5x
Inserted 1:1		
Gold Stars:		20x to 40x
Gold RCs:		4x to 10x
Production 99 sets		
1	Ben Grieve	.75
2	Kerry Wood	1.00
3	Ruben Rivera	.15
4	Sandy Alomar	.25
5	Cal Ripken Jr.	3.00
6	Mark McGwire	5.00
7	Vladimir Guerrero	1.50
8	Moises Alou	.25
9	Jim Edmonds	.15
10	Greg Maddux	2.50
11	Gary Sheffield	.25
12	John Valentin	.15
13	Chuck Knoblauch	.40
14	Tony Clark	.40
15	Rusty Greer	.15
16	Al Leiter	.15
17	Travis Lee	.75
18	Jose Cruz Jr.	.60
19	Pedro Martinez	.75
20	Paul O'Neill	.40
21	Todd Walker	.25
22	Vinny Castilla	.25
23	Barry Larkin	.40
24	Curt Schilling	.40
25	Jason Kendall	.25
26	Scott Erickson	.15
27	Andres Galarraga	.40
28	Jeff Shaw	.15
29	John Olerud	.25
30	Orlando Hernandez	1.00
31	Larry Walker	.75
32	Andruw Jones	1.00
33	Jeff Cirillo	.15
34	Barry Bonds	1.00
35	Manny Ramirez	2.00
36	Mark Kotsay	.15
37	Ivan Rodriguez	1.00
38	Jeff King	.15
39	Brian Hunter	.15
40	Ray Durham	.15
41	Bernie Williams	.75
42	Darin Erstad	1.00
43	Chipper Jones	2.50
44	Pat Hentgen	.15
45	Eric Young	.15
46	Jaret Wright	.50
47	Juan Guzman	.15
48	Jorge Posada	.25
49	Bobby Higginson	.15
50	Jose Guillen	.15
51	Trevor Hoffman	.15
52	Ken Griffey Jr.	4.00
53	David Justice	.40
54	Matt Williams	.40
55	Eric Karros	.25
56	Derek Bell	.15
57	Ray Lankford	.15
58	Mariano Rivera	.25
59	Brett Tomko	.15
60	Mike Mussina	.60
61	Kenny Lofton	1.00
62	Chuck Finley	.15
63	Alex Gonzalez	.15
64	Mark Grace	.30
65	Raul Mondesi	.30
66	David Cone	.25
67	Brad Fullmer	.25
68	Andy Benes	.15
69	John Smoltz	.25
70	Shane Reynolds	.25
71	Bruce Chen	.40
72	Adam Kennedy	.15
73	Jack Cust	.15
74	Matt Clement	.15
75	Derrick Gibson	.15
76	Darnell McDonald	.15
77	*Adam Everett*	2.00
78	Ricardo Aramboles	.15
79	*Mark Quinn*	1.00
80	Jason Rakers	.15
81	*Seth Etherton*	2.00
82	*Jeff Urban*	1.00
83	Manny Aybar	.15
84	*Mike Nannini*	1.50
85	Onan Masaoka	.15
86	Rod Barajas	.15
87	Mike Frank	.15
88	Scott Randall	.15
89	*Justin Bowles*	.50
90	Chris Haas	.15
91	*Arturo McDowell*	1.00
92	*Matt Belisle*	1.00
93	Scott Elarton	.15
94	Vernon Wells	.15
95	Pat Cline	.15
96	Ryan Anderson	1.00
97	Kevin Barker	.15
98	Ruben Mateo	2.00
99	Robert Fick	.15
100	Corey Koskie	.15
101	Ricky Ledee	.25
102	*Rick Elder*	3.00
103	*Jack Cressend*	.75
104	Joe Lawrence	.15
105	Mike Lincoln	.15
106	*Kit Pellow*	1.00
107	*Matt Burch*	2.00
108	Brent Butler	.15
109	Jason Dewey	.15
110	Cesar King	.15
111	Julio Ramirez	.15
112	Jake Westbrook	.15
113	*Eric Valent*	5.00
114	*Roosevelt Brown*	.75
115	*Choo Freeman*	1.50
116	Juan Melo	.15
117	Jason Grilli	.15
118	Jared Sandberg	.15
119	Glenn Davis	.15
120	*David Riske*	.75
121	Jacque Jones	.15
122	Corey Lee	.15
123	Michael Barrett	.40
124	Lariel Gonzalez	.15
125	Mitch Meluskey	.15
126	*Freddy Garcia*	2.00
127	*Tony Torcato*	1.00
128	Jeff Liefer	.15
129	Ntema Ndungidi	.15
130	*Andy Brown*	1.50
131	*Ryan Mills*	2.00
132	*Andy Abad*	.50
133	Carlos Febles	.15
134	*Jason Tyner*	1.00
135	Mark Osborne	.15
136	*Phil Norton*	1.00
137	Nathan Haynes	.15
138	Roy Halladay	.15
139	Juan Encarnacion	.15
140	Brad Penny	.15
141	Grant Roberts	.15
142	Aramis Ramirez	.15
143	Cristian Guzman	.15
144	*Mamon Tucker*	1.50
145	Ryan Bradley	.15
146	Brian Simmons	.15
147	Dan Reichert	.15

148	Russ Branyon	.15
149	*Victor Valencia*	2.00
150	Scott Schoeneweis	.15
151	*Sean Spencer*	.75
152	Odalis Perez	.15
153	Joe Fontenot	.15
154	Milton Bradley	.15
155	*Josh McKinley*	1.50
156	Terrence Long	.15
157	Danny Klassen	.15
158	*Paul Hoover*	1.00
159	Ron Belliard	.15
160	Armando Rios	.15
161	Ramon Hernandez	.15
162	Jason Conti	.15
163	Chad Hermansen	.15
164	Jason Standridge	.15
165	Jason Dellaero	.15
166	John Curtice	.15
167	*Clayton Andrews*	2.00
168	Jeremy Giambi	.25
169	Alex Ramirez	.15
170	*Gabe Molina*	.15
171	*Mario Encarnacion*	1.50
172	*Mike Zywica*	1.50
173	*Chip Ambres*	1.50
174	Trot Nixon	.15
175	*Pat Burrell*	10.00
176	Jeff Yoder	.15
177	*Chris Jones*	1.00
178	Kevin Witt	.15
179	*Keith Luuloa*	.50
180	Billy Koch	.15
181	*Damaso Marte*	1.00
182	*Ryan Glynn*	1.50
183	Calvin Pickering	.40
184	Michael Cuddyer	.15
185	*Nick Johnson*	5.00
186	*Doug Mientkiewicz*	1.00
187	*Nate Cornejo*	1.00
188	Octavio Dotel	.15
189	Wes Helms	.15
190	Nelson Lara	.15
191	*Chuck Abbott*	1.50
192	Tony Armas, Jr.	.15
193	Gil Meche	.15
194	Ben Petrick	.15
195	*Chris George*	1.50
196	*Scott Hunter*	.75
197	Ryan Brannan	.15
198	*Amaury Garcia*	.75
199	Chris Gissell	.15
200	*Austin Kearns*	3.00
201	Alex Gonzalez	.15
202	Wade Miller	.15
203	Scott Williamson	.15
204	Chris Enochs	.15
205	Fernando Seguignol	.50
206	Marlon Anderson	.15
207	Todd Sears	.75
208	*Nate Bump*	1.50
209	*J.M. Gold*	3.00
210	Matt LeCroy	.15
211	Alex Hernandez	.15
212	Luis Rivera	.15
213	Troy Cameron	.15
214	*Alex Escobar*	5.00
215	Jason LaRue	.15
216	Kyle Peterson	.15
217	Brent Butler	.15
218	Dernell Stenson	.40
219	Adrian Beltre	.75
220	Daryle Ward	.15
----	Series 1 Checklist Folder	.15
221	Jim Thome	.50
222	Cliff Floyd	.15
223	Rickey Henderson	.25
224	Garret Anderson	.15
225	Ken Caminiti	.25
226	Bret Boone	.15
227	Jeromy Burnitz	.15
228	Steve Finley	.15
229	Miguel Tejada	.15
230	Greg Vaughn	.25
231	Jose Offerman	.15
232	Andy Ashby	.15
233	Albert Belle	1.00
234	Fernando Tatis	.40
235	Todd Helton	.50
236	Sean Casey	.75
237	Brian Giles	.15
238	Andy Pettitte	.25
239	Fred McGriff	.25
240	Roberto Alomar	.75
241	Edgar Martinez	.15
242	Lee Stevens	.15
243	Shawn Green	.40
244	Ryan Klesko	.25
245	Sammy Sosa	2.50
246	Todd Hundley	.15
247	Shannon Stewart	.15
248	Randy Johnson	.75
249	Rondell White	.25
250	Mike Piazza	2.50
251	Craig Biggio	.50
252	David Wells	.15
253	Brian Jordan	.15
254	Edgar Renteria	.15
255	Bartolo Colon	.15
256	Frank Thomas	1.50
257	Will Clark	.50
258	Dean Palmer	.15
259	Dmitri Young	.15
260	Scott Rolen	1.00
261	Jeff Kent	.15
262	Dante Bichette	.40
263	Nomar Garciaparra	2.50
264	Tony Gwynn	2.00
265	Alex Rodriguez	2.50
266	Jose Canseco	.75
267	Jason Giambi	.15
268	Jeff Bagwell	1.50
269	Carlos Delgado	.50
270	Tom Glavine	.25
271	Eric Davis	.15
272	Edgardo Alfonzo	.25
273	Tim Salmon	.25
274	Johnny Damon	.15
275	Rafael Palmeiro	.75
276	Denny Neagle	.15
277	Neifi Perez	.15
278	Roger Clemens	1.50
279	Brant Brown	.15
280	Kevin Brown	.25
281	Jay Bell	.15
282	Jay Buhner	.25
283	Matt Lawton	.15
284	Robin Ventura	.25
285	Juan Gonzalez	1.50
286	Mo Vaughn	1.00
287	Kevin Millwood	.50
288	Tino Martinez	.50
289	Justin Thompson	.15
290	Derek Jeter	2.50
291	Ben Davis	.15
292	Mike Lowell	.15
293	*Joe Crede*	.40
294	*Micah Bowie*	1.00
295	Lance Berkman	.25
296	Jason Marquis	.15
297	Chad Green	.15
298	Dee Brown	.15
299	Jerry Hairston	.15
300	Gabe Kapler	.50
301	*Brent Stentz*	.50
302	*Scott Mullen*	.50
303	Brandon Reed	.15
304	*Shea Hillenbrand*	1.50
305	*J.D. Closser*	1.00
306	Gary Matthews Jr.	.15
307	*Toby Hall*	.75
308	*Jason Phillips*	.50
309	*Jose Macias*	.40
310	*Jung Bong*	2.00
311	*Ramon Soler*	.75
312	*Kelly Dransfeldt*	1.00
313	*Carlos Hernandez*	.50
314	Kevin Haverbusch	.15
315	*Aaron Myette*	1.50
316	*Chad Harville*	.50
317	*Kyle Farnsworth*	1.50
318	*Travis Dawkins*	1.00
319	Willie Martinez	.15
320	Carlos Lee	.15
321	*Carlos Pena*	3.00
322	*Peter Bergeron*	2.00
323	*A.J. Burnett*	3.00
324	*Bucky Jacobsen*	1.00
325	*Mo Bruce*	1.00
326	Reggie Taylor	.15
327	Jackie Rexrode	.15
328	*Alvin Morrow*	.50
329	Carlos Beltran	.50
330	Eric Chavez	.40
331	John Patterson	.15
332	Jayson Werth	.15
333	Richie Sexson	.15
334	Randy Wolf	.15
335	Eli Marrero	.15
336	Paul LoDuca	.15
337	J.D. Smart	.15
338	Ryan Minor	.15
339	Kris Benson	.15
340	George Lombard	.15
341	Troy Glaus	.75
342	Eddie Yarnell	.15
343	*Kip Wells*	2.50
344	*C.C. Sabathia*	3.00
345	*Sean Burroughs*	5.00
346	*Felipe Lopez*	.75
347	*Ryan Rupe*	1.00
348	*Orber Moreno*	.75
349	*Rafael Roque*	.75
350	*Alfonso Soriano*	6.00
351	Pablo Ozuna	.15
352	*Corey Patterson*	5.00
353	Braden Looper	.15
354	Robbie Bell	.15
355	*Mark Mulder*	2.50
356	Angel Pena	.15
357	Kevin McGlinchy	.15
358	*Michael Restovich*	4.00
359	Eric DuBose	.15
360	Geoff Jenkins	.15
361	*Mark Harriger*	1.00
362	*Junior Herndon*	.50
363	*Tim Raines, Jr.*	.75
364	*Rafael Furcal*	2.00
365	*Marcus Giles*	3.00
366	Ted Lilly	.15
367	*Jorge Toca*	2.00
368	*David Kelton*	.75
369	*Adam Dunn*	.75
370	*Guillermo Mota*	1.00
371	*Brett Laxton*	.50
372	*Travis Harper*	.50
373	*Tom Davey*	.50
374	*Darren Blakely*	.75
375	*Tim Hudson*	5.00
376	Jason Romano	.15
377	Dan Reichert	.15
378	*Julio Lugo*	.50
379	*Jose Garcia*	.50
380	*Erubiel Durazo*	10.00
381	Jose Jimenez	.15
382	Chris Fussell	.15
383	Steve Lomasney	.15
384	*Juan Pena*	1.00
385	*Allen Levrault*	.50
386	*Juan Rivera*	1.00
387	*Steve Colyer*	.50
388	*Joe Nathan*	1.50
389	*Ron Walker*	.75
390	Nick Bierbrodt	.15
391	*Luke Prokopec*	1.00
392	*Dave Roberts*	.75
393	Mike Darr	.15
394	*Abraham Nunez*	2.00
395	*Giuseppe Chiaramonte*	1.00
396	*Jermaine Van Buren*	.50
397	Mike Kusiewicz	.15
398	*Matt Wise*	.50
399	*Joe McEwing*	3.00
400	*Matt Holliday*	1.00
401	*Willi Mo Pena*	.75
402	*Ruben Quevedo*	.75
403	*Rob Ryan*	.50
404	*Freddy Garcia*	6.00
405	*Kevin Eberwein*	.50
406	*Jesus Colome*	.75
407	*Chris Singleton*	1.50
408	*Bubba Crosby*	.50
409	*Jesus Cordero*	.50
410	Donny Leon	.15
411	*Goefrey Tomlinson*	.50
412	*Jeff Winchester*	.50
413	*Adam Piatt*	4.00
414	Robert Stratton	.15
415	T.J. Tucker	.15
416	*Ryan Langerhans*	.50
417	*Anthony Shumaker*	.50
418	*Matt Miller*	.50
419	*Doug Clark*	.75
420	*Kory DeHaan*	1.00
421	*David Eckstein*	.50
422	*Brian Cooper*	.50
423	*Brady Clark*	.50
424	*Chris Magruder*	.50
425	*Bobby Seay*	1.50
426	*Aubrey Huff*	.15
427	Mike Jerzembeck	.15
428	*Matt Blank*	.50
429	*Benny Agbayani*	3.00
430	*Kevin Beirne*	.50
431	*Josh Hamilton*	6.00
432	*Josh Girdley*	.75
433	*Kyle Snyder*	1.50
434	*Mike Paradis*	1.00
435	*Jason Jennings*	.75
436	*David Walling*	2.00
437	*Omar Ortiz*	.50
438	*Jay Gehrke*	1.00
439	*Casey Burns*	.50
440	*Carl Crawford*	2.00

1999 Bowman Autographs

Autographs were randomly seeded in Series I and II packs, each card is stamped Topps Certified Autograph on the card fronts and each card is numbered with a "BA" prefix on the card back. Card rarity is differentiated by either a Blue, Silver or Gold foil stamping. Golds are the most difficult to find and are seeded 1:1,941, Silvers 1:485 and Blue 1:162.

		MT
	Common Player:	10.00
	Blues inserted 1:162	
	Silvers inserted 1:486	
	Golds inserted 1:1,954	
1	Ruben Mateo	50.00
2	Troy Glaus G	40.00
3	Ben Davis G	25.00
4	Jayson Werth	10.00
5	Jerry Hairston Jr. S	20.00
6	Darnell McDonald	10.00
7	Calvin Pickering S	25.00
8	Ryan Minor S	20.00
9	Alex Escobar	25.00
10	Grant Roberts	10.00
11	Carlos Guillen	10.00
12	Ryan Anderson S	25.00
13	Gil Meche S	15.00
14	Russell Branyan S	20.00
15	Alex Ramirez S	25.00
16	Jason Rakers S	20.00
17	Eddie Yarnall	10.00
18	Freddy Garcia	50.00
19	Jason Conti	10.00
20	Corey Koskie	10.00
21	Roosevelt Brown	10.00
22	Willie Martinez	10.00
23	Mike Jerzembeck	10.00
24	Lariel Gonzalez	10.00
25	Fernando Seguignol	20.00
26	Robert Fick S	20.00
27	J.D. Smart	10.00
28	Ryan Mills	10.00
29	Chad Hermansen G	50.00
30	Jason Grilli	10.00
31	Michael Cuddyer	10.00
32	Jacque Jones S	20.00
33	Reggie Taylor	10.00
34	Richie Sexson G	50.00
35	Michael Barrett	20.00
36	Paul LoDuca	10.00
37	Adrian Beltre G	40.00
38	Peter Bergeron	10.00
39	Joe Fontenot	10.00
40	Randy Wolf	10.00
41	Nick Johnson	40.00
42	Ryan Bradley	20.00
43	Mike Lowell S	15.00
44	Ricky Ledee	15.00
45	Mike Lincoln S	15.00
46	Jeremy Giambi	15.00
47	Dermal Brown S	20.00
48	Derrick Gibson	10.00
49	Scott Randall	10.00
50	Ben Petrick S	10.00
51	Jason LaRue	10.00
52	Cole Liniak	10.00
53	John Curtice	10.00
54	Jackie Rexrode	10.00
55	John Patterson	10.00
56	Brad Penny S	20.00
57	Jared Sandberg	10.00
58	Kerry Wood G	40.00
59	Eli Marrero	10.00
60	Jason Marquis	15.00
61	George Lombard S	15.00
62	Bruce Chen S	25.00
63	Kevin Witt S	10.00
64	Vernon Wells	25.00
65	Billy Koch	10.00
66	Roy Halladay	50.00
67	Nathan Haynes	10.00
68	Ben Grieve G	60.00
69	Eric Chavez G	30.00
70	Lance Berkman S	25.00

1999 Bowman Early Risers

This set features 11 current baseball superstars who have already won a Rookie of the Year award and who continue to excel. The insertion rate is 1:12.

		MT
	Complete Set (11):	30.00
	Common Player:	1.00
	Inserted 1:12	
1	Mike Piazza	5.00
2	Cal Ripken Jr.	6.00
3	Jeff Bagwell	2.50
4	Ben Grieve	1.50
5	Kerry Wood	1.00
6	Mark McGwire	10.00
7	Nomar Garciaparra	5.00
8	Derek Jeter	5.00
9	Scott Rolen	2.00
10	Jose Canseco	1.50
11	Raul Mondesi	1.00

1999 Bowman Late Bloomers

This 10-card set features late round picks from previous drafts who have emerged as stars on the field, including Mike Piazza and Jim Thome. These are seeded 1:12 packs.

		MT
	Complete Set (10):	12.00
	Common Player:	.50
	Inserted 1:12	
LB1	Mike Piazza	6.00
LB2	Jim Thome	2.00
LB3	Larry Walker	1.50
LB4	Vinny Castilla	.50
LB5	Andy Pettitte	.75
LB6	Jim Edmonds	.50
LB7	Kenny Lofton	2.50
LB8	John Smoltz	.50
LB9	Mark Grace	.75
LB10	Trevor Hoffman	.50

1999 Bowman Scout's Choice

Scout's Choice inserts were randomly inserted in series I packs and feature a borderless, double-etched design. The 21-card set focuses on prospects who have potential to win a future Rookie of the Year award. These are seeded 1:12 packs.

		MT
	Complete Set (21):	45.00
	Common Player:	1.00
	Inserted 1:12	
SC1	Ruben Mateo	6.00
SC2	Ryan Anderson	4.00
SC3	Pat Burrell	15.00
SC4	Troy Glaus	7.00
SC5	Eric Chavez	5.00
SC6	Adrian Beltre	2.50
SC7	Bruce Chen	1.50
SC8	Carlos Beltran	2.00
SC9	Alex Gonzalez	1.00
SC10	Carlos Lee	2.00
SC11	George Lombard	2.00
SC12	Matt Clement	1.00
SC13	Calvin Pickering	1.00
SC14	Marlon Anderson	1.00
SC15	Chad Hermansen	1.00
SC16	Russell Branyan	1.00
SC17	Jeremy Giambi	2.00
SC18	Ricky Ledee	1.00
SC19	John Patterson	1.00
SC20	Roy Halladay	2.00
SC21	Michael Barrett	1.50

1999 Bowman 2000 Rookie of the Year

Randomly inserted in series II packs at a rate of 1:12 packs, these have a borderless, double-etched foil design. The 10-card set focuses on players that have potential to win the 2000 Rookie of the Year award.

		MT
Complete Set (10):		15.00
Common Player:		.75
Inserted 1:12		
1	Ryan Anderson	.75
2	Pat Burrell	5.00
3	A.J. Burnett	1.50
4	Ruben Mateo	1.00
5	Alex Escobar	2.00
6	Pablo Ozuna	.75
7	Mark Mulder	1.00
8	Corey Patterson	2.50
9	George Lombard	.75
10	Nick Johnson	4.00

1999 Bowman Chrome

Bowman Chrome was released in two 220-card releases and is basically an upscaled chromium parallel version of Bowman Baseball. Like Bowman, each series set has 150 prospect cards that have blue foil, while veteran cards have red foil. Packs contain four cards and have an SRP of $3.00.

		MT
Complete Set (220):		150.00
Common Player:		.40
Intern. Stars:		1.5x to 2x
Intern. RCs:		1x to 1.5x
Inserted 1:4		
Golds:		3x to 6x
Inserted 1:12		
Refractors:		4x to 8x
Yng Stars & RCs:		2x to 5x
Inserted 1:12		
Intern. Refractor:		15x to 25x
Yng Stars & RCs:		8x to 15x
Production 100 sets		
1	Ben Grieve	1.50
2	Kerry Wood	1.50
3	Ruben Rivera	.40
4	Sandy Alomar	.50
5	Cal Ripken Jr.	6.00
6	Mark McGwire	10.00
7	Vladimir Guerrero	3.00
8	Moises Alou	.75
9	Jim Edmonds	.50
10	Greg Maddux	5.00
11	Gary Sheffield	.75
12	John Valentin	.40
13	Chuck Knoblauch	.75
14	Tony Clark	.75
15	Rusty Greer	.40
16	Al Leiter	.60
17	Travis Lee	1.50
18	Jose Cruz Jr.	1.00
19	Pedro Martinez	2.00
20	Paul O'Neill	.75
21	Todd Walker	.50
22	Vinny Castilla	.50
23	Barry Larkin	.75
24	Curt Schilling	.75
25	Jason Kendall	.50
26	Scott Erickson	.40
27	Andres Galarraga	.75
28	Jeff Shaw	.40
29	John Olerud	.50
30	Orlando Hernandez	2.00
31	Larry Walker	1.50
32	Andruw Jones	2.00
33	Jeff Cirillo	.40
34	Barry Bonds	2.00
35	Manny Ramirez	4.00
36	Mark Kotsay	.40
37	Ivan Rodriguez	2.00
38	Jeff King	.40
39	Brian Hunter	.40
40	Ray Durham	.40
41	Bernie Williams	1.50
42	Darin Erstad	1.50
43	Chipper Jones	5.00
44	Pat Hentgen	.40
45	Eric Young	.40
46	Jaret Wright	.75
47	Juan Guzman	.40
48	Jorge Posada	.50
49	Bobby Higginson	.40
50	Jose Guillen	.40
51	Trevor Hoffman	.40
52	Ken Griffey Jr.	8.00
53	David Justice	.75
54	Matt Williams	.75
55	Eric Karros	.50
56	Derek Bell	.40
57	Ray Lankford	.40
58	Mariano Rivera	.50
59	Brett Tomko	.40
60	Mike Mussina	1.50
61	Kenny Lofton	2.00
62	Chuck Finley	.40
63	Alex Gonzalez	.40
64	Mark Grace	.75
65	Raul Mondesi	.60
66	David Cone	.75
67	Brad Fullmer	.50
68	Andy Benes	.40
69	John Smoltz	.50
70	Shane Reynolds	.50
71	Bruce Chen	.75
72	Adam Kennedy	.40
73	Jack Cust	.40
74	Matt Clement	.40
75	Derrick Gibson	.40
76	Darnell McDonald	.40
77	*Adam Everett*	5.00
78	Ricardo Aramboles	.40
79	*Mark Quinn*	2.50
80	Jason Rakers	.40
81	*Seth Etherton*	5.00
82	*Jeff Urban*	2.50
83	Manny Aybar	.40
84	*Mike Nannini*	3.00
85	Onan Masaoka	.40
86	Rod Barajas	.40
87	Mike Frank	.40
88	Scott Randall	.40
89	*Justin Bowles*	1.00
90	Chris Haas	.40
91	*Arturo McDowell*	2.50
92	*Matt Belisle*	3.00
93	Scott Elarton	.40
94	Vernon Wells	.40
95	Pat Cline	.40
96	Ryan Anderson	2.00
97	Kevin Barker	.40
98	Ruben Mateo	4.00
99	Robert Fick	.40
100	Corey Koskie	.40
101	Ricky Ledee	.50
102	*Rick Elder*	8.00
103	*Jack Cressend*	2.00
104	Joe Lawrence	.40
105	Mike Lincoln	.40
106	*Kit Pellow*	2.50
107	*Matt Burch*	5.00
108	Brent Butler	.40
109	Jason Dewey	.40
110	Cesar King	.40
111	Julio Ramirez	.40
112	Jake Westbrook	.40
113	*Eric Valent*	12.00
114	*Roosevelt Brown*	2.00
115	*Choo Freeman*	4.00
116	Juan Melo	.40
117	Jason Grilli	.40
118	Jared Sandberg	.40
119	Glenn Davis	.40
120	*David Riske*	2.00
121	Jacque Jones	.40
122	Corey Lee	.40
123	Michael Barrett	.40
124	Lariel Gonzalez	.40
125	Mitch Meluskey	.40
126	*Freddy Garcia*	5.00
127	*Tony Torcato*	2.50
128	Jeff Liefer	.40
129	Ntema Ndungidi	.40
130	*Andy Brown*	5.00
131	*Ryan Mills*	5.00
132	*Andy Abad*	1.50
133	Carlos Febles	.40
134	*Jason Tyner*	2.50
135	Mark Osborne	.40
136	*Phil Norton*	2.50
137	Nathan Haynes	.40
138	Roy Halladay	.40
139	Juan Encarnacion	.75
140	Brad Penny	.40
141	Grant Roberts	.40
142	Aramis Ramirez	.40
143	Cristian Guzman	.40
144	*Mamon Tucker*	4.00
145	Ryan Bradley	.40
146	Brian Simmons	.40
147	Dan Reichert	.40
148	Russ Branyon	.40
149	*Victor Valencia*	5.00
150	Scott Schoeneweis	.40
151	*Sean Spencer*	2.00
152	Odalis Perez	.75
153	Joe Fontenot	.40
154	Milton Bradley	.40
155	*Josh McKinley*	4.00
156	Terrence Long	.40
157	Danny Klassen	.40
158	*Paul Hoover*	2.50
159	Ron Belliard	.40
160	Armando Rios	.40
161	Ramon Hernandez	.40
162	Jason Conti	.40
163	Chad Hermansen	.40
164	Jason Standridge	.40
165	Jason Dellaero	.40
166	John Curtice	.40
167	*Clayton Andrews*	5.00
168	Jeremy Giambi	.75
169	Alex Ramirez	.40
170	*Gabe Molina*	.40
171	*Mario Encarnacion*	4.00
172	*Mike Zywica*	4.00
173	*Chip Ambres*	4.00
174	Trot Nixon	.40
175	*Pat Burrell*	25.00
176	Jeff Yoder	.40
177	*Chris Jones*	2.50
178	Kevin Witt	.40
179	*Keith Luuloa*	1.50
180	Billy Koch	.40
181	*Damaso Marte*	2.50
182	*Ryan Glynn*	4.00
183	Calvin Pickering	.40
184	Michael Cuddyer	.40
185	*Nick Johnson*	12.00
186	*Doug Mientkiewicz*	2.50
187	*Nate Cornejo*	2.50
188	Octavio Dotel	.40
189	Wes Helms	.40
190	Nelson Lara	.40
191	*Chuck Abbott*	4.00
192	Tony Armas, Jr.	.40
193	Gil Meche	.40
194	Ben Petrick	.40
195	*Chris George*	4.00
196	*Scott Hunter*	2.00
197	Ryan Brannan	.40
198	*Amaury Garcia*	2.00
199	Chris Gissell	.40
200	*Austin Kearns*	6.00
201	Alex Gonzalez	.40
202	Wade Miller	.40
203	Scott Williamson	.40
204	Chris Enochs	.40
205	Fernando Seguignol	1.00
206	Marlon Anderson	.40
207	Todd Sears	1.50
208	*Nate Bump*	4.00
209	*J.M. Gold*	8.00
210	Matt LeCroy	.40
211	Alex Hernandez	.40
212	Luis Rivera	.40
213	Troy Cameron	.40
214	*Alex Escobar*	10.00
215	Jason LaRue	.40
216	Kyle Peterson	.40
217	Brent Butler	.40
218	Dernell Stenson	.40
219	Adrian Beltre	1.50
220	Daryle Ward	.40

1999 Bowman Chrome Diamond Aces

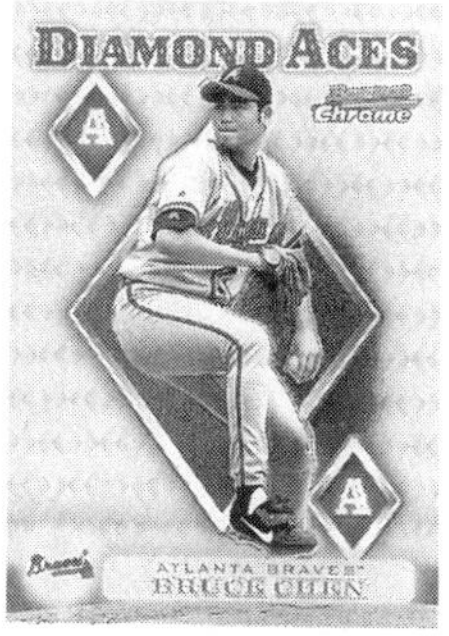

This 18-card set features nine emerging stars such as Troy Glaus as well as nine proven veterans. The cards have a prismatic look with Diamond Aces written across the top of the card. Diamond Aces are inserted in series I packs and are inserted 1:21 packs. A parallel Refractor version is also randomly inserted and found 1:84 packs.

		MT
Complete Set (18):		150.00
Common Player:		3.00
Inserted 1:21		
Refractors:		1.5x to 2x
Inserted 1:84		
DA1	Troy Glaus	5.00
DA2	Eric Chavez	4.00
DA3	Fernando Seguignol	3.00
DA4	Ryan Anderson	3.00
DA5	Ruben Mateo	6.00
DA6	Carlos Beltran	4.00
DA7	Adrian Beltre	4.00
DA8	Bruce Chen	3.00
DA9	Pat Burrell	25.00
DA10	Mike Piazza	12.00
DA11	Ken Griffey Jr.	20.00
DA12	Chipper Jones	10.00
DA13	Derek Jeter	12.00
DA14	Mark McGwire	25.00
DA15	Nomar Garciaparra	12.00
DA16	Sammy Sosa	12.00
DA17	Juan Gonzalez	10.00
DA18	Alex Rodriguez	12.00

1999 Bowman Chrome Scout's Choice

This is a chromium parallel of the inserts found in series I Bowman. The 21-card set is inserted in series I Bowman Chrome packs at a rate of 1:12 packs and showcases prospects that have potential to win a future Rookie of the Year award. A Refractor parallel is also randomly inserted 1:48 packs.

		MT
Complete Set (21):		75.00
Common Player:		2.00
Inserted 1:12		
Refractors:		1.5x to 2x
Inserted 1:48		
SC1	Ruben Mateo	8.00
SC2	Ryan Anderson	6.00
SC3	Pat Burrell	20.00
SC4	Troy Glaus	10.00
SC5	Eric Chavez	8.00
SC6	Adrian Beltre	4.00
SC7	Bruce Chen	3.00
SC8	Carlos Beltran	3.00
SC9	Alex Gonzalez	2.00
SC10	Carlos Lee	3.00
SC11	George Lombard	3.00
SC12	Matt Clement	2.00
SC13	Calvin Pickering	2.00
SC14	Marlon Anderson	2.00
SC15	Chad Hermansen	2.00
SC16	Russell Branyan	2.00
SC17	Jeremy Giambi	2.00
SC18	Ricky Ledee	2.00
SC19	John Patterson	2.00
SC20	Roy Halladay	2.00
SC21	Michael Barrett	3.00

1999 Bowman's Best

Bowman's Best consists of a base set of 200 cards, printed on 27-point stock. Within the base set there are 85 veteran stars printed on gold foil, 15 Best Performers on bronze foil, 50 Prospects on silver foil and 50 rookies on blue foil. The rookies are seeded one per pack. There are also two Refractor parallel versions: Atomic Refractors and Refractors. Atomic Refractors are inserted 1:62 packs and are sequentially numbered to 100, while Refractors are found 1:15 packs and are sequentially numbered to 400.

		MT
Complete Set (200):		150.00
Common Player:		.25
Common SP (151-200):		1.50
Inserted 1:1		
Refractors:		8x to 15x
SP Refractors:		3x to 5x
Production 400 sets		
Atomic Refractors:		25x to 40x
SP Atomic Refractors:		6x to 12x
Production 100 sets		
1	Chipper Jones	2.50
2	Brian Jordan	.25
3	David Justice	.50
4	Jason Kendall	.40
5	Mo Vaughn	1.25
6	Jim Edmonds	.25
7	Wade Boggs	.50
8	Jeromy Burnitz	.25
9	Todd Hundley	.25
10	Rondell White	.40
11	Cliff Floyd	.25
12	Sean Casey	.50
13	Bernie Williams	1.00
14	Dante Bichette	.50
15	Greg Vaughn	.40
16	Andres Galarraga	.75
17	Ray Durham	.25
18	Jim Thome	.75
19	Gary Sheffield	.40
20	Frank Thomas	2.50
21	Orlando Hernandez	1.00
22	Ivan Rodriguez	1.25
23	Jose Cruz Jr.	.50
24	Jason Giambi	.25
25	Craig Biggio	.75
26	Kerry Wood	1.00
27	Manny Ramirez	1.50
28	Curt Schilling	.40
29	Mike Mussina	1.00
30	Tim Salmon	.50
31	Mike Piazza	3.00
32	Roberto Alomar	1.00
33	Larry Walker	1.00
34	Barry Larkin	.75
35	Nomar Garciaparra	3.00
36	Paul O'Neill	.50
37	Todd Walker	.25
38	Eric Karros	.40
39	Brad Fullmer	.25
40	John Olerud	.40
41	Todd Helton	1.00
42	Raul Mondesi	.40
43	Jose Canseco	1.00
44	Matt Williams	.75
45	Ray Lankford	.25
46	Carlos Delgado	.50
47	Darin Erstad	1.00
48	Vladimir Guerrero	1.50
49	Robin Ventura	.40
50	Alex Rodriguez	3.00
51	Vinny Castilla	.25
52	Tony Clark	.50
53	Pedro Martinez	1.25
54	Rafael Palmeiro	.75
55	Scott Rolen	1.50
56	Tino Martinez	.75
57	Tony Gwynn	2.50
58	Barry Bonds	1.25
59	Kenny Lofton	1.25
60	Javy Lopez	.25
61	Mark Grace	.50
62	Travis Lee	1.00
63	Kevin Brown	.50
64	Al Leiter	.25
65	Albert Belle	1.25
66	Sammy Sosa	3.00
67	Greg Maddux	3.00
68	Mark Kotsay	.25
69	Dmitri Young	.25
70	Mark McGwire	6.00
71	Juan Gonzalez	2.50
72	Andruw Jones	1.25
73	Derek Jeter	3.00
74	Randy Johnson	1.00
75	Cal Ripken Jr.	4.00
76	Shawn Green	.50
77	Moises Alou	.40
78	Tom Glavine	.40
79	Sandy Alomar	.25
80	Ken Griffey Jr.	5.00
81	Ryan Klesko	.50
82	Jeff Bagwell	1.25
83	Ben Grieve	1.00
84	John Smoltz	.25
85	Roger Clemens	1.50
86	Ken Griffey Jr.	2.50
87	Roger Clemens	.75
88	Derek Jeter	1.50
89	Nomar Garciaparra	1.50
90	Mark McGwire	3.00
91	Sammy Sosa	1.50
92	Alex Rodriguez	1.50
93	Greg Maddux	1.50
94	Vladimir Guerrero	.75
95	Chipper Jones	1.25
96	Kerry Wood	.50
97	Ben Grieve	.50
98	Tony Gwynn	1.25
99	Juan Gonzalez	1.25
100	Mike Piazza	1.50
101	Eric Chavez	.75
102	Billy Koch	.25
103	Dernell Stenson	.25
104	Marlon Anderson	.25
105	Ron Belliard	.25
106	Bruce Chen	.25

107	Carlos Beltran	.75
108	Chad Hermansen	.25
109	Ryan Anderson	.75
110	Michael Barrett	1.00
111	Matt Clement	.25
112	Ben Davis	.25
113	Calvin Pickering	.25
114	Brad Penny	.25
115	Paul Konerko	.25
116	Alex Gonzalez	.25
117	George Lombard	.25
118	John Patterson	.25
119	Rob Bell	.25
120	Ruben Mateo	1.50
121	*Peter Bergeron*	1.00
122	Ryan Bradley	.25
123	Carlos Lee	.25
124	Gabe Kapler	1.50
125	Ramon Hernandez	.25
126	Carlos Febles	.75
127	Mitch Meluskey	.25
128	Michael Cuddyer	.25
129	Pablo Ozuna	.25
130	Jayson Werth	.25
131	Ricky Ledee	.25
132	Jeremy Giambi	.75
133	Danny Klassen	.25
134	Mark DeRosa	.25
135	Randy Wolf	.25
136	Roy Halladay	.50
137	Derrick Gibson	.25
138	Ben Petrick	.25
139	Warren Morris	.25
140	Lance Berkman	.25
141	Russell Branyan	.25
142	Adrian Beltre	.75
143	Juan Encarnacion	.50
144	Fernando Seguignol	.25
145	Corey Koskie	.25
146	Preston Wilson	.25
147	Homer Bush	.25
148	Daryle Ward	.25
149	*Joe McEwing*	6.00
150	Troy Glaus	1.50
151	*Pat Burrell*	15.00
152	*Choo Freeman*	3.00
153	*Matt Belisle*	2.50
154	*Carlos Pena*	5.00
155	*A.J. Burnett*	5.00
156	*Doug Mientkiewicz*	2.00
157	*Sean Burroughs*	5.00
158	*Mike Zywica*	3.00
159	*Corey Patterson*	8.00
160	*Austin Kearns*	5.00
161	*Chip Ambres*	3.00
162	*Kelly Dransfeldt*	1.50
163	*Mike Nannini*	3.00
164	*Mark Mulder*	4.00
165	*Jason Tyner*	2.50
166	*Bobby Seay*	2.50
167	*Alex Escobar*	10.00
168	*Nick Johnson*	10.00
169	*Alfonso Soriano*	15.00
170	*Clayton Andrews*	4.00
171	*C.C. Sabathia*	2.00
172	*Matt Holliday*	3.00
173	*Brad Lidge*	3.00
174	*Kit Pellow*	2.00
175	*J.M. Gold*	6.00
176	*Roosevelt Brown*	2.00
177	*Eric Valent*	8.00
178	*Adam Everett*	4.00
179	*Jorge Toca*	4.00
180	*Matt Roney*	3.00
181	*Andy Brown*	3.00
182	*Phil Norton*	2.00
183	*Mickey Lopez*	1.50
184	*Chris George*	3.00
185	*Arturo McDowell*	2.00
186	*Jose Fernandez*	1.50
187	*Seth Etherton*	4.00
188	*Josh McKinley*	3.00
189	*Nate Cornejo*	2.00
190	*Giuseppe Chiaramonte*	2.50
191	*Mamon Tucker*	3.00
192	*Ryan Mills*	5.00
193	*Chad Moeller*	3.00
194	*Tony Torcato*	2.00
195	*Jeff Winchester*	3.00
196	*Rick Elder*	6.00
197	*Matt Burch*	4.00
198	*Jeff Urban*	2.00
199	*Chris Jones*	2.00
200	*Masao Kida*	1.50

1999 Bowman's Best Franchise Favorites

This six-card set features retired legends and current stars in three versions. Version A features a current star, Version B features a retired player and Version C pairs the current star with the retired player. The insert rate is 1:40 packs.

		MT
Complete Set (6):		40.00
Common Player:		5.00
Inserted 1:75		
1A	Derek Jeter	15.00
1B	Don Mattingly	5.00
1C	Derek Jeter, Don Mattingly	10.00
2A	Scott Rolen	8.00
2B	Mike Schmidt	5.00
2C	Scott Rolen, Mike Schmidt	6.00

1999 Bowman's Best Franchise Favorites Autographs

This is a parallel autographed version of the regular Franchise Favorites inserts. The insert rate is 1:1,548 for Version A, 1:1,548 for Version B and 1:6,191 packs for Version C.

		MT
Common Player:		100.00
Version A & B 1:1,548		
Version C 1:6,191		
1A	Derek Jeter	200.00
1B	Don Mattingly	175.00
1C	Derek Jeter, Don Mattingly	400.00
2A	Scott Rolen	100.00
2B	Mike Schmidt	120.00
2C	Scott Rolen, Mike Schmidt	325.00

1999 Bowman's Best Franchise Best

Ten league leaders are featured on three different technologies. The three versions are Mach I, Mach II and Mach III. Mach I features die-cut Serillusion stock and are numbered to 3,000, Mach II features die-cut refractive styrene stock and are numbered to 1,000 and Mach III features die-cut polycarbonate stock and are limited to 500 numbered sets.

		MT
Complete Set (10):		100.00
Common Player:		5.00
Production 3,000 sets		
Mach II:		1.5x to 2x
Production 1,000 sets		
Mach III:		2x to 3x
Production 500 sets		
1	Mark McGwire	25.00
2	Ken Griffey Jr.	20.00
3	Sammy Sosa	12.00
4	Nomar Garciaparra	12.00
5	Alex Rodriguez	12.00
6	Derek Jeter	12.00
7	Mike Piazza	12.00
8	Frank Thomas	10.00
9	Chipper Jones	10.00
10	Juan Gonzalez	10.00

1999 Bowman's Best Future Foundations

Ten up-and-coming players are featured in this set that have the same technologies as the Franchise Best inserts and broken down the same way. The insert rates are 1:41 packs for Mach I, 1:124 for Mach II and 1:248 for Mach III.

		MT
Complete Set (10):		75.00
Common Player:		3.00
Production 3,000 sets		
Mach II:		1.5x to 2x
Production 1,000 sets		
Mach III:		2x to 3x
Production 500 sets		
1	Ruben Mateo	6.00
2	Troy Glaus	8.00
3	Eric Chavez	6.00
4	Pat Burrell	30.00
5	Adrian Beltre	5.00
6	Ryan Anderson	5.00
7	Alfonso Soriano	30.00
8	Brad Penny	3.00
9	Derrick Gibson	3.00
10	Bruce Chen	3.00

1999 Bowman's Best Mirror Image

These double-sided cards feature a veteran player on one side and a prospect on the other side for a total of 10 double-sided cards featuring 20 players. The insert rate is 1:24 packs. There are also two parallel versions: Atomic Refractors and Refractors. Refractors are inserted 1:96 packs while Atomic Refractors are seeded 1:192 packs.

		MT
Complete Set (10):		100.00
Common Player:		4.00
Inserted 1:24		
Refractors:		1.5x to 2x
Inserted 1:96		
Atomic Refractors:		2x to 4x
Inserted 1:192		
1	Alex Rodriguez, Alex Gonzalez	10.00
2	Ken Griffey Jr., Ruben Mateo	18.00
3	Derek Jeter, Alfonso Soriano	18.00
4	Sammy Sosa, Corey Patterson	10.00
5	Greg Maddux, Bruce Chen	10.00
6	Chipper Jones, Eric Chavez	8.00
7	Vladimir Guerrero, Carlos Beltran	6.00
8	Frank Thomas, Nick Johnson	8.00
9	Nomar Garciaparra, Pablo Ozuna	10.00
10	Mark McGwire, Pat Burrell	25.00

1999 Bowman's Best Rookie of the Year

This two card set salutes the 1998 AL and NL Rookie of Year award winners, Kerry Wood and Ben Grieve. They are inserted 1:95 packs and are numbered with a ROY prefix. Ben Grieve also autographed some of the inserts which feature a "Topps Certified Autograph Issue" stamp. Autographs are seeded 1:1,241 packs.

	MT
Complete Set (2):	12.00
ROY1Ben Grieve	8.00
ROY2Kerry Wood	6.00
ROYA1Ben Grieve (Auto.)	50.00

1999 Bowman's Best Rookie Locker Room Autographs

This five-card set features the autographs of baseball's current hot prospects, including Gabe Kapler. Each card is branded with a "Topps Certified Autograph Issue" stamp and are inserted 1:248 packs.

		MT
Complete Set (5):		180.00
Common Player:		25.00
Inserted 1:248		
1	Pat Burrell	75.00
2	Michael Barrett	25.00
3	Troy Glaus	50.00
4	Gabe Kapler	40.00
5	Eric Chavez	30.00

1999 Bowman's Best Rookie Locker Room Game-Used Lumber

This six-card set features actual pieces of each player's game-used bat embedded into each card. The insertion rate is 2 cards per 516 packs.

		MT
Complete Set (6):		400.00
Common Player:		50.00
Inserted 2:516		
1	Pat Burrell	150.00
2	Michael Barrett	50.00
3	Troy Glaus	90.00
4	Gabe Kapler	75.00
5	Eric Chavez	60.00
6	Richie Sexson	50.00

1999 Bowman's Best Rookie Locker Room Game-Worn Jerseys

This four card set spotlights hot prospects and has a swatch of game-used jersey from the featured player embedded into the card. These are inserted two cards per 539 packs.

		MT
Complete Set (4):		200.00
Common Player:		50.00
Inserted 2:539		
1	Richie Sexson	50.00
2	Michael Barrett	50.00
3	Troy Glaus	90.00
4	Eric Chavez	60.00

1999 Finest

Released in two series, with series I consisting of 100 veterans and 50 subset cards divided into three categories. The 50 subset cards are short-printed, seeded one per pack. Base cards are printed on 27 pt. stock utilizing chromium technology. There are two parallels of Finest Refractors and die-cut Gold Refractors. Refractors are seeded 1:12 packs, while Gold Refractors are numbered to 100 sets.

		MT
Complete Set (300):		275.00
Complete Series I (150):		150.00
Complete Series II (150):		125.00
Common Player:		.25
Common SP (101-150, 251-300):		.75
Star Refractors:		6x to 10x
SP's:		3x to 5x
Inserted 1:12		
Star Gold Refractors:		30x to 50x
SP's:		15x to 25x
Production 100 sets		
1	Darin Erstad	1.25
2	Javy Lopez	.40
3	Vinny Castilla	.25
4	Jim Thome	.75
5	Tino Martinez	.75
6	Mark Grace	.40
7	Shawn Green	.25
8	Dustin Hermanson	.25
9	Kevin Young	.25
10	Tony Clark	.75
11	Scott Brosius	.25
12	Craig Biggio	.75
13	Brian McRae	.25
14	Chan Ho Park	.50
15	Manny Ramirez	1.50
16	Chipper Jones	2.50
17	Rico Brogna	.25
18	Quinton McCracken	.25
19	J.T. Snow Jr.	.25
20	Tony Gwynn	2.50
21	Juan Guzman	.25
22	John Valentin	.25
23	Rick Helling	.25
24	Sandy Alomar	.25
25	Frank Thomas	3.00
26	Jorge Posada	.25
27	Dmitri Young	.25
28	Rick Reed	.25
29	Kevin Tapani	.25
30	Troy Glaus	1.50
31	Kenny Rogers	.25
32	Jeromy Burnitz	.25
33	Mark Grudzielanek	.25
34	Mike Mussina	1.00
35	Scott Rolen	1.25
36	Neifi Perez	.25
37	Brad Radke	.25
38	Darryl Strawberry	.50
39	Robb Nen	.25
40	Moises Alou	.50
41	Eric Young	.25
42	Livan Hernandez	.25
43	John Wetteland	.25
44	Matt Lawton	.25
45	Ben Grieve	1.25
46	Fernando Tatis	.25
47	Travis Fryman	.25
48	David Segui	.25
49	Bob Abreu	.25
50	Nomar Garciaparra	3.00
51	Paul O'Neill	.50
52	Jeff King	.25
53	Francisco Cordova	.25
54	John Olerud	.50
55	Vladimir Guerrero	1.50
56	Fernando Vina	.25
57	Shane Reynolds	.25
58	Chuck Finley	.25
59	Rondell White	.50
60	Greg Vaughn	.50
61	Ryan Minor	.75
62	Tom Gordon	.25
63	Damion Easley	.25
64	Ray Durham	.25
65	Orlando Hernandez	1.50
66	Bartolo Colon	.25
67	Jaret Wright	.50
68	Royce Clayton	.25
69	Tim Salmon	.75
70	Mark McGwire	6.00
71	Alex Gonzalez	.25
72	Tom Glavine	.50
73	David Justice	.50
74	Omar Vizquel	.25
75	Juan Gonzalez	2.50
76	Bobby Higginson	.25
77	Todd Walker	.25
78	Dante Bichette	.50

79	Kevin Millwood	.50
80	Roger Clemens	2.00
81	Kerry Wood	1.00
82	Cal Ripken Jr.	4.00
83	Jay Bell	.25
84	Barry Bonds	1.25
85	Alex Rodriguez	3.00
86	Doug Glanville	.25
87	Jason Kendall	.25
88	Sean Casey	.25
89	Aaron Sele	.25
90	Derek Jeter	3.00
91	Andy Ashby	.25
92	Rusty Greer	.25
93	Rod Beck	.25
94	Matt Williams	.75
95	Mike Piazza	3.00
96	Wally Joyner	.25
97	Barry Larkin	.75
98	Eric Milton	.25
99	Gary Sheffield	.50
100	Greg Maddux	3.00
101	Ken Griffey Jr. (Gem)	6.00
102	Frank Thomas (Gem)	4.00
103	Nomar Garciaparra (Gem)	4.00
104	Mark McGwire (Gem)	8.00
105	Alex Rodriguez (Gem)	4.00
106	Tony Gwynn (Gem)	3.00
107	Juan Gonzalez (Gem)	3.00
108	Jeff Bagwell (Gem)	1.50
109	Sammy Sosa (Gem)	4.00
110	Vladimir Guerrero (Gem)	2.00
111	Roger Clemens (Gem)	2.50
112	Barry Bonds (Gem)	1.50
113	Darin Erstad (Gem)	1.50
114	Mike Piazza (Gem)	4.00
115	Derek Jeter (Gem)	4.00
116	Chipper Jones (Gem)	3.00
117	Larry Walker (Gem)	1.00
118	Scott Rolen (Gem)	1.50
119	Cal Ripken Jr. (Gem)	5.00
120	Greg Maddux (Gem)	4.00
121	Troy Glaus (Sensations)	2.50
122	Ben Grieve (Sensations)	2.00
123	Ryan Minor (Sensations)	1.00
124	Kerry Wood (Sensations)	1.50
125	Travis Lee (Sensations)	1.00
126	Adrian Beltre (Sensations)	1.00
127	Brad Fullmer (Sensations)	.75
128	Aramis Ramirez (Sensations)	.75
129	Eric Chavez (Sensations)	2.00
130	Todd Helton (Sensations)	1.50
131	*Pat Burrell* (Finest Rookies)	20.00
132	*Ryan Mills* (Finest Rookies)	6.00
133	*Austin Kearns* (Finest Rookies)	6.00
134	*Josh McKinley* (Finest Rookies)	4.00
135	*Adam Everett* (Finest Rookies)	5.00
136	Marlon Anderson	2.00
137	Bruce Chen	1.50
138	Matt Clement	1.00
139	Alex Gonzalez	.75
140	Roy Halladay	2.00
141	Calvin Pickering	.75
142	Randy Wolf	2.50
143	Ryan Anderson	2.00
144	Ruben Mateo	3.00
145	*Alex Escobar*	12.00
146	Jeremy Giambi	2.00
147	Lance Berkman	3.00
148	Michael Barrett	2.00
149	Preston Wilson	.75
150	Gabe Kapler	5.00
151	Roger Clemens	2.00
152	Jay Buhner	.40
153	Brad Fullmer	.25
154	Ray Lankford	.25
155	Jim Edmonds	.25
156	Jason Giambi	.25
157	Bret Boone	.25
158	Jeff Cirillo	.25
159	Rickey Henderson	.40
160	Edgar Martinez	.25
161	Ron Gant	.40
162	Mark Kotsay	.25
163	Trevor Hoffman	.25
164	Jason Schmidt	.25
165	Brett Tomko	.25
166	David Ortiz	.25
167	Dean Palmer	.25
168	Hideki Irabu	.40
169	Mike Cameron	.25
170	Pedro Martinez	1.25
171	Tom Goodwin	.25
172	Brian Hunter	.25
173	Al Leiter	.25
174	Charles Johnson	.25
175	Curt Schilling	.40
176	Robin Ventura	.40
177	Travis Lee	1.00
178	Jeff Shaw	.25
179	Ugueth Urbina	.25
180	Roberto Alomar	1.00
181	Cliff Floyd	.25
182	Adrian Beltre	.75
183	Tony Womack	.25
184	Brian Jordan	.25
185	Randy Johnson	1.00
186	Mickey Morandini	.25
187	Todd Hundley	.25
188	Jose Valentin	.25
189	Eric Davis	.25
190	Ken Caminiti	.40
191	David Wells	.25
192	Ryan Klesko	.40
193	Garret Anderson	.25
194	Eric Karros	.25
195	Ivan Rodriguez	1.25
196	Aramis Ramirez	.25
197	Mike Lieberthal	.25
198	Will Clark	.75
199	Rey Ordonez	.25
200	Ken Griffey Jr.	5.00
201	Jose Guillen	.25
202	Scott Erickson	.25
203	Paul Konerko	.50
204	Johnny Damon	.25
205	Larry Walker	.75
206	Denny Neagle	.25
207	Jose Offerman	.25
208	Andy Pettitte	.50
209	Bobby Jones	.25
210	Kevin Brown	.40
211	John Smoltz	.40
212	Henry Rodriguez	.25
213	Tim Belcher	.25
214	Carlos Delgado	.50
215	Andruw Jones	1.00
216	Andy Benes	.25
217	Fred McGriff	.50
218	Edgar Renteria	.25
219	Miguel Tejada	.40
220	Bernie Williams	.75
221	Justin Thompson	.25
222	Marty Cordova	.25
223	Delino DeShields	.25
224	Ellis Burks	.25
225	Kenny Lofton	1.25
226	Steve Finley	.25
227	Eric Chavez	.75
228	Jose Cruz Jr.	.75
229	Marquis Grissom	.25
230	Jeff Bagwell	1.50
231	Jose Canseco	.75
232	Edgardo Alfonzo	.25
233	Richie Sexson	.50
234	Jeff Kent	.25
235	Rafael Palmeiro	.50
236	David Cone	.50
237	Gregg Jefferies	.25
238	Mike Lansing	.25
239	Mariano Rivera	.40
240	Albert Belle	1.25
241	Chuck Knoblauch	.50
242	Derek Bell	.25
243	Pat Hentgen	.25
244	Andres Galarraga	.75
245	Mo Vaughn	1.25
246	Wade Boggs	.50
247	Devon White	.25
248	Todd Helton	.75
249	Raul Mondesi	.50
250	Sammy Sosa	3.00
251	Nomar Garciaparra (Sterling)	4.00
252	Mark McGwire (Sterling)	8.00
253	Alex Rodriguez (Sterling)	4.00
254	Juan Gonzalez (Sterling)	3.00
255	Vladimir Guerrero (Sterling)	2.00
256	Ken Griffey Jr. (Sterling)	6.00
257	Mike Piazza (Sterling)	4.00
258	Derek Jeter (Sterling)	4.00
259	Albert Belle (Sterling)	1.50
260	Greg Vaughn (Sterling)	.75
261	Sammy Sosa (Sterling)	4.00
262	Greg Maddux (Sterling)	3.00
263	Frank Thomas (Sterling)	3.00
264	Mark Grace (Sterling)	.75
265	Ivan Rodriguez (Sterling)	1.50
266	Roger Clemens (Gamers)	2.00
267	Mo Vaughn (Gamers)	1.50
268	Jim Thome (Gamers)	1.00
269	Darin Erstad (Gamers)	1.00
270	Chipper Jones (Gamers)	3.00
271	Larry Walker (Gamers)	1.00
272	Cal Ripken Jr. (Gamers)	5.00
273	Scott Rolen (Gamers)	1.50
274	Randy Johnson (Gamers)	1.00
275	Tony Gwynn (Gamers)	3.00
276	Barry Bonds (Gamers)	1.50
277	*Sean Burroughs*	5.00
278	*J.M. Gold*	6.00
279	Carlos Lee	.75
280	George Lombard	.75
281	Carlos Beltran	1.00
282	Fernando Seguignol	.75
283	Eric Chavez	1.00
284	*Carlos Pena*	6.00
285	*Corey Patterson*	10.00
286	*Alfonso Soriano*	15.00
287	*Nick Johnson*	10.00
288	*Jorge Toca*	4.00
289	*A.J. Burnett*	6.00
290	*Andy Brown*	3.00
291	*Doug Mientkiewicz*	2.00
292	*Bobby Seay*	2.50
293	*Chip Ambres*	3.00
294	*C.C. Sabathia*	2.00
295	*Choo Freeman*	3.00
296	*Eric Valent*	8.00
297	*Matt Belisle*	2.50
298	*Jason Tyner*	2.50
299	*Masao Kida*	2.00
300	Hank Aaron, Mark McGwire (Homerun Kings)	5.00

1999 Finest Complements

This seven-card set pairs two players on a split screen card front. There are three different versions for each card, Non-Refractor/Refractor (1:56), Refractor/Non-Refractor (1:56) and Refractor/Refractor (1:168). Each card is numbered with a "C" prefix.

		MT
Complete Set (7):		70.00
Common Player:		5.00
Inserted 1:56		
Refractors:		1.5x to 2x
Inserted 1:168		
1	Mike Piazza, Ivan Rodriguez	12.00
2	Tony Gwynn, Wade Boggs	10.00
3	Kerry Wood, Roger Clemens	6.00
4	Juan Gonzalez, Sammy Sosa	12.00
5	Derek Jeter, Nomar Garciaparra	12.00
6	Mark McGwire, Frank Thomas	25.00
7	Vladimir Guerrero, Andruw Jones	6.00

1999 Finest Double Feature

Similar to Finest Complements, this seven card set utilizes split screen fronts to accommodate two players on a horizontal format. Each card has three versions: Non-Refractor/Refractor (1:56), Refractor/Non-Refractor (1:56) and Refractor/Refractor (1:168). Card numbers have an "DF" prefix.

		MT
Complete Set (7):		60.00
Common Player:		4.00
Inserted 1:56		
Refractors:		1.5x to 2x
Inserted 1:168		
1	Ken Griffey Jr., Alex Rodriguez	25.00
2	Chipper Jones, Andruw Jones	10.00
3	Darin Erstad, Mo Vaughn	5.00
4	Craig Biggio, Jeff Bagwell	6.00
5	Ben Grieve, Eric Chavez	4.00
6	Albert Belle, Cal Ripken Jr.	15.00
7	Scott Rolen, Pat Burrell	12.00

1999 Finest Franchise Records

This 10-card insert set focuses on players who led their teams in various statistical categories. They are randomly seeded in 1:129 packs, while a parallel Refractor version is inserted 1:378. Card numbers have an "FR" prefix.

		MT
Complete Set (10):		220.00
Common Player:		6.00
Inserted 1:129		
Refractors:		1.5x to 2x
Inserted 1:378		
1	Frank Thomas	20.00
2	Ken Griffey Jr.	40.00
3	Mark McGwire	50.00
4	Juan Gonzalez	20.00
5	Nomar Garciaparra	25.00
6	Mike Piazza	25.00
7	Cal Ripken Jr.	30.00
8	Sammy Sosa	25.00
9	Barry Bonds	10.00
10	Tony Gwynn	20.00

1999 Finest Future's Finest

This 10-card set focuses on young up-and-coming players who are primed to emerge as superstars, featuring Pat Burrell. These are seeded 1:171 packs and limited to 500 numbered sets. Card numbers have an "FF" prefix.

		MT
Complete Set (10):		150.00
Common Player:		8.00
Inserted 1:171		
1	Pat Burrell	50.00
2	Troy Glaus	25.00
3	Eric Chavez	15.00
4	Ryan Anderson	10.00
5	Ruben Mateo	20.00
6	Gabe Kapler	25.00
7	Alex Gonzalez	8.00
8	Michael Barrett	8.00
9	Lance Berkman	8.00
10	Fernando Seguignol	8.00

1999 Finest Hank Aaron Award Contenders

This insert set focuses on nine players who had the best chance to win baseball's newest award. Insertion odds vary from card to card, player nine's cards have nine times as many cards as card number one and so on. Card numbers have an "HA" prefix.

		MT
Complete Set (9):		80.00
Common Player:		8.00
varying odds for each #		
1	Juan Gonzalez	20.00
2	Vladimir Guerrero	10.00
3	Nomar Garciaparra	15.00
4	Albert Belle	8.00
5	Frank Thomas	8.00
6	Sammy Sosa	8.00
7	Alex Rodriguez	8.00
8	Ken Griffey Jr.	10.00
9	Mark McGwire	12.00

1999 Finest Hank Aaron Award Contenders Refractors

This is a nine-card parallel version of the base inserts. Insertion odds are as follows: card #1 (1:1,944), #2 (1:972), #3 (1:648), #4 (1:486), #5 (1:387), #6 (1:324), #7 (1:279), #8 (1:243), #9 (1:216).

		MT
Complete Set (9):		180.00
Common Player:		8.00
varying odds for each #		
1	Juan Gonzalez	40.00
2	Vladimir Guerrero	20.00
3	Nomar Garciaparra	25.00
4	Albert Belle	12.00
5	Frank Thomas	20.00
6	Sammy Sosa	20.00
7	Alex Rodriguez	20.00
8	Ken Griffey Jr.	30.00
9	Mark McGwire	30.00

1999 Finest Leading Indicators

Utilizing a heat-sensitive, thermal ink technology, these cards highlight the 1998 home run totals of 10 players. By touching the left, right or center field portion of the card behind each player's image, will reveal that player's '98 season home run total in that specific direction. These are seeded 1:24 packs.

		MT
Complete Set (10):		100.00
Common Player:		4.00
Inserted 1:24		
1	Mark McGwire	25.00
2	Sammy Sosa	18.00
3	Ken Griffey Jr.	20.00
4	Greg Vaughn	4.00
5	Albert Belle	6.00
6	Juan Gonzalez	10.00
7	Andres Galarraga	5.00
8	Alex Rodriguez	15.00
9	Barry Bonds	6.00
10	Jeff Bagwell	6.00

1999 Finest Milestones

This 40-card set is broken down into four 10-card sets, each focusing on a statistical category, Hits, Home Runs, RBIs and Doubles. The Hits category is limited to 3,000 numbered sets, Home Runs are limited to 500 numbered sets, RBIs are limited to 1,400 numbered sets and Doubles is limited to 500 numbered sets. Each card number carries an "M" prefix.

		MT
Complete Set (40):		700.00
Common Hits (1-10):		3.00
Production 3,000		
Common Homeruns (11-20):		
Production 500		
Common RBI (21-30):		
Common Doubles (31-40):		
Production 500		
1	Tony Gwynn (Hits)	10.00
2	Cal Ripken Jr. (Hits)	15.00
3	Wade Boggs (Hits)	3.00
4	Ken Griffey Jr. (Hits)	20.00
5	Frank Thomas (Hits)	10.00
6	Barry Bonds (Hits)	5.00
7	Travis Lee (Hits)	4.00
8	Alex Rodriguez (Hits)	12.00
9	Derek Jeter (Hits)	12.00
10	Vladimir Guerrero (Hits)	6.00
11	Mark McGwire (Home Runs)	70.00
12	Ken Griffey Jr. (Home Runs)	60.00
13	Vladimir Guerrero (Home Runs)	20.00
14	Alex Rodriguez (Home Runs)	40.00
15	Barry Bonds (Home Runs)	15.00
16	Sammy Sosa (Home Runs)	40.00
17	Albert Belle (Home Runs)	15.00
18	Frank Thomas (Home Runs)	30.00
19	Jose Canseco (Home Runs)	10.00
20	Mike Piazza (Home Runs)	40.00
21	Jeff Bagwell (RBI)	10.00
22	Barry Bonds (RBI)	8.00
23	Ken Griffey Jr. (RBI)	30.00
24	Albert Belle (RBI)	8.00
25	Juan Gonzalez (RBI)	15.00
26	Vinny Castilla (RBI)	4.00
27	Mark McGwire (RBI)	40.00
28	Alex Rodriguez (RBI)	20.00
29	Nomar Garciaparra (RBI)	20.00
30	Frank Thomas (RBI)	15.00
31	Barry Bonds (Doubles)	15.00
32	Albert Belle (Doubles)	15.00
33	Ben Grieve (Doubles)	12.00
34	Craig Biggio (Doubles)	10.00
35	Vladimir Guerrero (Doubles)	20.00
36	Nomar Garciaparra (Doubles)	40.00
37	Alex Rodriguez (Doubles)	40.00
38	Derek Jeter (Doubles)	40.00
39	Ken Griffey Jr. (Doubles)	60.00
40	Brad Fullmer (Doubles)	8.00

1999 Finest Peel & Reveal

20 players printed at varying levels of scarcity (common, uncommon and rare) with a protective coating on each card. By peeling the protective coating on the card front and back, the level will be revealed. Sparkle background is common (1:30), Hyperplaid background (uncommon, 1:60), Stadium Stars background (rare, 1:120).

		MT
Complete Set (20):		280.00
Common Player:		6.00
Inserted 1:30		
Hyperplaid:		1.5x to 2x
Inserted 1:60		
Stadium Stars:		2.5x to 3x
Inserted 1:120		
1	Kerry Wood	8.00
2	Mark McGwire	40.00
3	Sammy Sosa	25.00
4	Ken Griffey Jr.	30.00
5	Nomar Garciaparra	25.00
6	Greg Maddux	25.00
7	Derek Jeter	25.00
8	Andres Galarraga	6.00
9	Alex Rodriguez	25.00
10	Frank Thomas	25.00
11	Roger Clemens	12.00
12	Juan Gonzalez	15.00
13	Ben Grieve	8.00
14	Jeff Bagwell	8.00
15	Todd Helton	8.00
16	Chipper Jones	15.00
17	Barry Bonds	8.00
18	Travis Lee	8.00
19	Vladimir Guerrero	10.00
20	Pat Burrell	25.00

1999 Finest Prominent Figures

50 cards on Refractor technology highlights the superstars chasing the all-time records in five different statistical categories: Home Runs, Slugging Percentage, Batting Average, Runs Batted In and Total Bases. Ten players are featured in each category, each sequentially numbered to the all-time single season record statistic for that category. Home Run category is numbered to 70, Slugging Percentage to 847, Batting Average to 424, RBI's to 190 and Total Bases to 457.

		MT
Complete Set (50):		
Common Player:		10.00
Homeruns 1-10:		
Production 70 sets		
Slugging % 11-20:		
Production 847 sets		
Batting Ave. 21-30:		
Production 424 sets		
RBI's 31-40		
Production 190 sets		
Total Bases 41-50		
Production 457 sets		
1	Mark McGwire	300.00
2	Sammy Sosa	150.00
3	Ken Griffey Jr.	250.00
4	Mike Piazza	150.00
5	Juan Gonzalez	125.00
6	Greg Vaughn	25.00
7	Alex Rodriguez	150.00
8	Manny Ramirez	60.00
9	Jeff Bagwell	60.00
10	Andres Galarraga	40.00
11	Mark McGwire	60.00
12	Sammy Sosa	40.00
13	Juan Gonzalez	25.00
14	Ken Griffey Jr.	50.00
15	Barry Bonds	15.00
16	Greg Vaughn	8.00
17	Larry Walker	10.00
18	Andres Galarraga	10.00
19	Jeff Bagwell	15.00
20	Albert Belle	15.00
21	Tony Gwynn	40.00
22	Mike Piazza	50.00
23	Larry Walker	15.00
24	Alex Rodriguez	50.00
25	John Olerud	10.00
26	Frank Thomas	40.00
27	Bernie Williams	12.00
28	Chipper Jones	30.00
29	Jim Thome	12.00
30	Barry Bonds	15.00
31	Juan Gonzalez	70.00
32	Sammy Sosa	90.00
33	Mark McGwire	175.00
34	Albert Belle	35.00
35	Ken Griffey Jr.	140.00
36	Jeff Bagwell	35.00
37	Chipper Jones	70.00
38	Vinny Castilla	15.00
39	Alex Rodriguez	90.00
40	Andres Galarraga	25.00
41	Sammy Sosa	50.00
42	Mark McGwire	90.00
43	Albert Belle	20.00
44	Ken Griffey Jr.	75.00
45	Jeff Bagwell	20.00
46	Juan Gonzalez	40.00
47	Barry Bonds	20.00
48	Vladimir Guerrero	25.00
49	Larry Walker	15.00
50	Alex Rodriguez	50.00

1999 Finest Split Screen

Players who share a common bond are highlighted in this set, which includes 14 paired players. Each card is available in three variations, which are as follows: Non-Refractor/Refractor (1:28), Refractor/Non-Refractor (1:28) and Refractor/Refractor (1:84).

		MT
Complete Set (14):		160.00
Common Player:		6.00
Ref/non-Ref & non-Ref/Ref 1:28		
Ref/Ref:		2x to 2.5x
Inserted 1:84		
1	Mark McGwire, Sammy Sosa	30.00
2	Ken Griffey Jr., Alex Rodriguez	25.00
3	Nomar Garciaparra, Derek Jeter	15.00
4	Barry Bonds, Albert Belle	8.00
5	Cal Ripken Jr., Tony Gwynn	20.00
6	Manny Ramirez, Juan Gonzalez	12.00
7	Frank Thomas, Andres Galarraga	12.00
8	Scott Rolen, Chipper Jones	10.00
9	Ivan Rodriguez, Mike Piazza	15.00
10	Kerry Wood, Roger Clemens	12.00
11	Greg Maddux, Tom Glavine	12.00
12	Troy Glaus, Eric Chavez	8.00
13	Ben Grieve, Todd Helton	6.00
14	Travis Lee, Pat Burrell	20.00

1999 Finest Team Finest

The first 10 cards are showcased in series I while the last 10 cards are showcased in series II. Team Finest are available in three colors: Blue, Red and Gold. (Red and Gold are only available in Home Team Advantage packs.) All of Team Finest are serially numbered and are as follows: Blue, numbered to 1,500; Blue Refractors to 150; Red to 500; Red Refractors to 50; Gold to 250 and Gold Refractors to 25.

		MT
Complete Set (20):		275.00
Common Blue:		6.00
Production 1,500 sets		
Blue Refractors:		3x to 5x
Production 150 sets		
Reds:		1.5x to 2x
Production 500 sets HTA		
Red Refractors:		6x to 9x
Production 50 sets HTA		
Golds:		2x to 3x
Production 250 sets		
1	Greg Maddux	20.00
2	Mark McGwire	40.00
3	Sammy Sosa	20.00
4	Juan Gonzalez	15.00
5	Alex Rodriguez	20.00
6	Travis Lee	6.00
7	Roger Clemens	15.00
8	Darin Erstad	6.00
9	Todd Helton	6.00
10	Mike Piazza	20.00
11	Kerry Wood	8.00
12	Ken Griffey Jr.	30.00
13	Frank Thomas	15.00
14	Jeff Bagwell	8.00
15	Nomar Garciaparra	20.00
16	Derek Jeter	20.00
17	Chipper Jones	15.00
18	Barry Bonds	8.00
19	Tony Gwynn	15.00
20	Ben Grieve	6.00

1999 Flair Showcase Power

Power is one of three parallel levels in Showcase and has full-bleed, full holofoil treatment on the card fronts. Powers also have spot embossing over the player's name. Five-card packs of Flair Showcase have a $4.99 SRP. Each of the 432 total cards in Showcase are paralleled in blue foil and limited to 99 serially numbered sets and called Legacy Collection. A one-of-one Legacy Masterpiece parallel is also randomly seeded and has "The Only 1 of 1 Masterpiece" printed on the card backs.

		MT
Complete Set (144):		75.00
Common Player:		.25
Legacy Collection:		25x to 40x
Each player has 3 versions		
Production 99 sets		
1	Mark McGwire	6.00
2	Sammy Sosa	3.00
3	Ken Griffey Jr.	5.00
4	Chipper Jones	2.50
5	Ben Grieve	1.00
6	J.D. Drew	3.00
7	Jeff Bagwell	1.25
8	Cal Ripken Jr.	4.00
9	Tony Gwynn	2.50
10	Nomar Garciaparra	3.00
11	Travis Lee	1.00
12	Troy Glaus	2.00
13	Mike Piazza	3.00
14	Alex Rodriguez	3.00
15	Kevin Brown	.50
16	Darin Erstad	1.00
17	Scott Rolen	1.50
18	*Micah Bowie*	.75
19	Juan Gonzalez	2.50
20	Kerry Wood	1.00
21	Roger Clemens	2.00
22	Derek Jeter	3.00
23	*Pat Burrell*	10.00
24	Tim Salmon	.75
25	Barry Bonds	1.25
26	*Roosevelt Brown*	1.00
27	Vladimir Guerrero	2.00
28	Randy Johnson	1.00
29	Mo Vaughn	1.00
30	Fernando Seguignol	.25
31	Greg Maddux	3.00
32	Tony Clark	.75
33	Eric Chavez	.50
34	Kris Benson	.25
35	Frank Thomas	2.50
36	Mario Encarnacion	.25
37	Gabe Kapler	1.25
38	Jeremy Giambi	.40
39	*Peter Tucci*	.75
40	Manny Ramirez	2.00
41	Albert Belle	1.25
42	Warren Morris	.25
43	Michael Barrett	1.00
44	Andruw Jones	1.25
45	Carlos Delgado	.75
46	Jaret Wright	.50
47	Juan Encarnacion	.40
48	Scott Hunter	.75
49	Tino Martinez	.75
50	Craig Biggio	.75
51	Jim Thome	.75
52	Vinny Castilla	.40
53	Tom Glavine	.40
54	Bob Higginson	.25
55	Moises Alou	.40
56	Robin Ventura	.25
57	Bernie Williams	1.00
58	Pedro J. Martinez	1.25
59	Greg Vaughn	.40
60	Ray Lankford	.25
61	Jose Canseco	1.00
62	Ivan Rodriguez	1.25
63	Shawn Green	.75
64	Rafael Palmeiro	.75
65	Ellis Burks	.25

66	Jason Kendall	.50
67	David Wells	.25
68	Rondell White	.40
69	Gary Sheffield	.40
70	Ken Caminiti	.25
71	Cliff Floyd	.25
72	Larry Walker	1.00
73	Bartolo Colon	.25
74	Barry Larkin	.75
75	Calvin Pickering	.25
76	Jim Edmonds	.25
77	Henry Rodriguez	.25
78	Roberto Alomar	1.00
79	Andres Galarraga	.75
80	Richie Sexson	.50
81	Todd Helton	.75
82	Damion Easley	.25
83	Livan Hernandez	.25
84	Carlos Beltran	3.00
85	Todd Hundley	.25
86	Todd Walker	.25
87	Scott Brosius	.25
88	Bob Abreu	.25
89	Corey Koskie	.25
90	Ruben Rivera	.25
91	Edgar Renteria	.25
92	Quinton McCracken	.25
93	Bernard Gilkey	.25
94	Shannon Stewart	.25
95	Dustin Hermanson	.25
96	Mike Caruso	.25
97	Alex Gonzalez	.25
98	Raul Mondesi	.40
99	David Cone	.50
100	Curt Schilling	.40
101	Brian Giles	.25
102	Edgar Martinez	.25
103	Rolando Arrojo	.25
104	Derek Bell	.25
105	Denny Neagle	.25
106	Marquis Grissom	.25
107	Bret Boone	.25
108	Mike Mussina	1.00
109	John Smoltz	.25
110	Brett Tomko	.25
111	David Justice	.50
112	Andy Pettitte	.40
113	Eric Karros	.25
114	Dante Bichette	.75
115	Jeromy Burnitz	.25
116	Paul Konerko	.25
117	Steve Finley	.25
118	Ricky Ledee	.50
119	Edgardo Alfonzo	.25
120	Dean Palmer	.25
121	Rusty Greer	.25
122	Luis Gonzalez	.25
123	Randy Winn	.25
124	Jeff Kent	.25
125	Doug Glanville	.25
126	Justin Thompson	.25
127	Bret Saberhagen	.25
128	Wade Boggs	.75
129	Al Leiter	.25
130	Paul O'Neill	.75
131	Chan Ho Park	.50
132	Johnny Damon	.25
133	Darryl Kile	.25
134	Reggie Sanders	.25
135	Kevin Millwood	.75
136	Charles Johnson	.25
137	Ray Durham	.25
138	Rico Brogna	.25
139	Matt Williams	.75
140	Sandy Alomar	.25
141	Jeff Cirillo	.25
142	Devon White	.25
143	Andy Benes	.25
144	Mike Stanley	.25

1999 Flair Showcase Passion

Passions have the featured player's number in the background, which has textured embossing. Passion is stamped under the Flair Showcase logo as well. Card fronts also utilize holofoil and full bleed photos.

		MT
Common Player:		.50
Showdown (1-49):		1.5x to 2.5x
Inserted 1:3		
Showpiece (50-99):		1x
Inserted 1:1.3		
Showtime (100-144):		1x to 2x
Inserted 1:2		
1	Mark McGwire	15.00
2	Sammy Sosa	8.00
3	Ken Griffey Jr.	12.00
4	Chipper Jones	6.00
5	Ben Grieve	2.50
6	J.D. Drew	8.00
7	Jeff Bagwell	3.00
8	Cal Ripken Jr.	10.00
9	Tony Gwynn	6.00
10	Nomar Garciaparra	8.00
11	Travis Lee	2.50
12	Troy Glaus	5.00
13	Mike Piazza	8.00
14	Alex Rodriguez	8.00
15	Kevin Brown	1.00
16	Darin Erstad	2.00
17	Scott Rolen	4.00
18	*Micah Bowie*	1.50
19	Juan Gonzalez	6.00
20	Kerry Wood	2.50
21	Roger Clemens	5.00
22	Derek Jeter	8.00
23	Pat Burrell	20.00
24	Tim Salmon	1.50
25	Barry Bonds	3.00
26	Roosevelt Brown	2.00
27	Vladimir Guerrero	4.00
28	Randy Johnson	2.50
29	Mo Vaughn	2.50
30	Fernando Seguignol	.50
31	Greg Maddux	6.00
32	Tony Clark	1.50
33	Eric Chavez	1.00
34	Kris Benson	.50
35	Frank Thomas	6.00
36	Mario Encarnacion	.50
37	Gabe Kapler	3.00
38	Jeremy Giambi	1.00
39	*Peter Tucci*	1.50
40	Manny Ramirez	5.00
41	Albert Belle	3.00
42	Warren Morris	.50
43	Michael Barrett	2.00
44	Andruw Jones	3.00
45	Carlos Delgado	1.50
46	Jaret Wright	.75
47	Juan Encarnacion	.75
48	Scott Hunter	.75
49	Tino Martinez	2.00
50	Craig Biggio	2.00
51	Jim Thome	.75
52	Vinny Castilla	.40
53	Tom Glavine	.40
54	Bob Higginson	.50
55	Moises Alou	.40
56	Robin Ventura	.50
57	Bernie Williams	1.00
58	Pedro J. Martinez	1.25
59	Greg Vaughn	.40
60	Ray Lankford	.50
61	Jose Canseco	1.00
62	Ivan Rodriguez	1.25
63	Shawn Green	.75
64	Rafael Palmeiro	.75
65	Ellis Burks	.50
66	Jason Kendall	.50
67	David Wells	.50
68	Rondell White	.40
69	Gary Sheffield	.40
70	Ken Caminiti	.50
71	Cliff Floyd	.50
72	Larry Walker	1.00
73	Bartolo Colon	.50
74	Barry Larkin	.75
75	Calvin Pickering	.50
76	Jim Edmonds	.50
77	Henry Rodriguez	.50
78	Roberto Alomar	1.00
79	Andres Galarraga	.75
80	Richie Sexson	.50
81	Todd Helton	.75
82	Damion Easley	.50
83	Livan Hernandez	.50
84	Carlos Beltran	3.00
85	Todd Hundley	.50
86	Todd Walker	.50
87	Scott Brosius	.50
88	Bob Abreu	.50
89	Corey Koskie	.50
90	Ruben Rivera	.50
91	Edgar Renteria	.50
92	Quinton McCracken	.50
93	Bernard Gilkey	.50
94	Shannon Stewart	.50
95	Dustin Hermanson	.50
96	Mike Caruso	.50
97	Alex Gonzalez	.50
98	Raul Mondesi	.40
99	David Cone	.50
100	Curt Schilling	.75
101	Brian Giles	.50
102	Edgar Martinez	.50
103	Rolando Arrojo	.50
104	Derek Bell	.50
105	Denny Neagle	.50
106	Marquis Grissom	.50
107	Bret Boone	.50
108	Mike Mussina	2.00
109	John Smoltz	.75
110	Brett Tomko	.50
111	David Justice	1.00
112	Andy Pettitte	.75
113	Eric Karros	.50
114	Dante Bichette	1.50
115	Jeromy Burnitz	.50
116	Paul Konerko	.50
117	Steve Finley	.50
118	Ricky Ledee	.50
119	Edgardo Alfonzo	.50
120	Dean Palmer	.50
121	Rusty Greer	.50
122	Luis Gonzalez	.50
123	Randy Winn	.50
124	Jeff Kent	.50
125	Doug Glanville	.50
126	Justin Thompson	.50
127	Bret Saberhagen	.50
128	Wade Boggs	1.50
129	Al Leiter	.50
130	Paul O'Neill	1.50
131	Chan Ho Park	.50
132	Johnny Damon	.50
133	Darryl Kile	.50
134	Reggie Sanders	.50
135	Kevin Millwood	1.50
136	Charles Johnson	.50
137	Ray Durham	.50
138	Rico Brogna	.50
139	Matt Williams	1.50
140	Sandy Alomar	.50
141	Jeff Cirillo	.50
142	Devon White	.50
143	Andy Benes	.50
144	Mike Stanley	.50

1999 Flair Showcase Showcase

The Showcase level presents three photos on a plastic laminate, on a horizontal format. Gold foil stamping is also utilized, each card is serially numbered. Showpieces (1-49) are limited to 1,500 numbered sets, Showtimes (50-99) are limited to 3,000 sets and Showdowns (100-144) are numbered to 6,000 sets.

	MT
Showpiece (1-49):	6x to 10x
Production 1,500 sets	
Showtime (50-99):	3x to 5x
Production 3,000 sets	
Showdown (100-144):	2x to 3x
Production 6,000 sets	

1999 Flair Showcase Measure of Greatness

This 15-card set captures baseball's top superstars who are closing in on milestones, including McGwire's chase for 500 home runs. Each card is sequentially numbered to 500.

		MT
Complete Set (15):		350.00
Common Player:		15.00
Production 500 sets		
1	Roger Clemens	20.00
2	Nomar Garciaparra	40.00
3	Juan Gonzalez	30.00
4	Ken Griffey Jr.	60.00
5	Vladimir Guerrero	20.00
6	Tony Gwynn	30.00
7	Derek Jeter	40.00
8	Chipper Jones	30.00
9	Mark McGwire	75.00
10	Mike Piazza	40.00
11	Manny Ramirez	18.00
12	Cal Ripken Jr.	50.00
13	Alex Rodriguez	40.00
14	Sammy Sosa	40.00
15	Frank Thomas	30.00

1999 Flair Showcase Wave of the Future

This 15-card set spotlights young stars on the rise like Troy Glaus and J.D. Drew. These are limited to 1,000 serial numbered sets.

		MT
Complete Set (15):		170.00
Common Player:		6.00
Production 1,000 sets		
1	Kerry Wood	10.00
2	Ben Grieve	10.00
3	J.D. Drew	40.00
4	Juan Encarnacion	8.00
5	Travis Lee	10.00
6	Todd Helton	10.00
7	Troy Glaus	20.00
8	Ricky Ledee	6.00
9	Eric Chavez	15.00
10	Ben Davis	6.00
11	George Lombard	8.00
12	Jeremy Giambi	8.00
13	Roosevelt Brown	8.00
14	Pat Burrell	50.00
15	Preston Wilson	6.00

1999 Fleer

Released as a single series in 10-card packs with a suggested retail price of $1.59, the base set consists of 600 cards, including 10 checklists and a 15-card Franchise Futures subset. The cards are UV coated, with full bleed photos and gold foil stamping. Card backs have personal bio-information along with year-by-year career stats and a small photo. There are two parallels, Starting Nine, which are hobby-exclusive, numbered to nine sets with blue foil stamping and Warning Track. Found exclusively in retail packs, Warning Tracks can be identified by red foil stamping and a Warning Track logo.

		MT
Complete Set (600):		60.00
Common Player:		.10
Warning Track:		2x to 4x
Common Warning Track:		.25
Inserted 1:1 R		
1	Mark McGwire	4.00
2	Sammy Sosa	2.50
3	Ken Griffey Jr.	3.00
4	Kerry Wood	.75
5	Derek Jeter	2.00
6	Stan Musial	4.00
7	J.D. Drew	12.00
8	Cal Ripken Jr.	2.50
9	Alex Rodriguez	2.00
10	Travis Lee	.75
11	Andres Galarraga	.50
12	Nomar Garciaparra	2.00
13	Albert Belle	.75
14	Barry Larkin	.25
15	Dante Bichette	.25
16	Tony Clark	.40
17	Moises Alou	.20
18	Rafael Palmeiro	.25
19	Raul Mondesi	.25
20	Vladimir Guerrero	1.00
21	John Olerud	.20
22	Bernie Williams	.50
23	Ben Grieve	.75
24	Scott Rolen	.75
25	Jeromy Burnitz	.10
26	Ken Caminiti	.20
27	Barry Bonds	.75
28	Todd Helton	.50
29	Juan Gonzalez	1.50
30	Roger Clemens	1.25
31	Andruw Jones	.75
32	Mo Vaughn	.75
33	Larry Walker	.40
34	Frank Thomas	2.00
35	Manny Ramirez	1.00
36	Randy Johnson	.50
37	Vinny Castilla	.10
38	Juan Encarnacion	.10
39	Jeff Bagwell	.75
40	Gary Sheffield	.25
41	Mike Piazza	2.00
42	Richie Sexson	.10
43	Tony Gwynn	1.50
44	Chipper Jones	1.50
45	Jim Thome	.50
46	Craig Biggio	.30
47	Carlos Delgado	.25
48	Greg Vaughn	.25
49	Greg Maddux	2.00
50	Troy Glaus	.75
51	Roberto Alomar	.50
52	Dennis Eckersley	.10
53	Mike Caruso	.10
54	Bruce Chen	.10
55	Aaron Boone	.10
56	Bartolo Colon	.10
57	Derrick Gibson	.10
58	Brian Anderson	.10
59	Gabe Alvarez	.10
60	Todd Dunwoody	.10
61	Rod Beck	.10
62	Derek Bell	.10
63	Francisco Cordova	.10
64	Johnny Damon	.10
65	Adrian Beltre	.10
66	Garret Anderson	.10
67	Armando Benitez	.10
68	Edgardo Alfonzo	.10
69	Ryan Bradley	.10
70	Eric Chavez	1.00
71	Bobby Abreu	.10
72	Andy Ashby	.10
73	Ellis Burks	.10
74	Jeff Cirillo	.10
75	Jay Buhner	.25
76	Ron Gant	.20
77	Rolando Arrojo	.25
78	Will Clark	.40
79	Chris Carpenter	.10
80	Jim Edmonds	.10
81	Tony Batista	.10
82	Shane Andrews	.10
83	Mark DeRosa	.10
84	Brady Anderson	.10
85	Tony Gordon	.10
86	Brant Brown	.10
87	Ray Durham	.10
88	Ron Coomer	.10
89	Bret Boone	.10
90	Travis Fryman	.10
91	Darryl Kile	.10
92	Paul Bako	.10
93	Cliff Floyd	.10
94	Scott Elarton	.10
95	Jeremy Giambi	.10
96	Darren Dreifort	.10
97	Marquis Grissom	.10
98	Marty Cordova	.10
99	Fernando Seguignol	.25
100	Orlando Hernandez	1.00
101	Jose Cruz Jr.	.50
102	Jason Giambi	.10
103	Damion Easley	.10
104	Freddy Garcia	.10
105	Marlon Anderson	.10
106	Kevin Brown	.20
107	Joe Carter	.20
108	Russ Davis	.10
109	Brian Jordan	.10
110	Wade Boggs	.40
111	Tom Goodwin	.10
112	Scott Brosius	.10
113	Darin Erstad	.75
114	Jay Bell	.10
115	Tom Glavine	.25
116	Pedro Martinez	.50
117	Mark Grace	.25
118	Russ Ortiz	.10
119	Magglio Ordonez	.25
120	Sean Casey	.25
121	*Rafael Roque*	.25
122	Brian Giles	.10
123	Mike Lansing	.10
124	David Cone	.25
125	Alex Gonzalez	.10
126	Carl Everett	.10
127	Jeff King	.10
128	Charles Johnson	.10
129	Geoff Jenkins	.10
130	Corey Koskie	.10
131	Brad Fullmer	.25
132	Al Leiter	.20
133	Rickey Henderson	.25
134	Rico Brogna	.10
135	Jose Guillen	.25
136	Matt Clement	.20
137	Carlos Guillen	.10
138	Orel Hershiser	.10
139	Ray Lankford	.10
140	Miguel Cairo	.10
141	Chuck Finley	.10
142	Rusty Greer	.10
143	Kelvim Escobar	.10
144	Ryan Klesko	.25
145	Andy Benes	.20
146	Eric Davis	.10
147	David Wells	.10

148	Trot Nixon	.25
149	Jose Hernandez	.10
150	Mark Johnson	.10
151	Mike Frank	.10
152	Joey Hamilton	.10
153	David Justice	.30
154	Mike Mussina	.50
155	Neifi Perez	.10
156	Luis Gonzalez	.10
157	Livan Hernandez	.10
158	Dermal Brown	.10
159	Jose Lima	.10
160	Eric Karros	.20
161	Ronnie Belliard	.10
162	Matt Lawton	.10
163	Dustin Hermanson	.10
164	Brian McRae	.10
165	Mike Kinkade	.10
166	A.J. Hinch	.10
167	Doug Glanville	.10
168	Hideo Nomo	.20
169	Jason Kendall	.10
170	Steve Finley	.10
171	Jeff Kent	.10
172	Ben Davis	.10
173	Edgar Martinez	.10
174	Eli Marrero	.10
175	Quinton McCracken	.10
176	Rick Helling	.10
177	Tom Evans	.10
178	Carl Pavano	.10
179	Todd Greene	.10
180	Omar Daal	.10
181	George Lombard	.25
182	Ryan Minor	.40
183	Troy O'Leary	.10
184	Robb Nen	.10
185	Mickey Morandini	.10
186	Robin Ventura	.20
187	Pete Harnisch	.10
188	Kenny Lofton	.60
189	Eric Milton	.10
190	Bobby Higginson	.10
191	Jamie Moyer	.10
192	Mark Kotsay	.25
193	Shane Reynolds	.10
194	Carlos Febles	.10
195	Jeff Kubenka	.10
196	Chuck Knoblauch	.40
197	Kenny Rogers	.10
198	Bill Mueller	.10
199	Shane Monahan	.10
200	Matt Morris	.10
201	Fred McGriff	.30
202	Ivan Rodriguez	.75
203	Kevin Witt	.10
204	Troy Percival	.10
205	David Dellucci	.10
206	Kevin Millwood	.50
207	Jerry Hairston	.50
208	Mike Stanley	.10
209	Henry Rodriguez	.10
210	Trevor Hoffman	.10
211	Craig Wilson	.10
212	Reggie Sanders	.10
213	Carlton Loewer	.10
214	Omar Vizquel	.10
215	Gabe Kapler	1.00
216	Derrek Lee	.10
217	Billy Wagner	.10
218	Dean Palmer	.10
219	Chan Ho Park	.40
220	Fernando Vina	.10
221	Roy Halladay	.50
222	Paul Molitor	.50
223	Ugueth Urbina	.10
224	Rey Ordonez	.10
225	Ricky Ledee	.25
226	Scott Spiezio	.10
227	Wendell Magee Jr.	.10
228	Aramis Ramirez	.10
229	Brian Simmons	.10
230	Fernando Tatis	.10
231	Bobby Smith	.10
232	Aaron Sele	.10
233	Shawn Green	.10
234	Mariano Rivera	.25
235	Tim Salmon	.40
236	Andy Fox	.10
237	Denny Neagle	.10
238	John Valentin	.10
239	Kevin Tapani	.10
240	Paul Konerko	.25
241	Robert Fick	.10
242	Edgar Renteria	.10
243	Brett Tomko	.10
244	Daryle Ward	.10
245	Carlos Beltran	.10
246	Angel Pena	.10
247	Steve Woodard	.10
248	David Ortiz	.10
249	Justin Thompson	.10
250	Rondell White	.25
251	Jaret Wright	.50
252	Ed Sprague	.10
253	Jay Payton	.10
254	Mike Lowell	.25
255	Orlando Cabrera	.10
256	Jason Schmidt	.10
257	David Segui	.10
258	Paul Sorrento	.10
259	John Wetteland	.10
260	Devon White	.10
261	Odalis Perez	.40
262	Calvin Pickering	.10
263	Alex Ramirez	.10
264	Preston Wilson	.10
265	Brad Radke	.10
266	Walt Weiss	.10
267	Tim Young	.10
268	Tino Martinez	.40
269	Matt Stairs	.10
270	Curt Schilling	.20
271	Tony Womack	.10
272	Ismael Valdes	.10
273	Wally Joyner	.10
274	Armando Rios	.10
275	Andy Pettitte	.50
276	Bubba Trammell	.10
277	Todd Zeile	.10
278	Shannon Stewart	.10
279	Matt Williams	.40
280	John Rocker	.10
281	B.J. Surhoff	.10
282	Eric Young	.10
283	Dmitri Young	.10
284	John Smoltz	.25
285	Todd Walker	.25
286	Paul O'Neill	.25
287	Blake Stein	.10
288	Kevin Young	.10
289	Quilvio Veras	.10
290	Kirk Rueter	.10
291	Randy Winn	.10
292	Miguel Tejada	.10
293	J.T. Snow	.10
294	Michael Tucker	.10
295	Jay Tessmer	.10
296	Scott Erickson	.10
297	Tim Wakefield	.10
298	Jeff Abbott	.10
299	Eddie Taubensee	.10
300	Darryl Hamilton	.10
301	Kevin Orie	.10
302	Jose Offerman	.10
303	Scott Karl	.10
304	Chris Widger	.10
305	Todd Hundley	.10
306	Desi Relaford	.10
307	Sterling Hitchcock	.10
308	Delino DeShields	.10
309	Alex Gonzalez	.10
310	Justin Baughman	.10
311	Jamey Wright	.10
312	Wes Helms	.10
313	Dante Powell	.10
314	Jim Abbott	.10
315	Manny Alexander	.10
316	Harold Baines	.10
317	Danny Graves	.10
318	Sandy Alomar	.10
319	Pedro Astacio	.10
320	Jermaine Allensworth	.10
321	Matt Anderson	.10
322	Chad Curtis	.10
323	Antonio Osuna	.10
324	Brad Ausmus	.10
325	Steve Trachsel	.10
326	Mike Blowers	.10
327	Brian Bohanon	.10
328	Chris Gomez	.10
329	Valerio de los Santos	.10
330	Rich Aurilia	.10
331	Michael Barrett	.50
332	Rick Aguilera	.10
333	Adrian Brown	.10
334	Bill Spiers	.10
335	Matt Beech	.10
336	David Bell	.10
337	Juan Acevedo	.10
338	Jose Canseco	.40
339	Wilson Alvarez	.10
340	Luis Alicea	.10
341	Jason Dickson	.10
342	Mike Bordick	.10
343	Ben Ford	.10
344	Keith Lockhart	.10
345	Jason Christiansen	.10
346	Darren Bragg	.10
347	Doug Brocail	.10
348	Jeff Blauser	.10
349	James Baldwin	.10
350	Jeffrey Hammonds	.10
351	Ricky Bottalico	.10
352	Russ Branyon	.10
353	Mark Brownson	.75
354	Dave Berg	.10
355	Sean Bergman	.10
356	Jeff Conine	.10
357	Shayne Bennett	.10
358	Bobby Bonilla	.20
359	Bob Wickman	.10
360	Carlos Baerga	.10
361	Chris Fussell	.10
362	Chili Davis	.10
363	Jerry Spradlin	.10
364	Carlos Hernandez	.10
365	Roberto Hernandez	.10
366	Marvin Benard	.10
367	Ken Cloude	.10
368	Tony Fernandez	.10
369	John Burkett	.10
370	Gary DiSarcina	.10
371	Alan Benes	.10
372	Karim Garcia	.10
373	Carlos Perez	.10
374	Damon Buford	.10
375	Mark Clark	.10
376	*Edgard Clemente*	.10
377	Chad Bradford	.50
378	Frank Catalanotto	.10
379	Vic Darensbourg	.10
380	Sean Berry	.10
381	Dave Burba	.10
382	Sal Fasano	.10
383	Steve Parris	.10
384	Roger Cedeno	.10
385	Chad Fox	.10
386	Wilton Guerrero	.10
387	Dennis Cook	.10
388	Joe Girardi	.10
389	LaTroy Hawkins	.10
390	Ryan Christenson	.10
391	Paul Byrd	.10
392	Lou Collier	.10
393	Jeff Fassero	.10
394	Jim Leyritz	.10
395	Shawn Estes	.10
396	Mike Kelly	.10
397	Rich Croushore	.10
398	Royce Clayton	.10
399	Rudy Seanez	.10
400	Darrin Fletcher	.10
401	Shigetosi Hasegawa	.10
402	Bernard Gilkey	.10
403	Juan Guzman	.10
404	Jeff Frye	.10
405	Marino Santana	.10
406	Alex Fernandez	.10
407	Gary Gaetti	.10
408	Dan Miceli	.10
409	Mike Cameron	.10
410	Mike Remlinger	.10
411	Joey Cora	.10
412	Mark Gardner	.10
413	Aaron Ledesma	.10
414	Jerry Dipoto	.10
415	Ricky Gutierrez	.10
416	John Franco	.10
417	Mendy Lopez	.10
418	Hideki Irabu	.25
419	Mark Grudzielanek	.10
420	Bobby Hughes	.10
421	Pat Meares	.10
422	Jimmy Haynes	.10
423	Bob Henley	.10
424	Bobby Estalella	.10
425	Jon Lieber	.10
426	*Giomar Guevara*	.50
427	Jose Jimenez	.10
428	Deivi Cruz	.10
429	Jonathan Johnson	.10
430	Ken Hill	.10
431	Craig Grebeck	.10
432	Jose Rosado	.10
433	Danny Klassen	.10
434	Bobby Howry	.10
435	Gerald Williams	.10
436	Omar Olivares	.10
437	Chris Hoiles	.10
438	Seth Greisinger	.10
439	Scott Hatteberg	.10
440	Jeremi Gonzalez	.10
441	Wil Cordero	.10
442	Jeff Montgomery	.10
443	Chris Stynes	.10
444	Tony Saunders	.10
445	Einar Diaz	.10
446	Laril Gonzalez	.10
447	Ryan Jackson	.10
448	Mike Hampton	.10
449	Todd Hollandsworth	.10
450	Gabe White	.10
451	John Jaha	.10
452	Bret Saberhagen	.10
453	Otis Nixon	.10
454	Steve Kline	.10
455	Butch Huskey	.10
456	Mike Jerzembeck	.10
457	Wayne Gomes	.10
458	Mike Macfarlane	.10
459	Jesus Sanchez	.10
460	Al Martin	.10
461	Dwight Gooden	.20
462	Ruben Rivera	.10
463	Pat Hentgen	.10
464	Jose Valentin	.10
465	Vladimir Nunez	.10
466	Charlie Hayes	.10
467	Jay Powell	.10
468	Raul Ibanez	.10
469	Kent Mercker	.10
470	John Mabry	.10
471	Woody Williams	.10
472	Roberto Kelly	.10
473	Jim Mecir	.10
474	Dave Hollins	.10
475	Rafael Medina	.10
476	Darren Lewis	.10
477	Felix Heredia	.10
478	Brian Hunter	.10
479	Matt Mantei	.10
480	Richard Hidalgo	.10
481	Bobby Jones	.10
482	Hal Morris	.10
483	Ramiro Mendoza	.10
484	Matt Luke	.10
485	Esteban Loaiza	.10
486	Mark Loretta	.10
487	A.J. Pierzynski	.10
488	Charles Nagy	.10
489	Kevin Sefcik	.10
490	Jason McDonald	.10
491	Jeremy Powell	.10
492	Scott Servais	.10
493	Abraham Nunez	.10
494	Stan Spencer	.10
495	Stan Javier	.10
496	Jose Paniagua	.10
497	Gregg Jefferies	.10
498	Gregg Olson	.10
499	Derek Lowe	.10
500	Willis Otanez	.10
501	Brian Moehler	.10
502	Glenallen Hill	.10
503	Bobby Jones	.10
504	Greg Norton	.10
505	Mike Jackson	.10
506	Kirt Manwaring	.10
507	Eric Weaver	.75
508	Mitch Meluskey	.10
509	Todd Jones	.10
510	Mike Matheny	.10
511	Benj Sampson	.10
512	Tony Phillips	.10
513	Mike Thurman	.10
514	Jorge Posada	.10
515	Bill Taylor	.10
516	Mike Sweeney	.10
517	Jose Silva	.10
518	Mark Lewis	.10
519	Chris Peters	.10
520	Brian Johnson	.10
521	Mike Timlin	.10
522	Mark McLemore	.10
523	Dan Plesac	.10
524	Kelly Stinnett	.10
525	Sidney Ponson	.10
526	Jim Parque	.10
527	Tyler Houston	.10
528	John Thomson	.10
529	Mike Metcalfe	.10
530	Robert Person	.10
531	Marc Newfield	.10
532	Javier Vazquez	.10
533	Terry Steinbach	.10
534	Turk Wendell	.10
535	Tim Raines	.10
536	Brian Meadows	.10
537	Mike Lieberthal	.10
538	Ricardo Rincon	.10
539	Dan Wilson	.10
540	John Johnstone	.10
541	Todd Stottlemyre	.10
542	Kevin Stocker	.10
543	Ramon Martinez	.10
544	Mike Simms	.10
545	Paul Quantrill	.10
546	Matt Walbeck	.10
547	Turner Ward	.10
548	Bill Pulsipher	.10
549	Donnie Sadler	.10
550	Lance Johnson	.10
551	Bill Simas	.10
552	Jeff Reed	.10
553	Jeff Shaw	.10
554	Joe Randa	.10
555	Paul Shuey	.10
556	Mike Redmond	.50
557	Sean Runyan	.10
558	Enrique Wilson	.10
559	Scott Radinsky	.10
560	Larry Sutton	.10
561	Masato Yoshii	.10
562	David Nilsson	.10
563	Mike Trombley	.10
564	Darryl Strawberry	.25
565	Dave Mlicki	.10
566	Placido Polanco	.10
567	Yorkis Perez	.10
568	Esteban Yan	.10
569	Lee Stevens	.10
570	Steve Sinclair	.10
571	Jarrod Washburn	.10
572	Lenny Webster	.10
573	Mike Sirotka	.10
574	Jason Varitek	.10
575	Terry Mulholland	.10
576	Adrian Beltre (Franchise Futures)	.25
577	Eric Chavez (Franchise Futures)	.50
578	J.D. Drew (Franchise Futures)	6.00
579	Juan Encarnacion (Franchise Futures)	.10
580	Nomar Garciaparra (Franchise Futures)	1.00
581	Troy Glaus (Franchise Futures)	.40
582	Ben Grieve (Franchise Futures)	.40
583	Vladimir Guerrero (Franchise Futures)	.50
584	Todd Helton (Franchise Futures)	.40
585	Derek Jeter (Franchise Futures)	1.00
586	Travis Lee (Franchise Futures)	.40
587	Alex Rodriguez (Franchise Futures)	1.00
588	Scott Rolen (Franchise Futures)	.40
589	Richie Sexson (Franchise Futures)	.10
590	Kerry Wood (Franchise Futures)	.40
591	Ken Griffey Jr.	1.50
592	Chipper Jones	.75
593	Alex Rodriguez	1.00
594	Sammy Sosa	1.00
595	Mark McGwire	2.00
596	Cal Ripken Jr.	1.25
597	Nomar Garciaparra	1.00
598	Derek Jeter	1.00
599	Kerry Wood	.40
600	J.D. Drew	4.00

1999 Fleer Date With Destiny

This 10-card set takes a look at what Hall of Fame plaques might look like for some of today's great players, including Cal Ripken Jr. and Ken Griffey Jr. These are serially numbered to 100 sets.

		MT
Complete Set (10):		1000.
Common Player:		40.00
Production 100 sets		
1	Barry Bonds	50.00
2	Roger Clemens	75.00
3	Ken Griffey Jr.	200.00
4	Tony Gwynn	100.00
5	Greg Maddux	140.00
6	Mark McGwire	250.00
7	Mike Piazza	140.00
8	Cal Ripken Jr.	160.00
9	Alex Rodriguez	140.00
10	Frank Thomas	140.00

1999 Fleer Diamond Magic

A multi-layer card, where collectors turn a "wheel" for a kaleidoscope effect behind the player image, these are seeded 1:96 packs.

		MT
Complete Set (15):		250.00
Common Player:		8.00
Inserted 1:96		
1	Barry Bonds	10.00
2	Roger Clemens	15.00
3	Nomar Garciaparra	25.00
4	Ken Griffey Jr.	40.00
5	Tony Gwynn	20.00
6	Orlando Hernandez	12.00
7	Derek Jeter	20.00
8	Randy Johnson	8.00
9	Chipper Jones	20.00
10	Greg Maddux	25.00
11	Mark McGwire	50.00
12	Alex Rodriguez	25.00
13	Sammy Sosa	25.00
14	Bernie Williams	8.00
15	Kerry Wood	10.00

1999 Fleer Going Yard

This 15-card set features the top home run hitters from the '98 season. These 1:18 pack inserts unfold to be twice as wide as regular cards and takes an unorthodox look at how far the longest home runs went.

	MT
Complete Set (15):	45.00
Common Player:	.75

Inserted 1:18		
1	Moises Alou	.75
2	Albert Belle	2.50
3	Jose Canseco	1.50
4	Vinny Castilla	.75
5	Andres Galarraga	1.50
6	Juan Gonzalez	5.00
7	Ken Griffey Jr.	10.00
8	Chipper Jones	5.00
9	Mark McGwire	12.00
10	Rafael Palmeiro	1.00
11	Mike Piazza	6.00
12	Alex Rodriguez	6.00
13	Sammy Sosa	6.00
14	Greg Vaughn	.75
15	Mo Vaughn	2.50

1999 Fleer Golden Memories

This 15-card set pays tribute to the great moments from the 1998 season including David Wells, perfect game and McGwire's record breaking season. These are seeded 1:54 packs on an embossed frame design.

		MT
Complete Set (15):		160.00
Common Player:		4.00
Inserted 1:54		
1	Albert Belle	6.00
2	Barry Bonds	6.00
3	Roger Clemens	10.00
4	Nomar Garciaparra	15.00
5	Juan Gonzalez	12.00
6	Ken Griffey Jr.	25.00
7	Randy Johnson	4.00
8	Greg Maddux	15.00
9	Mark McGwire	30.00
10	Mike Piazza	15.00
11	Cal Ripken Jr.	20.00
12	Alex Rodriguez	15.00
13	Sammy Sosa	15.00
14	David Wells	4.00
15	Kerry Wood	6.00

1999 Fleer Rookie Flashback

This 15-card set features the impact rookies from the 1998 season. These are seeded 1:6 packs and feature sculpture embossing.

		MT
Complete Set (15):		18.00
Common Player:		.25
Inserted 1:6		
1	Matt Anderson	.25
2	Rolando Arrojo	.40
3	Adrian Beltre	.75
4	Mike Caruso	.25
5	Eric Chavez	1.50
6	J.D. Drew	10.00
7	Juan Encarnacion	.75
8	Brad Fullmer	.40
9	Troy Glaus	1.50
10	Ben Grieve	1.50
11	Todd Helton	1.00
12	Orlando Hernandez	1.50
13	Travis Lee	1.50
14	Richie Sexson	.50
15	Kerry Wood	1.00

1999 Fleer Stan Musial Monumental Moments

Great moments and insight from and about the St. Louis Cardinals great. This 10-card tribute set chronicles Musial's legendary career. These are seeded 1:36 packs with 500 autographed cards randomly seeded.

		MT
Complete Set (10):		40.00
Common Musial:		5.00
Autographed Card:		95.00
1	Life in Donora	6.00
2	Values	6.00
3	In the Beginning	6.00
4	In the Navy	6.00
5	The 1948 Season ((w/Red Schoendienst))	6.00
6	Success Stories (w/Pres. Kennedy)	6.00
7	Mr. Cardinal	6.00
8	Most Valuable Player	6.00
9	baseball's perfect knight	6.00
10	Hall of Fame	6.00

1999 Fleer Vintage '61

This 50-card set takes the first 50 cards from the base set and showcases them in the 1961 Fleer "Baseball Greats" card design. These are seeded one per hobby pack.

		MT
Complete Set (50):		25.00
Common Player:		.20
Inserted 1:1		
1	Mark McGwire	4.00
2	Sammy Sosa	2.50
3	Ken Griffey Jr.	3.00
4	Kerry Wood	.75
5	Derek Jeter	2.00
6	Stan Musial	4.00
7	J.D. Drew	8.00
8	Cal Ripken Jr.	2.50
9	Alex Rodriguez	2.00
10	Travis Lee	.75
11	Andres Galarraga	.50
12	Nomar Garciaparra	2.00
13	Albert Belle	.75
14	Barry Larkin	.40
15	Dante Bichette	.40
16	Tony Clark	.40
17	Moises Alou	.30
18	Rafael Palmeiro	.30
19	Raul Mondesi	.20
20	Vladimir Guerrero	1.00
21	John Olerud	.20
22	Bernie Williams	.40
23	Ben Grieve	.75
24	Scott Rolen	.75
25	Jeromy Burnitz	.20
26	Ken Caminiti	.20
27	Barry Bonds	.75
28	Todd Helton	.75
29	Juan Gonzalez	1.50
30	Roger Clemens	1.25
31	Andruw Jones	.75
32	Mo Vaughn	.75
33	Larry Walker	.50
34	Frank Thomas	2.00
35	Manny Ramirez	1.00
36	Randy Johnson	.50
37	Vinny Castilla	.20
38	Juan Encarnacion	.50
39	Jeff Bagwell	.75
40	Gary Sheffield	.30
41	Mike Piazza	2.00
42	Richie Sexson	.20
43	Tony Gwynn	1.50
44	Chipper Jones	1.50
45	Jim Thome	.50
46	Craig Biggio	.40
47	Carlos Delgado	.20
48	Greg Vaughn	.30
49	Greg Maddux	2.00
50	Troy Glaus	.75

1999 Fleer Brilliants

This 175-card set features a full bleed photo and complete silver foiled card fronts with a background swirl pattern. The featured player's name, team and posi tion are stamped in gold foil. Card backs have a small photo, vital information, 1998 statistics and a brief overview of the player's '98 season. Cards numbered 126-175 are part of a Rookies subset and are seeded 1:2 packs.

		MT
Complete Set (175):		180.00
Common Player:		.40
Common SP (126-175):		1.50
Blues:		2x to 3x
SP Blues:		1x to 1.5x
Inserted 1:3		
SP's inserted 1:6		
Golds:		15x to 30x
SP Golds:		3x to 6x
Production 99 sets		
24 Karat Golds:		50x to 100x
SP's:		10x to 20x
Production 24 sets		
1	Mark McGwire	8.00
2	Derek Jeter	4.00
3	Nomar Garciaparra	4.00
4	Travis Lee	1.00
5	Jeff Bagwell	1.50
6	Andres Galarraga	.75
7	Pedro Martinez	1.50
8	Cal Ripken Jr.	5.00
9	Vladimir Guerrero	2.00
10	Chipper Jones	3.00
11	Rusty Greer	.40
12	Omar Vizquel	.40
13	Quinton McCracken	.40
14	Jaret Wright	.60
15	Mike Mussina	1.00
16	Jason Giambi	.40
17	Tony Clark	.75
18	Troy O'Leary	.40
19	Troy Percival	.40
20	Kerry Wood	1.00
21	Vinny Castilla	.40
22	Chris Carpenter	.40
23	Richie Sexson	.40
24	Ken Griffey Jr.	6.00
25	Barry Bonds	1.50
26	Carlos Delgado	.75
27	Frank Thomas	3.00
28	Manny Ramirez	2.00
29	Shawn Green	.75
30	Mike Piazza	4.00
31	Tino Martinez	.75
32	Dante Bichette	.75
33	Scott Rolen	1.50
34	Gabe Alvarez	.40
35	Raul Mondesi	.60
36	Damion Easley	.40
37	Jeff Kent	.40
38	Al Leiter	.40
39	Alex Rodriguez	4.00
40	Jeff King	.40
41	Mark Grace	.75
42	Larry Walker	1.00
43	Moises Alou	.60
44	Juan Gonzalez	3.00
45	Rolando Arrojo	.40
46	Tom Glavine	.60
47	Johnny Damon	.40
48	Livan Hernandez	.40
49	Craig Biggio	.75
50	Dmitri Young	.40
51	Chan Ho Park	.60
52	Todd Walker	.40
53	Derrek Lee	.40
54	Todd Helton	1.00
55	Ray Lankford	.40
56	Jim Thome	.75
57	Matt Lawton	.40
58	Matt Anderson	.40
59	Jose Offerman	.40
60	Eric Karros	.40
61	Orlando Hernandez	1.50
62	Ben Grieve	1.00
63	Bobby Abreu	.40
64	Kevin Young	.40
65	John Olerud	.75
66	Sammy Sosa	4.00
67	Andy Ashby	.40
68	Juan Encarnacion	.40
69	Shane Reynolds	.40
70	Bernie Williams	1.00
71	Mike Cameron	.40
72	Troy Glaus	2.00
73	Gary Sheffield	.60
74	Jeromy Burnitz	.40
75	Mike Caruso	.40
76	Chuck Knoblauch	.75
77	Kenny Rogers	.40
78	David Cone	.60
79	Tony Gwynn	3.00
80	Aramis Ramirez	.40
81	Paul O'Neill	.75
82	Charles Nagy	.40
83	Javy Lopez	.60
84	Scott Erickson	.40
85	Trevor Hoffman	.40
86	Andruw Jones	1.50
87	Ray Durham	.40
88	Jorge Posada	.40
89	Edgar Martinez	.40
90	Tim Salmon	.75
91	Bobby Higginson	.40
92	Adrian Beltre	1.00
93	Jason Kendall	.60
94	Henry Rodriguez	.40
95	Greg Maddux	4.00
96	David Justice	.75
97	Ivan Rodriguez	1.50
98	Curt Schilling	.60
99	Matt Williams	.75
100	Darin Erstad	1.00
101	Rafael Palmeiro	.75
102	David Wells	.40
103	Barry Larkin	.75
104	Robin Ventura	.60
105	Edgar Renteria	.40
106	Andy Pettitte	.60
107	Albert Belle	1.50
108	Steve Finley	.40
109	Fernando Vina	.40
110	Rondell White	.60
111	Kevin Brown	.60
112	Jose Canseco	1.00
113	Roger Clemens	2.00
114	Todd Hundley	.40
115	Will Clark	1.00
116	Jim Edmonds	.40
117	Randy Johnson	1.00
118	Denny Neagle	.40
119	Brian Jordan	.40
120	Dean Palmer	.40
121	Roberto Alomar	1.00
122	Ken Caminiti	.60
123	Brian Giles	.40
124	Todd Stottlemyre	.40
125	Mo Vaughn	1.50
126	J.D. Drew	15.00
127	Ryan Minor	2.50
128	Gabe Kapler	8.00
129	Jeremy Giambi	2.00
130	Eric Chavez	5.00
131	Ben Davis	2.00
132	Rob Fick	1.50
133	George Lombard	2.00
134	Calvin Pickering	1.50
135	Preston Wilson	1.50
136	Corey Koskie	1.50
137	Russell Branyan	1.50
138	Bruce Chen	2.00
139	Matt Clement	1.50
140	*Pat Burrell*	15.00
141	*Freddy Garcia*	10.00
142	Brian Simmons	2.00
143	Carlos Febles	3.00
144	Carlos Guillen	1.50
145	Fernando Seguignol	2.00
146	Carlos Beltran	5.00
147	Edgard Clemente	1.50
148	Mitch Meluskey	1.50
149	Ryan Bradley	1.50
150	Marlon Anderson	1.50
151	*A.J. Burnett*	5.00
152	*Scott Hunter*	1.50
153	Mark Johnson	1.50
154	Angel Pena	3.00
155	Roy Halladay	2.00
156	*Chad Allen*	1.50
157	Trot Nixon	1.50
158	Ricky Ledee	1.50
159	*Gary Bennett*	1.50
160	*Micah Bowie*	1.50
161	Doug Mientkiewicz	1.50
162	Danny Klassen	1.50
163	Willis Otanez	1.50
164	Jin Ho Cho	1.50
165	Mike Lowell	2.00
166	Armando Rios	1.50
167	Tom Evans	1.50
168	Michael Barrett	3.00
169	Alex Gonzalez	2.00
170	*Masao Kida*	1.50
171	*Peter Tucci*	1.50
172	Luis Saturria	1.50
173	Kris Benson	1.50
174	Mario Encarnacion	5.00
175	*Roosevelt Brown*	2.00

1999 Fleer Brilliants Illuminators

This 15-card set highlights baseball's top young prospects on a team color-coded fully foiled front. Card backs are numbered with an "I" suffix and are inserted 1:10 packs.

		MT
Complete Set (15):		35.00
Common Player:		1.50
Inserted 1:10		
1	Kerry Wood	2.50
2	Ben Grieve	2.50
3	J.D. Drew	12.00
4	Juan Encarnacion	2.50
5	Travis Lee	2.50
6	Todd Helton	3.00
7	Troy Glaus	5.00
8	Ricky Ledee	1.50
9	Eric Chavez	3.00
10	Ben Davis	2.00
11	George Lombard	2.00
12	Jeremy Giambi	1.50
13	Richie Sexson	2.00
14	Corey Koskie	1.50
15		1.50

1999 Fleer Brilliants Shining Stars

Shining Stars is a 15-card set printed on styrene with two-sided mirrored foil. Card backs are numbered with an "S" suffix and are seeded 1:20 packs. Pulsars are a parallel set that are printed on two-sided rainbow holographic foil and styrene with an embossed star pattern in the background. Pulsars are seeded 1:400 packs.

		MT
Complete Set (15):		140.00
Common Player:		4.00
Inserted 1:20		
Pulsars:		4x to 8x
Inserted 1:400		
1	Ken Griffey Jr.	20.00
2	Mark McGwire	25.00
3	Sammy Sosa	12.00
4	Derek Jeter	12.00
5	Nomar Garciaparra	12.00
6	Alex Rodriguez	12.00
7	Mike Piazza	12.00
8	Juan Gonzalez	10.00
9	Chipper Jones	10.00
10	Cal Ripken Jr.	15.00
11	Frank Thomas	10.00
12	Greg Maddux	12.00
13	Roger Clemens	6.00
14	Vladimir Guerrero	6.00
15	Manny Ramirez	6.00

1999 Metal Universe

The 300-card base set offers 232 player cards and three subsets: Building Blocks, M.L.P.D. and Caught on the Fly. Base cards feature an action photo framed in an etched-foil and metallic embossed name plate. Packs consist of eight cards with an S.R.P. of $2.69. There are two parallels, Precious Metal Gems and Gem Masters. Metal Gems are numbered to 50 with gold-foil etching. Gem Masters are limited to only one set, with silver foil etching and serial numbered "one of one."

		MT
Complete Set (300):		35.00
Common Player:		.15
1	Mark McGwire	4.00
2	Jim Edmonds	.25
3	Travis Fryman	.15
4	Tom Gordon	.15
5	Jeff Bagwell	1.00
6	Rico Brogna	.15
7	Tom Evans	.15
8	John Franco	.15
9	Juan Gonzalez	1.50
10	Paul Molitor	.50
11	Roberto Alomar	.50
12	Mike Hampton	.15
13	Orel Hershiser	.15
14	Todd Stottlemyre	.15
15	Robin Ventura	.25
16	Todd Walker	.25
17	Bernie Williams	.50
18	Shawn Estes	.15
19	Richie Sexson	.25
20	Kevin Millwood	.40
21	David Ortiz	.15
22	Mariano Rivera	.25
23	Ivan Rodriguez	.75
24	Mike Sirotka	.15
25	David Justice	.30
26	Carl Pavano	.15
27	Albert Belle	.75
28	Will Clark	.40
29	Jose Cruz Jr.	.60
30	Trevor Hoffman	.15
31	Dean Palmer	.15
32	Edgar Renteria	.15
33	David Segui	.15
34	B.J. Surhoff	.15
35	Miguel Tejada	.30
36	Bob Wickman	.15
37	Charles Johnson	.15
38	Andruw Jones	.75
39	Mike Lieberthal	.15
40	Eli Marrero	.15
41	Neifi Perez	.15
42	Jim Thome	.50
43	Barry Bonds	.75
44	Carlos Delgado	.15
45	Chuck Finley	.15
46	Brian Meadows	.15
47	Tony Gwynn	1.50
48	Jose Offerman	.15
49	Cal Ripken Jr.	2.50
50	Alex Rodriguez	2.00
51	Esteban Yan	.15
52	Matt Stairs	.15
53	Fernando Vina	.15
54	Rondell White	.25
55	Kerry Wood	.75
56	Dmitri Young	.15
57	Ken Caminiti	.25
58	Alex Gonzalez	.15
59	Matt Mantei	.15
60	Tino Martinez	.30
61	Hal Morris	.15
62	Rafael Palmeiro	.30
63	Troy Percival	.15
64	Bobby Smith	.15
65	Ed Sprague	.15
66	Brett Tomko	.15
67	Steve Trachsel	.15
68	Ugueth Urbina	.15
69	Jose Valentin	.15
70	Kevin Brown	.25
71	Shawn Green	.15
72	Dustin Hermanson	.15
73	Livan Hernandez	.15
74	Geoff Jenkins	.15
75	Jeff King	.15
76	Chuck Knoblauch	.30
77	Edgar Martinez	.15
78	Fred McGriff	.25
79	Mike Mussina	.50
80	Dave Nilsson	.15
81	Kenny Rogers	.15
82	Tim Salmon	.30
83	Reggie Sanders	.15
84	Wilson Alvarez	.15
85	Rod Beck	.15
86	Jose Guillen	.25
87	Bob Higginson	.15
88	Gregg Olson	.15
89	Jeff Shaw	.15
90	Masato Yoshii	.25
91	Todd Helton	.75
92	David Dellucci	.15
93	Johnny Damon	.15
94	Cliff Floyd	.15
95	Ken Griffey Jr.	3.00
96	Juan Guzman	.15
97	Derek Jeter	2.00
98	Barry Larkin	.30
99	Quinton McCracken	.15
100	Sammy Sosa	2.50
101	Kevin Young	.15
102	Jay Bell	.15
103	Jay Buhner	.25
104	Jeff Conine	.15
105	Ryan Jackson	.15
106	Sidney Ponson	.15
107	Jeromy Burnitz	.15
108	Roberto Hernandez	.15
109	A.J. Hinch	.15
110	Hideki Irabu	.25
111	Paul Konerko	.25
112	Henry Rodriguez	.15
113	Shannon Stewart	.15
114	Tony Womack	.15
115	Wilton Guerrero	.15
116	Andy Benes	.15
117	Jeff Cirillo	.15
118	Chili Davis	.15
119	Eric Davis	.15
120	Vladimir Guerrero	1.00
121	Dennis Reyes	.15
122	Rickey Henderson	.25
123	Mickey Morandini	.15
124	Jason Schmidt	.15
125	J.T. Snow	.15
126	Justin Thompson	.15
127	Billy Wagner	.15
128	Armando Benitez	.15
129	Sean Casey	.25
130	Brad Fullmer	.25
131	Ben Grieve	.75
132	Robb Nen	.15
133	Shane Reynolds	.15
134	Todd Zeile	.15
135	Brady Anderson	.15
136	Aaron Boone	.15
137	Orlando Cabrera	.15
138	Jason Giambi	.15
139	Randy Johnson	.50
140	Jeff Kent	.15
141	John Wetteland	.15
142	Rolando Arrojo	.15
143	Scott Brosius	.15
144	Mark Grace	.30
145	Jason Kendall	.25
146	Travis Lee	.75
147	Gary Sheffield	.30
148	David Cone	.25
149	Jose Hernandez	.15
150	Todd Jones	.15
151	Al Martin	.15
152	Ismael Valdes	.15
153	Wade Boggs	.30
154	Garret Anderson	.15
155	Bobby Bonilla	.25
156	Darryl Kile	.15
157	Ryan Klesko	.25
158	Tim Wakefield	.15
159	Kenny Lofton	.60
160	Jose Canseco	.40
161	Doug Glanville	.15
162	Todd Hundley	.15
163	Brian Jordan	.15
164	Steve Finley	.15
165	Tom Glavine	.25
166	Al Leiter	.25
167	Raul Mondesi	.30
168	Desi Relaford	.15
169	Bret Saberhagen	.15
170	Omar Vizquel	.15
171	Larry Walker	.40
172	Bobby Abreu	.15
173	Moises Alou	.25
174	Mike Caruso	.15
175	Royce Clayton	.15
176	Bartolo Colon	.25
177	Marty Cordova	.15
178	Darin Erstad	.75
179	Nomar Garciaparra	2.00
180	Andy Ashby	.15
181	Dan Wilson	.15
182	Larry Sutton	.15
183	Tony Clark	.50
184	Andres Galarraga	.50
185	Ray Durham	.15
186	Hideo Nomo	.25
187	Steve Woodard	.15
188	Scott Rolen	.75
189	Mike Stanley	.15
190	Jaret Wright	.50
191	Vinny Castilla	.15
192	Jason Christiansen	.15
193	Paul Bako	.15
194	Carlos Perez	.15
195	Mike Piazza	2.00
196	Fernando Tatis	.15
197	Mo Vaughn	.75
198	Devon White	.15
199	Ricky Gutierrez	.15
200	Charlie Hayes	.15
201	Brad Radke	.15
202	Rick Helling	.15
203	John Smoltz	.25
204	Frank Thomas	2.00
205	David Wells	.15
206	Roger Clemens	1.25
207	Mark Grudzielanek	.15
208	Chipper Jones	1.50
209	Ray Lankford	.15
210	Pedro Martinez	.50
211	Manny Ramirez	1.00
212	Greg Vaughn	.25
213	Craig Biggio	.30
214	Rusty Greer	.15
215	Greg Maddux	2.00
216	Rick Aguilera	.15
217	Andy Pettitte	.50
218	Dante Bichette	.30
219	Damion Easley	.15
220	Matt Morris	.15
221	John Olerud	.25
222	Chan Ho Park	.40
223	Curt Schilling	.25
224	John Valentin	.15
225	Matt Williams	.40
226	Ellis Burks	.15
227	Tom Goodwin	.15
228	Javy Lopez	.25
229	Eric Milton	.15
230	Paul O'Neill	.30
231	Magglio Ordonez	.15
232	Derrek Lee	.15
233	Ken Griffey Jr. (Caught on the Fly)	1.50
234	Randy Johnson (Caught on the Fly)	.25
235	Alex Rodriguez (Caught on the Fly)	1.00
236	Darin Erstad (Caught on the Fly)	.40
237	Juan Gonzalez (Caught on the Fly)	.75
238	Derek Jeter (Caught on the Fly)	1.00
239	Tony Gwynn (Caught on the Fly)	.75
240	Kerry Wood (Caught on the Fly)	.40
241	Cal Ripken Jr. (Caught on the Fly)	1.25
242	Sammy Sosa (Caught on the Fly)	1.25
243	Greg Maddux (Caught on the Fly)	1.00
244	Mark McGwire (Caught on the Fly)	2.00
245	Chipper Jones (Caught on the Fly)	.75
246	Barry Bonds (Caught on the Fly)	.40
247	Ben Grieve (Caught on the Fly)	.40
248	Ben Davis (Building Blocks)	.15
249	Robert Fick (Building Blocks)	.25
250	Carlos Guillen (Building Blocks)	.15
251	Mike Frank (Building Blocks)	.25
252	Ryan Minor (Building Blocks)	.40
253	Troy Glaus (Building Blocks)	1.00
254	Matt Anderson (Building Blocks)	.25
255	Josh Booty (Building Blocks)	.15
256	Gabe Alvarez (Building Blocks)	.15
257	Gabe Kapler (Building Blocks)	1.50
258	Enrique Wilson (Building Blocks)	.15
259	Alex Gonzalez (Building Blocks)	.25
260	Preston Wilson (Building Blocks)	.15
261	Eric Chavez (Building Blocks)	.30
262	Adrian Beltre (Building Blocks)	.30
263	Corey Koskie (Building Blocks)	.25
264	*Robert Machado* (Building Blocks)	.50
265	Orlando Hernandez (Building Blocks)	2.00
266	Matt Clement (Building Blocks)	.15
267	Luis Ordaz (Building Blocks)	.15
268	Jeremy Giambi (Building Blocks)	.25
269	J.D. Drew (Building Blocks)	8.00
270	Cliff Politte (Building Blocks)	.15
271	Carlton Loewer (Building Blocks)	.15
272	Aramis Ramirez (Building Blocks)	.25
273	Ken Griffey Jr. (M.I.P.D.)	1.50
274	Randy Johnson (M.I.P.D.)	.25
275	Alex Rodriguez (M.I.P.D.)	1.00
276	Darin Erstad (M.I.P.D.)	.40
277	Scott Rolen (M.I.P.D.)	.40
278	Juan Gonzalez (M.I.P.D.)	.75
279	Jeff Bagwell (M.I.P.D.)	.40
280	Mike Piazza (M.I.P.D.)	1.00
281	Derek Jeter (M.I.P.D.)	1.00
282	Travis Lee (M.I.P.D.)	.40
283	Tony Gwynn (M.I.P.D.)	.75
284	Kerry Wood (M.I.P.D.)	.40
285	Albert Belle (M.I.P.D.)	.40
286	Sammy Sosa (M.I.P.D.)	1.25
287	Mo Vaughn (M.I.P.D.)	.40
288	Nomar Garciaparra (M.I.P.D.)	1.00
289	Frank Thomas (M.I.P.D.)	1.00
290	Cal Ripken Jr. (M.I.P.D.)	1.25
291	Greg Maddux (M.I.P.D.)	1.00
292	Chipper Jones (M.I.P.D.)	.75
293	Ben Grieve (M.I.P.D.)	.40
294	Andruw Jones (M.I.P.D.)	.40
295	Mark McGwire (M.I.P.D.)	2.00
296	Roger Clemens (M.I.P.D.)	.60
297	Barry Bonds (M.I.P.D.)	.40
298	Ken Griffey Jr.-Checklist (M.I.P.D.)	1.00
299	Kerry Wood-Checklist (M.I.P.D.)	.25
300	Alex Rodriguez-Checklist (M.I.P.D.)	.75

1999 Metal Universe Precious Metal Gems

A 300-card parallel of the base set, these cards feature gold foil etching and are inserted exclusively in hobby packs. Each card is serially numbered to 50.

		MT
Common Player:		15.00
Production 50 sets		
1	Mark McGwire	400.00
2	Jim Edmonds	25.00
3	Travis Fryman	25.00
4	Tom Gordon	15.00
5	Jeff Bagwell	100.00
6	Rico Brogna	15.00
7	Tom Evans	15.00
8	John Franco	15.00
9	Juan Gonzalez	175.00
10	Paul Molitor	60.00
11	Roberto Alomar	60.00
12	Mike Hampton	15.00
13	Orel Hershiser	15.00
14	Todd Stottlemyre	15.00
15	Robin Ventura	25.00
16	Todd Walker	25.00
17	Bernie Williams	70.00
18	Shawn Estes	15.00
19	Richie Sexson	25.00
20	Kevin Millwood	15.00
21	David Ortiz	15.00
22	Mariano Rivera	30.00
23	Ivan Rodriguez	90.00
24	Mike Sirotka	15.00
25	David Justice	35.00
26	Carl Pavano	15.00
27	Albert Belle	90.00
28	Will Clark	40.00
29	Jose Cruz Jr.	80.00
30	Trevor Hoffman	15.00
31	Dean Palmer	15.00
32	Edgar Renteria	15.00
33	David Segui	15.00
34	B.J. Surhoff	15.00
35	Miguel Tejada	25.00
36	Bob Wickman	15.00
37	Charles Johnson	15.00
38	Andruw Jones	90.00
39	Mike Lieberthal	15.00
40	Eli Marrero	15.00
41	Neifi Perez	15.00
42	Jim Thome	50.00
43	Barry Bonds	90.00
44	Carlos Delgado	15.00
45	Chuck Finley	15.00
46	Brian Meadows	15.00
47	Tony Gwynn	175.00
48	Jose Offerman	15.00
49	Cal Ripken Jr.	300.00
50	Alex Rodriguez	250.00
51	Esteban Yan	15.00
52	Matt Stairs	15.00
53	Fernando Vina	15.00
54	Rondell White	25.00
55	Kerry Wood	75.00
56	Dmitri Young	15.00
57	Ken Caminiti	25.00
58	Alex Gonzalez	15.00
59	Matt Mantei	15.00
60	Tino Martinez	40.00
61	Hal Morris	15.00
62	Rafael Palmeiro	30.00
63	Troy Percival	15.00
64	Bobby Smith	15.00
65	Ed Sprague	15.00
66	Brett Tomko	15.00
67	Steve Trachsel	15.00
68	Ugueth Urbina	15.00
69	Jose Valentin	15.00
70	Kevin Brown	25.00
71	Shawn Green	15.00
72	Dustin Hermanson	15.00
73	Livan Hernandez	15.00
74	Geoff Jenkins	15.00
75	Jeff King	15.00
76	Chuck Knoblauch	40.00
77	Edgar Martinez	15.00
78	Fred McGriff	25.00
79	Mike Mussina	60.00
80	Dave Nilsson	15.00
81	Kenny Rogers	15.00
82	Tim Salmon	30.00
83	Reggie Sanders	15.00
84	Wilson Alvarez	15.00
85	Rod Beck	15.00
86	Jose Guillen	25.00
87	Bob Higginson	15.00
88	Gregg Olson	15.00
89	Jeff Shaw	15.00
90	Masato Yoshii	25.00
91	Todd Helton	75.00
92	David Dellucci	15.00
93	Johnny Damon	15.00
94	Cliff Floyd	15.00
95	Ken Griffey Jr.	350.00
96	Juan Guzman	15.00
97	Derek Jeter	175.00
98	Barry Larkin	30.00
99	Quinton McCracken	15.00
100	Sammy Sosa	300.00
101	Kevin Young	15.00
102	Jay Bell	15.00
103	Jay Buhner	30.00
104	Jeff Conine	15.00
105	Ryan Jackson	15.00
106	Sidney Ponson	15.00
107	Jeromy Burnitz	15.00
108	Roberto Hernandez	15.00
109	A.J. Hinch	15.00
110	Hideki Irabu	20.00
111	Paul Konerko	25.00
112	Henry Rodriguez	15.00
113	Shannon Stewart	15.00
114	Tony Womack	15.00
115	Wilton Guerrero	15.00
116	Andy Benes	25.00
117	Jeff Cirillo	15.00
118	Chili Davis	15.00
119	Eric Davis	15.00
120	Vladimir Guerrero	120.00
121	Dennis Reyes	15.00
122	Rickey Henderson	25.00
123	Mickey Morandini	15.00
124	Jason Schmidt	15.00
125	J.T. Snow	15.00
126	Justin Thompson	15.00
127	Billy Wagner	15.00
128	Armando Benitez	15.00
129	Sean Casey	25.00
130	Brad Fullmer	25.00
131	Ben Grieve	90.00
132	Robb Nen	15.00
133	Shane Reynolds	15.00
134	Todd Zeile	15.00
135	Brady Anderson	15.00
136	Aaron Boone	15.00
137	Orlando Cabrera	15.00
138	Jason Giambi	15.00
139	Randy Johnson	75.00
140	Jeff Kent	15.00
141	John Wetteland	15.00
142	Rolando Arrojo	30.00
143	Scott Brosius	15.00
144	Mark Grace	30.00
145	Jason Kendall	25.00
146	Travis Lee	60.00
147	Gary Sheffield	30.00
148	David Cone	25.00
149	Jose Hernandez	15.00
150	Todd Jones	15.00
151	Al Martin	15.00
152	Ismael Valdes	15.00
153	Wade Boggs	30.00
154	Garret Anderson	15.00
155	Bobby Bonilla	25.00
156	Darryl Kile	15.00
157	Ryan Klesko	30.00
158	Tim Wakefield	15.00
159	Kenny Lofton	75.00
160	Jose Canseco	50.00
161	Doug Glanville	15.00
162	Todd Hundley	15.00
163	Brian Jordan	15.00
164	Steve Finley	15.00
165	Tom Glavine	25.00

166	Al Leiter	25.00
167	Raul Mondesi	30.00
168	Desi Relaford	15.00
169	Bret Saberhagen	15.00
170	Omar Vizquel	15.00
171	Larry Walker	40.00
172	Bobby Abreu	15.00
173	Moises Alou	25.00
174	Mike Caruso	15.00
175	Royce Clayton	15.00
176	Bartolo Colon	15.00
177	Marty Cordova	15.00
178	Darin Erstad	90.00
179	Nomar Garciaparra	250.00
180	Andy Ashby	15.00
181	Dan Wilson	15.00
182	Larry Sutton	15.00
183	Tony Clark	50.00
184	Andres Galarraga	60.00
185	Ray Durham	15.00
186	Hideo Nomo	30.00
187	Steve Woodard	15.00
188	Scott Rolen	90.00
189	Mike Stanley	15.00
190	Jaret Wright	50.00
191	Vinny Castilla	15.00
192	Jason Christiansen	15.00
193	Paul Bako	15.00
194	Carlos Perez	15.00
195	Mike Piazza	250.00
196	Fernando Tatis	15.00
197	Mo Vaughn	90.00
198	Devon White	15.00
199	Ricky Gutierrez	15.00
200	Charlie Hayes	15.00
201	Brad Radke	15.00
202	Rick Helling	15.00
203	John Smoltz	25.00
204	Frank Thomas	250.00
205	David Wells	15.00
206	Roger Clemens	150.00
207	Mark Grudzielanek	15.00
208	Chipper Jones	175.00
209	Ray Lankford	15.00
210	Pedro Martinez	70.00
211	Manny Ramirez	90.00
212	Greg Vaughn	25.00
213	Craig Biggio	30.00
214	Rusty Greer	15.00
215	Greg Maddux	250.00
216	Rick Aguilera	15.00
217	Andy Pettitte	50.00
218	Dante Bichette	35.00
219	Damion Easley	15.00
220	Matt Morris	15.00
221	John Olerud	25.00
222	Chan Ho Park	30.00
223	Curt Schilling	25.00
224	John Valentin	15.00
225	Matt Williams	40.00
226	Ellis Burks	15.00
227	Tom Goodwin	15.00
228	Javy Lopez	25.00
229	Eric Milton	15.00
230	Paul O'Neill	30.00
231	Magglio Ordonez	15.00
232	Derrek Lee	15.00
233	Ken Griffey Jr. (Caught on the Fly)	175.00
234	Randy Johnson (Caught on the Fly)	35.00
235	Alex Rodriguez (Caught on the Fly)	125.00
236	Darin Erstad (Caught on the Fly)	45.00
237	Juan Gonzalez (Caught on the Fly)	80.00
238	Derek Jeter (Caught on the Fly)	80.00
239	Tony Gwynn (Caught on the Fly)	80.00
240	Kerry Wood (Caught on the Fly)	40.00
241	Cal Ripken Jr. (Caught on the Fly)	150.00
242	Sammy Sosa (Caught on the Fly)	150.00
243	Greg Maddux (Caught on the Fly)	125.00
244	Mark McGwire (Caught on the Fly)	200.00
245	Chipper Jones (Caught on the Fly)	80.00
246	Barry Bonds (Caught on the Fly)	45.00
247	Ben Grieve (Caught on the Fly)	45.00
248	Ben Davis (Building Blocks)	15.00
249	Robert Fick (Building Blocks)	15.00
250	Carlos Guillen (Building Blocks)	15.00
251	Mike Frank (Building Blocks)	25.00
252	Ryan Minor (Building Blocks)	35.00
253	Troy Glaus (Building Blocks)	50.00
254	Matt Anderson (Building Blocks)	25.00
255	Josh Booty (Building Blocks)	15.00
256	Gabe Alvarez (Building Blocks)	15.00
257	Gabe Kapler (Building Blocks)	60.00
258	Enrique Wilson (Building Blocks)	15.00
259	Alex Gonzalez (Building Blocks)	15.00
260	Preston Wilson (Building Blocks)	15.00
261	Eric Chavez (Building Blocks)	35.00
262	Adrian Beltre (Building Blocks)	30.00
263	Corey Koskie (Building Blocks)	30.00
264	*Robert Machado* (Building Blocks)	25.00
265	Orlando Hernandez (Building Blocks)	60.00
266	Matt Clement (Building Blocks)	15.00
267	Luis Ordaz (Building Blocks)	15.00
268	Jeremy Giambi (Building Blocks)	25.00
269	J.D. Drew (Building Blocks)	250.00
270	Cliff Politte (Building Blocks)	15.00
271	Carlton Loewer (Building Blocks)	15.00
272	Aramis Ramirez (Building Blocks)	15.00
273	Ken Griffey Jr. (M.I.P.D.)	175.00
274	Randy Johnson (M.I.P.D.)	35.00
275	Alex Rodriguez (M.I.P.D.)	125.00
276	Darin Erstad (M.I.P.D.)	45.00
277	Scott Rolen (M.I.P.D.)	45.00
278	Juan Gonzalez (M.I.P.D.)	80.00
279	Jeff Bagwell (M.I.P.D.)	50.00
280	Mike Piazza (M.I.P.D.)	125.00
281	Derek Jeter (M.I.P.D.)	80.00
282	Travis Lee (M.I.P.D.)	30.00
283	Tony Gwynn (M.I.P.D.)	80.00
284	Kerry Wood (M.I.P.D.)	40.00
285	Albert Belle (M.I.P.D.)	45.00
286	Sammy Sosa (M.I.P.D.)	150.00
287	Mo Vaughn (M.I.P.D.)	45.00
288	Nomar Garciaparra (M.I.P.D.)	125.00
289	Frank Thomas (M.I.P.D.)	125.00
290	Cal Ripken Jr. (M.I.P.D.)	150.00
291	Greg Maddux (M.I.P.D.)	125.00
292	Chipper Jones (M.I.P.D.)	80.00
293	Ben Grieve (M.I.P.D.)	45.00
294	Andruw Jones (M.I.P.D.)	45.00
295	Mark McGwire (M.I.P.D.)	200.00
296	Roger Clemens (M.I.P.D.)	75.00
297	Barry Bonds (M.I.P.D.)	45.00
298	Ken Griffey Jr.-Checklist (M.I.P.D.)	125.00
299	Kerry Wood-Checklist (M.I.P.D.)	20.00
300	Alex Rodriguez-Checklist (M.I.P.D.)	75.00

1999 Metal Universe Boyz With The Wood

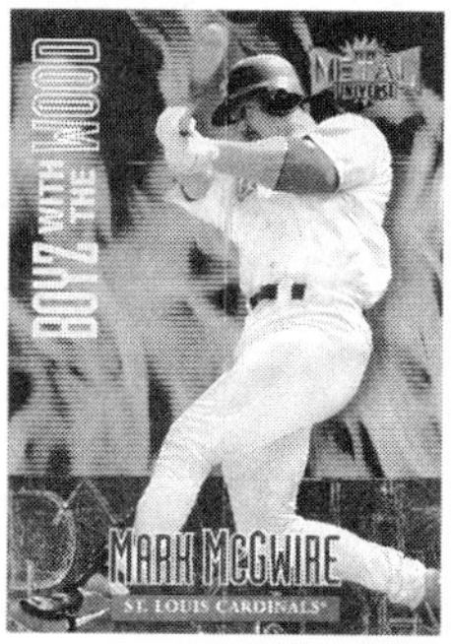

The top hitters in the game are featured on these folded cards with four sides. These are inserted 1:18.

		MT
Complete Set (15):		100.00
Common Player:		1.50
Inserted 1:18		
1	Ken Griffey Jr.	15.00
2	Frank Thomas	10.00
3	Jeff Bagwell	5.00
4	Juan Gonzalez	8.00
5	Mark McGwire	20.00
6	Scott Rolen	4.00
7	Travis Lee	3.00
8	Tony Gwynn	8.00
9	Mike Piazza	10.00
10	Chipper Jones	8.00
11	Nomar Garciaparra	10.00
12	Derek Jeter	10.00
13	Cal Ripken Jr.	12.00
14	Andruw Jones	4.00
15	Alex Rodriguez	10.00

1999 Metal Universe Diamond Soul

Utilizing lenticular technology these inserts showcase a soulful "galactic" design. The set consists of 15 cards which are seeded 1:72 packs.

		MT
Complete Set (15):		325.00
Common Player:		6.00
Inserted 1:72		
1	Cal Ripken Jr.	30.00
2	Alex Rodriguez	25.00
3	Chipper Jones	20.00
4	Derek Jeter	25.00
5	Frank Thomas	30.00
6	Greg Maddux	25.00
7	Juan Gonzalez	20.00
8	Ken Griffey Jr.	40.00
9	Kerry Wood	10.00
10	Mark McGwire	50.00
11	Mike Piazza	30.00
12	Nomar Garciaparra	30.00
13	Scott Rolen	10.00
14	Tony Gwynn	20.00
15	Travis Lee	8.00

1999 Metal Universe Linchpins

This 10-card set features a laser die-cut design and highlights key players who hold their teams together on the field and in the clubhouse. These are seeded 1:360 packs.

		MT
Complete Set (10):		600.00
Common Player:		25.00
Inserted 1:360		
1	Mike Piazza	60.00
2	Mark McGwire	120.00
3	Kerry Wood	25.00
4	Ken Griffey Jr.	100.00
5	Greg Maddux	60.00
6	Frank Thomas	60.00
7	Derek Jeter	60.00
8	Chipper Jones	50.00
9	Cal Ripken Jr.	75.00
10	Alex Rodriguez	60.00

1999 Metal Universe Neophytes

This 15-card insert set showcases young stars like J.D. Drew and Troy Glaus. The cards feature silver foil stamping on a horizontal format, found on an average of 1:6 packs.

		MT
Complete Set (15):		30.00
Common Player:		.50
Inserted 1:6		
1	Troy Glaus	4.00
2	Travis Lee	1.50
3	Scott Elarton	.50
4	Ricky Ledee	.50
5	Richard Hidalgo	.50
6	J.D. Drew	15.00
7	Paul Konerko	1.00
8	Orlando Hernandez	5.00
9	Mike Caruso	.50
10	Mike Frank	1.00
11	Miguel Tejada	1.00
12	Matt Anderson	.50
13	Kerry Wood	2.00
14	Gabe Alvarez	.50
15	Adrian Beltre	1.50

1999 Metal Universe Planet Metal

These die-cut cards feature a metallic view of the planet behind pop-out action photography. The 15-card set features the top players in the game and are seeded 1:36 packs.

		MT
Complete Set (15):		150.00
Common Player:		3.00
Inserted 1:36		
1	Alex Rodriguez	15.00
2	Andruw Jones	6.00
3	Cal Ripken Jr.	20.00
4	Chipper Jones	12.00
5	Darin Erstad	6.00
6	Derek Jeter	15.00
7	Frank Thomas	15.00
8	Travis Lee	5.00
9	Scott Rolen	6.00
10	Nomar Garciaparra	15.00
11	Mike Piazza	15.00
12	Mark McGwire	30.00
13	Ken Griffey Jr.	25.00
14	Juan Gonzalez	12.00
15	Jeff Bagwell	8.00

1999 Pacific

The 450-card base set features full bleed fronts enhanced with silver foil stamping. Card backs have year-by-year statistics, a small photo and a brief career highlight caption. There are two parallels, Platinum Blues and Reds. Platinum Blues have blue foil stamping and are seeded 1:73 packs. Reds are retail exclusive with red foil stamping and are seeded one per retail pack.

		MT
Complete Set (500):		40.00
Common Player:		.10
Platinum Blues:		30x to 50x
Yng Stars & RCs:		20x to 30x
Inserted 1:73		
Reds:		2x to 4x
Inserted 1:1 R		
1	Garret Anderson	.10
2	Jason Dickson	.10
3	Gary DiSarcina	.10
4	Jim Edmonds	.20
5	Darin Erstad	.75
6	Chuck Finley	.10
7	Shigetosi Hasegawa	.10
8	Ken Hill	.10
9	Dave Hollins	.10
10	Phil Nevin	.10
11	Troy Percival	.10
12	Tim Salmon (action)	.25
12	Tim Salmon (portrait)	.25
13	Brian Anderson	.10
14	Tony Batista	.10
15	Jay Bell	.10
16	Andy Benes	.10
17	Yamil Benitez	.10
18	Omar Daal	.10
19	David Dellucci	.10
20	Karim Garcia	.10
21	Bernard Gilkey	.10
22	Travis Lee (action)	.60
22	Travis Lee (portrait)	.60
23	Aaron Small	.10
24	Kelly Stinnett	.10
25	Devon White	.10
26	Matt Williams	.25
27	Bruce Chen (action)	.15
27	Bruce Chen (portrait)	.15
28	Andres Galarraga (action)	.35
28	Andres Galarraga (portrait)	.35
29	Tom Glavine	.20
30	Ozzie Guillen	.10
31	Andruw Jones	.75
32	Chipper Jones (action)	1.50
32	Chipper Jones (portrait)	1.50
33	Ryan Klesko	.25
34	George Lombard	.10
35	Javy Lopez	.10
36	Greg Maddux (action)	2.00
36	Greg Maddux (portrait)	2.00
37	Marty Malloy (action)	.10
37	Marty Malloy (portrait)	.10
38	Dennis Martinez	.10
39	Kevin Millwood	.25
40	Alex Rodriguez (action)	2.00
40	Alex Rodriguez (portrait)	2.00
41	Denny Neagle	.10
42	John Smoltz	.20
43	Michael Tucker	.10
44	Walt Weiss	.10
45	Roberto Alomar (action)	.50
45	Roberto Alomar (portrait)	.50
46	Brady Anderson	.10
47	Harold Baines	.10
48	Mike Bordick	.10
49	Danny Clyburn (action)	.10
49	Danny Clyburn (portrait)	.10
50	Eric Davis	.10
51	Scott Erickson	.10
52	Chris Hoiles	.10
53	Jimmy Key	.10
54	Ryan Minor (action)	.40
54	Ryan Minor (portrait)	.40
55	Mike Mussina	.50
56	Jesse Orosco	.10
57	Rafael Palmeiro (action)	.25
57	Rafael Palmeiro (portrait)	.25
58	Sidney Ponson	.10
59	Arthur Rhodes	.10
60	Cal Ripken Jr. (action)	2.00
60	Cal Ripken Jr. (portrait)	2.00
61	B.J. Surhoff	.10
62	Steve Avery	.10
63	Darren Bragg	.10
64	Dennis Eckersley	.10
65	Nomar Garciaparra (action)	2.00
65	Nomar Garciaparra (portrait)	2.00
66	Sammy Sosa (action)	2.50
66	Sammy Sosa (portrait)	2.50
67	Tom Gordon	.10
68	Reggie Jefferson	.10
69	Darren Lewis	.10
70	Mark McGwire (action)	4.00
70	Mark McGwire (portrait)	4.00
71	Pedro Martinez	.50

72	Troy O'Leary	.10
73	Bret Saberhagen	.10
74	Mike Stanley	.10
75	John Valentin	.10
76	Jason Varitek	.10
77	Mo Vaughn	.75
78	Tim Wakefield	.10
79	Manny Alexander	.10
80	Rod Beck	.10
81	Brant Brown	.10
82	Mark Clark	.10
83	Gary Gaetti	.10
84	Mark Grace	.25
85	Jose Hernandez	.10
86	Lance Johnson	.10
87	Jason Maxwell (action)	.10
87	Jason Maxwell (portrait)	.10
88	Mickey Morandini	.10
89	Terry Mulholland	.10
90	Henry Rodriguez	.10
91	Scott Servais	.10
92	Kevin Tapani	.10
93	Pedro Valdes	.10
94	Kerry Wood	.75
95	Jeff Abbott	.10
96	James Baldwin	.10
97	Albert Belle	.75
98	Mike Cameron	.10
99	Mike Caruso	.10
100	Wil Cordero	.10
101	Ray Durham	.10
102	Jaime Navarro	.10
103	Greg Norton	.10
104	Magglio Ordonez	.20
105	Mike Sirotka	.10
106	Frank Thomas (action)	2.00
106	Frank Thomas (portrait)	2.00
107	Robin Ventura	.10
108	Craig Wilson	.10
109	Aaron Boone	.10
110	Bret Boone	.10
111	Sean Casey	.20
112	Pete Harnisch	.10
113	John Hudek	.10
114	Barry Larkin	.25
115	Eduardo Perez	.10
116	Mike Remlinger	.10
117	Reggie Sanders	.10
118	Chris Stynes	.10
119	Eddie Taubensee	.10
120	Brett Tomko	.10
121	Pat Watkins	.10
122	Dmitri Young	.10
123	Sandy Alomar Jr.	.10
124	Dave Burba	.10
125	Bartolo Colon	.10
126	Joey Cora	.10
127	Brian Giles	.10
128	Dwight Gooden	.10
129	Mike Jackson	.10
130	David Justice	.25
131	Kenny Lofton	.60
132	Charles Nagy	.10
133	Chad Ogea	.10
134	Manny Ramirez (action)	1.00
134	Manny Ramirez (portrait)	1.00
135	Richie Sexson	.20
136	Jim Thome (action)	.40
136	Jim Thome (portrait)	.40
137	Omar Vizquel	.10
138	Jaret Wright	.40
139	Pedro Astacio	.10
140	Jason Bates	.10
141	Dante Bichette (action)	.25
141	Dante Bichette (portrait)	.25
142	Vinny Castilla (action)	.10
142	Vinny Castilla (portrait)	.10
143	Edgar Clemente (action)	.10
143	Edgar Clemente (portrait)	.10
144	Derrick Gibson (action)	.10
144	Derrick Gibson (portrait)	.10
145	Curtis Goodwin	.10
146	Todd Helton (action)	.60
146	Todd Helton (portrait)	.60
147	Bobby Jones	.10
148	Darryl Kile	.10
149	Mike Lansing	.10
150	Chuck McElroy	.10
151	Neifi Perez	.10
152	Jeff Reed	.10
153	John Thomson	.10
154	Larry Walker (action)	.30
154	Larry Walker (portrait)	.30
155	Jamey Wright	.10
156	Kimera Bartee	.10
157	Geronimo Berroa	.10
158	Raul Casanova	.10
159	Frank Catalanotto	.10
160	Tony Clark	.40
161	Deivi Cruz	.10
162	Damion Easley	.10
163	Juan Encarnacion	.10
164	Luis Gonzalez	.10
165	Seth Greisinger	.10
166	Bob Higginson	.10
167	Brian Hunter	.10
168	Todd Jones	.10
169	Justin Thompson	.10
170	Antonio Alfonseca	.10
171	Dave Berg	.10
172	John Cangelosi	.10
173	Craig Counsell	.10
174	Todd Dunwoody	.10
175	Cliff Floyd	.10
176	Alex Gonzalez	.10
177	Livan Hernandez	.10
178	Ryan Jackson	.10
179	Mark Kotsay	.20
180	Derrek Lee	.10
181	Matt Mantei	.10
182	Brian Meadows	.10
183	Edgar Renteria	.10
184	Moises Alou (action)	.25
184	Moises Alou (portrait)	.25
185	Brad Ausmus	.10
186	Jeff Bagwell (action)	.75
186	Jeff Bagwell (portrait)	.75
187	Derek Bell	.10
188	Sean Berry	.10
189	Craig Biggio	.25
190	Carl Everett	.10
191	Ricky Gutierrez	.10
192	Mike Hampton	.10
193	Doug Henry	.10
194	Richard Hidalgo	.10
195	Randy Johnson	.50
196	Russ Johnson (action)	.10
196	Russ Johnson (portrait)	.10
197	Shane Reynolds	.10
198	Bill Spiers	.10
199	Kevin Appier	.10
200	Tim Belcher	.10
201	Jeff Conine	.10
202	Johnny Damon	.10
203	Jermaine Dye	.10
204	Jeremy Giambi (batting stance)	.20
204	Jeremy Giambi (follow-through)	.20
205	Jeff King	.10
206	Shane Mack	.10
207	Jeff Montgomery	.10
208	Hal Morris	.10
209	Jose Offerman	.10
210	Dean Palmer	.10
211	Jose Rosado	.10
212	Glendon Rusch	.10
213	Larry Sutton	.10
214	Mike Sweeney	.10
215	Bobby Bonilla	.20
216	Alex Cora	.10
217	Darren Dreifort	.10
218	Mark Grudzielanek	.10
219	Todd Hollandsworth	.10
220	Trenidad Hubbard	.10
221	Charles Johnson	.10
222	Eric Karros	.20
223	Matt Luke	.10
224	Ramon Martinez	.20
225	Raul Mondesi	.25
226	Chan Ho Park	.20
227	Jeff Shaw	.10
228	Gary Sheffield	.25
229	Eric Young	.10
230	Jeromy Burnitz	.10
231	Jeff Cirillo	.10
232	Marquis Grissom	.10
233	Bobby Hughes	.10
234	John Jaha	.10
235	Geoff Jenkins	.10
236	Scott Karl	.10
237	Mark Loretta	.10
238	Mike Matheny	.10
239	Mike Myers	.10
240	Dave Nilsson	.10
241	Bob Wickman	.10
242	Jose Valentin	.10
243	Fernando Vina	.10
244	Rick Aguilera	.10
245	Ron Coomer	.10
246	Marty Cordova	.10
247	Denny Hocking	.10
248	Matt Lawton	.10
249	Pat Meares	.10
250	Paul Molitor (action)	.50
250	Paul Molitor (portrait)	.50
251	Otis Nixon	.10
252	Alex Ochoa	.10
253	David Ortiz	.20
254	A.J. Pierzynski	.10
255	Brad Radke	.10
256	Terry Steinbach	.10
257	Bob Tewksbury	.10
258	Todd Walker	.25
259	Shane Andrews	.10
260	Shayne Bennett	.10
261	Orlando Cabrera	.10
262	Brad Fullmer	.25
263	Vladimir Guerrero	1.00
264	Wilton Guerrero	.10
265	Dustin Hermanson	.10
266	Terry Jones	.10
267	Steve Kline	.10
268	Carl Pavano	.10
269	F.P. Santangelo	.10
270	Fernando Seguignol (action)	.25
270	Fernando Seguignol (portrait)	.25
271	Ugueth Urbina	.10
272	Jose Vidro	.10
273	Chris Widger	.10
274	Edgardo Alfonzo	.10
275	Carlos Baerga	.10
276	John Franco	.10
277	Todd Hundley	.10
278	Butch Huskey	.10
279	Bobby Jones	.10
280	Al Leiter	.20
281	Greg McMichael	.10
282	Brian McRae	.10
283	Hideo Nomo	.25
284	John Olerud	.20
285	Rey Ordonez	.10
286	Mike Piazza (action)	2.00
286	Mike Piazza (portrait)	2.00
287	Turk Wendell	.10
288	Masato Yoshii	.10
289	David Cone	.20
290	Chad Curtis	.10
291	Joe Girardi	.10
292	Orlando Hernandez	1.50
293	Hideki Irabu (action)	.20
293	Hideki Irabu (portrait)	.20
294	Derek Jeter (action)	2.00
294	Derek Jeter (portrait)	2.00
295	Chuck Knoblauch	.25
296	Mike Lowell (action)	.20
296	Mike Lowell (portrait)	.20
297	Tino Martinez	.25
298	Ramiro Mendoza	.20
299	Paul O'Neill	.25
300	Andy Pettitte	.40
301	Jorge Posada	.25
302	Tim Raines	.10
303	Mariano Rivera	.20
304	David Wells	.20
305	Bernie Williams (action)	.50
305	Bernie Williams (portrait)	.50
306	Mike Blowers	.10
307	Tom Candiotti	.10
308	Eric Chavez (action)	.40
308	Eric Chavez (portrait)	.40
309	Ryan Christenson	.10
310	Jason Giambi	.10
311	Ben Grieve (action)	.75
311	Ben Grieve (portrait)	.75
312	Rickey Henderson	.20
313	A.J. Hinch	.10
314	Jason McDonald	.10
315	Bip Roberts	.10
316	Kenny Rogers	.10
317	Scott Spiezio	.10
318	Matt Stairs	.10
319	Miguel Tejada	.25
320	Bob Abreu	.10
321	Alex Arias	.10
322	*Gary Bennett* (action)	.25
322	*Gary Bennett* (portrait)	.25
323	Ricky Bottalico	.10
324	Rico Brogna	.10
325	Bobby Estalella	.10
326	Doug Glanville	.10
327	Kevin Jordan	.10
328	Mark Leiter	.10
329	Wendell Magee	.10
330	Mark Portugal	.10
331	Desi Relaford	.10
332	Scott Rolen	.75
333	Curt Schilling	.20
334	Kevin Sefcik	.10
335	Adrian Brown	.10
336	Emil Brown	.10
337	Lou Collier	.10
338	Francisco Cordova	.10
339	Freddy Garcia	.10
340	Jose Guillen	.20
341	Jason Kendall	.20
342	Al Martin	.10
343	Abraham Nunez	.10
344	Aramis Ramirez	.20
345	Ricardo Rincon	.10
346	Jason Schmidt	.10
347	Turner Ward	.10
348	Tony Womack	.10
349	Kevin Young	.10
350	Juan Acevedo	.10
351	Delino DeShields	.10
352	J.D. Drew (action)	10.00
352	J.D. Drew (portrait)	10.00
353	Ron Gant	.20
354	Brian Jordan	.10
355	Ray Lankford	.20
356	Eli Marrero	.10
357	Kent Mercker	.10
358	Matt Morris	.10
359	Luis Ordaz	.10
360	Donovan Osborne	.10
361	Placido Polanco	.10
362	Fernando Tatis	.10
363	Andy Ashby	.10
364	Kevin Brown	.20
365	Ken Caminiti	.20
366	Steve Finley	.10
367	Chris Gomez	.10
368	Tony Gwynn (action)	1.50
368	Tony Gwynn (portrait)	1.50
369	Joey Hamilton	.10
370	Carlos Hernandez	.10
371	Trevor Hoffman	.10
372	Wally Joyner	.10
373	Jim Leyritz	.10
374	Ruben Rivera	.10
375	Greg Vaughn	.20
376	Quilvio Veras	.10
377	Rich Aurilla	.10
378	Barry Bonds (action)	.75
378	Barry Bonds (portrait)	.75
379	Ellis Burks	.10
380	Joe Carter	.20
381	Stan Javier	.10
382	Brian Johnson	.10
383	Jeff Kent	.10
384	Jose Mesa	.10
385	Bill Mueller	.10
386	Robb Nen	.10
387	Armando Rios (action)	.10
387	Armando Rios (portrait)	.10
388	Kirk Rueter	.10
389	Rey Sanchez	.10
390	J.T. Snow	.10
391	David Bell	.10
392	Jay Buhner	.25
393	Ken Cloude	.10
394	Russ Davis	.10
395	Jeff Fassero	.10
396	Ken Griffey Jr. (action)	3.00
396	Ken Griffey Jr. (portrait)	3.00
397	*Giomar Guevara*	.25
398	Carlos Guillen	.10
399	Edgar Martinez	.10
400	Shane Monahan	.10
401	Jamie Moyer	.10
402	David Segui	.10
403	Makoto Suzuki	.10
404	Mike Timlin	.10
405	Dan Wilson	.10
406	Wilson Alvarez	.10
407	Rolando Arrojo	.25
408	Wade Boggs	.25
409	Miguel Cairo	.10
410	Roberto Hernandez	.10
411	Mike Kelly	.10
412	Aaron Ledesma	.10
413	Albie Lopez	.10
414	Dave Martinez	.10
415	Quinton McCracken	.10
416	Fred McGriff	.25
417	Bryan Rekar	.10
418	Paul Sorrento	.10
419	Randy Winn	.10
420	John Burkett	.10
421	Will Clark	.25
422	Royce Clayton	.10
423	Juan Gonzalez (action)	1.50
423	Juan Gonzalez (portrait)	1.50
424	Tom Goodwin	.10
425	Rusty Greer	.10
426	Rick Helling	.10
427	Roberto Kelly	.10
428	Mark McLemore	.10
429	Ivan Rodriguez (action)	.75
429	Ivan Rodriguez (portrait)	.75
430	Aaron Sele	.10
431	Lee Stevens	.10
432	Todd Stottlemyre	.10
433	John Wetteland	.10
434	Todd Zeile	.10
435	Jose Canseco	.40
436	Roger Clemens (action)	1.50
436	Roger Clemens (portrait)	1.50
437	Felipe Crespo	.10
438	Jose Cruz Jr. (action)	.50
438	Jose Cruz Jr. (portrait)	.50
438	(portrait)	.50
439	Carlos Delgado	.10
440	Tom Evans (action)	.10
440	Tom Evans (portrait)	.10
441	Tony Fernandez	.10
442	Darrin Fletcher	.10
443	Alex Gonzalez	.10
444	Shawn Green	.10
445	Roy Halladay	.25
446	Pat Hentgen	.10
447	Juan Samuel	.10
448	Benito Santiago	.10
449	Shannon Stewart	.10
450	Woody Williams	.10

1999 Pacific Cramer's Choice

Pacific CEO/President Michael Cramer personally chose this 10-card set. Die-cut into a trophy shape, the cards are enhanced with silver holographic etching and gold foil stamping across the card bottom. These are seeded 1:721 packs.

		MT
Complete Set (10):		1200.
Common Player:		40.00
Inserted 1:721		
1	Cal Ripken Jr.	140.00
2	Nomar Garciaparra	125.00
3	Frank Thomas	125.00
4	Ken Griffey Jr.	200.00
5	Alex Rodriguez	125.00
6	Greg Maddux	125.00
7	Sammy Sosa	150.00
8	Kerry Wood	50.00
9	Mark McGwire	250.00
10	Tony Gwynn	100.00

1999 Pacific Dynagon Diamond

Dynagon Diamond captures 20 of baseball's biggest stars in action against a mirror-patterned full-foil background. These are seeded 4:37.

		MT
Complete Set (20):		75.00
Common Player:		1.00
Inserted 1:9		
1	Cal Ripken Jr.	5.00
2	Nomar Garciaparra	5.00
3	Frank Thomas	5.00
4	Derek Jeter	5.00
5	Ben Grieve	2.00
6	Ken Griffey Jr.	8.00
7	Alex Rodriguez	5.00
8	Juan Gonzalez	4.00
9	Travis Lee	1.50
10	Chipper Jones	4.00
11	Greg Maddux	5.00
12	Sammy Sosa	6.00
13	Kerry Wood	2.00
14	Jeff Bagwell	2.00
15	Hideo Nomo	1.00
16	Mike Piazza	5.00
17	J.D. Drew	10.00
18	Mark McGwire	10.00
19	Tony Gwynn	4.00
20	Barry Bonds	2.00

1999 Pacific Dynagon Diamond Titanium

A parallel to Dynagon Diamond, these are serially numbered to 99 sets and exclusive to hobby packs.

		MT
Complete Set (20):		2200.
Common Player:		25.00
Production 99 sets		
1	Cal Ripken Jr.	175.00
2	Nomar Garciaparra	150.00

3	Frank Thomas	150.00
4	Derek Jeter	125.00
5	Ben Grieve	60.00
6	Ken Griffey Jr.	250.00
7	Alex Rodriguez	150.00
8	Juan Gonzalez	125.00
9	Travis Lee	50.00
10	Chipper Jones	125.00
11	Greg Maddux	150.00
12	Sammy Sosa	200.00
13	Kerry Wood	60.00
14	Jeff Bagwell	60.00
15	Hideo Nomo	30.00
16	Mike Piazza	150.00
17	J.D. Drew	150.00
18	Mark McGwire	300.00
19	Tony Gwynn	125.00
20	Barry Bonds	60.00

1999 Pacific Gold Crown Die-Cuts

This 36-card die-cut set is shaped like a crown at the top and features dual foiling, 24-pt. stock and gold foil stamping. These are seeded 1:37 packs.

		MT
Complete Set (36):		500.00
Common Player:		4.00
Inserted 1:37		
1	Darin Erstad	10.00
2	Cal Ripken Jr.	25.00
3	Nomar Garciaparra	25.00
4	Pedro Martinez	8.00
5	Mo Vaughn	10.00
6	Frank Thomas	25.00
7	Kenny Lofton	8.00
8	Manny Ramirez	12.00
9	Jaret Wright	6.00
10	Paul Molitor	8.00
11	Derek Jeter	25.00
12	Bernie Williams	8.00
13	Ben Grieve	10.00
14	Ken Griffey Jr.	40.00
15	Alex Rodriguez	25.00
16	Rolando Arrojo	4.00
17	Wade Boggs	4.00
18	Juan Gonzalez	20.00
19	Ivan Rodriguez	10.00
20	Roger Clemens	20.00
21	Travis Lee	8.00
22	Chipper Jones	25.00
23	Greg Maddux	25.00
24	Sammy Sosa	30.00
25	Kerry Wood	10.00
26	Todd Helton	8.00
27	Jeff Bagwell	10.00
28	Craig Biggio	4.00
29	Vladimir Guerrero	12.00
30	Hideo Nomo	5.00
31	Mike Piazza	25.00
32	Scott Rolen	10.00
33	J.D. Drew	40.00
34	Mark McGwire	45.00
35	Tony Gwynn	20.00
36	Barry Bonds	10.00

1999 Pacific Team Checklists

This 30-card horizontal insert set features a star player from each team on the card front, with each team's complete checklist on the card back. Fronts feature a holographic silver-foiled and embossed logo of the player's respective team. These are seeded 2:37 packs.

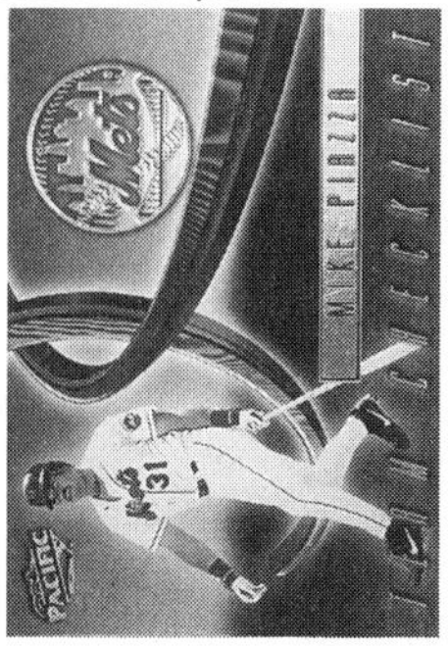

		MT
Complete Set (30):		100.00
Common Player:		1.50
Inserted 1:18		
1	Darin Erstad	3.00
2	Cal Ripken Jr.	8.00
3	Nomar Garciaparra	8.00
4	Frank Thomas	8.00
5	Manny Ramirez	3.00
6	Damion Easley	1.50
7	Jeff King	1.50
8	Paul Molitor	2.50
9	Derek Jeter	8.00
10	Ben Grieve	3.00
11	Ken Griffey Jr.	12.00
12	Wade Boggs	2.00
13	Juan Gonzalez	6.00
14	Roger Clemens	6.00
15	Travis Lee	2.00
16	Chipper Jones	6.00
17	Sammy Sosa	10.00
18	Barry Larkin	2.00
19	Todd Helton	2.50
20	Mark Kotsay	1.50
21	Jeff Bagwell	3.00
22	Raul Mondesi	2.00
23	Jeff Cirillo	1.50
24	Vladimir Guerrero	4.00
25	Mike Piazza	8.00
26	Scott Rolen	3.00
27	Jason Kendall	1.50
28	Mark McGwire	15.00
29	Tony Gwynn	6.00
30	Barry Bonds	3.00

1999 Pacific Timelines

Timelines features 20 superstars, giving a chronological history of each player complete with photos from early in their careers. Three photos of the player are on the card front. Inserted exclusively in hobby packs these are limited to 199 serially numbered sets.

		MT
Complete Set (20):		1200.
Common Player:		20.00
Inserted 1:181 H		
1	Cal Ripken Jr.	100.00
2	Frank Thomas	100.00
3	Jim Thome	20.00
4	Paul Molitor	30.00
5	Bernie Williams	30.00
6	Derek Jeter	90.00
7	Ken Griffey Jr.	140.00
8	Alex Rodriguez	100.00
9	Wade Boggs	20.00
10	Jose Canseco	20.00
11	Roger Clemens	80.00
12	Andres Galarraga	20.00
13	Chipper Jones	80.00
14	Greg Maddux	100.00
15	Sammy Sosa	120.00
16	Larry Walker	20.00
17	Randy Johnson	20.00
18	Mike Piazza	100.00
19	Mark McGwire	160.00
20	Tony Gwynn	80.00

1999 Pacific Aurora

The 200-card set features two photos on the card front and one on the back. Card backs also have '98 and career stats along with personal information. The player's name and Aurora logo are stamped with gold foil.

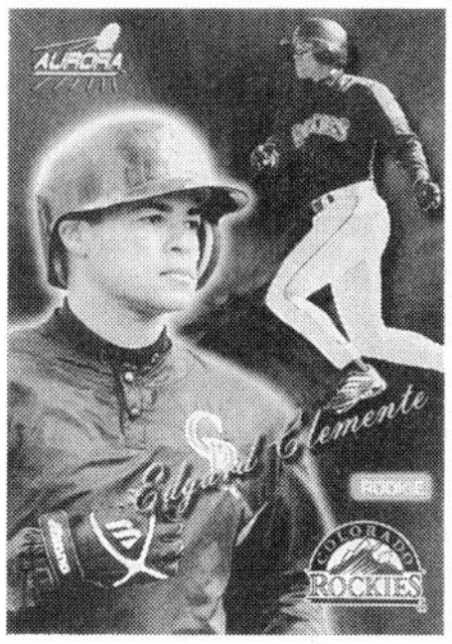

		MT
Complete Set (200):		55.00
Common Player:		.20
1	Garret Anderson	.20
2	Jim Edmonds	.40
3	Darin Erstad	1.00
4	Matt Luke	.20
5	Tim Salmon	.50
6	Mo Vaughn	1.00
7	Jay Bell	.20
8	David Dellucci	.20
9	Steve Finley	.20
10	Bernard Gilkey	.20
11	Randy Johnson	.75
12	Travis Lee	.75
13	Matt Williams	.50
14	Andres Galarraga	.50
15	Tom Glavine	.40
16	Andruw Jones	1.00
17	Chipper Jones	2.00
18	Brian Jordan	.20
19	Javy Lopez	.40
20	Greg Maddux	2.50
21	Albert Belle	1.00
22	Will Clark	.50
23	Scott Erickson	.20
24	Mike Mussina	.75
25	Cal Ripken Jr.	3.00
26	B.J. Surhoff	.20
27	Nomar Garciaparra	2.50
28	Reggie Jefferson	.20
29	Darren Lewis	.20
30	Pedro Martinez	.75
31	John Valentin	.20
32	Rod Beck	.20
33	Mark Grace	.40
34	Lance Johnson	.20
35	Mickey Morandini	.20
36	Sammy Sosa	2.50
37	Kerry Wood	1.00
38	James Baldwin	.20
39	Mike Caruso	.20
40	Ray Durham	.20
41	Magglio Ordonez	.40
42	Frank Thomas	2.00
43	Aaron Boone	.20
44	Sean Casey	.20
45	Barry Larkin	.40
46	Hal Morris	.20
47	Denny Neagle	.20
48	Greg Vaughn	.40
49	Pat Watkins	.20
50	Roberto Alomar	.75
51	Sandy Alomar Jr.	.30
52	David Justice	.40
53	Kenny Lofton	1.00
54	Manny Ramirez	1.00
55	Richie Sexson	.40
56	Jim Thome	.60
57	Omar Vizquel	.20
58	Dante Bichette	.50
59	Vinny Castilla	.40
60	*Edgard Clemente*	.50
61	Derrick Gibson	.20
62	Todd Helton	.75
63	Darryl Kile	.20
64	Larry Walker	.75
65	Tony Clark	.60
66	Damion Easley	.20
67	Bob Higginson	.40
68	Brian Hunter	.20
69	Dean Palmer	.20
70	Justin Thompson	.20
71	Craig Counsell	.20
72	Todd Dunwoody	.20
73	Cliff Floyd	.20
74	Alex Gonzalez	.20
75	Livan Hernandez	.20
76	Mark Kotsay	.20
77	Derrek Lee	.20
78	Moises Alou	.40
79	Jeff Bagwell	1.00
80	Derek Bell	.20
81	Craig Biggio	.75
82	Ken Caminiti	.40
83	Richard Hidalgo	.20
84	Shane Reynolds	.20
85	Jeff Conine	.20
86	Johnny Damon	.20
87	Jermaine Dye	.20
88	Jeff King	.20
89	Jeff Montgomery	.20
90	Mike Sweeney	.20
91	Kevin Brown	.40
92	Mark Grudzielanek	.20
93	Eric Karros	.20
94	Raul Mondesi	.40
95	Chan Ho Park	.40
96	Gary Sheffield	.40
97	Jeromy Burnitz	.20
98	Jeff Cirillo	.20
99	Marquis Grissom	.20
100	Geoff Jenkins	.20
101	Dave Nilsson	.20
102	Jose Valentin	.20
103	Fernando Vina	.20
104	Marty Cordova	.20
105	Matt Lawton	.20
106	David Ortiz	.20
107	Brad Radke	.20
108	Todd Walker	.40
109	Shane Andrews	.20
110	Orlando Cabrera	.20
111	Brad Fullmer	.40
112	Vladimir Guerrero	1.50
113	Wilton Guerrero	.20
114	Carl Pavano	.20
115	Fernando Seguignol	.50
116	Ugueth Urbina	.20
117	Edgardo Alfonzo	.20
118	Bobby Bonilla	.20
119	Rickey Henderson	.40
120	Hideo Nomo	.40
121	John Olerud	.40
122	Rey Ordonez	.20
123	Mike Piazza	2.50
124	Masato Yoshii	.20
125	Scott Brosius	.20
126	Orlando Hernandez	1.50
127	Hideki Irabu	.50
128	Derek Jeter	2.50
129	Chuck Knoblauch	.50
130	Tino Martinez	.50
131	Jorge Posada	.50
132	Bernie Williams	.75
133	Eric Chavez	.50
134	Ryan Christenson	.20
135	Jason Giambi	.20
136	Ben Grieve	1.00
137	A.J. Hinch	.20
138	Matt Stairs	.20
139	Miguel Tejada	.20
140	Bob Abreu	.20
141	*Gary Bennett*	.40
142	Desi Relaford	.20
143	Scott Rolen	1.00
144	Curt Schilling	.40
145	Kevin Sefcik	.20
146	Brian Giles	.20
147	Jose Guillen	.20
148	Jason Kendall	.40
149	Aramis Ramirez	.20
150	Tony Womack	.20
151	Kevin Young	.20
152	Eric Davis	.20
153	J.D. Drew	6.00
154	Ray Lankford	.20
155	Eli Marrero	.20
156	Mark McGwire	5.00
157	Luis Ordaz	.20
158	Edgar Renteria	.20
159	Andy Ashby	.20
160	Tony Gwynn	2.00
161	Trevor Hoffman	.20
162	Wally Joyner	.20
163	Jim Leyritz	.20
164	Ruben Rivera	.20
165	Reggie Sanders	.20
166	Quilvio Veras	.20
167	Rich Aurilia	.20
168	Marvin Benard	.20
169	Barry Bonds	1.00
170	Ellis Burks	.20
171	Jeff Kent	.40
172	Bill Mueller	.20
173	J.T. Snow	.20
174	Jay Buhner	.50
175	Jeff Fassero	.20
176	Ken Griffey Jr.	4.00
177	Carlos Guillen	.20
178	Edgar Martinez	.40
179	Alex Rodriguez	2.50
180	David Segui	.20
181	Dan Wilson	.20
182	Rolando Arrojo	.40
183	Wade Boggs	.50
184	Jose Canseco	1.00
185	Aaron Ledesma	.20
186	Dave Martinez	.20
187	Quinton McCracken	.20
188	Fred McGriff	.50
189	Juan Gonzalez	2.00
190	Tom Goodwin	.20
191	Rusty Greer	.20
192	Roberto Kelly	.20
193	Rafael Palmeiro	.75
194	Ivan Rodriguez	1.00
195	Roger Clemens	1.50
196	Jose Cruz Jr.	.75
197	Carlos Delgado	.50
198	Alex Gonzalez	.20
199	Roy Halladay	.50
200	Pat Hentgen	.20

1999 Pacific Aurora Complete Players

The 10 players featured in this serial numbered 20-card set each have two cards, designed to fit together. Card fronts feature a red border on the top and bottom with the rest of the card done in gold foil etching. Each card is serially numbered to 299.

		MT
Complete Set (10):		375.00
Common Player:		8.00
Production 299 sets		
1	Cal Ripken Jr.	50.00
2	Nomar Garciaparra	40.00
3	Sammy Sosa	40.00
4	Kerry Wood	15.00
5	Frank Thomas	40.00
6	Mike Piazza	40.00
7	Mark McGwire	75.00
8	Tony Gwynn	30.00
9	Ken Griffey Jr.	60.00
10	Alex Rodriguez	40.00

1999 Pacific Aurora Kings of the Major Leagues

The full foiled card fronts also utilize gold foil stamping. Pacific's crown as well as the featured player's team are shadow boxed in the background with the player's image in the foreground. These are seeded 1:361.

		MT
Complete Set (10):		1000.
Common Player:		40.00
Inserted 1:361		
1	Cal Ripken Jr.	120.00
2	Nomar Garciaparra	100.00
3	Sammy Sosa	100.00
4	Kerry Wood	40.00
5	Frank Thomas	80.00
6	Mike Piazza	100.00
7	Mark McGwire	200.00
8	Tony Gwynn	80.00
9	Ken Griffey Jr.	160.00
10	Alex Rodriguez	100.00

1999 Pacific Aurora On Deck

Twenty of the game's hottest players are featured in this laser-cut and silver foil stamped set. The player's team logo is laser cut into the bottom half of the card beneath the player photo. These are seeded 4:37 packs.

		MT
Complete Set (20):		100.00
Common Player:		2.00
Inserted 1:9		
1	Chipper Jones	6.00
2	Cal Ripken Jr.	10.00
3	Nomar Garciaparra	8.00
4	Sammy Sosa	8.00
5	Frank Thomas	6.00
6	Manny Ramirez	3.00
7	Todd Helton	2.50
8	Larry Walker	2.00
9	Jeff Bagwell	3.00
10	Vladimir Guerrero	4.00
11	Mike Piazza	8.00
12	Derek Jeter	8.00
13	Bernie Williams	2.50
14	J.D. Drew	12.00
15	Mark McGwire	15.00

16	Tony Gwynn	6.00
17	Ken Griffey Jr.	12.00
18	Alex Rodriguez	8.00
19	Juan Gonzalez	6.00
20	Ivan Rodriguez	3.00

1999 Pacific Aurora Pennant Fever

Regular Pennant Fever inserts feature gold foil stamping of 20 of the hottest players in the hobby. These are seeded 4:37 packs. There are also three parallel versions which consist of: Platinum Blue, Silver and Copper. Platinum Blues are limited to 100 serial numbered sets, Silvers are retail exclusive and limited to 250 numbered sets and Coppers are hobby exclusive and limited to 20 numbered sets.

		MT
Complete Set (20):		90.00
Common Player:		1.00
Inserted 1:9		
1	Chipper Jones	5.00
2	Greg Maddux	6.00
3	Cal Ripken Jr.	8.00
4	Nomar Garciaparra	6.00
5	Sammy Sosa	6.00
6	Kerry Wood	2.50
7	Frank Thomas	5.00
8	Manny Ramirez	2.50
9	Todd Helton	2.00
10	Jeff Bagwell	2.50
11	Mike Piazza	6.00
12	Derek Jeter	6.00
13	Bernie Williams	2.00
14	J.D. Drew	10.00
15	Mark McGwire	12.00
16	Tony Gwynn	5.00
17	Ken Griffey Jr.	10.00
18	Alex Rodriguez	6.00
19	Juan Gonzalez	5.00
20	Ivan Rodriguez	2.50

1999 Pacific Aurora Styrotechs

This 20-card set features styrene stock, which makes the cards more resilient. Fronts have a black border and stamped with gold foil. Backs have a photo and a brief career highlight caption. These are seeded 1:37 packs.

		MT
Complete Set (20):		300.00
Common Player:		5.00
Inserted 1:37		
1	Chipper Jones	15.00
2	Greg Maddux	20.00
3	Cal Ripken Jr.	25.00
4	Nomar Garciaparra	20.00
5	Sammy Sosa	20.00
6	Kerry Wood	8.00
7	Frank Thomas	15.00
8	Manny Ramirez	10.00
9	Larry Walker	5.00
10	Jeff Bagwell	8.00
11	Mike Piazza	20.00
12	Derek Jeter	20.00
13	Bernie Williams	6.00
14	J.D. Drew	30.00
15	Mark McGwire	40.00
16	Tony Gwynn	15.00
17	Ken Griffey Jr.	30.00
18	Alex Rodriguez	20.00
19	Juan Gonzalez	15.00
20	Ivan Rodriguez	8.00

1999 Pacific Crown Collection

Released in one series the 300-card set has white borders and gold foil stamping on the card fronts. Backs have a small photo along with english and spanish translation. There is one parallel to the base set Platinum Blues, which are stamped with a platinum blue holographic tint and are seeded 1:73. Packs consist of 12 cards with a S.R.P. of $2.49.

		MT
Complete Set (300):		30.00
Common Player:		.10
Platinum Blue Stars:		30x to 50x
Yng Stars & RCs:		20x to 40x
Inserted 1:73		
1	Garret Anderson	.10
2	Gary DiSarcina	.10
3	Jim Edmonds	.20
4	Darin Erstad	.75
5	Shigetosi Hasegawa	.10
6	Norberto Martin	.10
7	Omar Olivares	.10
8	Orlando Palmeiro	.10
9	Tim Salmon	.25
10	Randy Velarde	.10
11	Tony Batista	.10
12	Jay Bell	.10
13	Yamil Benitez	.10
14	Omar Daal	.10
15	David Dellucci	.10
16	Karim Garcia	.10
17	Travis Lee	.60
18	Felix Rodriguez	.10
19	Devon White	.10
20	Matt Williams	.25
21	Andres Galarraga	.50
22	Tom Glavine	.20
23	Ozzie Guillen	.10
24	Andruw Jones	.75
25	Chipper Jones	1.50
26	Ryan Klesko	.25
27	Javy Lopez	.20
28	Greg Maddux	2.00
29	Dennis Martinez	.10
30	Odaliz Perez	.10
31	Rudy Seanez	.10
32	John Smoltz	.20
33	Roberto Alomar	.50
34	Armando Benitez	.10
35	Scott Erickson	.10
36	Juan Guzman	.10
37	Mike Mussina	.50
38	Jesse Orosco	.10
39	Rafael Palmeiro	.30
40	Sidney Ponson	.10
41	Cal Ripken Jr.	2.50
42	B.J. Surhoff	.10
43	Lenny Webster	.10
44	Dennis Eckersley	.10
45	Nomar Garciaparra	2.00
46	Darren Lewis	.10
47	Pedro Martinez	.50
48	Troy O'Leary	.10
49	Bret Saberhagen	.10
50	John Valentin	.10
51	Mo Vaughn	.75
52	Tim Wakefield	.10
53	Manny Alexander	.10
54	Rod Beck	.10
55	Gary Gaetti	.10
56	Mark Grace	.25
57	Felix Heredia	.10
58	Jose Hernandez	.10
59	Henry Rodriguez	.10
60	Sammy Sosa	2.50
61	Kevin Tapani	.10
62	Kerry Wood	.75
63	James Baldwin	.10
64	Albert Belle	.75
65	Mike Caruso	.10
66	Carlos Castillo	.10
67	Wil Cordero	.10
68	Jaime Navarro	.10
69	Magglio Ordonez	.25
70	Frank Thomas	2.00
71	Robin Ventura	.10
72	Bret Boone	.10
73	Sean Casey	.25
74	*Guillermo Garcia*	.10
75	Barry Larkin	.25
76	Melvin Nieves	.10
77	Eduardo Perez	.10
78	Roberto Petagine	.10
79	Reggie Sanders	.10
80	Eddie Taubensee	.10
81	Brett Tomko	.10
82	Sandy Alomar Jr.	.10
83	Bartolo Colon	.10
84	Joey Cora	.10
85	Einar Diaz	.10
86	David Justice	.25
87	Kenny Lofton	.60
88	Manny Ramirez	1.00
89	Jim Thome	.40
90	Omar Vizquel	.10
91	Enrique Wilson	.10
92	Pedro Astacio	.10
93	Dante Bichette	.30
94	Vinny Castilla	.10
95	*Edgard Clemente*	.10
96	Todd Helton	.60
97	Darryl Kile	.10
98	Mike Munoz	.10
99	Neifi Perez	.10
100	Jeff Reed	.10
101	Larry Walker	.40
102	Gabe Alvarez	.10
103	Kimera Bartee	.10
104	Frank Castillo	.10
105	Tony Clark	.40
106	Deivi Cruz	.10
107	Damion Easley	.10
108	Luis Gonzalez	.10
109	Marino Santana	.10
110	Justin Thompson	.10
111	Antonio Alfonseca	.10
112	Alex Fernandez	.10
113	Cliff Floyd	.10
114	Alex Gonzalez	.10
115	Livan Hernandez	.10
116	Mark Kotsay	.20
117	Derrek Lee	.10
118	Edgar Renteria	.10
119	Jesus Sanchez	.10
120	Moises Alou	.20
121	Jeff Bagwell	1.00
122	Derek Bell	.10
123	Craig Biggio	.25
124	Tony Eusebio	.10
125	Ricky Gutierrez	.10
126	Richard Hidalgo	.10
127	Randy Johnson	.50
128	Jose Lima	.10
129	Shane Reynolds	.10
130	Johnny Damon	.10
131	Carlos Febles	.10
132	Jeff King	.10
133	Mendy Lopez	.10
134	Hal Morris	.10
135	Jose Offerman	.10
136	Jose Rosado	.10
137	Jose Santiago	.10
138	Bobby Bonilla	.20
139	Roger Cedeno	.10
140	Alex Cora	.10
141	Eric Karros	.20
142	Raul Mondesi	.25
143	Antonio Osuna	.10
144	Chan Ho Park	.20
145	Gary Sheffield	.25
146	Ismael Valdes	.10
147	Jeromy Burnitz	.10
148	Jeff Cirillo	.10
149	Valerio de los Santos	.10
150	Marquis Grissom	.10
151	Scott Karl	.10
152	Dave Nilsson	.10
153	Al Reyes	.10
154	Rafael Roque	.10
155	Jose Valentin	.10
156	Fernando Vina	.10
157	Rick Aguilera	.10
158	Hector Carrasco	.10
159	Marty Cordova	.10
160	Eddie Guardado	.10
161	Paul Molitor	.50
162	Otis Nixon	.10
163	Alex Ochoa	.10
164	David Ortiz	.10
165	Frank Rodriguez	.10
166	Todd Walker	.25
167	Miguel Batista	.10
168	Orlando Cabrera	.10
169	Vladimir Guerrero	1.00
170	Wilton Guerrero	.10
171	Carl Pavano	.10
172	Robert Perez	.10
173	F.P. Santangelo	.10
174	Fernando Seguignol	.25
175	Ugueth Urbina	.10
176	Javier Vazquez	.10
177	Edgardo Alfonzo	.10
178	Carlos Baerga	.10
179	John Franco	.10
180	Luis Lopez	.10
181	Hideo Nomo	.25
182	John Olerud	.20
183	Rey Ordonez	.10
184	Mike Piazza	2.00
185	Armando Reynoso	.10
186	Masato Yoshii	.10
187	David Cone	.20
188	Orlando Hernandez	2.00
189	Hideki Irabu	.20
190	Derek Jeter	2.00
191	Ricky Ledee	.25
192	Tino Martinez	.30
193	Ramiro Mendoza	.10
194	Paul O'Neill	.25
195	Jorge Posada	.20
196	Mariano Rivera	.20
197	Luis Sojo	.10
198	Bernie Williams	.50
199	Rafael Bournigal	.10
200	Eric Chavez	.40
201	Ryan Christenson	.10
202	Jason Giambi	.10
203	Ben Grieve	.75
204	Rickey Henderson	.20
205	A.J. Hinch	.10
206	Kenny Rogers	.10
207	Miguel Tejada	.20
208	Jorge Velandia	.10
209	Bobby Abreu	.10
210	Marlon Anderson	.10
211	Alex Arias	.10
212	Bobby Estalella	.10
213	Doug Glanville	.10
214	Scott Rolen	.75
215	Curt Schilling	.20
216	Kevin Sefcik	.10
217	Adrian Brown	.10
218	Francisco Cordova	.10
219	Freddy Garcia	.10
220	Jose Guillen	.20
221	Jason Kendall	.10
222	Al Martin	.10
223	Abraham Nunez	.10
224	Aramis Ramirez	.25
225	Ricardo Rincon	.10
226	Kevin Young	.10
227	J.D. Drew	8.00
228	Ron Gant	.10
229	Jose Jimenez	.10
230	Brian Jordan	.10
231	Ray Lankford	.10
232	Eli Marrero	.10
233	Mark McGwire	4.00
234	Luis Ordaz	.10
235	Placido Polanco	.10
236	Fernando Tatis	.10
237	Andy Ashby	.10
238	Kevin Brown	.10
239	Ken Caminiti	.20
240	Steve Finley	.10
241	Chris Gomez	.10
242	Tony Gwynn	1.50
243	Carlos Hernandez	.10
244	Trevor Hoffman	.10
245	Wally Joyner	.10
246	Ruben Rivera	.10
247	Greg Vaughn	.20
248	Quilvio Veras	.10
249	Rich Aurilia	.10
250	Barry Bonds	.75
251	Stan Javier	.10
252	Jeff Kent	.10
253	Ramon Martinez	.10
254	Jose Mesa	.10
255	Armando Rios	.10
256	Rich Rodriguez	.10
257	Rey Sanchez	.10
258	J.T. Snow	.10
259	Julian Tavarez	.10
260	Jeff Fassero	.10
261	Ken Griffey Jr.	3.00
262	*Giomar Guevara*	.10
263	Carlos Guillen	.10
264	Raul Ibanez	.10
265	Edgar Martinez	.10
266	Jamie Moyer	.10
267	Alex Rodriguez	2.00
268	David Segui	.10
269	Makoto Suzuki	.10
270	Wilson Alvarez	.10
271	Rolando Arrojo	.10
272	Wade Boggs	.25
273	Miguel Cairo	.10
274	Roberto Hernandez	.10
275	Aaron Ledesma	.10
276	Albie Lopez	.10
277	Quinton McCracken	.10
278	Fred McGriff	.25
279	Esteban Yan	.10
280	Luis Alicea	.10
281	Will Clark	.40
282	Juan Gonzalez	1.50
283	Rusty Greer	.10
284	Rick Helling	.10
285	Xavier Hernandez	.10
286	Roberto Kelly	.10
287	Esteban Loaiza	.10
288	Ivan Rodriguez	.75
289	Aaron Sele	.10
290	John Wetteland	.10
291	Jose Canseco	.40
292	Roger Clemens	1.00
293	Felipe Crespo	.10
294	Jose Cruz Jr.	.60
295	Carlos Delgado	.10
296	Kelvim Escobar	.10
297	Tony Fernandez	.10
298	Alex Gonzalez	.10
299	Tomas Perez	.10
300	Juan Samuel	.10

1999 Pacific Crown Collection In The Cage

These die-cut inserts have a netting like background with laser cutting, giving the look that the player is hitting in a batting cage. These are seeded 1:145 packs.

		MT
Complete Set (20):		600.00
Common Player:		10.00
Inserted 1:145		
1	Chipper Jones	30.00
2	Cal Ripken Jr.	50.00
3	Nomar Garciaparra	40.00
4	Sammy Sosa	50.00
5	Frank Thomas	40.00
6	Manny Ramirez	18.00
7	Todd Helton	15.00
8	Moises Alou	10.00
9	Vladimir Guerrero	20.00
10	Mike Piazza	40.00
11	Derek Jeter	35.00
12	Ben Grieve	15.00
13	J.D. Drew	90.00
14	Mark McGwire	80.00
15	Tony Gwynn	30.00
16	Ken Griffey Jr.	60.00
17	Edgar Martinez	10.00
18	Alex Rodriguez	40.00
19	Juan Gonzalez	30.00
20	Ivan Rodriguez	15.00

1999 Pacific Crown Collection Latinos/Major Leagues

This 36-card set salutes the many latino players in the major league including Roberto Alomar, Manny Ramirez and Juan Gonzalez. These are seeded 2:37 packs.

		MT
Complete Set (36):		160.00
Common Player:		2.50
Inserted 1:18		
1	Roberto Alomar	6.00
2	Rafael Palmeiro	4.00
3	Nomar Garciaparra	20.00
4	Pedro Martinez	8.00
5	Magglio Ordonez	4.00

6	Sandy Alomar Jr.	2.50
7	Bartolo Colon	2.50
8	Manny Ramirez	10.00
9	Omar Vizquel	2.50
10	Enrique Wilson	2.50
11	David Ortiz	2.50
12	Orlando Hernandez	20.00
13	Tino Martinez	4.00
14	Mariano Rivera	3.00
15	Bernie Williams	6.00
16	Edgar Martinez	2.50
17	Alex Rodriguez	20.00
18	David Segui	2.50
19	Rolando Arrojo	4.00
20	Juan Gonzalez	15.00
21	Ivan Rodriguez	8.00
22	Jose Canseco	6.00
23	Jose Cruz Jr.	6.00
24	Andres Galarraga	6.00
25	Andruw Jones	8.00
26	Javy Lopez	3.00
27	Sammy Sosa	20.00
28	Vinny Castilla	2.50
29	Alex Gonzalez	2.50
30	Moises Alou	4.00
31	Bobby Bonilla	2.50
32	Raul Mondesi	4.00
33	Fernando Vina	2.50
34	Vladimir Guerrero	10.00
35	Carlos Baerga	2.50
36	Rey Ordonez	2.50

1999 Pacific Crown Collection Pacific Cup

These die-cut inserts are shaped like a trophy with the featured player's photo in the foreground. These are seeded 1:721 packs.

		MT
Complete Set (10):		1000.
Common Player:		40.00
Inserted 1:721		
1	Cal Ripken Jr.	120.00
2	Nomar Garciaparra	100.00
3	Frank Thomas	100.00
4	Ken Griffey Jr.	150.00
5	Alex Rodriguez	100.00
6	Greg Maddux	100.00
7	Sammy Sosa	120.00
8	Kerry Wood	50.00
9	Mark McGwire	180.00
10	Tony Gwynn	75.00

1999 Pacific Crown Collection Tape Measure

This 20-card insert set is fully foiled in platinum blue with rainbow highlights in the background of the player photo. Saluting the top power hitters in the game today, these are seeded 1:73 packs.

		MT
Complete Set (20):		325.00
Common Player:		6.00
Inserted 1:73		
1	Andres Galarraga	8.00
2	Chipper Jones	20.00
3	Nomar Garciaparra	25.00
4	Sammy Sosa	30.00
5	Frank Thomas	25.00
6	Manny Ramirez	12.00
7	Vinny Castilla	6.00
8	Moises Alou	6.00
9	Jeff Bagwell	12.00
10	Raul Mondesi	6.00
11	Vladimir Guerrero	15.00
12	Mike Piazza	25.00
13	J.D. Drew	50.00
14	Mark McGwire	50.00
15	Greg Vaughn	6.00
16	Ken Griffey Jr.	40.00
17	Alex Rodriguez	25.00
18	Juan Gonzalez	20.00
19	Ivan Rodriguez	10.00
20	Jose Canseco	6.00

1999 Pacific Crown Collection Team Checklists

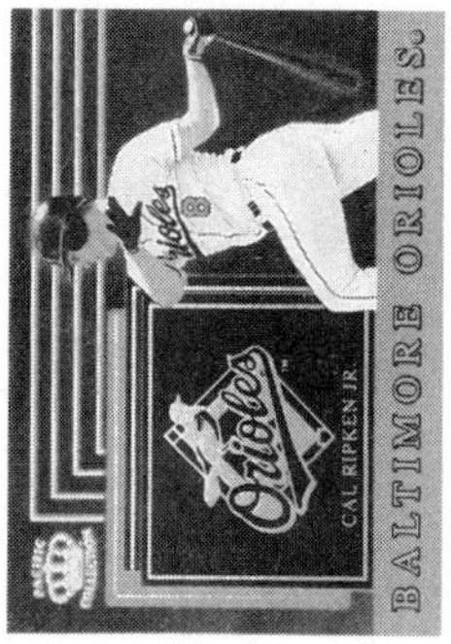

This 30-card set is highlighted with holographic silver foil stamping and done in a horizontal format. The backs have a complete team checklist for the featured player's team. These have an insertion rate of 1:37 packs.

		MT
Complete Set (30):		275.00
Common Player:		4.00
Inserted 1:37		
1	Darin Erstad	8.00
2	Travis Lee	6.00
3	Chipper Jones	15.00
4	Cal Ripken Jr.	25.00
5	Nomar Garciaparra	20.00
6	Sammy Sosa	25.00
7	Frank Thomas	20.00
8	Barry Larkin	5.00
9	Manny Ramirez	10.00
10	Larry Walker	6.00
11	Bob Higginson	4.00
12	Livan Hernandez	4.00
13	Moises Alou	5.00
14	Jeff King	4.00
15	Raul Mondesi	5.00
16	Marquis Grissom	4.00
17	David Ortiz	4.00
18	Vladimir Guerrero	10.00
19	Mike Piazza	20.00
20	Derek Jeter	15.00
21	Ben Grieve	8.00
22	Scott Rolen	8.00
23	Jason Kendall	4.00
24	Mark McGwire	40.00
25	Tony Gwynn	15.00
26	Barry Bonds	8.00
27	Ken Griffey Jr.	30.00
28	Wade Boggs	5.00
29	Juan Gonzalez	15.00
30	Jose Canseco	6.00

1999 Pacific Crown Royale

The Crown Royale 144-card base set has a horizontal format and are die-cut around a crown design at the top. The cards are double foiled and etched. There are two parallels: Limited Series and Opening Day. Limited Series is produced on 24-point stock with silver foil and limited to 99 numbered sets. Opening Day is limited to 72 numbered sets.

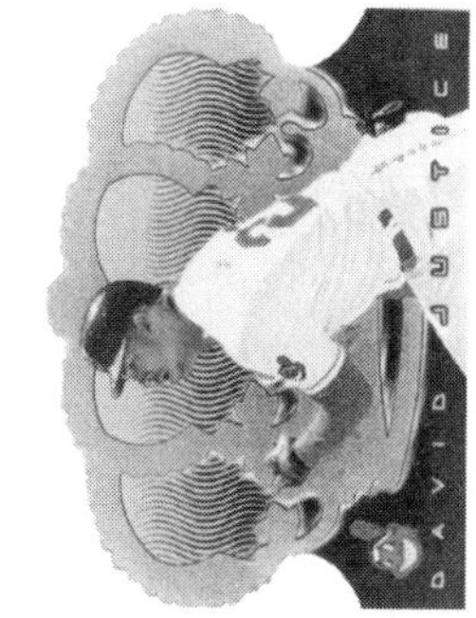

		MT
Complete Set (144):		275.00
Common Player:		.50
Common SP:		4.00
Limited Series:		5x to 10x
SP's:		1.5x to 2x
Production 99 sets		
Opening Day:		8x to 15x
SP's:		2x to 3x
Production 72 sets		
1	Jim Edmonds	.50
2	Darin Erstad	2.00
3	Troy Glaus	3.00
4	Tim Salmon	1.00
5	Mo Vaughn	2.50
6	Jay Bell	.50
7	Steve Finley	.50
8	Randy Johnson	2.00
9	Travis Lee	2.00
10	Matt Williams	1.00
11	Andruw Jones	2.50
12	Chipper Jones	5.00
13	Brian Jordan	.50
14	Ryan Klesko	.50
15	Javy Lopez	.75
16	Greg Maddux	6.00
17	Randall Simon	.50
18	Albert Belle	2.50
19	Will Clark	1.00
20	Delino DeShields	.50
21	Mike Mussina	2.00
22	Cal Ripken Jr.	8.00
23	Nomar Garciaparra	6.00
24	Pedro Martinez	2.50
25	Jose Offerman	.50
26	John Valentin	.50
27	Mark Grace	1.00
28	Lance Johnson	.50
29	Henry Rodriguez	.50
30	Sammy Sosa	6.00
31	Kerry Wood	2.50
32	Mike Caruso	.50
33	Ray Durham	.50
34	Magglio Ordonez	.75
35	Brian Simmons	.50
36	Frank Thomas	6.00
37	Mike Cameron	.50
38	Barry Larkin	.75
39	Greg Vaughn	.50
40	Dmitri Young	.50
41	Roberto Alomar	2.00
42	Sandy Alomar Jr.	.50
43	David Justice	.75
44	Kenny Lofton	2.50
45	Manny Ramirez	3.00
46	Jim Thome	1.00
47	Dante Bichette	1.00
48	Vinny Castilla	.50
49	Todd Helton	2.00
50	Larry Walker	2.00
51	Tony Clark	1.00
52	Damion Easley	.50
53	Bob Higginson	.50
54	Brian Hunter	.50
55	Gabe Kapler	8.00
56	*Jeff Weaver*	15.00
57	Cliff Floyd	.50
58	Alex Gonzalez	.50
59	Mark Kotsay	.50
60	Derrek Lee	.50
61	Preston Wilson	4.00
62	Moises Alou	.75
63	Jeff Bagwell	2.50
64	Derek Bell	.50
65	Craig Biggio	1.50
66	Ken Caminiti	.75
67	Carlos Beltran	10.00
68	Johnny Damon	.50
69	Carlos Febles	6.00
70	Jeff King	.50
71	Kevin Brown	.75
72	Todd Hundley	.50
73	Eric Karros	.50
74	Raul Mondesi	.75
75	Gary Sheffield	.75
76	Jeromy Burnitz	.50
77	Jeff Cirillo	.50
78	Marquis Grissom	.50
79	Fernando Vina	.50
80	*Chad Allen*	4.00
81	Matt Lawton	.50
82	Doug Mientkiewicz	4.00
83	Brad Radke	.50
84	Todd Walker	.50
85	Michael Barrett	6.00
86	Brad Fullmer	.50
87	Vladimir Guerrero	3.00
88	Wilton Guerrero	.50
89	Ugueth Urbina	.50
90	Bobby Bonilla	.50
91	Rickey Henderson	.75
92	Rey Ordonez	.50
93	Mike Piazza	6.00
94	Robin Ventura	.75
95	Roger Clemens	3.00
96	Orlando Hernandez	2.50
97	Derek Jeter	6.00
98	Chuck Knoblauch	1.00
99	Tino Martinez	1.00
100	Bernie Williams	1.50
101	Eric Chavez	5.00
102	Jason Giambi	.50
103	Ben Grieve	2.00
104	Tim Raines	.50
105	Marlon Anderson	4.00
106	Doug Glanville	.50
107	Scott Rolen	2.50
108	Curt Schilling	.75
109	Brian Giles	.50
110	Jose Guillen	.50
111	Jason Kendall	.75
112	Kevin Young	.50
113	J.D. Drew	20.00
114	Jose Jimenez	4.00
115	Ray Lankford	.50
116	Mark McGwire	12.00
117	Fernando Tatis	.50
118	Matt Clement	4.00
119	Tony Gwynn	5.00
120	Trevor Hoffman	.50
121	Wally Joyner	.50
122	Reggie Sanders	.50
123	Barry Bonds	2.50
124	Ellis Burks	.50
125	Jeff Kent	.50
126	J.T. Snow	.50
127	Freddy Garcia	25.00
128	Ken Griffey Jr.	10.00
129	Edgar Martinez	.50
130	Alex Rodriguez	6.00
131	David Segui	.50
132	Rolando Arrojo	.50
133	Wade Boggs	1.00
134	Jose Canseco	1.50
135	Quinton McCracken	.50
136	Fred McGriff	.75
137	Juan Gonzalez	5.00
138	Rusty Greer	.50
139	Rafael Palmeiro	1.00
140	Ivan Rodriguez	2.50
141	Jose Cruz Jr.	1.00
142	Carlos Delgado	.75
143	Shawn Green	.75
144	Roy Halladay	5.00

1999 Pacific Crown Royale Century 21

This 10-card set features some of baseball's most dominating players, on a full silver foil front. These are seeded 1:25 packs.

		MT
Complete Set (10):		
Common Player:		8.00
Inserted 1:25		
1	Cal Ripken Jr.	25.00
2	Nomar Garciaparra	20.00
3	Sammy Sosa	20.00
4	Frank Thomas	15.00
5	Mike Piazza	20.00
6	J.D. Drew	15.00
7	Mark McGwire	35.00
8	Tony Gwynn	15.00
9	Ken Griffey Jr.	30.00
10	Alex Rodriguez	20.00

1999 Pacific Crown Royale Living Legends

This 10-card set spotlights baseball's top stars on an full foiled card front. These are serial numbered to 375 sets.

		MT
Complete Set (10):		350.00
Common Player:		15.00
Production 375 sets		
1	Greg Maddux	40.00
2	Cal Ripken Jr.	40.00
3	Nomar Garciaparra	40.00
4	Sammy Sosa	40.00
5	Frank Thomas	30.00
6	Mike Piazza	40.00
7	Mark McGwire	70.00
8	Tony Gwynn	30.00
9	Ken Griffey Jr.	60.00
10	Alex Rodriguez	40.00

1999 Pacific Crown Royale Master Performers

This 20-card set features a full foiled front with the player photo in a frame like border. Master Performers are seeded 2:25 packs.

		MT
Complete Set (20):		250.00
Common Player:		4.00
Inserted 2:25		
1	Chipper Jones	15.00
2	Greg Maddux	20.00
3	Cal Ripken Jr.	25.00
4	Nomar Garciaparra	20.00
5	Sammy Sosa	20.00
6	Frank Thomas	15.00
7	Raul Mondesi	4.00
8	Vladimir Guerrero	10.00
9	Mike Piazza	20.00
10	Roger Clemens	10.00
11	Derek Jeter	20.00
12	Scott Rolen	8.00
13	J.D. Drew	15.00
14	Mark McGwire	35.00
15	Tony Gwynn	15.00
16	Barry Bonds	8.00
17	Ken Griffey Jr.	30.00
18	Alex Rodriguez	20.00
19	Juan Gonzalez	15.00
20	Ivan Rodriguez	8.00

1999 Pacific Crown Royale Pillars of the Game

This 25-card set features holographic silver foil fronts on a horizontal format. These are seeded one per pack.

	MT
Complete Set (25):	40.00
Common Player:	.75
Inserted 1:1	
1 Mo Vaughn	1.00
2 Chipper Jones	2.00
3 Greg Maddux	2.50
4 Albert Belle	1.00
5 Cal Ripken Jr.	3.00
6 Nomar Garciaparra	2.50
7 Sammy Sosa	2.50
8 Frank Thomas	2.00
9 Manny Ramirez	1.25
10 Jeff Bagwell	1.00
11 Raul Mondesi	.75
12 Vladimir Guerrero	1.50
13 Mike Piazza	2.50
14 Roger Clemens	1.50
15 Derek Jeter	2.50
16 Bernie Williams	.75
17 Ben Grieve	.75
18 J.D. Drew	3.00
19 Mark McGwire	5.00
20 Tony Gwynn	2.00
21 Barry Bonds	1.00
22 Ken Griffey Jr.	4.00
23 Alex Rodriguez	2.50
24 Juan Gonzalez	2.00
25 Ivan Rodriguez	1.00

1999 Pacific Crown Royale Pivotal Players

This 25-card set features holographic silver foil fronts with a flame in the background of the player photo. These are seeded one per pack.

	MT
Complete Set (25):	40.00
Common Player:	.75
Inserted 1:1	
1 Mo Vaughn	1.00
2 Chipper Jones	2.00
3 Greg Maddux	2.50
4 Albert Belle	1.00
5 Cal Ripken Jr.	3.00
6 Nomar Garciaparra	2.50
7 Sammy Sosa	2.50
8 Frank Thomas	2.00
9 Manny Ramirez	1.25
10 Craig Biggio	.75
11 Raul Mondesi	.75
12 Vladimir Guerrero	1.50
13 Mike Piazza	2.50
14 Roger Clemens	1.50
15 Derek Jeter	2.50
16 Bernie Williams	.75
17 Ben Grieve	.75
18 Scott Rolen	1.00
19 J.D. Drew	3.00
20 Mark McGwire	5.00
21 Tony Gwynn	2.00
22 Ken Griffey Jr.	4.00
23 Alex Rodriguez	2.50
24 Juan Gonzalez	2.00
25 Ivan Rodriguez	1.00

1999 Pacific Crown Royale Premium-Sized Cramer' Choice

This enlarged 10-card set is die-cut into a trophy shape, the cards are enhanced with silver holographic fronts with silver holographic etching and gold foil stamping across the card bottom. These are seeded one per box. Six serially numbered parallels are also randomly seeded: Dark Blue, Green, Red, Light Blue, Gold and Purple. Dark Blues are limited to 35 numbered sets, Greens 30 numbered sets, Reds 25 numbered sets, Light Blues 20 numbered sets, Gold 10 sets and Purple one set.

	MT
Complete Set (10):	120.00
Common Player:	8.00
Inserted 1:box	
Dark Blue:	3x to 6x
Production 35 sets	
Green:	3x to 6x
Production 30 sets	
Red:	4x to 8x
Production 25 sets	
Light Blue:	4x to 8x
Production 20 sets	
Gold:	6x to 12x
Production 10 sets	
Purple one set produced	
1 Cal Ripken Jr.	15.00
2 Nomar Garciaparra	12.00
3 Sammy Sosa	12.00
4 Frank Thomas	10.00
5 Mike Piazza	12.00
6 Derek Jeter	12.00
7 J.D. Drew	10.00
8 Mark McGwire	25.00
9 Tony Gwynn	10.00
10 Ken Griffey Jr.	20.00

1999 Pacific Crown Royale Prem.-Sized Gold Crown Die-Cu

This enlarged six-card set is identical to Crown Die-cuts besides their larger size. These were limited to 1,036 numbered sets.

	MT
Complete Set (6):	65.00
Common Player:	5.00
Inserted 6:10 boxes	
1 Cal Ripken Jr.	12.00
2 Mike Piazza	10.00
3 Ken Griffey Jr.	15.00
4 Tony Gwynn	8.00
5 Mark McGwire	20.00
6 J.D. Drew	8.00

1999 Pacific Invincible

The base set consists of 150 base cards and feature a player photo and a headshot in a cel window on the bottom right portion of the card. There are also two parallels to the base set: Opening Day and Platinum Blue. Both parallels are limited to 67 serial numbered sets.

	MT
Complete Set (150):	175.00
Common Player:	.75
Opening Day:	5x to 12x
Production 67 sets	
Platinum Blues:	5x to 12x
Production 67 sets	
1 Jim Edmonds	.75
2 Darin Erstad	3.00
3 Troy Glaus	4.00
4 Tim Salmon	1.50
5 Mo Vaughn	3.00
6 Steve Finley	.75
7 Randy Johnson	2.00
8 Travis Lee	2.50
9 Dante Powell	.75
10 Matt Williams	1.50
11 Bret Boone	.75
12 Andruw Jones	2.00
13 Chipper Jones	6.00
14 Brian Jordan	.75
15 Ryan Klesko	.75
16 Javy Lopez	.75
17 Greg Maddux	6.00
18 Brady Anderson	.75
19 Albert Belle	3.00
20 Will Clark	1.50
21 Mike Mussina	2.00
22 Cal Ripken Jr.	10.00
23 Nomar Garciaparra	8.00
24 Pedro Martinez	2.50
25 Trot Nixon	.75
26 Jose Offerman	.75
27 Donnie Sadler	.75
28 John Valentin	.75
29 Mark Grace	1.00
30 Lance Johnson	.75
31 Henry Rodriguez	.75
32 Sammy Sosa	8.00
33 Kerry Wood	3.00
34 McKay Christensen	.75
35 Ray Durham	.75
36 Jeff Liefer	.75
37 Frank Thomas	6.00
38 Mike Cameron	.75
39 Barry Larkin	1.50
40 Greg Vaughn	1.00
41 Dmitri Young	.75
42 Roberto Alomar	2.50
43 Sandy Alomar Jr.	.75
44 David Justice	1.00
45 Kenny Lofton	2.50
46 Manny Ramirez	4.00
47 Jim Thome	1.50
48 Dante Bichette	1.00
49 Vinny Castilla	1.00
50 Darryl Hamilton	.75
51 Todd Helton	2.00
52 Neifi Perez	.75
53 Larry Walker	2.00
54 Tony Clark	1.50
55 Damion Easley	.75
56 Bob Higginson	.75
57 Brian Hunter	.75
58 Gabe Kapler	4.00
59 Cliff Floyd	.75
60 Alex Gonzalez	.75
61 Mark Kotsay	.75
62 Derrek Lee	.75
63 Braden Looper	.75
64 Moises Alou	1.00
65 Jeff Bagwell	3.00
66 Craig Biggio	1.50
67 Ken Caminiti	1.00
68 Scott Elarton	.75
69 Mitch Meluskey	.75
70 Carlos Beltran	1.50
71 Johnny Damon	.75
72 Carlos Febles	1.00
73 Jeremy Giambi	.75
74 Kevin Brown	1.00
75 Todd Hundley	.75
76 Paul Loduca	.75
77 Raul Mondesi	1.00
78 Gary Sheffield	1.00
79 Geoff Jenkins	.75
80 Jeromy Burnitz	.75
81 Marquis Grissom	.75
82 Jose Valentin	.75
83 Fernando Vina	.75
84 Corey Koskie	.75
85 Matt Lawton	.75
86 Christian Guzman	.75
87 Torii Hunter	.75
88 Doug Mientkiewicz	.75
89 Michael Barrett	.75
90 Brad Fullmer	.75
91 Vladimir Guerrero	4.00
92 Fernando Seguignol	1.25
93 Ugueth Urbina	.75
94 Bobby Bonilla	.75
95 Rickey Henderson	1.00
96 Rey Ordonez	.75
97 Mike Piazza	8.00
98 Robin Ventura	.75
99 Roger Clemens	4.00
100 Derek Jeter	8.00
101 Chuck Knoblauch	1.25
102 Tino Martinez	1.50
103 Paul O'Neill	1.25
104 Bernie Williams	2.00
105 Eric Chavez	3.00
106 Ryan Christenson	.75
107 Jason Giambi	.75
108 Ben Grieve	3.00
109 Miguel Tejada	.75
110 Marlon Anderson	.75
111 Doug Glanville	.75
112 Scott Rolen	3.00
113 Curt Schilling	1.00
114 Brian Giles	.75
115 Warren Morris	.75
116 Jason Kendall	1.00
117 Kris Benson	.75
118 J.D. Drew	8.00
119 Ray Lankford	.75
120 Mark McGwire	15.00
121 Matt Clement	.75
122 Tony Gwynn	6.00
123 Trevor Hoffman	.75
124 Wally Joyner	.75
125 Reggie Sanders	.75
126 Barry Bonds	3.00
127 Ellis Burks	.75
128 Jeff Kent	.75
129 Stan Javier	.75
130 J.T. Snow	.75
131 Jay Buhner	1.00
132 Freddy Garcia	.75
133 Ken Griffey Jr.	12.00
134 Russ Davis	.75
135 Edgar Martinez	.75
136 Alex Rodriguez	8.00
137 David Segui	.75
138 Rolando Arrojo	.75
139 Wade Boggs	1.00
140 Jose Canseco	2.50
141 Quinton McCracken	.75
142 Fred McGriff	1.00
143 Juan Gonzalez	6.00
144 Tom Goodwin	.75
145 Rusty Greer	.75
146 Ivan Rodriguez	3.00
147 Jose Cruz Jr.	2.00
148 Carlos Delgado	1.00
149 Shawn Green	1.00
150 Roy Halladay	.75

1999 Pacific Invincible Diamond Magic

This 10-card set features a horizontal format with silver foil stamping on the front. Diamond Magic's are seeded 1:49 packs.

	MT
Complete Set (10):	175.00
Common Player:	15.00
Inserted 1:49	
1 Cal Ripken Jr.	25.00
2 Nomar Garciaparra	20.00
3 Sammy Sosa	20.00
4 Frank Thomas	15.00
5 Mike Piazza	20.00
6 J.D. Drew	20.00
7 Mark McGwire	40.00
8 Tony Gwynn	15.00
9 Ken Griffey Jr.	30.00
10 Alex Rodriguez	20.00

1999 Pacific Invincible Flash Point

This 20-card set features gold etching and gold foil stamping on the card front. These were seeded 1:25 packs.

	MT
Complete Set (20):	200.00
Common Player:	6.00
Inserted 1:25	
1 Mo Vaughn	6.00
2 Chipper Jones	12.00
3 Greg Maddux	15.00
4 Cal Ripken Jr.	20.00
5 Nomar Garciaparra	15.00
6 Sammy Sosa	15.00
7 Frank Thomas	12.00
8 Manny Ramirez	8.00
9 Vladimir Guerrero	8.00
10 Mike Piazza	15.00
11 Roger Clemens	8.00
12 Derek Jeter	15.00
13 Ben Grieve	6.00
14 Scott Rolen	6.00
15 J.D. Drew	15.00
16 Mark McGwire	30.00
17 Tony Gwynn	12.00
18 Ken Griffey Jr.	25.00
19 Alex Rodriguez	15.00
20 Juan Gonzalez	12.00

1999 Pacific Invincible Giants of the Game

This insert set features 10 of baseball's top stars and are limited to 10 serially numbered sets. Due to their scarcity no pricing is available.

	MT
Complete Set (10):	
Common Player:	
Production 10 sets	
1 Cal Ripken Jr.	
2 Nomar Garciaparra	
3 Sammy Sosa	
4 Frank Thomas	
5 Mike Piazza	
6 J.D. Drew	
7 Mark McGwire	
8 Tony Gwynn	
9 Ken Griffey Jr.	
10 Alex Rodriguez	

1999 Pacific Invincible Sandlot Heroes

Sandlot Heroes salutes baseball's top players on a horizontal format with holographic silver foil stamping on the card front. These were inserted one per pack.

	MT
Complete Set (20):	20.00
Common Player:	.50
Inserted 1:1	
1 Mo Vaughn	.75
2 Chipper Jones	1.50
3 Greg Maddux	2.00
4 Cal Ripken Jr.	2.50
5 Nomar Garciaparra	2.00
6 Sammy Sosa	2.00
7 Frank Thomas	1.50
8 Manny Ramirez	1.00
9 Vladimir Guerrero	1.00
10 Mike Piazza	2.00
11 Roger Clemens	1.00
12 Derek Jeter	2.00
13 Eric Chavez	.75
14 Ben Grieve	.75
15 J.D. Drew	2.00
16 Mark McGwire	4.00
17 Tony Gwynn	.50
18 Ken Griffey Jr.	.50
19 Alex Rodriguez	.50
20 Juan Gonzalez	.50

1999 Pacific Invincible Seismic Force

This 20-card set has a dot pattern behind the featured player with the left side and bottom of the card in a gold border. These were seeded one per pack.

		MT
Complete Set (20):		25.00
Common Player:		.50
Inserted 1:1		
1	Mo Vaughn	.75
2	Chipper Jones	1.50
3	Greg Maddux	2.00
4	Cal Ripken Jr.	2.50
5	Nomar Garciaparra	2.00
6	Sammy Sosa	2.00
7	Frank Thomas	1.50
8	Manny Ramirez	1.00
9	Vladimir Guerrero	1.00
10	Mike Piazza	2.00
11	Bernie Williams	.50
12	Derek Jeter	2.00
13	Ben Grieve	.75
14	J.D. Drew	2.50
15	Mark McGwire	4.00
16	Tony Gwynn	1.50
17	Ken Griffey Jr.	3.00
18	Alex Rodriguez	2.00
19	Juan Gonzalez	1.50
20	Ivan Rodriguez	.75

1999 Pacific Invincible Thunder Alley

Thunder Alley focuses on baseball's top power hitters. These were inserted 1:121 packs.

		MT
Complete Set (20):		800.00
Common Player:		15.00
Inserted 1:121		
1	Mo Vaughn	25.00
2	Chipper Jones	45.00
3	Cal Ripken Jr.	75.00
4	Nomar Garciaparra	60.00
5	Sammy Sosa	60.00
6	Frank Thomas	45.00
7	Manny Ramirez	30.00
8	Todd Helton	20.00
9	Vladimir Guerrero	30.00
10	Mike Piazza	60.00
11	Derek Jeter	60.00
12	Ben Grieve	20.00
13	Scott Rolen	25.00
14	J.D. Drew	60.00
15	Mark McGwire	100.00
16	Tony Gwynn	45.00
17	Ken Griffey Jr.	90.00
18	Alex Rodriguez	60.00
19	Juan Gonzalez	45.00
20	Ivan Rodriguez	25.00

1999 Pacific Paramount

The 250-card base set is highlighted by silver foil stamping and a white border. Card backs have a small photo along with 1998 statistics and career totals, along with a brief career note. There are four parallels to the base set: Copper, Platinum Blue, Holographic Silver and Opening Day Issue. Each parallel is stamped with the appropriate foil color as Coppers are found exclusively in hobby packs at a rate of one per pack. Platinum Blues are seeded one per 73 packs, Holographic Silvers are hobby only and limited to 99 serial numbered sets. Opening Day Issue is limited to 74 numbered sets.

		MT
Complete Set (250):		35.00
Common Player:		.10
Copper:		2x
Inserted 1:1 H		
Platinum Blue:		20x to 40x
Inserted 1:73		
Holographic Silver:		30x to 60x
Production 99 sets H		
Opening Day Issue:		40x to 75x
Production 74 sets		
1	Garret Anderson	.10
2	Gary DiSarcina	.10
3	Jim Edmonds	.20
4	Darin Erstad	.60
5	Chuck Finley	.10
6	Troy Glaus	.75
7	Troy Percival	.10
8	Tim Salmon	.25
9	Mo Vaughn	.60
10	Tony Batista	.10
11	Jay Bell	.10
12	Andy Benes	.10
13	Steve Finley	.10
14	Luis Gonzalez	.10
15	Randy Johnson	.50
16	Travis Lee	.60
17	Todd Stottlemyre	.10
18	Matt Williams	.25
19	David Dellucci	.10
20	Bret Boone	.10
21	Andres Galarraga	.40
22	Tom Glavine	.25
23	Andruw Jones	.50
24	Chipper Jones	1.25
25	Brian Jordan	.10
26	Ryan Klesko	.10
27	Javy Lopez	.20
28	Greg Maddux	1.50
29	John Smoltz	.20
30	Brady Anderson	.10
31	Albert Belle	.60
32	Will Clark	.30
33	Delino DeShields	.10
34	Charles Johnson	.10
35	Mike Mussina	.50
36	Cal Ripken Jr.	2.00
37	B.J. Surhoff	.10
38	Nomar Garciaparra	1.50
39	Reggie Jefferson	.10
40	Darren Lewis	.10
41	Pedro Martinez	.50
42	Troy O'Leary	.10
43	Jose Offerman	.10
44	Donnie Sadler	.10
45	John Valentin	.10
46	Rod Beck	.10
47	Gary Gaetti	.10
48	Mark Grace	.25
49	Lance Johnson	.10
50	Mickey Morandini	.10
51	Henry Rodriguez	.10
52	Sammy Sosa	1.50
53	Kerry Wood	.60
54	Mike Caruso	.10
55	Ray Durham	.10
56	Paul Konerko	.20
57	Jaime Navarro	.10
58	Greg Norton	.10
59	Magglio Ordonez	.10
60	Frank Thomas	1.25
61	Aaron Boone	.10
62	Mike Cameron	.10
63	Barry Larkin	.25
64	Hal Morris	.10
65	Pokey Reese	.10
66	Brett Tomko	.10
67	Greg Vaughn	.20
68	Dmitri Young	.10
69	Roberto Alomar	.50
70	Sandy Alomar Jr.	.20
71	Bartolo Colon	.10
72	Travis Fryman	.10
73	David Justice	.25
74	Kenny Lofton	.50
75	Manny Ramirez	.75
76	Richie Sexson	.10
77	Jim Thome	.25
78	Omar Vizquel	.10
79	Dante Bichette	.30
80	Vinny Castilla	.20
81	Darryl Hamilton	.10
82	Todd Helton	.50
83	Darryl Kile	.10
84	Mike Lansing	.10
85	Neifi Perez	.10
86	Larry Walker	.50
87	Tony Clark	.30
88	Damion Easley	.10
89	Bob Higginson	.10
90	Brian Hunter	.10
91	Dean Palmer	.10
92	Justin Thompson	.10
93	Todd Dunwoody	.10
94	Cliff Floyd	.10
95	Alex Gonzalez	.10
96	Livan Hernandez	.10
97	Mark Kotsay	.10
98	Derrek Lee	.10
99	Kevin Orie	.10
100	Moises Alou	.20
101	Jeff Bagwell	.75
102	Derek Bell	.10
103	Craig Biggio	.40
104	Ken Caminiti	.20
105	Ricky Gutierrez	.10
106	Richard Hidalgo	.10
107	Billy Wagner	.10
108	Jeff Conine	.10
109	Johnny Damon	.10
110	Carlos Febles	.20
111	Jeremy Giambi	.10
112	Jeff King	.10
113	Jeff Montgomery	.10
114	Joe Randa	.10
115	Kevin Brown	.25
116	Mark Grudzielanek	.10
117	Todd Hundley	.10
118	Eric Karros	.10
119	Raul Mondesi	.25
120	Chan Ho Park	.25
121	Gary Sheffield	.25
122	Devon White	.10
123	Eric Young	.10
124	Jeromy Burnitz	.10
125	Jeff Cirillo	.10
126	Marquis Grissom	.10
127	Geoff Jenkins	.10
128	Dave Nilsson	.10
129	Jose Valentin	.10
130	Fernando Vina	.10
131	Rick Aguilera	.10
132	Ron Coomer	.10
133	Marty Cordova	.10
134	Matt Lawton	.10
135	David Ortiz	.10
136	Brad Radke	.10
137	Terry Steinbach	.10
138	Javier Valentin	.10
139	Todd Walker	.10
140	Orlando Cabrera	.10
141	Brad Fullmer	.10
142	Vladimir Guerrero	.75
143	Wilton Guerrero	.10
144	Carl Pavano	.10
145	Ugueth Urbina	.10
146	Rondell White	.20
147	Chris Widger	.10
148	Edgardo Alfonzo	.10
149	Bobby Bonilla	.10
150	Rickey Henderson	.20
151	Brian McRae	.10
152	Hideo Nomo	.25
153	John Olerud	.25
154	Rey Ordonez	.10
155	Mike Piazza	1.50
156	Robin Ventura	.20
157	Masato Yoshii	.10
158	Roger Clemens	1.00
159	David Cone	.20
160	Orlando Hernandez	.75
161	Hideki Irabu	.10
162	Derek Jeter	1.50
163	Chuck Knoblauch	.25
164	Tino Martinez	.30
165	Paul O'Neill	.25
166	Darryl Strawberry	.20
167	Bernie Williams	.50
168	Eric Chavez	.60
169	Ryan Christenson	.10
170	Jason Giambi	.10
171	Ben Grieve	.60
172	Tony Phillips	.10
173	Tim Raines	.10
174	Scott Spiezio	.10
175	Miguel Tejada	.25
176	Bobby Abreu	.10
177	Rico Brogna	.10
178	Ron Gant	.20
179	Doug Glanville	.10
180	Desi Relaford	.10
181	Scott Rolen	.75
182	Curt Schilling	.25
183	Brant Brown	.10
184	Brian Giles	.10
185	Jose Guillen	.10
186	Jason Kendall	.20
187	Al Martin	.10
188	Ed Sprague	.10
189	Kevin Young	.10
190	Eric Davis	.10
191	J.D. Drew	1.50
192	Ray Lankford	.10
193	Eli Marrero	.10
194	Mark McGwire	3.00
195	Edgar Renteria	.10
196	Fernando Tatis	.10
197	Andy Ashby	.10
198	Tony Gwynn	1.25
199	Carlos Hernandez	.10
200	Trevor Hoffman	.10
201	Wally Joyner	.10
202	Jim Leyritz	.10
203	Ruben Rivera	.10
204	Matt Clement	.10
205	Quilvio Veras	.10
206	Rich Aurilia	.10
207	Marvin Benard	.10
208	Barry Bonds	.60
209	Ellis Burks	.10
210	Jeff Kent	.10
211	Bill Mueller	.10
212	Robb Nen	.10
213	J.T. Snow	.10
214	Jay Buhner	.20
215	Jeff Fassero	.10
216	Ken Griffey Jr.	2.50
217	Carlos Guillen	.10
218	Butch Huskey	.10
219	Edgar Martinez	.10
220	Alex Rodriguez	1.50
221	David Segui	.10
222	Dan Wilson	.10
223	Rolando Arrojo	.10
224	Wade Boggs	.25
225	Jose Canseco	.50
226	Roberto Hernandez	.10
227	Dave Martinez	.10
228	Quinton McCracken	.10
229	Fred McGriff	.20
230	Kevin Stocker	.10
231	Randy Winn	.10
232	Royce Clayton	.10
233	Juan Gonzalez	1.25
234	Tom Goodwin	.10
235	Rusty Greer	.10
236	Rick Helling	.10
237	Rafael Palmeiro	.25
238	Ivan Rodriguez	.60
239	Aaron Sele	.10
240	John Wetteland	.10
241	Todd Zeile	.10
242	Jose Cruz Jr.	.40
243	Carlos Delgado	.20
244	Tony Fernandez	.10
245	Cecil Fielder	.10
246	Alex Gonzalez	.10
247	Shawn Green	.20
248	Roy Halladay	.10
249	Shannon Stewart	.10
250	David Wells	.10

1999 Pacific Paramount Cooperstown Bound

This 10-card set focuses on players who seem destined for the Hall of Fame. These inserts feature silver foil stamping and are seeded 1:361 packs.

		MT
Complete Set (10):		575.00
Common Player:		20.00
Inserted 1:361		
1	Greg Maddux	60.00
2	Cal Ripken Jr.	75.00
3	Nomar Garciaparra	60.00
4	Sammy Sosa	60.00
5	Frank Thomas	50.00
6	Mike Piazza	60.00
7	Mark McGwire	100.00
8	Tony Gwynn	50.00
9	Ken Griffey Jr.	90.00
10	Alex Rodriguez	60.00

1999 Pacific Paramount Fielder's Choice

This 20-card set is die-cut into a glove shape and enhanced with gold foil stamping. These are seeded 1:73 packs.

		MT
Complete Set (20):		400.00
Common Player:		6.00
Inserted 1:73		
1	Chipper Jones	25.00
2	Greg Maddux	30.00
3	Cal Ripken Jr.	40.00
4	Nomar Garciaparra	30.00
5	Sammy Sosa	30.00
6	Kerry Wood	12.00
7	Frank Thomas	25.00
8	Manny Ramirez	15.00
9	Todd Helton	10.00
10	Jeff Bagwell	15.00
11	Mike Piazza	30.00
12	Derek Jeter	30.00
13	Bernie Williams	10.00
14	J.D. Drew	30.00
15	Mark McGwire	60.00
16	Tony Gwynn	25.00
17	Ken Griffey Jr.	50.00
18	Alex Rodriguez	30.00
19	Juan Gonzalez	25.00
20	Ivan Rodriguez	12.00

1999 Pacific Paramount Personal Bests

This 36-card set features holographic silver foil stamping on the card front. Card backs include a close-up photo of the featured player and a career note. These are seeded 1:37 packs.

		MT
Complete Set (36):		475.00
Common Player:		3.00
Inserted 1:37		
1	Darin Erstad	10.00
2	Mo Vaughn	10.00
3	Travis Lee	8.00
4	Chipper Jones	20.00
5	Greg Maddux	25.00
6	Albert Belle	10.00
7	Cal Ripken Jr.	30.00
8	Nomar Garciaparra	25.00
9	Sammy Sosa	25.00
10	Kerry Wood	10.00
11	Frank Thomas	20.00
12	Greg Vaughn	3.00
13	Manny Ramirez	12.00
14	Todd Helton	8.00
15	Larry Walker	8.00
16	Jeff Bagwell	12.00
17	Craig Biggio	5.00
18	Raul Mondesi	4.00
19	Vladimir Guerrero	12.00

20	Hideo Nomo	3.00
21	Mike Piazza	25.00
22	Roger Clemens	15.00
23	Derek Jeter	25.00
24	Bernie Williams	8.00
25	Eric Chavez	10.00
26	Ben Grieve	10.00
27	Scott Rolen	10.00
28	J.D. Drew	25.00
29	Mark McGwire	50.00
30	Tony Gwynn	20.00
31	Barry Bonds	10.00
32	Ken Griffey Jr.	40.00
33	Alex Rodriguez	25.00
34	Jose Canseco	6.00
35	Juan Gonzalez	20.00
36	Ivan Rodriguez	10.00

1999 Pacific Paramount Team Checklists

This 30-card set features gold foil etching and stamping on the card front. Card backs feature the featured player's team checklist for the main set. These were seeded 2:37 packs.

		MT
Complete Set (30):		150.00
Common Player:		1.50
Inserted 2:37		
1	Mo Vaughn	5.00
2	Travis Lee	4.00
3	Chipper Jones	10.00
4	Cal Ripken Jr.	15.00
5	Nomar Garciaparra	12.00
6	Sammy Sosa	12.00
7	Frank Thomas	10.00
8	Greg Vaughn	1.50
9	Manny Ramirez	5.00
10	Larry Walker	4.00
11	Damion Easley	1.50
12	Mark Kotsay	1.50
13	Jeff Bagwell	6.00
14	Jeremy Giambi	1.50
15	Raul Mondesi	2.50
16	Marquis Grissom	1.50
17	Brad Radke	1.50
18	Vladimir Guerrero	6.00
19	Mike Piazza	12.00
20	Roger Clemens	8.00
21	Ben Grieve	5.00
22	Scott Rolen	5.00
23	Brian Giles	1.50
24	Mark McGwire	25.00
25	Tony Gwynn	10.00
26	Barry Bonds	5.00
27	Ken Griffey Jr.	20.00
28	Jose Canseco	4.00
29	Juan Gonzalez	10.00
30	Jose Cruz Jr.	3.00

1999 Pacific Prism

This 150-card base set has a full, holographic silver card front. Card backs feature two more player photos along with 1998 and career statistics. Hobby packs consist of five cards. There are also three parallels including Holographic Gold, Holographic Mirror and Holographic Blue. Golds are limited to 480 serial numbered sets, Mirrors 160 sets and Blues 80 numbered sets.

		MT
Complete Set (150):		80.00
Common Player:		.50
Holographic Purples:		5x to 10x
Production 320 sets		
Holographic Gold:		3x to 6x
Production 480 sets		
Holographic Mirror:		12x to 20x
Production 160 sets		
Holographic Blue:		20x to 30x
Production 80 sets		
1	Garret Anderson	.50
2	Jim Edmonds	.50
3	Darin Erstad	1.50
4	Chuck Finley	.50
5	Tim Salmon	1.00
6	Jay Bell	.50
7	David Dellucci	.50
8	Travis Lee	1.00
9	Matt Williams	1.00
10	Andres Galarraga	1.00
11	Tom Glavine	.75
12	Andruw Jones	1.50
13	Chipper Jones	3.00
14	Ryan Klesko	.75
15	Javy Lopez	.75
16	Greg Maddux	4.00
17	Roberto Alomar	1.00
18	Ryan Minor	.50
19	Mike Mussina	1.25
20	Rafael Palmeiro	1.00
21	Cal Ripken Jr.	5.00
22	Nomar Garciaparra	4.00
23	Pedro Martinez	1.00
24	John Valentin	.50
25	Mo Vaughn	1.50
26	Tim Wakefield	.50
27	Rod Beck	.50
28	Mark Grace	.75
29	Lance Johnson	.50
30	Sammy Sosa	4.00
31	Kerry Wood	1.50
32	Albert Belle	1.50
33	Mike Caruso	.50
34	Magglio Ordonez	.75
35	Frank Thomas	4.00
36	Robin Ventura	.50
37	Aaron Boone	.50
38	Barry Larkin	.75
39	Reggie Sanders	.50
40	Brett Tomko	.50
41	Sandy Alomar Jr.	.50
42	Bartolo Colon	.50
43	David Justice	.75
44	Kenny Lofton	1.50
45	Manny Ramirez	2.00
46	Richie Sexson	.50
47	Jim Thome	1.00
48	Omar Vizquel	.50
49	Dante Bichette	.75
50	Vinny Castilla	.50
51	*Edgard Clemente*	.50
52	Todd Helton	1.50
53	Quinton McCracken	.50
54	Larry Walker	1.00
55	Tony Clark	1.00
56	Damion Easley	.50
57	Luis Gonzalez	.50
58	Bob Higginson	.50
59	Brian Hunter	.50
60	Cliff Floyd	.50
61	Alex Gonzalez	.50
62	Livan Hernandez	.50
63	Derrek Lee	.50
64	Edgar Renteria	.50
65	Moises Alou	.75
66	Jeff Bagwell	1.50
67	Derek Bell	.50
68	Craig Biggio	1.00
69	Randy Johnson	1.25
70	Johnny Damon	.50
71	Jeff King	.50
72	Hal Morris	.50
73	Dean Palmer	.50
74	Eric Karros	.75
75	Raul Mondesi	.75
76	Chan Ho Park	1.00
77	Gary Sheffield	.75
78	Jeromy Burnitz	.50
79	Jeff Cirillo	.50
80	Marquis Grissom	.50
81	Jose Valentin	.50
82	Fernando Vina	.50
83	Paul Molitor	1.00
84	Otis Nixon	.50
85	David Ortiz	.50
86	Todd Walker	.75
87	Vladimir Guerrero	2.00
88	Carl Pavano	.50
89	Fernando Seguignol	.50
90	Ugueth Urbina	.50
91	Carlos Baerga	.50
92	Bobby Bonilla	.75
93	Hideo Nomo	.50
94	John Olerud	.75
95	Rey Ordonez	.50
96	Mike Piazza	4.00
97	David Cone	.75
98	Orlando Hernandez	1.50
99	Hideki Irabu	.75
100	Derek Jeter	4.00
101	Tino Martinez	.75
102	Bernie Williams	1.00
103	Eric Chavez	.50
104	Jason Giambi	.50
105	Ben Grieve	1.50
106	Rickey Henderson	.75
107	Bob Abreu	.50
108	Doug Glanville	.50
109	Scott Rolen	1.50
110	Curt Schilling	.75
111	Emil Brown	.50
112	Jose Guillen	.50
113	Jason Kendall	.50
114	Al Martin	.50
115	Aramis Ramirez	.50
116	Kevin Young	.50
117	J.D. Drew	8.00
118	Ron Gant	.50
119	Brian Jordan	.50
120	Eli Marrero	.50
121	Mark McGwire	8.00
122	Kevin Brown	.75
123	Tony Gwynn	3.00
124	Trevor Hoffman	.50
125	Wally Joyner	.50
126	Greg Vaughn	.75
127	Barry Bonds	1.50
128	Ellis Burks	.50
129	Jeff Kent	.50
130	Robb Nen	.50
131	J.T. Snow	.50
132	Jay Buhner	.75
133	Ken Griffey Jr.	6.00
134	Edgar Martinez	.50
135	Alex Rodriguez	4.00
136	David Segui	.50
137	Rolando Arrojo	.75
138	Wade Boggs	.75
139	Aaron Ledesma	.50
140	Fred McGriff	.75
141	Will Clark	1.00
142	Juan Gonzalez	3.00
143	Rusty Greer	.50
144	Ivan Rodriguez	1.50
145	Aaron Sele	.50
146	Jose Canseco	1.00
147	Roger Clemens	2.00
148	Jose Cruz Jr.	1.25
149	Carlos Delgado	.75
150	Alex Gonzalez	.50

1999 Pacific Prism Ahead of the Game

Each card features full gold foil and etching with a close- up photo of baseball's top 20 stars. These are seeded 1:49 packs.

		MT
Complete Set (20):		400.00
Common Player:		5.00
Inserted 1:49		
1	Darin Erstad	12.00
2	Travis Lee	10.00
3	Chipper Jones	20.00
4	Cal Ripken Jr.	30.00
5	Nomar Garciaparra	25.00
6	Sammy Sosa	25.00
7	Kerry Wood	10.00
8	Frank Thomas	25.00
9	Manny Ramirez	12.00
10	Todd Helton	10.00
11	Jeff Bagwell	12.00
12	Mike Piazza	25.00
13	Derek Jeter	20.00
14	Bernie Williams	8.00
15	J.D. Drew	50.00
16	Mark McGwire	50.00
17	Tony Gwynn	20.00
18	Ken Griffey Jr.	40.00
19	Alex Rodriguez	25.00
20	Ivan Rodriguez	12.00

1999 Pacific Prism Ballpark Legends

This 10 card set salutes baseball's biggest stars. These inserts feature silver foil stamping and etching with an image of a ballpark in the background of the player photo. These are seeded 1:193 packs.

		MT
Complete Set (10):		450.00
Common Player:		30.00
Inserted 1:193		
1	Cal Ripken Jr.	60.00
2	Nomar Garciaparra	50.00
3	Frank Thomas	50.00
4	Ken Griffey Jr.	75.00
5	Alex Rodriguez	50.00
6	Greg Maddux	50.00
7	Sammy Sosa	50.00
8	Kerry Wood	30.00
9	Mark McGwire	90.00
10	Tony Gwynn	35.00

1999 Pacific Prism Diamond Glory

Card fronts feature full copper foil stamping with a star in the background of the player's photo. The 20-card set features 20 of baseball's most exciting players including several top 1999 rookies. These are seeded 2:25 packs.

		MT
Complete Set (20):		150.00
Common Player:		2.50
Inserted 2:25		
1	Darin Erstad	4.00
2	Travis Lee	3.00
3	Chipper Jones	8.00
4	Greg Maddux	10.00
5	Cal Ripken Jr.	12.00
6	Nomar Garciaparra	10.00
7	Sammy Sosa	10.00
8	Kerry Wood	4.00
9	Frank Thomas	10.00
10	Todd Helton	4.00
11	Jeff Bagwell	4.00
12	Mike Piazza	10.00
13	Derek Jeter	10.00
14	Bernie Williams	3.00
15	J.D. Drew	20.00
16	Mark McGwire	20.00
17	Tony Gwynn	8.00
18	Ken Griffey Jr.	15.00
19	Alex Rodriguez	10.00
20	Juan Gonzalez	8.00

1999 Pacific Prism Epic Performers

This hobby-only set features the 10 of the top hobby favorites and seeded at 1:97 packs.

		MT
Complete Set (10):		375.00
Common Player:		25.00
Inserted 1:97 H		
1	Cal Ripken Jr.	50.00
2	Nomar Garciaparra	40.00
3	Frank Thomas	40.00
4	Ken Griffey Jr.	60.00
5	Alex Rodriguez	40.00
6	Greg Maddux	40.00
7	Sammy Sosa	40.00
8	Kerry Wood	25.00
9	Mark McGwire	75.00
10	Tony Gwynn	30.00

1999 Pacific Private Stock

The premiere issue of Private Stock, base cards feature holographic silver foil on 30-pt. card stock. Card backs have selected box scores from the '98 season, with a brief commentary on the player. Packs consist of six cards.

		MT
Complete Set (150):		60.00
Common Player:		.25
1	Jeff Bagwell	1.50
2	Roger Clemens	2.00
3	J.D. Drew	15.00
4	Nomar Garciaparra	4.00
5	Juan Gonzalez	2.50
6	Ken Griffey Jr.	5.00
7	Tony Gwynn	2.50
8	Derek Jeter	3.00
9	Chipper Jones	2.50
10	Travis Lee	1.00
11	Greg Maddux	3.00
12	Mark McGwire	6.00
13	Mike Piazza	3.00
14	Manny Ramirez	1.50
15	Cal Ripken Jr.	4.00
16	Alex Rodriguez	3.00
17	Ivan Rodriguez	1.25
18	Sammy Sosa	4.00
19	Frank Thomas	3.00
20	Kerry Wood	1.50
21	Roberto Alomar	.75
22	Moises Alou	.40
23	Albert Belle	1.25
24	Craig Biggio	.25
25	Wade Boggs	.40
26	Barry Bonds	1.25
27	Jose Canseco	.75
28	Jim Edmonds	.25
29	Darin Erstad	1.25
30	Andres Galarraga	.75
31	Tom Glavine	.40
32	Ben Grieve	1.25
33	Vladimir Guerrero	1.50
34	Wilton Guerrero	.25
35	Todd Helton	1.25
36	Andruw Jones	1.25
37	Ryan Klesko	.40
38	Kenny Lofton	1.00
39	Javy Lopez	.40
40	Pedro Martinez	1.00

41	Paul Molitor	1.00
42	Raul Mondesi	.40
43	Rafael Palmeiro	.40
44	Tim Salmon	.40
45	Jim Thome	.75
46	Mo Vaughn	1.25
47	Larry Walker	.75
48	David Wells	.25
49	Bernie Williams	.75
50	Jaret Wright	.75
51	Bobby Abreu	.25
52	Garret Anderson	.25
53	Rolando Arrojo	.25
54	Tony Batista	.25
55	Rod Beck	.25
56	Derek Bell	.25
57	Marvin Benard	.25
58	Dave Berg	.25
59	Dante Bichette	.50
60	Aaron Boone	.25
61	Bret Boone	.25
62	Scott Brosius	.25
63	Brant Brown	.25
64	Kevin Brown	.40
65	Jeromy Burnitz	.25
66	Ken Caminiti	.40
67	Mike Caruso	.25
68	Sean Casey	.40
69	Vinny Castilla	.25
70	Eric Chavez	.75
71	Ryan Christenson	.25
72	Jeff Cirillo	.25
73	Tony Clark	.75
74	Will Clark	.50
75	*Edgard Clemente*	.25
76	David Cone	.40
77	Marty Cordova	.25
78	Jose Cruz Jr.	1.00
79	Eric Davis	.25
80	Carlos Delgado	.25
81	David Dellucci	.25
82	Delino DeShields	.25
83	Gary DiSarcina	.25
84	Damion Easley	.25
85	Dennis Eckersley	.25
86	Cliff Floyd	.25
87	Jason Giambi	.25
88	Doug Glanville	.25
89	Alex Gonzalez	.25
90	Mark Grace	.50
91	Rusty Greer	.25
92	Jose Guillen	.40
93	Carlos Guillen	.25
94	Jeffrey Hammonds	.25
95	Rick Helling	.25
96	Bob Henley	.25
97	Livan Hernandez	.25
98	Orlando Hernandez	2.00
99	Bob Higginson	.25
100	Trevor Hoffman	.25
101	Randy Johnson	.75
102	Brian Jordan	.25
103	Wally Joyner	.25
104	Eric Karros	.25
105	Jason Kendall	.40
106	Jeff Kent	.25
107	Jeff King	.25
108	Mark Kotsay	.40
109	Ray Lankford	.25
110	Barry Larkin	.40
111	Mark Loretta	.25
112	Edgar Martinez	.25
113	Tino Martinez	.50
114	Quinton McCracken	.25
115	Fred McGriff	.40
116	Ryan Minor	.75
117	Hal Morris	.25
118	Bill Mueller	.25
119	Mike Mussina	1.00
120	Dave Nilsson	.25
121	Otis Nixon	.25
122	Hideo Nomo	.50
123	Paul O'Neill	.50
124	Jose Offerman	.25
125	John Olerud	.40
126	Rey Ordonez	.25
127	David Ortiz	.25
128	Dean Palmer	.25
129	Chan Ho Park	.50
130	Aramis Ramirez	.50
131	Edgar Renteria	.25
132	Armando Rios	.25
133	Henry Rodriguez	.25
134	Scott Rolen	1.25
135	Curt Schilling	.40
136	David Segui	.25
137	Richie Sexson	.25
138	Gary Sheffield	.50
139	John Smoltz	.40
140	Matt Stairs	.25
141	Justin Thompson	.25
142	Greg Vaughn	.40
143	Omar Vizquel	.25
144	Tim Wakefield	.25
145	Todd Walker	.40
146	Devon White	.25
147	Rondell White	.40
148	Matt Williams	.50
149	*Enrique Wilson*	.25
150	Kevin Young	.25

1999 Pacific Private Stock Vintage Series

This insert set is a partial parallel of the first 50 cards in the base set and have a Vintage holographic stamp on the card fronts. These are limited to 99 numbered sets.

		MT
Common Player:		10.00
Production 99 sets		
1	Jeff Bagwell	50.00
2	Roger Clemens	75.00
3	J.D. Drew	160.00
4	Nomar Garciaparra	125.00
5	Juan Gonzalez	100.00
6	Ken Griffey Jr.	200.00
7	Tony Gwynn	100.00
8	Derek Jeter	125.00
9	Chipper Jones	100.00
10	Travis Lee	50.00
11	Greg Maddux	125.00
12	Mark McGwire	240.00
13	Mike Piazza	125.00
14	Manny Ramirez	50.00
15	Cal Ripken Jr.	160.00
16	Alex Rodriguez	125.00
17	Ivan Rodriguez	50.00
18	Sammy Sosa	125.00
19	Frank Thomas	100.00
20	Kerry Wood	50.00
21	Roberto Alomar	40.00
22	Moises Alou	10.00
23	Albert Belle	50.00
24	Craig Biggio	20.00
25	Wade Boggs	25.00
26	Barry Bonds	50.00
27	Jose Canseco	40.00
28	Jim Edmonds	10.00
29	Darin Erstad	50.00
30	Andres Galarraga	40.00
31	Tom Glavine	20.00
32	Ben Grieve	50.00
33	Vladimir Guerrero	75.00
34	Wilton Guerrero	10.00
35	Todd Helton	40.00
36	Andruw Jones	50.00
37	Ryan Klesko	15.00
38	Kenny Lofton	40.00
39	Javy Lopez	15.00
40	Pedro Martinez	40.00
41	Paul Molitor	40.00
42	Raul Mondesi	20.00
43	Rafael Palmeiro	25.00
44	Tim Salmon	20.00
45	Jim Thome	35.00
46	Mo Vaughn	50.00
47	Larry Walker	30.00
48	David Wells	10.00
49	Bernie Williams	50.00
50	Jaret Wright	30.00

1999 Pacific Private Stock PS-206

This 150-card set takes a reverent reach back into collecting history with its smaller format (1.5" x 2.5"). Card fronts have a white border with silver foil stamping and a blue back, these are found one per pack. A parallel also exists with a red back, which are seeded 1:25 packs.

		MT
Complete Set (150):		25.00
Common Player:		.25
Inserted 1:1		
parallels:		5x to 10x
Inserted 1:25		
1	Jeff Bagwell	.75
2	Roger Clemens	1.00
3	J.D. Drew	6.00
4	Nomar Garciaparra	2.00
5	Juan Gonzalez	1.50
6	Ken Griffey Jr.	3.00
7	Tony Gwynn	1.50
8	Derek Jeter	2.00
9	Chipper Jones	1.50
10	Travis Lee	.75
11	Greg Maddux	2.00
12	Mark McGwire	4.00
13	Mike Piazza	2.00
14	Manny Ramirez	1.00
15	Cal Ripken Jr.	2.50
16	Alex Rodriguez	2.00
17	Ivan Rodriguez	.75
18	Sammy Sosa	2.50
19	Frank Thomas	2.00
20	Kerry Wood	.75
21	Roberto Alomar	.50
22	Moises Alou	.25
23	Albert Belle	.75
24	Craig Biggio	.25
25	Wade Boggs	.25
26	Barry Bonds	.75
27	Jose Canseco	.40
28	Jim Edmonds	.25
29	Darin Erstad	.75
30	Andres Galarraga	.50
31	Tom Glavine	.40
32	Ben Grieve	.75
33	Vladimir Guerrero	1.00
34	Wilton Guerrero	.25
35	Todd Helton	.75
36	Andruw Jones	.75
37	Ryan Klesko	.25
38	Kenny Lofton	.75
39	Javy Lopez	.25
40	Pedro Martinez	.60
41	Paul Molitor	.50
42	Raul Mondesi	.35
43	Rafael Palmeiro	.35
44	Tim Salmon	.40
45	Jim Thome	.50
46	Mo Vaughn	.75
47	Larry Walker	.40
48	David Wells	.25
49	Bernie Williams	.60
50	Jaret Wright	.50
51	Bobby Abreu	.25
52	Garret Anderson	.25
53	Rolando Arrojo	.25
54	Tony Batista	.25
55	Rod Beck	.25
56	Derek Bell	.25
57	Marvin Benard	.25
58	Dave Berg	.25
59	Dante Bichette	.40
60	Aaron Boone	.25
61	Bret Boone	.25
62	Scott Brosius	.25
63	Brant Brown	.25
64	Kevin Brown	.35
65	Jeromy Burnitz	.25
66	Ken Caminiti	.25
67	Mike Caruso	.25
68	Sean Casey	.25
69	Vinny Castilla	.25
70	Eric Chavez	.50
71	Ryan Christenson	.25
72	Jeff Cirillo	.25
73	Tony Clark	.50
74	Will Clark	.40
75	Edgard Clemente	.25
76	David Cone	.25
77	Marty Cordova	.25
78	Jose Cruz Jr.	.60
79	Eric Davis	.25
80	Carlos Delgado	.25
81	David Dellucci	.25
82	Delino DeShields	.25
83	Gary DiSarcina	.25
84	Damion Easley	.25
85	Dennis Eckersley	.25
86	Cliff Floyd	.25
87	Jason Giambi	.25
88	Doug Glanville	.25
89	Alex Gonzalez	.25
90	Mark Grace	.40
91	Rusty Greer	.25
92	Jose Guillen	.25
93	Carlos Guillen	.25
94	Jeffrey Hammonds	.25
95	Rick Helling	.25
96	Bob Henley	.25
97	Livan Hernandez	.25
98	Orlando Hernandez	2.00
99	Bob Higginson	.25
100	Trevor Hoffman	.25
101	Randy Johnson	.50
102	Brian Jordan	.25
103	Wally Joyner	.25
104	Eric Karros	.25
105	Jason Kendall	.40
106	Jeff Kent	.25
107	Jeff King	.25
108	Mark Kotsay	.40
109	Ray Lankford	.25
110	Barry Larkin	.40
111	Mark Loretta	.25
112	Edgar Martinez	.25
113	Tino Martinez	.40
114	Quinton McCracken	.25
115	Fred McGriff	.40
116	Ryan Minor	.75
117	Hal Morris	.25
118	Bill Mueller	.25
119	Mike Mussina	.50
120	Dave Nilsson	.25
121	Otis Nixon	.25
122	Hideo Nomo	.40
123	Paul O'Neill	.40
124	Jose Offerman	.25
125	John Olerud	.40
126	Rey Ordonez	.25
127	David Ortiz	.25
128	Dean Palmer	.25
129	Chan Ho Park	.40
130	Aramis Ramirez	.40
131	Edgar Renteria	.25
132	Armando Rios	.25
133	Henry Rodriguez	.25
134	Scott Rolen	.75
135	Curt Schilling	.25
136	David Segui	.25
137	Richie Sexson	.25
138	Gary Sheffield	.40
139	John Smoltz	.25
140	Matt Stairs	.25
141	Justin Thompson	.25
142	Greg Vaughn	.40
143	Omar Vizquel	.25
144	Tim Wakefield	.25
145	Todd Walker	.40
146	Devon White	.25
147	Rondell White	.35
148	Matt Williams	.40
149	Enrique Wilson	.25
150	Kevin Young	.25

1999 Pacific Private Stock Exclusive Series

This 20-card set is a partial parallel to the base set. Taking the first 20 cards from the set and serially numbering them to 299 sets. These are inserted exclusively in hobby packs.

		MT
Complete Set (20):		750.00
Common Player:		8.00
Production 299 sets H		
1	Jeff Bagwell	20.00
2	Roger Clemens	30.00
3	J.D. Drew	75.00
4	Nomar Garciaparra	50.00
5	Juan Gonzalez	40.00
6	Ken Griffey Jr.	80.00
7	Tony Gwynn	40.00
8	Derek Jeter	50.00
9	Chipper Jones	40.00
10	Travis Lee	15.00
11	Greg Maddux	50.00
12	Mark McGwire	100.00
13	Mike Piazza	50.00
14	Manny Ramirez	20.00
15	Cal Ripken Jr.	60.00
16	Alex Rodriguez	50.00
17	Ivan Rodriguez	20.00
18	Sammy Sosa	50.00
19	Frank Thomas	40.00
20	Kerry Wood	20.00

1999 Pacific Private Stock Platinum Series

Another partial parallel of the first 50 cards in the base set. Cards have a platinum holographic sheen to them with a Platinum stamp on the front. These are limited to 199 numbered sets.

		MT
Common Player:		8.00
Production 199 sets		
1	Jeff Bagwell	50.00
2	Roger Clemens	50.00
3	J.D. Drew	90.00
4	Nomar Garciaparra	75.00
5	Juan Gonzalez	60.00
6	Ken Griffey Jr.	120.00
7	Tony Gwynn	60.00
8	Derek Jeter	80.00
9	Chipper Jones	60.00
10	Travis Lee	25.00
11	Greg Maddux	75.00
12	Mark McGwire	150.00
13	Mike Piazza	75.00
14	Manny Ramirez	30.00
15	Cal Ripken Jr.	100.00
16	Alex Rodriguez	75.00
17	Ivan Rodriguez	30.00
18	Sammy Sosa	75.00
19	Frank Thomas	60.00
20	Kerry Wood	30.00
21	Roberto Alomar	25.00
22	Moises Alou	10.00
23	Albert Belle	30.00
24	Craig Biggio	15.00
25	Wade Boggs	15.00
26	Barry Bonds	30.00
27	Jose Canseco	20.00
28	Jim Edmonds	10.00
29	Darin Erstad	30.00
30	Andres Galarraga	25.00
31	Tom Glavine	10.00
32	Ben Grieve	30.00
33	Vladimir Guerrero	40.00
34	Wilton Guerrero	8.00
35	Todd Helton	25.00
36	Andruw Jones	30.00
37	Ryan Klesko	10.00
38	Kenny Lofton	30.00
39	Javy Lopez	10.00
40	Pedro Martinez	25.00
41	Paul Molitor	25.00
42	Raul Mondesi	15.00
43	Rafael Palmeiro	15.00
44	Tim Salmon	15.00
45	Jim Thome	20.00
46	Mo Vaughn	30.00
47	Larry Walker	20.00
48	David Wells	8.00
49	Bernie Williams	25.00
50	Jaret Wright	20.00

1999 Pacific Private Stock Preferred Series

Another partial parallel of the first 20 base cards. Each card is stamped with a holographic Preferred logo and are numbered to 399 sets.

		MT
Complete Set (20):		500.00
Common Player:		5.00
Production 399 sets		
1	Jeff Bagwell	15.00
2	Roger Clemens	25.00
3	J.D. Drew	60.00
4	Nomar Garciaparra	40.00
5	Juan Gonzalez	30.00
6	Ken Griffey Jr.	60.00
7	Tony Gwynn	30.00
8	Derek Jeter	40.00
9	Chipper Jones	30.00
10	Travis Lee	12.00
11	Greg Maddux	40.00
12	Mark McGwire	75.00
13	Mike Piazza	40.00
14	Manny Ramirez	15.00
15	Cal Ripken Jr.	50.00
16	Alex Rodriguez	40.00
17	Ivan Rodriguez	15.00
18	Sammy Sosa	40.00
19	Frank Thomas	30.00
20	Kerry Wood	15.00

1999 Pacific Private Stock Homerun History

This holographic silver foiled commemorative set honors Mark McGwire and Sammy Sosa's historic '98 seasons. Two cards were added to the end of the set, which are Silver Crown Die-Cuts honoring Ripken Jr.'s consecutive games streak and McGwire's 70 home runs. These are inserted 2:25 packs.

		MT
Complete Set (22):		200.00
Common McGwire:		12.00
Common Sosa:		8.00
Inserted 1:12		
1	Home Run #61 (Mark McGwire)	15.00
2	Home Run #59 (Sammy Sosa)	10.00
3	Home Run #62 (Mark McGwire)	15.00
4	Home Run #60 (Sammy Sosa)	10.00
5	Home Run #63 (Mark McGwire)	15.00
6	Home Run #61 (Sammy Sosa)	10.00
7	Home Run #64 (Mark McGwire)	15.00
8	Home Run #62 (Sammy Sosa)	10.00
9	Home Run #65 (Mark McGwire)	15.00
10	Home Run #63 (Sammy Sosa)	10.00
11	Home Run #67 (Mark McGwire)	15.00
12	Home Run #64 (Sammy Sosa)	10.00
13	Home Run #68 Mark McGwire)	15.00
14	Home Run #65 (Sammy Sosa)	10.00
15	Home Run #70 (Mark McGwire)	15.00
16	Home Run #66 (Sammy Sosa)	10.00

17	A Season of Celebration (Mark McGwire)	15.00
18	A Season of Celebration (Sammy Sosa)	10.00
19	Awesome Power (Sammy Sosa, Mark McGwire)	15.00
20	Transcending Sports (Mark McGwire, Sammy Sosa)	15.00
21	Crown Die-Cut (Mark McGwire)	15.00
22	Crown Die-Cut (Cal Ripken Jr.)	10.00

1999 Pacific Revolution

The 150-card set features dual foiled etching and embossing enhanced by gold foil stamping. Card backs have year-by- year statistics along with a close-up photo. There are three parallels to the base set: Opening Day, Red and Shadow. Reds are retail exclusive and are limited to 299 numbered sets. Shadows have light blue foil stamping and are limited to 99 numbered sets. Opening Day are seeded exclusively in hobby packs at a rate of 1:25 packs.

		MT
Complete Set (150):		125.00
Common Player:		.50
Shadow:		5x to 10x
SP:		2x to 3x
Production 99 sets H		
Red:		2x to 4x
SP:		1x to 2x
Production 299 sets R		
Opening Day:		8x to 15x
SP:		3x to 4x
Production 49 sets H		
1	Jim Edmonds	.50
2	Darin Erstad	2.00
3	Troy Glaus	3.00
4	Tim Salmon	1.00
5	Mo Vaughn	2.50
6	Steve Finley	.50
7	Luis Gonzalez	.50
8	Randy Johnson	2.00
9	Travis Lee	2.00
10	Matt Williams	1.00
11	Andruw Jones	2.50
12	Chipper Jones	5.00
13	Brian Jordan	.50
14	Javy Lopez	.75
15	Greg Maddux	6.00
16	*Kevin McGlinchy*	.50
17	John Smoltz	.50
18	Brady Anderson	.50
19	Albert Belle	2.50
20	Will Clark	1.00
21	*Willis Otanez*	.50
23	*Calvin Pickering*	.50
23	Cal Ripken Jr.	8.00
24	Nomar Garciaparra	6.00
25	Pedro Martinez	2.50
26	Troy O'Leary	.50
27	Jose Offerman	.50
28	Mark Grace	.75
29	Mickey Morandini	.50
30	Henry Rodriguez	.50
31	Sammy Sosa	6.00
32	Ray Durham	.50
33	Carlos Lee	.50
34	*Jeff Liefer*	.50
35	Magglio Ordonez	.75
36	Frank Thomas	5.00
37	Mike Cameron	.50
38	Sean Casey	.75
39	Barry Larkin	1.00
40	Greg Vaughn	.75
41	Roberto Alomar	2.00
42	Sandy Alomar Jr.	.50
43	David Justice	.75
44	Kenny Lofton	2.50
45	Manny Ramirez	3.00
46	Richie Sexson	.50
47	Jim Thome	1.50
48	Dante Bichette	1.00
49	Vinny Castilla	.50
50	Darryl Hamilton	.50
51	Todd Helton	1.50
52	Larry Walker	2.00
53	Tony Clark	1.00
54	Damion Easley	.50
55	Bob Higginson	.50
56	*Gabe Kapler*	5.00
57	*Alex Gonzalez*	.50
58	Mark Kotsay	.50
59	Kevin Orie	.50
60	*Preston Wilson*	.50
61	Jeff Bagwell	2.50
62	Derek Bell	.50
63	Craig Biggio	1.00
64	Ken Caminiti	.50
65	Carlos Beltran	1.00
66	Johnny Damon	.50
67	Jermaine Dye	.50
68	Carlos Febles	.50
69	Kevin Brown	.75
70	Todd Hundley	.50
71	Eric Karros	.50
72	Raul Mondesi	.75
73	Gary Sheffield	.75
74	Jeromy Burnitz	.50
75	Jeff Cirillo	.50
76	Marquis Grissom	.50
77	Fernando Vina	.50
78	*Chad Allen*	.50
79	*Corey Koskie*	.50
80	*Doug Mientkiewicz*	.50
81	Brad Radke	.50
82	Todd Walker	.50
83	*Michael Barrett*	.75
84	Vladimir Guerrero	3.00
85	Wilton Guerrero	.50
86	*Guillermo Mota*	.50
87	Rondell White	.75
88	Edgardo Alfonzo	.50
89	Rickey Henderson	.75
90	John Olerud	.75
91	Mike Piazza	6.00
92	Robin Ventura	.75
93	Roger Clemens	3.00
94	Chili Davis	.50
95	Derek Jeter	6.00
96	Chuck Knoblauch	1.00
97	Tino Martinez	1.00
98	Paul O'Neill	.75
99	Bernie Williams	1.50
100	Eric Chavez	1.50
101	Jason Giambi	.50
102	Ben Grieve	2.00
103	John Jaha	.50
104	*Olmedo Saenz*	.50
105	Bobby Abreu	.50
106	Doug Glanville	.50
107	Desi Relaford	.50
108	Scott Rolen	2.50
109	Curt Schilling	.75
110	Brian Giles	.50
111	Jason Kendall	.75
112	Pat Meares	.50
113	Kevin Young	.50
114	J.D. Drew	5.00
115	Ray Lankford	.50
116	Eli Marrero	.50
117	*Joe McEwing*	.50
118	Mark McGwire	12.00
119	Fernando Tatis	.50
120	Tony Gwynn	5.00
121	Trevor Hoffman	.50
122	Wally Joyner	.50
123	Reggie Sanders	.50
124	Barry Bonds	2.50
125	Ellis Burks	.50
126	Jeff Kent	.50
127	*Ramon Martinez*	.50
128	*Joseph Nathan*	.50
129	*Freddy Garcia*	15.00
130	Ken Griffey Jr.	10.00
131	Brian Hunter	.50
132	Edgar Martinez	.50
133	Alex Rodriguez	6.00
134	David Segui	.50
135	Wade Boggs	1.00
136	Jose Canseco	1.50
137	Quinton McCracken	.50
138	Fred McGriff	.75
139	*Kelly Dransfeldt*	.50
140	Juan Gonzalez	5.00
141	Rusty Greer	.50
142	Rafael Palmeiro	1.00
143	Ivan Rodriguez	2.50
144	Lee Stevens	.50
145	Jose Cruz Jr.	1.50
146	Carlos Delgado	.75
147	Shawn Green	.75
148	*Roy Halladay*	.50
149	Shannon Stewart	.50
150	*Kevin Witt*	.50

1999 Pacific Revolution Diamond Legacy

This 36-card set features a holographic patterned foil card front. Card backs have a small close-up photo along with a career note. These were seeded 2:25 packs.

		MT
Complete Set (36):		250.00
Common Player:		2.00
Inserted 2:25		
1	Troy Glaus	8.00
2	Mo Vaughn	6.00
3	Matt Williams	3.00
4	Chipper Jones	12.00
5	Andruw Jones	6.00
6	Greg Maddux	15.00
7	Albert Belle	6.00
8	Cal Ripken Jr.	20.00
9	Nomar Garciaparra	15.00
10	Sammy Sosa	15.00
11	Frank Thomas	12.00
12	Manny Ramirez	8.00
13	Todd Helton	4.00
14	Larry Walker	4.00
15	Gabe Kapler	8.00
16	Jeff Bagwell	6.00
17	Craig Biggio	4.00
18	Raul Mondesi	2.00
19	Vladimir Guerrero	8.00
20	Mike Piazza	15.00
21	Roger Clemens	8.00
22	Derek Jeter	15.00
23	Bernie Williams	5.00
24	Ben Grieve	4.00
25	Scott Rolen	6.00
26	J.D. Drew	12.00
27	Mark McGwire	30.00
28	Fernando Tatis	2.00
29	Tony Gwynn	12.00
30	Barry Bonds	6.00
31	Ken Griffey Jr.	25.00
32	Alex Rodriguez	15.00
33	Jose Canseco	4.00
34	Juan Gonzalez	12.00
35	Ivan Rodriguez	6.00
36	Shawn Green	3.00

1999 Pacific Revolution Foul Pole Net-Fusions

This 20-card set features netting down the right side of each card, with the player photo on the left side. The player name, position and logo are stamped with gold foil. These were seeded 1:49 packs.

		MT
Complete Set (20):		400.00
Common Player:		10.00
Inserted 1:49		
1	Chipper Jones	25.00
2	Andruw Jones	15.00
3	Cal Ripken Jr.	40.00
4	Nomar Garciaparra	30.00
5	Sammy Sosa	30.00
6	Frank Thomas	25.00
7	Manny Ramirez	15.00
8	Jeff Bagwell	15.00
9	Raul Mondesi	10.00
10	Vladimir Guerrero	20.00
11	Mike Piazza	30.00
12	Derek Jeter	30.00
13	Bernie Williams	10.00
14	Scott Rolen	15.00
15	J.D. Drew	25.00
16	Mark McGwire	60.00
17	Tony Gwynn	25.00
18	Ken Griffey Jr.	50.00
19	Alex Rodriguez	30.00
20	Juan Gonzalez	25.00

1999 Pacific Revolution Icons

This 10-card set spotlights the top players, each card is die-cut in the shape of a shield with silver foil etching and stamping. These were seeded 1:121 packs.

		MT
Complete Set (10):		475.00
Common Player:		15.00
Inserted 1:121		
1	Cal Ripken Jr.	60.00
2	Nomar Garciaparra	50.00
3	Sammy Sosa	50.00
4	Frank Thomas	40.00
5	Mike Piazza	50.00
6	Derek Jeter	50.00
7	Mark McGwire	90.00
8	Tony Gwynn	40.00
9	Ken Griffey Jr.	80.00
10	Alex Rodriguez	50.00

1999 Pacific Revolution Thorn in the Side

This 20-card set features full holographic silver foil and is die-cut in the upper right portion. Card backs analyzes the featured player's success against a certain opponent over the years. These were seeded 1:25 packs.

		MT
Complete Set (20):		250.00
Common Player:		5.00
Inserted 1:25		
1	Mo Vaughn	8.00
2	Chipper Jones	15.00
3	Greg Maddux	20.00
4	Cal Ripken Jr.	25.00
5	Nomar Garciaparra	20.00
6	Sammy Sosa	20.00
7	Frank Thomas	15.00
8	Manny Ramirez	10.00
9	Jeff Bagwell	8.00
10	Mike Piazza	20.00
11	Derek Jeter	20.00
12	Bernie Williams	6.00
13	J.D. Drew	15.00
14	Mark McGwire	40.00
15	Tony Gwynn	15.00
16	Barry Bonds	8.00
17	Ken Griffey Jr.	30.00
18	Alex Rodriguez	20.00
19	Juan Gonzalez	15.00
20	Ivan Rodriguez	8.00

1999 Pacific Revolution Tripleheader

This 30-card set features spotted gold foil blotching around the player image with the name, postion, team and logo stamped in gold foil. These were seeded 4:25 hobby packs. The set is also broken down into three separate tiers of 10 cards. Tier 1 (cards 1-10) are limited to 99 numbered sets. Tier 2 (11-20) 199 numbered sets and Tier 3 (21-30) 299 numbered sets.

		MT
Complete Set (30):		120.00
Common Player:		2.00
Inserted 4:25 H		
Tier 1 (1-10):		3x to 6x
Production 99 sets H		
Tier 2 (11-20):		2x to 4x
Production 199 sets H		
Tier 3 (21-30):		1.5x to 2x
Production 299 sets H		
1	Greg Maddux	8.00
2	Cal Ripken Jr.	10.00
3	Nomar Garciaparra	8.00
4	Sammy Sosa	8.00
5	Frank Thomas	6.00
6	Mike Piazza	8.00
7	Mark McGwire	15.00
8	Tony Gwynn	6.00
9	Ken Griffey Jr.	12.00
10	Alex Rodriguez	8.00
11	Mo Vaughn	3.00
12	Chipper Jones	6.00
13	Manny Ramirez	4.00
14	Larry Walker	2.00
15	Jeff Bagwell	3.00
16	Vladimir Guerrero	4.00
17	Derek Jeter	8.00
18	J.D. Drew	6.00
19	Barry Bonds	3.00
20	Juan Gonzalez	6.00
21	Troy Glaus	4.00
22	Andruw Jones	3.00
23	Matt Williams	2.00
24	Craig Biggio	2.00
25	Raul Mondesi	2.00
26	Roger Clemens	4.00
27	Bernie Williams	2.00
28	Scott Rolen	3.00
29	Jose Canseco	2.00
30	Ivan Rodriguez	3.00

1999 SkyBox E-X Century

The 120-card base set features a clear plastic stock with the player name, logo and position stamped in holographic foil. Card backs have the featured player's vital information along with his '98

statistics and his major league totals. Cards 91-120 are part of a prospects subset and are short-printed, seeded 1:2 packs. Three-card packs have an S.R.P. of $5.99.

		MT
Complete Set (120):		140.00
Common Player:		.50
Common SP (91-120):		1.50
Inserted 1:2		
1	Scott Rolen	3.00
2	Nomar Garciaparra	6.00
3	Mike Piazza	6.00
4	Tony Gwynn	5.00
5	Sammy Sosa	6.00
6	Alex Rodriguez	6.00
7	Vladimir Guerrero	3.00
8	Chipper Jones	5.00
9	Derek Jeter	6.00
10	Kerry Wood	2.50
11	Juan Gonzalez	5.00
12	Frank Thomas	5.00
13	Mo Vaughn	2.50
14	Greg Maddux	6.00
15	Jeff Bagwell	3.00
16	Mark McGwire	12.00
17	Ken Griffey Jr.	10.00
18	Roger Clemens	3.00
19	Cal Ripken Jr.	8.00
20	Travis Lee	2.00
21	Todd Helton	2.00
22	Darin Erstad	2.50
23	Pedro Martinez	2.00
24	Barry Bonds	2.50
25	Andruw Jones	2.00
26	Larry Walker	1.50
27	Albert Belle	2.50
28	Ivan Rodriguez	2.50
29	Magglio Ordonez	.50
30	Andres Galarraga	1.00
31	Mike Mussina	2.00
32	Randy Johnson	2.00
33	Tom Glavine	.75
34	Barry Larkin	.75
35	Jim Thome	1.00
36	Gary Sheffield	.75
37	Bernie Williams	1.50
38	Carlos Delgado	.75
39	Rafael Palmeiro	.75
40	Edgar Renteria	.50
41	Brad Fullmer	.50
42	David Wells	.50
43	Dante Bichette	1.00
44	Jaret Wright	1.00
45	Ricky Ledee	.50
46	Ray Lankford	.50
47	Mark Grace	.75
48	Jeff Cirillo	.50
49	Rondell White	.50
50	Jeromy Burnitz	.50
51	Sean Casey	.75
52	Rolando Arrojo	.50
53	Jason Giambi	.50
54	John Olerud	.50
55	Will Clark	1.00
56	Raul Mondesi	.75
57	Scott Brosius	.50
58	Bartolo Colon	.50
59	Steve Finley	.50
60	Javy Lopez	.50
61	Tim Salmon	1.00
62	Roberto Alomar	1.50
63	Vinny Castilla	.50
64	Craig Biggio	1.50
65	Jose Guillen	.50
66	Greg Vaughn	.50
67	Jose Canseco	1.50
68	Shawn Green	.50
69	Curt Schilling	.75
70	Orlando Hernandez	2.00
71	Jose Cruz Jr.	1.50
72	Alex Gonzalez	.50
73	Tino Martinez	1.00
74	Todd Hundley	.50
75	Brian Giles	.50
76	Cliff Floyd	.50
77	Paul O'Neill	.75
78	Ken Caminiti	.75
79	Ron Gant	.50
80	Juan Encarnacion	.75
81	Ben Grieve	2.50
82	Brian Jordan	.50
83	Rickey Henderson	.75
84	Tony Clark	1.00
85	Shannon Stewart	.50
86	Robin Ventura	.50
87	Todd Walker	.50
88	Kevin Brown	.75
89	Moises Alou	.75
90	Manny Ramirez	3.00
91	Gabe Alvarez	1.50
92	Jeremy Giambi	2.00
93	Adrian Beltre	3.00
94	George Lombard	2.00
95	Ryan Minor	2.00
96	Kevin Witt	1.50
97	*Scott Hunter*	1.50
98	Carlos Guillen	1.50
99	Derrick Gibson	1.50
100	Trot Nixon	1.50
101	Troy Glaus	10.00
102	Armando Rios	2.00
103	Preston Wilson	1.50
104	*Pat Burrell*	20.00
105	J.D. Drew	20.00
106	Bruce Chen	2.00
107	Matt Clement	1.50
108	Carlos Beltran	5.00
109	Carlos Febles	2.50
110	Rob Fick	1.50
111	Russell Branyan	2.00
112	*Roosevelt Brown*	2.50
113	Corey Koskie	1.50
114	Mario Encarnacion	2.50
115	*Peter Tucci*	1.50
116	Eric Chavez	5.00
117	Gabe Kapler	8.00
118	Marlon Anderson	2.50
119	*A.J. Burnett*	5.00
120	Ryan Bradley	1.50
----	Checklist 1-96	.50
----	Checklist 97-120/ Inserts	.50

1999 SkyBox E-X Century Essential Credentials Future

A glossy silver design replaces where clear plastic was on the base cards. Production varied depending on the card number, with the exact production number of each player determined by subtracting his card number from 121.

		MT
Common Player:		.50
1	Scott Rolen (120)	75.00
2	Nomar Garciaparra (119)	125.00
3	Mike Piazza (118)	125.00
4	Tony Gwynn (117)	100.00
5	Sammy Sosa (116)	125.00
6	Alex Rodriguez (115)	125.00
7	Vladimir Guerrero (114)	60.00
8	Chipper Jones (113)	120.00
9	Derek Jeter (112)	125.00
10	Kerry Wood (111)	50.00
11	Juan Gonzalez (110)	75.00
12	Frank Thomas (109)	75.00
13	Mo Vaughn (108)	50.00
14	Greg Maddux (107)	100.00
15	Jeff Bagwell (106)	50.00
16	Mark McGwire (105)	250.00
17	Ken Griffey Jr. (104)	200.00
18	Roger Clemens (103)	100.00
19	Cal Ripken Jr. (102)	140.00
20	Travis Lee (101)	30.00
21	Todd Helton (100)	40.00
22	Darin Erstad (99)	30.00
23	Pedro Martinez (98)	60.00
24	Barry Bonds (97)	60.00
25	Andruw Jones (96)	40.00
26	Larry Walker (95)	40.00
27	Albert Belle (94)	50.00
28	Ivan Rodriguez (93)	50.00
29	Magglio Ordonez (92)	40.00
30	Andres Galarraga (91)	40.00
31	Mike Mussina (90)	60.00
32	Randy Johnson (89)	60.00
33	Tom Glavine (88)	30.00
34	Barry Larkin (87)	30.00
35	Jim Thome (86)	40.00
36	Gary Sheffield (85)	30.00
37	Bernie Williams (84)	60.00
38	Carlos Delgado (83)	40.00
39	Rafael Palmeiro (82)	40.00
40	Edgar Renteria (81)	15.00
41	Brad Fullmer (80)	15.00
42	David Wells (79)	15.00
43	Dante Bichette (78)	40.00
44	Jaret Wright (77)	25.00
45	Ricky Ledee (76)	20.00
46	Ray Lankford (75)	15.00
47	Mark Grace (74)	30.00
48	Jeff Cirillo (73)	15.00
49	Rondell White (72)	25.00
50	Jeromy Burnitz (71)	20.00
51	Sean Casey (70)	50.00
52	Rolando Arrojo (69)	15.00
53	Jason Giambi (68)	15.00
54	John Olerud (67)	30.00
55	Will Clark (66)	50.00
56	Raul Mondesi (65)	30.00
57	Scott Brosius (64)	15.00
58	Bartolo Colon (63)	15.00
59	Steve Finley (62)	15.00
60	Javy Lopez (61)	25.00
61	Tim Salmon (60)	40.00
62	Roberto Alomar (59)	75.00
63	Vinny Castilla (58)	25.00
64	Craig Biggio (57)	60.00
65	Jose Guillen (56)	20.00
66	Greg Vaughn (55)	30.00
67	Jose Canseco (54)	70.00
68	Shawn Green (53)	30.00
69	Curt Schilling (52)	25.00
70	Orlando Hernandez (51)	75.00
71	Jose Cruz Jr. (50)	25.00
72	Alex Gonzalez (49)	20.00
73	Tino Martinez (48)	50.00
74	Todd Hundley (47)	20.00
75	Brian Giles (46)	20.00
76	Cliff Floyd (45)	20.00
77	Paul O'Neill (44)	50.00
78	Ken Caminiti (43)	40.00
79	Ron Gant (42)	30.00
80	Juan Encarnacion (41)	40.00
81	Ben Grieve (40)	70.00
82	Brian Jordan (39)	15.00
83	Rickey Henderson (38)	30.00
84	Tony Clark (37)	50.00
85	Shannon Stewart (36)	20.00
86	Robin Ventura (35)	30.00
87	Todd Walker (34)	25.00
88	Kevin Brown (33)	50.00
89	Moises Alou (32)	40.00
90	Manny Ramirez (31)	125.00
91	Gabe Alvarez (30)	25.00
92	Jeremy Giambi (29)	25.00
93	Adrian Beltre (28)	40.00
94	George Lombard (27)	35.00
95	Ryan Minor (26)	40.00
96	Kevin Witt (25)	25.00
97	Scott Hunter (24)	25.00
98	Carlos Guillen (23)	25.00
99	Derrick Gibson (22)	25.00
100	Trot Nixon (21)	25.00
101	Troy Glaus (20)	125.00
102	Armando Rios (19)	30.00
103	Preston Wilson (18)	40.00
104	Pat Burrell (17)	300.00
105	J.D. Drew (16)	250.00
106	Bruce Chen (15)	40.00
107	Matt Clement (14)	40.00
108	Carlos Beltran (13)	75.00
109	Carlos Febles (12)	40.00
110	Rob Fick (11)	40.00
111	Russell Branyan (10)	40.00
112	Roosevelt Brown (9)	40.00
113	Corey Koskie (8)	40.00
114	Mario Encarnacion (7)	
115	Peter Tucci (6)	
116	Eric Chavez (5)	
117	Gabe Kapler (4)	
118	Marlon Anderson (3)	
119	A.J. Burnett (2)	
120	Ryan Bradley (1)	

1999 SkyBox E-X Century Essential Credentials Now

Like Future, this is a parallel of the base set, with production of each card limited to that player's card number. These cards have a glossy gold look.

		MT
Complete Set (120):		140.00
Common Player:		.50
1	Scott Rolen (1)	
2	Nomar Garciaparra (2)	
3	Mike Piazza (3)	
4	Tony Gwynn (4)	
5	Sammy Sosa (5)	
6	Alex Rodriguez (6)	
7	Vladimir Guerrero (7)	
8	Chipper Jones (8)	
9	Derek Jeter (9)	
10	Kerry Wood (10)	180.00
11	Juan Gonzalez (11)	300.00
12	Frank Thomas (12)	300.00
13	Mo Vaughn (13)	150.00
14	Greg Maddux (14)	400.00
15	Jeff Bagwell (15)	180.00
16	Mark McGwire (16)	800.00
17	Ken Griffey Jr. (17)	650.00
18	Roger Clemens (18)	275.00
19	Cal Ripken Jr. (19)	500.00
20	Travis Lee (20)	60.00
21	Todd Helton (21)	100.00
22	Darin Erstad (22)	60.00
23	Pedro Martinez (23)	150.00
24	Barry Bonds (24)	150.00
25	Andruw Jones (25)	120.00
26	Larry Walker (26)	120.00
27	Albert Belle (27)	120.00
28	Ivan Rodriguez (28)	150.00
29	Magglio Ordonez (29)	50.00
30	Andres Galarraga (30)	100.00
31	Mike Mussina (31)	120.00
32	Randy Johnson (32)	120.00
33	Tom Glavine (33)	40.00
34	Barry Larkin (34)	40.00
35	Jim Thome (35)	60.00
36	Gary Sheffield (36)	40.00
37	Bernie Williams (37)	100.00
38	Carlos Delgado (38)	50.00
39	Rafael Palmeiro (39)	75.00
40	Edgar Renteria (40)	25.00
41	Brad Fullmer (41)	25.00
42	David Wells (42)	25.00
43	Dante Bichette (43)	40.00
44	Jaret Wright (44)	25.00
45	Ricky Ledee (45)	25.00
46	Ray Lankford (46)	25.00
47	Mark Grace (47)	40.00
48	Jeff Cirillo (48)	25.00
49	Rondell White (49)	40.00
50	Jeromy Burnitz (50)	25.00
51	Sean Casey (51)	50.00
52	Rolando Arrojo (52)	25.00
53	Jason Giambi (53)	25.00
54	John Olerud (54)	40.00
55	Will Clark (55)	60.00
56	Raul Mondesi (56)	40.00
57	Scott Brosius (57)	25.00
58	Bartolo Colon (58)	20.00
59	Steve Finley (59)	20.00
60	Javy Lopez (60)	25.00
61	Tim Salmon (61)	40.00
62	Roberto Alomar (62)	75.00
63	Vinny Castilla (63)	25.00
64	Craig Biggio (64)	60.00
65	Jose Guillen (65)	15.00
66	Greg Vaughn (66)	25.00
67	Jose Canseco (67)	70.00
68	Shawn Green (68)	35.00
69	Curt Schilling (69)	25.00
70	Orlando Hernandez (70)	40.00
71	Jose Cruz Jr. (71)	25.00
72	Alex Gonzalez (72)	15.00
73	Tino Martinez (73)	40.00
74	Todd Hundley (74)	20.00
75	Brian Giles (75)	15.00
76	Cliff Floyd (76)	15.00
77	Paul O'Neill (77)	40.00
78	Ken Caminiti (78)	30.00
79	Ron Gant (79)	25.00
80	Juan Encarnacion (80)	30.00
81	Ben Grieve (81)	40.00
82	Brian Jordan (82)	15.00
83	Rickey Henderson (83)	30.00
84	Tony Clark (84)	40.00
85	Shannon Stewart (85)	15.00
86	Robin Ventura (86)	25.00
87	Todd Walker (87)	15.00
88	Kevin Brown (88)	30.00
89	Moises Alou (89)	30.00
90	Manny Ramirez (90)	60.00
91	Gabe Alvarez (91)	15.00
92	Jeremy Giambi (92)	15.00
93	Adrian Beltre (93)	25.00
94	George Lombard (94)	20.00
95	Ryan Minor (95)	25.00
96	Kevin Witt (96)	15.00
97	Scott Hunter (97)	15.00
98	Carlos Guillen (98)	15.00
99	Derrick Gibson (99)	15.00
100	Trot Nixon (100)	15.00
101	Troy Glaus (101)	40.00
102	Armando Rios (102)	15.00
103	Preston Wilson (103)	15.00
104	Pat Burrell (104)	125.00
105	J.D. Drew (105)	80.00
106	Bruce Chen (106)	15.00
107	Matt Clement (107)	15.00
108	Carlos Beltran (108)	40.00
109	Carlos Febles (109)	25.00
110	Rob Fick (110)	15.00
111	Russell Branyan (111)	25.00
112	Roosevelt Brown (112)	25.00
113	Corey Koskie (113)	15.00
114	Mario Encarnacion (114)	20.00
115	Peter Tucci (115)	15.00
116	Eric Chavez (116)	30.00
117	Gabe Kapler (117)	40.00
118	Marlon Anderson (118)	15.00
119	A.J. Burnett (119)	30.00
120	Ryan Bradley (120)	15.00

1999 SkyBox E-X Century Authen-Kicks

Authen-Kicks is a game-used insert that embeds game-worn shoe swatches from the featured player. Each is done in a horizontal format and is sequentially numbered. Due to the number of swatches differing from player to player, the numbers produced for each player varies.

		MT
Complete Set (9):		700.00
Common Player:		50.00
1	J.D. Drew	175.00
2	Travis Lee	75.00
3	Kevin Millwood	60.00
4	Bruce Chen	50.00
5	Troy Glaus	120.00
6	Todd Helton	75.00
7	Ricky Ledee	50.00
8	Scott Rolen	150.00
9	Jeremy Giambi	60.00

1999 SkyBox E-X Century E-X Quisite

15 of baseball's top young players are showcased, with a black background and interior die-cutting around the player image. These are seeded 1:18 packs.

		MT
Complete Set (15):		100.00
Common Player:		2.50
Inserted 1:18		
1	Troy Glaus	15.00
2	J.D. Drew	25.00
3	Pat Burrell	25.00
4	Russell Branyan	2.50
5	Kerry Wood	5.00
6	Eric Chavez	8.00
7	Ben Grieve	6.00
8	Gabe Kapler	15.00
9	Adrian Beltre	4.00
10	Todd Helton	5.00
11	Roosevelt Brown	3.00
12	Marlon Anderson	4.00
13	Jeremy Giambi	4.00
14	Magglio Ordonez	2.50
15	Travis Lee	6.00

1999 SkyBox E-X Century Favorites for Fenway

This 20-card set pays tribute to one of baseball's favorite ballparks, Fenway Park the venue for the 1999 All-Star

Game. These have a photo of the featured player with an image of Fenway Park in the background on a horizontal format. These are seeded 1:36 packs.

		MT
Complete Set (20):		325.00
Common Player:		5.00
Inserted 1:36		
1	Mo Vaughn	10.00
2	Nomar Garciaparra	25.00
3	Frank Thomas	20.00
4	Ken Griffey Jr.	40.00
5	Roger Clemens	15.00
6	Alex Rodriguez	25.00
7	Derek Jeter	25.00
8	Juan Gonzalez	20.00
9	Cal Ripken Jr.	30.00
10	Ivan Rodriguez	10.00
11	J.D. Drew	20.00
12	Barry Bonds	10.00
13	Tony Gwynn	20.00
14	Vladimir Guerrero	15.00
15	Chipper Jones	20.00
16	Kerry Wood	10.00
17	Mike Piazza	25.00
18	Sammy Sosa	25.00
19	Scott Rolen	12.00
20	Mark McGwire	45.00

1999 SkyBox E-X Century Milestones of the Century

This 10-card set spotlights the top statistical performances from the 1998 season, sequentially numbered to that performance in a multi-layered design.

		MT
Complete Set (10):		1350.
Common Player:		20.00
Numbered to featured milestone		
1	Kerry Wood (20)	120.00
2	Mark McGwire (70)	300.00
3	Sammy Sosa (66)	150.00
4	Ken Griffey Jr. (350)	75.00
5	Roger Clemens (98)	100.00
6	Cal Ripken Jr. (17)	500.00
7	Alex Rodriguez (40)	200.00
8	Barry Bonds (400)	20.00
9	N.Y. Yankees (114)	100.00
10	Travis Lee (98)	50.00

1999 SkyBox Molten Metal

Distributed exclusively to the hobby, the 150-card set consists of three subsets: Metal Smiths, Heavy Metal and Supernatural. Metal Smiths (1-100) show baseball's top players, Heavy Metal (101-130) focus on power hitters and Supernatural (131-150) focus on rookies. Base cards feature silver foil stamping on a 24-point stock with holo foil and wet-laminate overlays. Molten Metal was released in six-card packs with an S.R.P. of $4.99.

		MT
Complete Set (150):		120.00
Common Player (1-100):		.25
Inserted 4:1		
Common Player (101-130):		.50
Inserted 1:1		
Common Player (131-150):		1.50
Inserted 1:2		
1	Larry Walker	1.00
2	Jose Canseco	1.00
3	Brian Jordan	.25
4	Rafael Palmeiro	.75
5	Edgar Renteria	.25
6	Dante Bichette	.50
7	Mark Kotsay	.25
8	Denny Neagle	.25
9	Ellis Burks	.25
10	Paul O'Neill	.50
11	Miguel Tejada	.40
12	Ken Caminiti	.25
13	David Cone	.40
14	Jason Kendall	.40
15	Ruben Rivera	.25
16	Todd Walker	.25
17	Bobby Higginson	.25
18	Derrek Lee	.25
19	Rondell White	.40
20	Pedro J. Martinez	1.25
21	Jeff Kent	.25
22	Randy Johnson	1.00
23	Matt Williams	.75
24	Sean Casey	.40
25	Eric Davis	.25
26	Ryan Klesko	.40
27	Curt Schilling	.40
28	Geoff Jenkins	.25
29	Armand Abreu	.25
30	Vinny Castilla	.25
31	Will Clark	.75
32	Ray Durham	.25
33	Ray Lankford	.25
34	Richie Sexson	.25
35	Derrick Gibson	.25
36	Mark Grace	.50
37	Greg Vaughn	.25
38	Bartolo Colon	.25
39	Steve Finley	.25
40	Chuck Knoblauch	.50
41	Ricky Ledee	.25
42	John Smoltz	.25
43	Moises Alou	.40
44	Jim Edmonds	.25
45	Cliff Floyd	.25
46	Javy Lopez	.25
47	Jim Thome	.75
48	J.T. Snow	.25
49	Sandy Alomar Jr.	.25
50	Andy Pettitte	.25
51	Juan Encarnacion	.25
52	Travis Fryman	.25
53	Eli Marrero	.25
54	Jeff Cirillo	.25
55	Brady Anderson	.25
56	Jose Cruz Jr.	.50
57	Edgar Martinez	.25
58	Garret Anderson	.25
59	Paul Konerko	.25
60	Eric Milton	.25
61	Jason Giambi	.25
62	Tom Glavine	.40
63	Justin Thompson	.25
64	Brad Fullmer	.25
65	Marquis Grissom	.25
66	Fernando Tatis	.25
67	Carlos Beltran	1.50
68	Charles Johnson	.25
69	Raul Mondesi	.50
70	Richard Hildalgo	.25
71	Barry Larkin	.75
72	David Wells	.25
73	Jay Buhner	.40
74	Matt Clement	.25
75	Eric Karros	.25
76	Carl Pavano	.25
77	Mariano Rivera	.40
78	Livan Hernandez	.25
79	A.J. Hinch	.25
80	Tino Martinez	.75
81	Rusty Greer	.25
82	Jose Guillen	.25
83	Robin Ventura	.40
84	Kevin Brown	.40
85	Chan Ho Park	.25
86	John Olerud	.40
87	Johnny Damon	.25
88	Todd Hundley	.25
89	Fred McGriff	.50
90	Wade Boggs	.75
91	Mike Cameron	.25
92	Gary Sheffield	.40
93	Rickey Henderson	.40
94	Pat Hentgen	.25
95	Omar Vizquel	.25
96	Craig Biggio	.75
97	Mike Caruso	.25
98	Neifi Perez	.25
99	Mike Mussina	1.00
100	Carlos Delgado	.50
101	Andruw Jones (Heavy Metal)	1.50
102	*Pat Burrell* (Heavy Metal)	10.00
103	Orlando Hernandez (Heavy Metal)	1.00
104	Darin Erstad (Heavy Metal)	1.00
105	Roberto Alomar (Heavy Metal)	1.00
106	Tim Salmon (Heavy Metal)	.75
107	Albert Belle (Heavy Metal)	1.50
108	*Chad Allen* (Heavy Metal)	1.50
109	Travis Lee (Heavy Metal)	1.00
110	*Jesse Garcia* (Heavy Metal)	1.00
111	Tony Clark (Heavy Metal)	.50
112	Ivan Rodriguez (Heavy Metal)	1.50
113	Troy Glaus (Heavy Metal)	1.50
114	*A.J. Burnett* (Heavy Metal)	3.00
115	David Justice (Heavy Metal)	.50
116	Adrian Beltre (Heavy Metal)	.75
117	Eric Chavez (Heavy Metal)	.75
118	Kenny Lofton (Heavy Metal)	1.25
119	Michael Barrett (Heavy Metal)	.75
120	*Jeff Weaver* (Heavy Metal)	4.00
121	Manny Ramirez (Heavy Metal)	2.00
122	Barry Bonds (Heavy Metal)	1.50
123	Bernie Williams (Heavy Metal)	1.00
124	*Freddy Garcia* (Heavy Metal)	6.00
125	*Scott Hunter* (Heavy Metal)	1.00
126	Jeremy Giambi (Heavy Metal)	.50
127	*Masao Kida* (Heavy Metal)	1.00
128	Todd Helton (Heavy Metal)	1.00
129	Mike Figga (Heavy Metal)	.50
130	Mo Vaughn (Heavy Metal)	1.50
131	J.D. Drew (Supernaturals)	5.00
132	Cal Ripken Jr. (Supernaturals)	6.00
133	Ken Griffey Jr. (Supernaturals)	8.00
134	Mark McGwire (Supernaturals)	10.00
135	Nomar Garciaparra (Supernaturals)	6.00
136	Greg Maddux (Supernaturals)	6.00
137	Mike Piazza (Supernaturals)	6.00
138	Alex Rodriguez (Supernaturals)	6.00
139	Frank Thomas (Supernaturals)	5.00
140	Juan Gonzalez (Supernaturals)	5.00
141	Tony Gwynn (Supernaturals)	5.00
142	Derek Jeter (Supernaturals)	6.00
143	Chipper Jones (Supernaturals)	5.00
144	Scott Rolen (Supernaturals)	2.00
145	Sammy Sosa (Supernaturals)	5.00
146	Kerry Wood (Supernaturals)	2.00
147	Roger Clemens (Supernaturals)	3.00
148	Jeff Bagwell (Supernaturals)	2.00
149	Vladimir Guerrero (Supernaturals)	3.00
150	Ben Grieve (Supernaturals)	1.50

1999 SkyBox Molten Metal Xplosion

This is a 150-card parallel set, which is seeded 1:2 packs. These are made of actual metal that have added etching and some foil stamping.

	MT
Xplosion's (1-130):	2x to 5x
Supernaturals (131-150):	1.5x to 3x
Inserted 1:2	

1999 SkyBox Molten Metal Fusion

Fusion is a 50-card partial parallel that is paralleled three times: Fusion, Sterling Fusion and Titanium Fusion. The three parallels consist of the two subsets Heavy Metal and Supernatural. Fusion Heavy Metals (1-30) are seeded 1:12 packs and Supernatural Fusions are seeded 1:24 packs. Fusions are laser die-cut with additional silver-foil stamping. Sterling Fusions are limited to 500 numbered sets with each card laser die-cut with blue foil stamping. Titanium Fusions are limited to 50 sequentially numbered sets and enhanced with gold-foil stamping.

		MT
Complete Set (50):		500.00
Common Player (1-30):		2.00
Inserted 1:12		
Common (31-50):		5.00
Inserted 1:24		
Sterling (1-30):		1x to 2x
Sterling (31-50):		1x to 1.5x
Production 500 sets		
Titanium (1-30):		4x to 8x
Titanium (31-50):		3x to 8x
Production 50 sets		
1	Andruw Jones	6.00
2	Pat Burrell	25.00
3	Orlando Hernandez	5.00
4	Darin Erstad	5.00
5	Roberto Alomar	5.00
6	Tim Salmon	4.00
7	Albert Belle	6.00
8	Chad Allen	3.00
9	Travis Lee	4.00
10	Jesse Garcia	2.00
11	Tony Clark	2.00
12	Ivan Rodriguez	6.00
13	Troy Glaus	8.00
14	A.J. Burnett	5.00
15	David Justice	3.00
16	Adrian Beltre	3.00
17	Eric Chavez	3.00
18	Kenny Lofton	6.00
19	Michael Barrett	2.00
20	Jeff Weaver	12.00
21	Manny Ramirez	8.00
22	Barry Bonds	6.00
23	Bernie Williams	5.00
24	Freddy Garcia	15.00
25	Scott Hunter	2.00
26	Jeremy Giambi	2.00
27	Masao Kida	2.00
28	Todd Helton	5.00
29	Mike Figga	2.00
30	Mo Vaughn	6.00
31	J.D. Drew	25.00
32	Cal Ripken Jr.	30.00
33	Ken Griffey Jr.	40.00
34	Mark McGwire	50.00
35	Nomar Garciaparra	25.00
36	Greg Maddux	25.00
37	Mike Piazza	25.00
38	Alex Rodriguez	25.00
39	Frank Thomas	20.00
40	Juan Gonzalez	20.00
41	Tony Gwynn	20.00
42	Derek Jeter	25.00
43	Chipper Jones	20.00
44	Scott Rolen	10.00
45	Sammy Sosa	25.00
46	Kerry Wood	8.00
47	Roger Clemens	15.00
48	Jeff Bagwell	10.00
49	Vladimir Guerrero	15.00
50	Ben Grieve	8.00

1999 SkyBox Molten Metal Oh Atlanta!

This 30-card set features players who are either current or former Atlanta Braves like Chipper Jones and Dave Justice. These inserts are seeded one per pack and was produced in conjunction with the 20th annual National Sports Collectors Convention in Atlanta.

		MT
Complete Set (30):		25.00
Common Player:		.50
Inserted 1:1		
1	Kenny Lofton	3.00
2	Kevin Millwood	1.00
3	Bret Boone	.50
4	Otis Nixon	.50
5	Vinny Castilla	.50
6	Brian Jordan	.50
7	Chipper Jones	6.00
8	Dave Justice	1.00
9	Micah Bowie	.50
10	Fred McGriff	1.00
11	Ron Gant	.50
12	Andruw Jones	3.00
13	Kent Mercker	.50
14	Greg McMichael	.50
15	Steve Avery	.50
16	Marquis Grissom	.50
17	Jason Schmidt	.50
18	Ryan Klesko	.75
19	Charlie O'Brien	.50
20	Terry Pendleton	.50
21	Denny Neagle	.50
22	Greg Maddux	8.00
23	Tom Glavine	.75
24	Javy Lopez	.75
25	John Rocker	.75
26	Walt Weiss	.50
27	John Smoltz	.75
28	Michael Tucker	.50
29	Odalis Perez	1.00
30	Andres Galarraga	1.00

1999 SkyBox Premium

The base set consists of 300 cards, base cards feature full bleed fronts with gold-foil stamped player and team names. Card backs have complete year-by-year stats along with a close-up photo. The Rookie subset (223-272) also has a short-printed parallel version as well. Different photos are used but they have the same card number and card back. The short-print versions are seeded 1:8 packs and have an action photo front while the non-seeded cards have a close-up photo.

		MT
Complete Set (300):		30.00
Complete Set w/sp's (350):		160.00
Common Player:		.15
Common SP (223-272):		1.50
SP rookies inserted 1:8		
Star Rubies:		50x to 90x
Production 50 sets		
SP Star Rubies:		10x to 20x
Production 15 sets		
1	Alex Rodriguez	2.00
2	Sidney Ponson	.15
3	Shawn Green	.25
4	Dan Wilson	.15
5	Rolando Arrojo	.15
6	Roberto Alomar	.50
7	Matt Anderson	.15
8	David Segui	.15
9	Alex Gonzalez	.15
10	Edgar Renteria	.15

11 Benito Santiago .15
12 Todd Stottlemyre .15
13 Rico Brogna .15
14 Troy Glaus .75
15 Al Leiter .15
16 Pedro J. Martinez 1.00
17 Paul O'Neill .25
18 Manny Ramirez 1.00
19 Scott Rolen .75
20 Curt Schilling .25
21 Bobby Abreu .15
22 Robb Nen .15
23 Andy Pettitte .40
24 John Wetteland .15
25 Bobby Bonilla .15
26 Darin Erstad .60
27 Shawn Estes .15
28 John Franco .15
29 Nomar Garciaparra 2.00
30 Rick Helling .15
31 David Justice .25
32 Chuck Knoblauch .25
33 Quinton McCracken .15
34 Kenny Rogers .15
35 Brian Giles .15
36 Armando Benitez .15
37 Trevor Hoffman .15
38 Charles Johnson .15
39 Travis Lee .50
40 Tom Glavine .25
41 Rondell White .25
42 Orlando Hernandez .40
43 Mickey Morandini .15
44 Darryl Kile .15
45 Greg Vaughn .25
46 Gregg Jefferies .15
47 Mark McGwire 4.00
48 Kerry Wood .40
49 Jeromy Burnitz .15
50 Ron Gant .15
51 Vinny Castilla .15
52 Doug Glanville .15
53 Juan Guzman .15
54 Dustin Hermanson .15
55 Jose Hernandez .15
56 Bob Higginson .15
57 A.J. Hinch .15
58 Randy Johnson .50
59 Eli Marrero .15
60 Rafael Palmeiro .50
61 Carl Pavano .15
62 Brett Tomko .15
63 Jose Guillen .15
64 Mike Lieberthal .15
65 Jim Abbott .15
66 Dante Bichette .25
67 Jeff Cirillo .15
68 Eric Davis .25
69 Delino DeShields .15
70 Steve Finley .15
71 Mark Grace .25
72 Jason Kendall .25
73 Jeff Kent .15
74 Desi Relaford .15
75 Ivan Rodriguez .75
76 Shannon Stewart .15
77 Geoff Jenkins .15
78 Ben Grieve .60
79 Cliff Floyd .15
80 Jason Giambi .15
81 Rod Beck .15
82 Derek Bell .15
83 Will Clark .40
84 David Dellucci .15
85 Joey Hamilton .15
86 Livan Hernandez .15
87 Barry Larkin .30
88 Matt Mantei .15
89 Dean Palmer .15
90 Chan Ho Park .25
91 Jim Thome .40
92 Miguel Tejada .15
93 Justin Thompson .15
94 David Wells .15
95 Bernie Williams .50
96 Jeff Bagwell .75
97 Derrek Lee .15
98 Devon White .15
99 Jeff Shaw .15
100 Brad Radke .15
101 Mark Grudzielanek .15
102 Javy Lopez .25
103 Mike Sirotka .15
104 Robin Ventura .25
105 Andy Ashby .15
106 Juan Gonzalez 1.50
107 Albert Belle .75
108 Andy Benes .15
109 Jay Buhner .25
110 Ken Caminiti .25
111 Roger Clemens 1.25
112 Mike Hampton .15
113 Pete Harnisch .15
114 Mike Piazza 2.00
115 J.T. Snow .15
116 John Olerud .25
117 Tony Womack .15
118 Todd Zeile .15
119 Tony Gwynn 1.50
120 Brady Anderson .15
121 Sean Casey .50
122 Jose Cruz Jr. .25
123 Carlos Delgado .50
124 Edgar Martinez .15
125 Jose Mesa .15
126 Shane Reynolds .25
127 John Valentin .15
128 Mo Vaughn .60
129 Kevin Young .15
130 Jay Bell .15
131 Aaron Boone .15
132 John Smoltz .15
133 Mike Stanley .15
134 Bret Saberhagen .15
135 Tim Salmon .25
136 Mariano Rivera .25
137 Ken Griffey Jr. 3.00
138 Jose Offerman .15
139 Troy Percival .15
140 Greg Maddux 2.00
141 Frank Thomas 1.00
142 Steve Avery .15
143 Kevin Millwood .40
144 Sammy Sosa 2.00
145 Larry Walker .60
146 Matt Williams .40
147 Mike Caruso .15
148 Todd Helton .60
149 Andruw Jones .50
150 Ray Lankford .15
151 Craig Biggio .40
152 Ugueth Urbina .15
153 Wade Boggs .40
154 Derek Jeter 2.00
155 Wally Joyner .15
156 Mike Mussina .50
157 Gregg Olson .15
158 Henry Rodriguez .15
159 Reggie Sanders .15
160 Fernando Tatis .40
161 Dmitri Young .15
162 Rick Aguilera .15
163 Marty Cordova .15
164 Johnny Damon .15
165 Ray Durham .15
166 Brad Fullmer .15
167 Chipper Jones 2.00
168 Bobby Smith .15
169 Omar Vizquel .15
170 Todd Hundley .15
171 David Cone .25
172 Royce Clayton .15
173 Ryan Klesko .15
174 Jeff Montgomery .15
175 Magglio Ordonez .25
176 Billy Wagner .15
177 Masato Yoshii .15
178 Jason Christiansen .15
179 Chuck Finley .15
180 Tom Gordon .15
181 Wilton Guerrero .15
182 Rickey Henderson .25
183 Sterling Hitchcock .15
184 Kenny Lofton .75
185 Tino Martinez .40
186 Fred McGriff .30
187 Matt Stairs .15
188 Neifi Perez .15
189 Bob Wickman .15
190 Barry Bonds .75
191 Jose Canseco .50
192 Damion Easley .15
193 Jim Edmonds .15
194 Juan Encarnacion .25
195 Travis Fryman .25
196 Tom Goodwin .15
197 Rusty Greer .15
198 Roberto Hernandez .15
199 B.J. Surhoff .15
200 Scott Brosius .15
201 Brian Jordan .15
202 Paul Konerko .25
203 Ismael Valdes .15
204 Eric Milton .15
205 Adrian Beltre .40
206 Tony Clark .40
207 Bartolo Colon .15
208 Cal Ripken Jr. 2.50
209 Moises Alou .25
210 Wilson Alvarez .15
211 Kevin Brown .25
212 Orlando Cabrera .15
213 Vladimir Guerrero 1.00
214 Jose Rosado .15
215 Raul Mondesi .25
216 Dave Nilsson .15
217 Carlos Perez .15
218 Jason Schmidt .15
219 Richie Sexson .25
220 Gary Sheffield .25
221 Fernando Vina .15
222 Todd Walker .15
223 *Scott Sauerbeck* .25
223 *Scott Sauerbeck (sp)* 1.50
224 *Pascual Matos* .50
224 *Pascual Matos (sp)* 2.50
225 *Kyle Farnsworth* .25
225 *Kyle Farnsworth (sp)* 1.50
226 *Freddy Garcia* 5.00
226 *Freddy Garcia (sp)* 15.00
227 *David Lundquist* .25
227 *David Lundquist (sp)* 1.50
228 *Jolbert Cabrera* .25
228 *Jolbert Cabrera (sp)* 1.50
229 *Dan Perkins* .25
229 *Dan Perkins (sp)* 1.50
230 Warren Morris .15
230 Warren Morris (sp) 2.00
231 Carlos Febles .75
231 Carlos Febles (sp) 3.00
232 *Brett Hinchliffe* .25
232 *Brett Hinchliffe (sp)* 1.50
233 *Jason Phillips* .25
233 *Jason Phillips (sp)* 1.50
234 *Glen Barker* .25
234 *Glen Barker (sp)* 1.50
235 *Jose Macias* .50
235 *Jose Macias (sp)* 2.50
236 *Joe Mays* .40
236 *Joe Mays (sp)* 2.00
237 *Chad Allen* .25
237 *Chad Allen (sp)* 1.50
238 *Miguel Del Toro* .25
238 *Miguel Del Toro (sp)* 1.50
239 Chris Singleton .75
239 Chris Singleton (sp) 4.00
240 *Jesse Garcia* .25
240 *Jesse Garcia (sp)* 1.50
241 Kris Benson .25
241 Kris Benson (sp) 2.00
242 *Clay Bellinger* .40
242 *Clay Bellinger (sp)* 2.00
243 Scott Williamson .15
243 Scott Williamson (sp) 1.50
244 *Masao Kida* .50
244 *Masao Kida (sp)* 2.50
245 *Guillermo Garcia* .25
245 *Guillermo Garcia (sp)* 1.50
246 *A.J. Burnett* 2.00
246 *A.J. Burnett (sp)* 6.00
247 *Bo Porter* .25
247 *Bo Porter (sp)* 1.50
248 *Pat Burrell* 5.00
248 *Pat Burrell (sp)* 15.00
249 Carlos Lee .25
249 Carlos Lee (sp) 3.00
250 *Jeff Weaver* 2.50
250 *Jeff Weaver (sp)* 8.00
251 Ruben Mateo .50
251 Ruben Mateo (sp) 2.00
252 J.D. Drew 3.00
252 J.D. Drew (sp) 10.00
253 Jeremy Giambi .25
253 Jeremy Giambi (sp) 1.50
254 *Gary Bennett* .25
254 *Gary Bennett (sp)* 1.50
255 *Edwards Guzman* .25
255 *Edwards Guzman (sp)* 1.50
256 Ramon Martinez .15
256 Ramon Martinez (sp) 1.50
257 *Giomar Guevara* .40
257 *Giomar Guevara (sp)* 2.50
258 *Joe McEwing* 1.50
258 *Joe McEwing (sp)* 5.00
259 *Tom Davey* .25
259 *Tom Davey (sp)* 1.50
260 Gabe Kapler .75
260 Gabe Kapler (sp) 3.00
261 *Ryan Rupe* .25
261 *Ryan Rupe (sp)* 1.50
262 *Kelly Dransfeldt* .50
262 *Kelly Dransfeldt (sp)* 2.50
263 Michael Barrett .15
263 Michael Barrett (sp) 1.50
264 Eric Chavez .50
264 Eric Chavez (sp) 3.00
265 *Orber Moreno* .25
265 *Orber Moreno (sp)* 1.50
266 Marlon Anderson .15
266 Marlon Anderson (sp) 2.00
267 Carlos Beltran 2.00
267 Carlos Beltran (sp) 6.00
268 Doug Mientkiewicz .50
268 Doug Mientkiewicz (sp) 2.00
269 Roy Halladay .50
269 Roy Halladay (sp) 2.00
270 Torii Hunter .25
270 Torii Hunter (sp) 1.50
271 Stan Spencer .15
271 Stan Spencer (sp) 1.50
272 Alex Gonzalez .15
272 Alex Gonzalez (sp) 1.50
273 Mark McGwire (Spring Fling) 2.00
274 Scott Rolen (Spring Fling) .40
275 Jeff Bagwell (Spring Fling) .40
276 Derek Jeter (Spring Fling) 1.00
277 Tony Gwynn (Spring Fling) .75
278 Frank Thomas (Spring Fling) .50
279 Sammy Sosa (Spring Fling) 1.00
280 Nomar Garciaparra (Spring Fling) 1.00
281 Cal Ripken Jr. (Spring Fling) 1.25
282 Albert Belle (Spring Fling) .40
283 Kerry Wood (Spring Fling) .25
284 Greg Maddux (Spring Fling) 1.00
285 Barry Bonds (Spring Fling) .40
286 Juan Gonzalez (Spring Fling) .75
287 Ken Griffey Jr. (Spring Fling) 1.50
288 Alex Rodriguez (Spring Fling) 1.00
289 Ben Grieve (Spring Fling) .30
290 Travis Lee (Spring Fling) .25
291 Mo Vaughn (Spring Fling) .30
292 Mike Piazza (Spring Fling) 1.00
293 Roger Clemens (Spring Fling) .60
294 J.D. Drew (Spring Fling) .75
295 Randy Johnson (Spring Fling) .25
296 Chipper Jones (Spring Fling) 1.00
297 Vladimir Guerrero (Spring Fling) .50
298 Checklist (Nomar Garciaparra) .75
299 Checklist (Ken Griffey Jr.) 1.00
300 Checklist (Mark McGwire) 1.00

1999 SkyBox Premium Autographics

This 54-card autographed set feature an embossed SkyBox Seal of Authenticity stamp and are seeded 1:68 packs. We were unable to price before going to press.

MT
Complete Set (54):
Common Player:
Roberto Alomar
Paul Bako
Michael Barrett
Kris Benson
Micah Bowie
Roosevelt Brown
A.J. Burnett
Pat Burrell
Ken Caminiti
Jose Canseco
Royce Clayton
Edgard Clemente
Bartolo Colon
J.D. Drew
Damion Easley
Derrin Ebert
Mario Encarnacion
Juan Encarnacion
Troy Glaus
Tom Glavine
Juan Gonzalez
Shawn Green
Wilton Guerrero
Jose Guillen
Tony Gwynn
Mark Harriger
Bobby Higginson
Todd Hollandsworth
Scott Hunter
Gabe Kapler
Scott Karl
Mike Kinkade
Ray Lankford
Barry Larkin
Matt Lawton
Ricky Ledee
Travis Lee
Eli Marrero
Ruben Mateo
Joe McEwing
Doug Mientkiewicz
Russ Ortiz
Jim Parque
Robert Person
Alex Rodriguez
Scott Rolen
Benj Sampson
Luis Saturria
Curt Schilling
David Segui
Fernando Tatis
Peter Tucci
Javier Vasquez
Robin Ventura

1999 SkyBox Premium Diamond Debuts

This 15-card set features the best rookies of 1999 on a silver rainbow holo-foil card stock. These are seeded 1:49 packs. Card backs are numbered with a "DD" suffix.

		MT
Complete Set (15):		80.00
Common Player:		4.00
Inserted 1:49		
1	Eric Chavez	6.00
2	Kyle Farnsworth	4.00
3	Ryan Rupe	4.00
4	Jeremy Giambi	4.00
5	Marlon Anderson	4.00
6	J.D. Drew	25.00
7	Carlos Febles	5.00
8	Joe McEwing	6.00
9	Jeff Weaver	15.00
10	Alex Gonzalez	4.00
11	Chad Allen	4.00
12	Michael Barrett	6.00
13	Gabe Kapler	8.00
14	Carlos Lee	6.00
15	Edwards Guzman	4.00

1999 SkyBox Premium Intimidation Nation

This 15-card set highlights the top performers in baseball and features gold rainbow holo-foil stamping. These are limited to 99 sequentially numbered sets. Card backs are numbered with an "IN" suffix.

		MT
Complete Set (15):		1000.
Common Player:		25.00
Production 99 sets		
1	Cal Ripken Jr.	125.00
2	Tony Gwynn	75.00
3	Nomar Garciaparra	100.00
4	Frank Thomas	50.00
5	Mike Piazza	100.00
6	Mark McGwire	200.00
7	Scott Rolen	40.00
8	Chipper Jones	100.00
9	Greg Maddux	100.00
10	Ken Griffey Jr.	150.00
11	Juan Gonzalez	75.00
12	Derek Jeter	100.00
13	J.D. Drew	60.00
14	Roger Clemens	50.00
15	Alex Rodriguez	100.00

1999 SkyBox Premium Live Bats

This 15-card set spotlights baseball's top hitters and feature red foil stamping. Card backs are numbered with an "LB" suffix and are seeded 1:7 packs.

		MT
Complete Set (15):		40.00
Common Player:		.75
Inserted 1:7		
1	Juan Gonzalez	3.00
2	Mark McGwire	8.00
3	Jeff Bagwell	1.50
4	Frank Thomas	2.00
5	Mike Piazza	4.00
6	Nomar Garciaparra	4.00
7	Alex Rodriguez	4.00
8	Scott Rolen	1.50
9	Travis Lee	.75
10	Tony Gwynn	3.00
11	Derek Jeter	4.00
12	Ben Grieve	1.00
13	Chipper Jones	4.00
14	Ken Griffey Jr.	6.00
15	Cal Ripken Jr.	5.00

1999 SkyBox Premium Show Business

This 15-card set features some of the best players in the "show" on double foil-stamped card fronts. Card backs are numbered with an "SB" suffix and are seeded 1:70 packs.

		MT
Complete Set (15):		300.00
Common Player:		6.00
Inserted 1:70		
1	Mark McGwire	50.00
2	Tony Gwynn	20.00
3	Nomar Garciaparra	25.00
4	Juan Gonzalez	20.00
5	Roger Clemens	15.00
6	Chipper Jones	25.00
7	Cal Ripken Jr.	30.00
8	Alex Rodriguez	25.00
9	Orlando Hernandez	6.00
10	Greg Maddux	25.00
11	Mike Piazza	25.00
12	Frank Thomas	15.00
13	Ken Griffey Jr.	40.00
14	Scott Rolen	10.00
15	Derek Jeter	25.00

1999 SkyBox Premium Soul of The Game

This 15-card set features rainbow foil stamping and the name Soul of the Game prominently stamped, covering the entire card behind the player photo. Card backs are numbered with an "SG" suffix and are seeded 1:14 packs.

		MT
Complete Set (15):		90.00
Common Player:		1.50
Inserted 1:14		
1	Alex Rodriguez	8.00
2	Vladimir Guerrero	4.00
3	Chipper Jones	8.00
4	Derek Jeter	8.00
5	Tony Gwynn	6.00
6	Scott Rolen	3.00
7	Juan Gonzalez	6.00
8	Mark McGwire	15.00
9	Ken Griffey Jr.	12.00
10	Jeff Bagwell	3.00
11	Cal Ripken Jr.	10.00
12	Frank Thomas	4.00
13	Mike Piazza	8.00
14	Nomar Garciaparra	8.00
15	Sammy Sosa	8.00

1999 SkyBox Thunder

Skybox Thunder consists of a 300-card base set with three parallels and six inserts. The base set is inserted at varying odds. In hobby packs, regular-player cards #'s 1-140 come 4-5 per pack; veteran stars on cards #'s 141-240 come 2 per pack; and superstars on cards #'s 241-300 are seeded one per pack. For retail packs the odds were: #'s 1-141 (3-4 per pack); #'s 141-240 (2 per pack); and #'s 241-300 (1 per pack). The parallel sets include Rave (# to 150 sets) and Super Rave (# to 25), which are both hobby exclusive. The Rant parallel set is retail exclusive (1:2). The inserts are Unleashed (1:6), www.batterz.com (1:18), In Depth (1:24), Hip-No-Tized (1:36), Turbo-Charged (1:72), and Dial "1" (1:300).

		MT
Complete Set (300):		35.00
Common Player (1-140):		.10
Common Player (141-240):		.15
Common Player (241-300):		.25
Raves (1-140):		30x to 50x
Raves (141-240):		15x to 30x
Raves (241-300):		15x to 25x
Production 150 sets		
SuperRaves (1-140):		100x to 200x
SuperRaves (141-240):		50x to 120x
SuperRaves (241-300):		40x to 90x
Production 25 sets		
Rant (1-140):		4x to 8x
Rant (141-240):		2x to 5x
Rant (241-300):		1.5x to 3x
Inserted 1:2 R		
1	John Smoltz	.20
2	Garret Anderson	.10
3	Matt Williams	.25
4	Daryle Ward	.10
5	Andy Ashby	.10
6	Miguel Tejada	.20
7	Dmitri Young	.10
8	Roberto Alomar	.50
9	Kevin Brown	.20
10	Eric Young	.10
11	Odalis Perez	.10
12	Preston Wilson	.10
13	Jeff Abbott	.10
14	Bret Boone	.10
15	Mendy Lopez	.10
16	B.J. Surhoff	.10
17	Steve Woodard	.10
18	Ron Coomer	.10
19	Rondell White	.20
20	Edgardo Alfonzo	.10
21	Kevin Millwood	.50
22	Jose Canseco	.40
23	Blake Stein	.10
24	Quilvio Veras	.10
25	Chuck Knoblauch	.40
26	David Segui	.10
27	Eric Davis	.10
28	Francisco Cordova	.10
29	Randy Winn	.10
30	Will Clark	.30
31	Billy Wagner	.10
32	Kevin Witt	.10
33	Jim Edmonds	.20
34	Todd Stottlemyre	.10
35	Shane Andrews	.10
36	Michael Tucker	.10
37	Sandy Alomar Jr.	.10
38	Neifi Perez	.10
39	Jaret Wright	.25
40	Devon White	.10
41	Edgar Renteria	.10
42	Shane Reynolds	.10
43	Jeff King	.10
44	Darren Dreifort	.10
45	Fernando Vina	.10
46	Marty Cordova	.10
47	Ugueth Urbina	.10
48	Bobby Bonilla	.20
49	Omar Vizquel	.10
50	Tom Gordon	.10
51	Ryan Christenson	.10
52	Aaron Boone	.10
53	Jamie Moyer	.10
54	Brian Giles	.10
55	Kevin Tapani	.10
56	Scott Brosius	.10
57	Ellis Burks	.10
58	Al Leiter	.10
59	Royce Clayton	.10
60	Chris Carpenter	.10
61	Bubba Trammell	.10
62	Tom Glavine	.20
63	Shannon Stewart	.10
64	Todd Zeile	.10
65	J.T. Snow	.10
66	Matt Clement	.10
67	Matt Stairs	.10
68	Ismael Valdes	.10
69	Todd Walker	.10
70	Jose Lima	.10
71	Mike Caruso	.10
72	Brett Tomko	.10
73	Mike Lansing	.10
74	Justin Thompson	.10
75	Damion Easley	.10
76	Derrek Lee	.10
77	Derek Bell	.10
78	Brady Anderson	.10
79	Charles Johnson	.10
80	*Rafael Roque*	.10
81	Corey Koskie	.10
82	Fernando Seguignol	.50
83	Jay Tessmer	.10
84	Jason Giambi	.10
85	Mike Lieberthal	.10
86	Jose Guillen	.10
87	Jim Leyritz	.10
88	Shawn Estes	.10
89	Ray Lankford	.10
90	Paul Sorrento	.10
91	Javy Lopez	.20
92	John Wetteland	.10
93	Sean Casey	.10
94	Chuck Finley	.10
95	Trot Nixon	.10
96	Ray Durham	.10
97	Reggie Sanders	.10
98	Bartolo Colon	.10
99	Henry Rodriguez	.10
100	Rolando Arrojo	.10
101	Geoff Jenkins	.10
102	Darryl Kile	.10
103	Mark Kotsay	.10
104	Craig Biggio	.40
105	Omar Daal	.10
106	Carlos Febles	.10
107	Eric Karros	.10
108	Matt Lawton	.10
109	Carl Pavano	.10
110	Brian McRae	.10
111	Mariano Rivera	.20
112	Jay Buhner	.20
113	Doug Glanville	.10
114	Jason Kendall	.10
115	Wally Joyner	.10
116	Jeff Kent	.10
117	Shane Monahan	.10
118	Eli Marrero	.10
119	Bobby Smith	.10
120	Shawn Green	.10
121	Kirk Rueter	.10
122	Tom Goodwin	.10
123	Andy Benes	.10
124	Ed Sprague	.10
125	Mike Mussina	.50
126	Jose Offerman	.10
127	Mickey Morandini	.10
128	Paul Konerko	.25
129	Denny Neagle	.10
130	Travis Fryman	.10
131	John Rocker	.10
132	*Rob Fick*	.10
133	Livan Hernandez	.10
134	Ken Caminiti	.20
135	Johnny Damon	.10
136	Jeff Kubenka	.10
137	Marquis Grissom	.10
138	Doug Mientkiewicz	.10
139	Dustin Hermanson	.25
140	Carl Everett	.10
141	Hideo Nomo	.20
142	Jorge Posada	.15
143	Rickey Henderson	.25
144	Robb Nen	.15
145	Ron Gant	.25
146	Aramis Ramirez	.25
147	Trevor Hoffman	.15
148	Bill Mueller	.15
149	Edgar Martinez	.15
150	Fred McGriff	.30
151	Rusty Greer	.15
152	Tom Evans	.15
153	Todd Greene	.15
154	Jay Bell	.15
155	Mike Lowell	.25
156	Orlando Cabrera	.15
157	Troy O'Leary	.15
158	Jose Hernandez	.15
159	Magglio Ordonez	.25
160	Barry Larkin	.40
161	David Justice	.30
162	Derrick Gibson	.15
163	Luis Gonzalez	.15
164	Alex Gonzalez	.15
165	Scott Elarton	.15
166	Dermal Brown	.15
167	Eric Milton	.15
168	Raul Mondesi	.40
169	Jeff Cirillo	.15
170	Benj Sampson	.15
171	John Olerud	.25
172	Andy Pettitte	.40
173	A.J. Hinch	.15
174	Rico Brogna	.15
175	Jason Schmidt	.15
176	Dean Palmer	.25
177	Matt Morris	.15
178	Quinton McCracken	.15
179	Rick Helling	.15
180	Walt Weiss	.15
181	Troy Percival	.15
182	Tony Batista	.15
183	Brian Jordan	.15
184	Jerry Hairston	.15
185	Bret Saberhagen	.15
186	Mark Grace	.30
187	Brian Simmons	.15
188	Pete Harnisch	.15
189	Kenny Lofton	.75
190	Vinny Castilla	.25
191	Bobby Higginson	.15
192	Joey Hamilton	.15
193	Cliff Floyd	.15
194	Andres Galarraga	.50
195	Chan Ho Park	.40
196	Jeromy Burnitz	.15
197	David Ortiz	.15
198	Wilton Guerrero	.15
199	Rey Ordonez	.15
200	Paul O'Neill	.30
201	Kenny Rogers	.15
202	Marlon Anderson	.15
203	Tony Womack	.15
204	Robin Ventura	.25
205	Russ Ortiz	.15
206	Mike Frank	.15
207	Fernando Tatis	.15
208	Miguel Cairo	.15
209	Ivan Rodriguez	1.00
210	Carlos Delgado	.30
211	Tim Salmon	.40
212	Brian Anderson	.15
213	Ryan Klesko	.30
214	Scott Erickson	.15
215	Mike Stanley	.15
216	Brant Brown	.15
217	Rod Beck	.15
218	*Guillermo Garcia*	.15
219	David Wells	.15
220	Dante Bichette	.40
221	Armando Benitez	.15
222	Todd Dunwoody	.15
223	Kelvim Escobar	.15
224	Richard Hidalgo	.15
225	Angel Pena	.15
226	Ronnie Belliard	.15
227	Brad Radke	.15
228	Brad Fullmer	.30
229	Jay Payton	.15
230	Tino Martinez	.40
231	Scott Spiezio	.15
232	Bobby Abreu	.15
233	John Valentin	.15
234	Kevin Young	.15
235	Steve Finley	.15
236	David Cone	.30
237	Armando Rios	.15
238	Russ Davis	.15
239	Wade Boggs	.40
240	Aaron Sele	.15
241	Jose Cruz Jr.	.50
242	George Lombard	.25
243	Todd Helton	.75
244	Andruw Jones	1.25
245	Troy Glaus	1.25
246	Manny Ramirez	1.50
247	Ben Grieve	1.25
248	Richie Sexson	.25
249	Juan Encarnacion	.50
250	Randy Johnson	.75
251	Gary Sheffield	.40
252	Rafael Palmeiro	.50
253	Roy Halladay	.40
254	Mike Piazza	3.00
255	Tony Gwynn	2.50
256	Juan Gonzalez	2.50
257	Jeremy Giambi	.25
258	Ben Davis	.25
259	Russ Branyon	.25
260	Pedro Martinez	1.00
261	Frank Thomas	3.00
262	Calvin Pickering	.25
263	Chipper Jones	2.50
264	Ryan Minor	.25
265	Roger Clemens	2.00
266	Sammy Sosa	3.00
267	Mo Vaughn	1.25
268	Carlos Beltran	.25
269	Jim Thome	.75
270	Mark McGwire	6.00
271	Travis Lee	.60
272	Darin Erstad	1.25
273	Derek Jeter	3.00
274	Greg Maddux	3.00
275	Ricky Ledee	.50
276	Alex Rodriguez	3.00
277	Vladimir Guerrero	2.00
278	Greg Vaughn	.40
279	Scott Rolen	1.25
280	Carlos Guillen	.25
281	Jeff Bagwell	1.25
282	Bruce Chen	.25
283	Tony Clark	.75
284	Albert Belle	1.25
285	Cal Ripken Jr.	4.00
286	Barry Bonds	1.25
287	Curt Schilling	.40
288	Eric Chavez	1.00
289	Larry Walker	.75
290	Orlando Hernandez	1.50
291	Moises Alou	.50
292	Ken Griffey Jr.	5.00
293	Kerry Wood	.75
294	Nomar Garciaparra	3.00
295	Gabe Kapler	1.25
296	Bernie Williams	1.00
297	Matt Anderson	.25
298	Adrian Beltre	.50
299	J.D. Drew	6.00
300	Ryan Bradley	.25
---	Checklist 1-230	
---	Checklist 231-300 and inserts	
---	Video Game Sweepstakes form (Derek Jeter)	

1999 SkyBox Thunder Dial "1"

Designed to look like a mobile phone, this insert set featured 10 cards of long distance hitters. The set consisted of black plastic cards with rounded corners, and were seeded one card per every 300 packs.

		MT
Complete Set (10):		425.00
Common Player:		15.00
Inserted 1:300		
1D	Nomar Garciaparra	50.00
2D	Juan Gonzalez	40.00
3D	Ken Griffey Jr.	80.00
4D	Chipper Jones	40.00
5D	Mark McGwire	100.00
6D	Mike Piazza	50.00
7D	Manny Ramirez	25.00
8D	Alex Rodriguez	50.00
9D	Sammy Sosa	50.00
10D	Mo Vaughn	20.00

1999 SkyBox Thunder Hip-No-Tized

This insert set consisted of 15 cards, featuring both hitters and pitchers. The cards were seeded one card in every 36 packs, and consist of mesmerizing patterned holo-foil stamping.

		MT
Complete Set (15):		150.00
Common Player:		3.00
Inserted 1:36		
1H	J.D. Drew	25.00
2H	Nomar Garciaparra	12.00
3H	Juan Gonzalez	10.00
4H	Ken Griffey Jr.	20.00
5H	Derek Jeter	12.00
6H	Randy Johnson	4.00
7H	Chipper Jones	10.00
8H	Mark McGwire	25.00
9H	Mike Piazza	12.00
10H	Cal Ripken Jr.	15.00
11H	Alex Rodriguez	12.00
12H	Sammy Sosa	12.00
13H	Frank Thomas	12.00
14H	Jim Thome	3.00
15H	Kerry Wood	5.00

1999 SkyBox Thunder In Depth

This insert set consists of 10 cards, featuring baseball's elite players. The cards are highlighted with gold rainbow holo-foil and gold metallic ink.

The insertion rate for this insert was one card in every 24 packs.

		MT
Complete Set (10):		75.00
Common Player:		2.50
Inserted 1:240		
1ID	Albert Belle	4.00
2ID	Barry Bonds	4.00
3ID	Roger Clemens	6.00
4ID	Juan Gonzalez	8.00
5ID	Ken Griffey Jr.	15.00
6ID	Mark McGwire	18.00
7ID	Mike Piazza	10.00
8ID	Sammy Sosa	10.00
9ID	Mo Vaughn	4.00
10ID	Kerry Wood	4.00

1999 SkyBox Thunder Turbo Charged

This 10-card insert set consisted of the top home run hitters. The players were featured on plastic see-through cards with rainbow holofoil. One card was included in every 72 packs.

		MT
Complete Set (10):		125.00
Common Player:		5.00
Inserted 1:72		
1TC	Jose Canseco	5.00
2TC	Juan Gonzalez	12.00
3TC	Ken Griffey Jr.	25.00
4TC	Vladimir Guerrero	10.00
5TC	Mark McGwire	30.00
6TC	Mike Piazza	15.00
7TC	Manny Ramirez	10.00
8TC	Alex Rodriguez	15.00
9TC	Sammy Sosa	15.00
10TC	Mo Vaughn	8.00

1999 SkyBox Thunder Unleashed

This insert set contained 15 cards designed to resemble a cereal box. The players featured included the best young talent in baseball. The cards were silver-foil stamped, and offered facsimile signatures of each player. One card was included with every six packs.

		MT
Complete Set (15):		25.00
Common Player:		.75
Inserted 1:6		
1U	Carlos Beltran	.75
2U	Adrian Beltre	1.00
3U	Eric Chavez	2.00
4U	J.D. Drew	8.00
5U	Juan Encarnacion	1.50
6U	Jeremy Giambi	1.50
7U	Troy Glaus	2.00
8U	Ben Grieve	2.00
9U	Todd Helton	2.00
10U	Orlando Hernandez	3.00
11U	Gabe Kapler	3.00
12U	Travis Lee	1.50
13U	Calvin Pickering	.75
14U	Richie Sexson	.75
15U	Kerry Wood	2.00

1999 SkyBox Thunder www.Batterz.com

www.batterz.com is a 10-card insert set that was seeded one card per every 18 packs. The game's best hitters are in their own home site in this computer-inspired set.

		MT
Complete Set (10):		75.00
Common Player:		1.50
Inserted 1:18		
1WB	J.D. Drew	15.00
2WB	Nomar Garciaparra	8.00
3WB	Ken Griffey Jr.	12.00
4WB	Tony Gwynn	6.00
5WB	Derek Jeter	8.00
6WB	Mark McGwire	15.00
7WB	Alex Rodriguez	8.00
8WB	Scott Rolen	3.00
9WB	Sammy Sosa	8.00
10WB	Bernie Williams	2.00

1999 SP Authentic

SP Authentic Baseball was a 135-card set that sold in packs of 5 cards for $4.99 per pack. The set included a 30-card Future Watch subset and a 15-card Season to Remember subset. Both subsets were shorted-printed, with each card sequentially numbered to 2,700. The insert lineup included Ernie Banks 500 Club 'Piece of History' Bat cards. Each card features a piece of an Ernie Banks game-used bat. Only 350 of the cards were produced. Fourteen more of the cards were produced and autographed by Ernie Banks. Other insert sets included SP Chirography, The Home Run Chronicles, Epic Figures, Reflections, and SP Authentics.

		MT
Complete Set (135):		450.00
Common Player:		.25
Common Future Watch (91-120):		4.00
Production 2,700 sets		
Common Season to Remember (121-135):		4.00
Production 2,700 sets		
1	Mo Vaughn	1.25
2	Jim Edmonds	.25
3	Darin Erstad	1.25
4	Travis Lee	1.00
5	Matt Williams	.50
6	Randy Johnson	.75
7	Chipper Jones	2.50
8	Greg Maddux	3.00
9	Andruw Jones	1.25
10	Andres Galarraga	.75
11	Tom Glavine	.50
12	Cal Ripken Jr.	4.00
13	Brady Anderson	.25
14	Albert Belle	1.25
15	Nomar Garciaparra	3.00
16	Donnie Sadler	.25
17	Pedro Martinez	1.00
18	Sammy Sosa	3.00
19	Kerry Wood	.50
20	Mark Grace	.50
21	Mike Caruso	.25
22	Frank Thomas	3.00
23	Paul Konerko	.50
24	Sean Casey	.25
25	Barry Larkin	.50
26	Kenny Lofton	1.00
27	Manny Ramirez	1.50
28	Jim Thome	.75
29	Bartolo Colon	.25
30	Jaret Wright	.50
31	Larry Walker	.75
32	Todd Helton	1.00
33	Tony Clark	.75
34	Dean Palmer	.40
35	Mark Kotsay	.25
36	Cliff Floyd	.25
37	Ken Caminiti	.50
38	Craig Biggio	.75
39	Jeff Bagwell	1.25
40	Moises Alou	.50
41	Johnny Damon	.25
42	Larry Sutton	.25
43	Kevin Brown	.50
44	Gary Sheffield	.50
45	Raul Mondesi	.75
46	Jeromy Burnitz	.25
47	Jeff Cirillo	.25
48	Todd Walker	.50
49	David Ortiz	.25
50	Brad Radtke	.25
51	Vladimir Guerrero	1.50
52	Rondell White	.50
53	Brad Fullmer	.50
54	Mike Piazza	3.00
55	Robin Ventura	.40
56	John Olerud	.50
57	Derek Jeter	3.00
58	Tino Martinez	.75
59	Bernie Williams	1.00
60	Roger Clemens	4.00
61	Ben Grieve	1.25
62	Miguel Tejada	.25
63	A.J. Hinch	.25
64	Scott Rolen	1.25
65	Curt Schilling	.50
66	Doug Glanville	.25
67	Aramis Ramirez	.25
68	Tony Womack	.25
69	Jason Kendall	.25
70	Tony Gwynn	2.50
71	Wally Joyner	.25
72	Greg Vaughn	.50
73	Barry Bonds	1.25
74	Ellis Burks	.25
75	Jeff Kent	.25
76	Ken Griffey Jr.	5.00
77	Alex Rodriguez	3.00
78	Edgar Martinez	.40
79	Mark McGwire	6.00
80	Eli Marrero	.25
81	Matt Morris	.25
82	Rolando Arrojo	.25
83	Quinton McCracken	.25
84	Jose Canseco	.75
85	Ivan Rodriguez	1.25
86	Juan Gonzalez	2.50
87	Royce Clayton	.25
88	Shawn Green	.25
89	Jose Cruz Jr.	.75
90	Carlos Delgado	.50
91	Troy Glaus (Future Watch)	15.00
92	George Lombard (Future Watch)	4.00
93	Ryan Minor (Future Watch)	8.00
94	Calvin Pickering (Future Watch)	4.00
95	Jin Ho Cho (Future Watch)	10.00
96	Russ Branyon (Future Watch)	4.00
97	Derrick Gibson (Future Watch)	6.00
98	Gabe Kapler (Future Watch)	20.00
99	Matt Anderson (Future Watch)	6.00
100	Preston Wilson (Future Watch)	4.00
101	Alex Gonzalez (Future Watch)	6.00
102	Carlos Beltran (Future Watch)	6.00
103	Dee Brown (Future Watch)	4.00
104	Jeremy Giambi (Future Watch)	12.00
105	Angel Pena (Future Watch)	10.00
106	Geoff Jenkins (Future Watch)	4.00
107	Corey Koskie (Future Watch)	6.00
108	A.J. Pierzynski (Future Watch)	4.00
109	Michael Barrett (Future Watch)	8.00
110	Fernando Seguignol (Future Watch)	12.00
111	Mike Kinkade (Future Watch)	4.00
112	Ricky Ledee (Future Watch)	8.00
113	Mike Lowell (Future Watch)	6.00
114	Eric Chavez (Future Watch)	15.00
115	Matt Clement (Future Watch)	8.00
116	Shane Monahan (Future Watch)	8.00
117	J.D. Drew (Future Watch)	40.00
118	Bubba Trammell (Future Watch)	4.00
119	Kevin Witt (Future Watch)	6.00
120	Roy Halladay (Future Watch)	10.00
121	Mark McGwire (Season to Remember)	40.00
122	Mark McGwire, Sammy Sosa (Season to Remember)	30.00
123	Sammy Sosa (Season to Remember)	20.00
124	Ken Griffey Jr. (Season to Remember)	30.00
125	Cal Ripken Jr. (Season to Remember)	25.00
126	Juan Gonzalez (Season to Remember)	15.00
127	Kerry Wood (Season to Remember)	8.00
128	Trevor Hoffman (Season to Remember)	4.00
129	Barry Bonds (Season to Remember)	8.00
130	Alex Rodriguez (Season to Remember)	20.00
131	Ben Grieve (Season to Remember)	8.00
132	Tom Glavine (Season to Remember)	5.00
133	David Wells (Season to Remember)	4.00
134	Mike Piazza (Season to Remember)	20.00
135	Scott Brosius (Season to Remember)	4.00

1999 SP Authentic Chirography

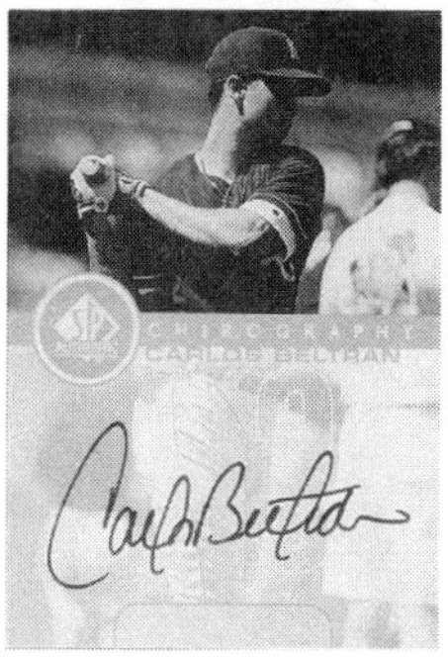

Baseball's top players and future stars are included in this 39-card autograph insert set. The set was split into Level 1 and Level 2 versions. Level 1 cards are not numbered, and were inserted one card per 24 packs. Level 2 cards are sequentially numbered to the featured player's jersey number.

		MT
Common Player:		20.00
Inserted 1:24		
EC	Eric Chavez	40.00
GK	Gabe Kapler	75.00
GMj	Gary Matthews Jr.	25.00
CP	Calvin Pickering	30.00
CK	Corey Koskie	25.00
SM	Shane Monahan	30.00
RH	Richard Hidalgo	40.00
MK	Mike Kinkade	30.00
CB	Carlos Beltran	25.00
AG	Alex Gonzalez	25.00
BC	Bruce Chen	35.00
MA	Matt Anderson	25.00
RM	Ryan Minor	35.00
RL	Ricky Ledee	35.00
RR	Ruben Rivera	30.00
BF	Brad Fullmer	30.00
RB	Russ Branyon	25.00
ML	Mike Lowell	25.00
JG	Jeremy Giambi	50.00
GL	George Lombard	40.00
KW	Kevin Witt	25.00
TW	Todd Walker	25.00
SR	Scott Rolen	75.00
KW	Kerry Wood	50.00
BG	Ben Grieve	60.00
JR	Ken Griffey Jr.	400.00
CJ	Chipper Jones	125.00
IR	Ivan Rodriguez	75.00
TGl	Troy Glaus	75.00
TL	Travis Lee	50.00
VG	Vladimir Guerrero	70.00
GV	Greg Vaughn	20.00
JT	Jim Thome	50.00
JD	J.D. Drew	180.00
TH	Todd Helton	40.00
GM	Greg Maddux	300.00
NG	Nomar Garciaparra	180.00
TG	Tony Gwynn	150.00
CR	Cal Ripken Jr.	300.00

1999 SP Authentic Chirography Gold

These are a parallel to Chirographies and can be identified by the gold tint on the card front and their sequential numbering; each featured player signed to his jersey number.

		MT
Common Player:		20.00
Inserted 1:24		
Autographed to player jersey #		
EC	Eric Chavez (30)	90.00
GK	Gabe Kapler (51)	40.00
GMj	Gary Matthews Jr. (68)	15.00
CP	Calvin Pickering (6)	
CK	Corey Koskie (47)	40.00
SM	Shane Monahan (12)	60.00
RH	Richard Hidalgo (15)	75.00
MK	Mike Kinkade (33)	40.00
CB	Carlos Beltran (36)	125.00
AG	Alex Gonzalez (22)	50.00
BC	Bruce Chen (48)	60.00
MA	Matt Anderson (14)	50.00
RM	Ryan Minor (10)	
RL	Ricky Ledee (38)	60.00
RR	Ruben Rivera (28)	40.00
BF	Brad Fullmer (20)	60.00
RB	Russ Branyon (66)	50.00
ML	Mike Lowell (60)	50.00
JG	Jeremy Giambi (15)	100.00
GL	George Lombard (26)	60.00
KW	Kevin Witt (6)	
TW	Todd Walker (12)	
SR	Scott Rolen (17)	300.00
KW	Kerry Wood (34)	90.00
BG	Ben Grieve (14)	200.00
JR	Ken Griffey Jr. (24)	1100.
CJ	Chipper Jones (10)	
IR	Ivan Rodriguez (7)	
TGl	Troy Glaus (14)	75.00
TL	Travis Lee (16)	125.00
VG	Vladimir Guerrero (27)	175.00
GV	Greg Vaughn (23)	50.00
JT	Jim Thome (25)	150.00
JD	J.D. Drew (8)	
TH	Todd Helton (17)	160.00

GM	Greg Maddux (31)	400.00
NG	Nomar Garciaparra (5)	
TG	Tony Gwynn (19)	500.00
CR	Cal Ripken Jr. (8)	

1999 SP Authentic Epic Figures

This 30-card set highlights baseball's biggest talents, including Mark McGwire and Derek Jeter. The card fronts have two photos, with the larger photo done with a shadow look in the background. Fronts also feature a holographic look, while the card backs feature the player's career highlights. These are seeded one per seven packs.

		MT
Complete Set (30):		150.00
Common Player:		1.50
Inserted 1:7		
E01	Mo Vaughn	5.00
E02	Travis Lee	4.00
E03	Andres Galarraga	4.00
E04	Andruw Jones	5.00
E05	Chipper Jones	10.00
E06	Greg Maddux	12.00
E07	Cal Ripken Jr.	15.00
E08	Nomar Garciaparra	12.00
E09	Sammy Sosa	12.00
E10	Frank Thomas	12.00
E11	Kerry Wood	8.00
E12	Kenny Lofton	4.00
E13	Manny Ramirez	6.00
E14	Larry Walker	3.00
E15	Jeff Bagwell	5.00
E16	Paul Molitor	4.00
E17	Vladimir Guerrero	6.00
E18	Derek Jeter	12.00
E19	Tino Martinez	3.00
E20	Mike Piazza	12.00
E21	Ben Grieve	5.00
E22	Scott Rolen	5.00
E23	Mark McGwire	25.00
E24	Tony Gwynn	10.00
E25	Barry Bonds	5.00
E26	Ken Griffey Jr.	20.00
E27	Alex Rodriguez	12.00
E28	J.D. Drew	20.00
E29	Juan Gonzalez	10.00
E30	Kevin Brown	1.50

1999 SP Authentic Home Run Chronicles

This two-tiered 70-card set focuses on the amazing seasons of McGwire, Sosa and Griffey Jr. Other players help round out the 70-card set, but special emphasis has been placed on the trio. These are seeded one per pack. A die-cut version also exists, with each card serially numbered to 70.

		MT
Complete Set (70):		140.00
Common Player:		.50
Inserted 1:1		
Die-Cuts:		8x to 20x
Production 70 sets		
HR01	Mark McGwire	10.00
HR02	Sammy Sosa	2.00
HR03	Ken Griffey Jr.	3.00
HR04	Mark McGwire	4.00
HR05	Mark McGwire	4.00
HR06	Albert Belle	.75
HR07	Jose Canseco	.50
HR08	Juan Gonzalez	1.50
HR09	Manny Ramirez	1.00
HR10	Rafael Palmeiro	.50
HR11	Mo Vaughn	.75
HR12	Carlos Delgado	.50
HR13	Nomar Garciaparra	2.00
HR14	Barry Bonds	.75
HR15	Alex Rodriguez	2.00
HR16	Tony Clark	.50
HR17	Jim Thome	.50
HR18	Edgar Martinez	.50
HR19	Frank Thomas	2.00
HR20	Greg Vaughn	.50
HR21	Vinny Castilla	.50
HR22	Andres Galarraga	.50
HR23	Moises Alou	.50
HR24	Jeromy Burnitz	.50
HR25	Vladimir Guerrero	1.00
HR26	Jeff Bagwell	.75
HR27	Chipper Jones	1.50
HR28	Javier Lopez	.50
HR29	Mike Piazza	2.00
HR30	Andruw Jones	.75
HR31	Henry Rodriguez	.50
HR32	Jeff Kent	.50
HR33	Ray Lankford	.50
HR34	Scott Rolen	.75
HR35	Raul Mondesi	.50
HR36	Ken Caminiti	.50
HR37	J.D. Drew	5.00
HR38	Troy Glaus	1.00
HR39	Gabe Kapler	1.00
HR40	Alex Rodriguez	2.00
HR41	Ken Griffey Jr.	3.00
HR42	Sammy Sosa	2.00
HR43	Mark McGwire	4.00
HR44	Sammy Sosa	2.00
HR45	Mark McGwire	4.00
HR46	Vinny Castilla	.50
HR47	Sammy Sosa	2.00
HR48	Mark McGwire	4.00
HR49	Sammy Sosa	2.00
HR50	Greg Vaughn	.50
HR51	Sammy Sosa	2.00
HR52	Mark McGwire	4.00
HR53	Sammy Sosa	2.00
HR54	Mark McGwire	4.00
HR55	Sammy Sosa	2.00
HR56	Ken Griffey Jr.	3.00
HR57	Sammy Sosa	2.00
HR58	Mark McGwire	4.00
HR59	Sammy Sosa	2.00
HR60	Mark McGwire	4.00
HR61	Mark McGwire	10.00
HR62	Mark McGwire	12.00
HR63	Mark McGwire	4.00
HR64	Mark McGwire	4.00
HR65	Mark McGwire	4.00
HR66	Sammy Sosa	10.00
HR67	Mark McGwire	4.00
HR68	Mark McGwire	4.00
HR69	Mark McGwire	4.00
HR70	Mark McGwire	20.00

1999 SP Authentic Reflections

Dot Matrix technology is utilized to provide a unique look at 30 of the best players in the game. Card fronts are horizontal with two small and one large photo. These are seeded 1:23 packs.

		MT
Complete Set (30):		475.00
Common Player:		4.00
Inserted 1:23		
R01	Mo Vaughn	10.00
R02	Travis Lee	8.00
R03	Andres Galarraga	8.00
R04	Andruw Jones	10.00
R05	Chipper Jones	20.00
R06	Greg Maddux	25.00
R07	Cal Ripken Jr.	30.00
R08	Nomar Garciaparra	25.00
R09	Sammy Sosa	25.00
R10	Frank Thomas	25.00
R11	Kerry Wood	10.00
R12	Kenny Lofton	8.00
R13	Manny Ramirez	12.00
R14	Larry Walker	6.00
R15	Jeff Bagwell	10.00
R16	Paul Molitor	8.00
R17	Vladimir Guerrero	12.00
R18	Derek Jeter	25.00
R19	Tino Martinez	6.00
R20	Mike Piazza	25.00
R21	Ben Grieve	10.00
R22	Scott Rolen	10.00
R23	Mark McGwire	50.00
R24	Tony Gwynn	20.00
R25	Barry Bonds	10.00
R26	Ken Griffey Jr.	40.00
R27	Alex Rodriguez	25.00
R28	J.D. Drew	40.00
R29	Juan Gonzalez	20.00
R30	Roger Clemens	15.00

1999 SP Authentic SP Authentics

These 1:864 pack inserts are redemption cards that can be redeemed for a special, unique piece of memorabilia from either Ken Griffey Jr. or Mark McGwire.

		MT
Complete Set (9):		
Common Player:		
1	Signed K. Griffey Jersey	
2	Signed K. Griffey Baseball	
3	Signed K. Griffey SI Cover	
4	Signed K. Griffey Mini Helmet	
5	McGwire Framed 62 HR Ticket	
6	McGwire Framed 70 HR Ticket	
7	K. Griffey Standee	
8	K. Griffey Gold Glove C-Card	
9	K. Griffey Facs. Sig. SI Cover	

1999 SP Authentic 500 Club Piece of History

These cards feature a piece of game-used bat once swung by Ernie Banks. Approximately 350 cards exist. An autographed version of this card also exists, only 14 were produced.

	MT
Ernie Banks	225.00
Production 350	
Ernie Banks Autographed Bat card	
Production 14	

1999 SPx

Formerly SPx Finite, this super-premium product showcases 80 of baseball's veteran players on regular cards and a 40-card rookie subset, which are serially numbered to 1,999. Two top rookies, J.D. Drew and Gabe Kapler autographed all 1,999 of their rookie subset cards. There are two parallels, SPx Radiance and SPx Spectrum. Radiance are serially numbered to 100 with Drew and Kapler signing all 100 of their cards. They are exclusive to Finite Radiance Hot Packs. Spectrums are limited to only one set and available only in Finite Spectrum Hot Packs. Packs consist of three cards with an S.R.P. of $5.99.

		MT
Complete Set (120):		575.00
Common Player:		.50
Common SPx Rookie (81-120):		4.00
Production 1,999 sets		
1	Mark McGwire #61	6.00
2	Mark McGwire #62	8.00
3	Mark McGwire #63	5.00
4	Mark McGwire #64	5.00
5	Mark McGwire #65	5.00
6	Mark McGwire #66	5.00
7	Mark McGwire #67	5.00
8	Mark McGwire #68	5.00
9	Mark McGwire #69	5.00
10	Mark McGwire #70	15.00
11	Mo Vaughn	2.50
12	Darin Erstad	2.50
13	Travis Lee	2.00
14	Randy Johnson	2.00
15	Matt Williams	1.50
16	Chipper Jones	5.00
17	Greg Maddux	6.00
18	Andruw Jones	2.50
19	Andres Galarraga	1.50
20	Cal Ripken Jr.	8.00
21	Albert Belle	2.50
22	Mike Mussina	2.00
23	Nomar Garciaparra	6.00
24	Pedro Martinez	2.00
25	John Valentin	.50
26	Kerry Wood	2.50
27	Sammy Sosa	6.00
28	Mark Grace	1.00
29	Frank Thomas	5.00
30	Mike Caruso	.50
31	Barry Larkin	1.00
32	Sean Casey	.75
33	Jim Thome	1.50
34	Kenny Lofton	2.00
35	Manny Ramirez	3.00
36	Larry Walker	1.50
37	Todd Helton	2.00
38	Vinny Castilla	.75
39	Tony Clark	1.50
40	Derrek Lee	.50
41	Mark Kotsay	.50
42	Jeff Bagwell	2.50
43	Craig Biggio	1.50
44	Moises Alou	.75
45	Larry Sutton	.50
46	Johnny Damon	.50
47	Gary Sheffield	.75
48	Raul Mondesi	1.00
49	Jeromy Burnitz	.50
50	Todd Walker	.75
51	David Ortiz	.50
52	Vladimir Guerrero	3.00
53	Rondell White	.75
54	Mike Piazza	6.00
55	Derek Jeter	6.00
56	Tino Martinez	1.50
57	David Wells	.50
58	Ben Grieve	2.00
59	A.J. Hinch	.50
60	Scott Rolen	2.50
61	Doug Glanville	.50
62	Aramis Ramirez	.50
63	Jose Guillen	.50
64	Tony Gwynn	5.00
65	Greg Vaughn	.75
66	Ruben Rivera	.50
67	Barry Bonds	2.50
68	J.T. Snow	.50
69	Alex Rodriguez	6.00
70	Ken Griffey Jr.	10.00
71	Jay Buhner	.75
72	Mark McGwire	12.00
73	Fernando Tatis	.50
74	Quinton McCracken	.50
75	Wade Boggs	1.00
76	Ivan Rodriguez	2.50
77	Juan Gonzalez	5.00
78	Rafael Palmeiro	1.50
79	Jose Cruz Jr.	1.50
80	Carlos Delgado	1.00
81	Troy Glaus	30.00
82	Vladimir Nunez	4.00
83	George Lombard	12.00
84	Bruce Chen	8.00
85	Ryan Minor	15.00
86	Calvin Pickering	6.00
87	Jin Ho Cho	6.00
88	Russ Branyon	6.00
89	Derrick Gibson	4.00
90	Gabe Kapler	75.00
91	Matt Anderson	8.00
92	Robert Fick	6.00
93	Juan Encarnacion	8.00
94	Preston Wilson	6.00
95	Alex Gonzalez	8.00
96	Carlos Beltran	12.00
97	Jeremy Giambi	15.00
98	Dee Brown	4.00
99	Adrian Beltre	10.00
100	Alex Cora	6.00
101	Angel Pena	12.00
102	Geoff Jenkins	6.00
103	Ronnie Belliard	6.00
104	Corey Koskie	6.00
105	A.J. Pierzynski	6.00
106	Michael Barrett	12.00
107	Fernando Seguignol	12.00
108	Mike Kinkade	10.00
109	Mike Lowell	8.00
110	Ricky Ledee	8.00
111	Eric Chavez	15.00
112	Abraham Nunez	6.00
113	Matt Clement	10.00
114	Ben Davis	6.00
115	Mike Darr	8.00
116	Ramon Martinez	8.00
117	Carlos Guillen	10.00
118	Shane Monahan	6.00
119	J.D. Drew	150.00
120	Kevin Witt	6.00

1999 SPx Dominance

This 20-card set showcases the most dominant MLB superstars, including Derek Jeter and Alex Rodriguez. These are seeded 1:17 packs and numbered with an "FB" prefix.

		MT
Complete Set (20):		250.00
Common Player:		3.00
Inserted 1:17		
1	Chipper Jones	15.00
2	Greg Maddux	20.00
3	Cal Ripken Jr.	25.00
4	Nomar Garciaparra	20.00
5	Mo Vaughn	8.00
6	Sammy Sosa	20.00
7	Albert Belle	8.00
8	Frank Thomas	12.00
9	Jim Thome	6.00
10	Jeff Bagwell	8.00
11	Vladimir Guerrero	10.00
12	Mike Piazza	20.00
13	Derek Jeter	20.00
14	Tony Gwynn	15.00
15	Barry Bonds	8.00
16	Ken Griffey Jr.	30.00
17	Alex Rodriguez	20.00
18	Mark McGwire	35.00
19	J.D. Drew	15.00
20	Juan Gonzalez	15.00

1999 SPx Power Explosion

This 30-card set salutes the top power hitters in the game today, including Mark McGwire and Sammy Sosa. These are seeded 1:3 packs, and numbered with a "PE" prefix.

		MT
Complete Set (30):		90.00
Common Player:		1.00
Inserted 1:3		
1	Troy Glaus	3.00
2	Mo Vaughn	2.50
3	Travis Lee	2.00
4	Chipper Jones	5.00
5	Andres Galarraga	2.00
6	Brady Anderson	1.00
7	Albert Belle	2.50
8	Nomar Garciaparra	6.00
9	Sammy Sosa	6.00
10	Frank Thomas	5.00
11	Jim Thome	2.00
12	Manny Ramirez	3.00
13	Larry Walker	2.00
14	Tony Clark	2.00
15	Jeff Bagwell	2.50
16	Moises Alou	1.00
17	Ken Caminiti	1.00
18	Vladimir Guerrero	3.00
19	Mike Piazza	6.00
20	Tino Martinez	2.00
21	Ben Grieve	2.50
22	Scott Rolen	2.50
23	Greg Vaughn	1.00
24	Barry Bonds	2.50
25	Ken Griffey Jr.	10.00
26	Alex Rodriguez	6.00
27	Mark McGwire	12.00
28	J.D. Drew	8.00
29	Juan Gonzalez	5.00
30	Ivan Rodriguez	2.50

1999 SPx Premier Stars

This 30-card set captures baseball's most dominant players, including Randy Johnson and Ken Griffey Jr. Featured on a rainbow-foil design, these are seeded 1:17 packs and numbered with a "PS" prefix.

		MT
Complete Set (30):		350.00
Common Player:		3.00
Inserted 1:17		
1	Mark McGwire	40.00
2	Sammy Sosa	20.00
3	Frank Thomas	15.00
4	J.D. Drew	20.00
5	Kerry Wood	8.00
6	Moises Alou	3.00
7	Kenny Lofton	8.00
8	Jeff Bagwell	8.00
9	Tony Clark	6.00
10	Roberto Alomar	6.00
11	Cal Ripken Jr.	25.00
12	Derek Jeter	20.00
13	Mike Piazza	20.00
14	Jose Cruz Jr.	6.00
15	Chipper Jones	15.00
16	Nomar Garciaparra	20.00
17	Greg Maddux	20.00
18	Scott Rolen	8.00
19	Vladimir Guerrero	10.00
20	Albert Belle	8.00
21	Ken Griffey Jr.	35.00
22	Alex Rodriguez	20.00
23	Ben Grieve	10.00
24	Juan Gonzalez	15.00
25	Barry Bonds	8.00
26	Larry Walker	6.00
27	Tony Gwynn	15.00
28	Randy Johnson	6.00
29	Travis Lee	6.00
30	Mo Vaughn	8.00

1999 SPx Star Focus

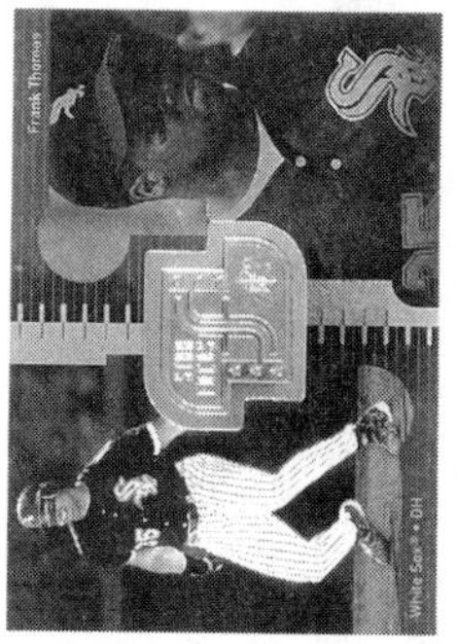

This 30-card set focuses on the 30 brightest stars in the game. These are seeded 1:8 packs and numbered with an "SF" prefix.

		MT
Complete Set (30):		150.00
Common Player:		2.00
Inserted 1:8		
1	Chipper Jones	8.00
2	Greg Maddux	10.00
3	Cal Ripken Jr.	12.00
4	Nomar Garciaparra	10.00
5	Mo Vaughn	4.00
6	Sammy Sosa	10.00
7	Albert Belle	4.00
8	Frank Thomas	8.00
9	Jim Thome	3.00
10	Kenny Lofton	4.00
11	Manny Ramirez	5.00
12	Larry Walker	3.00
13	Jeff Bagwell	4.00
14	Craig Biggio	3.00
15	Randy Johnson	3.00
16	Vladimir Guerrero	5.00
17	Mike Piazza	10.00
18	Derek Jeter	10.00
19	Tino Martinez	3.00
20	Bernie Williams	3.00
21	Curt Schilling	2.00
22	Tony Gwynn	8.00
23	Barry Bonds	4.00
24	Ken Griffey Jr.	15.00
25	Alex Rodriguez	10.00
26	Mark McGwire	20.00
27	J.D. Drew	10.00
28	Juan Gonzalez	8.00
29	Ivan Rodriguez	4.00
30	Ben Grieve	4.00

1999 SPx Winning Materials

This eight-card set includes a piece of the featured player's game-worn jersey and game-used bat on each card. These are seeded 1:251 packs.

		MT
Complete Set (8):		1300.
Common Player:		100.00
Inserted 1:251		
VC	Vinny Castilla	100.00
JD	J.D. Drew	175.00
JR	Ken Griffey Jr.	500.00
VG	Vladimir Guerrero	175.00
TG	Tony Gwynn	225.00
TH	Todd Helton	125.00
TL	Travis Lee	125.00
IR	Ivan Rodriguez	150.00

1999 SPx 500 Club Piece of History

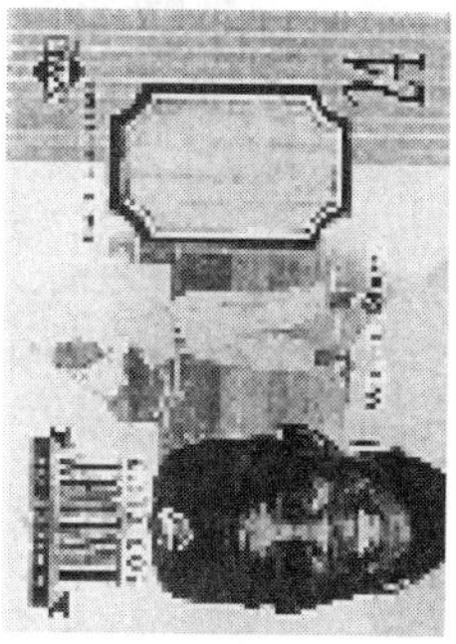

Each of these approximately 350 cards include a piece of game-used Louisville Slugger once swung by Wilie Mays. Mays also signed 24 of his Piece of History cards.

		MT
Complete Set (1):		350.00
Mays Auto. (24):		
WM	Willie Mays (350)	350.00

1999 Sports Illustrated

The Sports Illustrated Baseball by Fleer set consists of a 180-card base set. The base set is composed of 107 player cards, and four subsets. They include Team 2000, Postseason Review, Award Winners, and Season Highlights. Cards come in six-card packs with an S.R.P. of $1.99. The set also includes five insert sets, along with hobby exclusive autographed J.D. Drew cards numbered to 250. The insert sets include: Headliners (1:4), Ones to Watch (1:12), Fabulous 40's (1:20), Fabulous 40's Extra (hobby exclusive), and The Dominators (1:90 and 1:180).

		MT
Complete Set (180):		30.00
Common Player:		.10
1	Yankees (Postseason Review)	.25
2	Scott Brosius (Postseason Review)	.10
3	David Wells (Postseason Review)	.10
4	Sterling Hitchcock (Postseason Review)	.10
5	David Justice (Postseason Review)	.25
6	David Cone (Postseason Review)	.20
7	Greg Maddux (Postseason Review)	1.00
8	Jim Leyritz (Postseason Review)	.10
9	Gary Gaetti (Postseason Review)	.10
10	Mark McGwire (Award Winners)	2.00
11	Sammy Sosa (Award Winners)	1.00
12	Larry Walker (Award Winners)	.25
13	Tony Womack (Award Winners)	.10
14	Tom Glavine (Award Winners)	.20
15	Curt Schilling (Award Winners)	.10
16	Greg Maddux (Award Winners)	1.00
17	Trevor Hoffman (Award Winners)	.10
18	Kerry Wood (Award Winners)	.50
19	Tom Glavine (Award Winners)	.20
20	Sammy Sosa (Award Winners)	1.00
21	Travis Lee (Season Highlights)	.30
22	Roberto Alomar (Season Highlights)	.25
23	Roger Clemens (Season Highlights)	.75
24	Barry Bonds (Season Highlights)	.40
25	Paul Molitor (Season Highlights)	.30
26	Todd Stottlemyre (Season Highlights)	.10
27	Chris Hoiles (Season Highlights)	.10
28	Albert Belle (Season Highlights)	.40
29	Tony Clark (Season Highlights)	.25
30	Kerry Wood (Season Highlights)	.50
31	David Wells (Season Highlights)	.10
32	Dennis Eckersley (Season Highlights)	.10
33	Mark McGwire (Season Highlights)	2.00
34	Cal Ripken Jr. (Season Highlights)	1.25
35	Ken Griffey Jr. (Season Highlights)	1.50
36	Alex Rodriguez (Season Highlights)	1.00
37	Craig Biggio (Season Highlights)	.20
38	Sammy Sosa (Season Highlights)	1.00
39	Dennis Martinez (Season Highlights)	.10
40	Curt Schilling (Season Highlights)	.20
41	Orlando Hernandez (Season Highlights)	.50
42	Troy Glaus, *Ben Molina*, Todd Greene ("Team" 2000)	.50
43	Mitch Meluskey, Daryle Ward, Mike Grzanich ("Team" 2000)	.10
44	Eric Chavez, Mike Neill, *Steve Connelly* ("Team" 2000)	.50
45	Roy Halladay, Tom Evans, Kevin Witt ("Team" 2000)	.25
46	George Lombard, Adam Butler, Bruce Chen ("Team" 2000)	.10
47	Ronnie Belliard, Valerio de los Santos, *Rafael Roque* ("Team" 2000)	.25
48	J.D. Drew, Placido Polanco, *Mark Little* ("Team" 2000)	5.00
49	Jason Maxwell, *Jose Nieves*, Jeremi Gonzalez ("Team" 2000)	.20
50	Scott McClain, Kerry Robinson, *Mike Duvall* ("Team" 2000)	.25
51	Ben Ford, *Bryan Corey*, Danny Klassen ("Team" 2000)	.25
52	Angel Pena, Jeff Kubenka, Paul LoDuca ("Team" 2000)	.10
53	Kirk Bullinger, Fernando Seguignol, Tim Young ("Team" 2000)	.10
54	Ramon Martinez, Wilson Delgado, Armando Rios ("Team" 2000)	.10
55	Russ Branyon, *Jolbert Cabrera*, Jason Rakers ("Team" 2000)	.10
56	*Carlos Guillen*, *David Holdridge*, *Giomar Guevara* ("Team" 2000)	.25
57	Alex Gonzalez, Joe Fontenot, Preston Wilson ("Team" 2000)	.10
58	Mike Kinkade, Jay Payton, Masato Yoshii ("Team" 2000)	.10
59	Willis Otanez, Ryan Minor, Calvin Pickering ("Team" 2000)	.10
60	Ben Davis, Matt Clement, Stan Spencer ("Team" 2000)	.10
61	Marlon Anderson, Mike Welch, *Gary Bennett* ("Team" 2000)	.25
62	Abraham Nunez, *Sean Lawrence*, Aramis Ramirez ("Team" 2000)	.10
63	Jonathan Johnson, *Rob Sasser*, *Scott Sheldon* ("Team" 2000)	.25
64	*Keith Glauber*, *Guillermo Garcia*, Eddie Priest ("Team" 2000)	.25
65	Brian Barkley, Jin Ho Cho, Donnie Sadler ("Team" 2000)	.10
66	Derrick Gibson, Mark Strittmatter, *Edgard Clemente* ("Team" 2000)	.10
67	Jeremy Giambi, Dermal Brown, *Chris Hatcher* ("Team" 2000)	.25
68	*Rob Fick*, Gabe Kapler, Marino Santana ("Team" 2000)	.75
69	Corey Koskie, A.J. Pierzynski, Benj Sampson ("Team" 2000)	.10
70	Brian Simmons, Mark Johnson, Craig Wilson ("Team" 2000)	.10
71	Ryan Bradley, Mike Lowell, Jay Tessmer ("Team" 2000)	.10
72	Ben Grieve	.75
73	Shawn Green	.10
74	Rafael Palmeiro	.25
75	Juan Gonzalez	1.50
76	Mike Piazza	2.00
77	Devon White	.10
78	Jim Thome	.40
79	Barry Larkin	.25
80	Scott Rolen	.75
81	Raul Mondesi	.25
82	Jason Giambi	.10
83	Jose Canseco	.40
84	Tony Gwynn	1.50
85	Cal Ripken Jr.	2.50
86	Andy Pettitte	.40
87	Carlos Delgado	.20
88	Jeff Cirillo	.10
89	Bret Saberhagen	.10
90	John Olerud	.20
91	Ron Coomer	.10
92	Todd Helton	.60
93	Ray Lankford	.10
94	Tim Salmon	.40
95	Fred McGriff	.20
96	Matt Stairs	.10
97	Ken Griffey Jr.	3.00
98	Chipper Jones	1.50
99	Mark Grace	.20
100	Ivan Rodriguez	.75
101	Jeromy Burnitz	.10
102	Kenny Rogers	.10
103	Kevin Millwood	.40
104	Vinny Castilla	.20
105	Jim Edmonds	.20
106	Craig Biggio	.40
107	Andres Galarraga	.40
108	Sammy Sosa	2.00
109	Juan Encarnacion	.25
110	Larry Walker	.50
111	John Smoltz	.20
112	Randy Johnson	.50
113	Bobby Higginson	.10
114	Albert Belle	.75
115	Jaret Wright	.40
116	Edgar Renteria	.10
117	Andruw Jones	.75
118	Barry Bonds	.75
119	Rondell White	.20
120	Jamie Moyer	.10
121	Darin Erstad	.75
122	Al Leiter	.20
123	Mark McGwire	4.00
124	Mo Vaughn	.75
125	Livan Hernandez	.10
126	Jason Kendall	.10
127	Frank Thomas	1.50
128	Denny Neagle	.10
129	Johnny Damon	.10
130	Derek Bell	.10
131	Jeff Kent	.10
132	Tony Womack	.10
133	Trevor Hoffman	.10
134	Gary Sheffield	.25
135	Tino Martinez	.25
136	Travis Fryman	.10
137	Rolando Arrojo	.20
138	Dante Bichette	.25
139	Nomar Garciaparra	2.00
140	Moises Alou	.20
141	Chuck Knoblauch	.40
142	Robin Ventura	.10
143	Scott Erickson	.10
144	David Cone	.20
145	Greg Vaughn	.20

146	Wade Boggs	.25
147	Mike Mussina	.50
148	Tony Clark	.40
149	Alex Rodriguez	2.00
150	Javy Lopez	.20
151	Bartolo Colon	.10
152	Derek Jeter	2.00
153	Greg Maddux	2.00
154	Kevin Brown	.20
155	Curt Schilling	.20
156	Jeff King	.10
157	Bernie Williams	.50
158	Roberto Alomar	.50
159	Travis Lee	.60
160	Kerry Wood	.75
161	Jeff Bagwell	.75
162	Roger Clemens	1.00
163	Matt Williams	.25
164	Chan Ho Park	.25
165	Damion Easley	.10
166	Manny Ramirez	1.00
167	Quinton McCracken	.10
168	Todd Walker	.25
169	Eric Karros	.20
170	Will Clark	.40
171	Edgar Martinez	.10
172	Cliff Floyd	.10
173	Vladimir Guerrero	1.00
174	Tom Glavine	.25
175	Pedro Martinez	.50
176	Chuck Finley	.10
177	Dean Palmer	.10
178	Omar Vizquel	.10
179	Checklist	.10
180	Checklist	.10

1999 Sports Illustrated Diamond Dominators

This 10-card insert set features five hitters and five pitchers on embossed cards. The hitters are seeded 1 in every 180 packs, while the pitchers are seeded 1 in every 90 packs.

		MT
Complete Set (10):		475.00
Common Player:		10.00
Pitchers inserted 1:90		
Hitters inserted 1:180		
1DD	Kerry Wood	25.00
2DD	Roger Clemens	25.00
3DD	Randy Johnson	15.00
4DD	Greg Maddux	35.00
5DD	Pedro Martinez	15.00
6DD	Ken Griffey Jr.	100.00
7DD	Sammy Sosa	75.00
8DD	Nomar Garciaparra	60.00
9DD	Mark McGwire	120.00
10DD	Alex Rodriguez	75.00

1999 Sports Illustrated Fabulous 40s Extra

The insert set parallels the 13 cards in the Fabulous 40s insert set. The cards are hobby exclusive, and contained silver pattern holofoil. Each players cards are hand-numbered to the total number of home runs he hit in 1998.

		MT
Common Player:		40.00
Numbered to amount of HRs		
1FF	Mark McGwire (70)	350.00
2FF	Sammy Sosa (66)	200.00
3FF	Ken Griffey Jr. (56)	300.00
4FF	Greg Vaughn (50)	40.00
5FF	Albert Belle (49)	100.00
6FF	Jose Canseco (46)	75.00
7FF	Vinny Castilla (46)	40.00
8FF	Juan Gonzalez (45)	200.00
9FF	Manny Ramirez (45)	100.00
10FF	Andres Galarraga (44)	75.00
11FF	Rafael Palmeiro (43)	60.00
12FF	Alex Rodriguez (42)	250.00
13FF	Mo Vaughn (40)	125.00

1999 Sports Illustrated Fabulous 40s

This 13-card insert set consists of the players that hit 40 or more homers during the 1998 season. The cards are sculpture embossed and foil-stamped, with the player's home run total also on the card. One card comes with every 20 packs.

		MT
Complete Set (13):		100.00
Common Player:		3.00
Inserted 1:20		
1FF	Mark McGwire	30.00
2FF	Sammy Sosa	15.00
3FF	Ken Griffey Jr.	25.00
4FF	Greg Vaughn	3.00
5FF	Albert Belle	6.00
6FF	Jose Canseco	5.00
7FF	Vinny Castilla	3.00
8FF	Juan Gonzalez	12.00
9FF	Manny Ramirez	8.00
10FF	Andres Galarraga	5.00
11FF	Rafael Palmeiro	4.00
12FF	Alex Rodriguez	15.00
13FF	Mo Vaughn	6.00

1999 Sports Illustrated Headliners

Headliners is a 25-card insert set that features silver foil stamped, team-color coded cards. One card comes with every four packs.

		MT
Complete Set (25):		75.00
Common Player:		.75
Inserted 1:4		
1H	Vladimir Guerrero	3.00
2H	Randy Johnson	1.50
3H	Mo Vaughn	2.00
4H	Chipper Jones	4.00
5H	Jeff Bagwell	2.00
6H	Juan Gonzalez	4.00
7H	Mark McGwire	10.00
8H	Cal Ripken Jr.	6.00
9H	Frank Thomas	4.00
10H	Manny Ramirez	2.50
11H	Ken Griffey Jr.	8.00
12H	Scott Rolen	2.00
13H	Alex Rodriguez	6.00
14H	Barry Bonds	2.00
15H	Roger Clemens	3.00
16H	Darin Erstad	2.00
17H	Nomar Garciaparra	5.00
18H	Mike Piazza	5.00
19H	Greg Maddux	5.00
20H	Ivan Rodriguez	2.00
21H	Derek Jeter	5.00
22H	Sammy Sosa	5.00
23H	Andruw Jones	2.00
24H	Pedro Martinez	1.50
25H	Kerry Wood	2.00

1999 Sports Illustrated Ones To Watch

This 15-card insert set features the game's top rookies and young stars. The cards have 100%-foil background, and are team-color coded. One card was inserted in every 12 packs.

		MT
Complete Set (15):		50.00
Common Player:		1.50
Inserted 1:12		
1OW	J.D. Drew	20.00
2OW	Marlon Anderson	1.50
3OW	Roy Halladay	2.00
4OW	Ben Grieve	5.00
5OW	Todd Helton	3.00
6OW	Gabe Kapler	6.00
7OW	Troy Glaus	4.00
8OW	Ben Davis	1.50
9OW	Eric Chavez	5.00
10OW	Richie Sexson	1.50
11OW	Fernando Seguignol	3.00
12OW	Kerry Wood	5.00
13OW	Bobby Smith	1.50
14OW	Ryan Minor	1.50
15OW	Jeremy Giambi	2.50
	J.D. Drew Auto. (250)	100.00

1999 Sports Illustrated Greats of the Game

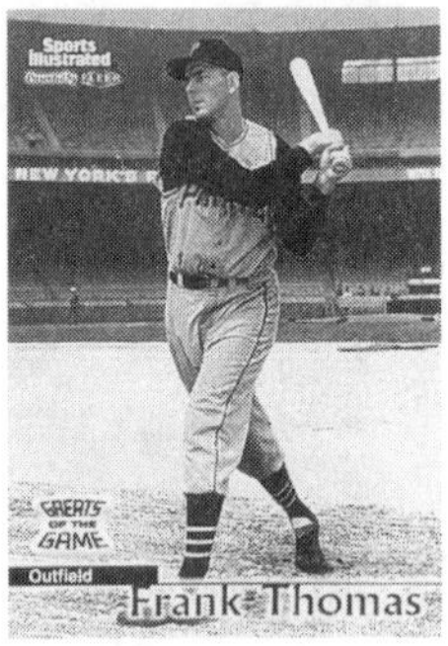

The 90-card base set includes many legendary major-leaguers including Babe Ruth and Cy Young. Card fronts feature a full bleed photo with the player name across the bottom and Greats of the Game printed on the bottom left portion of the card. Card backs have the player's vital information, along with career statistics and a few career highlights. Seven-card packs were issued with an S.R.P. of $15.

		MT
Complete Set (90):		60.00
Common Player:		.25
1	Jimmie Fox	2.00
2	Red Schoendienst	.25
3	Babe Ruth	5.00
4	Lou Gehrig	4.00
5	Mel Ott	1.50
6	Stan Musial	2.00
7	Mickey Mantle	5.00
8	Carl Yastrzemski	1.50
9	Enos Slaughter	.25
10	Andre Dawson	.25
11	Luis Aparicio	.75
12	Ferguson Jenkins	1.00
13	Christy Mathewson	1.00
14	Ernie Banks	2.00
15	Johnny Podres	.25
16	George Foster	.25
17	Jerry Koosman	.25
18	Curt Simmons	.25
19	Bob Feller	1.50
20	Frank Robinson	2.00
21	Gary Carter	.25
22	Frank Thomas	.25
23	Bill Lee	.25
24	Willie Mays	3.00
25	Tommie Agee	.25
26	Boog Powell	.25
27	Jimmy Wynn	.25
28	Sparky Lyle	.25
29	Bo Belinsky	.25
30	Maury Wills	.25
31	Bill Buckner	.25
32	Steve Carlton	1.50
33	Harmon Killebrew	2.00
34	Nolan Ryan	5.00
35	Randy Jones	.25
36	Robin Roberts	.25
37	Al Oliver	.25
38	Rico Petrocelli	.25
39	Dave Parker	.25
40	Eddie Mathews	1.50
41	Earl Weaver	.25
42	Jackie Robinson	4.00
43	Lou Brock	1.00
44	Reggie Jackson	2.00
45	Bob Gibson	1.50
46	Jeff Burroughs	.25
47	Jim Bouton	.25
48	Bob Forsch	.25
49	Ron Guidry	.25
50	Ty Cobb	3.00
51	Roy White	.25
52	Joe Rudi	.25
53	Moose Skowron	.25
54	Goose Gossage	.25
55	Ed Kranepool	.25
56	Paul Blair	.25
57	Kent Hrbek	.25
58	Orlando Cepeda	.75
59	Buck O'Neil	.50
60	Al Kaline	1.00
61	Vida Blue	.25
62	Sam McDowell	.25
63	Jesse Barfield	.25
64	Dave Kingman	.25
65	Ron Santo	.25
66	Steve Garvey	.25
67	Gaylord Perry	.75
68	Darrell Evans	.25
69	Rollie Fingers	.75
70	Walter Johnson	2.00
71	Al Hrabosky	.25
72	Mickey Rivers	.25
73	Mike Torrez	.25
74	Hank Bauer	.25
75	Tug McGraw	.25
76	David Clyde	.25
77	Jim Lonborg	.25
78	Clete Boyer	.25
79	Harry Walker	.25
80	Cy Young	2.50
81	Bud Harrelson	.25
82	Paul Splittorff	.25
83	Bert Campaneris	.25
84	Joe Niekro	.25
85	Bob Horner	.25
86	Jerry Royster	.25
87	Tommy John	.25
88	Mark Fidrych	.25
89	Dick Williams	.25
90	Graig Nettles	.25

1999 Sports Illus. Greats of the Game Autographs

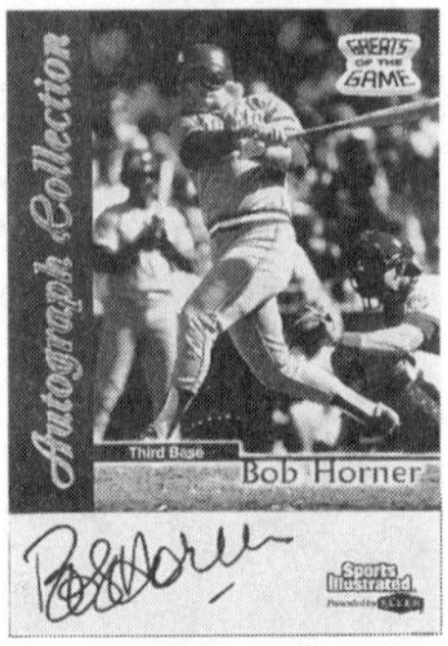

Each Greats of the Game pack has one autograph from the 80 card autograph checklist. Each card is autographed on the white portion on the bottom of the card, and is stamped "seal of authenticity". Card backs detail that the autograph is authentic and "has been embossed with the Fleer Mark of Authenticity."

		MT
Common Player:		8.00
Inserted 1:1		
1	Tommie Agee	8.00
2	Luis Aparicio	15.00
3	Ernie Banks	60.00
4	Jesse Barfield	8.00
5	Hank Bauer	8.00
6	Bo Belinsky	8.00
7	Paul Blair	8.00
8	Vida Blue	20.00
9	Jim Bouton	8.00
10	Clete Boyer	8.00
11	Lou Brock	25.00
12	Bill Buckner	8.00
13	Jeff Burroughs	8.00
14	Bert Campaneris	8.00
15	Steve Carlton	60.00
16	Gary Carter	20.00
17	Orlando Cepeda	15.00
18	David Clyde	8.00
19	Andre Dawson	15.00
20	Darrell Evans	8.00
21	Bob Feller	30.00
22	Mark Fidrych	8.00
23	Rollie Fingers	15.00
24	Bob Forsch	8.00
25	George Foster	8.00
26	Steve Garvey	15.00
27	Bob Gibson	30.00
28	Goose Gossage	8.00
29	Ron Guidry	8.00
30	Bud Harrelson	8.00
31	Bob Horner	8.00
32	Al Hrabosky	8.00
33	Kent Hrbek	8.00
34	Reggie Jackson	175.00
35	Ferguson Jenkins	20.00
36	Tommy John	8.00
37	Randy Jones	8.00
38	Al Kaline	40.00
39	Harmon Killebrew	50.00
40	Dave Kingman	8.00
41	Jerry Koosman	8.00
42	Ed Kranepool	8.00
43	Bill Lee	8.00
44	Jim Lonborg	8.00
45	Sparky Lyle	8.00
46	Eddie Mathews	50.00
47	Willie Mays	200.00
48	Sam McDowell	8.00
49	Tug McGraw	8.00
50	Stan Musial	180.00
51	Graig Nettles	15.00
52	Joe Niekro	8.00
53	Buck O'Neil	15.00
54	Al Oliver	8.00
55	Dave Parker	8.00
56	Gaylord Perry	8.00
57	Rico Petrocelli	8.00
58	Johnny Podres	8.00
59	Boog Powell	8.00
60	Mickey Rivers	8.00
61	Robin Roberts	8.00
62	Frank Robinson	40.00
63	Jerry Royster	8.00
64	Joe Rudi	8.00
65	Nolan Ryan	300.00
66	Ron Santo	8.00
67	Red Schoendienst	8.00
68	Curt Simmons	8.00
69	Moose Skowron	8.00
70	Enos Slaughter	8.00
71	Paul Splittorff	8.00
72	Frank Thomas	8.00
73	Mike Torrez	8.00
74	Harry Walker	8.00
75	Earl Weaver	8.00
76	Roy White	8.00
77	Dick Williams	8.00
78	Maury Wills	15.00
79	Jimmy Wynn	8.00
80	Carl Yastrzemski	125.00

1999 Sports Illus. Greats of the Game Cover Collection

Each pack features one of the 50 chosen baseball covers from the Sports Illustrated archives. Card fronts are a reprint of the actual cover, while the backs give a brief description of the cover article and date of the magazine cover. Each card is numbered with a "C" suffix.

		MT
Complete Set (50):		50.00
Common Player:		.25
Inserted 1:1		
1	Johnny Podres	.25
2	Mickey Mantle	8.00
3	Stan Musial	2.00
4	Eddie Mathews	1.50
5	Frank Thomas	.25
6	Willie Mays	3.00
7	Red Schoendienst	.25
8	Luis Aparicio	.25
9	Mickey Mantle	8.00
10	Al Kaline	1.00
11	Maury Wills	.25
12	Sam McDowell	.25
13	Harry Walker	.25
14	Carl Yastrzemski	1.00
15	Carl Yastrzemski	1.00
16	Lou Brock	1.00
17	Ron Santo	.25
18	Reggie Jackson	2.00
19	Frank Robinson	1.50
20	Jerry Koosman	.25
21	Bud Harrelson	.25
22	Vida Blue	.75
23	Ferguson Jenkins	.75
24	Sparky Lyle	.25
25	Steve Carlton	1.00
26	Bert Campaneris	.25
27	Jimmy Wynn	.25
28	Steve Garvey	.25
29	Nolan Ryan	5.00
30	Randy Jones	.25
31	Reggie Jackson	2.00
32	Joe Rudi	.25
33	Reggie Jackson	2.00
34	Dave Parker	.25
35	Mark Fidrych	.25
36	Earl Weaver	.25
37	Nolan Ryan	5.00
38	Steve Carlton	1.50
39	Reggie Jackson	2.00
40	Rollie Fingers	.50
41	Gary Carter	.25
42	Graig Nettles	.25
43	Gaylord Perry	.25
44	Kent Hrbek	.25
45	Gary Carter	.25
46	Steve Garvey	.25
47	Steve Carlton	1.50
48	Nolan Ryan	5.00
49	Nolan Ryan	5.00
50	Mickey Mantle	8.00

1999 Sports Illus. Greats of the Game Record Breakers

This 10-card set spotlights the top record breakers in the past century from Christy Mathewson to Nolan Ryan. Card fronts are full foiled with an oblong stamp on the bottom portion detailing the player's respective record. Card backs are numbered with an "RB" suffix and gives more detail on the featured player's record. These are seeded 1:12 packs. A Gold parallel is also randomly seeded 1:120 packs and have gold holo-foil.

		MT
Complete Set (10):		125.00
Common Player:		5.00
Inserted 1:12		
Golds:		2x to 4x
Inserted 1:120		
1	Mickey Mantle	25.00
2	Stan Musial	10.00
3	Babe Ruth	25.00
4	Christy Mathewson	5.00
5	Cy Young	10.00
6	Nolan Ryan	20.00
7	Jackie Robinson	20.00
8	Lou Gehrig	20.00
9	Ty Cobb	10.00
10	Walter Johnson	5.00

1999 Stadium Club

Released in two series with Series I 170-cards and Series II 185-cards. Base cards feature a full bleed design on 20 pt. stock with an embossed holographic logo. Draft Pick and Prospect subset cards are short-printed, seeded in every three packs. Card backs have 1998 statistics and personal information. Hobby packs consist of six cards with an S.R.P. of $2.00.

		MT
Complete Set (355):		115.00
Complete Series I Set (170):		65.00
Complete Series II Set (185):		50.00
Common Player:		.15
Common Prospect (141-148):		1.50
Inserted 1:3		
Common Draft Pick (149-160):		1.50
Inserted 1:3		
Common SP (311-335, 346-355):		1.00
Common SP (336-345):		2.00
1	Alex Rodriguez	2.00
2	Chipper Jones	1.50
3	Rusty Greer	.15
4	Jim Edmonds	.25
5	Ron Gant	.15
6	Kevin Polcovich	.15
7	Darryl Strawberry	.25
8	Bill Mueller	.15
9	Vinny Castilla	.15
10	Wade Boggs	.25
11	Jose Lima	.15
12	Darren Dreifort	.15
13	Jay Bell	.15
14	Ben Grieve	.75
15	Shawn Green	.15
16	Andres Galarraga	.60
17	Bartolo Colon	.15
18	Francisco Cordova	.15
19	Paul O'Neill	.30
20	Trevor Hoffman	.15
21	Darren Oliver	.15
22	John Franco	.15
23	Eli Marrero	.15
24	Roberto Hernandez	.15
25	Craig Biggio	.25
26	Brad Fullmer	.25
27	Scott Erickson	.15
28	Tom Gordon	.15
29	Brian Hunter	.15
30	Raul Mondesi	.25
31	Rick Reed	.15
32	Jose Canseco	.40
33	Robb Nen	.15
34	Turner Ward	.15
35	Bret Boone	.15
36	Jose Offerman	.15
37	Matt Lawton	.15
38	David Wells	.15
39	Bob Abreu	.15
40	Jeromy Burnitz	.15
41	Deivi Cruz	.15
42	Mike Cameron	.15
43	Rico Brogna	.15
44	Dmitri Young	.15
45	Chuck Knoblauch	.30
46	Johnny Damon	.15
47	Brian Meadows	.15
48	Jeremi Gonzalez	.15
49	Gary DiSarcina	.15
50	Frank Thomas	2.00
51	F.P. Santangelo	.15
52	Tom Candiotti	.15
53	Shane Reynolds	.15
54	Rod Beck	.15
55	Rey Ordonez	.15
56	Todd Helton	.75
57	Mickey Morandini	.15
58	Jorge Posada	.25
59	Mike Mussina	.50
60	Bobby Bonilla	.25
61	David Segui	.15
62	Brian McRae	.15
63	Fred McGriff	.25
64	Brett Tomko	.15
65	Derek Jeter	2.00
66	Sammy Sosa	2.50
67	Kenny Rogers	.15
68	Dave Nilsson	.15
69	Eric Young	.15
70	Mark McGwire	4.00
71	Kenny Lofton	.60
72	Tom Glavine	.20
73	Joey Hamilton	.15
74	John Valentin	.15
75	Mariano Rivera	.25
76	Ray Durham	.15
77	Tony Clark	.50
78	Livan Hernandez	.15
79	Rickey Henderson	.25
80	Vladimir Guerrero	1.00
81	J.T. Snow Jr.	.15
82	Juan Guzman	.15
83	Darryl Hamilton	.15
84	Matt Anderson	.25
85	Travis Lee	.75
86	Joe Randa	.15
87	Dave Dellucci	.15
88	Moises Alou	.20
89	Alex Gonzalez	.15
90	Tony Womack	.15
91	Neifi Perez	.15
92	Travis Fryman	.15
93	Masato Yoshii	.15
94	Woody Williams	.15
95	Ray Lankford	.15
96	Roger Clemens	1.00
97	Dustin Hermanson	.15
98	Joe Carter	.20
99	Jason Schmidt	.15
100	Greg Maddux	2.00
101	Kevin Tapani	.15
102	Charles Johnson	.15
103	Derrek Lee	.15
104	Pete Harnisch	.15
105	Dante Bichette	.40
106	Scott Brosius	.15
107	Mike Caruso	.15
108	Eddie Taubensee	.15
109	Jeff Fassero	.15
110	Marquis Grissom	.15
111	Jose Hernandez	.15
112	Chan Ho Park	.25
113	Wally Joyner	.15
114	Bobby Estalella	.15
115	Pedro Martinez	.50
116	Shawn Estes	.15
117	Walt Weiss	.15
118	John Mabry	.15
119	Brian Johnson	.15
120	Jim Thome	.40
121	Bill Spiers	.15
122	John Olerud	.25
123	Jeff King	.15
124	Tim Belcher	.15
125	John Wetteland	.15
126	Tony Gwynn	1.50
127	Brady Anderson	.15
128	Randy Winn	.15
129	Devon White	.15
130	Eric Karros	.25
131	Kevin Millwood	.40
132	Andy Benes	.20
133	Andy Ashby	.15
134	Ron Comer	.15
135	Juan Gonzalez	1.50
136	Randy Johnson	.50
137	Aaron Sele	.15
138	Edgardo Alfonzo	.15
139	B.J. Surhoff	.15
140	Jose Vizcaino	.15
141	*Chad Moeller* (Prospect)	2.00
142	*Mike Zwicka* (Prospect)	1.50
143	Angel Pena (Prospect)	3.00
144	*Nick Johnson* (Prospect)	5.00
145	*Giuseppe Chiaramonte* (Prospect)	2.50
146	*Kit Pellow* (Prospect)	2.50
147	*Clayton Andrews* (Prospect)	4.00
148	*Jerry Hairston Jr.* (Prospect)	3.00
149	*Jason Tyner* (Draft Pick)	1.50
150	*Chip Ambres* (Draft Pick)	3.00
151	*Pat Burrell* (Draft Pick)	12.00
152	*Josh McKinley* (Draft Pick)	4.00
153	*Choo Freeman* (Draft Pick)	3.00
154	*Rick Elder* (Draft Pick)	5.00
155	*Eric Valent* (Draft Pick)	4.00
156	*Jeff Winchester* (Draft Pick)	3.00
157	*Mike Nannini* (Draft Pick)	2.00
158	*Mamon Tucker* (Draft Pick)	2.00
159	*Nate Bump* (Draft Pick)	1.50
160	*Andy Brown* (Draft Pick)	1.50
161	Troy Glaus (Future Star)	1.00
162	Adrian Beltre (Future Star)	.40
163	Mitch Meluskey (Future Star)	1.00
164	Alex Gonzalez (Future Star)	.15
165	George Lombard (Future Star)	.15
166	Eric Chavez (Future Star)	.50
167	Ruben Mateo (Future Star)	.60
168	Calvin Pickering (Future Star)	.15
169	Gabe Kapler (Future Star)	1.50
170	Bruce Chen (Future Star)	.15
171	Darin Erstad	.75
172	Sandy Alomar	.25
173	Miguel Cairo	.15
174	Jason Kendall	.25
175	Cal Ripken Jr.	2.50
176	Darryl Kile	.15
177	David Cone	.25
178	Mike Sweeney	.15
179	Royce Clayton	.15
180	Curt Schilling	.30
181	Barry Larkin	.40
182	Eric Milton	.15
183	Ellis Burks	.15
184	A.J. Hinch	.15
185	Garret Anderson	.15
186	Sean Bergman	.15
187	Shannon Stewart	.15
188	Bernard Gilkey	.15
189	Jeff Blauser	.15
190	Andruw Jones	.75
191	Omar Daal	.15
192	Jeff Kent	.15
193	Mark Kotsay	.15
194	Dave Burba	.15
195	Bobby Higginson	.15
196	Hideki Irabu	.30
197	Jamie Moyer	.15
198	Doug Glanville	.15
199	Quinton McCracken	.15
200	Ken Griffey Jr.	3.00
201	Mike Lieberthal	.15
202	Carl Everett	.15
203	Omar Vizquel	.15
204	Mike Lansing	.15
205	Manny Ramirez	1.50
206	Ryan Klesko	.25
207	Jeff Montgomery	.15
208	Chad Curtis	.15
209	Rick Helling	.15
210	Justin Thompson	.15
211	Tom Goodwin	.15
212	Todd Dunwoody	.15
213	Kevin Young	.15
214	Tony Saunders	.15
215	Gary Sheffield	.25
216	Jaret Wright	.15
217	Quilvio Veras	.15
218	Marty Cordova	.15
219	Tino Martinez	.40
220	Scott Rolen	.75
221	Fernando Tatis	.15
222	Damion Easley	.15
223	Aramis Ramirez	.15
224	Brad Radke	.15
225	Nomar Garciaparra	2.00
226	Magglio Ordonez	.15
227	Andy Pettitte	.40
228	David Ortiz	.15
229	Todd Jones	.15
230	Larry Walker	.50
231	Tim Wakefield	.15
232	Jose Guillen	.15
233	Gregg Olson	.15
234	Ricky Gutierrez	.15
235	Todd Walker	.25
236	Abraham Nunez	.15
237	Sean Casey	.40
238	Greg Norton	.15
239	Bret Saberhagen	.15
240	Bernie Williams	.50
241	Tim Salmon	.40
242	Jason Giambi	.15
243	Fernando Vina	.15
244	Darrin Fletcher	.15
245	Greg Vaughn	.30
246	Dennis Reyes	.15
247	Hideo Nomo	.25
248	Reggie Sanders	.15
249	Mike Hampton	.15
250	Kerry Wood	.75
251	Ismael Valdes	.15
252	Pat Hentgen	.15
253	Scott Spiezio	.15
254	Chuck Finley	.15
255	Troy Glaus	.15
256	Bobby Jones	.15
257	Wayne Gomes	.15
258	Rondell White	.25
259	Todd Zeile	.15
260	Matt Williams	.40
261	Henry Rodriguez	.25
262	Matt Stairs	.15
263	Jose Valentin	.15
264	David Justice	.40
265	Javy Lopez	.25
266	Matt Morris	.15
267	Steve Trachsel	.15
268	Edgar Martinez	.15
269	Al Martin	.15
270	Ivan Rodriguez	.75
271	Carlos Delgado	.40
272	Mark Grace	.30
273	Ugueth Urbina	.15
274	Jay Buhner	.30
275	Mike Piazza	2.00
276	Rick Aguilera	.15
277	Javier Valentin	.15
278	Brian Anderson	.15
279	Cliff Floyd	.15
280	Barry Bonds	.75
281	Troy O'Leary	.15
282	Seth Greisinger	.15
283	Mark Grudzielanek	.15
284	Jose Cruz Jr.	.50
285	Jeff Bagwell	.75
286	John Smoltz	.25
287	Jeff Cirillo	.15
288	Richie Sexson	.15
289	Charles Nagy	.15
290	Pedro Martinez	.50
291	Juan Encarnacion	.25
292	Phil Nevin	.15
293	Terry Steinbach	.15
294	Miguel Tejada	.25
295	Dan Wilson	.15
296	Chris Peters	.15
297	Brian Moehler	.15
298	Jason Christiansen	.15
299	Kelly Stinnett	.15
300	Dwight Gooden	.25
301	Randy Velarde	.15
302	Kirt Manwaring	.15
303	Jeff Abbott	.15
304	Dave Hollins	.15
305	Kerry Ligtenberg	.15
306	Aaron Boone	.15
307	Carlos Hernandez	.15
308	Mike DiFelice	.15
309	Brian Meadows	.15
310	Tim Bogar	.15
311	Greg Vaughn (Transaction)	1.00
312	Brant Brown (Transaction)	1.00
313	Steve Finley (Transaction)	1.00
314	Bret Boone (Transaction)	1.00
315	Albert Belle (Transaction)	2.50
316	Robin Ventura (Transaction)	1.00
317	Eric Davis (Transaction)	1.00
318	Todd Hundley (Transaction)	1.00
319	Jose Offerman (Transaction)	1.00
320	Kevin Brown (Transaction)	1.50
321	Denny Neagle (Transaction)	1.00
322	Brian Jordan (Transaction)	1.00
323	Brian Giles (Transaction)	1.00
324	Bobby Bonilla (Transaction)	1.00
325	Roberto Alomar (Transaction)	1.50
326	Ken Caminiti (Transaction)	1.25
327	Todd Stottlemyre (Transaction)	1.00
328	Randy Johnson (Transaction)	1.50
329	Luis Gonzalez (Transaction)	1.00
330	Rafael Palmeiro (Transaction)	1.50
331	Devon White (Transaction)	1.00
332	Will Clark (Transaction)	1.50
333	Dean Palmer (Transaction)	1.00
334	Gregg Jefferies (Transaction)	1.00
335	Mo Vaughn (Transaction)	2.50
336	*Brad Lidge* (Draft Pick)	4.00
337	*Chris George* (Draft Pick)	2.00
338	*Austin Kearns* (Draft Pick)	4.00
339	*Matt Belisle* (Draft Pick)	2.00
340	*Nate Cornejo* (Draft Pick)	3.00
341	*Matt Holiday* (Draft Pick)	3.00
342	*J.M. Gold* (Draft Pick)	3.00
343	*Matt Roney* (Draft Pick)	3.00
344	*Seth Etherton* (Draft Pick)	2.00
345	*Adam Everett* (Draft Pick)	4.00
346	Marlon Anderson (Future Star)	1.00
347	Ron Belliard (Future Star)	1.00

348	Fernando Seguignol (Future Star)	1.50
349	Michael Barrett (Future Star)	1.00
350	Dernell Stenson (Future Star)	2.00
351	Ryan Anderson (Future Star)	2.50
352	Ramon Hernandez (Future Star)	1.00
353	Jeremy Giambi (Future Star)	1.50
354	Ricky Ledee (Future Star)	1.00
355	Carlos Lee (Future Star)	1.50

1999 Stadium Club First Day Issue

A parallel of the 355-card set. Inserted exclusively in retail packs, series I (1-170) are serially numbered to 170 at a rate of 1:75 retail packs. Series II (171-355) are serially numbered to 200 and inserted at a rate of 1:60 packs.

	MT
Common Player:	5.00
Ser. I Stars:	30x to 40x
Ser. I RCs:	10x to 20x
Ser. II Stars:	20x to 30x
Yng Stars & RCs:	8x to 15x
Ser. I Production 170 sets R	
Ser. II Prod. 200 sets R	

1999 Stadium Club One of a Kind

This insert set parallels the 355-card base set. Cards feature a mirrorboard look and are serially numbered to 150. Inserted exclusively in hobby packs, insertion rate for series I is 1:53 and series II 1:48 packs.

	MT
Common Player:	8.00
Stars:	30x to 50x
Yng Stars & RCs:	15x to 30x
Production 150 sets H	

1999 Stadium Club Autographs - Retail

This 10-card autographed set was issued in series I and series II, with five players signing in each series. Available exclusively in retail chains, series I autographs were seeded 1:1,107 packs, while series II were inserted in every 877 packs. Each autograph is marked with Topps Certified Autograph Issue stamp.

	MT
Complete Set (10):	600.00
Complete Series I (5):	350.00
Complete Series II (5):	250.00
Common Player:	25.00
Inserted 1:1,107	
SCA1Alex Rodriguez	150.00
SCA2Chipper Jones	80.00
SCA3Barry Bonds	60.00
SCA4Tino Martinez	40.00
SCA5Ben Grieve	60.00
SCA6Juan Gonzalez	80.00
SCA7Vladimir Guerrero	60.00
SCA8Albert Belle	60.00
SCA9Kerry Wood	40.00
SCA10Todd Helton	40.00

1999 Stadium Club Chrome

This 40-card set was inserted in series I and II packs, with 1-20 in series I packs and 21-40 in series II. Chrome appropriately utilizes chromium technology. The insertion rate is 1:24 packs with Refractor parallel versions also seeded 1:96 packs.

	MT
Complete Set (40):	220.00
Complete Ser. I Set (20):	100.00
Complete Ser. II Set (20):	120.00
Common Player:	3.00
Inserted 1:24	
Refractors:	2x
Inserted 1:96	
SCC1Nomar Garciaparra	12.00
SCC2Kerry Wood	5.00
SCC3Jeff Bagwell	6.00
SCC4Ivan Rodriguez	5.00
SCC5Albert Belle	5.00
SCC6Gary Sheffield	3.00
SCC7Andruw Jones	5.00
SCC8Kevin Brown	3.00
SCC9David Cone	3.00
SCC10Darin Erstad	5.00
SCC11Manny Ramirez	6.00
SCC12Larry Walker	4.00
SCC13Mike Piazza	12.00
SCC14Ken Caminiti	3.00
SCC15Pedro Martinez	4.00
SCC16Greg Vaughn	3.00
SCC17Barry Bonds	5.00
SCC18Mo Vaughn	5.00
SCC19Bernie Williams	4.00
SCC20Ken Griffey Jr.	20.00
SCC21Alex Rodriguez	12.00
SCC22Chipper Jones	10.00
SCC23Ben Grieve	5.00
SCC24Frank Thomas	10.00
SCC25Derek Jeter	12.00
SCC26Sammy Sosa	12.00
SCC27Mark McGwire	25.00
SCC28Vladimir Guerrero	6.00
SCC29Greg Maddux	12.00
SCC30Juan Gonzalez	10.00
SCC31Troy Glaus	5.00
SCC32Adrian Beltre	4.00
SCC33Mitch Meluskey	3.00
SCC34Alex Gonzalez	3.00
SCC35George Lombard	4.00
SCC36Eric Chavez	4.00
SCC37Ruben Mateo	5.00
SCC38Calvin Pickering	3.00
SCC39Gabe Kapler	5.00
SCC40Bruce Chen	3.00

1999 Stadium Club Co-Signers

Co-Signers feature two autographs on each card and also for the first time includes one level of four autographs per card. Co-Signers are grouped into four categories: A, B, C and D. Group A Co-Signers are autographed by four players, while B-D are signed by two players. Insertion odds are as follows: Group D, 1:254; C (1:3,014); B (1:9,043) and A (1:45,213). Each card features Topps Certified Autograph Issue stamp.

	MT
Complete Set (42):	
Common Group A (4 autos.):	
Inserted 1:18,085	
Common Group B:	
Inserted 1:9043	
Common Group C:	
Inserted 1:3,014	
Common Group D:	30.00
Inserted 1:254	
CS1 Ben Grieve (D), Richie Sexson	50.00
CS2 Todd Helton (D), Troy Glaus	50.00
CS3 Alex Rodriguez, Scott Rolen	200.00
CS4 Derek Jeter, Chipper Jones	200.00
CS5 Cliff Floyd (D), Eli Marrero	30.00
CS6 Jay Buhner (D), Kevin Young	40.00
CS7 Ben Grieve (C), Troy Glaus	75.00
CS8 Todd Helton (C), Richie Sexson	60.00
CS9 Alex Rodriguez (C), Chipper Jones	250.00
CS10Derek Jeter (C), Scott Rolen	200.00
CS11Cliff Floyd (C), Kevin Young	30.00
CS12Jay Buhner (B), Eli Marrero	50.00
CS13Ben Grieve (B), Todd Helton	100.00
CS14Richie Sexson (B), Troy Glaus	100.00
CS15Alex Rodriguez (B), Derek Jeter	400.00
CS16Chipper Jones (B), Scott Rolen	300.00
CS17Cliff Floyd (B), Jay Buhner	50.00
CS18Eli Marrero (B), Kevin Young	30.00
CS19Ben Grieve (A), Todd Helton, Richie Sexson, Troy Glaus	N/A
CS20Alex Rodriguez (A), Derek Jeter, Chipper Jones, Scott Rolen	N/A
CS21Cliff Floyd (A), Jay Buhner, Eli Marrero, Kevin Young	N/A
CS22Edgardo Alfonzo, Jose Guillen	30.00
CS23Mike Lowell, Ricardo Rincon	30.00
CS24Juan Gonzalez, Vinny Castilla	100.00
CS25Moises Alou, Roger Clemens	75.00
CS26Scott Spezio, Tony Womack	30.00
CS27Fernando Vina, Quilvio Veras	30.00
CS28Edgardo Alfonzo, Ricardo Rincon	N/A
CS29Jose Guillen, Mike Lowell	N/A
CS30Juan Gonzalez, Moises Alou	N/A
CS31Roger Clemens, Vinny Castilla	N/A
CS32Scott Spezio, Fernando Vina	N/A
CS33Tony Womack, Quilvio Veras	N/A
CS34Edgardo Alfonzo, Mike Lowell	N/A
CS35Jose Guillen, Ricardo Rincon	N/A
CS36Juan Gonzalez, Roger Clemens	N/A
CS37Moises Alou, Vinny Castilla	N/A
CS38Scott Spezio, Quilvio Veras	N/A
CS39Tony Womack, Fernando Vina	N/A
CS40Edgardo Alfonzo (ft), Jose Guillen (ft), Mike Lowell (bk), Ricardo Rincon (bk)	N/A
CS41Juan Gonzalez (ft), Moises Alou (ft), Roger Clemens(bk), Vinny Castilla (bk)	N/A
CS42Scott Spezio (ft), Tony Womack (ft), Fernando Vina (bk), Quilvio Veras (bk)	N/A

1999 Stadium Club Never Compromise

Topps selected players who bring hard work and devotion to the field every game are highlighted, including Cal Ripken Jr. The first 10 cards in the set are inserted in series I packs while the remaining 10 are seeded in series II at a rate of 1:12 packs.

	MT
Complete Set (20):	95.00
Complete Ser. I Set (10):	60.00
Complete Ser. II Set (10):	35.00
Common Player:	2.00
Inserted 1:12	
NC1 Mark McGwire	15.00
NC2 Sammy Sosa	10.00
NC3 Ken Griffey Jr.	12.00
NC4 Greg Maddux	8.00
NC5 Barry Bonds	3.00
NC6 Alex Rodriguez	8.00
NC7 Darin Erstad	3.00
NC8 Roger Clemens	5.00
NC9 Nomar Garciaparra	8.00
NC10Derek Jeter	8.00
NC11Cal Ripken Jr.	10.00
NC12Mike Piazza	8.00
NC13Greg Vaughn	2.00
NC14Andres Galarraga	2.50
NC15Vinny Castilla	2.00
NC16Jeff Bagwell	3.00
NC17Chipper Jones	6.00
NC18Eric Chavez	3.00
NC19Orlando Hernandez	3.00
NC20Troy Glaus	4.00

1999 Stadium Club Triumvirate

Three of these inserts "fuse" together to form a set of three cards, forming a Triumvirate. 48 players, 24 from each series, are available in three different technologies, Luminous, Luminescent and Illuminator. The insert ratio is as follows: Luminous (1:36), Luminescent (1:144) and Illuminator (1:288).

	MT
Complete Set (48):	425.00
Complete Ser. I Set (24):	200.00
Comp. Ser. II Set (24):	225.00
Common Player:	4.00
Inserted 1:36	
Luminescents:	1.5x to 3x
Inserted 1:144	
Illuminators:	3x to 5x
Inserted 1:288	
T1A Greg Vaughn	4.00
T1B Ken Caminiti	4.00
T1C Tony Gwynn	15.00
T2A Andruw Jones	8.00
T2B Chipper Jones	15.00
T2C Andres Galarraga	6.00
T3A Jay Buhner	4.00
T3B Ken Griffey Jr.	30.00
T3C Alex Rodriguez	20.00
T4A Derek Jeter	20.00
T4B Tino Martinez	6.00
T4C Bernie Williams	6.00
T5A Brian Jordan	4.00
T5B Ray Lankford	4.00
T5C Mark McGwire	40.00
T6A Jeff Bagwell	8.00
T6B Craig Biggio	6.00
T6C Randy Johnson	6.00
T7A Nomar Garciaparra	20.00
T7B Pedro Martinez	6.00
T7C Mo Vaughn	8.00
T8A Mark Grace	5.00
T8B Sammy Sosa	20.00
T8C Kerry Wood	8.00
T9A Alex Rodriguez	20.00
T9B Nomar Garciaparra	20.00
T9C Derek Jeter	20.00
T10ATodd Helton	8.00
T10BTravis Lee	6.00
T10CPat Burrell	4.00
T11AGreg Maddux	20.00
T11BKerry Wood	8.00
T11CTom Glavine	4.00
T12AChipper Jones	15.00
T12BVinny Castilla	4.00
T12CScott Rolen	8.00
T13AJuan Gonzalez	15.00
T13BKen Griffey Jr.	30.00
T13CBen Grieve	8.00
T14ASammy Sosa	20.00
T14BVladimir Guerrero	10.00
T14CBarry Bonds	8.00
T15AFrank Thomas	15.00
T15BJim Thome	6.00
T15CTino Martinez	6.00
T16AMark McGwire	40.00
T16BAndres Galarraga	6.00
T16CJeff Bagwell	8.00

1999 Stadium Club Video Replay

Utilizing lenticular technology, these inserts capture highlights, such as McGwire's 70th home run, from the '98 season. By tilting the card, successive images show the selected highlight almost come to life. Video Replays are inserted in series II packs at a rate of 1:12.

	MT
Complete Set (5):	25.00
Common Player:	3.00
Inserted 1:12	
VR1 Mark McGwire	10.00
VR2 Sammy Sosa	5.00
VR3 Ken Griffey Jr.	8.00
VR4 Kerry Wood	3.00
VR5 Alex Rodriguez	5.00

1999 Topps

Released in two series, the 462-card set featured two home run record subsets, featuring McGwire and Sosa. McGwire's subset card #220 has 70 different versions, commemorating each of his home runs, including where it was hit, the pitcher, date and estimated distance. Sosa's subset card #461 has 66 different versions. Other subsets include World Series Highlights, Prospects, Draft Picks and Season Highlights. Each pack contains 11 cards with an S.R.P. of $1.29. MVP's are the only parallel, which feature a special Topps MVP logo. 100 cards of each player exist, if the player on the card is named Topps MVP for a week, collectors can win prizes.

		MT
Complete Set (462):		55.00
Complete Series 1 (241):		30.00
Complete Series II (221):		25.00
Common Player:		.10
MVP Stars:		50x to 80x
Yng Stars & RCs:		30x to 60x
Production 100 sets		
1	Roger Clemens	1.00
2	Andres Galarraga	.30
3	Scott Brosius	.10
4	John Flaherty	.10
5	Jim Leyritz	.10
6	Ray Durham	.10
7	not issued	.10
8	Joe Vizcaino	.10
9	Will Clark	.25
10	David Wells	.10
11	Jose Guillen	.20
12	Scott Hatteberg	.10
13	Edgardo Alfonzo	.10
14	Mike Bordick	.10
15	Manny Ramirez	.75
16	Greg Maddux	1.50
17	David Segui	.10
18	Darryl Strawberry	.10
19	Brad Radke	.10
20	Kerry Wood	.75
21	Matt Anderson	.10
22	Derrek Lee	.10
23	Mickey Morandini	.10
24	Paul Konerko	.20
25	Travis Lee	.50
26	Ken Hill	.10
27	Kenny Rogers	.10
28	Paul Sorrento	.10
29	Quilvio Veras	.10
30	Todd Walker	.20
31	Ryan Jackson	.10
32	John Olerud	.20
33	Doug Glanville	.10
34	Nolan Ryan	2.50
35	Ray Lankford	.10
36	Mark Loretta	.10
37	Jason Dickson	.10
38	Sean Bergman	.10
39	Quinton McCracken	.10
40	Bartolo Colon	.10
41	Brady Anderson	.10
42	Chris Stynes	.10
43	Jorge Posada	.10
44	Justin Thompson	.10
45	Johnny Damon	.10
46	Armando Benitez	.10
47	Brant Brown	.10
48	Charlie Hayes	.10
49	Darren Dreifort	.10
50	Juan Gonzalez	1.25
51	Chuck Knoblauch	.25
52	Todd Helton (Rookie All-Star)	.50
53	Rick Reed	.10
54	Chris Gomez	.10
55	Gary Sheffield	.25
56	Rod Beck	.10
57	Rey Sanchez	.10
58	Garret Anderson	.10
59	Jimmy Haynes	.10
60	Steve Woodard	.10
61	Rondell White	.20
62	Vladimir Guerrero	.75
63	Eric Karros	.20
64	Russ Davis	.10
65	Mo Vaughn	.60
66	Sammy Sosa	2.00
67	Troy Percival	.10
68	Kenny Lofton	.50
69	Bill Taylor	.10
70	Mark McGwire	3.00
71	Roger Cedeno	.10
72	Javy Lopez	.10
73	Damion Easley	.10
74	Andy Pettitte	.40
75	Tony Gwynn	1.25
76	Ricardo Rincon	.10
77	F.P. Santangelo	.10
78	Jay Bell	.10
79	Scott Servais	.10
80	Jose Canseco	.25
81	Roberto Hernandez	.10
82	Todd Dunwoody	.10
83	John Wetteland	.10
84	Mike Caruso (Rookie All-Star)	.10
85	Derek Jeter	1.50
86	Aaron Sele	.10
87	Jose Lima	.10
88	Ryan Christenson	.10
89	Jeff Cirillo	.10
90	Jose Hernandez	.10
91	Mark Kotsay (Rookie All-Star)	.20
92	Darren Bragg	.10
93	Albert Belle	.60
94	Matt Lawton	.10
95	Pedro Martinez	.50
96	Greg Vaughn	.20
97	Neifi Perez	.10
98	Gerald Williams	.10
99	Derek Bell	.10
100	Ken Griffey Jr.	2.50
101	David Cone	.20
102	Brian Johnson	.10
103	Dean Palmer	.10
104	Javier Valentin	.10
105	Trevor Hoffman	.10
106	Butch Huskey	.10
107	Dave Martinez	.10
108	Billy Wagner	.10
109	Shawn Green	.10
110	Ben Grieve (Rookie All-Star)	.60
111	Tom Goodwin	.10
112	Jaret Wright	.40
113	Aramis Ramirez	.25
114	Dmitri Young	.10
115	Hideki Irabu	.20
116	Roberto Kelly	.10
117	Jeff Fassero	.10
118	Mark Clark	.10
119	Jason McDonald	.10
120	Matt Williams	.25
121	Dave Burba	.10
122	Bret Saberhagen	.10
123	Deivi Cruz	.10
124	Chad Curtis	.10
125	Scott Rolen	.60
126	Lee Stevens	.10
127	J.T. Snow Jr.	.10
128	Rusty Greer	.10
129	Brian Meadows	.10
130	Jim Edmonds	.20
131	Ron Gant	.20
132	A.J. Hinch (Rookie All-Star)	.10
133	Shannon Stewart	.10
134	Brad Fullmer	.25
135	Cal Eldred	.10
136	Matt Walbeck	.10
137	Carl Everett	.10
138	Walt Weiss	.10
139	Fred McGriff	.20
140	Darin Erstad	.60
141	Dave Nilsson	.10
142	Eric Young	.10
143	Dan Wilson	.10
144	Jeff Reed	.10
145	Brett Tomko	.10
146	Terry Steinbach	.10
147	Seth Greisinger	.10
148	Pat Meares	.10
149	Livan Hernandez	.10
150	Jeff Bagwell	.75
151	Bob Wickman	.10
152	Omar Vizquel	.10
153	Eric Davis	.10
154	Larry Sutton	.10
155	Maggio Ordonez (Rookie All-Star)	.20
156	Eric Milton	.10
157	Darren Lewis	.10
158	Rick Aguilera	.10
159	Mike Lieberthal	.10
160	Robb Nen	.10
161	Brian Giles	.10
162	Jeff Brantley	.10
163	Gary DiSarcina	.10
164	John Valentin	.10
165	David Dellucci	.10
166	Chan Ho Park	.20
167	Masato Yoshii	.10
168	Jason Schmidt	.10
169	LaTroy Hawkins	.10
170	Bret Boone	.10
171	Jerry DiPoto	.10
172	Mariano Rivera	.20
173	Mike Cameron	.10
174	Scott Erickson	.10
175	Charles Johnson	.10
176	Bobby Jones	.10
177	Francisco Cordova	.10
178	Todd Jones	.10
179	Jeff Montgomery	.10
180	Mike Mussina	.50
181	Bob Abreu	.10
182	Ismael Valdes	.10
183	Andy Fox	.10
184	Woody Williams	.10
185	Denny Neagle	.10
186	Jose Valentin	.10
187	Darrin Fletcher	.10
188	Gabe Alvarez	.10
189	Eddie Taubensee	.10
190	Edgar Martinez	.10
191	Jason Kendall	.20
192	Darryl Kile	.10
193	Jeff King	.10
194	Rey Ordonez	.10
195	Andruw Jones	.60
196	Tony Fernandez	.10
197	Jamey Wright	.10
198	B.J. Surhoff	.10
199	Vinny Castilla	.10
200	David Wells (Season Highlight)	.10
201	Mark McGwire (Season Highlight)	1.50
202	Sammy Sosa (Season Highlight)	1.00
203	Roger Clemens (Season Highlight)	.50
204	Kerry Wood (Season Highlight)	.50
205	Lance Berkman, Mike Frank, Gabe Kapler (Prospects)	1.50
206	*Alex Escobar*, Ricky Ledee, Mike Stoner (Prospects)	1.50
207	*Peter Bergeron*, Jeremy Giambi, George Lombard (Prospects)	.50
208	Michael Barrett, Ben Davis, Robert Fick (Prospects)	.25
209	Pat Cline, Ramon Hernandez, Jayson Werth (Prospects)	.75
210	Bruce Chen, Chris Enochs, Ryan Anderson (Prospects)	1.50
211	Mike Lincoln, Octavio Dotel, Brad Penny (Prospects)	.20
212	Chuck Abbott, Brent Butler, Danny Klassen (Prospects)	.25
213	Chris Jones, *Jeff Urban* (Draft Pick)	.10
214	*Arturo McDowell*, *Tony Torcato* (Draft Pick)	.10
215	*Josh McKinley*, *Jason Tyner* (Draft Pick)	.50
216	*Matt Burch*, *Seth Etherton* (Draft Pick)	.40
217	*Mamon Tucker*, *Rick Elder* (Draft Pick)	.50
218	*J.M. Gold*, *Ryan Mills* (Draft Pick)	1.50
219	*Adam Brown*, *Choo Freeman* (Draft Pick)	.40
220	Mark McGwire #1 (Record Breaker)	30.00
	McGwire 2-60	15.00
	McGwire 63-69	25.00
	McGwire 61-62	35.00
	McGwire #70	90.00
221	Larry Walker (League Leader)	.25
222	Bernie Williams (League Leader)	.30
223	Mark McGwire (League Leader)	2.00
224	Ken Griffey Jr. (League Leader)	1.50
225	Sammy Sosa (League Leader)	1.00
226	Juan Gonzalez (League Leader)	.75
227	Dante Bichette (League Leader)	.25
228	Alex Rodriguez (League Leader)	.75
229	Sammy Sosa (League Leader)	1.00
230	Derek Jeter (League Leader)	.75
231	Greg Maddux (League Leader)	.75
232	Roger Clemens (League Leader)	.50
233	Ricky Ledee (World Series)	.10
234	Chuck Knoblauch (World Series)	.20
235	Bernie Williams (World Series)	.40
236	Tino Martinez (World Series)	.20
237	Orlando Hernandez (World Series)	1.00
238	Scott Brosius (World Series)	.10
239	Andy Pettitte (World Series)	.25
240	Mariano Rivera (World Series)	.20
241	Checklist	.10
242	Checklist	.10
243	Tom Glavine	.25
244	Andy Benes	.10
245	Sandy Alomar	.20
246	Wilton Guerrero	.10
247	Alex Gonzalez	.10
248	Roberto Alomar	.40
249	Ruben Rivera	.10
250	Eric Chavez	.60
251	Ellis Burks	.10
252	Richie Sexson	.25
253	Steve Finley	.10
254	Dwight Gooden	.10
255	Dustin Hermanson	.10
256	Kirk Rueter	.10
257	Steve Trachsel	.10
258	Gregg Jefferies	.10
259	Matt Stairs	.10
260	Shane Reynolds	.10
261	Gregg Olson	.10
262	Kevin Tapani	.10
263	Matt Morris	.10
264	Carl Pavano	.10
265	Nomar Garciaparra	1.50
266	Kevin Young	.10
267	Rick Helling	.10
268	Mark Leiter	.10
269	Brian McRae	.10
270	Cal Ripken Jr.	2.00
271	Jeff Abbott	.10
272	Tony Batista	.10
273	Bill Simas	.10
274	Brian Hunter	.10
275	John Franco	.10
276	Devon White	.10
277	Rickey Henderson	.20
278	Chuck Finley	.10
279	Mike Blowers	.10
280	Mark Grace	.25
281	Randy Winn	.10
282	Bobby Bonilla	.20
283	David Justice	.25
284	Shane Monahan	.10
285	Kevin Brown	.25
286	Todd Zeile	.10
287	Al Martin	.10
288	Troy O'Leary	.10
289	Darryl Hamilton	.10
290	Tino Martinez	.40
291	David Ortiz	.10
292	Tony Clark	.40
293	Ryan Minor	.25
294	Reggie Sanders	.10
295	Wally Joyner	.10
296	Cliff Floyd	.10
297	Shawn Estes	.10
298	Pat Hentgen	.10
299	Scott Elarton	.10
300	Alex Rodriguez	1.50
301	Ozzie Guillen	.10
302	Manny Martinez	.10
303	Ryan McGuire	.10
304	Brad Ausmus	.10
305	Alex Gonzalez	.10
306	Brian Jordan	.10
307	John Jaha	.10
308	Mark Grudzielanek	.10
309	Juan Guzman	.10
310	Tony Womack	.10
311	Dennis Reyes	.10
312	Marty Cordova	.10
313	Ramiro Mendoza	.10
314	Robin Ventura	.10
315	Rafael Palmeiro	.25
316	Ramon Martinez	.10
317	John Mabry	.10
318	Dave Hollins	.10
319	Tom Candiotti	.10
320	Al Leiter	.10
321	Rico Brogna	.10
322	Jimmy Key	.10
323	Bernard Gilkey	.10
324	Jason Giambi	.10
325	Craig Biggio	.25
326	Troy Glaus	.75
327	Delino DeShields	.10
328	Fernando Vina	.10
329	John Smoltz	.20
330	Jeff Kent	.10
331	Roy Halladay	.25
332	Andy Ashby	.10
333	Tim Wakefield	.10
334	Tim Belcher	.10
335	Bernie Williams	.50
336	Desi Relaford	.10
337	John Burkett	.10
338	Mike Hampton	.10
339	Royce Clayton	.10
340	Mike Piazza	1.50
341	Jeremi Gonzalez	.10
342	Mike Lansing	.10
343	Jamie Moyer	.10
344	Ron Coomer	.10
345	Barry Larkin	.25
346	Fernando Tatis	.10
347	Chili Davis	.10
348	Bobby Higginson	.10
349	Hal Morris	.10
350	Larry Walker	.40
351	Carlos Guillen	.10
352	Miguel Tejada	.10
353	Travis Fryman	.10
354	Jarrod Washburn	.10
355	Chipper Jones	1.25
356	Todd Stottlemyre	.20
357	Henry Rodriguez	.10
358	Eli Marrero	.10
359	Alan Benes	.10
360	Tim Salmon	.25
361	Luis Gonzalez	.10
362	Scott Spiezio	.10
363	Chris Carpenter	.10
364	Bobby Howry	.10
365	Raul Mondesi	.25
366	Ugueth Urbina	.10
367	Tom Evans	.10
368	Kerry Ligtenberg	.25
369	Adrian Beltre	.40
370	Ryan Klesko	.25
371	Wilson Alvarez	.10
372	John Thomson	.10
373	Tony Saunders	.10
374	Mike Stanley	.10
375	Ken Caminiti	.20
376	Jay Buhner	.20
377	Bill Mueller	.10
378	Jeff Blauser	.10
379	Edgar Renteria	.10
380	Jim Thome	.40
381	Joey Hamilton	.10
382	Calvin Pickering	.20
383	Marquis Grissom	.10
384	Omar Daal	.10
385	Curt Schilling	.20
386	Jose Cruz Jr.	.50
387	Chris Widger	.10
388	Pete Harnisch	.10
389	Charles Nagy	.10
390	Tom Gordon	.10
391	Bobby Smith	.10
392	Derrick Gibson	.10
393	Jeff Conine	.10
394	Carlos Perez	.10
395	Barry Bonds	.60
396	Mark McLemore	.10
397	Juan Encarnacion	.20
398	Wade Boggs	.25
399	Ivan Rodriguez	.60
400	Moises Alou	.25
401	Jeromy Burnitz	.10
402	Sean Casey	.20
403	Jose Offerman	.10
404	Joe Fontenot	.10
405	Kevin Millwood	.20
406	Lance Johnson	.10
407	Richard Hidalgo	.10
408	Mike Jackson	.10
409	Brian Anderson	.10
410	Jeff Shaw	.10
411	Preston Wilson	.10
412	Todd Hundley	.10
413	Jim Parque	.10
414	Justin Baughman	.10
415	Dante Bichette	.30
416	Paul O'Neill	.30
417	Miguel Cairo	.10
418	Randy Johnson	.50
419	Jesus Sanchez	.10
420	Carlos Delgado	.30
421	Ricky Ledee	.25
422	Orlando Hernandez	.75
423	Frank Thomas	1.25
424	Pokey Reese	.10
425	Carlos Lee, Mike Lowell, *Kit Pellow* (Prospect)	.50
426	Michael Cuddyer, Mark DeRosa, Jerry Hairston (Prospect)	.10
427	Marlon Anderson, Ron Belliard, Orlando Cabrera (Prospect)	.10
428	*Micah Bowie, Phil Norton*, Randy Wolf (Prospect)	.25
429	Jack Cressend, Jason Rakers, John Rocker (Prospect)	.20
430	Ruben Mateo, Scott Morgan, *Mike Zywica* (Prospect)	.40
431	Jason LaRue, Matt LeCroy, Mitch Meluskey (Prospect)	.10
432	Gabe Kapler, Armando Rios, Fernando Seguignol (Prospect)	1.00
433	Adam Kennedy, *Mickey Lopez*, Jackie Rexrode (Prospect)	.25
434	*Jose Fernandez*, Jeff Liefer, Chris Truby (Prospect)	.25
435	Corey Koskie, Doug Mientkiewicz, Damon Minor (Prospect)	.40
436	*Roosevelt Brown*, Dernell Stenson, Vernon Wells (Prospect)	.40

437	*A.J. Burnett,* John Nicholson, Billy Koch (Prospect)	1.00
438	*Matt Belisle, Matt Roney* (Draft Pick)	.50
439	*Austin Kearns,* Chris George (Draft Pick)	.50
440	Nate Bump, *Nate Cornejo* (Draft Pick)	.50
441	*Brad Lidge,Mike Nannini* (Draft Pick)	.50
442	*Matt Holiday,Jeff Winchester* (Draft Pick)	.50
443	*Adam Everett, Chip Ambres* (Draft Pick)	.50
444	*Pat Burrell, Eric Valent* (Draft Pick)	2.50
445	Roger Clemens (Strikeout Kings)	.50
446	Kerry Wood (Strikeout Kings)	.20
447	Curt Schilling (Strikeout Kings)	.10
448	Randy Johnson (Strikeout Kings)	.10
449	Pedro Martinez (Strikeout Kings)	.20
450	Jeff Bagwell, Andres Galarraga, Mark McGwire (All-Topps)	1.00
451	John Olerud, Jim Thome, Tino Martinez (All-Topps)	.20
452	Alex Rodriguez, Nomar Garciaparra, Derek Jeter (All-Topps)	.40
453	Vinny Castilla, Chipper Jones, Scott Rolen (All-Topps)	.25
454	Sammy Sosa, Ken Griffey Jr., Juan Gonzalez (All-Topps)	.75
455	Barry Bonds, Manny Ramirez, Larry Walker (All-Topps)	.40
456	Frank Thomas, Tim Salmon, David Justice (All-Topps)	.40
457	Travis Lee, Todd Helton, Ben Grieve (All-Topps)	.20
458	Vladimir Guerrero, Greg Vaughn, Bernie Williams (All-Topps)	.25
459	Mike Piazza, Ivan Rodriguez, Jason Kendall (All-Topps)	.40
460	Roger Clemens, Kerry Wood, Greg Maddux (All-Topps)	.25
461	Sammy Sosa #1	15.00
461	Sosa 2-60	8.00
461	Sosa 61-62	25.00
461	Sosa #63-65	10.00
461	Sosa #66	40.00
462	Checklist	.10
463	Checklist	.10

1999 Topps All-Matrix

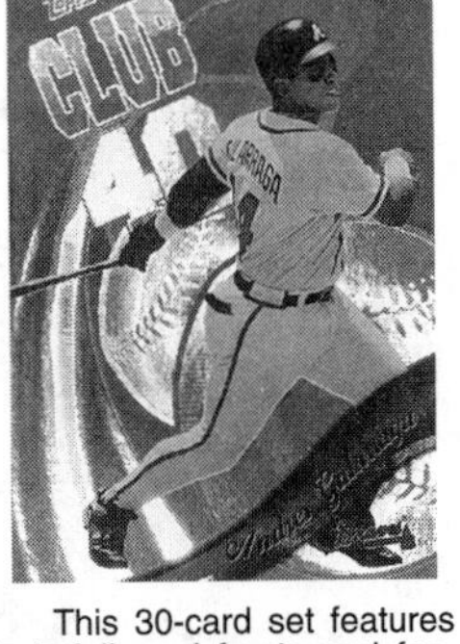

This 30-card set features holo-foil card fronts and features the top stars in the game. Each card is numbered with an "AM" prefix on card backs and are seeded 1:18 packs.

		MT
Complete Set (30):		100.00
Common Player:		2.00
Inserted 1:18		
AM1	Mark McGwire	20.00
AM2	Sammy Sosa	10.00
AM3	Ken Griffey Jr.	15.00
AM4	Greg Vaughn	2.00
AM5	Albert Belle	4.00
AM6	Vinny Castilla	2.00
AM7	Jose Canseco	3.00
AM8	Juan Gonzalez	8.00
AM9	Manny Ramirez	5.00
AM10	Andres Galarraga	3.00
AM11	Rafael Palmeiro	2.50
AM12	Alex Rodriguez	10.00
AM13	Mo Vaughn	4.00
AM14	Eric Chavez	4.00
AM15	Gabe Kapler	4.00
AM16	Calvin Pickering	2.00
AM17	Ruben Mateo	4.00
AM18	Roy Halladay	2.00
AM19	Jeremy Giambi	2.00
AM20	Alex Gonzalez	2.00
AM21	Ron Belliard	2.00
AM22	Marlon Anderson	2.00
AM23	Carlos Lee	2.00
AM24	Kerry Wood	4.00
AM25	Roger Clemens	6.00
AM26	Curt Schilling	2.00
AM27	Kevin Brown	3.00
AM28	Randy Johnson	3.00
AM29	Pedro Martinez	3.00
AM30	Orlando Hernandez	4.00

1999 Topps All-Topps Mystery Finest

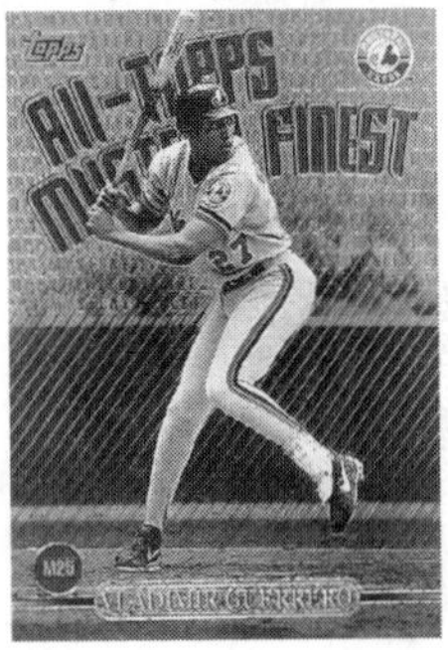

This 33-card set features a black opaque covering that collectors peel off to reveal the player. Each card is numbered with an "M" prefix and inserted 1:36 packs. A parallel Refractor version is also randomly seeded and inserted 1:144 packs.

		MT
Complete Set (33):		325.00
Common Player:		4.00
Inserted 1:36		
Refractors:		1.5x to 2x
Inserted 1:144		
M1	Jeff Bagwell	8.00
M2	Andres Galarraga	6.00
M3	Mark McGwire	40.00
M4	John Olerud	4.00
M5	Jim Thome	6.00
M6	Tino Martinez	6.00
M7	Alex Rodriguez	20.00
M8	Nomar Garciaparra	20.00
M9	Derek Jeter	20.00
M10	Vinny Castilla	4.00
M11	Chipper Jones	15.00
M12	Scott Rolen	8.00
M13	Sammy Sosa	20.00
M14	Ken Griffey Jr.	30.00
M15	Juan Gonzalez	15.00
M16	Barry Bonds	8.00
M17	Manny Ramirez	10.00
M18	Larry Walker	6.00
M19	Frank Thomas	15.00
M20	Tim Salmon	6.00
M21	David Justice	5.00
M22	Travis Lee	6.00
M23	Todd Helton	6.00
M24	Ben Grieve	8.00
M25	Bernie Williams	6.00
M26	Greg Vaughn	4.00
M27	Vladimir Guerrero	10.00
M28	Mike Piazza	20.00
M29	Ivan Rodriguez	8.00
M30	Jason Kendall	4.00
M31	Roger Clemens	12.00
M32	Kerry Wood	6.00
M33	Greg Maddux	20.00

1999 Topps Autographs

Autographs were inserted exclusively in hobby packs in both Topps series I and II. Each series had eight cards with each one carrying the Topps Certified Autograph Issue stamp. Series I Autographs were seeded 1:532 packs while Series II were found 1:501 packs.

		MT
Complete Set (16):		900.00
Complete Series I (8):		500.00
Complete Series II (8):		400.00
Common Player:		25.00
Ser. I Inserted 1:532 H		
Ser. II Inserted 1:501 H		
A1	Roger Clemens	120.00
A2	Chipper Jones	80.00
A3	Scott Rolen	50.00
A4	Alex Rodriguez	150.00
A5	Andres Galarraga	35.00
A6	Rondell White	25.00
A7	Ben Grieve	70.00
A8	Troy Glaus	50.00
A9	Moises Alou	25.00
A10	Barry Bonds	75.00
A11	Vladimir Guerrero	60.00
A12	Andruw Jones	55.00
A13	Darin Erstad	50.00
A14	Shawn Green	25.00
A15	Eric Chavez	50.00
A16	Pat Burrell	100.00

1999 Topps Hall of Fame

Found exclusively in hobby packs, Hall of Fame Collection is a ten-card set featured on cards that silhouette their images against their respective Hall of Fame plaques. Featured players include Yogi Berra, Reggie Jackson and Ernie Banks among others. These were seeded 1:12 packs.

		MT
Complete Set (10):		20.00
Common Player:		1.00
Inserted 1:12 H		
HOF1	Mike Schmidt	4.00
HOF2	Brooks Robinson	2.50
HOF3	Stan Musial	3.00
HOF4	Willie McCovey	1.00
HOF5	Eddie Mathews	2.00
HOF6	Reggie Jackson	4.00
HOF7	Ernie Banks	3.00
HOF8	Whitey Ford	1.00
HOF9	Bob Feller	1.00
HOF10	Yogi Berra	3.00

1999 Topps Lords of the Diamond

Inserted in every 18 packs this 15-card set features the top players in the game including Barry Bonds and Ken Griffey Jr. Card fronts include a holographic look with die-cutting across the top of the card on a silver background.

		MT
Complete Set (15):		60.00
Common Player:		1.00
Inserted 1:18		
LD1	Ken Griffey Jr.	10.00
LD2	Chipper Jones	5.00
LD3	Sammy Sosa	8.00
LD4	Frank Thomas	6.00
LD5	Mark McGwire	12.00
LD6	Jeff Bagwell	2.50
LD7	Alex Rodriguez	6.00
LD8	Juan Gonzalez	5.00
LD9	Barry Bonds	2.50
LD10	Nomar Garciaparra	6.00
LD11	Darin Erstad	2.50
LD12	Tony Gwynn	5.00
LD13	Andres Galarraga	1.00
LD14	Mike Piazza	6.00
LD15	Greg Maddux	6.00

1999 Topps New Breed

The next generation of stars are featured in this 15-card set that showcases the young talent on a silver foil card. These are seeded 1:18 packs.

		MT
Complete Set (15):		35.00
Common Player:		.50
Inserted 1:18		
NB1	Darin Erstad	2.50
NB2	Brad Fullmer	1.00
NB3	Kerry Wood	2.00
NB4	Nomar Garciaparra	6.00
NB5	Travis Lee	2.00
NB6	Scott Rolen	2.50
NB7	Todd Helton	1.00
NB8	Vladimir Guerrero	3.00
NB9	Derek Jeter	6.00
NB10	Alex Rodriguez	6.00
NB11	Ben Grieve	2.50
NB12	Andruw Jones	2.50
NB13	Paul Konerko	.50
NB14	Aramis Ramirez	.50
NB15	Adrian Beltre	.75

1999 Topps Nolan Ryan Reprints

Topps reprinted all 27 of Nolan Ryan's basic Topps cards, with 14 odd numbers appearing in Series I and the remaining 13 even cards inserted into Series II packs. Each card is stamped with a gold Topps commemorative stamp on the front for identification. Reprints were seeded in every 18 packs. Nolan Ryan also autographed a number of the reprints for both series. Series I Ryan autographs are seeded 1:4,260 with Series II autographs found 1:5,007 packs. Ryan autographs were inserted exclusively in hobby packs.

		MT
Complete Set (27):		150.00
Common Ryan:		6.00
Inserted 1:18		
Nolan Ryan Autograph:		300.00
1	Nolan Ryan (1968)	15.00
2	Nolan Ryan (1969)	10.00
3	Nolan Ryan (1970)	6.00
4	Nolan Ryan (1971)	6.00
5	Nolan Ryan (1972)	6.00
6	Nolan Ryan (1973)	6.00
7	Nolan Ryan (1974)	6.00
8	Nolan Ryan (1975)	6.00
9	Nolan Ryan (1976)	6.00
10	Nolan Ryan (1977)	6.00
11	Nolan Ryan (1978)	6.00
12	Nolan Ryan (1979)	6.00
13	Nolan Ryan (1980)	6.00
14	Nolan Ryan (1981)	6.00
15	Nolan Ryan (1982)	6.00
16	Nolan Ryan (1983)	6.00
17	Nolan Ryan (1984)	6.00
18	Nolan Ryan (1985)	6.00
19	Nolan Ryan (1986)	6.00
20	Nolan Ryan (1987)	6.00
21	Nolan Ryan (1988)	6.00
22	Nolan Ryan (1989)	6.00
23	Nolan Ryan (1990)	6.00
24	Nolan Ryan (1991)	6.00
25	Nolan Ryan (1992)	6.00
26	Nolan Ryan (1993)	6.00
27	Nolan Ryan (1994)	6.00

1999 Topps Nolan Ryan Finest Reprints

This 27-card set reprinted all 27 of Ryan's basic Topps cards. Odd numbers were distributed in Series I packs, with even numbers distributed in Series II packs. These are seeded 1:72 packs in both series I and II packs.

		MT
Complete Set (27):		250.00
Common Ryan:		12.00
Inserted 1:72		
Refractors:		2x to 3x
Inserted 1:288		
1	1968	20.00
2	1969	12.00
3	1970	12.00
4	1971	12.00
5	1972	12.00
6	1973	12.00
7	1974	12.00
8	1975	12.00
9	1976	12.00
10	1977	12.00
11	1978	12.00
12	1979	12.00
13	1980	12.00

14	1981	12.00
15	1982	12.00
16	1983	12.00
17	1984	12.00
18	1985	12.00
19	1986	12.00
20	1987	12.00
21	1988	12.00
22	1989	12.00
23	1990	12.00
24	1991	12.00
25	1992	12.00
26	1992	12.00
27	1992	12.00

1999 Topps Picture Perfect

This 10-card set features a full bleed photo of baseball's biggest stars, including Derek Jeter and Ken Griffey Jr. These are found one per eight packs.

	MT
Complete Set (10):	20.00
Common Player:	.50
Inserted 1:8	
P1 Ken Griffey Jr.	4.00
P2 Kerry Wood	1.00
P3 Pedro Martinez	1.00
P4 Mark McGwire	5.00
P5 Greg Maddux	2.50
P6 Sammy Sosa	3.00
P7 Greg Vaughn	.50
P8 Juan Gonzalez	2.00
P9 Jeff Bagwell	1.50
P10 Derek Jeter	2.50

1999 Topps Power Brokers

This 20-card set features baseball's biggest superstars including McGwire, Sosa and Chipper Jones. The cards are die-cut at the top and printed on Finest technology. Power Brokers are inserted in every 36 packs. A Refractor parallel version also exists, which are seeded 1:144 packs.

	MT
Complete Set (20):	180.00
Common Player:	2.00
Inserted 1:36	
Refractors:	2x to 3x
Inserted 1:144	
PB1 Mark McGwire	30.00
PB2 Andres Galarraga	3.00
PB3 Ken Griffey Jr.	25.00
PB4 Sammy Sosa	20.00
PB5 Juan Gonzalez	12.00
PB6 Alex Rodriguez	15.00
PB7 Frank Thomas	15.00
PB8 Jeff Bagwell	6.00
PB9 Vinny Castilla	2.00
PB10Mike Piazza	15.00
PB11Greg Vaughn	2.00
PB12Barry Bonds	6.00
PB13Mo Vaughn	6.00
PB14Jim Thome	4.00
PB15Larry Walker	3.00
PB16Chipper Jones	12.00
PB17Nomar Garciaparra	15.00
PB18Manny Ramirez	6.00
PB19Roger Clemens	10.00
PB20Kerry Wood	6.00

1999 Topps Record Numbers

This 10-card set highlights achievements from the game's current stars, including Nomar Garciaparra's 30 game hitting streak, the longest by a rookie in major league history. These inserts are randomly seeded 1:8 packs, each card is numbered on the back with an "RN" prefix.

	MT
Complete Set (10):	20.00
Common Player:	.75
Inserted 1:8	
RN1 Mark McGwire	5.00
RN2 Mike Piazza	2.50
RN3 Curt Schilling	.50
RN4 Ken Griffey Jr.	4.00
RN5 Sammy Sosa	3.00
RN6 Alex Rodriguez	3.00
RN7 Kerry Wood	1.00
RN8 Roger Clemens	1.50
RN9 Cal Ripken Jr.	3.00
RN10Mark McGwire	5.00

1999 Topps Record Numbers Gold

This is a parallel of the Record Numbers insert set, each card features the appropriate sequential numbering based on the featured players' highlighted record. Each card is numbered with an "RN" prefix on the card backs.

	MT
Complete Set (10):	1200.
Common Player:	8.00
RN1 Mark McGwire (70)	250.00
RN2 Mike Piazza (362)	40.00
RN3 Curt Schilling (319)	8.00
RN4 Ken Griffey Jr. (350)	60.00
RN5 Sammy Sosa (20)	350.00
RN6 Nomar Garciaparra (30)	300.00
RN7 Kerry Wood (20)	100.00
RN8 Roger Clemens (20)	250.00
RN9 Cal Ripken Jr. (2,632)	25.00
RN10Mark McGwire (162)	125.00

1999 Topps Chrome

The 462-card base set is a chromium parallel version of Topps baseball. Included are the Mark McGwire #220 and Sammy Sosa #461 home run subset cards, which commemorate each of their home runs. Each pack contains four cards with an S.R.P. of $3.00 per pack.

		MT
Complete Set (461):		280.00
Comp. Ser. I set (242):		160.00
Comp. Ser. II set (221):		125.00
Common Player:		.40
Star Refractors:		8x to 15x
Yng Stars & RCs:		3x to 8x
McGwire Refractors #220		4x to 6x
Sosa Refractors #461		4x to 6x
Inserted 1:12		
1	Roger Clemens	4.00
2	Andres Galarraga	1.50
3	Scott Brosius	.40
4	John Flaherty	.40
5	Jim Leyritz	.40
6	Ray Durham	.40
7	not issued	.40
8	Joe Vizcaino	.40
9	Will Clark	.75
10	David Wells	.40
11	Jose Guillen	.60
12	Scott Hatteberg	.40
13	Edgardo Alfonzo	.40
14	Mike Bordick	.40
15	Manny Ramirez	2.50
16	Greg Maddux	5.00
17	David Segui	.40
18	Darryl Strawberry	.75
19	Brad Radke	.40
20	Kerry Wood	2.00
21	Matt Anderson	.40
22	Derrek Lee	.40
23	Mickey Morandini	.40
24	Paul Konerko	.60
25	Travis Lee	1.50
26	Ken Hill	.40
27	Kenny Rogers	.40
28	Paul Sorrento	.40
29	Quilvio Veras	.40
30	Todd Walker	.75
31	Ryan Jackson	.40
32	John Olerud	.75
33	Doug Glanville	.40
34	Nolan Ryan	8.00
35	Ray Lankford	.40
36	Mark Loretta	.40
37	Jason Dickson	.40
38	Sean Bergman	.40
39	Quinton McCracken	.40
40	Bartolo Colon	.40
41	Brady Anderson	.40
42	Chris Stynes	.40
43	Jorge Posada	.60
44	Justin Thompson	.40
45	Johnny Damon	.40
46	Armando Benitez	.40
47	Brant Brown	.40
48	Charlie Hayes	.40
49	Darren Dreifort	.40
50	Juan Gonzalez	4.00
51	Chuck Knoblauch	.75
52	Todd Helton (Rookie All-Star)	2.00
53	Rick Reed	.40
54	Chris Gomez	.40
55	Gary Sheffield	.75
56	Rod Beck	.40
57	Rey Sanchez	.40
58	Garret Anderson	.40
59	Jimmy Haynes	.40
60	Steve Woodard	.40
61	Rondell White	.60
62	Vladimir Guerrero	3.00
63	Eric Karros	.60
64	Russ Davis	.40
65	Mo Vaughn	2.00
66	Sammy Sosa	6.00
67	Troy Percival	.40
68	Kenny Lofton	2.00
69	Bill Taylor	.40
70	Mark McGwire	10.00
71	Roger Cedeno	.40
72	Javy Lopez	.60
73	Damion Easley	.40
74	Andy Pettitte	1.00
75	Tony Gwynn	4.00
76	Ricardo Rincon	.40
77	F.P. Santangelo	.40
78	Jay Bell	.40
79	Scott Servais	.40
80	Jose Canseco	.75
81	Roberto Hernandez	.40
82	Todd Dunwoody	.40
83	John Wetteland	.40
84	Mike Caruso (Rookie All-Star)	.40
85	Derek Jeter	5.00
86	Aaron Sele	.40
87	Jose Lima	.40
88	Ryan Christenson	.40
89	Jeff Cirillo	.40
90	Jose Hernandez	.40
91	Mark Kotsay (Rookie All-Star)	.60
92	Darren Bragg	.40
93	Albert Belle	2.00
94	Matt Lawton	.40
95	Pedro Martinez	1.50
96	Greg Vaughn	.60
97	Neifi Perez	.40
98	Gerald Williams	.40
99	Derek Bell	.40
100	Ken Griffey Jr.	8.00
101	David Cone	.60
102	Brian Johnson	.40
103	Dean Palmer	.40
104	Javier Valentin	.40
105	Trevor Hoffman	.40
106	Butch Huskey	.40
107	Dave Martinez	.40
108	Billy Wagner	.40
109	Shawn Green	.40
110	Ben Grieve (Rookie All-Star)	2.00
111	Tom Goodwin	.40
112	Jaret Wright	1.00
113	Aramis Ramirez	.75
114	Dmitri Young	.40
115	Hideki Irabu	.50
116	Roberto Kelly	.40
117	Jeff Fassero	.40
118	Mark Clark	.40
119	Jason McDonald	.40
120	Matt Williams	.75
121	Dave Burba	.40
122	Bret Saberhagen	.40
123	Deivi Cruz	.40
124	Chad Curtis	.40
125	Scott Rolen	2.00
126	Lee Stevens	.40
127	J.T. Snow Jr.	.40
128	Rusty Greer	.40
129	Brian Meadows	.40
130	Jim Edmonds	.60
131	Ron Gant	.60
132	A.J. Hinch Rookie All-Star)	.40
133	Shannon Stewart	.40
134	Brad Fullmer	.60
135	Cal Eldred	.40
136	Matt Walbeck	.40
137	Carl Everett	.40
138	Walt Weiss	.40
139	Fred McGriff	.60
140	Darin Erstad	2.00
141	Dave Nilsson	.40
142	Eric Young	.40
143	Dan Wilson	.40
144	Jeff Reed	.40
145	Brett Tomko	.40
146	Terry Steinbach	.40
147	Seth Greisinger	.40
148	Pat Meares	.40
149	Livan Hernandez	.40
150	Jeff Bagwell	2.50
151	Bob Wickman	.40
152	Omar Vizquel	.40
153	Eric Davis	.40
154	Larry Sutton	.40
155	Magglio Ordonez (Rookie All-Star)	.75
156	Eric Milton	.40
157	Darren Lewis	.40
158	Rick Aguilera	.40
159	Mike Lieberthal	.40
160	Robb Nen	.40
161	Brian Giles	.40
162	Jeff Brantley	.40
163	Gary DiSarcina	.40
164	John Valentin	.40
165	David Dellucci	.40
166	Chan Ho Park	.60
167	Masato Yoshii	.40
168	Jason Schmidt	.40
169	LaTroy Hawkins	.40
170	Bret Boone	.40
171	Jerry DiPoto	.40
172	Mariano Rivera	.60
173	Mike Cameron	.40
174	Scott Erickson	.40
175	Charles Johnson	.40
176	Bobby Jones	.40
177	Francisco Cordova	.40
178	Todd Jones	.40
179	Jeff Montgomery	.40
180	Mike Mussina	1.50
181	Bob Abreu	.40
182	Ismael Valdes	.40
183	Andy Fox	.40
184	Woody Williams	.40
185	Denny Neagle	.40
186	Jose Valentin	.40
187	Darrin Fletcher	.40
188	Gabe Alvarez	.40
189	Eddie Taubensee	.40
190	Edgar Martinez	.40
191	Jason Kendall	.60
192	Darryl Kile	.40
193	Jeff King	.40
194	Rey Ordonez	.40
195	Andruw Jones	2.00
196	Tony Fernandez	.40
197	Jamey Wright	.40
198	B.J. Surhoff	.40
199	Vinny Castilla	.40
200	David Wells (Season Highlight)	.40
201	Mark McGwire (Season Highlight)	5.00
202	Sammy Sosa (Season Highlight)	3.00
203	Roger Clemens (Season Highlight)	1.50
204	Kerry Wood (Season Highlight)	1.00
205	Lance Berkman, Mike Frank, Gabe Kapler (Prospects)	4.00
206	*Alex Escobar*, Ricky Ledee, Mike Stoner (Prospects)	4.00
207	*Peter Bergeron*, Jeremy Giambi, George Lombard (Prospects)	5.00
208	Michael Barrett, Ben Davis, Robert Fick (Prospects)	1.00
209	Pat Cline, Ramon Hernandez, Jayson Werth (Prospects)	1.00
210	Bruce Chen, Chris Enochs, Ryan Anderson (Prospects)	3.00
211	Mike Lincoln, Octavio Dotel, Brad Penny (Prospects)	1.00
212	Chuck Abbott, Brent Butler, Danny Klassen (Prospects)	1.00
213	Chris Jones, *Jeff Urban* (Draft Pick)	1.50
214	*Arturo McDowell, Tony Torcato* (Draft Pick)	1.50
215	*Josh McKinley ,Jason Tyner* (Draft Pick)	1.50
216	*Matt Burch ,Seth Etherton* (Draft Pick)	2.00
217	*Mamon Tucker, Rick Elder* (Draft Pick)	5.00
218	*J.M. Gold, Ryan Mills* (Draft Pick)	10.00
219	*Adam Brown, Choo Freeman* (Draft Pick)	1.50
220	Mark McGwire (Record Breaker)	50.00
220	Mark McGwire #1	100.00
220	McGwire #25 & #50	75.00
220	McGwire #61	125.00
220	McGwire #62	150.00
220	McGwire #70	250.00
221	Larry Walker (League Leader)	.75
222	Bernie Williams (League Leader)	1.00
223	Mark McGwire (League Leader)	6.00
224	Ken Griffey Jr. (League Leader)	5.00
225	Sammy Sosa (League Leader)	4.00
226	Juan Gonzalez (League Leader)	2.50
227	Dante Bichette (League Leader)	.75
228	Alex Rodriguez (League Leader)	3.00
229	Sammy Sosa (League Leader)	4.00
230	Derek Jeter (League Leader)	3.00
231	Greg Maddux (League Leader)	3.00
232	Roger Clemens (League Leader)	2.00
233	Ricky Ledee (World Series)	1.00
234	Chuck Knoblauch (World Series)	.75
235	Bernie Williams (World Series)	1.00
236	Tino Martinez (World Series)	.75
237	Orlando Hernandez (World Series)	2.00
238	Scott Brosius (World Series)	.40
239	Andy Pettitte (World Series)	.75
240	Mariano Rivera (World Series)	.60
241	Checklist	.40
242	Checklist	.40
243	Tom Glavine	.60
244	Andy Benes	.40
245	Sandy Alomar	.60
246	Wilton Guerrero	.40

247	Alex Gonzalez	.40
248	Roberto Alomar	1.50
249	Ruben Rivera	.40
250	Eric Chavez	.40
251	Ellis Burks	.40
252	Richie Sexson	.75
253	Steve Finley	.40
254	Dwight Gooden	.60
255	Dustin Hermanson	.40
256	Kirk Rueter	.40
257	Steve Trachsel	.40
258	Gregg Jefferies	.40
259	Matt Stairs	.40
260	Shane Reynolds	.40
261	Gregg Olson	.40
262	Kevin Tapani	.40
263	Matt Morris	.40
264	Carl Pavano	.40
265	Nomar Garciaparra	5.00
266	Kevin Young	.40
267	Rick Helling	.40
268	Matt Franco	.40
269	Brian McRae	.40
270	Cal Ripken Jr.	6.00
271	Jeff Abbott	.40
272	Tony Batista	.40
273	Bill Simas	.40
274	Brian Hunter	.40
275	John Franco	.40
276	Devon White	.40
277	Rickey Henderson	.60
278	Chuck Finley	.40
279	Mike Blowers	.40
280	Mark Grace	.75
281	Randy Winn	.40
282	Bobby Bonilla	.60
283	David Justice	1.00
284	Shane Monahan	.40
285	Kevin Brown	.75
286	Todd Zeile	.40
287	Al Martin	.40
288	Troy O'Leary	.40
289	Darryl Hamilton	.40
290	Tino Martinez	1.00
291	David Ortiz	.40
292	Tony Clark	1.50
293	Ryan Minor	.60
294	Reggie Sanders	.40
295	Wally Joyner	.40
296	Cliff Floyd	.40
297	Shawn Estes	.40
298	Pat Hentgen	.40
299	Scott Elarton	.40
300	Alex Rodriguez	5.00
301	Ozzie Guillen	.40
302	Hideo Martinez	.40
303	Ryan McGuire	.40
304	Brad Ausmus	.40
305	Alex Gonzalez	.40
306	Brian Jordan	.40
307	John Jaha	.40
308	Mark Grudzielanek	.40
309	Juan Guzman	.40
310	Tony Womack	.40
311	Dennis Reyes	.40
312	Marty Cordova	.40
313	Ramiro Mendoza	.40
314	Robin Ventura	.40
315	Rafael Palmeiro	1.00
316	Ramon Martinez	.40
317	Pedro Astacio	.40
318	Dave Hollins	.40
319	Tom Candiotti	.40
320	Al Leiter	.60
321	Rico Brogna	.40
322	Reggie Jefferson	.40
323	Bernard Gilkey	.40
324	Jason Giambi	.40
325	Craig Biggio	1.00
326	Troy Glaus	3.00
327	Delino DeShields	.40
328	Fernando Vina	.40
329	John Smoltz	.75
330	Jeff Kent	.40
331	Roy Halladay	1.00
332	Andy Ashby	.40
333	Tim Wakefield	.40
334	Roger Clemens	4.00
335	Bernie Williams	1.50
336	Desi Relaford	.40
337	John Burkett	.40
338	Mike Hampton	.40
339	Royce Clayton	.40
340	Mike Piazza	5.00
341	Jeremi Gonzalez	.40
342	Mike Lansing	.40
343	Jamie Moyer	.40
344	Ron Coomer	.40
345	Barry Larkin	.75
346	Fernando Tatis	.75
347	Chili Davis	.40
348	Bobby Higginson	.40
349	Hal Morris	.40
350	Larry Walker	1.50
351	Carlos Guillen	.40
352	Miguel Tejada	.60
353	Travis Fryman	.60
354	Jarrod Washburn	.40
355	Chipper Jones	4.00
356	Todd Stottlemyre	.60
357	Henry Rodriguez	.40
358	Eli Marrero	.40
359	Alan Benes	.40
360	Tim Salmon	1.00
361	Luis Gonzalez	.40
362	Scott Spiezio	.40
363	Chris Carpenter	.40
364	Bobby Howry	.40
365	Raul Mondesi	1.00
366	Ugueth Urbina	.40
367	Tom Evans	.40
368	Kerry Ligtenberg	1.00
369	Adrian Beltre	1.50
370	Ryan Klesko	.75
371	Wilson Alvarez	.40
372	John Thomson	.40
373	Tony Saunders	.40
374	Mike Stanley	.40
375	Ken Caminiti	.75
376	Jay Buhner	.75
377	Bill Mueller	.40
378	Jeff Blauser	.40
379	Edgar Renteria	.40
380	Jim Thome	1.50
381	Joey Hamilton	.40
382	Calvin Pickering	.40
383	Marquis Grissom	.40
384	Omar Daal	.40
385	Curt Schilling	.75
386	Jose Cruz Jr.	1.50
387	Chris Widger	.40
388	Pete Harnisch	.40
389	Charles Nagy	.40
390	Tom Gordon	.40
391	Bobby Smith	.40
392	Derrick Gibson	.40
393	Jeff Conine	.40
394	Carlos Perez	.40
395	Barry Bonds	2.00
396	Mark McLemore	.40
397	Juan Encarnacion	.75
398	Wade Boggs	1.00
399	Ivan Rodriguez	2.00
400	Moises Alou	1.00
401	Jeromy Burnitz	.40
402	Sean Casey	.75
403	Jose Offerman	.40
404	Joe Fontenot	.40
405	Kevin Millwood	.75
406	Lance Johnson	.40
407	Richard Hidalgo	.40
408	Mike Jackson	.40
409	Brian Anderson	.40
410	Jeff Shaw	.40
411	Preston Wilson	.40
412	Todd Hundley	.40
413	Jim Parque	.40
414	Justin Baughman	.40
415	Dante Bichette	1.00
416	Paul O'Neill	1.00
417	Miguel Cairo	.40
418	Randy Johnson	1.50
419	Jesus Sanchez	.40
420	Carlos Delgado	1.00
421	Ricky Ledee	.75
422	Orlando Hernandez	2.00
423	Frank Thomas	4.00
424	Pokey Reese	.40
425	Carlos Lee, Mike Lowell, *Kit Pellow* (Prospect)	4.00
426	Michael Cuddyer, Mark DeRosa, *Jerry Hairston Jr.* (Prospect)	1.50
427	Marlon Anderson, Ron Belliard, Orlando Cabrera (Prospect)	1.50
428	*Micah Bowie, Phil Norton,* Randy Wolf (Prospect)	2.50
429	Jack Cressend, Jason Rakers, John Rocker (Prospect)	2.00
430	Ruben Mateo, Scott Morgan, *Mike Zywica* (Prospect)	6.00
431	Jason LaRue, Matt LeCroy, *Mitch Meluskey* (Prospect)	2.00
432	Gabe Kapler, *Armando Rios,* Fernando Seguignol (Prospect)	8.00
433	Adam Kennedy, *Mickey Lopez,* Jackie Rexrode (Prospect)	2.00
434	*Jose Fernandez,* Jeff Liefer, Chris Truby (Prospect)	2.00
435	Corey Koskie, *Doug Mientkiewicz,* Damon Minor (Prospect)	2.50
436	*Roosevelt Brown,* Dernell Stenson, Vernon Wells (Prospect)	3.00
437	*A.J. Burnett,* John Nicholson, Billy Koch (Prospect)	8.00
438	*Matt Belisle, Matt Roney* (Draft Pick)	4.00
439	*Austin Kearns, Chris George* (Draft Pick)	4.00
440	*Nate Bump, Nate Cornejo* (Draft Pick)	4.00
441	*Brad Lidge, Mike Nannini* (Draft Pick)	4.00
442	*Matt Holliday, Jeff Winchester* (Draft Pick)	5.00
443	*Adam Everett, Chip Ambres* (Draft Pick)	3.00
444	*Pat Burrell, Eric Valent* (Draft Pick)	20.00
445	Roger Clemens (Strikeout Kings)	1.50
446	Kerry Wood (Strikeout Kings)	.75
447	Curt Schilling (Strikeout Kings)	.40
448	Randy Johnson (Strikeout Kings)	.75
449	Pedro Martinez (Strikeout Kings)	.75
450	Jeff Bagwell, Andres Galarraga, Mark McGwire (All-Topps)	4.00
451	John Olerud, Jim Thome, Tino Martinez (All-Topps)	.40
452	Alex Rodriguez, Nomar Garciaparra, Derek Jeter (All-Topps)	2.50
453	Vinny Castilla, Chipper Jones, Scott Rolen (All-Topps)	2.00
454	Sammy Sosa, Ken Griffey Jr., Juan Gonzalez (All-Topps)	4.00
455	Barry Bonds, Manny Ramirez, Larry Walker (All-Topps)	1.50
456	Frank Thomas, Tim Salmon, David Justice (All-Topps)	1.50
457	Travis Lee, Todd Helton, Ben Grieve (All-Topps)	.75
458	Vladimir Guerrero, Greg Vaughn, Bernie Williams (All-Topps)	1.00
459	Mike Piazza, Ivan Rodriguez, Jason Kendall (All-Topps)	2.00
460	Roger Clemens, Kerry Wood, Greg Maddux (All-Topps)	1.00
461	Sammy Sosa #1 (Home Run Parade)	40.00
461	Sammy Sosa #2-60	20.00
461	S. Sosa #61-62	60.00
461	S. Sosa #63-65	25.00
461	S. Sosa #66	100.00
---	Checklist 1-100	.40
---	Checklist - inserts	.40

1999 Topps Chrome All-Etch

Inserted in Series II packs, All-Etch has three different levels of inserts, all printed on All-Etch technology. The three levels include '99 Rookie Rush which features rookies who have the best shot of winning '99 Rookie of the Year. Club 40 features 13 players who hit 40 homers or more from the '98 season and Club K features seven pitchers who are known for their strikeout abilities including Roger Clemens and Pedro Martinez. Each of these three levels are inserted 1:6 packs while the Refractor versions are all seeded 1:24 packs.

		MT
Complete Set (30):		60.00
Common Player:		1.00
Inserted 1:6		
Refractors:		2x
Inserted 1:24		
1	Mark McGwire	12.00
2	Sammy Sosa	6.00
3	Ken Griffey Jr.	10.00
4	Greg Vaughn	1.00
5	Albert Belle	2.50
6	Vinny Castilla	1.00
7	Jose Canseco	2.00
8	Juan Gonzalez	5.00
9	Manny Ramirez	3.00
10	Andres Galarraga	1.50
11	Rafael Palmeiro	1.50
12	Alex Rodriguez	6.00
13	Mo Vaughn	2.50
14	Eric Chavez	2.50
15	Gabe Kapler	3.00
16	Calvin Pickering	1.00
17	Ruben Mateo	2.50
18	Roy Halladay	1.50
19	Jeremy Giambi	1.50
20	Alex Gonzalez	1.00
21	Ron Belliard	1.00
22	Marlon Anderson	1.00
23	Carlos Lee	2.00
24	Kerry Wood	2.50
25	Roger Clemens	4.00
26	Curt Schilling	1.00
27	Kevin Brown	1.50
28	Randy Johnson	2.00
29	Pedro Martinez	2.00
30	Orlando Hernandez	2.50

1999 Topps Chrome Early Road to the Hall

This insert set spotlights 10 players with less than 10 years in the Majors but are gunning towards their respective spots in Cooperstown, New York. Utilizing Chromium technology, featured players include Alex Rodriguez and Derek Jeter, with an insert rate of 1:12 packs.

		MT
Complete Set (10):		75.00
Common Player:		3.00
Inserted 1:12		
ER1	Nomar Garciaparra	12.00
ER2	Derek Jeter	12.00
ER3	Alex Rodriguez	12.00
ER4	Juan Gonzalez	10.00
ER5	Ken Griffey Jr.	20.00
ER6	Chipper Jones	10.00
ER7	Vladimir Guerrero	6.00
ER8	Jeff Bagwell	6.00
ER9	Ivan Rodriguez	5.00
ER10	Frank Thomas	12.00

1999 Topps Chrome Early Road to the Hall Refractors

A parallel version of Early Road to the Hall inserts, these are limited to 100 serially numbered sets, utilizing Refractor technology. The insertion rate is 1:944 packs.

		MT
Complete Set (10):		1200.
Common Player:		3.00
Production 100 sets		
ER1	Nomar Garciaparra	200.00
ER2	Derek Jeter	150.00
ER3	Alex Rodriguez	200.00
ER4	Juan Gonzalez	150.00
ER5	Ken Griffey Jr.	300.00
ER6	Chipper Jones	150.00
ER7	Vladimir Guerrero	100.00
ER8	Jeff Bagwell	100.00
ER9	Ivan Rodriguez	75.00
ER10	Frank Thomas	200.00

1999 Topps Chrome Fortune 15

Fortune 15 showcases the baseball's best players such as Alex Rodriguez and Mike Piazza. Hot young rookies are also featured as well for their early dominance. These are inserted in Series II packs at a rate of 1:12 packs, a Refractor version also exists found exclusively in hobby packs at a rate of 1:627 packs. Refractors are sequentially numbered to 100.

		MT
Complete Set (15):		100.00
Common Player:		2.50
Inserted 1:12		
Refractors:		25x to 40x
Production 100 sets H		
1	Alex Rodriguez	10.00
2	Nomar Garciaparra	10.00
3	Derek Jeter	10.00
4	Troy Glaus	5.00
5	Ken Griffey Jr.	15.00
6	Vladimir Guerrero	5.00
7	Kerry Wood	4.00
8	Eric Chavez	4.00
9	Greg Maddux	10.00
10	Mike Piazza	10.00
11	Sammy Sosa	10.00
12	Mark McGwire	20.00
13	Ben Grieve	4.00
14	Chipper Jones	8.00
15	Manny Ramirez	5.00

1999 Topps Chrome Lords of the Diamond

Parallel to the Topps version, the 15-card set features die-cutting across the card top and are seeded 1:8 in series I packs. Refractor versions can be found 1:24 packs.

		MT
Complete Set (15):		60.00
Common Player:		1.00
Inserted 1:8		
Refractors:		2x
Inserted 1:24		
LD1	Ken Griffey Jr.	10.00
LD2	Chipper Jones	5.00

LD3 Sammy Sosa	8.00
LD4 Frank Thomas	6.00
LD5 Mark McGwire	12.00
LD6 Jeff Bagwell	2.50
LD7 Alex Rodriguez	6.00
LD8 Juan Gonzalez	5.00
LD9 Barry Bonds	2.50
LD10 Nomar Garciaparra	6.00
LD11 Darin Erstad	2.50
LD12 Tony Gwynn	5.00
LD13 Andres Galarraga	1.00
LD14 Mike Piazza	6.00
LD15 Greg Maddux	6.00

1999 Topps Chrome New Breed

A parallel version of Topps New Breed utilizing Chromium technology. The 15-card set features the top young stars in the game and are seeded 1:24 packs. A Refractor version also exists which is found 1:72 packs.

	MT
Complete Set (15):	35.00
Common Player:	.50
Inserted 1:24	
Refractors:	2x
Inserted 1:72	
NB1 Darin Erstad	2.50
NB2 Brad Fullmer	1.00
NB3 Kerry Wood	2.50
NB4 Nomar Garciaparra	6.00
NB5 Travis Lee	2.00
NB6 Scott Rolen	2.50
NB7 Todd Helton	1.00
NB8 Vladimir Guerrero	3.00
NB9 Derek Jeter	6.00
NB10 Alex Rodriguez	6.00
NB11 Ben Grieve	2.50
NB12 Andruw Jones	2.50
NB13 Paul Konerko	.50
NB14 Aramis Ramirez	.50
NB15 Adrian Beltre	.75

1999 Topps Chrome Record Numbers

This 10-card insert set salutes 10 record-setters who have earned a mark of distinction, including Cal Ripken Jr. for his record setting consecutive game streak. Inserted randomly in series II packs at a rate of 1:36 packs. Refractor parallel versions are seeded 1:144 packs.

	MT
Complete Set (10):	160.00
Common Player:	4.00
Inserted 1:36	
Refractors:	2x
Inserted 1:144	
1 Mark McGwire	35.00
2 Craig Biggio	4.00
3 Barry Bonds	8.00
4 Ken Griffey Jr.	30.00
5 Sammy Sosa	20.00
6 Alex Rodriguez	20.00
7 Kerry Wood	8.00
8 Roger Clemens	12.00
9 Cal Ripken Jr.	25.00
10 Mark McGwire	35.00

1999 Topps Gallery

This 150-card base set features a white textured border surrounding the player image with the player's name, team name and Topps Gallery logo stamped with gold foil. The first 100 cards in the set portray veteran players while the next 50 cards are broken down into three subsets: Masters, Artisans and Apprentices. Card backs have a monthly batting or pitching record from the '98 season, one player photo and vital information.

	MT
Complete Set (150):	120.00
Common Player (1-100):	.20
Common Player (101-150):	.50
Player's Private Issue:	20x to 30x
Priv Issue SP's:	15x to 25x
1 Mark McGwire	5.00
2 Jim Thome	.75
3 Bernie Williams	.75
4 Larry Walker	.75
5 Juan Gonzalez	2.50
6 Ken Griffey Jr.	5.00
7 Raul Mondesi	.50
8 Sammy Sosa	3.00
9 Greg Maddux	2.50
10 Jeff Bagwell	1.25
11 Vladimir Guerrero	1.50
12 Scott Rolen	1.25
13 Nomar Garciaparra	3.00
14 Mike Piazza	3.00
15 Travis Lee	.75
16 Carlos Delgado	.40
17 Darin Erstad	1.00
18 David Justice	.50
19 Cal Ripken Jr.	4.00
20 Derek Jeter	3.00
21 Tony Clark	.50
22 Barry Larkin	.40
23 Greg Vaughn	.40
24 Jeff Kent	.20
25 Wade Boggs	.40
26 Andres Galarraga	.50
27 Ken Caminiti	.20
28 Jason Kendall	.20
29 Todd Helton	.50
30 Chuck Knoblauch	.50
31 Roger Clemens	1.50
32 Jeromy Burnitz	.20
33 Javy Lopez	.20
34 Roberto Alomar	.75
35 Eric Karros	.20
36 Ben Grieve	1.25
37 Eric Davis	.20
38 Rondell White	.40
39 Dmitri Young	.20
40 Ivan Rodriguez	1.25
41 Paul O'Neill	.50
42 Jeff Cirillo	.20
43 Kerry Wood	1.00
44 Albert Belle	1.25
45 Frank Thomas	2.50
46 Manny Ramirez	2.00
47 Tom Glavine	.40
48 Mo Vaughn	1.25
49 Jose Cruz Jr.	.40
50 Sandy Alomar	.20
51 Edgar Martinez	.20
52 John Olerud	.40
53 Todd Walker	.40
54 Tim Salmon	.40
55 Derek Bell	.20
56 Matt Williams	.50
57 Alex Rodriguez	3.00
58 Rusty Greer	.20
59 Vinny Castilla	.40
60 Jason Giambi	.20
61 Mark Grace	.40
62 Jose Canseco	1.00
63 Gary Sheffield	.40
64 Brad Fullmer	.20
65 Trevor Hoffman	.20
66 Mark Kotsay	.20
67 Mike Mussina	.75
68 Johnny Damon	.20
69 Tino Martinez	.75
70 Curt Schilling	.40
71 Jay Buhner	.40
72 Kenny Lofton	1.00
73 Randy Johnson	1.00
74 Kevin Brown	.50
75 Brian Jordan	.20
76 Craig Biggio	.75
77 Barry Bonds	1.25
78 Tony Gwynn	2.50
79 Jim Edmonds	.20
80 Shawn Green	.20
81 Todd Hundley	.20
82 Cliff Floyd	.20
83 Jose Guillen	.20
84 Dante Bichette	.40
85 Moises Alou	.40
86 Chipper Jones	3.00
87 Ray Lankford	.20
88 Fred McGriff	.40
89 Rod Beck	.20
90 Dean Palmer	.20
91 Pedro Martinez	1.00
92 Andruw Jones	.75
93 Robin Ventura	.20
94 Ugueth Urbina	.20
95 Orlando Hernandez	1.50
96 Sean Casey	.50
97 Denny Neagle	.20
98 Troy Glaus	1.50
99 John Smoltz	.20
100 Al Leiter	.20
101 Ken Griffey Jr.	6.00
102 Frank Thomas	3.00
103 Mark McGwire	6.00
104 Sammy Sosa	4.00
105 Chipper Jones	4.00
106 Alex Rodriguez	4.00
107 Nomar Garciaparra	4.00
108 Juan Gonzalez	3.00
109 Derek Jeter	4.00
110 Mike Piazza	4.00
111 Barry Bonds	1.50
112 Tony Gwynn	3.00
113 Cal Ripken Jr.	5.00
114 Greg Maddux	4.00
115 Roger Clemens	2.00
116 Brad Fullmer	.50
117 Kerry Wood	1.50
118 Ben Grieve	1.50
119 Todd Helton	.75
120 Kevin Millwood	.50
121 Sean Casey	.75
122 Vladimir Guerrero	2.00
123 Travis Lee	1.00
124 Troy Glaus	2.00
125 Bartolo Colon	.50
126 Andruw Jones	1.00
127 Scott Rolen	1.50
128 *Alfonso Soriano*	10.00
129 *Nick Johnson*	6.00
130 *Matt Belisle*	1.00
131 *Jorge Toca*	3.00
132 *Masao Kida*	.50
133 *Carlos Pena*	4.00
134 Adrian Beltre	1.00
135 Eric Chavez	1.00
136 Carlos Beltran	1.50
137 Alex Gonzalez	.50
138 Ryan Anderson	1.00
139 Ruben Mateo	2.00
140 Bruce Chen	.50
141 *Pat Burrell*	10.00
142 Michael Barrett	.75
143 Carlos Lee	.75
144 *Mark Mulder*	4.00
145 Choo Freeman	1.50
146 Gabe Kapler	2.00
147 Juan Encarnacion	.50
148 Jeremy Giambi	.75
149 *Jason Tyner*	1.50
150 George Lombard	.50

1999 Topps Gallery Autograph Cards

Three of baseball's top young third baseman are featured in this autographed set, Eric Chavez, Troy Glaus and Adrian Beltre. The insertion odds are 1:209.

	MT
Complete Set (3):	150.00
Common Player:	40.00
Inserted 1:209	
GA1 Troy Glaus	75.00
GA2 Adrian Beltre	40.00
GA3 Eric Chavez	60.00

1999 Topps Gallery Awards Gallery

This 10-card set features players who have earned the highest honors in baseball. Each insert commemorates the player's award by stamping his achievement on the bottom of the card front. Card fronts have silver borders surrounding the player's image. These are seeded 1:12 and card numbers have an "AG" prefix.

	MT
Complete Set (10):	60.00
Common Player:	2.00
Inserted 1:12	
AG1 Kerry Wood	4.00
AG2 Ben Grieve	4.00
AG3 Roger Clemens	5.00
AG4 Tom Glavine	2.00
AG5 Juan Gonzalez	8.00
AG6 Sammy Sosa	10.00
AG7 Ken Griffey Jr.	15.00
AG8 Mark McGwire	15.00
AG9 Bernie Williams	3.00
AG10 Larry Walker	3.00

1999 Topps Gallery Exhibitions

This 20-card set is done on textured 24-point stock and features baseball's top stars. Exhibitions are seeded 1:48 packs.

	MT
Complete Set (20):	500.00
Common Player:	6.00
Inserted 1:48	
E1 Sammy Sosa	40.00
E2 Mark McGwire	60.00
E3 Greg Maddux	30.00
E4 Roger Clemens	20.00
E5 Ben Grieve	15.00
E6 Kerry Wood	15.00
E7 Ken Griffey Jr.	60.00
E8 Tony Gwynn	30.00
E9 Cal Ripken Jr.	50.00
E10 Frank Thomas	30.00
E11 Jeff Bagwell	15.00
E12 Derek Jeter	40.00
E13 Alex Rodriguez	40.00
E14 Nomar Garciaparra	40.00
E15 Manny Ramirez	18.00
E16 Vladimir Guerrero	20.00
E17 Darin Erstad	12.00
E18 Scott Rolen	15.00
E19 Mike Piazza	40.00
E20 Andres Galarraga	8.00

1999 Topps Gallery Gallery of Heroes

This 10-card set is done on card stock that simulates medieval stained glass. Gallery of Heroes are found 1:24 packs.

	MT
Complete Set (10):	120.00
Common Player:	3.00
Inserted 1:24	
GH1 Mark McGwire	25.00
GH2 Sammy Sosa	15.00
GH3 Ken Griffey Jr.	25.00
GH4 Mike Piazza	15.00
GH5 Derek Jeter	15.00
GH6 Nomar Garciaparra	15.00
GH7 Kerry Wood	6.00
GH8 Ben Grieve	6.00
GH9 Chipper Jones	12.00
GH10 Alex Rodriguez	15.00

1999 Topps Gallery 1953 Heritage

19 contemporary legends and Hall-of-Famer Hank Aaron are artistically depicted using the 1953 Topps design as a template. For a chance to bid on the original art used in the development of this insert set, collectors were able to enter the Topps Gallery Auction. Collectors could accumulate auction points found in Topps Gallery packs. Heritage's are seeded 1:12 packs. A parallel called Heritage Proofs are also randomly inserted 1:48 packs and have a chrome styrene finish.

	MT
Complete Set (20):	250.00
Common Player:	2.00
Inserted 1:12	
Heritage Proofs:	2x
Inserted 1:48	
TH1 Hank Aaron	15.00
TH2 Ben Grieve	6.00
TH3 Nomar Garciaparra	20.00
TH4 Roger Clemens	10.00
TH5 Travis Lee	5.00
TH6 Tony Gwynn	15.00
TH7 Alex Rodriguez	20.00
TH8 Ken Griffey Jr.	30.00
TH9 Derek Jeter	20.00
TH10 Sammy Sosa	20.00
TH11 Scott Rolen	6.00
TH12 Chipper Jones	15.00
TH13 Cal Ripken Jr.	25.00
TH14 Kerry Wood	6.00
TH15 Barry Bonds	6.00
TH16 Juan Gonzalez	15.00
TH17 Mike Piazza	20.00
TH18 Greg Maddux	15.00
TH19 Frank Thomas	12.00
TH20 Mark McGwire	35.00

1999 Topps Gallery 1953 Heritage Lithographs

Eight of the paintings used to create the Heritage inserts for 1999 Topps Gallery were reproduced as enlarged limited-edition offset lithographs. The paintings of Bill Purdom and James Fiorentino were reproduced in an 18" x 25" serially-numbered, artist-signed edition of 600 pieces each. The lithos were offered through Bill Goff Inc / Good Sports at $60 each unframed.

		MT
Complete Set (8):		480.00
Single Player:		60.00
1	Roger Clemens	60.00
2	Nomar Garciaparra	60.00
3	Ken Griffey Jr.	60.00
4	Derek Jeter	60.00
5	Mark McGwire	60.00
6	Mike Piazza	60.00
7	Cal Ripken Jr.	60.00
8	Sammy Sosa	60.00

1999 Topps Gold Label

This set consists of 100 cards on 35-point spectral-reflective rainbow stock with gold foil stamping. All cards are available in three versions each with the same foreground photo, but with different background photos that vary by category: Variation 1 (fielding), Variation 2 (running, 1:2), Variation 3 (hitting, 1:4), In addition each variation will have a different version of each player's team logo in the background. Variations for pitchers are #1 set position, #2 wind-up and #3 throwing. A One to One parallel version also exists and is limited to one numbered card for each variation and groupings (Gold, Black and Red) for a total of 900 cards.

		MT
Complete Set (100):		100.00
Common Player:		.50
Variation 2:		1x to 2x
Inserted 1:2		
Variation 3:		1.5x to 2x
Inserted 1:4		
1	Mike Piazza	6.00
2	Andres Galarraga	1.50
3	Mark Grace	.75
4	Tony Clark	1.00
5	Jim Thome	1.50
6	Tony Gwynn	5.00
7	*Kelly Dransfeldt*	1.00
8	Eric Chavez	2.50
9	Brian Jordan	.50
10	Todd Hundley	.50
11	Rondell White	.75
12	Dmitri Young	.50
13	Jeff Kent	.50
14	Derek Bell	.50
15	Todd Helton	1.50
16	Chipper Jones	5.00
17	Albert Belle	2.50
18	Barry Larkin	.75
19	Dante Bichette	.75
20	Gary Sheffield	.75
21	Cliff Floyd	.50
22	Derek Jeter	6.00
23	Jason Giambi	.50
24	Ray Lankford	.50
25	Alex Rodriguez	6.00
26	Ruben Mateo	1.50
27	Wade Boggs	1.00
28	Carlos Delgado	.75
29	Tim Salmon	.75
30	*Alfonso Soriano*	10.00
31	Javy Lopez	.50
32	Jason Kendall	.75
33	*Nick Johnson*	8.00
34	*A.J. Burnett*	1.50
35	Troy Glaus	3.00
36	*Pat Burrell*	15.00
37	Jeff Cirillo	.50
38	David Justice	1.00
39	Ivan Rodriguez	2.50
40	Bernie Williams	2.00
41	Jay Buhner	.75
42	Mo Vaughn	2.50
43	Randy Johnson	2.00
44	Pedro Martinez	2.00
45	Larry Walker	1.50
46	Todd Walker	.75
47	Roberto Alomar	2.00
48	Kevin Brown	.75
49	Mike Mussina	2.00
50	Tom Glavine	.75
51	Curt Schilling	.75
52	Ken Caminiti	.50
53	Brad Fullmer	.50
54	*Bobby Seay*	1.50
55	Orlando Hernandez	2.50
56	Sean Casey	.75
57	Al Leiter	.50
58	Sandy Alomar	.50
59	Mark Kotsay	.50
60	Matt Williams	.75
61	Raul Mondesi	.75
62	*Joe Crede*	1.00
63	Jim Edmonds	.50
64	Jose Cruz Jr.	1.00
65	Juan Gonzalez	5.00
66	Sammy Sosa	6.00
67	Cal Ripken Jr.	8.00
68	Vinny Castilla	.75
69	Craig Biggio	1.50
70	Mark McGwire	10.00
71	Greg Vaughn	.75
72	Greg Maddux	5.00
73	Paul O'Neill	.75
74	Scott Rolen	2.50
75	Ben Grieve	2.50
76	Vladimir Guerrero	3.00
77	John Olerud	.75
78	Eric Karros	.50
79	Jeromy Burnitz	.50
80	Jeff Bagwell	2.50
81	Kenny Lofton	2.00
82	Manny Ramirez	3.00
83	Andruw Jones	1.50
84	Travis Lee	2.00
85	Darin Erstad	2.00
86	Nomar Garciaparra	6.00
87	Frank Thomas	5.00
88	Moises Alou	.75
89	Tino Martinez	1.00
90	*Carlos Pena*	6.00
91	Shawn Green	.50
92	Rusty Greer	.50
93	*Matt Belisle*	1.00
94	Adrian Beltre	1.00
95	Roger Clemens	3.00
96	John Smoltz	.75
97	*Mark Mulder*	3.00
98	Kerry Wood	2.00
99	Barry Bonds	2.50
100	Ken Griffey Jr.	10.00

1999 Topps Gold Label Black

Blacks are a parallel of the 100-card base set and are identical besides the black foil stamping and their insertion ratio. Variation #1 is seeded 1:8 packs, #2 1:16 and #3 1:32.

	MT
Variation 1:	2x to 3x
Inserted 1:8	
Variation 2:	3x to 4x
Inserted 1:16	
Variation 3:	5x to 8x
Inserted 1:32	

1999 Topps Gold Label Red

A parallel to the 100-card base set these inserts can be idenified by their red foil stamping and sequential numbering. Variation #1 are numbered to 100, #2 numbered to 50 and #3 numbered to 25.

	MT
Variation 1:	25x to 30x
Production 100 sets	
Variation 2:	30x to 45x
Production 50 sets	
Variation 3:	50x to 75x
Production 25 sets	

1999 Topps Gold Label Race to Aaron

This 10-card set features the best current players who are chasing Hank Aaron's career home run and career RBI records. Each player is pictured in the foreground with Aaron silhouetted in the background on the card front. These are seeded 1:12 packs. Two parallel versions also exist: Black and Red. Blacks have black foil stamping and are seeded 1:48 packs. Reds have red foil stamping and are limited to 44 sequentially numbered sets.

		MT
Complete Set (10):		150.00
Common Player:		6.00
Inserted 1:12		
Blacks:		2x
Inserted 1:48		
Reds:		10x to 15x
Production 44 sets		
1	Mark McGwire	35.00
2	Ken Griffey Jr.	30.00
3	Alex Rodriguez	20.00
4	Vladimir Guerrero	10.00
5	Albert Belle	8.00
6	Nomar Garciaparra	20.00
7	Ken Griffey Jr.	30.00
8	Alex Rodriguez	20.00
9	Juan Gonzalez	15.00
10	Barry Bonds	8.00

1999 Topps Opening Day

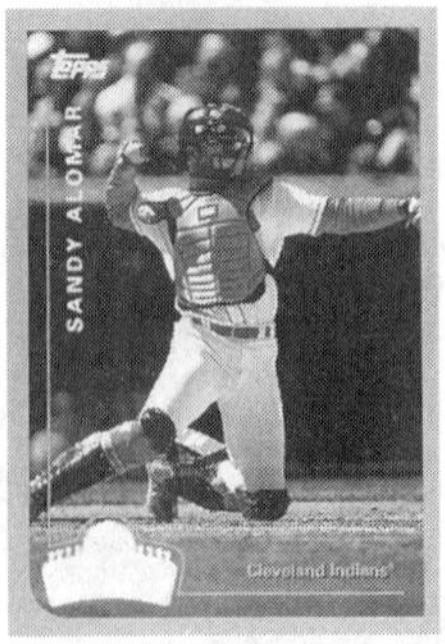

This retail exclusive product is comprised of 165 cards. Base cards have a silver border, and the Opening Day logo stamped with silver foil. Packs are pre-priced at $.99, each pack has seven cards. Hank Aaron autographs are randomly seeded and are stamped with the Topps "Certified Autograph Issue" stamp. The insertion rate for the autograph is 1:29,642 packs.

		MT
Complete Set (165):		30.00
Common Player:		.15
1	Hank Aaron	2.00
2a	Roger Clemens	1.00
2b	Andres Galarraga (should be #3)	.50
4	Scott Brosius	.15
5	Ray Durham	.15
6	Will Clark	.40
7	David Wells	.15
8	Jose Guillen	.15
9	Edgardo Alfonzo	.15
10	Manny Ramirez	1.00
11	Greg Maddux	2.00
12	David Segui	.15
13	Darryl Strawberry	.25
14	Brad Radke	.15
15	Kerry Wood	.75
16	Paul Konerko	.25
17	Travis Lee	.50
18	Kenny Rogers	.15
19	Todd Walker	.25
20	John Olerud	.25
21	Nolan Ryan	3.00
22	Ray Lankford	.15
23	Bartolo Colon	.15
24	Brady Anderson	.15
25	Jorge Posada	.15
26	Justin Thompson	.15
27	Juan Gonzalez	1.50
28	Chuck Knoblauch	.40
29	Todd Helton	.60
30	Gary Sheffield	.30
31	Rod Beck	.15
32	Garret Anderson	.15
33	Rondell White	.25
34	Vladimir Guerrero	1.00
35	Eric Karros	.15
36	Mo Vaughn	.75
37	Sammy Sosa	2.50
38	Kenny Lofton	.75
39	Mark McGwire	4.00
40	Javy Lopez	.25
41	Damion Easley	.15
42	Andy Pettitte	.40
43	Tony Gwynn	1.50
44	Jay Bell	.15
45	Jose Canseco	.40
46	John Wetteland	.15
47	Mike Caruso	.15
48	Derek Jeter	1.50
49	Aaron Sele	.15
50	Jeff Cirillo	.15
51	Mark Kotsay	.15
52	Albert Belle	.75
53	Matt Lawton	.15
54	Pedro Martinez	.50
55	Greg Vaughn	.25
56	Neifi Perez	.15
57	Derek Bell	.15
58	Ken Griffey Jr.	3.00
59	David Cone	.25
60	Dean Palmer	.15
61	Trevor Hoffman	.15
62	Billy Wagner	.15
63	Shawn Green	.15
64	Ben Grieve	.75
65	Tom Goodwin	.15
66	Jaret Wright	.40
67	Dmitri Young	.15
68	Hideki Irabu	.25
69	Jeff Fassero	.15
70	Matt Williams	.30
71	Bret Saberhagen	.15
72	Chad Curtis	.15
73	Scott Rolen	.75
74	J.T. Snow Jr.	.15
75	Rusty Greer	.15
76	Jim Edmonds	.15
77	Ron Gant	.15
78	A.J. Hinch	.15
79	Shannon Stewart	.15
80	Brad Fullmer	.25
81	Walt Weiss	.15
82	Fred McGriff	.25
83	Darin Erstad	.75
84	Eric Young	.15
85	Livan Hernandez	.15
86	Jeff Bagwell	.75
87	Omar Vizquel	.15
88	Eric Davis	.15
89	Magglio Ordonez	.15
90	John Valentin	.15
91	Dave Dellucci	.15
92	Chan Ho Park	.25
93	Masato Yoshii	.15
94	Bret Boone	.15
95	Mariano Rivera	.25
96	Bobby Jones	.15
97	Francisco Cordova	.15
98	Mike Mussina	.50
99	Denny Neagle	.15
100	Edgar Martinez	.15
101	Jason Kendall	.25
102	Jeff King	.15
103	Rey Ordonez	.15
104	Andruw Jones	.75
105	Vinny Castilla	.15
106	Troy Glaus	1.00
107	Tom Glavine	.25
108	Moises Alou	.25
109	Carlos Delgado	.15
110	Raul Mondesi	.25
111	Shane Reynolds	.15
112	Jason Giambi	.15
113	Jose Cruz Jr.	.50
114	Craig Biggio	.40
115	Tim Salmon	.40
116	Chipper Jones	1.50
117	Andy Benes	.15
118	John Smoltz	.25
119	Jeromy Burnitz	.15
120	Randy Johnson	.50
121	Mark Grace	.25
122	Henry Rodriguez	.15
123	Ryan Klesko	.25
124	Kevin Millwood	.50
125	Sean Casey	.15
126	Brian Jordan	.15
127	Kevin Brown	.25
128	Orlando Hernandez	1.50
129	Barry Bonds	.75
130	David Justice	.25
131	Carlos Perez	.15
132	Andy Ashby	.15
133	Paul O'Neill	.30
134	Curt Schilling	.25
135	Alex Rodriguez	2.00
136	Cliff Floyd	.15
137	Rafael Palmeiro	.30
138	Nomar Garciaparra	2.00
139	Mike Piazza	2.00
140	Roberto Alomar	.50
141	Todd Hundley	.15
142	Jeff Kent	.15
143	Barry Larkin	.25
144	Cal Ripken Jr.	2.50
145	Jay Buhner	.25
146	Kevin Young	.15
147	Ivan Rodriguez	.75
148	Al Leiter	.15
149	Sandy Alomar	.15
150	Bernie Williams	.50
151	Ellis Burks	.15
152	Wally Joyner	.15
153	Bobby Higginson	.15
154	Tony Clark	.50
155	Larry Walker	.40
156	Frank Thomas	2.00
157	Tino Martinez	.40
158	Jim Thome	.40
159	Dante Bichette	.25
160	David Wells (Season Highlights)	.15
161	Roger Clemens (Season Highlights)	.75
162	Kerry Wood (Season Highlights)	.50
163	Mark McGwire (HR Record#70)	5.00
164	Sammy Sosa (HR Record #66)	3.00
165	Checklist	.15

1999 Topps Stars

Topps Stars consists of 180 cards, on 20-point stock with foil stamping and metallic inks. Within the base set there are 150 base cards and 30 subset cards, Luminaries and Supernovas. Packs contain six cards; three base cards, two One-Star cards and one Two-Star card on the average.

		MT
Complete Set (180):		75.00
Common Player:		.25
Foils:		3x to 8x
Production 299 sets		
1	Ken Griffey Jr.	6.00
2	Chipper Jones	3.00
3	Mike Piazza	4.00
4	Nomar Garciaparra	4.00
5	Derek Jeter	4.00
6	Frank Thomas	2.00
7	Ben Grieve	1.00
8	Mark McGwire	8.00
9	Sammy Sosa	4.00
10	Alex Rodriguez	4.00
11	Troy Glaus	1.50
12	Eric Chavez	.75
13	Kerry Wood	.75
14	Barry Bonds	1.50
15	Vladimir Guerrero	2.00
16	Albert Belle	1.00
17	Juan Gonzalez	3.00
18	Roger Clemens	2.00
19	Ruben Mateo	1.00
20	Cal Ripken Jr.	5.00
21	Darin Erstad	1.00
22	Jeff Bagwell	1.50

23	Roy Halladay	.25
24	Todd Helton	1.00
25	Michael Barrett	.25
26	Manny Ramirez	1.50
27	Fernando Seguignol	.25
28	*Pat Burrell*	5.00
29	Andruw Jones	1.00
30	Randy Johnson	1.00
31	Jose Canseco	1.00
32	Brad Fullmer	.25
33	*Alex Escobar*	3.00
34	*Alfonso Soriano*	6.00
35	Larry Walker	1.00
36	Matt Clement	.25
37	Mo Vaughn	1.00
38	Bruce Chen	.25
39	Travis Lee	.75
40	Adrian Beltre	.50
41	Alex Gonzalez	.25
42	*Jason Tyner*	.75
43	George Lombard	.25
44	Scott Rolen	1.50
45	*Mark Mulder*	3.00
46	Gabe Kapler	1.50
47	*Choo Freeman*	.50
48	Tony Gwynn	3.00
49	*A.J. Burnett*	1.50
50	*Matt Belisle*	1.00
51	Greg Maddux	4.00
52	John Smoltz	.25
53	Mark Grace	.50
54	Wade Boggs	.50
55	Bernie Williams	1.00
56	Pedro Martinez	1.50
57	Barry Larkin	.50
58	Orlando Hernandez	.50
59	Jason Kendall	.25
60	Mark Kotsay	.25
61	Jim Thome	.75
62	Gary Sheffield	.40
63	Preston Wilson	.25
64	Rafael Palmeiro	1.00
65	David Wells	.25
66	Shawn Green	.75
67	Tom Glavine	.25
68	Jeromy Burnitz	.25
69	Kevin Brown	.50
70	Rondell White	.50
71	Roberto Alomar	1.00
72	Cliff Floyd	.25
73	Craig Biggio	.75
74	Greg Vaughn	.40
75	Ivan Rodriguez	1.50
76	Vinny Castilla	.25
77	Todd Walker	.25
78	Paul Konerko	.25
79	*Andy Brown*	.75
80	Todd Hundley	.25
81	Dmitri Young	.25
82	Tony Clark	.75
83	*Nick Johnson*	4.00
84	Mike Caruso	.25
85	David Ortiz	.25
86	Matt Williams	.75
87	Raul Mondesi	.40
88	Kenny Lofton	1.00
89	Miguel Tejada	.25
90	Dante Bichette	.50
91	Jorge Posada	.40
92	Carlos Beltran	1.50
93	Carlos Delgado	1.00
94	Javy Lopez	.25
95	Aramis Ramirez	.25
96	Neifi Perez	.25
97	Marlon Anderson	.25
98	David Cone	.25
99	Moises Alou	.25
100	John Olerud	.40
101	Tim Salmon	.40
102	Jason Giambi	.25
103	Sandy Alomar	.25
104	Curt Schilling	.40
105	Andres Galarraga	.75
106	Rusty Greer	.25
107	*Bobby Seay*	.75
108	Eric Young	.25
109	Brian Jordan	.25
110	Eric Davis	.25
111	Will Clark	.50
112	Andy Ashby	.25
113	Edgardo Alfonzo	.25
114	Paul O'Neill	.40
115	Denny Neagle	.25
116	Eric Karros	.25
117	Ken Caminiti	.40
118	Garret Anderson	.25
119	Todd Stottlemyre	.25
120	David Justice	.40
121	Francisco Cordova	.25
122	Robin Ventura	.40
123	Mike Mussina	1.00
124	Hideki Irabu	.25
125	Justin Thompson	.25
126	Mariano Rivera	.40
127	Delino DeShields	.25
128	Steve Finley	.25
129	Jose Cruz Jr.	.25
130	Ray Lankford	.25
131	Jim Edmonds	.25
132	Charles Johnson	.25
133	Al Leiter	.25
134	Jose Offerman	.25
135	Eric Milton	.25
136	Dean Palmer	.25
137	Johnny Damon	.25
138	Andy Pettitte	.40
139	Ray Durham	.25
140	Ugueth Urbina	.25
141	Marquis Grissom	.25
142	Ryan Klesko	.25
143	Brady Anderson	.25
144	Bobby Higginson	.25
145	Chuck Knoblauch	.50
146	Rickey Henderson	.40
147	Kevin Millwood	.50
148	Fred McGriff	.40
149	Damion Easley	.25
150	Tino Martinez	.50
151	Greg Maddux (Luminaries)	2.00
152	Scott Rolen (Luminaries)	.75
153	Pat Burrell (Luminaries)	2.50
154	Roger Clemens (Luminaries)	1.00
155	Albert Belle (Luminaries)	.50
156	Troy Glaus (Luminaries)	.75
157	Cal Ripken Jr. (Luminaries)	2.50
158	Alfonso Soriano (Luminaries)	3.00
159	Manny Ramirez (Luminaries)	.75
160	Eric Chavez (Luminaries)	.40
161	Kerry Wood (Luminaries)	.40
162	Tony Gwynn (Luminaries)	1.50
163	Barry Bonds (Luminaries)	.75
164	Ruben Mateo (Luminaries)	.50
165	Todd Helton (Luminaries)	.40
166	Darin Erstad (Luminaries)	.40
167	Jeff Bagwell (Luminaries)	.75
168	Juan Gonzalez (Luminaries)	1.50
169	Mo Vaughn (Luminaries)	.50
170	Vladimir Guerrero (Luminaries)	1.00
171	Nomar Garciaparra (Supernovas)	2.00
172	Derek Jeter (Supernovas)	2.00
173	Alex Rodriguez (Supernovas)	2.00
174	Ben Grieve (Supernovas)	.40
175	Mike Piazza (Supernovas)	2.00
176	Chipper Jones (Supernovas)	1.50
177	Frank Thomas (Supernovas)	1.00
178	Ken Griffey Jr. (Supernovas)	3.00
179	Sammy Sosa (Supernovas)	2.00
180	Mark McGwire (Supernovas)	4.00

1999 Topps Stars One Star

One Star inserts includes card numbers 1-100 from the base set and have silver foil stamping with one star on the bottom left portion of the card front. These are seeded two per pack. A foil one star parallel also is randomly seeded and sequentially numbered to 249 sets.

		MT
Complete Set (100):		40.00
Common Player:		.25
Foils:		6x to 12x
Production 249 sets		
1	Ken Griffey Jr.	4.00
2	Chipper Jones	2.00
3	Mike Piazza	2.50
4	Nomar Garciaparra	2.50
5	Derek Jeter	2.50
6	Frank Thomas	1.50
7	Ben Grieve	.75
8	Mark McGwire	5.00
9	Sammy Sosa	2.50
10	Alex Rodriguez	2.50
11	Troy Glaus	1.00
12	Eric Chavez	.50
13	Kerry Wood	.50
14	Barry Bonds	1.00
15	Vladimir Guerrero	1.50
16	Albert Belle	.75
17	Juan Gonzalez	2.00
18	Roger Clemens	1.50
19	Ruben Mateo	.75
20	Cal Ripken Jr.	3.00
21	Darin Erstad	.75
22	Jeff Bagwell	1.00
23	Roy Halladay	.25
24	Todd Helton	.75
25	Michael Barrett	.25
26	Manny Ramirez	1.00
27	Fernando Seguignol	.25
28	Pat Burrell	4.00
29	Andruw Jones	.75
30	Randy Johnson	.75
31	Jose Canseco	.75
32	Brad Fullmer	.25
33	Alex Escobar	2.00
34	Alfonso Soriano	4.00
35	Larry Walker	.75
36	Matt Clement	.25
37	Mo Vaughn	.75
38	Bruce Chen	.25
39	Travis Lee	.60
40	Adrian Beltre	.50
41	Alex Gonzalez	.25
42	*Jason Tyner*	.60
43	George Lombard	.25
44	Scott Rolen	1.00
45	*Mark Mulder*	2.00
46	Gabe Kapler	1.00
47	*Choo Freeman*	.50
48	Tony Gwynn	2.00
49	A.J. Burnett	1.00
50	*Matt Belisle*	.75
51	Greg Maddux	2.50
52	John Smoltz	.25
53	Mark Grace	.40
54	Wade Boggs	.40
55	Bernie Williams	.75
56	Pedro Martinez	1.00
57	Barry Larkin	.40
58	Orlando Hernandez	.40
59	Jason Kendall	.25
60	Mark Kotsay	.25
61	Jim Thome	.60
62	Gary Sheffield	.40
63	Preston Wilson	.25
64	Rafael Palmeiro	.75
65	David Wells	.25
66	Shawn Green	.60
67	Tom Glavine	.25
68	Jeromy Burnitz	.25
69	Kevin Brown	.40
70	Rondell White	.40
71	Roberto Alomar	.75
72	Cliff Floyd	.25
73	Craig Biggio	.60
74	Greg Vaughn	.40
75	Ivan Rodriguez	1.00
76	Vinny Castilla	.25
77	Todd Walker	.25
78	Paul Konerko	.25
79	*Andy Brown*	.50
80	Todd Hundley	.25
81	Dmitri Young	.25
82	Tony Clark	.50
83	*Nick Johnson*	2.00
84	Mike Caruso	.25
85	David Ortiz	.25
86	Matt Williams	.50
87	Raul Mondesi	.40
88	Kenny Lofton	.75
89	Miguel Tejada	.25
90	Dante Bichette	.40
91	Jorge Posada	.40
92	Carlos Beltran	1.00
93	Carlos Delgado	.75
94	Javy Lopez	.25
95	Aramis Ramirez	.25
96	Neifi Perez	.25
97	Marlon Anderson	.25
98	David Cone	.25
99	Moises Alou	.25
100	John Olerud	.40

1999 Topps Stars Two Star

Two-Stars are inserted one per pack and feature light gold metallic inks and foil stamping. Two-Stars include card numbers 1-50 from the base set. A Two-Star parallel is also randomly seeded and limited to 199 sequentially numbered sets.

		MT
Complete Set (50):		30.00
Common Player:		.25
Foils:		10x to 15x
Production 199 sets		
1	Ken Griffey Jr.	4.00
2	Chipper Jones	2.00
3	Mike Piazza	2.50
4	Nomar Garciaparra	2.50
5	Derek Jeter	2.50
6	Frank Thomas	1.50
7	Ben Grieve	.75
8	Mark McGwire	5.00
9	Sammy Sosa	2.50
10	Alex Rodriguez	2.50
11	Troy Glaus	1.00
12	Eric Chavez	.60
13	Kerry Wood	.50
14	Barry Bonds	1.00
15	Vladimir Guerrero	1.50
16	Albert Belle	.75
17	Juan Gonzalez	2.00
18	Roger Clemens	1.50
19	Ruben Mateo	.75
20	Cal Ripken Jr.	3.00
21	Darin Erstad	.75
22	Jeff Bagwell	1.00
23	Roy Halladay	.25
24	Todd Helton	.75
25	Michael Barrett	.25
26	Manny Ramirez	1.00
27	Fernando Seguignol	.25
28	Pat Burrell	3.00
29	Andruw Jones	.75
30	Randy Johnson	.75
31	Jose Canseco	.75
32	Brad Fullmer	.25
33	Alex Escobar	2.00
34	Alfonso Soriano	4.00
35	Larry Walker	.75
36	Matt Clement	.25
37	Mo Vaughn	.75
38	Bruce Chen	.25
39	Travis Lee	.50
40	Adrian Beltre	.40
41	Alex Gonzalez	.25
42	*Jason Tyner*	.50
43	George Lombard	.25
44	Scott Rolen	1.00
45	*Mark Mulder*	2.00
46	Gabe Kapler	1.00
47	*Choo Freeman*	.50
48	Tony Gwynn	2.00
49	A.J. Burnett	1.00
50	*Matt Belisle*	.75

1999 Topps Stars Three Star

Three-star inserts is a partial parallel from the base set including cards 1-20 from the base set. Inserted 1:5 packs, these cards feature refractive silver foil stamping along with gold metallic inks. A Three-star parallel also is randomly inserted featuring gold stamping and limited to 99 serial numbered sets.

		MT
Complete Set (20):		60.00
Common Player:		1.00
Foils:		8x to 20x
Production 99 sets		
1	Ken Griffey Jr.	8.00
2	Chipper Jones	4.00
3	Mike Piazza	5.00
4	Nomar Garciaparra	5.00
5	Derek Jeter	5.00
6	Frank Thomas	3.00
7	Ben Grieve	1.50
8	Mark McGwire	10.00
9	Sammy Sosa	5.00
10	Alex Rodriguez	5.00
11	Troy Glaus	2.00
12	Eric Chavez	1.00
13	Kerry Wood	1.00
14	Barry Bonds	2.00
15	Vladimir Guerrero	3.00
16	Albert Belle	1.50
17	Juan Gonzalez	4.00
18	Roger Clemens	3.00
19	Ruben Mateo	1.50
20	Cal Ripken Jr.	6.00

1999 Topps Stars Four Star

Four-Star inserts include cards numbered 1-10 from the base set and are seeded 1:10 packs, these cards feature dark metallic inks and refractive foil stamping on card fronts. A Four Star parallel is also randomly seeded and has gold metallic inks and sequentially numbered to 49.

		MT
Complete Set (10):		40.00
Common Player:		1.50
Foils:		15x to 25x
Production 49 sets		
1	Ken Griffey Jr.	8.00
2	Chipper Jones	4.00
3	Mike Piazza	5.00
4	Nomar Garciaparra	5.00
5	Derek Jeter	5.00
6	Frank Thomas	3.00
7	Ben Grieve	1.50
8	Mark McGwire	10.00
9	Sammy Sosa	5.00
10	Alex Rodriguez	5.00

1999 Topps Stars Bright Futures

This 10-card set features 10 top prospects who have a brilliant future ahead of them, including Pat Burrell. Each card features foil stamping and is sequentially numbered to 1,999. A metallized foil parallel version is also randomly seeded and limited to 30 numbered sets.

		MT
Complete Set (10):		60.00
Common Player:		3.00
Production 1,999 sets		
1	Troy Glaus	8.00
2	Eric Chavez	5.00
3	Adrian Beltre	4.00
4	Michael Barrett	4.00
5	Fernando Seguignol	3.00
6	Alex Gonzalez	3.00
7	Matt Clement	3.00
8	Pat Burrell	15.00
9	Ruben Mateo	8.00
10	Alfonso Soriano	20.00

1999 Topps Stars Galaxy

This 10-card set highlights the top players in baseball with foil stamping and limited to 1,999 numbered sets. Each card is numbered on the back with a "G" prefix. A Galaxy parallel version is randomly seeded and sequentially numbered to 30 sets.

		MT
Complete Set (10):		150.00
Common Player:		5.00
Production 1,999 sets		
1	Mark McGwire	40.00
2	Roger Clemens	10.00
3	Nomar Garciaparra	20.00

4	Alex Rodriguez	20.00
5	Kerry Wood	5.00
6	Ben Grieve	5.00
7	Derek Jeter	20.00
8	Vladimir Guerrero	10.00
9	Ken Griffey Jr.	30.00
10	Sammy Sosa	20.00

1999 Topps Stars Rookie Reprints

Topps reprinted five Hall of Famers Topps rookie cards. Each rookie reprint is inserted 1:65 packs and limited to 2,500 numbered sets.

		MT
Complete Set (5):		75.00
Common Player:		15.00
Production 2,500 sets		
1	Frank Robinson	15.00
2	Ernie Banks	20.00
3	Yogi Berra	20.00
4	Bob Gibson	15.00
5	Tom Seaver	25.00

1999 Topps Stars Rookie Reprints Autographs

These foil stamped inserts feature the "Topps Certified Autograph Issue" stamp and are inserted 1:406 packs. The Ernie Banks autograph is inserted 1:812 packs.

		MT
Complete Set (5):		400.00
Common Player:		60.00
Inserted 1:406		
Banks inserted 1:812		
1	Frank Robinson	75.00
2	Ernie Banks	120.00
3	Yogi Berra	90.00
4	Bob Gibson	60.00
5	Tom Seaver	125.00

1999 Topps Stars 'N Steel

Using Serilusion technology, each borderless card features a four-colored textured film laminate bonded to a sheet of strong 25-gauge metal. Each pack contains three cards, packaged in a stand-up tri-fold display unit, at an S.R.P. of $9.99. There are two parallels to the 44-card set, Gold and Holographics. Golds are seeded 1:12 packs, Holographics are found every 24 packs.

		MT
Complete Set (44):		150.00
Common Player:		2.00
Golds:		2x to 4x
Inserted 1:12		
Holographics:		4x to 8x
Inserted 1:24		
1	Kerry Wood	6.00
2	Ben Grieve	8.00
3	Chipper Jones	12.00
4	Alex Rodriguez	15.00
5	Mo Vaughn	6.00
6	Bernie Williams	5.00
7	Juan Gonzalez	12.00
8	Vinny Castilla	2.00
9	Tony Gwynn	12.00
10	Manny Ramirez	8.00
11	Raul Mondesi	3.00
12	Roger Clemens	10.00
13	Darin Erstad	6.00
14	Barry Bonds	6.00
15	Cal Ripken Jr.	20.00
16	Barry Larkin	3.00
17	Scott Rolen	6.00
18	Albert Belle	6.00
19	Craig Biggio	2.00
20	Tony Clark	4.00
21	Mark McGwire	30.00
22	Andres Galarraga	3.00
23	Kenny Lofton	6.00
24	Pedro Martinez	4.00
25	Paul O'Neill	3.00
26	Ken Griffey Jr.	25.00
27	Travis Lee	5.00
28	Tim Salmon	3.00
29	Frank Thomas	15.00
30	Larry Walker	3.00
31	Moises Alou	2.00
32	Vladimir Guerrero	8.00
33	Ivan Rodriguez	6.00
34	Derek Jeter	15.00
35	Greg Vaughn	3.00
36	Gary Sheffield	3.00
37	Carlos Delgado	2.00
38	Greg Maddux	15.00
39	Sammy Sosa	20.00
40	Mike Piazza	15.00
41	Nomar Garciaparra	15.00
42	Dante Bichette	3.00
43	Jeff Bagwell	8.00
44	Jim Thome	4.00

1999 Topps Super Chrome

Using identical photos from Topps Chrome Baseball, Topps supersized 36 players to 4-1/8" x 5-3/4" card size. The cards are done on standard chromium technology. Each pack contains three oversized cards and sells for an S.R.P. of $4.99. There also is a Refractor parallel set, which is seeded 1:12 packs.

		MT
Complete Set (36):		50.00
Common Player:		.50
Refractors:		5x to 10x
Inserted 1:12		
1	Roger Clemens	2.00
2	Andres Galarraga	.75
3	Manny Ramirez	1.50
4	Greg Maddux	3.00
5	Kerry Wood	1.50
6	Travis Lee	1.00
7	Nolan Ryan	5.00
8	Juan Gonzalez	2.50
9	Vladimir Guerrero	1.50
10	Sammy Sosa	3.00
11	Mark McGwire	6.00
12	Javy Lopez	.50
13	Tony Gwynn	2.50
14	Derek Jeter	3.00
15	Albert Belle	1.25
16	Pedro Martinez	1.00
17	Greg Vaughn	.50
18	Ken Griffey Jr.	5.00
19	Ben Grieve	1.25
20	Vinny Castilla	.50
21	Moises Alou	.50
22	Barry Bonds	1.25
23	Nomar Garciaparra	3.00
24	Chipper Jones	2.50
25	Mike Piazza	3.00
26	Alex Rodriguez	3.00
27	Ivan Rodriguez	1.25
28	Frank Thomas	3.00
29	Larry Walker	1.00
30	Troy Glaus	1.25
31	David Wells (Season Highlight)	.50
32	Roger Clemens (Season Highlight)	1.50
33	Kerry Wood (Season Highlight)	.75
34	Mark McGwire (Home Run Record)	8.00
35	Sammy Sosa (Home Run Parade)	4.00
36	World Series	.50

1999 Topps TEK

Topps TEK baseball contains 45 players, with all cards printed on a transparent, 27-point stock. Each player is featured in two different versions (A & B), which is noted on the card back. The versions are differentiated by type of player uniform (home is version A and away uniforms are version B). Each version also has 30 different baseball focused background patterns, as a result every player in the 45-card set has 60 total cards. There also is a Gold parallel set that has a gold design and all versions are paralleled. Each card is numbered to 10, with an insertion rate of 1:15 packs.

		MT
Complete Set (45):		80.00
Common Player:		.50
All Variations priced equally		
Golds:		5x to 8x
Each card is #'d to 10		
1	Ben Grieve	2.50
2	Andres Galarraga	1.50
3	Travis Lee	2.00
4	Larry Walker	1.50
5	Ken Griffey Jr.	10.00
6	Sammy Sosa	6.00
7	Mark McGwire	10.00
8	Roberto Alomar	2.00
9	Wade Boggs	1.00
10	Troy Glaus	3.00
11	Craig Biggio	1.50
12	Kerry Wood	2.50
13	Vladimir Guerrero	3.00
14	Albert Belle	2.50
15	Mike Piazza	6.00
16	Chipper Jones	5.00
17	Randy Johnson	2.00
18	Adrian Beltre	1.00
19	Barry Bonds	2.50
20	Jim Thome	1.50
21	Greg Vaughn	.75
22	Scott Rolen	2.50
23	Ivan Rodriguez	2.50
24	Derek Jeter	6.00
25	Cal Ripken Jr.	8.00
26	Mark Grace	.75
27	Bernie Williams	1.50
28	Darin Erstad	2.00
29	Eric Chavez	2.50
30	Tom Glavine	.75
31	Jeff Bagwell	2.50
32	Manny Ramirez	2.50
33	Tino Martinez	1.50
34	Todd Helton	1.50
35	Jason Kendall	.75
36	*Pat Burrell*	12.00
37	Tony Gwynn	5.00
38	Nomar Garciaparra	6.00
39	Frank Thomas	5.00
40	Orlando Hernandez	3.00
41	Juan Gonzalez	5.00
42	Alex Rodriguez	6.00
43	Greg Maddux	5.00
44	Mo Vaughn	2.50
45	Roger Clemens	3.00

1999 Topps TEK Fantastek Phenoms

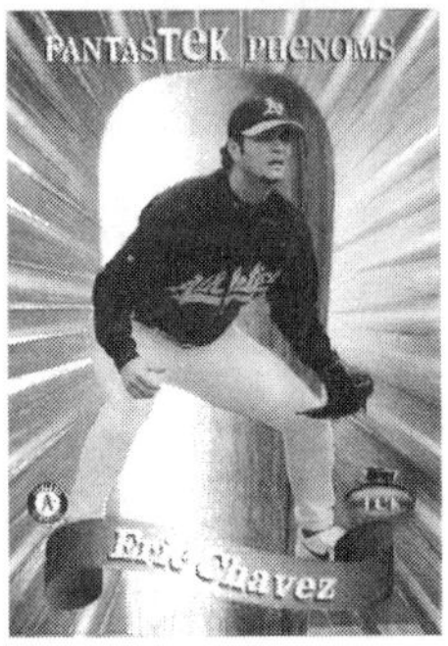

This 10-card set highlights top young prospects on a transparent plastic stock with silver and blue highlighting. These are inserted 1:18 packs.

		MT
Complete Set (10):		50.00
Common Player:		2.00
Inserted 1:18		
F1	Eric Chavez	5.00
F2	Troy Glaus	6.00
F3	Pat Burrell	20.00
F4	Alex Gonzalez	2.00
F5	Carlos Lee	4.00
F6	Ruben Mateo	5.00
F7	Carlos Beltran	3.00
F8	Adrian Beltre	4.00
F9	Bruce Chen	2.00
F10	Ryan Anderson	8.00

1999 Topps TEK Teknicians

This 10-card set focuses on baseball's top stars on a clear, plastic stock utilizing metallic blue, silver and red inks. These are inserted 1:18 packs.

		MT
Complete Set (10):		90.00
Common Player:		2.00
Inserted 1:18		
T1	Ken Griffey Jr.	20.00
T2	Mark McGwire	20.00
T3	Kerry Wood	5.00
T4	Ben Grieve	5.00
T5	Sammy Sosa	12.00
T6	Derek Jeter	12.00
T7	Alex Rodriguez	12.00
T8	Roger Clemens	6.00
T9	Nomar Garciaparra	12.00
T10	Vladimir Guerrero	6.00

1999 Ultra

Base cards feature the full career stats by year in 15 categories and career highlights. There are short-printed subsets including Season Crowns (216-225) found 1:8 packs and Prospects (226-250) found 1:4 packs. Card fronts feature full bleed photography, and metallic foil stamping. There are three parallel versions Gold Medallion seeded 1 per pack with Prospects 1:40 and Season Crowns 1:80. Platinum Medallions are numbered to 99 with Prospects numbered to 65 and Season Crowns numbered to 50 sets. One of One Masterpiece parallels also exist. Packs consist of 10 cards with an S.R.P. of $2.69.

		MT
Complete Set (250):		140.00
Common Player:		.10
Common Season Crown:		.50
Inserted 1:8		
Common Prospect:		.25
Inserted 1:4		
Gold Medallion (1-215):		1.5x to 2x
Inserted 1:1		
Gold Medall. Prospect:		2x to 4x
Inserted 1:40		
Gold Medall. Season Crown:		3x to 6x
Inserted 1:80		
Platinums (1-215):		25x to 50x
Production 99 sets		
Platinum Prospects:		5x to 10x
Production 65 sets		
Platinum Season Crowns:		15x to 30x
Production 50 sets		
1	Greg Maddux	2.00
2	Greg Vaughn	.20
3	John Wetteland	.10
4	Tino Martinez	.25
5	Todd Walker	.25
6	Troy O'Leary	.10
7	Barry Larkin	.25
8	Mike Lansing	.10
9	Delino DeShields	.10
10	Brett Tomko	.10
11	Carlos Perez	.10
12	Mark Langston	.10
13	Jamie Moyer	.10
14	Jose Guillen	.20
15	Bartolo Colon	.10
16	Brady Anderson	.10
17	Walt Weiss	.10
18	Shane Reynolds	.10
19	David Segui	.10
20	Vladimir Guerrero	1.00
21	Freddy Garcia	.10
22	Carl Everett	.10
23	Jose Cruz Jr.	.50
24	David Ortiz	.10
25	Andruw Jones	.75
26	Darren Lewis	.10
27	Ray Lankford	.10
28	Wally Joyner	.10
29	Charles Johnson	.10
30	Derek Jeter	2.00
31	Sean Casey	.10
32	Bobby Bonilla	.20
33	Todd Zelle	.10
34	Todd Helton	.75
35	David Wells	.10
36	Darin Erstad	.75
37	Ivan Rodriguez	.75
38	Antonio Osuna	.10
39	Mickey Morandini	.10
40	Rusty Greer	.10
41	Rod Beck	.10
42	Larry Sutton	.10
43	Edgar Renteria	.10
44	Otis Nixon	.10
45	Eli Marrero	.10
46	Reggie Jefferson	.10
47	Trevor Hoffman	.10
48	Andres Galarraga	.40
49	Scott Brosius	.10
50	Vinny Castilla	.10
51	Bret Boone	.10
52	Masato Yoshii	.10
53	Matt Williams	.25
54	Robin Ventura	.10
55	Jay Powell	.10
56	Dean Palmer	.10
57	Eric Milton	.10
58	Willie McGee	.10
59	Tony Gwynn	1.50
60	Tom Gordon	.10
61	Dante Bichette	.25
62	Jaret Wright	.40
63	Devon White	.10

64	Frank Thomas	2.00
65	Mike Piazza	2.00
66	Jose Offerman	.10
67	Pat Meares	.10
68	Brian Meadows	.10
69	Nomar Garciaparra	2.00
70	Mark McGwire	4.00
71	Tony Graffanino	.10
72	Ken Griffey Jr.	3.00
73	Ken Caminiti	.20
74	Todd Jones	.10
75	A.J. Hinch	.10
76	Marquis Grissom	.10
77	Jay Buhner	.25
78	Albert Belle	.75
79	Brian Anderson	.10
80	Quinton McCracken	.10
81	Omar Vizquel	.10
82	Todd Stottlemyre	.10
83	Cal Ripken Jr.	2.00
84	Magglio Ordonez	.10
85	John Olerud	.10
86	Hal Morris	.10
87	Derrek Lee	.10
88	Doug Glanville	.10
89	Marty Cordova	.10
90	Kevin Brown	.10
91	Kevin Young	.10
92	Rico Brogna	.10
93	Wilson Alvarez	.10
94	Bob Wickman	.10
95	Jim Thome	.50
96	Mike Mussina	.50
97	Al Leiter	.10
98	Travis Lee	.40
99	Jeff King	.10
100	Kerry Wood	.75
101	Cliff Floyd	.10
102	Jose Valentin	.10
103	Manny Ramirez	1.00
104	Butch Huskey	.10
105	Scott Erickson	.10
106	Ray Durham	.10
107	Johnny Damon	.10
108	Craig Counsell	.10
109	Rolando Arrojo	.10
110	Bob Abreu	.10
111	Tony Womack	.10
112	Mike Stanley	.10
113	Kenny Lofton	.60
114	Eric Davis	.10
115	Jeff Conine	.10
116	Carlos Baerga	.10
117	Rondell White	.20
118	Billy Wagner	.10
119	Ed Sprague	.10
120	Jason Schmidt	.10
121	Edgar Martinez	.10
122	Travis Fryman	.10
123	Armando Benitez	.10
124	Matt Stairs	.10
125	Roberto Hernandez	.10
126	Jay Bell	.10
127	Justin Thompson	.10
128	John Jaha	.10
129	Mike Caruso	.10
130	Miguel Tejada	.25
131	Geoff Jenkins	.10
132	Wade Boggs	.25
133	Andy Benes	.10
134	Aaron Sele	.10
135	Bret Saberhagen	.10
136	Mariano Rivera	.20
137	Neifi Perez	.10
138	Paul Konerko	.25
139	Barry Bonds	.75
140	Garret Anderson	.10
141	Bernie Williams	.60
142	Gary Sheffield	.25
143	Rafael Palmeiro	.25
144	Orel Hershiser	.10
145	Craig Biggio	.20
146	Dmitri Young	.10
147	Damion Easley	.10
148	Henry Rodriguez	.10
149	Brad Radke	.10
150	Pedro Martinez	.50
151	Mike Lieberthal	.10
152	Jim Leyritz	.10
153	Chuck Knoblauch	.25
154	Darryl Kile	.10
155	Brian Jordan	.10
156	Chipper Jones	1.50
157	Pete Harnisch	.10
158	Moises Alou	.20
159	Ismael Valdes	.10
160	Stan Javier	.10
161	Mark Grace	.25
162	Jason Giambi	.10
163	Chuck Finley	.10
164	Juan Encarnacion	.10
165	Chan Ho Park	.10
166	Randy Johnson	.50
167	J.T. Snow	.10
168	Tim Salmon	.25
169	Brian Hunter	.10
170	Rickey Henderson	.10
171	Cal Eldred	.10
172	Curt Schilling	.20
173	Alex Rodriguez	2.00
174	Dustin Hermanson	.10
175	Mike Hampton	.10
176	Shawn Green	.10
177	Roberto Alomar	.50
178	Sandy Alomar Jr.	.20
179	Larry Walker	.40
180	Mo Vaughn	.75
181	Raul Mondesi	.25
182	Hideki Irabu	.20
183	Jim Edmonds	.20
184	Shawn Estes	.10
185	Tony Clark	.40
186	Dan Wilson	.10
187	Michael Tucker	.10
188	Jeff Shaw	.10
189	Mark Grudzielanek	.10
190	Roger Clemens	1.50
191	Juan Gonzalez	1.50
192	Sammy Sosa	2.00
193	Troy Percival	.10
194	Robb Nen	.10
195	Bill Mueller	.10
196	Ben Grieve	.75
197	Luis Gonzalez	.10
198	Will Clark	.25
199	Jeff Cirillo	.10
200	Scott Rolen	.75
201	Reggie Sanders	.10
202	Fred McGriff	.25
203	Denny Neagle	.10
204	Brad Fullmer	.25
205	Royce Clayton	.10
206	Jose Canseco	.40
207	Jeff Bagwell	1.00
208	Hideo Nomo	.25
209	Karim Garcia	.10
210	Kenny Rogers	.10
211	Checklist (Kerry Wood)	.40
212	Checklist (Alex Rodriguez)	1.00
213	Checklist (Cal Ripken Jr.)	1.00
214	Checklist (Frank Thomas)	1.00
215	Checklist (Ken Griffey Jr.)	1.50
216	Alex Rodriguez (Season Crowns)	4.00
217	Greg Maddux (Season Crowns)	4.00
218	Juan Gonzalez (Season Crowns)	3.00
219	Ken Griffey Jr. (Season Crowns)	6.00
220	Kerry Wood (Season Crowns)	1.50
221	Mark McGwire (Season Crowns)	8.00
222	Mike Piazza (Season Crowns)	4.00
223	Rickey Henderson (Season Crowns)	.25
224	Sammy Sosa (Season Crowns)	4.00
225	Travis Lee (Season Crowns)	.75
226	Gabe Alvarez (Prospects)	.25
227	Matt Anderson (Prospects)	1.00
228	Adrian Beltre (Prospects)	.75
229	Orlando Cabrera (Prospects)	.10
230	Orlando Hernandez (Prospects)	8.00
231	Aramis Ramirez (Prospects)	.75
232	Troy Glaus (Prospects)	6.00
233	Gabe Kapler (Prospects)	6.00
234	Jeremy Giambi (Prospects)	1.50
235	Derrick Gibson (Prospects)	.25
236	Carlton Loewer (Prospects)	.25
237	Mike Frank (Prospects)	.50
238	Carlos Guillen (Prospects)	.25
239	Alex Gonzalez (Prospects)	.25
240	Enrique Wilson (Prospects)	.25
241	J.D. Drew (Prospects)	20.00
242	Bruce Chen (Prospects)	.25
243	Ryan Minor (Prospects)	3.00
244	Preston Wilson (Prospects)	.25
245	Josh Booty (Prospects)	.25
246	Luis Ordaz (Prospects)	.25
247	George Lombard (Prospects)	1.00
248	Matt Clement (Prospects)	.25
249	Eric Chavez (Prospects)	5.00
250	Corey Koskie (Prospects)	.75

1999 Ultra Book On

This 20-card set features insider scouting reports on the game's best players, utilizing embossing and gold foil stamping. These are found 1:6 packs.

		MT
Complete Set (20):		60.00
Common Player:		.50
Inserted 1:6		
1	Kerry Wood	2.00
2	Ken Griffey Jr.	8.00
3	Frank Thomas	5.00
4	Albert Belle	2.00
5	Juan Gonzalez	4.00
6	Jeff Bagwell	2.50
7	Mark McGwire	10.00
8	Barry Bonds	2.00
9	Andruw Jones	2.00
10	Mo Vaughn	2.00
11	Scott Rolen	2.00
12	Travis Lee	1.50
13	Tony Gwynn	4.00
14	Greg Maddux	5.00
15	Mike Piazza	5.00
16	Chipper Jones	4.00
17	Nomar Garciaparra	5.00
18	Cal Ripken Jr.	5.00
19	Derek Jeter	5.00
20	Alex Rodriguez	5.00

1999 Ultra Damage Inc.

This 15-card insert set has a buisness card design, for players who mean business. These are seeded 1:72 packs.

		MT
Complete Set (15):		300.00
Common Player:		5.00
Inserted 1:72		
1	Alex Rodriguez	25.00
2	Greg Maddux	25.00
3	Cal Ripken Jr.	25.00
4	Chipper Jones	20.00
5	Derek Jeter	25.00
6	Frank Thomas	25.00
7	Juan Gonzalez	20.00
8	Ken Griffey Jr.	40.00
9	Kerry Wood	10.00
10	Mark McGwire	50.00
11	Mike Piazza	25.00
12	Nomar Garciaparra	25.00
13	Scott Rolen	10.00
14	Tony Gwynn	20.00
15	Travis Lee	8.00

1999 Ultra Diamond Producers

This die-cut set uses full-foil plastic with custom embossing. Baseball's biggest stars comprise this 10-card set, which are seeded 1:288 packs.

		MT
Complete Set (10):		500.00
Common Player:		10.00
Inserted 1:288		
1	Ken Griffey Jr.	80.00
2	Frank Thomas	50.00
3	Alex Rodriguez	50.00
4	Cal Ripken Jr.	50.00
5	Mike Piazza	50.00
6	Mark McGwire	100.00
7	Greg Maddux	50.00
8	Kerry Wood	20.00
9	Chipper Jones	40.00
10	Derek Jeter	50.00

1999 Ultra RBI Kings

Found exclusively in retail packs, this 30-card set showcases baseball's top run producers. These are seeded one per retail pack.

		MT
Complete Set (30):		25.00
Common Player:		.25
Inserted 1:1 R		
1	Rafael Palmeiro	.25
2	Mo Vaughn	1.00
3	Ivan Rodriguez	1.00
4	Barry Bonds	1.00
5	Albert Belle	1.00
6	Jeff Bagwell	1.50
7	Mark McGwire	5.00
8	Darin Erstad	1.00
9	Manny Ramirez	1.50
10	Chipper Jones	2.00
11	Jim Thome	.50
12	Scott Rolen	1.00
13	Tony Gwynn	2.00
14	Juan Gonzalez	2.00
15	Mike Piazza	2.50
16	Sammy Sosa	3.00
17	Andruw Jones	1.00
18	Derek Jeter	3.00
19	Nomar Garciaparra	2.50
20	Alex Rodriguez	2.50
21	Frank Thomas	2.50
22	Cal Ripken Jr.	2.50
23	Ken Griffey Jr.	4.00
24	Travis Lee	.75
25	Paul O'Neill	.25
26	Greg Vaughn	.25
27	Andres Galarraga	.50
28	Tino Martinez	.40
29	Jose Canseco	.40
30	Ben Grieve	1.00

1999 Ultra Thunderclap

This set highlights the top hitters in the game, such as Nomar Garciaparra. Card fronts feature a lightning bolt in the background and are seeded 1:36 packs.

		MT
Complete Set (15):		160.00
Common Player:		4.00
Inserted 1:36		
1	Alex Rodriguez	15.00
2	Andruw Jones	6.00
3	Cal Ripken Jr.	15.00
4	Chipper Jones	12.00
5	Darin Erstad	6.00
6	Derek Jeter	15.00
7	Frank Thomas	15.00
8	Jeff Bagwell	8.00
9	Juan Gonzalez	12.00
10	Ken Griffey Jr.	25.00
11	Mark McGwire	30.00
12	Mike Piazza	15.00
13	Travis Lee	5.00
14	Nomar Garciaparra	15.00
15	Scott Rolen	6.00

1999 Ultra World Premiere

This 15-card set highlights rookies who made debuts in 1998, including J.D. Drew and Ben Grieve. These are seeded 1:18 packs.

		MT
Complete Set (15):		40.00
Common Player:		1.00
Inserted 1:18		
1	Gabe Alvarez	1.00
2	Kerry Wood	4.00
3	Orlando Hernandez	8.00
4	Mike Caruso	1.00
5	Matt Anderson	2.50
6	Randall Simon	1.00
7	Adrian Beltre	2.00
8	Scott Elarton	1.00
9	Karim Garcia	1.00
10	Mike Frank	1.00
11	Richard Hidalgo	1.00
12	Paul Konerko	2.00
13	Travis Lee	3.00
14	J.D. Drew	25.00
15	Miguel Tejada	2.00

1999 Upper Deck

Released in two series, card fronts feature a textured silver border along the left and right sides of the base card. The player name and Upper Deck logo also are stamped with silver foil. Card backs have a small photo, with year by year stats and a brief highlight caption of the player's career. Randomly seeded in packs are 100 Ken Griffey Jr. rookie cards that were bought back by Upper Deck from the hobby and autographed by Griffey Jr. Upper Deck also reinserted one pack of '89 Upper Deck inside every hobby box. 10-card hobby packs carry an S.R.P. of $2.99.

	MT
Complete Set (535):	80.00
Complete Series I set (255):	50.00
Complete Series II set (270):	30.00
Common Player:	.10
Production 100 sets	

1 Troy Glaus (Star Rookies) 4.00
2 Adrian Beltre (Star Rookies) 1.00
3 Matt Anderson (Star Rookies) .50
4 Eric Chavez (Star Rookies) 3.00
5 Jin Cho (Star Rookies) .50
6 *Robert Smith* (Star Rookies) .50
7 George Lombard (Star Rookies) 1.00
8 Mike Kinkade (Star Rookies) .75
9 Seth Greisinger (Star Rookies) .50
10 J.D. Drew (Star Rookies) 10.00
11 Aramis Ramirez (Star Rookies) .75
12 Carlos Guillen (Star Rookies) .50
13 Justin Baughman (Star Rookies) .50
14 Jim Parque (Star Rookies) .50
15 Ryan Jackson (Star Rookies) .50
16 Ramon Martinez (Star Rookies) .50
17 Orlando Hernandez (Star Rookies) 3.00
18 Jeremy Giambi (Star Rookies) 1.00
19 Gary DiSarcina .10
20 Darin Erstad .75
21 Troy Glaus 1.00
22 Chuck Finley .10
23 Dave Hollins .10
24 Troy Percival .10
25 Tim Salmon .25
26 Brian Anderson .10
27 Jay Bell .10
28 Andy Benes .10
29 Brent Brede .10
30 David Dellucci .10
31 Karim Garcia .10
32 Travis Lee .75
33 Andres Galarraga .30
34 Ryan Klesko .25
35 Keith Lockhart .10
36 Kevin Millwood .40
37 Denny Neagle .10
38 John Smoltz .25
39 Michael Tucker .10
40 Walt Weiss .10
41 Dennis Martinez .10
42 Javy Lopez .10
43 Brady Anderson .10
44 Harold Baines .10
45 Mike Bordick .10
46 Roberto Alomar .50
47 Scott Erickson .10
48 Mike Mussina .50
49 Cal Ripken Jr. 2.00
50 Darren Bragg .10
51 Dennis Eckersley .10
52 Nomar Garciaparra 2.00
53 Scott Hatteberg .10
54 Troy O'Leary .10
55 Bret Saberhagen .10
56 John Valentin .10
57 Rod Beck .10
58 Jeff Blauser .10
59 Brant Brown .10
60 Mark Clark .10
61 Mark Grace .25
62 Kevin Tapani .10
63 Henry Rodriguez .10
64 Mike Cameron .10
65 Mike Caruso .10
66 Ray Durham .10
67 Jaime Navarro .10
68 Maggilo Ordonez .25
69 Mike Sirotka .10
70 Sean Casey .20
71 Barry Larkin .25
72 Jon Nunnally .10
73 Paul Konerko .25
74 Chris Stynes .10
75 Brett Tomko .10
76 Dmitri Young .10
77 Sandy Alomar .10
78 Bartolo Colon .10
79 Travis Fryman .10
80 Brian Giles .10
81 David Justice .25
82 Omar Vizquel .10
83 Jaret Wright .50
84 Jim Thome .40
85 Charles Nagy .10
86 Pedro Astacio .10
87 Todd Helton .60
88 Darryl Kile .10
89 Mike Lansing .10
90 Neifi Perez .10
91 John Thomson .10
92 Larry Walker .40
93 Tony Clark .40
94 Deivi Cruz .10
95 Damion Easley .10
96 Brian L. Hunter .10
97 Todd Jones .10
98 Brian Moehler .10
99 Gabe Alvarez .10
100 Craig Counsell .10
101 Cliff Floyd .10
102 Livan Hernandez .10
103 Andy Larkin .10
104 Derrek Lee .10
105 Brian Meadows .10
106 Moises Alou .25
107 Sean Berry .10
108 Craig Biggio .25
109 Ricky Gutierrez .10
110 Mike Hampton .10
111 Jose Lima .10
112 Billy Wagner .10
113 Hal Morris .10
114 Johnny Damon .10
115 Jeff King .10
116 Jeff Montgomery .10
117 Glendon Rusch .10
118 Larry Sutton .10
119 Bobby Bonilla .20
120 Jim Eisenreich .10
121 Eric Karros .20
122 Matt Luke .10
123 Ramon Martinez .20
124 Gary Sheffield .25
125 Eric Young .10
126 Charles Johnson .10
127 Jeff Cirillo .10
128 Marquis Grissom .10
129 Jeremy Burnitz .10
130 Bob Wickman .10
131 Scott Karl .10
132 Mark Loretta .10
133 Fernando Vina .10
134 Matt Lawton .10
135 Pat Meares .10
136 Eric Milton .10
137 Paul Molitor .50
138 David Ortiz .10
139 Todd Walker .25
140 Shane Andrews .10
141 Brad Fullmer .25
142 Vladimir Guerrero 1.00
143 Dustin Hermanson .10
144 Ryan McGuire .10
145 Ugueth Urbina .10
146 John Franco .10
147 Butch Huskey .10
148 Bobby Jones .10
149 John Olerud .25
150 Rey Ordonez .10
151 Mike Piazza 2.00
152 Hideo Nomo .40
153 Masato Yoshii .10
154 Derek Jeter 2.00
155 Chuck Knoblauch .25
156 Paul O'Neill .25
157 Andy Pettitte .50
158 Mariano Rivera .20
159 Darryl Strawberry .25
160 David Wells .20
161 Jorge Posada .20
162 Ramiro Mendoza .20
163 Miguel Tejada .25
164 Ryan Christenson .10
165 Rickey Henderson .20
166 A.J. Hinch .10
167 Ben Grieve .75
168 Kenny Rogers .10
169 Matt Stairs .10
170 Bob Abreu .10
171 Rico Brogna .10
172 Doug Glanville .10
173 Mike Grace .10
174 Desi Relaford .10
175 Scott Rolen .75
176 Jose Guillen .20
177 Francisco Cordova .10
178 Al Martin .10
179 Jason Schmidt .10
180 Turner Ward .10
181 Kevin Young .10
182 Mark McGwire 4.00
183 Delino DeShields .10
184 Eli Marrero .10
185 Tom Lampkin .10
186 Ray Lankford .10
187 Willie McGee .10
188 Matt Morris .10
189 Andy Ashby .10
190 Kevin Brown .20
191 Ken Caminiti .20
192 Trevor Hoffman .10
193 Wally Joyner .10
194 Greg Vaughn .20
195 Danny Darwin .10
196 Shawn Estes .10
197 Orel Hershiser .10
198 Jeff Kent .10
199 Bill Mueller .10
200 Robb Nen .10
201 J.T. Snow .10
202 Ken Cloude .10
203 Russ Davis .10
204 Jeff Fassero .10
205 Ken Griffey Jr. 3.00
206 Shane Monahan .10
207 David Segui .10
208 Dan Wilson .10
209 Wilson Alvarez .10
210 Wade Boggs .25
211 Miguel Cairo .10
212 Bubba Trammell .10
213 Quinton McCracken .10
214 Paul Sorrento .10
215 Kevin Stocker .10
216 Will Clark .25
217 Rusty Greer .10
218 Rick Helling .10
219 Mike McLemore .10
220 Ivan Rodriguez .75
221 John Wetteland .10
222 Jose Canseco .40
223 Roger Clemens 1.50
224 Carlos Delgado .10
225 Darrin Fletcher .10
226 Alex Gonzalez .10
227 Jose Cruz Jr. .50
228 Shannon Stewart .10
229 Rolando Arrojo (Foreign Focus) .20
230 Livan Hernandez (Foreign Focus) .10
231 Orlando Hernandez (Foreign Focus) 1.00
232 Raul Mondesi (Foreign Focus) .20
233 Moises Alou (Foreign Focus) .20
234 Pedro Martinez (Foreign Focus) .40
235 Sammy Sosa (Foreign Focus) 1.25
236 Vladimir Guerrero (Foreign Focus) .50
237 Bartolo Colon (Foreign Focus) .10
238 Miguel Tejada (Foreign Focus) .10
239 Ismael Valdes (Foreign Focus) .10
240 Mariano Rivera (Foreign Focus) .10
241 Jose Cruz Jr. (Foreign Focus) .25
242 Juan Gonzalez (Foreign Focus) .75
243 Ivan Rodriguez (Foreign Focus) .40
244 Sandy Alomar (Foreign Focus) .10
245 Roberto Alomar (Foreign Focus) .25
246 Maggilo Ordonez (Foreign Focus) .20
247 Kerry Wood (Highlights Checklist) .75
248 Mark McGwire (Highlights Checklist) 2.00
249 David Wells (Highlights Checklist) .10
250 Rolando Arrojo (Highlights Checklist) .20
251 Ken Griffey Jr. (Highlights Checklist) 1.50
252 Trevor Hoffman (Highlights Checklist) .10
253 Travis Lee (Highlights Checklist) .40
254 Roberto Alomar (Highlights Checklist) .25
255 Sammy Sosa (Highlights Checklist) 1.25
266 *Pat Burrell* (Star Rookie) 5.00
267 Shea Hillenbrand (Star Rookie) .10
268 Robert Fick (Star Rookie) .10
269 Roy Halladay (Star Rookie) .25
270 Ruben Mateo (Star Rookie) 2.50
271 Bruce Chen (Star Rookie) .25
272 Angel Pena (Star Angel) .75
273 Michael Barrett (Star Rookie) .50
274 Kevin Witt (Star Rookie) .10
275 Damon Minor (Star Rookie) .10
276 Ryan Minor (Star Rookie) .40
277 A.J. Pierzynski (Star Rookie) .10
278 *A.J. Burnett* (Star Rookie) 2.00
279 Dermal Brown (Star Rookie) .10
280 Joe Lawrence (Star Rookie) .10
281 Derrick Gibson (Star Rookie) .10
282 Carlos Febles (Star Rookie) .75
283 Chris Haas (Star Rookie) .10
284 Cesar King (Star Rookie) .10
285 Calvin Pickering (Star Rookie) .10
286 Mitch Meluskey (Star Rookie) .10
287 Carlos Beltran (Star Rookie) 1.50
288 Ron Belliard (Star Rookie) .25
289 Jerry Hairston Jr. (Star Rookie) .10
290 Fernando Seguignol (Star Rookie) .50
291 Kris Benson (Star Rookie) .10
292 Chad Hutchinson (Star Rookie) 2.50
293 Jarrod Washburn .10
294 Jason Dickson .10
295 Mo Vaughn .75
296 Garrett Anderson .10
297 Jim Edmonds .10
298 Ken Hill .10
299 Shigetosi Hasegawa .10
300 Todd Stottlemyre .10
301 Randy Johnson .50
302 Omar Daal .10
303 Steve Finley .10
304 Matt Williams .25
305 Danny Klassen .10
306 Tony Batista .10
307 Brian Jordan .10
308 Greg Maddux 2.00
309 Chipper Jones 1.50
310 Bret Boone .10
311 Ozzie Guillen .10
312 John Rocker .10
313 Tom Glavine .20
314 Andruw Jones .75
315 Albert Belle .75
316 Charles Johnson .10
317 Will Clark .40
318 B.J. Surhoff .10
319 Delino DeShields .10
320 Heathcliff Slocumb .10
321 Sidney Ponson .10
322 Juan Guzman .10
323 Reggie Jefferson .10
324 Mark Portugal .10
325 Tim Wakefield .10
326 Jason Varitek .10
327 Jose Offerman .10
328 Pedro Martinez .75
329 Trot Nixon .10
330 Kerry Wood .40
331 Sammy Sosa 2.00
332 Glenallen Hill .10
333 Gary Gaetti .10
334 Mickey Morandini .10
335 Benito Santiago .10
336 Jeff Blauser .10
337 Frank Thomas 1.50
338 Paul Konerko .10
339 Jaime Navarro .10
340 Carlos Lee .10
341 Brian Simmons .10
342 Mark Johnson .10
343 Jeff Abbot .10
344 Steve Avery .10
345 Mike Cameron .10
346 Michael Tucker .10
347 Greg Vaughn .10
348 Hal Morris .10
349 Pete Harnisch .10
350 Denny Neagle .10
351 Manny Ramirez 1.00
352 Roberto Alomar .50
353 Dwight Gooden .10
354 Kenny Lofton .75
355 Mike Jackson .10
356 Charles Nagy .10
357 Enrique Wilson .10
358 Russ Branyan .10
359 Richie Sexson .10
360 Vinny Castilla .20
361 Dante Bichette .30
362 Kirt Manwaring .10
363 Darryl Hamilton .10
364 Jamey Wright .10
365 Curt Leskanic .10
366 Jeff Reed .10
367 Bobby Higginson .10
368 Justin Thompson .10
369 Brad Ausmus .10
370 Dean Palmer .10
371 Gabe Kapler 1.50
372 Juan Encarnacion .10
373 Karim Garcia .10
374 Alex Gonzalez .10
375 Braden Looper .10
376 Preston Wilson .10
377 Todd Dunwoody .10
378 Alex Fernandez .10
379 Mark Kotsay .10
380 Mark Mantei .10
381 Ken Caminiti .10
382 Scott Elarton .10
383 Jeff Bagwell .75
384 Derek Bell .10
385 Ricky Gutierrez .10
386 Richard Hildalgo .10
387 Shane Reynolds .10
388 Carl Everett .10
389 Scott Service .10
390 Jeff Suppan .10
391 Joe Randa .10
392 Kevin Appier .10
393 Shane Halter .10
394 Chad Kreuter .10
395 Mike Sweeney .10
396 Kevin Brown .25
397 Devon White .10
398 Todd Hollandsworth .10
399 Todd Hundley .10
400 Chan Ho Park .20
401 Mark Grudzielanek .10
402 Raul Mondesi .25
403 Ismael Valdes .10
404 Rafael Roque .10
405 Sean Berry .10
406 Kevin Barker .10
407 Dave Nilsson .10
408 Geoff Jenkins .10
409 Jim Abbott .10
410 Bobby Hughes .10
411 Corey Koskie .10
412 Rick Aguilera .10
413 LaTroy Hawkins .10
414 Ron Coomer .10
415 Denny Hocking .10
416 Marty Cordova .10
417 Terry Steinbach .10
418 Rondell White .20
419 Wilton Guerrero .10
420 Shane Andrews .10
421 Orlando Cabrerra .10
422 Carl Pavano .10
423 Jeff Vasquez .10
424 Chris Widger .10
425 Robin Ventura .20
426 Rickey Henderson .20
427 Al Leiter .20
428 Bobby Jones .10
429 Brian McRae .10
430 Roger Cedeno .10
431 Bobby Bonilla .10
432 Edgardo Alfonzo .10
433 Bernie Williams .50
434 Ricky Ledee .10
435 Chili Davis .10
436 Tino Martinez .40
437 Scott Brosius .10
438 David Cone .20
439 Joe Girardi .10
440 Roger Clemens 1.00
441 Chad Curtis .10
442 Hideki Irabu .10
443 Jason Giambi .10
444 Scott Spezio .10
445 Tony Phillips .10
446 Ramon Hernandez .10
447 Mike Macfarlane .10
448 Tom Candiotti .10
449 Billy Taylor .10
450 Bobby Estella .10
451 Curt Schilling .20
452 Carlton Loewer .10
453 Marlon Anderson .10
454 Kevin Jordan .10
455 Ron Gant .10
456 Chad Ogea .10
457 Abraham Nunez .10
458 Jason Kendall .20
459 Pat Meares .10
460 Brant Brown .10
461 Brian Giles .10
462 Chad Hermansen .10
463 Freddy Garcia 3.00
464 Edgar Renteria .10
465 Fernando Tatis .10
466 Eric Davis .10
467 Darren Bragg .10
468 Donovan Osborne .10
469 Manny Aybar .10
470 Jose Jimenez .10
471 Kent Mercker .10
472 Reggie Sanders .10
473 Ruben Rivera .10
474 Tony Gwynn 1.50
475 Jim Leyritz .10
476 Chris Gomez .10
477 Matt Clement .10
478 Carlos Hernandez .10
479 Sterling Hitchcock .10
480 Ellis Burks .10
481 Barry Bonds .75
482 Marvin Bernard .10
483 Kirk Rueter .10
484 F.P. Santangelo .10
485 Stan Javier .10
486 Jeff Kent .10

487	Alex Rodriguez	2.00
488	Tom Lampkin	.10
489	Jose Mesa	.10
490	Jay Buhner	.20
491	Edgar Martinez	.10
492	Butch Huskey	.10
493	John Mabry	.10
494	Jamie Moyer	.10
495	Roberto Hernandez	.10
496	Tony Saunders	.10
497	Fred McGriff	.25
498	Dave Martinez	.10
499	Jose Canseco	.50
500	Rolando Arrojo	.10
501	Esteban Yan	.10
502	Juan Gonzalez	1.50
503	Rafael Palmeiro	.40
504	Aaron Sele	.10
505	Royce Clayton	.10
506	Todd Zeile	.10
507	Tom Goodwin	.10
508	Lee Stevens	.10
509	Esteban Loaiza	.10
510	Joey Hamilton	.10
511	Homer Bush	.10
512	Willie Greene	.10
513	Shawn Green	.25
514	David Wells	.10
515	Kelvim Escobar	.10
516	Tony Fernandez	.10
517	Pat Hentgen	.10
518	Mark McGwire	2.00
519	Ken Griffey Jr.	1.50
520	Sammy Sosa	1.00
521	Juan Gonzalez	.75
522	J.D. Drew	.75
523	Chipper Jones	.75
524	Alex Rodriguez	1.00
525	Mike Piazza	1.00
526	Nomar Garciaparra	1.00
527	Season Highlights Checklist (Mark McGwire)	2.00
528	Season Highlights Checklist (Sammy Sosa)	1.00
529	Season Highlights Checklist (Scott Brosius)	.10
530	Season Highlights Checklist (Cal Ripken Jr.)	1.00
531	Season Highlights Checklist (Barry Bonds)	.40
532	Season Highlights Checklist (Roger Clemens)	.50
533	Season Highlights Checklist (Ken Griffey Jr.)	1.50
534	Season Highlights Checklist (Alex Rodriguez)	1.00
535	Season Highlights Checklist (Curt Schilling)	.10

1999 Upper Deck Exclusive

Randomly inserted into packs, this parallel issue is individually serial numbered on back from within an edition of 100 of each card. Besides the serial number, the inserts are readily apparent by the use of copper metallic foil graphic highlights on front. A parallel of this parallel with only one card of each player, was also issued but is not priced here because of rarity. Series 1 Exclusive cards have the serial number on back in gold foil; Series 2 Exclusives have the number ink-jetted in black.

	MT
Common Player:	6.00
Stars:	40-70X
Rookies:	20-40X

1999 Upper Deck Babe Ruth Piece of History Bat

Limited to approximately 400 cards, this unique card has a chip of a bat on it, from an actual game-used Louisville Slugger swung by the Bambino himself. A signed version of this card also exists, which incorporates both a "cut" signature of Ruth along with a piece of his game-used bat. Only three exist.

	MT
Babe Ruth Piece of History:	1600.
Babe Ruth Legendary Cutz.:	

1999 Upper Deck Crowning Glory

These double-sided cards feature players who reached milestones during the '98 season, including Roger Clemens, Kerry Wood and Mark McGwire. There are three cards in the set, with four different versions of each card. The regular version is seeded 1:23 packs. Doubles are numbered to 1,000, Triples numbered to 25 and Home Runs which are limited to one.

		MT
Complete Set (3):		60.00
Common Player:		10.00
Inserted 1:23		
Doubles:		4x to 8x
Production 1,000 sets		
CG1	Roger Clemens, Kerry Wood	15.00
CG2	Mark McGwire, Barry Bonds	25.00
CG3	Ken Griffey Jr., Mark McGwire	30.00

1999 Upper Deck Game Jersey-Hobby

This six-card set features a swatch of game-used jersey on each card and are available exclusively in hobby packs. The insert ratio is 1:288 packs.

		MT
Complete Set (14):		1800.
Common Player:		50.00
Inserted 1:288		
GJKG	Ken Griffey Jr.	400.00
GJAB	Adrian Beltre	60.00
GJBG	Ben Grieve	100.00
GJTL	Travis Lee	75.00
GJIV	Ivan Rodriguez	100.00
GJDE	Darin Erstad	90.00
GJKGs	Ken Griffey Jr. (Auto.)	4000.
BF	Brad Fullmer	50.00
BT	Bubba Trammell	50.00
EC	Eric Chavez	75.00
JD	J.D. Drew	150.00
MR	Manny Ramirez	160.00
NRa	Nolan Ryan	400.00
TGw	Tony Gwynn	200.00
CJ	Chipper Jones	200.00
JDs	J.D. Drew (auto)	50.00
NRaS	Nolan Ryan (auto)	50.00
TH	Todd Helton	75.00

1999 Upper Deck Game Jersey

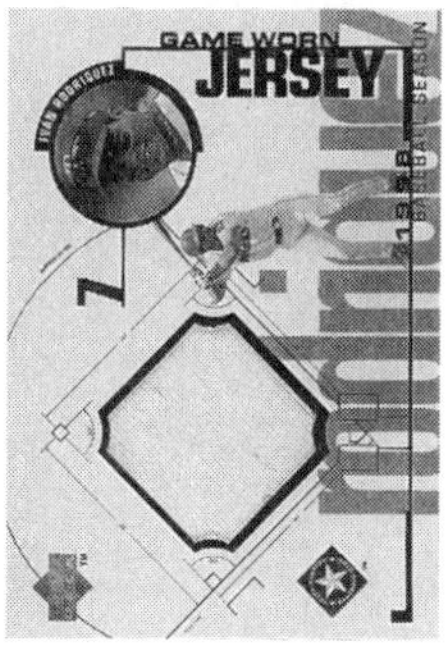

Inserted in both hobby and retail packs, this five-card set features a swatch of game-used jersey on each card. These are seeded 1:2,500 packs.

		MT
Complete Set (9):		2100.
Complete Series I set (5):		1000.
Complete Series II set (4):		1100.
Common Player:		100.00
Inserted 1:2,500		
GJKW	Kerry Wood	150.00
GJCJ	Charles Johnson	100.00
GJMP	Mike Piazza	350.00
GJAR	Alex Rodriguez	375.00
GJJG	Juan Gonzalez	250.00
GJKWs	Kerry Wood Auto.	1500.
GJKGs	Ken Griffey Jr. (Auto.)	4000.
GM	Greg Maddux	250.00
JR	Ken Griffey Jr.	400.00
NRb	Nolan Ryan	450.00
FT	Frank Thomas	220.00
JRS	Ken Griffey Jr. (auto)	100.00

1999 Upper Deck Forte

This 30-card set features the top players in the game, highlighted by blue holofoil treatment. Numbers on card backs have a "F" prefix and are seeded 1:23 packs. There are also three parallels to Forte: Double, Triple and Home Run. Doubles are sequentially numbered to 2,000 sets, Triples are limited to 100 numbered sets and Home Runs are limited to 10 numbered sets.

		MT
Complete Set (30):		250.00
Common Player:		3.00
Inserted 1:23		
Doubles:		1.5x to 2x
Production 2,000 sets		
Triples:		4x to 8x
Production 100 sets		
1	Darin Erstad	5.00
2	Troy Glaus	8.00
3	Mo Vaughn	6.00
4	Greg Maddux	15.00
5	Andres Galarraga	4.00
6	Chipper Jones	12.00
7	Cal Ripken Jr.	20.00
8	Albert Belle	6.00
9	Nomar Garciaparra	15.00
10	Sammy Sosa	15.00
11	Kerry Wood	5.00
12	Frank Thomas	12.00
13	Jim Thome	3.00
14	Jeff Bagwell	6.00
15	Vladimir Guerrero	8.00
16	Mike Piazza	15.00
17	Derek Jeter	15.00
18	Ben Grieve	5.00
19	Eric Chavez	5.00
20	Scott Rolen	6.00
21	Mark McGwire	30.00
22	J.D. Drew	12.00
23	Tony Gwynn	12.00
24	Barry Bonds	6.00
25	Alex Rodriguez	15.00
26	Ken Griffey Jr.	25.00
27	Ivan Rodriguez	6.00
28	JuLnzalez	12.00
29	Roger Clemens	8.00
30	Andruw Jones	6.00

1999 Upper Deck Immaculate Perception

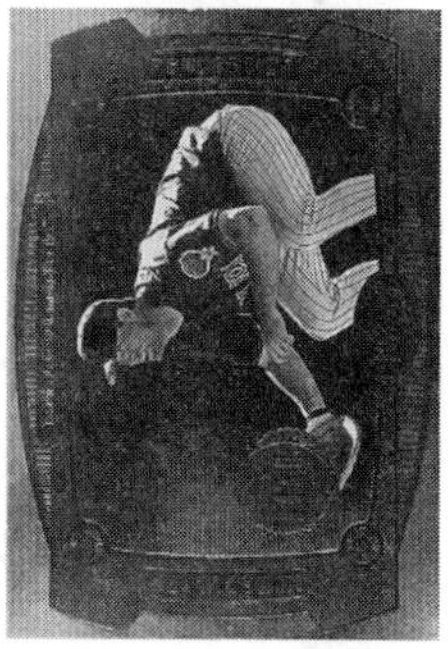

Done in a horizontal format, this 27-card set features baseball's most celebrated players. Card fronts are enhanced with copper and silver foil stamping, encasing the player's image. The cards are numbered with a I prefix and are seeded 1:23 packs. There are also three parallel versions: Doubles numbered to 1,000, Triples numbered to 25 and Home Runs which are limited to one.

		MT
Complete Set (27):		220.00
Common Player:		3.00
Inserted 1:23		
Doubles:		2x to 3x
Production 1,000 sets		
101	Jeff Bagwell	6.00
102	Craig Biggio	3.00
103	Barry Bonds	6.00
104	Roger Clemens	12.00
105	Jose Cruz Jr.	5.00
106	Nomar Garciaparra	20.00
107	Tony Clark	4.00
108	Ben Grieve	6.00
109	Ken Griffey Jr.	30.00
110	Tony Gwynn	15.00
111	Randy Johnson	5.00
112	Chipper Jones	15.00
113	Travis Lee	6.00
114	Kenny Lofton	5.00
115	Greg Maddux	20.00
116	Mark McGwire	35.00
117	Hideo Nomo	3.00
118	Mike Piazza	20.00
119	Manny Ramirez	8.00
120	Cal Ripken Jr.	20.00
121	Alex Rodriguez	20.00
122	Scott Rolen	6.00
123	Frank Thomas	20.00
124	Kerry Wood	8.00
125	Larry Walker	4.00
126	Vinny Castilla	3.00
127	Derek Jeter	15.00

1999 Upper Deck Textbook Excellence

This 30-card set features the game's most fundamentally sound performers. Card fronts have a photo of the featured player with a silver foil stamped grid surrounding the player. The left portion of the insert has the player name, team and his position on a brown background. These are seeded 1:23 packs. There are three parallels as well: Double, Triple and Home Run. Doubles are hobby exclusive and numbered to 2,000 sets, Triples are hobby-only and limited to 100 numbered sets and Home Runs are hobby-only and limited to 10 numbered sets.

		MT
Complete Set (30):		75.00
Common Player:		.75
Inserted 1:4		
Doubles:		4x to 6x
Production 2,000 sets H		
Triples:		15x to 25x
Production 100 sets H		
1	Mo Vaughn	2.00
2	Greg Maddux	5.00
3	Chipper Jones	4.00
4	Andruw Jones	2.00
5	Cal Ripken Jr.	6.00
6	Albert Belle	2.00
7	Roberto Alomar	1.50
8	Nomar Garciaparra	5.00
9	Kerry Wood	2.00
10	Sammy Sosa	5.00
11	Greg Vaughn	.75
12	Jeff Bagwell	2.00
13	Kevin Brown	.75
14	Vladimir Guerrero	2.50
15	Mike Piazza	5.00
16	Bernie Williams	1.50
17	Derek Jeter	5.00
18	Ben Grieve	1.50
19	Eric Chavez	1.50
20	Scott Rolen	2.00
21	Mark McGwire	10.00
22	David Wells	.75
23	J.D. Drew	4.00
24	Tony Gwynn	4.00
25	Barry Bonds	2.00
26	Alex Rodriguez	5.00
27	Ken Griffey Jr.	8.00
28	Juan Gonzalez	4.00
29	Ivan Rodriguez	2.00
30	Roger Clemens	3.00

1999 Upper Deck Wonder Years

These inserts look like a throwback to the groovin' '70s, with its bright, striped, green and pink border. Wonder Years is across the top of the card front in yellow lettering. Card backs have the player's three best seasons statistics along with a mention of a milestone. The cards are numbered with a WY prefix and are seeded 1:7 packs. There are three parallel versions: Doubles which are numbered to 1,000, Triples numbered to 25 and Home Runs which are limited to one.

	MT
Complete Set (30):	120.00
Common Player:	1.00
Inserted 1:7	
Doubles:	2x to 3x

Production 2,000 sets	
Triples:	20x to 40x
Production 50 sets	
W01 Kerry Wood	3.00
W02 Travis Lee	3.00
W03 Jeff Bagwell	3.00
W04 Barry Bonds	3.00
W05 Roger Clemens	6.00
W06 Jose Cruz Jr.	2.00
W07 Andres Galarraga	1.50
W08 Nomar Garciaparra	8.00
W09 Juan Gonzalez	6.00
W10 Ken Griffey Jr.	12.00
W11 Tony Gwynn	6.00
W12 Derek Jeter	6.00
W13 Randy Johnson	2.00
W14 Andruw Jones	3.00
W15 Chipper Jones	6.00
W16 Kenny Lofton	2.50
W17 Greg Maddux	8.00
W18 Tino Martinez	1.50
W19 Mark McGwire	15.00
W20 Paul Molitor	2.00
W21 Mike Piazza	8.00
W22 Manny Ramirez	4.00
W23 Cal Ripken Jr.	8.00
W24 Alex Rodriguez	8.00
W25 Sammy Sosa	10.00
W26 Frank Thomas	8.00
W27 Mo Vaughn	3.00
W28 Larry Walker	1.50
W29 Scott Rolen	3.00
W30 Ben Grieve	3.00

1999 Upper Deck View to a Thrill

This 30-card set focuses on baseball's best overall athletes. There are two photos of the featured player on the card front, highlighted by silver foil and some embossing. These are inserted 1:7 packs.

		MT
Complete Set (30):		100.00
Common Player:		1.00
Inserted 1:7		
Doubles:		2x to 4x
Production 2,000 sets		
Triples:		10x to 18x
Production 100 sets		
1	Mo Vaughn	3.00
2	Darin Erstad	2.00
3	Travis Lee	2.00
4	Chipper Jones	6.00
5	Greg Maddux	8.00
6	Gabe Kapler	4.00
7	Cal Ripken Jr.	10.00
8	Nomar Garciaparra	8.00
9	Kerry Wood	3.00
10	Frank Thomas	6.00
11	Manny Ramirez	4.00
12	Larry Walker	2.00
13	Tony Clark	1.00
14	Jeff Bagwell	3.00
15	Craig Biggio	1.50
16	Vladimir Guerrero	4.00
17	Mike Piazza	8.00
18	Bernie Williams	2.00
19	Derek Jeter	8.00
20	Ben Grieve	2.00
21	Eric Chavez	2.00
22	Scott Rolen	3.00
23	Mark McGwire	15.00
24	Tony Gwynn	6.00
25	Barry Bonds	3.00
26	Ken Griffey Jr.	12.00
27	Alex Rodriguez	8.00
28	J.D. Drew	6.00
29	Juan Gonzalez	6.00
30	Roger Clemens	4.00

1999 Upper Deck 10th Anniversary Team

This 30-card set commemorates Upper Deck's 10th Anniversary, as collectors selected their favorite players for this set. Regular versions are seeded 1:4 packs, Doubles numbered to 4,000, Triples numbered to 100 and Home Runs which are limited to one set.

		MT
Complete Set (30):		70.00
Common Player:		.50
Inserted 1:4		
Doubles:		2x to 3x
Production 4,000 sets		
Triples:		20x to 40x
Production 100 sets		
X1	Mike Piazza	5.00
X2	Mark McGwire	10.00
X3	Roberto Alomar	1.00
X4	Chipper Jones	4.00
X5	Cal Ripken Jr.	5.00
X6	Ken Griffey Jr.	8.00
X7	Barry Bonds	2.00
X8	Tony Gwynn	4.00
X9	Nolan Ryan	8.00
X10	Randy Johnson	1.50
X11	Dennis Eckersley	.50
X12	Ivan Rodriguez	2.00
X13	Frank Thomas	5.00
X14	Craig Biggio	.75
X15	Wade Boggs	.75
X16	Alex Rodriguez	5.00
X17	Albert Belle	2.00
X18	Juan Gonzalez	4.00
X19	Rickey Henderson	.75
X20	Greg Maddux	5.00
X21	Tom Glavine	.75
X22	Randy Myers	.50
X23	Sandy Alomar	.75
X24	Jeff Bagwell	2.00
X25	Derek Jeter	4.00
X26	Matt Williams	.75
X27	Kenny Lofton	1.50
X28	Sammy Sosa	6.00
X29	Larry Walker	.75
X30	Roger Clemens	4.00

1999 Upper Deck Black Diamond

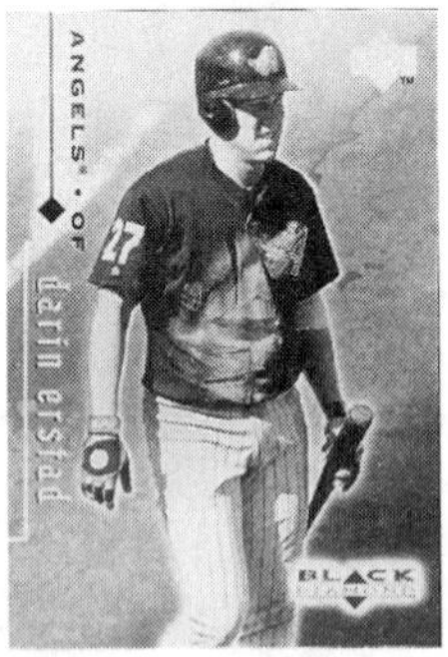

This 120-card base set features metallic foil fronts, while card backs have the featured player's vital information along with a close-up photo. The Diamond Debut subset (91-120) are short-printed and seeded 1:4 packs.

		MT
Complete Set (120):		140.00
Common Player:		.25
Common Diamond Debut (91-120):		1.00
Inserted 1:4		
Double Diamonds:		3x to 5x
Production 3,000 sets		
Double Diamond Debuts:		1.5x to 3x
Production 2,500 sets		
Triple Diamonds:		6x to 10x
Production 1,500 sets		
Triple Diamond Debuts:		3x to 5x
Production 1,000 sets		
1	Darin Erstad	1.25
2	Tim Salmon	.50
3	Jim Edmonds	.40
4	Matt Williams	.50
5	David Dellucci	.25
6	Jay Bell	.25
7	Andres Galarraga	.75
8	Chipper Jones	2.50
9	Greg Maddux	3.00
10	Andruw Jones	1.25
11	Cal Ripken Jr.	3.00
12	Rafael Palmeiro	.50
13	Brady Anderson	.25
14	Mike Mussina	1.00
15	Nomar Garciaparra	3.00
16	Mo Vaughn	1.25
17	Pedro Martinez	.75
18	Sammy Sosa	4.00
19	Henry Rodriguez	.25
20	Frank Thomas	3.00
21	Maggio Ordonez	.40
22	Albert Belle	1.25
23	Paul Konerko	.40
24	Sean Casey	.40
25	Jim Thome	.75
26	Kenny Lofton	1.25
27	Sandy Alomar Jr.	.25
28	Jaret Wright	.75
29	Larry Walker	.75
30	Todd Helton	1.25
31	Vinny Castilla	.25
32	Tony Clark	.75
33	Damion Easley	.25
34	Mark Kotsay	.25
35	Derrek Lee	.25
36	Moises Alou	.40
37	Jeff Bagwell	1.50
38	Craig Biggio	.50
39	Randy Johnson	.75
40	Dean Palmer	.25
41	Johnny Damon	.25
42	Chan Ho Park	.50
43	Raul Mondesi	.50
44	Gary Sheffield	.50
45	Jeromy Burnitz	.25
46	Marquis Grissom	.25
47	Jeff Cirillo	.25
48	Paul Molitor	1.00
49	Todd Walker	.50
50	Vladimir Guerrero	1.50
51	Brad Fullmer	.50
52	Mike Piazza	3.00
53	Hideo Nomo	.50
54	Carlos Baerga	.25
55	John Olerud	.40
56	Derek Jeter	3.00
57	Hideki Irabu	.50
58	Tino Martinez	.50
59	Bernie Williams	.75
60	Miguel Tejada	.50
61	Ben Grieve	1.50
62	Jason Giambi	.25
63	Scott Rolen	1.25
64	Doug Glanville	.25
65	Desi Relaford	.25
66	Tony Womack	.25
67	Jason Kendall	.25
68	Jose Guillen	.25
69	Tony Gwynn	2.50
70	Ken Caminiti	.40
71	Greg Vaughn	.40
72	Kevin Brown	.40
73	Barry Bonds	1.25
74	J.T. Snow	.25
75	Jeff Kent	.25
76	Ken Griffey Jr.	5.00
77	Alex Rodriguez	3.00
78	Edgar Martinez	.25
79	Jay Buhner	.50
80	Mark McGwire	6.00
81	Delino DeShields	.25
82	Brian Jordan	.25
83	Quinton McCracken	.25
84	Fred McGriff	.50
85	Juan Gonzalez	2.50
86	Ivan Rodriguez	1.25
87	Will Clark	.50
88	Roger Clemens	2.00
89	Jose Cruz Jr.	1.00
90	Babe Ruth	5.00
91	Troy Glaus (Diamond Debut)	8.00
92	Jarrod Washburn (Diamond Debut)	1.00
93	Travis Lee (Diamond Debut)	3.00
94	Bruce Chen (Diamond Debut)	1.00
95	Mike Caruso (Diamond Debut)	1.00
96	Jim Parque (Diamond Debut)	1.00
97	Kerry Wood (Diamond Debut)	1.00
98	Jeremy Giambi (Diamond Debut)	3.00
99	Matt Anderson (Diamond Debut)	2.00
100	Seth Greisinger (Diamond Debut)	1.00
101	Gabe Alvarez (Diamond Debut)	1.00
102	Rafael Medina (Diamond Debut)	1.00
103	Daryle Ward (Diamond Debut)	1.00
104	Alex Cora (Diamond Debut)	1.00
105	Adrian Beltre (Diamond Debut)	2.00
106	Geoff Jenkins (Diamond Debut)	1.50
107	Eric Milton (Diamond Debut)	1.00
108	Carl Pavano (Diamond Debut)	2.00
109	Eric Chavez (Diamond Debut)	6.00
110	Orlando Hernandez (Diamond Debut)	8.00
111	A.J. Hinch (Diamond Debut)	1.00
112	Carlton Loewer (Diamond Debut)	1.00
113	Aramis Ramirez (Diamond Debut)	1.50
114	Cliff Politte (Diamond Debut)	1.00
115	Matt Clement (Diamond Debut)	1.00
116	Alex Gonzalez (Diamond Debut)	3.00
117	J.D. Drew (Diamond Debut)	30.00
118	Shane Monahan (Diamond Debut)	1.00
119	Rolando Arrojo (Diamond Debut)	3.00
120	George Lombard (Diamond Debut)	1.00

1999 Upper Deck Black Diamond A Piece of History

This six-card set features green metallic foil fronts with a diamond-shaped piece of game-used bat from the featured player embedded on the card front. No insertion ratio was released.

		MT
Complete Set (6):		1200.
Common Player:		100.00
JG	Juan Gonzalez	250.00
TG	Tony Gwynn	250.00
BW	Bernie Williams	100.00
MM	Mark McGwire	500.00
MV	Mo Vaughn	150.00
SS	Sammy Sosa	300.00

1999 Upper Deck Black Diamond Diamond Dominance

This 30-card set features full-bleed metallic foil fronts and includes the top stars of the game along with Babe Ruth. Each card is numbered with a "D" prefix and is limited to 1,500 sequentially numbered sets.

	MT
Complete Set (30):	450.00
Common Player:	4.00
Production 1,500 sets	
D01 Kerry Wood	10.00
D02 Derek Jeter	20.00
D03 Alex Rodriguez	25.00
D04 Frank Thomas	25.00
D05 Jeff Bagwell	10.00
D06 Mo Vaughn	10.00
D07 Ivan Rodriguez	10.00
D08 Cal Ripken Jr.	30.00
D09 Rolando Arrojo	4.00
D10 Chipper Jones	20.00
D11 Kenny Lofton	10.00
D12 Paul Konerko	4.00
D13 Mike Piazza	25.00
D14 Ben Grieve	10.00
D15 Nomar Garciaparra	25.00
D16 Travis Lee	8.00
D17 Scott Rolen	10.00
D18 Juan Gonzalez	20.00
D19 Tony Gwynn	20.00
D20 Tony Clark	6.00
D21 Roger Clemens	18.00
D22 Sammy Sosa	30.00
D23 Larry Walker	6.00
D24 Ken Griffey Jr.	40.00
D25 Mark McGwire	50.00
D26 Barry Bonds	10.00
D27 Vladimir Guerrero	15.00
D28 Tino Martinez	6.00
D29 Greg Maddux	25.00
D30 Babe Ruth	50.00

1999 Upper Deck Black Diamond Mystery Numbers

The player's card number determines scarcity in this hobby-only insert set. The basic set has an action photo set against a silver-foil background of repeated numerals. Backs have a portrait photo and significant stat numbers from the 1998 season. Each base Mystery Numbers card is individually numbered within an edition of 100 cards times the card number within the 30-card set (i.e., card #24 has an edition of 2,400) for a total of 46,500 cards. An emerald version of the Mystery Numbers cards has a total issue of 465 cards, with cards issued to a limit of the player's card number multiplied by 100.

	MT
Complete Set (30):	1000.
Common Player:	4.00
M01 Babe Ruth (100)	250.00
M02 Ken Griffey Jr. (200)	200.00
M03 Kerry Wood (300)	40.00
M04 Mark McGwire (400)	100.00
M05 Alex Rodriguez (500)	60.00
M06 Chipper Jones (600)	40.00
M07 Nomar Garciaparra (700)	50.00
M08 Derek Jeter (800)	30.00
M09 Mike Piazza (900)	40.00
M10 Roger Clemens (1,000)	30.00
M11 Greg Maddux (1,100)	35.00
M12 Scott Rolen (1,200)	15.00
M13 Cal Ripken Jr. (1,300)	35.00
M14 Ben Grieve (1,400)	12.00
M15 Troy Glaus (1,500)	20.00
M16 Sammy Sosa (1,600)	30.00
M17 Darin Erstad (1,700)	10.00
M18 Juan Gonzalez (1,800)	20.00
M19 Pedro Martinez (1,900)	8.00
M20 Larry Walker (2,000)	8.00
M21 Vladimir Guerrero (2,100)	10.00
M22 Jeff Bagwell (2,200)	10.00

M23	Jaret Wright (2,300)	6.00
M24	Travis Lee (2,400)	8.00
M25	Barry Bonds (2,500)	8.00
M26	Orlando Hernandez (2,600)	20.00
M27	Frank Thomas (2,700)	15.00
M28	Tony Gwynn (2,800)	10.00
M29	Andres Galarraga (2,900)	6.00
M30	Craig Biggio (3,000)	4.00

1999 Upper Deck Black Diamond Quadruple Diamond

Quadruple Diamonds are the scarcest of the parallel inserts to the Black Diamond base cards. The regular player cards (#1-90) feature a green metallic foil background and are serially numbered on back from within an edition of 150 each. Diamond Debut cards (#91-120) also feature green foil highlights on front and are individually numbered within an edition of 100 each.

		MT
Common Player (1-90):		8.00
Production 150 sets		
Common Diamond Debut (91-120):		10.00
Production 100 sets		
1	Darin Erstad	60.00
2	Tim Salmon	30.00
3	Jim Edmonds	20.00
4	Matt Williams	25.00
5	David Dellucci	8.00
6	Jay Bell	8.00
7	Andres Galarraga	50.00
8	Chipper Jones	125.00
9	Greg Maddux	160.00
10	Andruw Jones	60.00
11	Cal Ripken Jr.	200.00
12	Rafael Palmeiro	25.00
13	Brady Anderson	10.00
14	Mike Mussina	50.00
15	Nomar Garciaparra	160.00
16	Mo Vaughn	60.00
17	Pedro Martinez	40.00
18	Sammy Sosa	200.00
19	Henry Rodriguez	10.00
20	Frank Thomas	160.00
21	Magglio Ordonez	20.00
22	Albert Belle	60.00
23	Paul Konerko	15.00
24	Sean Casey	15.00
25	Jim Thome	30.00
26	Kenny Lofton	60.00
27	Sandy Alomar Jr.	10.00
28	Jaret Wright	30.00
29	Larry Walker	30.00
30	Todd Helton	50.00
31	Vinny Castilla	10.00
32	Tony Clark	30.00
33	Damion Easley	8.00
34	Mark Kotsay	10.00
35	Derrek Lee	8.00
36	Moises Alou	15.00
37	Jeff Bagwell	60.00
38	Craig Biggio	20.00
39	Randy Johnson	40.00
40	Dean Palmer	8.00
41	Johnny Damon	8.00
42	Chan Ho Park	20.00
43	Raul Mondesi	20.00
44	Gary Sheffield	20.00
45	Jeromy Burnitz	8.00
46	Marquis Grissom	8.00
47	Jeff Cirillo	8.00
48	Paul Molitor	50.00
49	Todd Walker	20.00
50	Vladimir Guerrero	60.00
51	Brad Fullmer	20.00
52	Mike Piazza	160.00
53	Hideo Nomo	25.00
54	Carlos Baerga	8.00
55	John Olerud	15.00
56	Derek Jeter	125.00
57	Hideki Irabu	20.00
58	Tino Martinez	25.00
59	Bernie Williams	40.00
60	Miguel Tejada	20.00
61	Ben Grieve	60.00
62	Jason Giambi	8.00
63	Scott Rolen	60.00
64	Doug Glanville	8.00
65	Desi Relaford	8.00
66	Tony Womack	8.00
67	Jason Kendall	10.00
68	Jose Guillen	10.00
69	Tony Gwynn	125.00
70	Ken Caminiti	15.00
71	Greg Vaughn	15.00
72	Kevin Brown	15.00
73	Barry Bonds	60.00
74	J.T. Snow	8.00
75	Jeff Kent	10.00
76	Ken Griffey Jr.	250.00
77	Alex Rodriguez	160.00
78	Edgar Martinez	10.00
79	Jay Buhner	20.00
80	Mark McGwire	300.00
81	Delino DeShields	8.00
82	Brian Jordan	10.00
83	Quinton McCracken	8.00
84	Fred McGriff	20.00
85	Juan Gonzalez	125.00
86	Ivan Rodriguez	60.00
87	Will Clark	25.00
88	Roger Clemens	100.00
89	Jose Cruz Jr.	50.00
90	Babe Ruth	150.00
91	Troy Glaus (Diamond Debut)	100.00
92	Jarrod Washburn (Diamond Debut)	10.00
93	Travis Lee (Diamond Debut)	60.00
94	Bruce Chen (Diamond Debut)	15.00
95	Mike Caruso (Diamond Debut)	20.00
96	Jim Parque (Diamond Debut)	10.00
97	Kerry Wood (Diamond Debut)	60.00
98	Jeremy Giambi (Diamond Debut)	40.00
99	Matt Anderson (Diamond Debut)	25.00
100	Seth Greisinger (Diamond Debut)	10.00
101	Gabe Alvarez (Diamond Debut)	10.00
102	Rafael Medina (Diamond Debut)	10.00
103	Daryle Ward (Diamond Debut)	10.00
104	Alex Cora (Diamond Debut)	10.00
105	Adrian Beltre (Diamond Debut)	20.00
106	Geoff Jenkins (Diamond Debut)	15.00
107	Eric Milton (Diamond Debut)	10.00
108	Carl Pavano (Diamond Debut)	15.00
109	Eric Chavez (Diamond Debut)	50.00
110	Orlando Hernandez (Diamond Debut)	120.00
111	A.J. Hinch (Diamond Debut)	10.00
112	Carlton Loewer (Diamond Debut)	10.00
113	Aramis Ramirez (Diamond Debut)	20.00
114	Cliff Politte (Diamond Debut)	10.00
115	Matt Clement (Diamond Debut)	10.00
116	Alex Gonzalez (Diamond Debut)	30.00
117	J.D. Drew (Diamond Debut)	200.00
118	Shane Monahan (Diamond Debut)	10.00
119	Rolando Arrojo (Diamond Debut)	20.00
120	George Lombard (Diamond Debut)	10.00

1999 Upper Deck Century Legends

The first 47 cards in the 131-card set are taken from the Sporting News' list of Baseball's 100 Greatest Players. Each card bears a Sporting News photo of the featured player and his ranking in silver and copper foil. The next 50 cards tout Upper Deck's rankings of the Top 50 contemporary players. Rounding out the base set are two subsets: "21st Century Phenoms" and "Century Memories".

		MT
Complete Set (131):		50.00
Common Player:		.20
Century Collection:		25x to 50x
Production 100 sets H		
1	Babe Ruth (Sporting News Top 50)	4.00
2	Willie Mays (Sporting News Top 50)	2.00
3	Ty Cobb (Sporting News Top 50)	2.00
4	Walter Johnson (Sporting News Top 50)	.75
5	Hank Aaron (Sporting News Top 50)	1.50
6	Lou Gehrig (Sporting News Top 50)	3.00
7	Christy Mathewson (Sporting News Top 50)	.50
8	Ted Williams (Sporting News Top 50)	2.00
9	Rogers Hornsby (Sporting News Top 50)	.50
10	Stan Musial (Sporting News Top 50)	1.00
12	Grover Alexander (Sporting News Top 50)	.50
13	Honus Wagner (Sporting News Top 50)	.50
14	Cy Young (Sporting News Top 50)	.75
15	Jimmie Foxx (Sporting News Top 50)	.75
16	Johnny Bench (Sporting News Top 50)	.75
17	Mickey Mantle (Sporting News Top 50)	4.00
18	Josh Gibson (Sporting News Top 50)	.75
19	Satchel Paige (Sporting News Top 50)	1.00
20	Roberto Clemente (Sporting News Top 50)	2.00
21	Warren Spahn (Sporting News Top 50)	.75
22	Frank Robinson (Sporting News Top 50)	.75
23	Lefty Grove (Sporting News Top 50)	.50
24	Eddie Collins (Sporting News Top 50)	.50
27	Tris Speaker (Sporting News Top 50)	.50
28	Mike Schmidt (Sporting News Top 50)	.75
29	Napoleon LaJoie (Sporting News Top 50)	.50
30	Steve Carlton (Sporting News Top 50)	.50
31	Bob Gibson (Sporting News Top 50)	.75
32	Tom Seaver (Sporting News Top 50)	.75
33	George Sisler (Sporting News Top 50)	.50
34	Barry Bonds (Sporting News Top 50)	.75
35	Joe Jackson (Sporting News Top 50)	1.50
36	Bob Feller (Sporting News Top 50)	.50
37	Hank Greenberg (Sporting News Top 50)	.50
38	Ernie Banks (Sporting News Top 50)	.75
39	Greg Maddux (Sporting News Top 50)	1.50
40	Yogi Berra (Sporting News Top 50)	1.00
41	Nolan Ryan (Sporting News Top 50)	3.00
42	Mel Ott (Sporting News Top 50)	.50
43	Al Simmons (Sporting News Top 50)	.50
44	Jackie Robinson (Sporting News Top 50)	2.50
45	Carl Hubbell (Sporting News Top 50)	.50
46	Charley Gehringer (Sporting News Top 50)	.50
47	Buck Leonard (Sporting News Top 50)	.50
48	Reggie Jackson (Sporting News Top 50)	.75
49	Tony Gwynn (Sporting News Top 50)	1.00
50	Roy Campanella (Sporting News Top 50)	.75
51	Ken Griffey Jr. (Contemporaries)	3.00
52	Barry Bonds (Contemporaries)	.75
53	Roger Clemens (Contemporaries)	1.00
54	Tony Gwynn (Contemporaries)	1.50
55	Cal Ripken Jr. (Contemporaries)	2.50
56	Greg Maddux (Contemporaries)	1.50
57	Frank Thomas (Contemporaries)	1.50
58	Mark McGwire (Contemporaries)	4.00
59	Mike Piazza (Contemporaries)	2.00
60	Wade Boggs (Contemporaries)	.40
61	Alex Rodriguez (Contemporaries)	2.00
62	Juan Gonzalez (Contemporaries)	1.50
63	Mo Vaughn (Contemporaries)	.75
64	Albert Belle (Contemporaries)	.75
65	Sammy Sosa (Contemporaries)	2.00
66	Nomar Garciaparra (Contemporaries)	2.00
67	Derek Jeter (Contemporaries)	2.00
68	Kevin Brown (Contemporaries)	.30
69	Jose Canseco (Contemporaries)	.50
70	Randy Johnson (Contemporaries)	.50
71	Tom Glavine (Contemporaries)	.20
72	Barry Larkin (Contemporaries)	.30
73	Curt Schilling (Contemporaries)	.20
74	Moises Alou (Contemporaries)	.20
75	Fred McGriff (Contemporaries)	.20
76	Pedro Martinez (Contemporaries)	.50
77	Andres Galarraga (Contemporaries)	.30
78	Will Clark (Contemporaries)	.30
79	Larry Walker (Contemporaries)	.50
80	Ivan Rodriguez (Contemporaries)	.75
81	Chipper Jones (Contemporaries)	1.50
82	Jeff Bagwell (Contemporaries)	.75
83	Craig Biggio (Contemporaries)	.40
84	Kerry Wood (Contemporaries)	.75
85	Roberto Alomar (Contemporaries)	.50
86	Vinny Castilla (Contemporaries)	.20
87	Kenny Lofton (Contemporaries)	.75
88	Rafael Palmeiro (Contemporaries)	.30
89	Manny Ramirez (Contemporaries)	1.00
90	David Wells (Contemporaries)	.20
91	Mark Grace (Contemporaries)	.30
92	Bernie Williams (Contemporaries)	.50
93	David Cone (Contemporaries)	.20
94	John Olerud (Contemporaries)	.20
95	John Smoltz (Contemporaries)	.20
96	Tino Martinez (Contemporaries)	.40
97	Raul Mondesi (Contemporaries)	.30
98	Gary Sheffield (Contemporaries)	.30
99	Orel Hershiser (Contemporaries)	.20
100	Rickey Henderson (Contemporaries)	.30
101	J.D. Drew (21st Century Phenoms)	3.00
102	Troy Glaus (21st Century Phenoms)	1.00
103	Nomar Garciaparra (21st Century Phenoms)	2.00
104	Scott Rolen (21st Century Phenoms)	.75
105	Ryan Minor (21st Century Phenoms)	.20
106	Travis Lee (21st Century Phenoms)	.75
107	Roy Halladay (21st Century Phenoms)	.20
108	Carlos Beltran (21st Century Phenoms)	.75
109	Alex Rodriguez (21st Century Phenoms)	2.00
110	Eric Chavez (21st Century Phenoms)	.75
111	Vladimir Guerrero (21st Century Phenoms)	1.00
112	Ben Grieve (21st Century Phenoms)	.75
113	Kerry Wood (21st Century Phenoms)	.75
114	Alex Gonzalez (21st Century Phenoms)	.20
115	Darin Erstad (21st Century Phenoms)	.75
116	Derek Jeter (21st Century Phenoms)	2.00
117	Jaret Wright (21st Century Phenoms)	.40
118	Jose Cruz Jr. (21st Century Phenoms)	.40
119	Chipper Jones (21st Century Phenoms)	1.50
120	Gabe Kapler (21st Century Phenoms)	1.50
121	Satchel Paige (Century Memories)	1.00
122	Willie Mays (Century Memories)	1.50
123	Roberto Clemente (Century Memories)	1.50
124	Lou Gehrig (Century Memories)	2.50
125	Mark McGwire (Century Memories)	4.00
127	Bob Gibson (Century Memories)	.50
128	Johnny Vander Meer (Century Memories)	.20
129	Walter Johnson (Century Memories)	.50
130	Ty Cobb (Century Memories)	1.50
131	Don Larsen (Century Memories)	.40
132	Jackie Robinson (Century Memories)	2.00

133	Tom Seaver (Century Memories)	.75
134	Johnny Bench (Century Memories)	.50
135	Frank Robinson (Century Memories)	.75

1999 Upper Deck Century Legends All-Century Team

This 10-card set highlights Upper Deck's all-time all-star team. These were seeded 1:23 packs.

		MT
Complete Set (10):		50.00
Common Player:		4.00
Inserted 1:23		
1	Babe Ruth	15.00
2	Ty Cobb	6.00
3	Willie Mays	6.00
4	Lou Gehrig	10.00
5	Jackie Robinson	8.00
6	Mike Schmidt	4.00
7	Ernie Banks	4.00
8	Johnny Bench	4.00
9	Cy Young	4.00
10	Lineup Sheet	4.00

1999 Upper Deck Century Legends Century Artifacts

A total of nine cards were inserted, which were redeemable for memorabilia from some of the top players of the century. Due to the limited nature of these one-of-one inserts no pricing is available.

		MT
Complete Set (9):		
Common Player:		
1900's	Framed Cut of Cobb w/Cent. Card	
1910's	Framed Cut of Ruth w/Cent. Card	
1920's	Framed Cut of Hornsby w/Cent. Card	
1930's	Framed Cut of Paige w/Cent. Card	
1950's	Auto. Ball Coll. Aaron, Mays, Mantle	
1960's	Auto. Ball Coll. Banks, Gibson, Bench	
1970's	Auto. Ball Col. Seaver, Schmidt, Carlton	
1980's	Auto. Ball Coll. Nolan Ryan/Ken Griffey	
1990's	Ken Griffey Autographed Jersey	

1999 Upper Deck Century Legends Epic Signatures

This 30-card set features autographs from retired and current stars on a horizontal format. These autographed cards are seeded 1:24 packs.

		MT
Complete Set (30):		2000.
Common Player:		15.00
Inserted 1:24		
EB	Ernie Banks	50.00
JB	Johnny Bench	75.00
YB	Yogi Berra	60.00
BB	Barry Bonds	75.00
SC	Steve Carlton	40.00
BD	Bucky Dent	15.00
BF	Bob Feller	25.00
CF	Carlton Fisk	35.00
BG	Bob Gibson	30.00
JG	Juan Gonzalez	100.00
Jr.	Ken Griffey Jr.	250.00
Sr.	Ken Griffey Sr.	20.00
VG	Vladimir Guerrero	50.00
TG	Tony Gwynn	125.00
RJ	Reggie Jackson	125.00
HK	Harmon Killebrew	40.00
DL	Don Larsen	15.00
GM	Greg Maddux	150.00
EMa	Eddie Mathews	50.00
BM	Bill Mazeroski	15.00
WMc	Willie McCovey	30.00
SM	Stan Musial	80.00
FR	Frank Robinson	50.00
AR	Alex Rodriguez	180.00
NR	Nolan Ryan	350.00
MS	Mike Schmidt	60.00
TS	Tom Seaver	80.00
WS	Warren Spahn	50.00
FT	Frank Thomas	150.00
BT	Bobby Thomson	15.00

1999 Upper Deck Century Legends Century Epic Signatures

This 32-card autographed set features signatures from retired and current stars. The cards have a horizontal format and have gold foil stamping. Each card is hand numbered to 100.

		MT
Complete Set (32):		
Common Player:		50.00
Production 100 sets		
EB	Ernie Banks	140.00
JB	Johnny Bench	160.00
YB	Yogi Berra	160.00
BB	Barry Bonds	150.00
SC	Steve Carlton	125.00
BD	Bucky Dent	50.00
BF	Bob Feller	80.00
CF	Carlton Fisk	100.00
BG	Bob Gibson	120.00
JG	Juan Gonzalez	200.00
Jr.	Ken Griffey Jr.	500.00
Sr.	Ken Griffey Sr.	50.00
VG	Vladimir Guerrero	120.00
TG	Tony Gwynn	200.00
RJ	Reggie Jackson	250.00
HK	Harmon Killebrew	120.00
DL	Don Larsen	50.00
GM	Greg Maddux	250.00
EMa	Eddie Mathews	120.00
WM	Willie Mays	300.00
BM	Bill Mazeroski	50.00
WMc	Willie McCovey	75.00
SM	Stan Musial	200.00
FR	Frank Robinson	120.00
AR	Alex Rodriguez	350.00
NR	Nolan Ryan	500.00
MS	Mike Schmidt	150.00
TS	Tom Seaver	150.00
WS	Warren Spahn	120.00
FT	Frank Thomas	200.00
BT	Bobby Thomson	50.00
TW	Ted Williams	500.00

1999 Upper Deck Century Legends Epic Milestones

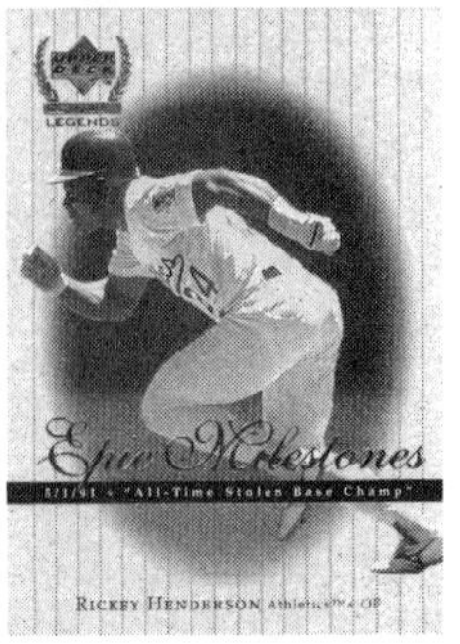

This nine-card set showcases nine of the most impressive milestones established in major league history. Each card is numbered with an "EM" prefix and is seeded 1:12 packs.

		MT
Complete Set (9):		45.00
Common Player:		2.00
Inserted 1:12		
2	Jackie Robinson	6.00
3	Nolan Ryan	10.00
4	Mark McGwire	12.00
5	Roger Clemens	4.00
6	Sammy Sosa	6.00
7	Cal Ripken Jr.	8.00
8	Rickey Henderson	2.00
9	Hank Aaron	4.00
10	Barry Bonds	3.00

1999 Upper Deck Century Legends Jerseys of the Century

This eight-card set features a swatch of game-worn jersey from the featured player, which includes current and retired players. These are seeded 1:418 packs.

		MT
Complete Set (10):		
Common Player:		125.00
Inserted 1:418		
GB	George Brett	250.00
RC	Roger Clemens	275.00
JR	Ken Griffey Jr.	125.00
TG	Tony Gwynn	250.00
GM	Greg Maddux	275.00
EM	Eddie Murray	125.00
NR	Nolan Ryan	650.00
MS	Mike Schmidt	250.00
OZ	Ozzie Smith	200.00
DW	Dave Winfield	125.00

1999 Upper Deck Century Legends Legendary Cuts

A total of nine of these inserts exist. These special inserts an actual "cut" signature from some of baseball's all-time greats, including Ty Cobb and Satchel Paige.

		MT
Complete Set (9):		
Common Player:		
RC	Roy Campanella	
TY	Ty Cobb	
XX	Jimmie Foxx	
LG	Lefty Grove	
WJ	Walter Johnson	
MO	Mel Ott	
SP	Satchel Paige	
BR	Babe Ruth	
CY	Cy Young	

1999 Upper Deck Century Legends Memorable Shots

This 10-card insert set focuses on the most memorable home runs launched during this century. The player's image is framed in an embossed foil, frame-like design. These are seeded 1:12 packs, each card back is numbered with an "HR" prefix.

		MT
Complete Set (10):		40.00
Common Player:		2.00
Inserted 1:12		
1	Babe Ruth	12.00
2	Bobby Thomson	2.00
3	Kirk Gibson	2.00
4	Carlton Fisk	2.00
5	Bill Mazeroski	2.00
6	Bucky Dent	2.00
7	Mark McGwire	10.00
8	Mickey Mantle	12.00
9	Joe Carter	2.00
10	Mark McGwire	10.00

1999 Upper Deck Century Legends 500 Club Piece History

This Jimmie Foxx insert has a piece of a game-used Louisville Slugger once swung by Foxx, embedded into the card front. An estimated 350 cards of this one exist.

		MT
Complete Set (1):		300.00
534 HR	Jimmie Foxx	300.00

1999 Upper Deck Encore

Encore is essentially a 180-card partial parallel of Upper Deck Series I, that utilizes a special holo-foil treatment on each card. The 180-card base set consists of 90 base cards and three short-printed subsets: 45 Star Rookie (1:4), 30 Homer Odyssey (1:6) and 15 Stroke of Genius (1:8).

		MT
Complete Set (180):		300.00
Common Player (1-90):		.20
Common Player (91-135):		1.50
Inserted 1:4		
Common Player (136-165):		.75
Inserted 1:6		
Common Player (166-180):		1.00
Inserted 1:8		
Gold (1-90):		15x to 30x
Gold (91-135):		2x to 4x
Gold (136-165):		4x to 6x
Gold (166-180):		5x to 8x
Production 125 sets		
1	Darin Erstad	.60
2	Mo Vaughn	.75
3	Travis Lee	.60
4	Randy Johnson	.75
5	Matt Williams	.40
6	John Smoltz	.20
7	Greg Maddux	2.50
8	Chipper Jones	2.00
9	Tom Glavine	.20
10	Andruw Jones	.75
11	Cal Ripken Jr.	3.00
12	Mike Mussina	.75
13	Albert Belle	.75
14	Nomar Garciaparra	2.50
15	Jose Offerman	.20
16	Pedro J. Martinez	1.00
17	Trot Nixon	.20
18	Kerry Wood	.50
19	Sammy Sosa	2.50
20	Frank Thomas	1.50
21	Paul Konerko	.20
22	Sean Casey	.75
23	Barry Larkin	.40
24	Greg Vaughn	.30
25	Travis Fryman	.20
26	Jaret Wright	.20
27	Jim Thome	.50
28	Manny Ramirez	1.00
29	Roberto Alomar	.75
30	Kenny Lofton	.75
31	Todd Helton	.75
32	Larry Walker	.75
33	Vinny Castilla	.20
34	Dante Bichette	.40
35	Tony Clark	.50
36	Dean Palmer	.20
37	Gabe Kapler	.75
38	Juan Encarnacion	.20
39	Alex Gonzalez	.20
40	Preston Wilson	.20
41	Mark Kotsay	.20
42	Moises Alou	.40
43	Craig Biggio	.50
44	Ken Caminiti	.30
45	Jeff Bagwell	1.00
46	Johnny Damon	.20
47	Gary Sheffield	.30
48	Kevin Brown	.40
49	Raul Mondesi	.30
50	Jeff Cirillo	.20
51	Jeromy Burnitz	.20
52	Todd Walker	.20
53	Corey Koskie	.20
54	Brad Fullmer	.20
55	Vladimir Guerrero	1.50
56	Mike Piazza	2.50
57	Robin Ventura	.30
58	Rickey Henderson	.30
59	Derek Jeter	2.50
60	Paul O'Neill	.40
61	Bernie Williams	.75
62	Tino Martinez	.50
63	Roger Clemens	1.50
64	Ben Grieve	.75
65	Jason Giambi	.20
66	Bob Abreu	.20
67	Scott Rolen	1.00
68	Curt Schilling	.40
69	Marlon Anderson	.20
70	Kevin Young	.20
71	Jason Kendall	.20
72	Brian Giles	.20
73	Mark McGwire	5.00
74	Fernando Tatis	.40
75	Eric Davis	.20
76	Trevor Hoffman	.20
77	Tony Gwynn	2.00
78	Matt Clement	.20
79	Robb Nen	.20
80	Barry Bonds	1.00
81	Ken Griffey Jr.	4.00
82	Alex Rodriguez	2.50
83	Wade Boggs	.40
84	Fred McGriff	.40
85	Jose Canseco	.75
86	Ivan Rodriguez	1.00
87	Juan Gonzalez	2.00
88	Rafael Palmeiro	.75
89	Carlos Delgado	.75
90	David Wells	.20
91	Troy Glaus (Star Rookies)	6.00
92	Adrian Beltre (Star Rookies)	3.00
93	Matt Anderson (Star Rookies)	2.00
94	Eric Chavez (Star Rookies)	4.00
95	*Jeff Weaver* (Star Rookies)	10.00
96	Warren Morris (Star Rookies)	2.00
97	George Lombard (Star Rookies)	2.00
98	Mike Kinkade (Star Rookies)	1.50
99	*Kyle Farnsworth* (Star Rookies)	2.00
100	J.D. Drew (Star Rookies)	15.00
101	*Joe McEwing* (Star Rookies)	10.00
102	Carlos Guillen (Star Rookies)	2.00
103	*Kelly Dransfeldt* (Star Rookies)	2.50
104	*Eric Munson* (Star Rookies)	18.00
105	Armando Rios (Star Rookies)	2.00

106	Ramon Martinez (Star Rookies)	1.50
107	Orlando Hernandez (Star Rookies)	2.50
108	Jeremy Giambi (Star Rookies)	2.00
109	*Pat Burrell* (Star Rookies)	20.00
110	Shea Hillenbrand (Star Rookies)	2.50
111	Billy Koch (Star Rookies)	2.00
112	Roy Halladay (Star Rookies)	2.50
113	Ruben Mateo (Star Rookies)	6.00
114	Bruce Chen (Star Rookies)	2.50
115	Angel Pena (Star Rookies)	2.50
116	Michael Barrett (Star Rookies)	3.00
117	Kevin Witt (Star Rookies)	1.50
118	Damon Minor (Star Rookies)	1.50
119	Ryan Minor (Star Rookies)	2.50
120	A.J. Pierzynski (Star Rookies)	2.50
121	*A.J. Burnett* (Star Rookies)	5.00
122	Christian Guzman (Star Rookies)	1.50
123	Joe Lawrence (Star Rookies)	1.50
124	Derrick Gibson (Star Rookies)	1.50
125	Carlos Febles (Star Rookies)	3.00
126	Chris Haas (Star Rookies)	1.50
127	Cesar King (Star Rookies)	2.00
128	Calvin Pickering (Star Rookies)	1.50
129	Mitch Meluskey (Star Rookies)	1.50
130	Carlos Beltran (Star Rookies)	6.00
131	Ron Belliard (Star Rookies)	3.00
132	Jerry Hairston Jr. (Star Rookies)	2.00
133	Fernando Seguignol (Star Rookies)	2.00
134	Kris Benson (Star Rookies)	2.00
135	Chad Hutchinson (Star Rookies)	8.00
136	Ken Griffey Jr. (Homer Odyssey)	8.00
137	Mark McGwire (Homer Odyssey)	10.00
138	Sammy Sosa (Homer Odyssey)	5.00
139	Albert Belle (Homer Odyssey)	1.50
140	Mo Vaughn (Homer Odyssey)	1.50
141	Alex Rodriguez (Homer Odyssey)	5.00
142	Manny Ramirez (Homer Odyssey)	2.00
143	J.D. Drew (Homer Odyssey)	4.00
144	Juan Gonzalez (Homer Odyssey)	4.00
145	Vladimir Guerrero (Homer Odyssey)	3.00
146	Fernando Tatis (Homer Odyssey)	.75
147	Mike Piazza (Homer Odyssey)	5.00
148	Barry Bonds (Homer Odyssey)	2.00
149	Ivan Rodriguez (Homer Odyssey)	2.00
150	Jeff Bagwell (Homer Odyssey)	2.00
151	Raul Mondesi (Homer Odyssey)	.75
152	Nomar Garciaparra (Homer Odyssey)	5.00
153	Jose Canseco (Homer Odyssey)	1.50
154	Greg Vaughn (Homer Odyssey)	.75
155	Scott Rolen (Homer Odyssey)	2.00
156	Vinny Castilla (Homer Odyssey)	.75
157	Troy Glaus (Homer Odyssey)	3.00
158	Craig Biggio (Homer Odyssey)	1.50
159	Tino Martinez (Homer Odyssey)	1.00
160	Jim Thome (Homer Odyssey)	1.50
161	Frank Thomas (Homer Odyssey)	3.00
162	Tony Clark (Homer Odyssey)	1.00
163	Ben Grieve (Homer Odyssey)	1.50
164	Matt Williams (Homer Odyssey)	1.00
165	Derek Jeter (Homer Odyssey)	5.00
166	Ken Griffey Jr. (Strokes of Genius)	6.00
167	Tony Gwynn (Strokes of Genius)	3.00
168	Mike Piazza (Strokes of Genius)	4.00
169	Mark McGwire (Strokes of Genius)	8.00
170	Sammy Sosa (Strokes of Genius)	4.00
171	Juan Gonzalez (Strokes of Genius)	3.00
172	Mo Vaughn (Strokes of Genius)	1.00
173	Derek Jeter (Strokes of Genius)	4.00
174	Bernie Williams (Strokes of Genius)	1.00
175	Ivan Rodriguez (Strokes of Genius)	1.50
176	Barry Bonds (Strokes of Genius)	1.50
177	Scott Rolen (Strokes of Genius)	1.50
178	Larry Walker (Strokes of Genius)	1.00
179	Chipper Jones (Strokes of Genius)	3.00
180	Alex Rodriguez (Strokes of Genius)	4.00

1999 Upper Deck Encore Batting Practice Caps

This 15-card set features actual swatch pieces of the highlighted players' batting practice cap embedded into each card. These are seeded 1:750 packs.

		MT
Complete Set (15):		
Common Player:		40.00
Inserted 1:750		
CB	Carlos Beltran	75.00
BB	Barry Bonds	120.00
VC	Vinny Castilla	50.00
EC	Eric Chavez	50.00
TC	Tony Clark	50.00
JD	J.D. Drew	125.00
VG	Vladimir Guerrero	160.00
TG	Tony Gwynn	150.00
TH	Todd Helton	60.00
GK	Gabe Kapler	50.00
JK	Jason Kendall	40.00
DP	Dean Palmer	40.00
BH	Frank Thomas	160.00
GV	Greg Vaughn	50.00
TW	Todd Walker	40.00

1999 Upper Deck Encore Driving Forces

This 15-card set is highlighted by holo-foil treatment on the card fronts on a thick card stock. Baseball's top performers are featured in this set and are seeded 1:23 packs. A Gold parallel exists and is limited to 10 sets.

		MT
Complete Set (15):		100.00
Common Player:		1.50
Inserted 1:23		
1	Ken Griffey Jr.	15.00
2	Mark McGwire	20.00
3	Sammy Sosa	10.00
4	Albert Belle	3.00
5	Alex Rodriguez	10.00
6	Mo Vaughn	3.00
7	Juan Gonzalez	8.00
8	Jeff Bagwell	4.00
9	Mike Piazza	10.00
10	Frank Thomas	5.00
11	Barry Bonds	4.00
12	Vladimir Guerrero	5.00
13	Chipper Jones	8.00
14	Tony Gwynn	8.00
15	J.D. Drew	8.00

1999 Upper Deck Encore McGwired!

This 10-card set salutes baseball's reigning single season home run king. These are seeded 1:23 packs. A gold parallel also is randomly seeded and is limited to 500 sequentially numbered sets. A small photo of the pitcher McGwire hit the historic home run off of is pictured as well.

		MT
Complete Set (10):		70.00
Common Player:		8.00
Inserted 1:23		
Parallel:		2x to 4x
Production 500 sets		
1	Mark McGwire, Carl Pavano	8.00
2	Mark McGwire, Michael Morgan	8.00
3	Mark McGwire, Steve Trachsel	8.00
4	Mark McGwire	8.00
5	Mark McGwire	8.00
6	Mark McGwire, Scott Elarton	8.00
7	Mark McGwire, Jim Parque	8.00
8	Mark McGwire	8.00
9	Mark McGwire, Rafael Roque	8.00
10	Mark McGwire, Jaret Wright	8.00

1999 Upper Deck Encore Pure Excitement

This 30-card set features Light F/X technology and includes the top players in baseball. These are seeded 1:7 packs.

		MT
Complete Set (30):		100.00
Common Player:		1.00
Inserted 1:7		
1	Mo Vaughn	2.00
2	Darin Erstad	1.50
3	Travis Lee	1.50
4	Chipper Jones	5.00
5	Greg Maddux	6.00
6	Gabe Kapler	1.50
7	Cal Ripken Jr.	8.00
8	Nomar Garciaparra	6.00
9	Kerry Wood	1.00
10	Frank Thomas	3.00
11	Manny Ramirez	2.50
12	Larry Walker	2.00
13	Tony Clark	1.00
14	Jeff Bagwell	2.50
15	Craig Biggio	1.50
16	Vladimir Guerrero	3.00
17	Mike Piazza	6.00
18	Bernie Williams	2.00
19	Derek Jeter	6.00
20	Ben Grieve	2.00
21	Eric Chavez	1.00
22	Scott Rolen	2.50
23	Mark McGwire	12.00
24	Tony Gwynn	5.00
25	Barry Bonds	2.50
26	Ken Griffey Jr.	10.00
27	Alex Rodriguez	6.00
28	J.D. Drew	5.00
29	Juan Gonzalez	5.00
30	Roger Clemens	3.00

1999 Upper Deck Encore Rookie Encore

This 10-card set highlights the top rookie prospects in 1999, including J.D. Drew and Gabe Kapler. These are seeded 1:23 packs. A parallel version is also randomly seeded and limited to 500 sequentially numbered sets.

		MT
Complete Set (10):		30.00
Common Player:		1.50
Inserted 1:23		
Parallel:		1.5x to 3x
Production 500 sets		
1	J.D. Drew	10.00
2	Eric Chavez	2.50
3	Gabe Kapler	3.00
4	Bruce Chen	1.50
5	Carlos Beltran	4.00
6	Troy Glaus	4.00
7	Roy Halladay	1.50
8	Adrian Beltre	2.00
9	Michael Barrett	1.50
10	Pat Burrell	12.00

1999 Upper Deck Encore Upper Realm

This 15-card set focuses on the top stars of the game. Card fronts utilize holo-foil treatment, with the initials UR lightly foiled. Card backs are numbered with a "U" prefix and are seeded 1:11 packs.

		MT
Complete Set (15):		60.00
Common Player:		1.00
Inserted 1:11		
1	Ken Griffey Jr.	8.00
2	Mark McGwire	10.00
3	Sammy Sosa	5.00
4	Tony Gwynn	4.00
5	Alex Rodriguez	5.00
6	Juan Gonzalez	4.00
7	J.D. Drew	4.00
8	Roger Clemens	3.00
9	Greg Maddux	5.00
10	Randy Johnson	1.50
11	Mo Vaughn	1.50
12	Derek Jeter	5.00
13	Vladimir Guerrero	3.00
14	Cal Ripken Jr.	6.00
15	Nomar Garciaparra	5.00

1999 Upper Deck Encore UD Authentics

This six-card autographed set features signatures of Griffey Jr. and Nomar Garciaparra. These are seeded 1:288 packs.

		MT
Complete Set (6):		500.00
Common Player:		20.00
MB	Michael Barrett	20.00
PB	Pat Burrell	50.00
JD	J.D. Drew	50.00
NG	Nomar Garciaparra	125.00
TG	Troy Glaus	25.00
JR	Ken Griffey Jr.	350.00

1999 Upper Deck Encore 2K Countdown

This set recognizes the countdown to the next century with a salute to baseball's next century of superstars including Derek Jeter and Alex Rodriguez. These are done on a horizontal format and inserted 1:11 packs.

		MT
Complete Set (10):		35.00
Common Player:		1.50
Inserted 1:11		
1	Ken Griffey Jr.	6.00
2	Derek Jeter	4.00
3	Mike Piazza	4.00
4	J.D. Drew	3.00
5	Vladimir Guerrero	2.00
6	Chipper Jones	3.00
7	Alex Rodriguez	4.00
8	Nomar Garciaparra	4.00
9	Mark McGwire	8.00
10	Sammy Sosa	4.00

1999 Upper Deck HoloGrFX

HoloGrFX was distributed exclusively to retail and the base set is comprised of 60 base cards, each utilizing holographic technology.

		MT
Complete Set (60):		30.00
Common Player:		.25
AUsome:		3x to 5x
Inserted 1:8		
1	Mo Vaughn	.75
2	Troy Glaus	1.00
3	Tim Salmon	.50
4	Randy Johnson	.75
5	Travis Lee	.60
6	Chipper Jones	2.00
7	Greg Maddux	2.50
8	Andruw Jones	.75
9	Tom Glavine	.25
10	Cal Ripken Jr.	3.00
11	Albert Belle	.75
12	Nomar Garciaparra	2.50
13	Pedro J. Martinez	1.00

14	Sammy Sosa	2.50
15	Frank Thomas	1.50
16	Greg Vaughn	.25
17	Kenny Lofton	.75
18	Jim Thome	.50
19	Manny Ramirez	1.00
20	Todd Helton	.50
21	Larry Walker	.75
22	Tony Clark	.50
23	Juan Encarnacion	.25
24	Mark Kotsay	.25
25	Jeff Bagwell	1.00
26	Craig Biggio	.60
27	Ken Caminiti	.40
28	Carlos Beltran	1.00
29	Jeremy Giambi	.25
30	Raul Mondesi	.40
31	Kevin Brown	.25
32	Jeromy Burnitz	.25
33	Corey Koskie	.25
34	Todd Walker	.25
35	Vladimir Guerrero	1.00
36	Mike Piazza	2.50
37	Robin Ventura	.25
38	Derek Jeter	2.50
39	Roger Clemens	1.50
40	Bernie Williams	.75
41	Orlando Hernandez	.50
42	Ben Grieve	.50
43	Eric Chavez	.50
44	Scott Rolen	1.00
45	*Pat Burrell*	4.00
46	Warren Morris	.25
47	Jason Kendall	.25
48	Mark McGwire	5.00
49	J.D. Drew	2.00
50	Tony Gwynn	2.00
51	Trevor Hoffman	.25
52	Barry Bonds	1.00
53	Ken Griffey Jr.	4.00
54	Alex Rodriguez	2.50
55	Jose Canseco	.75
56	Juan Gonzalez	2.00
57	Ivan Rodriguez	1.00
58	Rafael Palmeiro	.75
59	David Wells	.25
60	Carlos Delgado	.75

1999 Upper Deck HoloGrFX Future Fame

This six-card set focuses on players who are destined for Hall of Fame greatness. Card fronts feature a horizontal format on a die-cut design. These are seeded 1:34 packs. A parallel Gold (AU) version is also randomly seeded in every 1:432 packs.

		MT
Complete Set (6):		60.00
Common Player:		8.00
Inserted 1:34		
Golds:		2x to 4x
Inserted 1:210		
1	Tony Gwynn	8.00
2	Cal Ripken Jr.	12.00
3	Mark McGwire	20.00
4	Ken Griffey Jr.	15.00
5	Greg Maddux	10.00
6	Roger Clemens	6.00

1999 Upper Deck HoloGrFX Launchers

This 15-card set highlights the top home run hitters on holographic patterned foil fronts, including McGwire and Sosa. These are seeded 1:3 packs. A Gold (AU) parallel version is also seeded 1:105 packs.

		MT
Complete Set (15):		40.00
Common Player:		1.00
Inserted 1:3		
Golds		3x to 6x
Inserted 1:105		
1	Mark McGwire	8.00
2	Ken Griffey Jr.	6.00
3	Sammy Sosa	4.00
4	J.D. Drew	3.00
5	Mo Vaughn	1.00
6	Juan Gonzalez	3.00
7	Mike Piazza	4.00
8	Alex Rodriguez	4.00
9	Chipper Jones	3.00
10	Nomar Garciaparra	4.00
11	Vladimir Guerrero	2.00
12	Albert Belle	1.00
13	Barry Bonds	1.50
14	Frank Thomas	2.00
15	Jeff Bagwell	1.50

1999 Upper Deck HoloGrFX StarView

This nine-card set highlights the top players in the game on a rainbow foil, full bleed design. These are seeded 1:17 packs. A Gold parallel version is also randomly seeded 1:210 packs.

		MT
Complete Set (9):		50.00
Common Player:		4.00
Inserted 1:17		
Golds:		2x to 5x
Inserted 1:210		
1	Mark McGwire	12.00
2	Ken Griffey Jr.	10.00
3	Sammy Sosa	6.00
4	Nomar Garciaparra	6.00
5	Roger Clemens	4.00
6	Greg Maddux	6.00
7	Mike Piazza	6.00
8	Alex Rodriguez	6.00
9	Chipper Jones	5.00

1999 Upper Deck HoloGrFX UD Authentics

This 12-card autographed set is done on a horizontal format, with the player signature across the front of a shadow image, of the featured player in the background. These are inserted 1:431 packs.

		MT
Common Player:		10.00
Inserted 1:431		
CB	Carlos Beltran	50.00
BC	Bruce Chen	20.00
JD	J.D. Drew	100.00
AG	Alex Gonzalez	20.00
JR	Ken Griffey Jr.	300.00
CJ	Chipper Jones	150.00
GK	Gabe Kapler	40.00
MK	Mike Kinkade	10.00
CK	Corey Koskie	10.00
GL	George Lombard	20.00
RM	Ryan Minor	20.00
SM	Shane Monahan	10.00

1999 Upper Deck HoloGrFX 500 Club Piece of History

This twocard collection features game-used bat chips from bats swung by Willie McCovey and Eddie Mathews embedded into each card. 350 cards of each player exist. Each player also autographed these inserts to their respective jersey numbers: McCovey (44) and Mathews (41).

	MT
Willie McCovey	200.00
Production 350 cards	
McCovey Auto.	
Production 44 cards	
Eddie Mathews	250.00
Production 350 cards	

1999 Upper Deck MVP

Card fronts of the 220-card set feature silver foil stamping and a white border. Card backs feature year-by-year statistics, a small photo of the featured player and a brief career note. MVP was distributed in 24-pack boxes, with an S.R.P. of $1.59 for 10-card packs.

		MT
Complete Set (220):		30.00
Common Player:		.15
Silvers:		1.5x to 3x
Inserted 1:2		
Golds:		60x to 100x
Production 100 sets H		
Supers:		200x to 300x
Production 25 sets H		
1	Mo Vaughn	.75
2	Tim Belcher	.15
3	Jack McDowell	.15
4	Troy Glaus	.75
5	Darin Erstad	.75
6	Tim Salmon	.30
7	Jim Edmonds	.15
8	Randy Johnson	.50
9	Steve Finley	.15
10	Travis Lee	.75
11	Matt Williams	.25
12	Todd Stottlemyre	.15
13	Jay Bell	.15
14	David Dellucci	.15
15	Chipper Jones	1.50
16	Andruw Jones	.50
17	Greg Maddux	1.50
18	Tom Glavine	.25
19	Javy Lopez	.15
20	Brian Jordan	.15
21	George Lombard	.25
22	John Smoltz	.25
23	Cal Ripken Jr.	2.50
24	Charles Johnson	.15
25	Albert Belle	.75
26	Brady Anderson	.15
27	Mike Mussina	.60
28	Calvin Pickering	.15
29	Ryan Minor	.25
30	Jerry Hairston Jr.	.15
31	Nomar Garciaparra	2.00
32	Pedro Martinez	.60
33	Jason Varitek	.15
34	Troy O'Leary	.15
35	Donnie Sadler	.15
36	Mark Portugal	.15
37	John Valentin	.15
38	Kerry Wood	.75
39	Sammy Sosa	2.00
40	Mark Grace	.25
41	Henry Rodriguez	.15
42	Rod Beck	.15
43	Benito Santiago	.15
44	Kevin Tapani	.15
45	Frank Thomas	1.50
46	Mike Caruso	.15
47	Magglio Ordonez	.25
48	Paul Konerko	.25
49	Ray Durham	.15
50	Jim Parque	.15
51	Carlos Lee	.25
52	Denny Neagle	.15
53	Pete Harnisch	.15
54	Michael Tucker	.15
55	Sean Casey	.30
56	Eddie Taubenese	.15
57	Barry Larkin	.25
58	Pokey Reese	.15
59	Sandy Alomar	.25
60	Roberto Alomar	.60
61	Bartolo Colon	.15
62	Kenny Lofton	.60
63	Omar Vizquel	.15
64	Travis Fryman	.15
65	Jim Thome	.40
66	Manny Ramirez	1.00
67	Jaret Wright	.25
68	Darryl Kile	.15
69	Kirt Manwaring	.15
70	Vinny Castilla	.25
71	Todd Helton	.40
72	Dante Bichette	.25
73	Larry Walker	.50
74	Derrick Gibson	.15
75	Gabe Kapler	.75
76	Dean Palmer	.15
77	Matt Anderson	.15
78	Bobby Higginson	.15
79	Damion Easley	.15
80	Tony Clark	.40
81	Juan Encarnacion	.15
82	Livan Hernandez	.15
83	Alex Gonzalez	.15
84	Preston Wilson	.15
85	Derrek Lee	.15
86	Mark Kotsay	.15
87	Todd Dunwoody	.15
88	Cliff Floyd	.15
89	Ken Caminiti	.15
90	Jeff Bagwell	.75
91	Moises Alou	.25
92	Craig Biggio	.40
93	Billy Wagner	.15
94	Richard Hidalgo	.15
95	Derek Bell	.15
96	Hipolito Pichardo	.15
97	Jeff King	.15
98	Carlos Beltran	.20
99	Jeremy Giambi	.25
100	Larry Sutton	.15
101	Johnny Damon	.15
102	Dee Brown	.15
103	Kevin Brown	.25
104	Chan Ho Park	.25
105	Raul Mondesi	.30
106	Eric Karros	.15
107	Adrian Beltre	.30
108	Devon White	.15
109	Gary Sheffield	.30
110	Sean Berry	.15
111	Alex Ochoa	.15
112	Marquis Grissom	.15
113	Fernando Vina	.15
114	Jeff Cirillo	.15
115	Geoff Jenkins	.15
116	Jeromy Burnitz	.15
117	Brad Radke	.15
118	Eric Milton	.15
119	A.J. Pierzynski	.15
120	Todd Walker	.25
121	David Ortiz	.15
122	Corey Koskie	.15
123	Vladimir Guerrero	1.00
124	Rondell White	.25
125	Brad Fullmer	.25
126	Ugueth Urbina	.15
127	Dustin Hermanson	.15
128	Michael Barrett	.25
129	Fernando Seguignol	.40
130	Mike Piazza	2.00
131	Rickey Henderson	.25
132	Rey Ordonez	.15
133	John Olerud	.25
134	Robin Ventura	.15
135	Hideo Nomo	.25
136	Mike Kinkade	.15
137	Al Leiter	.25
138	Brian McRae	.15
139	Derek Jeter	2.00
140	Bernie Williams	.50
141	Paul O'Neill	.30
142	Scott Brosius	.15
143	Tino Martinez	.40
144	Roger Clemens	1.00
145	Orlando Hernandez	1.00
146	Mariano Rivera	.25
147	Ricky Ledee	.15
148	A.J. Hinch	.15
149	Ben Grieve	.75
150	Eric Chavez	.75
151	Miguel Tejada	.25
152	Matt Stairs	.15
153	Ryan Christenson	.15
154	Jason Giambi	.15
155	Curt Schilling	.25
156	Scott Rolen	.75
157	*Pat Burrell*	5.00
158	Doug Glanville	.15
159	Bobby Abreu	.15
160	Rico Brogna	.15
161	Ron Gant	.15
162	Jason Kendall	.25
163	Aramis Ramirez	.15
164	Jose Guillen	.15
165	Emil Brown	.15
166	Pat Meares	.15
167	Kevin Young	.15
168	Brian Giles	.15
169	Mark McGwire	3.00
170	J.D. Drew	3.00
171	Edgar Renteria	.15
172	Fernando Tatis	.15
173	Matt Morris	.15
174	Eli Marrero	.15
175	Ray Lankford	.15
176	Tony Gwynn	1.50
177	Sterling Hitchcock	.15
178	Ruben Rivera	.15
179	Wally Joyner	.15
180	Trevor Hoffman	.15
181	Jim Leyritz	.15
182	Carlos Hernandez	.15
183	Barry Bonds	.75
184	Ellis Burks	.15
185	F.P. Santangelo	.15
186	J.T. Snow	.15
187	Ramon Martinez	.15
188	Jeff Kent	.15
189	Robb Nen	.15
190	Ken Griffey Jr.	3.00
191	Alex Rodriguez	2.00
192	Shane Monahan	.15
193	Carlos Guillen	.15
194	Edgar Martinez	.15
195	David Segui	.15
196	Jose Mesa	.15
197	Jose Canseco	.75
198	Rolando Arrojo	.15
199	Wade Boggs	.25
200	Fred McGriff	.25
201	Quinton McCracken	.15
202	Bobby Smith	.15
203	Bubba Trammell	.15
204	Juan Gonzalez	1.50
205	Ivan Rodriguez	.75
206	Rafael Palmeiro	.30
207	Royce Clayton	.15
208	Rick Helling	.15
209	Todd Zeile	.15
210	Rusty Greer	.15
211	David Wells	.15
212	Roy Halladay	.25
213	Carlos Delgado	.25
214	Darrin Fletcher	.15
215	Shawn Green	.25
216	Kevin Witt	.15
217	Jose Cruz Jr.	.40
218	Ken Griffey Jr.	1.00
219	Sammy Sosa	.50
220	Mark McGwire	1.00

1999 Upper Deck MVP Dynamics

This 15-card set features holo-foil treatment on the card

fronts with silver foil stamping. Card backs are numbered with a "D" prefix and are inserted 1:28 packs.

		MT
Complete Set (15):		125.00
Common Player:		3.00
Inserted 1:28		
1	Ken Griffey Jr.	20.00
2	Alex Rodriguez	12.00
3	Nomar Garciaparra	12.00
4	Mike Piazza	12.00
5	Mark McGwire	20.00
6	Sammy Sosa	12.00
7	Chipper Jones	10.00
8	Mo Vaughn	5.00
9	Tony Gwynn	10.00
10	Vladimir Guerrero	6.00
11	Derek Jeter	12.00
12	Jeff Bagwell	5.00
13	Cal Ripken Jr.	15.00
14	Juan Gonzalez	10.00
15	J.D. Drew	10.00

1999 Upper Deck MVP Game Used Souvenirs

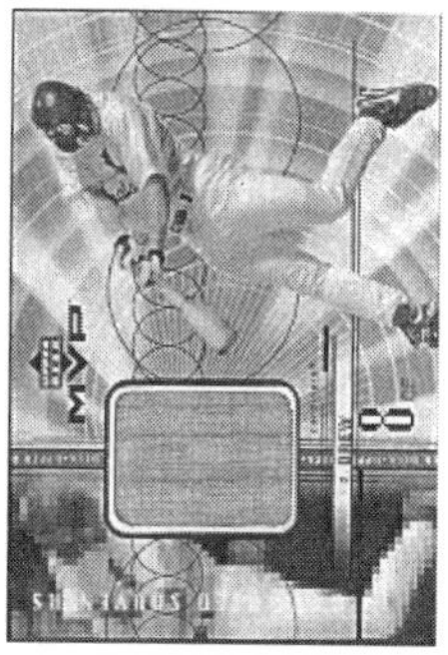

This 10-card set has a piece of game-used bat from the featured player embedded into each card. These are found exclusively in hobby packs at a rate of 1:144 packs.

		MT
Complete Set (9):		750.00
Common Player:		50.00
Inserted 1:144		
JB	Jeff Bagwell	60.00
BB	Barry Bonds	50.00
JD	J.D. Drew	100.00
KGj	Ken Griffey Jr.	200.00
CJ	Chipper Jones	100.00
MP	Mike Piazza	125.00
CR	Cal Ripken Jr.	160.00
SR	Scott Rolen	50.00
MV	Mo Vaughn	60.00

1999 Upper Deck MVP Signed Game Used Souvenirs

Ken Griffey Jr. and Chipper Jones both signed their Game Used Souvenir inserts to their jersey number, Griffey (24) and Jones (10). These were seeded exclusively in hobby packs.

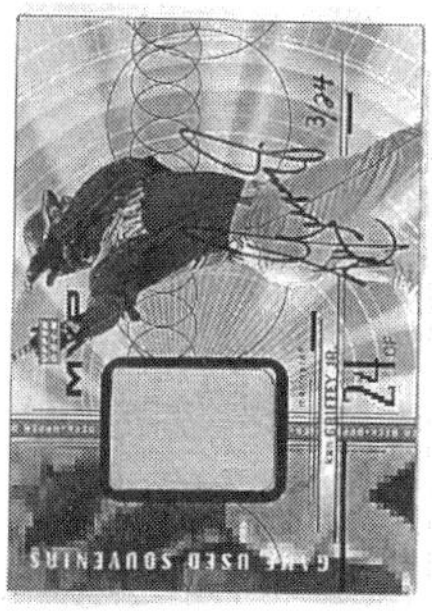

		MT
Complete Set (2):		1600.
KGj	Ken Griffey Jr.	1200.
CJ	Chipper Jones	500.00

1999 Upper Deck MVP Power Surge

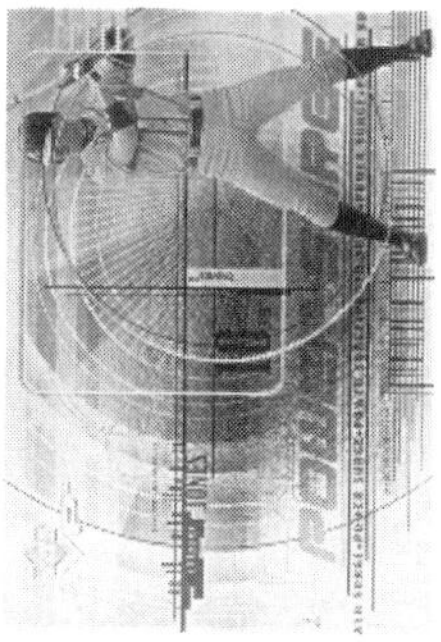

This 15-card set features baseball's top home run hitters, utilizing rainbow foil technology. Card backs are numbered with a "P" prefix and are seeded 1:9 packs.

		MT
Complete Set (15):		60.00
Common Player:		1.50
Inserted 1:9		
1	Mark McGwire	10.00
2	Sammy Sosa	6.00
3	Ken Griffey Jr.	10.00
4	Alex Rodriguez	6.00
5	Juan Gonzalez	5.00
6	Nomar Garciaparra	6.00
7	Vladimir Guerrero	3.00
8	Chipper Jones	5.00
9	Albert Belle	2.50
10	Frank Thomas	5.00
11	Mike Piazza	6.00
12	Jeff Bagwell	2.50
13	Manny Ramirez	3.00
14	Mo Vaughn	2.50
15	Barry Bonds	2.50

1999 Upper Deck MVP ProSign

This 30-card autographed set is randomly seeded, exclusively in retail packs at a rate of 1:216 packs. Card backs are numbered with the featured player's initials.

		MT
Common Player:		10.00
Inserted 1:216 R		
MA	Matt Anderson	15.00
CB	Carlos Beltran	50.00
RB	Russ Branyan	20.00
EC	Eric Chavez	30.00
BC	Bruce Chen	20.00
BF	Brad Fuller	15.00
NG	Nomar Garciaparra	140.00
JG	Jeremy Giambi	20.00
DG	Derrick Gibson	15.00
CG	Chris Gomez	10.00
AG	Alex Gonzalez	15.00
BG	Ben Grieve	40.00
JR.	Ken Griffey Jr.	10.00
RH	Richard Hidalgo	15.00
SH	Shea Hillenbrand	10.00
CJ	Chipper Jones	125.00
GK	Gabe Kapler	50.00
SK	Scott Karl	10.00
CK	Corey Koskie	15.00
RL	Ricky Ledee	15.00
ML	Mike Lincoln	10.00
GL	George Lombard	20.00
MLo	Mike Lowell	20.00
RM	Ryan Minor	20.00
SM	Shane Monahan	10.00
AN	Abraham Nunez	10.00
JP	Jim Parque	10.00
CP	Calvin Pickering	20.00
JRa	Jason Rakers	10.00
RR	Ruben Rivera	10.00
IR	Ivan Rodriguez	80.00
KW	Kevin Witt	10.00

1999 Upper Deck MVP Scout's Choice

Utilizing Light F/X technology, this 15-card set highlights the top young prospects in the game. Card backs are numbered with an "SC" prefix and are seeded 1:9 packs.

		MT
Complete Set (15):		40.00
Common Player:		1.00
Inserted 1:9		
1	J.D. Drew	10.00
2	Ben Grieve	2.50
3	Troy Glaus	3.00
4	Gabe Kapler	4.00
5	Carlos Beltran	1.00
6	Aramis Ramirez	1.00
7	Pat Burrell	10.00
8	Kerry Wood	2.50
9	Ryan Minor	1.00
10	Todd Helton	2.00
11	Eric Chavez	2.50
12	Russ Branyon	1.00
13	Travis Lee	2.50
14	Ruben Mateo	3.00
15	Roy Halladay	1.00

1999 Upper Deck MVP Super Tools

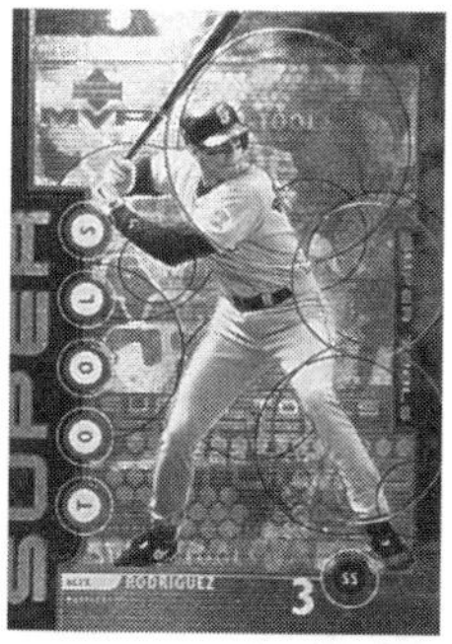

This 15-card insert set focuses on baseball's top stars and utilizes holo-foil technology on the card fronts. Card backs are numbered with a "T" prefix and are seeded 1:14 packs.

		MT
Complete Set (15):		75.00
Common Player:		1.50
Inserted 1:14		
1	Ken Griffey Jr.	15.00
2	Alex Rodriguez	10.00
3	Sammy Sosa	10.00
4	Derek Jeter	10.00
5	Vladimir Guerrero	4.00
6	Ben Grieve	3.00
7	Mike Piazza	10.00
8	Kenny Lofton	2.50
9	Barry Bonds	3.00
10	Darin Erstad	2.50
11	Nomar Garciaparra	10.00
12	Cal Ripken Jr.	12.00
13	J.D. Drew	8.00
14	Larry Walker	1.50
15	Chipper Jones	8.00

1999 Upper Deck MVP Swing Time

This 12-card set focuses on top hitters in the game and points out three aspects why the featured player is such a successful hitter. Printed on a full foiled front these are seeded 1:6 packs. Card backs are numbered with an "S" prefix.

		MT
Complete Set (12):		35.00
Common Player:		1.00
Inserted 1:6		
1	Ken Griffey Jr.	6.00
2	Mark McGwire	6.00
3	Sammy Sosa	4.00
4	Tony Gwynn	3.00
5	Alex Rodriguez	4.00
6	Nomar Garciaparra	4.00
7	Barry Bonds	1.50
8	Frank Thomas	3.00
9	Chipper Jones	3.00
10	Ivan Rodriguez	1.50
11	Mike Piazza	4.00
12	Derek Jeter	4.00

1999 Upper Deck MVP 500 Club Piece of History

This insert has a piece of game-used bat once swung by Mike Schmidt embedded into each card. A total of 350 of this insert was produced. Schmidt also signed 20 of the inserts.

	MT
Complete Set (1):	300.00
548HRMike Schmidt	300.00
548HRMike Schmidt Auto	

1999 Upper Deck Ovation

Cards 1-60 in the base set have the look and feel of an actual baseball. A player photo is in the foreground with a partial image of a baseball in the background on the card front. Cards 61-90 make up two subsets: World Premiere (61-80) is a 20-card collection consisting of 20 rookie prospects and Superstar Spotlight (81-90) is a 10-card lineup of baseball's biggest stars. Both subsets are short-printed, World Premiere are seeded 1:3.5 packs and Superstar Spotlight 1:6 packs. Five card packs carry an S.R.P. of $3.99 per pack.

		MT
Complete Set (90):		180.00
Common Player:		.40
Common World Premiere:		2.00
Inserted 1:3.5		
Common Superstar Spotlight:		4.00
Inserted 1:6		
1	Ken Griffey Jr.	5.00
2	Rondell White	.40
3	Tony Clark	.75
4	Barry Bonds	1.25
5	Larry Walker	.75
6	Greg Vaughn	.40
7	Mark Grace	.50
8	John Olerud	.50
9	Matt Williams	.75
10	Craig Biggio	1.00
11	Quinton McCracken	.40
12	Kerry Wood	1.00
13	Derek Jeter	3.00
14	Frank Thomas	3.00
15	Tino Martinez	.75
16	Albert Belle	1.25
17	Ben Grieve	1.25
18	Cal Ripken Jr.	4.00
19	Johnny Damon	.40
20	Jose Cruz Jr.	1.00
21	Barry Larkin	.75
22	Jason Giambi	.40
23	Sean Casey	.50
24	Scott Rolen	1.25
25	Jim Thome	.75
26	Curt Schilling	.50
27	Moises Alou	.75
28	Alex Rodriguez	3.00
29	Mark Kotsay	.50
30	Darin Erstad	1.25
31	Mike Mussina	1.00
32	Todd Walker	.50
33	Nomar Garciaparra	3.00
34	Vladimir Guerrero	1.50
35	Jeff Bagwell	1.25
36	Mark McGwire	6.00
37	Travis Lee	1.00
38	Dean Palmer	.40
39	Fred McGriff	.50
40	Sammy Sosa	3.00
41	Mike Piazza	3.00
42	Andres Galarraga	.75
43	Pedro Martinez	1.00
44	Juan Gonzalez	2.50
45	Greg Maddux	3.00
46	Jeromy Burnitz	.40
47	Roger Clemens	2.00
48	Vinny Castilla	.40
49	Kevin Brown	.50
50	Mo Vaughn	1.25
51	Raul Mondesi	.50
52	Randy Johnson	1.00
53	Ray Lankford	.40
54	Jaret Wright	.75
55	Tony Gwynn	2.50
56	Chipper Jones	2.50
57	Gary Sheffield	.75
58	Ivan Rodriguez	1.25
59	Kenny Lofton	1.00
60	Jason Kendall	.40
61	J.D. Drew (World Premiere)	35.00
62	Gabe Kapler (World Premiere)	8.00
63	Adrian Beltre (World Premiere)	4.00
64	Carlos Beltran (World Premiere)	3.00
65	Eric Chavez (World Premiere)	6.00
66	Mike Lowell (World Premiere)	3.00
67	Troy Glaus (World Premiere)	10.00
68	George Lombard (World Premiere)	4.00
69	Alex Gonzalez (World Premiere)	2.00
70	Mike Kinkade (World Premiere)	3.00

71 Jeremy Giambi (World Premiere) 8.00
72 Bruce Chen (World Premiere) 3.00
73 Preston Wilson (World Premiere) 2.00
74 Kevin Witt (World Premiere) 2.00
75 Carlos Guillen (World Premiere) 2.00
76 Ryan Minor (World Premiere) 3.00
77 Corey Koskie (World Premiere) 3.00
78 Robert Fick (World Premiere) 3.00
79 Michael Barrett (World Premiere) 3.00
80 Calvin Pickering (World Premiere) 3.00
81 Ken Griffey Jr. (Superstar Spotlight) 12.00
82 Mark McGwire (Superstar Spotlight) 15.00
83 Cal Ripken Jr. (Superstar Spotlight) 10.00
84 Derek Jeter (Superstar Spotlight) 8.00
85 Chipper Jones (Superstar Spotlight) 6.00
86 Nomar Garciaparra (Superstar Spotlight) 8.00
87 Sammy Sosa (Superstar Spotlight) 8.00
88 Juan Gonzalez (Superstar Spotlight) 6.00
89 Mike Piazza (Superstar Spotlight) 8.00
90 Alex Rodriguez (Superstar Spotlight) 8.00

1999 Upper Deck Ovation Curtain Calls

This 20-card set focuses on the most memorable accomplishments posted during the '98 season. Card fronts have two images of the player, one on the right half and a smaller image on the bottom left. Copper foil stamping is used to enhance the card front. These are numbered with an "R" prefix and are seeded 1:8 packs.

	MT
Complete Set (20):	120.00
Common Player:	2.00
Inserted 1:8	
R01 Mark McGwire	20.00
R02 Sammy Sosa	10.00
R03 Ken Griffey Jr.	15.00
R04 Alex Rodriguez	10.00
R05 Roger Clemens	6.00
R06 Cal Ripken Jr.	12.00
R07 Barry Bonds	4.00
R08 Kerry Wood	3.00
R09 Nomar Garciaparra	10.00
R10 Derek Jeter	10.00
R11 Juan Gonzalez	8.00
R12 Greg Maddux	10.00
R13 Pedro Martinez	3.00
R14 David Wells	2.00
R15 Moises Alou	2.00
R16 Tony Gwynn	8.00
R17 Albert Belle	4.00
R18 Mike Piazza	10.00
R19 Ivan Rodriguez	4.00
R20 Randy Johnson	3.00

1999 Upper Deck Ovation Major Production

This 20-card set utilizes thermography technology to simulate the look and feel of home plate and highlights some of the game's most productive players. These are inserted 1:45 packs and are numbered with an "S" prefix.

	MT
Complete Set (20):	500.00
Common Player:	8.00
Inserted 1:45	
S01 Mike Piazza	40.00
S02 Mark McGwire	75.00
S03 Chipper Jones	30.00
S04 Cal Ripken Jr.	50.00
S05 Ken Griffey Jr.	60.00
S06 Barry Bonds	15.00
S07 Tony Gwynn	30.00
S08 Randy Johnson	10.00
S09 Ivan Rodriguez	15.00
S10 Frank Thomas	40.00
S11 Alex Rodriguez	40.00
S12 Albert Belle	15.00
S13 Juan Gonzalez	30.00
S14 Greg Maddux	40.00
S15 Jeff Bagwell	15.00
S16 Derek Jeter	40.00
S17 Matt Williams	8.00
S18 Kenny Lofton	12.00
S19 Sammy Sosa	40.00
S20 Roger Clemens	20.00

1999 Upper Deck Ovation Piece of History

This 14-card set has actual pieces of game-used bat, from the featured player, imbedded into the card. These are inserted 1:247 packs. Ben Grieve autographed 25 versions of his Piece of History insert cards. Although there is no regular Piece of History Kerry Wood card, Upper Deck inserted 25 autographed Piece of History game-used baseball cards. These have a piece of one of Wood's game-hurled baseballs from the 1998 season.

	MT
Complete Set (14):	2500.
Common Player:	100.00
Inserted 1:247	
Ben Grieve Auto:	850.00
Production 25 cards	
Kerry Wood Auto:	600.00
Production 25 cards	
BB Barry Bonds	150.00
CJ Chipper Jones	200.00
BW Bernie Williams	100.00
KGj Ken Griffey Jr.	450.00
NG Nomar Garciaparra	250.00
JG Juan Gonzalez	200.00
DJ Derek Jeter	300.00
SS Sammy Sosa	300.00
TG Tony Gwynn	200.00
AR Alex Rodriguez	250.00
CR Cal Ripken Jr.	350.00
BG Ben Grieve	150.00
VG Vladimir Guerrero	160.00
MP Mike Piazza	250.00

1999 Upper Deck Ovation ReMarkable

This three-tiered 15-card insert showcases Mark McGwire's historic '98 season. Cards #1-5 are Bronze and inserted 1:9 packs; cards #6-10 are Silver and inserted 1:25 packs; and cards #11-15 are Gold and inserted 1:99 packs.

	MT
Complete Set (15):	200.00
Common #1-5:	6.00
Inserted 1:9	
Common #6-10:	12.00
Inserted 1:25	
Common # 11-15	35.00
Inserted 1:99	
MM01Mark McGwire	6.00
MM02Mark McGwire	6.00
MM03Mark McGwire	6.00
MM04Mark McGwire	6.00
MM05Mark McGwire	6.00
MM06Mark McGwire	12.00
MM07Mark McGwire	12.00
MM08Mark McGwire	12.00
MM09Mark McGwire	12.00
MM10Mark McGwire	12.00
MM11Mark McGwire	35.00
MM12Mark McGwire	35.00
MM13Mark McGwire	35.00
MM14Mark McGwire	35.00
MM15Mark McGwire	35.00

1999 Upper Deck Ovation Standing Ovation

This 90-card parallel of the base set, has gold foil stamping instead of copper foil for the subsets and gold foil instead of silver foil for cards 1-60, on the card fronts. 500 sequentially numbered sets were produced.

	MT
Common Player:	5.00
Production 500 sets	
1 Ken Griffey Jr.	60.00
2 Rondell White	8.00
3 Tony Clark	10.00
4 Barry Bonds	15.00
5 Larry Walker	10.00
6 Greg Vaughn	8.00
7 Mark Grace	8.00
8 John Olerud	8.00
9 Matt Williams	8.00
10 Craig Biggio	12.00
11 Quinton McCracken	5.00
12 Kerry Wood	15.00
13 Derek Jeter	40.00
14 Frank Thomas	40.00
15 Tino Martinez	10.00
16 Albert Belle	15.00
17 Ben Grieve	15.00
18 Cal Ripken Jr.	50.00
19 Johnny Damon	5.00
20 Jose Cruz Jr.	10.00
21 Barry Larkin	8.00
22 Jason Giambi	5.00
23 Sean Casey	8.00
24 Scott Rolen	15.00
25 Jim Thome	10.00
26 Curt Schilling	8.00
27 Moises Alou	10.00
28 Alex Rodriguez	40.00
29 Mark Kotsay	8.00
30 Darin Erstad	15.00
31 Mike Mussina	12.00
32 Todd Walker	10.00
33 Nomar Garciaparra	40.00
34 Vladimir Guerrero	20.00
35 Jeff Bagwell	15.00
36 Mark McGwire	75.00
37 Travis Lee	15.00
38 Dean Palmer	5.00
39 Fred McGriff	8.00
40 Sammy Sosa	40.00
41 Mike Piazza	40.00
42 Andres Galarraga	10.00
43 Pedro Martinez	12.00
44 Juan Gonzalez	30.00
45 Greg Maddux	40.00
46 Jeromy Burnitz	5.00
47 Roger Clemens	25.00
48 Vinny Castilla	5.00
49 Kevin Brown	8.00
50 Mo Vaughn	15.00
51 Raul Mondesi	8.00
52 Randy Johnson	12.00
53 Ray Lankford	5.00
54 Jaret Wright	10.00
55 Tony Gwynn	30.00
56 Chipper Jones	30.00
57 Gary Sheffield	8.00
58 Ivan Rodriguez	15.00
59 Kenny Lofton	12.00
60 Jason Kendall	5.00
61 J.D. Drew (World Premiere)	80.00
62 Gabe Kapler (World Premiere)	25.00
63 Adrian Beltre (World Premiere)	15.00
64 Carlos Beltran (World Premiere)	10.00
65 Eric Chavez (World Premiere)	25.00
66 Mike Lowell (World Premiere)	10.00
67 Troy Glaus (World Premiere)	30.00
68 George Lombard (World Premiere)	15.00
69 Alex Gonzalez (World Premiere)	5.00
70 Mike Kinkade (World Premiere)	8.00
71 Jeremy Giambi (World Premiere)	25.00
72 Bruce Chen (World Premiere)	10.00
73 Preston Wilson (World Premiere)	5.00
74 Kevin Witt (World Premiere)	5.00
75 Carlos Guillen (World Premiere)	5.00
76 Ryan Minor (World Premiere)	10.00
77 Corey Koskie (World Premiere)	10.00
78 Robert Fick (World Premiere)	10.00
79 Michael Barrett (World Premiere)	12.00
80 Calvin Pickering (World Premiere)	10.00
81 Ken Griffey Jr. (Superstar Spotlight)	40.00
82 Mark McGwire (Superstar Spotlight)	50.00
83 Cal Ripken Jr. (Superstar Spotlight)	30.00
84 Derek Jeter (Superstar Spotlight)	25.00
85 Chipper Jones (Superstar Spotlight)	20.00
86 Nomar Garciaparra (Superstar Spotlight)	25.00
87 Sammy Sosa (Superstar Spotlight)	25.00
88 Juan Gonzalez (Superstar Spotlight)	20.00
89 Mike Piazza (Superstar Spotlight)	25.00
90 Alex Rodriguez (Superstar Spotlight)	25.00

1999 Upper Deck Ovation 500 Club Piece of History

Each of these cards actually have a piece of game-used Louisville Slugger, once swung by Mickey Mantle, imbedded in them. Approximately 350 cards exist. There also is one card with a cut signature of Mantle and a piece of his game-used bat on it.

	MT
Mickey Mantle:	1200.
Production 350 cards	

1999 Upper Deck UD Choice

The 155-card base set consists of 110 regular player cards and two subsets, 27 Star Rookies and 18 Cover Glory subset cards. Card fronts have a white border, with the Upper Deck UD Choice logo on the bottom right of the front. Card backs have complete year-by-year stats along with some vital information. Each pack contains 12 cards. A parallel version also exists, called Prime Choice Reserve and are numbered to 100.

	MT
Complete Set (155):	15.00
Common Player:	.10
Prime Choice	
Reserve Stars:	60x to 100x
Yng Stars & RCs:	25x to 50x
Production 100 sets	
1 Gabe Kapler (Rookie Class)	.75
2 Jin Ho Cho (Rookie Class)	.10
3 Matt Anderson (Rookie Class)	.20
4 Ricky Ledee (Rookie Class)	.20
5 Bruce Chen (Rookie Class)	.10
6 Alex Gonzalez (Rookie Class)	.10
7 Ryan Minor (Rookie Class)	.25
8 Michael Barrett (Rookie Class)	.10
9 Carlos Beltran (Rookie Class)	.20
10 Ramon Martinez (Rookie Class)	.10
11 Dermal Brown (Rookie Class)	.10
12 Robert Fick (Rookie Class)	.10
13 Preston Wilson (Rookie Class)	.10
14 Orlando Hernandez (Rookie Class)	1.50
15 Troy Glaus (Rookie Class)	1.00
16 Calvin Pickering (Rookie Class)	.10

17	Corey Koskie (Rookie Class)	.10
18	Fernando Seguignol (Rookie Class)	.20
19	Carlos Guillen (Rookie Class)	.10
20	Kevin Witt (Rookie Class)	.10
21	Mike Kinkade (Rookie Class)	.10
22	Eric Chavez (Rookie Class)	.30
23	Mike Lowell (Rookie Class)	.10
24	Adrian Beltre (Rookie Class)	.25
25	George Lombard (Rookie Class)	.10
26	Jeremy Giambi (Rookie Class)	.10
27	J.D. Drew (Rookie Class)	4.00
28	Mark McGwire (Cover Glory)	1.25
29	Kerry Wood (Cover Glory)	.40
30	David Wells (Cover Glory)	.10
31	Juan Gonzalez (Cover Glory)	.50
32	Randy Johnson (Cover Glory)	.20
33	Derek Jeter (Cover Glory)	.50
34	Tony Gwynn (Cover Glory)	.50
35	Greg Maddux (Cover Glory)	.60
36	Cal Ripken Jr. (Cover Glory)	.75
37	Ken Griffey Jr. (Cover Glory)	1.00
38	Bartolo Colon (Cover Glory)	.10
39	Troy Glaus (Cover Glory)	.25
40	Ben Grieve (Cover Glory)	.25
41	Roger Clemens (Cover Glory)	.30
42	Chipper Jones (Cover Glory)	.50
43	Scott Rolen (Cover Glory)	.25
44	Nomar Garciaparra (Cover Glory)	.60
45	Sammy Sosa (Cover Glory)	.75
46	Tim Salmon	.20
47	Darin Erstad	.50
48	Chuck Finley	.10
49	Garrett Anderson	.10
50	Matt Williams	.20
51	Jay Bell	.10
52	Travis Lee	.50
53	Andruw Jones	.50
54	Andres Galarraga	.25
55	Chipper Jones	1.25
56	Greg Maddux	1.25
57	Javy Lopez	.15
58	Cal Ripken Jr.	1.50
59	Brady Anderson	.10
60	Rafael Palmeiro	.20
61	B.J. Surhoff	.10
62	Nomar Garciaparra	1.25
63	Troy O'Leary	.10
64	Pedro Martinez	.40
65	Jason Varitek	.10
66	Kerry Wood	.75
67	Sammy Sosa	1.50
68	Mark Grace	.20
69	Mickey Morandini	.10
70	Albert Belle	.50
71	Mike Caruso	.10
72	Frank Thomas	1.25
73	Sean Casey	.25
74	Pete Harnisch	.10
75	Dmitri Young	.10
76	Manny Ramirez	.75
77	Omar Vizquel	.10
78	Travis Fryman	.10
79	Jim Thome	.35
80	Kenny Lofton	.40
81	Todd Helton	.40
82	Larry Walker	.35
83	Vinny Castilla	.10
84	Gabe Alvarez	.10
85	Tony Clark	.40
86	Damion Easley	.10
87	Livan Hernandez	.10
88	Mark Kotsay	.20
89	Cliff Floyd	.10
90	Jeff Bagwell	.60
91	Moises Alou	.20
92	Randy Johnson	.40
93	Craig Biggio	.20
94	Larry Sutton	.10
95	Dean Palmer	.10
96	Johnny Damon	.10
97	Charles Johnson	.10
98	Gary Sheffield	.20
99	Raul Mondesi	.20
100	Mark Grudzielanek	.10
101	Jeromy Burnitz	.10
102	Jeff Cirillo	.10
103	Jose Valentin	.10
104	Mark Loretta	.10
105	Todd Walker	.20
106	David Ortiz	.10
107	Brad Radke	.10
108	Brad Fullmer	.20
109	Rondell White	.20
110	Vladimir Guerrero	.75
111	Mike Piazza	1.25
112	Brian McRae	.10
113	John Olerud	.20
114	Rey Ordonez	.10
115	Derek Jeter	1.00
116	Bernie Williams	.40
117	David Wells	.10
118	Paul O'Neill	.20
119	Tino Martinez	.25
120	A.J. Hinch	.10
121	Jason Giambi	.10
122	Miguel Tejada	.10
123	Ben Grieve	.50
124	Scott Rolen	.50
125	Desi Relaford	.10
126	Bobby Abreu	.10
127	Jose Guillen	.10
128	Jason Kendall	.15
129	Aramis Ramirez	.25
130	Mark McGwire	2.50
131	Ray Lankford	.10
132	Eli Marrero	.10
133	Wally Joyner	.10
134	Greg Vaughn	.10
135	Trevor Hoffman	.10
136	Kevin Brown	.15
137	Tony Gwynn	1.00
138	Bill Mueller	.10
139	Ellis Burks	.10
140	Barry Bonds	.50
141	Robb Nen	.10
142	Ken Griffey Jr.	2.00
143	Alex Rodriguez	1.25
144	Jay Buhner	.20
145	Edgar Martinez	.10
146	Rolando Arrojo	.20
147	Robert Smith	.10
148	Quinton McCracken	.10
149	Ivan Rodriguez	.50
150	Will Clark	.25
151	Mark McLemore	.10
152	Juan Gonzalez	1.00
153	Jose Cruz Jr.	.40
154	Carlos Delgado	.10
155	Roger Clemens	.75

1999 Upper Deck UD Choice Mini Bobbing Head

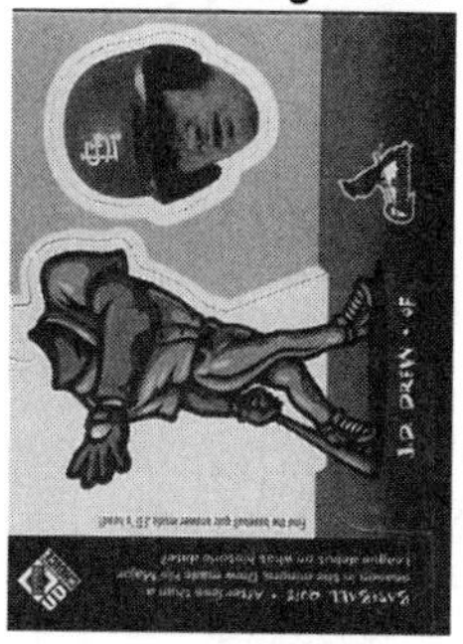

Inserted 1:5 packs, some of the game's best players can be assembled into a miniature bobbing head figure by following the instructions on the card backs.

		MT
Complete Set (30):		25.00
Common Player:		.40
Inserted 1:5		
B01	Randy Johnson	.60
B02	Troy Glaus	.75
B03	Chipper Jones	1.50
B04	Cal Ripken Jr.	2.50
B05	Nomar Garciaparra	2.00
B06	Pedro Martinez	.60
B07	Kerry Wood	.75
B08	Sammy Sosa	2.50
B09	Frank Thomas	2.00
B10	Paul Konerko	.40
B11	Omar Vizquel	.40
B12	Kenny Lofton	.60
B13	Gabe Kapler	1.50
B14	Adrian Beltre	.40
B15	Orlando Hernandez	1.50
B16	Derek Jeter	1.50
B17	Mike Piazza	2.00
B18	Tino Martinez	.40
B19	Ben Grieve	.75
B20	Rickey Henderson	.40
B21	Scott Rolen	.75
B22	Aramis Ramirez	.40
B23	Greg Vaughn	.40
B24	Tony Gwynn	1.50
B25	Barry Bonds	.75
B26	Alex Rodriguez	2.00
B27	Ken Griffey Jr.	3.00
B28	Mark McGwire	4.00
B29	J.D. Drew	6.00
B30	Juan Gonzalez	1.50

1999 Upper Deck UD Choice Piece of History 500 Club

A piece from an Eddie Murray game-used bat was incorporated into each of these cards, which are limited to 350.

		MT
Complete Set (1):		200.00
EM	Eddie Murray (350)	200.00

1999 Upper Deck UD Choice StarQuest

This four-tiered 30-card set features four different colors for each of the levels. Singles are seeded one per pack and have blue foil etching, Doubles (1:8) have green foil etching, Triples (1:23) have red foil etching and Home Runs are limited to 100 numbered sets with gold foil etching.

		MT
Complete Set (30):		18.00
Common Player:		.25
Inserted 1:1		
Greens:		2x to 3x
Inserted 1:8		
Reds:		4x to 8x
Inserted 1:23		
Golds:		50x to 100x
Production 100 sets		
SQ1	Ken Griffey Jr.	2.00
SQ2	Sammy Sosa	1.50
SQ3	Alex Rodriguez	1.25
SQ4	Derek Jeter	1.00
SQ5	Troy Glaus	.75
SQ6	Mike Piazza	1.25
SQ7	Barry Bonds	.50
SQ8	Tony Gwynn	1.00
SQ9	Juan Gonzalez	1.00
SQ10	Chipper Jones	1.00
SQ11	Greg Maddux	1.25
SQ12	Randy Johnson	.40
SQ13	Roger Clemens	.75
SQ14	Ben Grieve	.50
SQ15	Nomar Garciaparra	1.25
SQ16	Travis Lee	.50
SQ17	Frank Thomas	1.25
SQ18	Vladimir Guerrero	.75
SQ19	Scott Rolen	.50
SQ20	Ivan Rodriguez	.50
SQ21	Cal Ripken Jr.	1.50
SQ22	Mark McGwire	2.50
SQ23	Jeff Bagwell	.60
SQ24	Tony Clark	.40
SQ25	Kerry Wood	.50
SQ26	Kenny Lofton	.40
SQ27	Adrian Beltre	.40
SQ28	Larry Walker	.40
SQ29	Curt Schilling	.25
SQ30	Jim Thome	.40

1999 Upper Deck UD Choice Yard Work

This 30-card set showcases the top power hitters in the game. The right side of the card is covered in bronze foil and stamped with Yard Work. They are numbered with a "Y"prefix and seeded 1:13 packs.

		MT
Complete Set (30):		100.00
Common Player:		1.50
Inserted 1:13		
Y01	Andres Galarraga	2.50
Y02	Chipper Jones	6.00
Y03	Rafael Palmeiro	2.00
Y04	Nomar Garciaparra	8.00
Y05	Sammy Sosa	10.00
Y06	Frank Thomas	8.00
Y07	J.D. Drew	20.00
Y08	Albert Belle	3.00
Y09	Jim Thome	2.00
Y10	Manny Ramirez	4.00
Y11	Larry Walker	2.00
Y12	Vinny Castilla	1.50
Y13	Tony Clark	2.00
Y14	Jeff Bagwell	4.00
Y15	Moises Alou	1.50
Y16	Dean Palmer	1.50
Y17	Gary Sheffield	1.50
Y18	Vladimir Guerrero	4.00
Y19	Mike Piazza	8.00
Y20	Tino Martinez	2.00
Y21	Ben Grieve	3.00
Y22	Greg Vaughn	1.50
Y23	Ken Caminiti	1.50
Y24	Barry Bonds	3.00
Y25	Ken Griffey Jr.	12.00
Y26	Alex Rodriguez	8.00
Y27	Mark McGwire	15.00
Y28	Juan Gonzalez	6.00
Y29	Jose Canseco	2.00
Y30	Jose Cruz Jr.	3.00

1999 UD Retro

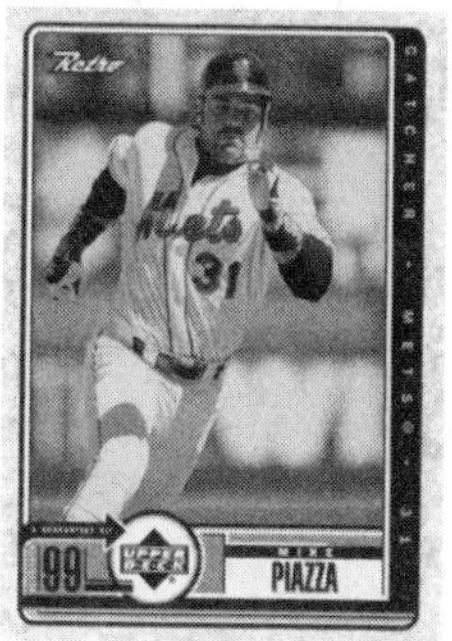

The 110-card base set is comprised of 88 current stars and 22 retired greats. Card fronts have a tan, speckled border while card backs have a year-by-year compilation of the player's stats along with a career note. Retro is packaged in lunch boxes, 24 packs to a box with an S.R.P. of $4.99 per six-card pack.

		MT
Complete Set (110):		40.00
Common Player:		.20
Golds (1-88):		6x to 12x
Golds (89-110):		10x to 20x
Production 250 sets		
Platinums one of one exist		
1	Mo Vaughn	.75
2	Troy Glaus	.75
3	Tim Salmon	.40
4	Randy Johnson	.75
5	Travis Lee	.40
6	Matt Williams	.50
7	Greg Maddux	2.00
8	Chipper Jones	2.50
9	Andruw Jones	.75
10	Tom Glavine	.40
11	Javy Lopez	.40
12	Albert Belle	1.00
13	Cal Ripken Jr.	3.00
14	Brady Anderson	.20
15	Nomar Garciaparra	2.50
16	Pedro J. Martinez	1.50
17	Sammy Sosa	2.50
18	Mark Grace	.50
19	Frank Thomas	1.50
20	Ray Durham	.20
21	Sean Casey	.50
22	Greg Vaughn	.40
23	Barry Larkin	.40
24	Manny Ramirez	1.00
25	Jim Thome	.50
26	Jaret Wright	.20
27	Kenny Lofton	.75
28	Larry Walker	.75
29	Todd Helton	.75
30	Vinny Castilla	.40
31	Tony Clark	.40
32	Juan Encarnacion	.20
33	Dean Palmer	.20
34	Mark Kotsay	.20
35	Alex Gonzalez	.20
36	Shane Reynolds	.20
37	Ken Caminiti	.40
38	Jeff Bagwell	1.00
39	Craig Biggio	.50
40	Carlos Febles	.40
41	Carlos Beltran	2.00
42	Jeremy Giambi	.20
43	Raul Mondesi	.40
44	Adrian Beltre	.40
45	Kevin Brown	.40
46	Jeromy Burnitz	.40
47	Jeff Cirillo	.20
48	Corey Koskie	.20
49	Todd Walker	.20
50	Vladimir Guerrero	1.50
51	Michael Barrett	.50
52	Mike Piazza	2.50
53	Robin Ventura	.50
54	Edgardo Alfonzo	.50
55	Derek Jeter	2.50
56	Roger Clemens	1.50
57	Tino Martinez	.75
58	Orlando Hernandez	.50
59	Chuck Knoblauch	.50
60	Bernie Williams	.75
61	Eric Chavez	.50
62	Ben Grieve	.50
63	Jason Giambi	.20
64	Scott Rolen	1.00
65	Curt Schilling	.40
66	Bobby Abreu	.20
67	Jason Kendall	.40
68	Kevin Young	.20
69	Mark McGwire	5.00
70	J.D. Drew	2.00
71	Eric Davis	.20
72	Tony Gwynn	2.00
73	Trevor Hoffman	.20
74	Barry Bonds	1.00
75	Robb Nen	.20
76	Ken Griffey Jr.	4.00
77	Alex Rodriguez	2.50
78	Jay Buhner	.40
79	Carlos Guillen	.20
80	Jose Canseco	1.00
81	Bobby Smith	.20
82	Juan Gonzalez	2.00
83	Ivan Rodriguez	1.00
84	Rafael Palmeiro	.75
85	Rick Helling	.20
86	Jose Cruz Jr.	.40
87	David Wells	.20
88	Carlos Delgado	.75
89	Nolan Ryan	4.00
90	George Brett	2.00
91	Robin Yount	1.00
92	Paul Molitor	1.00
93	Dave Winfield	.50
94	Steve Garvey	.20
95	Ozzie Smith	1.00
96	Ted Williams	4.00
97	Don Mattingly	.75
98	Mickey Mantle	4.00
99	Harmon Killebrew	.50
100	Rollie Fingers	.20
101	Kirk Gibson	.20
102	Bucky Dent	.20
103	Willie Mays	2.00
104	Babe Ruth	5.00
105	Gary Carter	.20
106	Reggie Jackson	1.50
107	Frank Robinson	1.50
108	Ernie Banks	1.50
109	Eddie Murray	.50
110	Mike Schmidt	1.50

1999 UD Retro Distant Replay

This 15-card set recounts the 15 most memorable plays from the 1998 season. Card fronts have a black and white photo of the player and along the bottom of the photo a date of the memorable play and brief description are given. These are seeded 1:8 packs. A parallel version, Level II is also randomly seeded, limited to 100 sequentially numbered sets.

	MT
Complete Set (15):	60.00
Common Player:	2.00
Inserted 1:8	
Level 2:	10x to 20x
Production 100 sets	
1 Ken Griffey Jr.	8.00
2 Mark McGwire	10.00
3 Cal Ripken Jr.	6.00
4 Greg Maddux	4.00
5 Nomar Garciaparra	5.00
6 Roger Clemens	3.00
7 Alex Rodriguez	5.00
8 Frank Thomas	3.00
9 Mike Piazza	5.00
10 Chipper Jones	5.00
11 Juan Gonzalez	4.00
12 Tony Gwynn	4.00
13 Barry Bonds	2.00
14 Ivan Rodriguez	2.00
15 Derek Jeter	5.00

1999 UD Retro INKredible

INKredible is an autographed insert set that consists of both current players and retired stars. Card fronts have a small photo in the upper left portion of the featured player and a large signing area. These are seeded 1:23 packs.

	MT
Common Player:	12.00
Inserted 1:23	
CBe Carlos Beltran	50.00
GB George Brett	125.00
PB Pat Burrell	50.00
SC Sean Casey	40.00
TC Tony Clark	25.00
BD Bucky Dent	15.00
DE Darin Erstad	30.00
RF Rollie Fingers	20.00
SG Steve Garvey	25.00
KG Kirk Gibson	25.00
RG Rusty Greer	15.00
JR Ken Griffey Jr.	350.00
TG Tony Gwynn	150.00
CJ Chipper Jones	125.00
GK Gabe Kapler	30.00
HK Harmon Killebrew	35.00
FL Fred Lynn	20.00
DM Don Mattingly	100.00
PM Paul Molitor	50.00
EM Eddie Murray	50.00
PO Paul O'Neill	25.00
AP Angel Pena	12.00
MR Manny Ramirez	75.00
IR Ivan Rodriguez	50.00
NR Nolan Ryan	250.00
OZ Ozzie Smith	75.00
DWe David Wells	15.00
BW Bernie Williams	50.00
DW Dave Winfield	40.00
RY Robin Yount	75.00

1999 UD Retro INKredible Level 2

A parallel to INKredible autographed inserts, these are hand-numbered to the featured player's jersey number.

	MT
Common Player:	12.00
Limited to player's jersey #	
CBe Carlos Beltran (36)	150.00
GB George Brett (5)	
PB Pat Burrell (76)	150.00
SC Sean Casey (21)	175.00
TC Tony Clark (17)	75.00
BD Bucky Dent (20)	75.00
DE Darin Erstad (17)	100.00
RF Rollie Fingers (34)	80.00
SG Steve Garvey (6)	
KG Kirk Gibson (23)	90.00
RG Rusty Greer (29)	75.00
JR Ken Griffey Jr. (24)	
TG Tony Gwynn (19)	500.00
CJ Chipper Jones (10)	
GK Gabe Kapler (23)	125.00
HK Harmon Killebrew (3)	
FL Fred Lynn (19)	90.00
DM Don Mattingly (23)	450.00
PM Paul Molitor (4)	
EM Eddie Murray (33)	150.00
PO Paul O'Neill (21)	100.00
AP Angel Pena (36)	40.00
MR Manny Ramirez (24)	250.00
IR Ivan Rodriguez (7)	
NR Nolan Ryan (34)	
OZ Ozzie Smith (1)	
DWe David Wells (33)	75.00
BW Bernie Williams (51)	100.00
DW Dave Winfield (31)	125.00
RY Robin Yount (19)	220.00

1999 UD Retro Lunchbox

Lunchboxes was the packaging for UD Retro. Each lunchbox contains 24 six-card packs and features 17 different current or retired baseball legends including Babe Ruth.

	MT
Complete Set (17):	300.00
Common lunchbox:	10.00
1 dual player per case	
Roger Clemens	12.00
Ken Griffey Jr.	20.00
Mickey Mantle	20.00
Mark McGwire	20.00
Mike Piazza	15.00
Alex Rodriguez	15.00
Babe Ruth	20.00
Sammy Sosa	15.00
Ted Williams	20.00
Ken Griffey Jr., Mark McGwire	30.00
Ken Griffey Jr., Babe Ruth	30.00
Ken Griffey Jr., Ted Williams	30.00
Mickey Mantle, Babe Ruth	30.00
Mark McGwire, Mickey Mantle	30.00
Mark McGwire, Babe Ruth	30.00
Mark McGwire, Ted Williams	30.00

1999 UD Retro Piece of History 500 Club

Each one of these inserts features a piece of game-used bat swung by Ted Williams embedded into each card. A total of 350 of these were issued. Williams also autographed nine of the 500 Club Piece of History cards.

	MT
Complete Set (2):	900.00
TW Ted Williams	900.00
TWA Ted Williams (9)	

1999 UD Retro Old/New School

This 30-card insert set captures 15 Old School players and 15 New School players. Each card is sequentially numbered to 1,000. A parallel version is also randomly seeded and is limited to 50 sequentially numbered sets.

	MT
Complete Set (30):	300.00
Common Player:	3.00
Production 1,000 sets	
Level 2:	5x to 10x
Production 50 sets	
1 Ken Griffey Jr.	30.00
2 Alex Rodriguez	20.00
3 Frank Thomas	10.00
4 Cal Ripken Jr.	25.00
5 Chipper Jones	20.00
6 Craig Biggio	6.00
7 Greg Maddux	15.00
8 Jeff Bagwell	8.00
9 Juan Gonzalez	15.00
10 Mark McGwire	40.00
11 Mike Piazza	20.00
12 Mo Vaughn	6.00
13 Roger Clemens	10.00
14 Sammy Sosa	20.00
15 Tony Gwynn	15.00
16 Gabe Kapler	6.00
17 J.D. Drew	12.00
18 Pat Burrell	15.00
19 Roy Halladay	3.00
20 Jeff Weaver	3.00
21 Troy Glaus	5.00
22 Vladimir Guerrero	10.00
23 Michael Barrett	3.00
24 Carlos Beltran	10.00
25 Scott Rolen	8.00
26 Nomar Garciaparra	20.00
27 Warren Morris	3.00
28 Alex Gonzalez	3.00
29 Kyle Farnsworth	3.00
30 Derek Jeter	20.00

1999 UD Retro Throwback Attack

This 15-card set has a "Retro" look, like trading cards from yesteryear. The set highlights the top players and feature card fronts with a player photo encircled, "throwback attack" across the top and a white border. Card backs are numbered with a "T" prefix and are seeded 1:5 packs. A parallel version is also randomly seeded and limited to 500 numbered sets.

	MT
Complete Set (15):	40.00
Common Player:	1.00
Inserted 1:5	
Level 2:	5x to 10x
Production 500 sets	
1 Ken Griffey Jr.	6.00
2 Mark McGwire	8.00
3 Sammy Sosa	4.00
4 Roger Clemens	2.00
5 J.D. Drew	3.00
6 Alex Rodriguez	4.00
7 Greg Maddux	3.00
8 Mike Piazza	4.00
9 Juan Gonzalez	2.00
10 Mo Vaughn	1.00
11 Cal Ripken Jr.	5.00
12 Frank Thomas	2.00
13 Nomar Garciaparra	4.00
14 Vladimir Guerrero	2.00
15 Tony Gwynn	3.00

1999 Upper Deck Victory

This 470-card base set is printed on 20-point stock and has a white border with UV coating. The set consists of a number of subsets including, 30-card Mark McGwire Magic, 30 team checklist cards, 50 '99 rookies, 15 Power Trip, 20 Rookie Flashback, 15 Big Play Makers and 10 History in the Making. Packs have an S.R.P. of $.99.

	MT
Complete Set (470):	40.00
Common Player:	.05
1 Anaheim Angels (Team Checklist)	.05
2 *Mark Harriger* (99 Rookie)	.25
3 Mo Vaughn (Power Trip)	.20
4 Darin Erstad (Big Play Makers)	.15
5 Troy Glaus	.25
6 Tim Salmon	.20
7 Mo Vaughn	.40
8 Darin Erstad	.25
9 Garret Anderson	.05
10 Todd Greene	.05
11 Troy Percival	.05
12 Chuck Finley	.05
13 Jason Dickson	.05
14 Jim Edmonds	.05
15 Arizona Diamondbacks (Team Checklist)	.05
16 Randy Johnson	.30
17 Matt Williams	.25
18 Travis Lee	.25
19 Jay Bell	.05
20 Tony Womack	.05
21 Steve Finley	.05
22 Bernard Gilkey	.05
23 Tony Batista	.05
24 Todd Stottlemyre	.05
25 Omar Daal	.05
26 Atlanta Braves (Team Checklist)	.05
27 Bruce Chen (99 Rookie)	.15
28 George Lombard (99 Rookie)	.05
29 Chipper Jones (Power Trip)	.50
30 Chipper Jones (Big Play Makers)	.50
31 Greg Maddux	1.00
32 Chipper Jones	1.00
33 Javy Lopez	.15
34 Tom Glavine	.20
35 John Smoltz	.15
36 Andruw Jones	.30
37 Brian Jordan	.05
38 Walt Weiss	.05
39 Bret Boone	.05
40 Andres Galarraga	.25
41 Baltimore Orioles (Team Checklist)	.05
42 Ryan Minor (99 Rookie)	.20
43 Jerry Hairston Jr. (99 Rookie)	.05
44 Calvin Pickering (99 Rookie)	.05
45 Cal Ripken Jr. (History in the Making)	.50
46 Cal Ripken Jr.	1.25
47 Charles Johnson	.05
48 Albert Belle	.40
49 Delino DeShields	.05
50 Mike Mussina	.30
51 Scott Erickson	.05
52 Brady Anderson	.10
53 B.J. Surhoff	.05
54 Harold Baines	.10
55 Will Clark	.25
56 Boston Red Sox (Team Checklist)	.05
57 Shea Hillenbrand (99 Rookie)	.05
58 Trot Nixon (99 Rookie)	.05
59 Jin Ho Cho (99 Rookie)	.05
60 Nomar Garciaparra (Power Trip)	.50
61 Nomar Garciaparra (Big Play Makers)	.50
62 Pedro Martinez	.40
63 Nomar Garciaparra	1.00
64 Jose Offerman	.05
65 Jason Varitek	.05
66 Darren Lewis	.05
67 Troy O'Leary	.05
68 Donnie Sadler	.05
69 John Valentin	.05
70 Tim Wakefield	.05
71 Bret Saberhagen	.05
72 Chicago Cubs (Team Checklist)	.05
73 *Kyle Farnsworth* (99 Rookie)	.20
74 Sammy Sosa (Power Trip)	.50
75 Sammy Sosa (Big Play Makers)	.50
76 Sammy Sosa (History in the Making)	.50
77 Kerry Wood (History in the Making)	.15
78 Sammy Sosa	1.00
79 Mark Grace	.20
80 Kerry Wood	.25
81 Kevin Tapani	.05
82 Benito Santiago	.05
83 Gary Gaetti	.05
84 Mickey Morandini	.05
85 Glenallen Hill	.05
86 Henry Rodriguez	.05
87 Rod Beck	.05
88 Chicago White Sox (Team Checklist)	.05
89 Carlos Lee (99 Rookie)	.15
90 Mark Johnson (99 Rookie)	.05
91 Frank Thomas (Power Trip)	.25
92 Frank Thomas	.50
93 Jim Parque	.05
94 Mike Sirotka	.05
95 Mike Caruso	.05
96 Ray Durham	.10
97 Magglio Ordonez	.20
98 Paul Konerko	.10
99 Bob Howry	.05
100 Brian Simmons	.05
101 Jaime Navarro	.05
102 Cincinnati Reds (Team Checklist)	.05
103 Denny Neagle	.05
104 Pete Harnisch	.05
105 Greg Vaughn	.15
106 Brett Tomko	.05
107 Mike Cameron	.05
108 Sean Casey	.25
109 Aaron Boone	.05
110 Michael Tucker	.05
111 Dmitri Young	.05
112 Barry Larkin	.25
113 Cleveland Indians (Team Checklist)	.05
114 Russ Branyan (99 Rookie)	.05
115 Jim Thome (Power Trip)	.15
116 Manny Ramirez (Power Trip)	.20
117 Manny Ramirez	.40
118 Jim Thome	.25
119 David Justice	.20
120 Sandy Alomar	.10
121 Roberto Alomar	.30
122 Jaret Wright	.10
123 Bartolo Colon	.10
124 Travis Fryman	.10
125 Kenny Lofton	.40
126 Omar Vizquel	.10
127 Colorado Rockies (Team Checklist)	.05
128 Derrick Gibson (99 Rookie)	.05
129 Larry Walker (Big Play Makers)	.15
130 Larry Walker	.30
131 Dante Bichette	.20
132 Todd Helton	.25
133 Neifi Perez	.05
134 Vinny Castilla	.10
135 Darryl Kile	.05
136 Pedro Astacio	.10
137 Darryl Hamilton	.05
138 Mike Lansing	.05
139 Kirt Manwaring	.05
140 Detroit Tigers (Team Checklist)	.05
141 *Jeff Weaver* (99 Rookie)	.50
142 Gabe Kapler (99 Rookie)	.30
143 Tony Clark (Power Trip)	.10
144 Tony Clark	.20
145 Juan Encarnacion	.05
146 Dean Palmer	.10
147 Damion Easley	.05
148 Bobby Higginson	.05
149 Karim Garcia	.05
150 Justin Thompson	.05
151 Matt Anderson	.05
152 Willie Blair	.05
153 Brian Hunter	.05

154	Florida Marlins (Team Checklist)	.05
155	Alex Gonzalez (99 Rookie)	.05
156	Mark Kotsay	.05
157	Livan Hernandez	.05
158	Cliff Floyd	.05
159	Todd Dunwoody	.05
160	Alex Fernandez	.05
161	Mark Mantei	.05
162	Derrek Lee	.05
163	Kevin Orie	.05
164	Craig Counsell	.05
165	Rafael Medina	.05
166	Houston Astros (Team Checklist)	.05
167	Daryle Ward (99 Rookie)	.05
168	Mitch Meluskey (99 Rookie)	.05
169	Jeff Bagwell (Power Trip)	.25
170	Jeff Bagwell	.50
171	Ken Caminiti	.15
172	Craig Biggio	.25
173	Derek Bell	.05
174	Moises Alou	.15
175	Billy Wagner	.10
176	Shane Reynolds	.10
177	Carl Everett	.05
178	Scott Elarton	.05
179	Richard Hidalgo	.05
180	Kansas City Royals (Team Checklist)	.05
181	Carlos Beltran (99 Rookie)	.40
182	Carlos Febles (99 Rookie)	.20
183	Jeremy Giambi (99 Rookie)	.15
184	Johnny Damon	.05
185	Joe Randa	.05
186	Jeff King	.05
187	Hipolito Pichardo	.05
188	Kevin Appier	.05
189	Chad Kreuter	.05
190	Rey Sanchez	.05
191	Larry Sutton	.05
192	Jeff Montgomery	.05
193	Jermaine Dye	.05
194	Los Angeles Dodgers (Team Checklist)	.05
195	Adam Riggs (99 Rookie)	.05
196	Angel Pena (99 Rookie)	.05
197	Todd Hundley	.05
198	Kevin Brown	.15
199	Ismael Valdes	.10
200	Chan Ho Park	.10
201	Adrian Beltre	.20
202	Mark Grudzielanek	.05
203	Raul Mondesi	.15
204	Gary Sheffield	.15
205	Eric Karros	.15
206	Devon White	.05
207	Milwaukee Brewers (Team Checklist)	.05
208	Ron Belliard (99 Rookie)	.10
209	Rafael Roque (99 Rookie)	.05
210	Jeromy Burnitz	.10
211	Fernando Vina	.05
212	Scott Karl	.05
213	Jim Abbott	.05
214	Sean Berry	.05
215	Marquis Grissom	.10
216	Geoff Jenkins	.05
217	Jeff Cirillo	.05
218	Dave Nilsson	.05
219	Jose Valentin	.05
220	Minnesota Twins (Team Checklist)	.05
221	Corey Koskie (99 Rookie)	.05
222	Christian Guzman (99 Rookie)	.05
223	A.J. Pierzynski (99 Rookie)	.05
224	David Ortiz	.05
225	Brad Radke	.05
226	Todd Walker	.05
227	Matt Lawton	.05
228	Rick Aguilera	.05
229	Eric Milton	.05
230	Marty Cordova	.05
231	Torii Hunter	.05
232	Ron Coomer	.05
233	LaTroy Hawkins	.05
234	Montreal Expos (Team Checklist)	.05
235	Fernando Seguignol (99 Rookie)	.15
236	Michael Barrett (99 Rookie)	.25
237	Vladimir Guerrero (Big Play Makers)	.25
238	Vladimir Guerrero	.50
239	Brad Fullmer	.05
240	Rondell White	.10
241	Ugueth Urbina	.05
242	Dustin Hermanson	.10
243	Orlando Cabrera	.05
244	Wilton Guerrero	.05
245	Carl Pavano	.05
246	Javier Vasquez	.05
247	Chris Widger	.05
248	New York Mets (Team Checklist)	.05
249	Mike Kinkade (99 Rookie)	.05
250	Octavio Dotel (99 Rookie)	.05
251	Mike Piazza (Power Trip)	.50
252	Mike Piazza	1.00
253	Rickey Henderson	.10
254	Edgardo Alfonzo	.10
255	Robin Ventura	.15
256	Al Leiter	.15
257	Brian McRae	.05
258	Rey Ordonez	.10
259	Bobby Bonilla	.10
260	Orel Hershiser	.10
261	John Olerud	.15
262	New York Yankees (Team Checklist)	.15
263	Ricky Ledee (99 Rookie)	.10
264	Bernie Williams (Big Play Makers)	.15
265	Derek Jeter (Big Play Makers)	.50
266	Scott Brosius (History in the Making)	.05
267	Derek Jeter	1.00
268	Roger Clemens	.50
269	Orlando Hernandez	.25
270	Scott Brosius	.05
271	Paul O'Neill	.15
272	Bernie Williams	.30
273	Chuck Knoblauch	.15
274	Tino Martinez	.25
275	Mariano Rivera	.15
276	Jorge Posada	.10
277	Oakland Athletics (Team Checklist)	.05
278	Eric Chavez (99 Rookie)	.15
279	Ben Grieve (History in the Making)	.20
280	Jason Giambi	.05
281	John Jaha	.05
282	Miguel Tejada	.15
283	Ben Grieve	.30
284	Matt Stairs	.05
285	Ryan Christenson	.05
286	A.J. Hinch	.05
287	Kenny Rogers	.05
288	Tom Candiotti	.05
289	Scott Spezio	.05
290	Philadelphia Phillies (Team Checklist)	.05
291	*Pat Burrell* (99 Rookie)	2.00
292	Marlon Anderson (99 Rookie)	.05
293	Scott Rolen (Big Play Makers)	.20
294	Scott Rolen	.40
295	Doug Glanville	.05
296	Rico Brogna	.05
297	Ron Gant	.15
298	Bobby Abreu	.05
299	Desi Relaford	.05
300	Curt Schilling	.15
301	Chad Ogea	.05
302	Kevin Jordan	.05
303	Carlton Loewer	.05
304	Pittsburgh Pirates (Team Checklist)	.05
305	Kris Benson (99 Rookie)	.15
306	Brian Giles	.05
307	Jason Kendall	.15
308	Jose Guillen	.05
309	Pat Meares	.05
310	Brant Brown	.05
311	Kevin Young	.05
312	Ed Sprague	.05
313	Francisco Cordova	.05
314	Aramis Ramirez	.05
315	Freddy Garcia	1.00
316	Saint Louis Cardinals (Team Checklist)	.05
317	J.D. Drew (99 Rookie)	1.00
318	Chad Hutchinson (99 Rookie)	.40
319	Mark McGwire (Power Trip)	1.00
320	J.D. Drew (Power Trip)	.50
321	Mark McGwire (Big Play Makers)	1.00
322	Mark McGwire (History in the Making)	1.00
323	Mark McGwire	2.00
324	Fernando Tatis	.15
325	Edgar Renteria	.05
326	Ray Lankford	.05
327	Willie McGee	.05
328	Ricky Bottalico	.05
329	Eli Marrero	.05
330	Matt Morris	.05
331	Eric Davis	.15
332	Darren Bragg	.05
333	Padres (Team Checklist)	.05
334	Matt Clement (99 Rookie)	.05
335	Ben Davis (99 Rookie)	.15
336	Gary Matthews Jr. (99 Rookie)	.05
337	Tony Gwynn (Big Play Makers)	.40
338	Tony Gwynn (History in the Making)	.40
339	Tony Gwynn	.75
340	Reggie Sanders	.05
341	Ruben Rivera	.05
342	Wally Joyner	.05
343	Sterling Hitchcock	.05
344	Carlos Hernandez	.05
345	Andy Ashby	.05
346	Trevor Hoffman	.05
347	Chris Gomez	.05
348	Jim Leyritz	.05
349	San Francisco Giants (Team Checklist)	.05
350	Armando Rios (99 Rookie)	.15
351	Barry Bonds (Power Trip)	.20
352	Barry Bonds (Big Play Makers)	.20
353	Barry Bonds (History in the Making)	.20
354	Robb Nen	.05
355	Bill Mueller	.05
356	Barry Bonds	.40
357	Jeff Kent	.15
358	J.T. Snow	.05
359	Ellis Burks	.10
360	F.P. Santangelo	.05
361	Marvin Benard	.05
362	Stan Javier	.05
363	Shawn Estes	.05
364	Seattle Mariners (Team Checklist)	.05
365	Carlos Guillen (99 Rookie)	.15
366	Ken Griffey Jr. (Power Trip)	.75
367	Alex Rodriguez (Power Trip)	.50
368	Ken Griffey Jr. (Big Play Makers)	.75
369	Alex Rodriguez (Big Play Makers)	.50
370	Ken Griffey Jr. (History in the Making)	.75
371	Alex Rodriguez (History in the Making)	.75
372	Ken Griffey Jr.	1.50
373	Alex Rodriguez	1.00
374	Jay Buhner	.15
375	Edgar Martinez	.15
376	Jeff Fassero	.05
377	David Bell	.05
378	David Segui	.05
379	Russ Davis	.05
380	Dan Wilson	.05
381	Jamie Moyer	.05
382	Tampa Bay Devil Rays (Team Checklist)	.05
383	Roberto Hernandez	.05
384	Bobby Smith	.05
385	Wade Boggs	.20
386	Fred McGriff	.20
387	Rolando Arrojo	.05
388	Jose Canseco	.40
389	Wilson Alvarez	.05
390	Kevin Stocker	.05
391	Miguel Cairo	.05
392	Quinton McCracken	.05
393	Texas Rangers (Team Checklist)	.05
394	Ruben Mateo (99 Rookie)	.40
395	Cesar King (99 Rookie)	.05
396	Juan Gonzalez (Power Trip)	.25
397	Juan Gonzalez (Big Play Makers)	.25
398	Ivan Rodriguez	.40
399	Juan Gonzalez	.50
400	Rafael Palmeiro	.25
401	Rick Helling	.05
402	Aaron Sele	.05
403	John Wetteland	.10
404	Rusty Greer	.10
405	Todd Zeile	.10
406	Royce Clayton	.05
407	Tom Goodwin	.05
408	Toronto Blue Jays (Team Checklist)	.05
409	Kevin Witt (99 Rookie)	.05
410	Roy Halladay (99 Rookie)	.15
411	Jose Cruz Jr.	.15
412	Carlos Delgado	.25
413	Willie Greene	.05
414	Shawn Green	.20
415	Homer Bush	.05
416	Shannon Stewart	.10
417	David Wells	.05
418	Kelvim Escobar	.05
419	Joey Hamilton	.05
420	Alex Gonzalez	.05
421	Mark McGwire (McGwire Magic)	.40
422	Mark McGwire (McGwire Magic)	.40
423	Mark McGwire (McGwire Magic)	.40
424	Mark McGwire (McGwire Magic)	.40
425	Mark McGwire (McGwire Magic)	.40
426	Mark McGwire (McGwire Magic)	.40
427	Mark McGwire (McGwire Magic)	.40
428	Mark McGwire (McGwire Magic)	.40
429	Mark McGwire (McGwire Magic)	.40
430	Mark McGwire (McGwire Magic)	.40
431	Mark McGwire (McGwire Magic)	.40
432	Mark McGwire (McGwire Magic)	.40
433	Mark McGwire (McGwire Magic)	.40
434	Mark McGwire (McGwire Magic)	.40
435	Mark McGwire (McGwire Magic)	.40
436	Mark McGwire (McGwire Magic)	.40
437	Mark McGwire (McGwire Magic)	.40
438	Mark McGwire (McGwire Magic)	.40
439	Mark McGwire (McGwire Magic)	.40
440	Mark McGwire (McGwire Magic)	.40
441	Mark McGwire (McGwire Magic)	.40
442	Mark McGwire (McGwire Magic)	.40
443	Mark McGwire (McGwire Magic)	.40
444	Mark McGwire (McGwire Magic)	.40
445	Mark McGwire (McGwire Magic)	.40
446	Mark McGwire (McGwire Magic)	.40
447	Mark McGwire (McGwire Magic)	.40
448	Mark McGwire (McGwire Magic)	.40
449	Mark McGwire (McGwire Magic)	.40
450	Mark McGwire (McGwire Magic)	.40
451	Chipper Jones '93 (Rookie Flashback)	.40
452	Cal Ripken Jr. '81 (Rookie Flashback)	.50
453	Roger Clemens '84 (Rookie Flashback)	.25
454	Wade Boggs '82 (Rookie Flashback)	.15
455	Greg Maddux '86 (Rookie Flashback)	.50
456	Frank Thomas '90 (Rookie Flashback)	.25
457	Jeff Bagwell '91 (Rookie Flashback)	.20
458	Mike Piazza '92 (Rookie Flashback)	.50
459	Randy Johnson '88 (Rookie Flashback)	.15
460	Mo Vaughn '91 (Rookie Flashback)	.15
461	Mark McGwire '86 (Rookie Flashback)	1.00
462	Rickey Henderson '79 (Rookie Flashback)	.10
463	Barry Bonds '86 (Rookie Flashback)	.20
464	Tony Gwynn '82 (Rookie Flashback)	.40
465	Ken Griffey Jr. '89 (Rookie Flashback)	.75
466	Alex Rodriquez '94 (Rookie Flashback)	.50
467	Sammy Sosa '89 (Rookie Flashback)	.50
468	Juan Gonzalez '89 (Rookie Flashback)	.25
469	Kevin Brown '86 (Rookie Flashback)	.05
470	Fred McGriff '86 (Rookie Flashback)	.10

1999 UD Ionix

Ionix is a 90-card set that includes a 30-card "Techno" subset that was short-printed (1:4 packs). Packs were sold for $4.99, and contain four cards. The first 60 cards of the set are included in a parallel set in which the photo from the back of the regular card was put on the front of a rainbow-foil Reciprocal card. These cards are sequentially numbered to 750. The remaining 30 cards in the set were also paralleled on a Reciprocal card sequentially numbered to 100. The set also includes 350 Frank Robinson "500 Club Piece of History" bat cards, with a piece of a Robinson game-used bat. Another version of the bat cards includes Robinson's autograph, and are hand-numbered to 20. Insert sets included Hyper, Nitro, Cyber, Warp Zone, and HoloGrFX.

		MT
Complete Set (90):		250.00
Common Player (1-60):		.75
Common Techno (61-90):		2.00
Inserted 1:4		
Reciprocals (1-60):		6x to 10x
Production 750 sets		
Techno Reciprocals (61-90):		10x to 15x
Production 100 sets		
1	Troy Glaus	1.50
2	Darin Erstad	1.50
3	Travis Lee	1.00
4	Matt Williams	1.00
5	Chipper Jones	3.00
6	Greg Maddux	4.00
7	Andruw Jones	1.50
8	Andres Galarraga	1.00
9	Tom Glavine	.75
10	Cal Ripken Jr.	5.00
11	Ryan Minor	.75
12	Nomar Garciaparra	4.00
13	Mo Vaughn	1.50
14	Pedro Martinez	1.25
15	Sammy Sosa	4.00
16	Kerry Wood	1.50
17	Albert Belle	1.50
18	Frank Thomas	4.00
19	Sean Casey	.75
20	Kenny Lofton	1.25
21	Manny Ramirez	2.00
22	Jim Thome	1.00
23	Bartolo Colon	.75
24	Jaret Wright	1.00
25	Larry Walker	1.00
26	Tony Clark	1.00
27	Gabe Kapler	2.00
28	Edgar Renteria	.75
29	Randy Johnson	1.00
30	Craig Biggio	.75
31	Jeff Bagwell	1.50
32	Moises Alou	.75
33	Johnny Damon	.75
34	Adrian Beltre	.75
35	Jeromy Burnitz	.75
36	Todd Walker	.75
37	Corey Koskie	.75
38	Vladimir Guerrero	2.00
39	Mike Piazza	4.00
40	Hideo Nomo	.75
41	Derek Jeter	4.00
42	Tino Martinez	1.00
43	Orlando Hernandez	2.00
44	Ben Grieve	1.50
45	Rickey Henderson	.75
46	Scott Rolen	1.50
47	Curt Schilling	.75

48	Aramis Ramirez	.75
49	Tony Gwynn	3.00
50	Kevin Brown	.75
51	Barry Bonds	1.50
52	Ken Griffey Jr.	6.00
53	Alex Rodriguez	4.00
54	Mark McGwire	8.00
55	J.D. Drew	10.00
56	Rolando Arrojo	.75
57	Ivan Rodriguez	1.50
58	Juan Gonzalez	3.00
59	Roger Clemens	2.50
60	Jose Cruz Jr.	1.25
61	Travis Lee (Techno)	3.00
62	Andres Galarraga (Techno)	2.50
63	Andruw Jones (Techno)	4.00
64	Chipper Jones (Techno)	8.00
65	Greg Maddux (Techno)	10.00
66	Cal Ripken Jr. (Techno)	12.00
67	Nomar Garciaparra (Techno)	10.00
68	Mo Vaughn (Techno)	4.00
69	Sammy Sosa (Techno)	10.00
70	Frank Thomas (Techno)	8.00
71	Kerry Wood (Techno)	3.00
72	Kenny Lofton (Techno)	3.00
73	Manny Ramirez (Techno)	5.00
74	Larry Walker (Techno)	3.00
75	Jeff Bagwell (Techno)	4.00
76	Randy Johnson (Techno)	3.00
77	Paul Molitor (Techno)	3.00
78	Derek Jeter (Techno)	10.00
79	Tino Martinez (Techno)	2.50
80	Mike Piazza (Techno)	10.00
81	Ben Grieve (Techno)	4.00
82	Scott Rolen (Techno)	4.00
83	Mark McGwire (Techno)	18.00
84	Tony Gwynn (Techno)	8.00
85	Barry Bonds (Techno)	4.00
86	Ken Griffey Jr. (Techno)	15.00
87	Alex Rodriguez (Techno)	10.00
88	Juan Gonzalez (Techno)	8.00
89	Roger Clemens (Techno)	6.00
90	J.D. Drew (Techno)	20.00

1999 UD Ionix Cyber

This insert set consisted of 25-cards of baseball's superstars and red-hot rookies. One card was inserted every 53 packs.

	MT
Complete Set (25):	750.00
Common Player:	10.00
C01 Ken Griffey Jr.	65.00
C02 Cal Ripken Jr.	50.00
C03 Frank Thomas	40.00
C04 Greg Maddux	45.00
C05 Mike Piazza	45.00
C06 Alex Rodriguez	45.00
C07 Chipper Jones	30.00
C08 Derek Jeter	40.00
C09 Mark McGwire	80.00
C10 Juan Gonzalez	30.00
C11 Kerry Wood	15.00
C12 Tony Gwynn	30.00
C13 Scott Rolen	15.00
C14 Nomar Garciaparra	45.00
C15 Roger Clemens	25.00
C16 Sammy Sosa	45.00
C17 Travis Lee	15.00
C18 Ben Grieve	15.00
C19 Jeff Bagwell	15.00
C20 Ivan Rodriguez	15.00
C21 Barry Bonds	15.00
C22 J.D. Drew	80.00
C23 Kenny Lofton	10.00
C24 Andruw Jones	15.00
C25 Vladimir Guerrero	20.00

1999 UD Ionix HoloGrFX

This insert set consisted of 10-cards, and featured only the best players in the game. The cards in this set were holographically enhanced. These cards were rare with one card inserted every 1,500 packs.

	MT
Complete Set (10):	2000.
Common Player:	175.00
Inserted 1:1,500	
HG01Ken Griffey Jr.	350.00
HG02Cal Ripken Jr.	275.00
HG03Frank Thomas	200.00
HG04Greg Maddux	200.00
HG05Mike Piazza	200.00
HG06Alex Rodriguez	200.00
HG07Chipper Jones	175.00
HG08Derek Jeter	200.00
HG09Mark McGwire	450.00
HG10Juan Gonzalez	175.00

1999 UD Ionix Hyper

This insert set featured the top players in baseball, and consisted of 20-cards. Hyper cards were inserted one per nine packs.

	MT
Complete Set (20):	150.00
Common Player:	3.00
Inserted 1:9	
H01 Ken Griffey Jr.	18.00
H02 Cal Ripken Jr.	12.00
H03 Frank Thomas	10.00
H04 Greg Maddux	10.00
H05 Mike Piazza	10.00
H06 Alex Rodriguez	10.00
H07 Chipper Jones	8.00
H08 Derek Jeter	10.00
H09 Mark McGwire	20.00
H10 Juan Gonzalez	8.00
H11 Kerry Wood	4.00
H12 Tony Gwynn	8.00
H13 Scott Rolen	4.00
H14 Nomar Garciaparra	10.00
H15 Roger Clemens	6.00
H16 Sammy Sosa	10.00
H17 Travis Lee	4.00
H18 Ben Grieve	4.00
H19 Jeff Bagwell	4.00
H20 J.D. Drew	25.00

1999 UD Ionix Nitro

Baseball's ten most collectible players are featured in this 10-card insert set. Each card features Ionix technology with rainbow foil and a unique color pattern. Nitro cards were inserted one per 18 packs.

	MT
Complete Set (10):	100.00
Common Player:	6.00
Inserted 1:18	
N01 Ken Griffey Jr.	18.00
N02 Cal Ripken Jr.	12.00
N03 Frank Thomas	10.00
N04 Greg Maddux	10.00
N05 Mike Piazza	10.00
N06 Alex Rodriguez	10.00
N07 Chipper Jones	8.00
N08 Derek Jeter	10.00
N09 Mark McGwire	20.00
N10 J.D. Drew	25.00

1999 UD Ionix Warp Zone

This 15-card insert set contained a special holographic foil enhancement. Warp Zone cards were inserted one per 216 packs.

	MT
Complete Set (15):	1000.
Common Player:	25.00
Inserted 1:216	
WZ01Ken Griffey Jr.	125.00
WZ02Cal Ripken Jr.	100.00
WZ03Frank Thomas	80.00
WZ04Greg Maddux	80.00
WZ05Mike Piazza	80.00
WZ06Alex Rodriguez	80.00
WZ07Chipper Jones	60.00
WZ08Derek Jeter	80.00
WZ09Mark McGwire	150.00
WZ10Juan Gonzalez	60.00
WZ11Kerry Wood	30.00
WZ12Tony Gwynn	60.00
WZ13Scott Rolen	30.00
WZ14Nomar Garciaparra	80.00
WZ15J.D. Drew	100.00

1999 UD Ionix 500 Club Piece of History

These cards feature an actual piece of game-used bat from one of Hall-of-Famer Frank Robinson's Louisville Sluggers. Approximately 350 were made. Robinson also autographed 20 of his Piece of History inserts.

	MT
Production 350	
Auto. Production 20	
FR Frank Robinson	200.00
FRA Frank Robinson (Auto)	800.00

Market Report

Top Rookies Like Vince Carter Lead The Way In Basketball Cards

When the 1998-99 NBA season didn't start on time due to the lockout, the league and card market faced a long road back. Players from the 1998 NBA Draft couldn't be used in products until they signed NBA contracts, which couldn't happen until a settlement occurred. This caused many card manufacturers to delay or cancel products until the lockout ended.

When the lockout finally ended in January, card manufacturers scrambled to get their products on the market, and since basketball popularity was at a low point, most spiced up their products any way they could in hope of winning collectors back.

Sales were strong immediately after the season began, but they suffered later in the season, with so many of the hobby's best products fighting for dollars with football and baseball. Of the 30 products released in 1998-99, 16 came out after the lockout ended, with most being super premium.

A strong rookie class, highlighted by Vince Carter, Jason Williams and Paul Pierce, helped sales throughout the season, but too many releases eventually took their toll, as nearly half the products sold below suggested retail price.

While Pierce and Williams got out of the gate quickly, it was Carter who dominated the second half and won Rookie of the Year honors. Carter averaged 18.8 ppg, 5.7 rebounds, 3.0 assists and 1.54 blocks as a rookie, and nearly led the Raptors to the playoffs.

Carter's top rookie cards continue to be among the hottest singles on the market. His SP Authentic rookie (#95) sells for $250, while his Topps Chrome (#199) books at $100.

Although Karl Malone won the MVP, the 1999 season belonged to Tim Duncan. Duncan led the San Antonio Spurs to the best regular-season record in the NBA, then to the NBA Championship as they plowed through Minnesota, Los Angeles, Portland and finally, New York in the Finals. Duncan, in only his second season, won the NBA Finals MVP.

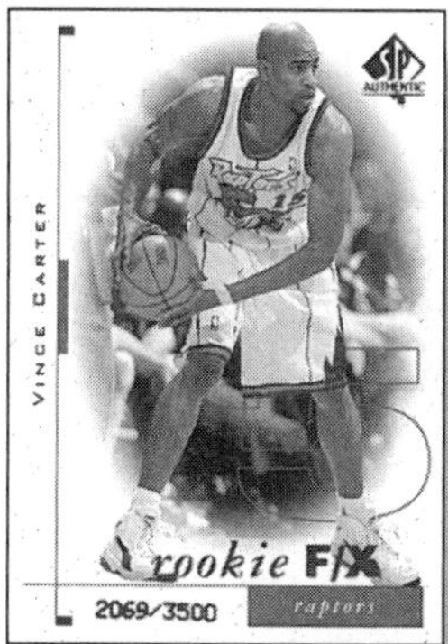

Collectors noticed Duncan's dominance also, as they chased his top rookie cards from 1997-98. These include: Topps Chrome (#115, $120), Finest (#101, $45) and SP Authentic (#128), which jumped from $20 to $50.

Another young player also distinguished himself among the NBA's elite. Kevin Garnett emerged to average 18.5 ppg, 10.5 rebounds, 4.3 assists and 1.7 blocks during the 1998-99. With his intense style of play and his flair for the dramatic, Garnett became the popular choice to lead the NBA into the millennium.

Garnett's 1995-96 rookie cards experienced increased interest, led by Finest (#115, $100), SP (#159, $15) and Flair (#206, $12).

Michael Jordan's popularity was also very evident during 1999. Upper Deck released two Jordan-only products (MJx and MJ A Living Legend), and featured Jordan inserts and subsets in most of its 1998-99 products. The company inserted 23 hand-numbered autographed Game Jersey cards ($11,000) in six different products early in the season to boost sales, then followed it up with such rarities as 23 hand-numbered Jordan autographs in Ionix ($7,000) and 50 Jordan autographs in Encore ($5,000).

THE CLASS OF 1996

If there were any questions concerning the strength of the 1996 NBA Draft, they were answered during 1999. Players like Kobe Bryant, Allen Iverson (led the NBA in scoring), Shareef Abdur-Rahim (finished fourth in scoring), Ray Allen and Stephon Marbury solidified their positions as NBA superstars, while Marcus Camby, Lorenzen Wright, Samaki Walker, Steve Nash, Derek Fisher, Jermaine O'Neal and Kerry Kittles offered plenty of potential for the future. Only the Celtics' Antoine Walker had a disappointing season.

Products from 1996-97, like Topps Chrome, Finest, E-X2000, SP and Bowman's Best were in high demand throughout the year, and with this kind of potential, seem destined to be collector favorites for a long time.

In addition, the 1996 rookie class was responsible for what was possibly the hottest set of the year. The 1996-97 Stadium Club Members Only 55 boxed set hadn't received much attention since its release, but quickly became a "must have" for collectors. The set consisted of 50 veterans and five rookies – Bryant, Iverson, Abdur-Rahim, Marbury and Kittles – on Finest technology. At the start of the year, Bryant's single sold for $20, but vaulted to $200 during the off-season. The others followed suit.

CERTIFIED CARD GRADING

The most popular trend of 1999 was certified card grading. In the past, primarily vintage cards from the 1960s and 1970s were the subject of professional grading, but now even new releases are immediately being graded. New releases got a nice boost from the graded card market, as singles from products like SP Authentic and Topps Chrome became plentiful in graded form.

Also reaping the benefits of card grading were rookies from products like 1997-98 SP Authentic and 1996-97 SP, which were hard to find in Gem Mint condition due to the foil printing techniques used on the cards. Wax boxes for SP shot up from around $100 to $175 within a few months.

Nearly every Jordan card was a target of professional grading. Any 1980s card, Fleer Stickers from 1986-87 through 1989-90, newer releases from super-premium products, and even "throwaway" cards like 1991-92 Fleer were hot items in Gem Mint Condition. Jordan's Gem Mint Fleer rookie now sells for $25,000, while his rookie sticker is valued at $20,000.

BRING ON THE WNBA

With Pinnacle's departure from the industry, Fleer/SkyBox took the opportunity to produce two WNBA products – Hoops and Ultra. Both products did quite well in the market, as WNBA fans and collectors searched for their favorite players. Rookie of the Year Chamique Holdsclaw drew much of the attention from collectors, while Autographics in Hoops and Fresh Ink autographs in Ultra also boosted product performance. Holdsclaw's Hoops rookie (#105) sells for $8, while her Ultra rookie (#102) books for $30.

THE FUTURE

Although the basketball card market had a down year in 1998-99, most of this can be attributed to the glut of products released once the lockout ended. However, led by players like Garnett, Duncan, Carter and Jordan, the basketball card market shows great potential for the future.

Adding to this is the draft class of 1999, with players like Lamar Odom, Steve Francis and Elton Brand. Pat Riley dubbed Odom "Magic Johnson with a jumpshot" before the draft, and his early season performances have done nothing to disprove that claim.

The chase for rookie cards from new releases, as well as the dollars that are still going into past year's products, give basketball plenty of promise for the future.

PLAYER OF THE YEAR

Full Name: Timothy Theodore Duncan
Hometown: St. Croix, Virgin Islands
Height: 7'0"
Weight: 248
College: Wake Forest
Birthdate: 4/25/76
Drafted: Selected in first round of 1997 draft by San Antonio, 1st pick overall

Tim Duncan

CARDS TO GET: Duncan's cards to get include: 1997-98 Finest (#101, $45), 1997-98 SP Authentic (#128, $50), 1997-98 Topps Chrome (#115, $120), 1997-98 Bowman's Best (#106, $25), 1997-98 E-X2001 (#75, $30), 1997-98 Ultra (#131, $70), 1997-98 Upper Deck (#114, $6), 1998-99 SkyBox Autographics ($300), 1998-99 Upper Deck Game Jersey (GJ15, $250).

TOP TENS

REGULAR-ISSUE SINGLES

1. Michael Jordan	1986-87 Fleer (#57)	$650
2. Kobe Bryant	1996-97 Topps Chrome (#138)	$325
3. Vince Carter	1998-99 SP Authentic (#95)	$250
4. Tim Duncan	1997-98 Topps Chrome (#115)	$125
5. Tim Duncan	1997-98 SP Authentic (#128)	$50
6. Allen Iverson	1996-97 Topps Chrome (#171)	$150
7. Kevin Garnett	1995-96 Finest (#115)	$100
8. Kobe Bryant	1996-97 Finest (#74)	$80
9. Kevin Garnett	1995-96 SP (#159	$15
10. C. Holdsclaw	1998-99 Ultra (#102)	$30

REGULAR-ISSUE SETS

1. 1996-97 Topps Chrome	$750/box	225-card set: $750
2. 1998-99 SP Authentic	$150	120-card set: $650
3. 1986-87 Fleer	$5,500	132-card set: $1,800
4. 1998-99 Topps Chrome	$125	220-card set: $325
5. 1996-97 Finest Series I	$375	100-card set: $190
6. 1999 Ultra WNBA	$65	125-card set: $100
7. 1999 UD Century Legends	$100	
8. 1998-99 Finest Series II	$90	125-card set: $125
9. 1996-97 SP	$175	146-card set: $65
10. 1998-99 UD MJ Access	$90	180-card set: $250

BASKETBALL

1998-99 Bowman's Best

This 125-card set included 100 veterans on gold foil and 25 rookies on silver foil seeded 1:4 packs. Refractor versions of each were sequentially numbered to 400 sets on the back, while Atomic Refractor versions were numbered to 100 and featured prismatic foil on the front. Inserts include: Refractors (1:25 packs), Atomic Refractors (1:100), Autographs, Mirror Image Fusion, Best Performers and Franchise Best.

		MT
Complete Set (125):		150.00
Common Player:		.20
Common Rookie:		2.00
Inserted 1:4		
Wax Box:		75.00
1	Jason Kidd	1.00
2	Dikembe Mutombo	.40
3	Chris Mullin	.40
4	Terrell Brandon	.40
5	Cedric Ceballos	.20
6	Rod Strickland	.40
7	Darrell Armstrong	.50
8	Anfernee Hardaway	1.50
9	Eddie Jones	.75
10	Allen Iverson	2.00
11	Kenny Anderson	.40
12	Toni Kukoc	.60
13	Lawrence Funderburke	.20
14	P.J. Brown	.20
15	Jeff Hornacek	.20
16	Mookie Blaylock	.20
17	Avery Johnson	.20
18	Donyell Marshall	.20
19	Detlef Schrempf	.20
20	Joe Dumars	.40
21	Charles Barkley	.75
22	Maurice Taylor	.60
23	Chauncey Billups	.60
24	Lee Mayberry	.20
25	Glen Rice	.40
26	John Stockton	.40
27	Rik Smits	.20
28	LaPhonso Ellis	.40
29	Kerry Kittles	.40
30	Damon Stoudamire	.60
31	Kevin Garnett	2.50
32	Chris Mills	.20
33	Kendall Gill	.20
34	Tim Thomas	1.00
35	Derek Anderson	.50
36	Billy Owens	.20
37	Bobby Jackson	.50
38	Allan Houston	.40
39	Horace Grant	.20
40	Ray Allen	.50
41	Shawn Bradley	.20
42	Arvydas Sabonis	.20
43	Rex Chapman	.20
44	Larry Johnson	.40
45	Jayson Williams	.40
46	Joe Smith	.50
47	Ron Mercer	1.00
48	Rodney Rogers	.20
49	Corliss Williamson	.20
50	Tim Duncan	2.50
51	Rasheed Wallace	.40
52	Vin Baker	.50
53	Reggie Miller	.40
54	Patrick Ewing	.40
55	Michael Finley	.40
56	Bryant Reeves	.40
57	Glenn Robinson	.40
58	Walter McCarty	.20
59	Brent Barry	.20
60	John Starks	.20
61	Clarence Weatherspoon	.20
62	Calbert Cheaney	.20
63	Lamond Murray	.20
64	Zydrunas Ilgauskas	.40
65	Anthony Mason	.20
66	Bryon Russell	.20
67	Dean Garrett	.20
68	Tom Gugliotta	.40
69	Dennis Rodman	1.00
70	Keith Van Horn	1.50
71	Jamal Mashburn	.40
72	Steve Smith	.40
73	David Wesley	.20
74	Chris Webber	1.00
75	Isaiah Rider	.40
76	Stephon Marbury	1.50
77	Tim Hardaway	.60
78	Jerry Stackhouse	.40
79	John Wallace	.40
80	Karl Malone	.75
81	Juwan Howard	.40
82	Antonio McDyess	.60
83	David Robinson	.75
84	Bobby Phills	.20
85	Scottie Pippen	1.00
86	Brevin Knight	.60
87	Alan Henderson	.20
88	Kobe Bryant	3.00
89	Shawn Kemp	1.00
90	Antoine Walker	1.50
91	Tracy McGrady	1.00
92	Hakeem Olajuwon	.75
93	Mark Jackson	.20
94	Bison Dele	.20
95	Gary Payton	.75
96	Ron Harper	.20
97	Shareef Abdur-Rahim	1.00
98	Alonzo Mourning	.40
99	Grant Hill	2.50
100	Shaquille O'Neal	1.50
101	*Michael Olowokandi*	6.00
102	*Mike Bibby*	10.00
103	*Raef LaFrentz*	6.00
104	*Antawn Jamison*	15.00
105	*Vince Carter*	35.00
106	*Robert Traylor*	6.00
107	*Jason Williams*	25.00
108	*Larry Hughes*	10.00
109	*Dirk Nowitzki*	3.00
110	*Paul Pierce*	20.00
111	*Bonzi Wells*	3.00
112	*Michael Doleac*	4.00
113	*Keon Clark*	4.00
114	*Michael Dickerson*	6.00
115	*Matt Harpring*	4.00
116	*Bryce Drew*	3.00
117	*Pat Garrity*	3.00
118	*Roshown McLeod*	3.00
119	*Ricky Davis*	4.00
120	*Brian Skinner*	2.00
121	*Tyronn Lue*	3.00
122	*Felipe Lopez*	5.00
123	*Al Harrington*	5.00
124	*Corey Benjamin*	2.00
125	*Nazr Mohammed*	2.00

1998-99 Bowman's Best Refractors

This 125-card set reprinted each card in Bowman's Best with a Refractor finish. Cards were inserted 1:25 packs and sequentially numbered to 400 sets. The cards were also distinguished by the word "Refractor" printed in small black letters below the card number.

	MT
Refractor Veterans:	8x-16x
Refractor Rookies:	3x-6x
Inserted 1:25	
Production 400 Sets	

1998-99 Bowman's Best Atomic Refractors

This 125-card parallel set reprinted each card in Bowman's Best with a prismatic Refractor front. Atomic Refractors were inserted 1:100 packs and sequentially numbered to 100 sets. The cards were also distinguished by the word "Atomic" above the card number and "Refractor" below the card number, both in small black print.

	MT
Atomic Ref. Veterans:	25x-50x
Atomic Ref. Rookies:	10x-20x
Inserted 1:100	
Production 100 Sets	

1998-99 Bowman's Best Autograph Cards

Five veteran and five rookie autographs were inserted into Bowman's Best. Each card arrived with a Topps "Certified Autograph Issue" stamp. Regular, Refractor and Atomic Refractor versions of each existed, with veterans seeded 1:628, 1:3,358 and 10,073 packs and rookies seeded 1:598, 1:4,172 and 1:12,515 packs, respectively.

		MT
Common Player:		20.00
Veterans Inserted 1:628		
Rookies Inserted 1:598		
Refractors:		2x
Veteran Refractors 1:3,358		
Rookie Refractors 1:4,172		
Atomic Refractors:		4x
Veteran Atomic Ref. 1:10,073		
Rookie Atomic Ref. 1:12,515		
Card No. 7 Does Not Exist		
1	Kobe Bryant	125.00
2	Tim Duncan	125.00
3	Eddie Jones	50.00
4	Gary Payton	50.00
5	Antoine Walker	60.00
6	Antawn Jamison	75.00
8	Mike Bibby	50.00
9	Vince Carter	200.00
10	Michael Doleac	20.00

1998-99 Bowman's Best Best Performers

This 10-card insert highlights five veterans and five rookies who have outstanding ability. Regular versions are seeded 1:12 packs, with Refractors 1:628 and numbered to 200 and Atomic Refractors numbered to 50 sets and seeded 1:2,504 packs. Best Performers are numbered with a "BP" prefix.

		MT
Complete Set (10):		50.00
Common Player:		1.00
Inserted 1:12		
Refractor Cards:		3x-6x
Inserted 1:628		
Production 200 Sets		
Atomic Ref. Cards:		10x-20x
Inserted 1:2,504		
Production 50 Sets		
1	Shaquille O'Neal	5.00
2	Kevin Garnett	10.00
3	Dikembe Mutombo	1.00
4	Grant Hill	10.00
5	Tim Duncan	10.00
6	Antawn Jamison	6.00
7	Raef LaFrentz	3.00
8	Mike Bibby	5.00
9	Paul Pierce	8.00
10	Jason Williams	10.00

1998-99 Bowman's Best Franchise Best

This 10-card insert was seeded 1:23 packs of Bowman's Best. Cards were printed on 26-point stock, featured a gold pin-striped background and were numbered with an "FB" prefix.

		MT
Complete Set (10):		90.00
Common Player:		3.00
Inserted 1:23		
1	Michael Jordan	30.00
2	Karl Malone	3.00
3	Antoine Walker	8.00
4	Grant Hill	15.00
5	Kevin Garnett	15.00
6	Shaquille O'Neal	8.00
7	Gary Payton	3.00
8	Keith Van Horn	8.00
9	Tim Duncan	15.00
10	Allen Iverson	10.00

1998-99 Bowman's Best Mirror Image Fusion

This insert featured the top eight players at each position with four veterans and four young stars from both conferences. Each double-sided die-cut card featured a tandem from either the Eastern or Western Conference. Regular Fusion cards were inserted 1:12 packs, Refractors sequentially numbered to 100 sets (1:628) and Atomic Refractors numbered to 25 sets (1:2,504).

		MT
Complete Set (20):		100.00
Common Player:		1.00
Inserted 1:12		
Refractor Cards:		3x-5x
Inserted 1:628		
Production 100 Sets		
Atomic Ref. Cards:		6x-12x
Inserted 1:2,504		
Production 25 Sets		
1	Tim Hardaway, Brevin Knight	3.00
2	Gary Payton, Damon Stoudamire	3.00
3	Anfernee Hardaway, Allen Iverson	12.00
4	John Stockton, Stephon Marbury	8.00
5	Ray Allen, Kerry Kittles	2.00
6	Eddie Jones, Kobe Bryant	12.00
7	Steve Smith, Ron Mercer	5.00
8	Isaiah Rider, Michael Finley	2.00
9	Latrell Sprewell, Antoine Walker	8.00
10	Detlef Schrempf, Shareef Abdur-Rahim	4.00
11	Grant Hill, Tim Thomas	12.00
12	Scottie Pippen, Kevin Garnett	12.00
13	Jayson Williams, Juwan Howard	2.00
14	Vin Baker, Antonio McDyess	3.00
15	Shawn Kemp, Keith Van Horn	10.00
16	Karl Malone, Tim Duncan	10.00
17	Alonzo Mourning, Zydrunas Ilgauskas	2.00
18	Shaquille O'Neal, Bryant Reeves	6.00
19	Dikembe Mutombo, Theo Ratliff	1.00
20	David Robinson, Greg Ostertag	2.00

1998-99 SkyBox E-X Century

E-X Century continued the SkyBox brand that started in 1994-95 as E-Motion. The 90-card set included 60 veterans and 30 rookies seeded 1:1.5 packs. Cards were printed on thick plastic, with a cut-out player's image and team color strip over the top of it. The player's name runs down the right side in holographic letters. Inserts include: Generation E-X, Dunk 'N' Go Nuts, Authen-Kicks and Autographics. All 90 cards are also paralleled in Essential Credentials Now (numbered to the player's card number) and Essential Credentials Future (numbered to the number that combined with Essential Credentials Now equals 91).

		MT
Complete Set (90):		150.00
Common Player:		.25
Wax Box:		90.00
1	Keith Van Horn	2.00
2	Scottie Pippen	1.50
3	Tim Thomas	1.00
4	Stephon Marbury	2.00
5	Allen Iverson	3.00
6	Grant Hill	5.00
7	Tim Duncan	5.00
8	Latrell Sprewell	.50
9	Ron Mercer	1.00
10	Kobe Bryant	6.00
11	Antoine Walker	2.00
12	Reggie Miller	.50
13	Kevin Garnett	5.00
14	Shaquille O'Neal	2.00
15	Karl Malone	.75
16	Dennis Rodman	1.00
17	Tracy McGrady	1.50
18	Anfernee Hardaway	2.00
19	Shareef Abdur-Rahim	1.00
20	Marcus Camby	.75
21	Eddie Jones	.75
22	Vin Baker	.50
23	Charles Barkley	.75
24	Patrick Ewing	.50
25	Jason Kidd	1.50
26	Mitch Richmond	.50
27	Tim Hardaway	.60
28	Glen Rice	.50
29	Shawn Kemp	1.00
30	John Stockton	.50
31	Ray Allen	.60
32	Brevin Knight	.50
33	David Robinson	.75
34	Juwan Howard	.50
35	Alonzo Mourning	.60
36	Hakeem Olajuwon	.75
37	Gary Payton	.75
38	Damon Stoudamire	.60
39	Steve Smith	.50
40	Chris Webber	1.50
41	Michael Finley	.60
42	Jayson Williams	.50
43	Maurice Taylor	.75
44	Jalen Rose	.25
45	Sam Cassell	.25
46	Jerry Stackhouse	.25
47	Toni Kukoc	.60
48	Charles Oakley	.25
49	Jim Jackson	.25
50	Dikembe Mutombo	.25
51	Wesley Person	.25
52	Antonio Daniels	.25
53	Isaiah Rider	.25
54	Tom Gugliotta	.50
55	Antonio McDyess	.75
56	Jeff Hornacek	.25
57	Joe Dumars	.50
58	Jamal Mashburn	.50
59	Donyell Marshall	.25
60	Glenn Robinson	.50
61	Jelani McCoy	1.00
62	Predrag Stojakovic	1.00
63	Randell Jackson	1.00
64	Brad Miller	1.00
65	Corey Benjamin	1.00
66	Toby Bailey	1.00
67	Nazr Mohammed	1.00
68	Dirk Nowitzki	3.00
69	Andrae Patterson	1.00
70	Michael Dickerson	5.00
71	Cory Carr	1.00
72	Brian Skinner	1.00
73	Pat Garrity	2.00
74	Ricky Davis	3.00
75	Roshown McLeod	2.00
76	Matt Harpring	3.00
77	Jason Williams	20.00
78	Keon Clark	3.00
79	Al Harrington	5.00
80	Felipe Lopez	4.00
81	Michael Doleac	3.00
82	Paul Pierce	20.00
83	Robert Traylor	8.00
84	Raef LaFrentz	8.00
85	Michael Olowokandi	8.00
86	Mike Bibby	10.00
87	Antawn Jamison	15.00
88	Bonzi Wells	2.00
89	Vince Carter	30.00
90	Larry Hughes	12.00

1998-99 SkyBox E-X Century Essential Credentials Future

This 90-card parallel set was sequentially numbered to a number that, when combined with "Now", equals total production of 91 cards. This parallel features gold color vs. the clear plastic used in regular-issue cards.

		MT
Common Player:		20.00
Cards 82-90 Unable to Price		
1	Keith Van Horn	100.00
2	Scottie Pippen	100.00
3	Tim Thomas	75.00
4	Stephon Marbury	100.00
5	Allen Iverson	125.00
6	Grant Hill	200.00
7	Tim Duncan	200.00
8	Latrell Sprewell	30.00
9	Ron Mercer	75.00
10	Kobe Bryant	300.00
11	Antoine Walker	100.00
12	Reggie Miller	30.00
13	Kevin Garnett	200.00
14	Shaquille O'Neal	120.00
15	Karl Malone	50.00
16	Dennis Rodman	100.00
17	Tracy McGrady	125.00
18	Anfernee Hardaway	175.00
19	Shareef Abdur-Rahim	125.00
20	Marcus Camby	65.00
21	Eddie Jones	75.00
22	Vin Baker	60.00
23	Charles Barkley	75.00
24	Patrick Ewing	50.00
25	Jason Kidd	125.00
26	Mitch Richmond	50.00
27	Tim Hardaway	60.00
28	Glen Rice	40.00
29	Shawn Kemp	100.00
30	John Stockton	40.00
31	Ray Allen	75.00
32	Brevin Knight	30.00
33	David Robinson	100.00
34	Juwan Howard	40.00
35	Alonzo Mourning	60.00
36	Hakeem Olajuwon	100.00
37	Gary Payton	100.00
38	Damon Stoudamire	60.00
39	Steve Smith	40.00
40	Chris Webber	150.00
41	Michael Finley	60.00
42	Jayson Williams	40.00
43	Maurice Taylor	75.00
44	Jalen Rose	30.00
45	Sam Cassell	30.00
46	Jerry Stackhouse	40.00
47	Toni Kukoc	125.00
48	Charles Oakley	20.00
49	Jim Jackson	20.00
50	Dikembe Mutombo	30.00
51	Wesley Person	20.00
52	Antonio Daniels	60.00
53	Isaiah Rider	40.00
54	Tom Gugliotta	40.00
55	Antonio McDyess	100.00
56	Jeff Hornacek	20.00
57	Joe Dumars	50.00
58	Jamal Mashburn	50.00
59	Donyell Marshall	20.00
60	Glenn Robinson	75.00
61	Jelani McCoy	40.00
62	Predrag Stojakovic	40.00
63	Randell Jackson	30.00
64	Brad Miller	30.00
65	Corey Benjamin	40.00
66	Toby Bailey	30.00
67	Nazr Mohammed	40.00
68	Dirk Nowitzki	50.00
69	Andrae Patterson	40.00
70	Michael Dickerson	100.00
71	Cory Carr	40.00
72	Brian Skinner	60.00
73	Pat Garrity	50.00
74	Ricky Davis	100.00
75	Roshown McLeod	50.00
76	Matt Harpring	150.00
77	Jason Williams	500.00
78	Keon Clark	100.00
79	Al Harrington	200.00
80	Felipe Lopez	150.00
81	Michael Doleac	100.00

1998-99 SkyBox E-X Century Essential Credentials Now

This 90-card parallel set was sequentially numbered to that player's card number on the back of the regular- issue card. Cards featured a silver foil finish vs. the clear plastic of the regular-issue cards.

		MT
Common Player:		20.00
Cards 1-9 Unable to Price		
10	Kobe Bryant	750.00
11	Antonie Walker	350.00
12	Reggie Miller	120.00
13	Kevin Garnett	600.00
14	Shaquille O'Neal	500.00
15	Karl Malone	250.00
16	Dennis Rodman	300.00
17	Tracy McGrady	350.00
18	Anfernee Hardaway	500.00
19	Shareef Abdur-Rahim	300.00
20	Marcus Camby	200.00
21	Eddie Jones	150.00
22	Vin Baker	100.00
23	Charles Barkley	150.00
24	Patrick Ewing	100.00
25	Jason Kidd	250.00
26	Mitch Richmond	100.00
27	Tim Hardaway	125.00
28	Glen Rice	100.00
29	Shawn Kemp	200.00
30	John Stockton	100.00
31	Ray Allen	100.00
32	Brevin Knight	60.00
33	David Robinson	150.00
34	Juwan Howard	60.00
35	Alonzo Mourning	100.00
36	Hakeem Olajuwon	150.00
37	Gary Payton	150.00
38	Damon Stoudamire	75.00
39	Steve Smith	50.00
40	Chris Webber	200.00
41	Michael Finley	75.00
42	Jayson Williams	50.00
43	Maurice Taylor	100.00
44	Jalen Rose	30.00
45	Sam Cassell	30.00
46	Jerry Stackhouse	40.00
47	Toni Kukoc	125.00
48	Charles Oakley	30.00
49	Jim Jackson	30.00
50	Dikembe Mutombo	30.00
51	Wesley Person	20.00
52	Antonio Daniels	50.00
53	Isaiah Rider	30.00
54	Tom Gugliotta	40.00
55	Antonio McDyess	75.00
56	Jeff Hornacek	20.00
57	Joe Dumars	30.00
58	Jamal Mashburn	30.00
59	Donyell Marshall	20.00
60	Glenn Robinson	50.00
61	Jelani McCoy	30.00
62	Predrag Stojakovic	30.00
63	Randell Jackson	20.00
64	Brad Miller	20.00
65	Corey Benjamin	30.00
66	Toby Bailey	20.00
67	Nazr Mohammed	20.00
68	Dirk Nowitzki	30.00
69	Andrae Patterson	20.00
70	Michael Dickerson	50.00
71	Cory Carr	20.00
72	Brian Skinner	30.00
73	Pat Garrity	30.00
74	Ricky Davis	40.00
75	Roshown McLeod	30.00
76	Matt Harpring	40.00
77	Jason Williams	200.00
78	Keon Clark	40.00
79	Al Harrington	50.00
80	Felipe Lopez	40.00
81	Michael Doleac	30.00
82	Paul Pierce	150.00
83	Robert Traylor	50.00
84	Raef LaFrentz	50.00
85	Michael Olowokandi	50.00
86	Mike Bibby	75.00
87	Antawn Jamison	100.00
88	Bonzi Wells	30.00
89	Vince Carter	300.00
90	Larry Hughes	75.00

1998-99 SkyBox E-X Century Authen-Kicks

Authen-Kicks was Fleer/SkyBox's first mainstream game-used material on a card insert. It included game-worn sneaker swatches from 12 top young players, with one version including a leather swatch and the other version offering a piece of shoe lace. Cards were thick and horizontal in the format, with each card hand-numbered on the front. Quantities varied between players depending on how many cards could be made from the player's shoe, and are listed next to the player's name below.

		MT
Complete Set (12):		1250.
Common Player:		75.00
1	Antawn Jamison (285)	150.00
2	Tracy McGrady (225)	125.00
3	Ron Mercer (180)	90.00
4	Antoine Walker (125)	125.00
5	Mike Bibby (165)	100.00
6	Michael Dickerson (230)	75.00
7	Larry Hughes (115)	150.00
8	Raef LaFrentz (160)	75.00
9	Keith Van Horn (125)	125.00
9A	Keith Van Horn Auto (44)	500.00
10	Tim Thomas (215)	75.00
11	Allen Iverson (165)	300.00
12	Robert Traylor (215)	75.00

1998-99 SkyBox E-X Century Dunk N'Go Nuts

This 20-card insert featured top athletes on thick plastic cards with the insert name, player's name and product logo printed in holographic letters in the background. Cards were inserted 1:36 packs and numbered with a "DG" suffix.

		MT
Complete Set (20):		225.00
Common Player:		3.00
Inserted 1:36		
1	Tim Thomas	8.00
2	Grant Hill	20.00
3	Shareef Abdur-Rahim	8.00
4	Tim Duncan	20.00
5	Allen Iverson	12.00
6	Kobe Bryant	30.00
7	Antoine Walker	10.00
8	Kevin Garnett	20.00
9	Shaquille O'Neal	12.00
10	Tracy McGrady	8.00
11	Antawn Jamison	12.00
12	Vince Carter	25.00
13	Robert Traylor	5.00
14	Scottie Pippen	10.00
15	Michael Jordan	50.00
16	Michael Olowokandi	5.00
17	Anfernee Hardaway	12.00
18	Michael Dickerson	3.00
19	Ron Mercer	8.00
20	Felipe Lopez	3.00

1998-99 SkyBox E-X Century Generation E-X

This 15-card insert was composed of players with three or less years of NBA experience. Each card featured an interior die-cut of the player's image surrounded by a black border. Generation E-X cards were inserted 1:18 packs and numbered with a "GE" suffix.

		MT
Complete Set (15):		90.00
Common Player:		2.00
Inserted 1:18		
1	Larry Hughes	8.00
2	Michael Olowokandi	6.00
3	Tim Duncan	12.00
4	Vince Carter	20.00
5	Antawn Jamison	10.00
6	Kevin Garnett	12.00
7	Al Harrington	2.00
8	Mike Bibby	8.00
9	Raef LaFrentz	6.00
10	Ron Mercer	5.00
11	Tracy McGrady	5.00
12	Kobe Bryant	15.00
13	Keith Van Horn	8.00
14	Stephon Marbury	8.00
15	Allen Iverson	10.00

1998-99 Flair Showcase Row 3

Row 3, or Power, included all 90 players in Flair Showcase and was the easiest version to obtain from packs. Fronts featured a larger close-up shot and a smaller action shot of the player over silver background. Showtime cards (1-30) were inserted 1:.82 packs, Showdown cards (31-

60) were inserted 1:1 pack and Showpiece cards (61-90) were inserted 1:1.2 packs.

		MT
Complete Set (90):		60.00
Common Player:		.25
Common Rookie:		.75
1-30 Inserted 1:.08		
31-60 Inserted 1:1		
61-90 Inserted 1:1.2		
Wax Box:		90.00
1	Keith Van Horn	1.50
2	Kobe Bryant	3.00
3	Tim Duncan	2.50
4	Kevin Garnett	2.50
5	Grant Hill	2.50
6	Allen Iverson	2.00
7	Shaquille O'Neal	1.50
8	Antoine Walker	1.50
9	Shareef Abdur-Rahim	1.00
10	Stephon Marbury	1.50
11	Ray Allen	.60
12	Shawn Kemp	1.00
13	Tim Thomas	1.00
14	Scottie Pippen	1.00
15	Latrell Sprewell	.50
16	*Dirk Nowitzki*	1.00
17	*Antawn Jamison*	6.00
18	Anfernee Hardaway	1.25
19	*Larry Hughes*	5.00
20	*Robert Traylor*	3.00
21	Kerry Kittles	.50
22	Ron Mercer	1.00
23	*Michael Olowokandi*	3.00
24	Jason Kidd	1.00
25	*Vince Carter*	15.00
26	Charles Barkley	.75
27	Antonio McDyess	.75
28	*Mike Bibby*	5.00
29	*Paul Pierce*	8.00
30	*Raef LaFrentz*	3.00
31	Reggie Miller	.50
32	Michael Finley	.50
33	Eddie Jones	.60
34	Tim Hardaway	.60
35	Glenn Robinson	.50
36	Brevin Knight	.60
37	Gary Payton	.75
38	David Robinson	.75
39	Karl Malone	.75
40	Derek Anderson	.50
41	Patrick Ewing	.50
42	Juwan Howard	.50
43	Jayson Williams	.50
44	Terrell Brandon	.50
45	Hakeem Olajuwon	.75
46	Isaac Austin	.25
47	Glen Rice	.50
48	Maurice Taylor	.60
49	Damon Stoudamire	.60
50	*Brian Skinner*	.75
51	*Nazr Mohammed*	.75
52	Tom Gugliotta	.50
53	*Al Harrington*	2.00
54	*Pat Garrity*	1.00
55	*Jason Williams*	10.00
56	Tracy McGrady	1.00
57	*Keon Clark*	1.50
58	Vin Baker	.60
59	*Bonzi Wells*	1.00
60	John Stockton	.50
61	Isaiah Rider	.50
62	Alonzo Mourning	.50
63	Allan Houston	.50
64	Dennis Rodman	1.00
65	*Felipe Lopez*	2.00
66	Joe Smith	.50
67	Chris Webber	1.00
68	Mitch Richmond	.50
69	Brent Barry	.25
70	Mookie Blaylock	.25
71	Donyell Marshall	.25
72	Anthony Mason	.25
73	Rod Strickland	.50
74	*Roshown McLeod*	1.50
75	*Matt Harpring*	2.00
76	Detlef Schrempf	.25
77	*Michael Dickerson*	3.00
78	*Michael Doleac*	1.50
79	John Starks	.25
80	*Ricky Davis*	1.50
81	Steve Smith	.50
82	Voshon Lenard	.25
83	Toni Kukoc	.60
84	Steve Nash	.50
85	Vlade Divac	.25
86	Rasheed Wallace	.50
87	Bryon Russell	.25
88	Antonio Daniels	.50
89	Rik Smits	.25
90	Joe Dumars	.50

1998-99 Flair Showcase Row 2

Row 2, or Passion, included all 90 cards in Flair Showcase and were identified by the player's uniform number shown prominently in the background. Showdown cards (1-30) were inserted 1:3 packs, Showpiece cards (31-60) were seeded 1:1:3 packs and Showtime cards (61-90) were inserted 1:2 packs.

	MT
Complete Set (90):	100.00
Common Player:	.50
Common Rookie:	1.50
Row 2 Cards:	1x-2x Row 3
1-30 Inserted 1:3	
31-60 Inserted 1:2	
61-90 Inserted 1:1.3	

1998-99 Flair Showcase Row 1

Row 1 featured all 90 players included in Flair Showcase on a horizontal format, with two close-up images divided by an action shot over the player's uniform number. Row 1 also included sequential numbering on the front in the upper left corner. Cards 1-30 were numbered to 1,500, cards 31-60 were numbered to 3,000 and cards 61-90 were numbered to 6,000.

		MT
Complete Set (90):		
1-30 Common:		3.00
1-30 Rookie:		3.00
1-30 Numbered to 1,500		
31-60 Common:		1.00
31-60 Rookie:		2.00
31-60 Numbered to 3,000		
61-90 Common:		.75
61-90 Rookie:		2.50
61-90 Numbered to 6,000		
1	Keith Van Horn	10.00
2	Kobe Bryant	25.00
3	Tim Duncan	20.00
4	Kevin Garnett	20.00
5	Grant Hill	20.00
6	Allen Iverson	15.00
7	Shaquille O'Neal	10.00
8	Antoine Walker	10.00
9	Shareef Abdur-Rahim	6.00
10	Stephon Marbury	10.00
11	Ray Allen	4.00
12	Shawn Kemp	6.00
13	Tim Thomas	6.00
14	Scottie Pippen	6.00
15	Latrell Sprewell	3.00
16	*Dirk Nowitzki*	3.00
17	*Antawn Jamison*	15.00
18	Anfernee Hardaway	8.00
19	*Larry Hughes*	12.00
20	*Robert Traylor*	8.00
21	Kerry Kittles	3.00
22	Ron Mercer	6.00
23	*Michael Olowokandi*	8.00
24	Jason Kidd	6.00
25	*Vince Carter*	40.00
26	Charles Barkley	5.00
27	Antonio McDyess	5.00
28	*Mike Bibby*	12.00
29	*Paul Pierce*	20.00
30	*Raef LaFrentz*	8.00
31	Reggie Miller	2.00
32	Michael Finley	2.00
33	Eddie Jones	2.50
34	Tim Hardaway	2.50
35	Glenn Robinson	2.00
36	Brevin Knight	2.50
37	Gary Payton	3.00
38	David Robinson	3.00
39	Karl Malone	3.00
40	Derek Anderson	2.00
41	Patrick Ewing	2.00
42	Juwan Howard	2.00
43	Jayson Williams	2.00
44	Terrell Brandon	2.00
45	Hakeem Olajuwon	3.00
46	Isaac Austin	1.00
47	Glen Rice	2.00
48	Maurice Taylor	2.50
49	Damon Stoudamire	2.50
50	*Brian Skinner*	2.00
51	*Nazr Mohammed*	2.00
52	Tom Gugliotta	2.00
53	*Al Harrington*	5.00
54	*Pat Garrity*	2.50
55	*Jason Williams*	25.00
56	Tracy McGrady	5.00
57	*Keon Clark*	3.00
58	Vin Baker	2.50
59	*Bonzi Wells*	2.50
60	John Stockton	1.50
61	Isaiah Rider	1.50
62	Alonzo Mourning	1.50
63	Allan Houston	1.50
64	Dennis Rodman	4.00
65	*Felipe Lopez*	3.00
66	Joe Smith	1.50
67	Chris Webber	4.00
68	Mitch Richmond	1.50
69	Brent Barry	.75
70	Mookie Blaylock	.75
71	Donyell Marshall	.75
72	Anthony Mason	.75
73	Rod Strickland	1.50
74	*Roshown McLeod*	2.50
75	*Matt Harpring*	3.00
76	Detlef Schrempf	.75
77	*Michael Dickerson*	5.00
78	*Michael Doleac*	2.50
79	John Starks	.75
80	*Ricky Davis*	2.50
81	Steve Smith	1.50
82	Voshon Lenard	.75
83	Toni Kukoc	2.00
84	Steve Nash	1.50
85	Vlade Divac	.75
86	Rasheed Wallace	1.50
87	Bryon Russell	.75
88	Antonio Daniels	1.50
89	Rik Smits	.75
90	Joe Dumars	1.50

1998-99 Flair Showcase Legacy Collection

Legacy Collection featured all 270 cards from Flair Showcase in a parallel version that added blue foil stamping and was sequentially numbered to 99 sets. All 90 cards from Row 1, Row 2 and Row 3 were paralleled so that each player had three Legacy Collection cards.

Common Player:	5.00
Common Rookie	10.00
Stars:	10x-20x
Rookies:	10x-15x
Production 99 Sets	
Each Player has 3 different cards.	

1998-99 Flair Showcase Class of '98

This 15-card insert featured the top rookies from the 1998 NBA Draft. Cards were sequentially numbered to 500 sets and featured full holofoil fronts with a sculptured embossed logo and player image. Class of '98 inserts were numbered with a "C" suffix.

		MT
Complete Set (15):		325.00
Commmon Player:		10.00
Production 500 Sets		
1	Michael Olowokandi	15.00
2	Mike Bibby	25.00
3	Raef LaFrentz	15.00
4	Antawn Jamison	40.00
5	Vince Carter	75.00
6	Robert Traylor	15.00
7	Jason Williams	55.00
8	Larry Hughes	25.00
9	Dirk Nowitzki	10.00
10	Paul Pierce	45.00
11	Bonzi Wells	10.00
12	Michael Doleac	10.00
13	Michael Dickerson	15.00
14	Pat Garrity	10.00
15	Al Harrington	12.00

1998-99 Flair Showcase takeit2.net

takeit2.net was a 15-card insert set in Flair Showcase. Top veterans were included on cards sequentially numbered to 1,000 sets. Card fronts featured multiple foils and a laser die-cut resembling a computer circuit board. takeit2.net cards were numbered with a "TN" suffix.

		MT
Complete Set (15):		300.00
Common Player:		10.00
Production 1,000 Sets		
1	Scottie Pippen	10.00
2	Tim Duncan	30.00
3	Keith Van Horn	20.00
4	Grant Hill	30.00
5	Kobe Bryant	35.00
6	Antoine Walker	20.00
7	Kevin Garnett	30.00
8	Allen Iverson	25.00
9	Shareef Abdur-Rahim	12.00
10	Anfernee Hardaway	18.00
11	Stephon Marbury	20.00
12	Ron Mercer	12.00
13	Michael Jordan	75.00
14	Shaquille O'Neal	20.00
15	Shawn Kemp	10.00

1998-99 Finest Promos

This six-card promotional set was distributed to dealers and members of the media to promote the 1998-99 Finest product. The cards were identical to the regular-issue cards except they were numbered PP1-PP6 on the back.

		MT
Complete Set (6):		4.00
Common Player:		.25
1	Dikembe Mutombo	.25
2	Antoine Walker	2.00
3	Reggie Miller	.50
4	John Stockton	.50
5	Eddie Jones	.75
6	Gary Payton	.75

1998-99 Finest

Finest was released in two 125-card series in 1998-99. Each card in the 250-card set was available in four versions - regular (with protective peel), No-Protector (1:4), Refractors (with protective peel, 1:12) and No-Protector Refractors (1:24). No-Protectors featured a foil-darkened background, while No-Protector Refractors featured the Refractor finish on both sides. Inserts in Series I included: Centurions, Hardwood Heroes, Mystery Finest and Oversized Finest. Inserts in Series II included: Mystery Finest, Arena Stars, Court Control and Oversized Finest.

		MT
Complete Set (250):		150.00
Complete Series 1 (125):		25.00
Complete Series 2 (125):		125.00
Common Player:		.25
Common Rookie:		2.00
Series I Wax Box:		60.00
Series 2 Wax Box:		90.00
1	Chris Mills	.25

2	Matt Maloney	.50
3	Sam Mitchell	.25
4	Corliss Williamson	.25
5	Bryant Reeves	.50
6	Juwan Howard	.50
7	Eddie Jones	1.25
8	Ray Allen	.50
9	Larry Johnson	.50
10	Travis Best	.25
11	Isaiah Rider	.25
12	Hakeem Olajuwon	1.00
13	Gary Trent	.25
14	Kevin Garnett	3.00
15	Dikembe Mutombo	.50
16	Brevin Knight	.75
17	Keith Van Horn	2.50
18	Theo Ratliff	.25
19	Tim Hardaway	.75
20	Blue Edwards	.25
21	David Wesley	.25
22	Jaren Jackson	.25
23	Nick Anderson	.25
24	Rodney Rogers	.25
25	Antonio Davis	.25
26	Clarence Weatherspoon	.25
27	Kelvin Cato	.25
28	Tracy McGrady	1.50
29	Mookie Blaylock	.25
30	Ron Harper	.25
31	Allan Houston	.50
32	Brian Williams	.25
33	John Stockton	.50
34	Hersey Hawkins	.25
35	Donyell Marshall	.25
36	Mark Strickland	.25
37	Rod Strickland	.25
38	Cedric Ceballos	.25
39	Danny Fortson	.25
40	Shaquille O'Neal	2.00
41	Kendall Gill	.25
42	Allen Iverson	1.50
43	Travis Knight	.25
44	Cedric Henderson	.50
45	Steve Kerr	.25
46	Antonio McDyess	.50
47	Darrick Martin	.25
48	Shandon Anderson	.25
49	Shareef Abdur-Rahim	1.25
50	Antoine Carr	.25
51	Jason Kidd	1.00
52	Calbert Cheaney	.25
53	Antoine Walker	2.00
54	Greg Anthony	.25
55	Jeff Hornacek	.25
56	Reggie Miller	.50
57	Lawrence Funderburke	.25
58	Derek Strong	.25
59	Robert Horry	.25
60	Shawn Bradley	.25
61	Matt Bullard	.25
62	Terrell Brandon	.50
63	Dan Majerle	.25
64	Jim Jackson	.25
65	Anthony Peeler	.25
66	Charles Outlaw	.25
67	Khalid Reeves	.25
68	Toni Kukoc	.50
69	Mario Elie	.25
70	Derek Anderson	.75
71	Jalen Rose	.25
72	Tyrone Corbin	.25
73	Anthony Mason	.50
74	Lamond Murray	.25
75	Tom Gugliotta	.50
76	Arvydas Sabonis	.25
77	Brian Shaw	.25
78	Rick Fox	.25
79	Danny Manning	.25
80	Lindsey Hunter	.25
81	Michael Jordan	6.00
82	LaPhonso Ellis	.25
83	David Robinson	.75
84	Christian Laettner	.50
85	Armon Gilliam	.25
86	Sherman Douglas	.25
87	Charlie Ward	.25
88	Shawn Kemp	1.25
89	Gary Payton	.75
90	Doug Christie	.25
91	Voshon Lenard	.25
92	Detlef Schrempf	.25
93	Walter McCarty	.25
94	Sam Cassell	.25
95	Jerry Stackhouse	.50
96	Billy Owens	.25
97	Matt Geiger	.25
98	Avery Johnson	.25
99	Bobby Jackson	.50
100	Rex Chapman	.25
101	Andrew DeClercq	.25
102	Vlade Divac	.25
103	Erick Strickland	.25
104	Dean Garrett	.25
105	Grant Long	.25
106	Adonal Foyle	.25
107	Isaac Austin	.25
108	Michael Curry	.25
109	Darrell Armstrong	.25
110	Aaron McKie	.25
111	Stacey Augmon	.25
112	Anthony Johnson	.25
113	Vinny Del Negro	.25
114	Reggie Slater	.25
115	Lee Mayberry	.25
116	Tracy Murray	.25
117	Scottie Pippen	1.50
118	Sam Perkins	.25
119	Derek Fisher	.25
120	Mark Bryant	.25
121	Dale Davis	.25
122	B.J. Armstrong	.25
123	Charles Barkley	.75
124	Horace Grant	.25
125	Checklist	.25
126	Alonzo Mourning	.50
127	Kerry Kittles	.50
128	Eldridge Recasner	.25
129	Dell Curry	.25
130	Jamal Mashburn	.50
131	Eric Piatkowski	.25
132	Othella Harrington	.25
133	Pete Chilcutt	.25
134	Corie Blount	.25
135	Patrick Ewing	.50
136	Danny Schayes	.25
137	John Williams	.25
138	Joe Smith	.50
139	Tariq Abdul-Wahad	.25
140	Vin Baker	1.00
141	Elden Campbell	.25
142	Chris Carr	.25
143	John Starks	.25
144	Felton Spencer	.25
145	Mark Jackson	.25
146	Dana Barros	.25
147	Eric Williams	.25
148	Wesley Person	.25
149	Joe Dumars	.50
150	Steve Smith	.50
151	Randy Brown	.25
152	A.C. Green	.25
153	Dee Brown	.25
154	Brian Grant	.25
155	Tim Thomas	1.50
156	Howard Eisley	.25
157	Malik Sealy	.25
158	Maurice Taylor	.75
159	Tyrone Hill	.25
160	Chris Gatling	.25
161	Rodrick Rhodes	.25
162	Muggsy Bogues	.25
163	Kenny Anderson	.50
164	Zydrunas Ilgauskas	.75
165	Grant Hill	3.00
166	Lorenzen Wright	.25
167	Tony Battie	.50
168	Bobby Phills	.25
169	Michael Finley	.75
170	Anfernee Hardaway	2.00
171	Terry Porter	.25
172	P.J. Brown	.25
173	Clifford Robinson	.25
174	Olden Polynice	.25
175	Kobe Bryant	5.00
176	Sean Elliott	.25
177	Latrell Sprewell	.50
178	Rik Smits	.25
179	Darrell Armstrong	.50
180	Stephon Marbury	2.00
181	Brent Price	.25
182	Danny Fortson	.25
183	Vitaly Potapenko	.25
184	Anthony Parker	.25
185	Glenn Robinson	.50
186	Erick Dampier	.25
187	George McCloud	.25
188	Rasheed Wallace	.50
189	Aaron Williams	.25
190	Tim Duncan	3.00
191	Chauncey Billups	.75
192	Jim McIlvaine	.25
193	Chris Mullin	.25
194	George Lynch	.25
195	Damon Stoudamire	.75
196	Bryon Russell	.25
197	Luc Longley	.25
198	Ron Mercer	1.50
199	Alan Henderson	.25
200	Jayson Williams	.50
201	Ben Wallace	.25
202	Elliot Perry	.25
203	Walt Williams	.25
204	Cherokee Parks	.25
205	Brent Barry	.25
206	Hubert Davis	.25
207	Terry Davis	.25
208	Loy Vaught	.25
209	Adam Keefe	.25
210	Karl Malone	1.00
211	Chuck Person	.25
212	Chris Childs	.25
213	Rony Seikaly	.25
214	Ervin Johnson	.25
215	Derrick McKey	.25
216	Jerome Williams	.25
217	Glen Rice	.50
218	Steve Nash	.25
219	Nick Van Exel	.50
220	Chris Webber	1.50
221	Marcus Camby	.75
222	Antonio Daniels	.25
223	Mitch Richmond	.50
224	Otis Thorpe	.25
225	Charles Oakley	.25
226	*Michael Olowokandi*	8.00
227	*Mike Bibby*	10.00
228	*Raef LaFrentz*	8.00
229	*Antawn Jamison*	12.00
230	*Vince Carter*	30.00
231	*Robert Traylor*	8.00
232	*Jason Williams*	20.00
233	*Larry Hughes*	10.00
234	*Dirk Nowitzki*	4.00
235	*Paul Pierce*	20.00
236	*Bonzi Wells*	3.00
237	*Michael Doleac*	4.00
238	*Keon Clark*	4.00
239	*Michael Dickerson*	8.00
240	*Matt Harpring*	5.00
241	*Bryce Drew*	2.00
242	*Pat Garrity*	2.00
243	*Roshown McLeod*	3.00
244	*Ricky Davis*	3.00
245	*Brian Skinner*	2.00
246	*Tyronn Lue*	3.00
247	*Felipe Lopez*	4.00
248	*Sam Jacobson*	2.00
249	*Corey Benjamin*	2.00
250	*Nazr Mohammed*	2.00

1998-99 Finest No Protector

This 250-card parallel set reprinted each card from Finest I and II with the absence of a Finest protector. Card fronts and backs featured a darkened, silver tint. No-Protector cards were inserted 1:4 packs.

	MT
Complete Set (250):	300.00
Complete Series 1 (125):	75.00
Complete Series 2 (125):	225.00
No Protector Cards:	3x
No Protector Rooies:	2x
Inserted 1:4	

1998-99 Finest Refractors

This 250-card parallel set reprinted each card from Finest I and II, but added a Refractor finish to the card front. Cards arrived with a protective peel and were inserted 1:12 packs. The word "Refractor" was printed in small black letters below the card number on the back.

	MT
Complete Set (250):	1150.
Complete Series 1 (125):	250.00
Complete Series 2 (125):	900.00
Refractor Cards:	5x-10x
Refractor Rookies:	2x-4x
Inserted 1:12	

1998-99 Finest No-Protector Refractors

This 250-card parallel set reprinted every card from Finest Series I and II, but added a Refractor finish to both the front and back. The word "Refractor" was also printed in small black letters below the card number. No-Protector Refractors were seeded 1:24 packs.

	MT
Complete Set (250):	1900.
Complete Series 1 (125):	500.00
Complete Series 2 (125):	1400.
NP Refractor Cards:	10x-20x
NP Refractor Rookies:	3x-6x
Inserted 1:24	

1998-99 Finest Arena Stars

Arena Stars was a 20-card insert exclusive to Series II Finest packs. They featured holo-foil printing on Finest technology with stars in the background. Cards were numbered with an "AS" prefix and were inserted 1:48 hobby packs and 1:20 HTA Collectors packs.

		MT
Complete Set (20):		225.00
Common Player:		3.00
Inserted 1:48 Series 2		
1	Shaquille O'Neal	15.00
2	Stephon Marbury	15.00
3	Allen Iverson	20.00
4	John Stockton	3.00
5	Kobe Bryant	35.00
6	Alonzo Mourning	3.00
7	Damon Stoudamire	6.00
8	Scottie Pippen	12.00
9	Tim Hardaway	4.00
10	Karl Malone	5.00
11	Tim Duncan	30.00
12	Gary Payton	6.00
13	Antoine Walker	15.00
14	Keith Van Horn	15.00
15	Juwan Howard	3.00
16	David Robinson	5.00
17	Michael Finley	3.00
18	Shareef Abdur-Rahim	12.00
19	Michael Jordan	60.00
20	Vin Baker	6.00

1998-99 Finest Centurions

Centurions featured 20 players that will lead the NBA into the millennium. Regular versions were numbered to 500 sets and inserted 1:91 packs, while Refrator versions were numbered to 75 and inserted 1:609 packs. Centurions were numbered with a "C" prefix and exclusive to Series I packs.

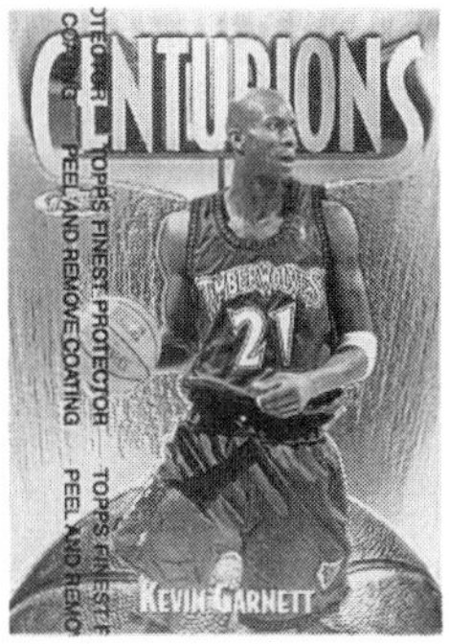

		MT
Complete Set (20):		450.00
Common Player:		10.00
Inserted 1:91 Series 1		
Production 500 Sets		
Refractor Cards:		2x-3x
Inserted 1:609 Series 1		
Production 75 Sets		
1	Grant Hill	60.00
2	Tim Thomas	20.00
3	Eddie Jones	20.00
4	Michael Finley	10.00
5	Shaquille O'Neal	35.00
6	Kobe Bryant	75.00
7	Keith Van Horn	45.00
8	Tim Duncan	60.00
9	Antoine Walker	40.00
10	Shareef Abdur-Rahim	25.00
11	Stephon Marbury	40.00
12	Kevin Garnett	60.00
13	Ray Allen	10.00
14	Kerry Kittles	10.00
15	Allen Iverson	30.00
16	Damon Stoudamire	10.00
17	Brevin Knight	15.00
18	Bryant Reeves	10.00
19	Ron Mercer	30.00
20	Zydrunas Ilgauskas	10.00

1998-99 Finest Court Control

Court Control was a 20-card insert that showcased top players over a basketball court background with a blue border on the right side featuring the insert name. Regular versions were inserted 1:76 hobby packs and 1:35 HTA Collector packs and numbered to 750 sets. Refractors were seeded 1:379 packs (1:175 HTA) and numbered to 150 sets. Court Control inserts were exclusive to Series II packs and numbered with a "CC" prefix.

		MT
Complete Set (20):		350.00
Common Player:		5.00
Inserted 1:76 Series 2		
Production 750 Sets		
Refractors		2x
Inserted 1:379 Series 2		
Production 150 Sets		
1	Shareef Abdur-Rahim	15.00
2	Keith Van Horn	20.00
3	Tim Duncan	35.00
4	Antoine Walker	20.00
5	Stephon Marbury	20.00
6	Kevin Garnett	35.00
7	Grant Hill	35.00
8	Michael Finley	5.00
9	Ron Mercer	15.00
10	Damon Stoudamire	10.00
11	Michael Olowokandi	15.00

12	Mike Bibby	20.00
13	Antawn Jamison	20.00
14	Vince Carter	40.00
15	Jason Williams	30.00
16	Larry Hughes	20.00
17	Paul Pierce	25.00
18	Michael Dickerson	12.00
19	Bryce Drew	5.00
20	Felipe Lopez	8.00

1998-99 Finest Hardwood Honors

Hardwood Heroes showcased 20 players who won awards during the 1997-98 season. Cards featured holo-foil printing on Finest technology and had basketballs in the background. Cards were exclusive to Series I packs, numbered with an "H" prefix and inserted 1:33 packs.

		MT
Complete Set (20):		130.00
Common Player:		5.00
Inserted 1:33 Series 1		
1	Michael Jordan	50.00
2	Shaquille O'Neal	15.00
3	Karl Malone	7.00
4	Eddie Jones	10.00
5	Dikembe Mutombo	5.00
6	Wesley Person	5.00
7	Glen Rice	5.00
8	David Robinson	8.00
9	Rik Smits	5.00
10	Steve Smith	5.00
11	Allen Iverson	12.00
12	Jayson Williams	5.00
13	Nick Anderson	5.00
14	Tim Duncan	25.00
15	Jason Kidd	10.00
16	Alonzo Mourning	5.00
17	Sam Cassell	5.00
18	Alan Henderson	5.00
19	Gary Payton	8.00
20	Scottie Pippen	12.00

1998-99 Finest Jumbo

This 14-card insert reprinted seven cards from each series on a 3-1/2" x 5" version. Jumbos were inserted as box toppers at a rate of one per box. Refractor versions were also available and seeded 1:12 packs (1:6 HTA).

		MT
Complete Set (14):		100.00
Complete Series 1 (7):		50.00
Complete Series 2 (7):		50.00
Common Player:		2.00
Inserted 1:3 Series 1/2 Boxes		
Refractor Cards:		2x
Inserted 1:12 Series 1/2 Boxes		
1	Kevin Garnett	15.00
2	Keith Van Horn	10.00
3	Shaquille O'Neal	10.00
4	Shareef Abdur-Rahim	5.00
5	Antoine Walker	8.00
6	Gary Payton	2.00
7	Scottie Pippen	8.00
8	Alonzo Mourning	2.00
9	Kerry Kittles	2.00
10	Kobe Bryant	20.00
11	Stephon Marbury	10.00
12	Tim Duncan	15.00
13	Ron Mercer	5.00
14	Karl Malone	2.00

1998-99 Finest Mystery Finest

20 Mystery Finest inserts were inserted into both series of Finest. This 40-card set featured double-sided Finest cards, with two stars matched up back-to-back. These were numbered with an "M" prefix and inserted 1:33 packs of Series I and 1:36 packs of Series II, while Refractor versions were seeded 1:133 Series I packs and 1:144 Series II packs. All Mystery Finest inserts arrived with a black opaque protector over both sides which had to be peeled off to reveal which players were on the card.

		MT
Complete Set (40):		500.00
Complete Series 1 (20):		250.00
Complete Series 2 (20):		250.00
Common Player:		5.00
Inserted 1:33 Series 1		
Inserted 1:36 Series 2		
Refractor Cards:		2x-4x
Inserted 1:133 Series 1		
Inserted 1:144 Series 2		
1	Michael Jordan, Kobe Bryant	50.00
2	Kobe Bryant, Shaquille O'Neal	30.00
3	Shaquille O'Neal, David Robinson	15.00
4	David Robinson, Tim Duncan	20.00
5	Tim Duncan, Keith Van Horn	25.00
6	Keith Van Horn, Scottie Pippen	15.00
7	Scottie Pippen, Shareef Abdur-Rahim	12.00
8	Shareef Abdur-Rahim, Grant Hill	20.00
9	Grant Hill, Kevin Garnett	25.00
10	Kevin Garnett, Stephon Marbury	20.00
11	Stephon Marbury, Gary Payton	15.00
12	Gary Payton, Vin Baker	5.00
13	Vin Baker, Karl Malone	5.00
14	Karl Malone, Shawn Kemp	10.00
15	Shawn Kemp, Tim Thomas	10.00
16	Tim Thomas, Antoine Walker	15.00
17	Antoine Walker, Ron Mercer	15.00
18	Ron Mercer, Kerry Kittles	10.00
19	Kerry Kittles, Eddie Jones	5.00
20	Eddie Jones, Michael Jordan	40.00
21	Alonzo Mourning, Scottie Pippen	10.00
22	Scottie Pippen, Antoine Walker	15.00
23	Antoine Walker, Shareef Abdur-Rahim	10.00
24	Shareef Abdur-Rahim, Kevin Garnett	18.00
25	Kevin Garnett, Keith Van Horn	25.00
26	Keith Van Horn, Tim Thomas	15.00
27	Tim Thomas, Grant Hill	15.00
28	Grant Hill, Anfernee Hardaway	20.00
29	Anfernee Hardaway, Kerry Kittles	10.00
30	Kerry Kittles, Jayson Williams	5.00
31	Jayson Williams, Karl Malone	6.00
32	Karl Malone, John Stockton	6.00
33	John Stockton, Gary Payton	6.00
34	Gary Payton, Ron Mercer	10.00
35	Ron Mercer, Stephon Marbury	20.00
36	Stephon Marbury, Allen Iverson	20.00
37	Allen Iverson, Kobe Bryant	30.00
38	Kobe Bryant, Tim Duncan	40.00
39	Tim Duncan, Shaquille O'Neal	25.00
40	Shaquille O'Neal, Alonzo Mourning	10.00

1998-99 Fleer Brilliants

Fleer Brilliants contained 125 cards, included a 25-card Rookies subset that was seeded 1:2 packs. Brilliants cards featured a radial-etched mirror foil laminate background and were printed on 24-point styrene card stock. Three parallel versions of each card were also printed. First, Brilliant Blue veterans (1-100) were seeded 1:3 packs, with Rookies every six packs. Next, all 125 cards were printed in Brilliant Gold versions numbered to 99 sets. Third, all 125 cards had 24-karat Gold versions numbered to 24 sets and featuring an actual 24-karat gold logo. Three insert sets were included in Brilliants: Illuminators, Shining Stars and Pulsars, which was a parallel to Shining Stars.

		MT
Complete Set (125):		200.00
Common Player:		.15
Common Rookie:		2.00
Inserted 1:2		
Wax Box:		70.00
1	Tim Duncan	6.00
2	Dikembe Mutombo	.30
3	Steve Nash	.15
4	Charles Barkley	1.00
5	Eddie Jones	1.50
6	Ray Allen	.50
7	Stephon Marbury	4.00
8	Anfernee Hardaway	4.00
9	Gary Payton	1.00
10	Ron Mercer	4.00
11	Nick Van Exel	.30
12	Brent Barry	.15
13	Allan Houston	.30
14	Avery Johnson	.15
15	Shareef Abdur-Rahim	2.00
16	Rod Strickland	.30
17	Vin Baker	1.50
18	Patrick Ewing	.50
19	Maurice Taylor	.50
20	Shawn Kemp	2.00
21	Michael Finley	.50
22	Reggie Miller	.30
23	Joe Smith	.50
24	Toni Kukoc	.30
25	Blue Edwards	.15
26	Joe Dumars	.30
27	Tom Gugliotta	.30
28	Terrell Brandon	.30
29	Erick Dampier	.15
30	Antonio McDyess	.75
31	Donyell Marshall	.15
32	Jeff Hornacek	.15
33	David Wesley	.15
34	Derek Anderson	.50
35	Ron Harper	.15
36	John Starks	.15
37	Kenny Anderson	.30
38	Anthony Mason	.15
39	Brevin Knight	.50
40	Antoine Walker	4.00
41	Mookie Blaylock	.30
42	LaPhonso Ellis	.30
43	Tim Hardaway	.50
44	Jim Jackson	.15
45	Matt Maloney	.15
46	Lamond Murray	.15
47	Voshon Lenard	.15
48	Isaiah Rider	.30
49	Tracy Murray	.15
50	Grant Hill	6.00
51	Vlade Divac	.30
52	Glenn Robinson	.30
53	Tony Battie	.30
54	Bobby Jackson	.15
55	Jayson Williams	.30
56	Doug Christie	.15
57	Glen Rice	.30
58	Tim Thomas	2.00
59	Lindsey Hunter	.15
60	Scottie Pippen	3.00
61	Marcus Camby	.50
62	Clifford Robinson	.15
63	John Wallace	.30
64	Larry Johnson	.30
65	Bryon Russell	.15
66	Isaac Austin	.15
67	Sam Cassell	.30
68	Allen Iverson	4.00
69	Chauncey Billups	.50
70	Kobe Bryant	8.00
71	Kevin Willis	.15
72	Jason Kidd	2.00
73	Chris Webber	2.00
74	Rasheed Wallace	.15
75	Karl Malone	1.00
76	Shawn Bradley	.15
77	Kerry Kittles	.30
78	Mitch Richmond	.30
79	Antonio Daniels	.15
80	Kevin Garnett	6.00
81	Nick Anderson	.15
82	David Robinson	1.00
83	Jamal Mashburn	.30
84	Rodney Rogers	.15
85	Michael Stewart	.15
86	Rik Smits	.30
87	Billy Owens	.15
88	Damon Stoudamire	.75
89	Theo Ratliff	.30
90	Keith Van Horn	5.00
91	Hakeem Olajuwon	1.50
92	Alonzo Mourning	.50
93	Steve Smith	.30
94	Mark Jackson	.15
95	Cedric Ceballos	.15
96	Bryant Reeves	.30
97	Juwan Howard	.30
98	Detlef Schrempf	.15
99	John Stockton	.30
100	Shaquille O'Neal	4.00
101	*Michael Olowokandi*	10.00
102	*Mike Bibby*	15.00
103	*Raef LaFrentz*	10.00
104	*Antawn Jamison*	12.00
105	*Vince Carter*	35.00
106	*Robert Traylor*	10.00
107	*Jason Williams*	25.00
108	*Larry Hughes*	10.00
109	*Dirk Nowitzki*	6.00
110	*Paul Pierce*	25.00
111	*Bonzi Wells*	3.00
112	*Michael Doleac*	4.00
113	*Keon Clark*	4.00
114	*Michael Dickerson*	8.00
115	*Matt Harpring*	6.00
116	*Bryce Drew*	2.00
117	*Pat Garrity*	3.00
118	*Roshown McLeod*	3.00
119	*Ricky Davis*	3.00
120	*Rashard Lewis*	3.00
121	*Tyronn Lue*	3.00
122	*Al Harrington*	3.00
123	*Corey Benjamin*	2.00
124	*Felipe Lopez*	6.00
125	*Korleone Young*	3.00

1998-99 Fleer Brilliants Blue

All 125 cards in Fleer Brilliants were reprinted in this Brilliant Blue parallel. Cards featured blue foil on the front and were numbered on the back with a "B" suffix. Brilliant Blue veterans (1-100) were inserted 1:3 packs, while Rookies (101-125) were inserted 1:6 packs.

	MT
Complete Set (125):	300.00
Blue Veterans:	2x-3x
Inserted 1:3	
Blue Rookies:	1.5x
Inserted 1:6	

1998-99 Fleer Brilliants Gold

All 125 cards in Fleer Brilliants were reprinted in this Brilliant Gold parallel, which featured gold foil on the front. Cards were sequentially numbered to 99 sets and numbered with a "G" suffix on the back.

	MT
Brilliant Gold Cards:	20x-40x
Brilliant Gold Rookies:	3x-5x
Production 99 Sets	

1998-99 Fleer Brilliants 24-Karat Gold

Each card in the 125-card Fleer Brilliants set was reprinted in a 24-Karat Gold version. Cards featured gold foil fronts and were sequentially numbered to just 24 sets.

	MT
24-Karat Gold Cards:	40x-80x
24-Karat Gold Rookies:	5x-10x
Production 24 Sets	

1998-99 Fleer Brilliants Illuminators

Illuminators was a 15-card insert set that was seeded 1:10 packs. This insert featured 15 top rookies on a starburst background, with the insert name printed in larger letters across the top and the player's name across the bottom. Cards were numbered with an "I" suffix.

		MT
Complete Set (15):		80.00
Common Player:		1.50
Inserted 1:10		
1	Michael Olowokandi	8.00
2	Mike Bibby	10.00
3	Antawn Jamison	8.00
4	Vince Carter	15.00
5	Robert Traylor	6.00
6	Larry Hughes	6.00
7	Paul Pierce	12.00
8	Raef LaFrentz	6.00
9	Dirk Nowitzki	4.00
10	Corey Benjamin	1.50
11	Michael Dickerson	5.00
12	Roshown McLeod	3.00
13	Ricky Davis	3.00
14	Tyronn Lue	3.00
15	Al Harrington	3.00

1998-99 Fleer Brilliants Shining Stars

Shining Stars was a 15-card insert that featured top NBA players on a mirror-foil background. The insert name ran up the left side, while backs were numbered with an "SS" suffix. Cards from this insert were seeded 1:20 packs.

		MT
Complete Set (15):		150.00
Common Player:		8.00
Inserted 1:20		
Pulsar Cards:		5x-10x
Inserted 1:400		
1	Tim Thomas	8.00
2	Antoine Walker	12.00
3	Tim Duncan	20.00
4	Keith Van Horn	15.00
5	Grant Hill	20.00
6	Shaquille O'Neal	12.00
7	Kevin Garnett	20.00
8	Allen Iverson	12.00
9	Shareef Abdur-Rahim	8.00
10	Shawn Kemp	8.00
11	Anfernee Hardaway	12.00
12	Scottie Pippen	10.00
13	Stephon Marbury	12.00
14	Kobe Bryant	25.00
15	Ron Mercer	12.00

1998-99 Metal Universe

Metal Universe was released in a single series, 125-card set in 1998-99 during the lockout. It contained 123 regular cards and two checklists, and was paralleled in Precious Metal Gems (numbered to 50) and Gem Masters (one of one) sets. What would have been Series II for this product was upgraded into the launch of Molten Metal. Inserts in Metal Universe include: Neophytes, Big Ups, Planet Metal, Two 4 Me, Zero 4 You, Linchpins and Autographics.

		MT
Complete Set (125):		25.00
Common Player:		.15
Wax Box:		45.00
1	Michael Jordan	5.00
2	Mario Elie	.15
3	Voshon Lenard	.15
4	John Starks	.15
5	Juwan Howard	.30
6	Michael Finley	.30
7	Bobby Jackson	.30
8	Glenn Robinson	.30
9	Antonio McDyess	.30
10	Marcus Camby	.30
11	Zydrunas Ilgauskas	.30
12	Tony Battie	.15
13	Terrell Brandon	.30
14	Kevin Johnson	.15
15	Rod Strickland	.15
16	Dennis Rodman	1.50
17	Clarence Weatherspoon	.15
18	P.J. Brown	.15
19	Anfernee Hardaway	1.50
20	Dikembe Mutombo	.30
21	Travis Best	.15
22	Patrick Ewing	.30
23	Sam Mack	.15
24	Scottie Pippen	1.25
25	Shaquille O'Neal	1.50
26	Donyell Marshall	.15
27	Bo Outlaw	.15
28	Isaiah Rider	.15
29	Detlef Schrempf	.15
30	Mark Price	.15
31	Jim Jackson	.15
32	Eddie Jones	.75
33	Allen Iverson	1.25
34	Corliss Williamson	.15
35	Tim Duncan	2.50
36	Ron Harper	.15
37	Tony Delk	.15
38	Derek Fisher	.15
39	Kendall Gill	.15
40	Theo Ratliff	.15
41	Kelvin Cato	.15
42	Antoine Walker	1.50
43	Lamond Murray	.15
44	Avery Johnson	.15
45	John Stockton	.30
46	David Wesley	.15
47	Brian Williams	.15
48	Elden Campbell	.15
49	Sam Cassell	.15
50	Grant Hill	2.50
51	Tracy McGrady	1.25
52	Glen Rice	.30
53	Kobe Bryant	3.00
54	Cherokee Parks	.15
55	John Wallace	.15
56	Bobby Phills	.15
57	Jerry Stackhouse	.30
58	Lorenzen Wright	.15
59	Stephon Marbury	1.50
60	Shandon Anderson	.15
61	Jeff Hornacek	.15
62	Joe Dumars	.15
63	Tom Gugliotta	.30
64	Johnny Newman	.15
65	Kevin Garnett	2.50
66	Clifford Robinson	.15
67	Dennis Scott	.15
68	Anthony Mason	.15
69	Rodney Rogers	.15
70	Bryon Russell	.15
71	Maurice Taylor	.30
72	Mookie Blaylock	.15
73	Shawn Bradley	.15
74	Matt Maloney	.15
75	Karl Malone	.50
76	Larry Johnson	.30
77	Calbert Cheaney	.15
78	Steve Smith	.15
79	Toni Kukoc	.15
80	Reggie Miller	.30
81	Jayson Williams	.15
82	Gary Payton	.50
83	George Lynch	.15
84	Wesley Person	.15
85	Charles Barkley	.50
86	Tim Hardaway	.30
87	Darrell Armstrong	.15
88	Rasheed Wallace	.15
89	Tariq Abdul-Wahad	.15
90	Kenny Anderson	.15
91	Chris Mullin	.15
92	Keith Van Horn	2.00
93	Hersey Hawkins	.15
94	Billy Owens	.15
95	Ron Mercer	1.50
96	Rik Smits	.15
97	David Robinson	.50
98	Derek Anderson	.50
99	Danny Fortson	.15
100	Jason Kidd	.50
101	Sean Elliott	.15
102	Chauncey Billups	.50
103	Tyrone Hill	.15
104	Alan Henderson	.15
105	Chris Anstey	.15
106	Hakeem Olajuwon	.75
107	Allan Houston	.30
108	Bryant Reeves	.15
109	Anthony Johnson	.15
110	Shawn Kemp	1.25
111	Brevin Knight	.50
112	A.C. Green	.15
113	Ray Allen	.30
114	Tim Thomas	1.25
115	Walter McCarty	.15
116	Jalen Rose	.15
117	Kerry Kittles	.30
118	Vin Baker	.50
119	Shareef Abdur-Rahim	1.25
120	Alonzo Mourning	.30
121	Joe Smith	.30
122	Tracy Murray	.15
123	Damon Stoudamire	.50
124	Checklist	.15
125	Checklist	.15

1998-99 Metal Universe Precious Metal Gems

This 123-card parallel set reprinted the Metal Universe set (excluding the two checklists). Cards were sequentially numbered to 50 sets on the back.

	MT
Precious Metal Gems:	50x-100x
Production 50 Sets	

1998-99 Metal Universe Big Ups

This 15-card insert featured the player over a planet background, and was inserted 1:18 packs. Cards were numbered with a "BU" suffix.

		MT
Complete Set (15):		65.00
Common Player:		1.25
Inserted 1:18		
1	Stephon Marbury	10.00
2	Shareef Abdur-Rahim	6.00
3	Scottie Pippen	6.00
4	Marcus Camby	1.25
5	Ray Allen	1.25
6	Allen Iverson	8.00
7	Kerry Kittles	1.25
8	Dennis Rodman	10.00
9	Damon Stoudamire	2.50
10	Antoine Walker	10.00
11	Anfernee Hardaway	10.00
12	Shawn Kemp	6.00
13	Juwan Howard	2.50
14	Gary Payton	4.00
15	Tim Duncan	15.00

1998-99 Metal Universe Linchpins

Linchpins was a 10-card insert set found only 1:360 packs of Metal Universe. The cards featured a player over a blue, explosive background with small laser-cut linchpins cut out of the card. These were numbered with an "LP" suffix.

		MT
Complete Set (10):		400.00
Common Player:		20.00
Inserted 1:360		
1	Shaquille O'Neal	40.00
2	Kobe Bryant	80.00
3	Kevin Garnett	60.00
4	Grant Hill	60.00
5	Shawn Kemp	30.00
6	Keith Van Horn	45.00
7	Antoine Walker	50.00
8	Michael Jordan	120.00
9	Gary Payton	20.00
10	Tim Duncan	60.00

1998-99 Metal Universe Neophytes

Neophytes included 15 top young stars over a foil background with gold highlights. These were seeded 1:6 packs and numbered with an "NE" suffix.

		MT
Complete Set (15):		25.00
Common Player:		.50
Inserted 1:6		
1	Antonio Daniels	1.00
2	Bobby Jackson	1.00
3	Brevin Knight	2.00
4	Chauncey Billups	2.00
5	Danny Fortson	.50
6	Derek Anderson	2.00
7	Jacque Vaughn	.50
8	Keith Van Horn	6.00
9	Maurice Taylor	2.00
10	Michael Stewart	.50
11	Ron Mercer	4.00
12	Tim Thomas	4.00
13	Tim Duncan	8.00
14	Tracy McGrady	3.00
15	Zydrunas Ilgauskas	1.00

1998-99 Metal Universe Planet Metal

Planet Metal featured 15 players on a die-cut planet background. These were inserted 1:36 packs of Metal and numbered with a "PM" suffix.

		MT
Complete Set (15):		160.00
Common Player:		3.00
Inserted 1:36		
1	Michael Jordan	45.00
2	Antoine Walker	20.00
3	Scottie Pippen	12.00
4	Grant Hill	25.00
5	Dennis Rodman	15.00
6	Kobe Bryant	30.00
7	Kevin Garnett	25.00
8	Shaquille O'Neal	15.00
9	Stephon Marbury	20.00
10	Kerry Kittles	3.00
11	Anfernee Hardaway	15.00
12	Allen Iverson	15.00
13	Damon Stoudamire	6.00
14	Marcus Camby	3.00
15	Shareef Abdur-Rahim	12.00

1998-99 Metal Universe Two for Me

Two 4 Me, Zero 4 You was a 15-card, double-sided insert that featured the player on offense on one side and playing defense on the other. These were inserted 1:96 packs of Metal Universe and numbered with a "TZ" suffix.

		MT
Complete Set (15):		250.00
Common Player:		10.00
Inserted 1:96		
1	Kobe Bryant	40.00
2	Anfernee Hardaway	20.00
3	Allen Iverson	15.00
4	Michael Jordan	60.00
5	Stephon Marbury	20.00
6	Ron Mercer	20.00
7	Shareef Abdur-Rahim	15.00
8	Marcus Camby	10.00
9	Damon Stoudamire	10.00
10	Kevin Garnett	30.00
11	Grant Hill	30.00
12	Scottie Pippen	15.00
13	Keith Van Horn	25.00
14	Dennis Rodman	20.00
15	Shaquille O'Neal	20.00

1998-99 Press Pass BK Authentics

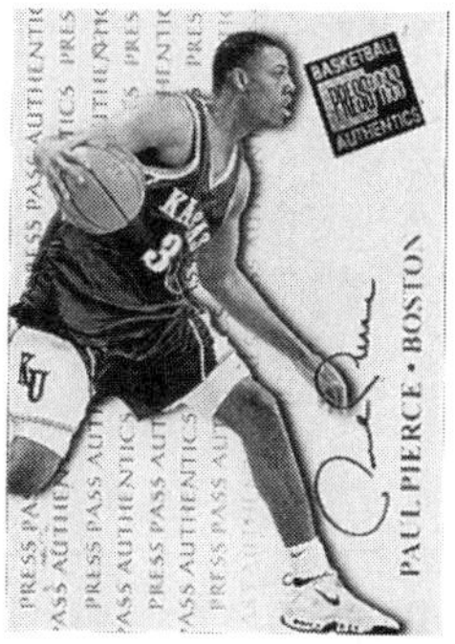

Press Pass' third basketball product of the 1998-99 season was hobby-only and oriented toward memorabilia. Boxes contained an average of three autographed cards and one authentic piece of memorabilia, available in the following forms: a signed 8" x 10" photo; or a redemption card valid for autographed basketballs, mini-balls or a Press Pass Game-Used Jersey Plaque. The set contained 45 cards, with each available in a holofoil-stamped parallel (one per pack). Inserts include: Lottery Club, Full Court Press, Certified Autographs and Sterlings, which were autographs limited to 10 numbered sets and inserted 1:720 packs.

		MT
Complete Set (45):		20.00
Common Player:		.25
Wax Box:		
1	Michael Olowokandi	3.00
2	Mike Bibby	4.00
3	Raef LaFrentz	2.00
4	Vince Carter	6.00
5	Robert Traylor	2.00
6	Jason Williams	5.00
7	Larry Hughes	2.00
8	Paul Pierce	5.00
9	Bonzi Wells	.50
10	Michael Doleac	1.00
11	Keon Clark	1.00
12	Michael Dickerson	1.50
13	Matt Harpring	.50
14	Bryce Drew	.50
15	Pat Garrity	.75
16	Roshown McLeod	.75
17	Brian Skinner	.25
18	Tyronn Lue	.75
19	Al Harrington	1.00
20	Sam Jacobson	.25
21	Nazr Mohammed	.25
22	Ruben Patterson	.50
23	Shammond Williams	.25
24	Casey Shaw	.25
25	DeMarco Johnson	.25
26	Miles Simon	.25
27	Jahidi White	.25
28	Sean Marks	.25
29	Toby Bailey	.25
30	Andrae Patterson	.25
31	Tyson Wheeler	.25
32	Cory Carr	.25
33	J.R. Henderson	.25
34	Torraye Braggs	.25
35	Tim Duncan	3.00
36	Keith Van Horn	2.00
37	Ron Mercer	1.50
38	Stephon Marbury	1.50
39	Ray Allen	.75
40	Glen Rice	.50
41	Brevin Knight	.75
42	Antoine Walker	1.50
43	Kerry Kittles	.50
44	Derek Anderson	.50
45	Checklist Michael Olowokandi	1.50

1998-99 Press Pass BK Authentics Hang Time

Hang Time paralleled all 45 cards from the base set, and were inserted one per pack. These cards were identical to the base set, but included prismatic silver foil on the card front.

	MT
Complete Set (45):	30.00
Hang Time Cards:	1.5x
Inserted 1:1	

1998-99 Press Pass BK Authentics Autographs

Thirty different players signed Certified Autograph cards in Authentics, and they were inserted one per eight packs. These cards were identical to the base cards except the real autographed replaced the facsimile autograph and most of the foil stamping was removed from the card front. Backs included the player's name and stated "Congratulations! You are now the proud owner of a Press Pass '98 Basketball Authentics Certified Autograph. Enjoy the card and collect the entire set!"

		MT
Common Player:		5.00
Inserted 1:8		
		15.00
1	Ray Allen	
2	Mike Bibby	25.00
3	Torraye Braggs	5.00
4	Cory Carr	5.00
5	Vince Carter	100.00
6	Michael Doleac	10.00
7	Bryce Drew	7.00
8	Tim Duncan	80.00
9	Pat Garrity	10.00
10	Matt Harpring	12.00
11	Al Harrington	15.00
12	J.R. Henderson	5.00
13	Larry Hughes	25.00
14	Sam Jacobson	5.00
15	DeMarco Johnson	5.00
16	Kerry Kittles	10.00
17	Raef LaFrentz	15.00
18	Tyronn Lue	10.00
19	Stephon Marbury	35.00
20	Sean Marks	5.00
21	Roshown McLeod	7.00
22	Nazr Mohammed	7.00
23	Ruben Patterson	7.00
24	Paul Pierce	50.00
25	Casey Shaw	5.00
26	Robert Traylor	5.00
27	Antoine Walker	30.00
28	Tyson Wheeler	5.00
29	Jason Williams	60.00

1998-99 Press Pass BK Authentics Full Court Press

Full Court Press was a 12-card insert featuring top rookies and five veterans on holofoil cards. The insert name and player's name are included in white letters running up the left side. Cards are insert 1:6 packs and numbered with an "FP" prefix.

		MT
Complete Set (12):		35.00
Common Player:		.50
Inserted 1:6		
1	Paul Pierce	8.00
2	Pat Garrity	1.00
3	Nazr Mohammed	.50
4	Vince Carter	10.00
5	Tim Duncan	5.00
6	Stephon Marbury	3.00
7	Ron Mercer	3.00
8	Antoine Walker	3.00
9	Keith Van Horn	4.00
10	Michael Olowokandi	5.00
11	Mike Bibby	6.00
12	Raef LaFrentz	4.00

1998-99 Press Pass BK Authentics Lottery Club

Lottery Club was a 12-card insert set that featured lottery picks from recent drafts on a foil card. The insert name, player's name and number pick were included on the left side. Inserted one per 12 packs, cards from this insert were numbered with an "LC" prefix.

		MT
Complete Set (12):		75.00
Common Player:		2.00
Inserted 1:12		
1	Michael Olowokandi	10.00
2	Tim Duncan	10.00
3	Mike Bibby	12.00
4	Keith Van Horn	8.00
5	Raef LaFrentz	8.00
6	Shareef Abdur-Rahim	4.00
7	Vince Carter	20.00
8	Stephon Marbury	6.00
9	Ray Allen	2.00
10	Robert Traylor	8.00
11	Antoine Walker	6.00
12	Jason Williams	15.00

1998-99 SkyBox Molten Metal

SkyBox Molten Metal made its debut with 150 cards in a three-tiered set. Cards 1-100 were considered the base cards and inserted four per pack. Cards 101-130 were inserted one per pack, while cards 131-150 were inserted one per two packs. The base tier contained most of the rookies, with five of the top picks included in the third tier. No rookies were found in the middle tier. Veterans were placed in tiers depending on their status in the league, with top players in the third tier and commons in the first. Inserts included every card in the set reprinted on metal in an Xplosion insert, and the second and third tiers reprinted in Fusion and Titanium Fusion parallels.

		MT
Complete Set (150):		200.00
Common Player (1-100):		.20
Inserted 4:1		
Common Player (101-130):		.25
Inserted 1:1		
Common Player (131-150):		1.50
Inserted 1:2		
Wax Box:		100.00
1	Maurice Taylor	.40
2	Brian Williams	.20
3	Anthony Mason	.20
4	John Starks	.20
5	Anthony Johnson	.20
6	Calbert Cheaney	.20
7	Roshown McLeod	3.00
8	Jalen Rose	.20
9	Kelvin Cato	.40
10	Walter McCarty	.20
11	Isaac Austin	.20
12	Arvydas Sabonis	.20
13	David Wesley	.20
14	Jim Jackson	.20
15	Elden Campbell	.20
16	*Michael Doleac*	3.00
17	Chris Webber	.75
18	Mitch Richmond	.40
19	Johnny Newman	.20
20	Jayson Williams	.20
21	George Lynch	.20
22	Ron Harper	.20
23	Donyell Marshall	.20
24	Derek Fisher	.20
25	*Matt Harpring*	4.00
26	*Jason Williams*	15.00
27	Toni Kukoc	.40
28	Clarence Weatherspoon	.20
29	Eddie Jones	.75
30	Charles Outlaw	.20
31	Zydrunas Ilgauskas	.40
32	*Michael Dickerson*	7.00
33	*Tyronn Lue*	3.00
34	Theo Ratliff	.20
35	*Dirk Nowitzki*	3.00
36	*Robert Traylor*	8.00
37	Gary Trent	.20
38	Wesley Person	.20
39	*Bryce Drew*	3.00
40	P.J. Brown	.20
41	Joe Smith	.40
42	Avery Johnson	.20
43	Chris Anstey	.20
44	Mario Elie	.20
45	Voshon Lenard	.20
46	Rex Chapman	.20
47	Hersey Hawkins	.20
48	Shawn Bradley	.20
49	Matt Maloney	.20
50	Dan Majerle	.20
51	*Pat Garrity*	3.00
52	Sam Perkins	.20
53	Mookie Blaylock	.20
54	*Al Harrington*	3.00
55	Clifford Robinson	.20
56	Alan Henderson	.20
57	Chris Mullin	.20
58	Dennis Scott	.20
59	A.C. Green	.20
60	Tyrone Hill	.20
61	Chauncey Billups	.40
62	Michael Finley	.40
63	Terrell Brandon	.40
64	Detlef Schrempf	.20
65	*Bonzi Wells*	3.00
66	Larry Johnson	.40
67	Bryant Reeves	.40
68	*Raef LaFrentz*	7.00
69	Kendall Gill	.20
70	Bryon Russell	.20
71	Bobby Phills	.20
72	Tony Delk	.20
73	Lorenzen Wright	.20
74	*Keon Clark*	3.00
75	Billy Owens	.20
76	Tracy Murray	.20
77	Bobby Jackson	.20
78	Sam Cassell	.20
79	Corliss Williamson	.20
80	Jeff Hornacek	.20
81	LaPhonso Ellis	.20
82	Sam Mitchell	.20
83	Sean Elliott	.20
84	John Wallace	.40
85	Dikembe Mutombo	.40
86	Rik Smits	.20
87	Isaiah Rider	.20
88	Joe Dumars	.20
89	Allan Houston	.40
90	Sam Mack	.20
91	*Paul Pierce*	15.00
92	Lamond Murray	.20
93	Rasheed Wallace	.20
94	Danny Fortson	.20
95	Cherokee Parks	.20
96	Antonio Daniels	.20
97	Shandon Anderson	.20
98	*Ricky Davis*	3.00
99	Rodney Rogers	.20
100	Tariq Abdul-Wahad	.20
101	Glenn Robinson	.50
102	Ron Mercer	2.00
103	Alonzo Mourning	.50
104	Marcus Camby	.50
105	Steve Smith	.50
106	Tim Hardaway	.75
107	Rod Strickland	.50
108	Reggie Miller	.50
109	Juwan Howard	.50
110	Hakeem Olajuwon	1.00
111	John Stockton	.50
112	Antonio McDyess	.75
113	Charles Barkley	.75
114	Karl Malone	.75
115	Jerry Stackhouse	.50
116	Tracy McGrady	1.50
117	Brevin Knight	.50
118	Gary Payton	.50
119	Derek Anderson	.50
120	Glen Rice	.50
121	David Robinson	.75
122	Vin Baker	.75
123	Tom Gugliotta	.50
124	Patrick Ewing	.50
125	Ray Allen	.50
126	Anfernee Hardaway	2.00
127	Jason Kidd	1.25
128	Kenny Anderson	.25
129	Kerry Kittles	.50
130	Tim Thomas	1.25
131	Shareef Abdur-Rahim	2.50
132	*Mike Bibby*	20.00
133	Kobe Bryant	10.00
134	*Vince Carter*	35.00
135	Tim Duncan	8.00
136	Kevin Garnett	8.00
137	Grant Hill	8.00
138	*Larry Hughes*	12.00
139	Allen Iverson	5.00
140	*Antawn Jamison*	15.00
141	Michael Jordan	15.00
142	Shawn Kemp	2.50
143	Stephon Marbury	5.00
144	*Michael Olowokandi*	15.00
145	Shaquille O'Neal	5.00
146	Scottie Pippen	4.00
147	Dennis Rodman	4.00
148	Damon Stoudamire	1.50
149	Keith Van Horn	5.00
150	Antoine Walker	5.00

1998-99 SkyBox Molten Metal Fusion

The final 50 cards in Molten Metal (the second and third tiers) were reprinted in a Fusion parallel. Cards 1-30 in the Fusion set (101-130 of the base set) were inserted 1:16 packs, while cards 31-50 (131-150 of the base set) were numbered to 250. Due to a production error, 15 of the 20 silver-fronted Fusion cards were incorrectly labeled Titanium Fusion on the front. The players printed correctly include: Grant Hill, Allen Iverson, Michael Jordan, Shawn Kemp and Stephon Marbury. Our guide lists all silver fronted and numbered to 250 sets under Fusion, regardless of whether the front label is correct or not.

	MT
Common Player (101-130):	1.50
Inserted 1:16	
Common Player (131-150):	30.00
Numbered to 250	

Due to a production error, 15 of the Supernatural Fusion cards were labeled "Titanium Fusion." We've priced all silver and numbered to 250 versions under Fusion.

1	Glenn Robinson	3.00
2	Ron Mercer	12.00
3	Alonzo Mourning	3.00
4	Marcus Camby	3.00
5	Steve Smith	3.00
6	Tim Hardaway	4.50
7	Rod Strickland	3.00
8	Reggie Miller	3.00
9	Juwan Howard	3.00
10	Hakeem Olajuwon	6.00
11	John Stockton	3.00
12	Antonio McDyess	4.50
13	Charles Barkley	4.50
14	Karl Malone	4.50
15	Jerry Stackhouse	3.00
16	Tracy McGrady	9.00
17	Brevin Knight	3.00
18	Gary Payton	3.00
19	Derek Anderson	3.00
20	Glen Rice	3.00
21	David Robinson	4.50
22	Vin Baker	4.50
23	Tom Gugliotta	3.00
24	Patrick Ewing	3.00
25	Ray Allen	3.00
26	Anfernee Hardaway	12.00
27	Jason Kidd	7.50
28	Kenny Anderson	1.50
29	Kerry Kittles	3.00
30	Tim Thomas	7.50
31	Shareef Abdur-Rahim	50.00
32	Mike Bibby	75.00
33	Kobe Bryant	200.00
34	Vince Carter	125.00
35	Tim Duncan	150.00
36	Kevin Garnett	150.00
37	Grant Hill	150.00
38	Larry Hughes	40.00
39	Allen Iverson	100.00
40	Antawn Jamison	60.00
41	Michael Jordan	300.00
42	Shawn Kemp	50.00
43	Stephon Marbury	100.00
44	Michael Olowokandi	60.00
45	Shaquille O'Neal	100.00
46	Scottie Pippen	75.00
47	Dennis Rodman	75.00
48	Damon Stoudamire	30.00
49	Keith Van Horn	100.00
50	Antoine Walker	100.00

1998-99 SkyBox Molten Metal Fusion Titanium Fusion

The entire Fusion insert was also available in a Titanium Fusion parallel. Cards 1-30 were inserted 1:96 packs, while 31-50 were numbered to 40 sets. As referenced in the Fusion set, 15 of the 20 cards are labeled incorrectly on the front as "Fusion." Our guide lists all Titanium colored fronts and numbered to 40 sets on the back cards under Titanium Fusion, regardless of what the front label indicates.

	MT
Common Player (101-130):	4.00
Inserted 1:96	
Common Player (131-150):	100.00
Numbered to 40	

Due to a production error, 15 of the Supernatural Titanium Fusion were labeleld "Fusion." We've priced all gold and numbered to 40 versions under Titanium Fusions, regardless of what the front says. Correct cards were Kemp, Jordan, Hill, Marbury and Iverson.

1	Glenn Robinson	8.00
2	Ron Mercer	30.00
3	Alonzo Mourning	8.00
4	Marcus Camby	8.00
5	Steve Smith	4.00
6	Tim Hardaway	12.00
7	Rod Strickland	8.00
8	Reggie Miller	8.00
9	Juwan Howard	8.00
10	Hakeem Olajuwon	15.00
11	John Stockton	8.00
12	Antonio McDyess	12.00
13	Charles Barkley	12.00
14	Karl Malone	12.00
15	Jerry Stackhouse	8.00
16	Tracy McGrady	25.00
17	Brevin Knight	8.00
18	Gary Payton	8.00
19	Derek Anderson	8.00
20	Glen Rice	8.00
21	David Robinson	12.00
22	Vin Baker	12.00
23	Tom Gugliotta	8.00
24	Patrick Ewing	8.00
25	Ray Allen	8.00
26	Anfernee Hardaway	30.00
27	Jason Kidd	20.00
28	Kenny Anderson	4.00
29	Kerry Kittles	8.00
30	Tim Thomas	20.00
31	Shareef Abdur-Rahim	200.00
32	Mike Bibby	300.00
33	Kobe Bryant	800.00
34	Vince Carter	500.00
35	Tim Duncan	600.00
36	Kevin Garnett	600.00
37	Grant Hill	600.00
38	Larry Hughes	160.00
39	Allen Iverson	400.00
40	Antawn Jamison	240.00
41	Michael Jordan	1200.
42	Shawn Kemp	200.00
43	Stephon Marbury	400.00
44	Michael Olowokandi	240.00
45	Shaquille O'Neal	400.00
46	Scottie Pippen	300.00
47	Dennis Rodman	300.00
48	Damon Stoudamire	100.00
49	Keith Van Horn	400.00
50	Antoine Walker	400.00

1998-99 SkyBox Molten Metal Xplosion

Xplosion reprinted all 150 cards from the base set on a metal card stock. Cards 1-100 were inserted 1:2.5 packs, 101-130 were inserted 1:18 packs and 131-150 were seeded 1:60 packs.

	MT
Veterans (1-100):	2x
Rookies (1-100):	1.5x
Inserted 1:2.5	
Veterans (101-130):	3x-6x
Inserted 1:18	
Veterans (131-150):	3x-6x
Rookies (131-150):	2x
Inserted 1:60)	

1998-99 SkyBox Premium

SkyBox Premium contained 265 cards, with 125 in Series I and 140 in Series II. Series II added a 40-card Rookies subset that was seeded 1:4 packs. Card fronts had a color shot of the player over a blurred background, with the player's name, team and position, as well as his initials in script, in holographic foil. Rubies paralleled each card in the set, with the first 225 cards, called Star Rubies, numbered to 50 sets, while the final 40 cards, called Star Rookies, were numbered to 25 sets. Series II also contained a 25-card Ninety Fine subset. Inserts in Series I included Smooth, Just Cookin', Soul of the Game, Net Set, 3-D's and Intimidation Nation. Inserts in Series II included: BPO, Mod Squad, Fresh Faces, That's Jam, and Slam Funk. In addition, Autographics cards were inserted in both series, at 1:68 in Series I and 1:24 in Series II.

	MT
Complete Set (265):	275.00
Complete Series 1 (125):	25.00
Complete Series 2 (140):	250.00
Common Player:	.10
Common Rookie:	1.50
Inserted 1:4	
Series 1 Wax Box:	45.00
Series 2 Wax Box:	65.00

1	Tim Duncan	2.50
2	Voshon Lenard	.10
3	John Starks	.10
4	Juwan Howard	.30
5	Michael Finley	.20
6	Bobby Jackson	.20
7	Glenn Robinson	.20
8	Antonio McDyess	.30
9	Eric Williams	.10
10	Zydrunas Ilgauskas	.20
11	Terrell Brandon	.20
12	Shandon Anderson	.10
13	Rod Strickland	.10
14	Dennis Rodman	1.50
15	Clarence Weatherspoon	.10
16	P.J. Brown	.10
17	Anfernee Hardaway	1.50
18	Dikembe Mutombo	.20
19	Patrick Ewing	.30
20	Scottie Pippen	1.25
21	Shaquille O'Neal	1.50
22	Donyell Marshall	.10
23	Michael Jordan	5.00
24	Mark Price	.10
25	Jim Jackson	.10
26	Isaiah Rider	.10
27	Eddie Jones	.75
28	Detlef Schrempf	.10
29	Corliss Williamson	.10
30	Bo Outlaw	.10
31	Allen Iverson	1.25
32	Luc Longley	.10
33	Theo Ratliff	.10
34	Antoine Walker	1.50
35	Lamond Murray	.10
36	Avery Johnson	.10
37	John Stockton	.30
38	David Wesley	.10
39	Elden Campbell	.10
40	Grant Hill	2.50
41	Sam Cassell	.10
42	Tracy McGrady	1.00
43	Glen Rice	.30
44	Kobe Bryant	3.00
45	John Wallace	.10
46	Bobby Phills	.10
47	Jerry Stackhouse	.20
48	Stephon Marbury	1.50
49	Jeff Hornacek	.10
50	Tom Gugliotta	.20
51	Joe Dumars	.10
52	Johnny Newman	.10
53	Kevin Garnett	2.50
54	Dennis Scott	.10
55	Anthony Mason	.10
56	Rodney Rogers	.10
57	Bryon Russell	.10
58	Maurice Taylor	.40
59	Mookie Blaylock	.10
60	Shawn Bradley	.10
61	Matt Maloney	.10
62	Karl Malone	.30
63	Larry Johnson	.20
64	Calbert Cheaney	.10
65	Steve Smith	.10
66	Toni Kukoc	.20
67	Reggie Miller	.30
68	Jayson Williams	.10
69	Gary Payton	.40
70	Sean Elliott	.10
71	Charles Barkley	.50
72	Tim Hardaway	.30
73	Rasheed Wallace	.10
74	Tariq Abdul-Wahad	.10
75	Kenny Anderson	.10
76	Chris Mullin	.10
77	Keith Van Horn	2.00
78	Hersey Hawkins	.10
79	Ron Mercer	1.50
80	Rik Smits	.10
81	David Robinson	.50
82	Derek Anderson	.50
83	Danny Fortson	.10
84	Jason Kidd	.75
85	Chauncey Billups	.40
86	Chris Anstey	.10
87	Hakeem Olajuwon	.75
88	Bryant Reeves	.10
89	Anthony Johnson	.10
90	Shawn Kemp	1.00
91	Brevin Knight	.50
92	Ray Allen	.30
93	Tim Thomas	1.00
94	Jalen Rose	.10
95	Kerry Kittles	.20
96	Vin Baker	.50
97	Shareef Abdur-Rahim	1.00
98	Alonzo Mourning	.30
99	Joe Smith	.20
100	Damon Stoudamire	.40
101	Alan Henderson	.10
102	Walter McCarty	.10
103	Vlade Divac	.10
104	Wesley Person	.10
105	A.C. Green	.10
106	Malik Sealy	.10
107	Carl Thomas	.10
108	Brent Price	.10
109	Mark Jackson	.10
110	Lorenzen Wright	.10
111	Derek Fisher	.10
112	Michael Smith	.10
113	Tyrone Hill	.10
114	Cherokee Parks	.10
115	Kendall Gill	.10
116	Darrell Armstrong	.10
117	Derrick Coleman	.10
118	Rex Chapman	.10
119	Arvydas Sabonis	.10
120	Billy Owens	.10
121	Sam Perkins	.10
122	Gary Trent	.10
123	Sam Mack	.10
124	Tracy Murray	.10
125	Allan Houston	.10
126	Mitch Richmond	.20
127	Carl Herrera	.10
128	Ron Harper	.10
129	Gary Trent	.10
130	Chris Webber	1.00
131	Antonio Daniels	.20
132	Charles Oakley	.10
133	Marcus Camby	.40
134	Tony Battie	.20
135	Otis Thorpe	.10
136	Dale Davis	.10
137	Chuck Person	.10
138	Ervin Johnson	.10
139	Jamal Mashburn	.20
140	Brian Grant	.10
141	Chris Mills	.10
142	Doug Christie	.10
143	George McCloud	.10
144	Todd Fuller	.10
145	Jerome Williams	.10
146	Chauncey Billups	.40
147	Dean Garrett	.10
148	Robert Pack	.10
149	Clarence Weatherspoon	.10
150	Tim Legler	.10
151	Bob Sura	.10
152	B.J. Armstrong	.10
153	Charlie Ward	.10
154	Rony Seikaly	.10
155	Chris Carr	.10
156	Eldridge Recasner	.10
157	Michael Stewart	.10
158	Jim McIlvaine	.10
159	Adam Keefe	.10
160	Antonio Davis	.10
161	Lawrence Funderburke	.10
162	Greg Ostertag	.10
163	Dan Majerle	.10
164	Dale Ellis	.10
165	Greg Anthony	.10
166	Chris Whitney	.10
167	Eric Piatkowski	.10
168	Tom Gugliotta	.20
169	Luc Longley	.10
170	Antonio McDyess	.40
171	George Lynch	.10
172	Dell Curry	.10
173	Johnny Newman	.10
174	Christian Laettner	.20
175	Steve Kerr	.10
176	Popeye Jones	.10
177	Brent Barry	.10
178	Billy Owens	.10
179	Cherokee Parks	.10
180	Derek Harper	.10
181	Howard Eisley	.10
182	Matt Geiger	.10
183	Darrick Martin	.10
184	Isaac Austin	.10
185	Dennis Scott	.10
186	Derrick Coleman	.20
187	Sam Perkins	.10
188	Latrell Sprewell	.20
189	Jud Buechler	.10
190	Jason Caffey	.10
191	Vlade Divac	.20
192	Travis Best	.10
193	Loy Vaught	.10
194	Mario Elie	.10
195	Ed Gray	.10
196	Joe Smith	.40
197	John Starks	.10
198	Anthony Johnson	.10
199	Kurt Thomas	.10
200	Chris Dudley	.10
201	Shareef Abdur-Rahim	.50
202	Ray Allen	.30
203	Vin Baker	.40
204	Charles Barkley	.30
205	Kobe Bryant	1.50
206	Tim Duncan	1.25
207	Anfernee Hardaway	.75
208	Grant Hill	1.25
209	Allen Iverson	.75
210	Jason Kidd	.50
211	Shawn Kemp	.50
212	Shaquille O'Neal	.75
213	Kerry Kittles	.20
214	Karl Malone	.30
215	Stephon Marbury	.75
216	Ron Mercer	.75
217	Reggie Miller	.10
218	Kevin Garnett	1.25
219	Gary Payton	.30
220	Scottie Pippen	.60
221	David Robinson	.30
222	Hakeem Olajuwon	.40
223	Damon Stoudamire	.30
224	Keith Van Horn	1.00
225	Antoine Walker	.75
226	*Cory Carr*	1.50
227	*Cuttino Mobley*	6.00
228	*Miles Simon*	1.50
229	*J.R. Henderson*	1.50
230	*Jason Williams*	40.00
231	*Felipe Lopez*	8.00
232	*Shammond Williams*	1.50
233	*Ricky Davis*	5.00
234	*Vince Carter*	50.00
235	*Antawn Jamison*	20.00
236	*Ryan Stack*	1.50
237	*Nazr Mohammed*	3.00
238	*Sam Jacobson*	3.00
239	*Larry Hughes*	18.00
240	*Ruben Patterson*	3.00
241	*Al Harrington*	5.00
242	*Ansu Sesay*	1.50
243	*Vladimir Stepania*	1.50
244	*Matt Harpring*	8.00
245	*Andrae Patterson*	1.50
246	*Pat Garrity*	4.00
247	*Bonzi Wells*	4.00
248	*Bryce Drew*	4.00
249	*Toby Bailey*	3.00
250	*Michael Doleac*	6.00
251	*Michael Dickerson*	12.00
252	*Predrag Stojakovic*	6.00
253	*Robert Traylor*	15.00
254	*Tyronn Lue*	3.00
255	*Dirk Nowitzki*	8.00
256	*Raef LaFrentz*	15.00
257	*Jelani McCoy*	1.50
258	*Michael Olowokandi*	15.00
259	*Brian Skinner*	3.00
260	*Keon Clark*	6.00

261	*Roshown McLeod*	3.00
262	*Mike Bibby*	25.00
263	*Paul Pierce*	40.00
264	*Tyson Wheeler*	1.50
265	*Corey Benjamin*	3.00

1998-99 SkyBox Premium Star Rubies

Star Rubies was a 265-card parallel set that was inserted into both Series I and II SkyBox Premium hobby packs. The cards featured ruby red foil stamping and sequentially numbered on the back, with 1-225 numbered to 50 sets and 226-265 numbered to 25 sets.

	MT
Star Ruby Cards:	75x-150x
Production 50 Sets	
Star Ruby Rookies:	10x-15x
Production 25 Sets	

1998-99 SkyBox Premium Autographics

The third season for NBA Autographics included over 120 veterans and 20 rookies. Cards were inserted into NBA Hoops I (1:144), Thunder I (1:112), Metal Universe I (1:68), SkyBox Premium I (1:68), SkyBox Premium II (1:24), Molten Metal (1:24) and E-X Century (1:18). Cards contained an embossed SkyBox seal of authenticity. Also, a parallel Century Marks version of each exists and is hand-numbered to 50.

	MT
Common Player:	10.00
Inserted 1:144 Hoops	
Inserted 1:68 Metal	
Inserted 1:68 SkyBox,	
Inserted 1:112 Thunder	
Inserted 1:24 Molten Metal	
Inserted 1:24 SkyBox II	
Blue Century Marks 4x	
Production 50 sets	
Iverson signed an equal amount in blue and black.	
Tariq Abdul-Wahad	25.00
Shareef Abdur-Rahim	120.00
Cory Alexander	10.00
Ray Allen	75.00
Kenny Anderson	20.00
Nick Anderson	15.00
Chris Anstey	10.00
Isaac Austin	10.00
Vin Baker	55.00
Dana Barros	10.00
Tony Battie	20.00
Travis Best	10.00
Mike Bibby	150.00
Chauncey Billups	35.00
Corie Blount	10.00
P.J. Brown	10.00
Scott Burrell	10.00
Jason Caffey	15.00
Marcus Camby	40.00
Elden Campbell	10.00
Chris Carr	10.00
Vince Carter	250.00
Kelvin Cato	20.00
Calbert Cheaney	10.00
Keith Closs	15.00
Antonio Daniels	30.00
Dale Davis	10.00
Ricky Davis	30.00
Andrew DeClerq	10.00
Tony Delk	10.00
Michael Dickerson	75.00
Michael Doleac	30.00
Bryce Drew	30.00
Tim Duncan	300.00
Howard Eisley	10.00
Danny Ferry	10.00
Derek Fisher	15.00
Danny Fortson	15.00
Adonal Foyle	10.00
Todd Fuller	10.00
Kevin Garnett	200.00
Pat Garrity	25.00
Brian Grant	10.00
Tom Gugliotta	40.00
Tom Hammonds	10.00
Tim Hardaway	60.00
Matt Harpring	25.00
Othella Harrington	15.00
Hersey Hawkins	10.00
Cedric Henderson	20.00
Grant Hill	250.00
Tyrone Hill	10.00
Allan Houston	25.00
Juwan Howard	60.00
Larry Hughes	100.00
Zydrunas Ilgauskus	20.00
Allen Iverson	200.00
Bobby Jackson	20.00
Antawn Jamison	160.00
Anthony Johnson	10.00
Ervin Johnson	10.00
Larry Johnson	30.00
Eddie Jones	100.00
Adam Keefe	10.00
Shawn Kemp	150.00
Steve Kerr	20.00
Jason Kidd	130.00
Kerry Kittles	40.00
Brevin Knight	40.00
Raef LaFrentz	100.00
Felipe Lopez	40.00
George Lynch	10.00
Karl Malone	175.00
Danny Manning	15.00
Donyell Marshall	15.00
Tony Massenberg	10.00
Walter McCarty	10.00
Jelani McCoy	25.00
Antonio McDyess	60.00
Tracy McGrady	75.00
Ron Mercer	100.00
Sam Mitchell	10.00
Nazr Mohammed	25.00
Alonzo Mourning	75.00
Chris Mullin	20.00
Dikembe Mutumbo	40.00
Hakeem Olajuwon	160.00
Michael Olowokandi	150.00
Elliot Perry	10.00
Bobby Phills	10.00
Eric Piatkowski	10.00
Paul Pierce	175.00
Scottie Pippen	200.00
Scot Pollard	20.00
Vitaly Potapenko	10.00
Brent Price	10.00
Theo Ratliff	10.00
Eldridge Recasner	10.00
Bryant Reeves	30.00
Glen Rice	50.00
Chris Robinson	10.00
David Robinson	160.00
Dennis Rodman	300.00
Bryon Russell	15.00
Danny Schayes	10.00
Detlef Schrempf	25.00
Brian Skinner	25.00
Reggie Slater	10.00
Joe Smith	45.00
Steve Smith	25.00
Rik Smits	15.00
Jerry Stackhouse	40.00
John Starks	25.00
Bryant Stith	10.00
Damon Stoudamire	100.00
Mark Strickland	10.00
Rod Strickland	35.00
Bob Sura	10.00
Tim Thomas	100.00
Robert Traylor	100.00
Gary Trent	10.00
Keith Van Horn	120.00
Jacque Vaughn	10.00
Antoine Walker	125.00
Eric Washington	10.00
Clarence Weatherspoon	15.00
David Wesley	10.00
Eric Williams	10.00
Jason Williams	175.00
Jayson Williams	25.00
Monty Williams	10.00
Walt Williams	15.00
Lorenzen Wright	10.00

1998-99 SkyBox Premium BPO

This 15-card insert was found in packs of Series II at a rate of one per six. Players were pictured over a dark background, with an orange flame trailing their body. Cards from this insert were numbered with a "BPO" suffix.

		MT
Complete Set (15):		30.00
Common Player:		.40
Inserted 1:6 Series 2		
1	Ron Mercer	2.50
2	Shareef Abdur-Rahim	1.00
3	Stephon Marbury	2.50
4	Tim Thomas	2.00
5	Tim Duncan	4.00
6	Mike Bibby	3.00
7	Ray Allen	1.00
8	Shawn Kemp	1.00
9	Vince Carter	5.00
10	Antoine Walker	2.00
11	Raef LaFrentz	1.00
12	Damon Stoudamire	.75
13	Keith Van Horn	3.00
14	Kerry Kittles	.40
15	Allen Iverson	2.50

1998-99 SkyBox Premium Fresh Faces

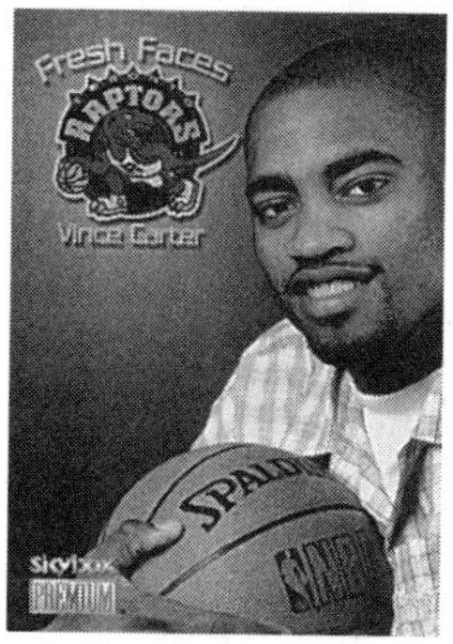

This 10-card insert featured portrait shots of top NBA rookies dressed in casual clothes. Cards added a silver rainbow holofoil finish, were seeded 1:36 packs of Series II and numbered with an "FF" suffix.

		MT
Complete Set (10):		55.00
Common Player:		2.00
Inserted 1:36 Series 2		
1	Mike Bibby	10.00
2	Vince Carter	15.00
3	Al Harrington	3.00
4	Larry Hughes	8.00
5	Antawn Jamison	8.00
6	Raef LaFrentz	6.00
7	Michael Olowokandi	6.00
8	Paul Pierce	12.00
9	Robert Traylor	6.00
10	Bonzi Wells	2.00

1998-99 SkyBox Premium Intimidation Nation

Intimidation Nation was a 10-card insert exclusive to Series I packs at a rate of one per 360. It featured close-up shots of 10 top NBA players over a blazing fire background. These inserts were numbered with an "IN" suffix.

		MT
Complete Set (10):		450.00
Common Player:		15.00
Inserted 1:360 Series 1		
1	Shaquille O'Neal	40.00
2	Kobe Bryant	80.00
3	Kevin Garnett	60.00
4	Grant Hill	60.00
5	Shawn Kemp	25.00
6	Keith Van Horn	45.00
7	Antoine Walker	40.00
8	Michael Jordan	125.00
9	Gary Payton	15.00
10	Tim Duncan	60.00

1998-99 SkyBox Premium Just Cookin'

This insert featured 10 rookies from the 1997-98 season over a silver background with a temperature gauge. Just Cookin' inserts were found in 1:12 packs of Series I and numbered with a "JC" suffix.

		MT
Complete Set (10):		30.00
Common Player:		1.50
Inserted 1:12 Series 1		
1	Maurice Taylor	4.00
2	Brevin Knight	4.00
3	Tim Thomas	8.00
4	Chauncey Billups	4.00
5	Chris Anstey	1.50
6	Tracy McGrady	8.00
7	Zydrunas Ilgauskas	3.00
8	Antonio Daniels	2.00
9	Bobby Jackson	2.00
10	Derek Anderson	4.00

1998-99 SkyBox Premium Mod Squad

Mod Squad was a Series II insert that captured how 15 top players dress off the court. The players were shown over a psychedelic background, while cards were numbered with an "MS" suffix and seeded 1:18 packs.

		MT
Complete Set (16):		80.00
Common Player:		2.00
Inserted 1:18 Series 2		
1	Tim Thomas	4.00
2	Shaquille O'Neal	6.00
3	Scottie Pippen	5.00
4	Kobe Bryant	12.00
5	Kevin Garnett	10.00
6	Grant Hill	10.00
7	Anfernee Hardaway	6.00
8	Antoine Walker	6.00
9	Stephon Marbury	6.00
10	Kerry Kittles	2.00
11	Allen Iverson	6.00
12	Gary Payton	3.00
13	Damon Stoudamire	3.00
14	Marcus Camby	2.00
15	Shareef Abdur-Rahim	4.00
16	Michael Jordan	20.00

1998-99 SkyBox Premium Net Set

Net Set featured 15 top players over a silver tinted game-action shot. The insert name, along with the player's name and team were included in right and left borders that were made of black and silver. Cards were numbered with an "NS" suffix and seeded 1:36 packs of Series I.

		MT
Complete Set (15):		70.00
Common Player:		2.00
Inserted 1:36 Series 1		
1	Ron Mercer	12.00
2	Shawn Kemp	10.00
3	Brevin Knight	5.00
4	Maurice Taylor	5.00
5	Ray Allen	2.00
6	Dennis Rodman	15.00
7	Kerry Kittles	2.00
8	Tim Thomas	8.00
9	Gary Payton	4.00
10	Marcus Camby	2.00
11	Karl Malone	4.00
12	Juwan Howard	3.00
13	Zydrunas Ilgauskas	3.00
14	Scottie Pippen	12.00
15	Anfernee Hardaway	15.00

1998-99 SkyBox Premium Slam Funk

Slam Funk was a 10-card insert that featured 10 players on plastic cards with rainbow holo lamination creating a sparkling background. These were inserted 1:360 Series II packs and numberd with an "SF" suffix.

		MT
Complete Set (10):		350.00
Common Player:		15.00
Inserted 1:360 Series 2		
1	Kobe Bryant	80.00
2	Kevin Garnett	60.00
3	Grant Hill	60.00
4	Shaquille O'Neal	35.00
5	Michael Olowokandi	20.00
6	Tim Duncan	60.00
7	Antawn Jamison	25.00
8	Keith Van Horn	35.00
9	Ron Mercer	30.00
10	Scottie Pippen	15.00

1998-99 SkyBox Premium Smooth

This 15-card insert was found in packs of Series I at a rate of 1:6. Smooth cards picture the player over a black background with the insert name printed across the bottom in large silver letters. Cards are numbered with an "SM" suffix.

		MT
Complete Set (15):		25.00
Common Player:		.75
Inserted 1:6 Series 1		
1	Stephon Marbury	4.00
2	Shareef Abdur-Rahim	2.50
3	Keith Van Horn	4.00
4	Marcus Camby	.75
5	Ray Allen	.75
6	Allen Iverson	3.00
7	Kerry Kittles	.75
8	Tim Thomas	2.00
9	Damon Stoudamire	1.50
10	Antoine Walker	4.00
11	Brevin Knight	1.50
12	Zydrunas Ilgauskas	.75
13	Ron Mercer	3.00
14	Maurice Taylor	1.50
15	Tim Duncan	6.00

1998-99 SkyBox Premium Soul of the Game

This 15-card insert featured the multi-colored words "Soul of the Game" over a white background, with the player's image over the words. These were seeded 1:18 packs of Series I and numbered with an "SG" suffix.

		MT
Complete Set (15):		75.00
Common Player:		2.00
Inserted 1:18 Series 1		
1	Michael Jordan	20.00
2	Antoine Walker	6.00
3	Scottie Pippen	5.00
4	Grant Hill	10.00
5	Dennis Rodman	6.00
6	Kobe Bryant	12.00
7	Kevin Garnett	10.00
8	Shaquille O'Neal	6.00
9	Stephon Marbury	6.00
10	Kerry Kittles	2.00
11	Anfernee Hardaway	6.00
12	Allen Iverson	5.00
13	Damon Stoudamire	3.00
14	Marcus Camby	2.00
15	Shareef Abdur-Rahim	4.00

1998-99 SkyBox Premium That's Jam!

That's Jam! included 15 players on plastic cards seeded 1:96 packs of Series II. Cards were numbered with a "TJ" suffix.

		MT
Complete Set (15):		225.00
Common Player:		5.00
Inserted 1:96 Series 2		
1	Tim Duncan	30.00
2	Stephon Marbury	15.00
3	Shareef Abdur-Rahim	12.00
4	Shaquille O'Neal	15.00
5	Ron Mercer	15.00
6	Scottie Pippen	12.00
7	Antawn Jamison	15.00
8	Anfernee Hardaway	15.00
9	Damon Stoudamire	5.00
10	Allen Iverson	15.00
11	Keith Van Horn	15.00
12	Grant Hill	30.00
13	Kevin Garnett	30.00
14	Kobe Bryant	40.00
15	Antoine Walker	15.00

1998-99 SkyBox Premium 3 D's

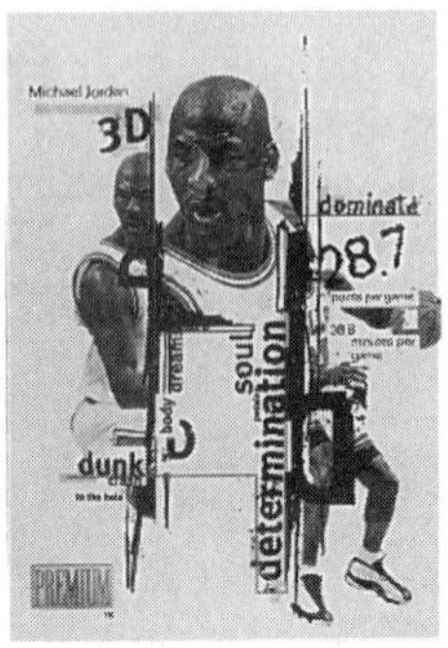

3-Ds was a 15-card insert devoted to the best at dunks, domination and determination. These were seeded 1:96 packs of Series I and numbered with a "DDD" suffix. Card fronts featured various pieces of photos of the player over a prismatic background.

		MT
Complete Set (15):		300.00
Common Player:		5.00
Inserted 1:96 Series 1		40.00
1	Kobe Bryant	
2	Anfernee Hardaway	20.00
3	Allen Iverson	15.00
4	Michael Jordan	60.00
5	Stephon Marbury	20.00
6	Ron Mercer	20.00
7	Shareef Abdur-Rahim	12.00
8	Tim Duncan	30.00
9	Damon Stoudamire	5.00
10	Kevin Garnett	30.00
11	Grant Hill	30.00
12	Scottie Pippen	20.00
13	Keith Van Horn	25.00
14	Dennis Rodman	20.00
15	Shaquille O'Neal	20.00

1998-99 SP Authentic

This 120-card set consisted of 90 veterans, including 10 Michael Jordan cards, and 30 rookies, which were sequentially numbered to 3,500 sets. The cards featured a color shot of the player over black-and-white background that faded into a white matte finish card. Inserts include: Authentics, First Class, MICHAEL, NBA 2K, and Sign of the Times (bronze, silver and gold).

		MT
Complete Set (120):		650.00
Common Player (1-90):		.25
Common MJ (1-10):		3.00
Common Rookie (91-120):		8.00
Production: 3,500 sets		
Wax Box:		175.00
1	Michael Jordan (Scoring Title #1 (86-87))	3.00
2	Michael Jordan (Scoring Title #2 (87-88))	3.00
3	Michael Jordan (Scoring Title #3 (88-89))	3.00
4	Michael Jordan (Scoring Title #4 (89-90))	3.00
5	Michael Jordan (Scoring Title #5 (90-91))	3.00
6	Michael Jordan (Scoring Title #6 (91-92))	3.00
7	Michael Jordan (Scoring Title #7 (92-93))	3.00
8	Michael Jordan (Scoring Title #8 (95-96))	3.00
9	Michael Jordan (Scoring Title #9 (96-97))	3.00
10	Michael Jordan (Scoring Title #10 (97-98))	3.00
11	Steve Smith	.40
12	Dikembe Mutombo	.25
13	Alan Henderson	.25
14	Antoine Walker	2.00
15	Ron Mercer	1.50
16	Kenny Anderson	.40
17	Derrick Coleman	.40
18	David Wesley	.25
19	Glen Rice	.40
20	Toni Kukoc	.50
21	Ron Harper	.25
22	Brent Barry	.25
23	Shawn Kemp	1.50
24	Zydrunas Ilgauskas	.40
25	Brevin Knight	.50
26	Michael Finley	.50
27	Steve Nash	.40
28	Cedric Ceballos	.25
29	Antonio McDyess	.75
30	Nick Van Exel	.40
31	Grant Hill	3.00
32	Jerry Stackhouse	.40
33	Bison Dele	.25
34	John Starks	.25
35	Chris Mills	.25
36	Hakeem Olajuwon	.75
37	Charles Barkley	.75
38	Scottie Pippen	1.50
39	Reggie Miller	.40
40	Chris Mullin	.25
41	Rik Smits	.25
42	Lamond Murray	.25
43	Maurice Taylor	.50
44	Kobe Bryant	4.00
45	Dennis Rodman	1.00
46	Shaquille O'Neal	2.00
47	Alonzo Mourning	.50
48	Tim Hardaway	.60
49	Jamal Mashburn	.40
50	Ray Allen	.40
51	Glenn Robinson	.40
52	Terrell Brandon	.40
53	Kevin Garnett	3.00
54	Stephon Marbury	2.00
55	Joe Smith	.40
56	Keith Van Horn	2.00
57	Kendall Gill	.25
58	Jayson Williams	.40
59	Patrick Ewing	.40
60	Allan Houston	.40
61	Larry Johnson	.40
62	Anfernee Hardaway	1.75
63	Horace Grant	.25
64	Allen Iverson	2.50
65	Tim Thomas	1.25
66	Jason Kidd	1.50
67	Tom Gugliotta	.40
68	Rex Chapman	.25
69	Damon Stoudamire	.60
70	Isaiah Rider	.40
71	Rasheed Wallace	.40
72	Chris Webber	1.50
73	Vlade Divac	.40
74	Corliss Williamson	.25
75	Tim Duncan	3.00
76	David Robinson	.75
77	Sean Elliott	.25
78	Detlef Schrempf	.25
79	Vin Baker	.60
80	Gary Payton	.75
81	Doug Christie	.25
82	Tracy McGrady	1.50
83	Karl Malone	.75
84	John Stockton	.40
85	Jeff Hornacek	.25
86	Shareef Abdur-Rahim	1.50
87	Bryant Reeves	.40
88	Juwan Howard	.50
89	Mitch Richmond	.40
90	Rod Strickland	.40
91	*Michael Olowokandi*	25.00
92	*Mike Bibby*	50.00
93	*Raef LaFrentz*	25.00
94	*Antawn Jamison*	60.00
95	*Vince Carter*	250.00
96	*Robert Traylor*	25.00
97	*Jason Williams*	100.00
98	*Larry Hughes*	50.00
99	*Dirk Nowitzki*	10.00
100	*Paul Pierce*	75.00
101	*Bonzi Wells*	10.00
102	*Michael Doleac*	12.00
103	*Keon Clark*	12.00
104	*Michael Dickerson*	15.00
105	*Matt Harpring*	15.00
106	*Bryce Drew*	8.00
107	*Pat Garrity*	10.00
108	*Roshown McLeod*	10.00
109	*Ricky Davis*	12.00
110	*Brian Skinner*	8.00
111	*Tyronn Lue*	12.00
112	*Felipe Lopez*	15.00
113	*Al Harrington*	20.00
114	*Sam Jacobson*	8.00
115	*Cory Carr*	8.00
116	*Corey Benjamin*	8.00
117	*Nazr Mohammed*	8.00
118	*Rashard Lewis*	12.00
119	*Predrag Stojakovic*	8.00
120	*Andrae Patterson*	8.00

1998-99 SP Authentic First Class

This 30-card insert captured some of the NBA's top stars on die-cut cards that were primarily white, with the player image over a rectangular box. SP First Class inserts were numbered with an "FC" prefix and inserted 1:7 packs.

		MT
Complete Set (30):		90.00
Common Player:		.50
Inserted 1:7		
1	Michael Jordan	15.00
2	Dikembe Mutombo	.50
3	Antoine Walker	3.00
4	Glen Rice	.75
5	Toni Kukoc	1.00
6	Shawn Kemp	2.00
7	Michael Finley	.75
8	Raef LaFrentz	2.00
9	Grant Hill	6.00
10	Antawn Jamison	6.00
11	Scottie Pippen	2.00
12	Reggie Miller	.75
13	Michael Olowokandi	2.00
14	Kobe Bryant	10.00
15	Tim Hardaway	1.50
16	Ray Allen	1.00
17	Kevin Garnett	6.00
18	Keith Van Horn	3.00
19	Allan Houston	.75
20	Anfernee Hardaway	3.00
21	Allen Iverson	4.00
22	Jason Kidd	2.00
23	Damon Stoudamire	1.00
24	Jason Williams	12.00
25	Tim Duncan	6.00
26	Gary Payton	1.00
27	Vince Carter	15.00
28	Karl Malone	1.00
29	Mike Bibby	4.00
30	Mitch Richmond	.75

1998-99 SP Authentic Michael

This 15-card insert feature Michael Jordan exclusively and utilized Ionix technology. "Michael" inserts were numbered with an "M" prefix and inserted 1:144 packs.

	MT
Complete Set (15):	500.00
Common Player:	40.00
Inserted 1:144	

1998-99 SP Authentic NBA 2K

NBA 2K was a 20-card insert showcasing top players that will lead the NBA into the year 2000. Cards were inserted 1:23 packs and numbered with a "2K" prefix.

		MT
Complete Set (20):		175.00
Common Player:		3.00
Inserted 1:23		
1	Michael Olowokandi	6.00
2	Mike Bibby	12.00
3	Raef LaFrentz	6.00
4	Antawn Jamison	15.00
5	Vince Carter	30.00
6	Robert Traylor	6.00
7	Jason Williams	25.00
8	Larry Hughes	12.00
9	Dirk Nowitzki	5.00
10	Paul Pierce	20.00
11	Cuttino Mobley	4.00
12	Michael Doleac	4.00
13	Corey Benjamin	3.00
14	Michael Dickerson	6.00
15	Allen Iverson	8.00
16	Kobe Bryant	15.00
17	Tim Duncan	12.00
18	Keith Van Horn	6.00
19	Kevin Garnett	12.00
20	Grant Hill	12.00

1998-99 SP Authentic Sign of the Times-Bronze

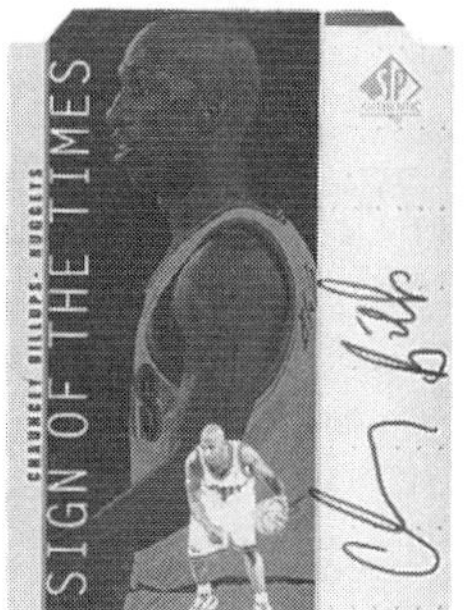

Sign of the Times - Bronze was a 45-card insert that featured autographs of NBA players. Silver and Gold Sign of the Times inserts were also available, with players signing in one of the three categories. Cards were unnumbered and identified by the player's initials (except in cases where two players had the same initials, then they would use the first two letters of the first name or some alternative identification), which appeared on the card back. Bronze level cards were inserted 1:23 packs of SP Authentic.

		MT
Common Player:		8.00
Inserted 1:23		
TQ	Tariq Abdul-Wahad	8.00
DA	Derek Anderson	12.00
KA	Kenny Anderson	12.00
NA	Nick Anderson	12.00
CB	Chauncey Billups	15.00
BL	Mookie Blaylock	8.00
TB	Terrell Brandon	12.00
PJ	P.J. Brown	8.00
CC	Chris Carr	8.00
CH	Calbert Cheaney	8.00
DC	Doug Christie	8.00
ED	Erick Dampier	8.00
BE	Blue Edwards	8.00
SE	Sean Elliott	12.00
MI	Michael Finley	15.00
DK	Derek Fisher	10.00
BG	Brian Grant	15.00
HG	Horace Grant	12.00
EG	Ed Gray	8.00
RH	Ron Harper	10.00
OH	Othella Harrington	8.00
JH	Jeff Hornacek	12.00
HW	Juwan Howard	15.00
LH	Lindsey Hunter	8.00
MK	Mark Jackson	8.00
AV	Avery Johnson	8.00
LJ	Larry Johnson	12.00
BK	Brevin Knight	12.00
TK	Toni Kukoc	25.00
DN	Danny Manning	15.00
DM	Donyell Marshall	8.00
WM	Walter McCarty	8.00
AM	Antonio McDyess	25.00
MG	Tracy McGrady	20.00
BP	Bobby Phills	8.00
TR	Theo Ratliff	12.00
RR	Rodrick Rhodes	8.00
GR	Glen Rice	25.00
JR	Jalen Rose	12.00
BR	Bryon Russell	8.00
DT	Detlef Schrempf	15.00
TY	Maurice Taylor	15.00
DV	David Wesley	8.00
JY	Jayson Williams	15.00
JW	Jerome Williams	8.00

1998-99 SP Authentic Sign of the Times-Gold

Four different players signed Gold level cards of Sign of the Times inserts. These die-cut cards were inserted 1:1,500 packs. Cards were identified by the player's initials on the card back.

		MT
Common Player:		75.00
TH	Tim Hardaway	75.00
AI	Allen Iverson	250.00
MJ	Michael Jordan	3000.
AW	Antoine Walker	100.00

1998-99 SP Authentic Sign of the Times-Silver

Thirteen different players autographed cards in the Silver level of Sign of the Times. These were inserted 1:115 packs and identified by the player's initials on the card back.

		MT
Common Player:		15.00
Inserted 1:115		
MB	Mike Bibby	25.00
VC	Vince Carter	250.00
PN	Anfernee Hardaway	75.00
LR	Larry Hughes	50.00
AJ	Antawn Jamison	60.00
SH	Shawn Kemp	30.00
RL	Raef LaFrentz	20.00
RM	Ron Mercer	20.00
MT	Dikembe Mutombo	15.00
HO	Hakeem Olajuwon	40.00
MO	Michael Olowokandi	20.00
DR	Dennis Rodman	100.00
RT	Robert Traylor	20.00

1998-99 SPx Finite

SPx Finite was a all-sequentially-numbered hobby-only set that consisted of 90 base cards (numbered to 10,000) and four different subsets. Subsets included: 60 Star Power (91-150, numbered to 5,400 sets), 30 SPx 2000 (151-180, numbered to 4,050 sets), 20 Top Flight (181-200, numbered to 3,390 sets) and 10 Finite Excellence (201-210, numbered to 1,770 sets). Upper Deck also made Rookie cards (211-240) as inserts in MJ Access later in the year, but those listings are included as an insert with that product. Each card was also paralleled in a Radiance and Spectrum level set with different sequential numbering. In addition, 23 hand-numbered Autographed Game-worn Jersey Cards of Jordan were available in this product.

		MT
Complete Set (210):		600.00
Common Player (1-90):		.50
Production 10,000 Sets		
Common Player (91-150):		1.00
Production 5,400 Sets		
Common Player (151-180):		1.50
Production 4,050 Sets		
Common Player (181-200):		1.50
Production 3,390 Sets		
Common Player (201-210):		7.00
Production 1,770 Sets		
Wax Box:		75.00
1	Michael Jordan	16.00
2	Hakeem Olajuwon	2.50
3	Keith Van Horn	6.00
4	Rasheed Wallace	.50
5	Mookie Blaylock	.50
6	Bobby Jackson	1.00
7	Detlef Schrempf	.50
8	Antonio McDyess	1.00
9	Lamond Murray	.50
10	Chris Mullin	.50
11	Zydrunas Ilgauskas	1.00
12	Tracy Murray	.50
13	Jerry Stackhouse	1.00
14	Avery Johnson	.50
15	Larry Johnson	1.00
16	Alan Henderson	.50
17	David Wesley	.50
18	Kevin Willis	.50
19	Eddie Jones	2.50
20	Horace Grant	.50
21	Ray Allen	1.00
22	Derrick Coleman	.50
23	Derek Anderson	1.50
24	Tim Hardaway	1.00
25	Danny Fortson	.50
26	Tariq Abdul-Wahad	.50
27	Charles Barkley	2.00
28	Sam Cassell	.50
29	Kevin Garnett	8.00
30	Jeff Hornacek	.50
31	Isaac Austin	.50
32	Allan Houston	1.00
33	David Robinson	2.00
34	Tracy McGrady	4.00
35	LaPhonso Ellis	.50
36	Shawn Kemp	4.00
37	Glenn Robinson	1.00
38	Shareef Abdur-Rahim	4.00
39	Vin Baker	2.00
40	Rik Smits	.50
41	Jason Kidd	2.50
42	Erick Dampier	.50
43	Shawn Bradley	.50
44	Anfernee Hardaway	5.00
45	John Stockton	1.00
46	Calbert Cheaney	.50
47	Terrell Brandon	1.00
48	Hubert Davis	.50
49	Patrick Ewing	1.00
50	Kobe Bryant	10.00
51	Gary Payton	1.50
52	Marcus Camby	1.00
53	Bryant Reeves	.50
54	Reggie Miller	1.00
55	Antoine Walker	5.00
56	Scottie Pippen	4.00
57	Hersey Hawkins	.50
58	John Starks	.50
59	Dikembe Mutombo	1.00
60	Damon Stoudamire	1.50
61	Rodney Rogers	.50
62	Nick Anderson	.50
63	Brian Williams	.50
64	Ron Mercer	5.00
65	Donyell Marshall	.50
66	Glen Rice	1.00
67	Michael Finley	1.00
68	Tim Duncan	8.00
69	Stephon Marbury	5.00
70	Antonio Daniels	1.00
71	Chauncey Billups	1.50
72	Kerry Kittles	1.00
73	Brian Grant	.50
74	Anthony Mason	.50
75	Allen Iverson	4.00
76	Juwan Howard	1.00
77	Grant Hill	8.00
78	Tony Delk	.50
79	Olden Polynice	.50
80	Alonzo Mourning	1.00
81	Karl Malone	1.50
82	Isaiah Rider	.50
83	Shaquille O'Neal	5.00
84	Steve Smith	.50
85	Kenny Anderson	.50
86	Toni Kukoc	.50
87	Anthony Peeler	.50
88	Tim Thomas	4.00
89	Nick Van Exel	1.00
90	Jamal Mashburn	.50
91	Reggie Miller	2.00
92	Juwan Howard	2.00
93	Glen Rice	2.00
94	Grant Hill	15.00
95	Maurice Taylor	2.00
96	Vin Baker	3.00
97	Tim Thomas	6.00
98	Bobby Jackson	1.00
99	Damon Stoudamire	2.00
100	Michael Jordan	30.00
101	Eddie Jones	4.00
102	Keith Van Horn	12.00
103	Dikembe Mutombo	2.00
104	Brevin Knight	3.00
105	Shawn Bradley	1.00
106	Lamond Murray	1.00
107	Tim Duncan	15.00
108	Bryant Reeves	1.00
109	Antoine Walker	8.00
110	John Stockton	2.00
111	Nick Anderson	1.00
112	Chris Mullin	1.00
113	Glenn Robinson	2.00
114	Kevin Garnett	15.00
115	Michael Stewart	1.00
116	Antonio McDyess	2.00
117	Jim Jackson	1.00
118	Chauncey Billups	3.00
119	Sam Cassell	1.00
120	Dennis Rodman	8.00
121	Rasheed Wallace	1.00
122	Brian Williams	1.00
123	Anfernee Hardaway	8.00
124	Scottie Pippen	6.00
125	Terrell Brandon	2.00
126	Michael Finley	2.00
127	Kerry Kittles	2.00
128	Toni Kukoc	1.00
129	Hakeem Olajuwon	4.00
130	Tim Hardaway	2.00
131	Shareef Abdur-Rahim	4.00
132	Donyell Marshall	1.00
133	David Robinson	3.00
134	LaPhonso Ellis	1.00
135	Ray Allen	2.00
136	Nick Van Exel	2.00
137	Patrick Ewing	2.00
138	Anthony Mason	1.00
139	Shaquille O'Neal	8.00
140	Shawn Kemp	6.00
141	Stephon Marbury	8.00
142	Karl Malone	2.00
143	Allen Iverson	6.00
144	Kenny Anderson	1.00
145	Marcus Camby	2.00
146	Steve Smith	1.00
147	Gary Payton	3.00
148	Jason Kidd	4.00
149	Alonzo Mourning	2.00
150	Charles Barkley	3.00
151	Kobe Bryant	25.00
152	Ron Mercer	12.00
153	Maurice Taylor	3.00
154	Tim Duncan	20.00
155	Shareef Abdur-Rahim	10.00
156	Eddie Jones	8.00
157	Chauncey Billups	4.00
158	Derek Anderson	4.00
159	Bobby Jackson	3.00
160	Stephon Marbury	12.00
161	Anfernee Hardaway	12.00
162	Zydrunas Ilgauskas	3.00
163	Allen Iverson	10.00
164	Antoine Walker	12.00
165	Tracy McGrady	8.00
166	Rasheed Wallace	1.50
167	Jason Kidd	7.00
168	Kevin Garnett	20.00
169	Damon Stoudamire	4.00
170	Brevin Knight	4.00
171	Tim Thomas	10.00
172	Danny Fortson	1.50
173	Jermaine O'Neal	1.50
174	Keith Van Horn	15.00
175	Ray Allen	3.00
176	Kerry Kittles	3.00
177	Vin Baker	4.00
178	Allan Houston	3.00
179	Alan Henderson	1.50
180	Bryon Russell	1.50
181	Michael Jordan	40.00
182	Maurice Taylor	4.00
183	Isaiah Rider	1.50
184	Antonio McDyess	3.00
185	Anfernee Hardaway	15.00
186	Glenn Robinson	3.00
187	Dikembe Mutombo	3.00
188	Shawn Kemp	12.00
189	Tracy McGrady	10.00
190	Reggie Miller	4.00
191	Derek Anderson	5.00
192	Allan Houston	3.00
193	Michael Finley	3.00
194	Nick Van Exel	3.00
195	Juwan Howard	3.00
196	LaPhonso Ellis	1.50
197	Ron Mercer	15.00
198	Glen Rice	4.00
199	Joe Smith	3.00
200	Kobe Bryant	30.00
201	Michael Jordan	85.00
202	Karl Malone	10.00
203	Hakeem Olajuwon	12.00
204	David Robinson	10.00
205	Shaquille O'Neal	25.00
206	John Stockton	7.00
207	Grant Hill	40.00
208	Tim Hardaway	7.00
209	Scottie Pippen	20.00
210	Gary Payton	10.00

1998-99 SPx Finite Radiance

Each card in SPx Finite was also available in a Radiance parallel version, which featured gold foil. Regular Radiance cards (1-90) were numbered to 5,000, Star Power cards were numbered to 2,700, SPx 2000 cards were numbered to 2,025, Top Flight cards were numbered to 1,130 and Finite Excellence cards were numbered to 590. Radiance cards were labeled as such on both the front and back of the card.

	MT
Cards (1-90):	2x
Production 5,000 Sets	
Cards (91-150):	2x
Production 2,700 Sets	
Cards (151-180):	2x
Production 2,025 Sets	
Cards (181-200):	2x
Production 1,130 Sets	
Cards (201-210):	2x
Production 590 Sets	

1998-99 SPx Finite Spectrum

Each card in the SPx Finite set was also available in a Spectrum version, which featured rainbow foil. Base Spectrum cards were numbered to 350, Star Power cards were numbered to 250, SPx 2000 cards were numbered to 75, Top Flight cards were numbered to 50 and Finite Excellence cards were numbered to 25 sets. Spectrum cards were labeled as such on both the front and the back. In addition, an Extreme level of Spectrum cards was also available and numbered 1 of 1.

	MT
Cards (1-90):	8x-16x
Production 350 Sets	
Cards (91-150):	6x-12x
Production 250 Sets	
Cards (151-180):	6x-12x
Production 75 Sets	
Cards (181-200):	10x-20x
Production 50 Sets	
Cards (201-210):	15x-30x
Production 25 Sets	

1998-99 Stadium Club Promos

This six-card promotional set was distributed to dealers and members of the media to promote the 1998-99 Stadium Club product. The cards were identical to the regular-issue cards except they were numbered PP1-PP6 on the back.

		MT
Complete Set (6):		5.00
Common Player:		.25
1	Shareef Abdur-Rahim	.50
2	Shaquille O'Neal	1.00
3	Keith Van Horn	1.00
4	Kevin Garnett	2.50
5	Tracy McGrady	.50
6	Tim Hardaway	.25

1998-99 Stadium Club

Stadium Club was released in two, 120-card series in 1998-99. Series I arrived during the lockout, but didn't allow that to diminish the product by including Draft Pick Redemption cards of the regular set numbered 101-120. Series I actually contains only 118 cards since cards 117 and 118 didn't exist because they were foreign players who didn't sign NBA contracts. Three parallels of Stadium Club existed - First Day Issue (numbered to 200, retail only), One of a Kind (numbered to 150, hobby only) and Printing Plates (four versions of each card, HTA packs only). While redemptions for cards 101-120 were in Series I, parallel versions of these cards were held until Series II. Inserts in Series I include: First Day Issue (200 numbered sets, retail only, 1:64), One of a Kind (150 numbered sets, hobby only, 1:56), Printing Plates (1:205 HTA), Co-Signers, Stadium Club Chrome, Triumvirates, Prime Rookies, Statliners and Never Compromise. Inserts in Series II include: First Day Issue (1:44), One of a Kind (1:55), Printing Plates (1:176), Co-Signers, Stadium Club Chrome, Triumvirate, Royal Court, Wing Men and Never Compromise Rookies.

		MT
Complete Set (240):		125.00
Complete Series 1 (120):		75.00
Complete Series 2 (120):		50.00
Common Player:		.15
Common Draft Picks:		1.00
Inserted 1:6		
Series 1 Wax Box:		50.00
Series 2 Wax Box:		40.00
1	Eddie Jones	1.00
2	Matt Geiger	.15
3	Ray Allen	.30
4	Billy Owens	.15
5	Larry Johnson	.30
6	Jerry Stackhouse	.30
7	Travis Best	.15
8	Sam Cassell	.15
9	Isaiah Rider	.15
10	Walter McCarty	.15
11	Hakeem Olajuwon	.75
12	Detlef Schrempf	.15
13	Chris Garner	.15
14	Voshon Lenard	.15
15	Kevin Garnett	2.50
16	Doug Christie	.15
17	Dikembe Mutombo	.30
18	Terrell Brandon	.30
19	Brevin Knight	.15
20	Dan Majerle	.15
21	Keith Van Horn	1.75
22	Jim Jackson	.30
23	Theo Ratliff	.15
24	Anthony Peeler	.15
25	Tim Hardaway	.40
26	Charles Outlaw	.15
27	Blue Edwards	.15
28	Khalid Reeves	.15
29	David Wesley	.15
30	Toni Kukoc	.30
31	Jaren Jackson	.15
32	Mario Elie	.15
33	Nick Anderson	.15
34	Derek Anderson	.50
35	Rodney Rogers	.15
36	Jalen Rose	.15
37	Corliss Williamson	.15
38	Tyrone Corbin	.15
39	Antonio Davis	.15
40	Chris Mills	.15
41	Clarence Weatherspoon	.15
42	George Lynch	.15
43	Kelvin Cato	.15
44	Anthony Mason	.15
45	Tracy McGrady	1.00
46	Lamond Murray	.15
47	Mookie Blaylock	.15
48	Tracy Murray	.15
49	Ron Harper	.15
50	Tom Gugliotta	.30
51	Allan Houston	.30
52	Arvydas Sabonis	.15
53	Brian Williams	.15
54	Brian Shaw	.15
55	John Stockton	.30
56	Rick Fox	.15
57	Hersey Hawkins	.15
58	Danny Manning	.15
59	Chris Carr	.15
60	Lindsey Hunter	.15
61	Donyell Marshall	.15
62	Michael Jordan	5.00
63	Mark Strickland	.15
64	LaPhonso Ellis	.15
65	Rod Strickland	.30
66	David Robinson	.50
67	Cedric Ceballos	.15
68	Christian Laettner	.30
69	Anthony Goldwire	.15
70	Armon Gilliam	.15
71	Shaquille O'Neal	1.50
72	Sherman Douglas	.15
73	Kendall Gill	.15
74	Charlie Ward	.15
75	Allen Iverson	1.25
76	Shawn Kemp	1.00
77	Travis Knight	.15
78	Gary Payton	.40
79	Cedric Henderson	.30
80	Matt Bullard	.15
81	Steve Kerr	.15
82	Shawn Bradley	.15
83	Antonio McDyess	.30
84	Robert Horry	.15
85	Darrick Martin	.15
86	Derek Strong	.15
87	Shandon Anderson	.15
88	Lawrence Funderburke	.15
89	Brent Price	.15
90	Reggie Miller	.30
91	Shareef Abdur-Rahim	1.00
92	Jeff Hornacek	.15
93	Antoine Carr	.15
94	Greg Anthony	.15
95	Rex Chapman	.15
96	Antoine Walker	1.50
97	Bobby Jackson	.30
98	Calbert Cheaney	.15
99	Avery Johnson	.15
100	Jason Kidd	.75
101	*Michael Olowokandi*	10.00
102	*Mike Bibby*	12.00
103	*Raef LaFrentz*	8.00
104	*Antawn Jamison*	12.00
105	*Vince Carter*	20.00
106	*Robert Traylor*	8.00
107	*Jason Williams*	15.00
108	*Larry Hughes*	10.00
109	*Dirk Nowitzki*	6.00
110	*Paul Pierce*	15.00
111	*Bonzi Wells*	3.00
112	*Michael Doleac*	4.00
113	*Keon Clark*	4.00
114	*Michael Dickerson*	6.00
115	*Matt Harpring*	4.00
116	*Bryce Drew*	3.00
117	*Pat Garrity*	1.50
118	*Roshown McLeod*	1.50
119	*Ricky Davis*	4.00
120	*Brian Skinner*	1.50
121	Dee Brown	.15
122	Hubert Davis	.15
123	Vitaly Potapenko	.15
124	Ervin Johnson	.15
125	Chris Gatling	.15
126	Darrell Armstrong	.15
127	Glen Rice	.30
128	Ben Wallace	.15
129	Sam Mitchell	.15
130	Joe Dumars	.30
131	Terry Davis	.15
132	A.C. Green	.15
133	Alan Henderson	.15
134	Ron Mercer	1.50
135	Brian Grant	.15
136	Chris Childs	.15
137	Rony Seikaly	.15
138	Pete Chilcutt	.15
139	Anfernee Hardaway	1.50
140	Bryon Russell	.15
141	Tim Thomas	1.00
142	Erick Dampier	.15
143	Charles Barkley	.50
144	Mark Jackson	.15
145	Bryant Reeves	.15
146	Tyrone Hill	.15
147	Rasheed Wallace	.15
148	Tim Duncan	2.50
149	Steve Smith	.30
150	Alonzo Mourning	.40
151	Danny Fortson	.30
152	Aaron Williams	.15
153	Andrew DeClercq	.15
154	Elden Campbell	.15
155	Don Reid	.15
156	Rik Smits	.15
157	Adonal Foyle	.15
158	Muggsy Bogues	.15
159	Chris Mullin	.15
160	Randy Brown	.15
161	Kenny Anderson	.30
162	Tariq Abdul-Wahad	.15
163	P.J. Brown	.15
164	Jayson Williams	.30
165	Grant Hill	2.50
166	Clifford Robinson	.15
167	Damon Stoudamire	.40
168	Aaron McKie	.15
169	Erick Strickland	.15
170	Kobe Bryant	4.00
171	Karl Malone	.50
172	Eric Piatkowski	.15
173	Rodrick Rhodes	.15
174	Sean Elliott	.15
175	John Wallace	.15
176	Derek Fisher	.15
177	Maurice Taylor	.40
178	Wesley Person	.15
179	Jamal Mashburn	.30
180	Patrick Ewing	.30
181	Howard Eisley	.15
182	Michael Finley	.30
183	Juwan Howard	.30
184	Matt Maloney	.15
185	Glenn Robinson	.30
186	Zydrunas Ilgauskas	.30
187	Dana Barros	.15
188	Stacey Augmon	.15
189	Bobby Phills	.15
190	Kerry Kittles	.30
191	Vin Baker	.75
192	Stephon Marbury	1.50
193	*Predrag Stojakovic*	2.00
194	Michael Olowokandi	3.00
195	Mike Bibby	5.00
196	Raef LaFrentz	3.00
197	Antawn Jamison	5.00
198	Vince Carter	8.00
199	Robert Traylor	3.00
200	Jason Williams	6.00
201	Larry Hughes	3.00
202	Dirk Nowitzki	2.00
203	Paul Pierce	6.00
204	Bonzi Wells	.50
205	Michael Doleac	1.00
206	Keon Clark	1.00
207	Michael Dickerson	3.00
208	Matt Harpring	1.00
209	Bryce Drew	.50
210	Pat Garrity	.75
211	Roshown McLeod	.75
212	Ricky Davis	1.00
213	Brian Skinner	.50
214	*Tyronn Lue*	2.00
215	*Felipe Lopez*	4.00
216	*Al Harrington*	4.00
217	*Sam Jacobson*	1.00
218	*Vladimir Stepania*	1.00
219	*Corey Benjamin*	1.00
220	*Nazr Mohammed*	1.00
221	Tom Gugliotta	.30
222	Derrick Coleman	.15
223	Mitch Richmond	.30
224	John Starks	.15
225	Antonio McDyess	.30
226	Joe Smith	.30
227	Bobby Jackson	.30
228	Luc Longley	.15
229	Isaac Austin	.15
230	Chris Webber	.50
231	Chauncey Billups	.30
232	Sam Perkins	.15
233	Christian Laettner	.15
234	Antonio Daniels	.15
235	Brent Barry	.15
236	Latrell Sprewell	.30
237	Vlade Divac	.15
238	Marcus Camby	.30
239	Charles Oakley	.15
240	Scottie Pippen	.60

1998-99 Stadium Club First Day Issue

This 240-card parallel set reprinted every card from Series I and II, but added the words "First Day Issue" in gold foil letters across the bottom. First Day Issue cards were exclusive to retail packs, seeded 1:44 packs and sequentially numbered to 200 sets. First Day Issue versions of the 20 rookie redemptions from Series I were included in Series II packs.

	MT
First Day Issue Cards:	15x-30x
FDI Series I Rookies:	4x-8x
FDI Series II Rookies:	8x-15x
Series I Inserted 1:64 Retail	
Series II Inserted 1:44 Retail	
Production 200 Retail Sets	

1998-99 Stadium Club One of a Kind

This 240-card parallel set reprinted all cards from Series I and II, but were printed on a plastic card stock and included the words "One of a Kind" within the Stadium Club oval on the front. Cards were hobby exclusive and sequentially numbered to 150 sets. Series I odds were 1:56 packs, while Series II odds were 1:55 packs. One of a Kind versions of the 20 rookie redemptions from Series I were included in Series II packs.

	MT
One Of A Kind Cards:	20x-40x
Series I Rookies:	5x-10x
Series II Rookies:	10x-20x
Series I Inserted 1:56 Hobby	
Series II Inserted 1:55 Hobby	
Production 150 Hobby Sets	

1998-99 Stadium Club Chrome

Stadium Club Chrome was a 40-card insert set that was distributed with 20 cards in both Series I and II. Cards reprinted the player's Stadium Club card, but added a chromium finish. These were inserted 1:12 packs in both series and were numbered with an "SCC" prefix. Refractor versions were seeded 1:48 packs.

		MT
Complete Set (40):		150.00
Complete Series 1 (20):		60.00
Complete Series 2 (20):		90.00
Common Player:		2.00
Inserted 1:12 Series 1/2		
Refractors:		2x
Inserted 1:48 Series 1/2		
1	Alonzo Mourning	2.00
2	Scottie Pippen	5.00
3	Patrick Ewing	2.00
4	Vin Baker	2.00
5	Glenn Robinson	2.00
6	Kobe Bryant	20.00
7	Charles Barkley	3.00
8	Chris Mullin	2.00
9	Steve Smith	2.00
10	Stephon Marbury	10.00
11	Zydrunas Ilgauskas	2.00
12	Jayson Williams	2.00
13	Juwan Howard	2.00
14	Grant Hill	15.00
15	Damon Stoudamire	3.00
16	Ron Mercer	5.00
17	Tim Duncan	15.00
18	Michael Finley	2.00
19	Glen Rice	2.00
20	Karl Malone	3.00
21	Eddie Jones	3.00
22	Dikembe Mutombo	2.00
23	Keith Van Horn	10.00
24	Jason Kidd	5.00
25	Shaquille O'Neal	10.00
26	Kevin Garnett	15.00
27	Allen Iverson	10.00
28	Shawn Kemp	5.00
29	Gary Payton	3.00
30	Shareef Abdur-Rahim	5.00
31	Mike Bibby	10.00
32	Raef LaFrentz	6.00
33	Jason Williams	15.00

34	Paul Pierce	15.00
35	Michael Doleac	3.00
36	Michael Dickerson	5.00
37	Bryce Drew	2.00
38	Roshown McLeod	2.00
39	Felipe Lopez	3.00
40	Al Harrington	3.00

1998-99 Stadium Club Co-Signers

Co-Signers was a 24-card insert set that ran through both Series I and II, with 12 cards in each. Cards featured two players on the front, split by a white strip that included the insert name. Both players autographed the card on their respective half. These were numbered with a "CO" prefix and inserted 1:209 Series I hobby packs and 1:290 Series II hobby packs.

		MT
	Common Player:	80.00
	Inserted 1:209 Series 1 Hobby	
	Inserted 1:290 Series 2 Hobby	
1	Tim Duncan, Kobe Bryant	900.00
2	Larry Johnson, Damon Stoudamire	200.00
3	Antoine Walker, Jason Kidd	400.00
4	Gary Payton, Shareef Abdur-Rahim	300.00
5	Kobe Bryant, Larry Johnson	400.00
6	Tim Duncan, Damon Stoudamire	275.00
7	Shareef Abdur-Rahim, Antoine Walker	200.00
8	Gary Payton, Jason Kidd	175.00
9	Damon Stoudamire, Kobe Bryant	225.00
10	Larry Johnson, Tim Duncan	150.00
11	Jason Kidd, Shareef Abdur-Rahim	80.00
12	Antoine Walker, Gary Payton	80.00
13	Tim Duncan, Eddie Jones	125.00
14	Jayson Williams, Vin Baker	100.00
15	Eddie Jones, Jayson Williams	60.00
16	Vin Baker, Tim Duncan	125.00
17	Eddie Jones, Vin Baker	40.00
18	Tim Duncan, Jayson Williams	125.00
19	Antawn Jamison, Michael Olowokandi	100.00
20	Vince Carter, Mike Bibby	250.00
21	Michael Olowokandi, Vince Carter	200.00
22	Mike Bibby, Antawn Jamison	150.00
23	Antawn Jamison, Vince Carter	500.00
24	Mike Bibby, Michael Olowokandi	80.00

1998-99 Stadium Club Never Compromise

Never Compromise was a 20-card insert with 10 cards in both Series I and II. Series I included veterans, while Series II featured rookies. Both were inserted 1:12 packs and numbered with an "NC" prefix.

		MT
	Complete Set (20):	80.00
	Complete Series 1 (10):	40.00
	Complete Series 2 (10):	40.00
	Common Series 1 (1-20):	1.00
	Inserted 1:12	
	Jumbo Cards:	1.5x
	Inserted 1:Series 1 Hobby Box	
	Jordan and Hill Do Not Exist in Jumbos	
1	Michael Jordan	15.00
2	Kobe Bryant	10.00
3	Vin Baker	2.00
4	Tim Duncan	8.00
5	Eddie Jones	2.00
6	Shawn Kemp	3.00
7	Grant Hill	8.00
8	Antoine Walker	5.00
9	Karl Malone	1.00
10	Scottie Pippen	4.00
11	Michael Olowokandi	5.00
12	Mike Bibby	6.00
13	Raef LaFrentz	4.00
14	Antawn Jamison	5.00
15	Vince Carter	10.00
16	Robert Traylor	4.00
17	Jason Williams	8.00
18	Larry Hughes	4.00
19	Paul Pierce	8.00
20	Felipe Lopez	3.00

1998-99 Stadium Club Prime Rookies

This 10-card set showcased the top 10 picks in the 1998 NBA Draft and was available through redemption cards inserted 1:16 packs of Series I. Cards were numbered with a "P" prefix and redemptions included the words "Prime Rookie Redemption" and the Draft Pick number over a shadowed image of a basketball player.

		MT
	Complete Set (10):	85.00
	Common Player:	8.00
	Inserted 1:16 Series 1	
1	Michael Olowokandi	12.00
2	Mike Bibby	12.00
3	Raef LaFrentz	8.00
4	Antawn Jamison	12.00
5	Vince Carter	20.00
6	Robert Traylor	8.00
7	Jason Williams	15.00
8	Larry Hughes	10.00
9	Dirk Nowitzki	8.00
10	Paul Pierce	15.00

1998-99 Stadium Club Royal Court

Royal Court was a 15-card insert set that was exclusive to Series II packs. Cards were numbered with an "RC" prefix and inserted 1:16 packs.

		MT
	Complete Set (15):	75.00
	Common Player:	2.00
	Inserted 1:16 Series 2	
1	Gary Payton	2.00
2	Kobe Bryant	15.00
3	Tim Duncan	10.00
4	Scottie Pippen	4.00
5	Allen Iverson	5.00
6	Shaquille O'Neal	5.00
7	Stephon Marbury	5.00
8	Antoine Walker	5.00
9	Michael Jordan	20.00
10	Keith Van Horn	5.00
11	Michael Olowokandi	3.00
12	Mike Bibby	6.00
13	Antawn Jamison	5.00
14	Robert Traylor	3.00
15	Roshown McLeod	2.00

1998-99 Stadium Club Statliners

Statliners was a 20-card insert exclusive to Series I packs. The top of each card in this die-cut featured a jagged die-cut set, with the insert name across the bottom. Cards were numbered with an "S" prefix and inserted 1:8 packs.

		MT
	Complete Set (20):	60.00
	Common Player:	1.00
	Inserted 1:8 Series 1	
1	Karl Malone	2.00
2	Michael Jordan	15.00
3	Antoine Walker	5.00
4	Tim Duncan	8.00
5	Grant Hill	8.00
6	Allen Iverson	5.00
7	Kevin Garnett	8.00
8	Gary Payton	2.00
9	Shareef Abdur-Rahim	3.00
10	Shawn Kemp	3.00
11	Stephon Marbury	5.00
12	Vin Baker	2.00
13	Ray Allen	1.00
14	Glen Rice	1.00
15	Dikembe Mutombo	1.00
16	Shaquille O'Neal	5.00
17	Kobe Bryant	10.00
18	Scottie Pippen	3.00
19	Keith Van Horn	5.00
20	David Robinson	2.00

1998-99 Stadium Club Triumvirate Luminous

Triumvirates was a 48-card insert set that was issued in both series, with 24 cards in each. These cards featured Finest technology and included eight different three-card or player panels that had some common link and fit together with die-cut edges. Series I linked three players from the same team, while Series II linked three players that play that same position. Cards were available in three different versions, with Luminous versions seeded 1:24 packs, Luminescent versions seeded 1:96 packs and Illuminators seeded 1:192 packs. Triumvirates were a hobby exclusive insert in both Series I and II.

		MT
	Complete Set (48):	250.00
	Complete Series 1 (24):	100.00
	Complete Series 2 (24):	150.00
	Common Player:	2.00
	Inserted 1:24 Series 1/2 Hobby	
	Luminescent Cards:	2x
	Inserted 1:96 Series 1/2 Hobby	
	Illuminator Cards:	3x
	Inserted 1:192 Series 1/2 Hobby	
1A	Kenny Anderson	2.00
1B	Antoine Walker	10.00
1C	Ron Mercer	8.00
2A	Kobe Bryant	20.00
2B	Shaquille O'Neal	10.00
2C	Eddie Jones	6.00
3A	Stephon Marbury	10.00
3B	Kevin Garnett	15.00
3C	Tom Gugliotta	4.00
4A	Jayson Williams	2.00
4B	Keith Van Horn	10.00
4C	Kerry Kittles	2.00
4A	Kevin Johnson	2.00
5B	Antonio McDyess	4.00
5C	Jason Kidd	6.00
6A	Avery Johnson	2.00
6B	David Robinson	6.00
6C	Tim Duncan	15.00
7A	Vin Baker	6.00
7B	Gary Payton	6.00
7C	Detlef Schrempf	2.00
8A	John Stockton	4.00
8B	Karl Malone	6.00
8C	Jeff Hornacek	2.00
9A	Shaquille O'Neal	10.00
9B	David Robinson	4.00
9C	Hakeem Olajuwon	5.00
10A	Dikembe Mutombo	2.00
10B	Alonzo Mourning	3.00
10C	Patrick Ewing	3.00
11A	Tim Duncan	15.00
11B	Kevin Garnett	15.00
11C	Shareef Abdur-Rahim	6.00
12A	Shawn Kemp	6.00
12B	Grant Hill	15.00
12C	Antoine Walker	10.00
13A	Kobe Bryant	20.00
13B	Gary Payton	4.00
13C	Stephon Marbury	10.00
14A	Ray Allen	3.00
14B	Allen Iverson	10.00
14C	Anfernee Hardaway	10.00
15A	Antawn Jamison	8.00
15B	Michael Olowokandi	8.00
15C	Raef LaFrentz	6.00
16A	Robert Traylor	6.00
16B	Larry Hughes	6.00
16C	Vince Carter	15.00

1998-99 Stadium Club Wingmen

Wingmen was a 20-card insert exclusive to Series II packs. Cards were numbered with a "W" prefix and inserted 1:8 packs.

		MT
	Complete Set (20):	60.00
	Common Player:	1.00
	Inserted 1:8 Series 2	
1	Kobe Bryant	10.00
2	Tim Duncan	8.00
3	Michael Finley	1.00
4	Kevin Garnett	8.00
5	Shawn Kemp	3.00
6	Grant Hill	8.00
7	Eddie Jones	2.00
8	Tim Thomas	3.00
9	Vin Baker	2.00
10	Antoine Walker	5.00
11	Steve Smith	1.00
12	Glen Rice	1.00
13	Ron Mercer	5.00
14	Allen Iverson	5.00
15	Ray Allen	1.00
16	Glenn Robinson	1.00
17	Kerry Kittles	1.00
18	Vince Carter	10.00
19	Larry Hughes	4.00
20	Paul Pierce	6.00

1998-99 Topps Series II

This 220-card set was released in two, 110-card series. Base cards featured the player with a gold border around the entire photo which included the team logo and player's name. Inserts in Series I include: Emmissaries, Roundball Royalty, Cornerstones, Autographs, Rookie Redemptions, Apparitions and Season's Best. Inserts in Series II include: Autographs, Kick Start, Gold Label, East/West, Legacies, Classic Collection, Topps Chrome and Coast to Coast.

		MT
	Complete Set (220):	35.00
	Complete Series 1 (110):	10.00
	Complete Series 2 (110):	25.00
	Common Player:	.10
	Series 1 Wax Box:	25.00
	Series 2 Wax Box:	40.00
111	Steve Smith	.20
112	Cedric Henderson	.10
113	*Raef Lafrentz*	2.50
114	Calbert Cheaney	.10
115	Rik Smits	.10
116	Rony Seikaly	.10
117	Lawrence Funderburke	.10
118	*Ricky Davis*	.75
119	Howard Eisley	.10
120	Kenny Anderson	.20
121	*Corey Benjamin*	.50
122	Maurice Taylor	.30
123	Eric Murdock	.10
124	Derek Fisher	.20
125	Kevin Garnett	1.50
126	Walt Williams	.10
127	*Bryce Drew*	.75
128	A.C. Green	.10
129	Ervin Johnson	.10
130	Christian Laettner	.10
131	Chauncey Billups	.10
132	Hakeem Olajuwon	.40
133	*Al Harrington*	.75
134	Danny Manning	.10
135	*Paul Pierce*	5.00
136	Terrell Brandon	.20
137	Bob Sura	.10
138	Chris Gatling	.10
139	Donyell Marshall	.10
140	Marcus Camby	.20
141	*Brian Skinner*	.50
142	Charles Oakley	.10
143	*Antawn Jamison*	3.00
144	*Nazr Mohammed*	.50
145	Karl Malone	.30
146	Chris Mills	.10
147	Bison Dele	.10
148	Gary Payton	.30

149 Terry Porter .10
150 Tim Hardaway .20
151 *Larry Hughes* 2.50
152 Derek Anderson .20
153 *Jason Williams* 5.00
154 *Dirk Nowitzki* 2.00
155 Juwan Howard .20
156 Avery Johnson .10
157 *Matt Harpring* 1.50
158 Reggie Miller .20
159 Walter McCarty .10
160 Allen Iverson 1.00
161 *Felipe Lopez* 1.50
162 Tracy McGrady .75
163 Damon Stoudamire .20
164 Antonio McDyess .20
165 Grant Hill 1.50
166 *Tyrron Lue* .30
167 P.J. Brown .10
168 Antonio Daniels .10
169 Mitch Richmond .20
170 David Robinson .40
171 Shawn Bradley .10
172 Shandon Anderson .10
173 Chris Childs .10
174 Shawn Kemp .60
175 Shaquille O'Neal 1.00
176 John Starks .10
177 Tyrone Hill .10
178 Jayson Williams .10
179 Anfernee Hardaway 1.00
180 Chris Webber .50
181 Don Reid .10
182 Stacey Augmon .10
183 Hersey Hawkins .10
184 Sam Mitchell .10
185 Jason Kidd .50
186 Nick Van Exel .20
187 Larry Johnson .20
188 Bryant Reeves .10
189 Glen Rice .20
190 Kerry Kittles .20
191 Toni Kukoc .20
192 Ron Harper .10
193 Bryon Russell .10
194 *Vladimir Stepania* .30
195 *Michael Olowokandi* 3.00
196 *Mike Bibby* 3.00
197 Dale Ellis .10
198 Muggsy Bogues .10
199 *Vince Carter* 5.00
200 *Robert Traylor* 2.00
201 *Predrag Stojakovic* 1.00
202 Aaron McKie .10
203 Hubert Davis .10
204 Dana Barros .10
205 *Bonzi Wells* .50
206 *Michael Doleac* 1.00
207 *Keon Clark* 1.00
208 *Michael Dickerson* 1.50
209 Nick Anderson .10
210 Brent Price .10
211 Cherokee Parks .10
212 *Sam Jacobson* .50
213 *Pat Garrity* .50
214 Tyrone Corbin .10
215 David Wesley .10
216 Rodney Rogers .10
217 Dean Garrett .10
218 *Roshown McLeod* .50
219 Dale Davis .10
220 Checklist 111-220 .10

1998-99 Topps Series II Autographs

This 16-card hobby exclusive insert features 18 cards each autographed and featuring the Topps "Certified Autograph Issue" stamp. Cards were numbered with an "AG" prefix, with cards 1-8 inserted 1:329 Series I packs and cards 9-18 inserted 1:378 packs of Series II.

MT
Complete Set (18): 1150.
Complete Series 1 (8): 500.00
Complete Series 2 (10): 650.00
Common Player: 25.00
Inserted 1:329 Series 1 Hobby
Inserted 1:378 Series 2 Hobby
9 Kobe Bryant 200.00
10 Ron Mercer 60.00
11 Glen Rice 25.00
12 Stephon Marbury 60.00
13 Kerry Kittles 25.00
14 Michael Olowokandi 50.00
15 Antawn Jamison 60.00
16 Mike Bibby 80.00
17 Robert Traylor 40.00
18 Paul Pierce 125.00

1998-99 Topps Series II Chrome Preview

This 10-card insert was found in Series II packs and previewed the upcoming release of Topps Chrome. Regular versions were seeded 1:36 packs, while Refractors were exclusive to Hobby Collector Packs at a rate of 1:40.

MT
Complete Set (10): 75.00
Common Player: 3.00
Inserted 1:36 Series 2
Refractor Cards: 2x-5x
Inserted 1:40 Series 2 HCP
6 Chris Mullin 6.00
10 Jerry Stackhouse 6.00
19 Detlef Schrempf 3.00
40 Patrick Ewing 6.00
43 Joe Dumars 6.00
60 Isaiah Rider 6.00
73 John Stockton 6.00
77 Michael Jordan 50.00
81 Michael Finley 8.00
100 Sean Elliot 3.00

1998-99 Topps Series II Classic Collection

This Series II insert contained 10 legends of the NBA. Cards featured the player in a framed image as well as an action shot on the front. Classic Collection cards were inserted 1:12 packs of Series II and are numbered with a "CL" prefix.

MT
Complete Set (10): 15.00
Common Player: .50
Inserted 1:12 Series 2
1 Larry Bird 5.00
2 Magic Johnson 5.00
3 Kareem Abdul-Jabbar 3.00
4 Julius Erving 2.00
5 Bill Russell 3.00
6 Wilt Chamberlain 3.00
7 Oscar Robertson 1.00
8 Jerry West 1.00
9 Elgin Baylor .50
10 Bob Cousy .50

1998-99 Topps Series II Coast to Coast

This 15-card insert featured 15 top players on a silver, brushed foil front. Coast to Coast cards were inserted 1:36 Series II packs and are numbered with a "CC" prefix.

MT
Complete Set (15): 125.00
Common Player: 1.50
Inserted 1:36 Series 1 Retail
1 Kobe Bryant 20.00
2 Scottie Pippen 8.00
3 Eddie Jones 5.00
4 Grant Hill 15.00
5 Michael Jordan 40.00
6 Antoine Walker 12.00
7 Michael Finley 3.00
8 Kevin Garnett 15.00
9 Allen Iverson 12.00
10 Shawn Kemp 6.00
11 Glenn Robinson 3.00
12 Anfernee Hardaway 10.00
13 Tim Hardaway 3.00
14 Ron Mercer 12.00
15 Kerry Kittles 1.50

1998-99 Topps Series II East/West

This 20-card, double-sided insert matched up two players one from the Eastern Conference and one from the West - on a Finest card. Players were pictured in front of a brushed globe with the words "East" or "West" running up the side of that respective player's background. Regular versions were seeded 1:36 Series II packs, with Refractor versions seeded 1:144 packs. East/West inserts were numbered with an "EW" prefix.

MT
Complete Set (20): 120.00
Common Player: 1.50
Inserted 1:36 Series 2
Refractor Cards: 2x
Inserted 1:144 Series 2
1 Antoine Walker, Shareef Abdur-Rahim 12.00
2 Alonzo Mourning, Shaquille O'Neal 10.00
3 Tim Hardaway, John Stockton 3.00
4 Scottie Pippen, Kevin Garnett 15.00
5 Michael Jordan, Kobe Bryant 35.00
6 Grant Hill, Michael Finley 12.00
7 Dikembe Mutombo, Hakeem Olajuwon 1.50
8 Keith Van Horn, Tim Duncan 18.00
9 Allen Iverson, Gary Payton 10.00
10 Patrick Ewing, David Robinson 3.00
11 Juwan Howard, Chris Webber 3.00
12 Brevin Knight, Stephon Marbury 8.00
13 Shawn Kemp, Vin Baker 6.00
14 Anthony Mason, Tom Gugliotta 1.50
15 Anfernee Hardaway, Damon Stoudamire 10.00
16 Ron Mercer, Eddie Jones 10.00
17 Rod Strickland, Jason Kidd 5.00
18 Tim Thomas, Antonio McDyess 6.00
19 Jayson Williams, Karl Malone 3.00
20 Reggie Miller, Jim Jackson 1.50

1998-99 Topps Series II Gold Label

This 10-card insert borrowed Topps' Gold Label brand and used it as an insert in Series II basketball. Regular versions were seeded 1:12 packs, while Black Label versions were seeded 1:96 packs and Red Label versions were numbered to 100 and inserted 1:4,967 packs. Gold Label inserts were numbered with a "GL" prefix.

MT
Complete Set (10): 45.00
Common Player: 1.00
Inserted 1:12 Series 2
Black Label Cards: 2x-3x
Inserted 1:96 Series 2
Red Label Cards: 8x-16x
Production 100 Series 2 Sets
1 Michael Jordan 15.00
2 Shaquille O'Neal 5.00
3 Kobe Bryant 10.00
4 Antoine Walker 5.00
5 Charles Barkley 1.00
6 Keith Van Horn 7.00
7 Tim Duncan 8.00
8 Stephon Marbury 5.00
9 Shareef Abdur-Rahim 3.00
10 Gary Payton 1.00

1998-99 Topps Series II Kick Start

Kick Start was a 15-card insert that focused on young players, and pictured them over a silver holographic background. Cards were numbered with a "KS" prefix and inserted 1:12 packs.

MT
Complete Set (15): 50.00
Common Player: 1.00
Inserted 1:12 Series 2
1 Tim Duncan 6.00
2 Kobe Bryant 8.00
3 Antoine Walker 4.00
4 Stephon Marbury 4.00
5 Allen Iverson 4.00
6 Shareef Abdur-Rahim 3.00
7 Keith Van Horn 5.00
8 Ray Allen 2.00
9 Vince Carter 6.00
10 Kevin Garnett 6.00
11 Kerry Kittles 1.00
12 Tim Thomas 3.00
13 Ron Mercer 4.00
14 Antawn Jamison 4.00
15 Mike Bibby 5.00

1998-99 Topps Legacies Series II

Legacies was a 15-card, hobby-only insert that was seeded 1:36 packs. Cards were numbered with an "L" prefix and featured the player over a silver holographic background that included a basketball and net.

MT
Complete Set (15): 70.00
Common Player: 1.50
Inserted 1:36 Series 2
1 Scottie Pippen 8.00
2 Grant Hill 15.00
3 Hakeem Olajuwon 4.00
4 Alonzo Mourning 3.00
5 Shaquille O'Neal 10.00
6 Shawn Kemp 6.00
7 Gary Payton 4.00
8 Karl Malone 3.00
9 Patrick Ewing 3.00
10 Tim Hardaway 3.00
11 Reggie Miller 3.00
12 Glen Rice 3.00
13 Dikembe Mutombo 1.50
14 John Stockton 3.00
15 Michael Jordan 30.00

1998-99 Topps Chrome

This 220-card set paralleled the regular-issue Topps Series I and II set, but added a chromium finish and a "Topps Chrome" logo to each card. Although the cards are numbered up to 235, there are only 220 cards in the set. The reason for this is that the 10 cards in a Chrome Preview insert included in Topps II are not in this set, and five players (#75 Mark Price, #89 Kevin Johnson, #90 Mahmoud Abdul-Rauf, #97 Buck Williams and #99 Nate McMillan) were not currently in the NBA and were not printed in Topps Chrome. In addition to a parallel Refractor set (1:12 packs), there are six different inserts in Topps Chrome.

	MT
Complete Set (220):	375.00
Common Player:	.25
The following cards do not exist: 75/89/90/97/99	
The following cards are in Preview: 6/10/19/40/43/60/73/77/81/100	
Wax Box:	110.00

1	Scottie Pippen	3.00
2	Shareef Abdur-Rahim	3.00
3	Rod Strickland	.50
4	Keith Van Horn	5.00
5	Ray Allen	.75
6	Anthony Parker	.25
7	Lindsey Hunter	.25
8	Mario Elie	.25
9	Eldridge Recasner	.25
10	Jeff Hornacek	.25
11	Chris Webber	3.00
12	Lee Mayberry	.25
13	Erick Strickland	.25
14	Arvydas Sabonis	.50
15	Tim Thomas	3.00
16	Luc Longley	.25
17	Alonzo Mourning	.75
18	Adonal Foyle	.25
19	Tony Battie	.50
20	Robert Horry	.25
21	Derek Harper	.25
22	Jamal Mashburn	.50
23	Elliot Perry	.25
24	Jalen Rose	.25
25	Joe Smith	.50
26	Henry James	.25
27	Travis Knight	.25
28	Tom Gugliotta	.50
29	Chris Anstey	.25
30	Antonio Daniels	.50
31	Elden Campbell	.25
32	Charlie Ward	.25
33	Eddie Johnson	.25
34	John Wallace	.25
35	Antonio Davis	.25
36	Antoine Walker	5.00
37	Doug Christie	.25
38	Andrew Lang	.25
39	Jaren Jackson	.25
40	Loy Vaught	.25
41	Allan Houston	.50
42	Mark Jackson	.25
43	Tracy Murray	.25
44	Tim Duncan	7.00
45	Micheal Williams	.25
46	Steve Nash	.50
47	Matt Maloney	.25
48	Sam Cassell	.25
49	Voshon Lenard	.25
50	Dikembe Mutombo	.50
51	Malik Sealy	.25
52	Dell Curry	.25
53	Stephon Marbury	5.00
54	Tariq Abdul-Wahad	.25
55	Kelvin Cato	.25
56	LaPhonso Ellis	.50
57	Jim Jackson	.25
58	Greg Ostertag	.25
59	Glenn Robinson	.50
60	Chris Carr	.25
61	Marcus Camby	.75
62	Kobe Bryant	10.00
63	Bobby Jackson	.25
64	B.J. Armstrong	.25
65	Alan Henderson	.25
66	Terry Davis	.25
67	Lamond Murray	.25
68	Rex Chapman	.25
69	Terry Cummings	.25
70	Dan Majerle	.25
71	Charles Outlaw	.25
72	Vin Baker	.25
73	Clifford Robinson	.25
74	Greg Anthony	.25
75	Brevin Knight	.50
76	Jacque Vaughn	.25
77	Bobby Phills	.25
78	Sherman Douglas	.25
79	Lorenzen Wright	.25
80	Eric Williams	.25
81	Will Perdue	.25
82	Charles Barkley	1.00
83	Kendall Gill	.25
84	Wesley Person	.25
85	Erick Dampier	.25
86	Rasheed Wallace	.50
87	Zydrunas Ilgauskas	.50
88	Eddie Jones	1.00
89	Ron Mercer	3.00
90	Horace Grant	.25
91	Corliss Williamson	.25
92	Anthony Mason	.25
93	Mookie Blaylock	.25
94	Dennis Rodman	3.00
95	Checklist	.25
96	Steve Smith	.50
97	Cedric Henderson	.25
98	*Raef LaFrentz*	15.00
99	Calbert Cheaney	.25
100	Rik Smits	.25
101	Rony Seikaly	.25
102	Lawrence Funderburke	.25
103	*Ricky Davis*	6.00
104	Howard Eisley	.25
105	Kenny Anderson	.50
106	*Corey Benjamin*	3.00
107	Maurice Taylor	.75
108	Eric Murdock	.25
109	Derek Fisher	.50
110	Kevin Garnett	7.00
111	Walt Williams	.25
112	*Bryce Drew*	3.00
113	A.C. Green	.25
114	Ervin Johnson	.25
115	Christian Laettner	.50
116	Chauncey Billups	.75
117	Hakeem Olajuwon	2.00
118	*Al Harrington*	10.00
119	Danny Manning	.25
120	*Paul Pierce*	40.00
121	Terrell Brandon	.50
122	Bob Sura	.25
123	Chris Gatling	.25
124	Donyell Marshall	.25
125	Marcus Camby	.75
126	*Brian Skinner*	2.00
127	Charles Oakley	.25
128	*Antawn Jamison*	30.00
129	*Nazr Mohammed*	2.00
130	Karl Malone	2.00
131	Chris Mills	.25
132	Bison Dele	.25
133	Gary Payton	2.00
134	Terry Porter	.25
135	Tim Hardaway	1.00
136	*Larry Hughes*	25.00
137	Derek Anderson	.50
138	*Jason Williams*	50.00
139	*Dirk Nowitzki*	6.00
140	Juwan Howard	.50
141	Avery Johnson	.25
142	*Matt Harpring*	8.00
143	Reggie Miller	.50
144	Walter McCarty	.25
145	Allen Iverson	5.00
146	*Felipe Lopez*	8.00
147	Tracy McGrady	3.00
148	Damon Stoudamire	1.00
149	Antonio McDyess	1.00
150	Grant Hill	7.00
151	*Tyronn Lue*	4.00
152	P.J. Brown	.25
153	Antonio Daniels	.50
154	Mitch Richmond	.50
155	David Robinson	2.00
156	Shawn Bradley	.25
157	Shandon Anderson	.25
158	Chris Childs	.25
159	Shawn Kemp	3.00
160	Shaquille O'Neal	5.00
161	John Starks	.25
162	Tyrone Hill	.25
163	Jayson Williams	.50
164	Anfernee Hardaway	5.00
165	Chris Webber	3.00
166	Don Reid	.25
167	Stacey Augmon	.25
168	Hersey Hawkins	.25
169	Sam Mitchell	.25
170	Jason Kidd	3.00
171	Nick Van Exel	.50
172	Larry Johnson	.50
173	Bryant Reeves	.25
174	Glen Rice	.50
175	Kerry Kittles	.50
176	Toni Kukoc	.50
177	Ron Harper	.25
178	Bryon Russell	.25
179	*Vladimir Stepania*	2.00
180	*Michael Olowokandi*	15.00
181	*Mike Bibby*	25.00
182	Dale Ellis	.25
183	Muggsy Bogues	.25
184	*Vince Carter*	100.00
185	*Robert Traylor*	15.00
186	*Predrag Stojakovic*	3.00
187	Aaron McKie	.25
188	Hubert Davis	.25
189	Dana Barros	.25
190	*Bonzi Wells*	3.00
191	*Michael Doleac*	6.00
192	*Keon Clark*	6.00
193	*Michael Dickerson*	15.00
194	Nick Anderson	.50
195	Brent Price	.25
196	Cherokee Parks	.25
197	*Sam Jacobson*	2.00
198	*Pat Garrity*	3.00
199	Tyrone Corbin	.25
200	David Wesley	.25
201	Rodney Rogers	.25
202	Dean Garrett	.25
203	*Roshown McLeod*	3.00
204	Dale Davis	.25
205	Checklist	.25
206	Scottie Pippen (Movin' On)	1.00
207	Antonio McDyess (Movin' On)	.50
208	Stephon Marbury (Movin' On)	2.00
209	Tom Gugliotta (Movin' On)	.25
210	Chris Webber (Movin' On)	1.00
211	Latrell Sprewell (Movin' On)	.25
212	Mitch Richmond (Movin' On)	.25
213	Joe Smith (Movin' On)	.50
214	John Starks (Movin' On)	.25
215	Charles Oakley (Movin' On)	.25
216	Dennis Rodman (Movin' On)	1.00
217	Eddie Jones (Movin' On)	.50
218	Nick Van Exel (Movin' On)	.25
219	Bobby Jackson (Movin' On)	.25
220	Glen Rice (Movin' On)	.25

1998-99 Topps Chrome Refractors

This 220-card parallel set reprinted every card from Topps Chrome in a Refractor version. These were seeded 1:12 packs and included the word "Refractor" in the white strip on the back that contained the team name.

	MT
Refractor Stars:	7x-14x
Refractor Rookies:	2x-4x
The following cards do not exist: 75/89/90/97/99	
The following cards are in Preview: 6/10/19/40/43/60/73/77/81/100	

1998-99 Topps Chrome Apparitions

Apparitions was a 14-card insert that was initially a retail-only Topps Series I insert, but was inserted 1:24 packs of Chrome. The set originally consisted of 15 players, however card #15, which was Michael Jordan, was not included in Chrome due to his retirement. Refractor versions were also printed and were sequentially numbered to 100 sets and inserted 1:1,105 packs. Cards were numbered with an "A" prefix.

		MT
Complete Set (14):		100.00
Common Player:		1.00
Inserted 1:24		
1	Kobe Bryant	15.00
2	Stephon Marbury	6.00
3	Brent Barry	1.00
4	Karl Malone	3.00
5	Shaquille O'Neal	8.00
6	Chris Webber	5.00
7	Shawn Kemp	4.00
8	Hakeem Olajuwon	3.00
9	Anfernee Hardaway	8.00
10	Michael Finley	2.00
11	Keith Van Horn	8.00
12	Kevin Garnett	12.00
13	Vin Baker	2.00
14	Tim Duncan	12.00

1998-99 Topps Chrome Apparitions Refractors

This 14-card parallel set reprinted each card from the Apparitions insert in a Refractor version. Cards were sequentially numbered to 100 sets and seeded 1:1,015 packs.

		MT
Refractors:		3x-6x
Inserted 1:1,015		
Production 100 Sets		
1	Kobe Bryant	90.00
2	Stephon Marbury	35.00
3	Brent Barry	5.00
4	Karl Malone	20.00
5	Shaquille O'Neal	50.00
6	Chris Webber	30.00
7	Shawn Kemp	25.00
8	Hakeem Olajuwon	20.00
9	Anfernee Hardaway	50.00
10	Michael Finley	15.00
11	Keith Van Horn	50.00
12	Kevin Garnett	75.00
13	Vin Baker	15.00
14	Tim Duncan	75.00

1998-99 Topps Chrome Back 2 Back

This seven-card insert was new for Chrome and inserted 1:12 packs. The insert name was printed in large letters across the top of the silver card, while backs were numbered with a "B" prefix.

		MT
Complete Set (7):		35.00
Common Player:		1.00
Inserted 1:12		
1	Michael Jordan	20.00
2	Scottie Pippen	5.00
3	Dennis Rodman	5.00
4	Hakeem Olajuwon	3.00
5	John Stockton	1.00
6	Dikembe Mutombo	1.00
7	Grant Hill	10.00

1998-99 Topps Chrome Championship Spirit

Championship Spirit was created specifically for Chrome and included seven players who have won championships, either on a collegiate or professional level. Cards were inserted 1:12 packs and numbered with a "CS" prefix.

		MT
Complete Set (7):		35.00
Common Player:		2.00
Inserted 1:12		
1	Michael Jordan	20.00
2	Hakeem Olajuwon	4.00
3	Ron Mercer	5.00
4	Mike Bibby	6.00
5	Michael Dickerson	5.00
6	Patrick Ewing	2.00
7	Scottie Pippen	5.00

1998-99 Topps Chrome Coast to Coast

This 15-card insert set featured players who excel on both ends of the court. Regular versions were seeded 1:24 packs, with Refractors seeded every 96 packs. Coast to Coast inserts were originally found in retail packs of Topps II, and were numbered with a "CC" prefix.

		MT
Complete Set (15):		100.00
Common Player:		1.50
Inserted 1:24		
Refractors:		3x
Inserted 1:96		
1	Kobe Bryant	20.00
2	Scottie Pippen	8.00
3	Eddie Jones	4.00
4	Grant Hill	15.00
5	Jason Kidd	8.00
6	Antoine Walker	12.00
7	Michael Finley	1.50
8	Kevin Garnett	1.50
9	Allen Iverson	1.50
10	Shawn Kemp	6.00
11	Glenn Robinson	1.50
12	Anfernee Hardaway	10.00
13	Tim Hardaway	3.00
14	Ron Mercer	8.00
15	Kerry Kittles	1.50

1998-99 Topps Chrome Instant Impact

Instant Impact was created specifically for Topps Chrome and featured 10 young players who have made a difference on their respective teams. Regular versions were seeded 1:36 packs, while Refractors were seeded 1:144 packs. Instant Impact cards were numbered with an "I" prefix.

		MT
Complete Set (10):		100.00
Common Player:		2.00
Inserted 1:36		
Refractors:		3x
Inserted 1:144		
1	Tim Duncan	20.00
2	Keith Van Horn	15.00
3	Stephon Marbury	15.00
4	Hakeem Olajuwon	2.00
5	Shaquille O'Neal	10.00
6	Michael Olowokandi	5.00
7	Raef LaFrentz	5.00
8	Vince Carter	25.00
9	Jason Williams	15.00
10	Paul Pierce	12.00

1998-99 Topps Chrome Season's Best

This 29-card set was reprinted from Topps I, and showcase five top players at each position, plus five top rookies from the 1997-98 season. The original set from Topps had 30 cards, but the Chrome version had 29 since Michael Jordan wasn't able to be used. Regular versions were seeded 1:6 packs, while Refractor versions were seeded every 24 packs. Cards were numbered with an "SB" prefix.

		MT
Complete Set (30):		85.00
Common Player:		1.00
Inserted 1:6		
Refractors:		3x
Inserted 1:24		
1	Rod Strickland	1.00
2	Gary Payton	3.00
3	Tim Hardaway	2.00
4	Stephon Marbury	8.00
5	Sam Cassell	1.00
7	Mitch Richmond	1.50
8	Steve Smith	1.50
9	Ray Allen	1.50
10	Isaiah Rider	1.00
11	Grant Hill	12.00
12	Kevin Garnett	12.00
13	Shareef Abdur-Rahim	5.00
14	Glenn Robinson	1.50
15	Michael Finley	1.50
16	Karl Malone	3.00
17	Tim Duncan	12.00
18	Antoine Walker	8.00
19	Chris Webber	5.00
20	Vin Baker	2.00
21	Shaquille O'Neal	6.00
22	David Robinson	3.00
23	Alonzo Mourning	1.50
24	Dikembe Mutombo	1.00
25	Hakeem Olajuwon	3.00
26	Tim Duncan	12.00
27	Keith Van Horn	8.00
28	Zydrunas Ilgauskas	1.50
29	Brevin Knight	1.50
30	Bobby Jackson	1.00

1998-99 Ultra

Ultra arrived in a 125-card, single series set in 1998-99. The product was delayed for several months until the NBA lockout ended, and due to lack of photography, didn't include Kings rookie Jason Williams in the 25-card Rookies subset, which was seeded 1:4 packs. Cards featured a borderless, full-color shot of the player with his name, team and position written in script in the bottom center. There were three hobby-only parallel sets in Ultra: Gold Medallions were one per pack, Platinum Medallions had the first 100 cards numbered to 99 and the Rookies numbered to 66 sets and Masterpieces were numbered one-of-one. Inserts included: NBAttitude, Give and Take, World Premiere, Unstoppable, Leading Performers and Exclamation Points.

		MT
Complete Set (125):		200.00
Common Player:		.15
Common Rookie:		2.00
Inserted 1:4		
Wax Box:		75.00
1	Keith Van Horn	2.00
2	Antonio Daniels	.15
3	Patrick Ewing	.30
4	Alonzo Mourning	.30
5	Isaac Austin	.15
6	Bryant Reeves	.15
7	Dennis Scott	.15
8	Damon Stoudamire	.50
9	Kenny Anderson	.15
10	Mookie Blaylock	.15
11	Mitch Richmond	.30
12	Jalen Rose	.15
13	Vin Baker	.75
14	Donyell Marshall	.15
15	Bryon Russell	.15
16	Rasheed Wallace	.15
17	Allan Houston	.30
18	Shawn Kemp	1.00
19	Nick Van Exel	.30
20	Theo Ratliff	.15
21	Jayson Williams	.15
22	Chauncey Billups	.50
23	Brent Barry	.15
24	David Wesley	.15
25	Joe Dumars	.30
26	Marcus Camby	.30
27	Juwan Howard	.30
28	Brevin Knight	.50
29	Reggie Miller	.30
30	Ray Allen	.50
31	Michael Finley	.30
32	Tom Gugliotta	.30
33	Allen Iverson	1.25
34	Toni Kukoc	.30
35	Tim Thomas	1.00
36	Jeff Hornacek	.15
37	Bobby Jackson	.15
38	Bo Outlaw	.15
39	Steve Smith	.30
40	Terrell Brandon	.30
41	Glen Rice	.30
42	Rik Smits	.15
43	Calbert Cheaney	.15
44	Stephon Marbury	1.50
45	Glenn Robinson	.30
46	Corliss Williamson	.15
47	Larry Johnson	.30
48	Antonio McDyess	.30
49	Detlef Schrempf	.15
50	Jerry Stackhouse	.30
51	Doug Christie	.15
52	Eddie Jones	.75
53	Karl Malone	.50
54	Anthony Mason	.15
55	Tim Duncan	2.50
56	Christian Laettner	.30
57	Isaiah Rider	.15
58	Shawn Bradley	.15
59	Jim Jackson	.15
60	Mark Jackson	.15
61	Kobe Bryant	3.00
62	Zydrunas Ilgauskas	.15
63	Ron Mercer	1.50
64	Hersey Hawkins	.15
65	John Wallace	.15
66	Avery Johnson	.15
67	Dikembe Mutombo	.30
68	Hakeem Olajuwon	.75
69	Tony Battie	.15
70	Jason Kidd	1.00
71	Latrell Sprewell	.30
72	Kevin Garnett	2.50
73	Voshon Lenard	.15
74	Gary Payton	.50
75	Cherokee Parks	.15
76	Antoine Walker	1.50
77	Anthony Johnson	.15
78	Danny Fortson	.15
79	Grant Hill	2.50
80	Dennis Rodman	1.50
81	Arvydas Sabonis	.15
82	Tracy McGrady	1.00
83	David Robinson	.50
84	Tariq Abdul-Wahad	.15
85	Michael Jordan	5.00
86	Kerry Kittles	.30
87	Maurice Taylor	.50
88	Cedric Ceballos	.15
89	Anfernee Hardaway	1.50
90	John Stockton	.30
91	Shareef Abdur-Rahim	.75
92	Tim Hardaway	.50
93	Shaquille O'Neal	1.50
94	Rodney Rogers	.15
95	Derek Anderson	.50
96	Kendall Gill	.15
97	Rod Strickland	.30
98	Charles Barkley	.50
99	Chris Webber	.75
100	Scottie Pippen	1.25
101	*Raef LaFrentz*	12.00
102	*Ricky Davis*	5.00
103	*Robert Traylor*	12.00
104	*Roshown McLeod*	2.00
105	*Tyronn Lue*	2.00
106	*Vince Carter*	40.00
107	*Miles Simon*	2.00
108	*Paul Pierce*	30.00
109	*Pat Garrity*	2.00
110	*Nazr Mohammed*	5.00
111	*Mike Bibby*	20.00
112	*Michael Dickerson*	12.00
113	*Michael Doleac*	7.00
114	*Matt Harpring*	7.00
115	*Larry Hughes*	20.00
116	*Keon Clark*	7.00
117	*Felipe Lopez*	5.00
118	*Dirk Nowitzki*	6.00
119	*Corey Benjamin*	5.00
120	*Bryce Drew*	5.00
121	*Brian Skinner*	2.00
122	*Bonzi Wells*	5.00
123	*Antawn Jamison*	25.00
124	*Al Harrington*	8.00
125	*Michael Olowokandi*	12.00

1998-99 Ultra Gold Medallion

This 125-card parallel set reprinted each card from Fleer Ultra using a gold foil background. Cards were inserted one per pack and numbered with a "G" suffix.

	MT
Complete Set (125):	400.00
Gold Cards:	2x
Inserted 1:1	
Gold Rookies:	1.5x
Inserted 1:35	

1998-99 Ultra Platinum Medallion

Platinum Medallions were a 125-card parallel set to Ultra. They utilized the same front as the base cards, but added a platinum finish to the entire card. The first 100 cards were sequentially numbered to 99 sets, while the 25-card Rookies subset was numbered to 66 sets. Platinum Medallion cards were exclusive to hobby packs.

		MT
Common Player:		10.00
Production 99 Sets		
Common Rookie:		20.00
Production 66 Sets		
1	Keith Van Horn	140.00
2	Antonio Daniels	10.00
3	Patrick Ewing	20.00
4	Alonzo Mourning	20.00
5	Isaac Austin	10.00
6	Bryant Reeves	10.00
7	Dennis Scott	10.00
8	Damon Stoudamire	35.00
9	Kenny Anderson	10.00
10	Mookie Blaylock	10.00
11	Mitch Richmond	20.00
12	Jalen Rose	10.00
13	Vin Baker	20.00
14	Donyell Marshall	10.00
15	Bryon Russell	10.00
16	Rasheed Wallace	10.00
17	Allan Houston	20.00
18	Shawn Kemp	70.00
19	Nick Van Exel	20.00
20	Theo Ratliff	10.00
21	Jayson Williams	10.00
22	Chauncey Billups	35.00
23	Brent Barry	10.00
24	David Wesley	10.00
25	Joe Dumars	20.00
26	Marcus Camby	20.00
27	Juwan Howard	20.00
28	Brevin Knight	35.00
29	Reggie Miller	20.00
30	Ray Allen	35.00
31	Michael Finley	20.00
32	Tom Gugliotta	20.00
33	Allen Iverson	90.00
34	Toni Kukoc	30.00
35	Tim Thomas	70.00
36	Jeff Hornacek	10.00
37	Bobby Jackson	10.00
38	Bo Outlaw	10.00
39	Steve Smith	20.00
40	Terrell Brandon	20.00
41	Glen Rice	20.00
42	Rik Smits	10.00
43	Calbert Cheaney	10.00
44	Stephon Marbury	100.00
45	Glenn Robinson	20.00
46	Corliss Williamson	10.00
47	Larry Johnson	20.00
48	Antonio McDyess	40.00
49	Detlef Schrempf	10.00
50	Jerry Stackhouse	20.00
51	Doug Christie	10.00
52	Eddie Jones	50.00
53	Karl Malone	35.00
54	Anthony Mason	10.00
55	Tim Duncan	175.00
56	Christian Laettner	20.00
57	Isaiah Rider	10.00
58	Shawn Bradley	10.00
59	Jim Jackson	10.00
60	Mark Jackson	10.00
61	Kobe Bryant	200.00
62	Zydrunas Ilgauskas	10.00
63	Ron Mercer	100.00
64	Hersey Hawkins	10.00
65	John Wallace	10.00
66	Avery Johnson	10.00
67	Dikembe Mutombo	20.00
68	Hakeem Olajuwon	50.00
69	Tony Battie	10.00
70	Jason Kidd	70.00
71	Latrell Sprewell	20.00
72	Kevin Garnett	175.00
73	Voshon Lenard	10.00
74	Gary Payton	35.00
75	Cherokee Parks	10.00
76	Antoine Walker	90.00
77	Anthony Johnson	10.00
78	Danny Fortson	10.00
79	Grant Hill	175.00
80	Dennis Rodman	70.00
81	Arvydas Sabonis	10.00
82	Tracy McGrady	70.00
83	David Robinson	35.00
84	Tariq Abdul-Wahad	10.00
85	Michael Jordan	350.00
86	Kerry Kittles	20.00
87	Maurice Taylor	35.00
88	Cedric Ceballos	10.00
89	Anfernee Hardaway	100.00
90	John Stockton	20.00
91	Shareef Abdur-Rahim	50.00
92	Tim Hardaway	35.00
93	Shaquille O'Neal	100.00
94	Rodney Rogers	10.00
95	Derek Anderson	35.00
96	Kendall Gill	10.00
97	Rod Strickland	20.00
98	Charles Barkley	35.00
99	Chris Webber	70.00
100	Scottie Pippen	90.00
101	*Raef LaFrentz*	70.00
102	*Ricky Davis*	25.00
103	*Robert Traylor*	60.00
104	*Roshown McLeod*	20.00
105	*Tyronn Lue*	20.00
106	*Vince Carter*	350.00
107	*Miles Simon*	10.00
108	*Paul Pierce*	200.00
109	*Pat Garrity*	20.00
110	*Nazr Mohammed*	20.00
111	*Mike Bibby*	100.00
112	*Michael Dickerson*	40.00
113	*Michael Doleac*	35.00
114	*Matt Harpring*	35.00
115	*Larry Hughes*	90.00
116	*Keon Clark*	35.00
117	*Felipe Lopez*	40.00
118	*Dirk Nowitzki*	20.00
119	*Corey Benjamin*	20.00
120	*Bryce Drew*	20.00
121	*Brian Skinner*	20.00
122	*Bonzi Wells*	25.00
123	*Antawn Jamison*	150.00
124	*Al Harrington*	40.00
125	*Michael Olowokandi*	70.00

1998-99 Ultra Exclamation Points

Exclamation Points was a 15-card insert seeded 1:288 packs. The cards featured a hardwood look on the front and included a pull-out card inside the exterior sleeve. Cards in this insert were numbered with an "EP" suffix.

		MT
Complete Set (15):		500.00
Common Player:		12.00
Inserted 1:288		
1	Vince Carter	50.00
2	Tim Duncan	50.00
3	Shawn Kemp	25.00

4	Shaquille O'Neal	35.00
5	Mike Bibby	45.00
6	Michael Jordan	100.00
7	Michael Olowokandi	40.00
8	Larry Hughes	35.00
9	Kobe Bryant	75.00
10	Kevin Garnett	50.00
11	Keith Van Horn	40.00
12	Grant Hill	50.00
13	Gary Payton	12.00
14	Antoine Walker	30.00
15	Antawn Jamison	40.00

1998-99 Ultra Leading Performers

Leading Performers was a 15-card insert in Ultra that was seeded 1:72 packs. The cards opened up like a book to reveal two additional shots of the player. The front photo was in black and white, while the insert name appeared in large black letters in a gold box across the top. Backs were numbered with an "LP" suffix.

		MT
Complete Set (15):		275.00
Common Player:		6.00
Inserted 1:72		
1	Allen Iverson	18.00
2	Anfernee Hardaway	20.00
3	Kobe Bryant	45.00
4	Michael Jordan	60.00
5	Ron Mercer	20.00
6	Stephon Marbury	20.00
7	Tim Duncan	30.00
8	Shareef Abdur-Rahim	12.00
9	Kevin Garnett	30.00
10	Grant Hill	30.00
11	Damon Stoudamire	6.00
12	Dennis Rodman	18.00
13	Keith Van Horn	25.00
14	Scottie Pippen	15.00
15	Shaquille O'Neal	20.00

1998-99 Ultra Give and Take

Give and Take was a 10-card insert that was exclusive to retail packs and inserted 1:18. These double-sided cards featured the player on offense on the front, and in a defensive pose on the back. Cards were numbered with a "GT" suffix.

		MT
Complete Set (10):		
Common Player:		1.50
Inserted 1:18 Retail		
1	Gary Payton	3.00
2	Shawn Kemp	5.00
3	Kerry Kittles	1.50
4	Ron Mercer	7.00
5	Scottie Pippen	6.00
6	Ray Allen	3.00
7	Anfernee Hardaway	8.00
8	Maurice Taylor	3.00
9	Brevin Knight	3.00
10	Karl Malone	3.00

1998-99 Ultra NBAttitude

This 20-card insert was seeded 1:6 packs of Ultra. It featured the player over a blurred background with the insert name across the middle. Cards were numbered with an "NA" suffix.

		MT
Complete Set (20):		20.00
Common Player:		.75
Inserted 1:6		
1	Allen Iverson	3.00
2	Chauncey Billups	.75
3	Keith Van Horn	5.00
4	Ray Allen	1.50
5	Shareef Abdur-Rahim	2.50
6	Stephon Marbury	4.00
7	Kerry Kittles	.75
8	Tim Thomas	1.50
9	Damon Stoudamire	1.50
10	Antoine Walker	4.00
11	Brevin Knight	1.50
12	Maurice Taylor	.75
13	Ron Mercer	3.00
14	Tim Duncan	6.00
15	Zydrunas Ilgauskas	.75
16	Michael Finley	.75
17	Bobby Jackson	.75
18	Tim Hardaway	1.50
19	David Robinson	2.00
20	Vin Baker	1.50

1998-99 Ultra Unstoppable

Unstoppable was a 15-card insert seeded 1:36 packs of Ultra. Fronts featured a metallized basketball and gave the appearance of metal held in place with bolts. Cards opened up to feature a shot of the player, while backs contained another shot and were numbered with a "US" suffix.

		MT
Complete Set (15):		150.00
Common Player:		4.00
Inserted 1:36		
1	Michael Jordan	40.00
2	Scottie Pippen	10.00
3	Grant Hill	20.00
4	Dennis Rodman	15.00
5	Stephon Marbury	15.00
6	Antoine Walker	15.00
7	Shareef Abdur-Rahim	8.00
8	Shaquille O'Neal	15.00
9	Damon Stoudamire	6.00
10	Kerry Kittles	4.00
11	Maurice Taylor	4.00
12	Kobe Bryant	30.00
13	Kevin Garnett	20.00
14	Anfernee Hardaway	15.00
15	Allen Iverson	12.00

1998-99 Ultra World Premiere

This 15-card insert was devoted to the top rookies from the 1998 NBA Draft and was seeded 1:20 packs. Cards featured a prismatic background with a globelike design and the embossed player image. World Premiere inserts were numbered with a "WP" suffix.

		MT
Complete Set (15):		85.00
Common Player:		2.00
Inserted 1:20		
1	Robert Traylor	7.00
2	Paul Pierce	20.00
3	Michael Olowokandi	12.00
4	Felipe Lopez	2.00
5	Raef LaFrentz	12.00
6	Antawn Jamison	12.00
7	Larry Hughes	10.00
8	Al Harrington	2.00
9	Pat Garrity	2.00
10	Bryce Drew	2.00
11	Michael Doleac	4.00
12	Michael Dickerson	6.00
13	Keon Clark	4.00
14	Vince Carter	20.00
15	Mike Bibby	12.00

1998-99 Upper Deck

Upper Deck Series I consisted of 175 cards, including 133 regular player cards, 30 Heart and Soul, 10 To the Net and two checklists. Later in the year, Upper Deck produced a Series II product called MJ Access, but that is listed separately. The entire 175-card set was paralleled in UD Exclusives, which were hobby-only and numbered to 100 sets, and a 1-of-1 version of UD Exclusives. Inserts included: Game Jerseys, Hobby Exclusive Game Jerseys, one MJ Autographed Game Jersey card, AeroDynamics, Intensity and Forces.

		MT
Complete Set (175):		75.00
Common Player:		.15
Common Heart & Soul:		.50
Inserted 1:4		
Common To The Net:		.50
Inserted 1:9		
Bronze Cards:		35x-70x
Bronze Heart & Soul:		10x-20x
Bronze To The Net:		10x-20x
Production 100 Sets		
Wax Box:		70.00
1	Mookie Blaylock	.15
2	Ed Gray	.15
3	Dikembe Mutombo	.30
4	Steve Smith	.15
5	Dikembe Mutombo, Steve Smith	.50
6	Kenny Anderson	.15
7	Dana Barros	.15
8	Travis Knight	.15
9	Walter McCarty	.15
10	Ron Mercer	1.50
11	Greg Minor	.15
12	Antoine Walker, Ron Mercer	3.50
13	B.J. Armstrong	.15
14	David Wesley	.15
15	Anthony Mason	.30
16	Glen Rice	.40
17	J.R. Reid	.15
18	Bobby Phills	.15
19	Glen Rice, Anthony Mason	1.00
20	Ron Harper	.15
21	Toni Kukoc	.30
22	Scottie Pippen	1.25
23	Michael Jordan	5.00
24	Dennis Rodman	1.50
25	Michael Jordan, Scottie Pippen	10.00
26	Michael Jordan, Michael Jordan	12.00
27	Shawn Kemp	1.00
28	Zydrunas Ilgauskas	.30
29	Cedric Henderson	.30
30	Vitaly Potapenko	.15
31	Derek Anderson	.50
32	Shawn Kemp, Zydrunas Ilgauskas	2.00
33	Shawn Bradley	.15
34	Khalid Reeves	.15
35	Robert Pack	.15
36	Michael Finley	.30
37	Erick Strickland	.15
38	Michael Finley, Shawn Bradley	1.00
39	Bryant Stith	.15
40	Dean Garrett	.15
41	Eric Williams	.15
42	Bobby Jackson	.30
43	Danny Fortson	.15
44	LaPhonso Ellis, Bryant Stith	.50
45	Grant Hill	2.50
46	Lindsey Hunter	.15
47	Brian Williams	.15
48	Scot Pollard	.15
49	Grant Hill, Brian Williams	5.00
50	Donyell Marshall	.15
51	Tony Delk	.15
52	Erick Dampier	.15
53	Felton Spencer	.15
54	Bimbo Coles	.15
55	Muggsy Bogues	.15
56	Donyell Marshall, Muggsy Bogues	.50
57	Charles Barkley	.50
58	Brent Price	.15
59	Hakeem Olajuwon	.75
60	Rodrick Rhodes	.15
61	Charles Barkley, Hakeem Olajuwon	1.50
62	Dale Davis	.15
63	Antonio Davis	.15
64	Chris Mullin	.15
65	Jalen Rose	.15
66	Reggie Miller	.30
67	Mark Jackson	.15
68	Reggie Miller, Mark Jackson	1.00
69	Rodney Rogers	.15
70	Lamond Murray	.15
71	Eric Piatkowski	.15
72	Lorenzen Wright	.15
73	Maurice Taylor	.50
74	Maurice Taylor, Lamond Murray	.50
75	Kobe Bryant	3.00
76	Shaquille O'Neal	1.50
77	Derek Fisher	.15
78	Elden Campbell	.15
79	Corie Blount	.15
80	Shaquille O'Neal, Kobe Bryant	7.00
81	Jamal Mashburn	.30
82	Alonzo Mourning	.30
83	Tim Hardaway	.40
84	Voshon Lenard	.15
85	Alonzo Mourning, Tim Hardaway	1.00
86	Ray Allen	.30
87	Terrell Brandon	.30
88	Elliot Perry	.15
89	Ervin Johnson	.15
90	Ray Allen, Glenn Robinson	1.00
91	Micheal Williams	.15
92	Anthony Peeler	.15
93	Chris Carr	.15
94	Kevin Garnett	2.50
95	Kevin Garnett, Stephon Marbury	5.00
96	Keith Van Horn	1.75
97	Kerry Kittles	.30
98	Kendall Gill	.15
99	Sam Cassell	.15
100	Chris Gatling	.15
101	Keith Van Horn, Sam Cassell	3.00
102	Patrick Ewing	.30
103	John Starks	.15
104	Allan Houston	.30
105	Chris Mills	.15
106	Chris Childs	.15
107	Charlie Ward	.15
108	Patrick Ewing, John Starks	1.00
109	Anfernee Hardaway	1.50
110	Horace Grant	.15
111	Nick Anderson	.15
112	Johnny Taylor	.15
113	Anfernee Hardaway, Horace Grant	3.50
114	Allen Iverson	1.25
115	Scott Williams	.15
116	Tim Thomas	1.25
117	Brian Shaw	.15
118	Anthony Parker	.15
119	Allen Iverson, Tim Thomas	2.50
120	Jason Kidd	.75
121	Rex Chapman	.15
122	Danny Manning	.15
123	Jason Kidd, Danny Manning	1.50
124	Rasheed Wallace	.15
125	Walt Williams	.15
126	Kelvin Cato	.15
127	Arvydas Sabonis	.15
128	Brian Grant	.15
129	Rasheed Wallace, Isaiah Rider	.50
130	Tariq Abdul-Wahad	.15
131	Corliss Williamson	.15
132	Olden Polynice	.15
133	Chris Robinson	.15
134	Tariq Abdul-Wahad, Olden Polynice	.50
135	Tim Duncan	2.50
136	Avery Johnson	.15
137	David Robinson	.50
138	Monty Williams	.15
139	Tim Duncan, David Robinson	5.00
140	Vin Baker	.50
141	Hersey Hawkins	.15
142	Detlef Schrempf	.15
143	Jim McIlvaine	.15
144	Gary Payton, Vin Baker	1.50
145	Chauncey Billups	.50
146	Tracy McGrady	1.00
147	John Wallace	.15
148	Doug Christie	.15
149	Dee Brown	.15
150	Tracy McGrady, Chauncey Billups	2.00
151	Karl Malone	.50
152	John Stockton	.30
153	Adam Keefe	.15
154	Howard Eisley	.15
155	Karl Malone, John Stockton	1.50
156	Bryant Reeves	.15
157	Lee Mayberry	.15
158	Michael Smith	.15
159	Shareef Abdur-Rahim, Bryant Reeves	2.00
160	Juwan Howard	.30
161	Calbert Cheaney	.15
162	Tracy Murray	.15
163	Juwan Howard, Calbert Cheaney	1.00
164	Shaquille O'Neal	3.50
165	Maurice Taylor	.50
166	Stephon Marbury	3.50
167	Tracy McGrady	2.00
168	Antoine Walker	3.50
169	Michael Jordan	10.00
170	Keith Van Horn	3.50
171	Shareef Abdur-Rahim	2.00
172	Kobe Bryant	7.00
173	Gary Payton	1.00
174	Checklist #1 Michael Jordan	2.00
175	Checklist #2 Michael Jordan	2.00

1998-99 Upper Deck AeroDynamics

This 30-card, multi-tiered insert is numbered with an "A" prefix. Regular versions are inserted 1:6 packs, while Tier 1 are numbered to 2,000, Tier

2 are numbered to 100 and Tier 3 are numbered to 25 sets.

		MT
Complete Set (30):		70.00
Common Player:		.75
Inserted 1:6		
Bronze Cards:		2x
Production 2,000 Sets		
Silver Cards:		10x-20x
Production 100 Sets		
Gold Cards:		20x-40x
Production 25 Sets		
1	Michael Jordan	15.00
2	Shawn Kemp	4.00
3	Anfernee Hardaway	5.00
4	Tracy McGrady	3.00
5	Glen Rice	1.50
6	Maurice Taylor	1.50
7	Kevin Garnett	7.50
8	Jason Kidd	2.50
9	Grant Hill	7.50
10	Kendall Gill	.75
11	Hakeem Olajuwon	2.50
12	Mookie Blaylock	.75
13	Toni Kukoc	1.50
14	Kobe Bryant	10.00
15	Corliss Williamson	.75
16	Ray Allen	1.50
17	Vin Baker	2.00
18	Reggie Miller	1.50
19	Allan Houston	.75
20	Shareef Abdur-Rahim	3.00
21	Tim Duncan	7.50
22	Michael Finley	1.50
23	Damon Stoudamire	1.50
24	Juwan Howard	1.50
25	Antoine Walker	5.00
26	Donyell Marshall	.75
27	Allen Iverson	3.50
28	Karl Malone	2.00
29	Bobby Jackson	.75
30	Tim Hardaway	1.50

1998-99 Upper Deck Forces

This 30-card, multi-tiered insert is numbered with an "F" prefix. Regular versions are inserted 1:24, while Tier 1 are numbered to 1,000, Tier 2 are numbered to 50 and Tier 3 are numbered to 25 sets.

		MT
Complete Set (30):		175.00
Common Player:		2.00
Inserted 1:24		
Bronze Cards:		2x
Production 1,000 Sets		
Silver Cards:		15x-30x
Production 50 Sets		
Gold Cards:		20x-40x
Production 25 Sets		
1	Michael Jordan	40.00
2	Shareef Abdur-Rahim	8.00
3	Shaquille O'Neal	12.00
4	Gary Payton	5.00
5	Allen Iverson	10.00
6	Allan Houston	2.00
7	LaPhonso Ellis	2.00
8	Kevin Garnett	20.00
9	Chauncey Billups	5.00
10	Tim Hardaway	4.00
11	Reggie Miller	4.00
12	Glen Rice	4.00
13	Damon Stoudamire	5.00
14	Lamond Murray	2.00
15	Shawn Kemp	8.00
16	Steve Smith	2.00
17	Tim Duncan	20.00
18	Hakeem Olajuwon	6.00
19	Karl Malone	5.00
20	Donyell Marshall	2.00
21	Anfernee Hardaway	12.00
22	Grant Hill	20.00
23	Antoine Walker	12.00
24	Toni Kukoc	4.00
25	Corliss Williamson	2.00
26	Glenn Robinson	4.00
27	Keith Van Horn	15.00
28	Jason Kidd	6.00
29	Juwan Howard	4.00
30	Michael Finley	4.00

1998-99 Upper Deck Game Jerseys

This 10-card insert featured a swatch of Game-Used Jersey from 10 different players on cards numbered GJ1-GJ10. These were inserted across both hobby and retail packs at a rate of 1:2,500.

		MT
Complete Set (10):		2500.
Common Player:		150.00
Inserted 1:2,500		
1	Glen Rice	200.00
2	Shawn Kemp	300.00
3	Reggie Miller	200.00
4	Shaquille O'Neal	400.00
5	Ray Allen	250.00
6	Keith Van Horn	500.00
7	Allen Iverson	350.00
8	David Robinson	250.00
9	Karl Malone	250.00
10	Shareef Abdur-Rahim	300.00

1998-99 Upper Deck Hobby Exclusive Game Jerseys

Hobby Exclusive Game Jersey cards were inserted 1:288 hobby packs of Upper Deck Series I. They were similar in design to the regular Game Jersey cards and numbered GJ11-GJ20.

		MT
Complete Set (10):		2500.
Common Player:		80.00
Inserted 1:288 Hobby		
11	Grant Hill	250.00
12	Hakeem Olajuwon	150.00
13	Kevin Garnett	250.00
14	Jayson Williams	80.00
15	Tim Duncan	250.00
16	Gary Payton	100.00
17	John Stockton	100.00
18	Bryant Reeves	80.00
19	Kobe Bryant	600.00
20	Michael Jordan	1600.

1998-99 Upper Deck Intensity

This 30-card, multi-tiered insert is numbered with an "I" prefix. Regular versions are inserted 1:12, while Tier 1 are numbered to 1,500, Tier 2 are numbered to 75 and Tier 3 are numbered to 25 sets.

		MT
Complete Set (30):		60.00
Common Player:		1.50
Inserted 1:12		
Bronze Cards:		2x
Production 1,500 Sets		
Silver Cards:		10x-20x
Production 75 Sets		
Gold Cards:		20x-40x
Production 25 Sets		
1	Michael Jordan	25.00
2	Tracy Murray	1.50
3	Ron Mercer	8.00
4	Terrell Brandon	3.00
5	Brevin Knight	3.00
6	Rasheed Wallace	1.50
7	Sam Cassell	1.50
8	Erick Dampier	1.50
9	LaPhonso Ellis	1.50
10	Tim Thomas	6.00
11	Anfernee Hardaway	8.00
12	Tariq Abdul-Wahad	1.50
13	Lorenzen Wright	1.50
14	Bryant Reeves	1.50
15	Charles Barkley	4.00
16	Chauncey Billups	3.00
17	John Starks	1.50
18	Jerry Stackhouse	3.00
19	Vlade Divac	1.50
20	Detlef Schrempf	1.50
21	John Stockton	3.00
22	Nick Anderson	1.50
23	Alonzo Mourning	3.00
24	Dikembe Mutombo	1.50
25	Jalen Rose	1.50
26	Robert Pack	1.50
27	Antonio McDyess	3.00
28	Eddie Jones	5.00
29	Stephon Marbury	8.00
30	David Robinson	4.00

1998-99 Upper Deck Michael Jordan Game Jersey Autographs

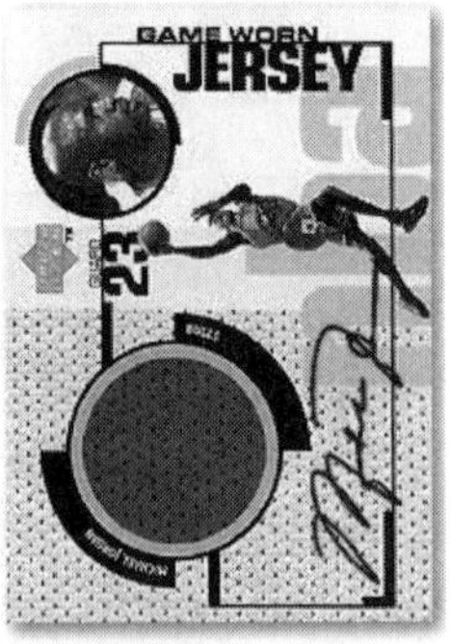

A total of 23 hand-numbered, autographed Game Jersey cards of Michael Jordan were each inserted into six different Upper Deck products throughout the 1998-99 season. The specific products are listed below.

	MT
Common Player:	11000.
Production 23 Cards	
Each Product Includes 23 Cards	
Randomly Inserted In MJ Access	
Randomly Inserted In MJ Living Legend	
Randomly Inserted In MJx	
Randomly Inserted In Ovation	
Randomly Inserted In SPx Finite 1	
Randomly Inserted In UD 1	

1998-99 Upper Deck MJ Access

This 180-card set was called MJ Access, but was actually Upper Deck Series II Basketball and is numbered 176-333. The set has 113 regular player cards and three subsets: 20 Highway 99, 22 Rookie Watch (seeded 1:4 packs) and 23 MJ regular player cards, which use the same card design but included a different photo on the front and are numbered 230a, 230b, 230c, etc. In addition, each hobby box has a two-card bonus pack of SPx Finite containing a 28-card SPx Finite Rookie Update set. These cards are numbered 211-240, and have regular cards numbered to 2,500 sets, Radiance level cards numbered to 1,500 sets and Spectrum level cards numbered to 25 sets. Cards 227 and 228 do not exist since these two rookies did not sign for the 1998-99 season. Inserts included: 23 hand-numbered Autographed Game-worn Jersey cards of Michael Jordan, 10 Rookie Jersey cards, 10 Game Jersey cards, nine hobby-only Game Jersey Exclusives, 180 Upper Deck Exclusives (parallel set with bronze cards numbered to 100 and gold versions numbered 1 of 1), 30 MJ 23, 30 Next Wave, 30 Super Powers and Quantum Parallels (parallels of MJ 23, Next Wave and Super Powers, with MJ23 Tier 1 numbered to 2,300, Tier 2 numbered to 23 and Tier 3 numbered to 1 set; Next Wave Tier 1 numbered to 1,500, Tier 2 numbered to 200 and Tier 3 numbered to 75; and Super Powers Tier 1 numbered to 1,000, Tier 2 numbered to 100 and Tier 3 numbered to 50 sets).

		MT
Complete Set (180):		250.00
Common Player:		.15
Jordan Regular Card:		4.00
Inserted 1:4		
Common Rookie:		2.00
Inserted 1:4		
Bronze Cards:		35x-70x
Bronze Jordan:		50x
Bronze Rookie:		5x
Production 100 Sets		
Wax Box:		90.00
176	Kevin Johnson	.30
177	Glenn Robinson	.30
178	Antoine Walker	1.50
179	Jerry Stackhouse	.30
180	Mark Price	.15
181	Stephon Marbury	1.50
182	Shareef Abdur-Rahim	.75
183	Wesley Person	.15
184	Keith Booth	.15
185	Sean Elliott	.15
186	Alan Henderson	.15
187	Bryon Russell	.15
188	Jermaine O'Neal	.30
189	Steve Nash	.30
190	Eldridge Recasner	.15
191	Damon Stoudamire	.50
192	Dell Curry	.15
193	Michael Stewart	.15
194	Bruce Bowen	.15
195	Steve Kerr	.15
196	Dale Ellis	.15
197	Shandon Anderson	.15
198	Larry Johnson	.30
199	Chris Webber	.75
200	Matt Geiger	.15
201	Chris Anstey	.15
202	Loy Vaught	.15
203	Aaron McKie	.15
204	A.C. Green	.15
205	Bo Outlaw	.15
206	Antonio McDyess	.50
207	Priest Lauderdale	.15
208	Greg Ostertag	.15
209	Dan Majerle	.15
210	Johnny Newman	.15
211	Tyrone Corbin	.15
212	Pervis Ellison	.15
213	Shawnelle Scott	.15
214	Travis Best	.15
215	Stacey Augmon	.15
216	Brevin Knight	.50
217	Jerome Williams	.15
218	Terry Mills	.15
219	Matt Maloney	.30
220	Dennis Scott	.15
221	John Thomas	.15
222	Nick Van Exel	.30
223	Duane Ferrell	.15
224	Chris Whitney	.15
225	Luc Longley	.15
226	Robert Horry	.15
227	Clifford Robinson	.15
228	Samaki Walker	.15
229	Derrick McKey	.15
230a	Michael Jordan	4.00
230b	Michael Jordan	4.00
230c	Michael Jordan	4.00
230d	Michael Jordan	4.00
230e	Michael Jordan	4.00
230f	Michael Jordan	4.00
230g	Michael Jordan	4.00
230h	Michael Jordan	4.00
230i	Michael Jordan	4.00
230j	Michael Jordan	4.00
230k	Michael Jordan	4.00
230l	Michael Jordan	4.00
230m	Michael Jordan	4.00
230n	Michael Jordan	4.00
230o	Michael Jordan	4.00
230p	Michael Jordan	4.00
230q	Michael Jordan	4.00
230r	Michael Jordan	4.00
230s	Michael Jordan	4.00
230t	Michael Jordan	4.00
230u	Michael Jordan	4.00
230v	Michael Jordan	4.00
230w	Michael Jordan	4.00
231	Armon Gilliam	.15
232	Andrew DeClercq	.15
233	Stojko Vrankovic	.15
234	Jayson Williams	.15
235	Vinny Del Negro	.15
236	Theo Ratliff	.30
237	Othella Harrington	.15
238	Mitch Richmond	.30
239	Vlade Divac	.30
240	Duane Causwell	.15
241	Todd Fuller	.15
242	Tom Gugliotta	.30
243	LaPhonso Ellis	.30
244	Brian Evans	.15
245	Jason Caffey	.15
246	Pooh Richardson	.15
247	George Lynch	.15
248	Bill Wennington	.15
249	Rik Smits	.15
250	Kevin Willis	.15
251	Mario Elie	.15
252	Austin Croshere	.15
253	Sharone Wright	.15
254	Danny Ferry	.15
255	Jacque Vaughn	.15
256	Adonal Foyle	.15
257	Billy Owens	.15
258	Randy Brown	.15
259	Joe Smith	.30
260	Joe Dumars	.30
261	Sean Rooks	.15
262	Eric Montross	.15
263	Hubert Davis	.15
264	Gary Payton	.50
265	Tyrone Hill	.15
266	John Crotty	.15
267	P.J. Brown	.15
268	Michael Cage	.15
269	Scott Burrell	.15
270	Marcus Camby	.30
271	Rod Strickland	.30
272	Jim Jackson	.15
273	Corey Beck	.15
274	James Robinson	.15
275	Cedric Ceballos	.15
276	Charles Oakley	.15
277	Anthony Johnson	.15
278	Bob Sura	.15
279	Isaiah Rider	.15
280	Jeff Hornacek	.15
281	Rony Seikaly	.15
282	Charles Smith	.15
283	Eddie Jones	.75
284	Lucious Harris	.15
285	Andrew Lang	.15
286	Terry Cummings	.15
287	Keith Closs	.15
288	Chris Anstey	.15
289	Clarence Weatherspoon	.15

290	Michael Jordan	2.50
291	Shawn Kemp	.50
292	Tracy McGrady	.30
293	Glen Rice	.15
294	David Robinson	.30
295	Antonio McDyess	.30
296	Vin Baker	.30
297	Juwan Howard	.15
298	Ron Mercer	.75
299	Michael Finley	.15
300	Scottie Pippen	.50
301	Tim Thomas	.30
302	Rasheed Wallace	.15
303	Alonzo Mourning	.15
304	Dikembe Mutombo	.15
305	Derek Anderson	.30
306	Ray Allen	.30
307	Patrick Ewing	.30
308	Sean Elliott	.15
309	Shaquille O'Neal	.75
310	Michael Jordan CL	1.50
311	Michael Jordan CL	1.50
312	*Michael Olowokandi*	20.00
313	*Mike Bibby*	20.00
314	*Raef LaFrentz*	15.00
315	*Antawn Jamison*	20.00
316	*Vince Carter*	40.00
317	*Robert Traylor*	15.00
318	*Jason Williams*	35.00
319	*Larry Hughes*	18.00
320	*Dirk Nowitzki*	10.00
321	*Paul Pierce*	35.00
322	*Bonzi Wells*	5.00
323	*Michael Doleac*	7.00
324	*Keon Clark*	7.00
325	*Michael Dickerson*	12.00
326	*Matt Harpring*	7.00
327	*Bryce Drew*	5.00
328	*Pat Garrity*	2.00
329	*Roshown McLeod*	2.00
330	*Ricky Davis*	5.00
331	*Predrag Stojakovic*	7.00
332	*Felipe Lopez*	7.00
333	*Al Harrington*	5.00
UDX1	Michael Jordan Extra	2.00

1998-99 Upper Deck MJ Access Game Jerseys

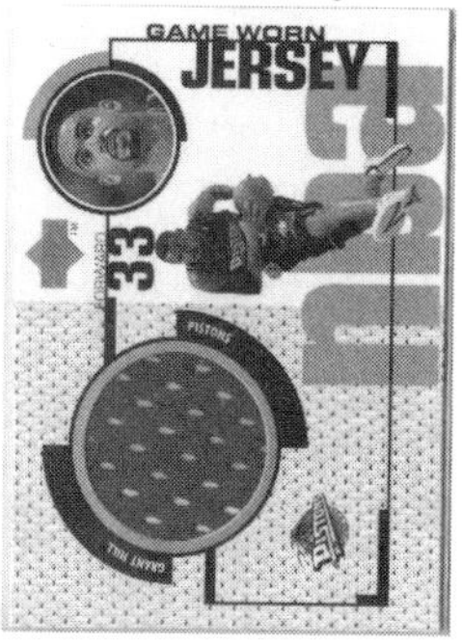

This 10-card insert was seeded 1:2,500 hobby and retail packs of MJ Access. Cards contained an actual swatch of game-worn jersey of the featured player. Game Jersey cards were numbered GJ21-GJ30.

		MT
Complete Set (10):		3000.
Common Player:		150.00
Inserted 1:2,500		
21	Kobe Bryant	1000.
22	Grant Hill	450.00
23	Anfernee Hardaway	400.00
24	Tim Thomas	150.00
25	Hakeem Olajuwon	175.00
26	Damon Stoudamire	175.00
27	Gary Payton	200.00
28	Jason Kidd	300.00
29	Reggie Miller	225.00
30	Kevin Garnett	450.00

1998-99 Upper Deck MJ Access Hobby Exclusive Game Jerseys

This nine-card insert featured game-worn jersey swatches from NBA veterans. They were exclusive to hobby packs and inserted 1:288. Hobby Exclusive Game Jerseys were inserted 1:288 packs and numbered with a "GJ" prefix. Card No. 38 does not exist; it was planned to be Charles Barkley, but was deleted.

		MT
Complete Set (9):		1400.
Common Player:		100.00
Inserted 1:288 Hobby		
#38 was never made		
31	Tim Duncan	250.00
32	Keith Van Horn	175.00
33	Stephon Marbury	175.00
34	Shaquille O'Neal	200.00
35	Allen Iverson	225.00
36	Antoine Walker	175.00
37	Karl Malone	175.00
39	Shareef Abdur-Rahim	150.00
40	David Robinson	100.00

1998-99 Upper Deck MJ Access MJ23

This 23-card set was devoted to Michael Jordan and was inserted 1:23 packs of MJ Access. Cards were numbered with an "MJ" prefix. Quantum parallel versions of each card were also available, with Bronze level cards numbered to 2,300 sets, Silver level cards were numbered to 23 sets and Gold level cards were numbered to one set.

	MT
Complete Set (30):	300.00
Common Player:	10.00
Inserted 1:23	
Bronze Cards:	2x
Production 2,300 Sets	
Silver Cards:	50x
Production 23 Sets	

1998-99 Upper Deck MJ Access Next Wave

Next Wave displayed 30 top young stars and was seeded 1:11 packs of MJ Access. Cards were numbered with an "NW" prefix. Quantum levels of this insert were also available, with Bronze level cards numbered to 1,500 sets, Silver levels numbered to 200 sets and Gold levels numbered to 75 sets.

		MT
Complete Set (30):		55.00
Common Player:		.50
Inserted 1:11		
Bronze Cards:		3x
Production 1,500 Sets		
Silver Cards:		5x-10x
Production 200 Sets		
Gold Cards:		8x-16x
Production 75 Sets		
1	Kobe Bryant	15.00
2	John Wallace	.50
3	Kerry Kittles	1.00
4	Tim Thomas	5.00
5	Maurice Taylor	2.00
6	Antonio McDyess	1.50
7	Jermaine O'Neal	1.00
8	Zydrunas Ilgauskas	1.00
9	Danny Fortson	.50
10	Tim Duncan	10.00
11	Derek Anderson	2.00
12	Ron Mercer	6.00
13	Joe Smith	1.50
14	Eddie Jones	4.00
15	Rodrick Rhodes	.50
16	Kevin Garnett	10.00
17	Ed Gray	.50
18	Bobby Jackson	1.00
19	Allan Houston	1.00
20	Chauncey Billups	2.00
21	Keith Booth	.50
22	Brevin Knight	2.00
23	Othella Harrington	.50
24	Keith Van Horn	8.00
25	Michael Finley	1.00
26	Tracy McGrady	5.00
27	Derek Fisher	.50
28	Ray Allen	1.50
29	Anthony Johnson	.50
30	Vin Baker	2.00

1998-99 Upper Deck MJ Access Rookie Game Jerseys

This 10-card insert featured swatches from jerseys used in the NBA Rookie Photo Shoot. Rookie Game Jerseys were inserted 1:2,500 packs of MJ Access and numbered GJ41-GJ50.

		MT
Complete Set (10):		2000.
Common Player:		100.00
Inserted 1:2,500		
41	Corey Benjamin	100.00
42	Mike Bibby	250.00
43	Vince Carter	600.00
44	Michael Doleac	125.00
45	Larry Hughes	250.00
46	Antawn Jamison	300.00
47	Raef LaFrentz	150.00
48	Robert Traylor	150.00
49	Bonzi Wells	100.00
50	Jason Williams	425.00

1998-99 Upper Deck MJ Access SPx Rookie

This 28-card insert was added to MJ Access since the rookies were not signed in time for the SPx Finite product. Cards from this insert were included in a special, two-card foil pack that was added as a hobby box topper. Cards were numbered 211-240, which simply added on to the SPx Finite numbering which left off at No. 210. Cards 227 and 228 of this insert do not exist since these players were unsigned for the 1998-99 season. Similar to SPx Finite, three levels of each rookie exist, with regular cards numbered to 2,500, Radiance levels numbered to 1,500 and Spectrum levels numbered to 25 sets.

		MT
Complete Set (28):		300.00
Common Player:		2.00
Production 2,500 Sets		
#227 & #228 were never made		
Radiance Cards:		2x
Production 1,500 Sets		
Spectrum Cards:		10x-20x
Production 25 Sets		
211	Michael Olowokandi	15.00
212	Mike Bibby	25.00
213	Raef LaFrentz	15.00
214	Antawn Jamison	40.00
215	Vince Carter	175.00
216	Robert Traylor	15.00
217	Jason Williams	60.00
218	Larry Hughes	30.00
219	Dirk Nowitzki	5.00
220	Paul Pierce	50.00
221	Bonzi Wells	5.00
222	Michael Doleac	5.00
223	Keon Clark	5.00
224	Michael Dickerson	10.00
225	Matt Harpring	10.00
226	Bryce Drew	5.00
229	Pat Garrity	4.00
230	Roshown McLeod	4.00
231	Ricky Davis	7.00
232	Brian Skinner	2.00
233	Tyronn Lue	4.00
234	Felipe Lopez	7.00
235	Al Harrington	10.00
236	Ruben Patterson	4.00
237	Vladimir Stepania	2.00
238	Corey Benjamin	4.00
239	Nazr Mohammed	2.00
240	Rashard Lewis	6.00

1998-99 Upper Deck MJ Access Super Powers

Super Powers was a 30-card insert that was seeded 1:5 packs of MJ Access. Cards were numbered with an "S" prefix. There were also Quantum parallel versions of Super Powers, with Bronze level cards numbered to 1,000, Silver levels numbered to 100 and Gold levels numbered to 50 sets.

		MT
Complete Set (30):		75.00
Common Player:		.50
Inserted 1:5		
Bronze Cards:		3x-6x
Production 1,000 Sets		
Silver Cards:		8x-16x
Production 100 Sets		
Gold Cards:		15x-30x
Production 50 Sets		
1	Dikembe Mutombo	.50
2	Ron Mercer	5.00
3	Glen Rice	1.00
4	Scottie Pippen	3.00
5	Shawn Kemp	3.00
6	Michael Finley	1.00
7	Bobby Jackson	.50
8	Grant Hill	8.00
9	Jim Jackson	.50
10	Hakeem Olajuwon	2.50
11	Reggie Miller	1.00
12	Maurice Taylor	1.50
13	Kobe Bryant	10.00
14	Tim Hardaway	1.50
15	Ray Allen	1.00
16	Stephon Marbury	5.00
17	Keith Van Horn	6.00
18	Allan Houston	.50
19	Anfernee Hardaway	5.00
20	Allen Iverson	4.00
21	Jason Kidd	3.00
22	Damon Stoudamire	2.00
23	Corliss Williamson	.50
24	Tim Duncan	8.00
25	Gary Payton	2.00
26	Tracy McGrady	4.00
27	Karl Malone	2.00
28	Shareef Abdur-Rahim	3.00
29	Juwan Howard	1.00
30	Michael Jordan	15.00

1998-99 Upper Deck Black Diamond

Black Diamond arrived in early April of 1999 after being cancelled initially in mid-December due to the lockout. Black Diamond arrived with 120 cards, including 90 short-printed rookies and the first 13 cards in the set featuring Michael Jordan. Upper Deck added several things to the product, including five UD Authentics autographs from top rookies and two hobby-only inserts - MJ Sheer Brilliance and MJ Extreme Brilliance. There were three parallel versions to the regular set - Double Diamond cards were all-red Light F/X with the first 90 numbered to 3,000 and the 30 rookies, called Futures, numbered to 2,500; Triple Diamonds were printed on all-gold Light F/X with veterans numbered to 1,500 and Futures numbered to 1,000; and Quadruple Diamonds printed on all-emerald Light F/X with veterans numbered to 150 and Futures numbered to 50 sets. The final insert in Black Diamond was Diamond Dominance, which had two versions with regular versions numbered to 1,000 and Emerald Edition versions numbered to 100 sets.

	MT
Complete Set (120):	200.00
Common Player:	.20
Common Rookie (91-120):	1.50
Inserted 1:4	
Wax Box:	65.00

1 Michael Jordan (1984-85) 3.00
2 Michael Jordan (1985-86) 3.00
3 Michael Jordan (1986-87) 3.00
4 Michael Jordan (1987-88) 3.00
5 Michael Jordan (1988-89) 3.00
6 Michael Jordan (1989-90) 3.00
7 Michael Jordan (1990-91) 3.00
8 Michael Jordan (1991-92) 3.00
9 Michael Jordan (1992-93) 3.00
10 Michael Jordan (1994-95) 3.00
11 Michael Jordan (1995-96) 3.00
12 Michael Jordan (1996-97) 3.00
13 Michael Jordan (1997-98) 3.00
14 Dikembe Mutombo .30
15 Steve Smith .30
16 Mookie Blaylock .20
17 Antoine Walker 1.50
18 Kenny Anderson .30
19 Ron Mercer 1.50
20 Glen Rice .30
21 Derrick Coleman .30
22 Michael Jordan 5.00
23 Toni Kukoc .30
24 Brent Barry .20
25 Brevin Knight .40
26 Derek Anderson .40
27 Shawn Kemp 1.00
28 Shawn Bradley .20
29 Michael Finley .40
30 Nick Van Exel .30
31 Chauncey Billups .40
32 Antonio McDyess .40
33 Grant Hill 2.50
34 Jerry Stackhouse .30
35 Bison Dele .20
36 John Starks .20
37 Chris Mills .20
38 Scottie Pippen 1.25
39 Hakeem Olajuwon .75
40 Charles Barkley .50
41 Antonio Davis .20
42 Reggie Miller .30
43 Mark Jackson .20
44 Eddie Jones .75
45 Shaquille O'Neal 1.50
46 Kobe Bryant 4.00
47 Rodney Rogers .20
48 Maurice Taylor .40
49 Tim Hardaway .40
50 Jamal Mashburn .30
51 Alonzo Mourning .40
52 Ray Allen .40
53 Terrell Brandon .30
54 Glenn Robinson .40
55 Joe Smith .40
56 Stephon Marbury 1.50
57 Kevin Garnett 2.50
58 Kerry Kittles .30
59 Jayson Williams .30
60 Keith Van Horn 2.00
61 Patrick Ewing .40
62 Allan Houston .30
63 Latrell Sprewell .30
64 Anfernee Hardaway 1.50
65 Horace Grant .20
66 Allen Iverson 1.50
67 Tim Thomas 1.00
68 Jason Kidd 1.00
69 Danny Manning .20
70 Tom Gugliotta .30
71 Damon Stoudamire .40
72 Rasheed Wallace .20
73 Isaiah Rider .20
74 Corliss Williamson .20
75 Chris Webber 1.00
76 Tim Duncan 2.50
77 David Robinson .50
78 Sean Elliott .20
79 Gary Payton .50
80 Vin Baker .75
81 John Wallace .20
82 Tracy McGrady 1.00
83 Jeff Hornacek .20
84 Karl Malone .50
85 John Stockton .30
86 Bryant Reeves .20
87 Shareef Abdur-Rahim 1.00
88 Rod Strickland .30
89 Juwan Howard .30
90 Mitch Richmond .30
91 *Michael Olowokandi* (Diamond Futures) 10.00
92 *Dirk Nowitzki* (Diamond Futures) 3.00
93 *Raef LaFrentz* (Diamond Futures) 10.00
94 *Mike Bibby* (Diamond Futures) 15.00
95 *Ricky Davis* (Diamond Futures) 3.00
96 *Jason Williams* (Diamond Futures) 30.00
97 *Al Harrington* (Diamond Futures) 8.00
98 *Bonzi Wells* (Diamond Futures) 3.00
99 *Keon Clark* (Diamond Futures) 3.00
100 *Rashard Lewis* (Diamond Futures) 5.00
101 *Paul Pierce* (Diamond Futures) 25.00
102 *Antawn Jamison* (Diamond Futures) 20.00
103 *Nazr Mohammed* (Diamond Futures) 1.50
104 *Brian Skinner* (Diamond Futures) 3.00
105 *Corey Benjamin* (Diamond Futures) 1.50
106 *Predrag Stojakovic* (Diamond Futures) 3.00
107 *Bryce Drew* (Diamond Futures) 3.00
108 *Matt Harpring* (Diamond Futures) 5.00
109 *Toby Bailey* (Diamond Futures) 1.50
110 *Tyronn Lue* (Diamond Futures) 3.00
111 *Michael Dickerson* (Diamond Futures) 8.00
112 *Roshown McLeod* (Diamond Futures) 3.00
113 *Felipe Lopez* (Diamond Futures) 8.00
114 *Michael Doleac* (Diamond Futures) 5.00
115 *Ruben Patterson* (Diamond Futures) 3.00
116 *Robert Traylor* (Diamond Futures) 10.00
117 *Sam Jacobson* (Diamond Futures) 1.50
118 *Larry Hughes* (Diamond Futures) 15.00
119 *Pat Garrity* (Diamond Futures) 3.00
120 *Vince Carter* (Diamond Futures) 40.00

1998-99 Upper Deck Black Diamond Double Diamond

This 120-card parallel set reprinted each card in Black Diamond, but added red foil to the card fronts. Double Diamond veterans (1-90) were sequentially numbered to 3,000 sets, while rookies (91-120) were numbered to 2,500 sets.

	MT
Complete Set (120):	300.00
Common Player:	.40
Common Rookie (91-120):	3.00
Double Diamond Cards:	2x
Production 3,000 Sets	
Double Diamond Rookies:	1.5x
Production 2,500 Sets	

1998-99 Upper Deck Black Diamond Triple Diamond

This 120-card parallel set reprinted each card in Black Diamond, but added gold foil to the card front. Triple Diamond veterans cards (1-90) were sequentially numbered to 1,500, while rookies (91-120) were numbered to 1,000 sets.

	MT
Complete Set (120):	500.00
Common Player:	.75
Common Rookie (91-120):	4.00
Triple Diamond Cards:	4x
Production 1,500 Sets	
Triple Diamond Rookies	3x
Production 1,000 Sets	

1998-99 Upper Deck Black Diamond Quadruple Diamond

This 120-card parallel set reprinted each card from Black Diamond, but added emerald foil to the card front. Quadruple Diamond veterans (1-90) were sequentially numbered to 150, while rookies (91-120) were numbered to 50 sets.

	MT
Common Player:	8.00
Common Rookie (91-120):	12.00
Quad. Diamond Cards	20x-40x
Production 150 Sets	
Quad. Diamond Rookies	4x-8x
Production 50 Sets	

1998-99 Upper Deck Black Diamond Diamond Dominance

This 30-card set featured top players printed on Light F/X technology. Cards were sequentially numbered to 1,000 sets and were numbered with a "D" prefix. Each card was also available in an Emerald Edition parallel, which was sequentially numbered to 100 sets.

	MT
Complete Set (30):	400.00
Common Player:	3.00
Production 1,000 Hobby Sets	
Emerald Cards	3x-6x
Production 100 Hobby Sets	

1 Steve Smith 3.00
2 Paul Pierce 30.00
3 Glen Rice 3.00
4 Toni Kukoc 5.00
5 Shawn Kemp 10.00
6 Michael Finley 5.00
7 Antonio McDyess 5.00
8 Grant Hill 30.00
9 Antawn Jamison 25.00
10 Scottie Pippen 15.00
11 Reggie Miller 3.00
12 Michael Olowokandi 10.00
13 Shaquille O'Neal 20.00
14 Alonzo Mourning 5.00
15 Ray Allen 5.00
16 Stephon Marbury 20.00
17 Keith Van Horn 20.00
18 Allan Houston 3.00
19 Anfernee Hardaway 20.00
20 Allen Iverson 20.00
21 Jason Kidd 15.00
22 Damon Stoudamire 5.00
23 Chris Webber 15.00
24 Tim Duncan 30.00
25 Gary Payton 8.00
26 Vince Carter 50.00
27 Karl Malone 8.00
28 Mike Bibby 15.00
29 Mitch Richmond 3.00
30 Michael Jordan 60.00

1998-99 Upper Deck Black Diamond MJ Sheer Brilliance

This 30-card insert exclusively featured Michael Jordan and was numbered with a "B" prefix. Regular versions were sequentially numbered to 230 sets, while a rarer Extreme Brilliance version was sequentially numbered to only 23 sets.

	MT
Complete Set (30):	2000.
Common Player:	75.00
Production 230 Hobby Sets	
Extreme Brilliance Cards:	500.00
Production 23 Hobby Sets	

1998-99 Upper Deck Black Diamond UD Authentics Autographs

Five different rookies signed cards for UD Authentics. The cards were unnumbered and checklisted by the player's initials. Each player signed only 475 sequentially numbered cards.

	MT
Complete Set (5):	225.00
Common Player:	25.00

MB Mike Bibby 60.00
LH Larry Hughes 60.00
AJ Antawn Jamison 80.00
RT Robert Traylor 40.00
BW Bonzi Wells 25.00

1998-99 Upper Deck Encore

Upper Deck Encore was comprised of 90 regular player cards and three shortprinted subsets - MJ Regular Players cards 91-113 (23 cards, 1:4 packs), Rookie Watch 114-143 (30 cards, 1:4 packs) and Bonus Regular Rookie cards 144-150 (seven cards, 1:8 packs). All of the cards except the seven Bonus Regular Rookie cards were reprinted cards from Upper Deck Series I and MJ Access (UD Series II) with the addition of a holographic finish and foil enhancements. Inserts included: nine PowerDeck, one UD Authentics Michael Jordan autographed hand-numbered to 50, 30 Intensity, 14 Driving Forces, 10 Rookie Encore, 20 MJ23 and 150 Upper Deck F/X parallel cards numbered to 125 sets.

	MT
Complete Set (150):	250.00
Common Player:	.20
Common Jordan (91-113):	3.00
Inserted 1:4	
Common Rookie Watch (114-143):	2.00
Inserted 1:4	
Common Rookie (144-150):	5.00
Inserted 1:8	
Wax Box:	75.00

1 Mookie Blaylock .20
2 Dikembe Mutombo .40
3 Steve Smith .40
4 Kenny Anderson .40
5 Antoine Walker 1.50
6 Ron Mercer 1.00
7 David Wesley .20
8 Elden Campbell .20
9 Eddie Jones .75
10 Ron Harper .20
11 Toni Kukoc .40
12 Brent Barry .20
13 Shawn Kemp 1.00
14 Brevin Knight .40
15 Derek Anderson .40
16 Shawn Bradley .20
17 Robert Pack .20
18 Michael Finley .40
19 Antonio McDyess .75
20 Nick Van Exel .40
21 Danny Fortson .20
22 Grant Hill 2.50
23 Jerry Stackhouse .40
24 Bison Dele .20
25 Donyell Marshall .20
26 Tony Delk .20
27 Erick Dampier .20
28 John Starks .20
29 Charles Barkley .75
30 Hakeem Olajuwon .75
31 Othella Harrington .20
32 Scottie Pippen 1.25
33 Rik Smits .20
34 Reggie Miller .40
35 Mark Jackson .20
36 Rodney Rogers .20
37 Lamond Murray .20
38 Maurice Taylor .40
39 Kobe Bryant 4.00
40 Shaquille O'Neal 1.50
41 Derek Fisher .20
42 Glen Rice .40
43 Jamal Mashburn .40
44 Alonzo Mourning .40
45 Tim Hardaway .60
46 Ray Allen .40
47 Vinny Del Negro .20
48 Glenn Robinson .40
49 Joe Smith .40
50 Terrell Brandon .40
51 Kevin Garnett 2.50
52 Keith Van Horn 1.50
53 Stephon Marbury 1.50
54 Jayson Williams .40
55 Patrick Ewing .40
56 Allan Houston .40
57 Latrell Sprewell .40
58 Anfernee Hardaway 1.50
59 Horace Grant .20
60 Nick Anderson .40
61 Allen Iverson 1.50
62 Matt Geiger .20
63 Theo Ratliff .20
64 Jason Kidd 1.00

65	Rex Chapman	.20
66	Tom Gugliotta	.20
67	Rasheed Wallace	.40
68	Arvydas Sabonis	.20
69	Damon Stoudamire	.60
70	Vlade Divac	.40
71	Corliss Williamson	.20
72	Chris Webber	1.00
73	Tim Duncan	2.50
74	Sean Elliott	.20
75	David Robinson	.75
76	Vin Baker	.60
77	Gary Payton	.75
78	Detlef Schrempf	.20
79	Tracy McGrady	1.00
80	John Wallace	.20
81	Doug Christie	.20
82	Karl Malone	.75
83	John Stockton	.40
84	Jeff Hornacek	.20
85	Bryant Reeves	.40
86	Michael Smith	.20
87	Shareef Abdur-Rahim	1.00
88	Juwan Howard	.40
89	Rod Strickland	.40
90	Mitch Richmond	.40
91	Michael Jordan	3.00
92	Michael Jordan	3.00
93	Michael Jordan	3.00
94	Michael Jordan	3.00
95	Michael Jordan	3.00
96	Michael Jordan	3.00
97	Michael Jordan	3.00
98	Michael Jordan	3.00
99	Michael Jordan	3.00
100	Michael Jordan	3.00
101	Michael Jordan	3.00
102	Michael Jordan	3.00
103	Michael Jordan	3.00
104	Michael Jordan	3.00
105	Michael Jordan	3.00
106	Michael Jordan	3.00
107	Michael Jordan	3.00
108	Michael Jordan	3.00
109	Michael Jordan	3.00
110	Michael Jordan	3.00
111	Michael Jordan	3.00
112	Michael Jordan	3.00
113	Michael Jordan	3.00
114	*Michael Olowokandi*	8.00
115	*Mike Bibby*	12.00
116	*Raef LaFrentz*	8.00
117	*Antawn Jamison*	15.00
118	*Vince Carter*	35.00
119	*Robert Traylor*	8.00
120	*Jason Williams*	25.00
121	*Larry Hughes*	12.00
122	*Dirk Nowitzki*	4.00
123	*Paul Pierce*	20.00
124	*Michael Doleac*	4.00
125	*Keon Clark*	4.00
126	*Michael Dickerson*	6.00
127	*Matt Harpring*	5.00
128	*Bryce Drew*	3.00
129	*Pat Garrity*	3.00
130	*Roshown McLeod*	3.00
131	*Ricky Davis*	3.00
132	*Predrag Stojakovic*	3.00
133	*Felipe Lopez*	6.00
134	*Al Harrington*	8.00
135	*Ruben Patterson*	3.00
136	*Cuttino Mobley*	3.00
137	*Tyronn Lue*	3.00
138	*Brian Skinner*	3.00
139	*Nazr Mohammed*	2.00
140	*Toby Bailey*	2.00
141	*Casey Shaw*	2.00
142	*Corey Benjamin*	2.00
143	*Rashard Lewis*	4.00
144	Jason Williams	15.00
145	Paul Pierce	12.00
146	Vince Carter	20.00
147	Antawn Jamison	10.00
148	Raef LaFrentz	5.00
149	Mike Bibby	8.00
150	Michael Olowokandi	5.00
MJ	Michael Jordan Auto	5000.

1998-99 Upper Deck Encore FX

This 150-card parallel set reprints each card from Encore, but replaces the silver foil from the regular-issue card with gold foil. Cards were sequentially numbered to 125 sets.

	MT
Common Player:	5.00
Common Jordan (91-113):	60.00
Common Rookie Watch (114-143):	10.00
Common Rookie (144-150):	25.00
F/X Cards:	15x-30x
F/X Jordans:	20x
F/X Rookies:	3x-6x
Production 125 Sets	

1998-99 Upper Deck Encore Driving Forces

Driving Forces was a 14-card insert that featured top offensive stars. The cards were numbered with an "F" prefix, and inserted 1:23 packs. A parallel version also existed and were sequentially numbered to 500 sets.

		MT
Complete Set (15):		125.00
Common Player:		2.00
Inserted 1:23		
F/X Parallel Cards:		3x
Production 500 Sets		
1	Michael Jordan	30.00
2	Kobe Bryant	20.00
3	Keith Van Horn	10.00
4	Kevin Garnett	15.00
5	Tim Duncan	15.00
6	Gary Payton	4.00
7	Antoine Walker	10.00
8	Grant Hill	15.00
9	Scottie Pippen	5.00
10	Tim Hardaway	3.00
11	Reggie Miller	2.00
12	Shareef Abdur-Rahim	5.00
13	Anfernee Hardaway	10.00
14	Allen Iverson	12.00
15	Ray Allen	3.00

1998-99 Upper Deck Encore Intensity

Intensity was a 30-card insert that was reprinted from Upper Deck Series I. This insert has rainbow foil added to the front and was inserted 1:11 packs. Cards were numbered with an "I" prefix.

		MT
Complete Set (30):		60.00
Common Player:		.50
Inserted 1:11		
1	Michael Jordan	15.00
2	Mitch Richmond	1.00
3	Ron Mercer	3.00
4	Terrell Brandon	1.00
5	Brevin Knight	1.00
6	Rasheed Wallace	.50
7	Keith Van Horn	5.00
8	Antawn Jamison	5.00
9	Antonio McDyess	1.00
10	Allen Iverson	6.00
11	Anfernee Hardaway	5.00
12	Chris Webber	3.00
13	Lorenzen Wright	.50
14	Bryant Reeves	.50
15	Charles Barkley	2.00
16	Tracy McGrady	3.00
17	Larry Johnson	.50
18	Jerry Stackhouse	.50
19	Derrick Coleman	.50
20	Detlef Schrempf	.50
21	John Stockton	1.00
22	Kobe Bryant	10.00
23	Alonzo Mourning	1.00
24	Dikembe Mutombo	.50
25	Jalen Rose	.50
26	Robert Pack	.50
27	Tom Gugliotta	1.00
28	Shaquille O'Neal	5.00
29	Stephon Marbury	5.00
30	David Robinson	2.00

1998-99 Upper Deck Encore MJ23

MJ23 featured 20 cards of Michael Jordan that were first issued in Upper Deck Series I (20 of the 30 original cards were reprinted), but rainbow Light F/X foil was added. Cards were numbered with an "MJ" prefix and inserted 1:23 packs. A parallel version also existed and was sequentially numbered to 23 sets.

	MT
Complete Set (20):	150.00
Common Player:	10.00
Inserted 1:23	
Common F/X Parallel:	400.00
Production 23 Sets	

1998-99 Upper Deck Encore PowerDeck

PowerDeck was a nine-card interactive insert that featured CD-Roms of top players with game-action footage, sound, photos and career highlights. These were numbered with a "PD" prefix and arrived in a protective sleeve out of the pack. PowerDeck cards were inserted 1:47 packs of Encore.

		MT
Complete Set (9):		225.00
Common Player:		10.00
Inserted 1:47		
1	Michael Jordan	65.00
2	Kobe Bryant	30.00
3	Charles Barkley	10.00
4	Shaquille O'Neal	15.00
5	Kevin Garnett	30.00
6	Jason Williams	30.00
7	Paul Pierce	20.00
8	Vince Carter	35.00
9	Julius Erving	15.00

1998-99 Upper Deck Encore Rookie Encore

This 10-card insert featured top players from the 1998 NBA Draft and was inserted 1:23 packs. Rookie Encore cards were numbered with an "RE" prefix. A parallel, gold foil version also existed and was sequentially numbered to 1,000 sets.

		MT
Complete Set (10):		100.00
Common Player:		2.00
Inserted 1:23		
F/X Parallel Cards:		2x
Production 1,000 Sets		
1	Jason Williams	20.00
2	Michael Olowokandi	6.00
3	Paul Pierce	15.00
4	Robert Traylor	6.00
5	Raef LaFrentz	6.00
6	Mike Bibby	10.00
7	Dirk Nowitzki	2.00
8	Antawn Jamison	12.00
9	Larry Hughes	10.00
10	Vince Carter	35.00

1998-99 Upper Deck Ionix

This 80-card set featured 53 veterans, seven Michael Jordan cards and 20 seeded rookies in an Electrix subset (1:4 packs). Each card was printed on a double-laminated, metalized stock. Inserts included: 23 hand-numbered Michael Jordan autographed cards, five UD Authentics, 60 Ionix Reciprocals (numbered to 750 sets), 20 Electrix Reciprocals (numbered to 100 sets), 20 Kinetix, 10 Area 23, 25 Skyonix, 15 Warp Zone and 10 MJ HoloGrFX.

		MT
Complete Set (80):		125.00
Common Player (1-60):		.20
Common Electrix Rookie (61-80):		3.00
Inserted 1:4		
Wax Box:		75.00
1	1991 NBA Championship Year Michael Jordan	2.00
2	1992 NBA Championship Year Michael Jordan	2.00
3	1993 NBA Championship Year Michael Jordan	2.00
4	1996 NBA Championship Year Michael Jordan	2.00
5	1997 NBA Championship Year Michael Jordan	2.00
6	1998 NBA Championship Year Michael Jordan	2.00
7	Steve Smith	.40
8	Dikembe Mutombo	.20
9	Ron Mercer	1.50
10	Antoine Walker	2.00
11	Derrick Coleman	.40
12	Glen Rice	.40
13	Michael Jordan	5.00
14	Toni Kukoc	.40
15	Derek Anderson	.40
16	Shawn Kemp	1.00
17	Michael Finley	.40
18	Steve Nash	.20
19	Antonio McDyess	1.00
20	Nick Van Exel	.40
21	Grant Hill	2.50
22	Jerry Stackhouse	.20
23	Donyell Marshall	.20
24	John Starks	.20
25	Charles Barkley	1.00
26	Hakeem Olajuwon	1.00
27	Scottie Pippen	1.50
28	Reggie Miller	.40
29	Rik Smits	.20
30	Maurice Taylor	.50
31	Kobe Bryant	4.00
32	Shaquille O'Neal	2.00
33	Tim Hardaway	.60
34	Alonzo Mourning	.40
35	Ray Allen	.40
36	Glenn Robinson	.40
37	Stephon Marbury	2.00
38	Kevin Garnett	2.50
39	Jayson Williams	.40
40	Keith Van Horn	1.50
41	Patrick Ewing	.40
42	Allan Houston	.40
43	Anfernee Hardaway	2.00
44	Isaac Austin	.20
45	Tim Thomas	1.50
46	Allen Iverson	2.00
47	Tom Gugliotta	.40
48	Jason Kidd	1.50
49	Damon Stoudamire	.50
50	Chris Webber	1.50
51	Tim Duncan	2.50
52	David Robinson	1.00
53	Gary Payton	1.00
54	Vin Baker	.40
55	Tracy McGrady	1.50
56	John Stockton	.40
57	Karl Malone	1.00
58	Shareef Abdur-Rahim	1.50
59	Juwan Howard	.40
60	Mitch Richmond	.40
61	*Michael Olowokandi* (Electrix)	8.00
62	*Mike Bibby* (Electrix)	10.00
63	*Raef LaFrentz* (Electrix)	8.00
64	*Antawn Jamison* (Electrix)	12.00
65	*Vince Carter* (Electrix)	30.00
66	*Robert Traylor* (Electrix)	8.00
67	*Jason Williams* (Electrix)	20.00
68	*Larry Hughes* (Electrix)	10.00
69	*Dirk Nowitzki* (Electrix)	4.00
70	*Paul Pierce* (Electrix)	15.00
71	*Cuttino Mobley* (Electrix)	3.00
72	*Corey Benjamin* (Electrix)	3.00
73	*Predrag Stojakovic* (Electrix)	3.00
74	*Michael Dickerson* (Electrix)	5.00
75	*Matt Harpring* (Electrix)	4.00
76	*Rashard Lewis* (Electrix)	4.00
77	*Pat Garrity* (Electrix)	3.00
78	*Roshown McLeod* (Electrix)	3.00
79	*Ricky Davis* (Electrix)	3.00
80	*Felipe Lopez* (Electrix)	5.00
J1A	Michael Jordan Auto	7000.

1998-99 Upper Deck Ionix Reciprocal

This 80-card parallel set reprinted each Ionix card, with the regular-issue front becoming the Reciprocal back and the regular-issue back becoming the Reciprocal front. Reciprocal versions of cards 1-60 (Veterans) were numbered to 750, while Reciprocal versions of cards 61-80 (Rookies) were sequentially numbered to 100 sets.

	MT
Common Player (1-60):	2.00
Common Electrix Rookie (61-80):	30.00
Reciprocals (1-60):	6x-10x
Production 750 sets	
Reciprocals (61-80):	8x-12x
Production 100 sets	

1998-99 Upper Deck Ionix Area 23

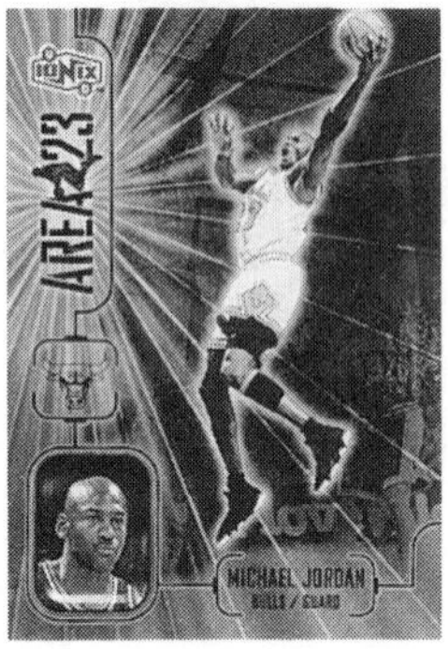

This 10-card set featured only Michael Jordan on cards enhanced with rainbow Ionix technology. The cards were numbered with an "A" prefix and inserted 1:18 packs.

	MT
Complete Set (10):	100.00
Common Player:	12.00
Inserted 1:18	

1998-99 Upper Deck Ionix Kinetix

Kinetix displayed 20 top young stars on a rainbow foil enhanced card. Each card was numbered with a "K" prefix and inserted 1:9 packs.

		MT
Complete Set (20):		125.00
Common Player:		2.00
Inserted 1:8		
1	Michael Jordan	20.00
2	Michael Olowokandi	5.00
3	Keith Van Horn	5.00
4	Grant Hill	10.00
5	Stephon Marbury	5.00
6	Larry Hughes	8.00
7	Vince Carter	20.00
8	Jason Kidd	3.00
9	Robert Traylor	5.00
10	Ron Mercer	3.00
11	Dirk Nowitzki	2.00
12	Antawn Jamison	10.00
13	Kobe Bryant	12.00
14	Jason Williams	12.00
15	Raef LaFrentz	4.00
16	Gary Payton	2.00
17	Tim Duncan	10.00
18	Paul Pierce	12.00
19	Mike Bibby	8.00
20	Scottie Pippen	3.00

1998-99 Upper Deck Ionix MJ HoloGrFX

Michael Jordan was featured on all 10 cards in this MJ HoloGrFx insert. Cards were numbered with an "MJ" prefix and inserted 1:1,500 packs.

	MT
Complete Set (10):	2500.
Common Player:	300.00
Inserted 1:1,500	

1998-99 Upper Deck Ionix Skyonix

Skyonix displayed 25 players who are known for flying through the air. Cards were numbered with an "S" prefix and inserted 1:53 packs.

		MT
Complete Set (25):		325.00
Common Player:		3.00
Inserted 1:53		
1	Michael Jordan	100.00
2	Scottie Pippen	15.00
3	Derek Anderson	3.00
4	Jason Kidd	15.00
5	Damon Stoudamire	5.00
6	Antoine Walker	15.00
7	Shaquille O'Neal	20.00
8	Tim Thomas	12.00
9	Reggie Miller	3.00
10	Allen Iverson	25.00
11	Antonio McDyess	8.00
12	Michael Finley	5.00
13	Charles Barkley	8.00
14	Shareef Abdur-Rahim	12.00
15	Gary Payton	8.00
16	David Robinson	8.00
17	Anfernee Hardaway	20.00
18	Ray Allen	5.00
19	Ron Mercer	15.00
20	Tim Hardaway	6.00
21	Chris Webber	15.00
22	Kevin Garnett	40.00
23	Juwan Howard	3.00
24	Karl Malone	8.00
25	Keith Van Horn	15.00

1998-99 Upper Deck Ionix Warp Zone

This 15-card insert set featured 15 top players with rainbow technology. Warp Zone inserts were numbered with a "Z" prefix and inserted 1:216 packs.

		MT
Complete Set (15):		800.00
Common Player:		6.00
Inserted 1:216		
1	Michael Jordan	200.00
2	Tim Duncan	100.00
3	Robert Traylor	20.00
4	Michael Olowokandi	20.00
5	Vince Carter	100.00
6	Dirk Nowitzki	6.00
7	Antawn Jamison	40.00
8	Jason Williams	60.00
9	Larry Hughes	30.00
10	Raef LaFrentz	20.00
11	Allen Iverson	50.00
12	Kobe Bryant	125.00
13	Grant Hill	100.00
14	Mike Bibby	30.00
15	Paul Pierce	50.00

1998-99 Upper Deck Ionix UD Authentics

Five different rookies signed cards for UD Authentics. The second installment of this insert was in Ionix, while the first appeared in Black Diamond. The cards were unnumbered and identified by the initials of the player, except in the case of Michael Doleac who was "numbered" "DO". Each player signed 475 sequentially numbered cards.

		MT
Complete Set (5):		250.00
Common Player:		30.00
Production 475 sets		
CB	Corey Benjamin	30.00
DO	Michael Doleac	35.00
RL	Raef LaFrentz	50.00
RM	Roshown McLeod	30.00
JW	Jason Williams	125.00

1998 UD Jordan Living Legend

This 165-card set was a retail-only Jordan set and released during the lockout. It contained 120 MJ Time Frames, along with two subsets - 15 The Elements of Style - Jordan, which took a look back at the varying styles MJ has sported over the years, and 30 The Jordan Files, which detailed his performance against each NBA franchise. Inserts include: 50 total Sign of Greatness Autographs, 23 hand-numbered Autographed Game-worn Jersey cards, 15 Jordan in Flight, 8 Cover Story and 30 Game Action.

	MT
Complete Set (165):	100.00
Common Player:	.75
Wax Box:	60.00

1998 UD Jordan Living Legend Autograph

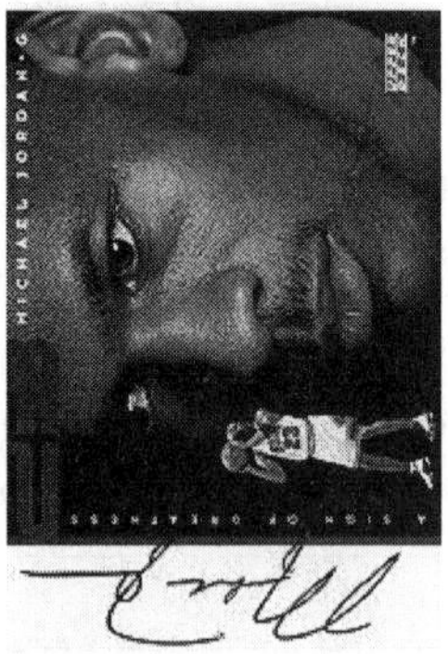

Michael Jordan autographed 50 hand-numbered cards for the Living Legend product. These cards were numbered "MJ1".

	MT
Complete Set (1):	5000.
Production 50 Cards	
MJ1 Michael Jordan	5000.

1998 UD Jordan Living Legend Cover Story

This eight-card insert featured magazine covers of Michael Jordan from Inside Stuff. The cards were numbered with a "C" prefix and inserted 1:14 packs.

	MT
Complete Set (8):	35.00
Common Player:	5.00
Inserted 1:14	

1998 UD Jordan Living Legend Game Action

This 30-card insert showcases some of the best action shots of Jordan, with each card containing Light F/X technology. Each card was available in three different versions, with Tier 1 sequentially numbered to 2,300 sets, Tier 2 featuring silver foil and numbered to 230 sets, and Tier 3 numbered to 23 sets.

	MT
Complete Set (30):	400.00
Common Player:	15.00
Production 2,300 Sets	
Common Silver:	125.00
Production 230 Sets	
Common Gold:	1000.
Production 23 Sets	

1998 UD Jordan Living Legend In-Flight

In-Flight was a 15-card insert featuring some of MJ's top flights to the basket. Cards were numbered with an "IF" prefix and inserted 1:5 packs.

	MT
Complete Set (15):	30.00
Common Player:	2.00
Inserted 1:5	

1998 Upper Deck MJx

MJx was a 135-card set featuring Michael Jordan and showcasing the future Hall of Famer's career. The product was released during the NBA lockout and capitalized on Jordan's popularity when he retired. The first 45 cards showcased his career from 1984-1990 (2:1 pack). Cards 46-55 were called "1st Quarter Highlights" and covered the years 1984-1987 (1:17). Cards 56-65 highlighted years 1988-1990 and were called "2nd Quarter Highlights" (1:12). Next, the second half lineup covered 1991-1998 with cards 66-110 (2:1). Cards 111-120 (1:7) were called "3rd Quarter Highlights" and covered 1991-1993. The "4th Quarter Highlights" were cards 121-130 (1:1) and covered 1995-1998. Cards 131-135 formed a subset called "The Best of Times" and were inserted 1:23 packs. Inserts included: 23 hand-numbered Autographed Game-worn Jersey cards, 50 hand-numbered MJ Autographed cards, 230 Game Commemorative Game-worn Shoe cards, 230 Game Commemorative Game-worn Warm-up cards, 90 MJ Timepiece parallels and 30 MJ Live inserts numbered to 100 sets.

	MT
Complete Set (135):	300.00
Common Player (1-45):	.50
Inserted 2:1	
Common Player (46-55):	15.00
Inserted 1:17	
Common Player (56-65):	10.00
Inserted 1:12	
Common Player (66-110):	.50
Inserted 1:2	
Common Player (111-120):	5.00
Inserted 1:7	
Common Player (121-130):	1.00
Inserted 1:1	
Common Player (131-135):	15.00
Inserted 1:23	

1998 Upper Deck MJx Autograph

This single card was signed by Jordan and limited to 50 hand-numbered versions. No odds were given for insertion and it was numbered "A1".

	MT
Complete Set (1):	5000.
Production 50 Cards	
A1 Michael Jordan Auto.	5000.

1998 Upper Deck MJx Game Commemoratives

Game Commemoratives featured two different pieces of game- worn Jordan merchandise. Next, there were 230 hand-numbered Game-Worn Shoe cards featuring a piece of shoe. Third, 230 sequentially numbered Game-worn Warm-up cards were inserted that featured an actual swatch of authentic warm-ups. Both cards were numbered with a "GC" prefix.

	MT
Complete Set (2):	2400.
Common Player:	1200.
Warm-Ups Production 230	
Shoes Production 230	
GC1 Michael Jordan Warm-Ups	1200.
GC2 Michael Jordan Shoes	1200.

1998 Upper Deck MJx Live

This 30-card insert features actual excerpts from interviews with MJ. Cards were sequentially numbered to 100 sets.

	MT
Complete Set (30):	3500.
Common Player:	125.00
Production 100 Sets	

1998 Upper Deck MJx Timepieces Red

This 90-card parallel set featured die-cut versions from MJ Timeline 1st Half and 2nd Half cards. MJ Timepiece Red cards were sequentially numbered to 2,300, Bronze cards were numbered to 230 and Gold versions were numbered to 23 sets.

	MT
Complete Set (90):	450.00
Common Player:	5.00
Production 2,300 Sets	
Common Bronze Player:	50.00
Production 230 Sets	
Common Gold Player:	300.00
Production 23 Sets	

1998-99 Upper Deck Ovation

Ovation arrived during the NBA lockout and included 80 cards in the base set, with the last 10 being redemption cards for the top 10 picks in the 1998 NBA Draft. The short-printed redemption cards were seeded 1:9 packs and numbered with a "T" suffix. Ovation featured cards printed on a basketball card stock, with Light F/X technology used in the background of the circular shot of the player. Inserts included: 23 hand-numbered Autographed Game-worn Jersey cards of Jordan, 90 Game-used Basketball cards of Jordan, 80 Gold Parallel cards, 15 Jordan Rules, 20 Superstars of the Court and 20 Future Forces.

		MT
Complete Set (80):		120.00
Common Player:		.20
Jordan Basketball Numbered to 90		
Wax Box:		50.00
1	Steve Smith	.20
2	Dikembe Mutombo	.40
3	Antoine Walker	3.00
4	Ron Mercer	3.00
5	Glen Rice	.50
6	Bobby Phills	.20
7	Michael Jordan	10.00
8	Toni Kukoc	.40
9	Dennis Rodman	2.50
10	Scottie Pippen	2.00
11	Shawn Kemp	1.50
12	Derek Anderson	.75
13	Brevin Knight	.75
14	Michael Finley	.50
15	Shawn Bradley	.20
16	LaPhonso Ellis	.20
17	Bobby Jackson	.40
18	Grant Hill	5.00
19	Jerry Stackhouse	.40
20	Donyell Marshall	.20
21	Erick Dampier	.20
22	Hakeem Olajuwon	1.25
23	Charles Barkley	1.00
24	Reggie Miller	.50
25	Chris Mullin	.20
26	Rik Smits	.20
27	Maurice Taylor	.75
28	Lorenzen Wright	.20
29	Kobe Bryant	6.00
30	Eddie Jones	1.50
31	Shaquille O'Neal	2.50
32	Alonzo Mourning	.50
33	Tim Hardaway	.50
34	Jamal Mashburn	.20
35	Ray Allen	.50
36	Terrell Brandon	.20
37	Glenn Robinson	.50
38	Kevin Garnett	5.00
39	Tom Gugliotta	.40
40	Stephon Marbury	3.00
41	Keith Van Horn	3.50
42	Kerry Kittles	.40
43	Jayson Williams	.20
44	Patrick Ewing	.40
45	Allan Houston	.40
46	Larry Johnson	.40
47	Anfernee Hardaway	2.50
48	Nick Anderson	.20
49	Allen Iverson	2.00
50	Joe Smith	.40
51	Tim Thomas	2.00
52	Jason Kidd	1.50
53	Antonio McDyess	.50
54	Damon Stoudamire	.75
55	Isaiah Rider	.20
56	Rasheed Wallace	.20
57	Tariq Abdul-Wahad	.20
58	Corliss Williamson	.20
59	Tim Duncan	5.00
60	David Robinson	1.00
61	Vin Baker	1.00
62	Gary Payton	.75
63	Chauncey Billups	.50
64	Tracy McGrady	1.75
65	Karl Malone	1.00
66	John Stockton	.75
67	Shareef Abdur-Rahim	1.50
68	Bryant Reeves	.20
69	Juwan Howard	.50
70	Rod Strickland	.20
71T	*Michael Olowokandi*	15.00
72T	*Mike Bibby*	15.00
73T	*Raef LaFrentz*	12.00
74T	*Antawn Jamison*	15.00
75T	*Vince Carter*	25.00
76T	*Robert Traylor*	12.00
77T	*Jason Williams*	20.00
78T	*Larry Hughes*	12.00
79T	*Dirk Nowitzki*	8.00
80T	*Paul Pierce*	20.00
NNO	Jordan Basketball	2000.

1998-99 Upper Deck Ovation Gold

This 80-card parallel set reprinted each card from Ovation, but replaced the silver foil on the front with gold foil. Gold foil versions were sequentially numbered to 1,000 sets.

	MT
Common Gold Cards:	2.00
Gold Cards:	5x-10x
Production 1,000 Sets	

1998-99 Upper Deck Ovation Future Forces

Future Forces was a 20-card insert that featured top young players on foil cards with a silver border on the right and left side. These were numbered with an "F" prefix and inserted 1:29 packs.

		MT
Complete Set (20):		175.00
Common Player:		2.50
Inserted 1:29		
1	Tim Duncan	25.00
2	Keith Van Horn	18.00
3	Kobe Bryant	30.00
4	Tracy McGrady	12.00
5	Maurice Taylor	5.00
6	Shareef Abdur-Rahim	10.00
7	Kevin Garnett	25.00
8	Brevin Knight	5.00
9	Ron Mercer	15.00
10	Tim Thomas	12.00
11	Antoine Walker	15.00
12	Michael Finley	2.50
13	Grant Hill	25.00
14	Jerry Stackhouse	2.50
15	Erick Dampier	2.50
16	Lorenzen Wright	2.50
17	Ray Allen	2.50
18	Stephon Marbury	15.00
19	Allen Iverson	12.00
20	Damon Stoudamire	5.00

1998-99 Upper Deck Ovation Jordan Rules

This 15-card insert featured only Michael Jordan on three different levels. Cards 1-5 were bronze in color and inserted 1:23 packs, cards 6-10 were silver in color and inserted 1:45 packs and cards 11-15 were die-cut and gold in color and inserted 1:99 packs. Cards were numbered with a "J" prefix.

	MT
Complete Set (15):	400.00
Common Player (J1-J5):	15.00
Inserted 1:23	
Common Player (J6-J10):	25.00
Inserted 1:45	
Common Player (J11-J15):	50.00
Inserted 1:99	

1998-99 Upper Deck Ovation Superstars of the Court

Superstars of the Court was a 20-card insert that featured top players on a holographic foil card. Cards were numbered with a "C" prefix and inserted 1:2 packs.

		MT
Complete Set (20):		75.00
Common Player:		1.00
Inserted 1:2		
1	Michael Jordan	15.00
2	Tim Duncan	8.00
3	Grant Hill	8.00
4	Karl Malone	2.00
5	Dennis Rodman	4.00
6	Hakeem Olajuwon	3.00
7	Keith Van Horn	6.00
8	Kobe Bryant	10.00
9	Jason Kidd	3.00
10	Stephon Marbury	5.00
11	Reggie Miller	1.00
12	Damon Stoudamire	2.00
13	Tracy McGrady	3.00
14	Scottie Pippen	4.00
15	Vin Baker	2.00
16	Shaquille O'Neal	5.00
17	Anfernee Hardaway	5.00
18	Charles Barkley	2.00
19	Kevin Garnett	8.00
20	Antoine Walker	5.00

1999-00 Fleer Tradition

Tradition contained 200 veterans and 20 rookies from the 1999 NBA Draft. Players from the Eastern Conference had blue foil stamping, while players from the Western Conference had red foil stamping and rookies had gold foil stamping. The set was paralleled twice - retail-only Roundball Collection and hobby-only Supreme Court Collection. Inserts included: Rookie Sensations, Masters of the Hardwood, Net Effect, Game Breakers and Fresh Ink.

		MT
Complete Set (220):		40.00
Common Player:		.10
Wax Box (36):		65.00
1	Vince Carter	1.50
2	Kobe Bryant	2.00
3	Keith Van Horn	.75
4	Tim Duncan	1.50
5	Grant Hill	1.50
6	Kevin Garnett	1.50
7	Anfernee Hardaway	1.00
8	Jason Williams	1.00
9	Paul Pierce	.75
10	Mookie Blaylock	.10
11	Shawn Bradley	.10
12	Kenny Anderson	.20
13	Chauncey Billups	.20
14	Elden Campbell	.10
15	Jason Caffey	.10
16	Brent Barry	.10
17	Charles Barkley	.40

18	Derek Anderson	.30
19	Darrick Martin	.10
20	Bison Dele	.10
21	Rick Fox	.10
22	Antonio Davis	.10
23	Terrell Brandon	.20
24	P.J. Brown	.10
25	Toby Bailey	.20
26	Ray Allen	.25
27	Brian Grant	.20
28	Scott Burrell	.10
29	Tariq Abdul-Wahad	.10
30	Marcus Camby	.25
31	John Stockton	.20
32	Nick Anderson	.20
33	Antonio Daniels	.20
34	Matt Geiger	.10
35	Vin Baker	.20
36	Dee Brown	.10
37	Shandon Anderson	.10
38	Calbert Cheaney	.10
39	Shareef Abdur-Rahim	.50
40	LaPhonso Ellis	.20
41	Cedric Ceballos	.10
42	Tony Battie	.20
43	Keon Clark	.20
44	Derrick Coleman	.20
45	Erick Dampier	.10
46	Corey Benjamin	.20
47	Michael Dickerson	.30
48	Cedric Henderson	.10
49	Lamond Murray	.10
50	Joe Dumars	.20
51	Shaquille O'Neal	1.00
52	Dale Davis	.10
53	Dean Garrett	.10
54	Tim Hardaway	.30
55	Gerald Brown	.10
56	Sam Cassell	.20
57	Jim Jackson	.10
58	Kendall Gill	.10
59	Eric Williams	.10
60	Chris Childs	.10
61	Vlade Divac	.20
62	Darrell Armstrong	.20
63	Mario Elie	.10
64	Tyrone Hill	.10
65	Dale Ellis	.10
66	Doug Christie	.10
67	Howard Eisley	.10
68	Juwan Howard	.20
69	Mike Bibby	.50
70	Alan Henderson	.10
71	Michael Finley	.25
72	Dana Barros	.10
73	Danny Fortson	.10
74	Ricky Davis	.20
75	Adonal Foyle	.10
76	Cory Carr	.20
77	Bryce Drew	.20
78	Shawn Kemp	.50
79	Tyrone Nesby	.20
80	Lindsey Hunter	.10
81	Ruben Patterson	.20
82	Al Harrington	.30
83	Bobby Jackson	.10
84	Dan Majerle	.10
85	Rex Chapman	.10
86	Dell Curry	.10
87	Walt Williams	.10
88	Kerry Kittles	.10
89	Isaiah Rider	.20
90	Patrick Ewing	.20
91	Lawrence Funderburke	.10
92	Isaac Austin	.10
93	Sean Elliott	.10
94	Larry Hughes	.40
95	Hersey Hawkins	.10
96	Tracy McGrady	.60
97	Jeff Hornacek	.10
98	Randell Jackson	.10
99	J.R. Henderson	.10
100	Roshown McLeod	.20
101	Steve Nash	.10
102	Ron Mercer	.50
103	Raef LaFrentz	.40
104	Eddie Jones	.30
105	Antawn Jamison	.60
106	Kornel David	.10
107	Othella Harrington	.10
108	Brevin Knight	.10
109	Michael Olowokandi	.40
110	Christian Laettner	.10
111	J.R. Reid	.10
112	Reggie Miller	.20
113	Andrae Patterson	.10
114	Jamal Mashburn	.20
115	Glenn Robinson	.20
116	Pat Garrity	.20
117	Stephon Marbury	1.00
118	Arvydas Sabonis	.10
119	Allan Houston	.20
120	Predrag Stojakovic	.10
121	Michael Doleac	.20
122	Avery Johnson	.10
123	Allen Iverson	1.25
124	Rashard Lewis	.25
125	Charles Oakley	.10
126	Karl Malone	.40
127	Tracy Murray	.10
128	Felipe Lopez	.30
129	Dikembe Mutombo	.20
130	Dirk Nowitzki	.20
131	Vitaly Potapenko	.10
132	Antonio McDyess	.40
133	Anthony Mason	.20
134	Donyell Marshall	.10
135	Ron Harper	.10
136	Cuttino Mobley	.20
137	Wesley Person	.10
138	Rodney Rogers	.10
139	Jerry Stackhouse	.20
140	Glen Rice	.20
141	Chris Mullin	.20
142	Anthony Peeler	.10
143	Alonzo Mourning	.30
144	Tom Gugliotta	.20
145	Tim Thomas	.50
146	Damon Stoudamire	.30
147	Jason Williams	.20
148	Larry Johnson	.20
149	Chris Webber	.60
150	Matt Harpring	.20
151	David Robinson	.40
152	George Lynch	.10
153	Gary Payton	.40
154	John Wallace	.10
155	Greg Ostertag	.10
156	Mitch Richmond	.20
157	Cherokee Parks	.10
158	Steve Smith	.20
159	Gary Trent	.20
160	Antoine Walker	.75
161	Johnny Taylor	.10
162	Brad Miller	.10
163	Chris Mills	.10
164	Charles R. Jones	.10
165	Hakeem Olajuwon	.40
166	Bob Sura	.10
167	Brian Skinner	.20
168	Korleone Young	.20
169	Dennis Rodman	.50
170	Jalen Rose	.20
171	Joe Smith	.20
172	Clarence Weatherspoon	.10
173	Jason Kidd	.60
174	Robert Traylor	.40
175	Rasheed Wallace	.20
176	Latrell Sprewell	.20
177	Corliss Williamson	.10
178	Charles Outlaw	.10
179	Malik Rose	.10
180	Nazr Mohammed	.20
181	Olden Polynice	.10
182	Kevin Willis	.10
183	Bryon Russell	.10
184	Bryant Reeves	.10
185	Rod Strickland	.20
186	Samaki Walker	.10
187	Nick Van Exel	.20
188	David Wesley	.10
189	John Starks	.10
190	Toni Kukoc	.30
191	Scottie Pippen	.60
192	Zydrunas Ilgauskas	.20
193	Maurice Taylor	.30
194	Rik Smits	.10
195	Clifford Robinson	.10
196	Bonzi Wells	.20
197	Charlie Ward	.10
198	Detlef Schrempf	.20
199	Theo Ratliff	.20
200	Rodrick Rhodes	.10
201	*Ron Artest*	1.00
202	*William Avery*	1.00
203	*Elton Brand*	5.00
204	*Baron Davis*	3.00
205	*Jumanie Jones*	.75
206	*Andre Miller*	1.00
207	*Lee Nailon*	.50
208	*James Posey*	.75
209	*Jason Terry*	1.00
210	*Kenny Thomas*	.50
211	*Steve Francis*	5.00
212	*Wally Szczerbiak*	3.00
213	*Richard Hamilton*	2.00
214	*Jonathan Bender*	2.00
215	*Shawn Marion*	1.00
216	*Aleksandar Radojevic*	.50
217	*Tim James*	.50
218	*Trajan Langdon*	1.00
219	*Lamar Odom*	5.00
220	*Corey Meggette*	2.00

1999-00 Fleer Tradition Roundball Collection

Roundball Collection was a 220-card parallel set to Fleer Tradition. The cards were identified by silver foil stamping on the front, and they were seeded one per retail pack.

	MT
Complete Set (220):	75.00
Roundball Cards:	2x-4x
Roundball Rookies:	1x-2x
Inserted 1:1 Retail	

1999-00 Fleer Tradition Supreme Court Collection

Supreme Court Collection was a hobby-exclusive parallel set to all 220 cards in Fleer Tradition. The cards were identified by green foil stamping on the front and were sequentially numbered to 20 sets.

	MT
Production 20 Hobby Sets	

1999-00 Fleer Tradition Fresh Ink

Fresh Ink featured autographs from 15 different players from the 1998 NBA Draft. These cards featured a color shot of the player, with a white space across the middle for the player's signature. Fresh Ink inserts were unnumbered on the back and hand-numbered to 400 sets.

	MT
Common Player:	15.00
Production 400 Sets	
Corey Benjamin	20.00
Mike Bibby	60.00
Michael Dickerson	40.00
Michael Doleac	30.00
Byrce Drew	25.00
Pat Garrity	25.00
Matt Harpring	35.00
Larry Hughes	60.00
Antawn Jamison	80.00
Raef LaFrentz	50.00
Felipe Lopez	35.00
Jelani McCoy	20.00
Brad Miller	15.00
Michael Olowokandi	50.00
Robert Traylor	50.00

1999-00 Fleer Tradition Game Breakers

Game Breakers featured 15 top players on a die-cut design. Cards were numbered with a "GB" suffix on the back and were sequentially numbered to just 100 sets.

		MT
Complete Set (15):		2000.
Common Player:		75.00
Production 100 Sets		
1	Shareef Abdur-Rahim	75.00
2	Kobe Bryant	250.00
3	Vince Carter	200.00
4	Tim Duncan	200.00
5	Kevin Garnett	200.00
6	Anfernee Hardaway	150.00
7	Grant Hill	200.00
8	Allen Iverson	175.00
9	Shawn Kemp	75.00
10	Stephon Marbury	125.00
11	Ron Mercer	75.00
12	Shaquille O'Neal	150.00
13	Keith Van Horn	100.00
14	Antoine Walker	125.00
15	Jason Williams	150.00

1999-00 Fleer Tradition Masters of the Hardwood

Masters of the Hardwood displayed 15 top players against a simulated wood background. Cards were numbered with an "MH" suffix and inserted 1:18 packs.

		MT
Complete Set (15):		55.00
Common Player:		2.00
Inserted 1:18		
1	Shareef Abdur-Rahim	3.00
2	Mike Bibby	2.00
3	Kobe Bryant	10.00
4	Tim Duncan	8.00
5	Kevin Garnett	8.00
6	Anfernee Hardaway	5.00
7	Grant Hill	8.00
8	Allen Iverson	6.00
9	Karl Malone	2.00
10	Stephon Marbury	4.00
11	Tracy McGrady	3.00
12	Ron Mercer	3.00
13	Scottie Pippen	3.00
14	Antoine Walker	4.00
15	Jason Williams	5.00

1999-00 Fleer Tradition Net Effect

This 10-card insert featured players on a die-cut design printed on opaque plastic. Cards were numbered with an "NE" suffix on the back and inserted 1:96 packs.

		MT
Complete Set (10):		225.00
Common Player:		15.00
Inserted 1:96		
1	Kobe Bryant	40.00
2	Vince Carter	30.00
3	Tim Duncan	30.00
4	Kevin Garnett	30.00
5	Grant Hill	30.00
6	Allen Iverson	25.00
7	Shaquille O'Neal	20.00
8	Paul Pierce	20.00
9	Scottie Pippen	15.00
10	Keith Van Horn	15.00

1999-00 Fleer Tradition Rookie Sensations

Rookie Sensations highlighted 20 rookies from the 1998-99 season over a white and gold foil background. This insert was numbered with an "RS" suffix and inserted 1:6 packs.

		MT
Complete Set (20):		20.00
Common Player:		.50
Inserted 1:6		
1	Mike Bibby	1.50
2	Vince Carter	5.00
3	Ricky Davis	.75
4	Michael Dickerson	.75
5	Michael Doleac	.50
6	Matt Harpring	.75
7	Larry Hughes	1.25
8	Randell Jackson	.50
9	Antawn Jamison	2.00
10	Raef LaFrentz	1.00
11	Felipe Lopez	.75
12	Roshown McLeod	.50
13	Brad Miller	.50
14	Cuttino Mobley	.60
15	Dirk Nowitzki	.60
16	Michael Olowokandi	1.00
17	Paul Pierce	3.00
18	Predrag Stojakovic	.50
19	Robert Traylor	1.00
20	Jason Williams	3.00

1999-00 Hoops

Hoops arrived in 1999-2000 with a 185-card single-series release that included 117 basic cards, 48 Sophomore Sensations and 20 Future Phenoms. Each card featured a full color front with a rough white border. The set was paralleled in a Starting Five insert, while insert sets included Name Plates, Calling Card, Y2K Corps, The Dunk Mob, Pure Players, 100% Pure Players, Build Your Own Card and Autographics.

		MT
Complete Set (185):		40.00
Common Player:		.10
Wax Box (36):		50.00
1	Paul Pierce	1.00
2	Ray Allen	.20
3	Jason Williams	1.00
4	Sean Elliott	.10
5	Al Harrington	.30
6	Bobby Phills	.10
7	Tyronn Lue	.25
8	James Cotton	.10
9	Anthony Peeler	.10
10	LaPhonso Ellis	.20
11	Voshon Lenard	.10
12	Kornel David	.20
13	Michael Finley	.30
14	Danny Fortson	.10
15	Antawn Jamison	.75
16	Reggie Miller	.20
17	Shaquille O'Neal	1.00
18	P.J. Brown	.10
19	Roshown McLeod	.20
20	Larry Johnson	.20
21	Rashard Lewis	.20
22	Tracy McGrady	.75
23	Predrag Stojakovic	.10
24	Tracy Murray	.10
25	Gary Payton	.50
26	Ricky Davis	.25
27	Kobe Bryant	2.00
28	Avery Johnson	.10
29	Kevin Garnett	1.50
30	Charles R. Jones	.20
31	Brevin Knight	.10
32	Lindsey Hunter	.10
33	Felipe Lopez	.30
34	Rik Smits	.10
35	Maurice Taylor	.30
36	Corey Benjamin	.20
37	Ervin Johnson	.10
38	Steve Smith	.20
39	Austin Croshere	.10
40	Matt Geiger	.10
41	Tom Gugliotta	.20

42	Radoslav Nesterovic	.20
43	Juwan Howard	.20
44	Keon Clark	.25
45	Latrell Sprewell	.20
46	George Lynch	.10
47	Greg Ostertag	.10
48	J.R. Henderson	.20
49	Kerry Kittles	.20
50	Matt Harpring	.25
51	Duane Causwell	.10
52	Andrae Patterson	.20
53	Jerry Stackhouse	.20
54	Adonal Foyle	.10
55	Bryce Drew	.20
56	Chris Childs	.10
57	Charles Smith	.10
58	Rony Seikaly	.10
59	Chauncey Billups	.20
60	Grant Hill	1.50
61	Marlon Garnett	.20
62	Tim Hardaway	.40
63	Vlade Divac	.20
64	Chris Gatling	.10
65	Glenn Robinson	.20
66	Michael Olowokandi	.40
67	Elliot Perry	.10
68	Howard Eisley	.10
69	Glen Rice	.20
70	Marcus Camby	.30
71	Theo Ratliff	.20
72	Brian Skinner	.20
73	Kenny Anderson	.20
74	Jamal Mashburn	.20
75	Vladimir Stepania	.20
76	Jayson Williams	.20
77	Brian Grant	.20
78	Raef LaFrentz	.40
79	John Starks	.10
80	Mike Bibby	.60
81	Stephon Marbury	1.00
82	Armen Gilliam	.10
83	Sam Jacobson	.20
84	Derrick Coleman	.20
85	Allan Houston	.20
86	Miles Simon	.20
87	Allen Iverson	1.25
88	Derek Anderson	.20
89	Chris Anstey	.10
90	Larry Hughes	.50
91	Vitaly Potapenko	.10
92	Cherokee Parks	.10
93	Donyell Marshall	.10
94	Danny Manning	.10
95	Bryon Russell	.10
96	Randell Jackson	.20
97	Antoine Walker	1.00
98	Dirk Nowitzki	.20
99	Karl Malone	.50
100	Vince Carter	1.50
101	Eddie Jones	.30
102	Bryant Stith	.10
103	Korleone Young	.20
104	Tim Duncan	1.50
105	Jerome Kersey	.10
106	Bonzi Wells	.20
107	Wesley Person	.10
108	Steve Nash	.10
109	Tyrone Nesby	.20
110	Doug Christie	.10
111	David Robinson	.50
112	Ruben Patterson	.20
113	Dikembe Mutombo	.20
114	Ron Mercer	.75
115	Elden Campbell	.10
116	Kevin Willis	.10
117	Hakeem Olajuwon	.50
118	Shawn Kemp	.75
119	Eric Montross	.10
120	Shareef Abdur-Rahim	.75
121	Bob Sura	.10
122	James Robinson	.10
123	Shawn Bradley	.10
124	Robert Traylor	.40
125	Dean Garrett	.10
126	Keith Van Horn	.75
127	Patrick Ewing	.20
128	Isaac Austin	.10
129	Jason Kidd	.75
130	Isaiah Rider	.20
131	Jerome James	.20
132	John Stockton	.20
133	Jason Caffey	.10
134	Bryant Reeves	.10
135	Michael Dickerson	.30
136	Chris Mullin	.20
137	Rasheed Wallace	.20
138	Cuttino Mobley	.20
139	Antonio McDyess	.40
140	Chris Webber	.75
141	Jelani McCoy	.20
142	Damon Stoudamire	.30
143	Gerald Brown	.20
144	Cory Carr	.20
145	Brent Barry	.10
146	Alan Henderson	.10
147	Nazr Mohammed	.20
148	Bison Dele	.10
149	Scottie Pippen	.75
150	Michael Doleac	.25
151	Nick Anderson	.20
152	Alonzo Mourning	.30
153	Jahidi White	.20
154	Jalen Rose	.20
155	Brad Miller	.20
156	Andrew DeClercq	.10
157	Erick Strickland	.10
158	Toni Kukoc	.30
159	Pat Garrity	.25
160	Bobby Jackson	.10
161	Steve Kerr	.10
162	Toby Bailey	.20
163	Charles Oakley	.10
164	Rod Strickland	.20
165	Rodrick Rhodes	.10
166	*Ron Artest*	1.00
167	*William Avery*	1.00
168	*Elton Brand*	5.00
169	*Baron Davis*	3.00
170	*John Celestand*	.25
171	*Jumanie Jones*	.75
172	*Andre Miller*	1.00
173	*Lee Nailon*	.50
174	*James Posey*	.75
175	*Jason Terry*	1.00
176	*Kenny Thomas*	.50
177	*Steve Francis*	5.00
178	*Wally Szczerbiak*	3.00
179	*Richard Hamilton*	2.00
180	*Jonathan Bender*	2.00
181	*Shawn Marion*	1.00
182	*Aleksandar Radojevic*	.50
183	*Tim James*	.50
184	*Trajan Langdon*	1.00
185	*Corey Maggette*	2.00

1999-00 Hoops Starting Five

Starting Five cards paralleled the entire 185-card set and were printed on silver foil. Each card was sequentially numbered to five.

	MT
Production 5 Sets	

1999-00 Hoops Build Your Own Card

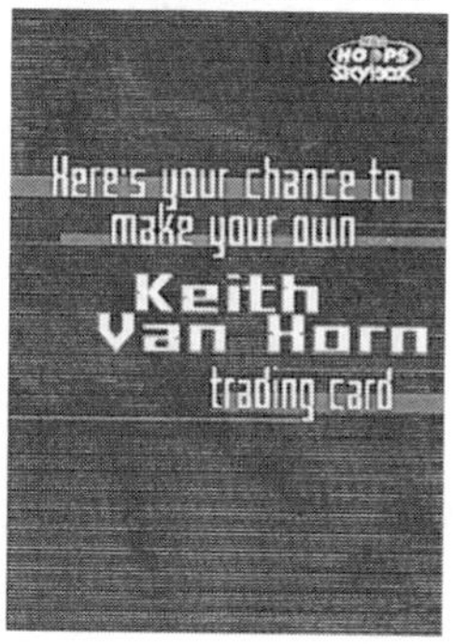

Build Your Own Card offer sheets were seeded 1:4 packs of Hoops. The offers opened like a book with a front displaying the player's name, the inside explaining the rules and showing the different front and back (three of each were available), and the back was a form to be filled out and sent in. Collectors could select the front and back of their choice, with six total versions available, each hand-numbered to 250. The requests were to be accompanied by a money order for $9.95. Ten different players were available in the set and the redemption cards were numbered with a "BC" suffix, while the offer sheets were unnumbered.

		MT
Complete Set (10):		10.00
Common Player:		.50
Inserted 1:4'		
1	Tim Duncan	2.00
2	Keith Van Horn	.50
3	Vince Carter	2.00
4	Grant Hill	2.00
5	Shaquille O'Neal	1.00
6	Kevin Garnett	2.00
7	Allen Iverson	1.50
8	Jason Williams	1.00
9	Kobe Bryant	2.50
10	Paul Pierce	1.00

1999-00 Hoops Calling Card

This 15-card insert highlighted players' top moves on a die-cut card that resembled a calling card. The signature move of the player was written up the right side of the card. Calling Card inserts were numbered with a "CC" suffix and inserted 1:8 packs.

		MT
Complete Set (15):		25.00
Common Player:		.50
Inserted 1:8		
1	Kobe Bryant	5.00
2	Kevin Garnett	4.00
3	Tim Hardaway	.75
4	Grant Hill	4.00
5	Allen Iverson	3.00
6	Karl Malone	1.00
7	Shawn Kemp	1.50
8	Stephon Marbury	2.00
9	Shaquille O'Neal	2.50
10	Hakeem Olajuwon	1.00
11	Ray Allen	.50
12	Damon Stoudamire	.75
13	Jason Williams	2.50
14	Keith Van Horn	1.50
15	Dikembe Mutombo	.50

1999-00 Hoops Dunk Mob

This 10-card insert captures top dunkers over a silver rainbow holofoil background. The insert name appears in both a graffiti-like background and in the lower right corner of each card. Dunk Mob inserts were numbered with a "DM" suffix and inserted 1:144 packs.

		MT
Complete Set (10):		150.00
Common Player:		5.00
Inserted 1:144		
1	Shaquille O'Neal	25.00
2	Stephon Marbury	25.00
3	Paul Pierce	25.00
4	Antawn Jamison	15.00
5	Michael Olowokandi	5.00
6	Scottie Pippen	15.00
7	Antonio McDyess	5.00
8	Vince Carter	35.00
9	Ron Mercer	15.00
10	Shawn Kemp	15.00

1999-00 Hoops Name Plates

This die-cut insert features 10 players on horizontal designs that resemble license plates. A color shot of the player on the left side, while his name is across the top and the insert name is across the bottom below the player's nickname in large letters through the middle. Name Plates were numbered with an "NP" suffix and inserted 1:4 packs.

		MT
Complete Set (10):		15.00
Common Player:		.40
Inserted 1:4		
1	Shareef Abdur-Rahim	1.50
2	Allen Iverson	3.00
3	Karl Malone	.75
4	Gary Payton	.75
5	Hakeem Olajuwon	.75
6	Glenn Robinson	.40
7	Kevin Garnett	5.00
8	Anfernee Hardaway	2.50
9	David Robinson	.75
10	Shaquille O'Neal	2.50

1999-00 Hoops Pure Players

This 10-card insert displayed top players on a silver plastic stock with orange foil stamping. Pure Players were numbered with a "PP" suffix and sequentially numbered to 500 sets. Parallel versions existed that featured purple foil stamping and were numbered to 100.

		MT
Complete Set (10):		325.00
Common Player:		15.00
Production 500 Sets		
100% Pure Players:		2x
Production 100 Sets		
1	Tim Duncan	50.00
2	Keith Van Horn	25.00
3	Stephon Marbury	25.00
4	Grant Hill	50.00
5	Kobe Bryant	60.00
6	Kevin Garnett	50.00
7	Allen Iverson	50.00
8	Antoine Walker	25.00
9	Shareef Abdur-Rahim	15.00
10	Anfernee Hardaway	30.00

1999-00 Hoops Y2K Corps

This 15-card insert featured top rookies from the 1998-99 season on embossed and silver foil-stamped back cards. Y2K inserts were numbered with a "Y2K" suffix and inserted 1:16 packs.

		MT
Complete Set (10):		30.00
Common Player:		1.00
Inserted 1:16		
1	Michael Olowokandi	2.00
2	Mike Bibby	3.00
3	Jason Williams	6.00
4	Dirk Nowitzki	1.00
5	Vince Carter	10.00
6	Robert Traylor	2.00
7	Larry Hughes	3.00
8	Paul Pierce	5.00
9	Matt Harpring	1.00
10	Michael Dickerson	2.00

1999 Hoops WNBA

This inaugural 110-card base set for Hoops WNBA featured 87 basic cards, seven Future Performers, eight League Leaders, six Postseason Rewind and two checklists. Cards featured a bleeding white border and arrived in 10-card packs. Inserts included: Autographics, Building Blocks, Award Winners and Talk of the Town.

		MT
Complete Set (110):		25.00
Common Player:		.05
Wax Box (36):		50.00
1	Cynthia Cooper	1.00
2	Game 3 - Houston vs. Phoenix	.75
3	Game 2 - Houston vs. Phoenix	.75
4	Game 1 - Houston vs. Phoenix	.25
5	Houston vs. Charlotte	.75
6	Phoenix vs. Cleveland	.10
7	League Leaders Scoring	1.00
8	League Leaders Rebounds	.50
9	League Leaders FG Pct.	.10
10	League Leaders 3-Pt. FG Pct.	.50
11	League Leaders FT Pct.	.50
12	League Leaders Assists	.30
13	League Leaders Steals	.50
14	League Leaders Blocks	.50
15	Andrea Kuklova	.05
16	Christy Smith	.10
17	Penny Moore	.15
18	Octavia Blue	.05
19	Vickie Johnson	.15
20	Latasha Byears	.15
21	Vicky Bullett	.15
22	Franthea Price	.05
23	Tina Thompson	.40
24	Teresa Weatherspoon	.50
25	Maria Stepanova	.05
26	Merlakia Jones	.20
27	Razija Mujanovic	.05
28	Rhonda Mapp	.10
29	Kristi Harrower	.05
30	Penny Toler	.10
31	*Margo Dydek*	.50
32	Kim Perrot	.60
33	Cindy Brown	1.00
34	Eva Nemcova	.20
35	Quacy Barnes	.10
36	*Tracy Reid*	.50
37	Chantel Tremitiere	.05
38	Lady Hardmon	.05
39	Michelle Griffiths	.05
40	Sheryl Swoopes	2.00
41	*Sandy Brondello*	1.50
42	Andrea Stinson	.50
43	*Marlies Askamp*	.50
44	*Rachael Sporn*	.30
45	Nikki McCray	1.50
46	Andrea Congreaves	.05
47	Toni Foster	.10
48	Kim Williams	.05

49	*Carla Porter*	.30
50	Jamila Wideman	.20
51	Isabelle Fijalkowski	.10
52	*Korie Hlede*	.30
53	Tora Suber	.10
54	Sue Wicks	.05
55	Coquese Washington	.05
56	Sharon Manning	.05
57	Tammy Jackson	.05
58	Tangela Smith	.10
59	Suzie McConnell Serio	.25
60	Lisa Leslie	1.50
61	Wendy Palmer	.50
62	Adia Barnes	.05
63	La'Shawn Brown	.05
64	Janeth Arcain	.05
65	Ruthie Bolton-Holifield	1.00
66	Bridget Pettis	.10
67	Pamela McGee	.10
68	Rebecca Lobo	1.00
69	*Cindy Blodgett*	.50
70	Rita Williams	.30
71	Mwadi Mabika	.05
72	Sophia Witherspoon	.20
73	Janice Braxton	.10
74	Cynthia Cooper	2.00
75	Tammi Reiss	.30
76	Umeki Webb	.05
77	Kym Hampton	.15
78	*LaTonya Johnson*	.30
79	Michele Timms	.75
80	Kisha Ford	.05
81	*Monica Lamb*	.30
82	Keri Chaconas	.05
83	Elena Baranova	.50
84	Linda Burgess	.05
85	Tamecka Dixon	.15
86	Heidi Burge	.05
87	Michelle Edwards	.30
88	Yolanda Moore	.05
89	*Ticha Penicheiro*	.50
90	*Ales Santos de Oliveiro*	.30
91	Rushia Brown	.05
92	Lynette Woodard	.50
93	Katrina Colleton	.05
94	Bridgette Gordon	.05
95	Jennifer Gillom	.50
96	Murriel Page	.25
97	Olympia Scott-Richardson	.05
98	*Adrienne Johnson*	.75
99	Gergana Branzova	.05
100	Allison Feaster	.05
101	*Brandy Reed*	1.00
102	*Katie Smith*	.75
103	*Natalie Williams*	2.00
104	*Jennifer Azzi*	3.00
105	*Clamnique Holdsclaw*	8.00
106	*Dawn Staley*	2.00
107	*Nykesha Sales*	1.00
108	*Kristin Folkl*	.50
109	Checklist	.05
110	Checklist	.05

1999 Hoops WNBA Autographics

This 13-card insert featured autographs from top players in the WNBA. Each card featured an embossed SkyBox seal of authenticity. These were unnumbered on the back and inserted 1:144 packs.

		MT
Complete Set (13):		1000.
Common Player:		40.00
Inserted 1:144		
1	Cynthia Cooper	200.00
2	Kristin Folkl	50.00
3	Bridgette Gordon	50.00
4	Lisa Leslie	125.00
5	Nikki McCray	75.00
6	Suzie McConnell Serio	90.00
7	Nykesha Sales	75.00
8	Dawn Staley	75.00
9	Andrea Stinson	60.00
10	Sheryl Swoopes	150.00
11	Michele Timms	125.00
12	Penny Toler	60.00
13	Teresa Weatherspoon	100.00

1999 Hoops WNBA Award Winners

This 10-card insert set featured All-WNBA First and Second Team players on a matte silver and holographic foil-stamped card. Award Winners were numbered with an "AW" suffix and inserted 1:24 packs.

		MT
Complete Set (10):		80.00
Common Player:		4.00
Inserted 1:24		
1	Tina Thompson	5.00
2	Sheryl Swoopes	20.00
3	Jennifer Gillom	12.00
4	Cynthia Cooper	20.00
5	Suzie McConnell Serio	5.00
6	Cindy Brown	8.00
7	Eva Nemcova	4.00
8	Lisa Leslie	15.00
9	Andrea Stinson	8.00
10	Teresa Weatherspoon	8.00

1999 Hoops WNBA Building Blocks

Building Blocks featured eight top WNBA players on a matte silver foil-stamped insert with a blue background. Cards were numbered with a "BB" prefix and inserted 1:4 packs.

		MT
Complete Set (8):		12.00
Common Player:		1.00
Inserted 1:4		
1	Dawn Staley	3.00
2	Rebecca Lobo	3.00
3	Tracy Reid	2.00
4	Korie Hlede	2.00
5	Ticha Penicheiro	1.00
6	Tammi Reiss	1.00
7	Nikki McCray	3.00
8	Jennifer Gillom	3.00

1999 Hoops WNBA Talk Of The Town

Talk of the Town captured a top star from each of the 12 WNBA cities on a gold foil-stamped card. Each player was pictured against a city-scape of her team's city. Cards were numbered with a "TT" suffix and inserted 1:12 packs.

		MT
Complete Set (12):		45.00
Common Player:		2.00
Inserted 1:12		
1	Cynthia Cooper	10.00
2	Michele Timms	4.00
3	Suzie McConnell Serio	3.00
4	Lisa Leslie	8.00
5	Andrea Stinson	4.00
6	Elena Baranova	4.00
7	Cindy Brown	4.00
8	Teresa Weatherspoon	6.00
9	Nikki McCray	6.00
10	Ruthie Bolton-Holifield	4.00
11	Nykesha Sales	3.00
12	Kristin Folkl	2.00

1999 Press Pass

This 45-card set featured players eligible to be drafted in the 1999 NBA Draft. Press Pass signed exclusive draft pick contracts with four of the top six picks - Elton Brand, Steve Francis, Lamar Odom and Wally Szczerbiak - to produce their cards and signatures in its 1999 product. The set featured 44 different players, and repeated Brand on the 45th card, which was a checklist. While regular cards featured silver foil, there was also a Gold Zone (hobby only, gold foil) and Torquers (retail only, blue foil) parallel, as well as Reflectors and Solos. Inserts included Y2K, Autographs, Standout Signatures, Jersey Cards, Net Burners, In Your Face, Crunch Time and On Fire.

		MT
Complete Set (45):		15.00
Common Player:		.10
Wax Box (24):		75.00
1	Elton Brand	3.00
2	Steve Francis	3.00
3	Baron Davis	2.00
4	Lamar Odom	3.00
5	Jonathan Bender	1.50
6	Wally Szczerbiak	2.00
7	Richard Hamilton	1.50
8	Andre Miller	.75
9	Jason Terry	1.00
10	Trajan Langdon	1.00
11	William Avery	.75
12	Ron Artest	.75
13	Cal Bowdler	.20
14	James Posey	.40
15	Quincy Lewis	.40
16	Jeff Foster	.20
17	Kenny Thomas	.20
18	Devean George	.20
19	Tim James	.20
20	Vonteego Cummings	.20
21	Jumanie Jones	.20
22	Scott Padgett	.20
23	John Celestand	.10
24	Rico Hill	.10
25	Michael Ruffin	.10
26	Chris Herren	.40
27	Evan Eschmeyer	.20
28	Calvin Booth	.10
29	Obinna Ekezie	.10
30	A.J. Bramlett	.20
31	Louis Bullock	.10
32	Lee Nailon	.10
33	Tyrone Washington	.10
34	Lari Ketner	.10
35	Venson Hamilton	.10
36	Roberto Bergersen	.10
37	Rodney Buford	.10
38	Melvin Levett	.20
39	Kris Clack	.10
40	Harold Jamison	.10
41	Heshimu Evans	.10
42	Ademola Okulaja	.10
43	Jamel Thomas	.10
44	Jason Miskiri	.10
45	Elton Brand (Checklist)	1.00

1999 Press Pass Gold Zone

This 45-card set paralleled every card in the base set and was inserted one per hobby pack. Gold Zone cards used gold foil stamping vs. the silver used on base cards.

	MT
Complete Set (45):	25.00
Gold Zone Cards:	2x
Inserted 1:1 Hobby	

1999 Press Pass Reflectors

Reflectors paralleled the 45-card base set in Press Pass, but added a holofoil finish to the front, which arrived protected by a laminate and peel-off covering. Cards were numbered with an "R" prefix and inserted 1:90 packs. Reflectors cards were also sequentially numbered to 250 on the back.

	MT
Complete Set (45):	350.00
Reflectors Cards:	15x-30x
Production 250 Sets	
Inserted 1:90	

1999 Press Pass Torquers

This 45-card set paralleled all 45 cards in the base set and was inserted one per retail pack. Torquers utilized blue foil stamping vs. the silver foil used on base cards.

	MT
Complete Set (45):	25.00
Torquers Cards:	2x
Inserted 1:1 Retail	

1999 Press Pass Certified Authentic

This insert featured autographed versions of player's base cards. Autographed versions featured a matte strip through the middle where the player signed. These were seeded 1:8 hobby packs and 1:36 retail packs. Redemption cards were issued for Lamar Odom, Jonathan Bender and Kenny Thomas, while John Celestand signed his on the back.

	MT
Common Player:	5.00
Inserted 1:8 Hobby, 1:36 Retail	
Elton Brand	75.00
Steve Francis	75.00
Baron Davis	40.00
Lamar Odom	75.00
Jonathan Bender	40.00
Wally Szczerbiak	50.00
Richard Hamilton	30.00
Andre Miller	15.00
Jason Terry	20.00
Trajan Langdon	20.00
William Avery	15.00
Ron Artest	15.00
Cal Bowdler	8.00
James Posey	10.00
Quincy Lewis	8.00
Kenny Thomas	8.00
Devean George	8.00
Tim James	10.00
Vonteego Cummings	8.00
John Celestand	5.00
Rico Hill	5.00
Michael Ruffin	5.00
Chris Herren	8.00
Evan Eschmeyer	8.00
Calvin Booth	8.00
A.J. Bramlett	8.00
Louis Bullock	5.00
Lee Nailon	5.00
Tyrone Washington	5.00
Lari Ketner	5.00
Venson Hamilton	5.00
Roberto Bergersen	5.00
Rodney Buford	5.00
Melvin Levett	8.00
Kris Clack	5.00

Harold Jamison	5.00
Heshimu Evans	8.00
Ademola Okulaja	5.00
Jamel Thomas	5.00
Jason Miskiri	5.00

1999 Press Pass Standout Signatures Parallel

Standout Signatures paralleled the Certified Authentic Autographs, but was sequentially numbered to 100 on the back. These parallel versions also included the insert name in gold foil up the left side.

	MT
Common Player:	10.00
Standout Signature Cards:	2x
Production 100 Sets	
Inserted 1:120 Hobby	

1999 Press Pass Crunch Time

This nine-card insert featured a color shot of the player over an action foil background. Crunch Time inserts were numbered with a "CT" prefix and inserted 1:18 packs.

		MT
Complete Set (9):		40.00
Common Player:		1.00
Inserted 1:18		
1	Elton Brand	10.00
2	Steve Francis	10.00
3	Baron Davis	5.00
4	Lamar Odom	10.00
5	Wally Szczerbiak	8.00
6	Richard Hamilton	4.00
7	Andre Miller	1.00
8	Jason Terry	2.00
9	William Avery	1.00

1999 Press Pass In Your Face

This six-card insert was printed on clear acetate stock and featured above-the-rim photography. Cards were numbered with an "IYF" prefix and inserted 1:24 packs.

		MT
Complete Set (6):		35.00
Common Player:		2.00
Inserted 1:24		
1	Elton Brand	20.00
2	Baron Davis	10.00
3	Andre Miller	4.00
4	Jason Terry	6.00
5	Ron Artest	6.00
6	Kenny Thomas	2.00

1999 Press Pass Jersey Cards

This five-card insert featured a swatch of game-worn college jersey from five different players. The cards are numbered with a "JC" prefix and inserted 1:480 hobby and 1:720 retail packs.

		MT
Complete Set (5):		400.00
Common Player:		30.00
Inserted 1:480 Hobby, 1:720 Retail		
1	Elton Brand	125.00
2	Steve Francis	125.00
3	Lamar Odom	125.00
4	James Posey	50.00
5	Evan Eschmeyer	30.00

1999 Press Pass Net Burners

This 36-card set was considered a set within a set since it featured nearly all of the players in the base set and was seeded one per pack. Cards were numbered with an "NB" prefix.

	MT
Complete Set (36):	25.00
Net Burners Cards:	1x-2x
Common Player:	.20
Inserted 1:1	

1999 Press Pass On Fire

This 12-card insert featured players on micro-etched Nitrokrome technology. Cards were numbered with an "OF" prefix on the back and inserted 1:12 packs.

		MT
Complete Set (12):		45.00
Common Player:		1.00
Inserted 1:12		
1	Elton Brand	10.00
2	Steve Francis	10.00
3	Baron Davis	6.00
4	Lamar Odom	10.00
5	Wally Szczerbiak	8.00
6	Richard Hamilton	5.00
7	Andre Miller	2.00
8	Jason Terry	3.00
9	William Avery	2.00
10	Ron Artest	2.00
11	James Posey	1.50
12	Kenny Thomas	1.00

1999 Press Pass Y2K

Y2K featured eight players on a die-cut format with a basketball background. The cards were printed on foil and sequentially numbered to 2000 sets. Cards were numbered with a "Y" prefix and inserted one per 24 hobby packs.

		MT
Complete Set (8):		60.00
Common Player:		3.00
Inserted 1:24 Hobby		
Production 2,000 Sets		
1	Elton Brand	15.00
2	Steve Francis	15.00
3	Baron Davis	10.00
4	Lamar Odom	15.00
5	Wally Szczerbiak	10.00
6	Richard Hamilton	6.00
7	Andre Miller	3.00
8	Jason Terry	4.00

1999 Upper Deck SP Top Prospects

This 38-card set highlighted players eligible to be drafted in the 1999 NBA Draft. The cards featured spot UV-coating on the player's image, with the action shot surrounded by a white border, then repeated the words "Top Prospects" in grey letters. The player's name and parts of the border were printed with silver foil. Cards #8, 15, 19 and 42 were not printed since Press Pass signed exclusive contracts with Brand, Francis, Odom and Szczerbiak to exclusive draft pick contracts. Inserts include: MJ Flight Mechanics 101, Vital Signs, Jordan's Scrapbook and College Legends. The entire set was also paralleled in an Upper Class parallel.

		MT
Complete Set (38):		20.00
Common Player:		.20
Cards 8/15/19/42 Do Not Exist		
Wax Box (24):		90.00
1	Lee Nailon	.40
2	A.J. Bramlett	.40
3	Jason Terry	3.00
4	Kareem Reid	.20
5	Melvin Levett	.40
6	Terrell McIntyre	.20
7	Trajan Langdon	3.00
9	Chris Herren	.75
10	Shawnta Rogers	.20
11	Corey Maggette	3.00
12	Wayne Turner	.40
13	Heshimu Evans	.40
14	Bobby Lazor	.20
16	Laron Profit	.75
17	Ron Artest	2.00
18	Tim James	1.00
20	Louis Bullock	.40
21	William Avery	2.00
22	Quincy Lewis	1.00
23	Kenny Thomas	1.00
24	Evan Eschmeyer	.40
25	Adrian Peterson	.20
26	Keith Carter	.20
27	Jelani Gardner	.20
28	Baron Davis	5.00
29	Jamel Thomas	.40
30	B.J. McKie	.20
31	Arthur Lee	.40
32	Tim Young	.20
33	Richard Hamilton	3.00
34	Calvin Booth	.40
35	Andre Miller	2.00
36	Todd MacCulloch	.40
37	James Posey	1.50
38	Lenny Brown	.20
39	Scott Padgett	1.00
40	Venson Hamilton	.40
41	Geno Carlisle	.20

1999 Upper Deck SP Top Prospects Upper Class

Upper Class was a 38-card parallel set of SP Top Prospects. Cards from this parallel were die-cut and sequentially numbered to 50 sets.

	MT
Upper Class Cards:	15x-30x
Production 50 Sets	

1999 Upper Deck SP Top Prospects College Legends

This 10-card insert focused on four of the top players ever at the college level. It includes three Jordan and Bird cards and two each of Erving and Anfernee Hardaway. College Legends are numbered with an "L" prefix and inserted 1:92 packs.

		MT
Complete Set (10):		125.00
Common Player:		5.00
Inserted 1:92		
1	Michael Jordan	25.00
2	Michael Jordan	25.00
3	Michael Jordan	25.00
4	Larry Bird	15.00
5	Larry Bird	15.00
6	Larry Bird	15.00
7	Julius Erving	10.00
8	Julius Erving	10.00
9	Anfernee Hardaway	5.00
10	Anfernee Hardaway	5.00

1999 Upper Deck SP Top Prospects Jordan's Scrapbook

This 20-card insert highlights Michael Jordan's top moments during his collegiate career at North Carolina. Cards were numbered with a "J" prefix and inserted 1:23 packs.

	MT
Complete Set (20):	100.00
Common Player:	6.00
Inserted 1:23	

1999 Upper Deck SP Top Prospects MJ Flight Mechanics

This 28-card insert features players over a blue foil background and was selected by Michael Jordan. The cards were numbered with an "FM" prefix and inserted 1:4 packs. Cards 4 and 25 were never printed.

		MT
Complete Set (30):		30.00
Common Player:		.50
Inserted 1:4		
1	Jason Terry	5.00
2	Geno Carlisle	.50
3	Heshimu Evans	.75
5	Keith Carter	.50
6	Trajan Langdon	5.00
7	Ron Artest	3.00
8	Kenny Thomas	1.00
9	Lenny Brown	.50
10	Kareem Reid	.50
11	Shawnta Rogers	.50
12	Quincy Lewis	1.50
13	Jamel Thomas	.75
14	James Posey	2.00
15	Lee Nailon	.75
16	Melvin Levett	.75
17	Laron Profit	.75
18	Louis Bullock	.50
19	Evan Eschmeyer	.75
20	B.J. McKie	.50
21	A.J. Bramlett	.75
22	Wayne Turner	.75
23	Jelani Gardner	.50
24	Terrell McIntyre	.50
26	Venson Hamilton	.75
27	Andre Miller	3.00
28	Chris Herren	.75
29	Adrian Peterson	.50
30	Tim James	1.50

1999 Upper Deck SP Top Prospects Vital Signs

Vital Signs included autographs from 39 players, including all 38 players in the base set and 23 numbered Michael Jordan autographs. The cards featured the same photograph as the base cards, but over a pure white background. In addition, the silver foil stamping was replaced by black and the grey photo border was replaced by blue. The player's signature was across the bottom of the card. Cards were numbered with a two-letter number on the back, usually involving the player's initials and inserted 1:4 packs.

		MT
Complete Set (39):		250.00
Common Player:		3.00
Inserted 1:4		
VC	Pat Bradley	3.00
AB	A.J. Bramlett	5.00
DG	Rasheed Brokenborough	5.00
LB	Lenny Brown	3.00
GC	Geno Carlisle	3.00
BD	Baron Davis	50.00
OE	Obinna Ekezie	3.00
EE	Evan Eschmeyer	5.00
HE	Heshimu Evans	5.00
DF	Damon Frierson	3.00
JG	Jelani Gardner	3.00
RH	Richard Hamilton	30.00
VH	Venson Hamilton	5.00
CH	Chris Herren	8.00
JK	Jermaine Jackson	3.00
TJ	Tim James	10.00
JA	Michael Jordan	3000.
TL	Trajan Langdon	25.00
AL	Arthur Lee	3.00
ML	Melvin Levett	5.00
QL	Quincy Lewis	8.00
GL	Gary Lumpkin	3.00
TM	Terrell McIntyre	3.00
BJ	B.J. McKie	3.00
AM	Andre Miller	20.00
LN	Lee Nailon	5.00
SP	Scott Padgett	10.00
AP	Adrian Peterson	3.00
JP	James Posey	10.00
LP	Laron Profit	8.00
KR	Kareem Reid	3.00
SR	Shawnta Rogers	5.00
TE	Jason Terry	20.00
JT	Jamel Thomas	5.00
KT	Kenny Thomas	10.00
WT	Wayne Turner	5.00
TY	Tim Young	3.00
DW	Donald Watts	3.00
OS	Kris Weems	3.00

1999-00 Topps Promos

This six-card promotional set was distributed to dealers and members of the media to promote the 1999-2000 Topps Basketball product. The cards were identical to the regular-issue cards except they were numbered PP1-PP6 on the back.

		MT
Complete Set (6):		1.00
Common Player:		.10
1	Bryant Reeves	.10
2	Isaiah Rider	.15
3	Sean Elliot	.15
4	Mark Jackson	.10
5	Voshon Lenard	.10
6	Juwan Howard	.50

1999-00 Topps

Topps included 120 cards in its Series I product, with 110 base cards featuring orange borders, and 10 1999 NBA Draft Picks seeded 1:5 packs. All 120 cards were paralleled in MVP Promotion, while inserts included: Patriarchs, Prodigy, Prodigy Refractors, Record Numbers, Season's Best, Picture Perfect, Highlight Reels, Autographs and Jumbos.

		MT
Complete Set (120):		40.00
Common Player:		.10
Common Rookie:		2.00
Inserted 1:5		
Wax Box (36):		50.00
1	Steve Smith	.20
2	Ron Harper	.10
3	Michael Dickerson	.30
4	LaPhonso Ellis	.20
5	Chris Webber	.75
6	Jason Caffey	.10
7	Bryon Russell	.10
8	Bison Dele	.10
9	Isaiah Rider	.20
10	Dean Garrett	.10
11	Eric Murdock	.10
12	Juwan Howard	.20
13	Latrell Sprewell	.20
14	Jalen Rose	.10
15	Larry Johnson	.20
16	Eric Williams	.10
17	Bryant Reeves	.10
18	Tony Battie	.10
19	Luc Longley	.10
20	Gary Payton	.50
21	Tariq Abdul-Wahad	.10
22	Armen Gilliam	.10
23	Shaquille O'Neal	1.00
24	Gary Trent	.20
25	John Stockton	.20
26	Mark Jackson	.10
27	Cherokee Parks	.10
28	Michael Olowokandi	.30
29	Raef LaFrentz	.30
30	Dell Curry	.10
31	Travis Best	.10
32	Shawn Kemp	.75
33	Voshon Lenard	.10
34	Brian Grant	.20
35	Alvin Williams	.10
36	Derek Fisher	.10
37	Allan Houston	.20
38	Arvydas Sabonis	.20
39	Terry Cummings	.10
40	Dale Ellis	.10
41	Maurice Taylor	.20
42	Grant Hill	1.50
43	Anthony Mason	.20
44	John Wallace	.10
45	David Wesley	.10
46	Nick Van Exel	.20
47	Cuttino Mobley	.20
48	Anfernee Hardaway	1.00
49	Terry Porter	.10
50	Brent Barry	.10
51	Derek Harper	.10
52	Antoine Walker	1.00
53	Karl Malone	.50
54	Ben Wallace	.10
55	Vlade Divac	.20
56	Sam Mitchell	.10
57	Joe Smith	.20
58	Shawn Bradley	.10
59	Darrell Armstrong	.20
60	Kenny Anderson	.20
61	Jason Williams	.75
62	Alonzo Mourning	.30
63	Matt Harpring	.20
64	Antonio Davis	.10
65	Lindsey Hunter	.10
66	Allen Iverson	1.25
67	Mookie Blaylock	.10
68	Wesley Person	.10
69	Bobby Phills	.10
70	Theo Ratliff	.10
71	Antonio Daniels	.10
72	P.J. Brown	.10
73	David Robinson	.50
74	Sean Elliott	.10
75	Zydrunas Ilgauskas	.20
76	Kerry Kittles	.10
77	Otis Thorpe	.10
78	John Starks	.10
79	Jaren Jackson	.10
80	Hersey Hawkins	.10
81	Glenn Robinson	.20
82	Paul Pierce	.75
83	Glen Rice	.20
84	Charlie Ward	.10
85	Dee Brown	.10
86	Danny Fortson	.10
87	Billy Owens	.10
88	Jason Kidd	.75
89	Brent Price	.10
90	Don Reid	.10
91	Mark Bryant	.10
92	Vinny Del Negro	.10
93	Stephon Marbury	1.00
94	Donyell Marshall	.10
95	Jim Jackson	.10
96	Horace Grant	.10
97	Calbert Cheaney	.10
98	Vince Carter	1.25
99	Bobby Jackson	.10
100	Alan Henderson	.10
101	Mike Bibby	.50
102	Cedric Henderson	.10
103	Lamond Murray	.10
104	A.C. Green	.10
105	Hakeem Olajuwon	.50
106	George Lynch	.10
107	Kendall Gill	.10
108	Rex Chapman	.10
109	Eddie Jones	.50
110	Kornel David	.10
111	*Jason Terry* (Draft Picks)	3.00
112	*Corey Maggette* (Draft Picks)	5.00
113	*Ron Artest* (Draft Picks)	3.00
114	*Richard Hamilton* (Draft Picks)	5.00
115	*Elton Brand* (Draft Picks)	10.00
116	*Baron Davis* (Draft Picks)	6.00
117	*Wally Szczerbiak* (Draft Picks)	6.00
118	*Steve Francis* (Draft Picks)	10.00
119	*James Posey* (Draft Picks)	2.00
120	*Shawn Marion* (Draft Picks)	2.00

1999-00 Topps MVP Promotion

MVP Promotion cards paralleled each card in Topps Series I, with identical fronts except for the addition of a gold foil stamp identifying the set. Card backs were white, unnumbered and explained the rules of the promotion. MVP Promotion cards were inserted 1:336 packs and limited to just 100 sets.

	MT
MVP Promotion Cards:	25x-50x
MVP Promotion Rookies:	3x-6x
Production 100 Sets	
Inserted 1:336 Hobby	

1999-00 Topps Autographs

Nine different Autographs were included in Series I, with each featuring the "Topps Certified Autograph Issue" stamp. These cards were hobby exclusive with Group A cards seeded 1:877 and Group B cards seeded 1:351.

		MT
Complete Set (9):		400.00
Common Player:		20.00
Inserted 1:934 Hobby		
SAR	Shareef Abdur-Rahim	60.00
JK	Jason Kidd	60.00
AM	Antonio McDyess	35.00
GP	Gary Payton	35.00
PP	Paul Pierce	75.00
SP	Scottie Pippen	100.00
MR	Mitch Richmond	20.00
SS	Steve Smith	20.00
DS	Damon Stoudamire	30.00

1999-00 Topps Jumbos

Eight different Jumbo cards were included in Series I and seeded one per hobby box as a box topper. The cards were identical to the regular-issue cards except they measured 3-1/4" x 4-1/2" and were numbered 1-8.

		MT
Complete Set (8):		25.00
Common Player:		1.00
Inserted 1:Hobby Box		
1	Gary Payton	2.00
2	Shaquille O'Neal	4.00
3	Antoine Walker	4.00
4	Jason Williams	3.00
5	Alonzo Mourning	1.00
6	Allen Iverson	6.00
7	Stephon Marbury	4.00
8	Vince Carter	6.00

1999-00 Topps Highlight Reels

Highlight Reels was a 15-card, retail exclusive insert found in packs of Topps Series I. They were numbered with an "HR" prefix and inserted 1:14 packs of Series I.

		MT
Complete Set (15):		35.00
Common Player:		.75
Inserted 1:14 Retail		
1	Stephon Marbury	2.00
2	Vince Carter	6.00
3	Kevin Garnett	6.00
4	Kobe Bryant	8.00
5	Chris Webber	1.50
6	Allen Iverson	4.00
7	Grant Hill	6.00
8	Antoine Walker	2.00
9	Jason Williams	4.00
10	Tim Duncan	6.00
11	Shareef Abdur-Rahim	1.50
12	Keith Van Horn	2.00
13	Antonio McDyess	.75
14	Jason Kidd	2.00
15	Ron Mercer	1.50

1999-00 Topps Patriarchs

This insert featured 15 players printed with dot matrix technology. Cards were numbered with a "P" prefix and inserted 1:22 packs of Series I.

		MT
Complete Set (15):		40.00
Common Player:		1.00
Inserted 1:22		
1	Patrick Ewing	1.00
2	Reggie Miller	1.00
3	Hakeem Olajuwon	3.00
4	Scottie Pippen	5.00
5	Grant Hill	12.00
6	Shaquille O'Neal	8.00
7	Mitch Richmond	1.00
8	Glen Rice	1.00
9	Charles Barkley	3.00
10	Karl Malone	3.00
11	John Stockton	1.00
12	Gary Payton	3.00
13	David Robinson	3.00
14	Tim Hardaway	2.00
15	Joe Dumars	1.00

1999-00 Topps Picture Perfect

This insert displayed 10 subjects printed with an intentional error somewhere in the picture. Backs were numbered with a "PIC" prefix and gave clues to what was wrong with the front photo. Picture Perfect cards were inserted 1:8 packs of Series I.

		MT
Complete Set (10):		10.00
Common Player:		.25
Inserted 1:8		
1	Shaquille O'Neal	2.00
2	Alonzo Mourning	1.00
3	Shareef Abdur-Rahim	1.50
4	Juwan Howard	.50
5	Keith Van Horn	2.00
6	Ron Mercer	1.50
7	Tim Hardaway	1.00
8	Kevin Garnett	3.00
9	David Robinson	1.00
10	Kerry Kittles	.25

1999-00 Topps Prodigy

This insert featured 20 players - 10 with less than five years of pro experience and 10 rookies - on die-cut chrome designs. Cards were numbered with a "PR" prefix and inserted 1:36 packs. Refractor versions of each card also existed and were seeded 1:144 packs of Series I.

		MT
Complete Set (20):		125.00
Common Player:		2.00
Inserted 1:36		
Refractors:		2x-3x
Inserted 1:144		
1	Stephon Marbury	10.00
2	Jason Kidd	6.00
3	Kevin Garnett	15.00
4	Kobe Bryant	20.00
5	Antoine Walker	10.00
6	Ron Mercer	6.00
7	Shareef Abdur-Rahim	6.00
8	Tim Duncan	15.00
9	Keith Van Horn	10.00
10	Ray Allen	2.00
11	Michael Doleac	2.00
12	Jason Williams	8.00
13	Michael Dickerson	3.00
14	Mike Bibby	4.00
15	Paul Pierce	8.00
16	Michael Olowokandi	3.00
17	Vince Carter	12.00
18	Antawn Jamison	6.00
19	Felipe Lopez	2.00
20	Matt Harpring	2.00

1999-00 Topps Record Numbers

This 10-card insert set featured record setting players over a blue, exploding background with a white border. Record Numbers were numbered with an "RN" prefix and inserted 1:12 packs of Series I.

		MT
Complete Set (10):		15.00
Common Player:		.50
Inserted 1:12		
1	Karl Malone	1.00
2	Kerry Kittles	.50
3	Reggie Miller	.75
4	Hakeem Olajuwon	1.00
5	John Stockton	.75
6	Dikembe Mutombo	.75
7	Kobe Bryant	6.00
8	Tim Duncan	5.00
9	Allen Iverson	4.00
10	Patrick Ewing	.75

1999-00 Topps Season's Best

Season's Best displayed 30 cards with the top five at each position and top five rookies from the 1998-99 season. Center Stage (centers), Mighty Men (power forwards), Gliders (small forwards), Shooting Stars (shooting guards), Conductors (point guards) and Fresh Foundations (rookies) were the six categories and each featured a different design. These inserts were numbered with an "SB" prefix and inserted 1:12 packs of Series I.

		MT
Complete Set (30):		65.00
Common Player:		1.00
Inserted 1:12		
1	David Robinson	3.00
2	Shaquille O'Neal	5.00
3	Patrick Ewing	1.00
4	Hakeem Olajuwon	3.00
5	Alonzo Mourning	2.00
6	Antonio McDyess	2.00
7	Tim Duncan	10.00
8	Keith Van Horn	5.00
9	Karl Malone	3.00
10	Chris Webber	4.00
11	Kevin Garnett	10.00
12	Juwan Howard	1.00
13	Shareef Abdur-Rahim	4.00
14	Glenn Robinson	1.00
15	Grant Hill	10.00
16	Michael Finley	1.00
17	Steve Smith	1.00
18	Mitch Richmond	1.00
19	Kobe Bryant	12.00
20	Ray Allen	1.00
21	Allen Iverson	6.00
22	Gary Payton	3.00
23	Stephon Marbury	5.00
24	Jason Kidd	4.00
25	Tim Hardaway	2.00
26	Jason Williams	5.00
27	Vince Carter	8.00
28	Paul Pierce	5.00
29	Mike Bibby	3.00
30	Michael Dickerson	1.00

1999 Ultra WNBA

Ultra marked Fleer/SkyBox's second WNBA card release of 1999. The set consisted of 125 total cards, with 90 basic player cards, 10 All-WNBA and 25 seeded rookies (1:2 packs). The cards featured a similar borderless design to other Ultra products, while the rookies had the same team color border at the bottom as the rookies from 1998-99 Ultra Basketball. The set was paralleled in Gold Medallion, Platinum Medallion and Masterpiece sets. Inserts include: WNBAttitude, World Premiere, Rock Talk and Fresh Ink.

		MT
Complete Set (125):		100.00
Common Player:		.15
Common Rookie:		3.00
Inserted 1:4		
Wax Box (24):		65.00
1	Sheryl Swoopes	4.00
2	Christy Smith	.15
3	Nikki McCray	2.50
4	Coquese Washington	.15
5	Vickie Johnson	.50
6	Toni Foster	.40
7	Allison Feaster	.15
8	Penny Toler	.40
9	*Brandy Reed*	2.00
10	Yolanda Moore	.30
11	Lisa Leslie	3.00
12	Kisha Ford	.15
13	Merlakia Jones	.50
14	Umeki Webb	.30
15	Tora Suber	.50
16	Octavia Blue	.15
17	Bridget Pettis	.15
18	*LaTonya Johnson*	.60
19	*Ales Santos de Oliveiro*	.60
20	Tia Paschal	.15
21	Jennifer Gillom	1.50
22	Wanda Guyton	.30
23	Franthea Price	.15
24	Andrea Kuklova	.15
25	Vicky Bullett	.50
26	Dena Head	.15
27	Isabelle Fijalkowski	.15
28	Michelle Edwards	1.00
29	Pamela McGee	.40
30	Elisabeth Cebrian	.15
31	Olympia Scott	.15
32	Murriel Page	.60
33	*Korie Hlede*	1.50
34	Andrea Stinson	1.50
35	Kristie Harrower	.15
36	Kym Hampton	.50
37	Gergana 1ranzova	.15
38	Teresa Weatherspoon	2.50
39	Rebecca Lobo	2.75
40	Michele Timms	2.50
41	Tamecka Dixon	.50
42	Tina Thompson	.50
43	Janice Braxton	.15
44	Elena Baranova	1.50
45	Adrienne Johnson	2.00
46	Adia Barnes	.15
47	Elaine Powell	.15
48	Lady Hardmon	.15
49	Kim Perrot	.75
50	*Marlies Askamp*	1.00
51	Deborah Carter	.15
52	*Sandy Brondello*	3.00
53	Heidi Burge	.15
54	Janeth Arcain	.15
55	Rushia Brown	.15
56	Suzie McConnell Serio	1.00
57	Penny Moore	.50
58	*Malgorzata Dydek*	.75
59	Angie Potthoff	.15
60	*Monica Lamb*	.40
61	Jamila Wideman	.60
62	*Ticha Penicheiro*	.75
63	Andrea Congreaves	.40
64	*Rachal Sporn*	.50
65	Chantel Tremitiere	.40
66	Carla McGhee	.15
67	Kim Williams	.30
68	Tangela Smith	.30
69	Quacy Barnes	.15
70	Sue Wicks	.50
71	*Tracy Reid*	.75
72	Linda Burgess	.15
73	Razija Brcaninovic	.15
74	Sharon Manning	.15
75	Tammy Jackson	.15
76	Rita Williams	.50
77	*Carla Porter*	.60
78	Michelle Griffiths	.30
79	Eva Nemcova	.75
80	Sophia Witherspoon	.60
81	*Sonja Tate*	.60
82	Cynthia Cooper	5.00
83	Wendy Palmer	1.50
84	Ruthie Bolton-Holifield	2.50
85	Tammi Reiss	1.00
86	Katrina Colleton	.15
87	Cindy Brown	2.00
88	Latasha Byears	.50
89	Mwadi Mabika	.15
90	Rhonda Mapp	.15
91	Tina Thompson (All-WNBA Team)	.30
92	Sheryl Swoopes (All-WNBA Team)	2.00
93	Jennifer Gillom (All-WNBA Team)	.75
94	Cynthia Cooper (All-WNBA Team)	2.50
95	Suzie McConnell Serio (All-WNBA Team)	.50
96	Cindy Brown (All-WNBA Team)	1.00
97	Eva Nemcova (All-WNBA Team)	.40
98	Lisa Leslie (All-WNBA Team)	1.50
99	Andrea Stinson (All-WNBA Team)	.75
100	Teresa Weatherspoon (All-WNBA Team)	1.25
101	*Dawn Staley*	10.00
102	*Clamnique Holdsclaw*	30.00
103	*Kristin Folkl*	8.00
104	*Nykesha Sales*	8.00
105	*Natalie Williams*	10.00
106	*Yolanda Griffith*	10.00
107	*Crystal Robinson*	5.00
108	*Edna Campbell*	3.00
109	*Tari Phillips*	5.00
110	*Tonya Edwards*	3.00
111	*Debbie Black*	3.00
112	*Kate Starbird*	3.00
113	*Adrienne Goodson*	3.00
114	*Sheri Sam*	3.00
115	*DeLisha Milton*	5.00
116	*Shannon Johnson*	3.00
117	*Katie Smith*	3.00
118	*Kara Wolters*	3.00
119	*Jennifer Azzi*	10.00
120	*Michele VanGorp*	3.00
121	*Stephanie White-McCarty*	3.00
122	*Ukari Figgs*	3.00
123	*Val Whiting*	3.00
124	*Mery Andrade*	3.00
125	*Charlotte Smith*	3.00

1999 Ultra WNBA Gold Medallion

Gold Medallion cards paralleled all 125 cards in Ultra WNBA and were seeded one per pack. Card fronts featured a gold tint, while backs included the words "Gold Medallion Edition" stamped in gold and were numbered with a "G" suffix.

	MT
Complete Set (125):	175.00
Gold Cards:	2x
Gold Rookies:	1x-2x
Inserted 1:1	

1999 Ultra WNBA Platinum Medallion

Platinum Medallion cards paralleled all 125 cards in Ultra WNBA. Cards 1-100 were sequentially numbered to 99 sets on the back, while the rookies (101-125) were numbered to 66 sets. Card fronts were distinguished by a platinum tint, while backs included the words "Platinum Medallion Edition" and were numbered with a "P" suffix.

	MT
Complete Set (125):	
Platinum Cards (1-100):	15x-30x
1-100 Production 99 Sets	
Platinum Rookies (101-125):	5x-10x

1999 Ultra WNBA Fresh Ink

Ultra WNBA marked the first installment of Fresh Ink, an autograph program exclusive to Ultra products. The insert featured autographs from 13 WNBA players on cards numbered to 400. Each card featured a color shot of the player, with a white border across the middle for the player's signature. The cards were hand-numbered to 400 in the bottom left corner.

		MT
Common Player:		45.00
Production 400 Sets		
1	Elana Baranova	45.00
2	Cynthia Cooper	175.00
3	Kristen Folkl	45.00

4	Lisa Leslie	100.00
5	Suzie McConnell Serio	75.00
6	Nikki McCray	75.00
7	Dawn Staley	75.00
8	Andrea Stinson	75.00
9	Sheryl Swoopes	150.00
10	Michele Timms	100.00
11	Penny Toler	45.00
12	Teresa Weatherspoon	90.00

1999 Ultra WNBA Rock Talk

Rock Talk inserts featured 10 different players over a silver holofoil pattern. Cards were numbered with an "RT" suffix and inserted 1:24 packs.

		MT
Complete Set (10):		80.00
Common Player:		5.00
Inserted 1:24		
1	Eva Nemcova	5.00
2	Cynthia Cooper	20.00
3	Ruthie Bolton-Holifield	10.00
4	Michele Timms	10.00
5	Jennifer Gillom	8.00
6	Cindy Brown	8.00
7	Lisa Leslie	15.00
8	Andrea Stinson	8.00
9	Teresa Weatherspoon	10.00
10	Rebecca Lobo	12.00

1999 Ultra WNBA WNBAttitude

This 10-card insert was seeded 1:6 packs of Ultra WNBA. Cards featured the player's image over the insert name background. Cards were numbered with a "WA" suffix.

		MT
Complete Set (10):		25.00
Common Player:		1.00
Inserted 1:6		
1	Lisa Leslie	4.00
2	Cynthia Cooper	5.00
3	Ruthie Bolton-Holifield	3.00
4	Rebecca Lobo	4.00
5	Sheryl Swoopes	4.00
6	Nikki McCray	4.00
7	Cindy Brown	3.00
8	Jennifer Gillom	2.00
9	Wendy Palmer	1.00
10	Michele Timms	3.00

1999 Ultra WNBA World Premiere

This insert featured 10 top rookies on a sculptured embossed card with a foil stamped background. World Premiere inserts were numbered with a "WP" suffix and inserted 1:12 packs.

		MT
Complete Set (10):		50.00
Common Player:		3.00
Inserted 1:12		
1	Clamnique Holdsclaw	20.00
2	Dawn Staley	6.00
3	Nykesha Sales	6.00
4	Kristin Folkl	5.00
5	Natalie Williams	8.00
6	Yolanda Griffith	10.00
7	Crystal Robinson	4.00
8	Edna Campbell	4.00
9	DeLisha Milton	4.00
10	Debbie Black	3.00

1999 UD Century Legends

Upper Deck released this 90-card set during the off-season of 1999. The first 50 cards highlight players selected on the Sporting News' list of Basketball's 100 Greatest Players, with each card bearing a Sporting News photo of the featured player and his ranking in silver and copper foil. The next 30 cards in the set feature Upper Deck's 21st Century Phenoms, while the final 10 cards profile Michael Jordan's career and are called Jordan - Player of the Century. The 90-card set is paralleled in Century Collection with sequential numbering to 100. Inserts include: Jerseys of the Century, Epic Signatures, Century Epic Signatures, All-Century Team, MJ's Most Memorable Shots, Epic Milestones and Generations.

		MT
Complete Set (90):		45.00
Common Player:		.10
Card #6 Does Not Exist		
Wax Box (24):		
1	Michael Jordan	5.00
2	Bill Russell	1.50
3	Wilt Chamberlain	1.50
4	George Mikan	1.00
5	Oscar Robertson	1.25
7	Larry Bird	3.00
8	Karl Malone	.40
9	Elgin Baylor	.40
10	Kareem Abdul-Jabbar	1.50
11	Jerry West	.60
12	Bob Cousy	.50
13	Julius Erving	1.50
14	Hakeem Olajuwon	.40
15	John Havlicek	.75
16	John Stockton	.20
17	Rick Barry	.10
18	Moses Malone	.25
19	Nate Thurmond	.10
20	Bob Pettit	.20
21	Pete Maravich	.75
22	Willis Reed	.20
23	Isiah Thomas	.30
24	Dolph Schayes	.10
25	Walt Frazier	.25
26	Wes Unseld	.20
27	Bill Sharman	.10
28	George Gervin	.30
29	Hal Greer	.10
30	Dave DeBusschere	.20
31	Earl Monroe	.25
32	Kevin McHale	.30
33	Charles Barkley	.40
34	Elvin Hayes	.20
35	Scottie Pippen	.75
36	Jerry Lucas	.10
37	Dave Bing	.10
38	Lenny Wilkens	.25
39	Paul Arizin	.10
40	Nate Archibald	.25
41	James Worthy	.30
42	Patrick Ewing	.20
43	Billy Cunningham	.20
44	Sam Jones	.10
45	Dave Cowens	.20
46	Robert Parish	.30
47	Bill Walton	.30
48	Shaquille O'Neal	1.50
49	David Robinson	.40
50	Dominique Wilkins	.20
51	Kobe Bryant	3.00
52	Vince Carter	2.50
53	Paul Pierce	1.25
54	Allen Iverson	2.00
55	Stephon Marbury	1.50
56	Mike Bibby	.50
57	Jason Williams	1.50
58	Kevin Garnett	2.50
59	Tim Duncan	2.50
60	Antawn Jamison	.75
61	Antoine Walker	1.00
62	Shareef Abdur-Rahim	.60
63	Michael Olowokandi	.40
64	Robert Traylor	.40
65	Keith Van Horn	1.00
66	Shaquille O'Neal	1.50
67	Ray Allen	.20
68	Gary Payton	.40
69	Raef LaFrentz	.40
70	Grant Hill	2.50
71	Anfernee Hardaway	1.50
72	Maurice Taylor	.30
73	Ron Mercer	.60
74	Michael Finley	.20
75	Jason Kidd	.75
76	Allan Houston	.20
77	Damon Stoudamire	.30
78	Antonio McDyess	.40
79	Eddie Jones	.30
80	Michael Dickerson	.30
81	Michael Jordan	2.00
82	Michael Jordan	2.00
83	Michael Jordan	2.00
84	Michael Jordan	2.00
85	Michael Jordan	2.00
86	Michael Jordan	2.00
87	Michael Jordan	2.00
88	Michael Jordan	2.00
89	Michael Jordan	2.00
90	Michael Jordan	2.00

1999 UD Century Legends Century Collection

Century Collection parallels all 90 cards of the base set, but adds a die-cut border on the left side and some holographic foil. Cards are also sequentially numbered to 100 on the front right.

	MT
Common Player:	5.00
Century Collection Cards:	25x-50x
Common Jordan Century Collection:	100.00
Production 100 Sets	

1999 UD Century Legends All-Century Team

This 12-card insert highlights Upper Deck's All-Time All-Star Team. The player's image is in black and white over a foil background. All-Century Team cards are numbered with an "A" prefix and seeded 1:11 packs.

		MT
Complete Set (12):		35.00
Common Player:		1.00
Inserted 1:11		
1	Michael Jordan	15.00
2	Oscar Robertson	3.00
3	Wilt Chamberlain	5.00
4	Larry Bird	8.00
5	Julius Erving	5.00
6	Jerry West	2.00
7	Charles Barkley	2.00
8	John Stockton	1.00
9	Hakeem Olajuwon	2.00
10	Karl Malone	2.00
11	Scottie Pippen	3.00
12	David Robinson	2.00

1999 UD Century Legends Epic Milestones

This 12-card insert showcases some of the most impressive milestones ever established in the NBA. Cards feature a black-and-white photo of the player over a foil background. Epic Milestones are numbered with an "EM" prefix and inserted 1:11 packs.

		MT
Cpmplete Set (12):		30.00
Common Player:		1.00
Inserted 1:11		
1	Michael Jordan	15.00
2	Jerry West	2.00
3	John Stockton	1.00
4	Wilt Chamberlain	5.00
5	Julius Erving	5.00
6	Reggie Miller	1.00
7	Hakeem Olajuwon	2.00
8	Robert Parish	1.00
9	Kobe Bryant	10.00
10	Rick Barry	1.00
11	Patrick Ewing	1.00
12	Charles Barkley	2.00

1999 UD Century Legends Epic Signatures

Epic Signatures was a collection of 33 autographed cards from current and retired players. The cards feature a photo of the player inside a television shape on the top half of the card, with the bottom featuring the player's signature over a white background. Cards were seeded 1:23 packs and numbered with two letters, usually corresponding to the player's initials.

		MT
Common Player:		20.00
Inserted 1:23		
KA	Kareem Abdul-Jabbar	150.00
NA	Nate Archibald	25.00
EB	Elgin Baylor	40.00
MB	Mike Bibby	30.00
LB	Larry Bird	400.00
WC	Wilt Chamberlain	250.00
BC	Bob Cousy	40.00
DC	Dave Cowens	25.00
CD	Clyde Drexler	40.00
AE	Alex English	20.00
DR	Julius Erving	250.00
WF	Walt Frazier	40.00
GG	George Gervin	30.00
TH	Tim Hardaway	40.00
JH	John Havlicek	40.00
EH	Elvin Hayes	25.00
AI	Allen Iverson	125.00
MJ	Michael Jordan	2500.
BL	Bob Lanier	20.00
JL	Jerry Lucas	20.00
MM	Moses Malone	25.00
EM	Earl Monroe	40.00
HK	Hakeem Olajuwon	75.00
MO	Michael Olowokandi	25.00
BP	Bob Pettit	25.00
WR	Willis Reed	25.00
OR	Oscar Robertson	75.00
BR	Bill Russell	400.00
BS	Bill Sharman	20.00
DT	David Thompson	25.00
WU	Wes Unseld	25.00
BW	Bill Walton	25.00
JW	Jerry West	60.00

1999 UD Century Legends Epic Signatures Century

Epic Signatures Century Collection was a parallel of Epic Signatures, but was limited and sequentially numbered to 100 sets. Players that do not have 100 of these include: Bill Russell (6), Julius Erving (6), Larry Bird (33) and Michael Jordan (23).

	MT
Common Player:	40.00
Century Signatures:	2x
Production 100 Sets	

1999 UD Century Legends Generations

This 12-card, double-sided insert featured a modern-day NBA star on the front printed on foil, with an NBA legend with comparable skills on the back printed in color. Generations were numbered with a "G" prefix and inserted 1:4 packs.

		MT
Complete Set (12):		25.00
Common Player:		1.00
Inserted 1:4		
1	Michael Jordan, Julius Erving	8.00
2	Kobe Bryant, Michael Jordan	8.00
3	Shaquille O'Neal, Wilt Chamberlain	4.00
4	Jason Williams, Pete Maravich	3.00
5	Stephon Marbury, Nate Archibald	1.00
6	Antoine Walker, Karl Malone	1.00
7	Grant Hill, George Gervin	2.00
8	Gary Payton, Isiah Thomas	2.00
9	Kevin Garnett, Dominique Wilkins	1.00
10	Hakeem Olajuwon, Moses Malone	1.00
11	Keith Van Horn, Larry Bird	3.00
12	Vince Carter, Oscar Robertson	3.00

1999 UD Century Legends Jerseys of the Century

Jerseys of the Century was an eight-card insert that featured a swatch of game-worn jersey from top current and retired players. These were inserted 1:475 packs and numbered with two letters corresponding to the player's initials except Erving's card is numbered "DR". In addition, Erving and Abdul-Jabbar autographed a limited amount of their cards, which are hand-numbered to the player's jersey number (6 and 33, respectively).

		MT
Complete Set (8):		3000.
Common Player:		150.00
Inserted 1:475		
KA	Kareem Abdul-Jabbar	250.00
KA-A	Kareem Abdul-Jabbar Auto (33)	1000.
LB	Larry Bird	400.00
CD	Clyde Drexler	150.00
DR	Julius Erving	300.00
DR-A	Julius Erving Auto (6)	3000.
MJ	Michael Jordan	2000.
KM	Karl Malone	150.00
SO	Shaquille O'Neal	150.00
JS	John Stockton	150.00

1999 UD Century Legends MJ's Most Memorable Shots

This six-card insert focuses on some of the most memorable shots made by Michael Jordan during his 13-year NBA career. MJ's Most Memorable Shots were numbered with an "MJ" prefix and inserted 1:23 packs.

	MT
Complete Set (6):	80.00
Common Player:	15.00
Inserted 1:23	

1999-00 Upper Deck MVP

Upper Deck MVP consisted of 220 cards, including 178 regular-player cards, 30 MJ Exclusives, 10 rookies and two checklists. The cards featured a color photo with a white border and some silver foil stamping. The first 218 cards (two checklists not included) were paralleled three times - Silver Script (1:2 packs), Gold Script (hobby-only, numbered to 100) and Super Script (hobby-only, numbered to 25). Insert sets include: Game-Used Souvenirs, ProSign, Draw Your Own Trading Card Winners, Jam Time, MVP Theatre, 21st Century NBA, Dynamics, Jordan's MVP Moments and Electrifying.

		MT
Complete Set (220):		45.00
Common Player:		.10
Common MJ Exclusives (179-208):		1.00
Wax Box (28):		45.00
1	Dikembe Mutombo	.20
2	Steve Smith	.20
3	Mookie Blaylock	.10
4	Alan Henderson	.10
5	LaPhonso Ellis	.20
6	Grant Long	.10
7	Kenny Anderson	.20
8	Antoine Walker	.75
9	Ron Mercer	.50
10	Paul Pierce	.75
11	Vitaly Potapenko	.10
12	Dana Barros	.10
13	Elden Campbell	.10
14	Eddie Jones	.40
15	David Wesley	.10
16	Bobby Phills	.10
17	Derrick Coleman	.20
18	Ricky Davis	.20
19	Toni Kukoc	.30
20	Brent Barry	.10
21	Ron Harper	.10
22	Kornel David	.10
23	Mark Bryant	.10
24	Dickey Simpkins	.10
25	Shawn Kemp	.50
26	Derek Anderson	.30
27	Brevin Knight	.20
28	Andrew DeClercq	.10
29	Zydrunas Ilgauskas	.20
30	Cedric Henderson	.10
31	Shawn Bradley	.10
32	A.C. Green	.10
33	Gary Trent	.20
34	Michael Finley	.25
35	Dirk Nowitzki	.20
36	Steve Nash	.10
37	Antonio McDyess	.40
38	Nick Van Exel	.20
39	Chauncey Billups	.20
40	Danny Fortson	.10
41	Eric Washington	.10
42	Raef LaFrentz	.40
43	Grant Hill	1.50
44	Bison Dele	.10
45	Lindsey Hunter	.10
46	Jerry Stackhouse	.20
47	Don Reid	.10
48	Christian Laettner	.10
49	John Starks	.10
50	Antawn Jamison	.60
51	Erick Dampier	.10
52	Donyell Marshall	.10
53	Chris Mills	.10
54	Bimbo Coles	.10
55	Charles Barkley	.40
56	Hakeem Olajuwon	.40
57	Scottie Pippen	.50
58	Othella Harrington	.10
59	Bryce Drew	.10
60	Michael Dickerson	.20
61	Rik Smits	.10
62	Reggie Miller	.20
63	Mark Jackson	.10
64	Antonio Davis	.10
65	Jalen Rose	.20
66	Dale Davis	.10
67	Chris Mullin	.20
68	Maurice Taylor	.30
69	Lamond Murray	.10
70	Rodney Rogers	.10
71	Darrick Martin	.10
72	Michael Olowokandi	.40
73	Tyrone Nesby	.10
74	Kobe Bryant	2.00
75	Shaquille O'Neal	1.00
76	Robert Horry	.10
77	Glen Rice	.20
78	J.R. Reid	.10
79	Rick Fox	.10
80	Derek Fisher	.10
81	Tim Hardaway	.40
82	Alonzo Mourning	.30
83	Jamal Mashburn	.20
84	P.J. Brown	.10
85	Terry Porter	.10
86	Dan Majerle	.10
87	Ray Allen	.20
88	Vinny Del Negro	.10
89	Glenn Robinson	.20
90	Dell Curry	.10
91	Sam Cassell	.20
92	Robert Traylor	.40
93	Kevin Garnett	1.50
94	Terrell Brandon	.20
95	Joe Smith	.20
96	Sam Mitchell	.10
97	Anthony Peeler	.10
98	Bobby Jackson	.10
99	Keith Van Horn	.75
100	Stephon Marbury	.75
101	Jayson Williams	.20
102	Kendall Gill	.10
103	Kerry Kittles	.10
104	Scott Burrell	.10
105	Patrick Ewing	.20
106	Allan Houston	.20
107	Latrell Sprewell	.20
108	Larry Johnson	.20
109	Marcus Camby	.20
110	Charlie Ward	.10
111	Anfernee Hardaway	1.00
112	Darrell Armstrong	.20
113	Nick Anderson	.20
114	Horace Grant	.10
115	Isaac Austin	.10
116	Matt Harpring	.20
117	Michael Doleac	.20
118	Allen Iverson	1.25
119	Theo Ratliff	.20
120	Matt Geiger	.10
121	Larry Hughes	.40
122	Tyrone Hill	.10
123	George Lynch	.10
124	Jason Kidd	.60
125	Tom Gugliotta	.20
126	Rex Chapman	.10
127	Clifford Robinson	.10
128	Luc Longley	.10
129	Danny Manning	.20
130	Rasheed Wallace	.20
131	Arvydas Sabonis	.10
132	Damon Stoudamire	.30
133	Brian Grant	.20
134	Isaiah Rider	.20
135	Walt Williams	.10
136	Jim Jackson	.10
137	Jason Williams	1.00
138	Vlade Divac	.20
139	Chris Webber	.60
140	Corliss Williamson	.10
141	Predrag Stojakovic	.10
142	Tariq Abdul-Wahad	.10
143	Tim Duncan	1.50
144	Sean Elliott	.10
145	David Robinson	.40
146	Mario Elie	.10
147	Avery Johnson	.10
148	Steve Kerr	.10
149	Gary Payton	.40
150	Vin Baker	.20
151	Detlef Schrempf	.20
152	Hersey Hawkins	.10
153	Dale Ellis	.10
154	Olden Polynice	.10
155	Vince Carter	1.50
156	John Wallace	.10
157	Doug Christie	.10
158	Tracy McGrady	.60
159	Kevin Willis	.10
160	Charles Oakley	.10
161	Karl Malone	.40
162	John Stockton	.20
163	Jeff Hornacek	.10
164	Bryon Russell	.10
165	Howard Eisley	.10
166	Shandon Anderson	.10
167	Shareef Abdur-Rahim	.50
168	Mike Bibby	.50
169	Bryant Reeves	.20
170	Felipe Lopez	.30
171	Cherokee Parks	.10
172	Michael Smith	.10
173	Juwan Howard	.20
174	Rod Strickland	.20
175	Mitch Richmond	.20
176	Otis Thorpe	.10
177	Calbert Cheaney	.10
178	Tracy Murray	.10
179	Michael Jordan (MJ Exclusives)	1.00
180	Michael Jordan (MJ Exclusives)	1.00
181	Michael Jordan (MJ Exclusives)	1.00
182	Michael Jordan (MJ Exclusives)	1.00
183	Michael Jordan (MJ Exclusives)	1.00
184	Michael Jordan (MJ Exclusives)	1.00
185	Michael Jordan (MJ Exclusives)	1.00
186	Michael Jordan (MJ Exclusives)	1.00
187	Michael Jordan (MJ Exclusives)	1.00
188	Michael Jordan (MJ Exclusives)	1.00
189	Michael Jordan (MJ Exclusives)	1.00
190	Michael Jordan (MJ Exclusives)	1.00
191	Michael Jordan (MJ Exclusives)	1.00
192	Michael Jordan (MJ Exclusives)	1.00
193	Michael Jordan (MJ Exclusives)	1.00
194	Michael Jordan (MJ Exclusives)	1.00
195	Michael Jordan (MJ Exclusives)	1.00
196	Michael Jordan (MJ Exclusives)	1.00
197	Michael Jordan (MJ Exclusives)	1.00
198	Michael Jordan (MJ Exclusives)	1.00
199	Michael Jordan (MJ Exclusives)	1.00
200	Michael Jordan (MJ Exclusives)	1.00
201	Michael Jordan (MJ Exclusives)	1.00
202	Michael Jordan (MJ Exclusives)	1.00
203	Michael Jordan (MJ Exclusives)	1.00
204	Michael Jordan (MJ Exclusives)	1.00
205	Michael Jordan (MJ Exclusives)	1.00
206	Michael Jordan (MJ Exclusives)	1.00
207	Michael Jordan (MJ Exclusives)	1.00
208	Michael Jordan (MJ Exclusives)	1.00
209	*Elton Brand*	5.00
210	*Steve Francis*	5.00
211	*Baron Davis*	3.00
212	*Wally Szczerbiak*	3.00
213	*Richard Hamilton*	2.00
214	*Andre Miller*	1.00
215	*Jason Terry*	1.50
216	*Corey Maggette*	2.00
217	*Shawn Marion*	1.00
218	*Lamar Odom*	5.00
219	Checklist	.10
220	Checklist	.10

1999-00 Upper Deck MVP Gold Script

This 218-card parallel set reprinted each card from MVP (except for the two checklists), but added a gold foil facsimile signature on the front. Gold Script cards were hobby exclusives and sequentially numbered to 100 sets.

	MT
Gold Script Cards:	30x-60x
Gold Script Rookies:	10x-20x
Gold MJ Exclusive (179-208):	50.00
Production 100 Sets	

1999-00 Upper Deck MVP Silver Script

This 218-card parallel set reprinted each card from MVP (except for the two checklists), but added a silver foil facsimile signature on the front. Silver Script cards were inserted 1:2 packs.

	MT
Complete Set (220):	150.00
Silver Script Cards:	2x-4x
Silver Script Rookies:	1x-2x
Silver MJ Exlusive (179-208):	4.00
Inserted 1:2	

1999-00 Upper Deck MVP Super Script

This 218-card parallel set reprinted each card from MVP (except for the two checklists), but added a holographic foil facsimile signature on the front. Super Script cards were hobby exclusives and sequentially numbered to 25 sets.

	MT
Super Script Cards:	75x-150x
Super Script Rookies:	20x-40x
Super Script MJ Exclusive (179-208):	150.00
Production 25 Sets	

1999-00 Upper Deck MVP Draw Your Own Trading Card

This 26-card insert featured winners to Upper Deck's Draw Your Own Trading Card promotion. Cards 1-8 were ages 5-8, cards 9-18 were ages 9-14 and cards 20-30 were ages 15 and up. Cards 11, 15, 19 and 27 were not printed. Cards from this insert are numbered with a "W" prefix and inserted 1:6 packs.

		MT
Complete Set (26):		18.00
Common Player:		.10
Inserted 1:6		
1	Michael Jordan	2.00
2	Grant Hill	1.00
3	Kobe Bryant	1.25
4	Michael Jordan	2.00
5	Glen Rice	.10
6	Michael Jordan	2.00
7	David Robinson	.20
8	Grant Hill	1.00
9	Stephon Marbury	.50
10	Michael Jordan	2.00
12	Charles Barkley	.20
13	Antoine Walker	.40
14	Shaquille O'Neal	.50
16	Michael Jordan	2.00
17	Stephon Marbury	.50
18	Michael Jordan	2.00
20	Allen Iverson	.75
21	Michael Jordan	2.00
22	Shareef Abdur-Rahim	.30
23	Reggie Miller	.10
24	Karl Malone	.20
25	Christian Laettner	.10
26	John Stockton	.10
28	Michael Jordan	2.00
29	Michael Jordan	2.00
30	Michael Jordan	2.00

1999-00 Upper Deck MVP Dynamics

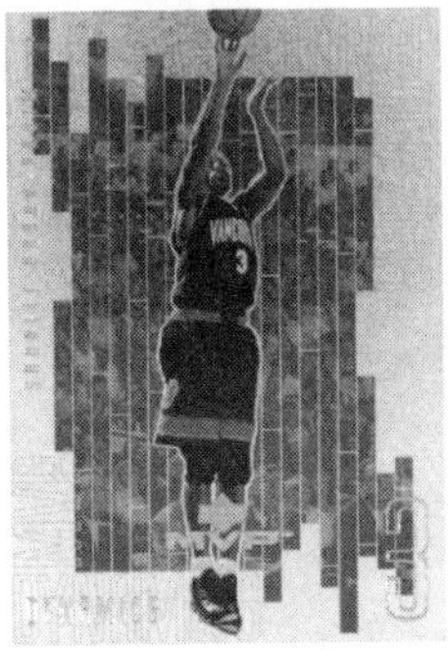

This six-card insert highlights players over a silver foil background and hardwood design. Cards were numbered with a "D" prefix and inserted 1:27 packs.

		MT
Complete Set (6):		35.00
Common Player:		2.00
Inserted 1:6		
1	Michael Jordan	15.00
2	Kobe Bryant	10.00
3	Grant Hill	8.00
4	Shareef Abdur-Rahim	2.00
5	Kevin Garnett	8.00
6	Vince Carter	6.00

1999-00 Upper Deck MVP Electrifying

This 15-card insert featured some of the most exciting players in the NBA on a foil background. Cards are numbered with an "E" prefix and inserted 1:9 packs.

		MT
Complete Set (15):		12.00
Common Player:		.50
Inserted 1:9		
1	Shaquille O'Neal	3.00
2	Steve Smith	.50
3	Toni Kukoc	.75
4	Ron Mercer	1.50
5	Damon Stoudamire	.75
6	Tim Hardaway	.75
7	Paul Pierce	2.50
8	Jason Kidd	1.50
9	Stephon Marbury	2.00
10	Terrell Brandon	.50
11	Reggie Miller	.50
12	Ray Allen	.50
13	Maurice Taylor	.75
14	Chris Webber	1.50
15	Charles Barkley	1.00

1999-00 Upper Deck MVP Game-used Souvenirs

This 15-card, hobby-only insert included a piece of a game-used basketball from some of the top players. Game-used Souvenirs were inserted 1:131 packs and cards were numbered with two letters followed by "-S," with the two letters corresponding to the player's initials in most cases. In addition, Anfernee Hardaway and Karl Malone autographed a number of their cards, which are hand-numbered to the player's jersey numbers. This means that Hardaway signed just one card and Malone signed 32. The autographed versions are numbered with the player's initials followed by "-A."

		MT
Complete Set (15):		900.00
Common Player:		30.00
Inserted 1:131 Hobby		
MB	Mike Bibby	40.00
KB	Kobe Bryant	125.00
TD	Tim Duncan	100.00
MF	Michael Finley	30.00
KG	Kevin Garnett	100.00
AH	Anfernee Hardaway	75.00
AH-A	Anfernee Hardaway Auto (1)	
AJ	Antawn Jamison	60.00
JK	Jason Kidd	60.00
KM	Karl Malone	50.00
KM-A	Karl Malone Auto (32)	
AM	Antonio McDyess	40.00
MO	Michael Olowokandi	30.00
SO	Shaquille O'Neal	75.00
GP	Gary Payton	40.00
SP	Scottie Pippen	60.00
JW	Jason Williams	90.00

1999-00 Upper Deck MVP Jam Time

This 12-card insert highlighted some of the best leapers in the NBA. Cards were printed on foil, with the left third displaying the insert name in silver foil over a black background and the rest showing the player. Jam Time inserts are numbered with an "JT" prefix and inserted 1:6 packs.

		MT
Complete Set (14):		10.00
Common Player:		.50
Inserted 1:6		
1	Michael Jordan	5.00
2	Alonzo Mourning	.50
3	Shawn Kemp	1.00
4	Juwan Howard	.50
5	Chris Webber	1.00
6	Tim Duncan	2.50
7	Keith Van Horn	1.25
8	Eddie Jones	.50
9	Michael Finley	.50
10	Anfernee Hardaway	1.50
11	Antonio McDyess	.75
12	Charles Barkley	.75
13	Latrell Sprewell	.50
14	Hakeem Olajuwon	.75

1999-00 Upper Deck MVP Jordan-MVP Moments

This 14-card insert set highlights all of MJ's MVP awards from his regular season awards to his All-Star game and post-season honors. Jordan's MVP Moments were numbered with an "MJ" prefix and inserted 1:27 packs.

		MT
Complete Set (14):		125.00
Common Player:		10.00
Inserted 1:27		
1	Michael Jordan (1988 MVP)	10.00
2	Michael Jordan (1991 MVP)	10.00
3	Michael Jordan (1992 MVP)	10.00
4	Michael Jordan (1996 MVP)	10.00
5	Michael Jordan (1998 MVP)	10.00
6	Michael Jordan (1988 All-Star MVP)	10.00
7	Michael Jordan (1996 All-Star MVP)	10.00
8	Michael Jordan (1998 All-Star MVP)	10.00
9	Michael Jordan (1991 Final MVP)	10.00
10	Michael Jordan (1992 Final MVP)	10.00
11	Michael Jordan (1993 Final MVP)	10.00
12	Michael Jordan (1996 Final MVP)	10.00
13	Michael Jordan (1997 Final MVP)	10.00
14	Michael Jordan (1998 Final MVP)	10.00

1999-00 Upper Deck MVP MVP Theatre

This 15-card, foil insert displays those players who have the best shot at winning the MVP. MVP Theatre inserts are numbered with a "M" prefix and seeded 1:9 packs.

		MT
Complete Set (15):		
Common Player:		.50
Inserted 1:9		
1	Karl Malone	1.00
2	Tom Gugliotta	.50
3	Shaquille O'Neal	2.50
4	Mitch Richmond	.50
5	David Robinson	1.00
6	Gary Payton	1.00
7	Allen Iverson	3.00
8	Glenn Robinson	.50
9	Antoine Walker	2.00
10	Hakeem Olajuwon	1.00
11	Patrick Ewing	.50
12	Antonio McDyess	1.00
13	Tim Hardaway	.75
14	Scottie Pippen	1.50
15	Anfernee Hardaway	3.00

1999-00 Upper Deck MVP ProSign

This 16-card, retail-only insert from MVP featured autographs from NBA players. Cards were numbered with two letters, usually corresponding to the player's initials, and inserted 1:144 packs.

		MT
Common Player:		6.00
Inserted 1:144 Retail		
DA	Darrell Armstrong	30.00
SA	Stacey Augmon	6.00
IA	Isaac Austin	6.00
VC	Vince Carter	175.00
TC	Terry Cummings	8.00
MD	Michael Dickerson	15.00
DF	Derek Fisher	12.00
JK	Jaren Jackson	8.00
JJ	Jim Jackson	10.00
MJ	Michael Jordan	—
TR	Theo Ratliff	8.00
JR	Jalen Rose	15.00
RT	Robert Traylor	15.00
NV	Nick Van Exel	20.00
CH	Charlie Ward	10.00
CW	Clarence Weatherspoon	8.00

1999-00 Upper Deck MVP 21st Century NBA

This 10-card insert featured the best young players in the NBA over a motion-foil background. 21st Century MVP cards were numbered with an "N" prefix and inserted 1:13 packs.

		MT
Complete Set (10):		25.00
Common Player:		2.00
Inserted 1:13		
1	Jason Williams	2.50
2	Paul Pierce	2.50
3	Antoine Walker	2.50
4	Keith Van Horn	2.00
5	Allen Iverson	4.00
6	Antawn Jamison	2.00
7	Kobe Bryant	8.00
8	Shareef Abdur-Rahim	2.00
9	Stephon Marbury	3.00
10	Grant Hill	6.00

1999-00 Upper Deck Victory

This 440-card release from Upper Deck was distributed exclusively in retail locations and arrived in 12-card packs for 99 cents. The cards featured a traditional white border, while the set was made up of eight different subsets, including: 33 Check It Out, 20 Rookie Flashback, 30 Dynamite Dunks, 15 Court Catalysts, 15 Power Corps, 15 Scoring Circle, 50 Jordan's Greatest Hits and 10 1999 Rookies. No inserts were available in this product, with the exception of a web promo card inserted into each pack.

		MT
Complete Set (440):		75.00
Common Player:		.10
Common Jordan (381-430):		.50
Wax Box (36):		35.00
1	Hawks Check It Out!	.10
2	Steve Smith	.20
3	Dikembe Mutombo	.20
4	Ed Gray	.10
5	Alan Henderson	.10
6	LaPhonso Ellis	.20
7	Roshown McLeod	.20
8	Bimbo Coles	.10
9	Chris Crawford	.10
10	Anthony Johnson	.10
11	Celtics Check It Out!	.50
12	Kenny Anderson	.20
13	Antoine Walker	1.00
14	Greg Minor	.10
15	Tony Battie	.10
16	Ron Mercer	.75
17	Paul Pierce	1.50
18	Vitaly Potapenko	.10
19	Dana Barros	.10
20	Walter McCarty	.10
21	Hornets Check It Out!	.10
22	Elden Campbell	.10
23	Eddie Jones	.30
24	David Wesley	.10
25	Bobby Phills	.10
26	Derrick Coleman	.20
27	Anthony Mason	.20
28	Brad Miller	.20
29	Eldridge Recasner	.10
30	Ricky Davis	.30
31	Bulls Check It Out!	.20
32	Michael Jordan	5.00
33	Brent Barry	.10
34	Randy Brown	.10
35	Keith Booth	.10
36	Kornel David	.10
37	Mark Bryant	.10
38	Toni Kukoc	.30
39	Rusty LaRue	.10
40	Cavaliers Check It Out!	.10
41	Shawn Kemp	.75
42	Wesley Person	.10
43	Johnny Newman	.10
44	Derek Anderson	.20
45	Brevin Knight	.10
46	Bob Sura	.10
47	Andrew DeClercq	.10
48	Zydrunas Ilgauskas	.20
49	Danny Ferry	.10
50	Mavericks Check It Out!	.10
51	Michael Finley	.25
52	Robert Pack	.10
53	Shawn Bradley	.10
54	John Williams	.10
55	Hubert Davis	.10
56	Dirk Nowitzki	.20
57	Steve Nash	.10
58	Chris Anstey	.10
59	Erick Strickland	.10
60	Nuggets Check It Out!	.10
61	Antonio McDyess	.40
62	Nick Van Exel	.20
63	Bryant Stith	.10
64	Chauncey Billups	.20
65	Danny Fortson	.10
66	Eric Williams	.10
67	Eric Washington	.10
68	Raef LaFrentz	.40
69	Johnny Taylor	.20
70	Pistons Check It Out!	.10
71	Grant Hill	2.00
72	Lindsey Hunter	.10
73	Bison Dele	.10
74	Loy Vaught	.10
75	Jerome Williams	.10
76	Jerry Stackhouse	.20
77	Christian Laettner	.20
78	Jud Buechler	.10
79	Don Reid	.10
80	Warriors Check It Out!	.40
81	John Starks	.10
82	Antawn Jamison	.75
83	Adonal Foyle	.10
84	Jason Caffey	.10
85	Donyell Marshall	.10
86	Chris Mills	.10
87	Tony Delk	.10
88	Mookie Blaylock	.10
89	Rockets Check It Out!	.20
90	Hakeem Olajuwon	.50
91	Scottie Pippen	.75
92	Charles Barkley	.40
93	Bryce Drew	.20
94	Cuttino Mobley	.20
95	Othella Harrington	.10
96	Matt Maloney	.10
97	Michael Dickerson	.30
98	Matt Bullard	.10
99	Pacers Check It Out!	.10
100	Reggie Miller	.20
101	Rik Smits	.10
102	Jalen Rose	.20
103	Antonio Davis	.10
104	Mark Jackson	.10
105	Sam Perkins	.10
106	Travis Best	.10
107	Dale Davis	.10
108	Chris Mullin	.20
109	Clippers Check It Out!	.20
110	Maurice Taylor	.30
111	Tyrone Nesby	.20
112	Lamond Murray	.10
113	Darrick Martin	.10
114	Michael Olowokandi	.40
115	Rodney Rogers	.10
116	Eric Piatkowski	.10
117	Lorenzen Wright	.10
118	Brian Skinner	.20
119	Lakers Check It Out!	1.25
120	Kobe Bryant	2.50
121	Shaquille O'Neal	1.50
122	Derek Fisher	.10
123	Tyronn Lue	.25
124	Travis Knight	.10
125	Glen Rice	.20
126	Derek Harper	.10
127	Robert Horry	.10
128	Rick Fox	.10
129	Heat Check It Out!	.20
130	Tim Hardaway	.30
131	Alonzo Mourning	.30
132	Keith Askins	.10
133	Jamal Mashburn	.20
134	P.J. Brown	.10
135	Clarence Weatherspoon	.10
136	Terry Porter	.10
137	Dan Majerle	.10
138	Voshon Lenard	.10
139	Bucks Check It Out!	.10
140	Ray Allen	.30
141	Vinny Del Negro	.10
142	Glenn Robinson	.20
143	Dell Curry	.10
144	Sam Cassell	.20
145	Haywoode Workman	.10
146	Armen Gilliam	.10
147	Robert Traylor	.40
148	Chris Gatling	.10
149	Timberwolves Check It Out!	1.00
150	Kevin Garnett	2.00
151	Malik Sealy	.10
152	Radoslav Nesterovic	.20
153	Joe Smith	.20
154	Sam Mitchell	.10
155	Dean Garrett	.10
156	Anthony Peeler	.10
157	Tom Hammonds	.10
158	Bobby Jackson	.10
159	Nets Check It Out!	.10
160	Keith Van Horn	1.00
161	Stephon Marbury	1.25
162	Jayson Williams	.20
163	Kendall Gill	.10
164	Kerry Kittles	.20
165	Jamie Feick	.10
166	Scott Burrell	.10
167	Lucious Harris	.10
168	Knicks Check It Out!	.20
169	Patrick Ewing	.20
170	Allan Houston	.20
171	Latrell Sprewell	.20
172	Kurt Thomas	.10
173	Larry Johnson	.10
174	Chris Childs	.10
175	Marcus Camby	.30
176	Charlie Ward	.10
177	Chris Dudley	.10
178	Magic Check It Out!	.10
179	Anfernee Hardaway	1.50
180	Darrell Armstrong	.20
181	Nick Anderson	.20
182	Horace Grant	.10
183	Isaac Austin	.10
184	Matt Harpring	.25
185	Michael Doleac	.25
186	Charles Outlaw	.10
187	76ers Check It Out!	.75
188	Allen Iverson	1.75
189	Theo Ratliff	.20
190	Matt Geiger	.10
191	Larry Hughes	.50
192	Tyrone Hill	.10
193	George Lynch	.10
194	Eric Snow	.10
195	Aaron McKie	.10
196	Harvey Grant	.10
197	Suns Check It Out!	.40
198	Jason Kidd	.75
199	Tom Gugliotta	.20
200	Rex Chapman	.10
201	Clifford Robinson	.10
202	Luc Longley	.10
203	Danny Manning	.10
204	Pat Garrity	.20
205	George McCloud	.10
206	Toby Bailey	.20
207	Trail Blazers Check It Out!	.10
208	Rasheed Wallace	.20
209	Arvydas Sabonis	.10
210	Damon Stoudamire	.25
211	Brian Grant	.20
212	Isaiah Rider	.20
213	Walt Williams	.10
214	Jim Jackson	.10
215	Greg Anthony	.10
216	Stacey Augmon	.10
217	Kings Check It Out!	.10
218	Jason Williams	1.50
219	Vlade Divac	.20
220	Chris Webber	.75
221	Nick Anderson	.10
222	Predrag Stojakovic	.20
223	Tariq Abdul-Wahad	.10
224	Vernon Maxwell	.10
225	Lawrence Funderburke	.10
226	Jon Barry	.10
227	Spurs Check It Out!	.20
228	Tim Duncan	2.00
229	Sean Elliott	.10
230	David Robinson	.40
231	Mario Elie	.10
232	Avery Johnson	.10
233	Steve Kerr	.10
234	Malik Rose	.10
235	Jaren Jackson	.10
236	SuperSonics Check It Out!	.10
237	Gary Payton	.40
238	Vin Baker	.25
239	Detlef Schrempf	.20
240	Hersey Hawkins	.10
241	Dale Ellis	.10
242	Rashard Lewis	.20
243	Billy Owens	.10
244	Aaron Williams	.10
245	Raptors Check It Out!	1.00
246	Vince Carter	2.00
247	John Wallace	.10
248	Doug Christie	.10
249	Tracy McGrady	.75
250	Kevin Willis	.10
251	Michael Stewart	.10
252	Dee Brown	.10
253	John Thomas	.10
254	Alvin Williams	.10
255	Jazz Check It Out!	.20
256	Karl Malone	.40
257	John Stockton	.20
258	Jacque Vaughn	.10
259	Bryon Russell	.10
260	Howard Eisley	.10
261	Greg Ostertag	.10
262	Adam Keefe	.10
263	Todd Fuller	.10
264	Grizzlies Check It Out!	.40
265	Shareef Abdur-Rahim	.75
266	Mike Bibby	.60
267	Bryant Reeves	.10
268	Felipe Lopez	.30
269	Cherokee Parks	.10
270	Michael Smith	.10
271	Tony Massenburg	.10
272	Rodrick Rhodes	.10
273	Wizards Check It Out!	.10
274	Juwan Howard	.20
275	Rod Strickland	.20
276	Mitch Richmond	.20
277	Otis Thorpe	.10
278	Calbert Cheaney	.10
279	Tracy Murray	.10
280	Ben Wallace	.10
281	Terry Davis	.10
282	Michael Jordan	2.00
283	Reggie Miller	.10
284	Dikembe Mutombo	.10
285	Patrick Ewing	.10
286	Allan Houston	.10
287	Danny Manning	.10
288	Jalen Rose	.10
289	Rasheed Wallace	.10
290	Jerry Stackhouse	.10
291	Damon Stoudamire	.10
292	Kenny Anderson	.10
293	Shawn Kemp	.40
294	Vlade Divac	.10
295	Larry Johnson	.10
296	Jamal Mashburn	.10
297	Ron Harper	.10
298	Steve Smith	.10
299	Kendall Gill	.10
300	Chris Mullin	.10
301	Robert Horry	.10
302	Dikembe Mutombo	.10
303	Ron Mercer	.40
304	Eddie Jones	.20
305	Toni Kukoc	.20
306	Derek Anderson	.10
307	Shawn Bradley	.10
308	Danny Fortson	.10
309	Bison Dele	.10
310	Antawn Jamison	.40
311	Scottie Pippen	.40
312	Reggie Miller	.10
313	Maurice Taylor	.20
314	Glen Rice	.10
315	Alonzo Mourning	.20
316	Glenn Robinson	.10
317	Anthony Peeler	.10
318	Kerry Kittles	.10
319	Latrell Sprewell	.10
320	Darrell Armstrong	.10
321	Larry Hughes	.25
322	Tom Gugliotta	.10
323	Brian Grant	.10
324	Chris Webber	.40
325	David Robinson	.20
326	Vin Baker	.10
327	Vince Carter	1.00
328	Bryon Russell	.10
329	Felipe Lopez	.20
330	Juwan Howard	.10
331	Michael Jordan	2.00
332	Jason Kidd	.40
333	Rod Strickland	.10
334	Stephon Marbury	.50
335	Gary Payton	.20
336	Mark Jackson	.10
337	John Stockton	.10
338	Brevin Knight	.10
339	Bobby Jackson	.10
340	Nick Van Exel	.10
341	Tim Hardaway	.10
342	Darrell Armstrong	.10
343	Avery Johnson	.10
344	Mike Bibby	.30
345	Damon Stoudamire	.10
346	Jason Williams	.75
347	Allen Iverson	.75
348	Kobe Bryant	1.50
349	Karl Malone	.20
350	Keith Van Horn	.40
351	Kevin Garnett	1.00
352	Antoine Walker	.50
353	Tim Duncan	1.00
354	Scottie Pippen	.40
355	Paul Pierce	.75
356	Michael Finley	.20
357	Shaquille O'Neal	.75
358	Grant Hill	1.00
359	Jason Williams	.75
360	Antonio McDyess	.20
361	Shareef Abdur-Rahim	.40
362	Allen Iverson	.75
363	Shaquille O'Neal	.75
364	Karl Malone	.20
365	Shareef Abdur-Rahim	.40
366	Keith Van Horn	.40
367	Tim Duncan	1.00
368	Gary Payton	.20
369	Stephon Marbury	.40
370	Antonio McDyess	.20
371	Grant Hill	1.00
372	Kevin Garnett	1.00
373	Shawn Kemp	.40
374	Kobe Bryant	1.50
375	Michael Finley	.20
376	Vince Carter	1.00
377	Checklist 1-110	.10
378	Checklist 111-220	.10
379	Checklist 221-330	.10
380	Checklist 331-440	.10
431	*Elton Brand*	10.00
432	*Steve Francis*	10.00
433	*Baron Davis*	6.00
434	*Lamar Odom*	10.00
435	*Wally Szczerbiak*	6.00
436	*Richard Hamilton*	4.00
437	*Andre Miller*	2.00
438	*Shawn Marion*	2.00
439	*Jason Terry*	2.00
440	*Corey Maggette*	4.00

Market Report

Manning, Moss And Taylor Lead The Way For NFL Cards

When the 1998 NFL season started, everyone wanted cards of Peyton Manning and Ryan Leaf. Why not? They were the No. 1 and 2 picks in the NFL Draft and were supposed to be franchise quarterbacks. Nineteen different teams passed on a troubled rookie named Randy Moss out of Marshall before the Minnesota Vikings snagged him with the 21st overall pick.

The football card market was relatively stable in 1998, with collectors chasing rookies from the 1997 season like Jake Plummer, Warrick Dunn and Corey Dillon.

When 1998's camp opened, Manning remained solid, Leaf immediately gave collectors reason to doubt he had the mental game to play quarterback, and there were rumblings about the things Moss was doing in Minnesota.

When the season opened, Moss took over the football card market. The rookie began with two touchdowns the opening week, while getting six TDs in his first five games. Moss won Rookie of the Year honors, ending the season with 69 receptions for 1,313 yards and 17 TDs, which was an NFL rookie record.

His 1998 Upper Deck rookie (#17) shot up to $70, while his Ultra (#207) also hit the $70 mark. Moss' hottest card of the season was his SP Authentic (#18), which was valued at $425, while his Bowman Chrome (#182) sold for $85 and his Topps Chrome (#35) booked at $85.

Another rookie, Fred Taylor, also emerged through the season. The running back stepped in when James Stewart was injured in the third game of the season and was dominant. He ended the season with 1,223 yards rushing and 14 TDs. He also had 421 yards receiving and three TDs.

Throughout the season, collectors searched for rookies of Moss, Taylor and Manning, while also speculating on others, including: Charlie Batch, Germane Crowell, Curtis Enis, Kevin Dyson and Brian Griese.

Football was back in full force in 1998, with 53 releases on the season, and most of them doing very well.

And if you thought 1998 football products did well, 1999 was even better. The stellar class of 1998 propelled new card sales to the top of the market, resulting in a 37 percent share during the year, which equalled baseball and was up considerably from 1997.

Led by a potentially better rookie class that included three quarterbacks being chosen with the first three picks, new card sales in 1999 were well on their way to topping the 1998 numbers.

At the beginning of the season, Ricky Williams and Tim Couch led the way, but there was also plenty of interest in Donovan McNabb, Edgerrin James and Akili Smith. By the end of the year, Couch and Williams were still doing well, but James had vaulted to the top of the class, while leading the NFL in rushing and helping the Colts to a 13-3 regular season record.

SHORT-PRINTED ROOKIES

Clearly the wave of 1998 card products was the addition of short-printed rookie cards. The short-printed cards completely revived interest in rookies, especially in the football card market.

Topps was the first company to seed rookies in football. '97 Topps Football featured 30 rookie cards, seeded one every three packs. The rookie wave was so successful that 15 products contained seeded rookies in 1998.

Products like SP Authentic even went a step further and sequentially numbered its rookies. The 1998 product contained 30 rookies, all of which were numbered to just 2,000. The cards shot up in price, while packs sold at $10.

The excitement continued through the first half of 1999, with seeded and sequentially numbered rookies of James, Couch and Williams. Through the first half of 1999, every single football product was selling above its suggested retail price.

In 1999, the trend continued to develop, to the point where products with seeded or sequentially numbered rookies outnumbered products without.

BYE, BYE BARRY

It was hard to believe that Barry Sanders would walk away from football at only 31 and within 1,457 yards of the all-time rushing record. Sanders averaged 1,526 yards per season during his 10-year career, but chose to retire rather than play for the Lions in 1999.

As for his cards, they had been on a steady rise with anticipation of the record. His 1989 Score rookie had risen $65 in the past year and $35 since the end of the 1998 season, to $165. His Gem Mint version of that rookie was selling for $1,200-$1,300, but those prices dropped quickly on the news of his retirement.

KURT WARNER CRAZE

Pacific enjoyed early season success when it was the first card company to issue a Kurt Warner card. The former Arena Football League star threw 15 touchdown passes during the season's first five games and was the talk of the NFL and the football card market.

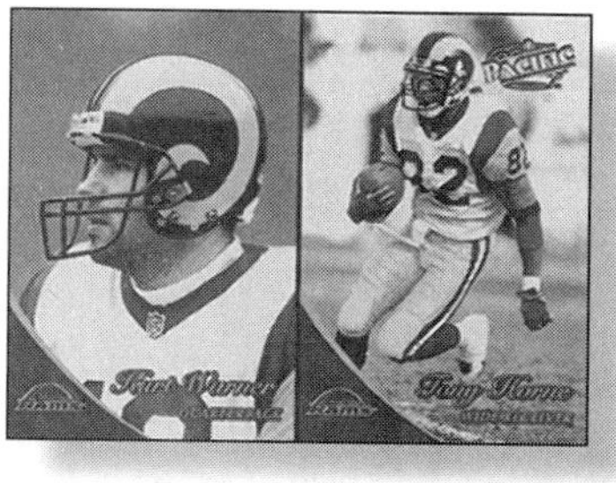

When collectors went searching for his rookie cards, they were led to 1999 Pacific (#343 with Tony Horne). The card jumped from $6 to $20 overnight and online auctions had sales of Mint cards at $30-$35. No other release during the next month had Warner on its checklist, so Pacific had Warner's only rookie card for quite some time.

THE FUTURE

The football card market had an enormous 1998 season and only got better in 1999. However, the flurry of releases by the end of the 1999 season had begun to take its toll. Collector dollars were spread among the releases and some products near the end began to slip some.

In 1998, it was Moss, Manning and Taylor who led the way. In 1999, the market got a huge boost from James, Couch and Williams, as well as Warner. The chances of a rookie class that potent for three years in a row are slim, but upcoming rookies like Peter Warrick, Ron Dayne and Chad Pennington might not agree.

The renewed interest in rookie cards throughout the past two seasons, along with the impressive rookie classes have placed football on top of the sports card market. It seems like each week of the NFL season a new star is born that sends collectors chasing their rookies. Names like Jeff George, Marcus Robinson and Warner consistently attract collectors to their rookie cards. As long as this continues, it's difficult to see how the football card market can struggle over the long term.

PLAYER OF THE YEAR

Full Name: Randy Moss
Hometown: Rand, West Virginia
Height: 6'4"
Weight: 194
College: Marshall
Birthdate: 2/13/77
Drafted: Selected in first round of 1998 draft by Minnesota, 21st pick overall

Randy Moss

CARDS TO GET: Moss' cards to get include: 1998 Bowman (#182, $30), Bowman Chrome (#182, $85), Bowman's Best (#109, $25), E-X2001 (#55, $40), Finest (#135, $50), Leaf Rookies & Stars (#199, $85), Pacific Crown Royale (#75, $30), Playoff Momentum (#131, $100), SkyBox (#240, $70), SP Authentic (#18, $425), SPx Finite (#239, $160), Topps Chrome (#35, $85), Topps Season Opener (#22, $50), Ultra (#207, $70) and Upper Deck (#17, $70).

TOP TENS

REGULAR-ISSUE SINGLES

1. Peyton Manning	1998 SP Authentic (#14)	$375
2. Edgerrin James	1999 SP Authentic (#94)	$250
3. Randy Moss	1998 SP Authentic (#18)	$425
4. Peyton Manning	1998 Topps Season Opener (#1)	$50
5. Marvin Harrison	1996 Topps Chrome (#156)	$50
6. Kurt Warner	1999 Playoff Momentum (#144)	$30
7. Walter Payton	1976 Topps (#148)	$200
8. Edgerrin James	1999 Topps Chrome (#145)	$100
9. Kurt Warner	1999 Kurt Warner (#343)	$30
10. Marvin Harrison	1999 Marvin Harrison (#18)	$15

REGULAR-ISSUE SETS

1. 1999 SP Authentic	$180/box	145-card set: $2,000
2. 1998 SP Authentic	$500	126-card set: $1,650
3. 1998 Topps Season Opener	$150	165-card set: $180
4. 1999 Leaf Certified	$150	225-card set: $850
5. 1999 Fleer Mystique	$100	160-card set: $650
6. 1999 Flair Showcase	$100	192-card set: $850
7. 1999 Topps Chrome	$150	165-card set: $700
8. 1999 SPx	$140	135-card set: $1,600
9. 1996 Topps Chrome	$230	165-card set: $250
10. 1999 E-X Century	$95	90-card set: $175

FOOTBALL

1998 Bowman's Best

This super-premium set has a 125-card base set that is made up of 100 veterans and 25 rookies. Each veteran card has a gold design, while the rookies are in silver. Each card has a Refractor version that is sequentially numbered to 400 and inserted 1:25 packs. Each player also has a parallel Atomic Refractor version that is numbered to 100 and inserted 1:103 packs.

		MT
Complete Set (125):		140.00
Common Player:		.25
Common Rookie:		2.00
Inserted 1:2		
Refractor Cards:		8x-16x
Refractor Rookies:		3x-6x
Inserted 1:25		
Production 400 Sets		
Atomic Ref. Cards:		25x-50x
Atomic Ref. Rookies:		10x-20x
Inserted 1:103		
Production 100 Sets		
Wax Box:		90.00
1	Emmitt Smith	4.00
2	Reggie White	.75
3	Jake Plummer	2.00
4	Ike Hilliard	.25
5	Isaac Bruce	.50
6	Trent Dilfer	.50
7	Ricky Watters	.50
8	Jeff George	.50
9	Wayne Chrebet	.50
10	Brett Favre	6.00
11	Terry Allen	.50
12	Bert Emanuel	.25
13	Andre Reed	.25
14	Andre Rison	.50
15	Jeff Blake	.50
16	Steve McNair	1.50
17	Joey Galloway	1.00
18	Irving Fryar	.25
19	Dorsey Levens	.75
20	Jerry Rice	3.00
21	Kerry Collins	.75
22	Michael Jackson	.25
23	Kordell Stewart	2.00
24	Junior Seau	.50
25	Jimmy Smith	.75
26	Michael Westbrook	.25
27	Eddie George	2.50
28	Cris Carter	1.00
29	Jason Sehorn	.25
30	Warrick Dunn	2.00
31	Garrison Hearst	.75
32	Erik Kramer	.25
33	Chris Chandler	.50
34	Michael Irvin	.50
35	Marshall Faulk	1.00
36	Warren Moon	.50
37	Rickey Dudley	.25
38	Drew Bledsoe	2.50
39	Antowain Smith	1.00
40	Terrell Davis	5.00
41	Gus Frerotte	.25
42	Robert Brooks	.25
43	Tony Banks	.50
44	Terrell Owens	1.50
45	Edgar Bennett	.25
46	Rob Moore	.50
47	J.J. Stokes	.50
48	Yancey Thigpen	.25
49	Elvis Grbac	.25
50	John Elway	3.00
51	Charles Johnson	.25
52	Karim Abdul-Jabbar	.75
53	Carl Pickens	.50
54	Peter Boulware	.25
55	Chris Warren	.25
56	Terance Mathis	.25
57	Andre Hastings	.25
58	Jake Reed	.25
59	Mike Alstott	1.00
60	Mark Brunell	2.50
61	Herman Moore	.75
62	Troy Aikman	3.00
63	Fred Lane	.50
64	Rod Smith	.75
65	Terry Glenn	.75
66	Jerome Bettis	.75
67	Derrick Thomas	.25
68	Marvin Harrison	.50
69	Adrian Murrell	.50
70	Curtis Martin	1.25
71	Bobby Hoying	.25
72	Darrell Green	.25
73	Sean Dawkins	.25
74	Robert Smith	.50
75	Antonio Freeman	1.50
76	Scott Mitchell	.25
77	Curtis Conway	.50
78	Rae Carruth	.25
79	Jamal Anderson	1.50
80	Dan Marino	4.00
81	Brad Johnson	1.00
82	Danny Kanell	.25
83	Charlie Garner	.25
84	Rob Johnson	.50
85	Natrone Means	.50
86	Tim Brown	.75
87	Keyshawn Johnson	1.00
88	Ben Coates	.50
89	Derrick Alexander	.25
90	Steve Young	2.00
91	Shannon Sharpe	.50
92	Corey Dillon	1.50
93	Bruce Smith	.25
94	Errict Rhett	.25
95	Jim Harbaugh	.50
96	Napoleon Kaufman	1.25
97	Glenn Foley	.50
98	Tony Gonzalez	.25
99	Keenan McCardell	.50
100	Barry Sanders	6.00
101	*Charles Woodson*	6.00
102	*Tim Dwight*	4.00
103	*Marcus Nash*	4.00
104	*Joe Jurevicius*	3.00
105	*Jacquez Green*	5.00
106	*Kevin Dyson*	4.00
107	*Keith Brooking*	2.00
108	*Andre Wadsworth*	2.50
109	*Randy Moss*	25.00
110	*Robert Edwards*	6.00
111	*Patrick Johnson*	2.50
112	*Peyton Manning*	15.00
113	*Duane Starks*	2.00
114	*Grant Wistrom*	2.00
115	*Anthony Simmons*	2.00
116	*Takeo Spikes*	2.00
117	*Tony Simmons*	3.00
118	*Jerome Pathon*	3.00
119	*Ryan Leaf*	8.00
120	*Skip Hicks*	3.00
121	*Curtis Enis*	5.00
122	*Germane Crowell*	4.00
123	*John Avery*	4.00
124	*Hines Ward*	3.00
125	*Fred Taylor*	12.00

1998 Bowman's Best Autographs

Ten players are in this set with each having two different cards. The only difference is the suffix "A" or "B" after the card number. Each of the 20 cards has a "Certified Autograph Issue" stamp on the fronts. Singles are found 1:158 packs, while Refractor versions are 1:840 and Atomic Refractors are 1:2,521.

		MT
Complete Set (20):		850.00
Common Player:		20.00
Inserted 1:158		
Refractor Cards:		2x
Inserted 1:840		
Atomic Ref. Cards:		3x
Inserted 1:2,521		
1A	Jake Plummer	100.00
1B	Jake Plummer	100.00
2A	Jason Sehorn	20.00
2B	Jason Sehorn	20.00
3A	Corey Dillon	80.00
3B	Corey Dillon	80.00
4A	Tim Brown	40.00
4B	Tim Brown	40.00
5A	Keenan McCardell	30.00
5B	Keenan McCardell	30.00
6A	Kordell Stewart	100.00
6B	Kordell Stewart	100.00
7A	Peyton Manning	150.00
7B	Peyton Manning	150.00
8A	Danny Kanell	20.00
8B	Danny Kanell	20.00
9A	Ryan Leaf	85.00
9B	Ryan Leaf	85.00
10A	Curtis Enis	50.00
10B	Curtis Enis	50.00

1998 Bowman's Best Mirror Image Fusion

This insert is made up of 20 double-sided cards that feature two top players at the same position. Singles are found 1:48 packs, while the parallel Refractors are sequentially numbered to 100 and inserted 1:630. Atomic Refractors are numbered to 25 and found 1:2,521.

		MT
Complete Set (20):		280.00
Common Player:		4.00
Inserted 1:48		
Refractor Cards:		3x-5x
Inserted 1:630		
Production 100 Sets		
Atomic Ref. Cards:		6x-12x
Inserted 1:2,521		
Production 25 Sets		
MI1	Terrell Davis, John Avery	35.00
MI2	Emmitt Smith, Curtis Enis	35.00
MI3	Barry Sanders, Skip Hicks	50.00
MI4	Eddie George, Robert Edwards	12.00
MI5	Jerome Bettis, Fred Taylor	20.00
MI6	Mark Brunell, Ryan Leaf	20.00
MI7	John Elway, Brian Griese	25.00
MI8	Dan Marino, Peyton Manning	25.00
MI9	Brett Favre, Charlie Batch	50.00
MI10	Drew Bledsoe, Jonathan Quinn	20.00
MI11	Tim Brown, Kevin Dyson	10.00
MI12	Herman Moore, Germane Crowell	10.00
MI13	Joey Galloway, Jerome Pathon	8.00
MI14	Cris Carter, Jacquez Green	12.00
MI15	Jerry Rice, Randy Moss	60.00
MI16	Junior Seau, Takeo Spikes	4.00
MI17	John Randle, Jason Peter	4.00
MI18	Reggie White, Andre Wadsworth	8.00
MI19	Peter Boulware, Anthony Simmons	4.00
MI20	Derrick Thomas, Brian Simmons	4.00

1998 Bowman's Best Performers

This insert showcases the top rookies who came up in '98. Singles were inserted 1:12 packs, while Refractors are numbered to 200 and can be found 1:630. Atomic Refractors are numbered to 50 and found 1:2,521.

		MT
Complete Set (10):		60.00
Common Player:		2.00
Inserted 1:12		
Refractor Cards:		3x-6x
Inserted 1:630		
Production 200 Sets		
Atomic Ref. Cards:		10x-20x
Inserted 1:2,521		
Production 50 Sets		
BP1	Peyton Manning	15.00
BP2	Charles Woodson	6.00
BP3	Skip Hicks	4.00
BP4	Andre Wadsworth	2.00
BP5	Randy Moss	25.00
BP6	Marcus Nash	5.00
BP7	Ahman Green	4.00
BP8	Anthony Simmons	2.00
BP9	Tavian Banks	4.00
BP10	Ryan Leaf	8.00

1998 Bowman Chrome

Bowman Chrome football is a 220-card base set that includes 150 veterans and 70 rookies. There are also Refractor parallel cards of every regular card in the set that are randomly inserted 1:12 packs. Rookies are designated with a silver and blue logo design, while the veteran cards are shown with a silver and red design.

		MT
Complete Set (220):		550.00
Common Player:		.30
Common Rookie:		3.50
Refractor Cards:		3x-6x
Refractor Rookies:		3x
Inserted 1:12		
Inter-State Cards:		3x
Inter-State Rookies:		1.2x
Inserted 1:4		
I.S. Refractor Cards:		5x-10x
I.S. Refractor Rookies:		3x
Inserted 1:24		
Golden Ann. Stars:		30x-60x
Golden Ann. Rookies:		2x-4x
Inserted 1:138		
Production 50 Sets		
Wax Box:		175.00
1	*Peyton Manning*	60.00
2	*Keith Brooking*	7.00
3	*Duane Starks*	5.00
4	*Takeo Spikes*	7.00
5	*Andre Wadsworth*	7.00
6	*Greg Ellis*	3.50
7	*Brian Griese*	25.00
8	*Germane Crowell*	15.00
9	*Jerome Pathon*	7.00
10	*Ryan Leaf*	30.00
11	*Fred Taylor*	45.00
12	*Robert Edwards*	10.00
13	*Grant Wistrom*	3.50
14	*Robert Holcombe*	10.00
15	*Tim Dwight*	10.00
16	*Jacquez Green*	10.00
17	*Marcus Nash*	10.00
18	*Jason Peter*	3.50
19	*Anthony Simmons*	3.50
20	*Curtis Enis*	15.00
21	*John Avery*	10.00
22	*Patrick Johnson*	7.00
23	*Joe Jurevicius*	7.00
24	*Brian Simmons*	4.00
25	*Kevin Dyson*	10.00
26	*Skip Hicks*	10.00
27	*Hines Ward*	10.00
28	*Tavian Banks*	7.00
29	*Ahman Green*	10.00
30	*Tony Simmons*	8.00
31	Charles Johnson	.30
32	Freddie Jones	.30
33	Joey Galloway	1.00
34	Tony Banks	.60
35	Jake Plummer	2.50
36	Reidel Anthony	.30
37	Steve McNair	1.00
38	Michael Westbrook	.60
39	Chris Sanders	.30
40	Isaac Bruce	.60
41	Charlie Garner	.30
42	Wayne Chrebet	.60
43	Michael Strahan	.30
44	Brad Johnson	1.00
45	Mike Alstott	1.00
46	Tony Gonzalez	.60
47	Johnnie Morton	.30
48	Darnay Scott	.30
49	Rae Carruth	.30
50	Terrell Davis	4.50
51	Jermaine Lewis	.30
52	Frank Sanders	.30
53	Byron Hanspard	.30
54	Gus Frerotte	.30
55	Terry Glenn	.60
56	J.J. Stokes	.60
57	Will Blackwell	.30
58	Keyshawn Johnson	1.00
59	Tiki Barber	.60
60	Dorsey Levens	.60
61	Zach Thomas	.30
62	Corey Dillon	1.50
63	Antowain Smith	1.00
64	Michael Sinclair	.30
65	Rod Smith	.60
66	Trent Dilfer	.60
67	Warren Sapp	.30
68	Charles Way	.30
69	Tamarick Vanover	.30
70	Drew Bledsoe	2.50
71	John Mobley	.30
72	Kerry Collins	.60
73	Peter Boulware	.30
74	Simeon Rice	.30
75	Eddie George	2.50
76	Fred Lane	.60
77	Jamal Anderson	1.50
78	Antonio Freeman	1.00
79	Jason Sehorn	.30
80	Curtis Martin	1.00
81	Bobby Hoying	.30
82	Garrison Hearst	1.00
83	Glenn Foley	.60
84	Danny Kanell	.30
85	Kordell Stewart	2.50
86	O.J. McDuffie	.30
87	Marvin Harrison	.60
88	Bobby Engram	.30
89	Chris Slade	.30
90	Warrick Dunn	2.00
91	Ricky Watters	.60
92	Rickey Dudley	.30
93	Terrell Owens	1.00
94	Karim Abdul-Jabbar	.60
95	Napoleon Kaufman	1.00
96	Darrell Green	.30
97	Levon Kirkland	.30

98	Jeff George	.60
99	Andre Hastings	.30
100	John Elway	3.00
101	John Randle	.30
102	Andre Rison	.30
103	Keenan McCardell	.30
104	Marshall Faulk	1.00
105	Emmitt Smith	4.50
106	Robert Brooks	.30
107	Scott Mitchell	.30
108	Shannon Sharpe	.60
109	Deion Sanders	1.00
110	Jerry Rice	3.00
111	Erik Kramer	.30
112	Michael Jackson	.30
113	Aeneas Williams	.30
114	Terry Allen	.60
115	Steve Young	1.75
116	Warren Moon	.60
117	Junior Seau	.60
118	Jerome Bettis	.60
119	Irving Fryar	.30
120	Barry Sanders	6.00
121	Tim Brown	.60
122	Chad Brown	.30
123	Ben Coates	.30
124	Robert Smith	.60
125	Brett Favre	6.00
126	Derrick Thomas	.30
127	Reggie White	1.00
128	Troy Aikman	3.00
129	Jeff Blake	.60
130	Mark Brunell	2.50
131	Curtis Conway	.60
132	Wesley Walls	.30
133	Thurman Thomas	.60
134	Chris Chandler	.30
135	Dan Marino	4.50
136	Larry Centers	.30
137	Shawn Jefferson	.30
138	Andre Reed	.30
139	Jake Reed	.30
140	Cris Carter	1.00
141	Elvis Grbac	.30
142	Mark Chmura	.60
143	Michael Irvin	.60
144	Carl Pickens	.60
145	Herman Moore	.60
146	Marvin Jones	.30
147	Terance Mathis	.30
148	Rob Moore	.60
149	Bruce Smith	.30
150	Checklist	.30
151	Leslie Shepherd	.30
152	Chris Spielman	.30
153	Tony McGee	.30
154	Kevin Smith	.30
155	Bill Romanowski	.30
156	Stephen Boyd	.30
157	James Stewart	.30
158	Jason Taylor	.30
159	Troy Drayton	.30
160	Mark Fields	.30
161	Jessie Armstead	.30
162	James Jett	.30
163	Bobby Taylor	.30
164	Kimble Anders	.30
165	Jimmy Smith	.60
166	Quentin Coryatt	.30
167	Bryant Westbrook	.30
168	Neil Smith	.30
169	Darren Woodson	.30
170	Ray Buchanan	.30
171	Earl Holmes	.30
172	Ray Lewis	.30
173	Steve Broussard	.30
174	Derrick Brooks	.30
175	Ken Harvey	.30
176	Darryll Lewis	.30
177	Derrick Rodgers	.30
178	James McKnight	.30
179	Cris Dishman	.30
180	Hardy Nickerson	.30
181	*Charles Woodson*	20.00
182	*Randy Moss*	85.00
183	*Stephen Alexander*	7.00
184	*Samari Rolle*	3.50
185	*Jamie Duncan*	3.50
186	*Lance Schulters*	3.50
187	*Tony Parrish*	3.50
188	*Corey Chavous*	3.50
189	*Jammi German*	7.00
190	*Sam Cowart*	3.50
191	*Donald Hayes*	6.00
192	*R.W. McQuarters*	6.00
193	*Az-Zahir Hakim*	6.00
194	*Chris Fuamatu-Ma'afala*	7.00
195	*Allen Rossum*	3.50
196	*Jon Ritchie*	7.00
197	*Blake Spence*	3.50
198	*Brian Alford*	3.50
199	*Fred Weary*	3.50
200	*Rod Rutledge*	3.50
201	*Michael Myers*	3.50
202	*Rashaan Shehee*	7.00
203	*Donovin Darius*	3.50
204	*E.G. Green*	7.00
205	*Vonnie Holliday*	7.00
206	*Charlie Batch*	35.00
207	*Michael Pittman*	7.00
208	*Artrell Hawkins*	3.50
209	*Jonathan Quinn*	10.00
210	*Kailee Wong*	3.50
211	*Deshea Townsend*	3.50
212	*Patrick Surtain*	3.50
213	*Brian Kelly*	3.50
214	*Tebucky Jones*	3.50
215	*Pete Gonzalez*	6.00
216	*Shaun Williams*	3.50
217	*Scott Frost*	6.00
218	*Leonard Little*	3.50
219	*Alonzo Mayes*	6.00
220	*Cordell Taylor*	3.50

1998 Collector's Edge First Place

Singles from this base set feature large action shots of each of the 250 players in this set. Each single has a parallel 50-Point card that are found one per pack. Also, each player has a 50-Point Silver issue that is sequentially numbered to 125 and found 1:24 packs.

		MT
Complete Set (250):		70.00
Common Player:		.10
50-Point Cards:		2x-4x
50-Point Rookies:		2x
Inserted 1:1		
50-Point Gold Cards:		15x-30x
50-Point Gold Rookies:		5x-10x
Inserted 1:24		
Production 125 Sets		
Wax Box:		80.00
1	Karim Abdul-Jabbar	.50
2	*Flozell Adams*	.50
3	Troy Aikman	1.50
4	Robert Smith	.20
5	*Stephen Alexander*	1.00
6	*Harold Shaw*	.50
7	Marcus Allen	.20
8	Terry Allen	.20
9	Mike Alstott	.50
10	Jamal Anderson	.50
11	Reidel Anthony	.20
12	Jamie Asher	.10
13	Darnell Autry	.10
14	*Phil Savoy*	.50
15	*Jon Ritchie*	1.00
16	Tony Banks	.20
17	Tiki Barber	.20
18	Pat Barnes	.20
19	*Charlie Batch*	8.00
20	*Mikhael Ricks*	2.00
21	Jerome Bettis	.20
22	Tim Biakabutuka	.10
23	*Roosevelt Blackmon*	.50
24	Jeff Blake	.20
25	Drew Bledsoe	1.50
26	Tony Boselli	.10
27	Peter Boulware	.10
28	Tony Brackens	.10
29	*Corey Bradford*	.50
30	*Michael Pittman*	1.00
31	*Keith Brooking*	1.00
32	Robert Brooks	.10
33	Derrick Brooks	.10
34	*Ken Oxendine*	.50
35	*R.W. McQuarters*	1.00
36	Tim Brown	.20
37	Chad Brown	.10
38	Isaac Bruce	.20
39	Mark Brunell	1.50
40	Chris Canty	.10
41	Mark Carrier	.10
42	Rae Carruth	.10
43	Ki-Jana Carter	.10
44	Cris Carter	.20
45	Larry Centers	.10
46	*Corey Chavous*	.50
47	Mark Chmura	.10
48	*Cameron Cleeland*	2.00
49	Dexter Coakley	.10
50	Ben Coates	.10
51	*Jonathon Linton*	1.00
52	Todd Collins	.10
53	Kerry Collins	.20
54	*Tebucky Jones*	.50
55	Curtis Conway	.20
56	*Sam Cowart*	.50
57	Bryan Cox	.10
58	Randall Cunningham	.50
59	Terrell Davis	2.00
60	Troy Davis	.10
61	*Patrick Johnson*	.50
62	Trent Dilfer	.20
63	*Vonnie Holliday*	2.00
64	Corey Dillon	1.00
65	Hugh Douglas	.10
66	Jim Druckenmiller	.20
67	Warrick Dunn	1.50
68	*Robert Edwards*	3.00
69	*Greg Ellis*	1.00
70	John Elway	1.50
71	Bert Emanuel	.10
72	Bobby Engram	.10
73	*Curtis Enis*	4.00
74	Marshall Faulk	.50
75	Brett Favre	3.00
76	Doug Flutie	1.50
77	Glenn Foley	.10
78	Antonio Freeman	.50
79	Gus Frerotte	.10
80	John Friesz	.10
81	Irving Fryar	.10
82	Joey Galloway	.50
83	Rich Gannon	.10
84	Charlie Garner	.10
85	Jeff George	.20
86	Eddie George	1.25
87	Sean Gilbert	.10
88	Terry Glenn	.20
89	Aaron Glenn	.10
90	Tony Gonzalez	.10
91	Jeff Graham	.10
92	Elvis Grbac	.10
93	*Jacquez Green*	3.00
94	Kevin Greene	.10
95	*Brian Griese*	5.00
96	Byron Hanspard	.10
97	Jim Harbaugh	.10
98	Kevin Hardy	.10
99	Walt Harris	.10
100	Marvin Harrison	.20
101	Rodney Harrison	.10
102	Jeff Hartings	.10
103	Ken Harvey	.10
104	Garrison Hearst	.20
105	Ike Hilliard	.10
106	Jeff Hostetler	.10
107	Bobby Hoying	.20
108	Michael Jackson	.10
109	Anthony Johnson	.10
110	Brad Johnson	.50
111	Keyshawn Johnson	.20
112	Charles Johnson	.10
113	Daryl Johnston	.10
114	Chris Jones	.10
115	George Jones	.10
116	*Donald Hayes*	1.50
117	Danny Kanell	.10
118	Napoleon Kaufman	.50
119	Cortez Kennedy	.10
120	Eddie Kennison	.20
121	Levon Kirkland	.10
122	Jon Kitna	.10
123	Erik Kramer	.10
124	David LaFleur	.10
125	Lamar Lathon	.10
126	Ty Law	.10
127	*Ryan Leaf*	6.00
128	Dorsey Levens	.20
129	Ray Lewis	.10
130	Darryll Lewis	.10
131	*Matt Hasselbeck*	.50
132	Greg Lloyd	.10
133	Kevin Lockett	.10
134	Keith Lyle	.10
135	*Peyton Manning*	10.00
136	Dan Marino	2.00
137	Wayne Martin	.10
138	*Ahman Green*	3.00
139	Tony Martin	.10
140	*E.G. Green*	1.50
141	Derrick Mayes	.10
142	Ed McCaffrey	.20
143	Keenan McCardell	.10
144	O.J. McDuffie	.10
145	Leeland McElroy	.10
146	Willie McGinest	.10
147	Chester McGlockton	.10
148	Steve McNair	.50
149	Natrone Means	.20
150	Eric Metcalf	.10
151	Anthony Miller	.10
152	Rick Mirer	.10
153	Scott Mitchell	.10
154	John Mobley	.10
155	Warren Moon	.50
156	Herman Moore	.50
157	*Randy Moss*	15.00
158	Eric Moulds	.20
159	Muhsin Muhammad	.10
160	Adrian Murrell	.10
161	*Marcus Nash*	3.00
162	Hardy Nickerson	.10
163	Ken Norton	.10
164	Neil O'Donnell	.10
165	Terrell Owens	.50
166	Orlando Pace	.10
167	*Jammi German*	1.50
168	Erric Pegram	.10
169	*Jason Peter*	.50
170	Carl Pickens	.20
171	Jake Plummer	1.50
172	John Randle	.10
173	Andre Reed	.10
174	Jake Reed	.10
175	Errict Rhett	.10
176	Simeon Rice	.10
177	Jerry Rice	1.50
178	Andre Rison	.20
179	Darrell Russell	.10
180	Rashaan Salaam	.10
181	Deion Sanders	.50
182	Barry Sanders	3.00
183	Chris Sanders	.10
184	Warren Sapp	.10
185	Junior Seau	.20
186	Jason Sehorn	.10
187	Shannon Sharpe	.20
188	Sedrick Shaw	.10
189	Heath Shuler	.10
190	*Chris Floyd*	.50
191	*Terry Fair*	1.50
192	*Kevin Dyson*	3.00
193	Torrance Small	.10
194	Antowain Smith	.75
195	Bruce Smith	.10
196	*Tarik Smith*	.50
197	Emmitt Smith	2.00
198	Neil Smith	.10
199	Jimmy Smith	.20
200	Chris Spielman	.10
201	Danny Wuerffel	.10
202	Irving Spikes	.10
203	Shawn Springs	.10
204	*Duane Starks*	.50
205	Kordell Stewart	1.50
206	J.J. Stokes	.20
207	Eric Swann	.10
208	Steve Tasker	.10
209	*Tim Dwight*	2.00
210	Jason Taylor	.10
211	Vinny Testaverde	.20
212	Thurman Thomas	.20
213	Broderick Thomas	.10
214	Derrick Thomas	.10
215	Zach Thomas	.10
216	*Germane Crowell*	2.50
217	Amani Toomer	.10
218	Tamarick Vanover	.10
219	Ross Verba	.10
220	*Andre Wadsworth*	1.50
221	Ray Zellars	.10
222	Chris Warren	.10
223	Steve Young	1.00
224	Tyrone Wheatley	.10
225	Reggie White	.50
226	*John Avery*	2.50
227	*Charles Woodson*	4.00
228	*Takeo Spikes*	1.50
229	Bryant Young	.10
230	*Tavian Banks*	2.50
231	*Fred Beasley*	.50
232	*Chris Ruhman*	.50

1998 Collector's Edge First Place Game Gear Jersey

Jerseys present at the NFL Draft Day Ceremonies and worn during the pre-season were used to make these cards. Singles were found 1:480 packs.

		MT
Complete Set (2):		300.00
Common Player:		100.00
Inserted 1:480		
1	Peyton Manning	200.00
2	Ryan Leaf	100.00

1998 Collector's Edge First Place Peyton Manning

Edge produced a five-card insert of Manning and inserted them 1:24 packs.

	MT
Complete Set (5):	40.00
Common Player:	8.00
Inserted 1:24	

1998 Collector's Edge First Place Rookie Ink

This set features autographed cards from the top 1998 rookies. Cards are enhanced with silver foil and each card back contains a certificate of authenticity. Singles are signed in blue ink and are found 1:24 packs. Red signatures also exist and are limited to 50 of each.

		MT
Complete Set (31):		750.00
Common Player:		8.00
Inserted 1:24		
Red Signatures:		3x
Production 50 Sets		
1	Brian Griese	45.00
2	Adrian Murrell	12.00
3	Marvin Harrison	20.00
4	Tavian Banks	25.00
5	Mike Alstott	18.00
6	Joe Jurevicius	12.00
7	Tim Dwight	18.00
8	Derrick Mayes	12.00
9	Kevin Greene	8.00
10	Marcus Nash	25.00
11	Charlie Batch	75.00
12	Cris Carter	25.00
13	Randy Moss	175.00
14	Tiki Barber	12.00
15	Ahman Green	25.00
16	Terrell Owens	20.00
17	Jim Druckenmiller	12.00
18	Reidel Anthony	12.00
19	Jacquez Green	25.00
20	Skip Hicks	20.00
21	Terry Allen	12.00
22	Fred Lane	12.00
23	Robert Holcombe	20.00
24	Jeremy Newberry	8.00
25	Fred Taylor	80.00
26	Mark Bruener	8.00
27	Hines Ward	20.00
28	Stephen Davis	12.00
29	Justin Armour	8.00
30	Peyton Manning	125.00
31	Ryan Leaf	50.00

1998 Collector's Edge First Place Rookie Markers

Each single in this 30-card set has a special embossed foil icon that recognizes the player's draft pick number. Singles were inserted 1:24 packs.

		MT
Complete Set (30):		175.00
Common Player:		2.00
Inserted 1:24		
1	Michael Pittman	2.00
2	Andre Wadsworth	4.00
3	Keith Brooking	2.00
4	Patrick Johnson	2.00
5	Jonathon Linton	2.00
6	Donald Hayes	4.00
7	Mark Chmura	2.00
8	Terry Allen	2.00
9	Brian Griese	8.00
10	Marcus Nash	8.00
11	Germane Crowell	8.00
12	Roosevelt Blackmon	2.00
13	Peyton Manning	30.00
14	Tavian Banks	8.00
15	Fred Taylor	20.00
16	Jim Druckenmiller	4.00
17	John Avery	8.00
18	Randy Moss	40.00
19	Robert Edwards	10.00
20	Cameron Cleeland	6.00
21	Joe Jurevicius	4.00
22	Charles Woodson	10.00
23	Terry Allen	2.00
24	Ryan Leaf	12.00
25	Chris Ruhman	2.00
26	Ahman Green	8.00
27	Jerome Pathon	4.00
28	Jacquez Green	8.00
29	Kevin Dyson	8.00
30	Skip Hicks	6.00

1998 Collector's Edge First Place Ryan Leaf

Edge produced a five-card insert set of Leaf and inserted them 1:24 packs.

	MT
Complete Set (5):	25.00
Common Player:	5.00
Inserted 1:24	

1998 Collector's Edge First Place Successors

Only the top players in the NFL are in this 25-card set. Singles are featured on mirror silver with gold foil. Cards were inserted 1:8 packs.

		MT
Complete Set (25):		75.00
Common Player:		1.00
Inserted 1:8		
1	Troy Aikman	4.00
2	Jerome Bettis	2.00
3	Drew Bledsoe	4.00
4	Tim Brown	1.00
5	Mark Brunell	4.00
6	Cris Carter	2.00
7	Terrell Davis	6.00
8	Robert Edwards	4.00
9	John Elway	4.00
10	Brett Favre	8.00
11	Eddie George	3.00
12	Brian Griese	3.00
13	Napoleon Kaufman	2.00
14	Ryan Leaf	5.00
15	Dorsey Levens	1.00
16	Peyton Manning	10.00
17	Dan Marino	6.00
18	Jim Druckenmiller	2.00
19	Herman Moore	2.00
20	Randy Moss	15.00
21	Jake Plummer	3.00
22	Barry Sanders	8.00
23	Emmitt Smith	6.00
24	Rod Smith	1.00
25	Fred Taylor	7.00

1998 Collector's Edge First Place Triple Threat

Three different levels to this 40-card insert. The first being Bronze that are found 1:12 packs. The next level is Silver that are inserted 1:24. The toughest is the Gold which are inserted 1:36.

		MT
Complete Set (40):		185.00
Common Bronze:		1.50
Inserted 1:12		
Common Silver:		2.50
Inserted 1:24		
Common Gold:		4.00
Inserted 1:36		
1	Robert Brooks	1.50
2	Troy Aikman	7.00
3	Randy Moss	20.00
4	Tim Brown	1.50
5	Brad Johnson	3.00
6	Kevin Dyson	4.00
7	Mark Chmura	1.50
8	Joey Galloway	3.00
9	Eddie George	6.00
10	Napoleon Kaufman	3.00
11	Dan Marino	12.00
12	Ed McCaffrey	3.00
13	Herman Moore	3.00
14	Carl Pickens	1.50
15	Emmitt Smith	12.00
16	Drew Bledsoe	7.00
17	Andre Wadsworth	3.00
18	Charles Woodson	7.00
19	Terrell Davis	12.00
20	Yancey Thigpen	2.50
21	Drew Bledsoe	7.00
22	Keith Brooking	2.50
23	Mark Brunell	7.00
24	Terrell Davis	12.00
25	Antonio Freeman	3.00
26	Peyton Manning	15.00
27	Jerry Rice	7.00
28	Takeo Spikes	3.00
29	Danny Wuerffel	1.50
30	Jerome Bettis	3.00
31	Cris Carter	4.00
32	Jim Druckenmiller	4.00
33	Warrick Dunn	8.00
34	John Elway	10.00
35	Brett Favre	20.00
36	Ryan Leaf	8.00
37	Dorsey Levens	4.00
38	Terrell Owens	6.00
39	Barry Sanders	20.00
40	Kordell Stewart	10.00

1998 Collector's Edge First Place Triumph

Each Triumph card is printed on clear acetate stock with a large action shot in the foreground with a head shot in the background. The 25 different singles were inserted 1:12 packs.

		MT
Complete Set (25):		85.00
Common Player:		2.00
Inserted 1:12		
1	Troy Aikman	5.00
2	Jerome Bettis	2.00
3	Drew Bledsoe	5.00
4	Tim Brown	2.00
5	Mark Brunell	4.00
6	Cris Carter	2.00
7	Terrell Davis	7.00
8	Jim Druckenmiller	2.00
9	Robert Edwards	4.00
10	John Elway	5.00
11	Brett Favre	10.00
12	Eddie George	4.00
13	Brian Griese	4.00
14	Napoleon Kaufman	2.00
15	Ryan Leaf	6.00
16	Dorsey Levens	2.00
17	Peyton Manning	10.00
18	Dan Marino	7.00
19	Herman Moore	2.00
20	Randy Moss	15.00
21	Jake Plummer	4.00
22	Barry Sanders	10.00
23	Emmitt Smith	7.00
24	Rod Smith	2.00
25	Fred Taylor	7.00

1998 Collector's Edge Masters

This is the first super-premium product that Edge has released. Every card in this set is sequentially numbered to 5,000, with double-thick parallel levels. The first being the 50-Point cards that are numbered to 3,000 and inserted one-per-pack. The 50-Point Gold singles are numbered to 150 and inserted 1:20 packs. HoloGold cards are numbered to 10 and found 1:300 packs.

		MT
Complete Set (199):		325.00
Common Player:		.25
Common Rookie:		1.50
Production 5,000 Sets		
50-Point Cards:		1.5x
Inserted 1:1		
Production 3,000 Sets		
50-Point Gold Cards:		7x-14x
50-Point Gold Rookies:		2x-4x
Inserted 1:20		
Production 150 Sets		
Hologold Cards:		50x-100x
Hologold Rookies:		8x-16x
Inserted 1:300		
Production 10 Sets		
Wax Box:		100.00
1	Rob Moore	.50
2	Adrian Murrell	.25
3	Jake Plummer	3.00
4	*Michael Pittman*	1.50
5	Frank Sanders	.50
6	*Andre Wadsworth*	3.00
7	Jamal Anderson	1.00
8	Chris Chandler	.50
9	*Tim Dwight*	7.50
10	Tony Martin	.25
11	Terance Mathis	.25
12	*Ken Oxendine*	1.50
13	Jim Harbaugh	.50
14	*Priest Holmes*	15.00
15	Michael Jackson	.25
16	*Pat Johnson*	3.00
17	Jermaine Lewis	.25
18	Eric Zeier	.25
19	Doug Flutie	2.00
20	Rob Johnson	.50
21	Eric Moulds	1.00
22	Andre Reed	.50
23	Antowain Smith	1.00
24	Bruce Smith	.25
25	Thurman Thomas	.50
26	Steve Beuerlein	.25
27	Kevin Greene	.25
29	Raghib Ismail	.25
30	Fred Lane	.25
31	Muhsin Muhammad	.25
32	Edgar Bennett	.25
33	Curtis Conway	.50
34	Bobby Engram	.25
35	*Curtis Enis*	7.50
36	Erik Kramer	.25
37	Chris Penn	.25
38	Jeff Blake	.50
39	Corey Dillon	2.00
40	Neil O'Donnell	.25
41	Carl Pickens	.50
42	Darnay Scott	.25
43	*Damon Gibson*	1.50
44	Troy Aikman	3.00
45	Billy Davis	.25
46	Michael Irvin	.50
47	Ernie Mills	.25
48	Deion Sanders	1.00
49	Emmitt Smith	4.50
50	Chris Warren	.50
51	Bubby Brister	.25
52	Terrell Davis	4.50
53	John Elway	4.50
54	*Brian Griese*	10.00
55	Ed McCaffrey	.75
56	*Marcus Nash*	5.00
57	Shannon Sharpe	.50
58	Rod Smith	.50
59	*Charlie Batch*	12.00
60	*Germane Crowell*	5.00
61	Scott Mitchell	.25
62	Johnnie Morton	.25
63	Herman Moore	.75
64	Barry Sanders	6.00
65	Robert Brooks	.25
66	Brett Favre	6.00
67	Antonio Freeman	1.00
68	Raymont Harris	.25
69	Dorsey Levens	1.00
70	Reggie White	1.00
71	Marshall Faulk	1.00
72	Marvin Harrison	.50
73	*Peyton Manning*	25.00
74	*Jerome Pathon*	3.00
75	*Tavian Banks*	4.00
76	Mark Brunell	3.00
77	Keenan McCardell	.25
78	Jimmy Smith	.75
79	*Fred Taylor*	20.00
80	Derrick Alexander	.25
81	Donnell Bennett	.25
82	Rich Gannon	.25
83	Elvis Grbac	.50
84	Andre Rison	.50
85	*Rashaan Shehee*	1.50
86	Karim Abdul	.75
87	*John Avery*	5.00
88	*Oronde Gadsden*	5.00
89	Dan Marino	4.50
90	O.J. McDuffie	.50
91	Zach Thomas	.50
92	Cris Carter	1.00
93	Randall Cunningham	1.00
94	Brad Johnson	.75
95	*Randy Moss*	50.00
96	Jake Reed	.25
97	Robert Smith	.50
98	Drew Bledsoe	3.00
99	Ben Coates	.50
100	*Robert Edwards*	7.50
101	Terry Glenn	.75
102	Shawn Jefferson	.25
103	Ty Law	.25
104	*Cameron Cleeland*	4.00
105	Kerry Collins	.50
106	Sean Dawkins	.25
107	Andre Hastings	.25
108	Lamar Smith	.25
109	Danny Wuerffel	.25
110	Gary Brown	.25
111	Chris Calloway	.25
112	Ike Hilliard	.25
113	*Joe Jurevicius*	3.00
114	Danny Kanell	.25
115	Wayne Chrebet	.75
116	Glenn Foley	.50
117	Keyshawn Johnson	1.00
118	Leon Johnson	.25
119	Curtis Martin	1.00
120	Vinny Testeverde	.50
121	Tim Brown	.50
122	Jeff George	.50
123	James Jett	.25
124	Napoleon Kaufman	1.00
125	*Charles Woodson*	7.50
126	Irving Fryar	.25
127	Jeff Graham	.25
128	Bobby Hoying	.25
129	Duce Staley	.25
130	Jerome Bettis	.75
131	*Chris Fuamatu-Ma'afala*	3.00
132	Courtney Hawkins	.25
133	Charles Johnson	.25
134	Kordell Stewart	2.00
135	*Hines Ward*	3.00
136	Tony Banks	.50
137	Isaac Bruce	.50
138	*Robert Holcombe*	5.00
139	Eddie Kennison	.50
140	*Ryan Leaf*	12.00
141	Natrone Means	.50
142	*Mikhael Ricks*	3.00
143	Junior Seau	.50
144	Bryan Still	.25
145	Garrison Hearst	.75
146	*R.W. McQuarters*	3.00
147	Terrell Owens	1.00
148	Jerry Rice	3.00
149	J.J. Stokes	.50
150	Steve Young	2.00
151	Joey Galloway	1.00
152	*Ahman Green*	5.00
153	Warren Moon	.50
154	Shawn Springs	.25
155	Ricky Watters	.50
156	Mike Alstott	.50
157	Reidel Anthony	.50
158	Trent Dilfer	.50
159	Warrick Dunn	2.00
160	*Jacquez Green*	5.00
161	*Kevin Dyson*	5.00
162	Eddie George	2.00
163	Steve McNair	1.00
164	Yancy Thigpen	.25
165	Frank Wycheck	.25
166	Terry Allen	.50
167	Gus Frerotte	.25
168	Trent Green	.50
169	*Skip Hicks*	5.00
170	Michael Westbrook	.50
171	Jamal Anderson	.50
172	Carl Pickens	.25
173	Deion Sanders	.50
174	Emmitt Smith	2.00
175	Terrell Davis	2.00
176	John Elway	2.00
177	Charlie Batch	7.50
178	Herman Moore	.25
179	Barry Sanders	3.00
180	Brett Favre	3.00
181	Antonio Freeman	.50
182	Marshall Faulk	.50
183	Peyton Manning	15.00
184	Mark Brunell	1.50
185	Dan Marino	2.00
186	Randy Moss	30.00
187	Drew Bledsoe	1.50
188	Robert Edwards	3.00
189	Curtis Martin	.50
190	Charles Woodson	3.00
191	Jerome Bettis	.25
192	Robert Holcombe	2.00
193	Ryan Leaf	7.50
194	Natrone Means	.50
195	Jerry Rice	1.50
196	Steve Young	1.00
197	Warrick Dunn	1.00
198	Eddie George	1.00
199	Peyton Manning CL	7.50
200	Ryan Leaf CL	4.00

1998 Collector's Edge Masters Legends

This 30-card set includes the top players from '98. Each card is sequentially numbered to 2,500 and inserted 1:8 packs.

		MT
Complete Set (30):		85.00
Common Player:		1.50
Inserted 1:8		
Production 2,500 Sets		
1	Jake Plummer	6.00
2	Doug Flutie	4.00
3	Corey Dillon	3.00
4	Carl Pickens	1.50
5	Troy Aikman	6.00
6	Deion Sanders	3.00
7	Emmitt Smith	10.00
8	Terrell Davis	10.00
9	John Elway	10.00
10	Herman Moore	3.00
11	Barry Sanders	12.00
12	Brett Favre	12.00
13	Antonio Freeman	3.00
14	Marshall Faulk	3.00
15	Mark Brunell	5.00
16	Dan Marino	10.00
17	Cris Carter	3.00
18	Drew Bledsoe	5.00
19	Keyshawn Johnson	3.00
20	Curtis Martin	3.00
21	Napoleon Kaufman	3.00
22	Jerome Bettis	3.00
23	Kordell Stewart	5.00
24	Natrone Means	3.00
25	Jerry Rice	6.00
26	Steve Young	4.00
27	Joey Galloway	3.00
28	Warrick Dunn	4.00
29	Eddie George	5.00
30	Terry Allen	1.50

1998 Collector's Edge Masters Main Event

Main Event singles are sequentially numbered to 2,000 and inserted 1:16 packs.

		MT
Complete Set (20):		160.00
Common Player:		2.50
Inserted 1:16		
Production 2,000 Sets		
1	Troy Aikman	8.00
2	Jamal Anderson	5.00
3	Charlie Batch	12.00
4	Jerome Bettis	2.50
5	Mark Brunell	6.00
6	Terrell Davis	12.00
7	Warrick Dunn	5.00
8	Robert Edwards	7.00
9	John Elway	12.00
10	Brett Favre	16.00
11	Doug Flutie	5.00
12	Eddie George	6.00
13	Dan Marino	12.00
14	Curtis Martin	5.00
15	Randy Moss	50.00
16	Carl Pickens	2.50
17	Jake Plummer	8.00
18	Barry Sanders	16.00
19	Emmitt Smith	12.00
20	Fred Taylor	25.00

1998 Collector's Edge Masters Rookie Masters

This 30-card set is made up of the top rookies from the class of '98. Each card is sequentially numbered to 2,500 and inserted 1:8 packs.

		MT
Complete Set (30):		125.00
Common Player:		1.50
Inserted 1:8		
Production 2,500 Sets		
1	Peyton Manning	25.00
2	Ryan Leaf	10.00
3	Charlie Batch	12.00
4	Brian Griese	8.00
5	Randy Moss	40.00
6	Jacquez Green	4.00
7	Kevin Dyson	4.00
8	Mikhael Ricks	3.00
9	Jerome Pathon	3.00
10	Joe Jurevicius	3.00
11	Germane Crowell	4.00
12	Tim Dwight	6.00
13	Pat Johnson	3.00
14	Hines Ward	3.00
15	Marcus Nash	4.00
16	Damon Gibson	1.50
17	Robert Edwards	5.00
18	Robert Holcombe	4.00
19	Tavian Banks	3.00
20	Fred Taylor	20.00
21	Skip Hicks	4.00
22	Curtis Enis	6.00
23	Ahman Green	4.00
24	John Avery	4.00
25	Chris Fuamatu-Ma'afala	3.00
26	Rashaan Shehee	1.50
27	Cameron Cleeland	4.00
28	Charles Woodson	6.00
29	R.W. McQuarters	3.00
30	Andre Wadsworth	3.00

1998 Collector's Edge Masters Sentinels

This 10-card set is made up of the top 10 most collectible superstars in the NFL. Each card is sequentially numbered to 500 and found 1:120 packs.

		MT
Complete Set (10):		275.00
Common Player:		15.00
Inserted 1:120		
Production 500 Sets		
1	John Elway	30.00
2	Brett Favre	40.00
3	Barry Sanders	40.00
4	Terrell Davis	30.00
5	Dan Marino	30.00
6	Emmitt Smith	30.00
7	Randy Moss	75.00
8	Peyton Manning	40.00
9	Robert Edwards	15.00
10	Fred Taylor	35.00

1998 Collector's Edge Masters Super Masters

We have the checklist at 23 players for a complete set. Ten of the players also have signed versions of their insert card. Insert odds are 1:10 packs for the regular insert and the Autographs vary.

	MT
Complete Set (23):	75.00
Common Player:	1.50
Inserted 1:10	
Production 2,000 Sets	
Set Price Doesn't Include Autographs	
Troy Aikman	8.00
Edgar Bennett	1.50
Robert Brooks	1.50
Dwight Clark	3.00
Dwight Clark AUTO	15.00
Roger Craig	3.00
Roger Craig AUTO	15.00
Terrell Davis	12.00
Len Dawson	3.00
Len Dawson AUTO	40.00
John Elway	12.00
Brett Favre	16.00
Antonio Freeman	3.00
Jack Ham	3.00
Jack Ham AUTO	15.00
Michael Irvin	3.00
Butch Johnson AUTO	10.00
Drew Pearson	3.00
Drew Pearson AUTO	15.00
Jerry Rice	8.00
Deion Sanders	3.00
Shannon Sharpe	3.00
Emmitt Smith	12.00
Rod Smith	3.00
John Stallworth	3.00
John Stallworth AUTO	15.00
Bart Starr	10.00
Bart Starr AUTO	325.00
Johnny Unitas	8.00
Johnny Unitas AUTO	300.00
Steve Young	5.00
Reggie White	3.00

1998 Collector's Edge Odyssey

The base set is made up of 250 cards and is broken down into four tiers or quarters. The first 150 cards are from the 1st Quarter subset. Cards 151-200 are 2nd Quarter and are inserted 1:1.5 packs. Cards 201-230 are 3rd Quarter and are found 1:3 packs. Cards 231-250 are the

4th Quarter singles and are the toughest to find at 1:18 packs.

		MT
Complete Set (250):		450.00
Common 1st Quarter:		.10
Common Rookie:		1.50
Common 2nd Quarter:		.50
Inserted 1:1.5		
Common 3rd Quarter:		.75
Inserted 1:3		
Common 4th Quarter:		3.00
Inserted 1:18		
Wax Box:		85.00
1	Terance Mathis	.10
2	Tony Martin	.10
3	Chris Chandler	.20
4	Jamal Anderson	.50
5	Jake Plummer	.75
6	Adrian Murrell	.10
7	Rob Moore	.10
8	Frank Sanders	.10
9	Larry Centers	.10
10	*Andre Wadsworth*	1.50
11	Jim Harbaugh	.20
12	Errict Rhett	.10
13	Jermaine Lewis	.10
14	Michael Jackson	.10
15	Eric Zeier	.10
16	Rob Johnson	.20
17	Antowain Smith	.50
18	Andre Reed	.10
19	Bruce Smith	.10
20	Doug Flutie	.50
21	Thurman Thomas	.20
22	Kerry Collins	.20
23	Fred Lane	.20
24	Muhsin Mohammed	.10
25	Rae Carruth	.10
26	Raghib Islmail	.10
27	Kevin Greene	.10
28	*Curtis Enis*	3.00
29	Curtis Conway	.20
30	Erik Kramer	.10
31	Edgar Bennett	.10
32	Neil O'Donnell	.20
33	Jeff Blake	.20
34	Carl Pickens	.20
35	Corey Dillon	.50
36	Troy Aikman	1.00
37	Jason Garrett	.10
38	Emmitt Smith	1.50
39	Deion Sanders	.50
40	Michael Irvin	.20
41	Chris Warren	.10
42	John Elway	1.00
43	Terrell Davis	1.50
44	Shannon Sharpe	.20
45	Rod Smith	.20
46	*Marcus Nash*	2.50
47	*Brian Griese*	4.00
48	Barry Sanders	2.00
49	Herman Moore	.20
50	Scott Mitchell	.10
51	Johnnie Morton	.10
52	*Rashaan Shehee*	1.50
53	*Charlie Batch*	5.00
54	Brett Favre	2.00
55	Dorsey Levens	.20
56	Antonio Freeman	.50
57	Reggie White	.50
58	Robert Brooks	.10
59	Raymont Harris	.10
60	*Peyton Manning*	10.00
61	Marshall Faulk	.50
62	*Jerome Pathon*	2.00
63	Marvin Harrison	.20
64	Mark Brunell	.75
65	*Fred Taylor*	5.00
66	Jimmy Smith	.20
67	James Stewart	.20
68	Keenan McCardell	.10
69	Andre Rison	.10
70	Elvis Grbac	.10
71	Donnell Bennett	.10
72	Rich Gannon	.10
73	Derrick Thomas	.10
74	Dan Marino	1.50
75	Karim Abdul-Jabbar	.50
76	*John Avery*	3.00
77	O.J. McDuffie	.10
78	*Oronde Gadsden*	2.00
79	Zach Thomas	.20
80	*Randy Moss*	15.00
81	Cris Carter	.50
82	Jake Reed	.10
83	Robert Smith	.20
84	Brad Johnson	.50
85	Drew Bledsoe	1.00
86	*Robert Edwards*	4.00
87	Terry Glenn	.50
88	Troy Brown	.10
89	Shawn Jefferson	.10
90	Danny Wuerffel	.10
91	Dana Stubblefield	.10
92	Derrick Alexander	.10
93	Ray Zellars	.10
94	Andre Hastings	.10
95	Danny Kanell	.10
96	Tiki Barber	.10
97	Ike Hilliard	.10
98	Charles Way	.10
99	Chris Calloway	.10
100	Curtis Martin	.50
101	Glenn Foley	.20
102	Vinny Testeverde	.20
103	Keyshawn Johnson	.50
104	Wayne Chrebet	.50
105	Leon Johnson	.10
106	Jeff George	.20
107	*Charles Woodson*	3.00
108	Tim Brown	.20
109	James Jett	.10
110	Napoleon Kaufman	.50
111	Charlie Garner	.10
112	Bobby Hoying	.10
113	Duce Staley	.10
114	Irving Fryar	.10
115	Kordell Stewart	.75
116	Jerome Bettis	.50
117	Charles Johnson	.10
118	Randall Cunningham	.50
119	Courtney Hawkins	.10
120	Tony Banks	.50
121	Isaac Bruce	.50
122	*Robert Holcombe*	2.50
123	Greg Hill	.10
124	*Ryan Leaf*	5.00
125	*Mikhael Ricks*	2.50
126	Natrone Means	.50
127	Junior Seau	.20
128	Jerry Rice	1.00
129	Terrell Owens	.75
130	Garrison Hearst	.20
131	Steve Young	.75
132	J.J. Stokes	.20
133	Warren Moon	.20
134	Joey Galloway	.50
135	Ricky Watters	.20
136	*Ahman Green*	2.50
137	Trent Dilfer	.20
138	Mike Alstott	.50
139	Warrick Dunn	.75
140	Reidel Anthony	.20
141	*Jacquez Green*	2.50
142	Steve McNair	.50
143	Eddie George	.75
144	Yancey Thigpen	.20
145	*Kevin Dyson*	2.50
146	Trent Green	.20
147	Gus Frerotte	.10
148	Terry Allen	.20
149	Michael Westbrook	.20
150	Jim Druckenmiller	.20
151	Jake Plummer	1.50
152	Adrian Murrell	.50
153	Rob Johnson	.50
154	Antowain Smith	.75
155	Kerry Collins	.50
156	Curtis Enis	5.00
157	Carl Pickens	.50
158	Corey Dillon	1.00
159	Troy Aikman	1.50
160	Emmitt Smith	2.00
161	Deion Sanders	.50
162	Michael Irvin	.50
163	John Elway	1.50
164	Terrell Davis	2.00
165	Shannon Sharpe	.50
166	Rod Smith	.50
167	Barry Sanders	3.00
168	Herman Moore	.50
169	Brett Favre	3.00
170	Dorsey Levens	.50
171	Antonio Freeman	.75
172	Peyton Manning	14.00
173	Marshall Faulk	.50
174	Mark Brunell	1.00
175	Fred Taylor	7.00
176	Dan Marino	2.00
177	Randy Moss	25.00
178	Cris Carter	.50
179	Drew Bledsoe	1.00
180	Robert Edwards	6.00
181	Curtis Martin	.50
182	Napoleon Kaufman	.50
183	Kordell Stewart	1.00
184	Jerome Bettis	.50
185	Tony Banks	.50
186	Isaac Bruce	.50
187	Ryan Leaf	8.00
188	Natrone Means	.50
189	Jerry Rice	1.50
190	Terrell Owens	.75
191	Garrison Hearst	.50
192	Steve Young	.75
193	Warren Moon	.50
194	Joey Galloway	.50
195	Trent Dilfer	.50
196	Mike Alstott	.50
197	Warrick Dunn	1.50
198	Steve McNair	.75
199	Eddie George	1.00
200	Terry Allen	.50
201	Jake Plummer	2.00
202	Curtis Enis	8.00
203	Carl Pickens	.75
204	Corey Dillon	1.00
205	Troy Aikman	2.00
206	Emmitt Smith	3.00
207	John Elway	2.00
208	Terrell Davis	3.00
209	Barry Sanders	4.00
210	Brett Favre	4.00
211	Antonio Freeman	.75
212	Peyton Manning	25.00
213	Mark Brunell	1.50
214	Fred Taylor	12.00
215	Dan Marino	3.00
216	Randy Moss	35.00
217	Drew Bledsoe	1.50
218	Robert Edwards	8.00
219	Curtis Martin	.75
220	Kordell Stewart	1.50
221	Jerome Bettis	.75
222	Tony Banks	.75
223	Ryan Leaf	12.00
224	Jerry Rice	2.00
225	Steve Young	1.00
226	Warren Moon	.75
227	Trent Dilfer	.75
228	Warrick Dunn	2.00
229	Steve McNair	1.00
230	Eddie George	1.50
231	Curtis Enis	15.00
232	Carl Pickens	3.00
233	Troy Aikman	6.00
234	Emmitt Smith	8.00
235	John Elway	6.00
236	Terrell Davis	10.00
237	Barry Sanders	12.00
238	Brett Favre	12.00
239	Peyton Manning	35.00
240	Fred Taylor	18.00
241	Dan Marino	8.00
242	Randy Moss	65.00
243	Drew Bledsoe	5.00
244	Kordell Stewart	5.00
245	Jerome Bettis	3.00
246	Ryan Leaf	20.00
247	Jerry Rice	6.00
248	Steve Young	4.00
249	Warren Moon	3.00
250	Eddie George	5.00

1998 Collector's Edge Odyssey Galvanized

Each base card has a parallel Galvanized single that is also tiered four ways. Each single has the letter "G" on the back and has a foil front. Cards 1-150 were inserted 1:3 packs, Cards 151-200 were found 1:15 packs, 201-230 at 1:29 and 231-250 at 1:59.

	MT
Complete Set (250):	1000.
1st Quarter Cards:	3x
1st Quarter Rookies:	1.5x
Inserted 1:3	
2nd Quarter Cards:	4x
2nd Quarter Rookies:	2x
Inserted 1:15	
3rd Quarter Cards:	3x
3rd Quarter Rookies:	1.5x
Inserted 1:29	
4th Quarter Cards:	4x
4th Quarter Rookies:	2x
Inserted 1:144	

1998 Collector's Edge Odyssey HoloGold

HoloGold is the second parallel set to the base and is also tiered four different ways. These singles have the letter "H" on the backs and also have foil fronts. Cards 1-150 are numbered to 150 and inserted 1:34 packs, cards 151-200 are numbered to 50 and found 1:307, cards 201-230 are limited to 30 and found 1:840 and the last tier are cards numbered 231-250 with a production run of 20 and inserted 1:1,920.

	MT
1st Quarter Cards:	20x-40x
1st Quarter Rookies:	5x-10x
Inserted 1:34	
Production 150 Sets	

1998 Collector's Edge Odyssey Double Edge

This 12-card set features photos of a veteran on one side and a rookie on the other. Each is printed on double-sided etched foil cards and inserted 1:15 packs.

		MT
Complete Set (12):		100.00
Common Player:		5.00
Inserted 1:15		
1	Jerry Rice, Randy Moss	30.00
2	Brett Favre, Ryan Leaf	15.00
3	Dan Marino, Bobby Hoying	12.00
4	Deion Sanders, Charles Woodson	8.00
5	Terrell Davis, Curtis Enis	12.00
6	Barry Sanders, Fred Taylor	15.00
7	Emmitt Smith, Robert Edwards	12.00
8	John Elway, Brian Griese	10.00
9	Reggie White, Andre Wadsworth	5.00
10	Drew Bledsoe, Charlie Batch	12.00
11	Doug Flutie, Glenn Foley	7.00
12	Napoleon Kaufman, Warrick Dunn	7.00

1998 Collector's Edge Odyssey Leading Edge

Leading Edge features 30 of the NFL's top stars in an attractive foil set. Singles were inserted 1:7 packs.

		MT
Complete Set (30):		75.00
Common Player:		1.00
Inserted 1:7		
1	Jake Plummer	2.00
2	Rob Johnson	1.00
3	Curtis Enis	3.00
4	Carl Pickens	1.00
5	Troy Aikman	3.00
6	Emmitt Smith	4.50
7	John Elway	3.00
8	Terrell Davis	4.50
9	Shannon Sharpe	1.00
10	Barry Sanders	6.00
11	Brett Favre	6.00
12	Antonio Freeman	1.50
13	Peyton Manning	10.00
14	Marshall Faulk	1.50
15	Mark Brunell	2.00
16	Dan Marino	4.50
17	Randy Moss	20.00
18	Cris Carter	1.50
19	Robert Edwards	4.00
20	Curtis Martin	1.50
21	Ryan Leaf	5.00
22	Terrell Owens	1.50
23	Garrison Hearst	1.00
24	Steve Young	1.50
25	Joey Galloway	1.50
26	Mike Alstott	1.50
27	Warrick Dunn	2.50
28	Eddie George	2.50
29	Kevin Dyson	2.00
30	Terry Allen	1.00

1998 Collector's Edge Odyssey Prodigies

The Prodigies insert is made up of autographs from young talent and rookies from '98. Singles were inserted 1:24 packs. A parallel of Red Signatures exist with most signing between 50 to 80.

	MT
Complete Set (32):	1000.
Common Player:	10.00
Inserted 1:24	
John Avery	30.00
Tavian Banks	20.00
Charlie Batch	75.00
Blaine Bishop	10.00
Robert Brooks	30.00
Tim Brown	50.00
Mark Brunell	100.00
Wayne Chrebet	30.00
Jim Druckenmiller	20.00
Robert Edwards	45.00
Doug Flutie	60.00
Glenn Foley	10.00
Oronde Gadsden	30.00
Joey Galloway	20.00
Garrison Hearst	20.00
Robert Holcombe	20.00
Joey Kent	10.00
Jon Kitna	30.00
Herman Moore	30.00
Randy Moss	200.00
Terrell Owens	30.00
Mikhael Ricks	20.00
Rashaan Shehee	30.00
Antowain Smith	20.00
Emmitt Smith	180.00
Robert Smith	20.00
Rod Smith	20.00
J.J. Stokes	20.00
Fred Taylor	60.00
Derrick Thomas	20.00
Chris Warren	10.00
Eric Zeier	10.00

1998 Collector's Edge Odyssey S.L. Edge

Super Limited Edge singles includes 12 of the game's most collectible superstars and were found 1:99 packs.

		MT
Complete Set (12):		275.00
Common Player:		10.00
Inserted 1:99		
1	Emmitt Smith	45.00
2	Deion Sanders	15.00
3	John Elway	30.00
4	Brett Favre	60.00
5	Antonio Freeman	15.00
6	Peyton Manning	30.00
7	Mark Brunell	25.00
8	Dan Marino	45.00
9	Randy Moss	70.00
10	Joey Galloway	10.00
11	Mike Alstott	10.00
12	Eddie George	25.00

1998 E-X2001

Each of the 60 base cards in this set are holographic and gold-foil stamped with player-specific die-cuts mounted on durable, see-thru plastic stock exposed along a large portion of the card. The Essential Credentials Now parallel cards differ from the base set in color, holo-foil and scarcity. Each card is sequentially numbered according to the player's card number in the base set. Card #1 has only one single and card #60 has cards numbered to 60. The Essential Credentials Future is similar to the Now set except in color, holo-foil and the sequentially numbering is opposite the player's card number. For example, card #1 has 60 cards and card #60 only has one.

		MT
Complete Set (60):		125.00
Common Player:		.30
Wax Box:		110.00
1	Kordell Stewart	3.00
2	Steve Young	2.50
3	Mark Brunell	3.00
4	Brett Favre	8.00
5	Barry Sanders	8.00
6	Warrick Dunn	3.00
7	Jerry Rice	4.00
8	Dan Marino	6.00
9	Emmitt Smith	6.00
10	John Elway	4.00
11	Eddie George	3.00
12	Jake Plummer	3.00
13	Terrell Davis	6.00
14	Curtis Martin	2.50
15	Troy Aikman	4.00
16	Terry Glenn	1.00
17	Mike Alstott	1.00
18	Drew Bledsoe	3.00
19	Keyshawn Johnson	.50
20	Dorsey Levens	.50
21	Elvis Grbac	.30
22	Ricky Watters	1.00
23	Robert Smith	1.00
24	Trent Dilfer	1.00
25	Joey Galloway	1.00
26	Rob Moore	.50
27	Steve McNair	1.50
28	Jim Harbaugh	.30
29	Troy Davis	.30
30	Rob Johnson	1.00
31	Shannon Sharpe	.50
32	Jerome Bettis	1.00
33	Jim Brown	.50
34	Kerry Collins	1.00
35	Garrison Hearst	.50
36	Antonio Freeman	1.00
37	Charlie Garner	.50
38	Glenn Foley	.50
39	Yatil Green	.30
40	Tiki Barber	.50
41	Bobby Hoying	.50
42	Corey Dillon	2.00
43	Antowain Smith	1.50
44	*Robert Edwards*	10.00
45	*Jammi German*	2.00
46	*Ahman Green*	6.00
47	*Hines Ward*	5.00
48	*Skip Hicks*	4.00
49	*Brian Griese*	10.00
50	*Charlie Batch*	12.00
51	*Jacquez Green*	6.00
52	*John Avery*	6.00
53	*Kevin Dyson*	6.00
54	*Peyton Manning*	25.00
55	*Randy Moss*	40.00
56	*Ryan Leaf*	12.00
57	*Curtis Enis*	10.00
58	*Charles Woodson*	10.00
59	*Robert Holcombe*	6.00
60	*Fred Taylor*	18.00

1998 E-X2001 Destination Honolulu

Hawaiian culture is celebrated on these wooden inserts, with five different statuesque die-cuts. Singles were inserted 1:720 packs.

		MT
Complete Set (10):		900.00
Common Player:		35.00
Inserted 1:720		
1	Peyton Manning	175.00
2	Terrell Davis	150.00
3	Corey Dillon	70.00
4	Eddie George	80.00
5	Emmitt Smith	150.00
6	Warrick Dunn	100.00
7	Brett Favre	200.00
8	Antowain Smith	35.00
9	Barry Sanders	200.00
10	Ryan Leaf	100.00

1998 E-X2001 Helmet Heroes

Each single is die-cut around the helmet at the top of the cards. These team color-coded, thick plastic inserts featured some of the NFL's most dynamic players. They were found 1:24 packs.

		MT
Complete Set (20):		200.00
Common Player:		3.00
Inserted 1:24		
1	Barry Sanders	25.00
2	Emmitt Smith	18.00
3	Brett Favre	25.00
4	Mark Brunell	10.00
5	Jerry Rice	12.00
6	Steve Young	8.00
7	Warrick Dunn	10.00
8	Kordell Stewart	10.00
9	John Elway	12.00
10	Troy Aikman	12.00
11	Dan Marino	18.00
12	Curtis Martin	8.00
13	Dorsey Levens	3.00
14	Jake Plummer	10.00
15	Corey Dillon	7.00
16	Yancey Thigpen	3.00
17	Randy Moss	35.00
18	Curtis Enis	10.00
19	Charles Woodson	10.00
20	Fred Taylor	18.00

1998 E-X2001 Star Date 2001

The idea behind this set was to include the stars of tomorrow on a thick, plastic stock with flecks of foil running through it and highlighted with etched silver foil stamping. Singles were inserted 1:12 packs.

		MT
Complete Set (15):		70.00
Common Player:		1.50
Inserted 1:12		
1	Randy Moss	20.00
2	Fred Taylor	10.00
3	Corey Dillon	6.00
4	Jake Plummer	8.00
5	Antowain Smith	4.00
6	Wilmont Perry	1.50
7	Donald Hayes	1.50
8	Tavian Banks	8.00
9	John Dutton	1.50
10	Kevin Dyson	6.00
11	Germane Crowell	3.00
12	Bobby Hoying	1.50
13	Jerome Pathon	3.00
14	Ryan Leaf	8.00
15	Peyton Manning	15.00

1998 Finest II

Finest was issued in two, 150-card series in 1998, with 150 in Series I and 120 in Series II. Each card was available in a Protector (base cards), No-Protector (1:2 packs), Protector Refractor (1:12) and No-Protector Refractor (1:24) version. An interesting twist to the releases was that the 30 rookies (121-150) were available in Protector and No-Protector Refractor versions in Series I, but the No-Protector and Protector Refractor versions were only issued in Series II packs. Series I inserts were: Double-Sided Mystery Finest, Centurions, Undergrads and Jumbos, while Series II inserts included Mystery Finest, Stadium Stars, Future's Finest, Jumbos (base cards), Jumbo Stadium Stars and Jumbo Mystery.

		MT
Complete Series 2 (120):		40.00
Common Player:		.25
Common Rookie:		1.50
Refractor Cards:		5x-10x
Refractor Rookies:		2x-4x
Inserted 1:12		
No-Protector Cards:		2x-4x
No-Protector Rookies:		2x
Inserted 1:2		
NP Refractor Cards:		10x-20x
NP Refractor Rookies:		3x-6x
Inserted 1:24		
Series 2 Wax Box:		75.00
151	Jerry Rice	2.50
152	Tony Martin	.25
153	Billy Joe Hobert	.25
154	Rob Johnson	.50
155	Shannon Sharpe	.50
156	Bert Emanuel	.25
157	Eric Metcalf	.25
158	Natrone Means	.75
159	Derrick Alexander	.25
160	Emmitt Smith	3.50
161	Jeff Burris	.25
162	Chris Warren	.25
163	Corey Fuller	.25
164	Courtney Hawkins	.25
165	James McKnight	.25
166	Shawn Springs	.25
167	Wayne Martin	.25
168	Michael Westbrook	.25
169	Michael Jackson	.25
170	Dan Marino	3.50
171	Amp Lee	.25
172	James Jett	.25
173	Ty Law	.25
174	Kerry Collins	.50
175	Robert Brooks	.50
176	Blaine Bishop	.25
177	Stephen Boyd	.25
178	Keyshawn Johnson	.75
179	Deon Figures	.25
180	Allen Aldridge	.25
181	Corey Miller	.25
182	Chad Lewis	.25
183	Derrick Rodgers	.25
184	Troy Drayton	.25
185	Darren Woodson	.25
186	Ken Dilger	.25
187	Elvis Grbac	.50
188	Terrell Fletcher	.25
189	Frank Sanders	.25
190	Curtis Martin	1.00
191	Derrick Brooks	.25
192	Darrien Gordon	.25
193	Andre Reed	.50
194	Darnay Scott	.25
195	Curtis Conway	.50
196	Tim McDonald	.25
197	Sean Dawkins	.25
198	Napoleon Kaufman	1.00
199	Willie Clay	.25
200	Terrell Davis	4.00
201	Wesley Walls	.25
202	Santana Dotson	.25
203	Frank Wycheck	.25
204	Wayne Chrebet	.75
205	Andre Rison	.50
206	Jason Sehorn	.25
207	Jessie Tuggle	.25
208	Kevin Turner	.25
209	Jason Taylor	.25
210	Yancey Thigpen	.25
211	Jake Reed	.50
212	Carnell Lake	.25
213	Joey Galloway	.75
214	Andre Hastings	.25
215	Terry Allen	.50
216	Jim Harbaugh	.50
217	Tony Banks	.50
218	Greg Clark	.25
219	Corey Dillon	1.25
220	Troy Aikman	2.50
221	Antowain Smith	1.00
222	Steve Atwater	.25
223	Trent Dilfer	.75
224	Junior Seau	.50
225	Garrison Hearst	.75
226	Eric Allen	.25
227	Chad Cota	.25
228	Vinny Testaverde	.50
229	Chris T. Jones	.25
230	Drew Bledsoe	2.00
231	Charles Johnson	.25
232	Jake Plummer	2.00
233	Errict Rhett	.25
234	Doug Evans	.25
235	Phillippi Sparks	.25
236	Ashley Ambrose	.25
237	Bryan Cox	.25
238	Kevin Smith	.25
239	Hardy Nickerson	.25
240	Terry Glenn	.75
241	Lee Woodall	.25
242	Andre Coleman	.25
243	Michael Bates	.25
244	Mark Fields	.25
245	Eddie Kennison	.50
246	Dana Stubblefield	.25
247	Bobby Hoying	.50
248	Mo Lewis	.25
249	Derrick Mayes	.25
250	Eddie George	2.00
251	Mike Alstott	1.00
252	J.J. Stokes	.50
253	Adrian Murrell	.50
254	Kevin Greene	.25
255	LeRoy Butler	.25
256	Glenn Foley	.50
257	Jimmy Smith	.50
258	Tiki Barber	.25
259	Irving Fryar	.25
260	Ricky Watters	.50
261	Jeff Graham	.25
262	Kordell Stewart	2.00
263	Rod Woodson	.25
264	Leslie Shepherd	.25
265	Ryan McNeil	.25
266	Ike Hilliard	.25
267	Keenan McCardell	.50
268	Marvin Harrison	.75
269	Dorsey Levens	.75
270	Barry Sanders	5.00

1998 Finest Future's Finest

This insert set features 20 players taking America's game into the next century. Singles were sequentially numbered to 500 and inserted 1:83 packs. Each card also had a parallel Refractor that was numbered to 75 and found 1:557 packs.

		MT
Complete Set (20):		325.00
Common Player:		7.00
Inserted 1:83		
Production 500 Sets		
Refractors:		2x-3x
Inserted 1:557		
Production 75 Sets		
F1	Peyton Manning	40.00
F2	Napoleon Kaufman	14.00
F3	Jake Plummer	25.00
F4	Terry Glenn	14.00
F5	Ryan Leaf	20.00
F6	Drew Bledsoe	25.00
F7	Dorsey Levens	14.00
F8	Andre Wadsworth	7.00
F9	Joey Galloway	14.00
F10	Curtis Enis	18.00
F11	Warrick Dunn	25.00
F12	Kordell Stewart	25.00
F13	Randy Moss	80.00
F14	Robert Edwards	15.00
F15	Eddie George	25.00
F16	Fred Taylor	25.00
F17	Corey Dillon	14.00
F18	Brett Favre	60.00
F19	Kevin Dyson	14.00
F20	Terrell Davis	45.00

1998 Finest Jumbos 2

Eight different Jumbo Finest cards were inserted as box toppers in both Series I and II. The 16-card set was inserted 1:3 boxes (1:2 hobby collector boxes), with Refractors every 12 boxes (1:6 hobby collector boxes).

		MT
Complete Set (7):		100.00
Common Player:		5.00
Inserted 1:3 Boxes		
Refractors:		2x
Inserted 1:12 Boxes		
151	Jerry Rice	15.00
160	Emmitt Smith	25.00
170	Dan Marino	25.00
213	Joey Galloway	5.00
230	Drew Bledsoe	12.00
250	Eddie George	12.00
270	Barry Sanders	30.00

1998 Finest Mystery Finest 2

Twenty different players were displayed either with one of three other players on the back, or by themselves on both sides in Mystery Finest. Each side has a Finest Opaque protector and is numbered with an "M" prefix. Regular versions are seeded one per 36 packs, while Refractors are found every 144 packs.

		MT
Complete Set (40):		550.00
Common Player:		7.00
Inserted 1:36		
Refractors:		1.5x
Inserted 1:144		
M1	Brett Favre, Dan Marino	30.00
M2	Brett Favre, Peyton Manning	35.00
M3	Brett Favre, Ryan Leaf	25.00
M4	Dan Marino, Peyton Manning	30.00
M5	Dan Marino, Ryan Leaf	25.00
M6	Peyton Manning, Ryan Leaf	25.00
M7	Barry Sanders, Emmitt Smith	30.00
M8	Barry Sanders, Curtis Enis	20.00
M9	Barry Sanders, Fred Taylor	30.00
M10	Emmitt Smith, Curtis Enis	15.00
M11	Emmitt Smith, Fred Taylor	20.00
M12	Curtis Enis, Fred Taylor	15.00
M13	John Elway, Jerry Rice	20.00
M14	John Elway, Randy Moss	40.00
M15	John Elway, Charles Woodson	20.00
M16	Jerry Rice, Randy Moss	40.00
M17	Jerry Rice, Charles Woodson	15.00
M18	Randy Moss, Charles Woodson	35.00
M19	Terrell Davis, Kordell Stewart	20.00
M20	Terrell Davis, Ricky Watters	15.00
M21	Terrell Davis, Kevin Dyson	15.00
M22	Kordell Stewart, Ricky Watters	12.00

M23 Kordell Stewart, Kevin Dyson 12.00
M24 Ricky Watters, Kevin Dyson 7.00
M25 Warrick Dunn, Eddie George 15.00
M26 Warrick Dunn, Curtis Martin 12.00
M27 Warrick Dunn, Robert Edwards 12.00
M28 Eddie George, Curtis Martin 12.00
M29 Eddie George, Robert Edwards 12.00
M30 Curtis Martin, Robert Edwards 12.00
M31 Peyton Manning, Peyton Manning 25.00
M32 Ryan Leaf, Ryan Leaf 15.00
M33 Curtis Enis, Curtis Enis 12.00
M34 Fred Taylor, Fred Taylor 15.00
M35 Randy Moss, Randy Moss 50.00
M36 Charles Woodson, Charles Woodson 12.00
M37 Ricky Watters, Ricky Watters 7.00
M38 Kevin Dyson, Kevin Dyson 10.00
M39 Curtis Martin, Curtis Martin 10.00
M40 Robert Edwards, Robert Edwards 12.00

1998 Finest Mystery Finest Jumbos 2

These singles measured 3-1/2" x 5", were inserted as box toppers and found 1:4 boxes. Refractor versions for each single were also produced and found 1:17 boxes.

	MT
Complete Set (3):	50.00
Common Player:	15.00
Inserted 1:4 Boxes	
Refractors:	2x
Inserted 1:17 Boxes	
M3 Brett Favre, Ryan Leaf	15.00
M8 Barry Sanders, Curtis Enis	15.00
M16 Jerry Rice, Randy Moss	30.00

1998 Finest Stadium Stars

Only 20 of the top players in the game were included in this 1:45 pack insert. Each single has the letter "S" prefixed to the card number.

	MT
Complete Set (20):	160.00
Common Player:	5.00
Inserted 1:45	
S1 Barry Sanders	30.00
S2 Steve Young	10.00
S3 Emmitt Smith	20.00
S4 Mark Brunell	10.00
S5 Curtis Martin	5.00
S6 Kordell Stewart	10.00
S7 Jerry Rice	15.00
S8 Warrick Dunn	10.00
S9 Peyton Manning	20.00
S10 Brett Favre	30.00
S11 Terrell Davis	25.00
S12 Cris Carter	5.00
S13 Herman Moore	5.00
S14 Troy Aikman	15.00
S15 Tim Brown	5.00
S16 Dan Marino	20.00
S17 Drew Bledsoe	10.00
S18 Jerome Bettis	5.00
S19 Ryan Leaf	10.00
S20 John Elway	15.00

1998 Finest Stadium Stars Jumbos

These cards were inserted as box toppers at 1:12 boxes. Each single measures 3-1/2" x 5".

	MT
Complete Set (6):	85.00
Common Player:	5.00
Inserted 1:12 Boxes	
9 Peyton Manning	25.00
10 Brett Favre	30.00
11 Terrell Davis	25.00
18 Jerome Bettis	5.00
19 Ryan Leaf	10.00
20 John Elway	20.00

1998 Flair Showcase Row 3

Row 3 is made up of 80 base cards with four different tiers. Cards 1-20 were inserted 1:0.9 packs, cards 21-40 at 1:1.1, cards 41-60 at 1:1.4 and cards 61-80 at 1:1.8.

	MT
Complete Set (80):	75.00
Common Player:	.25
Common Rookie:	1.00
1-20 Inserted 1:0.9	
21-40 Inserted 1:1.1	
41-60 Inserted 1:1.4	
61-80 Inserted 1:1.8	
Wax Box:	100.00
1 Brett Favre	3.00
2 Emmitt Smith	2.00
3 *Peyton Manning*	12.00
4 Mark Brunell	1.00
5 *Randy Moss*	20.00
6 Jerry Rice	1.50
7 John Elway	1.50
8 Troy Aikman	1.50
9 Warrick Dunn	1.00
10 Kordell Stewart	1.00
11 Drew Bledsoe	1.00
12 Eddie George	1.00
13 Dan Marino	2.00
14 Antowain Smith	.75
15 *Curtis Enis*	4.00
16 Jake Plummer	1.00
17 Steve Young	1.00
18 *Ryan Leaf*	6.00
19 Terrell Davis	2.00
20 Barry Sanders	3.00
21 Corey Dillon	1.00
22 *Fred Taylor*	6.00
23 Herman Moore	.50
24 Marshall Faulk	.75
25 *John Avery*	2.50
26 Terry Glenn	.50
27 Keyshawn Johnson	.50
28 *Charles Woodson*	3.00
29 Garrison Hearst	.50
30 Steve McNair	.75
31 Deion Sanders	.75
32 *Robert Holcombe*	2.50
33 Jerome Bettis	.50
34 *Robert Edwards*	3.00
35 *Skip Hicks*	2.50
36 *Marcus Nash*	2.50
37 Fred Lane	.25
38 *Kevin Dyson*	2.50
39 Dorsey Levens	.50
40 *Jacquez Green*	2.50
41 Shannon Sharpe	.50
42 Michael Irvin	.75
43 Jim Harbaugh	.25
44 Curtis Martin	.75
45 Bobby Hoying	.25
46 Trent Dilfer	.50
47 Yancey Thigpen	.25
48 Warren Moon	.50
49 Danny Kanell	.25
50 Rob Johnson	.50
51 Carl Pickens	.50
52 Scott Mitchell	.25
53 Tim Brown	.50
54 Tony Banks	.50
55 Jamal Anderson	1.00
56 Kerry Collins	.50
57 Elvis Grbac	.25
58 Mike Alstott	.75
59 Glenn Foley	.25
60 Brad Johnson	.75
61 Robert Brooks	.25
62 Irving Fryar	.25
63 Natrone Means	1.00
64 Rae Carruth	.25
65 Isaac Bruce	.75
66 Andre Rison	.50
67 Jeff George	.50
68 Charles Way	.25
69 Derrick Alexander	.25
70 Michael Jackson	.25
71 Rob Moore	.50
72 Ricky Watters	.50
73 Curtis Conway	.50
74 Antonio Freeman	1.25
75 Jimmy Smith	.75
76 Troy Davis	.25
77 Robert Smith	1.25
78 Terry Allen	.50
79 Joey Galloway	1.25
80 Charles Johnson	.25

1998 Flair Showcase Row 2

Row 2 is set up the same way that Row 3 is with 80 base cards and four tiers. It has different insert odds with cards 1-20 found 1:3 packs, cards 21-40 at 1:2.5 packs, cards 41-60 at 1:4 packs and cards 61-80 at 1:3.4 packs.

	MT
Complete Set (80):	150.00
Common Player:	.50
Common Rookie:	1.50
1-20 Inserted 1:3	
21-40 Inserted 1:2.5	
41-60 Inserted 1:4	
61-80 Inserted 1:3.4	
1 Brett Favre	6.00
2 Emmitt Smith	4.00
3 Peyton Manning	18.00
4 Mark Brunell	2.00
5 Randy Moss	35.00
6 Jerry Rice	3.00
7 John Elway	3.00
8 Troy Aikman	3.00
9 Warrick Dunn	2.00
10 Kordell Stewart	2.00
11 Drew Bledsoe	2.00
12 Eddie George	2.00
13 Dan Marino	4.00
14 Antowain Smith	1.50
15 Curtis Enis	6.00
16 Jake Plummer	2.00
17 Steve Young	2.00
18 Ryan Leaf	10.00
19 Terrell Davis	4.00
20 Barry Sanders	6.00
21 Corey Dillon	2.00
22 Fred Taylor	10.00
23 Herman Moore	1.00
24 Marshall Faulk	1.50
25 John Avery	4.00
26 Terry Glenn	1.00
27 Keyshawn Johnson	1.00
28 Charles Woodson	5.00
29 Garrison Hearst	1.00
30 Steve McNair	1.50
31 Deion Sanders	1.50
32 Robert Holcombe	4.00
33 Jerome Bettis	1.00
34 Robert Edwards	4.00
35 Skip Hicks	4.00
36 Marcus Nash	4.00
37 Fred Lane	.50
38 Kevin Dyson	4.00
39 Dorsey Levens	1.00
40 Jacquez Green	4.00
41 Shannon Sharpe	1.00
42 Michael Irvin	1.50
43 Jim Harbaugh	.50
44 Curtis Martin	1.50
45 Bobby Hoying	.50
46 Trent Dilfer	1.00
47 Yancey Thigpen	.50
48 Warren Moon	1.00
49 Danny Kanell	.50
50 Rob Johnson	1.00
51 Carl Pickens	1.00
52 Scott Mitchell	.50
53 Tim Brown	1.00
54 Tony Banks	1.00
55 Jamal Anderson	2.00
56 Kerry Collins	1.00
57 Elvis Grbac	.50
58 Mike Alstott	1.50
59 Glenn Foley	.50
60 Brad Johnson	1.50
61 Robert Brooks	.50
62 Irving Fryar	.50
63 Natrone Means	1.50
64 Rae Carruth	.50
65 Isaac Bruce	1.25
66 Andre Rison	1.00
67 Jeff George	1.00
68 Charles Way	.50
69 Derrick Alexander	.50
70 Michael Jackson	.50
71 Rob Moore	1.00
72 Ricky Watters	1.00
73 Curtis Conway	.50
74 Antonio Freeman	2.50
75 Jimmy Smith	1.50
76 Troy Davis	.50
77 Robert Smith	2.50
78 Terry Allen	1.00
79 Joey Galloway	2.50
80 Charles Johnson	.50

1998 Flair Showcase Row 1

Row 1 singles are much tougher to find than the previous Row 3 and 2 because of tougher insert odds. Same set up with 80 cards and four tiers. Cards 1-20 were inserted 1:16 packs, cards 21-40 at 1:24, cards 41-60 at 1:6 and the last tier of cards 61-80 at 1:9.6.

	MT
Complete Set (80):	600.00
Common Player:	1.50
Common Rookie:	4.00
1-20 Inserted 1:16	
21-40 Inserted 1:24	
41-60 Inserted 1:6	
61-80 Inserted 1:9.6	
1 Brett Favre	25.00
2 Emmitt Smith	16.00
3 Peyton Manning	45.00
4 Mark Brunell	8.00
5 Randy Moss	100.00
6 Jerry Rice	12.00
7 John Elway	12.00
8 Troy Aikman	12.00
9 Warrick Dunn	8.00
10 Kordell Stewart	8.00
11 Drew Bledsoe	8.00
12 Eddie George	8.00
13 Dan Marino	16.00
14 Antowain Smith	6.00
15 Curtis Enis	15.00
16 Jake Plummer	8.00
17 Steve Young	8.00
18 Ryan Leaf	25.00
19 Terrell Davis	16.00
20 Barry Sanders	25.00
21 Corey Dillon	8.00
22 Fred Taylor	25.00
23 Herman Moore	3.00
24 Marshall Faulk	6.00
25 John Avery	10.00
26 Terry Glenn	3.00
27 Keyshawn Johnson	3.00
28 Charles Woodson	12.00
29 Garrison Hearst	3.00
30 Steve McNair	6.00
31 Deion Sanders	6.00
32 Robert Holcombe	10.00
33 Jerome Bettis	3.00
34 Robert Edwards	12.00
35 Skip Hicks	10.00
36 Marcus Nash	10.00
37 Fred Lane	1.50
38 Kevin Dyson	10.00
39 Dorsey Levens	3.00
40 Jacquez Green	10.00
41 Shannon Sharpe	3.00
42 Michael Irvin	3.00
43 Jim Harbaugh	1.50
44 Curtis Martin	4.00
45 Bobby Hoying	1.50
46 Trent Dilfer	3.00
47 Yancey Thigpen	1.50
48 Warren Moon	3.00
49 Danny Kanell	1.50
50 Rob Johnson	3.00
51 Carl Pickens	3.00
52 Scott Mitchell	1.50
53 Tim Brown	3.00
54 Tony Banks	3.00
55 Jamal Anderson	5.00
56 Kerry Collins	3.00
57 Elvis Grbac	1.50
58 Mike Alstott	3.00
59 Glenn Foley	1.50
60 Brad Johnson	3.00
61 Robert Brooks	1.50
62 Irving Fryar	1.50
63 Natrone Means	4.00
64 Rae Carruth	1.50
65 Isaac Bruce	3.00
66 Andre Rison	3.00
67 Jeff George	3.00
68 Charles Way	1.50
69 Derrick Alexander	1.50
70 Michael Jackson	1.50
71 Rob Moore	3.00
72 Ricky Watters	3.00
73 Curtis Conway	1.50
74 Antonio Freeman	5.00
75 Jimmy Smith	3.00
76 Troy Davis	1.50
77 Robert Smith	5.00
78 Terry Allen	1.50
79 Joey Galloway	5.00
80 Charles Johnson	1.50

1998 Flair Showcase Row 0

The Row 0 set is made up of 80 cards and is tiered at four different levels. The first level includes cards 1-20 and each is sequentially numbered to 250. The next level includes cards 21-40 and are numbered to 500. Cards 41-60 are numbered to 1,000 and the last level of cards 61-80 are numbered to 2,000.

	MT
Complete Set (80):	3500.
Common Player (1-20):	7.00
Production 250 Sets	
Common Player (21-40):	5.00
Production 500 Sets	
Common Player (41-60):	3.00
Production 1000 Sets	
Common Player (61-80):	2.00
Production 2000 Sets	
1 Brett Favre	100.00
2 Emmitt Smith	70.00
3 Peyton Manning	120.00
4 Mark Brunell	35.00
5 Randy Moss	250.00
6 Jerry Rice	50.00
7 John Elway	50.00
8 Troy Aikman	50.00
9 Warrick Dunn	35.00
10 Kordell Stewart	35.00
11 Drew Bledsoe	35.00
12 Eddie George	35.00
13 Dan Marino	70.00
14 Antowain Smith	20.00
15 Curtis Enis	40.00
16 Jake Plummer	35.00
17 Steve Young	35.00
18 Ryan Leaf	60.00
19 Terrell Davis	70.00
20 Barry Sanders	100.00
21 Corey Dillon	20.00
22 Fred Taylor	50.00
23 Herman Moore	10.00
24 Marshall Faulk	15.00
25 John Avery	20.00
26 Terry Glenn	10.00
27 Keyshawn Johnson	10.00
28 Charles Woodson	25.00
29 Garrison Hearst	10.00
30 Steve McNair	15.00
31 Deion Sanders	15.00
32 Robert Holcombe	20.00
33 Jerome Bettis	10.00
34 Robert Edwards	20.00
35 Skip Hicks	20.00
36 Marcus Nash	20.00
37 Fred Lane	5.00
38 Kevin Dyson	20.00
39 Dorsey Levens	10.00
40 Jacquez Green	20.00

41	Shannon Sharpe	6.00
42	Michael Irvin	8.00
43	Jim Harbaugh	3.00
44	Curtis Martin	8.00
45	Bobby Hoying	3.00
46	Trent Dilfer	6.00
47	Yancey Thigpen	3.00
48	Warren Moon	6.00
49	Danny Kanell	3.00
50	Rob Johnson	6.00
51	Carl Pickens	6.00
52	Scott Mitchell	3.00
53	Tim Brown	6.00
54	Tony Banks	6.00
55	Jamal Anderson	15.00
56	Kerry Collins	6.00
57	Elvis Grbac	3.00
58	Mike Alstott	8.00
59	Glenn Foley	3.00
60	Brad Johnson	8.00
61	Robert Brooks	2.00
62	Irving Fryar	2.00
63	Natrone Means	10.00
64	Rae Carruth	2.00
65	Isaac Bruce	7.50
66	Andre Rison	4.00
67	Jeff George	4.00
68	Charles Way	2.00
69	Derrick Alexander	2.00
70	Michael Jackson	2.00
71	Rob Moore	4.00
72	Ricky Watters	4.00
73	Curtis Conway	4.00
74	Antonio Freeman	12.50
75	Jimmy Smith	7.50
76	Troy Davis	2.00
77	Robert Smith	12.50
78	Terry Allen	4.00
79	Joey Galloway	12.50
80	Charles Johnson	2.00

1998 Flair Showcase Legacy

Each of the 320 cards in this set has a parallel Legacy card. Each card has a foil front and is sequentially numbered to 100.

		MT
Common Player:		15.00
Production 100 Sets		
Each Player Has Four Different Cards		
1	Brett Favre	200.00
2	Emmitt Smith	150.00
3	Peyton Manning	175.00
4	Mark Brunell	85.00
5	Randy Moss	325.00
6	Jerry Rice	100.00
7	John Elway	100.00
8	Troy Aikman	100.00
9	Warrick Dunn	85.00
10	Kordell Stewart	85.00
11	Drew Bledsoe	85.00
12	Eddie George	85.00
13	Dan Marino	150.00
14	Antowain Smith	50.00
15	Curtis Enis	50.00
16	Jake Plummer	85.00
17	Steve Young	75.00
18	Ryan Leaf	90.00
19	Terrell Davis	150.00
20	Barry Sanders	200.00
21	Corey Dillon	60.00
22	Fred Taylor	100.00
23	Herman Moore	30.00
24	Marshall Faulk	40.00
25	John Avery	40.00
26	Terry Glenn	30.00
27	Keyshawn Johnson	30.00
28	Charles Woodson	50.00
29	Garrison Hearst	30.00
30	Steve McNair	40.00
31	Deion Sanders	40.00
32	Robert Holcombe	40.00
33	Jerome Bettis	30.00
34	Robert Edwards	50.00
35	Skip Hicks	45.00
36	Marcus Nash	45.00
37	Fred Lane	15.00
38	Kevin Dyson	40.00
39	Dorsey Levens	30.00
40	Jacquez Green	45.00
41	Shannon Sharpe	30.00
42	Michael Irvin	40.00
43	Jim Harbaugh	15.00
44	Curtis Martin	40.00
45	Bobby Hoying	15.00
46	Trent Dilfer	30.00
47	Yancey Thigpen	15.00
48	Warren Moon	30.00
49	Danny Kanell	15.00
50	Rob Johnson	30.00
51	Carl Pickens	30.00
52	Scott Mitchell	15.00
53	Tim Brown	30.00
54	Tony Banks	30.00
55	Jamal Anderson	40.00
56	Kerry Collins	30.00
57	Elvis Grbac	15.00
58	Mike Alstott	40.00
59	Glenn Foley	15.00
60	Brad Johnson	30.00
61	Robert Brooks	15.00
62	Irving Fryar	15.00
63	Natrone Means	30.00
64	Rae Carruth	15.00
65	Isaac Bruce	30.00
66	Andre Rison	15.00
67	Jeff George	30.00
68	Charles Way	15.00
69	Derrick Alexander	15.00
70	Michael Jackson	15.00
71	Rob Moore	30.00
72	Ricky Watters	30.00
73	Curtis Conway	15.00
74	Antonio Freeman	40.00
75	Jimmy Smith	30.00
76	Troy Davis	15.00
77	Robert Smith	30.00
78	Terry Allen	30.00
79	Joey Galloway	30.00
80	Charles Johnson	15.00

1998 Flair Showcase Feature Film

Each card in this set has an actual slide from the Showcase set mounted on it. Singles were inserted 1:60 packs.

		MT
Complete Set (10):		230.00
Common Player:		10.00
Inserted 1:60		
1	Terrell Davis	35.00
2	Brett Favre	50.00
3	Antowain Smith	10.00
4	Emmitt Smith	35.00
5	Dan Marino	35.00
6	Kordell Stewart	20.00
7	Warrick Dunn	15.00
8	Barry Sanders	50.00
9	Peyton Manning	40.00
10	Ryan Leaf	20.00

1998 Fleer Brilliants

This was the premier issue of Brilliants by Fleer. The 150-card set is made up of 100 veterans and 50 rookies (inserted 1:2 packs). The product also included three parallel sets. The easiest being the Brilliant Blues with veterans found 1:3 packs and the rookies 1:6. Each single from this series has a blue background with the letter "B" prefix on the card number. The Brilliant Golds have a sparkling gold background on super bright mirror foil and the letter "G" prefix on the card number. Each single is sequentially numbered to 99. The rarest parallel is the 24-Karat Gold set. Each single has a sparkling gold background on rainbow holographic reflective mirror foil with an actual 24-kt. gold logo. Each single is sequentially numbered to 24.

		MT
Complete Set (150):		250.00
Common Player:		.15
Common Rookie:		3.00
Inserted 1:2		
Blue Veterans:		2x-3x
Inserted 1:3		
Blue Rookies:		1.2x
Inserted 1:6		
Brilliant Gold Cards:		20x-40x
Brilliant Gold Rookies:		3x-5x
Production 99 Sets		
24-Karat Gold Cards:		40x-80x
24-Karat Gold Rookies:		5x-10x
Production 24 Sets		
Wax Box:		120.00
1	John Elway	3.00
2	Curtis Conway	.30
3	Danny Wuerffel	.15
4	Emmitt Smith	4.50
5	Marvin Harrison	.30
6	Antowain Smith	.75
7	James Stewart	.15
8	Junior Seau	.30
9	Herman Moore	.50
10	Drew Bledsoe	2.00
11	Rae Carruth	.15
12	Trent Dilfer	.30
13	Derrick Alexander	.15
14	Ike Hilliard	.15
15	Bruce Smith	.15
16	Warren Moon	.30
17	Jermaine Lewis	.15
18	Mike Alstott	.50
19	Robert Brooks	.15
20	Jerome Bettis	.50
21	Brett Favre	6.00
22	Garrison Hearst	.50
23	Neil O'Donnell	.15
24	Joey Galloway	.50
25	Barry Sanders	6.00
26	Donnell Bennett	.15
27	Jamal Anderson	.75
28	Isaac Bruce	.30
29	Chris Chandler	.30
30	Kordell Stewart	2.00
31	Corey Dillon	1.75
32	Troy Aikman	3.00
33	Frank Sanders	.15
34	Cris Carter	.50
35	Greg Hill	.15
36	Tony Martin	.15
37	Shannon Sharpe	.30
38	Wayne Chrebet	.30
39	Trent Green	.30
40	Warrick Dunn	2.00
41	Michael Irvin	.30
42	Eddie George	2.00
43	Carl Pickens	.30
44	Wesley Walls	.15
45	Steve McNair	.75
46	Bert Emanuel	.15
47	Terry Glenn	.30
48	Elvis Grbac	.15
49	Charles Way	.15
50	Steve Young	1.75
51	Deion Sanders	.75
52	Keyshawn Johnson	.50
53	Kerry Collins	.30
54	O.J. McDuffie	.15
55	Ricky Watters	.30
56	Scott Mitchell	.15
57	Antonio Freeman	.50
58	Jake Plummer	2.00
59	Andre Reed	.15
60	Jerry Rice	3.00
61	Dorsey Levens	.50
62	Eddie Kennison	.30
63	Marshall Faulk	.50
64	Michael Jackson	.15
65	Karim Abdul-Jabbar	.30
66	Andre Rison	.15
67	Glenn Foley	.30
68	Jake Reed	.15
69	Tony Banks	.30
70	Dan Marino	4.50
71	Bryan Still	.15
72	Tim Brown	.30
73	Charles Johnson	.30
74	Jeff George	.30
75	Jimmy Smith	.30
76	Ben Coates	.30
77	Rob Moore	.15
78	Johnnie Morton	.15
79	Peter Boulware	.15
80	Curtis Martin	.75
81	James McKnight	.15
82	Danny Kanell	.15
83	Brad Johnson	.30
84	Amani Toomer	.15
85	Terry Allen	.30
86	Rod Smith	.30
87	Keenan McCardell	.30
88	Leslie Shepherd	.15
89	Irving Fryar	.15
90	Terrell Davis	4.50
91	Robert Smith	.50
92	Duce Staley	.15
93	Rickey Dudley	.15
94	Bobby Hoying	.15
95	Terrell Owens	.75
96	Fred Lane	.30
97	Natrone Means	.30
98	Yancey Thigpen	.15
99	Reggie White	.50
100	Mark Brunell	2.00
101	*Ahman Green*	6.00
102	*Skip Hicks*	5.00
103	*Hines Ward*	5.00
104	*Marcus Nash*	6.00
105	*Terry Hardy*	3.00
106	*Patrick Johnson*	4.00
107	*Tremayne Stephens*	3.00
108	*Joe Jurevicius*	4.00
109	*Moses Moreno*	4.00
110	*Charles Woodson*	10.00
111	*Kevin Dyson*	6.00
112	*Alvis Whitted*	3.00
113	*Michael Pittman*	3.00
114	*Stephen Alexander*	4.00
115	*Tavian Banks*	6.00
116	*John Avery*	6.00
117	*Keith Brooking*	3.00
118	*Jerome Pathon*	5.00
119	*Terry Fair*	4.00
120	*Peyton Manning*	30.00
121	*R.W. McQuarters*	4.00
122	*Charlie Batch*	20.00
123	*Jonathan Quinn*	5.00
124	*Chris Fuamatu-Ma'afala*	5.00
125	*Jacquez Green*	8.00
126	*Germane Crowell*	6.00
127	*Oronde Gadsden*	5.00
128	*Koy Detmer*	4.00
129	*Robert Holcombe*	8.00
130	*Curtis Enis*	10.00
131	*Brian Griese*	15.00
132	*Tony Simmons*	5.00
133	*Vonnie Holliday*	4.00
134	*Alonzo Mayes*	3.00
135	*Jon Ritchie*	4.00
136	*Robert Edwards*	12.00
137	*Mike Vanderjagt*	3.00
138	*Jonathon Linton*	3.00
139	*Fred Taylor*	20.00
140	*Randy Moss*	50.00
141	*Rod Rutledge*	3.00
142	*Andre Wadsworth*	4.00
143	*Rashaan Shehee*	4.00
144	*Shaun Williams*	3.00
145	*Mikhael Ricks*	5.00
146	*Wade Richey*	3.00
147	*Carlos King*	3.00
148	*Tim Dwight*	6.00
149	*Scott Frost*	4.00
150	*Ryan Leaf*	15.00

1998 Fleer Brilliants Illuminators

Each card in this 15-card set has the players team color in super bright mirror foil on the front. Singles can be found 1:10 packs.

		MT
Complete Set (15):		70.00
Common Player:		1.50
Inserted 1:10		
1	Robert Edwards	6.00
2	Fred Taylor	10.00
3	Kordell Stewart	10.00
4	Troy Aikman	15.00
5	Curtis Enis	6.00
6	Drew Bledsoe	10.00
7	Curtis Martin	4.00
8	Joey Galloway	3.00
9	Jerome Bettis	3.00
10	Glenn Foley	1.50
11	Karim Abdul-Jabbar	3.00
12	Jake Plummer	8.00
13	Jerry Rice	15.00
14	Charlie Batch	12.00
15	Jacquez Green	4.00

1998 Fleer Brilliants Shining Stars

Singles in this insert are two-sided with super bright mirror foil and includes the top 15 players from the NFL. Singles were inserted 1:20 packs. A parallel version called Pulsars can also be found 1:400 packs.

		MT
Complete Set (15):		120.00
Common Player:		2.00
Inserted 1:20		
Pulsar Cards:		5x-10x
Inserted 1:400		
1	Terrell Davis	15.00
2	Emmitt Smith	15.00
3	Barry Sanders	20.00
4	Mark Brunell	8.00
5	Brett Favre	20.00
6	Ryan Leaf	10.00
7	Randy Moss	30.00
8	Warrick Dunn	8.00
9	Peyton Manning	20.00
10	Corey Dillon	4.00
11	Dan Marino	15.00
12	Keyshawn Johnson	2.00
13	John Elway	10.00
14	Eddie George	8.00
15	Antowain Smith	5.00

1998 Leaf Rookies & Stars

This is the first Leaf product released under Playoff. The 300-card set includes short-printed cards of 70 rookies and 30 Power Tools inserted 1:2 packs. Two parallel sets with the True Blue singles sequentially numbered to 500 and the Longevity parallel numbered to 50. The product also includes 13 other sequentially numbered inserts.

	MT
Complete Set (300):	450.00
Common Player:	.15
Common Rookie (171-240):	2.00
Common Power Tool (241-270):	2.00
Inserted 1:2	
Longevity Cards:	50x-100x
Longevity Rookies:	2x
Longevity PT Cards:	10x-20x
Longevity PT Rookies:	2x-4x
Production 50 Sets	
True Blue Cards:	7x-14x
True Blue Rookies:	1x
True Blue PT:	2x
Production 500 Sets	

Wax Box:		100.00
1	Keyshawn Johnson	.50
2	Marvin Harrison	.30
3	Eddie Kennison	.15
4	Bryant Young	.15
5	Darren Woodson	.15
6	Tyrone Wheatley	.15
7	Michael Westbrook	.15
8	Charles Way	.15
9	Ricky Watters	.30
10	Chris Warren	.15
11	Wesley Walls	.15
12	Tamarick Vanover	.15
13	Zach Thomas	.30
14	Derrick Thomas	.15
15	Yancey Thigpen	.15
16	Vinny Testaverde	.30
17	Dana Stubblefield	.15
18	J.J. Stokes	.30
19	James Stewart	.15
20	Jeff George	.30
21	John Randle	.15
22	Gary Brown	.15
23	Ed McCaffrey	.30
24	James Jett	.15
25	Rob Johnson	.30
26	Daryl Johnston	.15
27	Jermaine Lewis	.15
28	Tony Martin	.15
29	Derrick Mayes	.15
30	Keenan McCardell	.30
31	O.J. McDuffie	.30
32	Chris Chandler	.30
33	Doug Flutie	.75
34	Scott Mitchell	.30
35	Warren Moon	.30
36	Rob Moore	.30
37	Johnnie Morton	.15
38	Neil O'Donnell	.15
39	Rich Gannon	.15
40	Andre Reed	.15
41	Jake Reed	.15
42	Errict Rhett	.15
43	Simeon Rice	.15
44	Andre Rison	.30
45	Eric Moulds	.30
46	Frank Sanders	.15
47	Darnay Scott	.15
48	Junior Seau	.30
49	Shannon Sharpe	.30
50	Bruce Smith	.15
51	Jimmy Smith	.30
52	Robert Smith	.30
53	Derrick Alexander	.15
54	Kimble Anders	.15
55	Jamal Anderson	.75
56	Mario Bates	.15
57	Edgar Bennett	.15
58	Tim Biakabutuka	.15
59	Ki-Jana Carter	.15
60	Larry Centers	.15
61	Mark Chmura	.30
62	Wayne Chrebet	.30
63	Ben Coates	.30
64	Curtis Conway	.30
65	Randall Cunningham	.75
66	Rickey Dudley	.15
67	Bert Emanuel	.15
68	Bobby Engram	.15
69	William Floyd	.15
70	Irving Fryar	.15
71	Elvis Grbac	.15
72	Kevin Greene	.15
73	Jim Harbaugh	.30
74	Raymont Harris	.15
75	Garrison Hearst	.50
76	Greg Hill	.15
77	Desmond Howard	.15
78	Bobby Hoying	.30
79	Michael Jackson	.15
80	Terry Allen	.30
81	Jerome Bettis	.50
82	Jeff Blake	.30
83	Robert Brooks	.15
84	Tim Brown	.30
85	Isaac Bruce	.30
86	Cris Carter	.50
87	Ty Detmer	.30
88	Trent Dilfer	.30
89	Marshall Faulk	.50
90	Antonio Freeman	.75
91	Gus Frerotte	.30
92	Joey Galloway	.50
93	Michael Irvin	.30
94	Brad Johnson	.50
95	Danny Kanell	.15
96	Napoleon Kaufman	.50
97	Dorsey Levens	.50
98	Natrone Means	.50
99	Herman Moore	.50
100	Adrian Murrell	.30
101	Carl Pickens	.30
102	Rod Smith	.30
103	Thurman Thomas	.30
104	Reggie White	.50
105	Jim Druckenmiller	.30
106	Antowain Smith	.50
107	Reidel Anthony	.30
108	Ike Hilliard	.15
109	Rae Carruth	.15
110	Troy Davis	.15
111	Terrance Mathis	.15
112	Brett Favre	3.00
113	Dan Marino	2.00
114	Emmitt Smith	2.00
115	Barry Sanders	3.00
116	Eddie George	1.25
117	Drew Bledsoe	1.25
118	Troy Aikman	1.50
119	Terrell Davis	2.50
120	John Elway	1.75
121	Mark Brunell	1.25
122	Jerry Rice	1.50
123	Kordell Stewart	1.25
124	Steve McNair	.75
125	Curtis Martin	.75
126	Steve Young	1.00
127	Kerry Collins	.50
128	Terry Glenn	.50
129	Deion Sanders	.50
130	Mike Alstott	.50
131	Tony Banks	.30
132	Karim Abdul-Jabbar	.50
133	Terrell Owens	.75
134	Yatil Green	.30
135	Tony Gonzalez	.30
136	Byron Hanspard	.30
137	David LaFleur	.30
138	Danny Wuerffel	.30
139	Tiki Barber	.30
140	Peter Boulware	.15
141	Will Blackwell	.15
142	Warrick Dunn	1.00
143	Corey Dillon	.75
144	Jake Plummer	1.25
145	Neil Smith	.15
146	Charles Johnson	.30
147	Fred Lane	.30
148	Dan Wilkinson	.15
149	Ken Norton Jr.	.15
150	Stephen Davis	.15
151	Gilbert Brown	.15
152	Kenny Bynum	.15
153	Derrick Cullors	.15
154	Charlie Garner	.30
155	Jeff Graham	.15
156	Warren Sapp	.15
157	Jerald Moore	.15
158	Sean Dawkins	.15
159	Charlie Jones	.15
160	Kevin Lockett	.15
161	James McKnight	.15
162	Chris Penn	.15
163	Leslie Shepherd	.15
164	Karl Williams	.15
165	Mark Bruener	.15
166	Ernie Conwell	.15
167	Ken Dilger	.15
168	Troy Drayton	.15
169	Freddie Jones	.15
170	Dale Carter	.15
171	*Charles Woodson*	20.00
172	*Alonzo Mayes*	2.00
173	*Andre Wadsworth*	6.00
174	*Grant Winstrom*	4.00
175	*Greg Ellis*	4.00
176	*Chris Howard*	2.00
177	*Keith Brooking*	4.00
178	*Takeo Spikes*	6.00
179	*Anthony Simmons*	4.00
180	*Brian Simmons*	4.00
181	*Sam Cowart*	2.00
182	*Ken Oxendine*	2.00
183	*Vonnie Holliday*	6.00
184	*Terry Fair*	4.00
185	*Shaun Williams*	2.00
186	*Tremayne Stephens*	2.00
187	*Duane Starks*	6.00
188	*Jason Peter*	4.00
189	*Tebucky Jones*	2.00
190	*Donovin Darius*	2.00
191	*R.W. McQuarters*	4.00
192	*Corey Chavous*	4.00
193	*Cameron Cleeland*	8.00
194	*Stephen Alexander*	6.00
195	*Rod Rutledge*	2.00
196	*Scott Frost*	4.00
197	*Fred Beasley*	2.00
198	*Dorian Boose*	2.00
199	*Randy Moss*	85.00
200	*Jacquez Green*	15.00
201	*Marcus Nash*	15.00
202	*Hines Ward*	8.00
203	*Kevin Dyson*	15.00
204	*E.G. Green*	10.00
205	*Germane Crowell*	15.00
206	*Joe Jurevicius*	8.00
207	*Tony Simmons*	10.00
208	*Tim Dwight*	15.00
209	*Az-Zahir Hakim*	8.00
210	*Jerome Pathon*	8.00
211	*Patrick Johnson*	8.00
212	*Mikhael Ricks*	8.00
213	*Donald Hayes*	4.00
214	*Jammi German*	4.00
215	*Larry Shannon*	2.00
216	*Brian Alford*	4.00
217	*Curtis Enis*	15.00
218	*Fred Taylor*	40.00
219	*Robert Edwards*	15.00
220	*Ahman Green*	12.00
221	*Tavian Banks*	8.00
222	*Skip Hicks*	15.00
223	*Robert Holcombe*	12.00
224	*John Avery*	15.00
225	*Chris Fuamatu-Ma'afala*	8.00
226	*Michael Pittman*	4.00
227	*Rashaan Shehee*	6.00
228	*Jonathon Linton*	4.00
229	*Jon Ritchie*	4.00
230	*Chris Floyd*	4.00
231	*Wilmont Perry*	2.00
232	*Raymond Priester*	2.00
233	*Peyton Manning*	60.00
234	*Ryan Leaf*	30.00
235	*Brian Griese*	25.00
236	*Jeff Ogden*	4.00
237	*Charlie Batch*	40.00
238	*Moses Moreno*	4.00
239	*Jonathan Quinn*	6.00
240	*Flozell Adams*	2.00
241	Brett Favre PT	14.00
242	Dan Marino PT	10.00
243	Emmitt Smith PT	10.00
244	Barry Sanders PT	14.00
245	Eddie George PT	6.00
246	Drew Bledsoe PT	6.00
247	Troy Aikman PT	7.00
248	Terrell Davis PT	12.00
249	John Elway PT	8.00
250	Carl Pickens PT	2.00
251	Jerry Rice PT	7.00
252	Kordell Stewart PT	6.00
253	Steve McNair PT	4.00
254	Curtis Martin PT	4.00
255	Steve Young PT	5.00
256	Herman Moore PT	2.00
257	Dorsey Levens PT	2.00
258	Deion Sanders PT	3.00
259	Napoleon Kaufman PT	2.00
260	Warrick Dunn PT	5.00
261	Corey Dillon PT	4.00
262	Jerome Bettis PT	2.00
263	Tim Brown PT	2.00
264	Cris Carter PT	3.00
265	Antonio Freeman PT	3.00
266	Randy Moss PT	45.00
267	Curtis Enis PT	7.00
268	Fred Taylor PT	20.00
269	Robert Edwards PT	8.00
270	Peyton Manning PT	25.00
271	Barry Sanders TL	1.50
272	Eddie George TL	.50
273	Troy Aikman TL	.75
274	Mark Brunell TL	.50
275	Kordell Stewart TL	.50
276	Kerry Collins TL	.15
277	Terry Glenn TL	.30
278	Mike Alstott TL	.30
279	Tony Banks TL	.15
280	Karim Abdul TL	.30
281	Terrell Owens TL	.40
282	Byron Hanspard TL	.15
283	Jake Plummer TL	.50
284	Terry Allen TL	.15
285	Jeff Blake TL	.15
286	Brad Johnson TL	.30
287	Danny Kanell TL	.15
288	Natrone Means TL	.30
289	Rod Smith TL	.15
290	Thurman Thomas TL	.15
291	Reggie White TL	.30
292	Troy Davis TL	.15
293	Curtis Conway TL	.15
294	Irving Fryar TL	.15
295	Jim Harbaugh TL	.15
296	Andre Rison TL	.15
297	Ricky Watters TL	.15
298	Keyshawn Johnson TL	.30
299	Jeff George TL	.15
300	Marshall Faulk TL	.30

1998 Leaf Rookies & Stars Crosstraining

Each card in this 10-card set highlights the same player on front and back, demonstrating the different skills that make them great. All cards are printed on foil board and are sequentially numbered to 1,000.

		MT
Complete Set (10):		85.00
Common Player:		6.00
Production 1,000 Sets		
1	Brett Favre	30.00
2	Mark Brunell	12.00
3	Barry Sanders	30.00
4	John Elway	20.00
5	Jerry Rice	15.00
6	Kordell Stewart	12.00
7	Steve McNair	6.00
8	Deion Sanders	6.00
9	Jake Plummer	12.00
10	Steve Young	10.00

1998 Leaf Rookies & Stars Crusade

The 30-card set includes both stars and rookies from '98. Each of the Green singles are sequentially numbered to 250. A parallel Purple set is numbered to 100 and a parallel Red set is numbered to 25.

		MT
Complete Set (30):		650.00
Common Player:		10.00
Production 250 Sets		
Purple Cards:		2x
Production 100 Sets		
Red Cards:		2x-4x
Production 25 Sets		
1	Brett Favre	60.00
2	Dan Marino	45.00
3	Emmitt Smith	45.00
4	Barry Sanders	60.00
5	Eddie George	25.00
6	Drew Bledsoe	25.00
7	Troy Aikman	30.00
8	Terrell Davis	50.00
9	John Elway	40.00
10	Mark Brunell	25.00
11	Jerry Rice	30.00
12	Kordell Stewart	25.00
13	Steve McNair	10.00
14	Curtis Martin	10.00
16	Steve Young	20.00
18	Deion Sanders	10.00
22	Terrell Owens	10.00
23	Jamal Anderson	10.00
25	Jerome Bettis	10.00
30	Cris Carter	10.00
32	Marshall Faulk	10.00
33	Antonio Freeman	10.00
40	Dorsey Levens	10.00
49	Garrison Hearst	10.00
57	Warrick Dunn	20.00
59	Jake Plummer	25.00
66	Peyton Manning	50.00
69	Randy Moss	100.00
77	Fred Taylor	45.00
78	Robert Edwards	20.00

1998 Leaf Rookies & Stars Extreme Measures

This 10-card set takes the top players in the game and highlights an outstanding but extreme statistic for each. These cards are each printed on foil board and sequentially numbered to 1,000.

		MT
Complete Set (10):		135.00
Common Player:		5.00
1	Barry Sanders/918	30.00
2	Warrick Dunn/941	10.00
3	Curtis Martin/930	5.00
4	Terrell Davis/419	35.00
5	Troy Aikman/929	15.00
6	Drew Bledsoe/972	10.00
7	Eddie George/191	30.00
8	Emmitt Smith/888	20.00
9	Dan Marino/615	25.00
10	Brett Favre/965	30.00

1998 Leaf Rookies & Stars Extreme Measures Die Cuts

Each single in this set is sequentially numbered to a stat that was picked by the manufacturer. Each player in this set has a different amount of cards printed. Cards are identical to their Extreme Measures card except for being die cut in this set.

		MT
Complete Set (10):		725.00
Common Player:		15.00
1	Barry Sanders/82	150.00
2	Warrick Dunn/59	60.00
3	Curtis Martin/70	35.00
4	Terrell Davis/581	25.00
5	Troy Aikman/71	75.00
6	Drew Bledsoe/28	175.00
7	Eddie George/809	15.00
8	Emmitt Smith/112	100.00
9	Dan Marino/385	60.00
10	Brett Favre/35	300.00

1998 Leaf Rookies & Stars Freshman Orientation

This 20-card set not only features the future stars of the game, but also highlights which round and overall number each player was selected in the NFL draft. Each card is sequentially numbered to 2,500 and printed on holographic foil.

		MT
Complete Set (20):		100.00
Common Player:		2.50
Production 2,500 Sets		
1	Peyton Manning	20.00
2	Kevin Dyson	5.00
3	Joe Jurevicius	2.50
4	Tony Simmons	5.00
5	Marcus Nash	5.00
6	Ryan Leaf	10.00
7	Curtis Enis	6.00
8	Skip Hicks	5.00
9	Brian Griese	7.00
10	Jerome Pathon	2.50
11	John Avery	5.00
12	Fred Taylor	18.00
13	Robert Edwards	7.00
14	Robert Holcombe	5.00
15	Ahman Green	5.00
16	Hines Ward	2.50
17	Jacquez Green	5.00
18	Germane Crowell	5.00
19	Randy Moss	40.00
20	Charles Woodson	7.00

1998 Leaf Rookies & Stars Game Plan

Each card in this inside the game set is printed on foil board and sequentially numbered to 5,000. The first 500 of each card is treated with a "Master Game Plan" logo and unique color coating.

		MT
Complete Set (20):		45.00
Common Player:		1.50
Production 5,000 Sets		
Master Cards:		3x
Production First 500 Sets		
1	Ryan Leaf	5.00
2	Peyton Manning	12.00
3	Brett Favre	8.00
4	Mark Brunell	4.00
5	Isaac Bruce	1.50
6	Dan Marino	6.00

7	Jerry Rice	4.00
8	Cris Carter	3.00
9	Emmitt Smith	6.00
10	Kordell Stewart	4.00
11	Corey Dillon	3.00
12	Barry Sanders	8.00
13	Curtis Martin	3.00
14	Carl Pickens	1.50
15	Eddie George	4.00
16	Warrick Dunn	3.00
17	Jake Plummer	4.00
18	Curtis Enis	4.00
19	Drew Bledsoe	4.00
20	Terrell Davis	6.00

1998 Leaf Rookies & Stars Great American Heroes

The theme to this insert is players that have helped make the great American game of football. Each card in this set is stamped with holographic foil and sequentially numbered to 2,500.

		MT
Complete Set (20):		85.00
Common Player:		2.00
Production 2,500 Sets		
1	Brett Favre	12.00
2	Dan Marino	8.00
3	Emmitt Smith	8.00
4	Barry Sanders	12.00
5	Eddie George	5.00
6	Drew Bledsoe	5.00
7	Troy Aikman	6.00
8	Terrell Davis	10.00
9	John Elway	7.00
10	Mark Brunell	5.00
11	Jerry Rice	6.00
12	Kordell Stewart	5.00
13	Steve McNair	4.00
14	Curtis Martin	4.00
15	Steve Young	4.00
16	Dorsey Levens	2.00
17	Herman Moore	2.00
18	Deion Sanders	2.00
19	Thurman Thomas	2.00
20	Peyton Manning	18.00

1998 Leaf Rookies & Stars Greatest Hits

The top 20 players in the NFL are included in this insert and each card is sequentially numbered to 2,500.

		MT
Complete Set (20):		85.00
Common Player:		2.00
Production 2,500 Sets		
1	Brett Favre	12.00
2	Eddie George	5.00
3	John Elway	7.00
4	Steve Young	4.00
5	Napoleon Kaufman	2.00
6	Dan Marino	8.00
7	Drew Bledsoe	5.00
8	Mark Brunell	5.00
9	Warrick Dunn	4.00
10	Dorsey Levens	2.00
11	Emmitt Smith	8.00
12	Troy Aikman	6.00
13	Jerry Rice	6.00
14	Jake Plummer	5.00
15	Herman Moore	2.00
16	Barry Sanders	12.00
17	Terrell Davis	10.00
18	Kordell Stewart	5.00
19	Jerome Bettis	2.00
20	Isaac Bruce	2.00

1998 Leaf Rookies & Stars MVP Contenders

The set is made up of 20 of the league's top players who will contend for the MVP award. Each card is accented with holographic foil stamping and sequentially numbered to 2,500.

		MT
Complete Set (20):		85.00
Common Player:		2.00
Production 2,500 Sets		
1	Tim Brown	2.00
2	Herman Moore	2.00
3	Jake Plummer	5.00
4	Warrick Dunn	4.00
5	Dorsey Levens	2.00
6	Steve McNair	4.00
7	John Elway	7.00
8	Troy Aikman	6.00
9	Steve Young	5.00
10	Curtis Martin	4.00
11	Kordell Stewart	5.00
12	Jerry Rice	6.00
13	Mark Brunell	5.00
14	Terrell Davis	10.00
15	Drew Bledsoe	5.00
16	Eddie George	5.00
17	Barry Sanders	12.00
18	Emmitt Smith	8.00
19	Dan Marino	8.00
20	Brett Favre	12.00

1998 Leaf Rookies & Stars Standing Ovation

This 10-card set is printed with holographic foil stamping and sequentially numbered to 5,000. It features players who truly deserve a standing ovation for their accomplishments.

		MT
Complete Set (10):		40.00
Common Player:		1.50
Production 5,000 Sets		
1	Brett Favre	8.00
2	Dan Marino	6.00
3	Emmitt Smith	6.00
4	Barry Sanders	8.00
5	Terrell Davis	7.00
6	Jerry Rice	4.00
7	Steve Young	3.00
8	Reggie White	1.50
9	John Elway	5.00
10	Eddie George	3.00

1998 Leaf Rookies & Stars Ticket Masters

This double-sided 20-card set is printed on foil board and features players from the same team, like Terrell Davis and John Elway, that fill the seats for their franchise. Each card is sequentially numbered to 2,500 with the first 500 die-cut like a ticket.

		MT
Complete Set (20):		120.00
Common Player:		2.00
Production 2,500 Sets		
Die-Cut Cards:		3x
Production First 500 Sets		
1	Brett Favre, Dorsey Levens	12.00
2	Dan Marino, Karim Abdul	8.00
3	Troy Aikman, Deion Sanders	6.00
4	Barry Sanders, Herman Moore	12.00
5	Steve McNair, Eddie George	5.00
6	Drew Bledsoe, Robert Edwards	5.00
7	Terrell Davis, John Elway	10.00
8	Jerry Rice, Steve Young	6.00
9	Kordell Stewart, Jerome Bettis	5.00
10	Curtis Martin, Keyshawn Johnson	4.00
11	Warrick Dunn, Trent Dilfer	5.00
12	Corey Dillon, Carl Pickens	4.00
13	Tim Brown, Napoleon Kaufman	2.00
14	Jake Plummer, Frank Sanders	5.00
15	Ryan Leaf, Natrone Means	8.00
16	Peyton Manning, Marshall Faulk	15.00
17	Mark Brunell, Fred Taylor	10.00
18	Curtis Enis, Curtis Conway	5.00
19	Cris Carter, Randy Moss	30.00
20	Isaac Bruce, Tony Banks	2.00

1998 Leaf Rookies & Stars Touchdown Club

The 20 players showcased in this insert set are known for their ability to get into the end zone. Whether it's through the air, on the ground or both, these NFL stars get the job done. Each card is printed on foil board and sequentially numbered to 5,000.

		MT
Complete Set (20):		50.00
Common Player:		1.50
Production 5,000 Sets		
1	Brett Favre	8.00
2	Dan Marino	6.00
3	Emmitt Smith	6.00
4	Barry Sanders	8.00
5	Eddie George	3.00
6	Drew Bledsoe	4.00
7	Terrell Davis	7.00
8	Mark Brunell	4.00
9	Jerry Rice	4.00
10	Kordell Stewart	4.00
11	Curtis Martin	1.50
12	Karim Abdul	1.50
13	Warrick Dunn	3.00
14	Corey Dillon	3.00
15	Jerome Bettis	1.50
16	Antonio Freeman	1.50
17	Keyshawn Johnson	1.50
18	John Elway	5.00
19	Steve Young	3.00
20	Jake Plummer	4.00

1998 Pacific

The 450-card silver-foiled main set captures the NFL's pinpoint passes, touchdown runs and goal-line stands with the sharpest action photography. The set is designed with the die-hard football fan in mind, this set delivers outstanding player selection, including the strong crop of rookies from 1998. Each card back includes full year-by-year career stats. A parallel Red version can be found one per special retail pack and the Platinum Blue parallel singles can be found 1:73 packs.

		MT
Complete Set (450):		70.00
Common Player:		.10
Common Rookie:		1.00
Platinum Blue Cards:		60x-120x
Platinum Blue Rookies:		10x-20x
Inserted 1:73		
Wax Box:		60.00
1	Mario Bates	.10
2	Lomas Brown	.10
3	Larry Centers	.10
4	Chris Gedney	.10
5	Terry Irving	.10
6	Tom Knight	.10
7	Eric Metcalf	.10
8	Jamir Miller	.10
9	Rob Moore	.20
10	Joe Nedney	.10
11	Jake Plummer	1.00
12	Simeon Rice	.10
13	Frank Sanders	.10
14	Eric Swann	.10
15	Aeneas Williams	.10
16	Morten Andersen	.10
17	Jamal Anderson	.50
18	Michael Booker	.10
19	Keith Brooking	.10
20	Ray Buchanan	.10
21	Devin Bush	.10
22	Chris Chandler	.20
23	Tony Graziani	.10
24	Harold Green	.10
25	Byron Hanspard	.10
26	Todd Kinchen	.10
27	Tony Martin	.10
28	Terance Mathis	.10
29	Eugene Robinson	.10
30	O.J. Santiago	.10
31	Chuck Smith	.10
32	Jessie Tuggle	.10
33	Bob Whitfield	.10
34	Peter Boulware	.10
35	Jay Graham	.10
36	Eric Green	.10
37	Jim Harbaugh	.20
38	Michael Jackson	.10
39	Jermaine Lewis	.10
40	Ray Lewis	.10
41	Michael McCrary	.10
42	Stevon Moore	.10
43	Jonathan Ogden	.10
44	Errict Rhett	.10
45	Matt Stover	.10
46	Rod Woodson	.10
47	Eric Zeier	.10
48	Ruben Brown	.10
49	Steve Christie	.10
50	Quinn Early	.10
51	John Fina	.10
52	Doug Flutie	.75
53	Phil Hansen	.10
54	Lonnie Johnson	.10
55	Rob Johnson	.20
56	Henry Jones	.10
57	Eric Moulds	.20
58	Andre Reed	.10
59	Antowain Smith	.50
60	Bruce Smith	.10
61	Thurman Thomas	.20
62	Ted Washington	.10
63	Michael Bates	.10
64	Tim Biakabutuka	.10
65	Blake Brockermeyer	.10
66	Mark Carrier	.10
67	Rae Carruth	.10
68	Kerry Collins	.20
69	Doug Evans	.10
70	William Floyd	.10
71	Sean Gilbert	.10
72	Raghib Ismail	.10
73	John Kasay	.10
74	Fred Lane	.20
75	Lamar Lathon	.10
76	Muhsin Muhammad	.10
77	Wesley Walls	.10
78	Edgar Bennett	.10
79	Tom Carter	.10
80	Curtis Conway	.20
81	Bobby Engram	.10
82	*Curtis Enis*	3.00
83	Jim Flanigan	.10
84	Walt Harris	.10
85	Jeff Jaeger	.10
86	Erik Kramer	.10
87	John Mangum	.10
88	Glyn Milburn	.10
89	Barry Minter	.10
90	Chris Penn	.10
91	Todd Sauerbrun	.10
92	James Williams	.10
93	Ashley Ambrose	.10
94	Willie Anderson	.10
95	Eric Bieniemy	.10
96	Jeff Blake	.20
97	Ki-Jana Carter	.10
98	John Copeland	.10
99	Corey Dillon	.75
100	Tony McGee	.10
101	Neil O'Donnell	.20
102	Carl Pickens	.20
103	Kevin Sargent	.10
104	Darnay Scott	.20
105	*Takeo Spikes*	1.00
106	Troy Aikman	1.50
107	Larry Allen	.10
108	Eric Bjornson	.10
109	Billy Davis	.10
110	Jason Garrett	.10
111	Michael Irvin	.20
112	Daryl Johnston	.10
113	David LaFleur	.10
114	Everett McIver	.10
115	Ernie Mills	.10
116	Nate Newton	.10
117	Deion Sanders	.50
118	Emmitt Smith	2.00
119	Kevin Smith	.10
120	Erik Williams	.10
121	Steve Atwater	.10
122	Tyrone Braxton	.10
123	Ray Crockett	.10
124	Terrell Davis	2.00
125	Jason Elam	.10
126	John Elway	1.50
127	Willie Green	.10
128	*Brian Griese*	4.00
129	Tony Jones	.10
130	Ed McCaffrey	.20
131	John Mobley	.10
132	Tom Nalen	.10
133	*Marcus Nash*	2.00
134	Bill Romanowski	.10
135	Shannon Sharpe	.20
136	Neil Smith	.10
137	Rod Smith	.20
138	Keith Traylor	.10
139	Stephen Boyd	.10
140	Mark Carrier	.10
141	*Charlie Batch*	5.00
142	Jason Hanson	.10
143	Scott Mitchell	.20
144	Herman Moore	.50
145	Johnnie Morton	.10
146	Robert Porcher	.10
147	Ron Rivers	.10
148	Barry Sanders	3.00
149	Tracy Scroggins	.10
150	David Sloan	.10
151	Tommy Vardell	.10
152	Kerwin Waldroup	.10
153	Bryant Westbrook	.10

154	Robert Brooks	.10
155	Gilbert Brown	.10
156	LeRoy Butler	.10
157	Mark Chmura	.20
158	Earl Dotson	.10
159	Santana Dotson	.10
160	Brett Favre	3.00
161	Antonio Freeman	.50
162	Raymont Harris	.10
163	William Henderson	.10
164	*Vonnie Holliday*	1.50
165	George Koonce	.10
166	Dorsey Levens	.20
167	Derrick Mayes	.10
168	Craig Newsome	.10
169	Ross Verba	.10
170	Reggie White	.50
171	Elijah Alexander	.10
172	Aaron Bailey	.10
173	Jason Belser	.10
174	Robert Blackmon	.10
175	Zack Crockett	.10
176	Ken Dilger	.10
177	Marshall Faulk	.50
178	Tarik Glenn	.10
179	Marvin Harrison	.20
180	Tony Mandarich	.10
181	*Peyton Manning*	10.00
182	Marcus Pollard	.10
183	Lamont Warren	.10
184	*Tavian Banks*	2.00
185	Reggie Barlow	.10
186	Tony Boselli	.10
187	Tony Brackens	.10
188	Mark Brunell	1.00
189	Kevin Hardy	.10
190	Mike Hollis	.10
191	Jeff Lageman	.10
192	Keenan McCardell	.20
193	Pete Mitchell	.10
194	Bryce Paup	.10
195	Leon Searcy	.10
196	Jimmy Smith	.20
197	James Stewart	.10
198	*Fred Taylor*	5.00
199	Renaldo Wynn	.10
200	Derrick Alexander	.10
201	Kimble Anders	.10
202	Donnell Bennett	.10
203	Dale Carter	.10
204	Anthony Davis	.10
205	Rich Gannon	.10
206	Tony Gonzalez	.20
207	Elvis Grbac	.20
208	James Hasty	.10
209	Leslie O'Neal	.10
210	Andre Rison	.10
211	*Rashaan Shehee*	1.50
212	Will Shields	.10
213	Pete Stoyanovich	.10
214	Derrick Thomas	.20
215	Tamarick Vanover	.10
216	Karim Abdul-Jabbar	.20
217	Trace Armstrong	.10
218	*John Avery*	2.00
219	Tim Bowens	.10
220	Terrell Buckley	.10
221	Troy Drayton	.10
222	Daryl Gardener	.10
223	Damon Huard	.10
224	Charles Jordan	.10
225	Dan Marino	2.00
226	O.J. McDuffie	.10
227	Bernie Parmalee	.10
228	Stanley Pritchett	.10
229	Derrick Rodgers	.10
230	Lamar Thomas	.10
231	Zach Thomas	.20
232	Richmond Webb	.10
233	Derrick Alexander	.10
234	Jerry Ball	.10
235	Cris Carter	.50
236	Randall Cunningham	.50
237	Charles Evans	.10
238	Corey Fuller	.10
239	Andrew Glover	.10
240	Leroy Hoard	.10
241	Brad Johnson	.50
242	Ed McDaniel	.10
243	Randall McDaniel	.10
244	*Randy Moss*	15.00
245	John Randle	.10
246	Jake Reed	.10
247	Dwayne Rudd	.10
248	Robert Smith	.20
249	Bruce Armstrong	.10
250	Drew Bledsoe	1.00
251	Vincent Brisby	.10
252	Tedy Bruschi	.10
253	Ben Coates	.20
254	Derrick Cullors	.10
255	Terry Glenn	.20
256	Shawn Jefferson	.10
257	Ted Johnson	.10
258	Ty Law	.10
259	Willie McGinest	.10
260	Lawyer Milloy	.10
261	Sedrick Shaw	.10
262	Chris Slade	.10
263	Troy Davis	.10
264	Mark Fields	.10
265	Andre Hastings	.10
266	Billy Joe Hobert	.10
267	Qadry Ismail	.10
268	Tony Johnson	.10
269	Sammy Knight	.10
270	Wayne Martin	.10
271	Chris Naeole	.10
272	Keith Poole	.10
273	William Roaf	.10
274	Pio Sagapolutele	.10
275	Danny Wuerffel	.20
276	Ray Zellars	.10
277	Jessie Armstead	.10
278	Tiki Barber	.20
279	Chris Calloway	.10
280	Percy Ellsworth	.10
281	Sam Garnes	.10
282	Kent Graham	.10
283	Ike Hilliard	.10
284	Danny Kanell	.10
285	Corey Miller	.10
286	Phillippi Sparks	.10
287	Michael Strahan	.10
288	Amani Toomer	.10
289	Charles Way	.10
290	Tyrone Wheatley	.10
291	Tito Wooten	.10
292	Kyle Brady	.10
293	Keith Byars	.10
294	Wayne Chrebet	.20
295	John Elliott	.10
296	Glenn Foley	.20
297	Aaron Glenn	.10
298	Keyshawn Johnson	.50
299	Curtis Martin	.50
300	Otis Smith	.10
301	Vinny Testaverde	.20
302	Alex Van Dyke	.10
303	Dedric Ward	.10
304	Greg Biekert	.10
305	Tim Brown	.20
306	Rickey Dudley	.10
307	Jeff George	.20
308	Pat Harlow	.10
309	Desmond Howard	.10
310	James Jett	.10
311	Napoleon Kaufman	.50
312	Lincoln Kennedy	.10
313	Russell Maryland	.10
314	Darrell Russell	.10
315	Eric Turner	.10
316	Steve Wisniewski	.10
317	*Charles Woodson*	4.00
318	James Darling	.10
319	Jason Dunn	.10
320	Irving Fryar	.10
321	Charlie Garner	.20
322	Jeff Graham	.10
323	Bobby Hoying	.20
324	Chad Lewis	.10
325	Rodney Peete	.10
326	Freddie Solomon	.10
327	Duce Staley	.10
328	Bobby Taylor	.10
329	William Thomas	.10
330	Kevin Turner	.10
331	Troy Vincent	.10
332	Jerome Bettis	.50
333	Will Blackwell	.10
334	Mark Bruener	.10
335	Andre Coleman	.10
336	Dermontti Dawson	.10
337	Jason Gildon	.10
338	Courtney Hawkins	.10
339	Charles Johnson	.10
340	Levon Kirkland	.10
341	Carnell Lake	.10
342	Tim Lester	.10
343	Joel Steed	.10
344	Kordell Stewart	1.00
345	Will Wolford	.10
346	Tony Banks	.20
347	Isaac Bruce	.20
348	Ernie Conwell	.10
349	D'Marco Farr	.10
350	Wayne Gandy	.10
351	*Robert Holcombe*	2.00
352	Eddie Kennison	.20
353	Amp Lee	.10
354	Keith Lyle	.10
355	Ryan McNeil	.10
356	Jerald Moore	.20
357	Orlando Pace	.10
358	Roman Phifer	.10
359	David Thompson	.10
360	Darren Bennett	.10
361	John Carney	.10
362	Marco Coleman	.10
363	Terrell Fletcher	.10
364	William Fuller	.10
365	Charlie Jones	.10
366	Freddie Jones	.10
367	*Ryan Leaf*	4.00
368	Natrone Means	.50
369	Junior Seau	.20
370	Terrance Shaw	.10
371	Tremayne Stephens	.10
372	Bryan Still	.10
373	Aaron Taylor	.10
374	Greg Clark	.10
375	Ty Detmer	.10
376	Jim Druckenmiller	.20
377	Marc Edwards	.10
378	Merton Hanks	.10
379	Garrison Hearst	.20
380	Chuck Levy	.10
381	Ken Norton	.10
382	Terrell Owens	.75
383	Marquez Pope	.10
384	Jerry Rice	1.50
385	Irv Smith	.10
386	J.J. Stokes	.20
387	Iheanyi Uwaezuoke	.10
388	Bryant Young	.10
389	Steve Young	.75
390	Sam Adams	.10
391	Chad Brown	.10
392	Christian Fauria	.10
393	Joey Galloway	.50
394	*Ahman Green*	2.50
395	Walter Jones	.10
396	Cortez Kennedy	.10
397	Jon Kitna	.50
398	James McKnight	.10
399	Warren Moon	.20
400	Mike Pritchard	.10
401	Michael Sinclair	.10
402	Shawn Springs	.10
403	Ricky Watters	.20
404	Darryl Williams	.10
405	Mike Alstott	.50
406	Reidel Anthony	.20
407	Derrick Brooks	.10
408	Brad Culpepper	.10
409	Trent Dilfer	.50
410	Warrick Dunn	1.00
411	Bert Emanuel	.10
412	*Jacquez Green*	2.50
413	Paul Gruber	.10
414	Patrick Hape	.10
415	Dave Moore	.10
416	Hardy Nickerson	.10
417	Warren Sapp	.10
418	Robb Thomas	.10
419	Regan Upshaw	.10
420	Karl Williams	.10
421	Blaine Bishop	.10
422	Anthony Cook	.10
423	Willie Davis	.10
424	Al Del Greco	.10
425	*Kevin Dyson*	2.00
426	Henry Ford	.10
427	Eddie George	1.00
428	Jackie Harris	.10
429	Steve McNair	.75
430	Chris Sanders	.10
431	Mark Stepnoski	.10
432	Yancey Thigpen	.20
433	Barron Wortham	.10
434	Frank Wycheck	.10
435	Stephen Alexander	.10
436	Terry Allen	.20
437	Jamie Asher	.10
438	Bob Dahl	.10
439	Stephen Davis	.10
440	Cris Dishman	.10
441	Gus Frerotte	.10
442	Darrell Green	.10
443	Trent Green	.20
444	Ken Harvey	.10
445	*Skip Hicks*	2.00
446	Jeff Hostetler	.10
447	Brian Mitchell	.10
448	Leslie Shepherd	.10
449	Michael Westbrook	.20
450	Dan Wilkinson	.10

1998 Pacific Cramer's Choice Awards

Pacific President/CEO Michael Cramer selected and wrote about the 10 players that are on these die-cut awards. Each card is in the shape of a triangle and were inserted 1:721 packs.

		MT
Complete Set (10):		850.00
Common Player:		50.00
Inserted 1:721		
1	Terrell Davis	125.00
2	John Elway	100.00
3	Barry Sanders	150.00
4	Brett Favre	150.00
5	Peyton Manning	125.00
6	Mark Brunell	70.00
7	Dan Marino	125.00
8	Ryan Leaf	60.00
9	Jerry Rice	85.00
10	Warrick Dunn	50.00

1998 Pacific Dynagon Turf

This sparkling insert features action photography and a mirror-patterned full-foil background. Singles from this 20-card set were inserted 4:37 packs. A parallel Titanium Turf set was added for hobby-only packs. Each single is sequentially numbered to 99.

		MT
Complete Set (20):		100.00
Common Player:		2.00
Inserted 4:37		
Titanium Cards:		7x-14x
Production 99 Sets		
1	Corey Dillon	3.00
2	Troy Aikman	6.00
3	Emmitt Smith	10.00
4	Terrell Davis	10.00
5	John Elway	6.00
6	Barry Sanders	12.00
7	Brett Favre	12.00
8	Peyton Manning	12.00
9	Mark Brunell	5.00
10	Dan Marino	10.00
11	Drew Bledsoe	5.00
12	Curtis Martin	3.00
13	Napoleon Kaufman	2.00
14	Jerome Bettis	2.00
15	Kordell Stewart	5.00
16	Ryan Leaf	6.00
17	Jerry Rice	6.00
18	Steve Young	4.00
19	Warrick Dunn	4.00
20	Eddie George	4.00

1998 Pacific Gold Crown Die-Cuts

This die-cut dual-foiled insert honors 36 of football's elite players. These singles were created with Pacific's cutting-edge technology and feature super-thick 24-point stock. Singles were inserted 1:37 packs.

		MT
Complete Set (36):		425.00
Common Player:		5.00
Inserted 1:37		
1	Jake Plummer	15.00
2	Antowain Smith	10.00
3	Curtis Enis	12.00
4	Corey Dillon	10.00
5	Troy Aikman	20.00
6	Deion Sanders	10.00
7	Emmitt Smith	30.00
8	Terrell Davis	30.00
9	John Elway	20.00
10	Barry Sanders	40.00
11	Brett Favre	40.00
12	Dorsey Levens	5.00
13	Marshall Faulk	10.00
14	Peyton Manning	40.00
15	Mark Brunell	15.00
16	Fred Taylor	20.00
17	Derrick Thomas	5.00
18	Dan Marino	30.00
19	Brad Johnson	10.00
20	Robert Smith	10.00
21	Drew Bledsoe	15.00
22	Glenn Foley	5.00
23	Curtis Martin	10.00
24	Napoleon Kaufman	10.00
25	Charles Woodson	15.00
26	Jerome Bettis	10.00
27	Kordell Stewart	15.00
28	Ryan Leaf	20.00
29	Garrison Hearst	5.00
30	Jerry Rice	20.00
31	J.J. Stokes	5.00
32	Steve Young	12.00
33	Joey Galloway	10.00
34	Ricky Watters	5.00
35	Warrick Dunn	15.00
36	Eddie George	15.00

1998 Pacific Team Checklists

This uniquely-designed insert highlights a team leader side-by-side with the holographic silver-foiled NFL logo of his respective team. On the back you'll find another photo of that player and a complete team checklist. Singles were inserted 2:37 packs.

		MT
Complete Set (30):		150.00
Common Player:		2.00
Inserted 2:37		
1	Jake Plummer	7.00
2	Jamal Anderson	4.00
3	Eric Zeier	2.00
4	Rob Johnson	2.00
5	Fred Lane	2.00
6	Curtis Enis	8.00
7	Corey Dillon	4.00
8	Troy Aikman	10.00
9	John Elway	10.00
10	Barry Sanders	20.00
11	Brett Favre	20.00
12	Peyton Manning	20.00
13	Mark Brunell	8.00
14	Elvis Grbac	2.00
15	Dan Marino	15.00
16	Robert Smith	4.00
17	Drew Bledsoe	8.00
18	Danny Wuerffel	2.00
19	Tiki Barber	2.00
20	Curtis Martin	4.00
21	Napoleon Kaufman	4.00
22	Duce Staley	2.00
23	Kordell Stewart	8.00
24	Tony Banks	4.00
25	Ryan Leaf	10.00
26	Jerry Rice	10.00
27	Warren Moon	4.00
28	Warrick Dunn	7.00
29	Eddie George	7.00
30	Terry Allen	2.00

1998 Pacific Timelines

Timelines features 20 superstars, giving a chronological history of each player complete with photos from early in their careers. These singles could be found in hobby-only packs at a ratio of 1:181.

		MT
Complete Set (20):		750.00
Common Player:		10.00
Inserted 1:181 Hobby		
1	Troy Aikman	50.00
2	Deion Sanders	20.00
3	Emmitt Smith	75.00
4	Terrell Davis	75.00
5	John Elway	50.00

6	Barry Sanders	100.00
7	Brett Favre	100.00
8	Peyton Manning	100.00
9	Mark Brunell	35.00
10	Dan Marino	75.00
11	Drew Bledsoe	40.00
12	Curtis Martin	20.00
13	Jerome Bettis	10.00
14	Kordell Stewart	40.00
15	Ryan Leaf	50.00
16	Jerry Rice	50.00
17	Steve Young	30.00
18	Ricky Watters	10.00
19	Warrick Dunn	40.00
20	Eddie George	40.00

1998 Pacific Aurora

The Aurora main set shines its light on 200 of football's most exciting players, each featured on their own 24-point stock card. Each card back gives you the latest in-depth player information and statistics along with a trivia question.

		MT
Complete Set (200):		75.00
Common Player:		.20
Wax Box:		85.00
1	Rob Moore	.20
2	Jake Plummer	1.50
3	Frank Sanders	.20
4	Eric Swann	.20
5	Jamal Anderson	.75
6	Chris Chandler	.20
7	Byron Hanspard	.20
8	Terance Mathis	.20
9	O.J. Santiago	.20
10	Chuck Smith	.20
11	Jessie Tuggle	.20
12	Jay Graham	.20
13	Jim Harbaugh	.20
14	Michael Jackson	.20
15	*Patrick Johnson*	.40
16	Jermaine Lewis	.20
17	Errict Rhett	.20
18	Rod Woodson	.20
19	Quinn Early	.20
20	Andre Reed	.20
21	Antowain Smith	1.00
22	Bruce Smith	.20
23	Thurman Thomas	.40
24	Ted Washington	.20
25	Michael Bates	.20
26	Rae Carruth	.20
27	Kerry Collins	.40
28	Fred Lane	.40
29	Wesley Walls	.20
30	Edgar Bennett	.20
31	Curtis Conway	.40
32	*Curtis Enis*	5.00
33	Walt Harris	.20
34	Erik Kramer	.20
35	Barry Minter	.20
36	Jeff Blake	.40
37	Corey Dillon	1.25
38	Carl Pickens	.20
39	Darnay Scott	.20
40	Troy Aikman	2.00
41	Michael Irvin	.40
42	Deion Sanders	.75
43	Emmitt Smith	3.00
44	Chris Warren	.20
45	Terrell Davis	3.00
46	John Elway	2.00
47	*Brian Griese*	4.00
48	Ed McCaffrey	.20
49	John Mobley	.20
50	Shannon Sharpe	.40
51	Neil Smith	.20
52	Rod Smith	.20
53	Stephen Boyd	.20
54	Scott Mitchell	.20
55	Herman Moore	.75
56	Johnnie Morton	.20
57	Robert Porcher	.20
58	Barry Sanders	4.00
59	Robert Brooks	.20
60	Mark Chmura	.40
61	Brett Favre	4.00
62	Antonio Freeman	.75
63	*Vonnie Holliday*	1.00
64	Dorsey Levens	.40
65	Ross Verba	.20
66	Reggie White	.40
67	Elijah Alexander	.20
68	Ken Dilger	.20
69	Marshall Faulk	.75
70	Marvin Harrison	.40
71	*Peyton Manning*	12.00
72	Bryan Barker	.20
73	Mark Brunell	1.50
74	Keenan McCardell	.20
75	Jimmy Smith	.20
76	James Stewart	.20
77	Derrick Alexander	.20
78	Kimble Anders	.20
79	Donnell Bennett	.20
80	Elvis Grbac	.20
81	Andre Rison	.20
82	*Rashaan Shehee*	.75
83	Derrick Thomas	.20
84	Karim Abdul-Jabbar	.40
85	Trace Armstrong	.20
86	Charles Jordan	.20
87	Dan Marino	3.00
88	O.J. McDuffie	.20
89	Zach Thomas	.40
90	Cris Carter	.40
91	Charles Evans	.20
92	Andrew Glover	.20
93	Brad Johnson	.40
94	*Randy Moss*	15.00
95	John Randle	.20
96	Jake Reed	.20
97	Robert Smith	.40
98	Bruce Armstrong	.20
99	Drew Bledsoe	1.50
100	Ben Coates	.20
101	*Robert Edwards*	4.00
102	Terry Glenn	.40
103	Willie McGinest	.20
104	Sedrick Shaw	.20
105	*Tony Simmons*	2.00
106	Chris Slade	.20
107	Billy Joe Hobert	.20
108	Qadry Ismail	.20
109	Heath Shuler	.20
110	Lamar Smith	.20
111	Ray Zellars	.20
112	Tiki Barber	.40
113	Chris Calloway	.20
114	Ike Hilliard	.20
115	*Joe Jurevicius*	1.00
116	Danny Kanell	.20
117	Amani Toomer	.20
118	Charles Way	.20
119	Tyrone Wheatley	.20
120	Wayne Chrebet	.20
121	John Elliott	.20
122	Glenn Foley	.20
123	*Scott Frost*	.40
124	Aaron Glenn	.20
125	Keyshawn Johnson	.40
126	Curtis Martin	1.00
127	Vinny Testaverde	.20
128	Tim Brown	.40
129	Rickey Dudley	.20
130	Jeff George	.40
131	James Jett	.20
132	Napoleon Kaufman	.75
133	Darrell Russell	.20
134	*Charles Woodson*	5.00
135	James Darling	.20
136	Koy Detmer	.20
137	Irving Fryar	.20
138	Charlie Garner	.20
139	Bobby Hoying	.20
140	Chad Lewis	.20
141	Duce Staley	.20
142	Kevin Turner	.20
143	Jerome Bettis	.40
144	Will Blackwell	.20
145	Mark Bruener	.20
146	Dermontti Dawson	.20
147	Charles Johnson	.20
148	Levon Kirkland	.20
149	Tim Lester	.20
150	Kordell Stewart	1.50
151	Tony Banks	.75
152	Isaac Bruce	.40
153	*Robert Holcombe*	5.00
154	Eddie Kennison	.40
155	Amp Lee	.20
156	Jerald Moore	.20
157	Charlie Jones	.20
158	Freddie Jones	.20
159	*Ryan Leaf*	6.00
160	Natrone Means	.40
161	Junior Seau	.40
162	Bryan Still	.20
163	Marc Edwards	.20
164	Merton Hanks	.20
165	Garrison Hearst	.40
166	Terrell Owens	.40
167	Jerry Rice	2.00
168	J.J. Stokes	.20
169	Bryant Young	.20
170	Steve Young	1.00
171	Chad Brown	.20
172	Joey Galloway	.75
173	Walter Jones	.20
174	Cortez Kennedy	.20
175	Jon Kitna	.20
176	James McKnight	.20
177	Warren Moon	.40
178	Michael Sinclair	.20
179	Mike Alstott	.40
180	Reidel Anthony	.20
181	Derrick Brooks	.20
182	Trent Dilfer	.40
183	Warrick Dunn	1.50
184	Hardy Nickerson	.20
185	Warren Sapp	.20
186	Willie Davis	.20
187	Eddie George	1.25
188	Steve McNair	.75
189	Jon Runyan	.20
190	Chris Sanders	.20
191	Frank Wycheck	.20
192	Stephen Alexander	.20
193	Terry Allen	.20
194	Stephen Davis	.20
195	Cris Dishman	.20
196	Gus Frerotte	.20
197	Darrell Green	.20
198	*Skip Hicks*	1.50
199	Dana Stubblefield	.20
200	Michael Westbrook	.20

1998 Pacific Aurora Championship Fever

Each of the singles in this 50-card set are printed on gold foil and etched. Singles were inserted one-per-pack. This insert also has three parallel sets. The easiest being the Silvers that are found in retail packs and are sequentially numbered to 250. The Platinum Blues are numbered to 100 and can be found in both hobby and retail packs. The Copper cards are limited to 20 and are found in hobby packs.

		MT
Complete Set (50):		50.00
Common Player:		.30
Inserted 1:1		
Silver Cards:		15x-30x
Production 250 Sets		
Platinum Blue Cards:		25x-50x
Production 100 Sets		
Copper Cards:		75x-150x
Production 20 Sets		
1	Jake Plummer	2.00
2	Antowain Smith	1.00
3	Bruce Smith	.30
4	Kerry Collins	.60
5	Kevin Greene	.30
6	Jeff Blake	.30
7	Corey Dillon	1.50
8	Carl Pickens	.30
9	Troy Aikman	3.00
10	Michael Irvin	.60
11	Deion Sanders	.75
12	Emmitt Smith	4.00
13	Terrell Davis	4.00
14	John Elway	3.00
15	Shannon Sharpe	.30
16	Herman Moore	.60
17	Barry Sanders	6.00
18	Brett Favre	6.00
19	Antonio Freeman	.75
20	Dorsey Levens	.60
21	Marshall Faulk	.75
22	Peyton Manning	6.00
23	Mark Brunell	2.00
24	Elvis Grbac	.30
25	Andre Rison	.30
26	Rashaan Shehee	.60
27	Derrick Thomas	.30
28	Dan Marino	4.00
29	Cris Carter	.30
30	Robert Smith	.60
31	Drew Bledsoe	2.00
32	Robert Edwards	3.00
33	Terry Glenn	.60
34	Danny Kanell	.30
35	Keyshawn Johnson	.60
36	Tim Brown	.30
37	Napoleon Kaufman	.75
38	Bobby Hoying	.30
39	Jerome Bettis	.60
40	Kordell Stewart	2.00
41	Ryan Leaf	3.00
42	Jerry Rice	3.00
43	Steve Young	1.50
44	Joey Galloway	.75
45	Mike Alstott	.60
46	Trent Dilfer	.60
47	Warrick Dunn	2.00
48	Eddie George	2.00
49	Steve McNair	.75
50	Gus Frerotte	.30

1998 Pacific Aurora Cubes

The Cubes insert could only be found in hobby boxes and were inserted one per box. Only 20 of the top players from the NFL were included in this insert.

		MT
Complete Set (20):		170.00
Common Player:		4.00
One Per Box		
1	Corey Dillon	6.00
2	Troy Aikman	10.00
3	Emmitt Smith	15.00
4	Terrell Davis	15.00
5	John Elway	10.00
6	Barry Sanders	20.00
7	Brett Favre	20.00
8	Dorsey Levens	4.00
9	Peyton Manning	15.00
10	Mark Brunell	8.00
11	Dan Marino	15.00
12	Drew Bledsoe	8.00
13	Napoleon Kaufman	4.00
14	Jerome Bettis	4.00
15	Kordell Stewart	8.00
16	Ryan Leaf	8.00
17	Jerry Rice	10.00
18	Steve Young	6.00
19	Warrick Dunn	8.00
20	Eddie George	8.00

1998 Pacific Aurora Face Mask Cel-Fusions

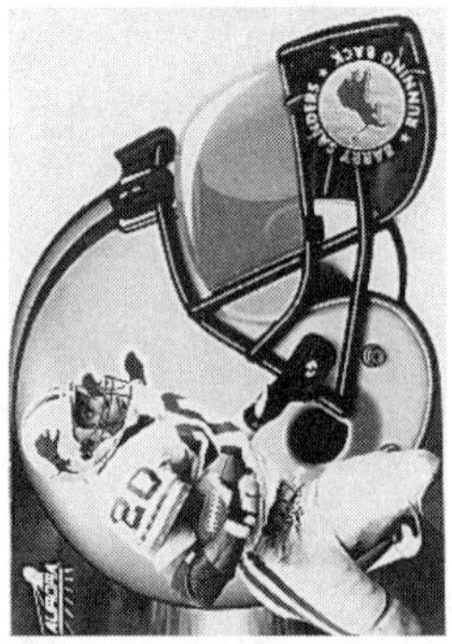

Each player in this 20-card foiled and etched set is profiled against a die-cut helmet that is fused to a cel-portion face mask. Singles were inserted 1:73 packs.

		MT
Complete Set (20):		550.00
Common Player:		10.00
Inserted 1:73		
1	Corey Dillon	15.00
2	Troy Aikman	35.00
3	Emmitt Smith	50.00
4	Terrell Davis	50.00
5	John Elway	35.00
6	Barry Sanders	70.00
7	Brett Favre	70.00
8	Antonio Freeman	10.00
9	Peyton Manning	60.00
10	Mark Brunell	25.00
11	Dan Marino	50.00
12	Drew Bledsoe	25.00
13	Napoleon Kaufman	10.00
14	Jerome Bettis	10.00
15	Kordell Stewart	25.00
16	Ryan Leaf	25.00
17	Jerry Rice	35.00
18	Steve Young	15.00
19	Warrick Dunn	20.00
20	Eddie George	20.00

1998 Pacific Aurora Gridiron Laser-Cuts

Each single in this 20-card set is laser cut and was inserted 4:37 packs. They could only be found in hobby packs.

		MT
Complete Set (20):		125.00
Common Player:		3.00
Inserted 4:37 Hobby		
1	Jake Plummer	6.00
2	Corey Dillon	5.00
3	Troy Aikman	8.00
4	Emmitt Smith	10.00
5	Terrell Davis	10.00
6	John Elway	8.00
7	Barry Sanders	15.00
8	Brett Favre	15.00
9	Peyton Manning	10.00
10	Mark Brunell	6.00
11	Dan Marino	10.00
12	Drew Bledsoe	6.00
13	Jerome Bettis	3.00
14	Kordell Stewart	6.00
15	Ryan Leaf	7.00
16	Jerry Rice	8.00
17	Steve Young	5.00
18	Warrick Dunn	6.00
19	Eddie George	6.00
20	Steve McNair	4.00

1998 Pacific Aurora NFL Command

This insert salutes 10 NFL stars with this coveted fully-foiled and etched insert. Singles were inserted 1:361 packs.

		MT
Complete Set (10):		650.00
Common Player:		50.00
Inserted 1:361		
1	Terrell Davis	100.00
2	John Elway	100.00
3	Barry Sanders	125.00
4	Brett Favre	125.00
5	Peyton Manning	100.00
6	Mark Brunell	50.00
7	Dan Marino	100.00
8	Drew Bledsoe	50.00
9	Ryan Leaf	50.00
10	Warrick Dunn	50.00

1998 Pacific Crown Royale

This 144-card base set features football's brightest stars and top rookies on the Crown Royale double-foiled, double-etched, all-die-cut format. The parallel Limited Series cards are printed on 24-point stock and are sequentially numbered to 99.

		MT
Complete Set (144):		180.00
Common Player:		.50
Common Rookie:		1.00
Limited Series Cards:		15x-30x
Limited Series Rookies:		3x-6x
Production 99 Sets		
Wax Box:		120.00
1	Larry Centers	.50
2	Rob Moore	.50
3	Adrian Murrell	.50
4	Jake Plummer	3.00
5	Jamal Anderson	1.50
6	Chris Chandler	.50
7	*Tim Dwight*	3.00
8	Tony Martin	.50
9	Jay Graham	.50
10	*Patrick Johnson*	2.00
11	Jermaine Lewis	.50
12	Eric Zeier	.50
13	Rob Johnson	1.00
14	Eric Moulds	1.00
15	Antowain Smith	1.50
16	Bruce Smith	.50
17	Steve Beuerlein	.50
18	Anthony Johnson	.50
19	Fred Lane	1.00
20	Muhsin Muhammad	.50

21 Curtis Conway 1.00
22 *Curtis Enis* 6.00
23 Erik Kramer .50
24 *Tony Parrish* 1.00
25 Corey Dillon 2.00
26 Neil O'Donnell .50
27 Carl Pickens 1.00
28 *Takeo Spikes* 2.00
29 Troy Aikman 4.00
30 Michael Irvin 1.00
31 Deion Sanders 1.50
32 Emmitt Smith 6.00
33 Chris Warren .50
34 Terrell Davis 6.00
35 John Elway 4.00
36 *Brian Griese* 10.00
37 Ed McCaffrey 1.00
38 Shannon Sharpe 1.00
39 Rod Smith 1.00
40 *Charlie Batch* 15.00
41 Herman Moore 1.00
42 Johnnie Morton .50
43 Barry Sanders 8.00
44 Bryant Westbrook .50
45 Robert Brooks .50
46 Brett Favre 8.00
47 Antonio Freeman 1.50
48 Raymont Harris .50
49 *Vonnie Holliday* 3.00
50 Reggie White 1.00
51 Marshall Faulk 1.50
52 *E.G. Green* 3.00
53 Marvin Harrison 1.00
54 *Peyton Manning* 20.00
55 *Jerome Pathon* 3.00
56 *Tavian Banks* 4.00
57 Mark Brunell 3.00
58 Keenan McCardell .50
59 Jimmy Smith 1.00
60 *Fred Taylor* 15.00
61 Derrick Alexander .50
62 Tony Gonzalez .50
63 Elvis Grbac .50
64 Andre Rison .50
65 *Rashaan Shehee* 2.00
66 Derrick Thomas 1.00
67 Karim Abdul-Jabbar 1.00
68 *John Avery* 4.00
69 *Oronde Gadsden* 3.00
70 Dan Marino 6.00
71 O.J. McDuffie .50
72 Cris Carter 1.50
73 Randall Cunningham 1.50
74 Brad Johnson 1.00
75 *Randy Moss* 30.00
76 John Randle .50
77 Jake Reed .50
78 Robert Smith 1.00
79 Drew Bledsoe 3.00
80 *Robert Edwards* 7.00
81 Terry Glenn 1.00
82 *Tebucky Jones* 1.00
83 *Tony Simmons* 3.00
84 Mark Fields .50
85 Andre Hastings .50
86 Danny Wuerffel 1.00
87 Ray Zellars .50
88 Tiki Barber 1.00
89 Ike Hilliard .50
90 *Joe Jurevicius* 2.00
91 Danny Kanell .50
92 Wayne Chrebet 1.00
93 Glenn Foley 1.00
94 Keyshawn Johnson 1.50
95 Leon Johnson .50
96 Curtis Martin 1.50
97 Tim Brown 1.00
98 Jeff George 1.00
99 Napoleon Kaufman 1.50
100 *Jon Ritchie* 1.50
101 *Charles Woodson* 7.00
102 Irving Fryar .50
103 Bobby Hoying 1.00
104 *Allen Rossum* 1.00
105 Duce Staley .50
106 Jerome Bettis 1.00
107 *Chris Fuamatu-Ma'afala* 3.00
108 Charles Johnson 1.00
109 Levon Kirkland .50
110 Kordell Stewart 3.00
111 *Hines Ward* 3.00
112 Tony Banks 1.00
113 *Tony Horne* 1.00
114 Eddie Kennison 1.00
115 Amp Lee .50
116 Freddie Jones .50
117 *Ryan Leaf* 7.00
118 Natrone Means 1.00
119 *Mikhael Ricks* 3.00
120 Bryan Still .50
121 Marc Edwards .50
122 Garrison Hearst 1.50
123 Terrell Owens 1.50
124 Jerry Rice 4.00
125 J.J. Stokes 1.00
126 Steve Young 2.50
127 Joey Galloway 1.50
128 *Ahman Green* 5.00
129 Warren Moon 1.00
130 Ricky Watters 1.00
131 Mike Alstott 1.50
132 Trent Dilfer 1.00
133 Warrick Dunn 3.00
134 *Jacquez Green* 6.00
135 Warren Sapp .50
136 *Kevin Dyson* 5.00
137 Eddie George 3.00
138 Steve McNair 2.00
139 Yancey Thigpen 1.00
140 *Stephen Alexander* 1.00
141 Terry Allen 1.00
142 Trent Green 1.00
143 *Skip Hicks* 4.00
144 Michael Westbrook 1.00

1998 Pacific Crown Royale Cramer's Choice Awards Jumbos

These singles are identical to the Cramer's Choice awards found in Pacific except for the size. Singles from this set are larger and found on top of boxes at one per. The twist to this insert is the six different parallels with varying foil colors and number of sets produced. The Dark Blues are numbered to 35, Greens are numbered to 30, Reds to 25, Light Blues to 20, Golds to 10 and only one Purple set.

	MT
Complete Set (10):	150.00
Common Player:	10.00
One Per Box	
Dark Blue Cards:	10x-20x
Production 35 Sets	
Green Cards:	10x-20x
Production 30 Sets	
Red Cards:	10x-20x
Production 25 Sets	
Light Blue Cards:	10x-20x
Production 20 Sets	
Gold Cards:	15x-30x
Production 10 Sets	
1 Terrell Davis	15.00
2 John Elway	12.00
3 Barry Sanders	20.00
4 Brett Favre	20.00
5 Peyton Manning	20.00
6 Mark Brunell	10.00
7 Dan Marino	15.00
8 Randy Moss	35.00
9 Jerry Rice	12.00
10 Warrick Dunn	10.00

1998 Pacific Crown Royale Living Legends

The players selected for this insert were based on the dozens of records, awards and championships that each player has earned. Each card in this insert is sequentially numbered to 375.

	MT
Complete Set (10):	300.00
Common Player:	20.00
Production 375 Sets	
1 Troy Aikman	30.00
2 Emmitt Smith	45.00
3 Terrell Davis	45.00
4 John Elway	30.00
5 Barry Sanders	60.00
6 Brett Favre	60.00
7 Mark Brunell	20.00
8 Dan Marino	45.00
9 Drew Bledsoe	25.00
10 Jerry Rice	30.00

1998 Pacific Crown Royale Master Performers

Master Performers includes the top 20 players from the NFL and was inserted 2:25 hobby packs.

	MT
Complete Set (20):	120.00
Common Player:	2.00
Inserted 2:25 Hobby	
1 Corey Dillon	2.00
2 Troy Aikman	7.00
3 Emmitt Smith	10.00
4 Terrell Davis	10.00
5 John Elway	7.00
6 Charlie Batch	8.00
7 Barry Sanders	14.00
8 Brett Favre	14.00
9 Peyton Manning	14.00
10 Mark Brunell	5.00
11 Fred Taylor	6.00
12 Dan Marino	10.00
13 Randy Moss	25.00
14 Drew Bledsoe	5.00
15 Curtis Martin	4.00
16 Kordell Stewart	5.00
17 Ryan Leaf	6.00
18 Jerry Rice	7.00
19 Steve Young	5.00
20 Warrick Dunn	5.00

1998 Pacific Crown Royale Pillars of the Game

These holographic gold foil cards served as the bottom card in every pack and featured a strong mix of NFL mainstays and rising stars. These could only be found in hobby packs.

	MT
Complete Set (25):	45.00
Common Player:	.50
Inserted 1:1 Hobby	
1 Antowain Smith	.50
2 Corey Dillon	1.00
3 Troy Aikman	1.50
4 Emmitt Smith	2.00
5 Terrell Davis	2.00
6 John Elway	1.50
7 Charlie Batch	4.00
8 Barry Sanders	3.00
9 Brett Favre	3.00
10 Antonio Freeman	1.00
11 Peyton Manning	6.00
12 Mark Brunell	1.25
13 Dan Marino	2.00
14 Randy Moss	14.00
15 Drew Bledsoe	1.25
16 Curtis Martin	1.00
17 Napoleon Kaufman	1.00
18 Jerome Bettis	1.00
19 Kordell Stewart	1.25
20 Ryan Leaf	4.00
21 Jerry Rice	1.50
22 Steve Young	1.00
23 Ricky Watters	.50
24 Eddie George	1.25
25 Warrick Dunn	1.25

1998 Pacific Crown Royale Pivotal Players

This 25-card holographic silver foil insert featured some of football's most dynamic superstars along with several top rookies from 1998. Singles were found one-per-pack in hobby packs only.

	MT
Complete Set (25):	30.00
Common Player:	.50
Inserted 1:1 Hobby	
1 Jake Plummer	1.00
2 Antowain Smith	.50
3 Corey Dillon	.75
4 Troy Aikman	1.50
5 Deion Sanders	.50
6 Emmitt Smith	2.00
7 Terrell Davis	2.00
8 John Elway	1.50
9 Charlie Batch	4.00
10 Barry Sanders	3.00
11 Brett Favre	3.00
12 Peyton Manning	6.00
13 Mark Brunell	1.00
14 Fred Taylor	3.00
15 Dan Marino	2.00
16 Randy Moss	14.00
17 Drew Bledsoe	1.25
18 Curtis Martin	.75
19 Napoleon Kaufman	.50
20 Jerome Bettis	.50
21 Kordell Stewart	1.25
22 Ryan Leaf	4.00
23 Jerry Rice	1.50
24 Eddie George	1.25
25 Warrick Dunn	1.00

1998 Pacific Crown Royale Rookie Paydirt

The fully foiled and etched Rookie Paydirt set gave collectors an early look at the top 20 rookies from 1998. Singles were inserted into hobby packs at a ratio of 1:25.

	MT
Complete Set (20):	175.00
Common Player:	3.00
Inserted 1:25 Hobby	
1 Curtis Enis	8.00
2 Marcus Nash	6.00
3 Charlie Batch	15.00
4 Vonnie Holliday	4.00
5 E.G. Green	3.00
6 Peyton Manning	30.00
7 Jerome Pathon	3.00
8 Tavian Banks	6.00
9 Fred Taylor	15.00
10 Rashaan Shehee	3.00
11 John Avery	6.00
12 Randy Moss	60.00
13 Robert Edwards	10.00
14 Charles Woodson	8.00
15 Hines Ward	5.00
16 Ryan Leaf	12.00
17 Mikhael Ricks	4.00
18 Ahman Green	6.00
19 Jacquez Green	8.00
20 Kevin Dyson	8.00

1998 Playoff Contenders Leather

Leather cards are one of three base sets found in Contenders. Each Leather card is printed on actual leather with three different foil stamps and are found one-per-pack. The 100-card set includes 70 veterans and 30 rookies from 1998. The parallel Red set has the players last name in red foil. Singles from this insert were found 1:9 hobby packs.

	MT
Complete Set (100):	225.00
Common Player:	.50
Common Rookie:	1.00
Inserted 1:1	
Red Cards:	3x
Red Rookies:	2x
Inserted 1:9	
Wax Box:	100.00
1 Adrian Murrell	.50
2 Michael Pittman	2.00
3 Jake Plummer	5.00
4 Andre Wadsworth	3.00
5 Jamal Anderson	2.00
6 Chris Chandler	1.00
7 Tim Dwight	6.00
8 Patrick Johnson	3.00
9 Jermaine Lewis	.50
10 Doug Flutie	3.00
11 Antowain Smith	2.00
12 Muhsin Muhammad	.50
13 Bobby Engram	.50
14 Curtis Enis	7.00
15 Alonzo Mayes	1.00
16 Corey Dillon	3.00
17 Carl Pickens	1.00
18 Troy Aikman	5.00
19 Michael Irvin	2.00
20 Deion Sanders	2.00
21 Emmitt Smith	7.00
22 Terrell Davis	8.00
23 John Elway	6.00
24 Brian Griese	8.00
25 Rod Smith	1.00
26 Charlie Batch	12.00
27 Germane Crowell	4.00
28 Terry Fair	3.00
29 Herman Moore	1.00
30 Barry Sanders	10.00
31 Brett Favre	10.00
32 Antonio Freeman	1.50
33 Vonnie Holliday	3.00
34 Reggie White	1.50
35 Marshall Faulk	1.50
36 Marvin Harrison	1.00
37 Peyton Manning	20.00
38 Jerome Pathon	3.00
39 Tavian Banks	3.00
40 Mark Brunell	4.00
41 Keenan McCardell	1.00
42 Fred Taylor	18.00
43 Elvis Grbac	.50
44 Andre Rison	1.00
45 Rashaan Shehee	2.00
46 Karim Abdul-Jabbar	1.00
47 John Avery	4.00
48 Dan Marino	7.00
49 O.J. McDuffie	1.00
50 Cris Carter	1.50
51 Brad Johnson	1.50
52 Randy Moss	40.00
53 Robert Smith	1.50
54 Drew Bledsoe	4.00
55 Ben Coates	1.00
56 Robert Edwards	7.00
57 Chris Floyd	2.00
58 Terry Glenn	1.50
59 Cameron Cleeland	4.00
60 Kerry Collins	1.00
61 Danny Kanell	.50
62 Charles Way	.50
63 Glenn Foley	1.00
64 Keyshawn Johnson	1.50
65 Curtis Martin	1.50
66 Tim Brown	1.00
67 Jeff George	1.00
68 Napoleon Kaufman	1.50
69 Charles Woodson	7.00
70 Irving Fryar	.50
71 Bobby Hoying	1.00
72 Jerome Bettis	1.00
73 Kordell Stewart	4.00
74 Hines Ward	3.00
75 Ryan Leaf	10.00
76 Natrone Means	1.00
77 Mikhael Ricks	3.00
78 Junior Seau	1.00
79 Garrison Hearst	1.00
80 Terrell Owens	1.50
81 Jerry Rice	5.00
82 Steve Young	3.00
83 Joey Galloway	1.50
84 Ahman Green	3.00
85 Warren Moon	1.00
86 Ricky Watters	1.00
87 Tony Banks	1.00
88 Isaac Bruce	1.00
89 Robert Holcombe	3.00
90 Mike Alstott	1.50
91 Trent Dilfer	1.00
92 Warrick Dunn	4.00
93 Jacquez Green	4.00
94 Kevin Dyson	4.00
95 Eddie George	4.00
96 Steve McNair	2.00
97 Yancey Thigpen	.50
98 Terry Allen	1.00
99 Skip Hicks	4.00
100 Michael Westbrook	.50

1998 Playoff Contenders Leather Gold

This insert parallel's the Leather set but each single is sequentially numbered to a player's featured stat. The cards look identical to the base Leather card except for the player's last name is in gold foil and the numbering is stamped on the back.

	MT
Common Player:	10.00
1 Adrian Murrell/27	30.00
2 Michael Pittman/32	30.00
3 Jake Plummer/53	100.00
4 Andre Wadsworth/29	50.00
5 Jamal Anderson/29	75.00
6 Chris Chandler/94	20.00
7 Tim Dwight/39	75.00
8 Patrick Johnson/55	20.00
9 Jermaine Lewis/42	20.00
10 Doug Flutie/38	75.00
11 Antowain Smith/28	75.00
12 Muhsin Muhammad/52	20.00
13 Bobby Engram/78	10.00
14 Curtis Enis/36	75.00
15 Alonzo Mayes/92	10.00
16 Corey Dillon/27	100.00
17 Carl Pickens/52	25.00
18 Troy Aikman/62	100.00
19 Michael Irvin/61	30.00
20 Deion Sanders/36	50.00

21	Emmitt Smith/40	200.00
22	Terrell Davis/35	275.00
23	John Elway/27	250.00
24	Brian Griese/33	125.00
25	Rod Smith/70	20.00
26	Charlie Batch/23	150.00
27	Germane Crowell/53	35.00
28	Terry Fair/42	30.00
29	Herman Moore/52	30.00
30	Barry Sanders/33	300.00
31	Brett Favre/35	300.00
32	Antonio Freeman/58	50.00
33	Vonnie Holliday/64	30.00
34	Reggie White/36	75.00
35	Marshall Faulk/47	50.00
36	Marvin Harrison/73	20.00
37	Peyton Manning/36	250.00
38	Jerome Pathon/69	20.00
39	Tavian Banks/33	45.00
40	Mark Brunell/52	85.00
41	Keenan McCardell/85	10.00
42	Fred Taylor/31	225.00
43	Elvis Grbac/29	35.00
44	Andre Rison/72	10.00
45	Rashaan Shehee/72	20.00
46	Karim Abdul-Jabbar/44	60.00
47	John Avery/26	60.00
48	Dan Marino/16	500.00
49	O.J. McDuffie/35	30.00
50	Cris Carter/89	20.00
51	Brad Johnson/37	50.00
52	Randy Moss/25	650.00
53	Robert Smith/90	20.00
54	Drew Bledsoe/28	175.00
55	Ben Coates/42	30.00
56	Robert Edwards/27	100.00
57	Chris Floyd/63	10.00
58	Terry Glenn/50	40.00
59	Cameron Cleeland/50	30.00
60	Kerry Collins/39	30.00
61	Danny Kanell/53	20.00
62	Charles Way/76	10.00
63	Glenn Foley/56	20.00
64	Keyshawn Johnson/70	25.00
65	Curtis Martin/41	40.00
66	Tim Brown/60	30.00
67	Jeff George/29	40.00
68	Napoleon Kaufman/40	50.00
69	Charles Woodson/27	120.00
70	Irving Fryar/75	10.00
71	Bobby Hoying/53	20.00
72	Jerome Bettis/31	65.00
73	Kordell Stewart/22	150.00
74	Hines Ward/55	30.00
75	Ryan Leaf/33	125.00
76	Natrone Means/78	20.00
77	Mikhael Ricks/47	25.00
78	Junior Seau/33	40.00
79	Garrison Hearst/74	25.00
80	Terrell Owens/60	35.00
81	Jerry Rice/16	325.00
82	Steve Young/19	175.00
83	Joey Galloway/72	25.00
84	Ahman Green/42	40.00
85	Warren Moon/25	85.00
86	Ricky Watters/56	25.00
87	Tony Banks/51	20.00
88	Isaac Bruce/56	30.00
89	Robert Holcombe/35	45.00
90	Mike Alstott/88	25.00
91	Trent Dilfer/38	45.00
92	Warrick Dunn/39	75.00
93	Jacquez Green/61	30.00
94	Kevin Dyson/60	30.00
95	Eddie George/30	150.00
96	Steve McNair/52	45.00
97	Yancey Thigpen/79	10.00
98	Terry Allen/58	30.00
99	Skip Hicks/48	45.00
100	Michael Westbrook/45	20.00

1998 Playoff Contenders Pennant

Pennant singles are printed on conventional stock with felt-like flocking and foil stamping. The 100-card set includes 70 veterans and 30 rookies from 1998. Pennant cards are found one-per-pack. Each player in the set has six different cards with each having a different color felt. The parallel Red singles are the same as the base except for the foil on the card is red. Singles are found 1:9 packs. The parallel Gold cards are in gold foil and are sequentially numbered to 98.

		MT
Complete Set (100):		225.00
Common Player:		.50
Common Rookie:		1.00
Each Card Issued In Six Colors		
Inserted 1:1		
Red Cards:		3x
Red Rookies:		2x
Inserted 1:9		
Gold Cards:		6x-12x
Gold Rookies:		4x-8x
Production 98 Sets		
1	Jake Plummer	5.00
2	Frank Sanders	.50
3	Jamal Anderson	2.00
4	Tim Dwight	6.00
5	Jammi German	2.00
6	Tony Martin	1.00
7	Jim Harbaugh	1.00
8	Rod Woodson	.50
9	Rob Johnson	1.00
10	Eric Moulds	1.50
11	Antowain Smith	1.50
12	Steve Beuerlein	.50
13	Fred Lane	1.00
14	Curtis Enis	5.00
15	Corey Dillon	3.00
16	Neil O'Donnell	.50
17	Carl Pickens	1.00
18	Darnay Scott	.50
19	Takeo Spikes	2.00
20	Troy Aikman	5.00
21	Michael Irvin	1.00
22	Deion Sanders	1.50
23	Emmitt Smith	7.00
24	Chris Warren	.50
25	Terrell Davis	8.00
26	John Elway	6.00
27	Brian Griese	6.00
28	Ed McCaffrey	1.50
29	Marcus Nash	3.00
30	Shannon Sharpe	1.00
31	Rod Smith	1.00
32	Charlie Batch	10.00
33	Germane Crowell	3.00
34	Herman Moore	1.00
35	Barry Sanders	10.00
36	Mark Chmura	1.00
37	Brett Favre	10.00
38	Antonio Freeman	1.50
39	Reggie White	1.00
40	Marshall Faulk	1.50
41	E.G. Green	2.50
42	Peyton Manning	15.00
43	Jerome Pathon	2.00
44	Mark Brunell	4.00
45	Jonathan Quinn	2.00
46	Fred Taylor	12.00
47	Tony Gonzalez	.50
48	Andre Rison	1.00
49	Karim Abdul-Jabbar	1.00
50	John Avery	3.00
51	Dan Marino	7.00
52	Cris Carter	1.50
53	Randall Cunningham	1.50
54	Brad Johnson	1.50
55	Randy Moss	30.00
56	Robert Smith	1.00
57	Drew Bledsoe	4.00
58	Robert Edwards	5.00
59	Terry Glenn	1.50
60	Tony Simmons	2.50
61	Tiki Barber	1.00
62	Joe Jurevicius	2.00
63	Danny Kanell	.50
64	Keyshawn Johnson	1.50
65	Curtis Martin	1.50
66	Vinny Testaverde	1.00
67	Tim Brown	1.00
68	Jeff George	1.00
69	Napoleon Kaufman	1.50
70	Jon Ritchie	2.00
71	Charles Woodson	5.00
72	Irving Fryar	.50
73	Duce Staley	1.00
74	Jerome Bettis	1.50
75	Chris Fuamatu-Ma'afala	2.00
76	Kordell Stewart	4.00
77	Hines Ward	2.50
78	Ryan Leaf	8.00
79	Natrone Means	1.50
80	Mikhael Ricks	2.00
81	Garrison Hearst	1.50
82	R.W. McQuarters	2.00
83	Jerry Rice	5.00
84	J.J. Stokes	1.00
85	Steve Young	3.00
86	Joey Galloway	1.50
87	Ahman Green	3.00
88	Warren Moon	1.00
89	Ricky Watters	1.00
90	Isaac Bruce	1.00
91	Robert Holcombe	2.50
92	Mike Alstott	1.50
93	Trent Dilfer	1.00
94	Warrick Dunn	3.00
95	Jacquez Green	3.00
96	Kevin Dyson	3.00
97	Eddie George	4.00
98	Steve McNair	2.00
99	Terry Allen	1.00
100	Skip Hicks	3.00

1998 Playoff Contenders Ticket

The 99-card Ticket set is made up 80 veterans and 19 rookies and was inserted one-per-pack. Each Ticket card was printed on conventional stock with foil stamping and has a ticket design to it. All of the rookie cards in this set are autographed. The quantities vary from player to player depending on how many they signed. A parallel Red and Gold insert was also produced. Red's were found 1:9 hobby packs and the Gold's were sequentially numbered to 25. The name on the fronts will either be in red or gold depending on which single you have.

		MT
Complete Set (99):		900.00
Common Player:		.50
Common Rookie Autograph:		25.00
Inserted 1:1		
Red Cards:		3x
Red Rookies: .		2x
Inserted 1:9		
Gold Cards:		35x-70x
Gold Rookies:		2x
Production 25 Sets		
1	Rob Moore	1.00
2	Jake Plummer	4.00
3	Jamal Anderson	1.50
4	Terance Mathis	.50
5	Priest Holmes	6.00
6	Michael Jackson	.50
7	Eric Zeier	.50
8	Andre Reed	.50
9	Antowain Smith	1.50
10	Bruce Smith	.50
11	Thurman Thomas	1.00
12	Raghib Ismail	.50
13	Wesley Walls	.50
14	Curtis Conway	1.00
15	Jeff Blake	1.00
16	Corey Dillon	2.00
17	Carl Pickens	1.00
18	Troy Aikman	5.00
19	Michael Irvin	1.00
20	Ernie Mills	.50
21	Deion Sanders	1.50
22	Emmitt Smith	7.00
23	Terrell Davis	8.00
24	John Elway	6.00
25	Neil Smith	.50
26	Rod Smith	1.00
27	Herman Moore	1.00
28	Johnnie Morton	.50
29	Barry Sanders	10.00
30	Robert Brooks	.50
31	Brett Favre	10.00
32	Antonio Freeman	1.50
33	Dorsey Levens	1.00
34	Reggie White	1.00
35	Marshall Faulk	1.50
36	Mark Brunell	4.00
37	Jimmy Smith	1.00
38	James Stewart	.50
39	Donnell Bennett	.50
40	Andre Rison	1.00
41	Derrick Thomas	1.00
42	Karim Abdul-Jabbar	1.00
43	Dan Marino	7.00
44	Cris Carter	1.50
45	Brad Johnson	1.50
46	Robert Smith	1.00
47	Drew Bledsoe	4.00
48	Terry Glenn	1.50
49	Lamar Smith	.50
50	Ike Hilliard	.50
51	Danny Kanell	.50
52	Wayne Chrebet	1.50
53	Keyshawn Johnson	1.50
54	Curtis Martin	1.50
55	Tim Brown	1.00
56	Rickey Dudley	.50
57	Jeff George	1.00
58	Napoleon Kaufman	1.50
59	Irving Fryar	.50
60	Jerome Bettis	1.50
61	Charles Johnson	.50
62	Kordell Stewart	4.00
63	Natrone Means	1.00
64	Bryan Still	.50
65	Garrison Hearst	1.50
66	Jerry Rice	5.00
67	Steve Young	3.00
68	Joey Galloway	1.50
69	Warren Moon	1.00
70	Ricky Watters	1.00
71	Isaac Bruce	1.00
72	Mike Alstott	1.50
73	Reidel Anthony	1.00
74	Trent Dilfer	1.00
75	Warrick Dunn	3.00
76	Warren Sapp	.50
77	Eddie George	4.00
78	Steve McNair	2.00
79	Terry Allen	1.00
80	Gus Frerotte	.50
81	Andre Wadsworth AUTO	25.00
82	Tim Dwight AUTO	50.00
83	Curtis Enis AUTO	50.00
85	Charlie Batch AUTO	85.00
86	Germane Crowell AUTO	40.00
87	Peyton Manning AUTO	200.00
88	Jerome Pathon AUTO	25.00
89	Fred Taylor AUTO	150.00
90	Tavian Banks AUTO	30.00
92	Randy Moss AUTO	300.00
93	Robert Edwards AUTO	35.00
94	Hines Ward AUTO	30.00
95	Ryan Leaf AUTO	50.00
96	Mikhael Ricks AUTO	25.00
97	Ahman Green AUTO	30.00
98	Jacquez Green AUTO	35.00
99	Kevin Dyson AUTO	45.00
100	Skip Hicks AUTO	35.00
103	Chris Fuamatu-Ma'afala AUTO	25.00

1998 Playoff Contenders Checklist

Each card in this 30-card set displays the top star from each club on the front and a checklist of each player from that team featured in our three base sets on the back. Each card measures 3" x 5" and was found one-per-box.

		MT
Complete Set (30):		150.00
Common Player:		2.50
Inserted 1:Box		
1	Jake Plummer	8.00
2	Jamal Anderson	5.00
3	Jermaine Lewis	2.50
4	Antowain Smith	5.00
5	Muhsin Muhammad	2.50
6	Curtis Enis	5.00
7	Corey Dillon	6.00
8	Deion Sanders	5.00
9	Terrell Davis	18.00
10	Barry Sanders	20.00
11	Brett Favre	20.00
12	Peyton Manning	15.00
13	Mark Brunell	8.00
14	Andre Rison	2.50
15	Dan Marino	15.00
16	Randy Moss	30.00
17	Drew Bledsoe	8.00
18	Kerry Collins	5.00
19	Danny Kanell	2.50
20	Curtis Martin	5.00
21	Tim Brown	2.50
22	Irving Fryar	2.50
23	Kordell Stewart	8.00
24	Natrone Means	5.00
25	Steve Young	6.00
26	Isaac Bruce	5.00
27	Warren Moon	5.00
28	Warrick Dunn	8.00
29	Eddie George	8.00
30	Terry Allen	5.00

1998 Playoff Contenders Honors

This is an insert that began with 1996 Playoff Prime and has continued throughout Playoff products over the past three years. Cards 19-21 can be found in this insert and are found 1:3,241 hobby packs.

		MT
Complete Set (3):		500.00
Common Player:		100.00
Inserted 1:3,241 Hobby		
19	Dan Marino	275.00
20	Jerry Rice	175.00
21	Mark Brunell	100.00

1998 Playoff Contenders MVP Contenders

This set showcases the players who are in contention for the league MVP. Each card is printed on holographic stock with an MVP graphic stamped in gold foil. Singles were inserted 1:19 hobby packs.

		MT
Complete Set (36):		160.00
Common Player:		4.00
Inserted 1:19		
1	Terrell Davis	18.00
2	Jerry Rice	10.00
3	Jerome Bettis	4.00
4	Brett Favre	20.00
5	Natrone Means	4.00
6	Steve Young	6.00
7	John Elway	12.00
8	Troy Aikman	10.00
9	Steve McNair	4.00
10	Kordell Stewart	8.00
11	Drew Bledsoe	8.00
12	Tim Brown	4.00
13	Dan Marino	15.00
14	Mark Brunell	8.00
15	Marshall Faulk	4.00
16	Jake Plummer	8.00
17	Corey Dillon	6.00
18	Carl Pickens	4.00
19	Keyshawn Johnson	4.00
20	Barry Sanders	20.00
21	Deion Sanders	4.00
22	Emmitt Smith	15.00
23	Antowain Smith	4.00
24	Curtis Martin	4.00
25	Cris Carter	4.00
26	Napoleon Kaufman	4.00
27	Eddie George	8.00
28	Warrick Dunn	8.00
29	Antonio Freeman	4.00
30	Joey Galloway	4.00
31	Herman Moore	4.00
32	Jamal Anderson	6.00
33	Terry Glenn	4.00
34	Garrison Hearst	4.00
35	Robert Smith	4.00
36	Mike Alstott	4.00

1998 Playoff Contenders Rookie of the Year

Playoff included the top 12 rookies from '98 who were battling for the rookie of the year award. Each card is printed on a wood-grain finish with two types of foil stamping. Singles were inserted 1:55 hobby packs.

		MT
Complete Set (12):		160.00
Common Player:		7.00
Inserted 1:55		
1	Tim Dwight	10.00
2	Curtis Enis	10.00
3	Charlie Batch	20.00
4	Peyton Manning	30.00
5	Fred Taylor	25.00
6	John Avery	7.00
7	Randy Moss	60.00
8	Robert Edwards	10.00
9	Charles Woodson	10.00
10	Ryan Leaf	12.00
11	Jacquez Green	7.00
12	Kevin Dyson	7.00

1998 Playoff Contenders Rookie Stallions

Only the top NFL draftees were featured in this 18-card set. Each card was printed on all micro-etched foil stock with silver foil stamping. Singles were inserted 1:19 hobby packs.

		MT
Complete Set (18):		100.00
Common Player:		2.50
Inserted 1:19		
1	Tim Dwight	6.00
2	Curtis Enis	6.00
3	Brian Griese	8.00
4	Charlie Batch	12.00
5	Germane Crowell	5.00
6	Peyton Manning	20.00
7	Tavian Banks	5.00
8	Fred Taylor	18.00
9	Rashaan Shehee	2.50
10	John Avery	5.00
11	Randy Moss	40.00
12	Robert Edwards	6.00
13	Charles Woodson	7.00
14	Ryan Leaf	10.00
15	Ahman Green	5.00
16	Jacquez Green	5.00
17	Kevin Dyson	5.00
18	Skip Hicks	5.00

1998 Playoff Contenders Super Bowl Leather

Each card in this set highlights a piece of an actual game-used football from Super Bowl XXXII. Each card back features a replica of the letter from the NFL verifying the authenticity of the ball. Cards are printed on conventional stock with foil stamping and were inserted 1:2,401 hobby packs.

		MT
Complete Set (6):		1000.
Common Player:		75.00
Inserted 1:2,401		
1	Brett Favre	350.00
2	John Elway	275.00
3	Robert Brooks	75.00
4	Rod Smith	100.00
5	Antonio Freeman	125.00
6	Terrell Davis	300.00

1998 Playoff Contenders Touchdown Tandems

Two teammates from over 20 NFL franchises were paired on the front of each card in this debut insert set. These cards, printed on holographic foil stock with foil stamping, show the players known for carrying the scoring load for their respective clubs. Singles were found 1:19 hobby packs.

		MT
Complete Set (24):		150.00
Common Player:		4.00
Inserted 1:19		
1	Brett Favre, Antonio Freeman	20.00
2	Dan Marino, Karim Abdul-Jabbar	15.00
3	Emmitt Smith, Troy Aikman	15.00
4	Barry Sanders, Herman Moore	20.00
5	Eddie George, Steve McNair	8.00
6	Robert Edwards, Drew Bledsoe	8.00
7	Terrell Davis, Rod Smith	15.00
8	Mark Brunell, Fred Taylor	12.00
9	Jerry Rice, Steve Young	10.00
10	Jerome Bettis, Kordell Stewart	8.00
11	Curtis Martin, Keyshawn Johnson	4.00
12	Mike Alstott, Warrick Dunn	6.00
13	Isaac Bruce, Tony Banks	4.00
14	Adrian Murrell, Jake Plummer	8.00
15	Tim Brown, Napoleon Kaufman	4.00
16	Cris Carter, Randy Moss	30.00
17	Joey Galloway, Ricky Watters	4.00
18	Peyton Manning, Marshall Faulk	15.00
19	Ryan Leaf, Natrone Means	8.00
20	Carl Pickens, Corey Dillon	4.00
21	Doug Flutie, Antowain Smith	6.00
22	Randall Cunningham, Robert Smith	4.00
23	Chris Chandler, Jamal Anderson	5.00
24	John Elway, Ed McCaffrey	12.00

1998 Playoff Momentum Hobby

Each card in this 250-card set was printed on premium doublesided metalized mylar with double micro-etching on both sides. The shortprinted Rookie subset included 48 rising NFL stars and were inserted 1:6 packs. Each card also has a Red and Gold parallel version. The Reds were inserted 1:4 hobby packs while the Golds were sequentially numbered to 25.

		MT
Complete Set (250):		750.00
Common Player:		.30
Common Rookie:		4.00
Inserted 1:6		
Red Cards:		2x-4x
Red Rookies:		1.2x
Inserted 1:4		
Gold Cards:		50x-100x
Gold Rookies:		3x-6x
Production 25 Sets		
Wax Box:		85.00
1	Jake Plummer	3.00
2	Eric Metcalf	.30
3	Adrian Murrell	.30
4	Larry Centers	.30
5	Frank Sanders	.30
6	Rob Moore	.60
7	*Andre Wadsworth*	8.00
8	Chris Chandler	.60
9	Jamal Anderson	1.00
10	Tony Martin	.30
11	Terrance Mathis	.30
12	*Tim Dwight*	15.00
13	*Jammi German*	8.00
14	O.J. Santiago	.30
15	Jim Harbaugh	.60
16	Eric Zeier	.30
17	*Duane Starks*	8.00
18	Rod Woodson	.30
19	Errict Rhett	.30
20	Jay Graham	.30
21	Ray Lewis	.30
22	Michael Jackson	.30
23	Jermaine Lewis	.30
24	*Patrick Johnson*	4.00
25	Eric Green	.30
26	Doug Flutie	3.00
27	Rob Johnson	.60
28	Antowain Smith	2.00
29	Thurman Thomas	.60
30	*Jonathon Linton*	4.00
31	Bruce Smith	.30
32	Eric Moulds	.60
33	Kevin Williams	.30
34	Andre Reed	.30
35	Steve Beurlein	.30
36	Kerry Collins	.60
37	Anthony Johnson	.30
38	Fred Lane	.60
39	William Floyd	.30
40	Raghib Ismail	.30
41	Wesley Walls	.30
42	Muhsin Muhammad	.30
43	Rae Carruth	.30
44	Kevin Greene	.30
45	Greg Lloyd	.30
46	*Moses Moreno*	8.00
47	Erik Kramer	.30
48	Edgar Bennett	.30
49	*Curtis Enis*	30.00
50	Curtis Conway	.60
51	Bobby Engram	.30
52	*Alonzo Mayes*	4.00
53	Jeff Blake	.60
54	Neil O'Donnell	.30
55	Corey Dillon	3.00
56	*Takeo Spikes*	4.00
57	Carl Pickens	.60
58	Tony McGee	.30
59	Darnay Scott	.30
60	Troy Aikman	4.00
61	Deion Sanders	1.00
62	Emmitt Smith	6.00
63	Darren Woodson	.30
64	Chris Warren	.30
65	Daryl Johnston	.30
66	Ernie Mills	.30
67	Billy Davis	.30
68	Michael Irvin	.60
69	David LaFleur	.30
70	John Elway	4.00
71	*Brian Griese*	30.00
72	Steve Atwater	.30
73	Terrell Davis	6.00
74	Rod Smith	.60
75	*Marcus Nash*	25.00
76	Shannon Sharpe	.60
77	Ed McCaffrey	.60
78	Neil Smith	.30
79	*Charlie Batch*	60.00
80	*Germane Crowell*	25.00
81	Scott Mitchell	.60
82	Barry Sanders	8.00
83	*Terry Fair*	8.00
84	Herman Moore	1.00
85	Johnnie Morton	.30
86	Brett Favre	8.00
87	Rick Mirer	.30
88	Dorsey Levens	.60
89	William Henderson	.30
90	Derrick Mayes	.30
91	Antonio Freeman	1.00
92	Robert Brooks	.30
93	Mark Chmura	.30
94	*Vonnie Holliday*	8.00
95	Reggie White	1.00
96	*E.G. Green*	8.00
97	*Jerome Pathon*	8.00
98	*Peyton Manning*	70.00
99	Marshall Faulk	1.00
100	Zack Crockett	.30
101	Ken Dilger	.30
102	Marvin Harrison	.60
103	Mark Brunell	3.00
104	*Jonathan Quinn*	8.00
105	*Tavian Banks*	20.00
106	*Fred Taylor*	60.00
107	James Stewart	.30
108	Jimmy Smith	.60
109	Keenan McCardell	.30
110	Elvis Grbac	.30
111	Rich Gannon	.30
112	*Rashaan Shehee*	8.00
113	Donnell Bennett	.30
114	Kimble Anders	.30
115	Derrick Thomas	.30
116	Kevin Lockett	.30
117	Derrick Alexander	.30
118	Tony Gonzalez	.60
119	Andre Rison	.30
120	Craig Erickson	.30
121	Dan Marino	6.00
122	*John Avery*	25.00
123	Karim Abdul-Jabbar	.60
124	Zach Thomas	.60
125	O.J. McDuffie	.30
126	Troy Drayton	.30
127	Randall Cunningham	1.00
128	Brad Johnson	.60
129	Robert Smith	.60
130	Cris Carter	1.00
131	*Randy Moss*	100.00
132	Jake Reed	.30
133	John Randle	.30
134	Drew Bledsoe	3.00
135	*Tony Simmons*	15.00
136	Sedrick Shaw	.30
137	*Chris Floyd*	4.00
138	*Robert Edwards*	25.00
139	*Rod Rutledge*	4.00
140	Shawn Jefferson	.30
141	Ben Coates	.60
142	Terry Glenn	.60
143	Heath Shuler	.30
144	Danny Wuerffel	.30
145	Troy Davis	.30
146	Qadry Ismail	.30
147	Ray Zellars	.30
148	Lamar Smith	.30
149	*Cameron Cleeland*	12.00
150	Sean Dawkins	.30
151	Andre Hastings	.30
152	Danny Kanell	.30
153	Tiki Barber	.60
154	Tyrone Wheatley	.30
155	Charles Way	.30
156	Gary Brown	.30
157	*Shaun Williams*	4.00
158	Chris Calloway	.30
159	Amani Toomer	.30
160	*Brian Alford*	4.00
161	*Joe Jurevicius*	8.00
162	Ike Hilliard	.30
163	Michael Strahan	.30
164	Glenn Foley	.60
165	Vinny Testaverde	.60
166	Keyshawn Johnson	.60
167	Curtis Martin	1.00
168	Leon Johnson	.30
169	Keith Byars	.30
170	Wayne Chrebet	.60
171	Kyle Brady	.30
172	Dedric Ward	.30
173	Jeff George	.60
174	*Charles Woodson*	30.00
175	Napoleon Kaufman	1.00
176	*Jon Ritchie*	4.00
177	Tim Brown	.60
178	James Jett	.30
179	Rickey Dudley	.30
180	Bobby Hoying	.30
181	Duce Staley	.30
182	Charlie Garner	.30
183	Irvin Fryar	.30
184	Jeff Graham	.30
185	Jason Dunn	.30
186	Kordell Stewart	3.00
187	Jerome Bettis	1.00
188	Andre Coleman	.30
189	*Chris Fuamatu-Ma'afala*	10.00
190	Charles Johnson	.30
191	*Hines Ward*	20.00
192	Mark Bruener	.30
193	Courtney Hawkins	.30
194	Will Blackwell	.30
195	Levon Kirkland	.30
196	*Mikhael Ricks*	15.00
197	*Ryan Leaf*	35.00
198	Natrone Means	.60
199	Junior Seau	.60
200	Bryan Still	.30
201	Freddie Jones	.30
202	Steve Young	2.00
203	Jim Druckenmiller	1.00
204	Garrison Hearst	.60
205	*R.W. McQuarters*	8.00
206	Merton Hanks	.30
207	Marc Edwards	.30
208	Jerry Rice	4.00
209	Terrell Owens	1.50
210	J.J. Stokes	.30
211	Tony Banks	.60
212	*Robert Holcombe*	20.00
213	Greg Hill	.30
214	Amp Lee	.30
215	Jerald Moore	.30
216	Isaac Bruce	.60
217	*Az-Zahir Hakim*	12.00
218	Eddie Kennison	.30
219	*Grant Wistrom*	4.00
220	Warren Moon	.60
221	*Ahman Green*	20.00
222	Steve Broussard	.30
223	Ricky Watters	.60
224	James McKnight	.30
225	Joey Galloway	1.00
226	Mike Pritchard	.30
227	Trent Dilfer	.60
228	Warrick Dunn	3.00
229	Mike Alstott	1.00
230	John Lynch	.30
231	*Jacquez Green*	25.00
232	Reidel Anthony	.60
233	Bert Emanuel	.30
234	Warren Sapp	.30
235	Steve McNair	1.50
236	Eddie George	3.00
237	Chris Sanders	.30
238	Yancey Thigpen	.30
239	Willie Davis	.30
240	*Kevin Dyson*	25.00
241	Frank Wycheck	.30
242	Trent Green	.60
243	Gus Frerotte	.30
244	*Skip Hicks*	25.00
245	Terry Allen	.30
246	Stephen Davis	.30
247	*Stephen Alexander*	4.00
248	Michael Westbrook	.60
249	Dana Stubblefield	.30
250	Dan Wilkinson	.30

1998 Playoff Momentum Hobby Class Reunion Quads

Each card in this set includes stars from every draft class since the famous one in 1983. Four players drafted in the same year appear on each card (two on the front, two on the back). Cards are printed on doublesided mirror foil stock with micro-etching on each side as well as gold foil stamping. Singles were inserted 1:81 hobby packs.

		MT
Complete Set (16):		700.00
Common Player:		20.00
Inserted 1:81		
1	1983 Dan Marino, John Elway, Bruce Matthews, Darrell Green	75.00
2	1984 Steve Young, Irving Fryar, Reggie White, Jeff Hostetler	35.00
3	1985 Jerry Rice, Bruce Smith, Andre Reed, Doug Flutie	50.00
4	1986 Keith Byars, Leslie O'Neal, Seth Joyner, Ray Brown	20.00
5	1987 Cris Carter, Vinny Testaverde, Jim Harbaugh, Rod Woodson	20.00
6	1988 Tim Brown, Chris Chandler, Michael Irvin, Neil Smith	20.00
7	1989 Troy Aikman, Barry Sanders, Deion Sanders, Andre Rison	100.00
8	1990 Emmitt Smith, Jeff George, Neil O'Donnell, Shannon Sharpe	75.00
9	1991 Brett Favre, Herman Moore, Yancey Thigpen, Ricky Watters	100.00
10	1992 Mark Chmura, Brad Johnson, Carl Pickens, Robert Brooks	20.00
11	1993 Drew Bledsoe, Jerome Bettis, Mark Brunell, Garrison Hearst	40.00
12	1994 Trent Dilfer, Dorsey Levens, Marshall Faulk, Isaac Bruce	25.00
13	1995 Terrell Davis, Kordell Stewart, Napoleon Kaufman, Curtis Martin	75.00
14	1996 Eddie George, Keyshawn Johnson, Karim Abdul-Jabbar, Terry Glenn	40.00
15	1997 Warrick Dunn, Corey Dillon, Jake Plummer, Antowain Smith	40.00
16	1998 Peyton Manning, Ryan Leaf, Curtis Enis, Randy Moss	125.00

1998 Playoff Momentum Hobby EndZone Xpress

This 29-card set spotlights the NFL's best who have a knack for getting into the end zone. Each card is printed on die-cut clear plastic with holographic foil stamping. Singles were found 1:9 hobby packs.

		MT
Complete Set (29):		250.00
Common Player:		2.00
Inserted 1:9		
1	Jake Plummer	10.00
2	Herman Moore	2.00
3	Terrell Davis	18.00
4	Antowain Smith	5.00
5	Curtis Enis	10.00
6	Corey Dillon	7.00
7	Troy Aikman	12.00
8	John Elway	12.00
9	Barry Sanders	25.00
10	Brett Favre	25.00
11	Peyton Manning	25.00
12	Mark Brunell	10.00
13	Andre Rison	2.00
14	Dan Marino	18.00
15	Randy Moss	35.00
16	Drew Bledsoe	10.00
17	Jerome Bettis	4.00
18	Tim Brown	2.00
19	Antonio Freeman	4.00
20	Napoleon Kaufman	4.00
21	Emmitt Smith	18.00
22	Kordell Stewart	10.00
23	Curtis Martin	6.00
24	Ryan Leaf	12.00
25	Jerry Rice	12.00
26	Joey Galloway	4.00
27	Warrick Dunn	10.00
28	Eddie George	10.00
29	Steve McNair	7.00

1998 Playoff Momentum Hobby Headliners

These cards cover the events and milestones that made these players great. Each is printed on holographic stock with foil stamping. Singles were inserted 1:49 hobby packs.

		MT
Complete Set (23):		650.00
Common Player:		15.00
Inserted 1:49		
1	Brett Favre	80.00
2	Jerry Rice	40.00
3	Barry Sanders	80.00
4	Troy Aikman	40.00
5	Warrick Dunn	30.00
6	Dan Marino	60.00
7	John Elway	40.00
8	Drew Bledsoe	30.00
9	Kordell Stewart	30.00
10	Mark Brunell	30.00
11	Eddie George	30.00
12	Terrell Davis	60.00
13	Emmitt Smith	60.00
14	Steve McNair	20.00
15	Mike Alstott	15.00
16	Peyton Manning	80.00
17	Antonio Freeman	15.00
18	Curtis Martin	20.00
19	Terry Glenn	15.00
20	Brad Johnson	15.00
21	Karim Abdul-Jabbar	15.00
22	Ryan Leaf	40.00
23	Jerome Bettis	15.00

1998 Playoff Momentum Hobby Marino Milestones

The final five cards (#11-15) of this chase set were inserted into Momentum packs at a ratio of 1:385. All cards are printed on premium card stock with film laminates and foil stamping designed to showcase the soon to be "Hall of Fame" autograph of Dan found on each.

	MT
Complete Set (11-15):	600.00
Common Player:	125.00
Inserted 1:385	

1998 Playoff Momentum Hobby NFL Rivals

Top NFL stars and rookie rivals were paired together on the front of these tough inserts. Each card in this 22-card set is printed on premium mirror foil board stock with gold foil stamping. Each was inserted 1:49 packs.

		MT
Complete Set (22):		650.00
Common Player:		15.00
Inserted 1:49		
1	Mark Brunell, John Elway	40.00
2	Jerome Bettis, Eddie George	30.00
3	Barry Sanders, Emmitt Smith	80.00
4	Dan Marino, Drew Bledsoe	60.00
5	Troy Aikman, Jake Plummer	40.00
6	Terrell Davis, Napoleon Kaufman	60.00
7	Cris Carter, Herman Moore	15.00
8	Warrick Dunn, Dorsey Levens	30.00
9	Kordell Stewart, Steve McNair	30.00
10	Curtis Martin, Antowain Smith	20.00
11	Jerry Rice, Michael Irvin	40.00
12	Steve Young, Brett Favre	80.00
13	Corey Dillon, Fred Taylor	50.00
14	Tim Brown, Andre Rison	15.00
15	Mike Alstott, Robert Smith	15.00
16	Brad Johnson, Scott Mitchell	15.00
17	Robert Edwards, John Avery	25.00
18	Deion Sanders, Rob Moore	15.00
19	Antonio Freeman, Randy Moss	100.00
20	Peyton Manning, Ryan Leaf	80.00
21	Curtis Enis, Jacquez Green	30.00
22	Keyshawn Johnson, Terry Glenn	15.00

1998 Playoff Momentum Hobby Playoff Honors

This insert has appeared in most Playoff products since it debuted in 1996 Prime. These singles (#16-18) were inserted 1:3,841 hobby packs.

	MT
Complete Set (3):	900.00
Common Player:	275.00
Inserted 1:3,841	
PH16Brett Favre	400.00
PH17Kordell Stewart	275.00
PH18Troy Aikman	300.00

1998 Playoff Momentum Hobby Rookie Double Feature

Each card in this set was printed on doublesided foil board with three patterned micro-etches on each side. Two rookies with similar styles of play are matched in this 20-card chase set. One on the front and one on the back. Singles were inserted 1:17 hobby packs.

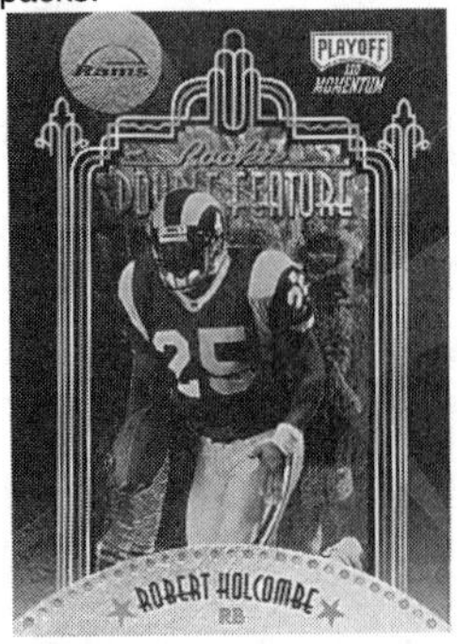

		MT
Complete Set (20):		200.00
Common Player:		4.00
Inserted 1:17		
1	Peyton Manning, Brian Griese	30.00
2	Ryan Leaf, Charlie Batch	25.00
3	Charles Woodson, Terry Fair	12.00
4	Curtis Enis, Tavian Banks	12.00
5	Fred Taylor, John Avery	20.00
6	Kevin Dyson, E.G. Green	10.00
7	Robert Edwards, Chris Fuamatu-Ma'afala	12.00
8	Randy Moss, Tim Dwight	40.00
9	Marcus Nash, Joe Jurevicius	10.00
10	Jerome Pathon, Az-Zahir Hakim	6.00
11	Jacquez Green, Mikhael Ricks	10.00
12	Robert Holcombe, Jon Ritchie	8.00
13	Cameron Cleeland, Alonzo Mayes	6.00
14	Patrick Johnson, Tony Simmons	4.00
15	Germane Crowell, Hines Ward	10.00
16	Skip Hicks, Chris Floyd	8.00
17	Brian Alford, Jammi German	4.00
18	Ahman Green, Rashaan Shehee	8.00
19	Jonathan Quinn, Moses Moreno	4.00
20	R.W. McQuarters, Duane Starks	4.00
		4.00

1998 Playoff Momentum Hobby Team Threads

Each card in this 20-card set showcased authentic team jerseys that the pros use. All the Home jerseys were in color while the parallel Away jerseys were in white. Home jerseys could be found 1:33 hobby packs while the Away singles were tougher at 1:65.

		MT
Complete Set (20):		350.00
Common Player:		7.00
Inserted 1:33		
Away Cards:		2x
Inserted 1:65		
1	Jerry Rice	20.00
2	Terrell Davis	30.00
3	Warrick Dunn	15.00
4	Brett Favre	40.00
5	Napoleon Kaufman	10.00
6	Corey Dillon	10.00
7	John Elway	20.00
8	Troy Aikman	20.00
9	Mark Brunell	15.00
10	Kordell Stewart	15.00
11	Drew Bledsoe	15.00
12	Curtis Martin	10.00
13	Dan Marino	30.00
14	Jerome Bettis	7.00
15	Eddie George	15.00
16	Ryan Leaf	20.00
17	Jake Plummer	15.00
18	Peyton Manning	40.00
19	Steve Young	12.00
20	Barry Sanders	40.00

1998 Playoff Momentum Retail

Each of the base cards in this set have a pigskin embossed style to them. Rookie cards are seeded at 1:3 retail packs. Each card has a parallel Red version with singles found 1:4 retail packs.

		MT
Complete Set (250):		150.00
Common Player:		.15
Common Rookie:		1.00
Inserted 1:3		
Red Cards:		3x
Red Rookies:		1.5x
Inserted 1:4		
Wax Box:		60.00
1	Karim Abdul	.50
2	Troy Aikman	1.50
3	Derrick Alexander	.15
4	*Stephen Alexander*	3.00
5	*Brian Alford*	2.00
6	Terry Allen	.30
7	Mike Alstott	.50
8	Kimble Anders	.15
9	Jamal Anderson	.75
10	Reidel Anthony	.30
11	Steve Atwater	.15
12	*John Avery*	4.00
13	*Tavian Banks*	3.50
14	Tony Banks	.30
15	Tiki Barber	.15
16	*Charlie Batch*	15.00
17	Donnell Bennett	.15
18	Edgar Bennett	.15
19	Jerome Bettis	.50
20	Steve Beuerlein	.15
21	Will Blackwell	.15
22	Jeff Blake	.30
23	Drew Bledsoe	1.25
24	Kyle Brady	.15
25	Robert Brooks	.30
26	Steve Broussard	.15
27	Gary Brown	.15
28	Tim Brown	.30
29	Isaac Bruce	.30
30	Mark Bruener	.15
31	Mark Brunell	1.25
32	Keith Byars	.15
33	Chris Calloway	.15
34	Rae Carruth	.15
35	Cris Carter	.50
36	Larry Centers	.15
37	Chris Chandler	.50
38	Mark Chmura	.30
39	Wayne Chrebet	.50
40	*Cameron Cleeland*	3.00
41	Ben Coates	.30
42	Kerry Collins	.30
43	Andre Coleman	.15
44	Curtis Conway	.30
45	Zack Crockett	.15
46	*Germane Crowell*	4.00
47	Randall Cunningham	1.00

48	Billy Davis	.15
49	Stephen Davis	.15
50	Terrell Davis	2.50
51	Troy Davis	.15
52	Willie Davis	.15
53	Sean Dawkins	.15
54	Trent Dilfer	.30
55	Ken Dilger	.15
56	Corey Dillon	1.00
57	Troy Drayton	.15
58	Jim Druckenmiller	.30
59	Rickey Dudley	.15
60	Jason Dunn	.15
61	Warrick Dunn	1.25
62	*Tim Dwight*	4.00
63	*Kevin Dyson*	4.00
64	Marc Edwards	.15
65	*Robert Edwards*	7.00
66	John Elway	1.75
67	Bert Emanuel	.15
68	Bobby Engram	.15
69	*Curtis Enis*	6.00
70	Craig Erickson	.15
71	*Terry Fair*	3.00
72	Marshall Faulk	.75
73	Brett Favre	3.00
74	*Chris Floyd*	1.00
75	William Floyd	.15
76	Doug Flutie	1.00
77	Glenn Foley	.30
78	Antonio Freeman	.50
79	Gus Frerotte	.30
80	Irving Fryar	.15
81	*Chris Fuamatu-Ma'afala*	2.00
82	Joey Galloway	.50
83	Rich Gannon	.15
84	Charlie Garner	.15
85	Eddie George	1.25
86	Jeff George	.30
87	*Jammi German*	3.00
88	Terry Glenn	.50
89	Tony Gonzalez	.30
90	Jay Graham	.15
91	Jeff Graham	.15
92	Elvis Grbac	.30
93	*Ahman Green*	3.00
94	*E.G. Green*	3.00
95	Eric Green	.15
96	*Jacquez Green*	4.00
97	Trent Green	.50
98	Kevin Greene	.15
99	*Brian Griese*	10.00
100	*Az-Zahir Hakim*	3.00
101	Merton Hanks	.15
102	Jim Harbaugh	.30
103	Marvin Harrison	.30
104	Andre Hastings	.15
105	Courtney Hawkins	.15
106	Garrison Hearst	.50
107	William Henderson	.15
108	*Skip Hicks*	5.00
109	Greg Hill	.15
110	Ike Hilliard	.15
111	*Robert Holcombe*	3.00
112	*Vonnie Holliday*	3.00
113	Bobby Hoying	.30
114	Michael Irvin	.30
115	Qadry Ismail	.15
116	Raghib Ismail	.15
117	Michael Jackson	.15
118	Shawn Jefferson	.15
119	James Jett	.15
120	Anthony Johnson	.15
121	Brad Johnson	.50
122	Charles Johnson	.15
123	Keyshawn Johnson	.50
124	Leon Johnson	.15
125	*Patrick Johnson*	3.00
126	Rob Johnson	.50
127	Daryl Johnston	.15
128	Freddie Jones	.15
129	*Joe Jurevicius*	3.00
130	Danny Kanell	.15
131	Napoleon Kaufman	.50
132	Eddie Kennison	.30
133	Levon Kirkland	.15
134	Erik Kramer	.15
135	David LaFleur	.15
136	Fred Lane	.30
137	*Ryan Leaf*	8.00
138	Amp Lee	.15
139	Dorsey Levens	.50
140	Jermaine Lewis	.30
141	Ray Lewis	.15
142	*Jonathon Linton*	2.00
143	Greg Lloyd	.15
144	Kevin Lockett	.15
145	John Lynch	.15
146	*Peyton Manning*	25.00
147	Dan Marino	2.00
148	Curtis Martin	.50
149	Tony Martin	.30
150	Terance Mathis	.15
151	*Alonzo Mayes*	1.00
152	Derrick Mayes	.15
153	Ed McCaffrey	.30
154	Keenan McCardell	.30
155	O.J. McDuffie	.30
156	Tony McGee	.15
157	James McKnight	.15
158	Steve McNair	.75
159	*R.W. McQuarters*	2.00
160	Natrone Means	.50
161	Eric Metcalf	.15
162	Ernie Mills	.15
163	Rick Mirer	.15
164	Scott Mitchell	.30
165	Warren Moon	.30
166	Herman Moore	.50
167	Jerald Moore	.15
168	Rob Moore	.30
169	*Moses Moreno*	2.00
170	Johnnie Morton	.15
171	*Randy Moss*	40.00
172	Eric Moulds	.75
173	Muhsin Muhammad	.15
174	Adrian Murrell	.30
175	*Marcus Nash*	4.00
176	Neil O'Donnell	.15
177	Terrell Owens	.75
178	*Jerome Pathon*	3.00
179	Carl Pickens	.50
180	Jake Plummer	1.25
181	Mike Pritchard	.15
182	*Jonathan Quinn*	3.00
183	John Randle	.15
184	Andre Reed	.30
185	Jake Reed	.30
186	Errict Rhett	.15
187	Jerry Rice	1.50
188	*Mikhael Ricks*	3.00
189	Andre Rison	.30
190	*John Ritchie*	2.00
191	*Rod Rutledge*	1.00
192	Barry Sanders	3.00
193	Chris Sanders	.15
194	Deion Sanders	.50
195	Frank Sanders	.15
196	O.J. Santiago	.30
197	Warren Sapp	.15
198	Darnay Scott	.15
199	Junior Seau	.30
200	Shannon Sharpe	.30
201	Sedrick Shaw	.15
202	*Rashaan Shehee*	2.00
203	Heath Shuler	.15
204	*Tony Simmons*	4.00
205	Antowain Smith	.50
206	Bruce Smith	.15
207	Emmitt Smith	2.00
208	Jimmy Smith	.50
209	Lamar Smith	.15
210	Neil Smith	.15
211	Robert Smith	.30
212	Rod Smith	.30
213	*Takeo Spikes*	2.00
214	Duce Staley	.30
215	*Duane Starks*	2.00
216	James Stewart	.15
217	Kordell Stewart	1.25
218	Bryan Still	.15
219	J.J. Stokes	.30
220	Michael Strahan	.15
221	Dana Stubblefield	.15
222	*Fred Taylor*	15.00
223	Vinny Testaverde	.30
224	Yancey Thigpen	.15
225	Derrick Thomas	.15
226	Thurman Thomas	.30
227	Zach Thomas	.30
228	Amani Toomer	.15
229	*Andre Wadsworth*	4.00
230	Wesley Walls	.15
231	Dedric Ward	.15
232	*Hines Ward*	3.00
233	Chris Warren	.30
234	Ricky Watters	.50
235	Charles Way	.15
236	Michael Westbrook	.15
237	Tyrone Wheatley	.15
238	Reggie White	.50
239	Dan Wilkinson	.15
240	Kevin Williams	.15
241	*Shaun Williams*	1.00
242	*Grant Wistrom*	2.00
243	*Charles Woodson*	7.00
244	Darren Woodson	.15
245	Rod Woolfolk	.15
246	Danny Wuerffel	.15
247	Frank Wycheck	.15
248	Steve Young	1.00
249	Eric Zeier	.15
250	Ray Zellars	.15

1998 Playoff Momentum Retail Class Reunion Tandems

The idea behind this insert was to pick two of the top players drafted from a specific season and picture one on the front and the other on the back. The set starts with the year 1983 and ends with 1998. Singles were inserted 1:121 retail packs.

		MT
Complete Set (16):		500.00
Common Player:		12.00
Inserted 1:121		
1	Dan Marino, John Elway	70.00
2	Steve Young, Reggie White	30.00
3	Jerry Rice, Bruce Smith	40.00
4	Keith Byars, Leslie O'Neal	12.00
5	Cris Carter, Vinny Testaverde	24.00
6	Tim Brown, Michael Irvin	24.00
7	Troy Aikman, Barry Sanders	80.00
8	Emmitt Smith, Jeff George	60.00
9	Brett Favre, Herman Moore	80.00
10	Brad Johnson, Carl Pickens	24.00
11	Drew Bledsoe, Mark Brunell	40.00
12	Dorsey Levens, Isaac Bruce	24.00
13	Terrell Davis, Kordell Stewart	70.00
14	Eddie George, Keyshawn Johnson	35.00
15	Warrick Dunn, Jake Plummer	35.00
16	Peyton Manning, Ryan Leaf	50.00

1998 Playoff Momentum Retail EndZone X-press

Each card in this set is similar to the hobby version except these singles aren't die cut. They are printed on plastic with gold foil and were inserted 1:13 retail packs.

		MT
Complete Set (29):		100.00
Common Player:		1.00
Inserted 1:13		
1	Jake Plummer	5.00
2	Herman Moore	2.00
3	Terrell Davis	8.00
4	Antowain Smith	2.00
5	Curtis Enis	3.00
6	Corey Dillon	3.00
7	Troy Aikman	6.00
8	John Elway	6.00
9	Barry Sanders	10.00
10	Brett Favre	10.00
11	Peyton Manning	10.00
12	Mark Brunell	6.00
13	Andre Rison	1.00
14	Dan Marino	8.00
15	Randy Moss	20.00
16	Drew Bledsoe	6.00
17	Jerome Bettis	2.00
18	Tim Brown	1.00
19	Antonio Freeman	2.00
20	Napoleon Kaufman	2.00
21	Emmitt Smith	8.00
22	Kordell Stewart	6.00
23	Curtis Martin	4.00
24	Ryan Leaf	5.00
25	Jerry Rice	6.00
26	Joey Galloway	2.00
27	Warrick Dunn	5.00
28	Eddie George	5.00
29	Steve McNair	3.00

1998 Playoff Momentum Retail Headliners

These red foil front cards highlight a record that the player had set in the past. Singles were found 1:73 retail packs.

		MT
Complete Set (23):		275.00
Common Player:		7.00
Inserted 1:73		
1	Brett Favre	40.00
2	Jerry Rice	20.00
3	Barry Sanders	40.00
4	Troy Aikman	20.00
5	Warrick Dunn	15.00
6	Dan Marino	30.00
7	John Elway	25.00
8	Drew Bledsoe	15.00
9	Kordell Stewart	15.00
10	Mark Brunell	15.00
11	Eddie George	15.00
12	Terrell Davis	35.00
13	Emmitt Smith	30.00
14	Steve McNair	10.00
15	Mike Alstott	7.00
16	Peyton Manning	30.00
17	Antonio Freeman	10.00
18	Curtis Martin	10.00
19	Terry Glenn	7.00
20	Brad Johnson	7.00
21	Karim Abdul	7.00
22	Ryan Leaf	15.00
23	Jerome Bettis	7.00

1998 Playoff Momentum Retail NFL Rivals

This set is identical to the hobby version except for the "R" prefix on these retail singles. Each card pictures two players who compete at the same position. Singles are found 1:73 retail packs.

		MT
Complete Set (22):		280.00
Common Player:		10.00
Inserted 1:73		
1	Mark Brunell, John Elway	20.00
2	Jerome Bettis, Eddie George	15.00
3	Barry Sanders, Emmitt Smith	40.00
4	Dan Marino, Drew Bledsoe	30.00
5	Troy Aikman, Jake Plummer	20.00
6	Terrell Davis, Napoleon Kaufman	30.00
7	Cris Carter, Herman Moore	10.00
8	Warrick Dunn, Dorsey Levens	15.00
9	Kordell Stewart, Steve McNair	15.00
10	Curtis Martin, Antowain Smith	10.00
11	Jerry Rice, Michael Irvin	20.00
12	Steve Young, Brett Favre	40.00
13	Corey Dillon, Fred Taylor	20.00
14	Tim Brown, Andre Rison	10.00
15	Mike Alstott, Robert Smith	10.00
16	Brad Johnson, Scott Mitchell	10.00
17	Robert Edwards, John Avery	15.00
18	Deion Sanders, Rob Moore	10.00
19	Antonio Freeman, Randy Moss	50.00
20	Peyton Manning, Ryan Leaf	35.00
21	Curtis Enis, Jacquez Green	15.00
22	Keyshawn Johnson, Terry Glenn	10.00

1998 Playoff Momentum Retail Rookie Double Feature

The hobby version of this set features two players on one card, where this set has the players on their own card. Each card also has the "R" prefix before the card number and were found 1:25 retail packs.

		MT
Complete Set (40):		220.00
Common Player:		2.00
Inserted 1:25		
1	Peyton Manning	30.00
2	Ryan Leaf	10.00
3	Charles Woodson	10.00
4	Curtis Enis	8.00
5	Fred Taylor	15.00
6	Kevin Dyson	6.00
7	Robert Edwards	8.00
8	Randy Moss	60.00
9	Marcus Nash	6.00
10	Jerome Pathon	4.00
11	Jacquez Green	6.00
12	Robert Holcombe	5.00
13	Cameron Cleeland	5.00
14	Patrick Johnson	4.00
15	Germane Crowell	6.00
16	Skip Hicks	6.00
17	Brian Alford	2.00
18	Ahman Green	5.00
19	Jonathan Quinn	4.00
20	R.W. McQuarters	4.00
21	Brian Griese	10.00
22	Charlie Batch	18.00
23	Terry Fair	4.00
24	Tavian Banks	5.00
25	John Avery	6.00
26	E.G. Green	4.00
27	Chris Fuamatu-Ma'afala	4.00
28	Tim Dwight	6.00
29	Joe Jurevicius	4.00
30	Az-Zahir Hakim	4.00
31	Tony Simmons	5.00
32	Jon Ritchie	4.00
33	Alonzo Mayes	2.00
34	Mikhael Ricks	4.00
35	Hines Ward	4.00
36	Chris Floyd	2.00
37	Jammi German	4.00
38	Rashaan Shehee	4.00
39	Moses Moreno	2.00
40	Duane Starks	4.00

1998 Playoff Momentum Retail Team Jerseys

Team Jersey cards feature a photo of the player on the front and a piece of an authentic jersey on the back. It isn't an actual game worn but a jersey that the pros use. The Home versions carry a colored swatch and were inserted 1:49 retail packs. The parallel Away versions feature the white jerseys and were inserted 1:97 packs.

		MT
Complete Set (20):		600.00
Common Player:		15.00
Inserted 1:49		
Away Cards:		1.5x
Inserted 1:97		
1	Jerry Rice	30.00
2	Terrell Davis	50.00
3	Warrick Dunn	25.00
4	Brett Favre	60.00
5	Napoleon Kaufman	15.00
6	Corey Dillon	15.00
7	John Elway	30.00
8	Troy Aikman	30.00
9	Mark Brunell	25.00
10	Kordell Stewart	25.00
11	Drew Bledsoe	25.00
12	Curtis Martin	15.00
13	Dan Marino	50.00
14	Jerome Bettis	15.00
15	Eddie George	25.00
16	Ryan Leaf	25.00
17	Jake Plummer	30.00
18	Peyton Manning	50.00
19	Steve Young	20.00
20	Barry Sanders	60.00

1998 Score

The 270-card base set is made up of 15 Off Season cards, 3 checklists, 20 rookies and 232 veterans. Three parallel sets that include Showcase, Artist's Proofs and One on One. The Showcase set includes only the top 110 players and were inserted 1:7 packs. The Artist's Proof set is made up of the best 50 players in the set and were found 1:35 packs. The last parallel set is the One on One set in which there is only one of each card in the 160-card set. A special hobby exclusive Ryan Leaf autographed card was added with only 200 signed.

		MT
Complete Set (270):		50.00
Common Player:		.10
Common Rookie:		1.00
Complete Showcase (110):		120.00
Showcase Cards:		2x-4x
Showcase Rookies:		2x
Inserted 1:7		
Complete Artist's Proof (50):		250.00
AP Cards:		5x-10x
Inserted 1:35		
Wax Box:		50.00
1	John Elway	1.00
2	Kordell Stewart	.75
3	Warrick Dunn	.75
4	Brad Johnson	.30
5	Kerry Collins	.20
6	Danny Kanell	.10
7	Emmitt Smith	1.50
8	Jamal Anderson	.50
9	Jim Harbaugh	.20
10	Tony Martin	.20
11	Rod Smith	.30
12	Dorsey Levens	.30
13	Steve McNair	.40
14	Derrick Thomas	.10
15	Rob Moore	.20
16	Peter Boulware	.10
17	Terry Allen	.20
18	Joey Galloway	.30
19	Jerome Bettis	.30
20	Carl Pickens	.20
21	Napoleon Kaufman	.30
22	Troy Aikman	1.00
23	Curtis Conway	.20
24	Adrian Murrell	.20
25	Elvis Grbac	.20
26	Garrison Hearst	.30
27	Chris Sanders	.10
28	Scott Mitchell	.20
29	Junior Seau	.20
30	Chris Chandler	.20
31	Kevin Hardy	.10
32	Terrell Davis	1.50
33	Keyshawn Johnson	.30
34	Natrone Means	.20
35	Antowain Smith	.30
36	Jake Plummer	.75
37	Isaac Bruce	.20
38	Tony Banks	.20
39	Reidel Anthony	.20
40	Darren Woodson	.10
41	Corey Dillon	.50
42	Antonio Freeman	.30
43	Eddie George	.75
44	Yancey Thigpen	.20
45	Tim Brown	.20
46	Wayne Chrebet	.30
47	Andre Rison	.20
48	Michael Strahan	.10
49	Deion Sanders	.30
50	Eric Moulds	.30
51	Mark Brunell	.75
52	Rae Carruth	.10
53	Warren Sapp	.10
54	Mark Chmura	.20
55	Darrell Green	.10
56	Quinn Early	.10
57	Barry Sanders	2.00
58	Neil O'Donnell	.20
59	Tony Brackens	.10
60	Willie Davis	.10
61	Shannon Sharpe	.30
62	Shawn Springs	.10
63	Tony Gonzalez	.10
64	Rodney Thomas	.10
65	Terance Mathis	.10
66	Brett Favre	2.00
67	Eric Swann	.10
68	Kevin Turner	.10
69	Tyrone Wheatley	.10
70	Trent Dilfer	.20
71	Bryan Cox	.10
72	Lake Dawson	.10
73	Will Blackwell	.10
74	Fred Lane	.20
75	Ty Detmer	.10
76	Eddie Kennison	.20
77	Jimmy Smith	.30
78	Chris Calloway	.10
79	Shawn Jefferson	.10
80	Dan Marino	1.50
81	LeRoy Butler	.10
82	William Roaf	.10
83	Rick Mirer	.10
84	Dermontti Dawson	.10
85	Errict Rhett	.10
86	Lamar Thomas	.10
87	Lamar Lathon	.10
88	John Randle	.10
89	Darryl Williams	.10
90	Keenan McCardell	.20
91	Erik Kramer	.10
92	Ken Dilger	.10
93	Dave Meggett	.10
94	Jeff Blake	.20
95	Ed McCaffrey	.20
96	Charles Johnson	.20
97	Irving Spikes	.10
98	Mike Alstott	.30
99	Vincent Brisby	.10
100	Michael Westbrook	.10
101	Rickey Dudley	.10
102	Bert Emanuel	.10
103	Daryl Johnston	.10
104	Lawrence Phillips	.10
105	Eric Bieniemy	.10
106	Bryant Westbrook	.10
107	Rob Johnson	.20
108	Ray Zellars	.10
109	Anthony Johnson	.10
110	Reggie White	.30
111	Wesley Walls	.10
112	Amani Toomer	.10
113	Gary Brown	.10
114	Brian Blades	.10
115	Alex Van Dyke	.10
116	Michael Haynes	.10
117	Jessie Armstead	.10
118	James Jett	.10
119	Troy Drayton	.10
120	Craig Heyward	.10
121	Steve Atwater	.10
122	Tiki Barber	.10
123	Karim Abdul	.20
124	Kimble Anders	.10
125	Frank Sanders	.10
126	David Sloan	.10
127	Andre Hastings	.10
128	Vinny Testaverde	.20
129	Robert Smith	.20
130	Horace Copeland	.10
131	Larry Centers	.10
132	J.J. Stokes	.20
133	Ike Hilliard	.10
134	Muhsin Muhammad	.10
135	Sean Dawkins	.10
136	Raymont Harris	.10
137	Lamar Smith	.10
138	David Palmer	.10
139	Steve Young	.75
140	Bryan Still	.10
141	Keith Byars	.10
142	Cris Carter	.30
143	Charlie Garner	.10
144	Drew Bledsoe	1.00
145	Simeon Rice	.10
146	Merton Hanks	.10
147	Aeneas Williams	.10
148	Rodney Hampton	.10
149	Zach Thomas	.20
150	Mark Bruener	.10
151	Jason Dunn	.10
152	Danny Wuerffel	.10
153	Jim Druckenmiller	.20
154	Greg Hill	.10
155	Earnest Byner	.10
156	Greg Lloyd	.10
157	John Mobley	.10
158	Tim Biakabutuka	.20
159	Terrell Owens	.50
160	O.J. McDuffie	.20
161	Glenn Foley	.20
162	Derrick Brooks	.10
163	Dave Brown	.10
164	Ki-Jana Carter	.10
165	Bobby Hoying	.20
166	Randal Hill	.10
167	Michael Irvin	.20
168	Bruce Smith	.10
169	Troy Davis	.10
170	Derrick Mayes	.10
171	Henry Ellard	.10
172	Dana Stubblefield	.10
173	Willie McGinest	.10
174	Leeland McElroy	.10
175	Edgar Bennett	.10
176	Robert Porcher	.10
177	Randall Cunningham	.30
178	Jim Everett	.10
179	Jake Reed	.10
180	Quentin Coryatt	.10
181	William Floyd	.10
182	Jason Sehorn	.10
183	Carnell Lake	.10
184	Dexter Coakley	.10
185	Derrick Alexander	.10
186	Johnnie Morton	.10
187	Irving Fryar	.10
188	Warren Moon	.20
189	Todd Collins	.10
190	Ken Norton Jr.	.10
191	Terry Glenn	.20
192	Rashaan Salaam	.20
193	Jerry Rice	1.00
194	James Stewart	.10
195	David LaFleur	.10
196	Eric Green	.10
197	Gus Frerotte	.20
198	Willie Green	.10
199	Marshall Faulk	.30
200	Brett Perriman	.10
201	Darnay Scott	.10
202	Marvin Harrison	.20
203	Joe Aska	.10
204	Darrien Gordon	.10
205	Herman Moore	.20
206	Curtis Martin	.30
207	Derek Loville	.10
208	Dale Carter	.10
209	Heath Shuler	.10
210	Jonathan Ogden	.10
211	Leslie Shepherd	.10
212	Tony Boselli	.10
213	Eric Metcalf	.10
214	Neil Smith	.10
215	Anthony Miller	.10
216	Jeff George	.20
217	Charles Way	.10
218	Mario Bates	.10
219	Ben Coates	.20
220	Michael Jackson	.10
221	Thurman Thomas	.20
222	Kyle Brady	.10
223	Marcus Allen	.20
224	Robert Brooks	.10
225	Yatil Green	.20
226	Byron Hanspard	.10
227	Andre Reed	.20
228	Chris Warren	.10
229	Jackie Harris	.10
230	Ricky Watters	.20
231	Bobby Engram	.10
232	Tamarick Vanover	.10
233	*Peyton Manning*	8.00
234	*Curtis Enis*	3.00
235	*Randy Moss*	12.00
236	*Charles Woodson*	3.00
237	*Robert Edwards*	3.00
238	*Jacquez Green*	2.00
239	*Keith Brooking*	1.00
240	*Jerome Pathon*	1.50
241	*Kevin Dyson*	2.00
242	*Fred Taylor*	6.00
243	*Tavian Banks*	1.50
244	*Marcus Nash*	2.00
245	*Brian Griese*	4.00
246	*Andre Wadsworth*	1.50
247	*Ahman Green*	2.00
248	*Joe Jurevicius*	1.00
249	*Germane Crowell*	2.00
250	*Skip Hicks*	2.00
251	*Ryan Leaf*	5.00
252	*Hines Ward*	1.50
253	John Elway	.50
254	Mark Brunell	.30
255	Brett Favre	1.00
256	Troy Aikman	.50
257	Warrick Dunn	.30
258	Barry Sanders	1.00
259	Eddie George	.30
260	Kordell Stewart	.30
261	Emmitt Smith	.75
262	Steve Young	.25
263	Terrell Davis	.75
264	Dorsey Levens	.10
265	Dan Marino	.75
266	Jerry Rice	.50
267	Drew Bledsoe	.30
268	Brett Favre	1.00
269	Barry Sanders	1.00
270	Terrell Davis	.75

1998 Score Complete Players

Only 10 of the NFL's all-around athletes are included in this set that has three different cards highlighting three specific attributes on special cards with holographic foil stamping. Singles were inserted 1:11 packs.

		MT
Complete Set (30):		100.00
Common Player:		2.50
Inserted 1:11		
1a	Brett Favre	8.00
1b	Brett Favre	8.00
1c	Brett Favre	8.00
2a	John Elway	5.00
2b	John Elway	5.00
2c	John Elway	5.00
3a	Emmitt Smith	6.00
3b	Emmitt Smith	6.00
3c	Emmitt Smith	6.00
4a	Kordell Stewart	2.50
4b	Kordell Stewart	2.50
4c	Kordell Stewart	2.50
5a	Dan Marino	6.00
5b	Dan Marino	6.00
5c	Dan Marino	6.00
6a	Mark Brunell	3.00
6b	Mark Brunell	3.00
6c	Mark Brunell	3.00
7a	Terrell Davis	7.00
7b	Terrell Davis	7.00
7c	Terrell Davis	7.00
8a	Barry Sanders	8.00
8b	Barry Sanders	8.00
8c	Barry Sanders	8.00
9a	Warrick Dunn	2.50
9b	Warrick Dunn	2.50
9c	Warrick Dunn	2.50
10a	Jerry Rice	4.00
10b	Jerry Rice	4.00
10c	Jerry Rice	4.00

1998 Score Rookie Autographs

The 33-card set includes all of the top rookies from 1998. Each is hand signed and limited to 500.

	MT
Complete Set (33):	1600.
Common Player:	20.00
Production 500 Sets	
Stephen Alexander	40.00
Tavian Banks	50.00
Charlie Batch	100.00
Keith Brooking	20.00
Thad Busby	20.00
John Dutton	20.00
Tim Dwight	50.00
Kevin Dyson	50.00
Robert Edwards	60.00
Greg Ellis	20.00
Curtis Enis	60.00
Chris Fuamatu-Ma'afala	40.00
Ahman Green	40.00
Jacquez Green	50.00
Brian Griese	70.00
Skip Hicks	50.00
Robert Holcombe	40.00
Tebucky Jones	20.00
Joe Jurevicius	30.00
Ryan Leaf	85.00
Leonard Little	20.00
Alonzo Mayes	20.00
Michael Myers	20.00
Randy Moss	250.00
Marcus Nash	50.00
Jerome Pathon	40.00
Jason Peter	20.00
Anthony Simmons	20.00
Tony Simmons	40.00
Takeo Spikes	30.00
Duane Starks	20.00
Fred Taylor	100.00
Hines Ward	40.00

1998 Score Star Salute

This set highlights the top 20 players in the NFL and puts each of them on a foil board with micro-etching. Singles were issued 1:35 packs.

		MT
Complete Set (20):		120.00
Common Player:		4.00
Inserted 1:35		
1	Terrell Davis	15.00
2	Barry Sanders	20.00
3	Steve Young	6.00
4	Drew Bledsoe	8.00
5	Kordell Stewart	8.00
6	Emmitt Smith	15.00
7	Dorsey Levens	4.00
8	Corey Dillon	5.00
9	Jerome Bettis	4.00
10	Herman Moore	4.00
11	Brett Favre	20.00
12	Antonio Freeman	5.00
13	Mark Brunell	8.00
14	John Elway	12.00
15	Terry Glenn	4.00
16	Warrick Dunn	7.00
17	Eddie George	8.00
18	Troy Aikman	10.00
19	Deion Sanders	4.00
20	Jerry Rice	10.00

1998 SP Authentic

The 126-card regular set features top-notch photography of the league's best players, along with subsets Future Watch and Time Warp. The 30-card Future Watch set is made up of the top rookies from 1998 and each player is sequentially numbered to 2,000. The 12-card Time Warp set pictures today's top stars shown in action during their respective rookie campaigns. This set is also numbered to 2,000. Each single in this set has a parallel Die-Cut card that is numbered to 500.

	MT
Complete Set (126):	1500.
Common Player:	.25
Die-Cut Cards:	5x-10x
Production 500 Sets	
Common Rookie (1-30):	15.00
Production 2,000 Sets	

Die-Cut Rookies:		1x
Production 500 Sets		
Common Time Warp (31-42):		5.00
Production 2,000 Sets		
Die-Cut Time Warps:		2x
Wax Box:		475.00
1	*Andre Wadsworth*	20.00
2	*Corey Chavous*	15.00
3	*Keith Brooking*	15.00
4	*Duane Starks*	15.00
5	*Patrick Johnson*	20.00
6	*Jason Peter*	15.00
7	*Curtis Enis*	75.00
8	*Takeo Spikes*	15.00
9	*Greg Ellis*	15.00
10	*Marcus Nash*	30.00
11	*Brian Griese*	185.00
12	*Germane Crowell*	45.00
13	*Vonnie Holliday*	25.00
14	*Peyton Manning*	325.00
15	*Jerome Pathon*	20.00
16	*Fred Taylor*	225.00
17	*John Avery*	40.00
18	*Randy Moss*	425.00
19	*Robert Edwards*	25.00
20	*Tony Simmons*	20.00
21	*Shaun Williams*	15.00
22	*Joe Jurevicius*	20.00
23	*Charles Woodson*	60.00
24	*Tre Thomas*	20.00
25	*Grant Wistrom*	15.00
26	*Ryan Leaf*	60.00
27	*Ahman Green*	40.00
28	*Jacquez Green*	40.00
29	*Kevin Dyson*	50.00
30	*Stephen Alexander*	25.00
31	John Elway	15.00
32	Jerry Rice	15.00
33	Emmitt Smith	20.00
34	Steve Young	10.00
35	Jerome Bettis	7.00
36	Deion Sanders	7.00
37	Andre Rison	5.00
38	Warren Moon	7.00
39	Mark Brunell	10.00
40	Ricky Watters	7.00
41	Dan Marino	20.00
42	Brett Favre	30.00
43	Jake Plummer	1.50
44	Adrian Murrell	.25
45	Eric Swann	.25
46	Jamal Anderson	.75
47	Chris Chandler	.50
48	Jim Harbaugh	.25
49	Michael Jackson	.25
50	Jermaine Lewis	.25
51	Rob Johnson	.50
52	Antowain Smith	.75
53	Thurman Thomas	.50
54	Kerry Collins	.50
55	Fred Lane	.25
56	Rae Carruth	.25
57	Erik Kramer	.25
58	Curtis Conway	.25
59	Corey Dillon	1.00
60	Neil O'Donnell	.25
61	Carl Pickens	.50
62	Troy Aikman	2.00
63	Emmitt Smith	3.00
64	Deion Sanders	.75
65	Terrell Davis	3.00
66	John Elway	2.00
67	Rod Smith	.50
68	Scott Mitchell	.25
69	Barry Sanders	4.00
70	Herman Moore	.50
71	Brett Favre	4.00
72	Dorsey Levens	.50
73	Antonio Freeman	.75
74	Marshall Faulk	.75
75	Marvin Harrison	.50
76	Mark Brunell	1.50
77	Keenan McCardell	.25
78	Jimmy Smith	.50
79	Andre Rison	.25
80	Elvis Grbac	.25
81	Derrick Alexander	.25
82	Dan Marino	3.00
83	Kareem Abdul-Jabbar	.50
84	O.J. McDuffie	.25
85	Brad Johnson	.75
86	Cris Carter	.75
87	Robert Smith	.50
88	Drew Bledsoe	1.50
89	Terry Glenn	.50
90	Ben Coates	.25
91	Lamar Smith	.25
92	Danny Wuerffel	.25
93	Tiki Barber	.50
94	Danny Kanell	.25
95	Ike Hilliard	.25
96	Curtis Martin	.75
97	Keyshawn Johnson	.75
98	Glenn Foley	.25
99	Jeff George	.50
100	Tim Brown	.50
101	Napoleon Kaufman	.75
102	Bobby Hoying	.25
103	Charlie Garner	.25
104	Irving Fryar	.25
105	Kordell Stewart	1.25
106	Jerome Bettis	.50
107	Charles Johnson	.25
108	Tony Banks	.50
109	Isaac Bruce	.50
110	Natrone Means	.50
111	Junior Seau	.50
112	Steve Young	1.00
113	Jerry Rice	2.00
114	Garrison Hearst	.50
115	Ricky Watters	.50
116	Warren Moon	.50
117	Joey Galloway	.75
118	Trent Dilfer	.50
119	Warrick Dunn	1.50
120	Mike Alstott	.75
121	Steve McNair	.75
122	Eddie George	1.50
123	Yancey Thigpen	.25
124	Gus Frerotte	.25
125	Terry Allen	.50
126	Michael Westbrook	.25

1998 SP Authentic Maximum Impact

This set was made up of the 30 players who provide the greatest contribution to their team's overall success. Singles were inserted 1:4 packs.

		MT
Complete Set (30):		75.00
Common Player:		.50
Inserted 1:4		
MI1	Brett Favre	6.00
MI2	Warrick Dunn	2.00
MI3	Junior Seau	.50
MI4	Steve Young	1.50
MI5	Herman Moore	.50
MI6	Antowain Smith	1.00
MI7	John Elway	3.00
MI8	Troy Aikman	3.00
MI9	Dorsey Levens	.50
MI10	Kordell Stewart	2.00
MI11	Peyton Manning	8.00
MI12	Eddie George	2.00
MI13	Dan Marino	4.50
MI14	Joey Galloway	1.00
MI15	Mark Brunell	2.00
MI16	Jake Plummer	2.00
MI17	Curtis Enis	4.00
MI18	Corey Dillon	1.50
MI19	Rob Johnson	1.00
MI20	Barry Sanders	6.00
MI21	Deion Sanders	1.25
MI22	Napoleon Kaufman	1.00
MI23	Ryan Leaf	5.00
MI24	Jerry Rice	3.00
MI25	Drew Bledsoe	2.00
MI26	Jerome Bettis	1.00
MI27	Emmitt Smith	4.50
MI28	Tim Brown	1.00
MI29	Curtis Martin	1.25
MI30	Terrell Davis	4.50

1998 SP Authentic Memorabilia

Each card appears in different quanities and could be redeemed for a special piece of autographed memorabilia from the NFL's top rookies.

		MT
Common Player:		50.00
Inserted 1:864		
M1	Curtis Enis Ball (signed NFL game football)	85.00
M2	Ryan Leaf Ball (signed NFL game football)	125.00
M3	Randy Moss Ball (signed NFL game football)	300.00
M4	Takeo Spikes Ball (signed NFL game football)	50.00
M5	Andre Wadsworth Ball (signed NFL game football)	65.00
M6	Marcus Nash Ball (signed NFL game football)	75.00
M7	Curtis Enis Mini FB (signed mini football)	60.00
M8	Ryan Leaf Mini FB (signed mini football)	90.00
M9	Randy Moss Mini FB (signed mini football)	200.00
M10	Takeo Spikes Mini FB (signed mini football)	50.00
M11	Andre Wadsworth Mini FB (signed mini football)	50.00
M12	Marcus Nash Mini FB (signed mini football)	50.00
M13	Curtis Enis Helmet (signed NFL helmet)	125.00
M14	Ryan Leaf Helmet (signed NFL helmet)	200.00
M15	Randy Moss Helmet (signed NFL helmet)	400.00
M16	Takeo Spikes Helmet (signed NFL helmet)	85.00
M17	Andre Wadsworth Helmet (signed NFL helmet)	85.00
M18	Marcus Nash Helmet (signed NFL helmet)	100.00
M19	Curtis Enis Mini Helmet (signed mini helmet)	60.00
M20	Ryan Leaf Mini Helmet (signed mini helmet)	85.00
M21	Randy Moss Mini Helmet (signed mini helmet)	200.00
M22	Takeo Spikes Mini Helmet (signed mini helmet)	50.00
M23	Andre Wadsworth Mini Helmet (signed mini helmet)	50.00
M24	Marcus Nash Mini Helmet (signed mini helmet)	50.00
M25	"Players Ink" Autograph Collection	50.00
M26	Brett Favre (game-worn authentics ("1-of-1's")	50.00
M27	Terrell Davis (game-worn authentics ("1-of-1's")	50.00
M28	Dan Marino (game-worn authentics ("1-of-1's")	50.00
M29	Jerry Rice (game-worn authentics ("1-of-1's")	50.00
M30	Mark Brunell (game-worn authentics ("1-of-1's")	50.00

1998 SP Authentic Player's Ink

This autographed insert comes in three versions. The base set has the green background, aren't numbered and were inserted 1:23 packs. The first parallel are the Silver cards and each single was sequentially numbered to 100. The last parallel was the Gold version in which each single was numbered to the players jersey number. Some singles were through redemption cards only.

		MT
Common Player:		20.00
Inserted 1:23		
Silver Cards:		2x
Production 100 Sets		
TA	Troy Aikman	120.00
BF	Brett Favre	240.00
RL	Ryan Leaf	75.00
DM	Dan Marino	200.00
JR	Jerry Rice	120.00
KS	Kordell Stewart	100.00
JP	Jake Plummer	70.00
KJ	Keyshawn Johnson	50.00
SS	Shannon Sharpe	40.00
MA	Mike Alstott	40.00
BH	Bobby Hoying	20.00
RM	Randy Moss	250.00
KM	Keenan McCardell	20.00
JM	Johnnie Morton	20.00
JA	Jamal Anderson	50.00
OE	Curtis Enis	50.00
MJ	Michael Jackson	20.00
AW	Andre Wadsworth	30.00
GC	Germane Crowell	40.00
BG	Brian Griese	80.00
SH	Skip Hicks	40.00
MN	Marcus Nash	40.00
JP	Jerome Pathon	25.00
TS	Takeo Spikes	25.00
FT	Fred Taylor	100.00
CD	Corey Dillon	30.00
RE	Robert Edwards	45.00
EG	Eddie George	60.00
DL	Dorsey Levens	30.00
TV	Tamarick Vanover	20.00

1998 SP Authentic Special Forces

The top specialists in the NFL were showcased in this premium collection set. Each single was sequentially numbered to 1,000.

		MT
Complete Set (30):		375.00
Common Player:		3.00
Production 1,000 Sets		
S1	Kordell Stewart	12.00
S2	Charles Woodson	15.00
S3	Terrell Davis	20.00
S4	Brett Favre	30.00
S5	Joey Galloway	6.00
S6	Warrick Dunn	10.00
S7	Ryan Leaf	20.00
S8	Drew Bledsoe	12.00
S9	Takeo Spikes	6.00
S10	Barry Sanders	30.00
S11	Troy Aikman	15.00
S12	John Elway	15.00
S13	Jerome Bettis	6.00
S14	Karim Abdul-Jabbar	6.00
S15	Tony Gonzalez	3.00
S16	Steve Young	10.00
S17	Napoleon Kaufman	6.00
S18	Andre Wadsworth	6.00
S19	Herman Moore	6.00
S20	Fred Taylor	25.00
S21	Deion Sanders	6.00
S22	Peyton Manning	45.00
S23	Jerry Rice	15.00
S24	Dan Marino	20.00
S25	Antonio Freeman	6.00
S26	Curtis Enis	12.00
S27	Jake Plummer	10.00
S28	Steve McNair	6.00
S29	Mark Brunell	12.00
S30	Robert Edwards	10.00

1998 SPx Finite

SPx Finite Series One consists of a 190-card base set built from five subsets. The base cards feature silver foil. The set consists of 90 regular cards (numbered to 7,600), 30 Playmakers (5,500), 30 Youth Movement (3,000), 20 Pure Energy (2,500) and 10 Heroes of the Game (1,250). Ten rookie cards were also added to SPx Finite, numbered to 1,998.

		MT
Complete Series 2 (180):		1300.
Common Player (191-280):		.50
Common Rookie (191-280):		1.00
Production 10,100 Sets		
Production 1,998 for #218,221,239		
Common Player (281-310):		.75
Production 7,200 Sets		
Common Player (311-340):		1.50
Production 4,000 Sets		
Production 1,700 for #321,338,339		
Common Player (341-360):		1.50
Production 2,700 Sets		
Common Player (361-370):		5.00
Production 1,620 Sets		
Series 2 Wax Box:		90.00
191	Adrian Murrell	1.00
192	Simeon Rice	.50
193	Frank Sanders	.50
194	Chris Chandler	1.00
195	Terrance Mathis	.50
196	*Keith Brooking*	1.50
197	Jim Harbaugh	1.00
198	Errict Rhett	.50
199	*Patrick Johnson*	2.00
200	Rob Johnson	1.00
201	Andre Reed	1.00
202	Thurman Thomas	1.00
203	Kerry Collins	1.00
204	William Floyd	.50
205	Sean Gilbert	.50
206	Bobby Engram	.50
207	Edgar Bennett	.50
208	Walt Harris	.50
209	Carl Pickens	1.00
210	Neil O'Donnell	1.00
211	Tony McGee	.50
212	Deion Sanders	1.50
213	Michael Irvin	1.00
214	*Greg Ellis*	1.50
215	Shannon Sharpe	1.00
216	Neil Smith	.50
217	*Marcus Nash*	4.00
218	*Brian Griese*	50.00
219	Johnnie Morton	.50
220	Herman Moore	1.00
221	*Charlie Batch*	40.00
222	Robert Brooks	.50
223	Mark Chmura	1.00
224	Brett Favre	6.00
225	*Jerome Pathon*	2.00
226	Zack Crockett	.50
227	Dan Footman	.50
228	Jimmy Smith	1.00
229	Bryce Paup	.50
230	James Stewart	.50
231	Derrick Thomas	.50
232	Derrick Alexander	.50
233	Tony Gonzalez	.50
234	Dan Marino	4.50
235	O.J. McDuffie	.50
236	Troy Drayton	.50
237	Cris Carter	1.00
238	Robert Smith	1.00
239	*Randy Moss*	160.00
240	Lamar Smith	.50
241	Sean Dawkins	.50
242	Alex Molden	.50
243	Ben Coates	1.00
244	Ted Johnson	.50
245	Sedrick Shaw	.50
246	Ike Hilliard	.50
247	Jason Sehorn	.50
248	Michael Strahan	.50
249	Keyshawn Johnson	1.00
250	Curtis Martin	1.50
251	Jeff George	1.00
252	Rickey Dudley	.50
253	James Jett	.50
254	Bobby Taylor	.50
255	Rodney Peete	.50
256	William Thomas	.50
257	Jerome Bettis	1.00
258	Charles Johnson	.50
259	*Chris Fuamatu-Ma'afala*	2.50
260	Eddie Kennison	.50
261	*Az-Zahir Hakim*	2.00
262	*Robert Holcombe*	3.00
263	Bryan Still	.50
264	*Mikhael Ricks*	2.00
265	Charlie Jones	.50
266	J.J. Stokes	1.00
267	Marc Edwards	.50
268	Steve Young	2.00
269	Ricky Watters	1.00
270	Cortez Kennedy	.50
271	Shawn Springs	.50
272	Trent Dilfer	1.00
273	Warren Sapp	.50
274	Reidel Anthony	1.00
275	Yancey Thigpen	.50
276	Chris Sanders	.50
277	Eddie George	2.50
278	Leslie Shepherd	.50
279	*Skip Hicks*	4.00
280	Dana Stubblefield	.50
281	John Elway	4.00
282	Brett Favre	8.00
283	Junior Seau	1.50

284	Barry Sanders	8.00
285	Jerry Rice	4.00
286	Antonio Freeman	1.50
287	Peyton Manning	20.00
288	Warrick Dunn	3.00
289	Steve Young	2.00
290	Dan Marino	6.00
291	Jerome Bettis	1.50
292	Ryan Leaf	8.00
293	Deion Sanders	1.50
294	Eddie George	3.00
295	Joey Galloway	1.50
296	Troy Aikman	4.00
297	Andre Wadsworth	1.50
298	Terrell Davis	6.00
299	Steve McNair	2.00
300	Jake Plummer	3.00
301	Emmitt Smith	6.00
302	Isaac Bruce	1.50
303	Kordell Stewart	3.00
304	Dorsey Levens	1.50
305	Antowain Smith	1.75
306	Drew Bledsoe	3.00
307	Marshall Faulk	1.50
308	Herman Moore	1.50
309	Mark Brunell	3.00
310	Charles Woodson	6.00
311	Peyton Manning	30.00
312	Curtis Enis	10.00
313	*Terry Fair*	7.00
314	Andre Wadsworth	5.00
315	*Anthony Simmons*	4.00
316	*Jacquez Green*	12.00
317	Takeo Spikes	4.00
318	*Vonnie Holliday*	7.00
319	*Kyle Turley*	2.00
320	Keith Brooking	4.00
321	Randy Moss	125.00
322	*Shaun Williams*	2.00
323	Greg Ellis	2.00
324	Mikhael Ricks	5.00
325	Charles Woodson	10.00
326	*Corey Chavous*	2.00
327	*Stephen Alexander*	7.00
328	Marcus Nash	7.00
329	*Tre Thomas*	2.00
330	*Duane Starks*	7.00
331	*John Avery*	12.00
332	Kevin Dyson	7.00
333	Fred Taylor	15.00
334	Grant Wistrom	2.00
335	Ryan Leaf	15.00
336	Robert Edwards	12.00
337	*Jason Peter*	4.00
338	Brian Griese	25.00
339	Charlie Batch	25.00
340	Patrick Johnson	4.00
341	John Elway	10.00
342	Curtis Enis	10.00
343	Antonio Freeman	3.00
344	Mark Brunell	6.00
345	Robert Edwards	12.00
346	Ryan Leaf	15.00
347	Steve Young	5.00
348	Jerome Bettis	3.00
349	Antowain Smith	3.00
350	Tim Brown	3.00
351	Peyton Manning	30.00
352	Troy Aikman	8.00
353	Natrone Means	3.00
354	Dan Marino	15.00
355	Junior Seau	1.50
356	Brad Johnson	3.00
357	Jerry Rice	8.00
358	Drew Bledsoe	6.00
359	Fred Taylor	15.00
360	Emmitt Smith	12.00
361	Terrell Davis	20.00
362	Kordell Stewart	10.00
363	Barry Sanders	25.00
364	Jake Plummer	10.00
365	Brett Favre	25.00
366	Curtis Enis	18.00
367	Eddie George	10.00
368	Napoleon Kaufman	5.00
369	Randy Moss	125.00
370	Warrick Dunn	10.00

1998 SPx Finite Radiance

Radiance is a gold-foil parallel of the SPx Finite base set. Regular cards are numbered to 3,800, Playmakers to 2,750, Youth Movement to 1,500, Pure Energy to 1,000 and Heroes of the Game to 100. The ten rookie cards are numbered to 50 in this set.

	MT
Cards (191-280):	2x
Production 5,050 Sets	
Production 500 for #218,221,239	
Cards (281-310):	2x
Production 3,600 Sets	
Cards (311-340):	2x
Production 1,885 Sets	
Production 350 for #321,338,339	
Cards (341-360):	2x
Production 900 Sets	
Cards (361-370):	2x
Production 540 Sets	

1998 SPx Finite Spectrum

Spectrum is a rainbow foil version of the SPx Finite base set. Regular cards are numbered to 1,900, Playmakers to 1,375, Youth Movement to 750, Pure Energy to 50 and Heroes of the Game is a 1-of-1 set. The ten rookie cards are also 1-of-1 in this parallel.

	MT
Cards (191-280):	4x-8x
Rookies (191-280):	1.5x-3x
Production 325 Sets	
Cards (281-310):	5x-10x
Rookies (281-310):	1.5x-3x
Production 150 Sets	
Cards (311-340):	4x-8x
#321,338,339:	2x-4x
Production 50 Sets	
Cards (341-360):	15x-30x
Rookies (341-360):	6x-12x
Production 25 Sets	
Cards (361-370):	
Production 1 Set	

1998 Topps Gold Label

Each card in this set was printed on 35 point spectra-reflective rainbow stock and was gold foiled-stamped with the player's name and the Gold Label logo. The backs of the cards reveal all relevant statistics, including career totals and career bests as well as insightful player commentary. Each card has a parallel Class 2 and a Class 3 card. The Class 2 cards have the name and logo in silver foil and were inserted 1:2 packs. The Class 3 singles were in prismatic gold foil and found 1:4 packs.

		MT
Complete Set (100):		125.00
Common Player:		.25
Class 2 Cards		2x
Class 2 Rookies:		1.5x
Name In Silver Foil		
Inserted 1:2		
Class 3 Cards:		3x
Class 3 Rookies:		2x
Name In Prismatic Gold Foil		
Inserted 1:4		
Wax Box:		110.00
1	John Elway	4.00
2	Rob Moore	.25
3	Jamal Anderson	1.50
4	*Patrick Johnson*	1.50
5	Troy Aikman	4.00
6	Antowain Smith	1.50
7	Wesley Walls	.25
8	*Curtis Enis*	5.00
9	Jimmy Smith	.50
10	Terrell Davis	6.00
11	Marshall Faulk	1.00
12	*Germane Crowell*	4.00
13	*Marcus Nash*	4.00
14	Deion Sanders	1.00
15	Dorsey Levens	.50
16	Corey Dillon	1.50
17	*Fred Taylor*	12.00
18	Derrick Thomas	.25
19	*Kevin Dyson*	4.00
20	*Peyton Manning*	15.00
21	Warren Sapp	.25
22	*Robert Holcombe*	3.00
23	Joey Galloway	1.00
24	Garrison Hearst	.50
25	Brett Favre	8.00
26	Aeneas Williams	.25
27	Danny Kanell	.25
28	Robert Smith	.50
29	Brad Johnson	1.00
30	Dan Marino	6.00
31	Elvis Grbac	.50
32	Terry Allen	.25
33	Frank Sanders	.25
34	Peter Boulware	.25
35	Tim Brown	.50
36	Thurman Thomas	.50
37	Rae Carruth	.25
38	Michael Irvin	.50
39	*Brian Griese*	8.00
40	Kordell Stewart	3.00
41	Johnnie Morton	.25
42	Robert Brooks	.25
43	Keenan McCardell	.25
44	Ben Coates	.50
45	Jerry Rice	4.00
46	*Tony Simmons*	2.50
47	Irving Fryar	.25
48	*Jerome Pathon*	2.00
49	Steve McNair	1.50
50	Warrick Dunn	3.00
51	*Skip Hicks*	4.00
52	*Andre Wadsworth*	2.00
53	Chris Chandler	.50
54	Curtis Conway	.50
55	Eddie George	3.00
56	Jeff Blake	.50
57	*Greg Ellis*	1.50
58	Scott Mitchell	.25
59	Antonio Freeman	1.00
60	Drew Bledsoe	4.00
61	Mark Brunell	3.00
62	Andre Rison	.50
63	Cris Carter	1.00
64	Jake Reed	.25
65	Napoleon Kaufman	1.50
66	Terry Glenn	1.00
67	Jason Sehorn	.25
68	Rickey Dudley	.25
69	Junior Seau	.50
70	Jerome Bettis	1.00
71	J.J. Stokes	.50
72	Warren Moon	.50
73	Isaac Bruce	.50
74	Mike Alstott	1.00
75	Steve Young	2.50
76	*Jacquez Green*	4.00
77	Gus Frerotte	.25
78	Michael Jackson	.25
79	Carl Pickens	.50
80	Bruce Smith	.25
81	Shannon Sharpe	.50
82	Herman Moore	.50
83	Reggie White	1.00
84	Marvin Harrison	.75
85	Jake Plummer	3.00
86	Karim Abdul-Jabbar	.75
87	John Randle	.25
88	*Robert Edwards*	6.00
89	Jeff George	.50
90	Emmitt Smith	6.00
91	Terrell Owens	1.50
92	Trent Dilfer	1.00
93	Darrell Green	.25
94	Andre Reed	.25
95	*Ryan Leaf*	7.00
96	Rod Smith	.50
97	O.J. McDuffie	.25
98	*John Avery*	4.00
99	Charles Way	.25
100	Barry Sanders	8.00

1998 Topps Gold Label Black Label

Each of the three versions in this set are the same as in the base Gold Label set except for the logo is in black. Class 1 singles have the name in gold foil and are found 1:8 packs. Class 2 cards are in silver foil and inserted 1:16 packs. Class 3 singles are in prismatic gold foil and inserted 1:32 packs.

	MT
Class 1 Cards:	5x
Class 1 Rookies:	3x
Name In Gold Foil	
Inserted 1:8	
Class 2 Cards:	8x
Class 2 Rookies:	5x
Name In Silver Foil	
Inserted 1:16	
Class 3 Cards:	12x
Class 3 Rookies:	7x
Name In Prismatic Gold Foil	
Inserted 1:32	

1998 Topps Gold Label Red Label

Red Label cards are the same as the base Gold Label set except for the logo is in red foil and each card is sequentially numbered. Class 1 singles have the name in gold foil (1:94) and are numbered to 100. Class 2 singles are in silver foil (1:187) and numbered to 50. Class 3 cards are in prismatic gold foil (1:375) and numbered to 25.

	MT
Class 1 Cards:	20x-40x
Class 1 Rookies:	10x-20x
Name In Gold Foil	
Inserted 1:94	
Production 100 Sets	
Class 2 Cards:	25x-50x
Class 2 Rookies:	12x-25x
Name In Silver Foil	
Inserted 1:187	
Production 50 Sets	
Class 3 Cards:	50x-100x
Class 3 Rookies:	25x-50x
Name In Prismatic Gold Foil	
Inserted 1:375	
Production 25 Sets	

1998 Topps Stars

Each borderless card is printed on 20-point stock and uses luminous diffraction technology with matte gold-foil stamping. Every card in this product is sequentially numbered. The Red and Bronze set are both considered base sets and are each numbered to 8,799. Three parallel sets include Silver, Gold and Gold Rainbow. The Silver singles were numbered to 3,999, the Gold cards are to 1,999 and inserted 1:2 packs, and the Gold Rainbow cards were numbered to 99 and found 1:41 packs.

		MT
Complete Set (150):		125.00
Common Red Player:		.20
Common Red Rookie:		1.00
Production 8,799 Sets		
Bronze Cards:		1x
Production 8,799 Sets		
Silver Cards:		1.5x
Production 3,999 Sets		
Gold Cards:		3x
Gold Rookies:		2x
Production 1,999 Sets		
Inserted 1:2		
Gold Rainbow Cards:		15x-30x
Gold Rainbow Rookies:		5x-10x
Production 99 Sets		
Inserted 1:41		
Wax Box:		90.00
1	John Elway	2.50
2	*Duane Starks*	2.00
3	Bruce Smith	.20
4	Jeff Blake	.40
5	Carl Pickens	.40
6	Shannon Sharpe	.40
7	*Jerome Pathon*	3.00
8	Jimmy Smith	.40
9	Elvis Grbac	.20
10	Mark Brunell	2.00
11	Karim Abdul-Jabbar	.75
12	Terry Glenn	.75
13	Larry Centers	.20
14	Jeff George	.40
15	Terry Allen	.20
16	Charles Johnson	.20
17	Chris Spielman	.20
18	*Ahman Green*	4.00
19	*Kevin Dyson*	4.00
20	Dan Marino	4.00
21	*Andre Wadsworth*	2.00
22	Chris Chandler	.20
23	Kerry Collins	.40
24	Erik Kramer	.20
25	Warrick Dunn	2.00
26	Michael Irvin	.40
27	Herman Moore	.40
28	Dorsey Levens	.40
29	Cris Carter	.40
30	Drew Bledsoe	2.00
31	Kevin Greene	.20
32	Charles Way	.20
33	Bobby Hoying	.20
34	Tony Banks	.40
35	Steve Young	1.50
36	Trent Dilfer	.40
37	Warren Sapp	.20
38	*Skip Hicks*	2.50
39	Michael Jackson	.20
40	Curtis Martin	1.00
41	Thurman Thomas	.40
42	Corey Dillon	1.50
43	*Brian Griese*	8.00
44	Marshall Faulk	.75
45	Isaac Bruce	.40
46	*Fred Taylor*	12.00
47	Andre Rison	.20
48	O.J. McDuffie	.20
49	*John Avery*	3.00
50	Terrell Davis	4.00
51	*Robert Edwards*	6.00
52	Keyshawn Johnson	.40
53	Rickey Dudley	.20
54	*Hines Ward*	2.50
55	Irving Fryar	.20
56	Freddie Jones	.20
57	Michael Sinclair	.20
58	Darnay Scott	.20
59	*Tim Dwight*	2.50
60	Tim Brown	.40

61 Ray Lewis .20
62 *Curtis Enis* 5.00
63 Emmitt Smith 4.00
64 Scott Mitchell .20
65 Antonio Freeman .75
66 *Randy Moss* 20.00
67 *Peyton Manning* 15.00
68 Danny Kanell .20
69 Charlie Garner .20
70 Mike Alstott .75
71 *Grant Wistrom* 1.00
72 *Jacquez Green* 3.50
73 Gus Frerotte .20
74 Peter Boulware .20
75 Jerry Rice 2.50
76 Antowain Smith 1.00
77 *Brian Simmons* 1.00
78 Rod Smith .40
79 Marvin Harrison .40
80 *Ryan Leaf* 7.00
81 Keenan McCardell .20
82 Derrick Thomas .20
83 Zach Thomas .40
84 Ben Coates .20
85 Rob Moore .20
86 Wayne Chrebet .20
87 Napoleon Kaufman .75
88 Levon Kirkland .20
89 Junior Seau .40
90 Eddie George 2.00
91 Warren Moon .40
92 *Anthony Simmons* 1.00
93 Steve McNair 1.25
94 Frank Sanders .20
95 Joey Galloway .75
96 Jamal Anderson .75
97 Rae Carruth .20
98 Curtis Conway .40
99 *Greg Ellis* 1.00
100 Kordell Stewart 2.00
101 *Germane Crowell* 3.50
102 Mark Chmura .40
103 Robert Smith .40
104 Andre Hastings .20
105 Reggie White .40
106 Jessie Armstead .20
107 Kevin Hardy .20
108 *Robert Holcombe* 3.50
109 Garrison Hearst .40
110 Jerome Bettis .40
111 Reidel Anthony .40
112 Michael Westbrook .20
113 *Patrick Johnson* 1.00
114 Andre Reed .20
115 *Charles Woodson* 5.00
116 *Takeo Spikes* 2.00
117 *Marcus Nash* 3.00
118 *Tavian Banks* 3.00
119 Tony Gonzalez .40
120 Jake Plummer 2.00
121 *Tony Simmons* 2.50
122 Aaron Glenn .20
123 Ricky Watters .40
124 Kimble Anders .20
125 Barry Sanders 5.00
126 Terance Mathis .20
127 Wesley Walls .20
128 Bobby Engram .20
129 Johnnie Morton .20
130 Brett Favre 5.00
131 Brad Johnson .40
132 John Randle .20
133 Chris Sanders .20
134 *Joe Jurevicius* 2.00
135 Deion Sanders 1.00
136 Terrell Owens 1.00
137 Darrell Green .20
138 Jermaine Lewis .20
139 James Stewart .20
140 Troy Aikman 2.50
141 Hardy Nickerson .20
142 Blaine Bishop .20
143 *Keith Brooking* 2.00
144 *Jason Peter* 1.00
145 Jake Reed .20
146 Jason Sehorn .20
147 Robert Brooks .20
148 J.J. Stokes .40
149 Michael Strahan .20
150 Glenn Foley .40

1998 Topps Stars Galaxy

Each single in this set has the bronze foil, was sequentially numbered to 100 and inserted 1:611 packs. Silver foil cards were numbered to 75 and found 1:814 packs. Gold foil cards were numbered to 50 and inserted 1:1,222. Gold Rainbow singles were the toughest to find with only five printed and inserted 1:12,215.

	MT
Complete Set (10):	750.00
Common Bronze Player:	25.00
Production 100 Sets	
Inserted 1:611	
Silver Cards:	1.5x
Production 75 Sets	
Inserted 1:814	
Gold Cards:	2x
Production 50 Sets	
Inserted 1:1,222	
G1 Brett Favre	200.00
G2 Barry Sanders	200.00
G3 Bruce Smith	25.00
G4 Herman Moore	50.00
G5 Tim Brown	50.00
G6 Steve Young	75.00
G7 Cris Carter	50.00
G8 John Elway	100.00
G9 Mark Brunell	100.00
G10 Terrell Davis	150.00

1998 Topps Stars Luminaries

Each card in this set has bronze foil stamping and is sequentially numbered to 100. Singles were tough to pull from packs at 1:407. The Silver parallel set has the foil stamping in silver and is numbered to 75 and was inserted 1:543 packs. The Gold parallel was numbered to 50 and inserted 1:814 packs. The last parallel set was the Gold Rainbow that was limited to five of each and found 1:8,144.

	MT
Complete Set (15):	850.00
Common Bronze Player:	25.00
Production 100 Sets	
Inserted 1:407	
Silver Cards:	1.5x
Production 75 Sets	
Inserted 1:543	
Gold Cards:	2x
Production 50 Sets	
Inserted 1:814	
L1 Brett Favre	120.00
L2 Steve Young	45.00
L3 John Elway	100.00
L4 Barry Sanders	120.00
L5 Terrell Davis	100.00
L6 Eddie George	50.00
L7 Herman Moore	25.00
L8 Tim Brown	25.00
L9 Jerry Rice	60.00
L10 Junior Seau	25.00
L11 Bruce Smith	25.00
L12 John Randle	25.00
L13 Peyton Manning	100.00
L14 Ryan Leaf	50.00
L15 Curtis Enis	35.00

1998 Topps Stars Rookie Reprints

Topps reprinted eight NFL Hall of Famers' rookie cards and inserted them 1:24 packs. Each card also has a parallel Autograph card with the odds at 1:153 packs.

	MT
Complete Set (8):	30.00
Common Player:	2.00
Inserted 1:24	
Autographs:	10x
Inserted 1:153	
1 Walter Payton	10.00
2 Don Maynard	4.00
3 Charlie Joiner	4.00
4 Fred Biletnikoff	4.00
5 Paul Hornung	4.00
6 Gale Sayers	6.00
7 John Hannah	2.00
8 Paul Warfield	4.00

1998 Topps Stars Supernova

Each single in this set has the bronze foil, was sequentially numbered to 100 and inserted 1:611 packs. Silver foil cards were numbered to 75 and found 1:814 packs. Gold foil cards were numbered to 50 and inserted 1:1,222. Gold Rainbow singles were the toughest to find with only five printed and inserted 1:12,215.

	MT
Complete Set (10):	750.00
Common Bronze Player:	25.00
Production 100 Sets	
Inserted 1:611	
Silver Cards:	1.5x
Production 75 Sets	
Inserted 1:814	
Gold Cards:	2x
Production 50 Sets	
Inserted 1:1,222	
S1 Ryan Leaf	50.00
S2 Curtis Enis	60.00
S3 Kevin Dyson	45.00
S4 Randy Moss	200.00
S5 Peyton Manning	100.00
S6 Duane Starks	25.00
S7 Grant Wistrom	25.00
S8 Charles Woodson	60.00
S9 Fred Taylor	100.00
S10 Andre Wadsworth	45.00

1998 UD Choice

UD Choice was released in two series. Series One consists of a 255-card base set. The set has 165 regular cards featuring white borders and 27 full-bleed regular cards. Subsets include 30 Rookie Class cards and 30 Draw Your Own Trading Card contest winners. Three checklists round out the set. The base set is paralleled in Choice Reserve and Prime Choice Reserve. Inserts include StarQuest and Mini Bobbing Head cards. A Draw Your Own Trading Card entry was inserted in each pack. UD Choice Series Two consists of a 183-card base set, featuring the 30-card Domination Next subset (1:4). Series Two also has Choice Reserve and Prime Choice Reserve parallels. Inserts include NFL GameDay '99, StarQuest-RookQuest and Domination Next SE.

	MT
Complete Series 2 (183):	35.00
Common Player:	.10
Common Domination Next:	.75
Inserted 1:4	
Domination Next SE:	3x
Production 2,000 Sets	
Choice Reserve Stars:	5x-10x
Choice Reserve Rookies:	3x
Inserted 1:6	
PC Reserve Stars:	40x-80x
PC Reserve Rookies:	12x-25x
Production 100 Sets	
Series 2 Wax Box:	40.00

256 Peyton Manning 6.00
257 Ryan Leaf 3.00
258 Andre Wadsworth 1.50
259 Charles Woodson 3.00
260 Curtis Enis 2.50
261 Grant Wistrom .75
262 Greg Ellis .75
263 Fred Taylor 3.00
264 Duane Starks 1.50
265 Keith Brooking .75
266 Takeo Spikes .75
267 Anthony Simmons .75
268 Kevin Dyson 2.00
269 Robert Edwards 2.00
270 Randy Moss 10.00
271 *John Avery* 4.00
272 *Marcus Nash* 4.00
273 *Jerome Pathon* 2.00
274 Jacquez Green 2.00
275 Robert Holcombe 2.00
276 *Patrick Johnson* .75
277 Germane Crowell 2.00
278 *Tony Simmons* 2.00
279 *Joe Jurevicius* 2.00
280 Skip Hicks 2.00
281 Sam Cowart .75
282 *Rashaan Shehee* 1.50
283 *Brian Griese* 10.00
284 *Tim Dwight* 4.00
285 Ahman Green 2.00
286 Adrian Murrell .20
287 Corey Chavous .10
288 Eric Swann .10
289 Frank Sanders .10
290 Eric Metcalf .10
291 *Jammi German* .50
292 Eugene Robinson .10
293 Chris Chandler .10
294 Tony Martin .10
295 Jessie Tuggle .10
296 Errict Rhett .10
297 Jim Harbaugh .10
298 Eric Green .10
299 Ray Lewis .10
300 Jamie Sharper .10
301 *Fred Coleman* .30
302 Rob Johnson .20
303 Quinn Early .10
304 Thurman Thomas .20
305 Andre Reed .10
306 Sean Gilbert .10
307 Kerry Collins .20
308 Jason Peter .10
309 Michael Bates .10
310 William Floyd .10
311 *Alonzo Mayes* .30
312 *Tony Parrish* .30
313 Walt Harris .10
314 Edgar Bennett .10
315 Jeff Jaeger .10
316 Brian Simmons .20
317 David Dunn .10
318 Ashley Ambrose .10
319 Darnay Scott .10
320 Neil O'Donnell .10
321 Flozell Adams .10
322 Stepfret Williams .10
323 Emmitt Smith 1.50
324 Michael Irvin .20
325 Chris Warren .10
326 *Eric Brown* .20
327 Rod Smith .20
328 Terrell Davis 1.50
329 Neil Smith .10
330 Darrien Gordon .10
331 *Curtis Alexander* .20
332 Barry Sanders 2.00
333 David Sloan .10
334 Johnnie Morton .10
335 Robert Porcher .10
336 Tommy Vardell .10
337 Vonnie Holliday .20
338 Dorsey Levens .20
339 Derrick Mayes .10
340 Robert Brooks .10
341 Raymont Harris .10
342 *E.G. Green* .75
343 Torrance Small .10
344 Carlton Gray .10
345 Aaron Bailey .10
346 Jeff Burris .10
347 *Donovin Darius* .20
348 *Tavian Banks* 1.50
349 *Aaron Beasley* .20
350 Tony Brackens .10
351 Bryce Paup .10
352 Chester McGlockton .10
353 Leslie O'Neal .10
354 Derrick Alexander .10
355 Kimble Anders .10
356 Tamarick Vanover .10
357 Brock Marion .10
358 *Larry Shannon* .20
359 Karim Abdul-Jabbar .30
360 Troy Drayton .10
361 O.J. McDuffie .10
362 John Randle .10
363 David Palmer .10
364 Robert Smith .20
365 *Kailee Wong* .20
366 Duane Clemons .10
367 *Kyle Turley* .20
368 Sean Dawkins .10
369 Lamar Smith .10
370 *Cameron Cleeland* 1.00
371 Keith Poole .10
372 *Tebucky Jones* .20
373 Willie McGinest .10
374 Ty Law .10
375 Lawyer Milloy .10
376 Tony Carter .10
377 *Shaun Williams* .20
378 *Brian Alford* .20
379 Tyrone Wheatley .10
380 Jason Sehorn .10
381 *David Patten* .20
382 *Scott Frost* .20
383 Mo Lewis .10
384 Kevin Williams .10
385 Curtis Martin .30
386 Vinny Testaverde .20
387 *Mo Collins* .20
388 James Jett .10
389 Eric Allen .10
390 *Jon Ritchie* .20
391 Harvey Williams .10
392 Tre Thomas .10
393 Rodney Peete .10
394 Hugh Douglas .10
395 Charlie Garner .10
396 *Karl Hankton* .20
397 Kordell Stewart .75
398 George Jones .10
399 Earl Holmes .10
400 *Hines Ward* 1.00
401 Jason Gildon .10
402 Ricky Proehl .10
403 Az-Zahir Hakim .20
404 Amp Lee .10
405 Eric Hill .10
406 *Leonard Little* .20
407 Charlie Jones .10
408 Craig Whelihan .10
409 Terrell Fletcher .10
410 *Kenny Bynum* .20
411 *Mikhael Ricks* .75
412 *R.W. McQuarters* .50
413 Jerry Rice 1.00
414 Garrison Hearst .20
415 Ty Detmer .10
416 Gabe Wilkins .10
417 *Michael Black* .20
418 James McKnight .10
419 Darrin Smith .10
420 Joey Galloway .20
421 Ricky Watters .20
422 Warrick Dunn .75
423 Brian Kelly .10
424 Bert Emanuel .10
425 John Lynch .10
426 Regan Upshaw .10
427 Yancey Thigpen .10
428 Kenny Holmes .10
429 Frank Wycheck .10
430 *Samari Rolle* .20
431 Brian Mitchell .10
432 Stephen Alexander .10
433 Jamie Asher .10
434 Michael Westbrook .10
435 Dana Stubblefield .10
436 Dan Wilkinson .10
437 Checklist Dan Marino .75
438 Checklist Jerry Rice .50

1998 UD Choice Starquest/Rookquest Blue

	MT
Complete Set (30):	30.00
Common Player:	.25
Inserted 1:1	
Green Cards:	3x
Inserted 1:7	
Red Cards:	3x-6x
Inserted 1:23	
Gold Cards:	20x-40x
Production 100 Sets	
SR1 John Elway, Peyton Manning	3.50

SR2	Drew Bledsoe, Ryan Leaf	2.50
SR3	Barry Sanders, Tavian Banks	2.50
SR4	Brett Favre, Vonnie Holliday	2.50
SR5	Junior Seau, Takeo Spikes	.50
SR6	Deion Sanders, Charles Woodson	1.00
SR7	Jerry Rice, Randy Moss	5.00
SR8	Reggie White, Andre Wadsworth	.50
SR9	Emmitt Smith, Fred Taylor	2.50
SR10	Michael Irvin, Kevin Dyson	.75
SR11	Troy Aikman, Shaun Williams	1.25
SR12	Jerome Bettis, Curtis Enis	1.00
SR13	Dan Marino, Brian Griese	2.50
SR14	Steve Young, R.W. McQuarters	.75
SR15	Dana Stubblefield, Greg Ellis	.25
SR16	Jake Plummer, Patrick Johnson	1.00
SR17	Corey Dillon, Rashaan Shehee	.75
SR18	Mark Brunell, Jerome Pathon	1.00
SR19	Andre Rison, Jacquez Green	.50
SR20	Mike Alstott, Jon Ritchie	.50
SR21	Dorsey Levens, Ahman Green	.50
SR22	Kordell Stewart, Hines Ward	1.00
SR23	Antowain Smith, Skip Hicks	.50
SR24	Herman Moore, Germane Crowell	.75
SR25	Kevin Greene, Jason Peter	.25
SR26	Keyshawn Johnson, Marcus Nash	.75
SR27	Eddie George, Robert Holcombe	1.00
SR28	Warrick Dunn, John Avery	1.00
SR29	Tamarick Vanover, Tim Dwight	.50
SR30	Terrell Davis, Robert Edwards	2.50

1998 Ultra

Ultra Football was released in two series in 1998 and contained a total of 425 cards. Series I had 197 veterans, three checklists and a 25-card 1998 Rookies subset seeded one per three packs. Series II had 132 player cards, 25 '98 Greats, three checklists and 40 rookies seeded one per three packs. Cards featured a full color shot of the player, with his name embossed foil writing in the lower right corner. Every card appears in three different parallels - Gold Medallion, Platinum Medallion and Masterpieces. Inserts in Series I include: Canton Classics, Flair Showcase Preview, Next Century, Sensational Sixty, Shots and Touchdown Kings. Inserts in Series II include: Rush Hour, Damage, Inc., Caught in the Draft, Indefensible and Exclamation Points.

		MT
Complete Series 2 (200):		130.00
Common Player:		.15
Common Rookie (386-425):		1.00
Inserted 1:3		
Gold Cards:		2x-4x
Inserted 1:1 Hobby		
Gold Rookies:		1.5x
Inserted 1:24 Hobby		
Platinum Cards:		40x-80x
Production 98 Sets		
Platinum Rookies:		4x-8x
Production 66 Sets		
Wax Box Series 2:		55.00
226	Doug Flutie	2.50
227	Ike Hillard	.15
228	Craig Heyward	.15
229	Kevin Hardy	.15
230	Jason Dunn	.15
231	Billy Davis	.15
232	Chester McGlockton	.15
233	Sean Gilbert	.15
234	Bert Emanuel	.15
235	Keith Byars	.15
236	Tyrone Wheatley	.15
237	Ricky Proehl	.15
238	Michael Bates	.15
239	Derrick Alexander	.15
240	Harvey Williams	.15
241	Mike Pritchard	.15
242	Paul Justin	.15
243	Jeff Hostetler	.15
244	Eric Moulds	.30
245	Jeff Burris	.15
246	Gary Brown	.15
247	Antwuan Wyatt	.15
248	Dan Wilkinson	.15
249	Chris Warren	.15
250	Lawrence Phillips	.15
251	Eric Metcalf	.15
252	Pat Swilling	.15
253	Lamar Smith	.15
254	Quinn Early	.15
255	Carlester Crumpler	.15
256	Eric Bieniemy	.15
257	Aaron Bailey	.15
258	Gabe Wilkins	.15
259	Rod Woodson	.15
260	Ricky Whittle	.15
261	Iheanyi Uwaezuoke	.15
262	Heath Shuler	.15
263	Darren Sharper	.15
264	John Henry Mills	.15
265	Marco Battaglia	.15
266	Yancey Thigpen	.15
267	Irv Smith	.15
268	Jamie Sharper	.15
269	Marcus Robinson	.15
270	Dorsey Levens	.30
271	Qadry Ismail	.15
272	Desmond Howard	.15
273	Webster Slaughter	.15
274	Eugene Robinson	.15
275	Bill Romanowski	.15
276	Vincent Brisby	.15
277	Errict Rhett	.15
278	Albert Connell	.15
279	Thomas Lewis	.15
280	John Farquhar	.15
281	Marc Edwards	.15
282	Tyrone Davis	.50
283	Eric Allen	.15
284	Aaron Glenn	.15
285	Roosevelt Potts	.15
286	Kez McCorvey	.15
287	Joey Kent	.15
288	Jim Druckenmiller	.30
289	Sean Dawkins	.15
290	Edgar Bennett	.15
291	Vinny Testaverde	.30
292	Chris Slade	.15
293	Lamar Lathon	.15
294	Jackie Harris	.15
295	Jim Harbaugh	.30
296	Rob Fredrickson	.15
297	Ty Detmer	.15
298	Karl Williams	.15
299	Troy Drayton	.15
300	Curtis Martin	.75
301	Tamarick Vanover	.15
302	Lorenzo Neal	.15
303	John Hall	.15
304	Kevin Greene	.15
305	Bryan Still	.15
306	Neil Smith	.15
307	Mark Rypien	.15
308	Shawn Jefferson	.15
309	Aaron Taylor	.15
310	Sedrick Shaw	.15
311	O.J. Santiago	.15
312	Kevin Abrams	.15
313	Dana Stubblefield	.15
314	Daryl Johnston	.15
315	Yatil Green	.15
316	Jeff Graham	.15
317	Mario Bates	.15
318	Adrian Murrell	.30
319	Larry Brown	.15
320	Jahine Arnold	.15
321	Justin Armour	.15
322	Ricky Watters	.30
323	Lamont Warren	.15
324	Mack Strong	.15
325	Darnay Scott	.15
326	Brian Mitchell	.15
327	Rob Johnson	.30
328	Kent Graham	.15
329	Hugh Douglas	.15
330	Simeon Rice	.15
331	Corey Holliday	.15
332	Randall Cunningham	.75
333	Steve Atwater	.15
334	Latario Rachel	.15
335	Tony Martin	.15
336	Leroy Hoard	.15
337	Howard Griffith	.15
338	Kevin Lockett	.15
339	William Floyd	.15
340	Jerry Ellison	.15
341	Kyle Brady	.15
342	Michael Westbrook	.15
343	Kevin Turner	.15
344	David LaFleur	.15
345	Robert Jones	.15
346	Dave Brown	.15
347	Kevin Williams	.15
348	Amani Toomer	.15
349	Amp Lee	.15
350	Bryce Paup	.15
351	DeWayne Washington	.15
352	Mercury Hayes	.15
353	Scottie Graham	.15
354	Ray Crockett	.15
355	Ted Washington	.15
356	Pete Mitchell	.15
357	Billy Jenkins	.15
358	Troy Aikman CL	.50
359	Drew Bledsoe CL	.50
360	Steve Young CL	.40
361	Antonio Freeman	.30
362	Antowain Smith	.50
363	Barry Sanders	3.00
364	Bobby Hoying	.15
365	Brett Favre	3.00
366	Corey Dillon	.75
367	Dan Marino	2.00
368	Drew Bledsoe	1.50
369	Eddie George	1.25
370	Emmitt Smith	2.00
371	Herman Moore	.30
372	Jake Plummer	1.00
373	Jerome Bettis	.30
374	Jerry Rice	1.50
375	Joey Galloway	.30
376	John Elway	1.50
377	Kordell Stewart	1.00
378	Mark Brunell	1.00
379	Keyshawn Johnson	.15
380	Steve Young	1.00
381	Steve McNair	.75
382	Terrell Davis	2.00
383	Tim Brown	.15
384	Troy Aikman	1.50
385	Warrick Dunn	1.00
386	Ryan Leaf	10.00
387	*Tony Simmons*	4.00
388	*Chris Howard*	1.00
389	*John Avery*	5.00
390	*Shaun Williams*	1.00
391	*Anthony Simmons*	2.00
392	*Rashaan Shehee*	2.00
393	Robert Holcombe	3.00
394	*Larry Shannon*	1.00
395	Skip Hicks	3.00
396	*Rod Rutledge*	1.00
397	*Donald Hayes*	2.00
398	Curtis Enis	5.00
399	*Mikhael Ricks*	3.00
400	*Brian Griese*	25.00
401	*Michael Pittman*	2.00
402	Jacquez Green	4.00
403	*Jerome Pathon*	3.00
404	*Ahman Green*	8.00
405	Marcus Nash	4.00
406	Randy Moss	30.00
407	*Terry Fair*	3.00
408	*Jammi German*	2.00
409	*Stephen Alexander*	3.00
410	*Grant Wistrom*	1.00
411	*Charlie Batch*	25.00
412	Fred Taylor	15.00
413	*Patrick Johnson*	2.00
414	Robert Edwards	7.00
415	*Keith Brooking*	2.00
416	Peyton Manning	20.00
417	*Duane Starks*	2.00
418	Andre Wadsworth	2.00
419	*Brian Alford*	2.00
420	*Brian Kelly*	1.00
421	*Joe Jurevicius*	3.00
422	*Tebucky Jones*	1.00
423	*R.W. McQuarters*	2.00
424	Kevin Dyson	4.00
425	Charles Woodson	6.00

1998 Ultra Caught in the Draft

Caught in the Draft singles were found in Series II packs and inserted 1:24. Only rookies who made an impact in '98 were included.

		MT
Complete Set (15):		100.00
Common Player:		3.00
Inserted 1:24		
1	Andre Wadsworth	3.00
2	Curtis Enis	7.00
3	Germane Crowell	5.00
4	Peyton Manning	20.00
5	Tavian Banks	5.00
6	Fred Taylor	15.00
7	John Avery	5.00
8	Randy Moss	30.00
9	Robert Edwards	6.00
10	Charles Woodson	8.00
11	Ryan Leaf	8.00
12	Ahman Green	5.00
13	Robert Holcombe	4.00
14	Jacquez Green	5.00
15	Skip Hicks	5.00

1998 Ultra Damage Inc.

Each single in this set has a business card look to it. Singles were found in Series II packs at 1:72.

		MT
Complete Set (15):		250.00
Common Player:		5.00
Inserted 1:72		
1	Terrell Davis	30.00
2	Joey Galloway	8.00
3	Kordell Stewart	15.00
4	Troy Aikman	20.00
5	Barry Sanders	40.00
6	Ryan Leaf	15.00
7	Antonio Freeman	8.00
8	Keyshawn Johnson	5.00
9	Eddie George	15.00
10	Warrick Dunn	15.00
11	Drew Bledsoe	20.00
12	Peyton Manning	40.00
13	Antowain Smith	8.00
14	Brett Favre	40.00
15	Emmitt Smith	30.00

1998 Ultra Exclamation Points

Exclamation Point cards can be found in Series II packs at 1:288. Each single in this 15-card set is printed on plastic and has a pattern holofoil front.

		MT
Complete Set (15):		550.00
Common Player:		15.00
Inserted 1:288		
1	Terrell Davis	50.00
2	Brett Favre	60.00
3	John Elway	50.00
4	Barry Sanders	60.00
5	Peyton Manning	60.00
6	Jerry Rice	30.00
7	Emmitt Smith	50.00
8	Dan Marino	50.00
9	Kordell Stewart	25.00
10	Mark Brunell	25.00
11	Ryan Leaf	30.00
12	Corey Dillon	20.00
13	Antowain Smith	15.00
14	Curtis Martin	15.00
15	Deion Sanders	15.00

1998 Ultra Indefensible

Each card in this 10-card set folds out from its original size and has embossed graphics on the front. Singles were inserted 1:144 packs.

		MT
Complete Set (10):		200.00
Common Player:		10.00
Inserted 1:144		
1	Jake Plummer	20.00
2	Mark Brunell	20.00
3	Terrell Davis	40.00
4	Jerry Rice	25.00
5	Barry Sanders	50.00
6	Curtis Martin	10.00
7	Warrick Dunn	20.00
8	Emmitt Smith	40.00
9	Dan Marino	40.00
10	Corey Dillon	15.00

1998 Ultra Rush Hour

Rush Hour singles were found in Series II packs at a

rate of 1:6. Fleer included both veterans and rookies from '98 in this 20-card set.

		MT
Complete Set (20):		35.00
Common Player:		1.00
Inserted 1:6		
1	Robert Edwards	4.00
2	John Elway	4.00
3	Mike Alstott	2.00
4	Robert Holcombe	2.00
5	Mark Brunell	3.00
6	Deion Sanders	2.00
7	Curtis Martin	2.50
8	Curtis Enis	3.00
9	Dorsey Levens	1.00
10	Fred Taylor	6.00
11	John Avery	3.00
12	Eddie George	3.00
13	Jake Plummer	3.00
14	Andre Wadsworth	1.00
15	Fred Lane	1.00
16	Corey Dillon	2.50
17	Brett Favre	8.00
18	Kordell Stewart	3.00
19	Steve McNair	3.00
20	Warrick Dunn	3.00

1998 Upper Deck Black Diamond Rookies

This 120-card set includes 90 regular player cards (all possessing Light F/X foil treatment) with each card sporting a Single Black Diamond, along with a 30-card, short-printed "Rookie Single Black Diamond" subset (1:4 packs). The parallel Double Black Diamond singles feature red Light F/X technology with veterans numbered to 3,000 and rookies to 2,500. The Triple Black Diamond parallel set has veterans numbered to 1,500 and rookies to 1,000. The Quadruple Black Diamond set has veterans numbered to 150 and rookies to 100.

		MT
Complete Set (120):		175.00
Common Player:		.15
Common Rookie (91-120):		1.00
Inserted 1:4		
Double Cards:		2x-4x
Production 3,000 Sets		
Double Rookies:		1x
Production 2,500 Sets		
Triple Cards:		4x-8x
Production 1,500 Sets		
Triple Rookies:		2x
Production 1,000 Sets		
Quad. Cards:		20x-40x
Production 150 Sets		
Quad. Rookies:		3x-6x
Production 100 Sets		
Wax Box:		100.00
1	Jake Plummer	1.25
2	Adrian Murrell	.15
3	Frank Sanders	.15
4	Jamal Anderson	.75
5	Chris Chandler	.30
6	Tony Martin	.15
7	Jim Harbaugh	.30
8	Errict Rhett	.15
9	Michael Jackson	.15
10	Rob Johnson	.30
11	Antowain Smith	.50
12	Thurman Thomas	.30
13	Fred Lane	.15
14	Kerry Collins	.30
15	Rae Carruth	.15
16	Erik Kramer	.15
17	Edgar Bennett	.15
18	Curtis Conway	.30
19	Corey Dillon	.75
20	Neil O'Donnell	.15
21	Carl Pickens	.30
22	Troy Aikman	1.50
23	Emmitt Smith	2.00
24	Deion Sanders	.50
25	John Elway	1.50
26	Terrell Davis	2.50
27	Rod Smith	.30
28	Barry Sanders	3.00
29	Johnnie Morton	.15
30	Herman Moore	.30
31	Brett Favre	3.00
32	Antonio Freeman	.50
33	Dorsey Levens	.30
34	Marshall Faulk	.50
35	Marvin Harrison	.30
36	Zack Crockett	.15
37	Mark Brunell	1.25
38	Jimmy Smith	.30
39	Keenan McCardell	.30
40	Elvis Grbac	.30
41	Andre Rison	.30
42	Derrick Alexander	.15
43	Dan Marino	2.00
44	Karim Abdul-Jabbar	.30
45	Zach Thomas	.30
46	Brad Johnson	.50
47	Cris Carter	.50
48	Robert Smith	.50
49	Drew Bledsoe	1.25
50	Terry Glenn	.30
51	Ben Coates	.30
52	Danny Wuerffel	.30
53	Lamar Smith	.15
54	Sean Dawkins	.15
55	Danny Kanell	.15
56	Tiki Barber	.15
57	Ike Hilliard	.15
58	Curtis Martin	.50
59	Vinny Testaverde	.30
60	Keyshawn Johnson	.50
61	Napoleon Kaufman	.50
62	Jeff George	.30
63	Tim Brown	.30
64	Bobby Hoying	.30
65	Charlie Garner	.15
66	Duce Staley	.15
67	Kordell Stewart	1.25
68	Jerome Bettis	.50
69	Charles Johnson	.30
70	Tony Banks	.30
71	Isaac Bruce	.30
72	Eddie Kennison	.30
73	Natrone Means	.30
74	Bryan Still	.15
75	Junior Seau	.30
76	Steve Young	1.00
77	Jerry Rice	1.50
78	Garrison Hearst	.50
79	Ricky Watters	.30
80	Joey Galloway	.50
81	Warren Moon	.30
82	Warrick Dunn	1.00
83	Trent Dilfer	.30
84	Bert Emanuel	.15
85	Steve McNair	.75
86	Eddie George	1.25
87	Yancey Thigpen	.15
88	Leslie Shepherd	.15
89	Terry Allen	.30
90	Michael Westbrook	.15
91	*Peyton Manning*	25.00
92	*Jacquez Green*	6.00
93	*Fred Taylor*	20.00
94	*Terry Fair*	3.00
95	*Patrick Johnson*	3.00
96	*Corey Chavous*	2.00
97	*Randy Moss*	50.00
98	*Curtis Enis*	10.00
99	*Rashaan Shehee*	3.00
100	*Kevin Dyson*	6.00
101	*Shaun Williams*	1.00
102	*Grant Wistrom*	2.00
103	*John Avery*	6.00
104	*Brian Griese*	12.00
105	*Ryan Leaf*	10.00
106	*Jerome Pathon*	4.00
107	*Sam Cowart*	1.00
108	*Germane Crowell*	6.00
109	*Ahman Green*	6.00
110	*Greg Ellis*	1.00
111	*Robert Holcombe*	6.00
112	*Marcus Nash*	6.00
113	*Duane Starks*	3.00
114	*Andre Wadsworth*	3.00
115	*Takeo Spikes*	3.00
116	*Eric Brown*	1.00
117	*Robert Edwards*	10.00
118	*Charlie Batch*	18.00
119	*Mikhael Ricks*	4.00
120	*Charles Woodson*	10.00

1998 Upper Deck Black Diamond Rookies Sheer Brilliance

Each of these hobby-only singles has the Quadruple Black Diamond stamp on the front and each is sequentially numbered to the player's uniform number multiplied by 100.

		MT
Complete Set (30):		325.00
Common Player:		4.00
B1	Dan Marino (1300)	25.00
B2	Troy Aikman (800)	20.00
B3	Brett Favre (400)	50.00
B4	Ryan Leaf (1600)	25.00
B5	Peyton Manning (1800)	45.00
B6	Barry Sanders (2000)	25.00
B7	Emmitt Smith (2200)	15.00
B8	John Elway (700)	30.00
B9	Steve Young (800)	15.00
B10	Steve McNair (900)	12.00
B11	Antowain Smith (2300)	4.00
B12	Corey Dillon (2800)	6.00
B13	Terrell Davis (3000)	10.00
B14	Mark Brunell (800)	15.00
B15	Charles Woodson (2400)	12.00
B16	Brian Griese (1400)	15.00
B17	Curtis Martin (2800)	4.00
B18	Keyshawn Johnson (1900)	6.00
B19	Kordell Stewart (1000)	15.00
B20	Eddie George (2700)	6.00
B21	Drew Bledsoe (1100)	15.00
B22	Jake Plummer (1600)	12.00
B23	Warren Moon (100)	30.00
B24	Curtis Enis (3900)	6.00
B25	John Avery (2000)	6.00
B26	Randy Moss (1800)	80.00
B27	Rob Johnson (1100)	6.00
B28	Warrick Dunn (2800)	4.00
B29	Terry Allen (2100)	4.00
B30	Robert Smith (2600)	4.00

1998 Upper Deck Black Diamond Rookies White Onyx

This insert incorporates a new design with Pearl Light F/X treatment and also has the Quadruple Black Diamond logo. Each is sequentially numbered to 2,250.

		MT
Complete Set (30):		200.00
Common Player:		2.00
Production 2,250 Sets		
ON1	Peyton Manning	30.00
ON2	Corey Dillon	6.00
ON3	Jerome Bettis	4.00
ON4	Brett Favre	20.00
ON5	Napoleon Kaufman	4.00
ON6	Joey Galloway	4.00
ON7	John Elway	10.00
ON8	Troy Aikman	10.00
ON9	Robert Smith	4.00
ON10	Kordell Stewart	8.00
ON11	Garrison Hearst	4.00
ON12	Curtis Enis	8.00
ON13	Dan Marino	15.00
ON14	Jimmy Smith	2.00
ON15	Steve Young	6.00
ON16	Ryan Leaf	12.00
ON17	Steve McNair	6.00
ON18	Randy Moss	60.00
ON19	Curtis Martin	4.00
ON20	Barry Sanders	20.00
ON21	Rob Johnson	4.00
ON22	Emmitt Smith	15.00
ON23	Jake Plummer	8.00
ON24	Antonio Freeman	4.00
ON25	Mark Brunell	8.00
ON26	Warrick Dunn	8.00
ON27	Eddie George	8.00
ON28	Jerry Rice	10.00
ON29	Drew Bledsoe	8.00
ON30	Terrell Davis	15.00

1998 Upper Deck Encore

Encore was a fine-tuned version of Upper Deck's 1998 NFL Series I product that utilized a special rainbow-foil treatment on 150 of the earlier set's 255 cards (120 regular player cards and 30 Star Rookie subset cards). The rookies could be found 1:4 packs. The F/X set is a direct parallel of the entire Encore set. The differentiation comes in a color shift with a special "Encore F/X" call-out featured on the card fronts and backs. Singles are sequentially numbered to 125.

		MT
Complete Set (150):		325.00
Common Player:		.20
Common Rookie:		2.00
Inserted 1:4		
F/X Gold Cards:		25x-50x
F/X Gold Rookies:		2x-4x
Production 125 Sets		
Wax Box:		135.00
1	*Peyton Manning*	50.00
2	*Ryan Leaf*	25.00
3	*Andre Wadsworth*	4.00
4	*Charles Woodson*	18.00
5	*Curtis Enis*	15.00
6	*Fred Taylor*	35.00
7	*Duane Starks*	4.00
8	*Keith Brooking*	4.00
9	*Takeo Spikes*	4.00
10	*Kevin Dyson*	10.00
11	*Robert Edwards*	10.00
12	*Randy Moss*	75.00
13	*John Avery*	8.00
14	*Marcus Nash*	10.00
15	*Jerome Pathon*	4.00
16	*Jacquez Green*	10.00
17	*Robert Holcombe*	8.00
18	*Pat Johnson*	4.00
19	*Skip Hicks*	10.00
20	*Ahman Green*	8.00
21	*Brian Griese*	20.00
22	*Hines Ward*	6.00
23	*Tavian Banks*	6.00
24	*Tony Simmons*	6.00
25	*Rashaan Shehee*	4.00
26	*R.W. McQuarters*	4.00
27	*Jon Ritchie*	2.00
28	*Ryan Sutter*	2.00
29	*Tim Dwight*	8.00
30	*Charlie Batch*	35.00
31	Chris Chandler	.40
32	Jamal Anderson	1.00
33	Terance Mathis	.20
34	Jake Plummer	2.00
35	Mario Bates	.20
36	Frank Sanders	.20
37	Adrian Murrell	.20
38	Jim Harbaugh	.40
39	Michael Jackson	.20
40	Jermaine Lewis	.20
41	Doug Flutie	1.50
42	Rob Johnson	.40
43	Antowain Smith	1.00
44	Eric Moulds	1.00
45	Thurman Thomas	.40
46	Kevin Greene	.20
47	Fred Lane	.40
48	Rae Carruth	.20
49	William Floyd	.20
50	Erik Kramer	.20
51	Edgar Bennett	.20
52	Curtis Conway	.40
53	Bobby Engram	.20
54	Jeff Blake	.40
55	Carl Pickens	.75
56	Darnay Scott	.20
57	Corey Dillon	1.50
58	Troy Aikman	2.50
59	Michael Irvin	.40
60	Emmitt Smith	3.50
61	Deion Sanders	1.00
62	John Elway	3.00
63	Terrell Davis	4.00
64	Rod Smith	.40
65	Shannon Sharpe	.40
66	Ed McCaffrey	.75
67	Barry Sanders	5.00
68	Scott Mitchell	.40
69	Herman Moore	.75
70	Johnnie Morton	.20
71	Brett Favre	5.00
72	Dorsey Levens	.40
73	Reggie White	1.00
74	Antonio Freeman	1.00
75	Robert Brooks	.20
76	Marshall Faulk	1.00
77	Marvin Harrison	.40
78	Mark Brunell	2.00
79	Keenan McCardell	.40
80	Jimmy Smith	.75
81	Elvis Grbac	.20
82	Andre Rison	.40
83	Tony Gonzalez	.20
84	Derrick Thomas	.20
85	Dan Marino	3.50
86	Karim Abdul	1.00
87	O.J. McDuffie	.40
88	Zach Thomas	.40
89	Brad Johnson	1.00
90	Cris Carter	1.00
91	Jake Reed	.20
92	Robert Smith	.40
93	John Randle	.20
94	Randall Cunningham	1.00
95	Drew Bledsoe	2.00
96	Terry Glenn	1.00
97	Ben Coates	.40
98	Danny Wuerffel	.20
99	Andre Hastings	.20
100	Troy Davis	.20
101	Danny Kanell	.20
102	Tiki Barber	.20
103	Amani Toomer	.20
104	Vinny Testaverde	.40
105	Glenn Foley	.40
106	Curtis Martin	1.00
107	Keyshawn Johnson	1.00
108	Wayne Chrebet	.75
109	Jeff George	.40
110	Napoleon Kaufman	1.00
111	Tim Brown	.40
112	James Jett	.20
113	Bobby Hoying	.20
114	Charlie Garner	.20
115	Irving Fryar	.20
116	Kordell Stewart	2.00
117	Jerome Bettis	1.00
118	Will Blackwell	.20
119	Charles Johnson	.20
120	Tony Banks	.40
121	Amp Lee	.20
122	Isaac Bruce	.40
123	Eddie Kennison	.40
124	Natrone Means	.75
125	Junior Seau	.40
126	Bryan Still	.20
127	Steve Young	1.50
128	Jerry Rice	2.50
129	Garrison Hearst	.75
130	J.J. Stokes	.40
131	Terrell Owens	1.00
132	Warren Moon	.40
133	Jon Kitna	.40
134	Ricky Watters	.40
135	Joey Galloway	1.00
136	Trent Dilfer	.40
137	Warrick Dunn	2.00
138	Mike Alstott	1.00
139	Bert Emanuel	.20
140	Reidel Anthony	.20
141	Steve McNair	1.25
142	Yancey Thigpen	.20
143	Eddie George	2.00
144	Chris Sanders	.20
145	Gus Frerotte	.20
146	Terry Allen	.40
147	Michael Westbrook	.20
148	Troy Aikman CL	1.25

149	Dan Marino CL	1.50
150	Randy Moss CL	5.00

1998 Upper Deck Encore Constant Threat

This lineup showcases high-impact players who could affect the outcome of a game in the blink of an eye. Singles have the prefix "CT" before the card number and were inserted 1:11 packs.

		MT
Complete Set (15):		85.00
Common Player:		2.00
Inserted 1:11		
CT1	Dan Marino	10.00
CT2	Peyton Manning	15.00
CT3	Randy Moss	25.00
CT4	Brett Favre	12.00
CT5	Mark Brunell	5.00
CT6	John Elway	8.00
CT7	Ryan Leaf	7.00
CT8	Jake Plummer	5.00
CT9	Terrell Davis	10.00
CT10	Barry Sanders	12.00
CT11	Emmitt Smith	10.00
CT12	Curtis Martin	2.00
CT13	Eddie George	5.00
CT14	Warrick Dunn	5.00
CT15	Curtis Enis	4.00

1998 Upper Deck Encore Driving Forces

This insert consists of 14 NFL superstars, including top QB's, running backs and wide receivers. Singles have the prefix "F" before the card number and were inserted 1:23. The parallel F/X Golds are in gold foil and were sequentially numbered to 1,500.

		MT
Complete Set (14):		85.00
Common Player:		3.00
Inserted 1:23		
F/X Golds:		2x
Production 1,500 Cards		
F1	Terrell Davis	15.00
F2	Barry Sanders	20.00
F3	Doug Flutie	7.00
F4	Mark Brunell	8.00
F5	Garrison Hearst	3.00
F6	Jamal Anderson	5.00
F7	Jerry Rice	10.00
F8	John Elway	12.00
F9	Robert Smith	3.00
F10	Kordell Stewart	8.00
F11	Eddie George	8.00
F12	Antonio Freeman	3.00
F13	Dan Marino	15.00
F14	Steve Young	7.00

1998 Upper Deck Encore Milestones

This collection includes cards that will boast special "UD Milestones" stamps. Designated sequential numbering for each gold-foil card signifies a remarkable milestone reached by that player for the '98 season. For example, Dan Marino (400th touchdown pass thrown on 11/28/98) will be crash-numbered to 400.

		MT
Complete Set (8):		1500.
Common Player:		50.00
1	Peyton Manning/26	325.00
12	Randy Moss/17	850.00
60	Emmitt Smith/124	75.00
62	John Elway/50	150.00
63	Terrell Davis/30	250.00
67	Barry Sanders/100	125.00
85	Dan Marino/400	60.00
128	Jerry Rice/184	50.00

1998 Upper Deck Encore Rookie Encore

The 1998 season produced a host of solid first-year players and this lineup captures the best of the best. Each card has the prefix "RE" before the number and were found 1:23 packs. The FX Gold parallel singles are in gold foil and are sequentially numbered to 500.

		MT
Complete Set (10):		80.00
Common Player:		2.00
Inserted 1:23		
F/X Golds:		2x-4x
Production 500 Sets		
RE1	Randy Moss	40.00
RE2	Peyton Manning	20.00
RE3	Charlie Batch	12.00
RE4	Fred Taylor	12.00
RE5	Robert Edwards	7.00
RE6	Curtis Enis	6.00
RE7	Robert Holcombe	2.00
RE8	Ryan Leaf	8.00
RE9	John Avery	4.00
RE10	Tim Dwight	4.00

1998 Upper Deck Encore Superstar Encore

This insert includes the top six players in the league including rookie Randy Moss. Each single has the prefix "RR" before the card number and were inserted 1:23 packs. The F/X Gold parallel singles were limited to only 25 of each.

		MT
Complete Set (6):		50.00
Common Player:		4.00
Inserted 1:23		
F/X Gold Cards:		20x-40x
F/X Gold Rookies:		10x-20x
Production 25 Sets		
1	Brett Favre	12.00
2	Barry Sanders	12.00
3	Mark Brunell	4.00
4	Emmitt Smith	8.00
5	Randy Moss	25.00
6	Terrell Davis	10.00

1998 Upper Deck Encore Super Powers

These cards feature the hottest players who are in pursuit of a Super Bowl ring. Singles are on rainbow-foil stock and were inserted 1:11 packs.

		MT
Complete Set (15):		85.00
Common Player:		2.00
Inserted 1:11		
S1	Dan Marino	10.00
S2	Napoleon Kaufman	2.00
S3	Brett Favre	12.00
S4	John Elway	8.00
S5	Randy Moss	25.00
S6	Kordell Stewart	5.00
S7	Mark Brunell	5.00
S8	Peyton Manning	15.00
S9	Emmitt Smith	10.00
S10	Jake Plummer	5.00
S11	Eddie George	5.00
S12	Warrick Dunn	5.00
S13	Jerome Bettis	2.00
S14	Terrell Davis	10.00
S15	Fred Taylor	10.00

1998 Upper Deck Encore UD Authentics

This collection includes autographed cards of five NFL superstars: Mark Brunell, Dan Marino, Randy Moss, Terrell Davis and Joe Montana. Singles were inserted 1:288 packs.

		MT
Complete Set (5):		750.00
Common Player:		75.00
Inserted 1:288		
MB	Mark Brunell	75.00
DM	Dan Marino	200.00
RM	Randy Moss	275.00
TD	Terrell Davis	150.00
JM	Joe Montana	150.00

1999 Collector's Edge Advantage

Edge Advantage is a 190-card set that is made up of 150 veterans, 38 draft pick rookies and 2 checklists. Each card has three different parallels that include Gold Ingot, Galvanized and HoloGold. Other inserts in the product include Rookie Autographs, Jumpstarters, Memorable Moments, Overture, Prime Connection, Shockwaves and Showtime.

		MT
Complete Set (190):		65.00
Common Player:		.15
Common Rookie:		.50
Wax Box:		75.00
1	Larry Centers	.15
2	Rob Moore	.30
3	Adrian Murrell	.15
4	Jake Plummer	1.25
5	Frank Sanders	.15
6	Jamal Anderson	.50
7	Chris Chandler	.30
8	Tim Dwight	.50
9	Tony Martin	.15
10	Terance Mathis	.15
11	O.J. Santiago	.15
12	Jim Harbaugh	.30
13	Priest Holmes	.75
14	Jermaine Lewis	.30
15	Rod Woodson	.15
16	Eric Zeier	.15
17	Doug Flutie	.75
18	Sam Gash	.15
19	Rob Johnson	.30
20	Eric Moulds	.50
21	Andre Reed	.30
22	Antowain Smith	.50
23	Bruce Smith	.15
24	Thurman Thomas	.30
25	Steve Beuerlein	.15
26	Kevin Greene	.15
27	Raghib Ismail	.15
28	Fred Lane	.15
29	Muhsin Muhammad	.15
30	Edgar Bennett	.15
31	Curtis Conway	.30
32	Bobby Engram	.15
33	Curtis Enis	.50
34	Erik Kramer	.15
35	Jeff Blake	.30
36	Corey Dillon	.75
37	Neil O'Donnell	.30
38	Carl Pickens	.30
39	Takeo Spikes	.15
40	Troy Aikman	1.25
41	Billy Davis	.15
42	Michael Irvin	.30
43	Deion Sanders	.50
44	Emmitt Smith	1.75
45	Darren Woodson	.15
46	Bubby Brister	.30
47	Terrell Davis	1.75
48	John Elway	1.75
49	Ed McCaffrey	.30
50	Bill Romanowski	.15
51	Shannon Sharpe	.30
52	Rod Smith	.30
53	Charlie Batch	1.00
54	Germane Crowell	.30
55	Herman Moore	.50
56	Johnnie Morton	.15
57	Barry Sanders	2.50
58	Robert Brooks	.15
59	Brett Favre	2.50
60	Antonio Freeman	.50
61	Darick Holmes	.15
62	Dorsey Levens	.50
63	Roell Preston	.15
64	Marshall Faulk	.50
65	E.G. Green	.15
66	Marvin Harrison	.30
67	Peyton Manning	2.00
68	Jerome Pathon	.15
69	Mark Brunell	1.00
70	Kevin Hardy	.15
71	Keenan McCardell	.15
72	Jimmy Smith	.30
73	Fred Taylor	1.25
74	Alvis Whitted	.15
75	Kimble Anders	.15
76	Donnell Bennett	.15
77	Rich Gannon	.15
78	Elvis Grbac	.15
79	Bam Morris	.15
80	Andre Rison	.30
81	Karim Abdul	.30
82	John Avery	.30
83	Oronde Gadsden	.30
84	Sam Madison	.15
85	Dan Marino	1.75
86	O.J. McDuffie	.30
87	Zach Thomas	.30
88	Cris Carter	.50
89	Randall Cunningham	.50
90	Brad Johnson	.50
91	Randy Moss	3.00
92	John Randle	.30
93	Jake Reed	.15
94	Robert Smith	.50
95	Drew Bledsoe	1.00
96	Ben Coates	.30
97	Robert Edwards	.50
98	Terry Glenn	.50
99	Ty Law	.15
100	Cam Cleeland	.30
101	Kerry Collins	.30
102	Gary Brown	.15
103	Kent Graham	.15
104	Ike Hilliard	.30
105	Joe Jurevicius	.30
106	Danny Kanell	.15
107	Wayne Chrebet	.50
108	Aaron Glenn	.15
109	Keyshawn Johnson	.50
110	Curtis Martin	.50
111	Vinny Testaverde	.30
112	Tim Brown	.30
113	Jeff George	.30
114	James Jett	.15
115	Napoleon Kaufman	.50
116	Charles Woodson	.50
117	Koy Detmer	.15
118	Duce Staley	.15
119	Jerome Bettis	.50
120	Charles Johnson	.15
121	Kordell Stewart	.75
122	Tony Banks	.30
123	Isaac Bruce	.30
124	June Henley	.15
125	Ryan Leaf	.75
126	Natrone Means	.50
127	Mikhael Ricks	.15
128	Craig Whelihan	.15
129	Garrison Hearst	.30
130	Terrell Owens	.75
131	Jerry Rice	1.25
132	J.J. Stokes	.30
133	Steve Young	1.00
134	Joey Galloway	.50
135	Ahman Green	.30
136	Jon Kitna	.75
137	Ricky Watters	.30
138	Mike Alstott	.50
139	Reidel Anthony	.30
140	Trent Dilfer	.30
141	Warrick Dunn	.75
142	Jacquez Green	.30
143	Kevin Dyson	.30
144	Eddie George	.75
145	Steve McNair	.75
146	Yancy Thigpen	.30
147	Terry Allen	.30
148	Trent Green	.50
149	Skip Hicks	.30
150	Michael Westbrook	.30
151	*Rahim Abdullah*	1.00
152	*Champ Bailey*	2.00
153	*Marlon Barnes*	1.00
154	*D'Wayne Bates*	1.00
155	*Michael Bishop*	2.50
156	*Dre' Bly*	1.00
157	*David Boston*	3.00
158	*Chris Claiborne*	1.50
159	*Tim Couch*	12.00
160	*Daunte Culpepper*	5.00
161	*Autrey Denson*	1.75
162	*Jared DeVries*	1.00
163	*Troy Edwards*	2.50
164	*Kris Farris*	.50
165	*Kevin Faulk*	3.00
166	*Martin Gramatica*	.50
167	*Torry Holt*	3.00
168	*Brock Huard*	2.00
169	*Sedrick Irvin*	1.75
170	*Edgerrin James*	7.00
171	*James Johnson*	2.00
172	*Kevin Johnson*	1.75
173	*Andy Katzenmoyer*	1.50
174	*Jevon Kearse*	1.00
175	*Shaun King*	2.00
176	*Rob Konrad*	1.00
177	*Chris McAlister*	1.00
178	*Darnell McDonald*	2.00
179	*Donovan McNabb*	6.00
180	*Cade McNown*	6.00
181	*Dat Nguyen*	1.50
182	*Peerless Price*	2.50
183	*Akili Smith*	5.00
184	*Tai Streets*	1.50
185	*Cuncho Brown*	1.00
186	*Ricky Williams*	12.00
187	*Craig Yeast*	1.00
188	*Amos Zereoue*	2.50
189	Checklist	.15
190	Checklist	.15

1999 Collector's Edge Advantage Gold Ingot

Each Gold Ingot single is identical to the base card except for the foil is in gold rather than silver and each has a Gold Ingot stamp on the fronts of the cards. It is a parallel to the base and singles were inserted 1:1 packs.

	MT
Complete Set (190):	100.00
Gold Ingot Cards:	2x
Gold Ingot Rookies:	1.5x
Inserted 1:1	

1999 Collector's Edge Advantage Galvanized

Galvanized singles are printed on silver foil board with gold foil stamping. Each has a Galvanized stamp on the front and are sequentially numbered on the back. Veterans are numbered to 500 and rookies to 200.

	MT
Galvanized Cards:	4x-8x
Production 500 Sets	
Galvanized Rookies:	3x-6x
Production 200 Sets	

1999 Collector's Edge Advantage HoloGold

HoloGold singles are printed on holographic foil board with veterans numbered to 50 and rookies to 20.

	MT
HoloGold Cards:	40x-80x
Production 50 Sets	
HoloGold Rookies:	20x-40x
Production 20 Sets	

1999 Collector's Edge Advantage Jumpstarters

Each of the singles in this set are printed on clear acetate and offer commentary of each player from Peyton Manning. Each card was sequentially numbered to 500.

		MT
Complete Set (10):		75.00
Common Player:		5.00
Production 500 Sets		
1	Champ Bailey	5.00
2	David Boston	10.00
3	Tim Couch	25.00
4	Daunte Culpepper	12.00
5	Torry Holt	10.00
6	Donovan McNabb	12.00
7	Cade McNown	12.00
8	Peerless Price	7.00
9	Brock Huard	5.00
10	Ricky Williams	25.00

1999 Collector's Edge Advantage Memorable Moments

Each card in this set highlights a memorable moment from 1998. Each is printed on silver foil and they were found 1:24 packs.

		MT
Complete Set (10):		85.00
Common Player:		5.00
Inserted 1:24		
1	Terrell Davis	12.00
2	Randy Moss	15.00
3	Peyton Manning	12.00
4	Emmitt Smith	12.00
5	Keyshawn Johnson	5.00
6	Dan Marino	12.00
7	John Elway	12.00
8	Doug Flutie	7.00
9	Jerry Rice	10.00
10	Steve Young	8.00

1999 Collector's Edge Advantage Overture

Ten of the NFL's superstars are featured in this foil set with gold foil stamping. Singles were inserted 1:24 packs.

		MT
Complete Set (10):		100.00
Common Player:		5.00
Inserted 1:24		
1	Jamal Anderson	5.00
2	Terrell Davis	12.00
3	John Elway	12.00
4	Brett Favre	15.00
5	Peyton Manning	12.00
6	Dan Marino	12.00
7	Randy Moss	15.00
8	Jerry Rice	10.00
9	Barry Sanders	15.00
10	Emmitt Smith	12.00

1999 Collector's Edge Advantage Prime Connection

Current and future NFL stars were included in this 20-card set. Singles were inserted 1:4 packs.

		MT
Complete Set (20):		65.00
Common Player:		1.50
Inserted 1:4		
1	Ricky Williams	12.00
2	Fred Taylor	4.00
3	Tim Couch	12.00
4	Peyton Manning	5.00
5	Daunte Culpepper	5.00
6	Drew Bledsoe	3.50
7	Torry Holt	4.00
8	Keyshawn Johnson	1.50
9	Champ Bailey	1.50
10	Charles Woodson	1.50
11	Brock Huard	1.50
12	Jake Plummer	4.00
13	Donovan McNabb	6.00
14	Steve Young	3.50
15	Edgerrin James	7.00
16	Jamal Anderson	1.50
17	Cade McNown	6.00
18	Mark Brunell	3.50
19	Peerless Price	3.50
20	Randy Moss	6.00

1999 Collector's Edge Advantage Rookie Autographs

Each of the autographs are printed on holographic foil board with the signature found on the fronts of each card. Singles were inserted on average of 1:24 packs.

		MT
Common Player:		6.00
Inserted 1:24		
151	Rahim Abdullah	12.00
152	Champ Bailey	15.00
153	Marlon Barnes	12.00
154	D'Wayne Bates	12.00
155	Michael Bishop	20.00
156	Dre Bly	6.00
157	David Boston	30.00
158	Cuncho Brown	6.00
159	Chris Claiborne	12.00
160	Tim Couch	100.00
161	Daunte Culpepper	45.00
162	Autry Denson	12.00
163	Jared DeVries	12.00
164	Troy Edwards	20.00
165	Kris Farris	6.00
166	Kevin Faulk	30.00
167	Martin Gramatica	6.00
168	Torry Holt	25.00
169	Brock Huard	15.00
170	Sedrick Irvin	15.00
171	Edgerrin James	60.00
172	James Johnson	15.00
173	Kevin Johnson	15.00
174	Andy Katzenmoyer	15.00
175	Jevon Kearse	12.00
176	Shaun King	15.00
177	Rob Konrad	12.00
178	Chris McAlister	12.00
179	Darnell McDonald	15.00
180	Donovan McNabb	45.00
181	Cade McNown	45.00
182	Dat Nguyen	12.00
183	Peerless Price	20.00
184	Akili Smith	40.00
185	Tai Streets	15.00
186	Ricky Williams	100.00
187	Craig Yeast	12.00
188	Amos Zereoue	20.00

1999 Collector's Edge Advantage Shockwaves

This 20-card set was printed on foil board with gold foil stamping. They were inserted 1:12 packs.

		MT
Complete Set (20):		120.00
Common Player:		3.50
Inserted 1:12		
1	Jamal Anderson	3.50
2	Jake Plummer	8.00
3	Eric Moulds	3.50
4	Troy Aikman	8.00
5	Emmitt Smith	12.00
6	Marshall Faulk	3.50
7	Jerome Bettis	3.50
8	Barry Sanders	16.00
9	Brett Favre	16.00
10	Peyton Manning	12.00
11	Mark Brunell	6.00
12	Fred Taylor	8.00
13	Randall Cunningham	3.50
14	Randy Moss	16.00
15	Drew Bledsoe	6.00
16	Keyshawn Johnson	3.50
17	Curtis Martin	3.50
18	Steve Young	5.00
19	Warrick Dunn	5.00
20	Eddie George	5.00

1999 Collector's Edge Advantage Showtime

Each of the 15 cards in this insert are printed on clear acetate with gold foil stamping. Each was sequentially numbered to 500.

		MT
Complete Set (15):		125.00
Common Player:		5.00
Production 500 Sets		
1	Troy Aikman	10.00
2	Jamal Anderson	5.00
3	Mark Brunell	8.00
4	Terrell Davis	15.00
5	Warrick Dunn	7.00
6	Brett Favre	20.00
7	Doug Flutie	7.00
8	Eddie George	7.00
9	Keyshawn Johnson	5.00
10	Peyton Manning	15.00
11	Dan Marino	15.00
12	Randy Moss	20.00
13	Jake Plummer	10.00
14	Jerry Rice	10.00
15	Barry Sanders	20.00

1999 Collector's Edge Fury

Edge Fury is a 200-card set with 148 veteran players, two checklists and 50 seeded rookies found one-per-pack. The product includes three parallel sets with Gold Ingot, Galvanized and HoloGold inserts. Other inserts include: Extreme Team, Fast and Furious, Forerunners, Game Ball, Heir Force and Xplosive.

		MT
Complete Set (200):		70.00
Common Player:		.15
Common Rookie:		.50
Inserted 1:1		
Wax Box:		60.00
1	Checklist	.15
2	Checklist	.15
3	Karim Abdul	.30
4	Troy Aikman	1.50
5	Derrick Alexander	.15
6	Mike Alstott	.50
7	Jamal Anderson	.50
8	Reidel Anthony	.30
9	Tiki Barber	.15
10	Charlie Batch	1.00
11	Edgar Bennett	.15
12	Jerome Bettis	.50
13	Steve Beuerlein	.15
14	Tim Biakabutuka	.30
15	Jeff Blake	.30
16	Drew Bledsoe	1.00
17	Bubby Brister	.30
18	Robert Brooks	.15
19	Gary Brown	.15
20	Tim Brown	.30
21	Isaac Bruce	.30
22	Mark Brunell	1.00
23	Chris Calloway	.15
24	Cris Carter	.50
25	Larry Centers	.15
26	Chris Chandler	.30
27	Wayne Chrebet	.50
28	Cam Cleeland	.30
29	Kerry Collins	.30
30	Curtis Conway	.30
31	Germane Crowell	.30
32	Randall Cunningham	.50
33	Terrell Davis	2.00
34	Koy Detmer	.15
35	Ty Detmer	.30
36	Trent Dilfer	.50
37	Corey Dillon	.50
38	Warrick Dunn	.75
39	Tim Dwight	.50
40	Kevin Dyson	.30
41	John Elway	2.00
42	Bobby Engram	.15
43	Curtis Enis	.50
44	Terry Fair	.15
45	Marshall Faulk	.50
46	Brett Favre	3.00
47	Doug Flutie	.75
48	Antonio Freeman	.50
49	Joey Galloway	.50
50	Rich Gannon	.15
51	Eddie George	.75
52	Jeff George	.30
53	Terry Glenn	.50
54	Elvis Grbac	.15
55	Ahman Green	.30
56	Jacquez Green	.30
57	Trent Green	.50
58	Kevin Greene	.15
59	Brian Griese	1.00
60	Az-Zahir Hakim	.30
61	Jim Harbaugh	.30
62	Marvin Harrison	.30
63	Courtney Hawkins	.15
64	Garrison Hearst	.50
65	Ike Hilliard	.30
66	Billy Joe Hobert	.15
67	Priest Holmes	.50
68	Michael Irvin	.30
69	Raghib Ismail	.15
70	Shawn Jefferson	.15
71	James Jett	.15
72	Brad Johnson	.50
73	Charles Johnson	.15
74	Keyshawn Johnson	.50
75	Pat Johnson	.15
76	Joe Jurevicius	.15
77	Napoleon Kaufman	.50
78	Eddie Kennison	.30
79	Terry Kirby	.15
80	Jon Kitna	.75
81	Erik Kramer	.15
82	Fred Lane	.15
83	Ty Law	.15
84	Ryan Leaf	.75
85	Amp Lee	.15
86	Dorsey Levens	.50
87	Jermaine Lewis	.30
88	Sam Madison	.15
89	Peyton Manning	2.00
90	Dan Marino	2.00
91	Curtis Martin	.75
92	Tony Martin	.15
93	Terance Mathis	.15
94	Ed McCaffrey	.30
95	Keenan McCardell	.15
96	O.J. McDuffie	.30
97	Steve McNair	.75
98	Natrone Means	.30
99	Herman Moore	.50
100	Rob Moore	.30
101	Bam Morris	.30
102	Johnnie Morton	.15
103	Randy Moss	3.50
104	Eric Moulds	.50
105	Muhsin Muhammad	.15
106	Adrian Murrell	.30
107	Terrell Owens	.50
108	Jerome Pathon	.15
109	Carl Pickens	.30
110	Jake Plummer	1.25
111	Andre Reed	.15
112	Jake Reed	.15
113	Jerry Rice	1.50
114	Mikhael Ricks	.15
115	Andre Rison	.30
116	Barry Sanders	3.00
117	Deion Sanders	.50
118	Frank Sanders	.30
119	O.J. Santiago	.15
120	Darnay Scott	.15
121	Junior Seau	.30
122	Shannon Sharpe	.30
123	Leslie Shepherd	.15
124	Antowain Smith	.50
125	Bruce Smith	.15
126	Emmitt Smith	2.00
127	Jimmy Smith	.30
128	Robert Smith	.50
129	Rod Smith	.30
130	Chris Spielman	.15
131	Takeo Spikes	.15
132	Duce Staley	.30
133	Kordell Stewart	.75
134	Bryan Still	.15
135	J.J. Stokes	.30
136	Fred Taylor	1.50

137	Vinny Testaverde	.30
138	Yancey Thigpen	.30
139	Thurman Thomas	.30
140	Zach Thomas	.30
141	Amani Toomer	.15
142	Hines Ward	.30
143	Chris Warren	.30
144	Ricky Watters	.30
145	Michael Westbrook	.30
146	Alvis Whitted	.15
147	Charles Woodson	.50
148	Rod Woodson	.15
149	Frank Wycheck	.15
150	Steve Young	1.00
151	*Rabih Abdullah*	1.00
152	*Champ Bailey*	2.00
153	*D'Wayne Bates*	1.50
154	*Michael Bishop*	2.50
155	*Dre' Bly*	1.50
156	*David Boston*	3.00
157	*Fernando Bryant*	.50
158	*Chris Claiborne*	1.50
159	Mike Cloud	1.50
160	*Cecil Collins*	3.00
161	*Tim Couch*	12.00
162	*Daunte Culpepper*	5.00
163	*Antwan Edwards*	.50
164	*Troy Edwards*	2.50
165	*Ebenezer Ekuban*	1.00
166	*Kevin Faulk*	3.00
167	*Joe Germaine*	2.00
168	*Aaron Gibson*	.50
169	*Martin Gramatica*	.50
170	*Torry Holt*	2.50
171	*Brock Huard*	2.00
172	*Sedrick Irvin*	1.50
173	*Edgerrin James*	8.00
174	*James Johnson*	1.75
175	*Kevin Johnson*	1.50
176	*Andy Katzenmoyer*	1.50
177	*Jevon Kearse*	1.00
178	*Patrick Kerney*	.50
179	*Lamar King*	.50
180	*Shaun King*	1.75
181	*Jim Kleinsasser*	.50
182	*Rob Konrad*	1.00
183	*Chris McAlister*	1.00
184	*Anthony McFarland*	1.00
185	*Karsten Bailey*	1.00
186	*Donovan McNabb*	5.00
187	*Cade McNown*	5.00
188	*Joe Montgomery*	1.50
189	*Dat Nguyen*	1.50
190	*Luke Petitgout*	.50
191	*Peerless Price*	2.00
192	*Akili Smith*	4.00
193	*Matt Stinchcomb*	.50
194	*John Tait*	.50
195	*Jermaine Fazande*	.50
196	*Ricky Williams*	12.00
197	*Al Wilson*	1.00
198	*Antoine Winfield*	1.00
199	*Damien Woody*	.50
200	*Amos Zereoue*	2.50

1999 Collector's Edge Fury Gold Ingot

This is a 200-card parallel to the base set that was inserted 1:1 packs. The photo is the same as the base except for it's printed on foil board and the foil on the front is gold rather than silver. Each also has a Gold Ingot gold stamp on the fronts of the cards.

	MT
Complete Set (200):	140.00
Gold Ingot Cards:	2x
Gold Ingot Rookies:	1.5x
Inserted 1:1	

1999 Collector's Edge Fury Galvanized

This 200-card parallel is identical to the Gold Ingot parallel except for the Galvanized stamp on the front of the card in silver and each card is sequentially numbered on the back. Veterans are numbered to 500 and rookies to 100.

	MT
Complete Set (200):	550.00
Galvanized Cards:	3x-6x
Production 500 Sets	
Galvanized Rookies:	5x-10x
Production 100 Sets	

1999 Collector's Edge Fury HoloGold

Each card in this 200-card parallel set are printed on prismatic silver foil board. Each card front has the HoloGold stamp in gold foil. Veterans are printed to 50 and rookies to 10.

	MT
HoloGold Cards:	40x-80x
Production 50 Sets	
HoloGold Rookies:	25x-50x
Production 10 Sets	

1999 Collector's Edge Fury Extreme Team

Each card in this 10-card set is printed on micro-etched gold holographic foil board. Singles were inserted 1:24 packs.

		MT
Complete Set (10):		60.00
Common Player:		4.00
Inserted 1:24		
1	Keyshawn Johnson	4.00
2	Emmitt Smith	12.00
3	John Elway	12.00
4	Terrell Davis	12.00
5	Barry Sanders	15.00
6	Brett Favre	15.00
7	Peyton Manning	12.00
8	Fred Taylor	8.00
9	Dan Marino	12.00
10	Randy Moss	15.00

1999 Collector's Edge Fury Fast and Furious

This 25-card insert is sequentially numbered to 500 and is printed on plastic card stock with gold foil stamping.

		MT
Complete Set (25):		100.00
Common Player:		2.00
Production 500 Sets		
1	Jake Plummer	8.00
2	Jamal Anderson	4.00
3	Eric Moulds	4.00
4	Curtis Enis	4.00
5	Emmitt Smith	12.00
6	Deion Sanders	4.00
7	Terrell Davis	12.00
8	Barry Sanders	15.00
9	Herman Moore	4.00
10	Charlie Batch	5.00
11	Marshall Faulk	4.00
12	Mark Brunell	6.00
13	Fred Taylor	8.00
14	Randy Moss	15.00
15	Cris Carter	4.00
16	Robert Edwards	2.00
17	Keyshawn Johnson	4.00
18	Curtis Martin	4.00
19	Charles Woodson	4.00
20	Jerome Bettis	4.00
21	Kordell Stewart	5.00
22	Steve Young	6.00
23	Jerry Rice	8.00
24	Warrick Dunn	5.00
25	Eddie George	5.00

1999 Collector's Edge Fury Forerunners

This 15-card set includes the top running backs in the NFL. Each card is printed on holographic foil board with gold foil stamping. Singles were inserted 1:8 packs.

		MT
Complete Set (15):		40.00
Common Player:		1.00
Inserted 1:8		
1	Jamal Anderson	2.00
2	Curtis Enis	2.00
3	Corey Dillon	2.00
4	Emmitt Smith	8.00
5	Barry Sanders	10.00
6	Terrell Davis	8.00
7	Marshall Faulk	2.00
8	Fred Taylor	6.00
9	Robert Smith	2.00
10	Curtis Martin	2.00
11	Jerome Bettis	2.00
12	Garrison Hearst	2.00
13	Warrick Dunn	4.00
14	Eddie George	4.00
15	Ricky Watters	1.00

1999 Collector's Edge Fury Game Ball

Each card in this 43-card set includes a piece of a game-used football that the player used. Singles were found 1:24 packs.

	MT
Complete Set (43):	600.00
Common Player:	6.00
Inserted 1:24	
Troy Aikman	25.00
Mike Alstott	12.00
Charlie Batch	20.00
Jerome Bettis	12.00
Mark Brunell	20.00
Cris Carter	12.00
Terrell Davis	40.00
Corey Dillon	12.00
Warrick Dunn	15.00
John Elway	40.00
Curtis Enis	12.00
Marshall Faulk	12.00
Brett Favre	50.00
Antonio Freeman	12.00
Joey Galloway	12.00
Eddie George	15.00
Garrison Hearst	12.00
Michael Irvin	6.00
Rob Johnson	12.00
Napoleon Kaufman	12.00
Ryan Leaf	15.00
Dorsey Levens	12.00
Peyton Manning	40.00
Curtis Martin	12.00
Steve McNair	15.00
Natrone Means	12.00
Warren Moon	12.00
Herman Moore	12.00
Randy Moss	50.00
Adrian Murrell	6.00
Terrell Owens	12.00
Carl Pickens	6.00
Jake Plummer	25.00
Jerry Rice	25.00
Barry Sanders	50.00
Deion Sanders	12.00
Shannon Sharpe	6.00
Antowain Smith	12.00
Emmitt Smith	35.00
Rod Smith	6.00
Kordell Stewart	15.00
Fred Taylor	25.00
Steve Young	20.00

1999 Collector's Edge Fury Heir Force

This 20-card set includes the top rookies and were inserted 1:6 packs. Each card was printed on holographic foil board with gold foil stamping.

		MT
Complete Set (20):		45.00
Common Player:		1.00
Inserted 1:6		
1	Rahim Abdullah	1.00
2	Champ Bailey	2.00
3	D'Wayne Bates	1.00
4	Michael Bishop	2.50
5	David Boston	3.00
6	Chris Claiborne	1.50
7	Tim Couch	12.00
8	Daunte Culpepper	5.00
9	Kevin Faulk	3.00
10	Torry Holt	2.50
11	Brock Huard	2.00
12	Edgerrin James	8.00
13	Andy Katzenmoyer	1.50
14	Shaun King	1.75
15	Rob Konrad	1.00
16	Donovan McNabb	5.00
17	Cade McNown	5.00
18	Peerless Price	2.00
19	Akili Smith	4.00
20	Ricky Williams	12.00

1999 Collector's Edge Fury X-Plosive

Each card is printed on explosive micro-etched holofoil with foil stamping. Singles from this 20-card set were found 1:12 packs.

		MT
Complete Set (20):		100.00
Common Player:		1.50
Inserted 1:12		
1	Jake Plummer	8.00
2	Doug Flutie	5.00
3	Eric Moulds	3.00
4	Troy Aikman	8.00
5	John Elway	12.00
6	Charlie Batch	6.00
7	Herman Moore	3.00
8	Brett Favre	15.00
9	Antonio Freeman	3.00
10	Peyton Manning	12.00
11	Mark Brunell	6.00
12	Dan Marino	12.00
13	Randy Moss	15.00
14	Drew Bledsoe	6.00
15	Keyshawn Johnson	3.00
16	Vinny Testaverde	1.50
17	Kordell Stewart	4.00
18	Terrell Owens	3.00
19	Jerry Rice	8.00
20	Steve Young	6.00

1999 Collector's Edge Supreme

The 170-card base set includes 40 rookie cards. A few errors in the set with two different Tim Couch cards #141. The error is the rarest to find without stats on the back. The corrected versions are numbered TC and include stats. Michael Wiley was suppose to be #166, but chose to stay in college and they had to be pulled from the set. Some still found their way into packs. The #166B Edgerrin James Trade card was inserted late and tough to find. Two parallel sets with Gold Ingot and Galvanized. Other inserts include: Future, Homecoming, Markers, PSA 10 Redemptions, Route XXXIII, Supremacy and T3.

		MT
Complete Set (170):		150.00
Common Player:		.20
Common Rookie:		1.00
Card #166A not part of set price		
Wax Box:		100.00
1	Randy Moss CL	1.50
2	Peyton Manning CL	.75
3	Rob Moore	.40
4	Adrian Murrell	.20
5	Jake Plummer	1.50
6	Andre Wadsworth	.20
7	Jamal Anderson	.75
8	Chris Chandler	.40
9	Tony Martin	.20
10	Terance Mathis	.20
11	Jim Harbaugh	.40
12	Priest Holmes	.75
13	Jermaine Lewis	.20
14	Eric Zeier	.20
15	Doug Flutie	.75
16	Eric Moulds	.75
17	Andre Reed	.40
18	Antowain Smith	.75
19	Steve Beuerlein	.20
20	Kevin Greene	.20
21	Raghib Ismail	.20
22	Fred Lane	.20
23	Edgar Bennett	.20
24	Curtis Conway	.40
25	Curtis Enis	.75
26	Erik Kramer	.20
27	Corey Dillon	.75
28	Neil O'Donnell	.20
29	Carl Pickens	.40
30	Darnay Scott	.20
31	Troy Aikman	1.50
32	Michael Irvin	.40
33	Deion Sanders	.75
34	Emmitt Smith	2.00
35	Chris Warren	.40
36	Terrell Davis	2.00
37	John Elway	2.00
38	Ed McCaffrey	.75
39	Shannon Sharpe	.40
40	Rod Smith	.40
41	Charlie Batch	1.25
42	Herman Moore	.40
43	Johnnie Morton	.20
44	Barry Sanders	3.00
45	Robert Brooks	.20
46	Brett Favre	3.00
47	Antonio Freeman	.75
48	Darick Holmes	.20
49	Dorsey Levens	.75
50	Reggie White	.40
51	Marshall Faulk	.75
52	Marvin Harrison	.40
53	Peyton Manning	2.50
54	Jerome Pathon	.40
55	Tavian Banks	.40
56	Mark Brunell	1.25
57	Keenan McCardell	.20
58	Fred Taylor	2.00
59	Derrick Alexander	.20
60	Donnell Bennett	.20
61	Rich Gannon	.20
62	Andre Rison	.40
63	Karim Abdul	.40
64	John Avery	.40
65	Oronde Gadsden	.40
66	Dan Marino	2.00
67	O.J. McDuffie	.20
68	Cris Carter	.75
69	Randall Cunningham	.75
70	Brad Johnson	.40
71	Randy Moss	5.00
72	Jake Reed	.20
73	Robert Smith	.40
74	Drew Bledsoe	1.25
75	Ben Coates	.40
76	Robert Edwards	.75
77	Terry Glenn	.40
78	Cameron Cleeland	.40
79	Kerry Collins	.40
80	Sean Dawkins	.20
81	Lamar Smith	.20
82	Gary Brown	.20
83	Chris Calloway	.20
84	Ike Hilliard	.20
85	Danny Kanell	.20
86	Wayne Chrebet	.75
87	Keyshawn Johnson	.75
88	Curtis Martin	.75
89	Vinny Testaverde	.40
90	Tim Brown	.40
91	Jeff George	.40
92	Napoleon Kaufman	.75
93	Charles Woodson	.75
94	Irving Fryar	.20
95	Bobby Hoying	.20
96	Duce Staley	.20
97	Jerome Bettis	.40
98	Courtney Hawkins	.20
99	Charles Johnson	.20
100	Kordell Stewart	1.00
101	Hines Ward	.40
102	Tony Banks	.40
103	Isaac Bruce	.40
104	Robert Holcombe	.40
105	Ryan Leaf	1.00
106	Natrone Means	.40
107	Mikhael Ricks	.40
108	Junior Seau	.40
109	Garrison Hearst	.40
110	Terrell Owens	.75
111	Jerry Rice	1.50
112	J.J. Stokes	.40
113	Steve Young	1.00
114	Joey Galloway	.75
115	Jon Kitna	1.00
116	Warren Moon	.40
117	Ricky Watters	.40
118	Mike Alstott	.40
119	Reidel Anthony	.40
120	Warrick Dunn	1.00
121	Trent Dilfer	.40
122	Jacquez Green	.40
123	Kevin Dyson	.40
124	Eddie George	1.00
125	Steve McNair	.75
126	Frank Wycheck	.20
127	Terry Allen	.40
128	Trent Green	.40
129	Skip Hicks	.40
130	Michael Westbrook	.20
131	*Rahim Abdullah*	2.00
132	*Champ Bailey*	4.00
133	*Marlon Barnes*	2.00
134	*D'Wayne Bates*	2.00
135	*Michael Bishop*	4.00
136	*Dre' Bly*	1.00
137	*David Boston*	5.00
138	*Cuncho Brown*	1.00
139	*Na Brown*	1.00
140	*Tony Bryant*	1.00
141	*Tim Couch ERROR*	85.00
141TC	*Tim Couch*	25.00
142	*Chris Claiborne*	3.00
143	*Daunte Culpepper*	7.00
144	*Jared DeVries*	1.00
145	*Troy Edwards*	4.00
146	*Kris Farris*	1.00
147	*Kevin Faulk*	3.00
148	*Joe Germaine*	4.00
149	*Aaron Gibson*	1.00
150	*Torry Holt*	5.00
151	*Brock Huard*	3.00
152	*Sedrick Irvin*	3.00
153	*James Johnson*	2.00
154	*Kevin Johnson*	3.00
155	*Andy Katzenmoyer*	3.00
156	*Jevon Kearse*	2.00
157	*Shaun King*	3.00
158	*Rob Konrad*	2.00
159	*Chris McAlister*	2.00
160	*Darnell McDonald*	2.00
161	*Donovan McNabb*	7.00
162	*Cade McNown*	7.00
163	*Peerless Price*	5.00
164	*Akili Smith*	10.00
165	*Matt Stinchcomb*	1.00
166A	Michael Wiley	300.00
166B	*Edgerrin James Trade*	100.00
167	*Ricky Williams*	20.00
168	*Antoine Winfield*	2.00
169	*Craig Yeast*	2.00
170	*Amos Zereoue*	2.00

1999 Collector's Edge Supreme Gold Ingot

The 169-card set is a parallel to the base minus the Michael Wiley and Edgerrin James cards #166. The cards are the same as the base except for the foil is in gold and the Gold Ingot stamp on the fronts. They were inserted one-per-pack.

	MT
Complete Set (169):	300.00
Gold Ingot Cards:	2x
Gold Ingot Rookies:	1x
Inserted 1:1	

1999 Collector's Edge Supreme Galvanized

This 169-card set is a parallel of the base minus the cards of Michael Wiley and Edgerrin James #166. Each card is printed on silver foil board and is sequentially numbered. Veterans are printed to 500 and rookies to 250.

	MT
Complete Set (169):	800.00
Galvanized Cards:	3x-6x
Production 500 Sets	
Galvanized Rookies:	5x
Production 250 Sets	

1999 Collector's Edge Supreme Future

Each card in this 10-card set is printed on micro-etched foil board and was inserted 1:24 packs.

		MT
Complete Set (10):		60.00
Common Player:		2.00
Inserted 1:24		
1	Ricky Williams	20.00
2	Tim Couch	20.00
3	Daunte Culpepper	7.00
4	Torry Holt	5.00
5	Edgerrin James	10.00
6	Brock Huard	2.00
7	Donovan McNabb	7.00
8	Joe Germaine	4.00
9	Cade McNown	7.00
10	Michael Bishop	4.00

1999 Collector's Edge Supreme Homecoming

Each card in this 20-card set includes two players on the front who went to the same college. A rookie from the 1999 draft and a veteran. Singles were inserted 1:12 packs.

		MT
Complete Set (20):		60.00
Common Player:		1.50
Inserted 1:12		
1	Ricky Williams, Priest Holmes	15.00
2	Andy Katzenmoyer, Eddie George	4.00
3	Daunte Culpepper, Shawn Jefferson	5.00
4	Torry Holt, Erik Kramer	4.00
5	Edgerrin James, Vinny Testaverde	8.00
6	Chris Claiborne, Junior Seau	1.50
7	Brock Huard, Mark Brunell	4.00
8	Champ Bailey, Terrell Davis	8.00
9	Donovan McNabb, Rob Moore	6.00
10	David Boston, Joey Galloway	4.00
11	Cade McNown, Troy Aikman	6.00
12	Kevin Faulk, Eddie Kennison	1.50
13	Sedrick Irvin, Andre Rison	1.50
14	Rob Konrad, Darryl Johnston	1.50
15	Amos Zereoue, Adrian Murrell	1.50
16	Peerless Price, Peyton Manning	10.00
17	Kevin Johnson, Marvin Harrison	3.00
18	Jevon Kearse, Emmitt Smith	7.00
19	Antoine Winfield, Shawn Springs	1.50
20	Tony Bryant, Andre Wadsworth	1.50

1999 Collector's Edge Supreme Markers

The cards are printed on clear vinyl stock with foil stamping. The set features 15 NFL stars and focuses on record-setting performances and milestones reached in the 1998 NFL season. They were sequentially numbered to 5,000.

		MT
Complete Set (15):		60.00
Common Player:		1.00
Production 5,000 Sets		
1	Terrell Davis	6.00
2	John Elway	5.00
3	Dan Marino	6.00
4	Peyton Manning	7.00
5	Barry Sanders	8.00
6	Emmitt Smith	6.00
7	Randy Moss	12.00
8	Jake Plummer	4.00
9	Cris Carter	1.00
10	Brett Favre	8.00
11	Drew Bledsoe	3.00
12	Charlie Batch	4.00
13	Curtis Martin	1.00
14	Mark Brunell	3.00
15	Jamal Anderson	2.00

1999 Collector's Edge Supreme PSA 10 Redemptions

Each card in this set was a redemption card for the player that was on it. You could then redeem it for a PSA 10 graded rookie of that player. The redemption cards were limited to 1,999.

		MT
Complete Set (3):		250.00
Common Player:		75.00
Production 1,999 Sets		
1	Ricky Williams	100.00
2	Tim Couch	100.00
3	Daunte Culpepper	75.00

1999 Collector's Edge Supreme Route XXXIII

This set includes the top stars from the 1998 NFL playoffs. Each player in the 10-card set is sequentially numbered to 1,000.

		MT
Complete Set (10):		150.00
Common Player:		8.00
Production 1,000 Sets		
1	Randy Moss	55.00
2	Jamal Anderson	8.00
3	Jake Plummer	15.00
4	Steve Young	12.00
5	Fred Taylor	20.00
6	Dan Marino	20.00
7	Keyshawn Johnson	8.00
8	Curtis Martin	12.00
9	John Elway	20.00
10	Terrell Davis	20.00

1999 Collector's Edge Supreme Supremacy

This set features 5 players from Super Bowl XXXIII. Each is printed on foil board with foil stamping and is sequentially numbered to 500.

		MT
Complete Set (5):		75.00
Common Player:		10.00
Production 500 Sets		
1	John Elway	25.00
2	Terrell Davis	25.00
3	Ed McCaffrey	10.00
4	Jamal Anderson	15.00
5	Chris Chandler	10.00

1999 Collector's Edge Supreme T3

This 30-card set is tiered into three levels with 10 wide receivers (foil board with bronze foil stamping), running backs (foil board with silver foil stamping) and quarterbacks (foil board with gold foil stamping). The receivers were the easiest to find at 1:8, running backs at 1:12 and the quarterbacks the toughest to get at 1:24.

		MT
Complete Set (30):		180.00
Common WR:		1.50
Inserted 1:8		
Common RB:		2.50
Inserted 1:12		
Common QB:		5.00
Inserted 1:24		
1	Doug Flutie (QB)	5.00
2	Troy Aikman (QB)	10.00
3	John Elway (QB)	15.00
4	Jake Plummer (QB)	10.00
5	Brett Favre (QB)	20.00
6	Mark Brunell (QB)	8.00
7	Peyton Manning (QB)	15.00
8	Dan Marino (QB)	15.00
9	Drew Bledsoe (QB)	8.00
10	Steve Young (QB)	7.00
11	Jamal Anderson (RB)	3.00
12	Emmitt Smith (RB)	8.00
13	Terrell Davis (RB)	10.00
14	Barry Sanders (RB)	10.00
15	Robert Smith (RB)	2.50
16	Robert Edwards (RB)	3.00
17	Curtis Martin (RB)	3.00
18	Jerome Bettis (RB)	2.50
19	Fred Taylor (RB)	10.00
20	Eddie George (RB)	5.00
21	Michael Irvin (WR)	1.50
22	Eric Moulds (WR)	3.00
23	Herman Moore (WR)	1.50
24	Reidel Anthony (WR)	1.50
25	Randy Moss (WR)	12.00
26	Cris Carter (WR)	1.50
27	Keyshawn Johnson (WR)	3.00
28	Jacquez Green (WR)	1.50
29	Jerry Rice (WR)	7.00
30	Terrell Owens (WR)	4.00

1999 Donruss Elite

This is a 200-card base set that includes 40 rookies. Cards #1-100 are printed on 20 point foil board with a foil stamped logo in red and full UV coating on both sides. They were inserted four-per-pack. Cards #101-200 are also printed on 20 point foil board with full UV coating and platinum blue tint on each side. They are found one-per-pack. Inserts include Common Threads, Field of Vision, Passing the Torch, Power Formulas and Primary Colors.

		MT
Complete Set (200):		300.00
Common Player (1-100):		.25
Common Player (101-200):		.50
Common Rookie (161-200):		3.00
#101-200 Inserted 1:1		
Wax Box:		125.00
1	Warren Moon	.50
2	Terry Allen	.50
3	Jeff George	.50
4	Brett Favre	3.00
5	Rob Moore	.50
6	Bubby Brister	.25
7	John Elway	2.50
8	Troy Aikman	1.50
9	Steve McNair	.75
10	Charlie Batch	1.00
11	Elvis Grbac	.25
12	Trent Dilfer	.50
13	Kerry Collins	.50
14	Neil O'Donnell	.25
15	Tony Simmons	.50
16	Ryan Leaf	1.00
17	Bobby Hoying	.25
18	Marvin Harrison	.50
19	Keyshawn Johnson	.75
20	Cris Carter	.75
21	Deion Sanders	.75
22	Emmitt Smith	2.50
23	Antowain Smith	.75
24	Terry Fair	.25
25	Robert Holcombe	.50
26	Napoleon Kaufman	.75
27	Eddie George	1.00
28	Corey Dillon	.75
29	Adrian Murrell	.25
30	Charles Way	.25
31	Amp Lee	.25
32	Ricky Watters	.50
33	Gary Brown	.25
34	Thurman Thomas	.50
35	Patrick Johnson	.25
36	Jerome Bettis	.75
37	Muhsin Muhammad	.25
38	Kimble Anders	.25
39	Curtis Enis	.75
40	Mike Alstott	.75
41	Charles Johnson	.25
42	Chris Warren	.25
43	Tony Banks	.50
44	Leroy Hoard	.25
45	Chris Fuamatu-Ma'afala	.25
46	Michael Irvin	.75
47	Robert Edwards	.75
48	Hines Ward	.50
49	Trent Green	.50
50	Eric Zeier	.25
51	Sean Dawkins	.25
52	Yancey Thigpen	.50
53	Jacquez Green	.50
54	Zach Thomas	.50
55	Junior Seau	.50
56	Darnay Scott	.25
57	Kent Graham	.25
58	O.J. Santiago	.25
59	Tony Gonzalez	.25
60	Ty Detmer	.25
61	Albert Connell	.25
62	James Jett	.25
63	Bert Emanuel	.25
64	Derrick Alexander	.25
65	Wesley Walls	.25
66	Jake Reed	.25
67	Randall Cunningham	.75
68	Leslie Shepherd	.25
69	Mark Chmura	.25
70	Bobby Engram	.25
71	Rickey Dudley	.25
72	Darick Holmes	.25
73	Andre Reed	.50
74	Az-Zahir Hakim	.50
75	Cameron Cleeland	.25
76	Lamar Thomas	.25
77	Oronde Gadsden	.50
78	Ben Coates	.50
79	Bruce Smith	.25
80	Jerry Rice	1.50
81	Tim Brown	.50
82	Michael Westbrook	.50
83	J.J. Stokes	.50
84	Shannon Sharpe	.50
85	Reidel Anthony	.25
86	Antonio Freeman	.75
87	Keenan McCardell	.50
88	Terry Glenn	.75
89	Andre Rison	.50
90	Neil Smith	.25
91	Terrance Mathis	.25
92	Raghib Ismail	.25
93	Bam Morris	.25
94	Ike Hillard	.25
95	Eddie Kennison	.25
96	Tavian Banks	.50
97	Yatil Green	.25
98	Frank Wycheck	.25
99	Warren Sapp	.25
100	Germane Crowell	1.00
101	Curtis Martin	2.00
102	John Avery	1.00
103	Eric Moulds	2.00
104	Randy Moss	12.00
105	Terrell Owens	2.00
106	Vinny Testaverde	1.00
107	Doug Flutie	2.50
108	Mark Brunell	3.00
109	Isaac Bruce	1.00
110	Kordell Stewart	2.50
111	Drew Bledsoe	3.00
112	Chris Chandler	.50
113	Dan Marino	6.00
114	Brian Griese	4.00
115	Carl Pickens	.50
116	Jake Plummer	4.00
117	Natrone Means	1.00
118	Peyton Manning	8.00
119	Garrison Hearst	1.00
120	Barry Sanders	8.00
121	Steve Young	3.00
122	Rashaan Shehee	.50
123	Ed McCaffrey	1.50
124	Charles Woodson	2.00
125	Dorsey Levens	1.50
126	Robert Smith	1.50
127	Greg Hill	.50
128	Fred Taylor	5.00
129	Marcus Nash	1.00
130	Terrell Davis	6.00
131	Ahman Green	1.00
132	Jamal Anderson	2.00
133	Karim Abdul	1.00
134	Jermaine Lewis	.50
135	Jerome Pathon	.50
136	Brad Johnson	1.00
137	Herman Moore	1.50
138	Tim Dwight	2.00
139	Johnnie Morton	.50
140	Marshall Faulk	2.00
141	Frank Sanders	1.00
142	Kevin Dyson	1.00
143	Curtis Conway	1.00
144	Derrick Mayes	.50
145	O.J. McDuffie	1.00
146	Joe Jurevicius	.50
147	Jon Kitna	2.00
148	Joey Galloway	1.50
149	Jimmy Smith	1.00
150	Skip Hicks	1.00
151	Rod Smith	1.00
152	Duce Staley	.50
153	James O. Stewart	.50
154	Rob Johnson	1.00
155	Mikhael Ricks	.50
156	Wayne Chrebet	1.50
157	Robert Brooks	.50
158	Tim Biakabutuka	.50
159	Priest Holmes	2.00
160	Warrick Dunn	2.00
161	*Champ Bailey*	10.00
162	*D'Wayne Bates*	3.00
163	*Michael Bishop*	8.00
164	*David Boston*	10.00
165	*Na Brown*	3.00
166	*Chris Claiborne*	5.00
167	*Joe Montgomery*	3.00
168	*Mike Cloud*	3.00
169	*Travis McGriff*	3.00
170	*Tim Couch*	50.00
171	*Daunte Culpepper*	15.00
172	*Autry Denson*	5.00
173	*Jermaine Fazande*	3.00
174	*Troy Edwards*	8.00
175	*Kevin Faulk*	10.00
176	*Dee Miller*	3.00
177	*Brock Huard*	6.00
178	*Torry Holt*	10.00
179	*Sedrick Irvin*	5.00
180	*Edgerrin James*	25.00
181	*Joe Germaine*	6.00
182	*James Johnson*	5.00
183	*Kevin Johnson*	8.00
184	*Andy Katzenmoyer*	5.00
185	*Jevon Kearse*	3.00
186	*Shaun King*	6.00
187	*Rob Konrad*	3.00
188	*Jim Kleinsasser*	3.00
189	*Chris McAlister*	4.00
190	*Donovan McNabb*	20.00
191	*Cade McNown*	15.00
192	*De'Mond Parker*	3.00
193	*Craig Yeast*	3.00
194	*Shawn Bryson*	3.00
195	*Peerless Price*	8.00
196	*Darnell McDonald*	3.00
197	*Akili Smith*	20.00
198	*Tai Streets*	5.00
199	*Ricky Williams*	50.00
200	*Amos Zereoue*	6.00

1999 Donruss Elite Common Threads

Each card is printed on conventional board with foil and game-used jersey swatches. Twelve players are featured with six cards with one player on it and the other six are combo cards. Each is sequentially numbered to 150.

		MT
Complete Set (18):		3000.
Common Player:		100.00
Production 150 Sets		
1	Randy Moss, Randall Cunningham	400.00
2	Randy Moss	350.00
3	Randall Cunningham	125.00
4	John Elway, Terrell Davis	350.00
5	John Elway	275.00
6	Terrell Davis	225.00
7	Jerry Rice, Steve Young	300.00
8	Jerry Rice	250.00
9	Steve Young	150.00
10	Mark Brunell, Fred Taylor	175.00
11	Mark Brunell	125.00
12	Fred Taylor	150.00
13	Kordell Stewart, Jerome Bettis	150.00
14	Kordell Stewart	125.00
15	Jerome Bettis	100.00
16	Dan Marino, Karim Abdul	300.00
17	Dan Marino	300.00
18	Karim Abdul	100.00

1999 Donruss Elite Field of Vision

Each card is printed on clear plastic with holo-foil stamping. Twelve players are featured on three seperate cards, with each representing a section of the playing field (left-middle-right). Each card is then sequentially numbered to the yards the player gained in that area of the field in 1998.

		MT
Common Player:		5.00
Production #'d to a Season Stat		
1A	Dan Marino 1712	12.00
1B	Dan Marino 834	20.00
1C	Dan Marino 951	20.00
2A	Emmitt Smith 640	20.00
2B	Emmitt Smith 202	35.00
2C	Emmitt Smith 490	20.00
3A	Jake Plummer 1165	10.00
3B	Jake Plummer 624	15.00
3C	Jake Plummer 1948	5.00
4A	Brett Favre 1408	14.00
4B	Brett Favre 983	25.00
4C	Brett Favre 1820	12.00
5A	Fred Taylor 486	10.00
5B	Fred Taylor 400	12.00
5C	Fred Taylor 337	15.00
6A	Drew Bledsoe 1355	5.00
6B	Drew Bledsoe 689	10.00
6C	Drew Bledsoe 1589	5.00
7A	Terrell Davis 1283	12.00
7B	Terrell Davis 306	25.00
7C	Terrell Davis 419	20.00
8A	Jerry Rice 611	10.00
8B	Jerry Rice 234	25.00
8C	Jerry Rice 312	20.00
9A	Randy Moss 639	30.00
9B	Randy Moss 16	350.00
9C	Randy Moss 658	30.00
10A	John Elway 1320	12.00
10B	John Elway 615	25.00
10C	John Elway 871	20.00
11A	Peyton Manning 1141	15.00
11B	Peyton Manning 1020	15.00
11C	Peyton Manning 1578	12.00
12A	Barry Sanders 556	20.00
12B	Barry Sanders 373	30.00
12C	Barry Sanders 562	20.00

1999 Donruss Elite Field of Vision Die Cuts

This is similar to the Field of Vision cards except each card is die-cut and sequentially numbered to the number of attempts, receptions or completions of that particular player.

		MT
Common Player:		25.00
Production #'d to a Season Stat		
1A	Dan Marino 164	45.00
1B	Dan Marino 56	100.00
1C	Dan Marino 90	70.00
2A	Emmitt Smith 158	30.00
2B	Emmitt Smith 64	75.00
2C	Emmitt Smith 97	45.00
3A	Jake Plummer 89	35.00
3B	Jake Plummer 44	60.00
3C	Jake Plummer 191	25.00
4A	Brett Favre 112	60.00
4B	Brett Favre 67	100.00
4C	Brett Favre 168	40.00
5A	Fred Taylor 103	35.00
5B	Fred Taylor 79	45.00
5C	Fred Taylor 82	45.00
6A	Drew Bledsoe 90	30.00
6B	Drew Bledsoe 48	45.00
6C	Drew Bledsoe 125	25.00
7A	Terrell Davis 217	35.00
7B	Terrell Davis 66	70.00
7C	Terrell Davis 109	50.00
8A	Jerry Rice 50	70.00
8B	Jerry Rice 11	325.00
8C	Jerry Rice 21	200.00
9A	Randy Moss 34	225.00
9B	Randy Moss 2	
9C	Randy Moss 33	225.00
10A	John Elway 98	50.00
10B	John Elway 35	150.00
10C	John Elway 77	75.00
11A	Peyton Manning 110	45.00
11B	Peyton Manning 79	60.00
11C	Peyton Manning 137	35.00
12A	Barry Sanders 137	45.00
12B	Barry Sanders 83	85.00
12C	Barry Sanders 123	45.00

1999 Donruss Elite Passing the Torch

Each card is printed with holo-foil board on the front and back with UV coating on both sides and sequentially numbered to 1,500. Twelve players were used with each having an individual card as well as six cards pairing two players together. The first 100 of each card are autographed.

		MT
Complete Set (18):		175.00
Common Player:		5.00
Production 1,500 Sets		
1	Johnny Unitas, Peyton Manning	15.00
2	Johnny Unitas	8.00
3	Peyton Manning	12.00
4	Walter Payton, Barry Sanders	20.00
5	Walter Payton	10.00
6	Barry Sanders	15.00
7	Earl Campbell, Ricky Williams	20.00
8	Earl Campbell	5.00
9	Ricky Williams	25.00
10	Jim Brown, Terrell Davis	15.00
11	Jim Brown	10.00
12	Terrell Davis	15.00
13	Emmitt Smith, Fred Taylor	15.00
14	Emmitt Smith	10.00
15	Fred Taylor	10.00
16	Cris Carter, Randy Moss	20.00
17	Cris Carter	5.00
18	Randy Moss	20.00

1999 Donruss Elite Passing the Torch Autographs

This is the same as the regular Passing the Torch cards except for each one of these are autographed. They are each sequentially numbered to 100.

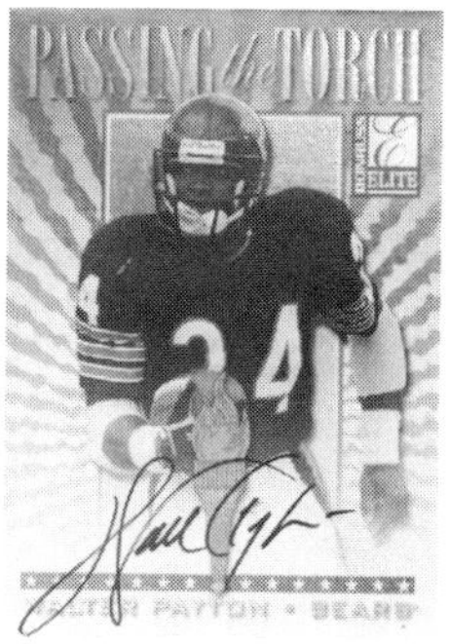

		MT
Complete Set (18):		4000.
Common Player:		75.00
Production 100 Sets		
1	Johnny Unitas, Peyton Manning	400.00
2	Johnny Unitas	150.00
3	Peyton Manning	200.00
4	Walter Payton, Barry Sanders	775.00
5	Walter Payton	275.00
6	Barry Sanders	400.00
7	Earl Campbell, Ricky Williams	350.00
8	Earl Campbell	100.00
9	Ricky Williams	250.00
10	Jim Brown, Terrell Davis	400.00
11	Jim Brown	200.00
12	Terrell Davis	250.00
13	Emmitt Smith, Fred Taylor	350.00
14	Emmitt Smith	300.00
15	Fred Taylor	125.00
16	Cris Carter, Randy Moss	325.00
17	Cris Carter	75.00
18	Randy Moss	300.00

1999 Donruss Elite Power Formulas

This 30-card set spotlights the NFL's most powerful players and the statistical formulas behind their greatness. Each is sequentially numbered to 3,500.

		MT
Complete Set (30):		120.00
Common Player:		1.50
Production 3,500 Sets		
1	Randy Moss	15.00
2	Terrell Davis	10.00
3	Brett Favre	12.00
4	Dan Marino	8.00
5	Barry Sanders	12.00
6	Peyton Manning	8.00
7	John Elway	8.00
8	Fred Taylor	6.00
9	Emmitt Smith	8.00
10	Steve Young	5.00
11	Jerry Rice	6.00
12	Jake Plummer	5.00
13	Kordell Stewart	5.00
14	Mark Brunell	5.00
15	Drew Bledsoe	5.00
16	Eddie George	5.00
17	Troy Aikman	6.00
18	Warrick Dunn	4.00
19	Keyshawn Johnson	3.00
20	Jamal Anderson	3.00
21	Randall Cunningham	3.00
22	Doug Flutie	4.00
23	Jerome Bettis	3.00
24	Garrison Hearst	1.50
25	Curtis Martin	3.00
26	Corey Dillon	3.00
27	Antowain Smith	3.00
28	Antonio Freeman	3.00
29	Terrell Owens	3.00
30	Carl Pickens	1.50

1999 Donruss Elite Primary Colors

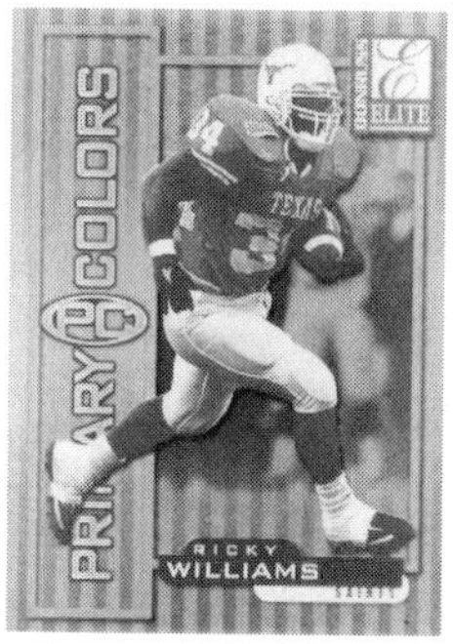

The 40-card set is printed on holo-foil board and is sequentially numbered to 1,875. This insert has five different parallel sets with a Blue (#'d to 950), Red (#'d to 25), Blue Die-Cut (#'d to 50), Red Die-Cut (#'d to 75) and a Yellow Die-Cut (#'d to 25) version.

		MT
Complete Set (40):		160.00
Common Yellow:		3.00
Production 1,875 Sets		
Blue Cards:		1.5x
Production 950 Sets		
Red Cards:		15x-30x
Red Rookies:		7x-14x
Production 25 Sets		
Blue Die-Cut Cards:		10x-20x
Blue Die-Cut Rookies:		5x-10x
Production 50 Sets		
Red Die-Cut Cards:		7x-14x
Red Die-Cut Rookies:		3x-6x
Production 75 Sets		
Yellow Die-Cut Cards:		15x-30x
Yellow Die-Cut Rookies:		7x-14x
Production 25 Sets		
1	Herman Moore	3.00
2	Marshall Faulk	3.00
3	Dorsey Levens	3.00
4	Napoleon Kaufman	3.00
5	Jamal Anderson	3.00
6	Edgerrin James	10.00
7	Troy Aikman	6.00
8	Cris Carter	3.00
9	Eddie George	4.00
10	Donovan McNabb	10.00
11	Drew Bledsoe	5.00
12	Daunte Culpepper	8.00
13	Mark Brunell	5.00
14	Corey Dillon	3.00
15	Kordell Stewart	5.00
16	Curtis Martin	3.00
17	Jake Plummer	5.00
18	Charlie Batch	4.00
19	Jerry Rice	6.00
20	Antonio Freeman	3.00
21	Steve Young	4.00
22	Steve McNair	3.00
23	Emmitt Smith	8.00
24	Terrell Owens	3.00
25	Fred Taylor	6.00
26	Joey Galloway	3.00
27	John Elway	8.00
28	Ryan Leaf	3.00
29	Barry Sanders	12.00
30	Ricky Williams	20.00
31	Dan Marino	8.00
32	Tim Couch	20.00
33	Brett Favre	12.00
34	Eric Moulds	3.00
35	Peyton Manning	8.00
36	Deion Sanders	3.00
37	Terrell Davis	8.00
38	Tim Brown	3.00
39	Randy Moss	15.00
40	Mike Alstott	3.00

1999 Fleer

The 300-card set includes 50 unseeded rookies. The card fronts include the player's name and conference logo in blue foil for the NFC and red for the AFC. Inserts include: Trophy Case, Aerial Assault, Rookie Sensations, Under Pressure and Unsung Heroes.

		MT
Complete Set (300):		50.00
Common Player:		.10
Common Rookie:		.40
Wax Box:		60.00
1	Randy Moss	2.00
2	Peyton Manning	1.50
3	Barry Sanders	2.00
4	Terrell Davis	1.50
5	Brett Favre	2.00
6	Fred Taylor	1.00
7	Jake Plummer	1.00
8	John Elway	1.50
9	Emmitt Smith	1.50
10	Kerry Collins	.20
11	Peter Boulware	.10
12	Jamal Anderson	.50
13	Doug Flutie	.75
14	Michael Bates	.10
15	Corey Dillon	.50
16	Curtis Conway	.20
17	Ty Detmer	.20
18	Robert Brooks	.10
19	Dale Carter	.10
20	Charlie Batch	.75
21	Ken Dilger	.10
22	Troy Aikman	1.00
23	Tavian Banks	.20
24	Cris Carter	.50
25	Derrick Alexander	.10
26	Chris Bordano	.10
27	Karim Abdul	.30
28	Jessie Armstead	.10
29	Drew Bledsoe	.75
30	Brian Dawkins	.10
31	Wayne Chrebet	.50
32	Garrison Hearst	.30
33	Eric Allen	.10
34	Tony Banks	.20
35	Jerome Bettis	.50
36	Stephen Alexander	.10
37	Rodney Harrison	.10
38	Mike Alstott	.50
39	Chad Brown	.10
40	Johnny McWilliams	.10
41	Kevin Dyson	.20
42	Keith Brooking	.10
43	Jim Harbaugh	.20
44	Bobby Engram	.10
45	John Holecek	.10
46	Steve Beuerlein	.10
47	Tony McGee	.10
48	Greg Ellis	.10
49	Corey Fuller	.10
50	Stephen Boyd	.10
51	Marshall Faulk	.50
52	Leroy Butler	.10
53	Reggie Barlow	.10
54	Randall Cunningham	.50
55	Aeneas Williams	.10
56	Kimble Anders	.10
57	Cameron Cleeland	.20
58	John Avery	.20
59	Gary Brown	.10
60	Ben Coates	.20
61	Koy Detmer	.10
62	Bryan Cox	.10
63	Edgar Bennett	.10
64	Tim Brown	.20
65	Isaac Bruce	.30
66	Eddie George	.75
67	Reidel Anthony	.20
68	Charlie Jones	.10
69	Terry Allen	.20
70	Joey Galloway	.50
71	Jamir Miller	.10
72	Will Blackwell	.10
73	Ray Buchanan	.10
74	Priest Holmes	.50
75	Michael Irvin	.20
76	Jonathon Linton	.10
77	Curtis Enis	.50
78	Neil O'Donnell	.20
79	Tim Biakabutuka	.20
80	Terry Kirby	.10
81	Germane Crowell	.20
82	Jason Elam	.10
83	Mark Chmura	.20
84	Marvin Harrison	.30
85	Jimmy Hitchcock	.10
86	Tony Brackens	.10
87	Sean Dawkins	.10
88	Tony Gonzalez	.20
89	Kent Graham	.10
90	Oronde Gadsden	.20
91	Hugh Douglas	.10
92	Robert Edwards	.30
93	R.W. McQuarters	.10
94	Aaron Glenn	.10
95	Kevin Carter	.10
96	Rickey Dudley	.10
97	Derrick Brooks	.10
98	Mark Bruener	.10
99	Darrell Green	.10
100	Jessie Tuggle	.10
101	Freddie Jones	.10
102	Rob Moore	.20
103	Ahman Green	.20
104	Chris Chandler	.20
105	Steve McNair	.50
106	Kevin Greene	.10
107	Jermaine Lewis	.20
108	Erik Kramer	.10
109	Eric Moulds	.50
110	Terry Fair	.10
111	Carl Pickens	.20
112	La'Roi Glover	.10
113	Chris Spielman	.10
114	Leroy Hoard	.10
115	Mark Brunell	.75
116	Patrick Jeffers	.10
117	Elvis Grbac	.20
118	Ike Hilliard	.20
119	Sam Madison	.10
120	Terrell Owens	.50
121	Rich Gannon	.10
122	Skip Hicks	.50
123	Eric Green	.10
124	Trent Dilfer	.50
125	Terry Glenn	.30
126	Trent Green	.50
127	Charles Johnson	.10
128	Adrian Murrell	.20
129	Jason Gildon	.10
130	Tim Dwight	.50
131	Ryan Leaf	.50
132	Raghib Ismail	.10
133	Jon Kitna	.50
134	Alonzo Mayes	.10
135	Yancey Thigpen	.20
136	David LaFleur	.10
137	Ray Lewis	.10
138	Herman Moore	.50
139	Brian Griese	.30
140	Antonio Freeman	.50
141	Darnay Scott	.10
142	Ed McDaniel	.10
143	Andre Reed	.10
144	Andre Hastings	.10
145	Chris Warren	.10
146	Kevin Hardy	.10
147	Joe Jurevicius	.10
148	Jerome Pathon	.10
149	Duce Staley	.20
150	Dan Marino	1.50
151	Jerry Rice	1.00
152	Bam Morris	.20
153	Az-Zahir Hakim	.20
154	Ty Law	.10
155	Warrick Dunn	.50
156	Keyshawn Johnson	.50
157	Brian Mitchell	.10
158	James Jett	.10
159	Fred Lane	.10
160	Courtney Hawkins	.10
161	Andre Wadsworth	.20
162	Natrone Means	.30
163	Andrew Glover	.10
164	Anthony Simmons	.10
165	Leon Lett	.10
166	Frank Wycheck	.10
167	Barry Minter	.10
168	Michael McCrary	.10
169	Johnnie Morton	.10
170	Jay Riemersma	.10
171	Vonnie Holliday	.20
172	Brian Simmons	.10
173	Joe Johnson	.10
174	Ed McCaffrey	.30
175	Jason Sehorn	.10
176	Keenan McCardell	.10
177	Bobby Taylor	.10
178	Andre Rison	.20
179	Greg Hill	.10
180	O.J. McDuffie	.20
181	Darren Woodson	.10
182	Willie McGinest	.10
183	J.J. Stokes	.20
184	Leon Johnson	.10
185	Bert Emanuel	.10
186	Napoleon Kaufman	.50
187	Leslie Shepherd	.10
188	Levon Kirkland	.10
189	Simeon Rice	.10
190	Mikhael Ricks	.10
191	Robert Smith	.50
192	Michael Sinclair	.10
193	Muhsin Muhammad	.10
194	Duane Starks	.10
195	Terance Mathis	.10
196	Antowain Smith	.50
197	Tony Parrish	.10
198	Takeo Spikes	.10
199	Ernie Mills	.10
200	John Mobley	.10
201	Robert Porcher	.10
202	Pete Mitchell	.10
203	Darick Holmes	.10
204	Derrick Thomas	.20
205	David Palmer	.10
206	Jason Taylor	.10
207	Sammy Knight	.10
208	Dwayne Rudd	.10
209	Lawyer Milloy	.10
210	Michael Strahan	.10
211	Mo Lewis	.10
212	William Thomas	.10
213	Darrell Russell	.10
214	Brad Johnson	.50
215	Kordell Stewart	.50
216	Robert Holcombe	.20
217	Junior Seau	.20
218	Jacquez Green	.20
219	Shawn Springs	.10
220	Michael Westbrook	.20
221	Rod Woodson	.10
222	Frank Sanders	.20
223	Bruce Smith	.10
224	Eugene Robinson	.10
225	Bill Romanowski	.10
226	Wesley Walls	.10
227	Jimmy Smith	.20
228	Deion Sanders	.50
229	Lamar Thomas	.10
230	Dorsey Levens	.50
231	Tony Simmons	.20
232	John Randle	.10
233	Curtis Martin	.50
234	Bryant Young	.10
235	Charles Woodson	.50
236	Charles Way	.10
237	Zack Thomas	.20
238	Ricky Proehl	.10
239	Ricky Watters	.20
240	Hardy Nickerson	.10
241	Shannon Sharpe	.20
242	O.J. Santiago	.10
243	Vinny Testaverde	.20
244	Preston Roell	.10
245	James Stewart	.10
246	Jake Reed	.10
247	Steve Young	.75
248	Shaun Williams	.10
249	Rod Smith	.20
250	Warren Sapp	.10
251	*Champ Bailey*	1.50
252	*Karsten Bailey*	.40
253	*D'Wayne Bates*	.75
254	*Michael Bishop*	1.50
255	*David Boston*	3.00
256	*Na Brown*	.40
257	*Fernando Bryant*	.40
258	*Shawn Bryson*	.40
259	*Darrin Chiaverini*	.40
260	*Chris Claiborne*	1.00
261	*Mike Cloud*	.40
262	*Cecil Collins*	2.50
263	*Tim Couch*	10.00
264	*Scott Covington*	.40
265	*Daunte Culpepper*	4.00
266	*Antwan Edwards*	.40
267	*Troy Edwards*	2.50
268	*Ebenezer Ekuban*	.75
269	*Kevin Faulk*	3.00
270	*Jermaine Fazande*	.40
271	*Joe Germaine*	1.25
272	*Martin Gramatica*	.40
273	*Torry Holt*	2.50
274	*Brock Huard*	1.50
275	*Sedrick Irvin*	1.50
276	*Sheldon Jackson*	.40
277	*Edgerrin James*	6.00
278	*James Johnson*	1.50
279	*Kevin Johnson*	1.50
280	*Malcolm Johnson*	.40
281	*Andy Katzenmoyer*	1.00
282	*Jevon Kearse*	.75
283	*Patrick Kerney*	.40
284	*Shaun King*	1.50
285	*Jim Kleinsasser*	.40
286	*Rob Konrad*	.75
287	*Chris McAlister*	.75
288	*Donovan McNabb*	4.00
289	*Cade McNown*	4.00
290	*Dee Miller*	.40
291	*Joe Montgomery*	1.00
292	*De'Mond Parker*	.40
293	*Peerless Price*	2.00
294	*Akili Smith*	4.00
295	*Justin Swift*	.40
296	*Jerame Tuman*	.40
297	*Ricky Williams*	10.00
298	*Antoine Winfield*	.75
299	*Craig Yeast*	.40
300	*Amos Zereoue*	2.00

1999 Fleer Aerial Assault

Each card is printed on plastic with silver holofoil featuring the NFL's top throwers and their targets. The 15 different singles were inserted 1:24 packs.

		MT
Complete Set (15):		85.00
Common Player:		2.00
Inserted 1:24		
1	Troy Aikman	8.00
2	Jamal Anderson	2.00
3	Charlie Batch	5.00
4	Mark Brunell	6.00
5	Terrell Davis	10.00
6	John Elway	10.00
7	Brett Favre	15.00
8	Keyshawn Johnson	4.00
9	Jon Kitna	5.00
10	Peyton Manning	10.00
11	Dan Marino	10.00
12	Randy Moss	15.00
13	Eric Moulds	2.00
14	Jake Plummer	8.00
15	Jerry Rice	8.00

1999 Fleer Rookie Sensations

Rookies from the 1999 season are featured against team color backgrounds and glistening on silver foil fronts. The 20 different singles can be found 1:6 packs.

		MT
Complete Set (20):		50.00
Common Player:		1.00
Inserted 1:6		
1	Champ Bailey	2.00
2	Michael Bishop	2.50
3	David Boston	3.00
4	Chris Claiborne	1.00
5	Tim Couch	10.00
6	Daunte Culpepper	4.00
7	Troy Edwards	3.00
8	Kevin Faulk	3.00
9	Torry Holt	3.00
10	Brock Huard	2.00
11	Edgerrin James	6.00
12	Kevin Johnson	2.00
13	Shaun King	2.00
14	Rob Konrad	1.00
15	Chris McAlister	1.00
16	Donovan McNabb	4.00
17	Cade McNown	4.00
18	Peerless Price	2.50
19	Akili Smith	4.00
20	Ricky Williams	10.00

1999 Fleer Under Pressure

This 15-card set spotlights a sculpture embossed player image on patterned holofoil. Each is die- cut and found 1:96 packs.

		MT
Complete Set (15):		250.00
Common Player:		8.00
Inserted 1:96		
1	Charlie Batch	12.00
2	Terrell Davis	30.00
3	Warrick Dunn	12.00
4	John Elway	30.00
5	Brett Favre	40.00
6	Keyshawn Johnson	8.00
7	Peyton Manning	30.00
8	Dan Marino	30.00
9	Curtis Martin	12.00
10	Randy Moss	40.00
11	Jake Plummer	20.00
12	Barry Sanders	40.00
13	Emmitt Smith	30.00
14	Fred Taylor	20.00
15	Charles Woodson	8.00

1999 Fleer Unsung Heroes

This 30-card set picks one under-recognized star from each team and highlights him on cardboard. Singles were inserted 1:3 packs.

		MT
Complete Set (30):		7.00
Common Player:		.25
Inserted 1:3		
1	Tommy Bennett	.25
2	Lester Archambeau	.25
3	James Jones	.25
4	Phil Hansen	.25
5	Anthony Johnson	.25
6	Bobby Engram	.25
7	Eric Bienemy	.25
8	Daryl Johnston	.25
9	Maa Tanuvasa	.25
10	Stephen Boyd	.25
11	Adam Timmerman	.25
12	Ken Dilger	.25
13	Bryan Barker	.25
14	Rich Gannon	.25
15	O.J. Brigance	.25
16	Jeff Christy	.25
17	Shawn Jefferson	.25
18	Aaron Craver	.25
19	Chris Calloway	.25
20	Pepper Johnson	.25
21	Greg Biekert	.25
22	Duce Staley	.50
23	Courtney Hawkins	.25
24	Rodney Harrison	.25
25	Ray Brown	.25
26	Jon Kitna	1.50
27	D'Marco Farr	.25
28	Brad Culpepper	.25
29	Steve Jackson	.25
30	Brian Mitchell	.25

1999 Metal Universe

The 250-card base set features each player's name stamped in a steel-look foil across the top and stats laid into another steel motif on the card backs. The 182 player cards are joined by the 25 all-foil "N.F.L.P.D." subset. The base set also includes forty non-seeded rookies and three checklists. Top inserts include: Precious Metal, Gem Masters, Autographics, Linchpins, Planet Metal, Quasars and Starchild.

		MT
Complete Set (250):		50.00
Common Player:		.10
Common Rookie:		.50
Wax Box:		50.00
1	Eric Moulds	.50
2	David Palmer	.10
3	Ricky Watters	.20
4	Antonio Freeman	.50
5	Hugh Douglas	.10
6	Johnnie Morton	.10
7	Corey Fuller	.10
8	J.J. Stokes	.20
9	Keith Poole	.10
10	Steve Beuerlein	.10
11	Keenan McCardell	.10
12	Carl Pickens	.20
13	Mark Bruener	.10
14	Warren Sapp	.10
15	Rich Gannon	.10
16	Bruce Smith	.10
17	Mark Chmura	.20
18	Drew Bledsoe	.75
19	Charles Woodson	.50
20	Ahman Green	.20
21	Ricky Proehl	.10
22	Corey Dillon	.50
23	Terry Fair	.10
24	Mark Brunell	.75
25	Leroy Hoard	.10
26	La'Roi Glover	.10
27	Tim Brown	.20
28	Kevin Turner	.10
29	Terrell Owens	.50
30	Mike Alstott	.50
31	Rob Moore	.20
32	Troy Aikman	1.00
33	Derrick Alexander	.10
34	Chris Calloway	.10
35	Kordell Stewart	.75
36	Reidel Anthony	.20
37	Michael Westbrook	.20
38	Ray Lewis	.10
39	Alonzo Mayes	.10
40	Rod Smith	.20
41	Reggie Barlow	.10
42	Sean Dawkins	.10
43	Duce Staley	.10
44	R.W. McQuarters	.10
45	Robert Holcombe	.10
46	Priest Holmes	.50
47	Erik Kramer	.10
48	Shannon Sharpe	.20
49	Mike Vanderjagt	.10
50	Cris Carter	.50
51	Billy Joe Tolliver	.10
52	Vinny Testaverde	.20
53	Antonio Langham	.10
54	Damon Gibson	.10
55	Garrison Hearst	.30
56	Brad Johnson	.50
57	Randall Cunningham	.50
58	Jim Harbaugh	.20
59	Curtis Enis	.50
60	Bill Romanowski	.10
61	Marcus Pollard	.10
62	Zach Thomas	.20
63	Cameron Cleeland	.20
64	Curtis Martin	.50
65	Charlie Garner	.10
66	Jerris McPhail	.10
67	Jon Kitna	.75
68	Chris Chandler	.20
69	Emmitt Smith	1.50
70	Andre Rison	.20
71	Wayne Chrebet	.50
72	Mikhael Ricks	.10
73	Yancey Thigpen	.20
74	Peter Boulware	.10
75	Bobby Engram	.10
76	John Mobley	.10
77	Peyton Manning	1.50
78	O.J. McDuffie	.20
79	Tony Simmons	.20
80	Mo Lewis	.10
81	Bryan Still	.10
82	Eugene Robinson	.10
83	Curtis Conway	.20
84	Ed McCaffrey	.30
85	Marvin Harrison	.30
86	Dan Marino	1.50
87	Ty Law	.10
88	Leon Johnson	.10
89	Junior Seau	.20
90	Terance Mathis	.10
91	Wesley Walls	.10
92	John Elway	1.50
93	Marshall Faulk	.50
94	Oronde Gadsden	.20
95	Keyshawn Johnson	.50
96	Muhsin Muhammad	.10
97	Dorsey Levens	.50
98	Shawn Jefferson	.10
99	Rocket Ismail	.10
100	Vonnie Holliday	.20
101	Terry Glenn	.30
102	Shawn Springs	.10
103	Tim Dwight	.50
104	Terrell Davis	1.50
105	Karim Abdul	.30
106	Bryan Cox	.10
107	Steve McNair	.75
108	Tony Martin	.10
109	Jason Elam	.10
110	John Avery	.20
111	Aaron Glenn	.10
112	Eddie George	.75
113	Larry Centers	.10
114	Darnay Scott	.10
115	Jimmy Smith	.20
116	Tiki Barber	.10
117	Charles Johnson	.10
118	Mike Archie	.10
119	Adrian Murrell	.10
120	Dexter Coakley	.10
121	Dale Carter	.10
122	Kent Graham	.10
123	Hines Ward	.20
124	Greg Hill	.10
125	Skip Hicks	.50
126	Doug Flutie	.75
127	Leslie Shepherd	.10
128	Neil O'Donnell	.20
129	Herman Moore	.50
130	Kevin Hardy	.10
131	Randy Moss	2.00
132	Andre Hastings	.10
133	Rickey Dudley	.10
134	Jerome Bettis	.50
135	Jerry Rice	1.00
136	Jake Plummer	1.00
137	Billy Davis	.10
138	Tony Gonzalez	.20
139	Ike Hilliard	.20
140	Freddie Jones	.10
141	Isaac Bruce	.30
142	Darrell Green	.10
143	Trent Green	.50
144	Jamal Anderson	.50
145	Deion Sanders	.50
146	Bam Morris	.20
147	Charles Way	.10
148	Natrone Means	.30
149	Frank Wycheck	.10
150	Brett Favre	2.00
151	Michael Bates	.10
152	Ben Coates	.20
153	Koy Detmer	.10
154	Eddie Kennison	.10
155	Eric Metcalf	.10
156	Takeo Spikes	.10
157	Fred Taylor	1.00
158	Gary Brown	.10
159	Levon Kirkland	.10
160	Trent Dilfer	.30
161	Antowain Smith	.50
162	Robert Brooks	.10
163	Robert Smith	.50
164	Napoleon Kaufman	.50
165	Chad Brown	.10
166	Warrick Dunn	.75
167	Joey Galloway	.50
168	Frank Sanders	.20
169	Michael Irvin	.20
170	Elvis Grbac	.20
171	Michael Strahan	.10
172	Ryan Leaf	.50
173	Stephen Alexander	.10
174	Andre Reed	.10
175	Barry Sanders	2.00
176	Jake Reed	.10
177	James Jett	.10
178	Steve Young	.75
179	Jermaine Lewis	.20
180	Charlie Batch	.75
181	Jacquez Green	.20
182	Kevin Dyson	.20
183	Roell Preston	.10
184	Randall Cunningham	.20
185	Charlie Batch	.20
186	Kordell Stewart	.20
187	Bennie Thompson	.10
188	Deion Sanders	.20
189	Jake Plummer	.50
190	Eric Moulds	.20
191	Derrick Brooks	.10
192	Steve McNair	.20
193	Ryan Leaf	.20
194	Keyshawn Johnson	.20
195	Eddie George	.20
196	Warrick Dunn	.20
197	Jessie Tuggle	.10
198	Rodney Harrison	.10
199	Vinny Testaverde	.10
200	Marshall Faulk	.20
201	Ray Buchanon	.10
202	Garrison Hearst	.10
203	John Randle	.10
204	Drew Bledsoe	.50
205	Sam Gash	.10
206	Troy Aikman	.50
207	Michael McCrary	.10
208	*Chris Claiborne*	1.00
209	*Ricky Williams*	10.00
210	*Tim Couch*	10.00
211	*Champ Bailey*	1.50
212	*Torry Holt*	2.50
213	*Donovan McNabb*	4.00
214	*David Boston*	3.00
215	*Chris McAlister*	.75
216	*Aaron Gibson*	.50
217	*Daunte Culpepper*	4.00
218	*Matt Stinchcomb*	.50
219	*Edgerrin James*	6.00
220	*Jevon Kearse*	.75
221	*Ebenezer Ekuban*	.50
222	*Kris Farris*	.50
223	*Chris Terry*	.50
224	*Cecil Collins*	2.50
225	*Akili Smith*	4.00
226	*Shaun King*	1.50
227	*Rahim Abdullah*	.50
228	*Peerless Price*	1.50
229	*Antoine Winfield*	.50
230	*Antwan Edwards*	.50
231	*Rob Konrad*	.75
232	*Troy Edwards*	2.00
233	*John Thornton*	.50
234	*Fred Vinson*	.50
235	*Gary Stills*	.50
236	*Desmond Clark*	.50
237	*Lamar King*	.50
238	*Jared DeVries*	.50
239	*Martin Gramatica*	.50
240	*Montae Reagor*	.50
241	*Andy Katzenmoyer*	1.00
242	*Rufus French*	.50
243	*D'Wayne Bates*	.75
244	*Amos Zereoue*	2.00
245	*Dre' Bly*	.75
246	*Kevin Johnson*	1.00
247	*Cade McNown*	4.00
248	Kordell Stewart	.20
249	Deion Sanders	.20
250	Vinny Testaverde	.10

1999 Metal Universe Precious Metal Gem

This is a 250-card parallel to the base that is sequentially numbered to 50.

	MT
Precious Metal Cards:	75x-150x
Precious Metal Rookies:	15x-30x
Production 50 Sets	

1999 Metal Universe Linchpins

This 10-card set spotlights a laser die-cut design and highlights key players who hold their teams together on the field and in the clubhouse. Singles were found 1:360 packs.

		MT
Complete Set (10):		400.00
Common Player:		25.00
Inserted 1:360		
1	Emmitt Smith	60.00
2	Charlie Batch	25.00
3	Fred Taylor	60.00
4	Jake Plummer	40.00
5	Brett Favre	80.00
6	Barry Sanders	80.00
7	Mark Brunell	35.00
8	Peyton Manning	60.00
9	Randy Moss	80.00
10	Terrell Davis	60.00

1999 Metal Universe Planet Metal

Each player in this 15-card set is printed on a die-cut card that features a metallic view of the planet. Singles were inserted 1:36 packs.

		MT
Complete Set (15):		135.00
Common Player:		4.00
Inserted 1:36		
1	Terrell Davis	15.00
2	Troy Aikman	10.00
3	Peyton Manning	15.00
4	Mark Brunell	8.00
5	John Elway	15.00
6	Doug Flutie	8.00
7	Dan Marino	15.00
8	Brett Favre	20.00
9	Barry Sanders	20.00
10	Emmitt Smith	15.00
11	Fred Taylor	10.00
12	Jerry Rice	10.00
13	Jamal Anderson	4.00
14	Randall Cunningham	4.00
15	Randy Moss	20.00

1999 Metal Universe Quasars

This 15-card set features the top rookies from 1999 and puts them on a silver rainbow holofoil card. They were inserted 1:18 packs.

		MT
Complete Set (15):		85.00
Common Player:		2.00
Inserted 1:18		
1	Ricky Williams	25.00
2	Tim Couch	25.00
3	Shaun King	3.00
4	Champ Bailey	3.00
5	Torry Holt	5.00
6	Donovan McNabb	8.00
7	David Boston	6.00
8	Andy Katzenmoyer	2.00
9	Daunte Culpepper	8.00
10	Edgerrin James	15.00
11	Cade McNown	8.00
12	Troy Edwards	4.00
13	Akili Smith	8.00
14	Peerless Price	4.00
15	Amos Zereoue	4.00

1999 Metal Universe Starchild

This 20-card insert has a young star theme to it and prints each player on a silver rainbow holofoil background. Singles were found 1:6 packs.

		MT
Complete Set (20):		30.00
Common Player:		1.00
Inserted 1:6		
1	Skip Hicks	2.00
2	Mike Alstott	2.00
3	Joey Galloway	2.00
4	Tony Simmons	1.00
5	Jamal Anderson	2.00
6	John Avery	1.00
7	Charles Woodson	2.00
8	Jon Kitna	3.00
9	Marshall Faulk	2.00
10	Eric Moulds	2.00
11	Keyshawn Johnson	3.00
12	Ryan Leaf	3.00
13	Curtis Enis	2.00
14	Steve McNair	2.00
15	Corey Dillon	2.00
16	Tim Dwight	2.00
17	Brian Griese	4.00
18	Drew Bledsoe	5.00
19	Eddie George	4.00
20	Terrell Owens	3.00

1999 Pacific

Pacific Football is a 450-card set that includes more than 30 unseeded rookie cards. Copper, Gold, Opening Day and Platinum Blue are the four different parallel sets. Other inserts include: Cramer's Choice, Dynagon Turf, Gold Crown Die Cuts, Pro Bowl Die Cuts, Record Breakers and Team Checklists.

		MT
Complete Set (450):		75.00
Common Player:		.15
Common Rookie:		.50
Wax Box:		60.00
1	Mario Bates	.15
2	Larry Centers	.15
3	Chris Gedney	.15
4	Kwamie Lassiter	.15
5	Johnny McWilliams	.15
6	Eric Metcalf	.15
7	Rob Moore	.30
8	Adrian Murrell	.15
9	Jake Plummer	1.00
10	Simeon Rice	.15
11	Frank Sanders	.30
12	Andre Wadsworth	.30
13	Aeneas Williams	.15
14	Michael Pittman, Ronnie Anderson	.15
15	Morten Andersen	.15
16	Jamal Anderson	.50
17	Lester Archambeau	.15
18	Chris Chandler	.15
19	Bob Christian	.15
20	Steve DeBerg	.15
21	Tim Dwight	.50
22	Tony Martin	.15
23	Terance Mathis	.15
24	Eugene Robinson	.15
25	O.J. Santiago	.15
26	Chuck Smith	.15
27	Jessie Tuggle	.15
28	Jammi German, Ken Oxendine	.15
29	Peter Boulware	.15
30	Jay Graham	.15
31	Jim Harbaugh	.30
32	Priest Holmes	.75
33	Michael Jackson	.15
34	Jermaine Lewis	.15
35	Ray Lewis	.15
36	Michael McCrary	.15
37	Jonathan Ogden	.15
38	Errict Rhett	.15
39	James Roe	.15
40	Floyd Turner	.15
41	Rod Woodson	.15
42	Eric Zeier	.15
43	Wally Richardson, Patrick Johnson	.15
44	Ruben Brown	.15
45	Quinn Early	.15
46	Doug Flutie	.50
47	Sam Gash	.15
48	Phil Hansen	.15
49	Lonnie Johnson	.15
50	Rob Johnson	.30
51	Eric Moulds	.50
52	Andre Reed	.15
53	Jay Riemersma	.15
54	Antowain Smith	.30
55	Bruce Smith	.15
56	Thurman Thomas	.30
57	Ted Washington	.15
58	Jonathon Linton, Kamil Loud	.15
59	Michael Bates	.15
60	Steve Beuerlein	.15
61	Tshimanga Biakabutuka	.15
62	Mark Carrier	.15
63	Eric Davis	.15
64	William Floyd	.15
65	Sean Gilbert	.15
66	Kevin Greene	.15
67	Raghib Ismail	.15
68	Anthony Johnson	.15
69	Fred Lane	.15
70	Muhsin Muhammad	.15
71	Winslow Oliver	.15
72	Wesley Walls	.15
73	Dameyune Craig, Shane Matthews	.15
74	Edgar Bennett	.15
75	Curtis Conway	.30
76	Bobby Engram	.15
77	Curtis Enis	.50
78	Ty Hallock	.15
79	Walt Harris	.15
80	Jeff Jaeger	.15
81	Erik Kramer	.15
82	Glyn Milburn	.15
83	Chris Penn	.15
84	Steve Stenstrom	.15
85	Ryan Wetnight	.15
86	Moses Moreno, James Allen	.15
87	Ashley Ambrose	.15
88	Brandon Bennett	.15
89	Eric Bieniemy	.15
90	Jeff Blake	.30
91	Corey Dillon	.50
92	Paul Justin	.15
93	Eric Kresser	.15
94	Tremain Mack	.15
95	Tony McGee	.15
96	Neil O'Donnell	.15
97	Carl Pickens	.30
98	Darnay Scott	.15
99	Takeo Spikes	.15
100	Ty Detmer	.15
101	Chris Gardocki	.15
102	Damon Gibson	.15
103	Antonio Langham	.15
104	Jerris McPhail	.15
105	Irv Smith	.15
106	Freddie Solomon	.15
107	Scott Milanovich, Fred Brock	.15
108	Troy Aikman	1.25
109	Larry Allen	.15
110	Eric Bjornson	.15
111	Billy Davis	.15
112	Michael Irvin	.30
113	David LaFleur	.15
114	Ernie Mills	.15
115	Nate Newton	.15
116	Deion Sanders	.50
117	Emmitt Smith	1.75
118	Chris Warren	.15
119	Bubby Brister	.15
120	Terrell Davis	2.00
121	Jason Elam	.15
122	John Elway	2.00
123	Willie Green	.15
124	Howard Griffith	.15
125	Vaughn Hebron	.15
126	Ed McCaffrey	.30
127	John Mobley	.15
128	Bill Romanowski	.15
129	Shannon Sharpe	.30
130	Neil Smith	.15
131	Rod Smith	.30
132	Brian Griese, Marcus Nash	.50
133	Charlie Batch	1.00
134	Stephen Boyd	.15
135	Mark Carrier	.15
136	Germane Crowell	.30
137	Terry Fair	.15
138	Jason Hanson	.15
139	Greg Jeffries	.15
140	Herman Moore	.30
141	Johnnie Morton	.15
142	Robert Porcher	.15
143	Ron Rivers	.15
144	Barry Sanders	2.50
145	Tommy Vardell	.15
146	Bryant Westbrook	.15
147	Robert Brooks	.15
148	LeRoy Butler	.15
149	Mark Chmura	.15
150	Tyrone Davis	.15
151	Brett Favre	2.50
152	Antonio Freeman	.50
153	Raymont Harris	.15
154	Vonnie Holliday	.30
155	Darick Holmes	.15
156	Dorsey Levens	.30
157	Brian Manning	.15
158	Derrick Mayes	.15
159	Roell Preston	.15
160	Jeff Thomason	.15
161	Tyrone Williams	.15
162	Corey Bradford, Michael Blair	.15
163	Aaron Bailey	.15
164	Ken Dilger	.15
165	Marshall Faulk	.50
166	E.G. Green	.30
167	Marvin Harrison	.30
168	Craig Heyward	.15
169	Peyton Manning	2.50
170	Jerome Pathon	.30
171	Marcus Pollard	.15
172	Torrance Small	.15
173	Mike Vanderjagt	.15
174	Lamont Warren	.15
175	Tavian Banks	.30
176	Reggie Barlow	.15
177	Tony Boselli	.15
178	Tony Brackens	.15
179	Mark Brunell	1.00
180	Kevin Hardy	.15
181	Damon Jones	.15
182	Jamie Martin	.15
183	Keenan McCardell	.15
184	Pete Mitchell	.15
185	Bryce Paup	.15
186	Jimmy Smith	.30
187	Fred Taylor	1.50
188	Alvis Whitted, Chris Howard	.15
189	Derrick Alexander	.15
190	Kimble Anders	.15
191	Donnell Bennett	.15
192	Dale Carter	.15
193	Rich Gannon	.15
194	Tony Gonzalez	.15
195	Elvis Grbac	.15
196	Joe Horn	.15
197	Kevin Lockett	.15
198	Bam Morris	.15
199	Andre Rison	.30
200	Derrick Thomas	.15
201	Tamarick Vanover	.15
202	Gregory Favors, Rashaan Shehee	.15
203	Karim Abdul	.30
204	Trace Armstrong	.15
205	John Avery	.30
206	Lorenzo Bromell	.15
207	Terrell Buckley	.15
208	Oronde Gadsden	.30
209	Sam Madison	.15
210	Dan Marino	1.75
211	O.J. McDuffie	.15
212	Ed Perry	.15
213	Jason Taylor	.15
214	Lamar Thomas	.15
215	Zach Thomas	.30
216	Henry Lusk, Nate Jacquet	.15
217	Damon Huard, Todd Doxzon	.15
218	Gary Anderson	.15
219	Cris Carter	.50
220	Randall Cunningham	.50
221	Andrew Glover	.15
222	Matthew Hatchette	.15
223	Brad Johnson	.50
224	Ed McDaniel	.15
225	Randall McDaniel	.15
226	Randy Moss	4.00
227	David Palmer	.15
228	John Randle	.15
229	Jake Reed	.15
230	Robert Smith	.30
231	Todd Steussie	.15
232	Stalin Colinet, Kivuusama Mays	.15
233	Jay Fiedler, Todd Bouman	.15
234	Drew Bledsoe	1.00
235	Troy Brown	.15
236	Ben Coates	.30
237	Derrick Cullors	.15
238	Robert Edwards	.30
239	Terry Glenn	.30
240	Shawn Jefferson	.15
241	Ty Law	.15
242	Lawyer Milloy	.15
243	Lovett Purnell	.15
244	Sedrick Shaw	.15
245	Tony Simmons	.30
246	Chris Slade	.15
247	Rod Rutledge, Anthony Ladd	.15
248	Chris Floyd, Harold Shaw	.15
249	Ink Aleaga	.15
250	Cameron Cleeland	.30
251	Kerry Collins	.30
252	Troy Davis	.15
253	Sean Dawkins	.15
254	Mark Fields	.15
255	Andre Hastings	.15
256	Sammy Knight	.15
257	Keith Poole	.15
258	William Roaf	.15
259	Lamar Smith	.15
260	Danny Wuerffel	.15
261	Josh Wilcox, Brett Bech	.15
262	Chris Bordeleau, Wilmont Perry	.15
263	Jessie Armstead	.15
264	Tiki Barber	.15
265	Chad Bratzke	.15
266	Gary Brown	.15
267	Chris Calloway	.15
268	Howard Cross	.15
269	Kent Graham	.15
270	Ike Hilliard	.15
271	Danny Kanell	.15
272	Michael Strahan	.15
273	Amani Toomer	.15
274	Charles Way	.15
275	Mike Cherry, Greg Comella	.15
276	Kyle Brady	.15
277	Keith Byars	.15
278	Chad Cascadden	.15
279	Wayne Chrebet	.30
280	Bryan Cox	.15
281	Glenn Foley	.30
282	Aaron Glenn	.15
283	Keyshawn Johnson	.50
284	Leon Johnson	.15
285	Mo Lewis	.15
286	Curtis Martin	.50
287	Otis Smith	.15
288	Vinny Testaverde	.30
289	Dedric Ward	.15
290	Tim Brown	.30
291	Rickey Dudley	.15
292	Jeff George	.30
293	Desmond Howard	.15
294	James Jett	.15
295	Lance Johnstone	.15
296	Randy Jordan	.15
297	Napoleon Kaufman	.50
298	Lincoln Kennedy	.15
299	Terry Mickens	.15
300	Darrell Russell	.15
301	Harvey Williams	.15
302	Jon Ritchie, Charles Woodson	.30
303	Rodney Williams, Jermaine Williams	.15
304	Koy Detmer	.15
305	Hugh Douglas	.15
306	Jason Dunn	.15
307	Irving Fryar	.15
308	Charlie Garner	.15
309	Jeff Graham	.15
310	Bobby Hoying	.15
311	Rodney Peete	.15
312	Allen Rossum	.15
313	Duce Staley	.15
314	William Thomas	.15
315	Kevin Turner	.15
316	Kaseem Sinceno, Corey Walker	.15
317	Jahine Arnold	.15
318	Jerome Bettis	.30
319	Will Blackwell	.15
320	Mark Bruener	.15
321	Dermontti Dawson	.15
322	Chris Fuamatu-Ma'afala	.15
323	Courtney Hawkins	.15
324	Richard Huntley	.15
325	Charles Johnson	.15
326	Levon Kirkland	.15
327	Kordell Stewart	.75
328	Hines Ward	.30
329	DeWayne Washington	.15
330	Tony Banks	.30
331	Steve Bono	.15
332	Isaac Bruce	.30
333	June Henley	.15
334	Robert Holcombe	.30
335	Mike Jones	.15
336	Eddie Kennison	.15
337	Amp Lee	.15
338	Jerald Moore	.15
339	Ricky Proehl	.15
340	J.T. Thomas	.15
341	Derrick Harris, Az-Zahir Hakim	.15
✓ 342	Roland Williams, Grant Wistrom	.15
343	*Kurt Warner, Tony Horne*	35.00
344	Terrell Fletcher	.15
345	Greg Jackson	.15
346	Charlie Jones	.15
347	Freddie Jones	.15
348	Ryan Leaf	1.00
349	Natrone Means	.30
350	Mikhael Ricks	.15
351	Junior Seau	.30
352	Bryan Still	.15
353	Tremayne Stephens, Ryan Thelwell	.15
354	Greg Clark	.15

355	Marc Edwards	.15
356	Merton Hanks	.15
357	Garrison Hearst	.30
358	R.W. McQuarters	.15
359	Ken Norton Jr.	.15
360	Terrell Owens	.50
361	Jerry Rice	1.25
362	J.J. Stokes	.30
363	Bryant Young	.15
364	Steve Young	1.00
365	Chad Brown	.15
366	Christian Fauria	.15
367	Joey Galloway	.50
368	Ahman Green	.30
369	Cortez Kennedy	.15
370	Jon Kitna	.75
371	James McKnight	.15
372	Mike Pritchard	.15
373	Michael Sinclair	.15
374	Shawn Springs	.15
375	Ricky Watters	.30
376	Darryl Williams	.15
377	Robert Wilson, Kerry Joseph	.15
378	Mike Alstott	.30
379	Reidel Anthony	.15
380	Derrick Brooks	.15
381	Trent Dilfer	.30
382	Warrick Dunn	.75
383	Bert Emanuel	.15
384	Jacquez Green	.30
385	Patrick Hape	.15
386	John Lynch	.15
387	Dave Moore	.15
388	Hardy Nickerson	.15
389	Warren Sapp	.15
390	Karl Williams	.15
391	Blaine Bishop	.15
392	Joe Bowden	.15
393	Isaac Byrd	.15
394	Willie Davis	.15
395	Al Del Greco	.15
396	Kevin Dyson	.30
397	Eddie George	.75
398	Jackie Harris	.15
399	Dave Krieg	.15
400	Steve McNair	.50
401	Michael Roan	.15
402	Yancey Thigpen	.15
403	Frank Wycheck	.15
404	Derrick Mason, Steve Matthews	.15
405	Stephen Alexander	.15
406	Terry Allen	.30
407	Jamie Asher	.15
408	Stephen Davis	.15
409	Darrell Green	.15
410	Trent Green	.30
411	Skip Hicks	.30
412	Brian Mitchell	.15
413	Leslie Shepherd	.15
414	Michael Westbrook	.15
415	Terry Hardy, Rabih Abdullah	.15
416	Corey Thomas, Mike Quinn	.15
417	Jonathan Quinn, Kelly Holcomb	.15
418	Brian Alford, Blake Spence	.15
419	Andy Haase, Carlos King	.15
420	Karl Hankton, James Thrash	.15
421	Fred Beasley, Itula Mili	.15
422	*Champ Bailey*	2.50
423	*D'Wayne Bates*	1.00
424	*Michael Bishop*	3.00
425	*David Boston*	3.00
426	*Shawn Bryson*	.50
427	*Tim Couch*	12.00
428	*Scott Covington*	1.00
429	*Daunte Culpepper*	4.00
430	*Autry Denson*	1.00
431	*Troy Edwards*	3.00
432	*Kevin Faulk*	3.00
433	*Joe Germaine*	2.00
434	*Torry Holt*	3.00
435	*Brock Huard*	2.00
436	*Sedrick Irvin*	1.50
437	*Edgerrin James*	6.00
438	*Andy Katzenmoyer*	1.00
439	*Shaun King*	2.00
440	*Rob Konrad*	.50
441	*Donovan McNabb*	5.00
442	*Cade McNown*	5.00
443	*Billy Miller*	1.00
444	*Dee Miller*	1.00
445	*Sirr Parker*	1.00
446	*Peerless Price*	3.00
447	*Akili Smith*	5.00
448	*Tai Streets*	1.00
449	*Ricky Williams*	10.00
450	*Amos Zereoue*	2.00

1999 Pacific Copper

This 450-card parallel was a hobby-only release and was sequentially numbered to 99.

	MT
Copper Cards:	30x-60x
Copper Rookies:	5x-10x
Production 99 Sets	

1999 Pacific Gold

This 450-card set is a parallel to the base and was hobby only and is sequentially numbered to 199.

	MT
Gold Cards:	15x-30x
Gold Rookies:	3x-6x
Production 199 Sets	

1999 Pacific Opening Day

This 450-card set is a parallel to the base and each card is sequentially numbered to 45.

	MT
Opening Day Cards:	50x-100x
Opening Day Rookies:	10x-20x
Production 45 Sets	

1999 Pacific Platinum Blue

This is a 450-card set that is a parallel to the base with each single sequentially numbered to 75.

	MT
Platinum Blue Cards:	40x-80x
Platinum Blue Rookies:	8x-16x
Production 75 Sets	

1999 Pacific Cramer's Choice Awards

This insert includes the top ten players in the NFL and captures them on a dual-foiled trophy card. Each is die cut in the shape of a pyramid and is sequentially numbered to 299.

		MT
Complete Set (10):		950.00
Common Player:		40.00
Production 299 Sets		
1	Jamal Anderson	40.00
2	Terrell Davis	125.00
3	John Elway	125.00
4	Barry Sanders	150.00
5	Brett Favre	150.00
6	Peyton Manning	100.00
7	Fred Taylor	85.00
8	Dan Marino	125.00
9	Randall Cunningham	40.00
10	Randy Moss	175.00

1999 Pacific Dynagon Turf

Each card in this 20-card set is printed on a silver-foil card and is horizontal. Singles were inserted 2:25 packs. A parallel Titanium Turf was made and is sequentially numbered to 99.

		MT
Complete Set (20):		85.00
Common Player:		.75
Inserted 2:25		
Titanium Turf Singles:		6x-12x
Production 99 Sets		
1	Jake Plummer	6.00
2	Jamal Anderson	1.50
3	Doug Flutie	1.50
4	Emmitt Smith	10.00
5	Terrell Davis	10.00
6	John Elway	10.00
7	Barry Sanders	12.00
8	Brett Favre	12.00
9	Peyton Manning	8.00
10	Mark Brunell	4.00
11	Fred Taylor	6.00
12	Dan Marino	10.00
13	Randall Cunningham	1.50
14	Randy Moss	15.00
15	Drew Bledsoe	4.00
16	Curtis Martin	1.50
17	Jerome Bettis	.75
18	Jerry Rice	6.00
19	Jon Kitna	1.50
20	Eddie George	3.00

1999 Pacific Gold Crown Die-Cuts

Each card in this 36-card set is printed on dual-foil board and is die cut in the shape of a gold crown. Singles were inserted 1:25 packs.

		MT
Complete Set (36):		300.00
Common Player:		3.00
Inserted 1:25		
1	Jake Plummer	12.00
2	Jamal Anderson	6.00
3	Priest Holmes	6.00
4	Doug Flutie	6.00
5	Antowain Smith	3.00
6	Corey Dillon	6.00
7	Troy Aikman	15.00
8	Emmitt Smith	20.00
9	Terrell Davis	20.00
10	John Elway	20.00
11	Brian Griese	8.00
12	Charlie Batch	12.00
13	Barry Sanders	30.00
14	Brett Favre	30.00
15	Antonio Freeman	6.00
16	Marshall Faulk	6.00
17	Peyton Manning	20.00
18	Mark Brunell	12.00
19	Fred Taylor	18.00
20	Dan Marino	20.00
21	Randall Cunningham	6.00
22	Randy Moss	35.00
23	Drew Bledsoe	12.00
24	Keyshawn Johnson	6.00
25	Curtis Martin	6.00
26	Napoleon Kaufman	6.00
27	Jerome Bettis	6.00
28	Kordell Stewart	10.00
29	Terrell Owens	8.00
30	Jerry Rice	15.00
31	Steve Young	10.00
32	Joey Galloway	6.00
33	Jon Kitna	6.00
34	Trent Dilfer	3.00
35	Warrick Dunn	8.00
36	Eddie George	8.00

1999 Pacific Pro Bowl Die-Cuts

The 20 players in this set are printed on a die-cut card with an erupting volcano in the background. Singles were inserted 1:49 packs.

		MT
Complete Set (20):		150.00
Common Player:		4.00
Inserted 1:49		
1	Jamal Anderson	6.00
2	Chris Chandler	4.00
3	Doug Flutie	6.00
4	Deion Sanders	6.00
5	Emmitt Smith	20.00
6	Terrell Davis	20.00
7	John Elway	20.00
8	Barry Sanders	30.00
9	Antonio Freeman	6.00
10	Marshall Faulk	6.00
11	Randall Cunningham	6.00
12	Randy Moss	35.00
13	Robert Smith	4.00
14	Ty Law	4.00
15	Keyshawn Johnson	6.00
16	Curtis Martin	6.00
17	Jerry Rice	15.00
18	Steve Young	10.00
19	Mike Alstott	6.00
20	Eddie George	8.00

1999 Pacific Record Breakers

This was a hobby only insert that included record-breaking achievements from 1998. Singles from this 20-card insert were sequentially numbered to 199.

		MT
Complete Set (20):		1250.
Common Player:		40.00
Production 199 Sets		
1	Jake Plummer	75.00
2	Jamal Anderson	40.00
3	Doug Flutie	40.00
4	Troy Aikman	75.00
5	Emmitt Smith	125.00
6	Terrell Davis	125.00
7	John Elway	125.00
8	Barry Sanders	150.00
9	Brett Favre	150.00
10	Marshall Faulk	40.00
11	Peyton Manning	100.00
12	Mark Brunell	60.00
13	Fred Taylor	85.00
14	Dan Marino	125.00
15	Randall Cunningham	40.00
16	Randy Moss	175.00
17	Drew Bledsoe	60.00
18	Curtis Martin	40.00
19	Jerry Rice	75.00
20	Steve Young	50.00

1999 Pacific Team Checklists

Each card in this 31-card set includes each team with a star player from that team on the fronts of the horizontal card. The backs include the team checklist for each player in the base set. Singles were inserted 2:25 packs.

		MT
Complete Set (31):		100.00
Common Player:		1.25
Inserted 2:25		
1	Jake Plummer	8.00
2	Jamal Anderson	2.50
3	Priest Holmes	2.50
4	Doug Flutie	2.50
5	Muhsin Muhammad	1.25
6	Curtis Enis	2.50
7	Corey Dillon	2.50
8	Ty Detmer	1.25
9	Emmitt Smith	12.00
10	John Elway	12.00
11	Barry Sanders	16.00
12	Brett Favre	16.00
13	Peyton Manning	10.00
14	Fred Taylor	8.00
15	Andre Rison	1.25
16	Dan Marino	12.00
17	Randy Moss	20.00
18	Drew Bledsoe	6.00
19	Cameron Cleeland	1.25
20	Ike Hilliard	1.25
21	Curtis Martin	2.50
22	Napoleon Kaufman	2.50
23	Duce Staley	1.25
24	Jerome Bettis	2.50
25	Isaac Bruce	2.50
26	Ryan Leaf	4.00
27	Steve Young	4.00
28	Joey Galloway	2.50
29	Warrick Dunn	4.00
30	Eddie George	4.00
31	Michael Westbrook	1.25

1999 Pacific Aurora

Each card in this 200-card set has a large posed photo and a smaller action photo in a vintage looking sepia color. A total of 150 players were used with 50 star players and rookies duplicated with a pinstripe background and posed photo on front. Inserts include: Premiere Date, Canvas Creations, Championship Fever, Complete Players, Leather Bound and Styrotechs.

		MT
Complete Set (200):		85.00
Common Player:		.15
Wax Box:		75.00
1	*David Boston*	3.00
2	Larry Centers	.15
3	Rob Moore	.30
4	Adrian Murrell	.15
5C	Jake Plummer	1.00
5D	Jake Plummer	1.00
6C	Jamal Anderson	.50
6D	Jamal Anderson	.50
7	Chris Chandler	.30
8	Tim Dwight	.50
9	Terance Mathis	.15
10	O.J. Santiago	.15
11C	Priest Holmes	.50
11D	Priest Holmes	.50
12	Michael Jackson	.15
13	Jermaine Lewis	.30
14	Ray Lewis	.15

15	Michael McCrary	.15
16C	Doug Flutie	.75
16D	Doug Flutie	.75
17C	Eric Moulds	.50
17D	Eric Moulds	.50
18	*Peerless Price*	2.50
19	Antowain Smith	.50
20	Bruce Smith	.15
21	Steve Beuerlein	.15
22	Tshimanga Biakabutuka	.15
23	Kevin Greene	.15
24	Muhsin Muhammad	.15
25	Wesley Walls	.15
26	Curtis Conway	.30
27	Bobby Engram	.15
28	Curtis Enis	.30
29	Erik Kramer	.15
30C	*Cade McNown*	5.00
30D	*Cade McNown*	5.00
31	Jeff Blake	.30
32C	Corey Dillon	.50
32D	Corey Dillon	.50
33	Carl Pickens	.30
34	Darnay Scott	.15
35C	*Akili Smith*	4.00
35D	*Akili Smith*	4.00
36C	*Tim Couch*	12.00
36D	*Tim Couch*	12.00
37	Ty Detmer	.15
38	*Kevin Johnson*	3.00
39	Terry Kirby	.15
40C	Troy Aikman	1.00
40D	Troy Aikman	1.00
41	Michael Irvin	.30
42	Raghib Ismail	.15
43C	Deion Sanders	.50
43D	Deion Sanders	.50
44C	Emmitt Smith	1.50
44D	Emmitt Smith	1.50
45	Bubby Brister	.30
46C	Terrell Davis	1.50
46D	Terrell Davis	1.50
47	Brian Griese	1.00
48	Ed McCaffrey	.30
49C	Shannon Sharpe	.30
49D	Shannon Sharpe	.30
50	Rod Smith	.30
51C	Charlie Batch	.75
51D	Charlie Batch	.75
52	*Sedrick Irvin*	2.00
53C	Herman Moore	.50
53D	Herman Moore	.50
54	Johnnie Morton	.15
55C	Barry Sanders	2.00
55D	Barry Sanders	2.00
56	Robert Brooks	.15
57C	Brett Favre	2.00
57D	Brett Favre	2.00
58C	Antonio Freeman	.50
58D	Antonio Freeman	.50
59	Dorsey Levens	.50
60	Derrick Mayes	.30
61	Marvin Harrison	.50
62C	*Edgerrin James*	7.00
62D	*Edgerrin James*	7.00
63C	Peyton Manning	1.50
63D	Peyton Manning	1.50
64	Jerome Pathon	.15
65	Tavian Banks	.30
66C	Mark Brunell	.75
66D	Mark Brunell	.75
67	Keenan McCardell	.15
68	Jimmy Smith	.30
69C	Fred Taylor	1.00
69D	Fred Taylor	1.00
70	Derrick Alexander	.15
71	Kimble Anders	.15
72	*Michael Cloud*	1.50
73	Elvis Grbac	.30
74	Andre Rison	.30
75	Karim Abdul	.30
76	*James Johnson*	2.00
77C	Dan Marino	1.50
77D	Dan Marino	1.50
78	O.J. McDuffie	.30
79	Lamar Thomas	.15
80C	Cris Carter	.50
80D	Cris Carter	.50
81	*Daunte Culpepper*	5.00
82C	Randall Cunningham	.50
82D	Randall Cunningham	.50
83C	Randy Moss	2.50
83D	Randy Moss	2.50
84	John Randle	.15
85C	Robert Smith	.50
85D	Robert Smith	.50
86C	Drew Bledsoe	.75
86D	Drew Bledsoe	.75
87	Ben Coates	.30
88	*Kevin Faulk*	3.00
89C	Terry Glenn	.50
89D	Terry Glenn	.50
90	Ty Law	.15
91	Cameron Cleeland	.30
92	Andre Hastings	.15
93	Billy Joe Hobert	.15
94C	*Ricky Williams*	12.00
94D	*Ricky Williams*	12.00
95	Tiki Barber	.15
96	Kent Graham	.15
97	Ike Hilliard	.15
98	Charles Way	.15
99	Wayne Chrebet	.50
100C	Keyshawn Johnson	.50
100D	Keyshawn Johnson	.50
101C	Curtis Martin	.50
101D	Curtis Martin	.50
102C	Vinny Testaverde	.30
102D	Vinny Testaverde	.30
103	Dedric Ward	.15
104C	Tim Brown	.30
104D	Tim Brown	.30
105	Rickey Dudley	.15
106	James Jett	.15
107	Napoleon Kaufman	.50
108	Charles Woodson	.50
109	Jeff Graham	.15
110	Charles Johnson	.15
111C	*Donovan McNabb*	5.00
111D	*Donovan McNabb*	5.00
112	Duce Staley	.30
113C	Jerome Bettis	.50
113D	Jerome Bettis	.50
114	*Troy Edwards*	3.00
115	Courtney Hawkins	.15
116C	Kordell Stewart	.50
116D	Kordell Stewart	.50
117	*Amos Zereoue*	2.50
118	Isaac Bruce	.30
119C	Marshall Faulk	.50
119D	Marshall Faulk	.50
120	*Joe Germaine*	2.00
121C	*Torry Holt*	3.00
121D	*Torry Holt*	3.00
122	Amp Lee	.15
123	Charlie Jones	.15
124	Ryan Leaf	.50
125	Natrone Means	.30
126	Junior Seau	.30
127	Garrison Hearst	.50
128C	Terrell Owens	.50
128D	Terrell Owens	.50
129C	Jerry Rice	1.00
129D	Jerry Rice	1.00
130	J.J. Stokes	.30
131C	Steve Young	.75
131D	Steve Young	.75
132	Chad Brown	.15
133C	Joey Galloway	.50
133D	Joey Galloway	.50
134	*Brock Huard*	2.00
135C	Jon Kitna	.50
135D	Jon Kitna	.50
136C	Ricky Watters	.30
136D	Ricky Watters	.30
137C	Mike Alstott	.50
137D	Mike Alstott	.50
138	Reidel Anthony	.30
139	Trent Dilfer	.30
140C	Warrick Dunn	.50
140D	Warrick Dunn	.50
141	Jacquez Green	.30
142	*Shaun King*	2.00
143C	Eddie George	.50
143D	Eddie George	.50
144C	Steve McNair	.50
144D	Steve McNair	.50
145	Yancey Thigpen	.30
146	Frank Wycheck	.15
147	*Champ Bailey*	2.00
148	Skip Hicks	.50
149	Brad Johnson	.50
150	Michael Westbrook	.30

1999 Pacific Aurora Premiere Date

This 200-card set is a parallel to the base and is sequentially numbered to 77. Singles were only found in hobby product and were inserted 1:25 packs.

	MT
Premiere Date Cards:	30x-60x
Premiere Date Rookies:	8x-16x
Production 77 Sets	

1999 Pacific Aurora Canvas Creations

Each player in this 10-card set was printed on real canvas. Singles were inserted 1:193 packs.

		MT
Complete Set (10):		275.00
Common Player:		15.00
Inserted 1:193		
1	Troy Aikman	30.00
2	Terrell Davis	45.00
3	Barry Sanders	60.00
4	Brett Favre	60.00
5	Peyton Manning	45.00
6	Dan Marino	45.00
7	Randy Moss	60.00
8	Drew Bledsoe	25.00
9	Steve Young	20.00
10	Jon Kitna	15.00

1999 Pacific Aurora Championship Fever

This 20-card set was issued at 4:25 packs. Each card has a parallel Copper issue that was only found in hobby product and are sequentially numbered to 20. A Platinum Blue parallel was also made and are numbered to 100. The retail only Silver parallel are numbered to 250.

		MT
Complete Set (20):		35.00
Common Player:		1.00
Inserted 4:25		
Copper Cards:		25x-50x
Production 20 Sets		
Platinum Blue Cards:		8x-16x
Production 100 Sets		
1	Jake Plummer	2.50
2	Jamal Anderson	1.00
3	Tim Couch	6.00
4	Troy Aikman	2.50
5	Emmitt Smith	3.50
6	Terrell Davis	3.50
7	Barry Sanders	5.00
8	Brett Favre	5.00
9	Peyton Manning	3.50
10	Fred Taylor	2.50
11	Dan Marino	3.50
12	Randy Moss	5.00
13	Drew Bledsoe	2.00
14	Ricky Williams	6.00
15	Keyshawn Johnson	1.00
16	Terrell Owens	1.00
17	Jerry Rice	2.50
18	Steve Young	1.50
19	Jon Kitna	1.00
20	Eddie George	1.25

1999 Pacific Aurora Complete Players

Ten players were used in this insert with two different cards. One in hobby product and the other in retail. Each product has a 10-card set with each single sequentially numbered to 299. Each card is printed on 10-point double laminated stock with full foil on both sides. A parallel Hologold set was made and inserted into both products and are sequentially numbered to 25.

		MT
Complete Set (10):		125.00
Common Player:		10.00
Production 299 Sets		
Hologold Cards:		4x-8x
Production 25 Sets		
1	Troy Aikman	15.00
2	Terrell Davis	20.00
3	Barry Sanders	30.00
4	Brett Favre	30.00
5	Peyton Manning	20.00
6	Dan Marino	20.00
7	Randy Moss	30.00
8	Drew Bledsoe	10.00
9	Jerry Rice	15.00
10	Steve Young	10.00

1999 Pacific Aurora Leather Bound

This hobby-only insert features 20 players on a laminated leather football card with white foil embossed laces. They were found 2:25 packs.

		MT
Complete Set (20):		85.00
Common Player:		2.00
Inserted 2:25		
1	Jake Plummer	5.00
2	Jamal Anderson	2.00
3	Tim Couch	12.00
4	Troy Aikman	5.00
5	Emmitt Smith	7.00
6	Terrell Davis	7.00
7	Barry Sanders	10.00
8	Brett Favre	10.00
9	Peyton Manning	7.00
10	Fred Taylor	5.00
11	Dan Marino	7.00
12	Randy Moss	10.00
13	Drew Bledsoe	4.00
14	Ricky Williams	12.00
15	Curtis Martin	2.00
16	Jerome Bettis	2.00
17	Jerry Rice	5.00
18	Steve Young	4.00
19	Jon Kitna	3.00
20	Eddie George	3.00

1999 Pacific Aurora Styrotechs

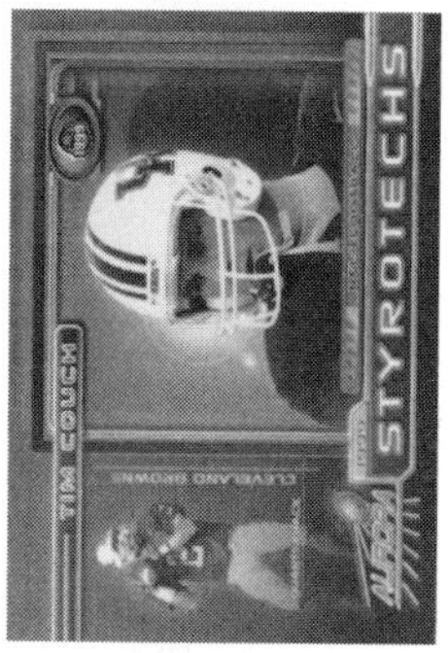

Each card in this 20-card set is horizontal with two photos of the player. One in color and the other a smaller photo of the player in black and white. Singles are printed on styrene and were inserted 1:25.

		MT
Complete Set (20):		125.00
Common Player:		3.00
Inserted 1:25		
1	Jake Plummer	8.00
2	Jamal Anderson	3.00
3	Tim Couch	16.00
4	Troy Aikman	8.00
5	Emmitt Smith	12.00
6	Terrell Davis	12.00
7	Barry Sanders	16.00
8	Brett Favre	16.00
9	Peyton Manning	12.00
10	Fred Taylor	8.00
11	Dan Marino	12.00
12	Randy Moss	16.00
13	Drew Bledsoe	5.00
14	Ricky Williams	16.00
15	Curtis Martin	3.00
16	Jerry Rice	8.00
17	Steve Young	5.00
18	Joey Galloway	3.00
19	Jon Kitna	4.00
20	Eddie George	4.00

1999 Pacific Aurora Terrell Owens Autograph

Owens signed a total of 197 cards for Aurora Football. Each card is full foil and hand sequentially numbered.

		MT
Production 197 Sets		
AU1	Terrell Owens Auto	85.00

1999 Pacific Paramount

Pacific Paramount Football is a 250-card set that includes all of the top rookies from 1999. The base has six different parallel sets with Copper, Gold, Premiere Date, HoloGold, HoloSilver and Platinum Blue. Other inserts include: Canton Bound, End Zone Net-Fusions, Personal Bests and Team Checklists.

		MT
Complete Set (250):		60.00
Common Player:		.10
Common Rookie:		.50
Wax Box:		50.00
1	*David Boston*	3.00
2	Larry Centers	.10
3	*Joel Makovicka*	1.00
4	Eric Metcalf	.10
5	Rob Moore	.20
6	Adrian Murrell	.20
7	Jake Plummer	1.00
8	Frank Sanders	.20
9	Aeneas Williams	.10
10	Morten Anderson	.10
11	Jamal Anderson	.50
12	Chris Chandler	.20
13	Tim Dwight	.50
14	Terance Mathis	.10
15	*Jeff Paulk*	1.00
16	O.J. Santiago	.10
17	Chuck Smith	.10
18	Peter Boulware	.10
19	Priest Holmes	.50
20	Michael Jackson	.10
21	Jermaine Lewis	.20
22	Ray Lewis	.10
23	Michael McCrary	.10
24	Bennie Thompson	.10
25	Rod Woodson	.10
26	*Shawn Bryson*	.50
27	Doug Flutie	.75
28	Eric Moulds	.50
29	*Peerless Price*	1.50
30	Andre Reed	.10
31	Jay Riemersma	.10
32	Antowain Smith	.50
33	Bruce Smith	.10
34	Michael Bates	.10
35	Steve Beuerlein	.10
36	Tshimanga Biakabutuka	.10
37	Kevin Greene	.10
38	Anthony Johnson	.10
39	Fred Lane	.10
40	Muhsin Muhammad	.10
41	Wesley Walls	.10
42	*D'Wayne Bates*	.75
43	Edgar Bennett	.10
44	*Marty Booker*	.50
45	Curtis Conway	.20
46	Bobby Engram	.10
47	Curtis Enis	.50
48	Erik Kramer	.10
49	*Cade McNown*	4.00
50	Jeff Blake	.20
51	*Scott Covington*	1.00

52 Corey Dillon .50
53 *Quincy Jackson* .50
54 Carl Pickens .20
55 Darnay Scott .10
56 *Akili Smith* 4.00
57 *Craig Yeast* .50
58 Jerry Ball .10
59 *Darrin Chiaverini* .50
60 *Tim Couch* 12.00
61 Ty Detmer .10
62 *Kevin Johnson* 1.25
63 Terry Kirby .10
64 *Daylon McCutcheon* .50
65 Irv Smith .10
66 Troy Aikman 1.00
67 *Ebenezer Ekuban* .50
68 Michael Irvin .20
69 Daryl Johnston .10
70 *Wayne McGarity* .75
71 *Dat Nguyen* 1.00
72 Deion Sanders .50
73 Emmitt Smith 1.50
74 Bubby Brister .30
75 Terrell Davis 1.50
76 Jason Elam .10
77 *Olandis Gary* .50
78 Brian Griese .75
79 Ed McCaffrey .30
80 *Travis McGriff* 1.00
81 Shannon Sharpe .20
82 Rod Smith .20
83 Charlie Batch .75
84 *Chris Claiborne* 1.00
85 Germane Crowell .20
86 *Sedrick Irvin* 1.50
87 Herman Moore .50
88 Johnnie Morton .10
89 Barry Sanders 2.00
90 Robert Brooks .10
91 *Aaron Brooks* 1.50
92 Mark Chmura .20
93 Brett Favre 2.00
94 Antonio Freeman .50
95 Vonnie Holliday .20
96 Dorsey Levens .50
97 *De'Mond Parker* .75
98 Ken Dilger .10
99 Marvin Harrison .30
100 *Edgerrin James* 6.00
101 Peyton Manning 1.50
102 Jerome Pathon .10
103 *Mike Peterson* .50
104 Marcus Pollard .10
105 Tavian Banks .20
106 Reggie Barlow .10
107 Tony Boselli .10
108 Mark Brunell .75
109 Keenan McCardell .10
110 Bryce Paup .10
111 Jimmy Smith .20
112 Fred Taylor 1.00
113 Dave Thomas .10
114 Kimble Anders .10
115 Donnell Bennett .10
116 *Mike Cloud* 1.00
117 Tony Gonzalez .20
118 Elvis Grbac .20
119 *Larry Parker* .50
120 Andre Rison .20
121 *Brian Shay* .50
122 Karim Abdul .30
123 Oronde Gadsden .20
124 *James Johnson* 1.50
125 *Rob Konrad* 1.00
126 Dan Marino 1.50
127 O.J. McDuffie .20
128 Zach Thomas .20
129 Cris Carter .50
130 *Daunte Culpepper* 4.00
131 Randall Cunningham .50
132 Matthew Hatchette .10
133 Leroy Hoard .10
134 Randy Moss 2.00
135 John Randle .10
136 Jake Reed .10
137 Robert Smith .50
138 *Michael Bishop* 2.00
139 Drew Bledsoe .75
140 Ben Coates .20
141 *Kevin Faulk* 2.50
142 Terry Glenn .30
143 Shawn Jefferson .10
144 *Andy Katzenmoyer* 1.00
145 Tony Simmons .20
146 *Cuncho Brown* .50
147 Cameron Cleeland .20
148 Mark Fields .10
149 La'Roi Glover .10
150 Andre Hastings .10
151 Billy Joe Hobert .10
152 William Roaf .10
153 Billy Joe Tolliver .10
154 *Ricky Williams* 12.00
155 Jessie Armstead .10
156 Tiki Barber .20
157 Gary Brown .10
158 Kent Graham .10
159 Ike Hilliard .20
160 *Joe Montgomery* 1.25
161 Amani Toomer .10
162 Charles Way .10
163 Wayne Chrebet .50
164 Bryan Cox .10
165 Aaron Glenn .10
166 Keyshawn Johnson .50
167 Leon Johnson .10
168 Curtis Martin .50
169 Vinny Testaverde .20
170 Dedric Ward .10
171 Tim Brown .20
172 *Dameane Douglas* .75
173 Rickey Dudley .20
174 James Jett .10
175 Napoleon Kaufman .50
176 Darrell Russell .10
177 Harvey Williams .10
178 Charles Woodson .50
179 *Na Brown* .50
180 Hugh Douglas .10
181 *Cecil Martin* .50
182 *Donovan McNabb* 4.00
183 Duce Staley .10
184 Kevin Turner .10
185 Jerome Bettis .50
186 *Troy Edwards* 2.00
187 Jason Gildon .10
188 Courtney Hawkins .10
189 *Malcolm Johnson* .50
190 Kordell Stewart .75
191 *Jerame Tuman* .50
192 *Amos Zereoue* 2.00
193 Isaac Bruce .30
194 Kevin Carter .10
195 *Jeremaine Copeland* .50
196 *Joe Germaine* 1.75
197 Az-Zahir Hakim .20
198 *Torry Holt* 2.50
199 Amp Lee .10
200 Ricky Proehl .10
201 Charlie Jones .10
202 Freddie Jones .10
203 Ryan Leaf .50
204 Natrone Means .30
205 Mikhael Ricks .10
206 Junior Seau .20
207 Bryan Still .10
208 Garrison Hearst .30
209 *Terry Jackson* .50
210 R.W. McQuarters .10
211 Ken Norton Jr. .10
212 Terrell Owens .50
213 Jerry Rice 1.00
214 J.J. Stokes .20
215 *Tai Streets* 1.00
216 Steve Young .75
217 *Karsten Bailey* 1.00
218 Chad Brown .10
219 Joey Galloway .50
220 Ahman Green .20
221 *Brock Huard* 1.50
222 Cortez Kennedy .10
223 Jon Kitna .75
224 Shawn Springs .10
225 Ricky Watters .20
226 Mike Alstott .50
227 Reidel Anthony .20
228 Trent Dilfer .30
229 Warrick Dunn .75
230 Bert Emanuel .10
231 *Martin Gramatica* .50
232 Jacquez Green .20
233 *Shaun King* 1.50
234 *Anthony McFarland* 1.00
235 Warren Sapp .10
236 Willie Davis .10
237 Kevin Dyson .20
238 Eddie George .75
239 *Darran Hall* .50
240 Jackie Harris .10
241 Steve McNair .50
242 Yancey Thigpen .20
243 Frank Wycheck .10
244 Stephen Alexander .10
245 *Champ Bailey* 1.50
246 Stephen Davis .10
247 Darrell Green .10
248 Skip Hicks .50
249 Brian Mitchell .10
250 Michael Westbrook .20

1999 Pacific Paramount Copper

This is a parallel to the base and could only be found in hobby product at one-per-pack.

	MT
Complete Set (250):	135.00
Copper Cards:	3x
Copper Rookies:	1.5x
Inserted 1:1	

1999 Pacific Paramount Premiere Date

This is a parallel to the base that was found 1:37 hobby packs and each is sequentially numbered to 62.

	MT
Premiere Date Cards:	50x-100x
Premiere Date Rookies:	9x-18x
Inserted 1:37	

1999 Pacific Paramount Holographic Silver

This is a parallel to the base and was inserted into hobby product. Each card was sequentially numbered to 99.

	MT
Silver Cards:	40x-80x
Silver Rookies:	7x-14x
Production 99 Sets	

1999 Pacific Paramount HoloGold

This is a parallel to the base set and was only found in retail product. Each card was sequentially numbered to 199.

	MT
HoloGold Cards:	20x-40x
HoloGold Rookies:	5x-10x
Production 199 Sets	

1999 Pacific Paramount Platinum Blue

This is a parallel to the base and was inserted in both hobby and retail product. Cards were found 1:73 packs.

	MT
Blue Cards:	40x-80x
Blue Rookies:	7x-14x
Inserted 1:73	

1999 Pacific Paramount Canton Bound

Each card is fully foiled and etched with just ten of the top players heading to Canton. Each card is horizontal and were inserted 1:361 packs. A parallel Proof set was also issued with each card sequentially numbered to 20.

	MT
Complete Set (10):	550.00
Common Player:	40.00
Inserted 1:361	
Proofs:	4x
Production 20 Sets	

1 Troy Aikman 60.00
2 Emmitt Smith 80.00
3 Terrell Davis 80.00
4 Barry Sanders 100.00
5 Brett Favre 100.00
6 Dan Marino 80.00
7 Randy Moss 100.00
8 Drew Bledsoe 50.00
9 Jerry Rice 60.00
10 Steve Young 40.00

1999 Pacific Paramount End Zone Net-Fusions

Each card in this 20-card set has a die-cut design that includes actual netting from behind the goal posts. Singles were inserted 1:73 packs.

	MT
Complete Set (20):	325.00
Common Player:	10.00
Inserted 1:73	

1 Jake Plummer 20.00
2 Jamal Anderson 10.00
3 Doug Flutie 15.00
4 Tim Couch 40.00
5 Troy Aikman 20.00
6 Emmitt Smith 30.00
7 Terrell Davis 30.00
8 Barry Sanders 40.00
9 Brett Favre 40.00
10 Peyton Manning 30.00
11 Mark Brunell 15.00
12 Fred Taylor 15.00
13 Dan Marino 30.00
14 Randy Moss 40.00
15 Drew Bledsoe 15.00
16 Ricky Williams 40.00
17 Jerry Rice 20.00
18 Steve Young 15.00
19 Jon Kitna 10.00
20 Eddie George 12.00

1999 Pacific Paramount Personal Bests

Thirty-six of the NFL's top players are featured on these holographic patterned foil cards. Singles were inserted 1:37 packs.

	MT
Complete Set (36):	225.00
Common Player:	4.00
Inserted 1:37	

1 Jake Plummer 10.00
2 Jamal Anderson 4.00
3 Priest Holmes 6.00
4 Doug Flutie 8.00
5 Antowain Smith 4.00
6 Corey Dillon 4.00
7 Akili Smith 10.00
8 Tim Couch 25.00
9 Troy Aikman 10.00
10 Emmitt Smith 15.00
11 Terrell Davis 15.00
12 Barry Sanders 20.00
13 Brett Favre 20.00
14 Antonio Freeman 4.00
15 Edgerrin James 15.00
16 Peyton Manning 15.00
17 Mark Brunell 8.00
18 Fred Taylor 10.00
19 Dan Marino 15.00
20 Randall Cunningham 4.00
21 Randy Moss 20.00
22 Drew Bledsoe 8.00
23 Kevin Faulk 6.00
24 Ricky Williams 25.00
25 Curtis Martin 4.00
26 Napoleon Kaufman 4.00
27 Donovan McNabb 10.00
28 Jerome Bettis 4.00
29 Kordell Stewart 6.00
30 Terrell Owens 6.00
31 Jerry Rice 10.00
32 Steve Young 8.00
33 Jon Kitna 6.00
34 Warrick Dunn 6.00
35 Eddie George 6.00
36 Steve McNair 4.00

1999 Pacific Paramount Team Checklists

Each card in this 31-card set highlights one player from each team and uses his photo on the front with his name in gold foil. The back has a smaller photo with a checklist of players from that team. Singles were inserted 2:37 packs.

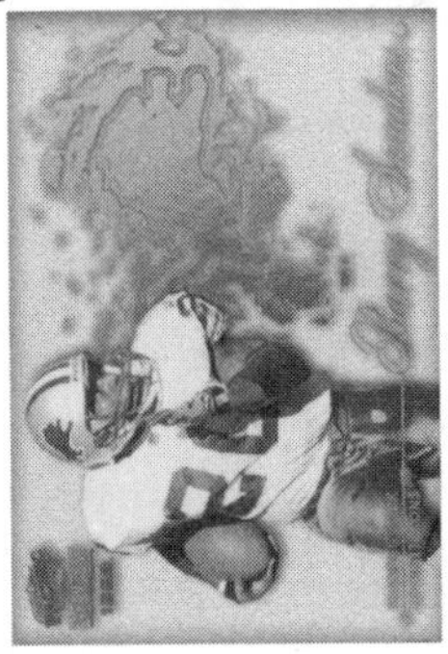

	MT
Complete Set (31):	125.00
Common Player:	1.50
Inserted 2:37	

1 Jake Plummer 6.00
2 Jamal Anderson 3.00
3 Priest Holmes 3.00
4 Doug Flutie 5.00
5 Muhsin Muhammad 1.50
6 Cade McNown 6.00
7 Corey Dillon 3.00
8 Tim Couch 15.00
9 Troy Aikman 6.00
10 Terrell Davis 8.00
11 Barry Sanders 12.00
12 Brett Favre 12.00
13 Peyton Manning 8.00
14 Fred Taylor 6.00
15 Elvis Grbac 1.50
16 Dan Marino 8.00
17 Randy Moss 12.00
18 Drew Bledsoe 5.00
19 Ricky Williams 15.00
20 Ike Hilliard 1.50
21 Curtis Martin 3.00
22 Napoleon Kaufman 3.00
23 Donovan McNabb 6.00
24 Jerome Bettis 3.00
25 Torry Holt 4.00
26 Natrone Means 1.50
27 Jerry Rice 6.00
28 Jon Kitna 4.00
29 Warrick Dunn 4.00
30 Eddie George 4.00
31 Skip Hicks 3.00

1999 Pacific Revolution

Pacific Revolution is a 175-card set that includes 50 seeded rookies at 1:4 packs. Each card includes dual foiling, etching and embossing. Opening Day, Shadow and Red are three parallel sets. Other inserts include: Chalk Talk, Icons, Showstoppers and Thorn in the Side.

	MT
Complete Set (175):	75.00
Common Player:	.25
Common Rookie:	1.00
Inserted 1:4	
Wax Box:	80.00

1 *David Boston* 5.00
2 *Joel Makovicka* 2.00
3 Rob Moore .50
4 Adrian Murrell .25
5 Jake Plummer 2.00
6 Frank Sanders .25
7 Jamal Anderson 1.00
8 Chris Chandler .50
9 Tim Dwight .75
10 Terance Mathis .25
11 *Jeff Paulk* 2.00
12 O.J. Santiago .25
13 Peter Boulware .25

14	Priest Holmes	1.00
15	Michael Jackson	.25
16	Jermaine Lewis	.25
17	Doug Flutie	1.50
18	Eric Moulds	1.00
19	*Peerless Price*	4.00
20	Andre Reed	.50
21	Antowain Smith	1.00
22	Bruce Smith	.25
23	Steve Beuerlein	.25
24	Kevin Greene	.25
25	Fred Lane	.25
26	Muhsin Muhammad	.25
27	Wesley Walls	.25
28	*Marty Booker*	1.00
29	Curtis Conway	.50
30	Bobby Engram	.25
31	Curtis Enis	1.00
32	Erik Kramer	.25
33	*Cade McNown*	8.00
34	*Scott Covington*	2.00
35	Corey Dillon	1.25
36	Carl Pickens	.50
37	Darnay Scott	.25
38	*Akili Smith*	7.00
39	*Craig Yeast*	2.00
40	*Darrin Chiaverini*	2.00
41	*Tim Couch*	20.00
42	Ty Detmer	.25
43	*Kevin Johnson*	3.00
44	Terry Kirby	.25
45	*Daylon McCutcheon*	1.00
46	Irv Smith	.25
47	Troy Aikman	2.00
48	Michael Irvin	.75
49	*Wayne McGarity*	2.00
50	*Dat Nguyen*	2.00
51	Deion Sanders	1.00
52	Emmitt Smith	3.00
53	Terrell Davis	3.00
54	John Elway	3.00
55	Brian Griese	1.50
56	Ed McCaffrey	.75
57	*Travis McGriff*	2.00
58	Shannon Sharpe	.50
59	Rod Smith	.50
60	Charlie Batch	1.50
61	*Chris Claiborne*	3.00
62	*Sedrick Irvin*	3.00
63	Herman Moore	1.00
64	Johnnie Morton	.25
65	Barry Sanders	4.00
66	*Aaron Brooks*	2.00
67	Mark Chmura	.50
68	Brett Favre	4.00
69	Antonio Freeman	1.00
70	Dorsey Levens	.75
71	*De'Mond Parker*	1.00
72	Marvin Harrison	.50
73	*Edgerrin James*	10.00
74	Peyton Manning	3.00
75	Jerome Pathon	.25
76	*Mike Peterson*	2.00
77	Reggie Barlow	.25
78	Mark Brunell	1.50
79	Keenan McCardell	.50
80	Jimmy Smith	.75
81	Fred Taylor	2.00
82	*Mike Cloud*	2.00
83	Tony Gonzalez	.50
84	Elvis Grbac	.25
85	*Larry Parker*	1.00
86	Andre Rison	.50
87	*Brian Shay*	1.00
88	Karim Abdul	.75
89	Oronde Gadsden	.50
90	*James Johnson*	3.00
91	*Rob Konrad*	2.00
92	Dan Marino	3.00
93	O.J. McDuffie	.50
94	Cris Carter	1.00
95	*Daunte Culpepper*	8.00
96	Randall Cunningham	1.00
97	*Jim Kleinsasser*	2.00
98	Randy Moss	5.00
99	Jake Reed	.25
100	Robert Smith	.75
101	Drew Bledsoe	1.50
102	Ben Coates	.50
103	*Kevin Faulk*	5.00
104	Terry Glenn	.75
105	Shawn Jefferson	.25
106	*Andy Katzenmoyer*	3.00
107	Cameron Cleeland	.50
108	Andre Hastings	.25
109	Billy Joe Tolliver	.25
110	*Ricky Williams*	18.00
111	Gary Brown	.25
112	Kent Graham	.25
113	Ike Hilliard	.25
114	*Joe Montgomery*	2.00
115	Amani Toomer	.25
116	Wayne Chrebet	.75
117	Keyshawn Johnson	1.00
118	Leon Johnson	.25
119	Curtis Martin	1.00
120	Vinny Testaverde	.50
121	Dedric Ward	.25
122	Tim Brown	.75
123	*Dameane Douglas*	2.00
124	Rickey Dudley	.50
125	James Jett	.25
126	Napoleon Kaufman	1.00
127	Charles Woodson	1.00
128	*Na Brown*	2.00
129	*Cecil Martin*	2.00
130	*Donovan McNabb*	8.00
131	Duce Staley	.25
132	Kevin Turner	.25
133	Jerome Bettis	1.00
134	*Troy Edwards*	4.00
135	Courtney Hawkins	.25
136	*Malcolm Johnson*	2.00
137	Kordell Stewart	1.25
138	*Jerame Tuman*	1.00
139	*Amos Zereoue*	4.00
140	Isaac Bruce	1.00
141	*Joe Germaine*	4.00
142	*Torry Holt*	5.00
143	Amp Lee	.25
144	Ricky Proehl	.25
145	Freddie Jones	.25
146	Ryan Leaf	1.50
147	Natrone Means	1.00
148	Mikhael Ricks	.25
149	Garrison Hearst	.75
150	*Terry Jackson*	2.00
151	Terrell Owens	1.00
152	Jerry Rice	2.00
153	J.J. Stokes	.50
154	Steve Young	1.50
155	*Karsten Bailey*	2.00
156	Joey Galloway	1.00
157	Ahman Green	.50
158	*Brock Huard*	3.00
159	Jon Kitna	1.00
160	Ricky Watters	.75
161	Mike Alstott	1.00
162	Reidel Anthony	.50
163	Trent Dilfer	.75
164	Warrick Dunn	1.25
165	*Shaun King*	3.00
166	*Anthony McFarland*	2.00
167	Kevin Dyson	.50
168	Eddie George	1.25
169	*Darran Hall*	2.00
170	Steve McNair	1.00
171	Frank Wycheck	.25
172	Stephen Alexander	.25
173	*Champ Bailey*	2.50
174	Skip Hicks	.50
175	Michael Westbrook	.25

1999 Pacific Revolution Opening Day

This is a parallel to the base set and each single is sequentially numbered to 68.

	MT
Opening Day Cards:	20x-40x
Opening Day Rookies:	5x-10x
Production 68 Sets	

1999 Pacific Revolution Red

This is a parallel to the base set and each single is sequentially numbered to 299.

	MT
Red Cards:	3x-6x
Red Rookies:	2x
Production 299 Sets	

1999 Pacific Revolution Shadow

This is a parallel to the base set and each single is sequentially numbered to 99.

	MT
Shadow Cards:	15x-30x
Shadow Rookies:	4x-8x
Production 99 Sets	

1999 Pacific Revolution Chalk Talk

Each card in this 20-card set has the player pictured on a chalk board with a diagram of an offensive play. Singles were inserted 1:49 packs.

		MT
Complete Set (20):		200.00
Common Player:		5.00
Inserted 1:49		
1	Jake Plummer	10.00
2	Jamal Anderson	5.00
3	Doug Flutie	7.00
4	Tim Couch	25.00
5	Troy Aikman	10.00
6	Emmitt Smith	15.00
7	Terrell Davis	15.00
8	John Elway	15.00
9	Barry Sanders	20.00
10	Brett Favre	20.00
11	Peyton Manning	15.00
12	Mark Brunell	8.00
13	Fred Taylor	10.00
14	Dan Marino	15.00
15	Randy Moss	25.00
16	Drew Bledsoe	8.00
17	Ricky Williams	25.00
18	Jerry Rice	10.00
19	Jon Kitna	5.00
20	Eddie George	7.00

1999 Pacific Revolution Icons

Each card is silver foiled, etched and die-cut. The 10 players in the set were found 1:121 packs.

		MT
Complete Set (10):		275.00
Common Player:		15.00
Inserted 1:121		
1	Emmitt Smith	35.00
2	Terrell Davis	35.00
3	John Elway	35.00
4	Barry Sanders	50.00
5	Brett Favre	50.00
6	Peyton Manning	35.00
7	Dan Marino	35.00
8	Randy Moss	60.00
9	Jerry Rice	25.00
10	Jon Kitna	15.00

1999 Pacific Revolution Showstoppers

The top 36 players in the NFL are in this insert that is etched and includes silver foil on the fronts. Singles were inserted 2:25 packs.

		MT
Complete Set (36):		160.00
Common Player:		2.50
Inserted 2:25		
1	Jake Plummer	7.50
2	Jamal Anderson	2.50
3	Priest Holmes	5.00
4	Doug Flutie	6.00
5	Antowain Smith	5.00
6	Cade McNown	7.00
7	Tim Couch	20.00
8	Corey Dillon	5.00
9	Akili Smith	7.00
10	Troy Aikman	7.50
11	Emmitt Smith	10.00
12	Terrell Davis	10.00
13	John Elway	10.00
14	Charlie Batch	6.00
15	Barry Sanders	15.00
16	Brett Favre	15.00
17	Antonio Freeman	2.50
18	Edgerrin James	10.00
19	Peyton Manning	10.00
20	Mark Brunell	6.00
21	Fred Taylor	7.50
22	Dan Marino	10.00
23	Randall Cunningham	5.00
24	Randy Moss	15.00
25	Drew Bledsoe	6.00
26	Ricky Williams	20.00
27	Curtis Martin	5.00
28	Napoleon Kaufman	5.00
29	Donovan McNabb	7.00
30	Kordell Stewart	6.00
31	Terrell Owens	5.00
32	Jerry Rice	7.50
33	Steve Young	6.00
34	Jon Kitna	5.00
35	Warrick Dunn	6.00
36	Eddie George	6.00

1999 Pacific Revolution Thorn in the Side

Each card is die cut and on the back includes an analysis of how that player has hurt an opposing team. A total of 20 players were used for this insert and were found 1:25 packs.

		MT
Complete Set (20):		125.00
Common Player:		2.50
Inserted 1:25		
1	Jake Plummer	7.50
2	Jamal Anderson	2.50
3	Doug Flutie	6.00
4	Tim Couch	20.00
5	Troy Aikman	7.50
6	Emmitt Smith	10.00
7	Terrell Davis	10.00
8	John Elway	10.00
9	Barry Sanders	15.00
10	Brett Favre	15.00
11	Peyton Manning	10.00
12	Fred Taylor	7.50
13	Dan Marino	10.00
14	Randy Moss	15.00
15	Drew Bledsoe	6.00
16	Ricky Williams	20.00
17	Curtis Martin	5.00
18	Jerome Bettis	2.50
19	Jerry Rice	7.50
20	Jon Kitna	5.00

1999 Playoff Prestige EXP

This 200-card set was a retail only release that included 40 unseeded rookie cards. It had two parallel sets with Reflections Gold and Reflections Silver. Other inserts include: Alma Maters, Checklists, Crowd Pleasers, Terrell Davis Salute, Draft Picks, Performers and Stars of the NFL.

		MT
Complete Set (200):		70.00
Common Player:		.20
Common Rookie:		.50
Wax Box:		60.00
1	*Anthony McFarland*	1.00
2	*Al Wilson*	1.00
3	*Jevon Kearse*	1.00
4	*Aaron Brooks*	1.50
5	*Travis McGriff*	1.00
6	*Jeff Paulk*	1.00
7	*Shawn Bryson*	.50
8	*Karsten Bailey*	1.00
9	*Mike Cloud*	1.00
10	*James Johnson*	2.00
11	*Tai Streets*	1.00
12	*Jermaine Fazande*	.50
13	*Ebenezer Ekuban*	.50
14	*Joe Montgomery*	1.50
15	*Craig Yeast*	1.00
16	*Joe Germaine*	2.00
17	*Andy Katzenmoyer*	1.50
18	*Kevin Faulk*	3.00
19	*Chris McAlister*	1.00
20	*Sedrick Irvin*	2.00
21	*Brock Huard*	2.00
22	*Cade McNown*	5.00
23	*Shaun King*	2.50
24	*Amos Zereoue*	2.50
25	*Dameane Douglas*	1.00
26	*D'Wayne Bates*	1.00
27	*Kevin Johnson*	3.00
28	*Rob Konrad*	1.50
29	*Troy Edwards*	3.00
30	*Peerless Price*	2.50
31	*Daunte Culpepper*	5.00
32	*Akili Smith*	4.00
33	*David Boston*	3.00
34	*Chris Claiborne*	1.50
35	*Torry Holt*	3.00
36	*Champ Bailey*	2.00
37	*Edgerrin James*	8.00
38	*Donovan McNabb*	5.00
39	*Ricky Williams*	12.00
40	*Tim Couch*	12.00
41	Charles Woodson (Repeat Performers)	.20
42	Skip Hicks (Repeat Performers)	.20
43	Brian Griese (Repeat Performers)	.75
44	Tim Dwight (Repeat Performers)	.20
45	Ryan Leaf (Repeat Performers)	.50
46	Curtis Enis (Repeat Performers)	.20
47	Charlie Batch (Repeat Performers)	.75
48	Fred Taylor (Repeat Performers)	1.00
49	Peyton Manning (Repeat Performers)	1.50

50	Randy Moss (Repeat Performers)	2.00
51	Jim Harbaugh (Trading Places)	.20
52	Warren Moon (Trading Places)	.75
53	Jeff George (Trading Places)	.20
54	Rich Gannon (Trading Places)	.20
55	Scott Mitchell (Trading Places)	.20
56	Kerry Collins (Trading Places)	.20
57	Brad Johnson (Trading Places)	.75
58	Charles Johnson (Trading Places)	.20
59	Chris Calloway (Trading Places)	.20
60	Tyrone Wheatley (Trading Places)	.20
61	Michael Westbrook	.40
62	Skip Hicks	.75
63	Terry Allen	.20
64	Albert Connell	.20
65	Kevin Dyson	.40
66	Frank Wycheck	.20
67	Yancey Thigpen	.40
68	Steve McNair	.75
69	Eddie George	1.00
70	Eric Zeier	.20
71	Jacquez Green	.40
72	Reidel Anthony	.40
73	Warren Sapp	.20
74	Mike Alstott	.75
75	Warrick Dunn	1.00
76	Trent Dilfer	.40
77	Ahman Green	.40
78	Joey Galloway	.75
79	Ricky Watters	.40
80	Jon Kitna	1.00
81	Amp Lee	.20
82	Isaac Bruce	.40
83	Robert Holcombe	.20
84	Greg Hill	.20
85	Marshall Faulk	.75
86	Trent Green	.75
87	J.J. Stokes	.40
88	Terrell Owens	.75
89	Jerry Rice	2.00
90	Garrison Hearst	.75
91	Steve Young	1.25
92	Junior Seau	.40
93	Mikhael Ricks	.20
94	Natrone Means	.40
95	Ryan Leaf	.75
96	Courtney Hawkins	.20
97	Chris Fuamatu-Ma'afala	.20
98	Jerome Bettis	.75
99	Kordell Stewart	.75
100	Bobby Hoying	.40
101	Charlie Garner	.40
102	Duce Staley	.40
103	Charles Woodson	.75
104	James Jett	.20
105	Rickey Dudley	.20
106	Tim Brown	.50
107	Napoleon Kaufman	.75
108	Wayne Chrebet	.50
109	Keyshawn Johnson	.75
110	Vinny Testaverde	.40
111	Curtis Martin	.75
112	Joe Jurevicius	.20
113	Tiki Barber	.20
114	Ike Hilliard	.20
115	Kent Graham	.20
116	Gary Brown	.20
117	Lamar Smith	.20
118	Eddie Kennison	.20
119	Cameron Cleeland	.20
120	Tony Simmons	.20
121	Ben Coates	.40
122	Darick Holmes	.20
123	Terry Glenn	.75
124	Drew Bledsoe	1.50
125	Leroy Hoard	.20
126	Jake Reed	.20
127	Randy Moss	4.00
128	Cris Carter	.75
129	Robert Smith	.75
130	Randall Cunningham	.75
131	Lamar Thomas	.20
132	John Avery	.40
133	O.J. McDuffie	.40
134	Dan Marino	3.00
135	Karim Abdul	.40
136	Rashaan Shehee	.20
137	Derrick Alexander	.20
138	Bam Morris	.20
139	Andre Rison	.40
140	Elvis Grbac	.40
141	Tavian Banks	.20
142	Keenan McCardell	.20
143	Jimmy Smith	.40
144	Fred Taylor	2.00
145	Mark Brunell	1.50
146	Jerome Pathon	.20
147	Marvin Harrison	.40
148	Peyton Manning	3.00
149	Robert Brooks	.20
150	Mark Chmura	.40
151	Antonio Freeman	.75
152	Dorsey Levens	.75
153	Brett Favre	4.00
154	Johnnie Morton	.20
155	Germane Crowell	.40
156	Barry Sanders	4.00
157	Herman Moore	.75
158	Charlie Batch	1.25
159	Marcus Nash	.20
160	Shannon Sharpe	.40
161	Rod Smith	.40
162	Ed McCaffrey	.40
163	Terrell Davis	3.00
164	John Elway	3.00
165	Ernie Mills	.20
166	Michael Irvin	.40
167	Deion Sanders	.75
168	Emmitt Smith	3.00
169	Troy Aikman	2.00
170	Chris Spielman	.20
171	Terry Kirby	.20
172	Ty Detmer	.20
173	Leslie Shepherd	.20
174	Darnay Scott	.20
175	Jeff Blake	.40
176	Carl Pickens	.40
177	Corey Dillon	.75
178	Bobby Engram	.20
179	Curtis Conway	.40
180	Curtis Enis	.75
181	Muhsin Muhammad	.20
182	Steve Beuerlein	.20
183	Tim Biakabutuka	.20
184	Bruce Smith	.20
185	Andre Reed	.20
186	Thurman Thomas	.40
187	Eric Moulds	.75
188	Antowain Smith	.75
189	Doug Flutie	1.25
190	Jermaine Lewis	.20
191	Priest Holmes	.75
192	O.J. Santiago	.20
193	Tim Dwight	.75
194	Terrance Mathis	.20
195	Chris Chandler	.40
196	Jamal Anderson	.75
197	Rob Moore	.40
198	Frank Sanders	.20
199	Adrian Murrell	.20
200	Jake Plummer	1.50

1999 Playoff Prestige EXP Reflections Silver

This is a parallel to the base set and is identical to the base card except each single is printed on a silver foil card and is sequentially numbered to 3,250.

	MT
Complete Set (200):	140.00
Silver Cards:	2x
Silver Rookies:	1.5x
Production 3,250 Sets	

1999 Playoff Prestige EXP Reflections Gold

This is a parallel to the base set and each single is the same as the base card except for these singles are printed on a gold foil card and are sequentially numbered to 1,000.

	MT
Complete Set (200):	280.00
Gold Cards:	3x-6x
Gold Rookies:	3x
Production 1,000 Sets	

1999 Playoff Prestige EXP Alma Maters

Each card in this 30-card set pictures two players that went to the same college. Singles were inserted 1:25 packs.

		MT
	Complete Set (30):	100.00
	Common Player:	2.00
	Inserted 1:25	
1	Priest Holmes, Ricky Williams	12.00
2	Tim Couch, Dermonti Dawson	12.00
3	Terrell Davis, Garrison Hearst	8.00
4	Troy Brown, Randy Moss	10.00
5	Barry Sanders, Thurman Thomas	10.00
6	Emmitt Smith, Fred Taylor	8.00
7	Doug Flutie, Bill Romanowski	5.00
8	Brett Favre, Michael Jackson	10.00
9	Charlie Batch, Ron Rice	5.00
10	Mark Brunell, Chris Chandler	5.00
11	Warrick Dunn, Deion Sanders	4.00
12	Cris Carter, Eddie George	4.00
13	Drew Bledsoe, Ryan Leaf	5.00
14	Corey Dillon, Napoleon Kaufman	2.00
15	Jerome Bettis, Tim Brown	2.00
16	Marshall Faulk, Darnay Scott	2.00
17	Tiki Barber, Herman Moore	2.00
18	Jamal Anderson, Chris Fuamatu-Ma'afala	2.00
19	Troy Aikman, Cade McNown	7.00
20	Brian Griese, Charles Woodson	6.00
21	Charles Johnson, Kordell Stewart	4.00
22	Kevin Faulk, Eddie Kennison	4.00
23	Donovan McNabb, Rob Moore	5.00
24	Steve McNair, John Thierry	4.00
25	Michael Irvin, Vinny Testaverde	2.00
26	Randall Cunningham, Keenan McCardell	4.00
27	Keyshawn Johnson, Junior Seau	2.00
28	Karim Abdul, Skip Hicks	2.00
29	Curtis Enis, O.J. McDuffie	2.00
30	Joey Galloway, Robert Smith	2.00

1999 Playoff Prestige EXP Checklists

This 31-card set includes a card for each NFL team and highlights one player on the front of these silver foil singles. The backs include photos of each player on that team in the base set and includes their card number. Singles were inserted 1:25 packs.

		MT
	Complete Set (31):	85.00
	Common Player:	1.50
	Inserted 1:25	
1	Jake Plummer	6.00
2	Chris Chandler	1.50
3	Priest Holmes	3.00
4	Doug Flutie	4.00
5	Wesley Walls	1.50
6	Curtis Enis	3.00
7	Corey Dillon	3.00
8	Kevin Johnson	3.00
9	Troy Aikman	6.00
10	Terrell Davis	8.00
11	Barry Sanders	12.00
12	Antonio Freeman	3.00
13	Peyton Manning	8.00
14	Fred Taylor	6.00
15	Andre Rison	1.50
16	Dan Marino	8.00
17	Randy Moss	12.00
18	Kevin Faulk	4.00
19	Ricky Williams	12.00
20	Joe Montgomery	3.00
21	Vinny Testaverde	1.50
22	Tim Brown	3.00
23	Duce Staley	1.50
24	Jerome Bettis	3.00
25	Natrone Means	3.00
26	Terrell Owens	3.00
27	Joey Galloway	3.00
28	Isaac Bruce	3.00
29	Mike Alstott	3.00
30	Eddie George	4.00
31	Skip Hicks	3.00

1999 Playoff Prestige EXP Crowd Pleasers

Each card in this 30-card set highlights the hottest players who fill the stadiums. Singles were inserted 1:49 packs.

		MT
	Complete Set (30):	200.00
	Common Player:	2.50
	Inserted 1:49	
1	Terrell Davis	15.00
2	Fred Taylor	10.00
3	Corey Dillon	5.00
4	Eddie George	6.00
5	Napoleon Kaufman	5.00
6	Jamal Anderson	5.00
7	Tim Couch	20.00
8	Emmitt Smith	15.00
9	Deion Sanders	5.00
10	Garrison Hearst	2.50
11	Peyton Manning	15.00
12	Ricky Williams	20.00
13	Barry Sanders	20.00
14	Jerry Rice	10.00
15	Jake Plummer	8.00
16	Tim Brown	2.50
17	Terrell Owens	5.00
18	Dan Marino	15.00
19	Chris Chandler	2.50
20	Drew Bledsoe	7.00
21	Charlie Batch	6.00
22	Mark Brunell	7.00
23	Troy Aikman	10.00
24	John Elway	15.00
25	Jon Kitna	5.00
26	Jerome Bettis	5.00
27	Brett Favre	20.00
28	Steve Young	6.00
29	Randy Moss	20.00
30	Antonio Freeman	5.00

1999 Playoff Prestige EXP Terrell Davis Salute

This 5-card set highlights 15 milestones in Davis' career. Each single is sequentially numbered to 750 and the first 150 of each single were autographed.

		MT
	Complete Set (5):	60.00
	Common Player:	12.00
	Production 750 Sets	
	Common Autographs:	85.00
	First 150-cards were signed	
1	Terrell Davis	12.00
2	Terrell Davis	12.00
3	Terrell Davis	12.00
4	Terrell Davis	12.00
5	Terrell Davis	12.00

1999 Playoff Prestige EXP Draft Picks

This insert includes the top 30 players drafted in 1999. It pictures each player in their college uniform on a silver foil card. Singles were inserted 1:13 packs.

		MT
	Complete Set (30):	60.00
	Common Player:	1.00
	Inserted 1:13	
1	Tim Couch	12.00
2	Ricky Williams	12.00
3	Donovan McNabb	5.00
4	Edgerrin James	7.00
5	Champ Bailey	2.50
6	Torry Holt	4.00
7	Chris Claiborne	2.00
8	David Boston	4.00
9	Akili Smith	5.00
10	Daunte Culpepper	5.00
11	Peerless Price	3.00
12	Troy Edwards	4.00
13	Rob Konrad	1.00
14	Kevin Johnson	4.00
15	D'Wayne Bates	2.00
16	Cecil Collins	5.00
17	Amos Zereous	3.00
18	Shaun King	3.00
19	Cade McNown	5.00
20	Brock Huard	2.50
21	Sedrick Irvin	2.50
22	Chris McAlister	1.00
23	Kevin Faulk	3.00
24	Jevon Kearse	1.00
25	Joe Germaine	2.50
26	Andy Katzenmoyer	2.00
27	Joe Montgomery	2.00
28	Al Wilson	1.00
29	Jermaine Fazande	1.00
30	Ebenezer Ekuban	1.00

1999 Playoff Prestige EXP Performers

This 24-card insert includes the top performers from 1998. Singles were inserted 1:97 packs.

		MT
Complete Set (24):		200.00
Common Player:		3.00
Inserted 1:97		
1	Marshall Faulk	6.00
2	Jake Plummer	15.00
3	Antonio Freeman	6.00
4	Brett Favre	30.00
5	Troy Aikman	15.00
6	Randy Moss	30.00
7	John Elway	20.00
8	Mark Brunell	10.00
9	Jamal Anderson	6.00
10	Doug Flutie	8.00
11	Drew Bledsoe	12.00
12	Barry Sanders	30.00
13	Dan Marino	20.00
14	Randall Cunningham	6.00
15	Steve Young	8.00
16	Carl Pickens	3.00
17	Peyton Manning	20.00
18	Herman Moore	6.00
19	Eddie George	7.00
20	Fred Taylor	15.00
21	Garrison Hearst	6.00
22	Emmitt Smith	20.00
23	Jerry Rice	15.00
24	Terrell Davis	20.00

1999 Playoff Prestige EXP Barry Sanders Commemorative

This was a special insert found 1:289 packs that was commemorating Sanders run for the record.

		MT
Inserted 1:289		
RR1	Barry Sanders	20.00

1999 Playoff Prestige EXP Stars of the NFL

Each card in this 20-card set is printed on clear plastic and is die cut. Singles were inserted 1:73 packs.

		MT
Complete Set (20):		160.00
Common Player:		5.00
Inserted 1:73		
1	Jerry Rice	12.00
2	Steve Young	8.00
3	Drew Bledsoe	10.00
4	Jamal Anderson	5.00
5	Eddie George	6.00
6	Keyshawn Johnson	5.00
7	Kordell Stewart	6.00
8	Barry Sanders	25.00
9	Tim Brown	5.00
10	Mark Brunell	8.00
11	Fred Taylor	12.00
12	Randy Moss	25.00
13	Peyton Manning	18.00
14	Emmitt Smith	18.00
15	Deion Sanders	5.00
16	Troy Aikman	12.00
17	Brett Favre	25.00
18	Dan Marino	18.00
19	Terrell Davis	18.00
20	John Elway	18.00

1999 Playoff Prestige SSD

Prestige SSD was a 200-card set that was a hobby-only product. It had 50 short prints with 40 rookies and 10 Repeat Performers that were inserted 1:2 packs. It has a parallel Spectrum insert in five different colors that include Blue, Gold, Green, Purple and Red. Other inserts include: Alma Maters, Checklists, Checklists Autographs, Draft Picks, For the Record, Gridiron Heritage, Inside the Numbers and Barry Sanders Run for the Record.

		MT
Complete Set (200):		250.00
Common Player:		.25
Common RP (151-160):		1.00
Common Rookie:		2.00
Inserted 1:2		
Wax Box:		100.00
1	Jake Plummer	2.50
2	Adrian Murrell	.25
3	Frank Sanders	.50
4	Rob Moore	.50
5	Jamal Anderson	1.00
6	Chris Chandler	.50
7	Terrance Mathis	.25
8	Tim Dwight	1.00
9	O.J. Santiago	.25
10	Priest Holmes	1.50
11	Jermaine Lewis	.50
12	Doug Flutie	1.50
13	Antowain Smith	1.00
14	Eric Moulds	1.00
15	Thurman Thomas	.50
16	Andre Reed	.25
17	Bruce Smith	.25
18	Tim Biakabutuka	.50
19	Steve Beuerlein	.25
20	Muhsin Muhammed	.25
21	Curtis Enis	1.00
22	Curtis Conway	.25
23	Bobby Engram	.25
24	Corey Dillon	1.00
25	Carl Pickens	.50
26	Jeff Blake	.50
27	Darnay Scott	.25
28	Leslie Shepherd	.25
29	Ty Detmer	.25
30	Terry Kirby	.25
31	Chris Spielman	.25
32	Troy Aikman	2.50
33	Emmitt Smith	4.00
34	Deion Sanders	1.00
35	Michael Irvin	.50
36	Ernie Mills	.25
37	John Elway	4.00
38	Terrell Davis	4.00
39	Ed McCaffrey	.50
40	Rod Smith	.50
41	Shannon Sharpe	.50
42	Marcus Nash	.50
43	Charlie Batch	2.00
44	Herman Moore	1.00
45	Barry Sanders	5.00
46	Germane Crowell	.50
47	Johnnie Morton	.25
48	Brett Favre	5.00
49	Dorsey Levens	1.00
50	Antonio Freeman	1.00
51	Mark Chmura	.50
52	Robert Brooks	.25
53	Peyton Manning	4.00
54	Marvin Harrison	.50
55	Jerome Pathon	.25
56	Mark Brunell	2.00
57	Fred Taylor	2.50
58	Jimmy Smith	.50
59	Keenan McCardell	.25
60	Tavian Banks	.50
61	Elvis Grbac	.50
62	Andre Rison	.50
63	Bam Morris	.50
64	Derrick Alexander	.25
65	Rashaan Shehee	.25
66	Karim Abdul	.75
67	Dan Marino	4.00
68	O.J. McDuffie	.50
69	John Avery	.50
70	Lamar Thomas	.25
71	Randall Cunningham	1.00
72	Robert Smith	.75
73	Cris Carter	1.00
74	Randy Moss	6.00
75	Jake Reed	.25
76	Leroy Hoard	.25
77	Drew Bledsoe	2.00
78	Terry Glenn	.75
79	Darick Holmes	.25
80	Ben Coates	.50
81	Tony Simmons	.50
82	Cam Cleeland	.50
83	Eddie Kennison	.25
84	Lamar Smith	.25
85	Gary Brown	.25
86	Kent Graham	.25
87	Ike Hilliard	.50
88	Tiki Barber	.25
89	Joe Jurevicius	.25
90	Curtis Martin	1.00
91	Vinny Testeverde	.50
92	Keyshawn Johnson	1.00
93	Wayne Chrebet	1.00
94	Napoleon Kaufman	1.00
95	Tim Brown	.50
96	Rickey Dudley	.25
97	James Jett	.25
98	Charles Woodson	1.00
99	Duce Staley	.25
100	Charlie Garner	.25
101	Bobby Hoying	.25
102	Kordell Stewart	1.50
103	Jerome Bettis	1.00
104	Chris Fuamatu-Ma'afala	.25
105	Courtney Hawkins	.25
106	Ryan Leaf	1.50
107	Natrone Means	.75
108	Mikhael Ricks	.25
109	Junior Seau	.50
110	Steve Young	2.00
111	Garrison Hearst	1.00
112	Jerry Rice	2.50
113	Terrell Owens	1.00
114	J.J. Stokes	.50
115	Trent Green	1.00
116	Marshall Faulk	1.00
117	Greg Hill	.25
118	Robert Holcombe	.50
119	Isaac Bruce	.75
120	Amp Lee	.25
121	Jon Kitna	1.50
122	Ricky Watters	.75
123	Joey Galloway	1.00
124	Ahman Green	.50
125	Trent Dilfer	.75
126	Warrick Dunn	1.50
127	Mike Alstott	1.00
128	Warren Sapp	.25
129	Reidel Anthony	.50
130	Jacquez Green	.50
131	Eric Zeier	.25
132	Eddie George	1.50
133	Steve McNair	1.00
134	Yancey Thigpen	.50
135	Frank Wycheck	.25
136	Kevin Dyson	.50
137	Albert Connell	.25
138	Terry Allen	.50
139	Skip Hicks	1.00
140	Michael Westbrook	.50
141	Tyrone Wheatley (Trading Places)	.25
142	Chris Calloway (Trading Places)	.25
143	Charles Johnson (Trading Places)	.25
144	Brad Johnson (Trading Places)	.50
145	Kerry Collins (Trading Places)	.25
146	Scott Mitchell (Trading Places)	.25
147	Rich Gannon (Trading Places)	.25
148	Jeff George (Trading Places)	.25
149	Warren Moon (Trading Places)	.25
150	Jim Harbaugh (Trading Places)	.25
151	Randy Moss (Repeat Performers)	10.00
152	Peyton Manning (Repeat Performers)	8.00
153	Fred Taylor (Repeat Performers)	6.00
154	Charlie Batch (Repeat Performers)	3.00
155	Curtis Enis (Repeat Performers)	1.00
156	Ryan Leaf (Repeat Performers)	2.00
157	Tim Dwight (Repeat Performers)	2.00
158	Brian Griese (Repeat Performers)	3.00
159	Skip Hicks (Repeat Performers)	1.00
160	Charles Woodson (Repeat Performers)	2.00
161	*Tim Couch*	40.00
162	*Ricky Williams*	40.00
163	*Donovan McNabb*	15.00
164	*Edgerrin James*	25.00
165	*Champ Bailey*	6.00
166	*Torry Holt*	10.00
167	*Chris Claiborne*	4.00
168	*David Boston*	12.00
169	*Akili Smith*	15.00
170	*Peerless Price*	8.00
171	*Troy Edwards*	8.00
172	*Rob Konrad*	4.00
173	*Kevin Johnson*	5.00
174	*D'Wayne Bates*	4.00
175	*Daunte Culpepper*	15.00
176	*Dameane Douglas*	4.00
177	*Amos Zereoue*	8.00
178	*Shaun King*	6.00
179	*Cade McNown*	15.00
180	*Brock Huard*	6.00
181	*Sedrick Irvin*	5.00
182	*Chris McAlister*	4.00
183	*Kevin Faulk*	10.00
184	*Andy Katzenmoyer*	5.00
185	*Joe Germaine*	6.00
186	*Craig Yeast*	4.00
187	*Joe Montgomery*	5.00
188	*Ebenezer Ekuban*	4.00
189	*Jermaine Fazande*	4.00
190	*Tai Streets*	4.00
191	*James Johnson*	6.00
192	*Mike Cloud*	5.00
193	*Karsten Bailey*	4.00
194	*Shawn Bryson*	2.00
195	*Jeff Paulk*	4.00
196	*Travis McGriff*	4.00
197	*Aaron Brooks*	5.00
198	*Jevon Kearse*	4.00
199	*Al Wilson*	4.00
200	*Anthony McFarland*	4.00

1999 Playoff Prestige SSD Spectrum Blue

This is a 200-card parallel to the base and is the same except for the background color is in blue and the foil on the fronts are also in blue. Each card is sequentially numbered on the back to 500. There is also a Gold, Green, Purple and Red version that are also numbered to 500 and are only different by the colors on the fronts of the cards.

	MT
Complete Set (200):	600.00
Spectrum Blue Cards:	4x
Spectrum Blue Rookies:	1x
Production 500 Sets	

Prices and production are the same for Gold, Green, Purple and Red.

1999 Playoff Prestige SSD Alma Maters

Each of these horizontal cards picture two players that went to the same college and put them on a foil card. Singles were inserted 1:17 packs. A parallel Jumbo version was also produced and inserted as a box topper.

		MT
Complete Set (30):		185.00
Common Player:		4.00
Inserted 1:17		
Jumbos:		1x
One Per Box		
1	Priest Holmes, Ricky Williams	30.00
2	Tim Couch, Dermontti Dawson	30.00
3	Terrell Davis, Garrison Hearst	15.00
4	Troy Brown, Randy Moss	25.00
5	Barry Sanders, Thurman Thomas	25.00
6	Emmitt Smith, Fred Taylor	15.00
7	Doug Flutie, Bill Romanowski	8.00
8	Brett Favre, Michael Jackson	25.00
9	Charlie Batch, Ron Rice	8.00
10	Mark Brunell, Chris Chandler	8.00
11	Warrick Dunn, Deion Sanders	7.00
12	Cris Carter, Eddie George	7.00
13	Drew Bledsoe, Ryan Leaf	8.00
14	Corey Dillon, Napoleon Kaufman	4.00
15	Jerome Bettis, Tim Brown	4.00
16	Marshall Faulk, Darnay Scott	4.00
17	Tiki Barber, Herman Moore	4.00
18	Jamal Anderson, Chris Fuamatu-Ma'afala	4.00
19	Troy Aikman, Cade McNown	12.00
20	Brian Griese, Charles Woodson	8.00
21	Charles Johnson, Kordell Stewart	6.00
22	Kevin Faulk, Eddie Kennison	7.00
23	Donovan McNabb, Rob Moore	8.00
24	Steve McNair, John Thierry	6.00
25	Michael Irvin, Vinny Testaverde	4.00
26	Randall Cunningham, Keenan McCardell	4.00
27	Keyshawn Johnson, Junior Seau	6.00
28	Karim Abdul, Skip Hicks	4.00
29	Curtis Enis, O.J. McDuffie	4.00
30	Joey Galloway, Robert Smith	4.00

1999 Playoff Prestige SSD Barry Sanders

This is a 10-card set that celebrates Sanders ten years of pursuit for the rushing record. Singles were found 1:161 packs.

	MT
Complete Set (10):	750.00
Common Player:	75.00
Inserted 1:161	

1999 Playoff Prestige SSD Checklist

Each NFL team has a card in this 31-card insert with a player from each team on the fronts of the foil singles. The backs have a small picture from each player on that team with their card number next to it. Singles were found 1:17 packs.

		MT
Complete Set (31):		200.00
Common Player:		2.50
Inserted 1:17		
1	Jake Plummer	12.00
2	Chris Chandler	2.50
3	Priest Holmes	6.00
4	Doug Flutie	8.00
5	Wesley Walls	2.50
6	Curtis Enis	5.00
7	Corey Dillon	5.00
8	Kevin Johnson	5.00
9	Troy Aikman	12.00
10	Terrell Davis	18.00

11	Barry Sanders	25.00
12	Antonio Freeman	5.00
13	Peyton Manning	18.00
14	Fred Taylor	12.00
15	Andre Rison	2.50
16	Dan Marino	18.00
17	Randy Moss	25.00
18	Kevin Faulk	8.00
19	Ricky Williams	25.00
20	Joe Montgomery	5.00
21	Vinny Testaverde	2.50
22	Tim Brown	5.00
23	Duce Staley	2.50
24	Jerome Bettis	5.00
25	Natrone Means	2.50
26	Terrell Owens	5.00
27	Joey Galloway	5.00
28	Isaac Bruce	5.00
29	Mike Alstott	5.00
30	Eddie George	6.00
31	Skip Hicks	5.00

1999 Playoff Prestige SSD Checklist Autographs

These cards are identical to the Checklist insert except for that each of these singles are autographed on the fronts. Each is sequentially numbered to 250.

		MT
Complete Set (31):		2000.
Common Player:		20.00
Production 250 Sets		
1	Jake Plummer	85.00
2	Chris Chandler	20.00
3	Priest Holmes	40.00
4	Doug Flutie	60.00
5	Wesley Walls	20.00
6	Curtis Enis	40.00
7	Corey Dillon	40.00
8	Kevin Johnson	40.00
9	Troy Aikman	120.00
10	Terrell Davis	150.00
11	Barry Sanders	250.00
12	Antonio Freeman	40.00
13	Peyton Manning	150.00
14	Fred Taylor	100.00
15	Andre Rison	20.00
16	Dan Marino	200.00
17	Randy Moss	250.00
18	Kevin Faulk	60.00
19	Ricky Williams	250.00
20	Joe Montgomery	40.00
21	Vinny Testaverde	20.00
22	Tim Brown	40.00
23	Duce Staley	20.00
24	Jerome Bettis	40.00
25	Natrone Means	20.00
26	Terrell Owens	50.00
27	Joey Galloway	50.00
28	Isaac Bruce	40.00
29	Mike Alstott	40.00
30	Eddie George	50.00
31	Skip Hicks	40.00

1999 Playoff Prestige SSD Draft Picks

Each card in this 30-card set is printed on a silver-foiled card with a blue foil background. Singles were inserted 1:9 packs.

		MT
Complete Set (30):		135.00
Common Player:		2.00
Inserted 1:9		
1	Tim Couch	30.00
2	Ricky Williams	30.00
3	Donovan McNabb	10.00
4	Edgerrin James	15.00
5	Champ Bailey	5.00
6	Torry Holt	8.00
7	Chris Claiborne	4.00
8	David Boston	8.00
9	Akili Smith	10.00
10	Daunte Culpepper	10.00
11	Peerless Price	5.00
12	Troy Edwards	6.00
13	Rob Konrad	2.00
14	Kevin Johnson	4.00
15	D'Wayne Bates	2.00
16	Cecil Collins	8.00
17	Amos Zereous	6.00
18	Shaun King	5.00
19	Cade McNown	10.00
20	Brock Huard	5.00
21	Sedrick Irvin	4.00
22	Chris McAlister	2.00
23	Kevin Faulk	8.00
24	Jevon Kearse	2.00
25	Joe Germaine	5.00
26	Andy Katzenmoyer	4.00
27	Joe Montgomery	4.00
28	Al Wilson	2.00
29	Jermaine Fazande	2.00
30	Ebenezer Ekuban	2.00

1999 Playoff Prestige SSD For the Record

Each card in this set has a player that broke a record in 1998 or projections for a player in 1999. They were printed on a holographic foil board with the name in gold foil. Singles were found 1:161 packs.

		MT
Complete Set (30):		750.00
Common Player:		15.00
Inserted 1:161		
1	Mark Brunell	30.00
2	Jerry Rice	40.00
3	Peyton Manning	50.00
4	Barry Sanders	70.00
5	Deion Sanders	15.00
6	Eddie George	20.00
7	Corey Dillon	15.00
8	Jerome Bettis	15.00
9	Curtis Martin	15.00
10	Ricky Williams	70.00
11	Jake Plummer	40.00
12	Emmitt Smith	50.00
13	Dan Marino	50.00
14	Terrell Davis	50.00
15	Fred Taylor	40.00
16	Warrick Dunn	20.00
17	Steve McNair	15.00
18	Cris Carter	15.00
19	Mike Alstott	15.00
20	Steve Young	25.00
21	Charlie Batch	25.00
22	Tim Couch	70.00
23	Jamal Anderson	15.00
24	Randy Moss	70.00
25	Brett Favre	70.00
26	Drew Bledsoe	30.00
27	Troy Aikman	40.00
28	John Elway	50.00
29	Kordell Stewart	20.00
30	Keyshawn Johnson	15.00

1999 Playoff Prestige SSD Gridiron Heritage

Each card in this 24-card set tracks the players career from high school to the NFL. Each is printed on actual leather and were inserted 1:33 packs.

		MT
Complete Set (24):		375.00
Common Player:		10.00
Inserted 1:33		
1	Randy Moss	40.00
2	Terrell Davis	30.00
3	Brett Favre	40.00
4	Barry Sanders	30.00
5	Peyton Manning	30.00
6	John Elway	30.00
7	Fred Taylor	20.00
8	Cris Carter	10.00
9	Jamal Anderson	10.00
10	Jake Plummer	20.00
11	Steve Young	15.00
12	Mark Brunell	15.00
13	Dan Marino	30.00
14	Emmitt Smith	30.00
15	Deion Sanders	10.00
16	Troy Aikman	20.00
17	Drew Bledsoe	15.00
18	Jerry Rice	20.00
19	Ricky Williams	40.00
20	Tim Couch	40.00
21	Jerome Bettis	10.00
22	Eddie George	12.00
23	Marshall Faulk	10.00
24	Terrell Owens	12.00

1999 Playoff Prestige SSD Inside the Numbers

Each card in this 20-card set is printed on clear plastic and each is sequentially numbered to a different number. Overall odds for these cards were 1:49 packs.

		MT
Complete Set (20):		300.00
Common Player:		10.00
Inserted 1:49		
1	Tim Brown 1012	10.00
2	Charlie Batch 2178	10.00
3	Deion Sanders 226	15.00
4	Eddie George 1294	15.00
5	Keyshawn Johnson 1131	10.00
6	Jamal Anderson 1846	10.00
7	Steve Young 4170	12.00
8	Tim Couch 4275	30.00
9	Ricky Williams 6279	25.00
10	Jerry Rice 1157	25.00
11	Randy Moss 1313	50.00
12	Edgerrin James 1416	30.00
13	Peyton Manning 3739	20.00
14	John Elway 2803	25.00
15	Terrell Davis 2008	25.00
16	Fred Taylor 1213	20.00
17	Brett Favre 4212	25.00
18	Jake Plummer 3737	12.00
19	Mark Brunell 2601	12.00
20	Barry Sanders 1491	50.00

1999 Press Pass

This 45-card set includes all of the top draft picks from 1999. Each is pictured in his college uniform and each name is in gold foil. Three parallel sets were made with Paydirt, Torquers and Reflectors. Other inserts include: Autographs, Big Numbers, Game Jerseys, Goldenarm, Hardware and X's and O's.

		MT
Complete Set (45):		20.00
Common Player:		.10
Paydirt Cards:		2x
Inserted 1:1 Hobby		
Torquer Cards:		2x
Inserted 1:1 Mass		
Reflector Cards:		25x-50x
Inserted 1:180		
Wax Box:		75.00
1	Ricky Williams	4.00
2	Tim Couch	5.00
3	Champ Bailey	1.50
4	Chris Claiborne	.75
5	Donovan McNabb	2.50
6	Edgerrin James	2.50
7	Akili Smith	2.50
8	John Tait	.10
9	Jevon Kearse	.20
10	Torry Holt	1.25
11	Troy Edwards	1.00
12	Chris McAlister	.20
13	Daunte Culpepper	2.00
14	Andy Katzenmoyer	.50
15	David Boston	1.25
16	Ebenezer Ekuban	.10
17	Peerless Price	1.00
18	Shaun King	.75
19	Joe Germaine	.75
20	Brock Huard	.75
21	Michael Bishop	1.00
22	Amos Zereoue	.75
23	Sedrick Irvin	.50
24	Autry Denson	.50
25	Kevin Faulk	1.25
26	James Johnson	.20
27	D'Wayne Bates	.50
28	Kevin Johnson	1.00
29	Tai Streets	.50
30	Craig Yeast	.50
31	Dre Bly	.10
32	Anthony Poindexter	.10
33	Jared DeVries	.10
34	Rob Konrad	.20
35	Dat Nguyen	.10
36	Cade McNown	2.00
37	Scott Covington	.50
38	Jon Jansen	.10
39	Rufus French	.20
40	Mike Rucker	.10
41	Aaron Gibson	.10
42	Kris Farris	.10
43	Anthony McFarland	.10
44	Matt Stinchcomb	.10
45	Checklist Dee Miller	.10

1999 Press Pass Autographs

Each autographed card in this set has the same photo as his base card but the name is in smaller type and the autograph is above it. Singles were inserted 1:16 packs.

	MT
Complete Set (50):	750.00
Common Player:	6.00
Inserted 1:16 Hobby	
Inserted 1:36 Retail	
Champ Bailey	40.00
D'Wayne Bates	15.00
Michael Bishop	25.00
Dre Bly	6.00
David Boston	35.00
Chris Claiborne	20.00
Mike Cloud	6.00
Tim Couch	125.00
Scott Covington	15.00
Daunte Culpepper	50.00
Autry Denson	15.00
Jared DeVries	6.00
Antwan Edwards	6.00
Troy Edwards	25.00
Ebenezer Ekuban	6.00
Kris Farris	6.00
Kevin Faulk	35.00
Rufus French	12.00
Joe Germaine	20.00
Aaron Gibson	6.00
Torry Holt	35.00
Brock Huard	20.00
Sedrick Irvin	15.00
Edgerrin James	60.00
Jon Jansen	6.00
James Johnson	12.00
Kevin Johnson	25.00
Andy Katzenmoyer	15.00
Jevon Kearse	12.00
Shaun King	20.00
Rob Konrad	12.00
Chris McAlister	12.00
Darnell McDonald	6.00
Anthony McFarland	6.00
Donovan McNabb	60.00
Cade McNown	50.00
Dee Miller	6.00
Dat Nguyen	6.00
Mike Peterson	6.00
Anthony Poindexter	6.00
Peerless Price	25.00
Mike Rucker	6.00
Akili Smith	60.00
Matt Stinchcomb	6.00
Tai Streets	15.00
John Tait	6.00
Jerame Tuman	6.00
Ricky Williams	100.00
Craig Yeast	15.00
Amos Zereoue	20.00

1999 Press Pass Big Numbers

Each card in this 9-card set is printed on foil board with a photo of the player and the number that he was drafted in the background. Singles were inserted 1:16 packs. A parallel Die Cut version was also made with each single the same except for die cut. Those were found 1:32 packs.

		MT
Complete Set (9):		60.00
Common Player:		2.50
Inserted 1:16		
Die-Cut Cards:		2x
Inserted 1:32		
1	Tim Couch	20.00
2	Ricky Williams	18.00
3	Donovan McNabb	10.00
4	Edgerrin James	10.00
5	Peerless Price	5.00
6	Amos Zereoue	2.50
7	Daunte Culpepper	8.00
8	Tai Streets	2.50
9	Akili Smith	10.00

1999 Press Pass Goldenarm

Each card in this 9-card set is horizontal and includes the top quarterbacks drafted in 1999. They were printed on foil board and were inserted 1:10 packs.

		MT
Complete Set (9):		40.00
Common Player:		1.50
Inserted 1:10		
1	Tim Couch	18.00
2	Donovan McNabb	10.00
3	Akili Smith	10.00
4	Daunte Culpepper	8.00
5	Cade McNown	8.00
6	Brock Huard	1.50
7	Joe Germaine	1.50
8	Shaun King	1.50
9	Michael Bishop	4.00

1999 Press Pass Hardware

Only the top rookies were included in this 12-card insert that was inserted 1:8 packs.

		MT
Complete Set (12):		55.00
Common Player:		2.00
Inserted 1:8		
1	Cade McNown	8.00
2	Ricky Williams	16.00
3	Torry Holt	6.00
4	Tim Couch	18.00
5	David Boston	6.00
6	Troy Edwards	4.00
7	Michael Bishop	4.00
8	Mike Cloud	2.00
9	Champ Bailey	5.00
10	Kevin Faulk	6.00
11	Autry Denson	2.00
12	Donovan McNabb	10.00

1999 Press Pass Jersey Cards

Each single in this 6-card set features a piece of game-used jersey on the card. Singles were found 1:640 packs.

		MT
Complete Set (6):		550.00
Common Player:		60.00
Inserted 1:640 Hobby		
Inserted 1:720 Mass		
TC	Tim Couch (redemption)	175.00
DC	Daunte Culpepper	100.00
TH	Torry Holt	75.00
AS	Akili Smith	125.00
CM	Cade McNown	100.00
PP	Peerless Price	60.00

1999 Press Pass "X's and O's"

The top 36 players from the base set were included in this insert that was found one-per-pack. Each is die cut and embossed on extra thick stock.

		MT
Complete Set (36):		40.00
Common Player:		.15
Inserted 1:1		
1	Ricky Williams	6.00
2	Tim Couch	7.50
3	Champ Bailey	2.00
4	Donovan McNabb	4.00
5	Edgerrin James	4.00
6	Akili Smith	4.00
7	Torry Holt	2.00
8	Troy Edwards	1.50
9	Daunte Culpepper	3.00
10	Andy Katzenmoyer	.75
11	David Boston	2.00
12	Peerless Price	1.50
13	Shaun King	1.00
14	Joe Germaine	1.00
15	Brock Huard	1.00
16	Michael Bishop	1.50
17	Amos Zereoue	1.00
18	Sedrick Irvin	.75
19	Autry Denson	.75
20	Kevin Faulk	2.00
21	James Johnson	.30
22	D'Wayne Bates	.75
23	Kevin Johnson	1.50
24	Tai Streets	.75
25	Cade McNown	3.00
26	Scott Covington	.75
27	Chris Claiborne	1.00
28	Jevon Kearse	.30
29	Rob Konrad	.30
30	Dat Nguyen	.15
31	Chris McAlister	.30
32	Craig Yeast	.75
33	Anthony Poindexter	.15
34	Dre Bly	.15
35	Mike Rucker	.15
36	Checklist Tim Couch	3.00

1999 Sage

This was the premiere issue of Sage Football. It released a 50-card prospect set that included all of the top picks from 1999 except for Ricky Williams. Only 4,200 of each player was produced. Inserts included five different levels of autographs with Red, Bronze, Silver, Gold and Platinum.

		MT
Complete Set (50):		30.00
Common Player:		.25
Wax Box:		120.00
1	Rahim Abdullah	.50
2	Jerry Azumah	.50
3	Champ Bailey	1.00
4	D'Wayne Bates	.50
5	Michael Bishop	1.50
6	David Boston	2.00
7	Fernando Bryant	.50
8	Tony Bryant	.25
9	Chris Claiborne	.75
10	Mike Cloud	.75
11	Cecil Collins	1.25
12	Tim Couch	7.50
13	Daunte Culpepper	2.50
14	Jared DeVries	.25
15	Adrian Dingle	.25
16	Antwan Edwards	.50
17	Troy Edwards	1.50
18	Kevin Faulk	2.00
19	Rufus French	.25
20	Martin Gramatica	.25
21	Torry Holt	1.75
22	Sedrick Irvin	.75
23	Edgerrin James	4.00
24	Jon Jansen	.25
25	Andy Katzenmoyer	1.00
26	Jevon Kearse	.25
27	Patrick Kerney	.25
28	Lamar King	.25
29	Shaun King	1.00
30	Jim Kleinsasser	.25
31	Rob Konrad	.50
32	Brian Kuklick	.50
33	Chris McAlister	.50
34	Darnell McDonald	1.00
35	Reggie McGrew	.50
36	Donovan McNabb	3.00
37	Cade McNown	2.50
38	Dat Nguyen	.50
39	Solomon Page	.25
40	Mike Peterson	.25
41	Anthony Poindexter	.25
42	Peerless Price	1.50
43	Michael Rucker	.25
44	L.J. Shelton	.25
45	Akili Smith	3.00
46	John Tait	.25
47	Fred Vinson	.25
48	Al Wilson	.25
49	Antoine Winfield	.25
50	Damien Woody	.25

1999 Sage Autographs

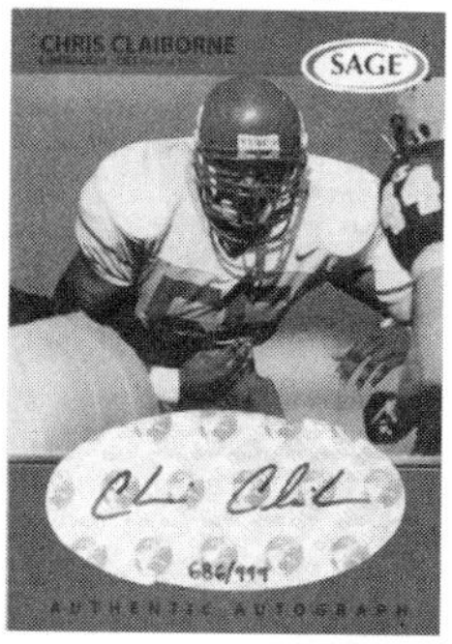

This is a 50-card Autograph insert that has red borders and a hologram on the front with the player's autograph and sequentially numbered. Most players signed a total of 999 except for ten players.

		MT
Complete Set (50):		525.00
Common Player:		4.00
1	Rahim Abdullah 999	8.00
2	Jerry Azumah 999	8.00
3	Champ Bailey 999	12.00
4	D'Wayne Bates 999	8.00
5	Michael Bishop 999	18.00
6	David Boston 869	25.00
7	Fernando Bryant 999	8.00
8	Tony Bryant 999	4.00
9	Chris Claiborne 999	10.00
10	Mike Cloud 434	15.00
11	Cecil Collins 999	18.00
12	Tim Couch 999	60.00
13	Daunte Culpepper 419	45.00
14	Jared DeVries 887	4.00
15	Adrian Dingle 999	4.00
16	Antwan Edwards 999	8.00
17	Troy Edwards 999	18.00
18	Kevin Faulk 999	20.00
19	Rufus French 999	4.00
20	Martin Gramatica 999	4.00
21	Torry Holt 999	18.00
22	Sedrick Irvin 999	10.00
23	Edgerrin James 859	45.00
24	Jon Jansen 999	4.00
25	Andy Katzenmoyer 209	30.00
26	Jevon Kearse 999	4.00
27	Patrick Kerney 879	4.00
28	Lamar King 999	4.00
29	Shaun King 999	12.00
30	Jim Kleinsasser 999	4.00
31	Rob Konrad 999	8.00
32	Brian Kuklick 999	8.00
33	Chris McAlister 999	8.00
34	Darnell McDonald 999	12.00
35	Reggie McGrew 999	8.00
36	Donovan McNabb 999	30.00
37	Cade McNown 209	50.00
38	Dat Nguyen 999	8.00
39	Solomon Page 999	4.00
40	Mike Peterson 999	4.00
41	Anthony Poindexter 999	4.00
42	Peerless Price 232	35.00
43	Michael Rucker 999	4.00
44	L.J. Shelton 999	4.00
45	Akili Smith 419	40.00
46	John Tait 999	4.00
47	Fred Vinson 999	4.00
48	Al Wilson 999	4.00
49	Antoine Winfield 999	4.00
50	Damien Woody 999	4.00

1999 Sage Autographs Bronze

This insert is the same as the Red Autographs except for the borders are Bronze and the players only signed a total of 650. A few of the players signed less.

		MT
Complete Set (50):		725.00
Common Player:		6.00
1	Rahim Abdullah 650	12.00
2	Jerry Azumah 650	12.00
3	Champ Bailey 650	15.00
4	D'Wayne Bates 650	12.00
5	Michael Bishop 650	20.00
6	David Boston 565	30.00
7	Fernando Bryant 650	12.00
8	Tony Bryant 650	6.00
9	Chris Claiborne 650	15.00
10	Mike Cloud 280	25.00
11	Cecil Collins 650	20.00
12	Tim Couch 650	75.00
13	Daunte Culpepper 285	60.00
14	Jared DeVries 575	6.00
15	Adrian Dingle 650	6.00
16	Antwan Edwards 650	12.00
17	Troy Edwards 650	20.00
18	Kevin Faulk 650	25.00
19	Rufus French 650	6.00
20	Martin Gramatica 650	6.00
21	Torry Holt 650	25.00
22	Sedrick Irvin 650	15.00
23	Edgerrin James 570	60.00
24	Jon Jansen 650	6.00
25	Andy Katzenmoyer 140	40.00
26	Jevon Kearse 650	6.00
27	Patrick Kerney 585	10.00
28	Lamar King 650	6.00
29	Shaun King 650	15.00
30	Jim Kleinsasser 650	6.00
31	Rob Konrad 650	12.00
32	Brian Kuklick 650	12.00
33	Chris McAlister 650	12.00
34	Darnell McDonald 650	15.00
35	Reggie McGrew 650	12.00
36	Donovan McNabb 650	40.00
37	Cade McNown 140	65.00
38	Dat Nguyen 650	12.00
39	Solomon Page 650	6.00
40	Mike Peterson 650	6.00
41	Anthony Poindexter 650	6.00
42	Peerless Price 150	40.00
43	Michael Rucker 650	6.00
44	L.J. Shelton 650	6.00
45	Akili Smith 285	50.00
46	John Tait 650	6.00
47	Fred Vinson 650	6.00
48	Al Wilson 650	6.00
49	Antoine Winfield 650	6.00
50	Damien Woody 650	6.00

1999 Sage Autographs Silver

This insert is the same as the Red Autographs except most of the players signed a total of 400 cards and the borders are in silver.

		MT
Common Player:		10.00
1	Rahim Abdullah 400	15.00
2	Jerry Azumah 400	15.00
3	Champ Bailey 400	20.00
4	D'Wayne Bates 400	15.00
5	Michael Bishop 400	30.00
6	David Boston 348	45.00
7	Fernando Bryant 400	15.00
8	Tony Bryant 400	10.00
9	Chris Claiborne 400	20.00
10	Mike Cloud 175	30.00
11	Cecil Collins 400	30.00
12	Tim Couch 400	100.00
13	Daunte Culpepper 180	75.00
14	Jared DeVries 355	10.00
15	Adrian Dingle 400	10.00
16	Antwan Edwards 400	15.00
17	Troy Edwards 400	30.00
18	Kevin Faulk 400	35.00
19	Rufus French 400	10.00
20	Martin Gramatica 400	10.00
21	Torry Holt 400	35.00
22	Sedrick Irvin 400	20.00
23	Edgerrin James 350	75.00
24	Jon Jansen 400	10.00
25	Andy Katzenmoyer 90	55.00
26	Jevon Kearse 400	10.00
27	Patrick Kerney 365	10.00
28	Lamar King 400	10.00
29	Shaun King 400	20.00
30	Jim Kleinsasser 400	10.00
31	Rob Konrad 400	15.00
32	Brian Kuklick 400	15.00
33	Chris McAlister 400	15.00
34	Darnell McDonald 400	20.00
35	Reggie McGrew 400	15.00
36	Donovan McNabb 400	50.00
37	Cade McNown 90	80.00
38	Dat Nguyen 400	15.00
39	Solomon Page 400	10.00
40	Mike Peterson 400	10.00
41	Anthony Poindexter 400	10.00
42	Peerless Price 93	50.00
43	Michael Rucker 400	10.00
44	L.J. Shelton 400	10.00
45	Akili Smith 180	65.00
46	John Tait 400	10.00
47	Fred Vinson 400	10.00
48	Al Wilson 400	10.00
49	Antoine Winfield 400	10.00
50	Damien Woody 400	10.00

1999 Sage Autographs Gold

This insert is the same as the Red set except for the borders are in gold and most players in the set signed only 200.

		MT
	Common Player:	15.00
1	Rahim Abdullah 200	20.00
2	Jerry Azumah 200	20.00
3	Champ Bailey 200	30.00
4	D'Wayne Bates 200	20.00
5	Michael Bishop 200	40.00
6	David Boston 174	60.00
7	Fernando Bryant 200	20.00
8	Tony Bryant 200	15.00
9	Chris Claiborne 200	30.00
10	Mike Cloud 88	40.00
11	Cecil Collins 200	45.00
12	Tim Couch 200	150.00
13	Daunte Culpepper 90	100.00
14	Jared DeVries 185	20.00
15	Adrian Dingle 200	15.00
16	Antwan Edwards 200	20.00
17	Troy Edwards 200	40.00
18	Kevin Faulk 200	45.00
19	Rufus French 200	15.00
20	Martin Gramatica 200	15.00
21	Torry Holt 200	45.00
22	Sedrick Irvin 200	30.00
23	Edgerrin James 175	100.00
24	Jon Jansen 200	15.00
25	Andy Katzenmoyer 45	70.00
26	Jevon Kearse 200	15.00
27	Patrick Kerney 175	15.00
28	Lamar King 200	15.00
29	Shaun King 200	30.00
30	Jim Kleinsasser 200	15.00
31	Rob Konrad 200	20.00
32	Brian Kuklick 200	20.00
33	Chris McAlister 200	20.00
34	Darnell McDonald 200	30.00
35	Reggie McGrew 200	20.00
36	Donovan McNabb 200	60.00
37	Cade McNown 45	120.00
38	Dat Nguyen 200	20.00
39	Solomon Page 200	15.00
40	Mike Peterson 200	15.00
41	Anthony Poindexter 200	15.00
42	Peerless Price 46	65.00
43	Michael Rucker 200	15.00
44	L.J. Shelton 200	15.00
45	Akili Smith 90	80.00
46	John Tait 200	15.00
47	Fred Vinson 200	15.00
48	Al Wilson 200	15.00
49	Antoine Winfield 200	15.00
50	Damien Woody 200	15.00

1999 Sage Autographs Platinum

This insert is the same as the Red Autographs except most of the players only signed 50 cards and the borders are in platinum.

		MT
	Common Player:	25.00
1	Rahim Abdullah 50	40.00
2	Jerry Azumah 50	40.00
3	Champ Bailey 50	50.00
4	D'Wayne Bates 50	40.00
5	Michael Bishop 50	65.00
6	David Boston 43	75.00
7	Fernando Bryant 50	40.00
8	Tony Bryant 50	25.00
9	Chris Claiborne 50	40.00
10	Mike Cloud 22	50.00
11	Cecil Collins 50	60.00
12	Tim Couch 50	200.00
13	Daunte Culpepper 25	130.00
14	Jared DeVries 47	25.00
15	Adrian Dingle 50	25.00
16	Antwan Edwards 50	40.00
17	Troy Edwards 50	55.00
18	Kevin Faulk 50	60.00
19	Rufus French 50	25.00
20	Martin Gramatica 50	25.00
21	Torry Holt 50	60.00
22	Sedrick Irvin 50	40.00
23	Edgerrin James 45	150.00
24	Jon Jansen 50	25.00
25	Andy Katzenmoyer 15	100.00
26	Jevon Kearse 50	25.00
27	Patrick Kerney 45	25.00
28	Lamar King 50	25.00
29	Shaun King 50	45.00
30	Jim Kleinsasser 50	25.00
31	Rob Konrad 50	40.00
32	Brian Kuklick 50	40.00
33	Chris McAlister 50	40.00
34	Darnell McDonald 50	40.00
35	Reggie McGrew 50	40.00
36	Donovan McNabb 50	80.00
37	Cade McNown 15	150.00
38	Dat Nguyen 50	40.00
39	Solomon Page 50	25.00
40	Mike Peterson 50	25.00
41	Anthony Poindexter 50	25.00
42	Peerless Price 13	100.00
43	Michael Rucker 50	25.00
44	L.J. Shelton 50	25.00
45	Akili Smith 25	120.00
46	John Tait 50	25.00
47	Fred Vinson 50	25.00
48	Al Wilson 50	25.00
49	Antoine Winfield 50	25.00
50	Damien Woody 50	25.00

1999 Score

This is a 275-card set that had 55 short-printed cards found 1:3 hobby packs and 1:9 retail packs. The short-prints were of 40 Rookies, 10 All-Pros and 5 Great Combos. The base set is divided into three colors like the first set was in 1989. Red, blue and green borders with the short-prints in green. Inserts include: Showcase, Artist's Proofs, Reprints, Reprint Autographs, Complete Players, Franchise, Future Franchise, Millenium Men, Numbers Game, Rookie Preview Autographs, Scoring Core and Settle the Score.

		MT
	Complete Set (275):	150.00
	Common Player:	.10
	Common Rookie (221-260):	1.00
	Common All-Pros (261-270):	1.00
	Inserted 1:3	
	Wax Box:	80.00
1	Randy Moss	2.50
2	Randall Cunningham	.50
3	Cris Carter	.50
4	Robert Smith	.20
5	Jake Reed	.10
6	Leroy Hoard	.10
7	John Randle	.10
8	Brett Favre	2.00
9	Antonio Freeman	.50
10	Dorsey Levens	.20
11	Robert Brooks	.20
12	Derrick Mayes	.10
13	Mark Chmura	.20
14	Darick Holmes	.10
15	Vonnie Holliday	.20
16	Mike Alstott	.50
17	Warrick Dunn	.75
18	Trent Dilfer	.20
19	Jacquez Green	.20
20	Reidel Anthony	.20
21	Warren Sapp	.10
22	Bert Emanuel	.10
23	Curtis Enis	.50
24	Curtis Conway	.20
25	Bobby Engram	.10
26	Erik Kramer	.10
27	Moses Moreno	.10
28	Edgar Bennett	.10
29	Barry Sanders	2.00
30	Charlie Batch	.75
31	Herman Moore	.50
32	Johnnie Morton	.10
33	Germane Crowell	.20
34	Terry Fair	.10
35	Gary Brown	.10
36	Kent Graham	.10
37	Kerry Collins	.20
38	Charles Way	.10
39	Tiki Barber	.20
40	Ike Hilliard	.10
41	Joe Jurevicius	.20
42	Michael Strahan	.10
43	Jason Sehorn	.10
44	Brad Johnson	.50
45	Terry Allen	.20
46	Skip Hicks	.50
47	Michael Westbrook	.20
48	Leslie Shepherd	.10
49	Stephen Alexander	.10
50	Albert Connell	.10
51	Darrell Green	.10
52	Jake Plummer	1.00
53	Adrian Murrell	.20
54	Frank Sanders	.20
55	Rob Moore	.20
56	Larry Centers	.10
57	Simeon Rice	.10
58	Andre Wadsworth	.20
59	Duce Staley	.10
60	Charles Johnson	.10
61	Charlie Garner	.10
62	Bobby Hoying	.20
63	Darryl Johnston	.10
64	Emmitt Smith	1.50
65	Troy Aikman	1.00
66	Michael Irvin	.20
67	Deion Sanders	.50
68	Chris Warren	.20
69	Darren Woodson	.10
70	Rod Woodson	.10
71	Travis Jervey	.10
72	Jerry Rice	1.00
73	Terrell Owens	.50
74	Steve Young	.75
75	Garrison Hearst	.20
76	J.J. Stokes	.20
77	Ken Norton	.10
78	R.W. McQuarters	.10
79	Bryant Young	.10
80	Jamal Anderson	.50
81	Chris Chandler	.20
82	Terrance Mathis	.10
83	Tim Dwight	.50
84	O.J. Santiago	.10
85	Chris Calloway	.10
86	Keith Brooking	.10
87	Eddie Kennison	.10
88	Willie Roaf	.10
89	Cameron Cleeland	.20
90	Lamar Smith	.10
91	Sean Dawkins	.10
92	Tim Biakabutuka	.20
93	Muhsin Muhammad	.10
94	Steve Beuerlein	.10
95	Rae Carruth	.10
96	Wesley Walls	.10
97	Kevin Greene	.10
98	Trent Green	.50
99	Tony Banks	.20
100	Greg Hill	.10
101	Robert Holcombe	.20
102	Isaac Bruce	.30
103	Amp Lee	.10
104	Az-Zahir Hakim	.20
105	Warren Moon	.20
106	Jeff George	.20
107	Raghib Ismail	.10
108	Kordell Stewart	.75
109	Jerome Bettis	.20
110	Courtney Hawkins	.10
111	Chris Fuamatu-Ma'afala	.20
112	Levon Kirkland	.10
113	Hines Ward	.20
114	Will Blackwell	.10
115	Corey Dillon	.50
116	Carl Pickens	.20
117	Neil O'Donnell	.20
118	Jeff Blake	.20
119	Darnay Scott	.20
120	Takeo Spikes	.10
121	Steve McNair	.75
122	Frank Wycheck	.10
123	Eddie George	.75
124	Chris Sanders	.10
125	Yancy Thigpen	.20
126	Kevin Dyson	.20
127	Blaine Bishop	.10
128	Fred Taylor	1.00
129	Mark Brunell	.75
130	Jimmy Smith	.20
131	Keenan McCardell	.10
132	Kyle Brady	.10
133	Tavian Banks	.20
134	James Stewart	.10
135	Kevin Hardy	.10
136	Jonathan Quinn	.10
137	Jermaine Lewis	.20
138	Priest Holmes	.50
139	Scott Mitchell	.20
140	Eric Zeier	.10
141	Patrick Johnson	.20
142	Ray Lewis	.10
143	Terry Kirby	.10
144	Ty Detmer	.10
145	Irv Smith	.10
146	Chris Spielman	.10
147	Antonio Langham	.10
148	Dan Marino	1.50
149	O.J. McDuffie	.20
150	Oronde Gadsden	.20
151	Karim Abdul	.30
152	Yatil Green	.10
153	Zach Thomas	.20
154	John Avery	.20
155	Lamar Thomas	.10
156	Drew Bledsoe	.75
157	Terry Glenn	.30
158	Ben Coates	.20
159	Shawn Jefferson	.10
160	Cedric Shaw	.10
161	Tony Simmons	.20
162	Ty Law	.10
163	Robert Edwards	.30
164	Curtis Martin	.50
165	Keyshawn Johnson	.50
166	Vinny Testaverde	.20
167	Aaron Glenn	.10
168	Wayne Chrebet	.30
169	Dedric Ward	.10
170	Peyton Manning	1.50
171	Marshall Faulk	.50
172	Marvin Harrison	.20
173	Jerome Pathon	.20
174	Ken Dilger	.10
175	E.G. Green	.20
176	Doug Flutie	.75
177	Thurman Thomas	.20
178	Andre Reed	.20
179	Eric Moulds	.50
180	Antowain Smith	.30
181	Bruce Smith	.10
182	Rob Johnson	.20
183	Terrell Davis	1.50
184	John Elway	1.50
185	Ed McCaffrey	.20
186	Rod Smith	.20
187	Shannon Sharpe	.20
188	Marcus Nash	.20
189	Brian Griese	.50
190	Neil Smith	.10
191	Bubby Brister	.20
192	Ryan Leaf	.50
193	Natrone Means	.50
194	Mikhael Ricks	.20
195	Junior Seau	.20
196	Jim Harbaugh	.20
197	Bryan Still	.10
198	Freddie Jones	.10
199	Andre Rison	.20
200	Elvis Grbac	.20
201	Bam Morris	.20
202	Rashaan Shehee	.10
203	Kimble Anders	.10
204	Donnell Bennett	.10
205	Tony Gonzalez	.20
206	Derrick Alexander	.10
207	Jon Kitna	.50
208	Ricky Watters	.20
209	Joey Galloway	.50
210	Ahman Green	.20
211	Shawn Springs	.10
212	Michael Sinclair	.10
213	Napoleon Kaufman	.50
214	Tim Brown	.20
215	Charles Woodson	.50
216	Harvey Williams	.10
217	Jon Ritchie	.10
218	Rich Gannon	.10
219	Rickey Dudley	.20
220	James Jett	.10
221	*Tim Couch*	30.00
222	*Ricky Williams*	30.00
223	*Donovan McNabb*	12.00
224	*Edgerrin James*	15.00
225	*Torry Holt*	6.00
226	*Daunte Culpepper*	12.00
227	*Akili Smith*	10.00
228	*Champ Bailey*	5.00
229	*Chris Claiborne*	2.50
230	*Chris McAlister*	2.00
231	*Troy Edwards*	5.00
232	*Jevon Kearse*	2.00
233	*Shaun King*	4.00
234	*David Boston*	7.00
235	*Peerless Price*	5.00
236	*Cecil Collins*	6.00
237	*Rob Konrad*	2.00
238	*Cade McNown*	12.00
239	*Shawn Bryson*	1.00
240	*Kevin Faulk*	7.00
241	*Scott Covington*	2.00
242	*James Johnson*	4.00
243	*Mike Cloud*	2.00
244	*Aaron Brooks*	2.00
245	*Sedrick Irvin*	4.00
246	*Amos Zereoue*	5.00
247	*Jermaine Fazande*	1.00
248	*Joe Germaine*	4.00
249	*Brock Huard*	3.00
250	*Craig Yeast*	1.00
251	*Travis McGriff*	2.00
252	*D'Wayne Bates*	2.00
253	*Na Brown*	1.00
254	*Tai Streets*	2.00
255	*Andy Katzenmoyer*	2.00
256	*Kevin Johnson*	3.00
257	*Joe Montgomery*	2.00
258	*Karsten Bailey*	2.00
259	*De'Mond Parker*	2.00
260	*Reg Kelly*	1.00
261	Eddie George	2.00
262	Jamal Anderson	1.00
263	Barry Sanders	5.00
264	Fred Taylor	3.00
265	Keyshawn Johnson	1.00
266	Jerry Rice	3.50
267	Doug Flutie	2.50
268	Deion Sanders	1.00
269	Randall Cunningham	1.00
270	Steve Young	2.50
271	Terrell Davis, John Elway	5.00
272	Marshall Faulk, Peyton Manning	4.00
273	Brett Favre, Antonio Freeman	5.00
274	Troy Aikman, Emmitt Smith	4.00
275	Cris Carter, Randy Moss	6.00

1999 Score Anniversary Showcase

This is a parallel to the base with each card the same except for a gold foil border around the photo and a gold foil stamp on the front. The backs are sequentially numbered to 1989 and say Anniversary Showcase next to it.

	MT
Complete Set (275):	450.00
Showcase Cards:	3x-6x
Showcase Rookies:	1.5x
Showcase AP/GC:	2x
Production 1,989 Sets	

1999 Score Anniversary Artist Proof

This is a parallel to the base and each card is sequentially numbered to 10.

	MT
Production 10 Sets	

1999 Score Complete Players

These singles were found in both hobby (1:17) and retail (1:35) product. Each of the 30 cards are printed on foil board with foil stamping and have one large color photo of the player on the front along with four smaller shots in black and white on the side.

		MT
	Complete Set (30):	75.00
	Common Player:	1.50
	Inserted 1:17	
1	Antonio Freeman	1.50
2	Troy Aikman	5.00
3	Jerry Rice	5.00
4	Brett Favre	10.00
5	Cris Carter	3.00
6	Jamal Anderson	1.50
7	John Elway	7.50
8	Mark Brunell	4.00
9	Steve McNair	3.00
10	Kordell Stewart	3.00
11	Drew Bledsoe	4.00
12	Tim Couch	12.00
13	Dan Marino	7.50
14	Akili Smith	5.00
15	Peyton Manning	5.00
16	Jake Plummer	4.00
17	Jerome Bettis	1.50
18	Randy Moss	10.00
19	Keyshawn Johnson	1.50
20	Barry Sanders	10.00

21	Ricky Williams	12.00
22	Emmitt Smith	7.50
23	Corey Dillon	1.50
24	Dorsey Levens	1.50
25	Donovan McNabb	5.00
26	Curtis Martin	1.50
27	Eddie George	3.00
28	Fred Taylor	3.50
29	Steve Young	3.50
30	Terrell Davis	7.50

1999 Score Franchise

This 31-card set was a retail exclusive (1:35) and picked a star player from each team. Each card is printed on holographic foil board and has a large color photo of the player on the front along with a smaller black and white next to it.

		MT
Complete Set (31):		125.00
Common Player:		2.00
Inserted 1:35		
1	Brett Favre	15.00
2	Randy Moss	15.00
3	Mike Alstott	4.00
4	Barry Sanders	15.00
5	Curtis Enis	4.00
6	Ike Hilliard	2.00
7	Emmitt Smith	10.00
8	Jake Plummer	8.00
9	Brad Johnson	4.00
10	Duce Staley	2.00
11	Jamal Anderson	4.00
12	Steve Young	6.00
13	Eddie Kennison	2.00
14	Isaac Bruce	4.00
15	Muhsin Muhammad	2.00
16	Dan Marino	15.00
17	Drew Bledsoe	7.00
18	Curtis Martin	4.00
19	Doug Flutie	6.00
20	Peyton Manning	10.00
21	Kordell Stewart	5.00
22	Ty Detmer	2.00
23	Corey Dillon	4.00
24	Mark Brunell	7.00
25	Priest Holmes	4.00
26	Eddie George	5.00
27	John Elway	10.00
28	Natrone Means	4.00
29	Tim Brown	2.00
30	Andre Rison	2.00
31	Joey Galloway	4.00

1999 Score Future Franchise

This 31-card set was a hobby exclusive and included a rookie on one side and a star player on the other from the same team. Singles were found 1:35 packs and each were printed on holographic foil board.

		MT
Complete Set (31):		160.00
Common Player:		2.00
Inserted 1:35		
1	Aaron Brooks, Brett Favre	12.00
2	Daunte Culpepper, Randy Moss	15.00
3	Shaun King, Mike Alstott	4.00
4	Sedrick Irvin, Barry Sanders	12.00
5	Cade McNown, Curtis Enis	10.00
6	Joe Montgomery, Ike Hilliard	2.00
7	Wayne McGarity, Emmitt Smith	8.00
8	David Boston, Jake Plummer	6.00
9	Champ Bailey, Brad Johnson	4.00
10	Donovan McNabb, Duce Staley	10.00
11	Reg Kelly, Jamal Anderson	2.00
12	Tai Streets, Steve Young	5.00
13	Ricky Williams, Eddie Kennison	25.00
14	Torry Holt, Isaac Bruce	6.00
15	Mike Rucker, Muhsin Muhammad	2.00
16	James Johnson, Dan Marino	8.00
17	Kevin Faulk, Drew Bledsoe	6.00
18	Randy Thomas, Curtis Martin	4.00
19	Peerless Price, Doug Flutie	5.00
20	Edgerrin James, Peyton Manning	12.00
21	Troy Edwards, Kordell Stewart	5.00
22	Tim Couch, Ty Detmer	25.00
23	Akili Smith, Corey Dillon	10.00
24	Fernando Bryant, Mark Brunell	5.00
25	Chris McAlister, Priest Holmes	4.00
26	Jevon Kearse, Eddie George	4.00
27	Travis McGriff, John Elway	8.00
28	Jermaine Fazande, Natrone Means	2.00
29	Dameane Douglas, Tim Brown	2.00
30	Mike Cloud, Andre Rison	2.00
31	Brock Huard, Joey Galloway	4.00

1999 Score Millenium Men

The Millennium Men set has Barry Sanders, representing ten years of NFL excellence with Ricky Williams, representing the outstanding future generation of running backs. Each player has an individual card and a back-to-back single in this 3-card set. Each is sequentially numbered to 1,000 and the first 100 of each are autographed. These were only found in retail product.

		MT
Complete Set (3):		60.00
Common Player:		20.00
1	Barry Sanders	20.00
2	Ricky Williams	25.00
3	Barry Sanders, Ricky Williams	20.00

1999 Score Numbers Game

This was a 30-card set that was printed on holographic foil board with gold foil stamping. Each card is sequentially numbered to the player's specific stat.

		MT
Complete Set (30):		75.00
Common Player:		1.50
Numbered to Stat		
1	Brett Favre 4212	7.00
2	Steve Young 4170	3.00
3	Jake Plummer 3737	3.50
4	Drew Bledsoe 3633	3.00
5	Dan Marino 3497	6.00
6	Peyton Manning 3739	6.00
7	Randall Cunningham 3704	1.50
8	John Elway 2806	8.00
9	Doug Flutie 2711	3.00
10	Mark Brunell 2601	3.00
11	Troy Aikman 2330	5.00
12	Terrell Davis 2008	8.00
13	Jamal Anderson 1846	1.50
14	Garrison Hearst 1570	1.50
15	Barry Sanders 1491	12.00
16	Emmitt Smith 1332	7.00
17	Marshall Faulk 1319	3.00
18	Eddie George 1294	4.00
19	Curtis Martin 1287	3.00
20	Fred Taylor 1223	6.00
21	Corey Dillon 1130	3.00
22	Antonio Freeman 1424	3.00
23	Eric Moulds 1368	3.00
24	Randy Moss 1313	12.00
25	Rod Smith 1222	1.50
26	Jerry Rice 1157	7.00
27	Keyshawn Johnson 1131	3.00
28	Terrell Owens 1097	3.00
29	Tim Brown 1012	1.50
30	Cris Carter 1011	3.00

1999 Score Rookie Preview Autographs

Each of these singles were randomly inserted into hobby packs with each player signing a total of 600 cards. Each card is printed on foil board with the signature on the bottom of the card.

	MT
Common Player:	10.00
Production 600 Sets	
Ricky Williams	150.00
Donovan McNabb	75.00
Edgerrin James	85.00
Torry Holt	50.00
Daunte Culpepper	75.00
Akili Smith	60.00
Champ Bailey	30.00
Chris Claiborne	20.00
Chris McAlister	20.00
Troy Edwards	40.00
Jevon Kearse	20.00
David Boston	50.00
Peerless Price	40.00
Cecil Collins	40.00
Rob Konrad	20.00
Cade McNown	75.00
Shawn Bryson	10.00
Kevin Faulk	50.00
Corby Jones	20.00
James Johnson	30.00
Mike Cloud	20.00
Autrey Denson	25.00
Sedrick Irvin	30.00
Michael Bishop	40.00
Joe Germaine	30.00
De'Mond Parker	20.00
Shaun King	30.00
D'Wayne Bates	20.00
Na Brown	10.00
Tai Streets	25.00
Kevin Johnson	30.00
Jim Kleinsasser	20.00
Darnell McDonald	25.00
Travis McGriff	20.00

1999 Score Scoring Core

Scoring Core's holographic foil design highlights 30 players who find their way into the end zone. Singles were found 1:17 hobby packs and 1:35 retail.

		MT
Complete Set (30):		75.00
Common Player:		1.50
Inserted 1:17		
1	Antonio Freeman	1.50
2	Troy Aikman	5.00
3	Jerry Rice	5.00
4	Brett Favre	10.00
5	Cris Carter	3.00
6	Jamal Anderson	1.50
7	John Elway	7.50
8	Tim Brown	1.50
9	Mark Brunell	4.00
10	Terrell Owens	3.00
11	Drew Bledsoe	4.00
12	Tim Couch	12.00
13	Dan Marino	7.50
14	Marshall Faulk	1.50
15	Peyton Manning	5.00
16	Jake Plummer	4.00
17	Jerome Bettis	1.50
18	Randy Moss	10.00
19	Charlie Batch	3.00
20	Barry Sanders	10.00
21	Ricky Williams	12.00
22	Emmitt Smith	7.50
23	Joey Galloway	1.50
24	Herman Moore	1.50
25	Natrone Means	1.50
26	Mike Alstott	1.50
27	Eddie George	3.00
28	Fred Taylor	3.50
29	Steve Young	3.50
30	Terrell Davis	7.50

1999 Score Settle the Score

This retail exclusive insert is a dual-sided foil set that matches two players who need to settle the score between each other. Singles were inserted 1:17 packs.

		MT
Complete Set (30):		70.00
Common Player:		1.50
Inserted 1:17 Retail		
1	Randall Cunningham, Brett Favre	10.00
2	Doug Flutie, Dan Marino	7.50
3	Terry Allen, Emmitt Smith	7.50
4	Warrick Dunn, Barry Sanders	10.00
5	Corey Dillon, Eddie George	3.00
6	Drew Bledsoe, Vinny Testaverde	4.00
7	Troy Aikman, Jake Plummer	5.00
8	Jamal Anderson, Terrell Davis	7.50
9	Chris Chandler, John Elway	7.50
10	Mark Brunell, Steve Young	4.00
11	Cris Carter, Herman Moore	1.50
12	Steve McNair, Kordell Stewart	3.00
13	Napoleon Kaufman, Natrone Means	1.50
14	Marshall Faulk, Curtis Martin	1.50
15	Antonio Freeman, Terrell Owens	3.00
16	Wayne Chrebet, Terry Glenn	1.50
17	Garrison Hearst, Dorsey Levens	1.50
18	Jon Kitna, Ryan Leaf	3.00
19	Mike Alstott, Robert Smith	1.50
20	Randy Moss, Jerry Rice	10.00
21	Charlie Batch, Peyton Manning	6.00
22	Jerome Bettis, Fred Taylor	4.00
23	Keyshawn Johnson, Eric Moulds	3.00
24	Tim Couch, Ricky Williams	20.00
25	Isaac Bruce, Carl Pickens	1.50
26	Deion Sanders, Charles Woodson	1.50
27	Tim Brown, Rod Smith	1.50
28	Daunte Culpepper, Donovan McNabb	8.00
29	Joey Galloway, Ed McCaffrey	1.50
30	Karim Abdul, Antowain Smith	1.50

1999 Score 1989 Score Reprints

This was a 20-card reprint of the 1989 Score cards that included all of the top rookies and stars from the premiere release. These were only found in hobby product and were sequentially numbered to 1989. The first 150 of each card were autographed.

		MT
Complete Set (20):		80.00
Common Player:		3.00
Production 1,989 Sets		
1	Barry Sanders	20.00
2	Troy Aikman	10.00
3	John Elway	15.00
4	Cris Carter	8.00
5	Tim Brown	6.00
6	Doug Flutie	5.00
7	Chris Chandler	3.00
8	Thurman Thomas	3.00
9	Steve Young	6.00
10	Dan Marino	12.00
11	Derrick Thomas	3.00

12	Bubby Brister	5.00
13	Jerry Rice	10.00
14	Andre Rison	3.00
15	Randall Cunningham	5.00
16	Vinny Testaverde	3.00
17	Michael Irvin	3.00
18	Rod Woodson	3.00
19	Neil Smith	3.00
20	Deion Sanders	6.00

1999 Score 1989 Score Reprints Autographs

These are the same cards as the Reprint set except for each is autographed and has the words "Authentic Signature" down the side of the fronts of the cards. Only 150 of each were signed.

		MT
Complete Set (20):		1700.
Common Player:		40.00
Production 150 Sets		
1	Barry Sanders	375.00
2	Troy Aikman	200.00
3	John Elway	300.00
4	Cris Carter	80.00
5	Tim Brown	60.00
6	Doug Flutie	85.00
7	Chris Chandler	40.00
8	Thurman Thomas	40.00
9	Steve Young	85.00
10	Dan Marino	300.00
11	Derrick Thomas	40.00
12	Bubby Brister	60.00
13	Jerry Rice	200.00
14	Andre Rison	40.00
15	Randall Cunningham	75.00
16	Vinny Testaverde	50.00
17	Michael Irvin	40.00
18	Rod Woodson	40.00
19	Neil Smith	40.00
20	Deion Sanders	80.00

1999 Sports Illustrated

This was a 150-card release that included 90 stars of yesterday and today, 30 Fresh Faces (impact rookies of 1998) and 30 Super Bowl MVP's. Top inserts include: Autographs, Canton Calling and SI Covers.

		MT
Complete Set (150):		100.00
Common Player:		.15
Common Rookie:		1.00
Wax Box:		210.00
1	Bart Starr	.50
2	Bart Starr	.50
3	Joe Namath	.50
4	Len Dawson	.30
5	Chuck Howley	.15
6	Roger Staubach	.50
7	Jake Scott	.15
8	Larry Csonka	.30
9	Franco Harris	.30
10	Fred Biletnikoff	.15
11	Harvey Martin, Randy White	.15
12	Terry Bradshaw	.50
13	Terry Bradshaw	.50
14	Jim Plunkett	.30
15	Joe Montana	1.00
16	Marcus Allen	.50
17	Joe Montana	1.00
18	Richard Dent	.15
19	Phil Simms	.30
20	Doug Williams	.15
21	Jerry Rice	1.00
22	Joe Montana	1.00
23	Ottis Anderson	.30
24	Mark Rypien	.15
25	Troy Aikman	1.00
26	Emmitt Smith	1.50
27	Steve Young	.50
28	Larry Brown	.15
29	Desmond Howard	.15
30	Terrell Davis	1.50
31	Y.A. Tittle	.30
32	Paul Hornung	.50
33	Gale Sayers	.50
34	Garo Yepremian	.15
35	Bert Jones	.30
36	Joe Washington	.15
37	Joe Theismann	.30
38	Roger Craig	.30
39	Mike Singletary	.30
40	Bobby Bell	.15
41	Ken Houston	.15
42	Lenny Moore	.15
43	Mark Moseley	.15
44	Chuck Bednarik	.15
45	Ted Hendricks	.15
46	Steve Largent	.50
47	Bob Lilly	.15
48	Don Maynard	.50
49	John Mackey	.15
50	Anthony Munoz	.15
51	Bobby Mitchell	.15
52	Jim Brown	.50
53	Otto Graham	.50
54	Earl Morrall	.15
55	Danny White	.30
56	Karim Abdul-Jabbar	.50
57	Charlie Garner	.15
58	Jeff Blake	.30
59	Reggie White	.50
60	Derrick Thomas	.15
61	Duce Staley	.15
62	Tim Brown	.30
63	Elvis Grbac	.30
64	Tony Banks	.30
65	Rob Johnson	.30
66	Danny Kanell	.15
67	Marshall Faulk	.50
68	Warrick Dunn	1.25
69	Dan Marino	3.00
70	Jimmy Smith	.50
71	John Elway	2.50
72	Charles Way	.15
73	Ricky Watters	.30
74	Terry Glenn	.50
75	Bobby Hoying	.30
76	Curtis Martin	.50
77	Trent Dilfer	.30
78	Emmitt Smith	3.00
79	Irving Fryar	.15
80	Troy Aikman	2.00
81	Barry Sanders	4.00
82	Brett Favre	4.00
83	Robert Smith	.50
84	Dorsey Levens	.50
85	Cris Carter	.50
86	Jeff George	.30
87	Jerome Bettis	.30
88	Warren Moon	.30
89	Steve Young	.75
90	Fred Lane	.30
91	Jerry Rice	2.00
92	Natrone Means	.50
93	Mike Alstott	.50
94	Kordell Stewart	1.50
95	Jake Plummer	1.75
96	Jamal Anderson	.75
97	Corey Dillon	1.00
98	Deion Sanders	.50
99	Mark Brunell	1.50
100	Garrison Hearst	.50
101	Andre Rison	.15
102	Antowain Smith	.75
103	Drew Bledsoe	1.50
104	Eddie George	1.50
105	Keyshawn Johnson	.50
106	Isaac Bruce	.30
107	Rob Moore	.30
108	Steve McNair	.75
109	Terrell Davis	3.00
110	Carl Pickens	.30
111	Wayne Chrebet	.50
112	Kerry Collins	.30
113	Eric Metcalf	.15
114	Joey Galloway	.50
115	Shannon Sharpe	.30
116	Robert Brooks	.15
117	Glenn Foley	.30
118	Yancey Thigpen	.30
119	Frank Sanders	.30
120	Herman Moore	.50
121	Antonio Freeman	.75
122	Michael Irvin	.30
123	Brad Johnson	.50
124	James Stewart	.15
125	Jim Harbaugh	.30
126	Peyton Manning	12.00
127	Ryan Leaf	6.00
128	Curtis Enis	4.00
129	Fred Taylor	10.00
130	Randy Moss	25.00
131	John Avery	3.00
132	Charles Woodson	5.00
133	Robert Edwards	3.50
134	Charlie Batch	8.00
135	Brian Griese	5.00
136	Skip Hicks	3.00
137	Jacquez Green	3.00
138	Robert Holcombe	2.00
139	Kevin Dyson	3.00
140	Rodney Williams	1.00
141	Ahman Green	2.00
142	Tavian Banks	2.00
143	Donald Hayes	1.00
144	Tony Simmons	3.00
145	Patrick Johnson	2.00
146	Marcus Nash	3.00
147	Germane Crowell	3.00
148	R.W. McQuarters	2.00
149	Jonathan Quinn	2.00
150	Andre Wadsworth	2.00

1999 Sports Illustrated Autographs

A total of 35 players from the past signed cards in this insert with numbers unknown. Singles were found one-per-pack.

	MT
Complete Set (35):	3000.
Common Player:	10.00
Inserted 1:1	
Ottis Anderson	20.00
Chuck Bednarik	10.00
Bobby Bell	10.00
Terry Bradshaw	400.00
Jim Brown	250.00
Roger Craig	25.00
Len Dawson	175.00
Otto Graham	30.00
Franco Harris	175.00
Ted Hendricks	10.00
Paul Hornung	185.00
Ken Houston	10.00
Bert Jones	10.00
Steve Largent	35.00
Bob Lilly	10.00
John Mackey	10.00
Don Maynard	20.00
Bobby Mitchell	10.00
Joe Montana	425.00
Lenny Moore	10.00
Earl Morrall	10.00
Mark Moseley	10.00
Anthony Munoz	20.00
Joe Namath	450.00
Jim Plunkett	20.00
Gale Sayers	35.00
Mike Singletary	100.00
Bart Starr	400.00
Roger Staubach	200.00
Joe Theismann	85.00
Y.A. Tittle	100.00
Joe Washington	10.00
Danny White	10.00
Doug Williams	100.00
Garo Yepremian	10.00

1999 Sports Illustrated Canton Calling

This was an 8-card set that included players who are on their way to the Hall of Fame. Singles were inserted 1:12 packs and a parallel Gold insert was also produced and found 1:120 packs.

		MT
Complete Set (8):		60.00
Common Player:		3.00
Inserted 1:12		
Gold Cards:		3x-6x
Inserted 1:120		
1	Warren Moon	3.00
2	Emmitt Smith	10.00
3	Jerry Rice	8.00
4	Brett Favre	15.00
5	Barry Sanders	15.00
6	Dan Marino	10.00
7	John Elway	10.00
8	Troy Aikman	8.00

1999 Sports Illustrated Covers

This was a 60-card set that took the best covers from the past and reproduced them on a card. Singles were found one-per-pack.

		MT
Complete Set (60):		30.00
Common Player:		.25
Inserted 1:1		
1	Jim Brown	.50
2	Y.A. Tittle	.25
3	Dallas Cowboys	.25
4	Joe Namath	.75
5	Bart Starr	.50
6	Earl Morrall	.25
7	Minnesota Vikings	.25
8	Kansas City Chiefs	.25
9	Len Dawson	.25
10	Monday Night Football	.25
11	Jim Plunkett	.25
12	Garo Yepremian	.25
13	Larry Csonka	.25
14	Terry Bradshaw	.50
15	Franco Harris	.25
16	Bert Jones	.25
17	Harvey Martin, Randy White	.25
18	Roger Staubach	.50
19	Marcus Allen	.50
20	Joe Washington	.25
21	Dan Marino	2.50
22	Joe Theismann	.25
23	Roger Craig	.25
24	Mike Singletary	.25
25	Chicago Bears	.25
26	Phil Simms	.25
27	Vinny Testaverde	.25
28	Doug Williams	.25
29	Jerry Rice	1.50
30	Hershel Walker	.25
31	Joe Montana	1.75
32	Ottis Anderson	.25
33	Rocket Ismail	.25
34	Bruce Smith	.25
35	Thurman Thomas	.25
36	Mark Rypien	.25
37	Jim Harbaugh	.25
38	Randall Cunningham	.50
39	Troy Aikman	1.50
40	Reggie White	.50
41	Junior Seau	.25
42	Emmitt Smith	2.50
43	Natrone Means	.25
44	Ricky Watters	.25
45	Pittsburgh Steelers	.25
46	Steve Young, Troy Aikman	1.00
47	Steve Young	1.00
48	Deion Sanders	.50
49	Elvis Grbac	.25
50	Green Bay Packers	.25
51	Brett Favre	3.00
52	Mark Brunell, Kerry Collins	1.00
53	Antonio Freeman	.75
54	Desmond Howard	.25
55	AFC Central Quarterbacks	.25
56	Warrick Dunn	.50
57	Jerome Bettis	.25
58	John Elway	2.00
59	Brent Jones	.25
60	Terrell Davis	3.00

1999 SP Signature

This 180-card release from Upper Deck includes both past and present stars from the NFL. The last 10 cards in the set never made it into the product and were later released to dealers from the manufacturer. Inserts include: Autographs and Montana Great Performances.

		MT
Complete Set (180):		500.00
Common Player:		.50
Wax Box:		200.00
1	Jake Plummer	2.50
2	Mario Bates	.50
3	Adrian Murrell	.50
4	Jamal Anderson	1.50
5	Chris Chandler	1.00
6	Bob Christian	.50
7	O.J. Santiago	.50
8	Jim Harbaugh	1.00
9	Priest Holmes	1.50
10	Ray Lewis	.50
11	Michael Jackson	.50
12	Tony Siragusa	.50
13	Doug Flutie	2.00
14	Antowain Smith	1.25
15	Eric Moulds	1.25
16	William Floyd	.50
17	Fred Lane	.50
18	Muhsin Muhammad	.50
19	Bobby Engram	.50
20	Curtis Enis	1.50
21	Curtis Conway	1.00
22	Corey Dillon	1.50
23	Carl Pickens	1.00
24	Ashley Ambrose	.50
25	Darnay Scott	.50
26	Troy Aikman	3.00
27	Jason Garrett	.50
28	Emmitt Smith	4.50
29	Deion Sanders	1.25
30	John Elway	4.50
31	Terrell Davis	4.50
32	Ed McCaffrey	1.00
33	John Mobley	.50
34	Maa Tanuvasa	.50
35	Ray Crockett	.50
36	Barry Sanders	6.00
37	Herman Moore	1.00
38	Charlie Batch	2.00
39	Robert Porcher	.50
40	Tommy Vardell	.50
41	Brett Favre	6.00
42	Antonio Freeman	1.50
43	Darick Holmes	.50
44	Robert Brooks	.50
45	Peyton Manning	5.00
46	Marshall Faulk	1.25
47	Torrance Small	.50
48	Lamont Warren	.50
49	Zack Crockett	.50
50	Mark Brunell	2.00
51	Pete Mitchell	.50
52	Fred Taylor	4.00
53	Jimmy Smith	1.00
54	Andre Rison	1.00
55	Rich Gannon	.50
56	Donnell Bennett	.50

57	Dan Marino	4.50
58	Karim Abdul	1.00
59	Troy Drayton	.50
60	Jason Taylor	.50
61	Cris Carter	1.25
62	Randy Moss	8.00
63	Robert Smith	1.00
64	Leroy Hoard	.50
65	Randall Cunningham	1.25
66	Derrick Alexander	.50
67	Drew Bledsoe	2.00
68	Robert Edwards	1.25
69	Willie McGinest	.50
70	Chris Slade	.50
71	Terry Glenn	1.00
72	Ty Law	.50
73	Kerry Collins	1.00
74	Sean Dawkins	.50
75	Cameron Cleeland	1.00
76	Sammy Knight	.50
77	Danny Kanell	.50
78	Gary Brown	.50
79	Chris Calloway	.50
80	Curtis Martin	1.25
81	Keyshawn Johnson	1.25
82	Vinny Testaverde	1.00
83	Leon Johnson	.50
84	Kyle Brady	.50
85	Tim Brown	1.00
86	Jeff George	1.00
87	Rickey Dudley	.50
88	Napoleon Kaufman	1.25
89	James Jett	.50
90	Harvey Williams	.50
91	Koy Detmer	.50
92	Duce Staley	.50
93	Charlie Garner	.50
94	Jerome Bettis	1.00
95	Kordell Stewart	1.75
96	Courtney Hawkins	.50
97	Hines Ward	1.00
98	Isaac Bruce	1.00
99	Tony Banks	1.00
100	Greg Hill	.50
101	Keith Lyle	.50
102	Ryan Leaf	2.00
103	Craig Whelihan	.50
104	Charlie Jones	.50
105	Junior Seau	1.00
106	Natrone Means	1.00
107	Rodney Harrison	.50
108	Steve Young	2.00
109	Garrison Hearst	1.00
110	Jerry Rice	3.00
111	Chris Doleman	.50
112	Roy Barker	.50
113	Ricky Watters	1.00
114	Jon Kitna	1.50
115	Joey Galloway	1.25
116	Chad Brown	.50
117	Michael Sinclair	.50
118	Warrick Dunn	1.50
119	Mike Alstott	1.25
120	Bert Emanuel	.50
121	Hardy Nickerson	.50
122	Eddie George	1.50
123	Steve McNair	1.25
124	Yancey Thigpen	.50
125	Frank Wycheck	.50
126	Jackie Harris	.50
127	Terry Allen	1.00
128	Trent Green	1.25
129	Jamie Asher	.50
130	Brian Mitchell	.50
131	Lance Alworth	1.00
132	Fred Biletnikoff	1.25
133	Mel Blount	.50
134	Cliff Branch	.50
135	Harold Carmichael	.50
136	Larry Csonka	1.25
137	Eric Dickerson	1.00
138	Randy Gradishar	.50
139	Joe Greene	1.00
140	Jack Ham	.50
141	Ted Hendricks	.50
142	Charlie Joiner	1.00
143	Ed Jones	.50
144	Billy Kilmer	.50
145	Paul Krause	.50
146	James Lofton	.50
147	Archie Manning	1.00
148	Don Maynard	1.00
149	Ozzie Newsome	.50
150	Jim Otto	.50
151	Lee Roy Selmon	.50
152	Billy Sims	1.00
153	Mike Singletary	1.00
154	Ken Stabler	1.50
155	John Stallworth	1.00
156	Roger Staubach	2.00
157	Charley Taylor	.50
158	Paul Warfield	1.25
159	Kellen Winslow	1.00
160	Jack Youngblood	.50
161	Bill Bergey	.50
162	Raymond Berry	.50
163	Chuck Howley	.50
164	Rocky Bleier	.50
165	Russ Francis	.50
166	Drew Pearson	.50
167	Mercury Morris	.50
168	Dick Anderson	.50
169	Earl Morrall	.50
170	Jim Hart	.50
171	*Ricky Williams*	100.00
172	*Cade McNown*	50.00
173	*Tim Couch*	100.00
174	*Daunte Culpepper*	50.00
175	*Akili Smith*	40.00
176	*Brock Huard*	20.00
177	*Donovan McNabb*	50.00
178	*Michael Bishop*	20.00
179	*Shaun King*	25.00
180	*Tory Holt*	30.00

1999 SP Signature Autographs

Cards in this insert are the same as the base except for the signature on the front. The backs are different than the regular base card. Singles were inserted one-per-pack. A Gold parallel was produced and inserted 1:59 packs.

		MT
Common Player:		10.00
Inserted 1:1		
Gold Cards:		2x
Inserted 1:59		
KA	Karim Abdul	20.00
TA	Troy Aikman	250.00
DA	Derrick Alexander	10.00
MA	Mike Alstott	50.00
AA	Ashley Ambrose	10.00
AN	Dick Anderson	10.00
TE	Jamie Asher	10.00
DE	Roy Barker	10.00
CB	Charlie Batch	60.00
MB	Mario Bates	10.00
DB	Donnell Bennett	10.00
BB	Bill Bergey	10.00
RY	Raymond Berry	25.00
MI	Michael Bishop	150.00
ML	Mel Blount	20.00
KB	Kyle Brady	10.00
RB	Robert Brooks	30.00
LB	Chad Brown	10.00
GB	Gary Brown	10.00
TB	Tim Brown	35.00
IB	Isaac Bruce	35.00
MK	Mark Brunell	125.00
CY	Chris Calloway	10.00
HC	Harold Carmichael	20.00
CC	Chris Chandler	30.00
BC	Bob Christian	10.00
CL	Cameron Cleeland	20.00
CW	Curtis Conway	20.00
TC	Tim Couch	325.00
CK	Ray Crockett	10.00
ZC	Zack Crockett	10.00
DC	Daunte Culpepper	175.00
NO	Sean Dawkins	10.00
KD	Koy Detmer	10.00
CD	Corey Dillon	35.00
TR	Troy Drayton	10.00
RD	Rickey Dudley	10.00
RE	Robert Edwards	25.00
JE	John Elway	300.00
BT	Bert Emanuel	20.00
BE	Bobby Engram	10.00
CE	Curtis Enis	30.00
MF	Marshall Faulk	40.00
BF	Brett Favre	300.00
WF	William Floyd	10.00
RF	Russ Francis	10.00
AF	Antonio Freeman	75.00
GA	Joey Galloway	70.00
CG	Charlie Garner	20.00
JG	Jason Garrett	10.00
EG	Eddie George	85.00
GE	Jeff George	20.00
GR	Randy Gradishar	10.00
GN	Trent Green	25.00
JH	Jack Ham	20.00
JK	Jackie Harris	10.00
RH	Rodney Harrison	10.00
HT	Jim Hart	20.00
GH	Garrison Hearst	25.00
TH	Ted Hendricks	20.00
HL	Greg Hill	10.00
LH	Leroy Hoard	10.00
DH	Darick Holmes	10.00
PH	Priest Holmes	30.00
WP	Torry Holt	150.00
HY	Chuck Howley	20.00
BH	Brock Huard	85.00
MJ	Michael Jackson	20.00
JJ	James Jett	20.00
KJ	Keyshawn Johnson	50.00
LJ	Leon Johnson	10.00
CJ	Charlie Joiner	20.00
SD	Charlie Jones	20.00
EJ	Ed Jones	20.00
NK	Napoleon Kaufman	50.00
SH	Shaun King	60.00
KI	Jon Kitna	30.00
SK	Sammy Knight	20.00
PK	Paul Krause	20.00
FL	Fred Lane	20.00
TL	Ty Law	10.00
RL	Ray Lewis	10.00
JL	James Lofton	20.00
KL	Keith Lyle	10.00
MG	Archie Manning	30.00
DM	Dan Marino	375.00
NY	Don Maynard	20.00
WM	Willie McGinest	10.00
MN	Donovan McNabb	175.00
QB	Cade McNown	175.00
NM	Natrone Means	30.00
KR	Brian Mitchell	10.00
PT	Pete Mitchell	10.00
JM	John Mobley	10.00
HM	Herman Moore	35.00
MO	Earl Morrall	20.00
MY	Mercury Morris	20.00
RM	Randy Moss	350.00
EM	Eric Moulds	40.00
MM	Muhsin Muhammad	10.00
AM	Adrian Murrell	20.00
HN	Hardy Nickerson	10.00
OZ	Ozzie Newsome	25.00
DP	Drew Pearson	25.00
JP	Jake Plummer	100.00
RP	Robert Porcher	10.00
OJ	O.J. Santiago	10.00
JR	Junior Seau	25.00
LS	Lee Roy Selmon	20.00
MS	Michael Sinclair	10.00
SY	Mike Singletary	25.00
TS	Tony Siragusa	10.00
CS	Chris Slade	10.00
TO	Torrance Small	10.00
AK	Akili Smith	150.00
AS	Antowain Smith	25.00
ES	Emmitt Smith	250.00
JS	Jimmy Smith	20.00
KS	Ken Stabler	40.00
ST	Duce Staley	10.00
SW	John Stallworth	25.00
MT	Maa Tanuvasa	10.00
CT	Charley Taylor	20.00
FT	Fred Taylor	125.00
JT	Jason Taylor	10.00
TV	Tommy Vardell	10.00
HW	Hines Ward	20.00
PW	Paul Warfield	25.00
LW	Lamont Warren	10.00
ND	Ricky Watters	40.00
WH	Craig Whelihan	10.00
HV	Harvey Williams	10.00
RW	Ricky Williams	325.00
KW	Kellen Winslow	25.00
FW	Frank Wycheck	10.00
JY	Jack Youngblood	20.00

1999 SP Signature Montana Great Performances

This was a 10-card set that highlights the career of Montana. Singles were randomly inserted. A parallel Autographed version was also produced and found 1:47 packs and a Gold Autographed parallel was made and found 1:880 packs.

		MT
Complete Set (10):		50.00
Common Player:		5.00
Randomly Inserted		
Signature Cards:		25x
Inserted 1:47		
Gold Signature Cards:		160x
Inserted 1:880		
1	Joe Montana	5.00
2	Joe Montana	5.00
3	Joe Montana	5.00
4	Joe Montana	5.00
5	Joe Montana	5.00
6	Joe Montana	5.00
7	Joe Montana	5.00
8	Joe Montana	5.00
9	Joe Montana	5.00
10	Joe Montana	5.00

1999 Topps

Each card in this 357-card set was printed on 16-pt. stock, with green borders and gold foil stamping. Included are 27 rookies that were seeded 1:5 packs. Other subsets include 10 Season Highlights and five Cleveland Browns Expansion Draft cards. Top inserts include: MVP Promotion, All Matrix, Autographs, Hall of Fame Autographs, Mystery Chrome, Picture Perfect, Record Numbers and Season's Best.

		MT
Complete Set (357):		75.00
Common Player:		.10
Common Rookie:		1.00
Inserted 1:5		
Wax Box:		50.00
1	Terrell Davis	1.50
2	Adrian Murrell	.10
3	Ernie Mills	.10
4	Jimmy Hitchcock	.10
5	Charlie Garner	.10
6	Blaine Bishop	.10
7	Junior Seau	.20
8	Andre Rison	.20
9	Jake Reed	.10
10	Cris Carter	.40
11	Torrance Small	.10
12	Ronald McKinnon	.10
13	Tyrone Davis	.10
14	Warren Moon	.20
15	Joe Johnson	.10
16	Bert Emanuel	.10
17	Brad Culpepper	.10
18	Henry Jones	.10
19	Jonathan Ogden	.10
20	Terrell Owens	.40
21	Derrick Mason	.10
22	Jon Ritchie	.10
23	Eric Metcalf	.10
24	Kevin Carter	.10
25	Fred Taylor	1.00
26	DeWayne Washington	.10
27	William Thomas	.10
28	Raghib Ismail	.10
29	Jason Taylor	.10
30	Doug Flutie	.50
31	Michael Sinclair	.10
32	Yancey Thigpen	.10
33	Darnay Scott	.10
34	Amani Toomer	.10
35	Edgar Bennett	.10
36	LeRoy Butler	.10
37	Jessie Tuggle	.10
38	Andrew Glover	.10
39	Tim McDonald	.10
40	Marshall Faulk	.40
41	Ray Mickens	.10
42	Kimble Anders	.10
43	Trent Green	.40
44	Dermontti Dawson	.10
45	Greg Ellis	.10
46	Hugh Douglas	.10
47	Amp Lee	.10
48	Lamar Thomas	.10
49	Curtis Conway	.20
50	Emmitt Smith	1.50
51	Elvis Grbac	.10
52	Tony Simmons	.20
53	Darrin Smith	.10
54	Donovin Darius	.10
55	Corey Chavous	.10
56	Phillippi Sparks	.10
57	Luther Elliss	.10
58	Tim Dwight	.40
59	Andre Hastings	.10
60	Dan Marino	1.50
61	Micheal Barrow	.10
62	Corey Fuller	.10
63	Bill Romanowski	.10
64	Derrick Rodgers	.10
65	Natrone Means	.30
66	Peter Boulware	.10
67	Brian Mitchell	.10
68	Cornelius Bennett	.10
69	Dedric Ward	.10
70	Drew Bledsoe	.75
71	Freddie Jones	.10
72	Derrick Thomas	.10
73	Willie Davis	.10
74	Larry Centers	.10
75	Mark Brunell	.75
76	Chuck Smith	.10
77	Desmond Howard	.10
78	Sedrick Shaw	.10
79	Tiki Barber	.10
80	Curtis Martin	.40
81	Barry Minter	.10
82	Skip Hicks	.20
83	O.J. Santiago	.10
84	Ed McCaffrey	.30
85	Terrell Buckley	.10
86	Charlie Jones	.10
87	Pete Mitchell	.10
88	La'Roi Glover	.10
89	Eric Davis	.10
90	John Elway	1.50
91	Kavika Pittman	.10
92	Fred Lane	.10
93	Warren Sapp	.10
94	Lorenzo Bromell	.10
95	Lawyer Milloy	.10
96	Aeneas Williams	.10
97	Michael McCrary	.10
98	Rickey Dudley	.10
99	Bryce Paup	.10
100	Jamal Anderson	.50
101	D'Marco Farr	.10
102	Johnnie Morton	.10
103	Jeff Graham	.10
104	Sam Cowart	.10
105	Bryant Young	.10
106	Jermaine Lewis	.10
107	Chad Bratzke	.10
108	Jeff Burris	.10
109	Roell Preston	.10
110	Vinny Testaverde	.20
111	Ruben Brown	.10
112	Darryll Lewis	.10
113	Billy Davis	.10
114	Bryant Westbrook	.10
115	Stephen Alexander	.10
116	Terrell Fletcher	.10
117	Terry Glenn	.30
118	Rod Smith	.20
119	Carl Pickens	.20
120	Tim Brown	.20
121	Mikhael Ricks	.10
122	Jason Gildon	.10
123	Charles Way	.10
124	Rob Moore	.20
125	Jerome Bettis	.30
126	Kerry Collins	.20
127	Bruce Smith	.10
128	James Hasty	.10
129	Ken Norton Jr.	.10
130	Charles Woodson	.40
131	Tony McGee	.10
132	Kevin Turner	.10
133	Jerome Pathon	.10
134	Garrison Hearst	.30
135	Craig Newsome	.10
136	Hardy Nickerson	.10
137	Ray Lewis	.10
138	Derrick Alexander	.10
139	Phil Hansen	.10
140	Joey Galloway	.50
141	Oronde Gadsden	.20
142	Herman Moore	.30
143	Bobby Taylor	.10
144	Mario Bates	.10
145	Kevin Dyson	.20
146	Aaron Glenn	.10
147	Ed McDaniel	.10
148	Terry Allen	.20
149	Ike Hilliard	.10
150	Steve Young	.50
151	Eugene Robinson	.10
152	John Mobley	.10
153	Kevin Hardy	.10
154	Lance Johnstone	.10
155	Willie McGinest	.10
156	Gary Anderson	.10
157	Dexter Coakley	.10
158	Mark Fields	.10
159	Steve McNair	.50
160	Corey Dillon	.50
161	Zach Thomas	.30
162	Kent Graham	.10
163	Tony Parrish	.10
164	Sam Gash	.10
165	Kyle Brady	.10
166	Donnell Bennett	.10
167	Tony Martin	.10
168	Michael Bates	.10
169	Bobby Engram	.10
170	Jimmy Smith	.20
171	Vonnie Holliday	.20
172	Simeon Rice	.10
173	Kevin Greene	.10
174	Mike Alstott	.40
175	Eddie George	.50
176	Michael Jackson	.10
177	Neil O'Donnell	.10
178	Sean Dawkins	.10

179	Courtney Hawkins	.10
180	Michael Irvin	.20
181	Thurman Thomas	.20
182	Cameron Cleeland	.20
183	Ellis Johnson	.10
184	Will Blackwell	.10
185	Ty Law	.10
186	Merton Hanks	.10
187	Dan Wilkinson	.10
188	Andre Wadsworth	.20
189	Troy Vincent	.10
190	Frank Sanders	.20
191	Stephen Boyd	.10
192	Jason Elam	.10
193	Kordell Stewart	.50
194	Ted Johnson	.10
195	Glyn Milburn	.10
196	Gary Brown	.10
197	Travis Hall	.10
198	John Randle	.10
199	Jay Riemersma	.10
200	Barry Sanders	2.00
201	Chris Spielman	.10
202	Rod Woodson	.10
203	Darrell Russell	.10
204	Tony Boselli	.10
205	Darren Woodson	.10
206	Muhsin Muhammad	.10
207	Jim Harbaugh	.20
208	Isaac Bruce	.30
209	Mo Lewis	.10
210	Dorsey Levens	.30
211	Frank Wycheck	.10
212	Napoleon Kaufman	.40
213	Walt Harris	.10
214	Leon Lett	.10
215	Karim Abdul	.20
216	Carnell Lake	.10
217	Byron Morris	.10
218	John Avery	.20
219	Chris Slade	.10
220	Robert Smith	.20
221	Mike Pritchard	.10
222	Ty Detmer	.10
223	Randall Cunningham	.40
224	Alonzo Mayes	.10
225	Jake Plummer	1.00
226	Derrick Mayes	.10
227	Jeff Brady	.10
228	John Lynch	.10
229	Steve Atwater	.10
230	Warrick Dunn	.50
231	Shawn Jefferson	.10
232	Erik Kramer	.10
233	Ken Dilger	.10
234	Ryan Leaf	.40
235	Ray Buchanan	.10
236	Kevin Williams	.10
237	Ricky Watters	.20
238	Dwayne Rudd	.10
239	Duce Staley	.10
240	Charlie Batch	.50
241	Tim Biakabutuka	.20
242	Tony Gonzalez	.20
243	Bryan Still	.10
244	Donnie Edwards	.10
245	Troy Aikman	1.00
246	Az-Zahir Hakim	.20
247	Curtis Enis	.40
248	Chris Chandler	.20
249	James Jett	.10
250	Brett Favre	2.00
251	Keith Poole	.10
252	Ricky Proel	.10
253	Shannon Sharpe	.20
254	Robert Jones	.10
255	Chad Brown	.10
256	Ben Coates	.20
257	Jacquez Green	.20
258	Jessie Armstead	.10
259	Dale Carter	.10
260	Antowain Smith	.40
261	Mark Chmura	.20
262	Michael Westbrook	.20
263	Marvin Harrison	.20
264	Darrien Gordon	.10
265	Rodney Harrison	.10
266	Charles Johnson	.10
267	Roman Pfifer	.10
268	Reidel Anthony	.20
269	Jerry Rice	1.00
270	Eric Moulds	.50
271	Robert Porcher	.10
272	Deion Sanders	.40
273	Germane Crowell	.20
274	Randy Moss	2.00
275	Antonio Freeman	.40
276	Trent Dilfer	.30
277	Eric Turner	.10
278	Jeff George	.20
279	Levon Kirkland	.10
280	O.J. McDuffie	.10
281	Takeo Spikes	.10
282	Jim Flanigan	.10
283	Chris Warren	.10
284	J.J. Stokes	.20
285	Bryan Cox	.10
286	Sam Madison	.10
287	Priest Holmes	.40
288	Keenan McCardell	.10
289	Michael Strahan	.10
290	Robert Edwards	.30
291	Tommy Vardell	.10
292	Wayne Chrebet	.40
293	Chris Calloway	.10
294	Wesley Walls	.10
295	Derrick Brooks	.10
296	Trace Armstrong	.10
297	Brian Simmons	.10
298	Darrell Green	.10
299	Robert Brooks	.10
300	Peyton Manning	1.50
301	Dana Stubblefield	.10
302	Shawn Springs	.10
303	Leslie Shepherd	.10
304	Ken Harvey	.10
305	Jon Kitna	.50
306	Terance Mathis	.10
307	Andre Reed	.20
308	Jackie Harris	.10
309	Rich Gannon	.10
310	Keyshawn Johnson	.50
311	Victor Green	.10
312	Eric Allen	.10
313	Terry Fair	.10
314	Season Highlights Jason Elam	.10
315	Season Highlights Garrison Hearst	.10
316	Season Highlights Jake Plummer	.50
317	Season Highlights Randall Cunningham	.20
318	Season Highlights Randy Moss	1.00
319	Season Highlights Jamal Anderson	.20
320	Season Highlights John Elway	.75
321	Season Highlights Doug Flutie	.20
322	Season Highlights Emmitt Smith	.50
323	Season Highlights Terrell Davis	.75
324	Jerris McPhail	.10
325	Damon Gibson	.10
326	Jim Pyne	.10
327	Antonio Langham	.10
328	Freddie Solomon	.10
329	*Ricky Williams*	15.00
330	*Daunte Culpepper*	6.00
331	*Chris Claiborne*	1.75
332	*Amos Zereoue*	3.00
333	*Chris McAlister*	1.00
334	*Kevin Faulk*	4.00
335	*James Johnson*	2.50
336	*Mike Cloud*	1.75
337	*Jevon Kearse*	1.00
338	*Akili Smith*	6.00
339	*Edgerrin James*	8.00
340	*Cecil Collins*	4.00
341	*Donovan McNabb*	6.00
342	*Kevin Johnson*	1.75
343	*Torry Holt*	4.00
344	*Rob Konrad*	1.00
345	*Tim Couch*	15.00
346	*David Boston*	5.00
347	*Karsten Bailey*	1.75
348	*Troy Edwards*	3.00
349	*Sedrick Irvin*	1.75
350	*Shaun King*	2.50
351	*Peerless Price*	3.00
352	*Brock Huard*	2.50
353	*Cade McNown*	6.00
354	*Champ Bailey*	2.50
355	*D'Wayne Bates*	1.00
356	Checklist	.10
357	Checklist	.10

1999 Topps All Matrix

This 30-card insert is divided into three different subsets. 1200 Yard Club (10 running backs who rushed for 1200 yards or more), 3000 Yard Club (quarterbacks with rocket-arms) and '99 Rookie Rush (9 players from the 1999 NFL draft). Each is printed on dot matrix cards and were inserted 1:14 packs.

		MT
Complete Set (30):		120.00
Common Player:		1.00
Inserted 1:14		
1	1200 Yard Club Fred Taylor	6.00
2	1200 Yard Club Ricky Watters	2.00
3	1200 Yard Club Curtis Martin	3.00
4	1200 Yard Club Eddie George	4.00
5	1200 Yard Club Marshall Faulk	2.00
6	1200 Yard Club Emmitt Smith	8.00
7	1200 Yard Club Barry Sanders	12.00
8	1200 Yard Club Garrison Hearst	2.00
9	1200 Yard Club Jamal Anderson	2.00
10	1200 Yard Club Terrell Davis	10.00
11	3000 Yard Club Chris Chandler	1.00
12	3000 Yard Club Steve McNair	3.00
13	3000 Yard Club Vinny Testaverde	1.00
14	3000 Yard Club Trent Green	2.00
15	3000 Yard Club Dan Marino	8.00
16	3000 Yard Club Drew Bledsoe	5.00
17	3000 Yard Club Randall Cunningham	2.00
18	3000 Yard Club Jake Plummer	6.00
19	3000 Yard Club Peyton Manning	10.00
20	3000 Yard Club Steve Young	4.00
21	3000 Yard Club Brett Favre	12.00
22	99 Rookie Rush Tim Couch	15.00
23	99 Rookie Rush Edgerrin James	8.00
24	99 Rookie Rush David Boston	4.00
25	99 Rookie Rush Akili Smith	5.00
26	99 Rookie Rush Troy Edwards	2.00
27	99 Rookie Rush Torry Holt	3.00
28	99 Rookie Rush Donovan McNabb	5.00
29	99 Rookie Rush Daunte Culpepper	6.00
30	99 Rookie Rush Ricky Williams	15.00

1999 Topps Autographs

This 10-card set was a hobby exclusive that included 8 current stars and 2 top draft picks. Singles were found 1:509 packs except for the Ricky Williams single which was harder to find at 1:18,372.

		MT
Complete Set (10):		900.00
Common Player:		25.00
Inserted 1:509		
#A5 Inserted 1:18,372		
1	Randy Moss	200.00
2	Wayne Chrebet	35.00
3	Tim Couch	150.00
4	Joey Galloway	35.00
5	Ricky Williams	425.00
6	Doug Flutie	50.00
7	Terrell Owens	50.00
8	Marshall Faulk	35.00
9	Rod Smith	25.00
10	Dan Marino	150.00

1999 Topps Hall of Fame Autographs

The five inductees into the Hall of Fame for 1999 are included in this autographed set. Singles were inserted 1:1,832 packs.

		MT
Complete Set (5):		185.00
Common Player:		25.00
Inserted 1:1,832		
1	Eric Dickerson	50.00
2	Billy Shaw	25.00
3	Lawrence Taylor	80.00
4	Tom Mack	25.00
5	Ozzie Newsome	40.00

1999 Topps Mystery Chrome

Each card in this 20-card set is printed on chrome technology and inserted 1:36 packs. A parallel Refractor version was also made and inserted 1:144 packs.

		MT
Complete Set (20):		135.00
Common Player:		3.00
Inserted 1:36		
Mystery Chrome Refractor:		3x
Inserted 1:144		
1	Terrell Davis	15.00
2	Steve Young	6.00
3	Fred Taylor	10.00
4	Chris Claiborne	3.00
5	Terrell Davis	15.00
6	Randall Cunningham	5.00
7	Charlie Batch	7.00
8	Fred Taylor	10.00
9	Vinny Testaverde	3.00
10	Jamal Anderson	3.00
11	Randy Moss	20.00
12	Keyshawn Johnson	5.00
13	Vinny Testaverde	3.00
14	Chris Chandler	3.00
15	Fred Taylor	10.00
16	Ricky Williams	25.00
17	Chris Chandler	3.00
18	John Elway	15.00
19	Randy Moss	20.00
20	Troy Edwards	6.00

1999 Topps Picture Perfect

Each card in this 10-card set has an intentional error for collectors to find. A hint is printed on the back of each card and singles were inserted 1:14 packs.

		MT
Complete Set (10):		25.00
Common Player:		1.00
Inserted 1:14		
1	Steve Young	1.00
2	Brett Favre	6.00
3	Terrell Davis	4.00
4	Peyton Manning	4.00
5	Jake Plummer	3.00
6	Fred Taylor	3.00
7	Barry Sanders	6.00
8	Dan Marino	4.00
9	John Elway	4.00
10	Randy Moss	6.00

1999 Topps Record Numbers

This set features 10 NFL Record Holders on a white stock card with silver foil. Singles were inserted 1:18 packs.

		MT
Complete Set (10):		35.00
Common Player:		1.00
Inserted 1:18		
1	Randy Moss	7.00
2	Terrell Davis	5.00
3	Emmitt Smith	5.00
4	Barry Sanders	7.00
5	Dan Marino	5.00
6	Brett Favre	7.00
7	Doug Flutie	2.00
8	Jerry Rice	3.50
9	Peyton Manning	4.00
10	Jason Elam	1.00

1999 Topps Season's Best

Thirty dominate players show their mettle in six categories printed on metallic foilboard. The following categories are: Bull Rushers (Running Backs), Rocket Launchers (Quarterbacks), Deep Threats (Wide Receivers), Power Packed (Defensive stars), Strike Force (Special Teams) and Career Best (top players). Singles were found 1:18 packs.

		MT
Complete Set (30):		100.00
Common Player:		1.00
Inserted 1:18		
1	Bull Rushers Terrell Davis	12.00
2	Bull Rushers Jamal Anderson	2.00
3	Bull Rushers Garrison Hearst	2.00
4	Bull Rushers Barry Sanders	15.00
5	Bull Rushers Emmitt Smith	10.00
6	Rocket Launchers Randall Cunningham	2.00
7	Rocket Launchers Brett Favre	15.00
8	Rocket Launchers Steve Young	5.00
9	Rocket Launchers Jake Plummer	8.00
10	Rocket Launchers Peyton Manning	12.00
11	Deep Threats Antonio Freeman	2.00
12	Deep Threats Eric Moulds	2.00
13	Deep Threats Randy Moss	15.00
14	Deep Threats Rod Smith	1.00
15	Deep Threats Jimmy Smith	1.00
16	Power Packed Michael Sinclair	1.00

17	Power Packed Kevin Greene	1.00
18	Power Packed Michael Strahan	1.00
19	Power Packed Michael McCrary	1.00
20	Power Packed Hugh Douglas	1.00
21	Strike Force Deion Sanders	3.00
22	Strike Force Terry Fair	1.00
23	Strike Force Jacquez Green	2.00
24	Strike Force Corey Harris	1.00
25	Strike Force Tim Dwight	3.00
26	Career Best Dan Marino	10.00
27	Career Best Barry Sanders	15.00
28	Career Best Jerry Rice	8.00
29	Career Best Bruce Smith	1.00
30	Career Best Darrien Gordon	1.00

1999 Topps Chrome

This 165-card set is the same as the regular Topps set except each card is printed on a chromium card. For the first time in Topps Chrome the rookies were seeded 1:8 packs. Top inserts include: Refractors, All-Etch, Hall of Fame, Record Numbers and Season's Best. Each of the inserts also has a parallel Refractor version.

		MT
Complete Set (165):		650.00
Common Player:		.25
Common Rookie:		6.00
Inserted 1:8		
Wax Box:		150.00
1	Randy Moss	5.00
2	Keyshawn Johnson	1.00
3	Priest Holmes	1.25
4	Warren Moon	.50
5	Joey Galloway	1.00
6	Zach Thomas	.50
7	Cameron Cleeland	.50
8	Jim Harbaugh	.50
9	Napoleon Kaufman	1.00
10	Fred Taylor	2.50
11	Mark Brunell	2.00
12	Shannon Sharpe	.50
13	Jacquez Green	.50
14	Adrian Murrell	.50
15	Cris Carter	1.00
16	Marshall Faulk	1.00
17	Drew Bledsoe	2.00
18	Curtis Martin	1.25
19	Johnnie Morton	.25
20	Doug Flutie	1.50
21	Carl Pickens	.50
22	Jerome Bettis	1.00
23	Derrick Alexander	.25
24	Antowain Smith	1.00
25	Barry Sanders	5.00
26	Reidel Anthony	.50
27	Wayne Chrebet	1.00
28	Terance Mathis	.25
29	Shawn Springs	.25
30	Emmitt Smith	3.50
31	Robert Smith	1.00
32	Charles Johnson	.50
33	Mike Alstott	1.00
34	Ike Hilliard	.25
35	Ricky Watters	.75
36	Charles Woodson	1.00
37	Rod Smith	.50
38	Pete Mitchell	.25
39	Derrick Thomas	.50
40	Dan Marino	3.50
41	Darnay Scott	.50
42	Jake Reed	.50
43	Chris Chandler	.50
44	Dorsey Levens	1.00
45	Kordell Stewart	1.25
46	Eddie George	1.25
47	Corey Dillon	1.00
48	Rich Gannon	.25
49	Chris Spielman	.25
50	Jerry Rice	2.50
51	Trent Dilfer	.75
52	Mark Chmura	.50
53	Jimmy Smith	.50
54	Isaac Bruce	.50
55	Karim Abdul	.75
56	Sedrick Shaw	.25
57	Jake Plummer	2.50
58	Tony Gonzalez	.50
59	Ben Coates	.50
60	John Elway	3.50
61	Bruce Smith	.25
62	Tim Brown	.50
63	Tim Dwight	1.00
64	Yancey Thigpen	.50
65	Terrell Owens	1.00
66	Kyle Brady	.25
67	Tony Martin	.25
68	Michael Strahan	.25
69	Deion Sanders	1.00
70	Steve Young	1.50
71	Dale Carter	.25
72	Ty Law	.25
73	Frank Wycheck	.25
74	Marshall Faulk	1.00
75	Vinny Testaverde	.50
76	Chad Brown	.25
77	Natrone Means	.75
78	Bert Emanuel	.25
79	Kerry Collins	.50
80	Randall Cunningham	1.00
81	Garrison Hearst	1.00
82	Curtis Enis	1.00
83	Steve Atwater	.25
84	Kevin Greene	.25
85	Steve McNair	1.25
86	Andre Reed	.50
87	J.J. Stokes	.50
88	Eric Moulds	1.00
89	Marvin Harrison	.75
90	Troy Aikman	2.50
91	Herman Moore	.75
92	Michael Irvin	.50
93	Frank Sanders	.50
94	Duce Staley	.50
95	James Jett	.25
96	Ricky Proehl	.25
97	Andre Rison	.50
98	Leslie Shepherd	.25
99	Trent Green	.75
100	Terrell Davis	3.50
101	Freddie Jones	.25
102	Skip Hicks	1.00
103	Jeff Graham	.25
104	Rob Moore	.50
105	Torrance Small	.25
106	Antonio Freeman	1.00
107	Robert Brooks	.25
108	Jon Kitna	1.25
109	Curtis Conway	.50
110	Brett Favre	5.00
111	Warrick Dunn	1.25
112	Elvis Grbac	.50
113	Corey Fuller	.25
114	Rickey Dudley	.25
115	Jamal Anderson	1.00
116	Terry Glenn	.75
117	Raghib Ismail	.25
118	John Randle	.25
119	Chris Calloway	.25
120	Peyton Manning	3.50
121	Keenan McCardell	.25
122	O.J. McDuffie	.50
123	Ed McCaffrey	.50
124	Charlie Batch	1.25
125	Jason Elam (Season Highlights)	.25
126	Randy Moss (Season Highlights)	2.50
127	John Elway (Season Highlights)	1.50
128	Emmitt Smith (Season Highlights)	1.50
129	Terrell Davis (Season Highlights)	1.50
130	Jerris McPhail	.25
131	Damon Gibson	.25
132	Jim Pyne	.25
133	Antonio Langham	.25
134	Freddie Solomon	.25
135	*Ricky Williams*	110.00
136	*Daunte Culpepper*	40.00
137	*Chris Claiborne*	8.00
138	*Amos Zereoue*	20.00
139	*Chris McAlister*	6.00
140	*Kevin Faulk*	25.00
141	*James Johnson*	12.00
142	*Mike Cloud*	8.00
143	*Jevon Kearse*	6.00
144	*Akili Smith*	40.00
145	*Edgerrin James*	75.00
146	*Cecil Collins*	30.00
147	*Donovan McNabb*	40.00
148	*Kevin Johnson*	12.00
149	*Torry Holt*	20.00
150	*Rob Konrad*	8.00
151	*Tim Couch*	110.00
152	*David Boston*	25.00
153	*Karsten Bailey*	8.00
154	*Troy Edwards*	20.00
155	*Sedrick Irvin*	12.00
156	*Shaun King*	15.00
157	*Peerless Price*	15.00
158	*Brock Huard*	12.00
159	*Cade McNown*	40.00
160	*Champ Bailey*	15.00
161	*D'Wayne Bates*	6.00
162	*Joe Germaine*	12.00
163	*Andy Katzenmoyer*	8.00
164	*Antoine Winfield*	6.00
165	Checklist	.25

1999 Topps Chrome Refractors

This is a parallel to the base with each single having a mirror shine to them. Singles were inserted 1:12 packs and rookies were found 1:32 packs.

	MT
Complete Set (165):	1800.
Refractor Cards:	6x-12x
Inserted 1:12	
Refractor Rookies:	2x
Inserted 1:32	

1999 Topps Chrome All Etch

This 30-card insert is divided into three tiers with 1,200 Yard Club, 3,000 Yard Club and '99 Rookie Rush. Singles were inserted 1:24 packs and a Refractor version was also produced and found 1:120 packs.

		MT
Complete Set (30):		170.00
Common Player:		3.00
Inserted 1:24		
Refractors:		2x
Inserted 1:120		
1	Fred Taylor (1200 Yard Club)	12.00
2	Ricky Watters (1200 Yard Club)	3.00
3	Curtis Martin (1200 Yard Club)	6.00
4	Eddie George (1200 Yard Club)	6.00
5	Marshall Faulk (1200 Yard Club)	3.00
6	Emmitt Smith (1200 Yard Club)	18.00
7	Barry Sanders (1200 Yard Club)	25.00
8	Garrison Hearst (1200 Yard Club)	3.00
9	Jamal Anderson (1200 Yard Club)	3.00
10	Terrell Davis (1200 Yard Club)	18.00
11	Chris Chandler (3000 Yard Club)	3.00
12	Steve McNair (3000 Yard Club)	6.00
13	Vinny Testaverde (3000 Yard Club)	3.00
14	Trent Green (3000 Yard Club)	3.00
15	Dan Marino (3000 Yard Club)	18.00
16	Drew Bledsoe (3000 Yard Club)	10.00
17	Randall Cunningham (3000 Yard Club)	6.00
18	Jake Plummer (3000 Yard Club)	12.00
19	Peyton Manning (3000 Yard Club)	18.00
20	Steve Young (3000 Yard Club)	8.00
21	Brett Favre (3000 Yard Club)	25.00
22	Tim Couch (99 Rookie Rushers)	30.00
23	Edgerrin James (99 Rookie Rushers)	15.00
24	David Boston (99 Rookie Rushers)	8.00
25	Akili Smith (99 Rookie Rushers)	10.00
26	Troy Edwards (99 Rookie Rushers)	8.00
27	Torry Holt (99 Rookie Rushers)	8.00
28	Donovan McNabb (99 Rookie Rushers)	10.00
29	Daunte Culpepper (99 Rookie Rushers)	10.00
30	Ricky Williams (99 Rookie Rushers)	30.00

1999 Topps Chrome Hall of Fame

This is a 30-card set of players that are gunning for a spot in Canton, Ohio. The set is divided into three categories (Hall Bound, Early Road to the Hall and Hall Hopefuls) each with a different card design. Hall Bound showcases veterans, Early Road to the Hall features young stars and Hall Hopefuls contains '99 draft picks. Singles were found 1:29 packs and Refractors were sequentially numbered to 100.

		MT
Complete Set (30):		200.00
Common Player:		3.00
Inserted 1:29		
Refractors:		4x
Inserted 1:485		
Production 100 Sets		
1	Akili Smith (Hall Hopefuls)	10.00
2	Troy Edwards (Hall Hopefuls)	8.00
3	Donovan McNabb (Hall Hopefuls)	10.00
4	Cade McNown (Hall Hopefuls)	10.00
5	Ricky Williams (Hall Hopefuls)	30.00
6	David Boston (Hall Hopefuls)	8.00
7	Daunte Culpepper (Hall Hopefuls)	10.00
8	Edgerrin James (Hall Hopefuls)	15.00
9	Torry Holt (Hall Hopefuls)	8.00
10	Tim Couch (Hall Hopefuls)	30.00
11	Terrell Davis (Early Road To)	18.00
12	Fred Taylor (Early Road To)	12.00
13	Antonio Freeman (Early Road To)	3.00
14	Jamal Anderson (Early Road To)	3.00
15	Randy Moss (Early Road To)	25.00
16	Joey Galloway (Early Road To)	3.00
17	Eddie George (Early Road To)	3.00
18	Jake Plummer (Early Road To)	12.00
19	Curtis Martin (Early Road To)	3.00
20	Peyton Manning (Early Road To)	18.00
21	Barry Sanders (Hall Bound)	25.00
22	Steve Young (Hall Bound)	8.00
23	Cris Carter (Hall Bound)	3.00
24	Emmitt Smith (Hall Bound)	18.00
25	John Elway (Hall Bound)	18.00
26	Drew Bledsoe (Hall Bound)	10.00
27	Troy Aikman (Hall Bound)	12.00
28	Brett Favre (Hall Bound)	25.00
29	Jerry Rice (Hall Bound)	12.00
30	Dan Marino (Hall Bound)	18.00

1999 Topps Chrome Record Numbers

		MT
Complete Set (10):		120.00
Common Player:		4.00
Inserted 1:72		
Refractors:		2x
Inserted 1:360		
1	Randy Moss	25.00
2	Terrell Davis	18.00
3	Emmitt Smith	18.00
4	Barry Sanders	25.00
5	Dan Marino	18.00
6	Brett Favre	25.00
7	Doug Flutie	8.00
8	Jerry Rice	12.00
9	Peyton Manning	15.00
10	Jason Elam	4.00

1999 Topps Chrome Season's Best

The 30-card set is divided into six categories. Bull Rushers, Rocket Launchers, Deep Threats, Power Packed, Strike Force and Career Best. Each has a different design and was inserted 1:24 packs. A Refractor version was also produced and inserted 1:120 packs.

		MT
Complete Set (30):		125.00
Common Player:		3.00
Inserted 1:24		
Refractors:		2x
Inserted 1:120		
1	Terrell Davis (Bull Rushers)	18.00
2	Jamal Anderson (Bull Rushers)	6.00
3	Garrison Hearst (Bull Rushers)	6.00
4	Barry Sanders (Bull Rushers)	25.00
5	Emmitt Smith (Bull Rushers)	18.00
6	Randall Cunningham (Rocket Launchers)	6.00
7	Brett Favre (Rocket Launchers)	25.00
8	Steve Young (Rocket Launchers)	8.00
9	Jake Plummer (Rocket Launchers)	12.00
10	Peyton Manning (Rocket Launchers)	18.00
11	Antonio Freeman (Deep Threats)	6.00
12	Eric Moulds (Deep Threats)	6.00
13	Randy Moss (Deep Threats)	25.00
14	Rod Smith (Deep Threats)	3.00
15	Jimmy Smith (Deep Threats)	3.00
16	Michael Sinclair (Power Packed)	3.00
17	Kevin Greene (Power Packed)	3.00
18	Michael Strahan (Power Packed)	3.00
19	Michael McCrary (Power Packed)	3.00
20	Hugh Douglas (Power Packed)	3.00
21	Deion Sanders (Strike Force)	6.00
22	Terry Fair (Strike Force)	3.00
23	Jacquez Green (Strike Force)	3.00
24	Corey Harris (Strike Force)	3.00
25	Tim Dwight (Stike Force)	6.00
26	Dan Marino (Career Best)	18.00
27	Barry Sanders (Career Best)	25.00
28	Jerry Rice (Career Best)	12.00
29	Bruce Smith (Career Best)	3.00
30	Darrien Gordon (Career Best)	3.00

1999 Topps Season Opener

Topps Season Opener Football was a retail exclusive 165-card set that used the same photos as the regular Topps set but had blue borders and a Season Opener stamp in silver foil rather than green borders in the regular issue.

		MT
Complete Set (165):		60.00
Common Player:		.10
Common Rookie:		1.50
Wax Box:		50.00
1	Jerry Rice	1.00
2	Emmitt Smith	1.50
3	Curtis Martin	.30
4	Ed McCaffrey	.20
5	Oronde Gadsden	.20
6	Byron Morris	.20
7	Michael Irvin	.20
8	Shannon Sharpe	.20
9	Levon Kirkland	.10
10	Fred Taylor	1.00
11	Andre Reed	.20
12	Chad Brown	.10
13	Skip Hicks	.20
14	Tim Dwight	.30
15	Michael Sinclair	.10
16	Carl Pickens	.20
17	Derrick Alexander	.10
18	Kevin Green	.10
19	Duce Staley	.20
20	Dan Marino	1.50
21	Frank Sanders	.20
22	Ricky Proehl	.10
23	Frank Wycheck	.10
24	Andre Rison	.20
25	Natrone Means	.20
26	Steve McNair	.30
27	Vonnie Holliday	.20
28	Charles Woodson	.30
29	Rob Moore	.20
30	John Elway	1.50
31	Derrick Thomas	.20
32	Jake Plummer	.75
33	Mike Alstott	.30
34	Keenan McCardell	.20
35	Mark Chmura	.20
36	Keyshawn Johnson	.30
37	Priest Holmes	.30
38	Antonio Freeman	.30
39	Ty Law	.10
40	Jamal Anderson	.30
41	Courtney Hawkins	.10
42	James Jett	.10
43	Aaron Glenn	.10
44	Jimmy Smith	.20
45	Michael McCrary	.10
46	Junior Seau	.20
47	Bill Romanowski	.10
48	Mark Brunell	.75
49	Yancey Thigpen	.20
50	Steve Young	.75
51	Cris Carter	.30
52	Vinny Testaverde	.20
53	Zach Thomas	.20
54	Kordell Stewart	.50
55	Tim Biakabutuka	.10
56	J.J. Stokes	.10
57	Jon Kitna	.30
58	Jacquez Green	.20
59	Marvin Harrison	.20
60	Barry Sanders	2.00
61	Darrell Green	.10
62	Terance Mathis	.10
63	Ricky Watters	.20
64	Chris Chandler	.20
65	Cameron Cleeland	.20
66	Rod Smith	.20
67	Freddie Jones	.10
68	Adrian Murrell	.20
69	Terrell Owens	.30
70	Troy Aikman	1.00
71	John Mobley	.10
72	Corey Dillon	.30
73	Rickey Dudley	.10
74	Randall Cunningham	.30
75	Muhsin Muhammed	.10
76	Stephen Boyd	.10
77	Tony Gonzalez	.20
78	Deion Sanders	.30
79	Ben Coates	.20
80	Brett Favre	2.00
81	Shawn Springs	.10
82	Dorsey Levens	.30
83	Ray Buchanan	.10
84	Charlie Batch	.50
85	John Randle	.10
86	Eddie George	.50
87	Ray Lewis	.10
88	Johnnie Morton	.10
89	Kevin Hardy	.10
90	O.J. McDuffie	.20
91	Herman Moore	.30
92	Tim Brown	.30
93	Bert Emanuel	.10
94	Elvis Grbac	.20
95	Peter Boulware	.10
96	Curtis Conway	.20
97	Doug Flutie	.50
98	Jake Reed	.10
99	Ike Hilliard	.10
100	Randy Moss	2.00
101	Warren Sapp	.10
102	Bruce Smith	.10
103	Joey Galloway	.30
104	Napoleon Kaufman	.30
105	Warrick Dunn	.30
106	Wayne Chrebet	.30
107	Robert Brooks	.10
108	Antowain Smith	.30
109	Trent Dilfer	.20
110	Peyton Manning	1.50
111	Isaac Bruce	.20
112	John Lynch	.10
113	Terry Glenn	.30
114	Garrison Hearst	.30
115	Jerome Bettis	.30
116	Darnay Scott	.10
117	Lamar Thomas	.10
118	Chris Spielman	.10
119	Robert Smith	.20
120	Drew Bledsoe	.75
121	Reidel Anthony	.10
122	Wesley Walls	.10
123	Eric Moulds	.30
124	Terrell Davis	1.50
125	Dale Carter	.10
126	Charles Johnson	.10
127	Steve Atwater	.10
128	Jim Harbaugh	.20
129	Tony Martin	.10
130	Kerry Collins	.20
131	Trent Green	.30
132	Marshall Faulk	.30
133	Raghib Ismail	.10
134	Warren Moon	.30
135	Jerris McPhail	.10
136	Damon Gibson	.10
137	Jim Pyne	.10
138	Antonio Langham	.10
139	Freddie Solomon	.10
140	Randy Moss SH	1.00
141	John Elway SH	.75
142	Doug Flutie SH	.25
143	Emmitt Smith SH	.75
144	Terrell Davis SH	.75
145	*Troy Edwards*	3.00
146	*Torry Holt*	3.00
147	*Tim Couch*	12.00
148	*Sedrick Irvin*	2.00
149	*Ricky Williams*	12.00
150	*Peerless Price*	3.00
151	*Mike Cloud*	1.50
152	*Kevin Faulk*	3.00
153	*Kevin Johnson*	2.50
154	*James Johnson*	2.50
155	*Edgerrin James*	7.00
156	*D'Wayne Bates*	2.00
157	*Donovan McNabb*	5.00
158	*David Boston*	3.00
159	*Daunte Culpepper*	5.00
160	*Champ Bailey*	2.00
161	*Cecil Collins*	5.00
162	*Cade McNown*	5.00
163	*Brock Huard*	2.00
164	*Akili Smith*	4.00
165	Checklist	.10

1999 Topps Season Opener Autographs

Only two players signed in this insert and were inserted 1:7,126 packs.

		MT
Complete Set (2):		475.00
Common Player:		200.00
Inserted 1:7,126		
1	Tim Couch	275.00
2	Peyton Manning	200.00

1999 UD Ionix

UD Ionix is a 90-card set with 30 seeded rookies found 1:4 packs. Each card is super thick, double laminated and metalized. Inserts include: Reciprocal, Astronomix, Electric Forces, HoloGrFX, Power F/X, UD Authentics and Warp Zone.

		MT
Complete Set (90):		160.00
Common Player:		.25
Common Rookie:		2.50
Inserted 1:4		
Wax Box:		85.00
1	Jake Plummer	2.00
2	Adrian Murrell	.25
3	Jamal Anderson	1.00
4	Chris Chandler	.50
5	Priest Holmes	1.00
6	Michael Jackson	.50
7	Antowain Smith	1.00
8	Doug Flutie	1.50
9	Tshimanga Biakabutuka	.25
10	Muhsin Muhammad	.25
11	Erik Kramer	.25
12	Curtis Enis	1.00
13	Corey Dillon	1.00
14	Ty Detmer	.50
15	Justin Armour	.25
16	Troy Aikman	2.00
17	Emmitt Smith	3.00
18	John Elway	3.00
19	Terrell Davis	3.00
20	Barry Sanders	4.00
21	Charlie Batch	1.50
22	Brett Favre	4.00
23	Dorsey Levens	1.00
24	Marshall Faulk	1.00
25	Peyton Manning	3.00
26	Mark Brunell	1.50
27	Fred Taylor	2.00
28	Elvis Grbac	.50
29	Andre Rison	.50
30	Dan Marino	3.00
31	Karim Abdul	.75
32	Randall Cunningham	1.00
33	Randy Moss	5.00
34	Drew Bledsoe	1.50
35	Terry Glenn	.75
36	Danny Wuerffel	.25
37	Kent Graham	.25
38	Gary Brown	.25
39	Vinny Testaverde	.50
40	Keyshawn Johnson	1.00
41	Napoleon Kaufman	1.00
42	Tim Brown	.50
43	Koy Detmer	.25
44	Duce Staley	.25
45	Kordell Stewart	1.25
46	Jerome Bettis	1.00
47	Isaac Bruce	.75
48	Robert Holcombe	.25
49	Jim Harbaugh	.50
50	Natrone Means	.75
51	Steve Young	1.50
52	Jerry Rice	2.00
53	Jon Kitna	1.25
54	Joey Galloway	1.00
55	Warrick Dunn	1.25
56	Trent Dilfer	.75
57	Steve McNair	1.25
58	Eddie George	1.25
59	Skip Hicks	1.00
60	Michael Westbrook	.50
61	*Tim Couch*	30.00
62	*Ricky Williams*	30.00
63	*Daunte Culpepper*	10.00
64	*Akili Smith*	10.00
65	*Donovan McNabb*	10.00
66	*Michael Bishop*	7.00
67	*Brock Huard*	5.00
68	*Torry Holt*	8.00
69	*Cade McNown*	10.00
70	*Shaun King*	5.00
71	*Champ Bailey*	5.00
72	*Chris Claiborne*	4.00
73	*Jevon Kearse*	2.50
74	*D'Wayne Bates*	2.50
75	*David Boston*	8.00
76	*Edgerrin James*	18.00
77	*Sedrick Irvin*	4.00
78	*Dameane Douglas*	4.00
79	*Troy Edwards*	6.00
80	*Ebenezer Ekuban*	2.50
81	*Kevin Faulk*	8.00
82	*Joe Germaine*	5.00
83	*Kevin Johnson*	4.00
84	*Andy Katzenmoyer*	4.00
85	*Rob Konrad*	2.50
86	*Chris McAlister*	2.50
87	*Peerless Price*	5.00
88	*Tai Streets*	2.50
89	*Autry Denson*	4.00
90	*Amos Zereoue*	6.00

1999 UD Ionix Reciprocal

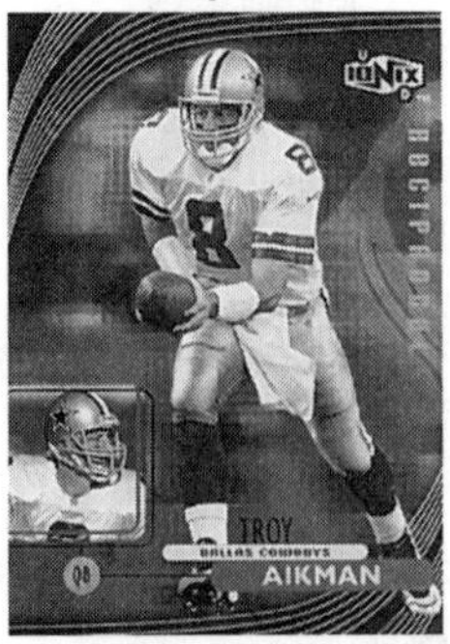

This is a parallel to the base and has the prefix "R" before the card number. Cards #1-60 were found 1:6 packs and the rookies #61-90 were inserted 1:19 packs. The word "Reciprocal" is printed on the front of each card.

	MT
Complete Set (90):	400.00
Reciprocal Cards:	2x-4x
Inserted 1:6	
Reciprocal Rookies:	2x
Inserted 1:19	

1999 UD Ionix Astronomix

Each card in this 25-card set highlights a statistical achievement by that particular player. Singles were inserted 1:23 packs.

		MT
Complete Set (25):		200.00
Common Player:		5.00
Inserted 1:23		
1	Keyshawn Johnson	5.00
2	Emmitt Smith	18.00
3	Eddie George	6.00
4	Fred Taylor	12.00
5	Peyton Manning	18.00
6	John Elway	18.00
7	Brett Favre	25.00
8	Terrell Davis	18.00
9	Mark Brunell	8.00
10	Dan Marino	18.00
11	Randall Cunningham	5.00
12	Steve McNair	5.00
13	Jamal Anderson	5.00
14	Barry Sanders	25.00
15	Jake Plummer	12.00
16	Drew Bledsoe	8.00
17	Jerome Bettis	5.00
18	Jerry Rice	12.00
19	Warrick Dunn	6.00
20	Steve Young	8.00
21	Terrell Owens	5.00
22	Ricky Williams	30.00
23	Akili Smith	12.00
24	Cade McNown	12.00
25	David Boston	10.00

1999 UD Ionix Electric Forces

This 20-card set includes the most collectible NFL stars of today. Singles were inserted 1:6 packs.

		MT
Complete Set (20):		60.00
Common Player:		2.00
Inserted 1:6		
1	Ricky Williams	15.00
2	Tim Couch	15.00
3	Daunte Culpepper	5.00
4	Akili Smith	5.00
5	Cade McNown	5.00
6	Donovan McNabb	5.00
7	Brock Huard	2.00
8	Michael Bishop	3.00
9	Torry Holt	4.00
10	Peerless Price	3.00
11	Peyton Manning	6.00
12	Jake Plummer	4.00
13	John Elway	6.00
14	Mark Brunell	3.00
15	Steve Young	2.50
16	Jamal Anderson	2.00
17	Kordell Stewart	2.50
18	Eddie George	2.50
19	Fred Taylor	4.00
20	Brett Favre	8.00

1999 UD Ionix HoloGrFX

The top NFL stars and rookies are included in this 10-card set. Singles were issued at 1:1,500 packs.

		MT
Complete Set (10):		1200.
Common Player:		75.00
Inserted 1:1,500		
1	Ricky Williams	250.00
2	Tim Couch	250.00
3	Cade McNown	100.00
4	Peyton Manning	150.00
5	Jake Plummer	125.00
6	Randy Moss	250.00
7	Barry Sanders	250.00
8	Jamal Anderson	75.00
9	Terrell Davis	175.00
10	Brett Favre	250.00

1999 UD Ionix Power F/X

The game's most impressive talents, with a mix of rookies and veterans are highlighted in this 9-card set. Singles were inserted 1:11 packs.

		MT
Complete Set (9):		40.00
Common Player:		2.00
Inserted 1:11		
1	Peyton Manning	7.00
2	Randy Moss	10.00
3	Terrell Davis	8.00
4	Steve Young	3.00
5	Dan Marino	8.00
6	Warrick Dunn	2.00
7	Keyshawn Johnson	2.00
8	Barry Sanders	10.00
9	Tim Couch	12.00

1999 UD Ionix UD Authentics

This 10-card set includes autographs from the top rookies from the 1999 draft. Each player signed 100 cards each except for Ricky Williams who signed only 50.

		MT
Complete Set (10):		1300.
Common Player:		60.00
Production 100 Sets		
Ricky Williams Only Signed 50		
MB	Michael Bishop	75.00
TC	Tim Couch	250.00
DC	Daunte Culpepper	125.00
TH	Torry Holt	85.00
BH	Brock Huard	60.00
SK	Shaun King	60.00
DM	Donovan McNabb	125.00
CM	Cade McNown	125.00
AS	Akili Smith	125.00
RW	Ricky Williams	500.00

1999 UD Ionix Warp Zone

A mix of stars and rookies from the NFL make up this 15-card set that was inserted 1:108 packs.

		MT
Complete Set (15):		375.00
Common Player:		10.00
Inserted 1:108		
1	Ricky Williams	75.00
2	Tim Couch	75.00
3	Cade McNown	25.00
4	Daunte Culpepper	25.00
5	Akili Smith	25.00
6	Brock Huard	10.00
7	Donovan McNabb	25.00
8	Jake Plummer	25.00
9	Jamal Anderson	10.00
10	John Elway	40.00
11	Randy Moss	50.00
12	Terrell Davis	40.00
13	Troy Aikman	25.00
14	Barry Sanders	50.00
15	Fred Taylor	25.00

1999 Ultra

Ultra Football is a 300-card set with 50 short-printed cards. The short prints are 40 Rookies (1:4) and 10 Super Bowl XXXIII (1:8). Ultra has two parallel sets with Gold and Platinum Medallions. Other inserts include: As Good As It Gets, Caught in the Draft, Counterparts, Damage Inc. and Over the Top.

		MT
Complete Set (300):		300.00
Common Player:		.15
Common Rookie (261-300):		3.00
Inserted 1:4		
Common Back 2 Back:		3.00
Inserted 1:8		
Wax Box:		75.00
1	Terrell Davis	2.50
2	Courtney Hawkins	.15
3	Cris Carter	.50
4	Darnay Scott	.15
5	Darrell Green	.15
6	Jimmy Smith	.30
7	Doug Flutie	.75
8	Michael Jackson	.15
9	Warren Sapp	.15
10	Greg Hill	.15
11	Karim Abdul	.50
12	Greg Ellis	.15
13	Dan Marino	2.00
14	Napoleon Kaufman	.50
15	Peyton Manning	2.50
16	Simeon Rice	.15
17	Tony Simmons	.30
18	Carlester Crumpler	.15
19	Charles Johnson	.15
20	Derrick Alexander	.15
21	Kent Graham	.15
22	Randall Cunningham	.50
23	Trent Green	.50
24	Chris Spielman	.15
25	Carl Pickens	.30
26	Bill Romanowski	.15
27	Jermaine Lewis	.15
28	Ahman Green	.30
29	Bryan Still	.15
30	Dorsey Levens	.50
31	Frank Wycheck	.15
32	Jerome Bettis	.50
33	Reidel Anthony	.30
34	Robert Jones	.15
35	Terry Glenn	.50
36	Tim Brown	.50
37	Eric Metcalf	.15
38	Kevin Greene	.15
39	Takeo Spikes	.15
40	Brian Mitchell	.15
41	Duane Starks	.15
42	Eddie George	1.00
43	Joe Jurevicius	.15
44	Kimble Anders	.15
45	Kordell Stewart	1.00
46	Leroy Hoard	.15
47	Rod Smith	.30
48	Terrell Owens	.75
49	Tony McGee	.15
50	Charles Woodson	.50
51	Andre Rison	.15
52	Chris Slade	.15
53	Frank Sanders	.30
54	Michael Irvin	.30
55	Jerome Pathon	.15
56	Desmond Howard	.15
57	Billy Davis	.15
58	Anthony Simmons	.15
59	James Jett	.15
60	Jake Plummer	1.50
61	John Avery	.30
62	Marvin Harrison	.50
63	Merton Hanks	.15
64	Ricky Proehl	.15
65	Steve Beuerlein	.15
66	Willie McGinest	.15
67	Bryce Paup	.15
68	Brett Favre	3.00
69	Brian Griese	1.00
70	Curtis Martin	.75
71	Drew Bledsoe	1.25
72	Jim Harbaugh	.30
73	Joey Galloway	.50
74	Natrone Means	.50
75	O.J. McDuffie	.15
76	Tiki Barber	.15
77	Wesley Walls	.15
78	Will Blackwell	.15
79	Bert Emanuel	.15
80	J.J. Stokes	.30
81	Steve McNair	1.00
82	Adrian Murrell	.15
83	Dexter Coakley	.15
84	Jeff George	.30
85	Marshall Faulk	.50
86	Tim Biakabutuka	.30
87	Troy Drayton	.15
88	Ty Law	.15
89	Brian Simmons	.15
90	Eric Allen	.15
91	Jon Kitna	.75
92	Junior Seau	.30
93	Kevin Turner	.15
94	Larry Centers	.15
95	Robert Edwards	.50
96	Rocket Ismail	.15
97	Sam Madison	.15
98	Stephen Alexander	.15
99	Trent Dilfer	.30
100	Vonnie Holliday	.30
101	Charlie Garner	.15
102	Deion Sanders	.75
103	Jamal Anderson	.75
104	Mike Vanderjagt	.15
105	Aeneas Williams	.15
106	Daryl Johnston	.15
107	Hugh Douglas	.15
108	Torrance Small	.15
109	Amani Toomer	.15
110	Amp Lee	.15
111	Germane Crowell	.30
112	Marco Battaglia	.15
113	Michael Westbrook	.15
114	Randy Moss	4.00
115	Ricky Watters	.50
116	Rob Johnson	.30
117	Tony Gonzalez	.30
118	Charles Way	.15
119	Chris Penn	.15
120	Eddie Kennison	.15
121	Elvis Grbac	.15
122	Eric Moulds	.50
123	Terry Fair	.15
124	Tony Banks	.30
125	Chris Chandler	.30
126	Emmitt Smith	2.00
127	Herman Moore	.50
128	Irv Smith	.15
129	Kyle Brady	.15
130	Lamont Warren	.15
131	Troy Davis	.15
132	Andre Reed	.30
133	Justin Armour	.15
134	James Hasty	.15
135	Johnnie Morton	.15
136	Reggie Barlow	.15
137	Robert Holcombe	.30
138	Sean Dawkins	.15
139	Steve Atwater	.15
140	Tim Dwight	.50
141	Wayne Chrebet	.50
142	Alonzo Mayes	.15
143	Mark Brunell	1.25
144	Antowain Smith	.50
145	Bam Morris	.15
146	Isaac Bruce	.50
147	Bryan Cox	.15
148	Bryant Westbrook	.15
149	Duce Staley	.15
150	Barry Sanders	3.00
151	La'Roi Glover	.15
152	Ray Crockett	.15
153	Tony Brackens	.15
154	Roy Barker	.15
155	Kerry Collins	.30
156	Andre Wadsworth	.30
157	Cameron Cleeland	.30
158	Koy Detmer	.15
159	Marcus Pollard	.15
160	Patrick Jeffers	.15
161	Aaron Glenn	.15
162	Andre Hastings	.15
163	Bruce Smith	.15
164	David Palmer	.15
165	Erik Kramer	.15
166	Orlando Pace	.15
167	Robert Brooks	.30
168	Shawn Springs	.15
169	Terance Mathis	.15
170	Chris Calloway	.15
171	Gilbert Brown	.15
172	Charlie Jones	.15
173	Curtis Enis	.75
174	Eugene Robinson	.15
175	Garrison Hearst	.50
176	Jason Elam	.15
177	John Randle	.15
178	Keith Poole	.15
179	Kevin Hardy	.15
180	Keyshawn Johnson	.75
181	O.J. Santiago	.15
182	Jacquez Green	.30
183	Bobby Engram	.15
184	Damon Jones	.15
185	Freddie Jones	.15
186	Jake Reed	.15
187	Jerry Rice	1.50
188	Joey Kent	.15
189	Lamar Smith	.15
190	John Elway	2.00
191	Leon Johnson	.15
192	Mark Chmura	.30
193	Peter Boulware	.15
194	Zach Thomas	.30
195	Marc Edwards	.15
196	Mike Alstott	.75
197	Yancey Thigpen	.30
198	Oronde Gadsden	.30
199	Rae Carruth	.15
200	Troy Aikman	1.50
201	Shawn Jefferson	.15
202	Rob Moore	.30
203	Rickey Dudley	.15
204	Jason Taylor	.15
205	Curtis Conway	.30
206	Darrien Gordon	.15
207	Eric Green	.15
208	Jesse Armstead	.15
209	Keenan McCardell	.30
210	Robert Smith	.50
211	Mo Lewis	.15
212	Ryan Leaf	1.00
213	Steve Young	1.00
214	Tyrone Davis	.15
215	Chad Brown	.15
216	Ike Hilliard	.15
217	Jimmy Hitchcock	.15
218	Kevin Dyson	.30
219	Levon Kirkland	.15
220	Neil O'Donnell	.15
221	Ray Lewis	.15
222	Shannon Sharpe	.50
223	Skip Hicks	.50
224	Brad Johnson	.50
225	Charlie Batch	1.00
226	Corey Dillon	.75
227	Dale Carter	.15
228	John Mobley	.15
229	Hines Ward	.30
230	Leslie Shepherd	.15
231	Michael Strahan	.15
232	R.W. McQuarters	.15
233	Mike Pritchard	.15
234	Antonio Freeman	.75
235	Ben Coates	.50
236	Michael Bates	.15
237	Ed McCaffrey	.50
238	Gary Brown	.15
239	Mark Bruener	.15
240	Mikhael Ricks	.15
241	Muhsin Muhammad	.15
242	Priest Holmes	.75
243	Stephen Davis	.15
244	Vinny Testaverde	.50
245	Warrick Dunn	1.00
246	Derrick Mayes	.15
247	Fred Taylor	1.50
248	Drew Bledsoe CL	.50
249	Eddie George CL	.50
250	Steve Young CL	.50
251	Back-2-Back - Super Bowl XXXIII	3.00
252	Back-2-Back - Super Bowl XXXIII	3.00
253	Back-2-Back - Super Bowl XXXIII	3.00
254	Back-2-Back - Super Bowl XXXIII	3.00
255	Back-2-Back - Super Bowl XXXIII	3.00
256	Back-2-Back - Super Bowl XXXIII	3.00
257	Back-2-Back - Super Bowl XXXIII	3.00
258	Back-2-Back - Super Bowl XXXIII	3.00
259	Back-2-Back - Super Bowl XXXIII	3.00
260	Back-2-Back - Super Bowl XXXIII	3.00
261	*Ricky Williams*	55.00
262	*Tim Couch*	55.00
263	*Chris Claiborne*	10.00
264	*Champ Bailey*	12.00
265	*Torry Holt*	15.00
266	*Donovan McNabb*	25.00
267	*David Boston*	15.00
268	*Chris McAlister*	3.00
269	*Brock Huard*	10.00
270	*Daunte Culpepper*	20.00
271	*Matt Stinchcomb*	3.00
272	*Edgerrin James*	30.00
273	*Jevon Kearse*	3.00
274	*Ebenezer Ekuban*	3.00
275	*Kris Farris*	3.00
276	*Chris Terry*	3.00
277	*Jerame Tuman*	3.00
278	*Akili Smith*	25.00
279	*Aaron Gibson*	3.00
280	*Rahim Abdullah*	3.00
281	*Peerless Price*	15.00
282	*Antoine Winfield*	3.00
283	*Antwan Edwards*	3.00
284	*Rob Konrad*	3.00
285	*Troy Edwards*	15.00
286	*John Thornton*	3.00
287	*James Johnson*	6.00
288	*Gary Stills*	3.00
289	*Mike Peterson*	3.00
290	*Kevin Faulk*	15.00
291	*Jared DeVries*	3.00
292	*Martin Gramatica*	3.00
293	*Montae Reagor*	3.00
294	*Andy Katzenmoyer*	6.00
295	*Sedrick Irvin*	8.00
296	*D'Wayne Bates*	3.00
297	*Amos Zereoue*	10.00
298	*Dre' Bly*	3.00
299	*Kevin Johnson*	8.00
300	*Cade McNown*	25.00

1999 Ultra Gold Medallion

This is a 300-card parallel to the base and is the same except each card is printed on gold foil and stamped Gold Medallion Edition on the back. Veterans were inserted 1:1, Rookies 1:25 and Super Bowl singles at 1:50.

	MT
Complete Set (300):	600.00
Gold Cards:	2x-4x
Inserted 1:1	
Gold Rookies:	1.5x
Inserted 1:25	
Gold Back 2 Back:	5x-10x
Inserted 1:50	

1999 Ultra Platinum Medallion

This is a parallel to the base and is the same except each card is printed on a silver stock and on the backs are sequentially numbered and have a Platinum Medallion stamp. Veterans are numbered to 99, Rookies to 65 and Super Bowl singles to 40.

	MT
Platinum Cards:	35x-70x
Production 99 Sets	
Platinum Rookies:	3x-6x
Production 65 Sets	
Platinum Back 2 Back:	25x-50x
Production 40 Sets	

1999 Ultra As Good As It Gets

Each of the 15 players in this set are the best in the NFL. Each is on a die-cut felt stock with silver and gold holo-foil. Singles were inserted 1:288 packs.

		MT
Complete Set (15):		500.00
Common Player:		12.00
Inserted 1:288		
1	Warrick Dunn	12.00
2	Terrell Davis	50.00
3	Robert Edwards	12.00
4	Randy Moss	75.00
5	Peyton Manning	50.00
6	Mark Brunell	20.00
7	John Elway	50.00
8	Jerry Rice	30.00
9	Jake Plummer	25.00
10	Fred Taylor	30.00
11	Emmitt Smith	50.00
12	Dan Marino	50.00
13	Charlie Batch	20.00
14	Brett Favre	60.00
15	Barry Sanders	60.00

1999 Ultra Caught In The Draft

This 15-card set includes the top rookies from 1999 and captures them on a silver pattern holo-foil card. They were inserted 1:18 packs.

		MT
Complete Set (15):		75.00
Common Player:		1.50
Inserted 1:18		
1	Ricky Williams	20.00
2	Tim Couch	25.00
3	Chris Claiborne	3.00
4	Champ Bailey	4.00
5	Torry Holt	6.00
6	Donovan McNabb	10.00
7	David Boston	6.00
8	Andy Katzenmoyer	1.50
9	Daunte Culpepper	8.00
10	Edgerrin James	12.00
11	Cade McNown	10.00
12	Troy Edwards	6.00
13	Akili Smith	10.00
14	Peerless Price	6.00
15	Amos Zereoue	3.00

1999 Ultra Counterparts

Each card in this 15-card set highlights two players from the same team and puts them on an embossed silver holo-foil card. Singles were found 1:36 packs.

		MT
Complete Set (15):		100.00
Common Player:		4.00
Inserted 1:36		
1	Troy Aikman, Michael Irvin	10.00
2	Drew Bledsoe, Ben Coates	8.00
3	Terrell Davis, Howard Griffith	15.00
4	Warrick Dunn, Mike Alstott	6.00
5	Brett Favre, Antonio Freeman	20.00
6	Jake Plummer, Frank Sanders	8.00
7	Randy Moss, Randall Cunningham	25.00
8	Eddie George, Steve McNair	8.00
9	Keyshawn Johnson, Wayne Chrebet	4.00
10	Ryan Leaf, Mikhael Ricks	6.00
11	Peyton Manning, Marshall Faulk	15.00
12	Barry Sanders, Tommy Vardell	20.00
13	Charlie Batch, Herman Moore	8.00
14	Emmitt Smith, Daryl Johnston	15.00
15	Kordell Stewart, Jerome Bettis	8.00

1999 Ultra Damage Inc.

This 15-card set includes the top players in the league and showcases them on a sculpted special silver foil card. Singles were found 1:72 packs.

		MT
Complete Set (15):		180.00
Common Player:		6.00
Inserted 1:72		
1	Brett Favre	30.00
2	Dan Marino	20.00
3	John Elway	20.00
4	Mark Brunell	12.00
5	Peyton Manning	20.00
6	Robert Edwards	6.00
7	Terrell Davis	20.00
8	Troy Aikman	15.00
9	Randy Moss	35.00
10	Kordell Stewart	10.00
11	Jerry Rice	15.00
12	Fred Taylor	15.00
13	Emmitt Smith	20.00
14	Charlie Batch	10.00
15	Barry Sanders	30.00

1999 Ultra Over The Top

This was a 20-card set that included gold foil stamping and was inserted 1:6 packs.

		MT
Complete Set (20):		40.00
Common Player:		1.00
Inserted 1:6		
1	Troy Aikman	5.00
2	Drew Bledsoe	4.00
3	Mark Brunell	4.00
4	Randall Cunningham	2.00
5	Jamal Anderson	2.00
6	Warrick Dunn	3.00
7	Robert Edwards	2.00
8	John Elway	8.00
9	Eddie George	4.00
10	Eric Moulds	1.00
11	Keyshawn Johnson	2.00
12	Ryan Leaf	1.00
13	Dan Marino	8.00
14	Steve McNair	3.00
15	Jake Plummer	4.00
16	Jerry Rice	5.00
17	Deion Sanders	2.00
18	Kordell Stewart	4.00
19	Fred Taylor	8.00
20	Steve Young	3.00

1999 Upper Deck

Upper Deck is a 270-card set that includes 45 seeded rookies found 1:4 packs. Each base card has a parallel Exclusive Silver and Exclusive Gold. Other inserts include: 21 TD Salute, Game Jersey, Game Jersey Patch, Highlight Zone, Livewires, PowerDeck, Quarterback Class and Strike Force.

		MT
Complete Set (270):		300.00
Common Player:		.15
Common Rookie:		2.00
Inserted 1:4		
Wax Box:		80.00
1	Jake Plummer	1.25
2	Adrian Murrell	.15
3	Rob Moore	.30
4	Larry Centers	.15
5	Simeon Rice	.15
6	Andre Wadsworth	.15
7	Frank Sanders	.30
8	Tim Dwight	.50
9	Ray Buchanan	.15
10	Chris Chandler	.30
11	Jamal Anderson	.50
12	O.J. Santiago	.15
13	Danny Kanell	.15
14	Terance Mathis	.15
15	Priest Holmes	.50
16	Tony Banks	.30
17	Ray Lewis	.15
18	Patrick Johnson	.15
19	Michael Jackson	.15
20	Michael McCrary	.15
21	Jermaine Lewis	.30
22	Eric Moulds	.50
23	Doug Flutie	.75
24	Antowain Smith	.50
25	Rob Johnson	.30
26	Bruce Smith	.15
27	Andre Reed	.15
28	Thurman Thomas	.15
29	Fred Lane	.15
30	Wesley Walls	.15
31	Tshimanga Biakabutuka	.15
32	Kevin Greene	.15
33	Steve Beuerlein	.15
34	Muhsin Muhammad	.15
35	Rae Carruth	.15
36	Bobby Engram	.15
37	Curtis Enis	.30
38	Edgar Bennett	.15
39	Erik Kramer	.15
40	Steve Stenstrom	.15
41	Alonzo Mayes	.15
42	Curtis Conway	.30
43	Tony McGee	.15
44	Darnay Scott	.15
45	Jeff Blake	.30
46	Corey Dillon	.50
47	Ki-Jana Carter	.15
48	Takeo Spikes	.15
49	Carl Pickens	.30
50	Ty Detmer	.15
51	Leslie Shepherd	.15
52	Terry Kirby	.15
53	Marquez Pope	.15
54	Antonio Langham	.15
55	Jamir Miller	.15
56	Derrick Alexander	.15
57	Troy Aikman	1.25
58	Raghib Ismail	.15
59	Emmitt Smith	2.00
60	Michael Irvin	.30
61	David LaFleur	.15
62	Chris Warren	.15
63	Deion Sanders	.50
64	Greg Ellis	.15
65	John Elway	2.00
66	Bubby Brister	.30
67	Terrell Davis	2.00
68	Ed McCaffrey	.30
69	John Mobley	.15
70	Bill Romanowski	.15
71	Rod Smith	.30
72	Shannon Sharpe	.30
73	Charlie Batch	.75
74	Germane Crowell	.30
75	Johnnie Morton	.15
76	Barry Sanders	2.50
77	Robert Porcher	.15
78	Stephen Boyd	.15
79	Herman Moore	.50
80	Brett Favre	2.50
81	Mark Chmura	.30
82	Antonio Freeman	.50
83	Robert Brooks	.15
84	Vonnie Holliday	.15
85	Bill Schroeder	.15
86	Dorsey Levens	.50
87	Santana Dotson	.15
88	Peyton Manning	2.00
89	Jerome Pathon	.15
90	Marvin Harrison	.30
91	Ellis Johnson	.15
92	Ken Dilger	.15
93	E.G. Green	.15
94	Jeff Burris	.15
95	Mark Brunell	1.00
96	Fred Taylor	1.25
97	Jimmy Smith	.30
98	James Stewart	.15
99	Kyle Brady	.15
100	Dave Thomas	.15
101	Keenan McCardell	.15
102	Elvis Grbac	.30
103	Tony Gonzalez	.30
104	Andre Rison	.30
105	Donnell Bennett	.15
106	Derrick Thomas	.15
107	Warren Moon	.30
108	Derrick Alexander	.15
109	Dan Marino	2.00
110	O.J. McDuffie	.30
111	Karim Abdul	.30
112	John Avery	.30
113	Sam Madison	.15
114	Jason Taylor	.15
115	Zach Thomas	.30
116	Randall Cunningham	.50
117	Randy Moss	3.00
118	Cris Carter	.50
119	Jake Reed	.15
120	Matthew Hatchette	.15
121	John Randle	.15
122	Robert Smith	.30
123	Drew Bledsoe	1.00
124	Ben Coates	.30
125	Terry Glenn	.30
126	Ty Law	.15
127	Tony Simmons	.30
128	Ted Johnson	.15
129	Tony Carter	.15
130	Willie McGinest	.15
131	Danny Wuerffel	.15
132	Cameron Cleeland	.15
133	Eddie Kennison	.15
134	Joe Johnson	.15
135	Andre Hastings	.15
136	La'Roi Glover	.15
137	Kent Graham	.15
138	Tiki Barber	.15
139	Gary Brown	.15
140	Ike Hilliard	.15
141	Jason Sehorn	.15
142	Michael Strahan	.15
143	Amani Toomer	.15
144	Kerry Collins	.30
145	Vinny Testaverde	.30
146	Wayne Chrebet	.30
147	Curtis Martin	.50
148	Mo Lewis	.15
149	Aaron Glenn	.15
150	Steve Atwater	.15
151	Keyshawn Johnson	.50
152	James Farrior	.15
153	Rich Gannon	.15
154	Tim Brown	.30
155	Darrell Russell	.15
156	Rickey Dudley	.15
157	Charles Woodson	.50
158	James Jett	.15
159	Napoleon Kaufman	.50
160	Duce Staley	.30
161	Doug Pederson	.15
162	Bobby Hoying	.15
163	Koy Detmer	.15
164	Kevin Turner	.15
165	Charles Johnson	.15
166	Mike Mamula	.15
167	Jerome Bettis	.50
168	Courtney Hawkins	.15
169	Will Blackwell	.15
170	Kordell Stewart	.75
171	Richard Huntley	.15
172	Levon Kirkland	.15
173	Hines Ward	.30
174	Trent Green	.30
175	Marshall Faulk	.50
176	Az-Zahir Hakim	.15
177	Amp Lee	.15
178	Robert Holcombe	.30
179	Isaac Bruce	.30
180	Kevin Carter	.15
181	Jim Harbaugh	.30
182	Junior Seau	.30
183	Natrone Means	.50
184	Ryan Leaf	.50
185	Charlie Jones	.15
186	Rodney Harrison	.15
187	Mikhael Ricks	.15
188	Steve Young	.75
189	Terrell Owens	.50
190	Jerry Rice	1.25
191	J.J. Stokes	.30
192	Irv Smith	.15
193	Bryant Young	.15
194	Garrison Hearst	.30
195	Jon Kitna	.75
196	Ahman Green	.30
197	Joey Galloway	.50
198	Ricky Watters	.30
199	Chad Brown	.15
200	Shawn Springs	.15
201	Mike Pritchard	.15
202	Trent Dilfer	.30
203	Reidel Anthony	.30
204	Bert Emanuel	.15
205	Warrick Dunn	.50
206	Jacquez Green	.30
207	Hardy Nickerson	.15
208	Mike Alstott	.50
209	Eddie George	.75
210	Steve McNair	.75
211	Kevin Dyson	.30
212	Frank Wycheck	.15
213	Jackie Harris	.15
214	Blaine Bishop	.15
215	Yancey Thigpen	.15
216	Brad Johnson	.50
217	Rodney Peete	.15
218	Michael Westbrook	.30
219	Skip Hicks	.50
220	Brian Mitchell	.15
221	Dan Wilkinson	.15
222	Dana Stubblefield	.15
223	Set Checklist #1	.15
224	Checklist #2	.15
225	Checklist #3	.15
226	*Champ Bailey*	6.00
227	*Chris McAlister*	4.00
228	*Jevon Kearse*	2.00
229	*Ebenezer Ekuban*	2.00
230	*Chris Claiborne*	4.00
231	*Andy Katzenmoyer*	5.00
232	*Tim Couch*	50.00
233	*Daunte Culpepper*	15.00
234	*Akili Smith*	15.00
235	*Donovan McNabb*	15.00
236	*Sean Bennett*	5.00
237	*Brock Huard*	6.00
238	*Cade McNown*	15.00
239	*Shaun King*	6.00
240	*Joe Germaine*	6.00
241	*Ricky Williams*	50.00
242	*Edgerrin James*	25.00
243	*Sedrick Irvin*	6.00
244	*Kevin Faulk*	10.00
245	*Rob Konrad*	4.00
246	*James Johnson*	4.00
247	*Amos Zereoue*	8.00
248	*Torry Holt*	10.00
249	*D'Wayne Bates*	4.00
250	*David Boston*	12.00
251	*Dameane Douglas*	2.00
252	*Troy Edwards*	8.00
253	*Kevin Johnson*	5.00
254	*Peerless Price*	6.00
255	*Antoine Winfield*	4.00
256	*Michael Cloud*	4.00
257	*Joe Montgomery*	5.00
258	*Jermaine Fazande*	2.00
259	*Scott Covington*	2.00
260	*Aaron Brooks*	4.00
261	*Patrick Kerney*	2.00
262	*Cecil Collins*	15.00
263	*Chris Greisen*	2.00
264	*Craig Yeast*	2.00
265	*Karsten Bailey*	4.00
266	*Reginald Kelly*	2.00
267	*Travis McGriff*	2.00
268	*Jeff Paulk*	4.00
269	*Jim Kleinsasser*	2.00
270	*Darrin Chiaverini*	2.00

1999 Upper Deck Exclusives Silver

This is a parallel to the base set and is the same card except for on the bottom of the card the words "UD Exclusives" are printed on it along with the sequential numbering to 100 on gold foil.

	MT
UDE Cards:	20x-40x
UDE Rookies:	3x
Production 100 Sets	

1999 Upper Deck Exclusives Gold

This is a parallel to the base set with each single sequentially numbered to only 1.

	MT
Production 1 Set	

1999 Upper Deck Game Jersey

Singles from this 11-card set were inserted in both hobby and retail product at 1:2,500 packs. Each single has a piece of actual game-used (or rookie photo shoot-used) jersey on the fronts of the cards. Both Terrell Davis and Cade McNown signed cards to their jersey numbers of 30 and 8.

		MT
Complete Set (11):		2500.
Common Player:		100.00
Inserted 1:2,500		
JA	Jamal Anderson	100.00
DB	Drew Bledsoe	225.00
TC	Tim Couch	425.00
TC-A	Tim Couch Auto.	
TD	Terrell Davis	400.00
TD-A	Terrell Davis Auto.	
DF	Doug Flutie	175.00
EJ	Edgerrin James	350.00
KJ	Keyshawn Johnson	150.00
DM	Dan Marino	400.00
RM	Randy Moss	500.00
AS	Akili Smith	200.00
SY	Steve Young	175.00

1999 Upper Deck Game Jersey Hobby

This 12-card insert could only be found in hobby products at 1:288 packs. Each single includes a piece of game-used (or rookie photo shoot-used) jersey on the fronts of the cards. Both Tim Couch and Brock Huard signed cards to their jersey number of 2 and 5.

		MT
Complete Set (12):		1700.
Common Player:		60.00
Inserted 1:288		
TA	Troy Aikman	200.00
DV	David Boston	100.00
DC	Daunte Culpepper	150.00
JE	John Elway	250.00
BH	Brock Huard	60.00
BH-A	Brock Huard Auto.	
PM	Peyton Manning	250.00
MC	Donovan McNabb	150.00
CM	Cade McNown	150.00
CM-A	Cade McNown Auto.	
EM	Eric Moulds	60.00
JP	Jake Plummer	200.00
JR	Jerry Rice	200.00
BS	Barry Sanders	300.00

1999 Upper Deck Game Jersey Patch

Each single in this 20-card set has a piece of the team logo from the jersey on the card. Singles were inserted 1:7,500 packs.

		MT
Common Player:		150.00
Inserted 1:7,500		
TA	Troy Aikman	450.00
JA	Jamal Anderson	150.00
DB	Drew Bledsoe	400.00
DV	David Boston	200.00
TC	Tim Couch	800.00
DC	Daunte Culpepper	300.00
TD	Terrell Davis	600.00
JE	John Elway	700.00
DF	Doug Flutie	350.00
BH	Brock Huard	150.00
EJ	Edgerrin James	600.00
PM	Peyton Manning	600.00
DM	Dan Marino	600.00
DV	Donovan McNabb	300.00
CM	Cade McNown	300.00
RM	Randy Moss	850.00
JR	Jerry Rice	450.00
BS	Barry Sanders	750.00
AS	Akili Smith	300.00
SY	Steve Young	375.00

1999 Upper Deck Highlight Zone

This 20-card insert spotlights the top players in the NFL. Singles were printed on a foil board and found 1:23 packs. A Silver parallel was printed and sequentially numbered to 100, along with a Gold numbered to only 1.

		MT
Complete Set (20):		170.00
Common Player:		2.00
Inserted 1:23		
Quantum Silver:		5x-10x
Production 100 Sets		
Quantum Gold		
Production 1 Set		
1	Terrell Davis	15.00
2	Ricky Williams	20.00
3	Akili Smith	8.00
4	Charlie Batch	4.00
5	Jake Plummer	10.00
6	Emmitt Smith	15.00
7	Dan Marino	15.00
8	Tim Couch	20.00
9	Randy Moss	20.00
10	Troy Aikman	10.00
11	Barry Sanders	20.00
12	Jerry Rice	10.00
13	Mark Brunell	8.00
14	Jamal Anderson	2.00
15	Peyton Manning	12.00
16	Jerome Bettis	2.00
17	Donovan McNabb	8.00
18	Steve Young	6.00
19	Keyshawn Johnson	4.00
20	Brett Favre	20.00

1999 Upper Deck Livewires

Each card in this 15-card set has actual printed transcripts of statements made by big-name players during games. Singles were inserted 1:10 packs. A Silver parallel was produced and numbered to 100, along with a Gold that was limited to only one set.

		MT
Complete Set (15):		50.00
Common Player:		1.00
Inserted 1:10		
Quantum Silver:		10x-20x
Production 100 Sets		
Quantum Gold:		
Production 1 Set		
1	Jake Plummer	4.00
2	Jamal Anderson	1.00
3	Emmitt Smith	6.00
4	John Elway	6.00
5	Barry Sanders	8.00
6	Brett Favre	8.00
7	Mark Brunell	3.00
8	Fred Taylor	4.00
9	Randy Moss	8.00
10	Drew Bledsoe	3.00
11	Keyshawn Johnson	2.00
12	Jerome Bettis	2.00
13	Kordell Stewart	2.00
14	Terrell Owens	2.00
15	Eddie George	2.00

1999 Upper Deck PowerDeck I

Each of these singles are an interactive card that comes to life with game-action footage, sound, photos and career highlights of the featured player. Singles were found 1:288 packs.

	MT
Complete Set (8):	325.00
Common Player:	25.00
Inserted 1:288	
TC-PDTim Couch	60.00
DC-PDDaunte Culpepper	25.00
JE-PDJohn Elway	60.00
PM-PDPeyton Manning	60.00
DM-PDDan Marino	60.00
CM-PDCade McNown	25.00
BS-PDBarry Sanders	75.00
AS-PDAkili Smith	25.00

1999 Upper Deck PowerDeck II

Each single in this set is an interactive card with game-action footage, sound, photos and career highlights of that featured player. Singles were found 1:24 packs.

	MT
Complete Set (8):	45.00
Common Player:	2.00
Inserted 1:24	
TA-PDTroy Aikman	8.00
TD-PDTerrell Davis	12.00
JG-PDJoe Germaine	2.00
BH-PDBrock Huard	2.00
SK-PDShaun King	4.00
Mc-PDDonovan McNabb	8.00
JM-PDJoe Montana	8.00
RM-PDRandy Moss	16.00

1999 Upper Deck Quarterback Class

This 15-card insert includes the top QB's in the NFL along with rookies from 1999. Singles were found 1:10 packs. A parallel Silver was numbered to 100 and a parallel Gold was limited to only one set.

		MT
Complete Set (15):		50.00
Common Player:		1.00
Inserted 1:10		
Quantum Silver		10x-20x
Production 100 Sets		
Quantum Gold		
Production 1 Set		
1	Tim Couch	10.00
2	Akili Smith	4.00
3	Daunte Culpepper	4.00
4	Cade McNown	4.00
5	Donovan McNabb	4.00
6	Brock Huard	1.00
7	John Elway	6.00
8	Dan Marino	6.00
9	Brett Favre	8.00
10	Charlie Batch	2.00
11	Steve Young	2.50
12	Jake Plummer	4.00
13	Peyton Manning	6.00
14	Mark Brunell	3.00
15	Troy Aikman	4.00

1999 Upper Deck Strike Force

This 30-card set includes the top scoring threats in the NFL and brings them to life on a silver-foil board card. Singles were inserted 1:4 packs. A parallel Silver was sequentially numbered to 100 and a Gold parallel was issued with only one set made.

		MT
Complete Set (30):		50.00
Common Player:		1.00
Inserted 1:4		
1	Jamal Anderson	1.00
2	Keyshawn Johnson	2.00
3	Eddie George	2.50
4	Steve Young	2.50
5	Emmitt Smith	4.00
6	Karim Abdul	1.00
7	Kordell Stewart	2.50
8	Cade McNown	3.50
9	Tim Couch	8.00
10	Corey Dillon	2.00
11	Peyton Manning	5.00
12	Curtis Martin	2.00
13	Jerome Bettis	2.00
14	Jon Kitna	2.00
15	Dan Marino	5.00
16	Eric Moulds	2.00
17	Charlie Batch	2.50
18	Ricky Williams	8.00
19	Terrell Owens	2.00
20	Ty Detmer	1.00
21	Curtis Enis	2.00
22	Doug Flutie	2.50
23	Randall Cunningham	2.00
24	Donovan McNabb	3.50
25	Steve McNair	2.50
26	Terrell Davis	5.00
27	Daunte Culpepper	3.50
28	Warrick Dunn	2.00
29	Akili Smith	3.50
30	Barry Sanders	6.00

1999 Upper Deck 21 TD Salute

This 10-card insert is a salute to Denver running back Terrell Davis for becoming the fourth NFL player in history to run for more than 2,000 yards in a single season. He also set a Broncos' franchise record with 21 rushing touchdowns. Singles were found 1:23 packs. A parallel Silver set was made and sequentially numbered to 100 and a Gold limited to only one.

		MT
Complete Set (10):		60.00
Common Player:		6.00
Inserted 1:23		
Quantum Silver:		8x-16x
Production 100 Sets		
Quantum Gold		
Production 1 Set		
1	Terrell Davis	6.00
2	Terrell Davis	6.00
3	Terrell Davis	6.00
4	Terrell Davis	6.00
5	Terrell Davis	6.00
6	Terrell Davis	6.00
7	Terrell Davis	6.00
8	Terrell Davis	6.00
9	Terrell Davis	6.00
10	Terrell Davis	6.00

1999 Upper Deck MVP

MVP Football is a 220-card set that includes 20 unseeded rookie cards. Three different parallel sets were made with Gold Script, Silver Script and Super Script. Other inserts include: Draw Your Own Card, Drive Time, Dynamics, Game Used Souvenirs, Power Surge, Strictly Business and Theatre.

		MT
Complete Set (220):		40.00
Common Player:		.10
Wax Box:		45.00
1	Jake Plummer	1.00
2	Adrian Murrell	.10
3	Larry Centers	.10
4	Frank Sanders	.10
5	Andre Wadsworth	.20
6	Rob Moore	.20
7	Simeon Rice	.10
8	Jamal Anderson	.50
9	Chris Chandler	.20
10	Chuck Smith	.10
11	Terance Mathis	.10
12	Tim Dwight	.50
13	Ray Buchanan	.10
14	O.J. Santiago	.10
15	Eric Zeier	.10
16	Priest Holmes	.50
17	Michael Jackson	.10
18	Jermaine Lewis	.20
19	Michael McCrary	.10
20	Rob Johnson	.20
21	Antowain Smith	.50
22	Thurman Thomas	.20
23	Doug Flutie	.75
24	Eric Moulds	.30
25	Bruce Smith	.10
26	Andre Reed	.20
27	Fred Lane	.10
28	Tshimanga Biakabutuka	.20
29	Rae Carruth	.10
30	Wesley Walls	.10
31	Steve Beuerlein	.10
32	Muhsin Muhammad	.10
33	Erik Kramer	.10
34	Edgar Bennett	.10
35	Curtis Conway	.20
36	Curtis Enis	.50
37	Bobby Engram	.10
38	Alonzo Mayes	.10
39	Corey Dillon	.50
40	Jeff Blake	.20
41	Carl Pickens	.20
42	Darnay Scott	.10
43	Tony McGee	.10
44	Ki-Jana Carter	.20
45	Ty Detmer	.20
46	Terry Kirby	.10
47	Justin Armour	.10
48	Freddie Solomon	.10
49	Marquez Pope	.10
50	Antonio Langham	.10
51	Troy Aikman	1.00
52	Emmitt Smith	1.50
53	Deion Sanders	.50
54	Raghib Ismail	.10
55	Michael Irvin	.20
56	Chris Warren	.20
57	Greg Ellis	.10
58	John Elway	1.50
59	Terrell Davis	1.50
60	Rod Smith	.20
61	Shannon Sharpe	.20
62	Ed McCaffrey	.20
63	John Mobley	.10
64	Bill Romanowski	.10
65	Barry Sanders	2.00
66	Johnnie Morton	.10
67	Herman Moore	.50
68	Charlie Batch	.75
69	Germane Crowell	.20
70	Robert Porcher	.10
71	Brett Favre	2.00
72	Antonio Freeman	.50
73	Dorsey Levens	.50
74	Mark Chmura	.20
75	Vonnie Holliday	.20
76	Bill Schroeder	.10
77	Marshall Faulk	.50
78	Marvin Harrison	.20
79	Peyton Manning	1.50
80	Jerome Pathon	.10
81	E.G. Green	.10
82	Ellis Johnson	.10
83	Mark Brunell	.75
84	Jimmy Smith	.20
85	Keenan McCardell	.10
86	Fred Taylor	1.00
87	James Stewart	.10
88	Kevin Hardy	.10
89	Elvis Grbac	.10
90	Andre Rison	.20
91	Derrick Alexander	.10
92	Tony Gonzalez	.20
93	Donnell Bennett	.10
94	Derrick Thomas	.20
95	Tamarick Vanover	.10
96	Dan Marino	1.50
97	Karim Abdul	.50
98	Zach Thomas	.20
99	O.J. McDuffie	.20
100	John Avery	.20
101	Sam Madison	.10
102	Randall Cunningham	.50
103	Cris Carter	.50
104	Robert Smith	.50
105	Randy Moss	2.00
106	Jake Reed	.10
107	Matthew Hatchette	.10
108	John Randle	.20
109	Drew Bledsoe	.75
110	Terry Glenn	.50
111	Ben Coates	.20
112	Ty Law	.10
113	Tony Simmons	.20
114	Ted Johnson	.10
115	Danny Wuerffel	.20
116	Lamar Smith	.10
117	Sean Dawkins	.10
118	Cameron Cleeland	.20
119	Joe Johnson	.10
120	Andre Hastings	.10
121	Kent Graham	.10
122	Gary Brown	.10
123	Amani Toomer	.10
124	Tiki Barber	.20
125	Ike Hilliard	.20
126	Jason Sehorn	.10
127	Vinny Testeverde	.20
128	Curtis Martin	.50
129	Keyshawn Johnson	.50
130	Wayne Chrebet	.50
131	Mo Lewis	.10
132	Steve Atwater	.10
133	Donald Hollas	.10
134	Napoleon Kaufman	.50
135	Tim Brown	.20
136	Darrell Russell	.10
137	Rickey Dudley	.20
138	Charles Woodson	.50
139	Koy Detmer	.10
140	Duce Staley	.10
141	Charlie Garner	.10
142	Doug Pederson	.10
143	Jeff Graham	.10
144	Charles Johnson	.10
145	Kordell Stewart	.75
146	Jerome Bettis	.50
147	Hines Ward	.20
148	Courtney Hawkins	.10
149	Will Blackwell	.10
150	Richard Huntley	.10
151	Levon Kirkland	.10
152	Trent Green	.30
153	Tony Banks	.20
154	Isaac Bruce	.30
155	Eddie Kennison	.20
156	Az-Zahir Hakim	.20
157	Amp Lee	.10
158	Robert Holcombe	.20
159	Ryan Leaf	.75
160	Natrone Means	.50
161	Jim Harbaugh	.20
162	Junior Seau	.20
163	Charlie Jones	.10
164	Rodney Harrison	.10
165	Steve Young	.75
166	Jerry Rice	1.00
167	Garrison Hearst	.30
168	Terrell Owens	.50
169	J.J. Stokes	.20
170	Bryant Young	.10
171	Ricky Watters	.30
172	Joey Galloway	.50
173	Jon Kitna	.50
174	Ahman Green	.20
175	Mike Pritchard	.10
176	Chad Brown	.10
177	Warrick Dunn	.75
178	Trent Dilfer	.20
179	Mike Alstott	.50
180	Reidel Anthony	.20
181	Bert Emanuel	.10
182	Jacquez Green	.20
183	Hardy Nickerson	.10
184	Steve McNair	.50
185	Eddie George	.75
186	Yancey Thigpen	.20
187	Frank Wycheck	.10
188	Kevin Dyson	.20
189	Jackie Harris	.10
190	Blaine Bishop	.10
191	Skip Hicks	.20
192	Michael Westbrook	.20
193	Stephen Alexander	.10
194	Leslie Shepherd	.10
195	Casey Weldon	.10
196	Brian Mitchell	.10
197	Dan Wilkinson	.10
198	Checklist Card #1 Terrell Davis CL	.50
199	Checklist Car #2 Troy Aikman CL	.30
200	Checklist Card #3 Tim Couch CL	3.00
201	*Ricky Williams*	10.00
202	*Tim Couch*	10.00
203	*Akili Smith*	4.00
204	*Daunte Culpepper*	4.00
205	*Torry Holt*	2.50
206	*Edgerrin James*	5.00
207	*David Boston*	2.50
208	*Peerless Price*	1.75
209	*Chris Claiborne*	1.00
210	*Champ Bailey*	1.25
211	*Cade McNown*	3.50
212	*Jevon Kearse*	.50
213	*Joe Germaine*	1.50
214	*D'Wayne Bates*	.75
215	*Dameane Douglas*	.75
216	*Troy Edwards*	1.75
217	*Sedrick Irvin*	1.25
218	*Brock Huard*	1.50
219	*Amos Zereoue*	1.75
220	*Donovan McNabb*	4.00

1999 Upper Deck MVP Gold Script

This is a parallel to the base set and is the same except for the players facsimile signature on the front in gold foil along with all the other foil in gold too. On the back the hologram is in gold foil and each single is sequentially numbered to 100.

	MT
Gold Cards:	30x-60x
Gold Rookies:	10x-20x
Production 100 Sets	

1999 Upper Deck MVP Silver Script

This is a parallel to the base and is the same except for the players facsimile autograph on the front in silver foil and the words Silver Script on the back. Singles were inserted 1:2 packs.

	MT
Complete Set (220):	120.00
Silver Cards:	4x
Silver Rookies:	2x
Inserted 1:2	

1999 Upper Deck MVP Super Script

This is a parallel to the base set and each single has a holo foil facsimile signature of the player on the front and each is sequentially numbered to 25.

	MT
Super Cards:	75x-150x
Super Rookies:	20x-40x
Production 25 Sets	

1999 Upper Deck MVP Draw Your Own

Each single from this 30-card set is a drawing from a young collector from a previous contest winner. Singles were inserted 1:6 packs.

		MT
Complete Set (30):		18.00
Common Player:		.20
Inserted 1:6		
1	Brett Favre	2.00
2	Emmitt Smith	1.50
3	John Elway	1.50
4	Emmitt Smith	1.50
5	Randy Moss	2.00
6	Terrell Davis	1.50
7	Steve Young	.75
8	Drew Bledsoe	.75
9	Troy Aikman	1.00
10	Terry Allen	.20
11	Warrick Dunn	.75
12	Kimble Anders	.20
13	Joey Galloway	.40
14	Barry Sanders	2.00
15	Mark Brunell	.75
16	Bruce Smith	.20
17	Randy Moss	2.00
18	Jerome Bettis	.40
19	John Elway	1.50
20	Jerome Bettis	.40
21	Brett Favre	2.00
22	Troy Aikman	1.00
23	Cris Carter	.75
24	Jason Gildon	.20
25	Randall Cunningham	.75
26	Thurman Thomas	.40
27	Jerry Rice	1.00
28	Jerome Bettis	.40
29	Steve Young	.75
30	Reggie White	.40

1999 Upper Deck MVP Drive Time

Each card in this 14-card set pays tribute to a star player who led the best offensive drive during the 1998 season. Singles were found 1:6 packs.

		MT
Complete Set (14):		10.00
Common Player:		.50
Inserted 1:6		
1	Steve Young	1.50
2	Kordell Stewart	1.25
3	Eric Moulds	1.00
4	Corey Dillon	1.00
5	Doug Flutie	1.50
6	Charlie Batch	1.50
7	Curtis Martin	1.00
8	Marshall Faulk	1.00
9	Terrell Owens	1.25
10	Antowain Smith	1.00
11	Troy Aikman	2.50
12	Drew Bledsoe	1.50
13	Keyshawn Johnson	1.00
14	Steve McNair	1.25

1999 Upper Deck MVP Dynamics

This 15-card set includes the top players in the NFL and puts them on a holo foil card. Singles were inserted 1:28 packs.

		MT
Complete Set (15):		65.00
Common Player:		2.00
Inserted 1:28		
1	John Elway	10.00
2	Steve Young	6.00
3	Jake Plummer	7.50
4	Fred Taylor	7.50
5	Mark Brunell	6.00
6	Joey Galloway	2.00
7	Terrell Davis	10.00
8	Randy Moss	15.00
9	Charlie Batch	5.00
10	Peyton Manning	10.00
11	Barry Sanders	15.00
12	Eddie George	5.00
13	Warrick Dunn	4.00
14	Jamal Anderson	2.00
15	Brett Favre	15.00

1999 Upper Deck MVP Game-Used Souvenirs

Each card in this 21-card set includes a piece of a game-used football by that player pictured on the card. Singles were inserted 1:130 packs.

		MT
Complete Set (21):		1400.
Common Player:		50.00
Inserted 1:130		
BS	Barry Sanders	160.00
ES	Emmitt Smith	120.00
DF	Doug Flutie	65.00
KJ	Keyshawn Johnson	60.00
JP	Jake Plummer	85.00
JE	John Elway	150.00
PM	Peyton Manning	125.00

RM	Randy Moss	175.00
TD	Terrell Davis	125.00
JA	Jamal Anderson	60.00
MC	Donovan McNabb	75.00
AS	Akili Smith	65.00
EJ	Edgerrin James	85.00
BH	Brock Huard	50.00
TH	Torry Holt	60.00
CB	Champ Bailey	50.00
DB	David Boston	60.00
DC	Daunte Culpepper	80.00
CM	Cade McNown	80.00
DM	Dan Marino	150.00

1999 Upper Deck MVP Power Surge

The game's most impressive talents are highlighted in this 15-card set. Each foil card was inserted 1:9 packs.

		MT
Complete Set (15):		20.00
Common Player		.75
Inserted 1:9		
1	Jerome Bettis	1.50
2	Eddie George	2.00
3	Karim Abdul	.75
4	Curtis Martin	1.50
5	Antowain Smith	1.75
6	Kordell Stewart	1.75
7	Curtis Enis	1.50
8	Joey Galloway	1.50
9	Mark Brunell	2.50
10	Peyton Manning	4.00
11	Antonio Freeman	1.50
12	Jerry Rice	3.50
13	Eric Moulds	1.50
14	Drew Bledsoe	2.00
15	Fred Taylor	3.50

1999 Upper Deck MVP Strictly Business

Only the top players in the game were included in this 13-card insert. Singles were found 1:14 packs.

		MT
Complete Set (15):		45.00
Common Player:		2.00
Inserted 1:14		
1	Eddie George	3.00
2	Curtis Martin	2.00
3	Fred Taylor	5.00
4	Steve Young	3.00
5	Kordell Stewart	3.00
6	Corey Dillon	2.00
7	Dan Marino	7.50
8	Jake Plummer	4.00
9	Jerry Rice	5.00
10	Warrick Dunn	3.00
11	Jerome Bettis	2.00
12	John Elway	7.50
13	Randy Moss	10.00
14	Troy Aikman	5.00
15	Brett Favre	10.00

1999 Upper Deck MVP Theatre

Each card in this 15-card set pictures a star player in action. Singles were inserted 1:9 packs.

		MT
Complete Set (15):		20.00
Common Player:		.75
Inserted 1:9		
1	Terrell Davis	5.00
2	Corey Dillon	1.50
3	Brett Favre	6.00
4	Jerry Rice	3.00
5	Emmitt Smith	4.00
6	Dan Marino	4.00
7	Jerome Bettis	.75
8	Napoleon Kaufman	1.50
9	Keyshawn Johnson	1.50
10	Warrick Dunn	1.50
11	Barry Sanders	6.00
12	Troy Aikman	3.00
13	Jamal Anderson	1.50
14	Randall Cunningham	.75
15	Doug Flutie	1.75

1999 Victory

This was the premiere edition of Victory Football. The 440-card set included 60 rookie cards found one-per-pack. This was a retail-only release that didn't include any inserts. Subsets included: All-Victory, Season Leaders, Victory Parade, Rookie Flashback and '99 Rookie Class.

		MT
Complete Set (440):		70.00
Common Player:		.10
Common Rookie:		.50
Inserted 1:1		
Wax Box:		35.00
1	Arizona Cardinals visit	.10
2	Jake Plummer	.75
3	Adrian Murrell	.10
4	Michael Pittman	.10
5	Frank Sanders	.20
6	Andre Wadsworth	.10
7	Rob Moore	.20
8	Simeon Rice	.10
9	Kwamie Lassiter	.10
10	Mario Bates	.10
11	Atlanta Falcons visit	.10
12	Jamal Anderson	.30
13	Chris Chandler	.20
14	Chuck Smith	.10
15	Terance Mathis	.10
16	Tim Dwight	.30
17	Ray Buchanan	.10
18	O.J. Santiago	.10
19	Lester Archambeau	.10
20	Baltimore Ravens visit	.10
21	Tony Banks	.20
22	Priest Holmes	.30
23	Michael Jackson	.10
24	Jermaine Lewis	.20
25	Michael McCrary	.10
26	Rod Woodson	.10
27	Buffalo Bills visit	.10
28	Rob Johnson	.20
29	Antowain Smith	.30
30	Thurman Thomas	.20
31	Doug Flutie	.50
32	Eric Moulds	.30
33	Bruce Smith	.10
34	Andre Reed	.20
35	Phil Hansen	.10
36	Carolina Panthers visit	.10
37	Fred Lane	.10
38	Tshimanga Biakabutuka	.10
39	Rae Carruth	.10
40	Wesley Walls	.10
41	Steve Beuerlein	.10
42	Muhsin Muhammad	.10
43	Kevin Greene	.10
44	Chicago Bears visit	.10
45	Erik Kramer	.10
46	Edgar Bennett	.10
47	Curtis Conway	.20
48	Curtis Enis	.30
49	Bobby Engram	.10
50	Alonzo Mayes	.10
51	Tony Parrish	.10
52	Glyn Milburn	.10
53	Cincinnati Bengals visit	.10
54	Corey Dillon	.30
55	Jeff Blake	.20
56	Carl Pickens	.20
57	Darnay Scott	.10
58	Tony McGee	.10
59	Ki-Jana Carter	.10
60	Takeo Spikes	.10
61	Cleveland Browns visit	.10
62	Ty Detmer	.10
63	Terry Kirby	.10
64	Derrick Alexander	.10
65	Leslie Shepherd	.10
66	Marquez Pope	.10
67	Antonio Langham	.10
68	Marc Edwards	.10
69	Dallas Cowboys visit	.10
70	Troy Aikman	1.00
71	Emmitt Smith	1.50
72	Deion Sanders	.30
73	Raghib Ismail	.10
74	Michael Irvin	.20
75	Chris Warren	.10
76	Greg Ellis	.10
77	Kavika Pittman	.10
78	David LaFleur	.10
79	Denver Broncos visit	.10
80	John Elway	1.50
81	Terrell Davis	1.50
82	Rod Smith	.20
83	Shannon Sharpe	.20
84	Ed McCaffrey	.20
85	John Mobley	.10
86	Bill Romanowski	.10
87	Jason Elam	.10
88	Howard Griffith	.10
89	Detroit Lions visit	.10
90	Barry Sanders	2.00
91	Johnnie Morton	.10
92	Herman Moore	.30
93	Charlie Batch	.50
94	Germane Crowell	.20
95	Robert Porcher	.10
96	Stephen Boyd	.10
97	Green Bay Packers visit	.10
98	Brett Favre	2.00
99	Antonio Freeman	.30
100	Dorsey Levens	.30
101	Mark Chmura	.20
102	Vonnie Holliday	.20
103	Bill Schroeder	.10
104	LeRoy Butler	.10
105	William Henderson	.10
106	Indianapolis Colts visit	.10
107	Peyton Manning	1.50
108	Marvin Harrison	.30
109	Ken Dilger	.10
110	Jerome Pathon	.10
111	E.G. Green	.10
112	Ellis Johnson	.10
113	Jeff Burris	.10
114	Jacksonville Jaguars visit	.10
115	Mark Brunell	.75
116	Jimmy Smith	.20
117	Keenan McCardell	.10
118	Fred Taylor	1.00
119	James Stewart	.10
120	Dave Thomas	.10
121	Kyle Brady	.10
122	Bryce Paup	.10
123	Kansas City Chiefs visit	.10
124	Elvis Grbac	.20
125	Andre Rison	.20
126	Derrick Alexander	.10
127	Tony Gonzalez	.20
128	Donnell Bennett	.10
129	Derrick Thomas	.20
130	Tamarick Vanover	.10
131	Donnie Edwards	.10
132	Miami Dolphins visit	.10
133	Dan Marino	1.50
134	Karim Abdul	.30
135	Zach Thomas	.20
136	O.J. McDuffie	.20
137	John Avery	.20
138	Sam Madison	.10
139	Terrell Buckley	.10
140	Jason Taylor	.10
141	Oronde Gadsden	.20
142	Minnesota Vikings visit	.10
143	Randall Cunningham	.30
144	Cris Carter	.30
145	Robert Smith	.20
146	Randy Moss	2.00
147	Jake Reed	.10
148	Leroy Hoard	.10
149	Matthew Hatchette	.10
150	John Randle	.10
151	Gary Anderson	.10
152	New England Patriots visit	.10
153	Drew Bledsoe	.75
154	Terry Glenn	.30
155	Ben Coates	.20
156	Ty Law	.10
157	Tony Simmons	.20
158	Ted Johnson	.10
159	Willie McGinest	.10
160	Tony Carter	.10
161	Shawn Jefferson	.10
162	New Orleans Saints visit	.10
163	Danny Wuerffel	.20
164	Lamar Smith	.10
165	Keith Poole	.10
166	Cameron Cleeland	.20
167	Joe Johnson	.10
168	Andre Hastings	.10
169	La'Roi Glover	.10
170	Aaron Craver	.10
171	New York Giants visit	.10
172	Kent Graham	.20
173	Gary Brown	.20
174	Amani Toomer	.10
175	Tiki Barber	.10
176	Ike Hilliard	.10
177	Jason Sehorn	.10
178	Michael Strahan	.10
179	Charles Way	.10
180	New York Jets visit	.10
181	Vinny Testaverde	.20
182	Curtis Martin	.30
183	Keyshawn Johnson	.30
184	Wayne Chrebet	.30
185	Mo Lewis	.10
186	Steve Atwater	.10
187	Leon Johnson	.10
188	Bryan Cox	.10
189	Oakland Raiders visit	.10
190	Rich Gannon	.10
191	Napoleon Kaufman	.30
192	Tim Brown	.30
193	Darrell Russell	.10
194	Rickey Dudley	.10
195	Charles Woodson	.30
196	Harvey Williams	.10
197	James Jett	.10
198	Philadelphia Eagles visit	.10
199	Koy Detmer	.10
200	Duce Staley	.20
201	Bobby Taylor	.10
202	Doug Pederson	.10
203	Karl Hankton	.10
204	Charles Johnson	.10
205	Kevin Turner	.10
206	Hugh Douglas	.10
207	Pittsburgh Steelers visit	.10
208	Kordell Stewart	.50
209	Jerome Bettis	.30
210	Hines Ward	.20
211	Courtney Hawkins	.10
212	Will Blackwell	.10
213	Richard Huntley	.10
214	Levon Kirkland	.10
215	Jason Gildon	.10
216	St. Louis Rams visit	.10
217	Trent Green	.30
218	Isaac Bruce	.20
219	Az Hakim	.20
220	Amp Lee	.10
221	Robert Holcombe	.20
222	Ricky Proehl	.10
223	Kevin Carter	.10
224	Marshall Faulk	.30
225	San Diego Chargers visit	.10
226	Ryan Leaf	.30
227	Natrone Means	.30
228	Jim Harbaugh	.20
229	Junior Seau	.20
230	Charlie Jones	.10
231	Rodney Harrison	.10
232	Terrell Fletcher	.10
233	Tremayne Stephens	.10
234	San Francisco 49ers visit	.10
235	Steve Young	.75
236	Jerry Rice	1.00
237	Garrison Hearst	.30
238	Terrell Owens	.30
239	J.J. Stokes	.20
240	Bryant Young	.10
241	Tim McDonald	.10
242	Merton Hanks	.10
243	Travis Jervey	.10
244	Seattle Seahawks visit	.10
245	Ricky Watters	.20
246	Joey Galloway	.30
247	Jon Kitna	.30
248	Ahman Green	.20
249	Mike Pritchard	.10
250	Chad Brown	.10
251	Christian Fauria	.10
252	Michael Sinclair	.10
253	Tampa Bay Bucs visit	.10
254	Warrick Dunn	.30
255	Trent Dilfer	.20
256	Mike Alstott	.30
257	Reidel Anthony	.20
258	Bert Emanuel	.10
259	Jacquez Green	.20
260	Hardy Nickerson	.10
261	Derrick Brooks	.10
262	Dave Moore	.10
263	Tennessee Titans visit	.10
264	Steve McNair	.30
265	Eddie George	.50
266	Yancey Thigpen	.20
267	Frank Wycheck	.10
268	Kevin Dyson	.20
269	Jackie Harris	.10
270	Blaine Bishop	.10
271	Willie Davis	.10
272	Washington 'Skins visit	.10
273	Skip Hicks	.20
274	Michael Westbrook	.20
275	Stephen Alexander	.10
276	Dana Stubblefield	.10
277	Brad Johnson	.30
278	Brian Mitchell	.10
279	Dan Wilkinson	.10
280	Stephen Davis	.20
281	John Elway (All-Victory Team)	.50
282	Dan Marino (All-Victory Team)	.50
283	Troy Aikman (All-Victory Team)	.30
284	Vinny Testaverde (All-Victory Team)	.10
285	Corey Dillon (All-Victory Team)	.10
286	Steve Young (All-Victory Team)	.20
287	Randy Moss (All-Victory Team)	.75
288	Drew Bledsoe (All-Victory Team)	.30
289	Jerome Bettis (All-Victory Team)	.10
290	Antonio Freeman (All-Victory Team)	.10
291	Fred Taylor (All-Victory Team)	.30
292	Doug Flutie (All-Victory Team)	.10
293	Jerry Rice (All-Victory Team)	.30
294	Peyton Manning (All-Victory Team)	.50
295	Brett Favre (All-Victory Team)	.50
296	Barry Sanders (All-Victory Team)	.50
297	Keyshawn Johnson (All-Victory Team)	.10
298	Mark Brunell (All-Victory Team)	.20
299	Jamal Anderson (All-Victory Team)	.10
300	Terrell Davis (All-Victory Team)	.50
301	Randall Cunningham (All-Victory Team)	.10
302	Kordell Stewart (All-Victory Team)	.10
303	Warrick Dunn (All-Victory Team)	.10
304	Jake Plummer (All-Victory Team)	.20
305	Junior Seau (All-Victory Team)	.10
306	Antowain Smith (All-Victory Team)	.10
307	Charlie Batch (All-Victory Team)	.20
308	Eddie George (All-Victory Team)	.20
309	Michael Irvin (All-Victory Team)	.10
310	Joey Galloway (All-Victory Team)	.10
311	Randall Cunningham (Season Leaders)	.10
312	Vinny Testaverde (Season Leaders)	.10
313	Steve Young (Season Leaders)	.20
314	Chris Chandler (Season Leaders)	.10
315	John Elway (Season Leaders)	.50
316	Steve Young (Season Leaders)	.20
317	Randall Cunningham (Season Leaders)	.10
318	Brett Favre (Season Leaders)	.50
319	Vinny Testaverde (Season Leaders)	.10

320 Peyton Manning (Season Leaders) .50
321 Terrell Davis (Season Leaders) .50
322 Jamal Anderson (Season Leaders) .10
323 Garrison Hearst (Season Leaders) .10
324 Barry Sanders (Season Leaders) .50
325 Emmitt Smith (Season Leaders) .30
326 Terrell Davis (Season Leaders) .50
327 Fred Taylor (Season Leaders) .30
328 Jamal Anderson (Season Leaders) .10
329 Emmitt Smith (Season Leaders) .30
330 Ricky Watters (Season Leaders) .10
331 O.J. McDuffie (Season Leaders) .10
332 Frank Sanders (Season Leaders) .10
333 Rod Smith (Season Leaders) .10
334 Marshall Faulk (Season Leaders) .10
335 Antonio Freeman (Season Leaders) .10
336 Randy Moss (Season Leaders) .75
337 Antonio Freeman (Season Leaders) .10
338 Terrell Owens (Season Leaders) .10
339 Cris Carter (Season Leaders) .10
340 Terance Mathis (Season Leaders) .10
341 Jake Plummer (Victory Parade) .20
342 Steve McNair (Victory Parade) .10
343 Randy Moss (Victory Parade) .75
344 Peyton Manning (Victory Parade) .50
345 Mark Brunell (Victory Parade) .20
346 Terrell Owens (Victory Parade) .10
347 Antowain Smith (Victory Parade) .10
348 Jerry Rice (Victory Parade) .30
349 Troy Aikman (Victory Parade) .30
350 Fred Taylor (Victory Parade) .30
351 Charlie Batch (Victory Parade) .10
352 Dan Marino (Victory Parade) .50
353 Eddie George (Victory Parade) .20
354 Drew Bledsoe (Victory Parade) .20
355 Kordell Stewart (Victory Parade) .10
356 Doug Flutie (Victory Parade) .10
357 Deion Sanders (Victory Parade) .10
358 Keyshawn Johnson (Victory Parade) .10
359 Jerome Bettis (Victory Parade) .10
360 Warrick Dunn (Victory Parade) .10
361 John Elway (Rookie Flashback) .50
362 Dan Marino (Rookie Flashback) .50
363 Brett Favre (Rookie Flashback) .50
364 Andre Rison (Rookie Flashback) .10
365 Rod Woodson (Rookie Flashback) .10
366 Jerry Rice (Rookie Flashback) .30
367 Barry Sanders (Rookie Flashback) .50
368 Thurman Thomas (Rookie Flashback) .10
369 Troy Aikman (Rookie Flashback) .30
370 Ricky Watters (Rookie Flashback) .10
371 Jerome Bettis (Rookie Flashback) .10
372 Reggie White (Rookie Flashback) .10
373 Junior Seau (Rookie Flashback) .10
374 Deion Sanders (Rookie Flashback) .10
375 Chris Chandler (Rookie Flashback) .10
376 Curtis Martin (Rookie Flashback) .10
377 Kordell Stewart (Rookie Flashback) .10
378 Mark Brunell (Rookie Flashback) .20
379 Cris Carter (Rookie Flashback) .10
380 Emmitt Smith (Rookie Flashback) .30
381 *Tim Couch* 12.00
382 *Donovan McNabb* 5.00
383 *Akili Smith* 4.00
384 *Edgerrin James* 7.00
385 *Ricky Williams* 12.00
386 *Torry Holt* 3.00
387 *Champ Bailey* 2.00
388 *David Boston* 3.00
389 *Chris Claiborne* 1.00
390 *Chris McAlister* 1.00
391 *Daunte Culpepper* 5.00
392 *Cade McNown* 5.00
393 *Troy Edwards* 3.00
394 *John Tait* .50
395 *Anthony McFarland* 1.00
396 *Jevon Kearse* 1.00
397 *Damien Woody* .50
398 *Matt Stinchcomb* .50
399 *Luke Petitgout* .50
400 *Ebenezer Ekuban* 1.00
401 *L.J. Shelton* .50
402 *Marty Booker* .50
403 *Antoine Winfield* 1.00
404 *Scott Covington* 1.00
405 *Antwan Edwards* 1.00
406 *Fernando Bryant* .50
407 *Aaron Gibson* .50
408 *Andy Katzenmoyer* 1.50
409 *Dimitrius Underwood* 1.00
410 *Patrick Kerney* .50
411 *Al Wilson* .50
412 *Kevin Johnson* 2.00
413 *Joel Makovicka* 1.00
414 *Reginald Kelly* .50
415 *Jeff Paulk* 1.00
416 *Brandon Stokley* 1.00
417 *Peerless Price* 3.00
418 *D'Wayne Bates* 1.50
419 *Travis McGriff* 1.50
420 *Sedrick Irvin* 2.00
421 *Aaron Brooks* 1.50
422 *Michael Cloud* 1.50
423 *Joe Montgomery* 1.50
424 *Shaun King* 2.50
425 *Dameane Douglas* 1.00
426 *Joe Germaine* 2.00
427 *James Johnson* 2.00
428 *Michael Bishop* 2.50
429 *Karsten Bailey* 1.00
430 *Craig Yeast* 1.00
431 *Jim Kleinsasser* 1.00
432 *Martin Gramatica* 1.00
433 *Jermaine Fazande* 1.00
434 *Dre' Bly* 1.00
435 *Brock Huard* 2.00
436 *Rob Konrad* 1.50
437 *Tony Bryant* 1.00
438 *Sean Bennett* 2.00
439 *Kevin Faulk* 3.00
440 *Amos Zereoue* 2.50

Market Report

The Great One Says Goodbye, Stars Win The Stanley Cup

The 1998-99 season will be remembered as the farewell season of Wayne Gretzky. The Great One didn't announce his retirement until shortly prior to the last game of the season. He capped off his incomparable career with his 1,963rd assist and 2,857th point in his final game April 18. There was no farewell tour, but the unassuming Great One wanted it that way.

Now the question remains: who will lead hockey into the next century? Most fingers point to Jaromir Jagr, who took home the Hart Trophy (MVP) and Art Ross Trophy (leading scorer) after the 1998-99 season. As great a player as Gretzky was, his role as hockey's ambassador in helping expand the game to bigger markets in the southern U.S. is immeasurable. Without Gretzky, the NHL still has plenty of great stars. But whether those stars will put together the kind of performance that drives sales of hockey card products in the future remains to be seen.

It's unfair to expect any player to duplicate Gretzky's achievements, both in terms of statistics and hobby stature. No player will ever fill the skates of the Great One, but Jagr has emerged as the most dominant player in game. No player has the power and ability to influence a game's outcome more than Jagr. Other young superstars who will be counted on to help carry the torch into the next century include Mike Modano, Eric Lindros and Paul Kariya.

STARS WIN STANLEY CUP

The Stanley Cup left hockey's heartland for Dallas as the Stars took home the hardware after beating the Buffalo Sabres 4-2 in the Finals. The Stars were led by Modano, Brett Hull and Ed Belfour. The Stars became the first southern market team to win the Stanley Cup.

Modano's rookie cards received a boost as his 1990-91 O-Pee-Chee Premier (No. 74) jumped from a $6 card to $15 over the course of the season. Post-season success also led to increased activity for Hull's 1988-89 Topps (No. 66, $25) and O-Pee-Chee (No. 66, $50) rookie cards and Belfour's 1990-91 Upper Deck rookie (No. 55, $3).

ROOKIE SEARCH

Although the past several seasons haven't produced an impact rookie season like Teemu Selanne's rookie record-breaking season with the Winnipeg Jets in 1992-93, when he scored an incredible 76 goals in 84 games, hockey collectors will always pursue rookie cards of hockey's most promising prospects. The 1998-99 season produced a number of rookie prospects that collectors sought after, including the 1998-99 Calder Trophy winner and former Hobey Baker award winner Chris Drury, who recorded a modest 20 goals and 44 points with the Colorado Avalanche. His only rookie card, 1995-96 Upper Deck (No. 569) catapaulted from 50 cents to $10 over the course of the season.

Another Avalanche rookie who caught the eye of collectors was Milan Hejduk, who finished the 1998-99 season with 48 points. His short-printed 1998-99 SP Authentic rookie (No. 95) jumped from $3 to $15 over the course of the season. His other key rookie cards include 1998-99 Bowman's Best (No. 110, $6), Upper Deck (No. 247, $1.50) and Topps Gold Label (No. 90, $2).

FEWER BRANDS, MORE SALES

As the 1998-99 NHL season began, many card dealers were cautiously hoping for an upswing in sales. With the NBA lockout continuing, but after a disappointing 1997-98 season, there was only cautious optimism. Due to the absence of Pinnacle/Donruss, overall sales could be expected to be down. But according to Ted Saskin, the NHLPA's senior director/business affairs and licensing, sales were up on a per-manufacturer basis.

"I'm very pleased with the performance of our licensees this year," Saskin said. "With the departure of Pinnacle/Donruss, it was clear that there would be some transitional issues and inventory issues that needed to be addressed in the marketplace. It's good to see that our current licensees are having a better year than they did last year. We want to continue to approach the market cautiously and assess things after we see the full-season results."

Some eyebrows were raised in the industry when Fleer/SkyBox issued a statement saying it didn't feel the hockey card market was strong enough to warrant another try at a hockey license. "I certainly disagree with that assessment," Saskin said. "The performance of our current licensees is up this year. In terms of the health of the marketplace, I'm very comfortable. Sales are down, but it's only a little, and in light of how much Pinnacle and Donruss were into the marketplace, the fact that our other licensees were able to pick up that slack is very encouraging."

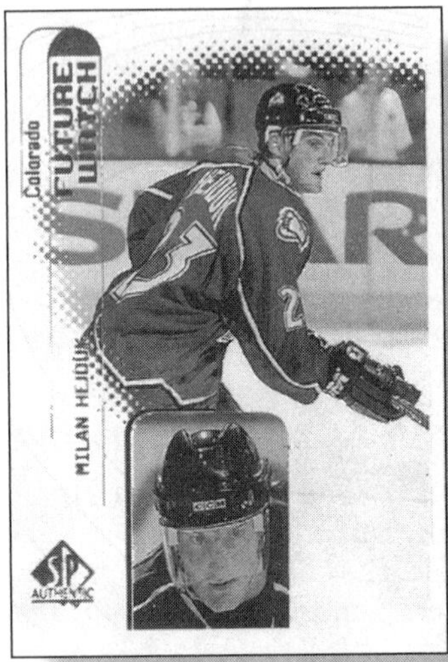

TOPPS RE-ENTERS THE HOBBY

After a one-year absence from the hockey market, Topps re-entered the market producing five different brands (Bowman's Best, Finest, O-Pee-Chee Chrome, Topps and Topps Gold Label). Topps rejoined Upper Deck, In The Game and Pacific as the only licensees to produce hockey cards in 1998-99.

THE FUTURE

Hockey has always taken a backseat to the other three major sports for collectors. With the absence of the "Great One," hockey must find a way to attract more collectors and fans. A lack of scoring and impact rookies has been a problem, although the NHL addressed the scoring issue by eliminating the instant replay on crease violations and going four-on-four in overtime periods. Overall, scoring for the 1999-00 season is slightly up, so the changes seem to be having some impact, though it's still too early to tell. The NHL also needs to infuse youth and more excitement into the game to attract the more casual fan. Hopefully young prospects like Patrik Stefan, Vincent Lecavalier, Hejduk, Chris Drury and Steve Kariya can live up to the billing placed on their

PLAYER OF THE YEAR

Full Name: Wayne Douglas Gretzky
Hometown: Brantford, Ontario
Height: 6'0"
Weight: 170
College: None
Birthdate: 1/26/61
Drafted: Signed as an underage free agent by Indianapolis (WHA), June 12, 1978.

Wayne Gretzky

CARDS TO GET: Gretzky has two rookie cards: 1979-80 O-Pee-Chee (#18, $800) and Topps (#18, $550). He also has a number of desirable autographed inserts including 1998-99 SP Authentic Sign of the Times (#WG, $400), 1999-00 UD Retro Inkredible (#WG, $400) and 1999-00 Upper Deck MVP Pro Sign (#WG, $300) to name a few.

TOP TENS

REGULAR-ISSUE SINGLES

1. Wayne Gretzky	1979-80 O-Pee-Chee (#18)	$800
2. Wayne Gretzky	1979-80 Topps (#18)	$550
3. Jaromir Jagr	1990-91 O-Pee-Chee Premier (#50)	$30
4. Mike Modano	1990-91 O-Pee-Chee Premier (#74)	$15
5. Steve Yzerman	1984-85 O-Pee-Chee (#67)	$90
6. Brett Hull	1988-89 O-Pee-Chee (#66)	$50
7. Chris Drury	1995-96 Upper Deck (#569)	$10
8. Dominik Hasek	1991-92 Upper Deck (#335)	$8
9. Milan Hejduk	1998-99 SP Authentic (#95)	$15
10. Dominik Hasek	1991-92 Parkhurst (#263)	$8

REGULAR-ISSUE SETS

1. 1979-80 O-Pee-Chee		396-card set: $900
2. 1979-80 Topps		264-card set: $575
3. 1998-99 SP Authentic	$100/box	135-card set: $240
4. 1990-91 O-Pee-Chee Premier	$125	132-card set: $100
5. 1998-99 Bowman's Best	$100	150-card set: $90
6. 1998-99 Be A Player All-Star	$120	150-card set: $75
7. 1984-85 O-Pee-Chee	$100	396-card set: $230
8. 1998-99 O-Pee-Chee Chrome	$65	242-card set: $150
9. 1988-89 O-Pee-Chee		264-card set: $175
10. 1998-99 Upper Deck	$55	420-card set: $165

HOCKEY

1998-99 Be A Player

Be A Player was issued in two 150-card series: All-Star and Playoff. The base cards are printed on silver foil with a touch of silver etching. Backs have a small player photo, career highlight, 1997-98 statistics and career totals. A Gold parallel version is randomly inserted and have gold tinted fronts and a touch of gold etching.

		MT
	Complete Set (300):	105.00
	Complete Series I (150):	75.00
	Complete Series II (150):	30.00
	Common Player:	.40
	Golds:	1.5x to 3x
1	Jason Marshall	.40
2	Paul Kariya	6.00
3	Teemu Selanne	2.50
4	Guy Hebert	1.00
5	Ted Drury	.40
6	Byron Dafoe	1.00
7	Rob Dimaio	.40
8	Ray Bourque	1.50
9	Joe Thornton	1.00
10	Sergei Samsonov	2.50
11	Dimitri Khristich	.40
12	Michael Peca	.40
13	Jason Woolley	.40
14	Matthew Barnaby	.40
15	Brian Holzinger	.40
16	Dixon Ward	.40
17	Tyler Moss	.40
18	Jarome Iginla	.40
19	Marty McInnis	.40
20	Andrew Cassels	.40
21	Jason Wiemer	.40
22	Trevor Kidd	1.00
23	Keith Primeau	1.00
24	Sami Kapanen	.75
25	Robert Kron	.40
26	Glen Wesley	.40
27	Jeff Hackett	1.00
28	Tony Amonte	1.00
29	Alexei Zhamnov	.40
30	Eric Weinrich	.40
31	Jeff Shantz	.40
32	Christian Laflamme	.40
33	Adam Foote	.40
34	Patrick Roy	8.00
35	Peter Forsberg	5.00
36	Adam Deadmarsh	.75
37	Joe Sakic	3.00
38	Eric Lacroix	.40
39	Guy Carbonneau	.40
40	Mike Modano	2.50
41	Roman Turek	.40
42	Mike Keane	.40
43	Sergei Zubov	.40
44	Jere Lehtinen	.40
45	Sergei Fedorov	2.50
46	Steve Yzerman	5.00
47	Chris Osgood	1.50
48	Larry Murphy	.40
49	Vyacheslav Kozlov	.40
50	Darren McCarty	.40
51	Boris Mironov	.40
52	Roman Hamrlik	.40
53	Bill Guerin	.40
54	Mike Grier	.40
55	Todd Marchant	.40
56	Ray Whitney	.40
57	Dave Gagner	.40
58	Scott Mellanby	.40
59	Robert Svehla	.40
60	Viktor Kozlov	.40
61	Luc Robitaille	.75
62	Yanic Perreault	.40
63	Jozef Stumpel	.40
64	Sandy Moger	.40
65	Ian Laperriere	.40
66	Jocelyn Thibault	1.00
67	Dave Manson	.40
68	Mark Recchi	.40
69	Patrick Poulin	.40
70	Benoit Brunet	.40
71	Turner Stevenson	.40
72	Mike Dunham	.75
73	Tom Fitzgerald	.40
74	Darren Turcotte	.40
75	Brad Smyth	.40
76	J.J. Daigneault	.40
77	Dave Andreychuk	.75
78	Jason Arnott	.40
79	Martin Brodeur	3.00
80	Randy McKay	.40
81	Patrik Elias	.40
82	Kevin Dean	.40
83	Tommy Salo	1.00
84	Scott Lachance	.40
85	Bryan Berard	.75
86	Robert Reichel	.40
87	Kenny Jonsson	.40
88	Kevin Stevens	.40
89	Mike Richter	1.50
90	Wayne Gretzky	10.00
91	Adam Graves	.75
92	Alexei Kovalev	.40
93	Ulf Samuelsson	.40
94	Radek Bonk	.40
95	Wade Redden	.40
96	Damian Rhodes	1.00
97	Bruce Gardiner	.40
98	Daniel Alfredsson	.75
99	Ron Hextall	1.00
100	Eric Lindros	6.00
101	Chris Gratton	.40
102	Dainius Zubrus	.40
103	Luke Richardson	.40
104	Petr Svoboda	.40
105	Rick Tocchet	.40
106	Teppo Numminen	.40
107	Jeremy Roenick	1.50
108	Nikolai Khabibulin	1.50
109	Brad Isbister	.40
110	Peter Skudra	.40
111	Alexei Morozov	.40
112	Kevin Hatcher	.40
113	Darius Kasparaitis	.40
114	Stu Barnes	.40
115	Martin Straka	.75
116	Andrei Zyuzin	.40
117	Marcus Ragnarsson	.40
118	Murray Craven	.40
119	Marco Sturm	.40
120	Patrick Marleau	2.00
121	Shawn Burr	.40
122	Grant Fuhr	1.50
123	Chris Pronger	1.00
124	Geoff Courtnall	.40
125	Jim Campbell	.40
126	Pavol Demitra	1.00
127	Todd Gill	.40
128	Cory Cross	.40
129	Daymond Langkow	.40
130	Alexander Selivanov	.40
131	Mikael Renberg	.40
132	Rob Zamuner	.40
133	Stephane Richer	.40
134	Fredrik Modin	.40
135	Derek King	.40
136	Mats Sundin	2.00
137	Mike Johnson	.40
138	Alyn McCauley	.40
139	Jason Smith	.40
140	Markus Naslund	.75
141	Alexander Mogilny	1.50
142	Mattias Ohlund	.40
143	Donald Brashear	.40
144	Garth Snow	1.00
145	Brian Bellows	.40
146	Peter Bondra	2.00
147	Joe Juneau	.40
148	Steve Konowalchuk	.40
149	Ken Klee	.40
150	Michal Pivonka	.40
151	Steve Rucchin	.40
152	Stu Grimson	.40
153	Tomas Sandstrom	.40
154	Fredrik Olausson	.40
155	Travis Green	.40
156	Jason Allison	.75
157	Steve Heinze	.40
158	Rob Tallas	.40
159	Darren Van Impe	.40
160	Ken Baumgartner	.40
161	Peter Ferraro	.40
162	Dominik Hasek	3.00
163	Geoff Sanderson	.40
164	Miroslav Satan	.40
165	Rob Ray	.40
166	Alexei Zhitnik	.40
167	Phil Housley	.40
168	Theoren Fleury	.75
169	Ken Wregget	.40
170	Valeri Bure	.40
171	Rico Fata	1.50
172	Arturs Irbe	.75
173	Sean Hill	.40
174	Ron Francis	.75
175	Jeff O'Neill	.40
176	Paul Ranheim	.40
177	Paul Coffey	.75
178	Doug Gilmour	.75
179	Eric Daze	.40
180	Chris Chelios	1.00
181	Bob Probert	.40
182	Mark Fitzpatrick	.40
183	Alexei Gusarov	.40
184	Sylvain Lefebvre	.40
185	Craig Billington	.75
186	Valeri Kamensky	.40
187	Milan Hejduk	2.50
188	Sandis Ozolinsh	.40
189	Brett Hull	2.00
190	Ed Belfour	1.50
191	Darryl Sydor	.40
192	Sergey Gusev	.40
193	Joe Nieuwendyk	.75
194	Derian Hatcher	.40
195	Brendan Shanahan	2.50
196	Tomas Holmstrom	.40
197	Nicklas Lidstrom	1.00
198	Martin Lapointe	.40
199	Igor Larionov	.40
200	Kris Draper	.40
201	Kelly Buchberger	.40
202	Andrei Kovalenko	.40
203	Josef Beranek	.40
204	Mikhail Shtalenkov	.75
205	Pat Falloon	.40
206	Mark Parrish	4.00
207	Terry Carkner	.40
208	Rob Niedermayer	.40
209	Sean Burke	.75
210	*Oleg Kvasha*	2.00
211	Pavel Bure	2.50
212	Rob Blake	.40
213	Vladimir Tsyplakov	.40
214	Stephane Fiset	.75
215	Steve Duchesne	.40
216	Patrice Brisebois	.40
217	Vincent Damphousse	.40
218	Saku Koivu	.75
219	Jose Theodore	.75
220	Bret Clark	.40
221	Martin Rucinsky	.40
222	Vladimir Malakhov	.40
223	Sergei Krivokrasov	.40
224	Scott Walker	.40
225	Greg Johnson	.40
226	Cliff Ronning	.40
227	Eric Fichaud	.75
228	Bob Carpenter	.40
229	Scott Daniels	.40
230	Brian Rolston	.40
231	Sergei Bylin	.40
232	Scott Niedermayer	.40
233	Bryan Smolinski	.40
234	Trevor Linden	.40
235	Eric Brewer	.40
236	Zigmund Palffy	1.50
237	Sergei Nemchinov	.40
238	Brian Leetch	1.00
239	Mathieu Schneider	.40
240	Niklas Sundstrom	.40
241	Manny Malhotra	1.00
242	Jeff Beukeboom	.40
243	Peter Nedved	.40
244	Ron Tugnutt	.75
245	Shaun Van Allen	.40
246	Alexei Yashin	.75
247	Jason York	.40
248	Shawn McEachern	.40
249	Marian Hossa	.40
250	John LeClair	2.50
251	Rod Brind'Amour	.75
252	John Vanbiesbrouck	2.00
253	Eric Desjardins	.40
254	Valeri Zelepukin	.40
255	Karl Dykhuis	.40
256	Keith Tkachuk	1.50
257	Dallas Drake	.40
258	Oleg Tverdovsky	.40
259	Jyrki Lumme	.40
260	Jimmy Waite	.40
261	Jaromir Jagr	6.00
262	German Titov	.40
263	Robert Lang	.40
264	Brad Werenka	.40
265	Rob Brown	.40
266	Bobby Dollas	.40
267	Jeff Friesen	.40
268	Andy Sutton	.40
269	Steve Shields	.75
270	Mike Ricci	.40
271	Joe Murphy	.40
272	Tony Granato	.40
273	Jamie McLennan	.75
274	Al MacInnis	.75
275	Pierre Turgeon	.75
276	Kelly Chase	.40
277	Craig Conroy	.40
278	Scott Young	.40
279	Vincent Lecavalier	6.00
280	Wendel Clark	.40
281	Daren Puppa	.40
282	Sandy McCarthy	.40
283	Daniil Markov	.40
284	Curtis Joseph	1.50
285	Sergei Berezin	.40
286	Steve Sullivan	.40
287	Thomas Kaberle	.40
288	Kris King	.40
289	Igor Korolev	.40
290	Mark Messier	2.00
291	Bill Muckalt	2.00
292	Todd Bertuzzi	.40
293	Brad May	.40
294	Peter Zezel	.40
295	Dmitri Mironov	.40
296	Adam Oates	.75
297	Calle Johansson	.40
298	Craig Berube	.40
299	Sergei Gonchar	.40
300	Andrei Nikolishin	.40

1998-99 Be A Player Autographs

Autographs are seeded one per pack and have identical fronts to the base cards besides the autograph. Card backs have a small photo and on the bottom half has "Congratulations ..." written. A Gold parallel was also randomly seeded with gold foil fronts and limited to a stated production of 50 sets for short-printed players.

		MT
	Complete Set (300):	
	Common Player:	5.00
	Golds:	1.5x to 3x
1	Jason Marshall	5.00
2	Paul Kariya	275.00
3	Teemu Selanne	150.00
4	Guy Hebert	15.00
5	Ted Drury	5.00
6	Byron Dafoe	15.00
7	Rob Dimaio	5.00
8	Ray Bourque	85.00
9	Joe Thornton	20.00
10	Sergei Samsonov	40.00
11	Dimitri Khristich	10.00
12	Michael Peca	10.00
13	Jason Woolley	5.00
14	Matthew Barnaby	10.00
15	Brian Holzinger	5.00
16	Dixon Ward	5.00
17	Tyler Moss	5.00
18	Jarome Iginla	15.00
19	Marty McInnis	5.00
20	Andrew Cassels	5.00
21	Jason Wiemer	5.00
22	Trevor Kidd	15.00
23	Keith Primeau	25.00
24	Sami Kapanen	15.00
25	Robert Kron	5.00
26	Glen Wesley	5.00
27	Jeff Hackett	20.00
28	Tony Amonte	25.00
29	Alexei Zhamnov	5.00
30	Eric Weinrich	5.00
31	Jeff Shantz	5.00
32	Christian Laflamme	5.00
33	Adam Foote	10.00
34	Patrick Roy	275.00
35	Peter Forsberg	200.00
36	Adam Deadmarsh	10.00
37	Joe Sakic	140.00
38	Eric Lacroix	5.00
39	Guy Carbonneau	5.00
40	Mike Modano	70.00
41	Roman Turek	15.00
42	Mike Keane	5.00
43	Sergei Zubov	10.00
44	Jere Lehtinen	10.00
45	Sergei Fedorov	125.00
46	Steve Yzerman	225.00
47	Chris Osgood	25.00
48	Larry Murphy	10.00
49	Vyacheslav Kozlov	10.00
50	Darren McCarty	10.00
51	Boris Mironov	5.00
52	Roman Hamrlik	10.00
53	Bill Guerin	10.00
54	Mike Grier	10.00
55	Todd Marchant	5.00
56	Ray Whitney	5.00
57	Dave Gagner	5.00
58	Scott Mellanby	5.00
59	Robert Svehla	5.00
60	Viktor Kozlov	10.00
61	Luc Robitaille	20.00
62	Yanic Perreault	5.00
63	Jozef Stumpel	10.00
64	Sandy Moger	5.00
65	Ian Laperriere	5.00
66	Jocelyn Thibault	15.00
67	Dave Manson	5.00
68	Mark Recchi	10.00
69	Patrick Poulin	5.00
70	Benoit Brunet	5.00
71	Turner Stevenson	5.00
72	Mike Dunham	15.00
73	Tom Fitzgerald	5.00
74	Darren Turcotte	5.00
75	Brad Smyth	5.00
76	J.J. Daigneault	5.00
77	Dave Andreychuk	10.00
78	Jason Arnott	10.00
79	Martin Brodeur	140.00
80	Randy McKay	5.00
81	Patrik Elias	10.00
82	Kevin Dean	5.00
83	Tommy Salo	15.00
84	Scott Lachance	5.00
85	Bryan Berard	15.00
86	Robert Reichel	5.00
87	Kenny Jonsson	10.00
88	Kevin Stevens	10.00
89	Mike Richter	30.00
90	Wayne Gretzky	700.00
91	Adam Graves	10.00
92	Alexei Kovalev	10.00
93	Ulf Samuelsson	10.00
94	Radek Bonk	10.00
95	Wade Redden	5.00
96	Damian Rhodes	20.00
97	Bruce Gardiner	5.00
98	Daniel Alfredsson	15.00
99	Ron Hextall	15.00
100	Eric Lindros	225.00
101	Chris Gratton	10.00
102	Dainius Zubrus	10.00
103	Luke Richardson	5.00
104	Petr Svoboda	5.00
105	Rick Tocchet	15.00
106	Teppo Numminen	10.00
107	Jeremy Roenick	40.00
108	Nikolai Khabibulin	25.00
109	Brad Isbister	5.00
110	Peter Skudra	5.00
111	Alexei Morozov	5.00
112	Kevin Hatcher	5.00
113	Darius Kasparaitis	5.00
114	Stu Barnes	5.00
115	Martin Straka	10.00
116	Andrei Zyuzin	5.00
117	Marcus Ragnarsson	5.00
118	Murray Craven	5.00
119	Marco Sturm	5.00
120	Patrick Marleau	30.00
121	Shawn Burr	5.00
122	Grant Fuhr	25.00
123	Chris Pronger	15.00
124	Geoff Courtnall	5.00
125	Jim Campbell	5.00
126	Pavol Demitra	15.00
127	Todd Gill	5.00
128	Cory Cross	5.00
129	Daymond Langkow	5.00
130	Alexander Selivanov	5.00
131	Mikael Renberg	10.00
132	Rob Zamuner	5.00
133	Stephane Richer	5.00
134	Fredrik Modin	5.00
135	Derek King	5.00
136	Mats Sundin	75.00

137	Mike Johnson	10.00
138	Alyn McCauley	5.00
139	Jason Smith	5.00
140	Markus Naslund	10.00
141	Alexander Mogilny	15.00
142	Mattias Ohlund	10.00
143	Donald Brashear	10.00
144	Garth Snow	15.00
145	Brian Bellows	5.00
146	Peter Bondra	40.00
147	Joe Juneau	10.00
148	Steve Konowalchuk	5.00
149	Ken Klee	5.00
150	Michal Pivonka	5.00
151	Steve Rucchin	5.00
152	Stu Grimson	5.00
153	Tomas Sandstrom	8.00
154	Fredrik Olausson	5.00
155	Travis Green	10.00
156	Jason Allison	15.00
157	Steve Heinze	5.00
158	Rob Tallas	5.00
159	Darren Van Impe	5.00
160	Ken Baumgartner	5.00
161	Peter Ferraro	5.00
162	Dominik Hasek	125.00
163	Geoff Sanderson	5.00
164	Miroslav Satan	10.00
165	Rob Ray	10.00
166	Alexei Zhitnik	5.00
167	Phil Housley	8.00
168	Theoren Fleury	25.00
169	Ken Wregget	10.00
170	Valeri Bure	8.00
171	Rico Fata	10.00
172	Arturs Irbe	15.00
173	Sean Hill	5.00
174	Ron Francis	20.00
175	Jeff O'Neill	5.00
176	Paul Ranheim	5.00
177	Paul Coffey	15.00
178	Doug Gilmour	15.00
179	Eric Daze	10.00
180	Chris Chelios	50.00
181	Bob Probert	8.00
182	Mark Fitzpatrick	5.00
183	Alexei Gusarov	5.00
184	Sylvain Lefebvre	5.00
185	Craig Billington	8.00
186	Valeri Kamensky	5.00
187	Milan Hejduk	10.00
188	Sandis Ozolinsh	8.00
189	Brett Hull	70.00
190	Ed Belfour	50.00
191	Darryl Sydor	10.00
192	Sergey Gusev	5.00
193	Joe Nieuwendyk	10.00
194	Derian Hatcher	10.00
195	Brendan Shanahan	90.00
196	Tomas Holmstrom	5.00
197	Nicklas Lidstrom	15.00
198	Martin Lapointe	5.00
199	Igor Larionov	5.00
200	Kris Draper	5.00
201	Kelly Buchberger	5.00
202	Andrei Kovalenko	5.00
203	Josef Beranek	5.00
204	Mikhail Shtalenkov	5.00
205	Pat Falloon	5.00
206	Mark Parrish	15.00
207	Terry Carkner	5.00
208	Rob Niedermayer	5.00
209	Sean Burke	10.00
210	*Oleg Kvasha*	12.00
211	Pavel Bure	100.00
212	Rob Blake	10.00
213	Vladimir Tsyplakov	5.00
214	Stephane Fiset	10.00
215	Steve Duchesne	8.00
216	Patrice Brisebois	5.00
217	Vincent Damphousse	8.00
218	Saku Koivu	15.00
219	Jose Theodore	10.00
220	Bret Clark	5.00
221	Martin Rucinsky	5.00
222	Vladimir Malakhov	5.00
223	Sergei Krivokrasov	5.00
224	Scott Walker	5.00
225	Greg Johnson	5.00
226	Cliff Ronning	5.00
227	Eric Fichaud	8.00
228	Bob Carpenter	5.00
229	Scott Daniels	5.00
230	Brian Rolston	5.00
231	Sergei Bylin	5.00
232	Scott Niedermayer	5.00
233	Bryan Smolinski	5.00
234	Trevor Linden	8.00
235	Eric Brewer	5.00
236	Zigmund Palffy	40.00
237	Sergei Nemchinov	5.00
238	Brian Leetch	40.00
239	Mathieu Schneider	5.00
240	Niklas Sundstrom	5.00
241	Manny Malhotra	15.00
242	Jeff Beukeboom	5.00
243	Peter Nedved	8.00
244	Ron Tugnutt	10.00
245	Shaun Van Allen	5.00
246	Alexei Yashin	20.00
247	Jason York	5.00
248	Shawn McEachern	5.00
249	Marian Hossa	5.00
250	John LeClair	90.00
251	Rod Brind'Amour	15.00
252	John Vanbiesbrouck	50.00
253	Eric Desjardins	5.00
254	Valeri Zelepukin	5.00
255	Karl Dykhuis	5.00
256	Keith Tkachuk	70.00
257	Dallas Drake	5.00
258	Oleg Tverdovsky	8.00
259	Jyrki Lumme	5.00
260	Jimmy Waite	5.00
261	Jaromir Jagr	150.00
262	German Titov	5.00
263	Robert Lang	5.00
264	Brad Werenka	5.00
265	Rob Brown	5.00
266	Bobby Dollas	5.00
267	Jeff Friesen	5.00
268	Andy Sutton	5.00
269	Steve Shields	10.00
270	Mike Ricci	8.00
271	Joe Murphy	8.00
272	Tony Granato	8.00
273	Jamie McLennan	10.00
274	Al MacInnis	20.00
275	Pierre Turgeon	12.00
276	Kelly Chase	5.00
277	Craig Conroy	5.00
278	Scott Young	5.00
279	Vincent Lecavalier	20.00
280	Wendel Clark	8.00
281	Daren Puppa	8.00
282	Sandy McCarthy	5.00
283	Daniil Markov	5.00
284	Curtis Joseph	40.00
285	Sergei Berezin	8.00
286	Steve Sullivan	5.00
287	Thomas Kaberle	5.00
288	Kris King	5.00
289	Igor Korolev	5.00
290	Mark Messier	80.00
291	Bill Muckalt	10.00
292	Todd Bertuzzi	5.00
293	Brad May	5.00
294	Peter Zezel	5.00
295	Dmitri Mironov	5.00
296	Adam Oates	40.00
297	Calle Johansson	5.00
298	Craig Berube	5.00
299	Sergei Gonchar	8.00
300	Andrei Nikolishin	5.00

1998-99 Be A Player All-Star Jersey

These inserts feature a piece of game-used All-Star jerseys from the featured player embedded into the card front. An announced production run of 100 sets was issued. Card backs are numbered with a "AS" prefix.

		MT
Complete Set (25):		7000.
Common Player:		150.00
AS-1	Eric Lindros	500.00
AS-2	Peter Forsberg	450.00
AS-3	Teemu Selanne	275.00
AS-4	Mike Modano	250.00
AS-5	Mats Sundin	250.00
AS-6	Patrick Roy	500.00
AS-7	Paul Kariya	600.00
AS-8	Martin Brodeur	300.00
AS-9	Steve Yzerman	500.00
AS-10	Mark Messier	250.00
AS-11	Paul Coffey	150.00
AS-12	Brett Hull	250.00
AS-13	Joe Sakic	400.00
AS-14	Alexander Mogilny	150.00
AS-15	Sergei Fedorov	250.00
AS-16	Ray Bourque	200.00
AS-17	Jeremy Roenick	200.00
AS-18	Jaromir Jagr	450.00
AS-19	Pavel Bure	250.00
AS-20	Dominik Hasek	300.00
AS-21	Chris Chelios	200.00
AS-22	John LeClair	300.00
AS-23	Brendan Shanahan	275.00
AS-24	Ed Belfour	250.00
AS-25	Wayne Gretzky	700.00

1998-99 Be A Player Game Used Jerseys

This 24-card set has a swatch from the featured player's game-used jersey embedded into the card front. A stated production run of 100 sets was announced. The Gretzky jersey is from a 1982-83 Edmonton Oilers jersey. Card backs are numbered with a "G" prefix.

		MT
Complete Set (24):		7500.
Common Player:		150.00
1	Wayne Gretzky	1000.
2	Mats Sundin	200.00
3	Jeremy Roenick	200.00
4	Eric Lindros	500.00
5	John LeClair	300.00
6	Joe Sakic	350.00
7	Peter Forsberg	500.00
8	Patrick Roy	600.00
9	Martin Brodeur	350.00
10	Pavel Bure	300.00
11	Teemu Selanne	300.00
12	Paul Kariya	600.00
13	Ray Bourque	150.00
14	Brendan Shanahan	300.00
15	Steve Yzerman	500.00
16	Sergei Fedorov	300.00
17	Mike Modano	300.00
18	Brett Hull	250.00
19	Ed Belfour	200.00
20	Mark Messier	250.00
21	Alexander Mogilny	150.00
22	Alexei Yashin	150.00
23	Jaromir Jagr	600.00
24	Tony Amonte	150.00

1998-99 Be A Player Game-Used Stick

Inserted in the first series (All-Star) these have a piece of game-used stick from the featured player embedded into the card front. An announced production of 100 sets was issued. Card backs are numbered with a "S" prefix.

		MT
Complete Set (23):		4000.
Common Player:		100.00
S-1	Eric Lindros	350.00
S-2	Peter Forsberg	200.00
S-3	Teemu Selanne	175.00
S-4	Mike Modano	150.00
S-5	Mats Sundin	150.00
S-6	Patrick Roy	400.00
S-7	Paul Kariya	400.00
S-8	Martin Brodeur	200.00
S-9	Steve Yzerman	300.00
S-10	Mark Messier	200.00
S-11	Brett Hull	150.00
S-12	Joe Sakic	200.00
S-13	Alexander Mogilny	100.00
S-14	Sergei Fedorov	150.00
S-15	Ray Bourque	125.00
S-16	Jeremy Roenick	125.00
S-17	Jaromir Jagr	250.00
S-18	Dominik Hasek	200.00
S-19	Chris Chelios	125.00
S-20	John LeClair	175.00
S-21	Brendan Shanahan	150.00
S-22	Ed Belfour	125.00
S-23	Wayne Gretzky	500.00

1998-99 Be A Player Legend Gordie Howe

Inserted in All-Star series packs, this set has a Gordie Howe game jersey card autographed and one Gordie Howe autographed card. A total of 90 of each card was issued.

		MT
Complete Set (2):		2500.
GH1	Gordie Howe G. Jer. Auto.	1700.
GH2	Gordie Howe Auto.	800.00

1998-99 Be A Player Legend Mario Lemieux

Randomly inserted in Playoff Series packs each of the cards in the four-card set are autographed and limited to 66 of each card. Card backs are numbered with a "L" prefix.

		MT
Common Lemieux:		1500.
1	Penguins jersey card	1500.
2	All-Star jersey card	1500.
3	Penguins jersey and stick card	2000.
4	All-Star jersey and stick card	2000.

1998-99 Be A Player Milestones

This set highlights players who reached a key career milestone of either 1,000 points or 500 goals. The card has perimeter die-cutting with rounded corners. The 1,000 point milestone cards have full silver foil fronts with a lightly etched 1000 throughout the background of the card. The 500 goal milestone cards have full gold foil fronts with a lightly etched 500 throughout the background. Card backs are numbered with a "M" prefix.

		MT
Complete Set (22):		100.00
Common Player:		3.00
M-1	Wayne Gretzky	25.00
M-2	Mark Messier	6.00
M-3	Dino Ciccarelli	3.00
M-4	Steve Yzerman	15.00
M-5	Dave Andreychuk	3.00
M-6	Brett Hull	6.00
M-7	Wayne Gretzky	25.00
M-8	Mark Messier	6.00
M-9	Dino Ciccarelli	3.00
M-10	Steve Yzerman	15.00
M-11	Bernie Nicholls	3.00
M-12	Ron Francis	4.00
M-13	Ray Bourque	5.00
M-14	Paul Coffey	4.00
M-15	Adam Oates	5.00
M-16	Phil Housley	3.00
M-17	Dale Hunter	3.00
M-18	Luc Robitaille	4.00
M-19	Doug Gilmour	4.00
M-20	Larry Murphy	3.00
M-21	Dave Andreychuk	3.00
M-22	Al MacInnis	4.00

1998-99 Be A Player Playoff Hilites

This 18-card set highlights a key playoff performance for the featured player. They are printed on a full foil front and are random inserts in packs.

		MT
Complete Set (18):		150.00
Common Player:		3.00
1	Mark Messier	6.00
2	Peter Forsberg	15.00
3	Wayne Gretzky	30.00
4	Martin Brodeur	8.00
5	Jaromir Jagr	20.00
6	Mike Richter	4.00
7	Steve Yzerman	15.00
8	Patrick Roy	25.00
9	Paul Coffey	3.00
10	Joe Sakic	10.00
11	John Vanbiesbrouck	6.00
12	Pavel Bure	8.00
13	Chris Osgood	4.00
14	Chris Chelios	4.00
15	Curtis Joseph	4.00
16	Brian Leetch	4.00
17	Sergei Fedorov	8.00
18	Doug Gilmour	3.00

1998-99 Be A Player Practice Used Jerseys

These inserts have a swatch from the featured player's practice jersey embedded into the card front. An announced production of 100 sets was produced. Card backs were numbered with a "P" prefix.

		MT
Complete Set (24):		6000.
Common Player:		100.00
1	Brett Hull	200.00
2	Alexander Mogilny	100.00
3	Ray Bourque	150.00
4	Pavel Bure	250.00
5	Steve Yzerman	400.00
6	Ed Belfour	200.00
7	Sergei Fedorov	250.00
8	Teemu Selanne	250.00
9	Eric Lindros	400.00
10	Jeremy Roenick	150.00
11	John LeClair	250.00
12	Mike Modano	250.00
13	Joe Sakic	300.00
14	Patrick Roy	500.00
15	Mark Messier	200.00
16	Paul Kariya	500.00
17	Martin Brodeur	300.00
18	Mats Sundin	200.00
19	Brendan Shanahan	250.00
20	Peter Forsberg	400.00
21	Alexei Yashin	100.00
22	Wayne Gretzky	750.00
23	Jaromir Jagr	500.00
24	Tony Amonte	100.00

1998-99 Bowman's Best

This 150-card set consists of 100 veteran stars with a gold foil design and 35 rookies and 14 CHL prospects on a silver foil design. Base cards are printed on 26-point stock. Card backs have a small photo, the featured player's 1997-98 stats along with his career totals. A brief career highlight is also given. Six-card packs have a $5 SRP.

		MT
Complete Set (150):		90.00
Common Player:		.25
Star Refractors:		10x to 20x
Yng Stars & RCs:		6x to 12x
Production 400 sets		
Atomic Star Refractors:		50x to 75x
Yng Stars & RCs:		25x to 40x
Production 100 sets		
1	Steve Yzerman	2.50
2	Paul Kariya	3.00
3	Wayne Gretzky	5.00
4	Jaromir Jagr	3.00
5	Mark Messier	1.00
6	Keith Tkachuk	1.00
7	John LeClair	1.25
8	Martin Brodeur	1.50
9	Rob Blake	.25
10	Brett Hull	1.00
11	Dominik Hasek	2.00
12	Peter Forsberg	2.50
13	Doug Gilmour	.50
14	Vincent Damphousse	.25
15	Zigmund Palffy	.75
16	Daniel Alfredsson	.25
17	Mike Vernon	.50
18	Chris Pronger	.50
19	Wendel Clark	.25
20	Curtis Joseph	.75
21	Peter Bondra	.75
22	Grant Fuhr	.75
23	Nikolai Khabibulin	.50
24	Kevin Hatcher	.25
25	Brian Leetch	.75
26	Patrik Elias	.25
27	Chris Osgood	.75
28	Patrick Roy	4.00
29	Chris Chelios	.75
30	Trevor Kidd	.50
31	Theoren Fleury	.40
32	Michael Peca	.25
33	Ray Bourque	.75
34	Ed Belfour	.75
35	Sergei Fedorov	1.25
36	Adrian Aucoin	.25
37	Alexei Yashin	.50
38	Rick Tocchet	.25
39	Mats Sundin	.75
40	Alexander Mogilny	.50
41	Jeff Friesen	.25
42	Eric Lindros	3.00
43	Mike Richter	.75
44	Saku Koivu	.50
45	Teemu Selanne	1.25
46	Doug Weight	.40
47	Nicklas Lidstrom	.50
48	Mike Modano	1.00
49	Joe Sakic	2.00

50	Ron Francis	.40
51	Jason Allison	.40
52	Brendan Shanahan	1.25
53	Bobby Holik	.25
54	Damian Rhodes	.50
55	Jeremy Roenick	.75
56	Tom Barrasso	.50
57	Al MacInnis	.50
58	Pavel Bure	1.25
59	Olaf Kolzig	.50
60	Patrick Marleau	1.00
61	Cliff Ronning	.25
62	Joe Nieuwendyk	.40
63	Jeff Hackett	.50
64	Keith Primeau	.50
65	Jarome Iginla	.25
66	Sergei Samsonov	1.00
67	Rod Brind'Amour	.40
68	Dino Ciccarelli	.25
69	Ryan Smyth	.25
70	Owen Nolan	.25
71	Mike Johnson	.25
72	Adam Oates	.50
73	Mattias Ohlund	.25
74	*Jamie Heward*	.75
75	Mike Dunham	.50
76	Jere Lehtinen	.25
77	Tony Amonte	.40
78	Derek Morris	.25
79	Darren McCarty	.40
80	Bryan Berard	.40
81	Adam Graves	.40
82	John Vanbiesbrouck	1.00
83	Marco Sturm	.25
84	Joe Thornton	.75
85	Wade Redden	.25
86	Pierre Turgeon	.40
87	Bill Ranford	.40
88	Alexei Zhitnik	.25
89	Valeri Kamensky	.25
90	Dean McAmmond	.25
91	Jozef Stumpel	.25
92	Jocelyn Thibault	.50
93	Joe Juneau	.25
94	Craig Janney	.25
95	Robert Reichel	.25
96	Mark Recchi	.25
97	Sami Kapanen	.40
98	Shayne Corson	.25
99	Scott Niedermayer	.25
100	Trevor Linden	.25
101	Olli Jokinen	.25
102	Chris Drury	.50
103	Dan Cleary	.25
104	Yan Golubovsky	.25
105	Brendan Morrison	.40
106	Manny Malhotra	1.50
107	Marian Hossa	.25
108	Daniel Briere	.25
109	Vincent Lecavalier	10.00
110	*Milan Hejduk*	6.00
111	Tom Poti	.25
112	*Mike Maneluk*	6.00
113	Marty Reasoner	.25
114	Rico Fata	2.00
115	Eric Brewer	.25
116	Dan Cloutier	.75
117	Mike Leclerc	.25
118	*Dimitri Tertyshny*	.50
119	*Josh Green*	1.00
120	*Mark Parrish*	10.00
121	Jamie Wright	.25
122	*Fred Lindquist*	1.50
123	*Daniil Markov*	.75
124	*Bill Muckalt*	.25
125	Johan Davidsson	.25
126	*Oleg Kvasha*	5.00
127	Cameron Mann	.25
128	*Pascal Trepanier*	.75
129	*Clark Wilm*	.75
130	*Alain Nasreddine*	.75
131	*Bryan Helmer*	.75
132	*Michal Handzus*	3.00
133	*Pavel Kubina*	1.00
134	*Matt Cooke*	.75
135	*Matt Higgins*	.75
136	David Legwand	10.00
137	*Brad Stuart*	1.00
138	*Mark Bell*	8.00
139	Eric Chouinard	2.00
140	Simon Gagne	.25
141	*Ramzi Abid*	6.00
142	Sergei Varlamov	5.00
143	*Mike Ribiero*	4.00
144	*Derrick Walser*	.50
145	Mathieu Garon	.25
146	Daniel Tkaczuk	2.00
147	*Jeff Heerema*	6.00
148	Sebastien Roger	.25
149	*Brett DeCecco*	.50
150	Checklist	.25

1998-99 Bowman's Best Refractors

Refractors are a parallel to the base set and have a mirror like sheen. To help identify the word "Refractor" is written under the card number on the back. They are limited to 400 sequentially numbered sets. Atomic Refractors are another parallel and appear to have a prism sheen. "Atomic Refractor" is written under the card number on the back to eliminate any doubt and they are also limited to 100 sequentially numbered sets.

	MT
Star Refractors:	10x to 20x
Yng Stars & RC's:	6x to 12x
Production 400 sets	
Atomic Star Refractors:	50x to 75x
Yng Stars & RC's:	25x to 40x
Production 100 sets	

1998-99 Bowman's Best Autograph Cards

Each of the ten players in this set have two different autographed versions and are numbered with a "A" or "B" suffix on the card back to identify each version. Each card has a Topps "Certified Autograph Issue" stamp for authenticity. They are seeded 1:97 packs. There are two parallel versions randomly seeded: Refractors and Atomic Refractors. Refractors are seeded 1:516 packs, while Atomic Refractors are seeded 1:1,549.

		MT
Common Player:		20.00
Inserted 1:97		
Refractors:		1.5x to 2x
Inserted 1:516		
Atomic Refractors:		2x to 3x
Inserted 1:1,549		
A1A	Dominik Hasek	90.00
A1B	Dominik Hasek	90.00
A2A	Jaromir Jagr	100.00
A2B	Jaromir Jagr	100.00
A3A	Peter Bondra	30.00
A3B	Peter Bondra	30.00
A4A	Sergei Fedorov	70.00
A4B	Sergei Fedorov	70.00
A5A	Ray Bourque	65.00
A5B	Ray Bourque	65.00
A6A	Bill Muckalt	20.00
A6B	Bill Muckalt	20.00
A7A	Brendan Morrison	25.00
A7B	Brendan Morrison	25.00
A8A	Chris Drury	25.00
A8B	Chris Drury	25.00
A9A	Mark Parrish	30.00
A9B	Mark Parrish	30.00
A10A	Manny Malhotra	30.00
A10B	Manny Malhotra	30.00

1998-99 Bowman's Best Mirror Image Fusion

Each card features a tandem of a veteran player and a rising prospect on the card front and back. These are numbered on the back with a "F" prefix and are seeded 1:12 packs. Two parallel versions are also randomly seeded: Refractor and Atomic Refractor. Refractors are limited to 100 numbered sets and have "Refractor" written under the card number. Atomic Refractors are limited to 25 numbered sets and have "Atomic Refractor" written under the card number.

		MT
Complete Set (20):		150.00
Common Player:		2.00
Inserted 1:12		
Refractors:		5x to 10x
Production 100 sets		
Atomic Refractors:		15x to 25x
Production 25 sets		
F1	John LeClair, Bates Battaglia	6.00
F2	Paul Kariya, Mike Leclerc	15.00
F3	Jaromir Jagr, Mark Parrish	15.00
F4	Teemu Selanne, Fred Lindquist	6.00
F5	Eric Lindros, Vincent Lecavalier	18.00
F6	Peter Forsberg, Olli Jokinen	12.00
F7	Brian Leetch, Daniil Markov	2.00
F8	Nicklas Lidstrom, Yan Golubovsky	2.00
F9	Dominik Hasek, Dan Cloutier	10.00
F10	Patrick Roy, Tyler Moss	20.00
F11	Sergei Samsonov, Mike Watt	6.00
F12	Keith Tkachuk, Jamie Wright	5.00
F13	Peter Bondra, Marian Hossa	3.00
F14	Pavel Bure, Bill Muckalt	6.00
F15	Wayne Gretzky, Brendan Morrison	25.00
F16	Sergei Fedorov, Marty Reasoner	6.00
F17	Ray Bourque, Eric Brewer	3.00
F18	Chris Pronger, Tom Poti	2.00
F19	Martin Brodeur, Jose Theodore	10.00
F20	Chris Osgood, Jamie Storr	4.00

1998-99 Bowman's Best Performers

Ten of hockey's young stars, including five rookies are spotlighted. Card backs are numbered with a "BP" prefix and are seeded 1:12 packs. There are also two parallels randomly seeded: Refractors and Atomic Refractors. Refractors are limited to 200 sequentially numbered sets and marked "Refractor" under the card number on the back. Atomic Refractors are limited to 50 numbered sets.

		MT
Complete Set (10):		20.00
Common Player:		1.50
Inserted 1:12		
Refractors:		5x to 10x
Production 200 sets		
Atomic Refractors:		10x to 20x
Production 50 sets		
BP1	Mike Johnson	1.50
BP2	Sergei Samsonov	4.00
BP3	Patrik Elias	1.50
BP4	Patrick Marleau	5.00
BP5	Mattias Ohlund	1.50
BP6	Manny Malhotra	3.00
BP7	Chris Drury	2.00
BP8	Daniel Briere	1.50
BP9	Brendan Morrison	1.50
BP10	Vincent Lecavalier	8.00

1998-99 Bowman's Best Scotty Bowman's Best

This set spotlights ten players selected by Detroit Red Wing coach Scotty Bowman. These are seeded 1:6 packs. Two parallels are randomly seeded: Refractors and Atomic Refractors. Refractors are limited to 200 numbered sets and marked "Refractor" under the card number on the back. Atomic Refractors are limited to 50 numbered sets and are marked "Atomic Refractor" under the card number to ensure identification. Cards are numbered on the back with a "BF" prefix.

		MT
Complete Set (11):		35.00
Common Player:		1.00
Inserted 1:6		
Refractors:		5x to 10x
Production 200 sets		
Atomic Refractors:		10x to 25x
Production 50 sets		
SB1	Dominik Hasek	4.00
SB2	Martin Brodeur	4.00
SB3	Chris Osgood	2.00
SB4	Nicklas Lidstrom	1.00
SB5	Eric Lindros	6.00
SB6	Jaromir Jagr	6.00
SB7	Steve Yzerman	5.00
SB8	Peter Forsberg	5.00
SB9	Paul Kariya	6.00
SB10	Ray Bourque	1.50
SB11	Scotty Bowman	1.00

1998-99 Finest

The 150-card set features a chromium foil finish on a full bleed card front. Backs have a small photo along with the featured player's 1997-98 statistics and his career totals on a 29-point stock. A No-Protector parallel version is randomly seeded without the Finest Protector and have Finest technology on the back and seeded 1:4 packs.

		MT
Complete Set (150):		50.00
Common Player:		.25
No Protector:		2x to 3x
Inserted 1:4		
Refractors:		5x to 10x
Inserted 1:12		
No Prot. Refractor:		8x to 15x
Inserted 1:24		
1	Teemu Selanne	1.25
2	Theoren Fleury	.40
3	Ed Belfour	.75
4	Dominik Hasek	2.00
5	Dino Ciccarelli	.25
6	Peter Forsberg	2.50
7	Rob Blake	.25
8	Martin Gelinas	.25
9	Vincent Damphousse	.25
10	Doug Brown	.25
11	Dave Andreychuk	.25
12	Bill Guerin	.25
13	Daniel Alfredsson	.40
14	Dainius Zubrus	.25
15	Nikolai Khabibulin	.75
16	Sergei Nemchinov	.25
17	Rod Brind'Amour	.40
18	Patrick Marleau	1.00
19	Brett Hull	1.00
20	Rob Zamuner	.25
21	Anson Carter	.25
22	Chris Pronger	.40
23	Owen Nolan	.25
24	Alexandre Daigle	.25
25	Darius Kasparaitis	.25
26	Steve Rucchin	.25
27	Grant Fuhr	.75
28	Mike Sillinger	.25
29	Tony Amonte	.40
30	Jeremy Roenick	1.00
31	Garry Galley	.25
32	Jeff Friesen	.25
33	Alexei Zhitnik	.25
34	Sergei Fedorov	1.25
35	Martin Brodeur	1.50
36	Curtis Joseph	.75
37	Mike Johnson	.25
38	Mattias Ohlund	.40
39	Derian Hatcher	.25
40	Zigmund Palffy	.75
41	Rob Niedermayer	.25
42	Keith Primeau	.50
43	Valeri Kamensky	.25
44	Cliff Ronning	.25
45	Saku Koivu	.75
46	Jiri Slegr	.25
47	Igor Korolev	.25
48	Sergei Samsonov	1.25
49	Vaclav Prospal	.25
50	Ron Francis	.40
51	John LeClair	1.25
52	Peter Bondra	.75
53	Matt Cullen	.25
54	Doug Gilmour	.50
55	John Vanbiesbrouck	1.25
56	Kevin Stevens	.25
57	Vladimir Malakhov	.25
58	Guy Hebert	.50
59	Patrik Elias	.40
60	Boris Mironov	.25
61	Rob DiMaio	.25
62	Pavol Demitra	.40
63	Michael Nylander	.25
64	Wayne Gretzky	5.00
65	Miroslav Satan	.25
66	Eric Daze	.25
67	Jozef Stumpel	.25
68	Mark Messier	1.00
69	Pat Verbeek	.25
70	Felix Potvin	.75
71	Ethan Moreau	.25
72	Steve Yzerman	2.50
73	Paul Ysebaert	.25
74	Jaromir Jagr	3.00
75	Mike Modano	1.25
76	Chris Osgood	.75
77	Robert Svehla	.25
78	Joe Juneau	.25
79	Adam Deadmarsh	.40
80	Keith Tkachuk	1.00
81	Mark Recchi	.25
82	Andrew Cassels	.25
83	Mike Hough	.25
84	Rem Murray	.25
85	Trevor Kidd	.75
86	Jeff Hackett	.50
87	Mikael Renberg	.25
88	Al MacInnis	.40
89	Mike Richter	.75
90	Markus Naslund	.25
91	Joe Sakic	2.00
92	Michael Peca	.25
93	Scott Thornton	.25
94	Vyacheslav Kozlov	.25
95	Bobby Holik	.25
96	Alexei Yashin	.50
97	Robert Kron	.25
98	Adam Oates	.75
99	Chris Simon	.25

100	Paul Kariya	3.00
101	Ray Bourque	.75
102	Eric Desjardins	.25
103	Glen Murray	.25
104	Oleg Tverdovsky	.25
105	Pavel Bure	1.25
106	Mats Sundin	1.00
107	Bryan Berard	.40
108	Janne Niinimaa	.25
109	Wade Redden	.25
110	Trevor Linden	.25
111	Jarome Iginla	.40
112	Joe Nieuwendyk	.40
113	Alexei Kovalev	.25
114	Dave Gagner	.25
115	Dimitri Yushkevich	.25
116	Sandis Ozolinsh	.25
117	Dimitri Khristich	.25
118	Jim Campbell	.25
119	Nicklas Lidstrom	.50
120	Scott Niedermayer	.25
121	Niklas Sundstrom	.25
122	Karl Dykhuis	.25
123	Brendan Shanahan	1.25
124	Sandy McCarthy	.25
125	Pierre Turgeon	.40
126	Olaf Kolzig	.75
127	Chris Chelios	.75
128	Luc Robitaille	.40
129	Alexander Mogilny	.50
130	Sami Kapanen	.25
131	Stu Barnes	.25
132	Scott Stevens	.25
133	Doug Weight	.25
134	Alexei Zhamnov	.25
135	Mike Vernon	.50
136	Derek Morris	.25
137	Brian Leetch	.50
138	Ray Whitney	.25
139	Chris Gratton	.25
140	Patrick Roy	4.00
141	Jason Allison	.40
142	Tom Barrasso	.50
143	Derek Plante	.25
144	Denis Pederson	.25
145	Mike Ricci	.25
146	Damian Rhodes	.50
147	Marco Sturm	.25
148	Darryl Sydor	.25
149	Eric Lindros	3.00
150	Checklist	.25

1998-99 Finest Centurions

This 20-card set highlight young players who are destined for stardom. Card fronts utilize Finest's chromium technology. Card backs have a small photo along with a career note. Card backs are numbered with a "C" prefix and limited to 500 sequentially numbered sets. A parallel Refractor version is also randomly seeded and is labeled "Refractor" under the card number and limited to 75 sequentially numbered sets.

		MT
Complete Set (20):		400.00
Common Player:		10.00
Production 500 sets		
Refractors:		1.5x to 3x
Production 75 sets		
C1	Patrik Elias	10.00
C2	Bryan Berard	10.00
C3	Chris Osgood	20.00
C4	Saku Koivu	20.00
C5	Alexei Yashin	15.00
C6	Zigmund Palffy	20.00
C7	Peter Forsberg	50.00
C8	Jason Allison	15.00
C9	Wade Redden	10.00
C10	Paul Kariya	60.00
C11	Martin Brodeur	30.00
C12	Patrick Marleau	20.00
C13	Jaromir Jagr	60.00
C14	Mattias Ohlund	10.00
C15	Teemu Selanne	25.00
C16	Mike Johnson	10.00
C17	Joe Thornton	20.00
C18	Jocelyn Thibault	15.00
C19	Daniel Alfredsson	10.00
C20	Sergei Samsonov	25.00

1998-99 Finest Future,s Finest

This set focuses on 20 of the NHL's top prospects and CHL players. Future's Finest feature Finest's chromium technology and are numbered with a "F" prefix on the card back. They are limited to 500 sequentially numbered sets. A Refractor parallel version is also randomly seeded and can easily be identified with "Refractor" written under the card number. Refractors are limited to 150 serially numbered sets.

		MT
Complete Set (20):		250.00
Common Player:		6.00
Production 500 sets		
Refractors:		1x to 2x
Production 150 sets		
F1	David Legwand	30.00
F2	Manny Malhotra	15.00
F3	Vincent Lecavalier	40.00
F4	Brad Stuart	6.00
F5	Bryan Allen	6.00
F6	Rico Fata	25.00
F7	Mark Bell	20.00
F8	Michael Rupp	15.00
F9	Jeff Heerema	15.00
F10	Alex Tanguay	25.00
F11	Patrick Desrochers	20.00
F12	Mathieu Chouinard	20.00
F13	Eric Chouinard	10.00
F14	Martin Skoula	10.00
F15	Robyn Regehr	6.00
F16	Marian Hossa	10.00
F17	Dan Cleary	6.00
F18	Olli Jokinen	10.00
F19	Brendan Morrison	10.00
F20	Erik Rasmussen	6.00

1998-99 Finest Mystery Finest

This set features 20 players; of which both sides are covered with a Finest opaque protector. Collectors remove the protector to reveal the player underneath. They are seeded 1:36 packs. A Refractor parallel version is also randomly seeded 1:144 packs.

		MT
Complete Set (50):		1100.
Common Player:		8.00
Inserted 1:36		
Refractors:		1.5x to 2.5x
Inserted 1:144		
1	Jaromir Jagr, Wayne Gretzky	50.00
2	Jaromir Jagr, Dominik Hasek	40.00
3	Jaromir Jagr, Eric Lindros	40.00
4	Jaromir Jagr, Jaromir Jagr	40.00
5	Dominik Hasek, Wayne Gretzky	50.00
6	Dominik Hasek, Eric Lindros	40.00
7	Dominik Hasek, Dominik Hasek	20.00
8	Wayne Gretzky, Eric Lindros	50.00
9	Wayne Gretzky, Wayne Gretzky	60.00
10	Eric Lindros, Eric Lindros	40.00
11	Paul Kariya, Teemu Selanne	40.00
12	Paul Kariya, Ray Bourque	30.00
13	Paul Kariya, Sergei Samsonov	30.00
14	Paul Kariya, Paul Kariya	40.00
15	Teemu Selanne, Ray Bourque	30.00
16	Teemu Selanne, Sergei Samsonov	15.00
17	Teemu Selanne, Teemu Selanne	15.00
18	Ray Bourque, Sergei Samsonov	12.00
19	Ray Bourque, Ray Bourque	10.00
20	Sergei Samsonov, Sergei Samsonov	15.00
21	Martin Brodeur, Peter Forsberg	30.00
22	Martin Brodeur, Patrick Roy	40.00
23	Martin Brodeur, Joe Sakic	20.00
24	Martin Brodeur, Martin Brodeur	20.00
25	Peter Forsberg, Patrick Roy	40.00
26	Peter Forsberg, Joe Sakic	25.00
27	Peter Forsberg, Peter Forsberg	30.00
28	Patrick Roy, Joe Sakic	40.00
29	Patrick Roy, Patrick Roy	50.00
30	Joe Sakic, Joe Sakic	20.00
31	Mike Modano, Steve Yzerman	25.00
32	Mike Modano, Sergei Fedorov	15.00
33	Mike Modano, Brendan Shanahan	15.00
34	Mike Modano, Mike Modano	15.00
35	Steve Yzerman, Sergei Fedorov	25.00
36	Steve Yzerman, Brendan Shanahan	25.00
37	Steve Yzerman, Steve Yzerman	30.00
38	Sergei Fedorov, Brendan Shanahan	15.00
39	Sergei Fedorov, Sergei Fedorov	15.00
40	Brendan Shanahan, Brendan Shanahan	15.00
41	Mark Messier, John Leclair	15.00
42	Mark Messier, Keith Tkachuk	15.00
43	Mark Messier, Pavel Bure	15.00
44	Mark Messier, Mark Messier	15.00
45	John Leclair, Keith Tkachuk	15.00
46	John Leclair, Pavel Bure	15.00
47	John Leclair, John Leclair	15.00
48	Pavel Bure, Keith Tkachuk	15.00
49	Pavel Bure, Pavel Bure	15.00
50	Keith Tkachuk, Keith Tkachuk	12.00

1998-99 Finest Oversize

The cards in this seven-card set are 3 1/4 x 4 9/16 in size. One oversize card is inserted into every box. A Refractor parallel version is also randomly seeded one per six boxes.

		MT
Complete Set (7):		40.00
Common Player:		4.00
One per box		
Refractors: 2x to 3x		
Inserted 1:6 boxes		
1	Teemu Selanne	4.00
2	Dominik Hasek	5.00
3	Martin Brodeur	4.00
4	Wayne Gretzky	12.00
5	Steve Yzerman	6.00
6	Jaromir Jagr	8.00
7	Eric Lindros	8.00

1998-99 Finest Red Lighters

This 20-card collection highlights the NHL's top scorers. Each card is die-cut on Finest's chromium technology. These are seeded 1:24 packs. A Refractor parallel version is also randomly seeded 1:72 packs.

		MT
Complete Set (20):		160.00
Common Player:		4.00
Inserted 1:24		
Refractors:		1.5x to 2x
Inserted 1:72		
R1	Jaromir Jagr	20.00
R2	Mike Modano	8.00
R3	Paul Kariya	20.00
R4	Pavel Bure	8.00
R5	Peter Bondra	6.00
R6	Sergei Fedorov	8.00
R7	Steve Yzerman	15.00
R8	Teemu Selanne	8.00
R9	Wayne Gretzky	30.00
R10	Brendan Shanahan	8.00
R11	Eric Lindros	20.00
R12	Alexei Yashin	4.00
R13	Jason Allison	4.00
R14	Joe Nieuwendyk	4.00
R15	Joe Sakic	12.00
R16	John Leclair	8.00
R17	Keith Tkachuk	6.00
R18	Mark Messier	6.00
R19	Mats Sundin	6.00
R20	Zigmund Palffy	6.00

1998-99 O-Pee-Chee Chrome

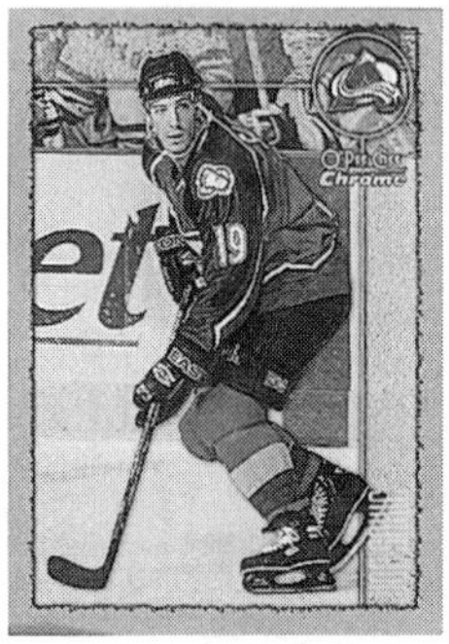

This base set consists of 242-cards printed on chromium stock with a brown border. Card backs have a small photo, year-by-year statistics, playoff statistics and a brief career note. A Refractor parallel version was also randomly seeded, which can be distinguished by their mirror-like sheen. "Refractor" is also written underneath the card number on the card back, they were seeded 1:12 packs.

		MT
Complete Set (242):		150.00
Common Player:		.25
Refractors:		5x to 10x
Inserted 1:12		
1	Peter Forsberg	5.00
2	Petr Sykora	.25
3	Byron Dafoe	.75
4	Ron Francis	.50
5	Alexei Yashin	.50
6	Dave Ellett	.25
7	Jamie Langenbrunner	.25
8	Doug Weight	.40
9	Jason Woolley	.25
10	Paul Coffey	.40
11	Uwe Krupp	.25
12	Tomas Sandstrom	.25
13	Scott Mellanby	.25
14	Vladimir Tsyplakov	.25
15	Martin Rucinsky	.25
16	Mikael Renberg	.25
17	Marco Sturm	.50
18	Eric Lindros	6.00
19	Sean Burke	.50
20	Martin Brodeur	4.00
21	Boyd Devereaux	.25
22	Kelly Buchberger	.25
23	Scott Stevens	.25
24	Jamie Storr	.50
25	Anders Eriksson	.25
26	Gary Suter	.25
27	Theoren Fleury	.50
28	Steve Leach	.25
29	Felix Potvin	.75
30	Brett Hull	2.00
31	Mike Grier	.25
32	Cale Hulse	.25
33	Larry Murphy	.25
34	Rick Tocchet	.25
35	Eric Desjardins	.25
36	Igor Kravchuk	.25
37	Rob Niedermayer	.25
38	Bryan Smolinski	.25
39	Valeri Kamensky	.25
40	Ryan Smyth	.25
41	Bruce Driver	.25
42	Mike Johnson	.40
43	Rob Zamuner	.25
44	Steve Duchesne	.40
45	Martin Straka	.25
46	Bill Houlder	.25
47	Craig Conroy	.25
48	Guy Hebert	.50
49	Colin Forbes	.25
50	Mike Modano	2.50
51	Jamie Pushor	.25
52	Jarome Iginla	.40
53	Paul Kariya	6.00
54	Mattias Ohlund	.50
55	Sergei Berezin	.50
56	Peter Zezel	.25
57	Teppo Numminen	.40
58	Dale Hunter	.25
59	Sandy Moger	.25
60	John LeClair	2.50
61	Wade Redden	.25
62	Patrik Elias	.50
63	Rob Blake	.40
64	Todd Marchant	.25
65	Claude Lemieux	.25
66	Trevor Kidd	.75
67	Sergei Fedorov	2.50
68	Joe Sakic	3.00
69	Derek Morris	.25
70	Alexei Morozov	.25
71	Mats Sundin	1.50
72	Daymond Langkow	.25
73	Kevin Hatcher	.25
74	Damian Rhodes	.50
75	Brian Leetch	.50
76	Saku Koivu	1.50
77	Rick Tabaracci	.25
78	Bernie Nicholls	.25
79	Alyn McCauley	.25
80	Patrice Brisebois	.25
81	Bret Hedican	.25
82	Sandy McCarthy	.25
83	Viktor Kozlov	.25
84	Derek King	.25
85	Alexander Selivanov	.25
86	Mike Vernon	.50
87	Jeff Beukeboom	.25
88	Tommy Salo	.50
89	Adam Graves	.40
90	Randy McKay	.25
91	Rich Pilon	.25
92	Richard Zednik	.25
93	Jeff Hackett	.50
94	Mike Peca	.25
95	Brent Gilchrist	.25
96	Stu Grimson	.25
97	Bob Probert	.25
98	Stu Barnes	.25
99	Ruslan Salei	.25
100	Al MacInnis	.50
101	Ken Daneyko	.25
102	Paul Ranheim	.25
103	Marty McInnis	.25
104	Marian Hossa	.50
105	Darren McCarty	.25
106	Guy Carbonneau	.25
107	Dallas Drake	.25
108	Sergei Samsonov	2.50
109	Teemu Selanne	2.50
110	Checklist	.25
111	Jaromir Jagr	6.00
112	Joe Thornton	2.00
113	Jon Klemm	.25
114	Grant Fuhr	.75
115	Nikolai Khabibulin	.50
116	Rod Brind'Amour	.40
117	Trevor Linden	.25
118	Vincent Damphousse	.25
119	Dino Ciccarelli	.25
120	Pat Verbeek	.40
121	Sandis Ozolinsh	.40
122	Garth Snow	.50
123	Ed Belfour	1.00
124	Keith Primeau	.40
125	Jason Allison	.40
126	Peter Bondra	2.00
127	Ulf Samuelsson	.25
128	Jeff Friesen	.40
129	Jason Bonsignore	.25
130	Daniel Alfredsson	.40
131	Bobby Holik	.25
132	Jozef Stumpel	.25
133	Brian Bellows	.25
134	Chris Osgood	1.00
135	Alexei Zhamnov	.25
136	Mattias Norstrom	.25
137	Drake Berehowsky	.25
138	Mark Messier	2.00
139	Geoff Courtnall	.25
140	Marc Bureau	.25
141	Don Sweeney	.25
142	Wendel Clark	.25
143	Scott Niedermayer	.25
144	Chris Therien	.25
145	Kirk Muller	.25
146	Wayne Primeau	.25
147	Tony Granato	.25
148	Derian Hatcher	.25
149	Daniel Briere	.25
150	Fredrik Olausson	.25
151	Joe Juneau	.25
152	Michal Grosek	.25
153	Janne Laukkanen	.25
154	Keith Tkachuk	2.00

155	Marty McSorley	.25
156	Owen Nolan	.25
157	Mark Tinordi	.25
158	Steve Washburn	.25
159	Luke Richardson	.25
160	Kris King	.25
161	Joe Nieuwendyk	.50
162	Travis Green	.25
163	Dominik Hasek	4.00
164	Dimitri Khristich	.25
165	Dave Manson	.25
166	Chris Chelios	.75
167	Claude LaPointe	.25
168	Kris Draper	.25
169	Brad Isbister	.25
170	Patrick Marleau	2.00
171	Jeremy Roenick	.75
172	Darren Langdon	.25
173	Kevin Dineen	.25
174	Luc Robitaille	.40
175	Steve Yzerman	5.00
176	Sergei Zubov	.25
177	Ed Jovanovski	.25
178	Sami Kapanen	.40
179	Adam Oates	.60
180	Pavel Bure	2.50
181	Chris Pronger	.40
182	Pat Falloon	.25
183	Darcy Tucker	.25
184	Zigmund Palffy	1.50
185	Curtis Brown	.25
186	Curtis Joseph	.75
187	Valeri Zelepukin	.25
188	Russ Courtnall	.25
189	Adam Foote	.25
190	Patrick Roy	8.00
191	Cory Stillman	.25
192	Alexei Zhitnik	.25
193	Olaf Kolzig	1.00
194	Mark Fitzpatrick	.25
195	James Black	.25
196	Zarley Zalapski	.25
197	Niklas Sundstrom	.25
198	Bryan Berard	.50
199	Jason Arnott	.25
200	Mike Richter	.75
201	Ken Baumgartner	.25
202	Jason Dawe	.25
203	Nicklas Lidstrom	.50
204	Tony Amonte	.50
205	Kjell Samuelsson	.25
206	Ray Bourque	.75
207	Alexander Mogilny	.50
208	Pierre Turgeon	.40
209	Tom Barrasso	.60
210	Richard Matvichuk	.25
211	Sergei Krivokrasov	.25
212	Ted Drury	.25
213	Matthew Barnaby	.25
214	Denis Pederson	.25
215	John Vanbiesbrouck	2.00
216	Brendan Shanahan	2.50
217	Jocelyn Thibault	.50
218	Nelson Emerson	.25
219	Wayne Gretzky	10.00
220	Checklist	.25
221	*Ramzi Abid*	6.00
222	*Mark Bell*	6.00
223	*Mike Henrich*	6.00
224	Vincent Lecavalier	10.00
225	Rico Fata	6.00
226	Bryan Allen	.25
227	Daniel Tkaczuk	.50
228	*Brad Stuart*	.50
229	*Derrick Walser*	.40
230	*Jonathan Cheechoo*	4.00
231	Sergei Varlamov	2.50
232	*Scott Gomez*	3.00
233	*Jeff Heerema*	4.00
234	David Legwand	8.00
235	Manny Malhotra	4.00
236	*Michael Rupp*	3.00
237	Alex Tanguay	6.00
238	*Mathieu Biron*	2.50
239	*Bujar Amidovski*	.75
240	*Brian Finley*	6.00
241	*Philippe Sauve*	4.00
242	*Jiri Fischer*	.50

1998-99 O-Pee-Chee Chrome Board Members

This 15-card set focuses on the NHL's top defensemen and is printed on a chromium card stock. Card backs have a small photo and are numbered with a "B" prefix. These were seeded 1:12 packs. A Refractor parallel version was also randomly seeded and have a mirror-like sheen associated with Refractors and also have "Refractor" written underneath the card number on the card back. Refractors are seeded 1:36 packs.

		MT
Complete Set (15):		50.00
Common Player:		2.50
Inserted 1:12		
Refractors:		1.5x to 2x
Inserted 1:36		
B1	Chris Pronger	4.00
B2	Chris Chelios	8.00
B3	Brian Leetch	8.00
B4	Ray Bourque	8.00
B5	Mattias Ohlund	4.00
B6	Nicklas Lidstrom	8.00
B7	Sergei Zubov	5.00
B8	Scott Niedermayer	2.50
B9	Larry Murphy	2.50
B10	Sandis Ozolinsh	5.00
B11	Rob Blake	4.00
B12	Scott Stevens	2.50
B13	Derian Hatcher	2.50
B14	Kevin Hatcher	2.50
B15	Wade Redden	2.50

1998-99 O-Pee-Chee Chrome Reprints

This 10-card set features retired greats like Wayne Gretzky and Gordie Howe as well as six current stars. Each card is a reprint of the featured player's Topps rookie card on a chromium stock and seeded 1:28 packs. A Refractor parallel version was also randomly seeded and have a mirror-like sheen and "Refractor" written beside the card number on the card back. Refractors were inserted 1:112 packs.

		MT
Complete Set (10):		100.00
Common Player:		4.00
Inserted 1:28		
Refractors:		1.5x to 2x
Inserted 1:112		
1	Wayne Gretzky	30.00
2	Mark Messier	10.00
3	Ray Bourque	8.00
4	Patrick Roy	20.00
5	Grant Fuhr	8.00
6	Brett Hull	10.00
7	Gordie Howe	20.00
8	Stan Mikita	10.00
9	Bobby Hull	15.00
10	Phil Esposito	8.00

1998-99 O-Pee-Chee Chrome Season's Best

This 30-card set is broken down into 5 statistical categories: Goaltenders, goal scorers, assists, Plus/Minus and rookies. Each category consists of six cards, card backs are numbered with a "SB" prefix and were inserted 1:8 packs. A Refractor parallel version was also randomly seeded, and has a mirror-like sheen and "Refractor" written beside the number on the card back. Refractors were inserted 1:24 packs.

		MT
Complete Set (30):		50.00
Common Player:		.50
Inserted 1:8		
Refractors:		1.5x to 2x
Inserted 1:24		
SB1	Dominik Hasek	5.00
SB2	Martin Brodeur	5.00
SB3	Ed Belfour	1.50
SB4	Curtis Joseph	1.50
SB5	Jeff Hackett	1.00
SB6	Tom Barrasso	1.00
SB7	Mike Johnson	.50
SB8	Sergei Samsonov	4.00
SB9	Patrik Elias	.50
SB10	Patrick Marleau	2.50
SB11	Mattias Ohlund	1.00
SB12	Marco Sturm	.50
SB13	Teemu Selanne	4.00
SB14	Peter Bondra	2.00
SB15	Pavel Bure	4.00
SB16	John LeClair	4.00
SB17	Zigmund Palffy	2.00
SB18	Keith Tkachuk	2.00
SB19	Jaromir Jagr	8.00
SB20	Wayne Gretzky	15.00
SB21	Peter Forsberg	8.00
SB22	Ron Francis	1.00
SB23	Adam Oates	1.50
SB24	Jozef Stumpel	.50
SB25	Chris Pronger	1.00
SB26	Larry Murphy	.50
SB27	Jason Allison	1.00
SB28	John LeClair	4.00
SB29	Randy McKay	.50
SB30	Dainius Zubrus	.50

1998-99 Pacific Aurora

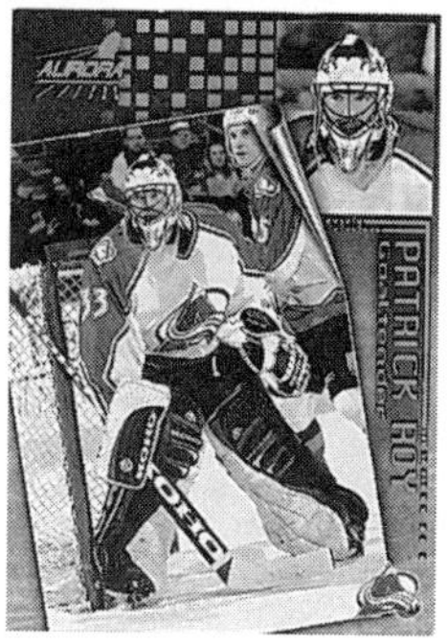

The 200-card base set features 24-point card stock with two photos of the featured player on the card front highlighted by gold foil stamping. Card backs have a small photo, a career highlight, 1997-98 statistics along with career totals.

		MT
Complete Set (200):		35.00
Common Player:		.15
1	Travis Green	.15
2	Guy Hebert	.25
3	Paul Kariya	2.50
4	Steve Rucchin	.15
5	Tomas Sandstrom	.15
6	Teemu Selanne	1.00
7	Jason Allison	.25
8	Ray Bourque	.40
9	Anson Carter	.15
10	Byron Dafoe	.40
11	Ted Donato	.15
12	Dave Ellett	.15
13	Dimitri Khristich	.15
14	Sergei Samsonov	1.00
15	Matthew Barnaby	.15
16	Michal Grosek	.15
17	Dominik Hasek	1.25
18	Brian Holzinger	.15
19	Mike Peca	.15
20	Miroslav Satan	.15
21	Dixon Ward	.15
22	Alexei Zhitnik	.15
23	Andrew Cassels	.15
24	Theoren Fleury	.30
25	Jarome Iginla	.15
26	Marty McInnis	.15
27	Derek Morris	.15
28	Michael Nylander	.15
29	Cory Stillman	.15
30	Kevin Dineen	.15
31	Nelson Emerson	.15
32	Martin Gelinas	.15
33	Sami Kapanen	.25
34	Trevor Kidd	.40
35	Robert Kron	.15
36	Jeff O'Neill	.15
37	Keith Primeau	.30
38	Tony Amonte	.40
39	Chris Chelios	.40
40	Eric Daze	.25
41	Jeff Hackett	.40
42	Jean-Yves Leroux	.15
43	Jeff Shantz	.15
44	Alexei Zhamnov	.15
45	Adam Deadmarsh	.25
46	Peter Forsberg	2.00
47	Valeri Kamensky	.15
48	Claude Lemieux	.15
49	Eric Messier	.15
50	Sandis Ozolinsh	.25
51	Patrick Roy	3.00
52	Joe Sakic	1.50
53	Ed Belfour	.50
54	Derian Hatcher	.15
55	Brett Hull	.75
56	Jamie Langenbrunner	.15
57	Jere Lehtinen	.15
58	Mike Modano	1.00
59	Joe Nieuwendyk	.30
60	Darryl Sydor	.15
61	Sergei Zubov	.25
62	Sergei Fedorov	1.00
63	Vyacheslav Kozlov	.15
64	Igor Larionov	.15
65	Nicklas Lidstrom	.30
66	Darren McCarty	.15
67	Chris Osgood	.50
68	Brendan Shanahan	1.00
69	Steve Yzerman	2.50
70	Kelly Buchberger	.15
71	Mike Grier	.15
72	Bill Guerin	.15
73	Roman Hamrlik	.15
74	Boris Mironov	.15
75	Janne Niinimaa	.15
76	Ryan Smyth	.15
77	Doug Weight	.30
78	Dino Ciccarelli	.15
79	Dave Gagner	.15
80	Ed Jovanovski	.15
81	Viktor Kozlov	.15
82	Paul Laus	.15
83	Scott Mellanby	.15
84	Ray Whitney	.15
85	Rob Blake	.15
86	Stephane Fiset	.30
87	Yanic Perreault	.15
88	Luc Robitaille	.25
89	Jamie Storr	.30
90	Jozef Stumpel	.15
91	Vladimir Tsyplakov	.15
92	Shayne Corson	.15
93	Vincent Damphousse	.25
94	Saku Koivu	.50
95	Mark Recchi	.25
96	Martin Rucinsky	.15
97	Brian Savage	.15
98	Jocelyn Thibault	.40
99	Andrew Brunette	.15
100	Mike Dunham	.40
101	Tom Fitzgerald	.15
102	Sergei Krivokrasov	.15
103	Denny Lambert	.15
104	Mikhail Shtalenkov	.30
105	Darren Turcotte	.15
106	Dave Andreychuk	.15
107	Jason Arnott	.15
108	Martin Brodeur	1.25
109	Patrik Elias	.25
110	Bobby Holik	.15
111	Randy McKay	.15
112	Scott Niedermayer	.15
113	Scott Stevens	.15
114	Bryan Berard	.25
115	Jason Dawe	.15
116	Trevor Linden	.15
117	Zigmund Palffy	.75
118	Robert Reichel	.15
119	Tommy Salo	.40
120	Bryan Smolinski	.15
121	Adam Graves	.15
122	Wayne Gretzky	4.00
123	Alexei Kovalev	.15
124	Brian Leetch	.30
125	Mike Richter	.50
126	Ulf Samuelsson	.15
127	Kevin Stevens	.15
128	Daniel Alfredsson	.30
129	Andreas Dackell	.15
130	Igor Kravchuk	.15
131	Shawn McEachern	.15
132	Chris Phillips	.15
133	Damian Rhodes	.40
134	Alexei Yashin	.40
135	Rod Brind'Amour	.30
136	Alexandre Daigle	.15
137	Eric Desjardins	.15
138	Chris Gratton	.15
139	Ron Hextall	.30
140	John LeClair	1.00
141	Eric Lindros	2.50
142	John Vanbiesbrouck	1.00
143	Dainius Zubrus	.15
144	Brad Isbister	.15
145	Nikolai Khabibulin	.40
146	Jeremy Roenick	.50
147	Cliff Ronning	.15
148	Keith Tkachuk	.75
149	Rick Tocchet	.15
150	Oleg Tverdovsky	.15
151	Stu Barnes	.15
152	Tom Barrasso	.40
153	Kevin Hatcher	.15
154	Jaromir Jagr	2.50
155	Darius Kasparaitis	.15
156	Alexei Morozov	.15
157	Martin Straka	.15
158	Jim Campbell	.15
159	Geoff Courtnall	.15
160	Grant Fuhr	.50
161	Al MacInnis	.40
162	Jamie McLennan	.40
163	Chris Pronger	.30
164	Pierre Turgeon	.30
165	Tony Twist	.15
166	Jeff Friesen	.15
167	Tony Granato	.15
168	Patrick Marleau	1.00
169	Marty McSorley	.15
170	Owen Nolan	.15
171	Marco Sturm	.15
172	Mike Vernon	.40
173	Karl Dykhuis	.15
174	Mikael Renberg	.15
175	Stephane Richer	.15
176	Alexander Selivanov	.15
177	Paul Ysebaert	.15
178	Rob Zamuner	.15
179	Sergei Berezin	.15
180	Tie Domi	.15
181	Mike Johnson	.15
182	Curtis Joseph	.75
183	Igor Korolev	.15
184	Mathieu Schneider	.15
185	Mats Sundin	.75
186	Todd Bertuzzi	.15
187	Donald Brashear	.15
188	Pavel Bure	1.00
189	Mark Messier	1.00
190	Alexander Mogilny	.50
191	Mattias Ohlund	.50
192	Garth Snow	.40
193	Brian Bellows	.15
194	Peter Bondra	.75
195	Sergei Gonchar	.15
196	Calle Johansson	.15
197	Joe Juneau	.15
198	Olaf Kolzig	.75
199	Adam Oates	.50
200	Richard Zednik	.15

1998-99 Pacific Aurora Atomic Laser-Cuts

This 20-card set highlights the NHL's top stars on a horizontal format with gold foil stamping and an atomic symbol and small circles laser cut into the card. These were seeded 1:9 packs.

		MT
Complete Set (20):		90.00
Common Player:		1.50
Inserted 1:9		
1	Paul Kariya	10.00
2	Teemu Selanne	4.00
3	Sergei Samsonov	4.00
4	Dominik Hasek	5.00
5	Peter Forsberg	6.00
6	Patrick Roy	10.00
7	Joe Sakic	5.00
8	Mike Modano	4.00
9	Sergei Fedorov	4.00
10	Brendan Shanahan	4.00

11	Steve Yzerman	8.00
12	Martin Brodeur	5.00
13	Wayne Gretzky	15.00
14	John LeClair	4.00
15	Eric Lindros	10.00
16	Jaromir Jagr	10.00
17	Mats Sundin	2.00
18	Pavel Bure	4.00
19	Mark Messier	3.00
20	Peter Bondra	2.00

1998-99 Pacific Aurora Championship Fever

This 50-card insert set captures NHL players on a horizontal format with a full gold etched image of the featured player on the right hand side of the card. Gold foil stamping is used throughout as well. Card backs have a small photo along with a career highlight. They were seeded one per pack.

		MT
Complete Set (50):		35.00
Common Player:		.25
Inserted 1:1		
Silvers:		30x to 50x
Production 250 sets		
Martin Brodeur Auto.		120.00
1	Paul Kariya	2.50
2	Teemu Selanne	1.00
3	Ray Bourque	.50
4	Byron Dafoe	.40
5	Sergei Samsonov	1.00
6	Dominik Hasek	1.50
7	Mike Peca	.25
8	Theoren Fleury	.40
9	Keith Primeau	.40
10	Chris Chelios	.50
11	Peter Forsberg	2.00
12	Patrick Roy	3.00
13	Joe Sakic	1.50
14	Ed Belfour	.50
15	Mike Modano	1.00
16	Sergei Fedorov	1.00
17	Nicklas Lidstrom	.50
18	Chris Osgood	.50
19	Brendan Shanahan	1.00
20	Steve Yzerman	2.00
21	Doug Weight	.25
22	Dino Ciccarelli	.25
23	Rob Blake	.25
24	Saku Koivu	.50
25	Mark Recchi	.25
26	Martin Brodeur	1.50
27	Patrik Elias	.25
28	Trevor Linden	.25
29	Zigmund Palffy	.50
30	Wayne Gretzky	4.00
31	Mike Richter	.50
32	Daniel Alfredsson	.25
33	Damian Rhodes	.25
34	Alexei Yashin	.25
35	John LeClair	1.00
36	Eric Lindros	2.50
37	Dainius Zubrus	.25
38	Keith Tkachuk	.75
39	Tom Barrasso	.40
40	Jaromir Jagr	2.50
41	Grant Fuhr	.50
42	Pierre Turgeon	.25
43	Patrick Marleau	1.00
44	Mike Vernon	.50
45	Rob Zamuner	.25
46	Mats Sundin	.75
47	Pavel Bure	1.00
48	Mark Messier	.75
49	Peter Bondra	.75
50	Olaf Kolzig	.60

1998-99 Pacific Aurora Championship Fever Blue

A parallel to Championship Fever, these inserts are identical besides the blue foiled design and limited to 100 numbered sets. Silvers are limited to 250 numbered sets.

		MT
Common Player:		40.00
Stars:		50x to 90x
Production 100 sets		
1	Paul Kariya	200.00
2	Teemu Selanne	90.00
3	Ray Bourque	60.00
4	Byron Dafoe	50.00
5	Sergei Samsonov	90.00
6	Dominik Hasek	125.00
7	Mike Peca	40.00
8	Theoren Fleury	50.00
9	Keith Primeau	50.00
10	Chris Chelios	60.00
11	Peter Forsberg	175.00
12	Patrick Roy	250.00
13	Joe Sakic	125.00
14	Ed Belfour	60.00
15	Mike Modano	90.00
16	Sergei Fedorov	90.00
17	Nicklas Lidstrom	50.00
18	Chris Osgood	60.00
19	Brendan Shanahan	90.00
20	Steve Yzerman	200.00
21	Doug Weight	40.00
22	Dino Ciccarelli	40.00
23	Rob Blake	40.00
24	Saku Koivu	60.00
25	Mark Recchi	40.00
26	Martin Brodeur	125.00
27	Patrik Elias	40.00
28	Trevor Linden	40.00
29	Zigmund Palffy	60.00
30	Wayne Gretzky	350.00
31	Mike Richter	60.00
32	Daniel Alfredsson	40.00
33	Damian Rhodes	50.00
34	Alexei Yashin	50.00
35	John LeClair	90.00
36	Eric Lindros	200.00
37	Dainius Zubrus	40.00
38	Keith Tkachuk	75.00
39	Tom Barrasso	50.00
40	Jaromir Jagr	200.00
41	Grant Fuhr	60.00
42	Pierre Turgeon	50.00
43	Patrick Marleau	75.00
44	Mike Vernon	60.00
45	Rob Zamuner	40.00
46	Mats Sundin	75.00
47	Pavel Bure	90.00
48	Mark Messier	75.00
49	Peter Bondra	75.00
50	Olaf Kolzig	60.00

1998-99 Pacific Aurora Cubes

Cubes were inserted one per box and are an actual miniature cube, wrapped in clear plastic. Three of the four sides have a photo of the featured player and the fourth side has year- by-year statistics.

		MT
Complete Set (20):		120.00
Common Player:		3.00
Inserted one per box		
1	Paul Kariya	12.00
2	Teemu Selanne	5.00
3	Dominik Hasek	6.00
4	Peter Forsberg	10.00
5	Patrick Roy	15.00
6	Joe Sakic	6.00
7	Mike Modano	5.00
8	Sergei Fedorov	5.00
9	Brendan Shanahan	5.00
10	Steve Yzerman	10.00
11	Martin Brodeur	6.00
12	Wayne Gretzky	20.00
13	John LeClair	5.00
14	Eric Lindros	12.00
15	Jaromir Jagr	12.00
16	Mats Sundin	4.00
17	Pavel Bure	5.00
18	Mark Messier	4.00
19	Peter Bondra	3.00
20	Olaf Kolzig	3.00

1998-99 Pacific Aurora Man Advantage

This 20-card set captures each player on a full foil, die-cut card which is fused to a plastic portion resembling half of a hockey puck. They were seeded 1:73 packs.

		MT
Complete Set (20):		350.00
Common Player:		8.00
Inserted 1:73		
1	Paul Kariya	40.00
2	Teemu Selanne	15.00
3	Ray Bourque	10.00
4	Mike Peca	8.00
5	Peter Forsberg	30.00
6	Joe Sakic	20.00
7	Mike Modano	15.00
8	Joe Nieuwendyk	8.00
9	Brendan Shanahan	15.00
10	Steve Yzerman	30.00
11	Shayne Corson	8.00
12	Zigmund Palffy	12.00
13	Wayne Gretzky	60.00
14	John LeClair	15.00
15	Eric Lindros	40.00
16	Jaromir Jagr	40.00
17	Mats Sundin	10.00
18	Pavel Bure	15.00
19	Mark Messier	12.00
20	Peter Bondra	12.00

1998-99 Pacific Aurora NHL Command

This 10-card set features a full foiled design on a horizontal format, highlighted by gold foil stamping. These were inserted 1:361 packs.

		MT
Complete Set (10):		650.00
Common Player:		20.00
Inserted 1:361		
1	Teemu Selanne	40.00
2	Dominik Hasek	50.00
3	Peter Forsberg	75.00
4	Patrick Roy	120.00
5	Mike Modano	40.00
6	Steve Yzerman	75.00
7	Martin Brodeur	50.00
8	Wayne Gretzky	150.00
9	Eric Lindros	100.00
10	Jaromir Jagr	100.00

1998-99 Pacific Crown Royale

The 144-card base set features dual foil, dual etching on a die-cut crown design. Limited Series is a parallel to the base set featuring a 24-point stock and limited to 99 serial numbered sets.

		MT
Complete Set (144):		125.00
Common Player:		.50
Limited Series Stars:		20x to 35x
Yng Stars & RCs:		10x to 20x
Production 99 sets		
1	Travis Green	.50
2	Guy Hebert	.75
3	Paul Kariya	6.00
4	Tomas Sandstrom	.50
5	Teemu Selanne	2.50
6	Jason Allison	.75
7	Ray Bourque	1.50
8	Byron Dafoe	1.00
9	Dimitri Khristich	.50
10	Sergei Samsonov	2.00
11	Matthew Barnaby	.50
12	Michal Grosek	.50
13	Dominik Hasek	3.00
14	Michael Peca	.50
15	Miroslav Satan	.50
16	Andrew Cassels	.50
17	Rico Fata	.75
18	Theoren Fleury	1.00
19	Jarome Iginla	.50
20	*Martin St. Louis*	1.00
21	Ken Wregget	.75
22	Ron Francis	.75
23	Arturs Irbe	.75
24	Sami Kapanen	.75
25	Trevor Kidd	1.00
26	Keith Primeau	1.00
27	Tony Amonte	.75
28	Chris Chelios	1.00
29	Eric Daze	.50
30	Doug Gilmour	.75
31	Jocelyn Thibault	.75
32	Chris Drury	.50
33	Peter Forsberg	5.00
34	*Milan Hejduk*	1.00
35	Patrick Roy	8.00
36	Joe Sakic	3.00
37	Ed Belfour	1.50
38	Brett Hull	2.00
39	Jamie Langenbrunner	.75
40	Jere Lehtinen	.50
41	Mike Modano	2.00
42	Joe Nieuwendyk	.75
43	Darryl Sydor	.50
44	Sergei Fedorov	2.50
45	Nicklas Lidstrom	1.00
46	Darren McCarty	.50
47	Chris Osgood	1.50
48	Brendan Shanahan	2.50
49	Steve Yzerman	5.00
50	Bob Essensa	.75
51	Bill Guerin	.50
52	Janne Niinimaa	.50
53	Tom Poti	.50
54	Ryan Smyth	.50
55	Doug Weight	.75
56	Sean Burke	.75
57	Dino Ciccarelli	.50
58	Ed Jovanovski	.50
59	Viktor Kozlov	.50
60	*Oleg Kvasha*	3.00
61	*Mark Parrish*	2.50
62	Rob Blake	.50
63	Manny Legace	.50
64	Yanic Perreault	.50
65	Luc Robitaille	.75
66	Jozef Stumpel	.50
67	Shayne Corson	.50
68	Vincent Damphousse	.50
69	Jeff Hackett	1.00
70	Saku Koivu	1.00
71	Mark Recchi	.50
72	Andrew Brunette	.50
73	Mike Dunham	.75
74	Tom Fitzgerald	.50
75	Greg Johnson	.50
76	Sergei Krivokrasov	.50
77	Jason Arnott	.50
78	Martin Brodeur	3.00
79	Patrik Elias	.50
80	Bobby Holik	.50
81	Brendan Morrison	.50
82	Bryan Berard	.50
83	Trevor Linden	.50
84	Zigmund Palffy	1.00
85	Robert Reichel	.50
86	Tommy Salo	1.00
87	Adam Graves	.75
88	Wayne Gretzky	10.00
89	Brian Leetch	1.00
90	Manny Malhotra	1.00
91	Mike Richter	1.50
92	Daniel Alfredsson	.50
93	Igor Kravchuk	.50
94	Shawn McEachern	.50
95	Damian Rhodes	.75
96	Alexei Yashin	.75
97	Rod Brind'Amour	.75
98	Ron Hextall	.75
99	John LeClair	2.50
100	Eric Lindros	6.00
101	John Vanbiesbrouck	2.00
102	Dainius Zubrus	.50
103	Nikolai Khabibulin	1.00
104	Jeremy Roenick	1.50
105	Keith Tkachuk	1.50
106	Rick Tocchet	.50
107	Oleg Tverdovsky	.50
108	Tom Barrasso	.75
109	*Jan Hrdina*	.75
110	Jaromir Jagr	6.00
111	Alexei Morozov	.50
112	German Titov	.50
113	Jim Campbell	.50
114	Grant Fuhr	1.00
115	Al MacInnis	.75
116	Chris Pronger	.75
117	Pierre Turgeon	.75
118	Jeff Friesen	.50
119	Patrick Marleau	1.50
120	Owen Nolan	.50
121	Marco Sturm	.50
122	Mike Vernon	.75
123	Wendel Clark	.50
124	Vincent Lecavalier	3.00
125	Bill Ranford	.50
126	Stephane Richer	.50
127	Rob Zamuner	.50
128	Sergei Berezin	.50
129	Tie Domi	.50
130	Mike Johnson	.50
131	Curtis Joseph	1.00
132	Mats Sundin	1.50
133	Donald Brashear	.50
134	Pavel Bure	2.50
135	Mark Messier	2.00
136	Alexander Mogilny	1.00
137	*Bill Muckalt*	.50
138	Mattias Ohlund	.50
139	Garth Snow	.75
140	Peter Bondra	1.00
141	*Matthew Herr*	.75
142	Joe Juneau	.50
143	Olaf Kolzig	1.00
144	Adam Oates	1.00

1998-99 Pacific Crown Royale Cramer's Choice Awards

This 10-card set features an enlarged, jumbo-sized format with a holographic silver foil front with gold foil stamping and etching on the card bottom. They are seeded one per box. Six different serial numbered parallels with varying foil colors are also randomly seeded. Dark Blue 35 numbered sets, Green 30 sets, Red 25 sets, Light Blue 20 sets, Gold 10 sets.

		MT
Complete Set (10):		90.00
Common Player:		5.00
Inserted 1:box		
Dark Blue:		10x to 20x
Production 35 sets		
Green:		10x to 20x
Production 30 sets		
Red:		10x to 20x
Production 25 sets		
Light Blue:		10x to 20x
Production 20 sets		
Gold:		15x to 30x
Production 10 sets		
1	Paul Kariya	12.00
2	Teemu Selanne	5.00
3	Dominik Hasek	6.00
4	Peter Forsberg	10.00
5	Patrick Roy	15.00
6	Steve Yzerman	10.00
7	Martin Brodeur	6.00
8	Wayne Gretzky	20.00
9	Eric Lindros	12.00
10	Jaromir Jagr	12.00

1998-99 Pacific Crown Royale Living Legends

Ten of the NHL's top stars are spotlighted in this gold foiled set, with 375 total serial numbered sets produced.

		MT
Complete Set (10):		700.00
Common Player:		25.00
Production 375 sets		
1	Paul Kariya	100.00
2	Teemu Selanne	40.00
3	Dominik Hasek	50.00
4	Peter Forsberg	75.00
5	Patrick Roy	120.00
6	Steve Yzerman	75.00
7	Martin Brodeur	50.00
8	Wayne Gretzky	150.00
9	Eric Lindros	100.00
10	Jaromir Jagr	90.00

1998-99 Pacific Crown Royale Master Performers

Card fronts feature full gold foil etching on a design resembling a marquee. These are seeded 2:25 packs.

		MT
Complete Set (20):		180.00
Common Player:		4.00
Inserted 1:12		
1	Paul Kariya	20.00

2	Teemu Selanne	8.00
3	Dominik Hasek	10.00
4	Peter Forsberg	15.00
5	Patrick Roy	25.00
6	Joe Sakic	10.00
7	Brett Hull	6.00
8	Mike Modano	6.00
9	Sergei Fedorov	8.00
10	Brendan Shanahan	8.00
11	Steve Yzerman	15.00
12	Saku Koivu	4.00
13	Martin Brodeur	10.00
14	Wayne Gretzky	30.00
15	John LeClair	8.00
16	Eric Lindros	20.00
17	Jaromir Jagr	20.00
18	Mats Sundin	6.00
19	Mark Messier	6.00
20	Peter Bondra	5.00

1998-99 Pacific Crown Royale Pillars of the Game

This 25-card set profiled some of the NHL's established fan favorites on a holographic gold foil design on a horizontal format. They were seeded one per pack.

		MT
Complete Set (25):		25.00
Common Player:		.50
Inserted 1:1		
1	Teemu Selanne	1.25
2	Ray Bourque	.75
3	Michael Peca	.50
4	Theoren Fleury	.75
5	Chris Chelios	.75
6	Doug Gilmour	.75
7	Patrick Roy	4.00
8	Joe Sakic	1.50
9	Ed Belfour	.75
10	Brett Hull	1.00
11	Mike Modano	1.00
12	Sergei Fedorov	1.25
13	Brendan Shanahan	1.25
14	Steve Yzerman	2.50
15	Saku Koivu	.50
16	Martin Brodeur	1.50
17	John LeClair	1.25
18	Eric Lindros	3.00
19	John Vanbiesbrouck	1.00
20	Keith Tkachuk	1.00
21	Jaromir Jagr	3.00
22	Curtis Joseph	.75
23	Mats Sundin	.75
24	Mark Messier	1.00
25	Peter Bondra	.50

1998-99 Pacific Crown Royale Pivotal Players

This 25-card insert set features holographic silver foil fronts and are seeded one per pack.

		MT
Complete Set (25):		25.00
Common Player:		.50
Inserted 1:1		
1	Paul Kariya	3.00
2	Dominik Hasek	1.50
3	Michael Peca	.50
4	Peter Forsberg	2.50
5	Joe Sakic	1.50
6	Brett Hull	1.00
7	Mike Modano	1.25
8	Sergei Fedorov	1.25
9	Chris Osgood	.75
10	Brendan Shanahan	1.25
11	Ryan Smyth	.50
12	Mark Parrish	.50
13	Saku Koivu	.50
14	Martin Brodeur	1.50
15	Trevor Linden	.50
16	Wayne Gretzky	5.00
17	Alexei Yashin	.50
18	John LeClair	1.25
19	John Vanbiesbrouck	1.00
20	Keith Tkachuk	1.00
21	Vincent Lecavalier	1.50
22	Mats Sundin	1.00
23	Mark Messier	1.00
24	Peter Bondra	.75
25	Olaf Kolzig	.75

1998-99 Pacific Crown Royale Rookie Class

This 10-card set spotlighted hockey's top newcomers that debuted in 1998-99. Card fronts feature an all-foil design and card backs offer a brief highlight on the featured rookie. These are seeded 1:25.

		MT
Complete Set (10):		50.00
Common Player:		3.00
Inserted 1:25		
1	Chris Drury	4.00
2	Milan Hejduk	5.00
3	Mark Parrish	8.00
4	Manny Legace	3.00
5	Brendan Morrison	5.00
6	Manny Malhotra	10.00
7	Daniel Briere	5.00
8	Vincent Lecavalier	20.00
9	Tomas Kaberle	3.00
10	Bill Muckalt	3.00

1998-99 Pacific Dynagon Ice

The 200-card set is printed on blue foil with gold foil etching and stamping. Card backs have a photo, 1997-98 statistics and career totals. Two parallels to the base set are randomly seeded: Red and Ice Blue. Reds feature red foil stamping and etching and Ice Blues have stamping and etching in blue foil. Reds are inserted in treat retail packs at a rate of 4:37 packs and a total of 67 Ice Blue sets were produced.

		MT
Complete Set (200):		40.00
Common Player:		.15
Reds:		4x to 8x
Inserted 4:37 Treat		
Ice Blue stars:		40x to 80x
Yng Stars & RCs: 20x to 40x		
Production 67 sets		
1	Travis Green	.15
2	Guy Hebert	.25
3	Paul Kariya	2.50
4	Steve Rucchin	.15
5	Tomas Sandstrom	.15
6	Teemu Selanne	1.00
7	Jason Allison	.25
8	Ray Bourque	.50
9	Byron Dafoe	.40
10	Anson Carter	.15
11	Dimitri Khristich	.15
12	*Antti Laaksonen*	.40
13	*Peter Nordstrom*	.40
14	Sergei Samsonov	1.00
15	Joe Thornton	.50
16	Matthew Barnaby	.15
17	Michal Grosek	.15
18	Dominik Hasek	1.50
19	Brian Holzinger	.15
20	Michael Peca	.15
21	Miroslav Satan	.15
22	Vaclav Varada	.15
23	Andrew Cassels	.15
24	Rico Fata	.40
25	Theoren Fleury	.40
26	Phil Housley	.15
27	Jarome Iginla	.25
28	*Martin St. Louis*	.40
29	Ken Wregget	.40
30	Kevin Dineen	.15
31	Ron Francis	.40
32	Martin Gelinas	.15
33	Arturs Irbe	.40
34	Sami Kapanen	.15
35	Trevor Kidd	.50
36	Robert Kron	.15
37	Keith Primeau	.40
38	Tony Amonte	.50
39	Chris Chelios	.50
40	Eric Daze	.15
41	Doug Gilmour	.40
42	Jeff Hackett	.40
43	Ty Jones	.15
44	Bob Probert	.15
45	Adam Deadmarsh	.15
46	Chris Drury	.15
47	Peter Forsberg	2.00
48	*Milan Hejduk*	.75
49	Valeri Kamensky	.15
50	Claude Lemieux	.15
51	Patrick Roy	3.00
52	Joe Sakic	1.50
53	Ed Belfour	.50
54	*Sergey Gusev*	.40
55	Derian Hatcher	.15
56	Brett Hull	.75
57	Jamie Langenbrunner	.25
58	Jere Lehtinen	.15
59	Mike Modano	1.00
60	Joe Nieuwendyk	.40
61	Sergei Zubov	.15
62	Sergei Fedorov	1.00
63	Vyacheslav Kozlov	.15
64	Uwe Krupp	.15
65	Nicklas Lidstrom	.40
66	Darren McCarty	.15
67	Chris Osgood	.50
68	Brendan Shanahan	1.00
69	Steve Yzerman	2.00
70	Bob Essensa	.40
71	Mike Grier	.15
72	Bill Guerin	.15
73	Roman Hamrlik	.15
74	Janne Niinimaa	.15
75	Tom Poti	.15
76	Ryan Smyth	.15
77	Doug Weight	.15
78	Sean Burke	.40
79	Dino Ciccarelli	.15
80	Dave Gagner	.15
81	Ed Jovanovski	.15
82	Viktor Kozlov	.15
83	*Oleg Kvasha*	1.50
84	Paul Laus	.15
85	*Mark Parrish*	1.50
86	Rob Blake	.15
87	Stephane Fiset	.15
88	*Josh Green*	.25
89	Yanic Perreault	.15
90	Luc Robitaille	.15
91	Jozef Stumpel	.15
92	Vladimir Tsyplakov	.15
93	Brad Brown	.15
94	Shayne Corson	.15
95	Vincent Damphousse	.15
96	Saku Koivu	.50
97	Mark Recchi	.15
98	Jocelyn Thibault	.40
99	Sergei Zholtok	.15
100	Andrew Brunette	.15
101	Mike Dunham	.40
102	Tom Fitzgerald	.15
103	Patrik Kjellberg	.15
104	Sergei Krivokrasov	.15
105	Darren Turcotte	.15
106	Dave Andreychuk	.15
107	Jason Arnott	.15
108	Martin Brodeur	1.25
109	Patrik Elias	.15
110	Bobby Holik	.15
111	Brendan Morrison	.15
112	Scott Stevens	.15
113	Bryan Berard	.25
114	Eric Brewer	.15
115	Trevor Linden	.15
116	Zigmund Palffy	.60
117	Robert Reichel	.15
118	Tommy Salo	.40
119	Bryan Smolinski	.15
120	Adam Graves	.15
121	Wayne Gretzky	4.00
122	Alexei Kovalev	.15
123	Brian Leetch	.30
124	Manny Malhotra	.15
125	Mike Richter	.60
126	Daniel Alfredsson	.25
127	Igor Kravchuk	.15
128	Shawn McEachern	.15
129	Vaclav Prospal	.15
130	Damian Rhodes	.40
131	*Sami Salo*	.40
132	Alexei Yashin	.40
133	Rod Brind'Amour	.25
134	Alexandre Daigle	.15
135	Chris Gratton	.15
136	Ron Hextall	.40
137	John LeClair	1.00
138	Eric Lindros	2.50
139	*Mike Maneluk*	.75
140	John Vanbiesbrouck	1.00
141	Dainius Zubrus	.15
142	Brad Isbister	.15
143	Nikolai Khabibulin	.60
144	Jeremy Roenick	.75
145	Keith Tkachuk	.75
146	Rick Tocchet	.15
147	Oleg Tverdovsky	.15
148	Tom Barrasso	.40
149	Kevin Hatcher	.15
150	*Jan Hrdina*	.40
151	Jaromir Jagr	2.50
152	Alexei Morozov	.15
153	Jiri Slegr	.15
154	Martin Straka	.15
155	Jim Campbell	.15
156	Geoff Courtnall	.15
157	Grant Fuhr	.60
158	*Michal Handzus*	.40
159	Al MacInnis	.40
160	Jamie McLennan	.40
161	Chris Pronger	.40
162	Marty Reasoner	.15
163	Pierre Turgeon	.25
164	Jeff Friesen	.15
165	Tony Granato	.15
166	*Scott Hannan*	.40
167	Patrick Marleau	.75
168	Owen Nolan	.15
169	Marco Sturm	.15
170	Mike Vernon	.40
171	Wendel Clark	.25
172	John Cullen	.15
173	Vincent Lecavalier	1.50
174	Stephane Richer	.15
175	Paul Ysebaert	.15
176	Rob Zamuner	.15
177	Sergei Berezin	.15
178	Tie Domi	.15
179	Mike Johnson	.15
180	Curtis Joseph	.60
181	*Tomas Kaberle*	.50
182	Igor Korolev	.15
183	Alyn McCauley	.15
184	Mats Sundin	.75
185	Todd Bertuzzi	.15
186	Donald Brashear	.15
187	Pavel Bure	1.00
188	*Matt Cooke*	.25
189	Mark Messier	.75
190	Alexander Mogilny	.40
191	Mattias Ohlund	.15
192	Garth Snow	.40
193	Peter Bondra	.60
194	*Matthew Herr*	.25
195	Calle Johansson	.15
196	Joe Juneau	.15
197	Olaf Kolzig	.60
198	Adam Oates	.50
199	Jaroslav Svejkovsky	.15
200	Richard Zednik	.15

1998-99 Pacific Dynagon Ice Forward Thinking

Forward Thinking are printed on a blue foil board and highlighted by blue foil stamping. Card backs have a small photo and a career note. These were inserted 1:37 packs.

		MT
Complete Set (20):		175.00
Common Player:		4.00
Inserted 1:37		
1	Paul Kariya	20.00
2	Teemu Selanne	8.00
3	Michael Peca	4.00
4	Doug Gilmour	5.00
5	Peter Forsberg	15.00
6	Joe Sakic	10.00
7	Brett Hull	6.00
8	Mike Modano	8.00
9	Sergei Fedorov	8.00
10	Brendan Shanahan	8.00
11	Steve Yzerman	15.00
12	Saku Koivu	6.00
13	Wayne Gretzky	30.00
14	John LeClair	8.00
15	Eric Lindros	20.00
16	Jaromir Jagr	20.00
17	Vincent Lecavalier	12.00
18	Mats Sundin	6.00
19	Mark Messier	7.00
20	Peter Bondra	6.00

1998-99 Pacific Dynagon Ice Watchmen

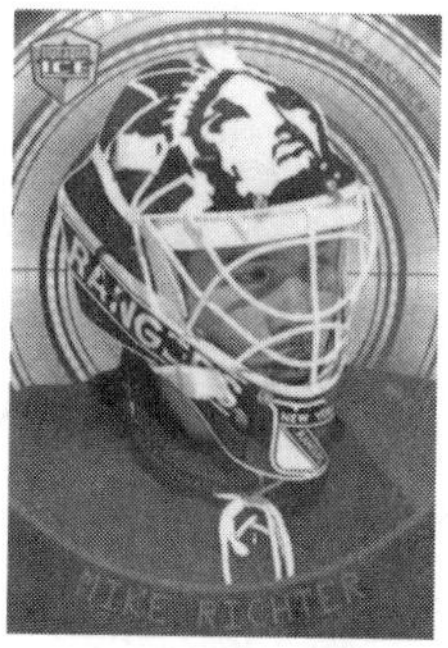

This insert set spotlights ten of the NHL's top goalies. Cards are printed utilizing styrotech technology. Card fronts have a close-up photo of the goalie and is enhanced with red foil etching. Card backs have an action shot along with a career note. These were inserted 1:73 packs.

		MT
Complete Set (10):		80.00
Common Goalie:		6.00
Inserted 1:73		
1	Dominik Hasek	15.00
2	Patrick Roy	30.00
3	Ed Belfour	8.00
4	Chris Osgood	8.00
5	Martin Brodeur	12.00
6	Mike Richter	8.00
7	John Vanbiesbrouck	10.00
8	Grant Fuhr	8.00
9	Curtis Joseph	6.00
10	Olaf Kolzig	6.00

1998-99 Pacific Dynagon Ice Preeminent Players

This 10-card set highlights the NHL's top performers including Gretzky and Yzerman. These were seeded 1:181 packs.

	MT
Complete Set (10):	375.00
Common Player:	20.00

Inserted 1:181		
1	Paul Kariya	50.00
2	Dominik Hasek	30.00
3	Peter Forsberg	40.00
4	Patrick Roy	60.00
5	Mike Modano	20.00
6	Steve Yzerman	40.00
7	Martin Brodeur	25.00
8	Wayne Gretzky	80.00
9	Eric Lindros	50.00
10	Jaromir Jagr	50.00

1998-99 Pacific Dynagon Ice Rookies

The card fronts were printed on an emerald colored foil board on a horizontal format and enhanced with light blue etching and foil stamping. Card backs have a close-up photo along with a career highlight of the featured rookie. They were seeded exclusively in hobby packs at a rate of 1:73 packs.

		MT
Complete Set (10):		60.00
Common Player:		4.00
Inserted 1:73 H		
1	Chris Drury	6.00
2	Milan Hejduk	8.00
3	Mark Parrish	10.00
4	Brendan Morrison	6.00
5	Mike Maneluk	8.00
6	Jan Hrdina	4.00
7	Marty Reasoner	4.00
8	Vincent Lecavalier	20.00
9	Tomas Kaberle	4.00
10	Bill Muckalt	4.00

1998-99 Pacific Dynagon Ice Team Checklists

Card fronts utilize a holographic, prismatic gold foil design, with the featured team's logo prominent beside the player photo. Card backs have a checklist of the featured team from the base set as well as the insert sets. They were inserted 1:18 packs.

		MT
Complete Set (27):		120.00
Common Player:		2.00
Inserted 1:18		
1	Paul Kariya	12.00
2	Ray Bourque	3.00
3	Dominik Hasek	6.00
4	Theoren Fleury	2.00
5	Keith Primeau	2.00
6	Chris Chelios	3.00
7	Patrick Roy	15.00
8	Mike Modano	5.00
9	Steve Yzerman	10.00
10	Ryan Smyth	2.00
11	Dino Ciccarelli	2.00
12	Rob Blake	2.00
13	Saku Koivu	3.00
14	Mike Dunham	3.00
15	Martin Brodeur	6.00
16	Trevor Linden	2.00
17	Wayne Gretzky	20.00
18	Alexei Yashin	3.00
19	Eric Lindros	12.00
20	Keith Tkachuk	4.00
21	Jaromir Jagr	12.00
22	Grant Fuhr	4.00
23	Mike Vernon	3.00
24	Vincent Lecavalier	10.00
25	Mats Sundin	4.00
26	Mark Messier	4.00
27	Peter Bondra	4.00

1998-99 Pacific Omega

Omega's 250-card base set features a horizontal format with silver foil stamping. Card backs feature a small photo along with career totals.

		MT
Complete Set (250):		30.00
Common Player:		.10
1	Travis Green	.10
2	Stu Grimson	.10
3	Guy Hebert	.25
4	Paul Kariya	2.00
5	Marty McInnis	.10
6	Fredrik Olausson	.10
7	Steve Rucchin	.10
8	Teemu Selanne	.75
9	Johan Davidsson, Antti Aalto	.10
10	Jason Allison	.25
11	Ken Belanger	.10
12	Ray Bourque	.40
13	Anson Carter	.10
14	Byron Dafoe	.50
15	Steve Heinze	.10
16	Dimitri Khristich	.10
17	Sergei Samsonov	.75
18	Robbie Tallas	.10
19	Joe Thornton	.50
20	Matthew Barnaby	.10
21	Curtis Brown	.10
22	Michal Grosek	.10
23	Dominik Hasek	1.00
24	Brian Holzinger	.10
25	Michael Peca	.10
26	Rob Ray	.10
27	Geoff Sanderson	.10
28	Miroslav Satan	.20
29	Dixon Ward	.10
30	Valeri Bure	.20
31	Theoren Fleury	.40
32	Jean-Sebastien Giguere	.10
33	Jarome Iginla	.10
34	Tyler Moss	.10
35	Cory Stillman	.10
36	Jason Wiemer	.10
37	Clark Wilm	.10
38	Martin St. Louis, Rico Fata	.75
39	Paul Coffey	.25
40	Ron Francis	.25
41	Martin Gelinas	.10
42	Arturs Irbe	.25
43	Sami Kapanen	.25
44	Trevor Kidd	.25
45	Keith Primeau	.40
46	Gary Roberts	.20
47	Ray Sheppard	.20
48	Tony Amonte	.40
49	Chris Chelios	.40
50	Eric Daze	.20
51	Nelson Emerson	.10
52	Doug Gilmour	.25
53	Mike Maneluk	.50
54	Bob Probert	.20
55	Jocelyn Thibault	.25
56	Alexei Zhamnov	.10
57	Todd White, Brad Brown	.10
58	Adam Deadmarsh	.10
59	Marc Denis	.40
60	Peter Forsberg	1.50
61	Claude Lemieux	.10
62	Jeff Odgers	.10
63	Sandis Ozolinsh	.20
64	Patrick Roy	2.50
65	Joe Sakic	1.00
66	Wade Belak, Scott Parker	.10
67	Chris Drury, Milan Hejduk	.75
68	Ed Belfour	.50
69	Derian Hatcher	.10
70	Brett Hull	.50
71	Jamie Langenbrunner	.10
72	Jere Lehtinen	.10
73	Mike Modano	.75
74	Joe Nieuwendyk	.25
75	Darryl Sydor	.10
76	Roman Turek	.25
77	Sergei Zubov	.10
78	Sergey Gusev, Jamie Wright	.10
79	Sergei Fedorov	.75
80	Joey Kocur	.10
81	Martin LaPointe	.10
82	Igor Larionov	.10
83	Nicklas Lidstrom	.25
84	Darren McCarty	.20
85	Larry Murphy	.10
86	Chris Osgood	.40
87	Brendan Shanahan	.75
88	Steve Yzerman	1.50
89	*Norm Maracle*, Stacy Roest	.75
90	Josef Beranek	.10
91	Sean Brown	.10
92	Bill Guerin	.10
93	Roman Hamrlik	.10
94	Janne Niinimaa	.10
95	Mikhail Shtalenkov	.25
96	Ryan Smyth	.10
97	Doug Weight	.20
98	Tom Poti, Craig Millar	.10
99	Pavel Bure	.75
100	Sean Burke	.25
101	Dino Ciccarelli	.10
102	Bret Hedican	.10
103	Viktor Kozlov	.10
104	Paul Laus	.10
105	Rob Niedermayer	.10
106	*Mark Parrish*	1.50
107	Ray Whitney	.10
108	*Oleg Kvasha*, Peter Worrell	.75
109	Rob Blake	.10
110	Stephane Fiset	.25
111	Glen Murray	.10
112	Luc Robitaille	.25
113	Jamie Storr	.25
114	Jozef Stumpel	.10
115	Vladimir Tsyplakov	.10
116	Mark Visheau, Josh Green	.10
117	Olli Jokinen, Pavel Rosa	.10
118	Benoit Brunet	.10
119	Shayne Corson	.10
120	Vincent Damphousse	.10
121	Jeff Hackett	.25
122	Matt Higgins	.10
123	Saku Koivu	.25
124	Mark Recchi	.20
125	Martin Rucinsky	.10
126	Brian Savage	.10
127	Andrew Brunette	.10
128	Mike Dunham	.25
129	Greg Johnson	.10
130	Sergei Krivokrasov	.10
131	Denny Lambert	.10
132	Cliff Ronning	.10
133	Tomas Vokoun	.10
134	Patrick Cote, Kimmo Timonen	.10
135	Jason Arnott	.10
136	Martin Brodeur	.75
137	Patrik Elias	.10
138	Bobby Holik	.10
139	Brendan Morrison	.40
140	Krzysztof Oliwa	.10
141	Brian Rolston	.10
142	Vadim Sharifijanov	.10
143	Scott Stevens	.10
144	Petr Sykora	.10
145	Ted Donato	.10
146	Kenny Jonsson	.10
147	Trevor Linden	.10
148	Gino Odjick	.10
149	Zigmund Palffy	.40
150	Felix Potvin	.25
151	Robert Reichel	.10
152	Tommy Salo	.40
153	Mike Watt, Eric Brewer	.10
154	Dan Cloutier	.25
155	Adam Graves	.25
156	Wayne Gretzky	3.00
157	Todd Harvey	.10
158	Brian Leetch	.25
159	Manny Malhotra	.40
160	Petr Nedved	.10
161	Mike Richter	.40
162	Esa Tikkanen	.10
163	Daniel Alfredsson	.25
164	Marian Hossa	.10
165	Andreas Johansson	.10
166	Shawn McEachern	.10
167	Wade Redden	.10
168	Damian Rhodes	.25
169	Ron Tugnutt	.25
170	Alexei Yashin	.40
171	Patrick Traverse, Sami Salo	.10
172	Rod Brind'Amour	.25
173	Eric Desjardins	.10
174	Ron Hextall	.25
175	Keith Jones	.10
176	John LeClair	.75
177	Eric Lindros	2.00
178	Mikael Renberg	.10
179	Dimitri Tertyshny	.10
180	John Vanbiesbrouck	.50
181	Dainius Zubrus	.10
182	Daniel Briere	.25
183	Dallas Drake	.10
184	Nikolai Khabibulin	.40
185	Jyrki Lumme	.10
186	Teppo Numminen	.10
187	Jeremy Roenick	.50
188	Keith Tkachuk	.50
189	Rick Tocchet	.10
190	Oleg Tverdovsky	.10
191	Jim Waite	.10
192	Jean-Sebastien Aubin	.10
193	Stu Barnes	.10
194	Tom Barrasso	.25
195	Jaromir Jagr	2.00
196	Alexei Kovalev	.10
197	Robert Lang	.10
198	Alexei Morozov	.10
199	Martin Straka	.10
200	Jan Hrdina, Maxim Galanov	.10
201	Pavol Demitra	.25
202	Grant Fuhr	.40
203	Al MacInnis	.25
204	Jamie McLennan	.25
205	Chris Pronger	.25
206	Pierre Turgeon	.25
207	Tony Twist	.20
208	Marty Reasoner, Lubos Bartecko	.10
209	Jeff Friesen	.10
210	Bryan Marchment	.10
211	Patrick Marleau	.50
212	Owen Nolan	.10
213	Mike Ricci	.10
214	Steve Shields	.25
215	Marco Sturm	.10
216	Mike Vernon	.25
217	Wendel Clark	.20
218	Chris Gratton	.10
219	Vincent Lecavalier	1.00
220	Sandy McCarthy	.10
221	Stephane Richer	.10
222	Darcy Tucker	.10
223	Rob Zamuner	.10
224	Pavel Kubina, Zac Bierk	.10
225	Bryan Berard	.25
226	Tie Domi	.10
227	Mike Johnson	.10
228	Curtis Joseph	.50
229	Igor Korolev	.10
230	Alyn McCauley	.10
231	Mats Sundin	.50
232	Steve Thomas	.10
233	Tomas Kaberle, Daniil Markov	.10
234	Adrian Aucoin	.10
235	Corey Hirsch	.10
236	Mark Messier	.60
237	Alexander Mogilny	.25
238	Bill Muckalt	.10
239	Markus Naslund	.25
240	Mattias Ohlund	.10
241	Garth Snow	.25
242	Matt Cooke, Peter Schaefer	.10
243	Brian Bellows	.10
244	Craig Berube	.10
245	Peter Bondra	.50
246	Matt Herr	.10
247	Joe Juneau	.10
248	Olaf Kolzig	.50
249	Adam Oates	.40
250	Richard Zednik	.10

1998-99 Pacific Omega Online

This 36-card set features full foiled fronts with a brief career highlight on the back. Each card also has the web-site addresses for NHLPA and NHL on the card front and back. These were inserted 4:37.

		MT
Complete Set (36):		150.00
Common Player:		1.50
Inserted 4:37		
1	Paul Kariya	12.00
2	Teemu Selanne	5.00
3	Ray Bourque	3.00
4	Dominik Hasek	6.00
5	Theoren Fleury	2.50
6	Chris Chelios	3.00
7	Doug Gilmour	2.00
8	Peter Forsberg	10.00
9	Patrick Roy	15.00
10	Joe Sakic	6.00
11	Ed Belfour	3.00
12	Brett Hull	4.00
13	Mike Modano	5.00
14	Sergei Fedorov	5.00
15	Brendan Shanahan	5.00
16	Steve Yzerman	10.00
17	Pavel Bure	5.00
18	Saku Koivu	2.50
19	Martin Brodeur	6.00
20	Brendan Morrison	1.50
21	Zigmund Palffy	2.50
22	Felix Potvin	2.00
23	Wayne Gretzky	20.00
24	Alexei Yashin	2.50
25	John LeClair	5.00
26	Eric Lindros	12.00
27	John Vanbiesbrouck	4.00
28	Nikolai Khabibulin	2.00
29	Keith Tkachuk	3.00
30	Jaromir Jagr	12.00
31	Vincent Lecavalier	5.00
32	Curtis Joseph	3.00
33	Mats Sundin	3.00
34	Mark Messier	4.00
35	Bill Muckalt	1.50
36	Peter Bondra	3.00

1998-99 Pacific Omega Prism

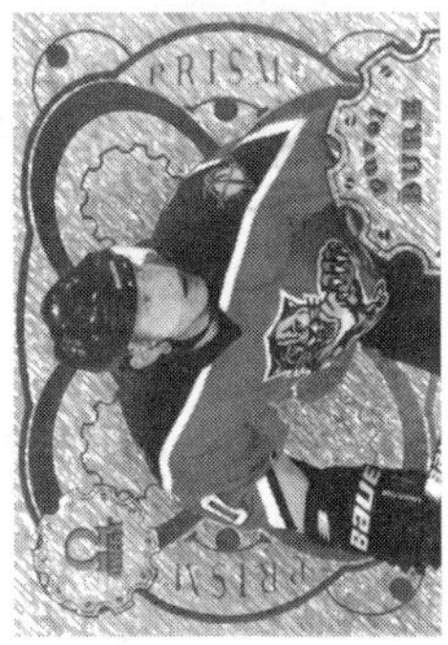

		MT
Complete Set (20):		200.00
Common Player:		4.00
Inserted 1:37		
1	Paul Kariya	20.00
2	Teemu Selanne	8.00
3	Dominik Hasek	10.00
4	Peter Forsberg	15.00
5	Patrick Roy	25.00
6	Joe Sakic	10.00
7	Mike Modano	8.00
8	Sergei Fedorov	8.00
9	Brendan Shanahan	8.00
10	Steve Yzerman	18.00
11	Pavel Bure	8.00
12	Martin Brodeur	10.00
13	Wayne Gretzky	35.00
14	Alexei Yashin	4.00
15	John LeClair	8.00
16	Eric Lindros	20.00
17	Keith Tkachuk	6.00
18	Jaromir Jagr	20.00
19	Mats Sundin	6.00
20	Mark Messier	6.00

1998-99 Pacific Omega EO Portraits

This 20-card insert set features gold foil stamping and utilizes Electro-Optical technology to laser-cut the featured player image into every card. These are seeded 1:73 packs.

		MT
Complete Set (20):		400.00
Common Player:		8.00
Inserted 1:73		
1	Paul Kariya	40.00
2	Teemu Selanne	15.00
3	Dominik Hasek	20.00
4	Peter Forsberg	30.00
5	Patrick Roy	45.00
6	Joe Sakic	20.00
7	Brett Hull	12.00
8	Mike Modano	15.00
9	Sergei Fedorov	15.00
10	Brendan Shanahan	15.00
11	Steve Yzerman	30.00
12	Pavel Bure	15.00
13	Martin Brodeur	20.00
14	Wayne Gretzky	60.00
15	John LeClair	15.00
16	Eric Lindros	40.00
17	Keith Tkachuk	10.00
18	Jaromir Jagr	40.00
19	Mats Sundin	10.00
20	Mark Messier	12.00

1998-99 Pacific Omega Face To Face

This 10-card set matches two of the NHL's top players on a horizontal format. Card fronts also feature silver foil stamping. Card backs have a small photo of each of the featured player's along with a brief career highlight. These were seeded 1:145 packs.

		MT
Complete Set (10):		200.00
Common Player:		10.00
Inserted 1:145		
1	Patrick Roy Martin Brodeur	35.00
2	Wayne Gretzky, Paul Kariya	50.00
3	Dominik Hasek, Jaromir Jagr	30.00
4	Sergei Fedorov, Pavel Bure	15.00
5	Keith Tkachuk, Brendan Shanahan	12.00
6	Steve Yzerman, Joe Sakic	25.00
7	Teemu Selanne, Saku Koivu	12.00
8	Peter Forsberg, Mats Sundin	20.00
9	Mike Modano, John LeClair	15.00
10	Eric Lindros, Mark Messier	30.00

1998-99 Pacific Omega Planet Ice

This 30-card set spotlights the NHL's top players on a horizontal format with silver foil stamping. They were seeded 4:37. The set is also spun off into five different tiers of six cards, each tier is foiled in its own unique color and serial numbered in varying amounts. Tier 1 (1-6) is blue foiled and limited to 100 numbered sets. Tier 2 (7-12) is red foil and limited to 75 sets. Tier 3 (13-18) is green foil and limited to 50 sets. Tier 4 (19-24) is purple foil and limited to 25 sets and Tier 5 (25-30) is gold foil and limited to one set.

		MT
Common Tier 1 Blue (1-6):		30.00
Production 100 sets H		
Common Tier 2 Red (7-12):		60.00
Production 75 sets H		
Common Tier 3 Green (13-18):		75.00
Production 50 sets H		
Tier 4 Purple (19-24):		
Production 25 sets H		
Tier 5 Gold (25-30):		
Production 1 set		
1	Ray Bourque	50.00
2	Chris Chelios	50.00
3	Vincent Lecavalier	60.00
4	Mark Parrish	30.00
5	Felix Potvin	30.00
6	Alexei Yashin	30.00
7	Ed Belfour	75.00
8	Peter Bondra	60.00
9	Brett Hull	75.00
10	Mark Messier	75.00
11	Mats Sundin	75.00
12	John Vanbiesbrouck	75.00
13	Sergei Fedorov	125.00
14	Curtis Joseph	100.00
15	John LeClair	125.00
16	Mike Modano	125.00
17	Brendan Shanahan	125.00
18	Keith Tkachuk	90.00
19	Martin Brodeur	N/A
20	Pavel Bure	N/A
21	Dominik Hasek	N/A
22	Joe Sakic	N/A
23	Teemu Selanne	N/A
24	Steve Yzerman	N/A
25	Peter Forsberg	N/A
26	Wayne Gretzky	N/A
27	Jaromir Jagr	N/A
28	Paul Kariya	N/A
29	Eric Lindros	N/A
30	Patrick Roy	N/A

1998-99 Pacific Paramount

This 250-card set features full bleed photos highlighted by holographic gold foil. Card backs have a small photo along with 1997-98 statistics along with career totals. There are five parallel versions of the base set also randomly seeded: Silver, Copper, Ice Blue, Emerald and Holo-electric. Silvers are retail only and seeded 1:1. Copper are U.S. hobby exclusive and seeded 1:1. Ice Blue are seeded 1:73. Emerald are Canadian hobby exclusive and seeded 1:1 and Holo-electric are limited to 99 serial numbered sets.

		MT
Complete Set (250):		20.00
Common Player:		.10
Coppers:		1.5x to 3x
Inserted 1:1 H		
Holo-electric Stars:		90x to 150x
Yng Stars & Rookies:		50x to 90x
Production 99 sets		
Silver:		1.5x to 2x
Inserted 1:1 R		
Ice Blue:		50x to 100x
Inserted 1:73		
Emerald:		2x to 3x
Inserted 1:1 Can. H		
1	Travis Green	.10
2	Guy Hebert	.25
3	Paul Kariya	1.50
4	Josef Marha	.10
5	Steve Rucchin	.10
6	Tomas Sandstrom	.10
7	Teemu Selanne	.60
8	Jason Allison	.20
9	Per Axelsson	.10
10	Ray Bourque	.25
11	Anson Carter	.10
12	Byron Dafoe	.25
13	Ted Donato	.10
14	Dave Ellett	.10
15	Dimitri Khristich	.10
16	Sergei Samsonov	.75
17	Matthew Barnaby	.10
18	Michal Grosek	.10
19	Dominik Hasek	.75
20	Brian Holzinger	.10
21	Mike Peca	.10
22	Miroslav Satan	.10
23	Vaclav Varada	.10
24	Dixon Ward	.10
25	Alexei Zhitnik	.10
26	Andrew Cassels	.10
27	Theoren Fleury	.25
28	Jarome Iginla	.10
29	Marty McInnis	.10
30	Derek Morris	.10
31	Michael Nylander	.10
32	Cory Stillman	.10
33	Rick Tabaracci	.10
34	Kevin Dineen	.10
35	Nelson Emerson	.10
36	Martin Gelinas	.10
37	Sami Kapanen	.20
38	Trevor Kidd	.25
39	Robert Kron	.10
40	Jeff O'Neill	.10
41	Keith Primeau	.20
42	Gary Roberts	.10
43	Tony Amonte	.25
44	Chris Chelios	.25
45	Paul Coffey	.25
46	Eric Daze	.20
47	Doug Gilmour	.25
48	Jeff Hackett	.30
49	Jean-Yves Leroux	.10
50	Eric Weinrich	.10
51	Alexei Zhamnov	.10
52	Craig Billington	.20
53	Adam Deadmarsh	.10
54	Adam Foote	.10
55	Peter Forsberg	1.25
56	Valeri Kamensky	.10
57	Claude Lemieux	.10
58	Eric Messier	.10
59	Sandis Ozolinsh	.20
60	Patrick Roy	2.00
61	Joe Sakic	.75
62	Ed Belfour	.30
63	Derian Hatcher	.10
64	Brett Hull	.50
65	Jamie Langenbrunner	.10
66	Jere Lehtinen	.10
67	Juha Lind	.10
68	Mike Modano	.60
69	Joe Nieuwendyk	.20
70	Darryl Sydor	.10
71	Roman Turek	.10
72	Sergei Zubov	.20
73	Anders Eriksson	.10
74	Sergei Fedorov	.60
75	Kevin Hodson	.25
76	Vyacheslav Kozlov	.10
77	Igor Larionov	.10
78	Nicklas Lidstrom	.25
79	Darren McCarty	.10
80	Larry Murphy	.10
81	Chris Osgood	.30
82	Brendan Shanahan	.60
83	Steve Yzerman	1.25
84	Kelly Buchberger	.10
85	Mike Grier	.10
86	Bill Guerin	.10
87	Roman Hamrlik	.10
88	Todd Marchant	.10
89	Dean McAmmond	.10
90	Boris Mironov	.10
91	Janne Niinimaa	.20
92	Ryan Smyth	.10
93	Doug Weight	.20
94	Dino Ciccarelli	.10
95	Dave Gagner	.10
96	Ed Jovanovski	.10
97	Viktor Kozlov	.10
98	Paul Laus	.10
99	Scott Mellanby	.10
100	Robert Svehla	.10
101	Ray Whitney	.10
102	Rob Blake	.10
103	Russ Courtnall	.10
104	Stephane Fiset	.20
105	Glen Murray	.10
106	Yanic Perreault	.10
107	Luc Robitaille	.20
108	Jamie Storr	.25
109	Jozef Stumpel	.10
110	Vladimir Tsyplakov	.10
111	Shayne Corson	.10
112	Vincent Damphousse	.10
113	Saku Koivu	.40
114	Vladimir Malakhov	.10
115	Dave Manson	.10
116	Mark Recchi	.10
117	Martin Rucinsky	.10
118	Brian Savage	.10
119	Jocelyn Thibault	.25
120	Blair Atcheynum	.10
121	Andrew Brunette	.10
122	Mike Dunham	.10
123	Tom Fitzgerald	.10
124	Sergei Krivokrasov	.10
125	Denny Lambert	.10
126	*Jay More*	.25
127	Mikhail Shtalenkov	.10
128	Darren Turcotte	.10
129	Scott Walker	.10
130	Dave Andreychuk	.10
131	Jason Arnott	.20
132	Martin Brodeur	.75
133	Patrik Elias	.10
134	Bobby Holik	.10
135	Randy McKay	.10
136	Scott Niedermayer	.10
137	Krzysztof Oliwa	.10
138	*Sheldon Souray*	.10
139	Scott Stevens	.10
140	Bryan Berard	.20
141	Mariusz Czerkawski	.10
142	Jason Dawe	.10
143	Kenny Jonsson	.10
144	Trevor Linden	.10
145	Zigmund Palffy	.50
146	Richard Pilon	.10
147	Robert Reichel	.10
148	Tommy Salo	.25
149	Bryan Smolinski	.10
150	Dan Cloutier	.25
151	Adam Graves	.10
152	Wayne Gretzky	2.50
153	Alexei Kovalev	.10
154	Pat LaFontaine	.20
155	Brian Leetch	.25
156	Mike Richter	.30
157	Ulf Samuelsson	.10
158	Kevin Stevens	.10
159	Niklas Sundstrom	.10
160	Daniel Alfredsson	.20
161	Magnus Arvedson	.10
162	Andreas Dackell	.10
163	Igor Kravchuk	.10
164	Shawn McEachern	.10
165	Chris Phillips	.10
166	Damian Rhodes	.25
167	Ron Tugnutt	.20
168	Alexei Yashin	.25
169	Rod Brind'Amour	.20
170	Alexandre Daigle	.10
171	Eric Desjardins	.10
172	Colin Forbes	.10
173	Chris Gratton	.10
174	Ron Hextall	.20
175	Trent Klatt	.10
176	John LeClair	.60
177	Eric Lindros	1.50
178	John Vanbiesbrouck	.60
179	Dainius Zubrus	.20
180	Dallas Drake	.10
181	Brad Isbister	.10
182	Nikolai Khabibulin	.25
183	Teppo Numminen	.10
184	Jeremy Roenick	.30
185	Cliff Ronning	.10
186	Keith Tkachuk	.50
187	Rick Tocchet	.10
188	Oleg Tverdovsky	.20
189	Stu Barnes	.10
190	Tom Barrasso	.25
191	Kevin Hatcher	.10
192	Jaromir Jagr	1.50
193	Darius Kasparaitis	.10
194	Alexei Morozov	.10
195	Fredrik Olausson	.10
196	Jiri Slegr	.10
197	Martin Straka	.10
198	Jim Campbell	.10
199	Kelly Chase	.10
200	Craig Conroy	.10
201	Geoff Courtnall	.10
202	Pavol Demitra	.10
203	Grant Fuhr	.25
204	Al MacInnis	.20
205	Jamie McLennan	.10
206	Chris Pronger	.20
207	Pierre Turgeon	.25
208	Tony Twist	.10
209	Jeff Friesen	.10
210	Tony Granato	.10
211	Patrick Marleau	.50
212	Stephane Matteau	.10
213	Marty McSorley	.10
214	Owen Nolan	.10
215	Marco Sturm	.10
216	Mike Vernon	.25
217	Karl Dykhuis	.10
218	Sandy McCarthy	.10
219	Mikael Renberg	.10
220	Stephane Richer	.10
221	Alexander Selivanov	.10
222	Paul Ysebaert	.10
223	Rob Zamuner	.10
224	Sergei Berezin	.20
225	Tie Domi	.10
226	Mike Johnson	.10
227	Curtis Joseph	.30
228	Derek King	.10
229	Igor Korolev	.10
230	Mathieu Schneider	.10
231	Mats Sundin	.40
232	Todd Bertuzzi	.10
233	Donald Brashear	.10
234	Pavel Bure	.60
235	Arturs Irbe	.20
236	Mark Messier	.50
237	Alexander Mogilny	.25
238	Mattias Ohlund	.25
239	Dave Scatchard	.10
240	Garth Snow	.20
241	Brian Bellows	.10
242	Peter Bondra	.40
243	Jeff Brown	.10
244	Sergei Gonchar	.10
245	Calle Johansson	.10
246	Joe Juneau	.10
247	Olaf Kolzig	.40
248	Steve Konowalchuk	.10
249	Adam Oates	.30
250	Richard Zednik	.10

1998-99 Pacific Paramount Glove Side

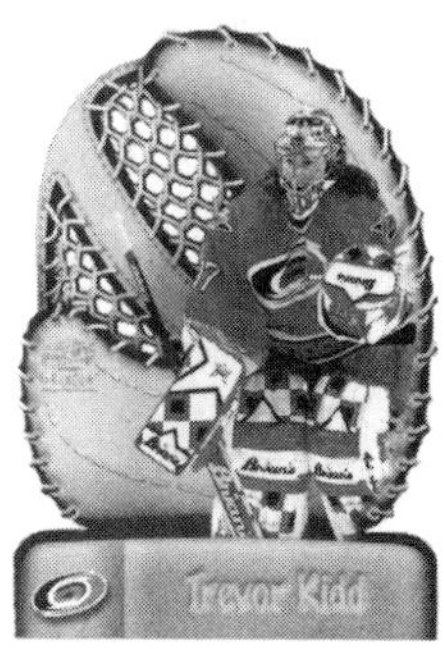

This insert set focuses on twenty of the NHL's top goalies on a die-cut design shaped like a goalie catching glove. These were seeded 1:73 packs.

		MT
Complete Set (20):		180.00
Common Player:		6.00
Inserted 1:73		
1	Guy Hebert	6.00
2	Byron Dafoe	6.00
3	Dominik Hasek	25.00
4	Trevor Kidd	6.00
5	Jeff Hackett	8.00
6	Patrick Roy	40.00
7	Ed Belfour	12.00
8	Chris Osgood	15.00
9	Mike Dunham	10.00
10	Martin Brodeur	25.00
11	Tommy Salo	6.00
12	Mike Richter	12.00
13	Damian Rhodes	6.00
14	Ron Hextall	6.00
15	Nikolai Khabibulin	8.00
16	Tom Barrasso	10.00
17	Grant Fuhr	12.00
18	Mike Vernon	10.00
19	Curtis Joseph	15.00
20	Olaf Kolzig	15.00

1998-99 Pacific Paramount Hall of Fame Bound

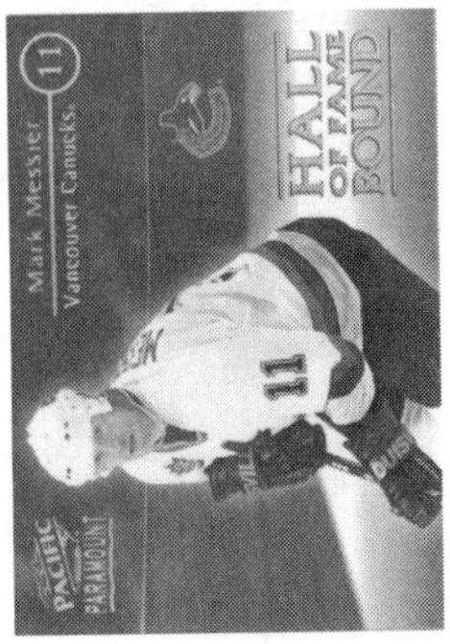

This set focuses on ten players destined for the Hall of Fame on a horizontal format with gold foil stamping. They were seeded 1:361 packs.

		MT
Complete Set (10):		550.00
Common Player:		25.00
Inserted 1:361		
1	Teemu Selanne	30.00
2	Dominik Hasek	40.00
3	Peter Forsberg	60.00
4	Patrick Roy	85.00
5	Steve Yzerman	60.00
6	Martin Brodeur	40.00
7	Wayne Gretzky	125.00
8	Eric Lindros	75.00
9	Jaromir Jagr	75.00
10	Mark Messier	25.00

1998-99 Pacific Paramount Ice Galaxy

Found exclusively in Canadian retail packs these inserts feature bronze foiled fronts and are limited to 140 serial numbered sets, seeded 1:97 packs. Two parallel versions are also randomly seeded: Silver and Gold. Silvers have silver foil fronts and are limited to 50 numbered sets. Gold have gold foil fronts and are limited to 10 numbered sets.

		MT
Complete Set (10):		600.00
Common Player:		25.00
Inserted 1:97 Canada R		
Silver: 1.		5x to 2.5x
Production 50 sets		
Gold:		3x to 6x
Production 10 sets		
1	Paul Kariya	100.00
2	Peter Forsberg	75.00
3	Patrick Roy	120.00
4	Joe Sakic	50.00
5	Steve Yzerman	75.00
6	Martin Brodeur	40.00
7	Wayne Gretzky	150.00
8	Alexei Yashin	25.00
9	Eric Lindros	75.00
10	Curtis Joseph	25.00

1998-99 Pacific Paramount Special Delivery

This 20-card insert set highlights the NHL's top offensive talents on an all die-cut border design. Card fronts are fully foiled with some gold foil stamping. These were seeded 1:37 packs.

		MT
Complete Set (20):		125.00
Common Player:		4.00
Inserted 1:37		
1	Paul Kariya	15.00
2	Teemu Selanne	6.00
3	Sergei Samsonov	8.00
4	Peter Forsberg	12.00
5	Joe Sakic	8.00
6	Mike Modano	6.00
7	Sergei Fedorov	6.00
8	Brendan Shanahan	6.00
9	Steve Yzerman	12.00
10	Saku Koivu	4.00
11	Zigmund Palffy	4.00
12	Wayne Gretzky	25.00
13	John LeClair	6.00
14	Eric Lindros	15.00
15	Keith Tkachuk	5.00
16	Jaromir Jagr	15.00
17	Mats Sundin	4.00
18	Pavel Bure	6.00
19	Mark Messier	5.00
20	Peter Bondra	4.00

1998-99 Pacific Paramount Team Checklists

This 27-card insert set represents each NHL team, on a die-cut fully foiled design. The featured team's top player is featured on the card front. Card backs have the team's complete main set checklist. These were seeded 2:37 packs.

		MT
Complete Set (27):		100.00
Common Player:		2.50
Inserted 1:18		
1	Teemu Selanne	5.00
2	Sergei Samsonov	6.00
3	Dominik Hasek	6.00
4	Theoren Fleury	2.50
5	Keith Primeau	2.50
6	Chris Chelios	2.50
7	Patrick Roy	15.00
8	Mike Modano	5.00
9	Steve Yzerman	10.00
10	Ryan Smyth	2.50
11	Dino Ciccarelli	2.50
12	Rob Blake	2.50
13	Saku Koivu	4.00
14	Tom Fitzgerald	2.50
15	Martin Brodeur	6.00
16	Zigmund Palffy	4.00
17	Wayne Gretzky	20.00
18	Alexei Yashin	2.50
19	Eric Lindros	12.00
20	Keith Tkachuk	4.00
21	Jaromir Jagr	12.00
22	Grant Fuhr	4.00
23	Patrick Marleau	5.00
24	Rob Zamuner	2.50
25	Mats Sundin	4.00
26	Mark Messier	4.00
27	Peter Bondra	4.00

1998-99 Pacific Revolution

The base set consists of 150-cards with dual foiling, etching, embossing and gold foil stamping. Card backs have a small photo along with complete year-by-year statistics. Two parallel versions are also randomly seeded: Shadows and Reds. Shadows are hobby exclusive and limited to 99 serial numbered sets. Reds are a retail exclusive parallel, which have red foil stamping and limited to 299 serial numbered sets.

		MT
Complete Set (150):		100.00
Common Player:		.50
Shadows:		15x to 30x
Production 99 sets H		
Red:		3x to 6x
Production 299 sets R		
1	Guy Hebert	1.00
2	Paul Kariya	6.00
3	Marty McInnis	.50
4	Steve Rucchin	.50
5	Teemu Selanne	2.50
6	Jason Allison	.75
7	Ray Bourque	1.50
8	Anson Carter	.50
9	Byron Dafoe	1.00
10	Dimitri Khristich	.50
11	Sergei Samsonov	2.50
12	Matthew Barnaby	.50
13	Michal Grosek	.50
14	Dominik Hasek	3.00
15	Michael Peca	.50
16	Miroslav Satan	.75
17	Dixon Ward	.50
18	Theoren Fleury	1.00
19	Jean-Sebastien Giguere	.50
20	Jarome Iginla	.50
21	Tyler Moss	.50
22	Cory Stillman	.50
23	Ron Francis	.75
24	Arturs Irbe	1.00
25	Trevor Kidd	1.00
26	Keith Primeau	.75
27	Ray Sheppard	.50
28	Tony Amonte	1.00
29	Chris Chelios	1.50
30	Eric Daze	.50
31	Doug Gilmour	.75
32	Jocelyn Thibault	1.00
33	Adam Deadmarsh	.50
34	Chris Drury	.50
35	Peter Forsberg	5.00
36	*Milan Hejduk*	1.50
37	Claude Lemieux	.50
38	Patrick Roy	8.00
39	Joe Sakic	3.00
40	Ed Belfour	1.50
41	Brett Hull	2.00
42	Jamie Langenbrunner	.50
43	Jere Lehtinen	.50
44	Mike Modano	2.50
45	Joe Nieuwendyk	.75
46	Darryl Sydor	.50
47	Sergei Fedorov	2.50
48	Nicklas Lidstrom	1.00
49	*Norm Maracle*	2.50
50	Darren McCarty	.75
51	Chris Osgood	1.50
52	Brendan Shanahan	2.50
53	Steve Yzerman	5.00
54	Bill Guerin	.50
55	Andrei Kovalenko	.50
56	Mikhail Shtalenkov	.75
57	Ryan Smyth	.50
58	Doug Weight	.50
59	Pavel Bure	2.50
60	Sean Burke	1.00
61	Dino Ciccarelli	.50
62	Viktor Kozlov	.50
63	Rob Niedermayer	.50
64	*Mark Parrish*	2.50
65	Rob Blake	.50
66	Stephane Fiset	1.00
67	Olli Jokinen	.50
68	Luc Robitaille	.75
69	*Pavel Rosa*	1.00
70	Jozef Stumpel	.50
71	Shayne Corson	.50
72	Vincent Damphousse	.50
73	Jeff Hackett	1.00
74	Saku Koivu	1.00
75	Mark Recchi	.50
76	Brian Savage	.50
77	Andrew Brunette	.50
78	Mike Dunham	1.00
79	Sergei Krivokrasov	.50
80	Cliff Ronning	.50
81	Tomas Vokoun	.50
82	Jason Arnott	.50
83	Martin Brodeur	3.00
84	Patrik Elias	.50
85	Bobby Holik	.50
86	Brendan Morrison	.50
87	Kenny Jonsson	.50
88	Trevor Linden	.50
89	Zigmund Palffy	1.50
90	Tommy Salo	1.00
91	Mike Watt	.50
92	Wayne Gretzky	10.00
93	Todd Harvey	.50
94	Brian Leetch	1.00
95	Manny Malhotra	.50
96	Petr Nedved	.50
97	Mike Richter	1.50
98	Daniel Alfredsson	.75
99	Marian Hossa	.50
100	Shawn McEachern	.50
101	Damian Rhodes	1.00
102	Alexei Yashin	1.50
103	Rod Brind'Amour	.75
104	Ron Hextall	1.00
105	John LeClair	2.50
106	Eric Lindros	6.00
107	John Vanbiesbrouck	2.00
108	Dainius Zubrus	.50
109	Daniel Briere	.50
110	Nikolai Khabibulin	1.00
111	Jeremy Roenick	1.50
112	Keith Tkachuk	2.00
113	Rick Tocchet	.50
114	Jim Waite	.50
115	*Jean-Sebastien Aubin*	1.00
116	Stu Barnes	.50
117	Tom Barrasso	1.00
118	Jaromir Jagr	6.00
119	Alexei Kovalev	.50
120	Martin Straka	.50
121	Pavol Demitra	.75
122	Grant Fuhr	1.50
123	Al MacInnis	.75
124	Chris Pronger	.75
125	Pierre Turgeon	.75
126	Jeff Friesen	.50
127	Patrick Marleau	1.00
128	Owen Nolan	.50
129	Marco Sturm	.50
130	Mike Vernon	1.00
131	Wendel Clark	.50
132	Daren Puppa	.75
133	Vincent Lecavalier	3.00
134	Stephane Richer	.50
135	Rob Zamuner	.50
136	Tie Domi	.50
137	Mike Johnson	.50
138	Curtis Joseph	1.50
139	*Tomas Kaberle*	.75
140	Mats Sundin	2.00
141	Mark Messier	2.00
142	Alexander Mogilny	1.00
143	*Bill Muckalt*	.50
144	Mattias Ohlund	.50
145	Garth Snow	1.00
146	Peter Bondra	1.50
147	Joe Juneau	.50
148	Olaf Kolzig	1.00
149	Adam Oates	1.00
150	Richard Zednik	.50

1998-99 Pacific Revolution All-Stars

This 30-card set is a full-foil insert with a die-cut top in the shape of a star. All-Stars feature players in the 1999 All-Star Game and are seeded 1:25 packs.

		MT
Complete Set (30):		280.00
Common Player:		6.00
Inserted 1:25		
1	Tony Amonte	6.00
2	Ed Belfour	8.00
3	Peter Bondra	8.00
4	Ray Bourque	8.00
5	Martin Brodeur	15.00
6	Theo Fleury	6.00
7	Peter Forsberg	25.00
8	Wayne Gretzky	50.00
9	Dominik Hasek	15.00
10	Bobby Holik	6.00
11	Arturs Irbe	8.00
12	Jaromir Jagr	30.00
13	Paul Kariya	30.00
14	Nikolai Khabibulin	8.00
15	Sergei Krivokrasov	6.00
16	John LeClair	12.00
17	Nicklas Lidstrom	8.00
18	Eric Lindros	30.00
19	Al MacInnis	6.00
20	Mike Modano	12.00
21	Mattias Ohlund	6.00
22	Keith Primeau	6.00
23	Chris Pronger	6.00
24	Mark Recchi	6.00
25	Jeremy Roenick	8.00
26	Teemu Selanne	12.00
27	Brendan Shanahan	12.00
28	Mats Sundin	10.00
29	Keith Tkachuk	8.00
30	Alexei Yashin	6.00

1998-99 Pacific Revolution Chalk Talk

Chalk Talk inserts have a diagrammed play on the left portion of the card front with a player photo on the right side. Chalk Talks are inserted 1:49 packs.

		MT
Complete Set (20):		360.00
Common Player:		8.00
Inserted 1:49		
1	Paul Kariya	40.00
2	Teemu Selanne	15.00
3	Theoren Fleury	8.00
4	Peter Forsberg	30.00
5	Joe Sakic	20.00
6	Brett Hull	12.00
7	Mike Modano	15.00
8	Sergei Fedorov	15.00
9	Brendan Shanahan	15.00
10	Steve Yzerman	30.00
11	Wayne Gretzky	60.00
12	Alexei Yashin	8.00
13	John LeClair	15.00
14	Eric Lindros	40.00
15	Keith Tkachuk	10.00
16	Jaromir Jagr	40.00
17	Vincent Lecavalier	20.00
18	Mats Sundin	12.00
19	Mark Messier	12.00
20	Peter Bondra	10.00

1998-99 Pacific Revolution NHL Icons

Ten of hockey's biggest stars are featured on a die-cut silver foil etched design. These are seeded 1:121 packs.

		MT
Complete Set (10):		375.00
Common Player:		20.00
Inserted 1:121		

1	Paul Kariya	50.00
2	Dominik Hasek	30.00
3	Peter Forsberg	40.00
4	Patrick Roy	60.00
5	Mike Modano	20.00
6	Steve Yzerman	40.00
7	Martin Brodeur	30.00
8	Wayne Gretzky	80.00
9	Eric Lindros	50.00
10	Jaromir Jagr	50.00

1998-99 Pacific Revolution Showstoppers

Hockey's top stars renown for their game-winning heroics are profiled on this holographic silver foil design. The set consists of 36-cards, inserted 2:25 packs.

		MT
Complete Set (36):		200.00
Common Player:		3.00
Inserted 2:25		
1	Paul Kariya	20.00
2	Teemu Selanne	8.00
3	Ray Bourque	5.00
4	Dominik Hasek	10.00
5	Michael Peca	3.00
6	Theoren Fleury	4.00
7	Tony Amonte	4.00
8	Chris Chelios	5.00
9	Doug Gilmour	4.00
10	Peter Forsberg	15.00
11	Patrick Roy	20.00
12	Joe Sakic	10.00
13	Ed Belfour	5.00
14	Brett Hull	6.00
15	Mike Modano	8.00
16	Sergei Fedorov	8.00
17	Brendan Shanahan	8.00
18	Steve Yzerman	15.00
19	Mark Parrish	3.00
20	Saku Koivu	4.00
21	Martin Brodeur	10.00
22	Zigmund Palffy	5.00
23	Wayne Gretzky	30.00
24	Alexei Yashin	3.00
25	John LeClair	8.00
26	Eric Lindros	20.00
27	John Vanbiesbrouck	6.00
28	Nikolai Khabibulin	5.00
29	Jeremy Roenick	5.00
30	Keith Tkachuk	6.00
31	Jaromir Jagr	20.00
32	Vincent Lecavalier	10.00
33	Curtis Joseph	5.00
34	Mats Sundin	6.00
35	Mark Messier	6.00
36	Peter Bondra	5.00

1998-99 Pacific Revolution Three-Pronged Attack

Three-Pronged Attack features 30 of the NHL's top players and is seeded exclusively in hobby packs at a rate of 4:25. A parallel version is also randomly seeded. The 30-card set is broken down into three separate tiers of 10 cards, each tier is serially numbered in varying amounts. Tier 1 (1-10) is limited to 99 numbered sets. Tier 2 (11-20) are limited to 199 numbered sets. Tier 3 (21-30) are limited to 299 numbered sets.

		MT
Complete Set (30):		90.00
Common Player:		1.50
Inserted 1:6		
1	Matthew Barnaby	1.50
2	Theo Fleury	2.00
3	Chris Chelios	2.50
4	Darren McCarty	1.50
5	Brendan Shanahan	4.00
6	Eric Lindros	10.00
7	Keith Tkachuk	3.00
8	Tony Twist	1.50
9	Tie Domi	1.50
10	Donald Brashear	1.50
11	Dominik Hasek	5.00
12	Patrick Roy	10.00
13	Ed Belfour	2.50
14	Chris Osgood	2.50
15	Martin Brodeur	5.00
16	Mike Richter	2.50
17	John Vanbiesbrouck	3.00
18	Nikolai Khabibulin	2.00
19	Curtis Joseph	2.00
20	Olaf Kolzig	2.00
21	Paul Kariya	10.00
22	Teemu Selanne	4.00
23	Peter Forsberg	7.00
24	Joe Sakic	5.00
25	Mike Modano	4.00
26	Steve Yzerman	7.00
27	Wayne Gretzky	15.00
28	John LeClair	4.00
29	Jaromir Jagr	10.00
30	Pavel Bure	4.00

1998-99 Pacific Revolution Three-Pronged Attack Parallel

The 30-card set is broken down into three separate tiers of 10 cards, each tier is serially numbered in varying amounts. Tier 1 (1-10) is limited to 99 numbered sets. Tier 2 (11-20) are limited to 199 numbered sets. Tier 3 (21-30) are limited to 299 numbered sets.

		MT
Complete Set (30):		1250.
Common Tier 1 (1-10):		25.00
Production 99 sets		
Common Tier 2 (11-20):		15.00
Production 199 sets		15.00
Common Tier 3 (21-30):		20.00
Production 299 sets		
1	Matthew Barnaby	25.00
2	Theo Fleury	50.00
3	Chris Chelios	60.00
4	Darren McCarty	30.00
5	Brendan Shanahan	80.00
6	Eric Lindros	200.00
7	Keith Tkachuk	60.00
8	Tony Twist	25.00
9	Tie Domi	25.00
10	Donald Brashear	25.00
11	Dominik Hasek	60.00
12	Patrick Roy	140.00
13	Ed Belfour	30.00
14	Chris Osgood	30.00
15	Martin Brodeur	60.00
16	Mike Richter	30.00
17	John Vanbiesbrouck	40.00
18	Nikolai Khabibulin	25.00
19	Curtis Joseph	30.00
20	Olaf Kolzig	25.00
21	Paul Kariya	60.00
22	Teemu Selanne	25.00
23	Peter Forsberg	50.00
24	Joe Sakic	30.00
25	Mike Modano	25.00
26	Steve Yzerman	50.00
27	Wayne Gretzky	100.00
28	John LeClair	25.00
29	Jaromir Jagr	60.00
30	Pavel Bure	25.00

1998-99 SP Authentic

The 135-card set consists of 90 current NHL players, along with 45 short-printed "Future Watch" subset cards, which are sequentially numbered to 2,000. Card fronts have blue foil stamping and card backs have a small photo, a career note and up to the last five seasons of statistics. A parallel to the base set called Power Shift are randomly seeded, limited to 500 numbered sets. Power Shift is stamped in red foil on the card front.

		MT
Complete Set (135):		240.00
Common Player:		.25
Common SP (91-135):		4.00
SP Production 2,000 sets		
Common Powershift:		3.00
Powershifts:		5x to 10x
SP's:		1.5x
Production 500 sets		
1	Paul Kariya	3.00
2	Teemu Selanne	1.25
3	Guy Hebert	.50
4	Sergei Samsonov	1.25
5	Joe Thornton	.75
6	Jason Allison	.50
7	Ray Bourque	.75
8	Dominik Hasek	2.00
9	Michael Peca	.25
10	Michal Grosek	.25
11	Derek Morris	.25
12	Theoren Fleury	.50
13	Jarome Iginla	.25
14	Ron Francis	.40
15	Keith Primeau	.50
16	Sami Kapanen	.40
17	Tony Amonte	.40
18	Doug Gilmour	.40
19	Chris Chelios	.75
20	Peter Forsberg	2.50
21	Patrick Roy	3.00
22	Joe Sakic	1.50
23	Adam Deadmarsh	.40
24	Brett Hull	1.00
25	Mike Modano	1.25
26	Ed Belfour	.75
27	Jere Lehtinen	.25
28	Sergei Fedorov	1.25
29	Brendan Shanahan	1.25
30	Chris Osgood	.75
31	Steve Yzerman	2.50
32	Nicklas Lidstrom	.75
33	Doug Weight	.40
34	Bill Guerin	.25
35	Tom Poti	.25
36	Rob Niedermayer	.25
37	Ed Jovanovski	.25
38	Luc Robitaille	.50
39	Rob Blake	.25
40	Glen Murray	.25
41	Saku Koivu	.50
42	Mark Recchi	.25
43	Vincent Damphousse	.25
44	Mike Dunham	.50
45	Sergei Krivokrasov	.25
46	Andrew Brunette	.25
47	Brendan Morrison	.25
48	Martin Brodeur	1.50
49	Scott Stevens	.25
50	Patrik Elias	.25
51	Trevor Linden	.25
52	Zigmund Palffy	.75
53	Bryan Berard	.25
54	Robert Reichel	.25
55	Mike Richter	.75
56	Wayne Gretzky	5.00
57	Brian Leetch	.50
58	Wade Redden	.25
59	Alexei Yashin	.75
60	Daniel Alfredsson	.40
61	Eric Lindros	3.00
62	John Vanbiesbrouck	1.00
63	John LeClair	1.25
64	Rod Brind'Amour	.50
65	Jeremy Roenick	.75
66	Keith Tkachuk	1.00
67	Nikolai Khabibulin	.75
68	German Titov	.25
69	Martin Straka	.50
70	Jaromir Jagr	3.00
71	Chris Pronger	.50
72	Al MacInnis	.50
73	Pierre Turgeon	.40
74	Pavol Demitra	.40
75	Patrick Marleau	.75
76	Jeff Friesen	.25
77	Owen Nolan	.25
78	Bill Ranford	.50
79	Wendel Clark	.25
80	Craig Janney	.25
81	Mike Johnson	.25
82	Curtis Joseph	.75
83	Mats Sundin	1.00
84	Mattias Ohlund	.25
85	Mark Messier	1.00
86	Pavel Bure	1.25
87	Olaf Kolzig	.75
88	Peter Bondra	.75
89	Joe Juneau	.25
90	Adam Oates	.75
91	Johan Davidsson (Future Watch)	4.00
92	Rico Fata (Future Watch)	10.00
93	Mike Maneluk (Future Watch)	12.00
94	J.P. Dumont (Future Watch)	4.00
95	*Milan Hejduk* (Future Watch)	25.00
96	Chris Drury (Future Watch)	12.00
97	*Mark Parrish* (Future Watch)	20.00
98	*Oleg Kvasha* (Future Watch)	12.00
99	Josh Green (Future Watch)	4.00
100	Olli Jokinen (Future Watch)	5.00
101	Manny Malhotra (Future Watch)	10.00
102	Eric Brewer (Future Watch)	4.00
103	Mike Watt (Future Watch)	4.00
104	Daniel Briere (Future Watch)	5.00
105	*Jean-Sebastien Aubin* (Future Watch)	8.00
106	Jan Hrdina (Future Watch)	10.00
107	Marty Reasoner (Future Watch)	4.00
108	Michal Handzus (Future Watch)	10.00
109	Vincent LaCavalier (Future Watch)	25.00
110	*Tomas Kaberle* (Future Watch)	4.00
111	*Bill Muckalt* (Future Watch)	15.00
112	Josh Holden (Future Watch)	4.00
113	Matthew Herr (Future Watch)	4.00
114	Brian Finley (Future Watch)	15.00
115	Maxime Ouellet (Future Watch)	8.00
116	Kurtis Foster (Future Watch)	4.00
117	Barrett Jackman (Future Watch)	4.00
118	Ross Lupaschuk (Future Watch)	6.00
119	Steven McCarthy (Future Watch)	8.00
120	Peter Reynolds (Future Watch)	4.00
121	Bart Rushmer (Future Watch)	4.00
122	Jonathon Zion (Future Watch)	6.00
123	Kris Beech (Future Watch)	15.00
124	Brandin Cote (Future Watch)	4.00
125	Scott Kelman (Future Watch)	8.00
126	Jamie Lundmark (Future Watch)	8.00
127	Derek MacKenzie (Future Watch)	4.00
128	Rory McDade (Future Watch)	4.00
129	David Morisset (Future Watch)	8.00
130	Mirko Murovic (Future Watch)	8.00
131	Taylor Pyatt (Future Watch)	12.00
132	Charlie Stephens (Future Watch)	4.00
133	Kyle Wanvig (Future Watch)	8.00
134	Krzystof Wieckowski (Future Watch)	6.00
135	Michael Zigomanis (Future Watch)	10.00

1998-99 SP Authentic Authentics

Authentics are redemption cards good for a piece of autographed hockey memorabilia. Autographed items include pucks, sticks and jerseys and were inserted 1:864.

		MT
Common Redemption:		25.00
Inserted 1:864		
1	Rob Blake (puck, 75)	25.00
2	Rob Blake (8x10, 100)	25.00
3	Chris Chelios (8x10, 75)	60.00
4	Chris Chelios (puck, 75)	60.00
5	Wayne Gretzky (puck, 50)	250.00
6	Wayne Gretzky (8x10, 50)	250.00
7	Brett Hull (puck, 90)	75.00
8	Keith Tkachuk (8x10, 75)	75.00
9	Keith Tkachuk (puck, 75)	75.00
10	Steve Yzerman (card, 50)	100.00
11	Steve Yzerman (2-card, 50)	125.00
12	Steve Yzerman (BD card, 50)	125.00
13	Doug Gilmour (1-of-1)	
14	Wayne Gretzky (1-of-1)	
15	Patrick Roy (1-of-1)	
16	Doug Weight (1-of-1)	
17	Steve Yzerman (1-of-1)	

1998-99 SP Authentic Snap Shots

This 30-card set spotlighted the NHL's top stars on a horizontal format, with silver foil etching and stamping. They were seeded 1:11 packs. Card backs are numbered with a "SS" prefix.

		MT
Complete Set (30):		110.00
Common Player:		2.00
Inserted 1:11		
SS01	Wayne Gretzky	15.00
SS02	Patrick Roy	10.00
SS03	Steve Yzerman	8.00
SS04	Brett Hull	3.00
SS05	Jaromir Jagr	10.00
SS06	Peter Forsberg	8.00
SS07	Dominik Hasek	6.00
SS08	Paul Kariya	10.00
SS09	Eric Lindros	10.00
SS10	Teemu Selanne	4.00
SS11	John LeClair	4.00
SS12	Mike Modano	4.00
SS13	Martin Brodeur	5.00
SS14	Brendan Shanahan	4.00
SS15	Ray Bourque	3.00
SS16	John Vanbiesbrouck	3.00
SS17	Brian Leetch	2.00
SS18	Vincent LaCavalier	4.00
SS19	Joe Sakic	5.00
SS20	Chris Drury	2.00
SS21	Eric Brewer	2.00
SS22	Jeremy Roenick	3.00
SS23	Mats Sundin	3.00
SS24	Zigmund Palffy	3.00
SS25	Keith Tkachuk	3.00
SS26	Sergei Samsonov	4.00
SS27	Curtis Joseph	3.00
SS28	Peter Bondra	3.00
SS29	Sergei Fedorov	4.00
SS30	Doug Gilmour	2.50

1998-99 SP Authentic StatMasters

This 30-card set focuses on the NHL's top players with each card sequentially numbered to the featured player's key accomplishment. Sequential numbering appears on the card front along with gold foil stamping. Card backs are numbered with a "S" prefix.

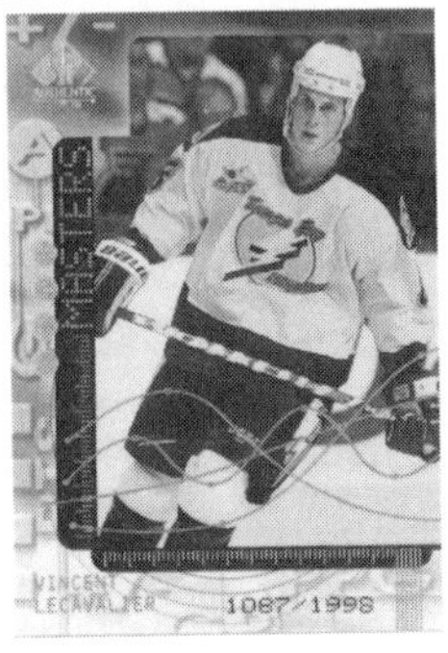

MT
Complete Set (30): 1500.
Common Player: 6.00
Numbered to featured stat
S01 Brendan Shanahan (400) 30.00
S02 Brett Hull (1,000) 15.00
S03 Dominik Hasek (200) 75.00
S04 Doug Gilmour (1,200) 6.00
S05 Doug Weight (500) 12.00
S06 Eric Lindros (115) 250.00
S07 Jaromir Jagr (301) 75.00
S08 Joe Sakic (900) 25.00
S09 John LeClair (500) 25.00
S10 John Vanbiesbrouck (306) 30.00
S11 Keith Tkachuk (250) 30.00
S12 Mark Messier (600) 20.00
S13 Martin Brodeur (200) 90.00
S14 Mike Modano (650) 20.00
S15 Patrick Roy (400) 60.00
S16 Paul Kariya (108) 250.00
S17 Pavel Bure (500) 30.00
S18 Peter Bondra (300) 20.00
S19 Peter Forsberg (400) 40.00
S20 Ray Bourque (1,500) 10.00
S21 Ron Francis (1,500) 6.00
S22 Sergei Fedorov (600) 25.00
S23 Steve Yzerman (1,500) 25.00
S24 Steve Yzerman (900) 35.00
S25 Steve Yzerman (500) 50.00
S26 Teemu Selanne (300) 40.00
S27 Vincent Lecavalier (1,998) 15.00
S28 Wayne Gretzky (92) 350.00
S29 Wayne Gretzky (900) 45.00
S30 Wayne Gretzky (2,000) 25.00

1998-99 SP Authentic Sign of the Times

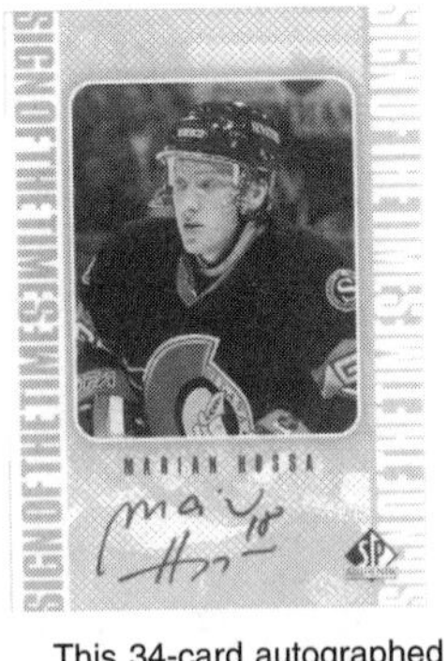

This 34-card autographed set has Sign of the Times written down the left and right border, a photo and the autograph underneath the photo. These were inserted 1:23 packs.

MT
Complete Set (35): 1200.
Common Player: 10.00
Inserted 1:23
DA Daniel Alfredsson 15.00
JA Jason Allison 20.00
MB Matthew Barnaby 12.00
BB Bates Battaglia 10.00
RB Rob Blake 15.00
PBo Peter Bondra 25.00
PB Pavel Bure 50.00
BD Byron Dafoe 25.00
AD Adam Deadmarsh 15.00
SG Sergei Gonchar 10.00
WG Wayne Gretzky 400.00
TH Thomas Holstrom 12.00
MH Marian Hossa 12.00
BH Brett Hull 60.00
CJ Curtis Joseph 30.00
EJ Ed Jovanovski 10.00
JJ Joe Juneau 12.00
VL Vincent Lecavalier 50.00
NL Nicklas Lidstrom 25.00
MM Manny Malhotra 20.00
MMc Marty McSorley 10.00
AM Alexander Mogilny 25.00
RN Rumun Ndur 15.00
ON Owen Nolan 12.00
MO Mattias Ohlund 12.00
PR Patrick Roy 175.00
TS Teemu Selanne 10.00
AS Alexander Selivanov 10.00
RS Ryan Smyth 12.00
JS Jozef Stumpel 12.00
MS Mats Sundin 50.00
JT Joe Thornton 20.00
KT Keith Tkachuk 35.00
DW Doug Weight 15.00
SY Steve Yzerman 160.00

1998-99 SP Authentic Sign of the Times-Prospect

This 15-card autographed set included 15 Canadian "Under 18" National Team members. Identical in design to regular Sign of the Times inserts, these were seeded 1:23 packs.

MT
Complete Set (15): 220.00
Common Player: 10.00
Inserted 1:23
KB Kris Beech 25.00
BF Brian Finley 30.00
KF Kurtis Foster 10.00
BJ Barrett Jackman 20.00
SK Scott Kelman 20.00
RL Ross Lupaschuk 15.00
DM Derek MacKenzie 15.00
SM Steven McCarthy 15.00
RM Rory McDade 15.00
MiM Mirko Murovic 20.00
MaO Maxime Ouellet 15.00
TP Taylor Pyatt 25.00
PR Peter Reynolds 15.00
CS Charlie Stephens 15.00
MZ Michael Zigomanis 25.00

1998-99 SP Authentic YOTGO Auto. Game Jersey

This Wayne Gretzky Game Jersey has a game-used piece of Gretzky's jersey embedded into each card along with Gretzky's autograph. 40 total cards were produced.

MT
Complete Set (1):
Wayne Gretzky (40)

1998-99 SPx Finite

Each card in the 180-card set is sequentially numbered. The overall set consists of 90 regular player cards with bronze foil stamping, serially numbered to 9,500. The rest of the set consists of four subsets: Global Impact (30 cards, numbered to 6,950); NHL Sure Shots (30 cards, 3,900 sets); Marquee Performers (20 cards, 2,625 sets); and Living Legends (10 cards, 1,620 sets). There are also two 180-card parallel sets: Radiance and Spectrum. Radiance feature silver foiled fronts and varying levels of serial numbering. Spectrums utilize holographic rainbow technology and also have varying levels of serial numbering.

MT
Common Reg. Card (1-90): .40
Radiance Reg. Card: 1.5x to 2x
Production 4,750 sets
Spectrum Reg. Card: 8x to 12x
Production 300 sets
Common Global Impact (91-120): .75
Radiance GI: 1.5x to 2x
Production 3,475 sets
Spectrum GI: 8x to 12x
Production 225 sets
Common NHL Sure Shots (121-150): 1.50
Radiance Sure Shots: 2x to 3x
Production 1,300 sets
Spectrum Sure Shots: 8x to 12x
Production 75 sets
Common Marquee Performers (151-170): 3.00
Radiance MP: 2x to 3x
Production 875 sets
Common Living Legends (171-180): 5.00
Radiance LL: 2x to 3x
Production 540 sets
1 Teemu Selanne 2.50
2 Guy Hebert .75
3 Josef Marha .40
4 Travis Green .40
5 Sergei Samsonov 2.50
6 Jason Allison .60
7 Byron Dafoe .75
8 Dominik Hasek 3.00
9 Mike Peca .40
10 Erik Rasmussen .40
11 Miroslav Satan .40
12 Theoren Fleury .75
13 Derek Morris .40
14 Valeri Bure .40
15 Trevor Kidd .75
16 Sami Kapanen .75
17 Bates Battaglia .40
18 Tony Amonte .75
19 Dmitri Nabokov .40
20 Daniel Cleary .40
21 Jeff Hackett 1.00
22 Joe Sakic 3.00
23 Valeri Kamensky .40
24 Patrick Roy 8.00
25 Wade Belak .40
26 Joe Nieuwendyk .75
27 Mike Keane .40
28 Jere Lehtinen .40
29 Ed Belfour 1.50
30 Steve Yzerman 5.00
31 Dmitri Mironov .40
32 Brendan Shanahan 2.50
33 Nicklas Lidstrom .75
34 Doug Weight .60
35 Janne Niinimaa .40
36 Bill Guerin .40
37 Ray Whitney .40
38 Robert Svehla .40
39 Ed Jovanovski .40
40 Donald MacLean .40
41 Jozef Stumpel .40
42 Rob Blake .40
43 Mark Recchi .40
44 Andy Moog .75
45 Matt Higgins .40
46 Martin Brodeur 3.00
47 Doug Gilmour 1.00
48 Brendan Morrison 1.50
49 Patrik Elias 1.00
50 Trevor Linden .40
51 Bryan Berard .60
52 Zdeno Chara .40
53 Wayne Gretzky 10.00
54 Marc Savard .40
55 Daniel Goneau .40
56 Pat LaFontaine .40
57 Alexei Yashin .75
58 Marian Hossa .75
59 Wade Redden .40
60 John LeClair 2.50
61 Alexandre Daigle .40
62 Rod Brind'Amour .75
63 Chris Therien .40
64 Keith Tkachuk 2.00
65 Brad Isbister .40
66 Nikolai Khabibulin 1.00
67 Robert Dome .40
68 Alexei Morozov .40
69 Stu Barnes .40
70 Tom Barrasso 1.00
71 Owen Nolan .40
72 Marco Sturm .40
73 Patrick Marleau 2.50
74 Pierre Turgeon .75
75 Chris Pronger .75
76 Pavol Demitra .40
77 Grant Fuhr 1.50
78 Stephane Richer .40
79 *Zac Bierk* .75
80 Alexander Selivanov .40
81 Mike Johnson .40
82 Mats Sundin 1.50
83 Alyn McAuley .40
84 Pavel Bure 2.50
85 Todd Bertuzzi .40
86 Garth Snow .75
87 Peter Bondra 2.00
88 Olaf Kolzig 1.50
89 Jan Bulis .40
90 Sergei Gonchar .40
91 Pavel Bure 4.00
92 Joe Sakic 5.00
93 Steve Yzerman 8.00
94 Jaromir Jagr 10.00
95 Peter Forsberg 8.00
96 Brendan Shanahan 4.00
97 Brett Hull 3.00
98 Alexei Yashin 1.00
99 Wayne Gretzky 15.00
100 Eric Lindros 10.00
101 Sergei Samsonov 4.00
102 John LeClair 4.00
103 Dominik Hasek 5.00
104 Teemu Selanne 4.00
105 Martin Brodeur 5.00
106 Tony Amonte 1.00
107 Theoren Fleury 1.50
108 Rob Blake .75
109 Mike Modano 4.00
110 Peter Bondra 3.00
111 Brian Leetch 1.50
112 Nicklas Lidstrom 1.50
113 Doug Weight 1.00
114 Zigmund Palffy 3.00
115 Saku Koivu 2.50
116 Paul Kariya 10.00
117 Ray Bourque 1.50
118 Mats Sundin 2.50
119 Patrick Roy 10.00
120 Chris Chelios 1.50
121 Sergei Samsonov 8.00
122 Mike Johnson 1.50
123 Patrik Elias 2.00
124 Josef Marha 1.50
125 Dan Cloutier 3.00
126 Cameron Mann 1.50
127 Mattias Ohlund 3.00
128 Daniel Cleary 1.50
129 Anders Eriksson 1.50
130 Patrick Marleau 8.00
131 Jan Bulis 2.50
132 Alyn McAuley 1.50
133 Joe Thornton 8.00
134 Andrei Zyuzin 1.50
135 Richard Zednik 1.50
136 Derek Morris 1.50
137 Bates Battaglia 1.50
138 Mike Watt 1.50
139 Olli Jokinen 4.00
140 Marian Hossa 3.00
141 Daniel Goneau 1.50
142 Erik Rasmussen 1.50
143 Daniel Briere 2.50
144 *Norm Maracle* 6.00
145 Brendan Morrison 6.00
146 Brad Isbister 1.50
147 Robert Dome 1.50
148 Zac Bierk 1.50
149 Alexei Morozov 2.00
150 Marco Sturm 3.00
151 Wayne Gretzky 40.00
152 Eric Lindros 25.00
153 Paul Kariya 25.00
154 Patrick Roy 30.00
155 Sergei Samsonov 10.00
156 Steve Yzerman 20.00
157 Teemu Selanne 10.00
158 Brendan Shanahan 10.00
159 Dominik Hasek 12.00
160 Mark Messier 8.00
161 Martin Brodeur 12.00
162 Mats Sundin 5.00
163 Joe Sakic 12.00
164 John LeClair 10.00
165 Jaromir Jagr 25.00
166 Peter Forsberg 20.00
167 Theoren Fleury 3.00
168 Peter Bondra 5.00
169 Mike Modano 10.00
170 Pavel Bure 10.00
171 Patrick Roy 40.00
172 Eric Lindros 30.00
173 Dominik Hasek 15.00
174 Jaromir Jagr 30.00
175 Steve Yzerman 25.00
176 Martin Brodeur 15.00
177 Ray Bourque 5.00
178 Peter Forsberg 25.00
179 Paul Kariya 30.00
180 Wayne Gretzky 50.00

1998-99 SPx Prospects

This product features 90 regular player cards, including a short-printed rookie subset (61-90)which are sequentially numbered to 1,999. In addition prospects Daniel and Henrik Sedin, autographed all 1,999 of their rookie cards. There are two parallels to the base set: Radiance and Spectrum. Radiance are limited to 100 sequentially numbered sets and found only in Finite Radiance hot packs. Spectrums are limited on one numbered set and are found only in hot packs.

MT
Complete Set (90): 350.00
Common Player: .25
Common SP (61-90): 4.00
Production 1,999 sets
Radiance Stars: 20x to 35x
Radiance SP: 4x to 8x
Production 100 sets
1 Paul Kariya 6.00
2 Teemu Selanne 2.50
3 Ray Bourque 1.00
4 Sergei Samsonov 2.00
5 Joe Thornton .50
6 Dominik Hasek 3.00
7 Theoren Fleury .50
8 Keith Primeau .50
9 Tony Amonte .40
10 Doug Gilmour .40
11 J.P. Dumont .25
12 Chris Chelios 1.00
13 Peter Forsberg 5.00
14 Patrick Roy 8.00
15 Joe Sakic 3.00
16 Milan Hedjuk 2.00
17 Chris Drury 1.50
18 Mike Modano 2.00
19 Brett Hull 2.00
20 Ed Belfour 1.50
21 Steve Yzerman 5.00
22 Brendan Shanahan 2.50
23 Sergei Fedorov 2.50
24 Chris Osgood 1.50
25 Nicklas Lidstrom .75
26 Bill Guerin .25
27 Doug Weight .50
28 Tom Poti .25
29 Mark Parrish 3.00
30 Rob Blake .25
31 Pavel Rosa .25
32 Vincent Damphousse .25
33 Saku Koivu .50
34 Mike Dunham .75
35 Martin Brodeur 3.00
36 Zigmund Palffy 1.00
37 Eric Brewer .25
38 Wayne Gretzky 10.00
39 Brian Leetch .75
40 Manny Malhotra .50
41 Petr Nedved .25
42 Alexei Yashin .50
43 Eric Lindros 6.00
44 John LeClair 2.50
45 John Vanbiesbrouck 2.00
46 Keith Tkachuk 1.50
47 Jeremy Roenick 1.50
48 Daniel Briere .25
49 Jaromir Jagr 6.00
50 Patrick Marleau 1.00
51 Al MacInnis .50
52 Chris Pronger .50
53 Vincent Lecavalier 2.50
54 Curtis Joseph 1.50
55 Mats Sundin 1.50
56 Tomas Kaberle .25
57 Mark Messier 2.00
58 Pavel Bure 2.50
59 Bill Muckalt 2.00
60 Peter Bondra 1.00
61 Brian Finley (World Juniors) 10.00
62 Roberto Luongo (World Juniors) 8.00
63 Mike Van Ryn (World Juniors) 4.00
64 Harold Druken (World Juniors) 4.00
65 Daniel Tkaczuk (World Juniors) 4.00
66 Brenden Morrow (World Juniors) 6.00
67 Jani Rita (World Juniors) 15.00
68 Tommi Santala (World Juniors) 4.00

69	Teemu Virkkunnen (World Juniors)	4.00
70	Arto Laaktikainen (World Juniors)	4.00
71	Ilkka Mikkola (World Juniors)	4.00
72	Miko Jokela (World Juniors)	4.00
73	Kirill Safronov (World Juniors)	10.00
74	Denis Shvidki (World Juniors)	6.00
75	Denis Arkhipov (World Juniors)	8.00
76	Maxim Afinogenov (World Juniors)	6.00
77	Alexander Zevakhin (World Juniors)	4.00
78	Alexei Volkov (World Juniors)	6.00
79	Daniel Sedin Auto. (World Juniors)	80.00
80	Henrik Sedin Auto. (World Juniors)	60.00
81	Jimmie Olvestad (World Juniors)	4.00
82	Mattias Weinhandl (World Juniors)	4.00
83	Mathias Tjarnqvist (World Juniors)	4.00
84	Jakob Johansson (World Juniors)	4.00
85	Barrett Heisten (World Juniors)	4.00
86	Tim Connolly (World Juniors)	6.00
87	Andy Hilbert (World Juniors)	4.00
88	David Legwand (World Juniors)	10.00
89	Joe Blackburn (World Juniors)	4.00
90	Dave Tanabe (World Juniors)	4.00

1998-99 SPx Prospects Highlight Heroes

This 30-card set spotlights top NHL players most likely to appear on the nightly highlight reels. These were seeded 1:8 packs. Card backs are numbered with a "H" prefix.

		MT
Complete Set (30):		180.00
Common Player:		2.50
Inserted 1:8		
1	Paul Kariya	15.00
2	Teemu Selanne	6.00
3	Ray Bourque	4.00
4	Sergei Samsonov	4.00
5	Dominik Hasek	8.00
6	Theoren Fleury	3.00
7	Doug Gilmour	2.50
8	Joe Sakic	8.00
9	Patrick Roy	20.00
10	Peter Forsberg	12.00
11	Mike Modano	5.00
12	Brett Hull	5.00
13	Brendan Shanahan	6.00
14	Steve Yzerman	12.00
15	Sergei Fedorov	6.00
16	Saku Koivu	3.00
17	Martin Brodeur	8.00
18	Wayne Gretzky	25.00
19	Zigmund Palffy	4.00
20	John Vanbiesbrouck	5.00
21	Eric Lindros	15.00
22	John LeClair	6.00
23	Keith Tkachuk	5.00
24	Jeremy Roenick	5.00
25	Jaromir Jagr	15.00
26	Vincent Lecavalier	8.00
27	Mats Sundin	5.00
28	Curtis Joseph	4.00
29	Pavel Bure	6.00
30	Peter Bondra	4.00

1998-99 SPx Prospects Lasting Impressions

This card collection features 30 of the top players on a full foiled front with gold foil stamping. Backs are numbered with a "L" prefix. These were seeded 1:3 packs.

		MT
Complete Set (30):		100.00
Common Player:		2.00
Inserted 1:3		
1	Vincent Lecavalier	4.00
2	John Vanbiesbrouck	3.00
3	Paul Kariya	8.00
4	Keith Tkachuk	3.00
5	Mike Modano	3.00
6	Dominik Hasek	5.00
7	Teemu Selanne	4.00
8	Mats Sundin	3.00
9	Brendan Shanahan	4.00
10	Pavel Bure	4.00
11	Theoren Fleury	2.00
12	Curtis Joseph	3.00
13	Joe Sakic	5.00
14	Eric Lindros	8.00
15	Peter Bondra	2.50
16	Brett Hull	3.00
17	Ray Bourque	2.50
18	Jaromir Jagr	8.00
19	Steve Yzerman	10.00
20	Jeremy Roenick	3.00
21	Martin Brodeur	5.00
22	Saku Koivu	2.50
23	Patrick Roy	12.00
24	John LeClair	4.00
25	Doug Gilmour	2.00
26	Sergei Fedorov	4.00
27	Wayne Gretzky	15.00
28	Peter Forsberg	8.00
29	Zigmund Palffy	2.50
30	Sergei Samsonov	3.00

1998-99 SPx Prospects Premier Stars

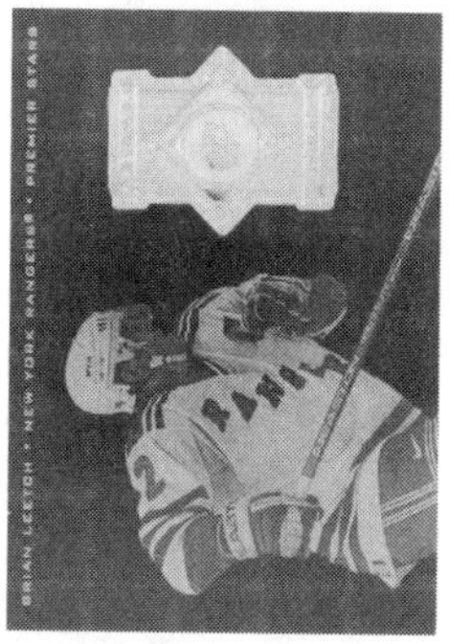

This 30-card set is done on a horizontal format utilizing holographic technology and gold foil stamping. Card backs are numbered with a "PS" prefix and are seeded 1:17 packs.

		MT
Complete Set (30):		325.00
Common Player:		4.00
Inserted 1:17		
1	Wayne Gretzky	40.00
2	Sergei Samsonov	8.00
3	Ray Bourque	6.00
4	Dominik Hasek	15.00
5	Martin Brodeur	12.00
6	Brian Leetch	6.00
7	Mike Richter	6.00
8	Eric Lindros	25.00
9	John LeClair	10.00
10	John Vanbiesbrouck	8.00
11	Jaromir Jagr	25.00
12	Vincent Lecavalier	10.00
13	Mats Sundin	6.00
14	Curtis Joseph	6.00
15	Peter Bondra	6.00
16	Wayne Gretzky	40.00
17	Teemu Selanne	10.00
18	Paul Kariya	25.00
19	Theoren Fleury	4.00
20	Tony Amonte	4.00
21	Patrick Roy	30.00
22	Joe Sakic	15.00
23	Peter Forsberg	20.00
24	Mike Modano	8.00
25	Brett Hull	8.00
26	Steve Yzerman	20.00
27	Brendan Shanahan	10.00
28	Doug Weight	4.00
29	Keith Tkachuk	8.00
30	Mark Messier	8.00

1998-99 SPx Prospects SP Winning Materials

This 10-card set has a game-used piece of the featured player's jersey or stick embedded into the front of each card. These were seeded 1:251 packs.

		MT
Complete Set (12):		2500.
Common Player:		100.00
Inserted 1:251		
RB	Ray Bourque	200.00
JJ	Jaromir Jagr	400.00
CJ	Curtis Joseph	200.00
JL	John LeClair	275.00
EL	Eric Lindros	400.00
CO	Chris Osgood	225.00
FP	Felix Potvin	175.00
MR	Mike Richter	200.00
PR	Patrick Roy	500.00
JS	Joe Sakic	300.00
MS	Mats Sundin	200.00
JV	John Vanbiesbrouck	240.00

1998-99 SPx Prospects YOTGO Quotables

This 30-card set pays tribute to Wayne Gretzky and features a photo of Gretzky with notable quotes about his career on the card backs. These were seeded 1:17 packs.

		MT
Complete Set (30):		260.00
Common Gretzky:		10.00
Inserted 1:17		
1	Wayne Gretzky	10.00
2	Wayne Gretzky	10.00
3	Wayne Gretzky	10.00
4	Wayne Gretzky	10.00
5	Wayne Gretzky	10.00
6	Wayne Gretzky	10.00
7	Wayne Gretzky	10.00
8	Wayne Gretzky	10.00
9	Wayne Gretzky	10.00
10	Wayne Gretzky	10.00
11	Wayne Gretzky	10.00
12	Wayne Gretzky	10.00
13	Wayne Gretzky	10.00
14	Wayne Gretzky	10.00
15	Wayne Gretzky	10.00
16	Wayne Gretzky	10.00
17	Wayne Gretzky	10.00
18	Wayne Gretzky	10.00
19	Wayne Gretzky	10.00
20	Wayne Gretzky	10.00
21	Wayne Gretzky	10.00
22	Wayne Gretzky	10.00
23	Wayne Gretzky	10.00
24	Wayne Gretzky	10.00
25	Wayne Gretzky	10.00
26	Wayne Gretzky	10.00
27	Wayne Gretzky	10.00
28	Wayne Gretzky	10.00
29	Wayne Gretzky	10.00
30	Wayne Gretzky	10.00

1998-99 SPx Prospects YOTGO Auto. Game Jersey

This Wayne Gretzky Game Jersey has a game-used piece of Gretzky's jersey embedded into each card along with Gretzky's autograph. 40 total cards were produced.

	MT
Complete Set (1):	
Wayne Gretzky (40)	

1998-99 Topps

Card fronts of the 242-card set have a brown border with the logo and player name stamped in gold foil. Card backs have a small close-up photo, complete year-by-year statistics and playoff statistics. An O-Pee-Chee parallel of the base set was also randomly inserted exclusively in Canadian hobby packs at a rate of one per pack. They can be identified by a O-Pee-Chee foil stamp logo.

		MT
Complete Set (242):		20.00
Common Player:		.10
OPC:		5x to 10x
Inserted 1:1 Can. H		
1	Peter Forsberg	1.25
2	Petr Sykora	.10
3	Byron Dafoe	.25
4	Ron Francis	.20
5	Alexei Yashin	.20
6	Dave Ellett	.10
7	Jamie Langenbrunner	.10
8	Doug Weight	.20
9	Jason Woolley	.10
10	Paul Coffey	.20
11	Uwe Krupp	.10
12	Tomas Sandstrom	.10
13	Scott Mellanby	.10
14	Vladimir Tsyplakov	.10
15	Martin Rucinsky	.10
16	Mikael Renberg	.10
17	Marco Sturm	.25
18	Eric Lindros	1.50
19	Sean Burke	.25
20	Martin Brodeur	.75
21	Boyd Devereaux	.10
22	Kelly Buchberger	.10
23	Scott Stevens	.10
24	Jamie Storr	.25
25	Anders Eriksson	.10
26	Gary Suter	.10
27	Theoren Fleury	.20
28	Steve Leach	.10
29	Felix Potvin	.30
30	Brett Hull	.50
31	Mike Grier	.10
32	Cale Hulse	.10
33	Larry Murphy	.10
34	Rick Tocchet	.10
35	Eric Desjardins	.10
36	Igor Kravchuk	.10
37	Rob Niedermayer	.10
38	Bryan Smolinski	.10
39	Valeri Kamensky	.10
40	Ryan Smyth	.10
41	Bruce Driver	.10
42	Mike Johnson	.20
43	Rob Zamuner	.10
44	Steve Duchesne	.20
45	Martin Straka	.10
46	Bill Houlder	.10
47	Craig Conroy	.10
48	Guy Hebert	.25
49	Colin Forbes	.10
50	Mike Modano	.50
51	Jamie Pushor	.10
52	Jarome Iginla	.20
53	Paul Kariya	1.50
54	Mattias Ohlund	.25
55	Sergei Berezin	.10
56	Peter Zezel	.10
57	Teppo Numminen	.10
58	Dale Hunter	.10
59	Sandy Moger	.10
60	John LeClair	.50
61	Wade Redden	.10
62	Patrik Elias	.10
63	Rob Blake	.10
64	Todd Marchant	.10
65	Claude Lemieux	.10
66	Trevor Kidd	.25
67	Sergei Fedorov	.60
68	Joe Sakic	.75
69	Derek Morris	.10
70	Alexei Morozov	.10
71	Mats Sundin	.40
72	Daymond Langkow	.10
73	Kevin Hatcher	.10
74	Damian Rhodes	.20
75	Brian Leetch	.25
76	Saku Koivu	.40
77	Rick Tabaracci	.10
78	Bernie Nicholls	.10
79	Alyn McCauley	.10
80	Patrice Brisebois	.10
81	Bret Hedican	.10
82	Sandy McCarthy	.10
83	Viktor Kozlov	.10
84	Derek King	.10
85	Alexander Selivanov	.10
86	Mike Vernon	.25
87	Jeff Beukeboom	.10
88	Tommy Salo	.25
89	Adam Graves	.10
90	Randy McKay	.10
91	Rich Pilon	.10
92	Richard Zednik	.10
93	Jeff Hackett	.25
94	Mike Peca	.10
95	Brent Gilchrist	.10
96	Stu Grimson	.10
97	Bob Probert	.10
98	Stu Barnes	.10
99	Ruslan Salei	.10
100	Al MacInnis	.20
101	Ken Daneyko	.10
102	Paul Ranheim	.10
103	Marty McInnis	.10
104	Marian Hossa	.10
105	Darren McCarty	.10
106	Guy Carbonneau	.10
107	Dallas Drake	.10
108	Sergei Samsonov	.75
109	Teemu Selanne	.60
110	Checklist	.10
111	Jaromir Jagr	1.50
112	Joe Thornton	.50
113	Jon Klemm	.10
114	Grant Fuhr	.35
115	Nikolai Khabibulin	.25
116	Rod Brind'Amour	.20
117	Trevor Linden	.10
118	Vincent Damphousse	.10
119	Dino Ciccarelli	.10
120	Pat Verbeek	.20
121	Sandis Ozolinsh	.20
122	Garth Snow	.20
123	Ed Belfour	.40
124	Keith Primeau	.20
125	Jason Allison	.20
126	Peter Bondra	.50
127	Ulf Samuelsson	.10
128	Jeff Friesen	.10
129	Jason Bonsignore	.10
130	Daniel Alfredsson	.20
131	Bobby Holik	.10
132	Jozef Stumpel	.10
133	Brian Bellows	.10
134	Chris Osgood	.30
135	Alexei Zhamnov	.10
136	Mattias Norstrom	.10
137	Drake Berehowsky	.10
138	Mark Messier	.50
139	Geoff Courtnall	.10
140	Marc Bureau	.10
141	Don Sweeney	.10
142	Wendel Clark	.10
143	Scott Niedermayer	.10
144	Chris Therien	.10
145	Kirk Muller	.10
146	Wayne Primeau	.10
147	Tony Granato	.10
148	Derian Hatcher	.10
149	Daniel Briere	.10
150	Fredrik Olausson	.10
151	Joe Juneau	.10
152	Michal Grosek	.10
153	Janne Laukkanen	.10
154	Keith Tkachuk	.50
155	Marty McSorley	.10
156	Owen Nolan	.10
157	Mark Tinordi	.10
158	Steve Washburn	.10
159	Luke Richardson	.10
160	Kris King	.10
161	Joe Nieuwendyk	.25
162	Travis Green	.10
163	Dominik Hasek	.75
164	Dimitri Khristich	.10
165	Dave Manson	.10
166	Chris Chelios	.25
167	Claude LaPointe	.10
168	Kris Draper	.10
169	Brad Isbister	.10
170	Patrick Marleau	.50
171	Jeremy Roenick	.30
172	Darren Langdon	.10
173	Kevin Dineen	.10
174	Luc Robitaille	.20
175	Steve Yzerman	1.50
176	Sergei Zubov	.10
177	Ed Jovanovski	.10
178	Sami Kapanen	.20
179	Adam Oates	.25

180	Pavel Bure	.60
181	Chris Pronger	.20
182	Pat Falloon	.10
183	Darcy Tucker	.10
184	Zigmund Palffy	.50
185	Curtis Brown	.10
186	Curtis Joseph	.30
187	Valeri Zelepukin	.10
188	Russ Courtnall	.10
189	Adam Foote	.10
190	Patrick Roy	2.00
191	Cory Stillman	.10
192	Alexei Zhitnik	.10
193	Olaf Kolzig	.40
194	Mark Fitzpatrick	.10
195	James Black	.10
196	Zarley Zalapski	.10
197	Niklas Sundstrom	.10
198	Bryan Berard	.10
199	Jason Arnott	.10
200	Mike Richter	.30
201	Ken Baumgartner	.10
202	Jason Dawe	.10
203	Nicklas Lidstrom	.20
204	Tony Amonte	.20
205	Kjell Samuelsson	.10
206	Ray Bourque	.25
207	Alexander Mogilny	.20
208	Pierre Turgeon	.20
209	Tom Barrasso	.25
210	Richard Matvichuk	.10
211	Sergei Krivokrasov	.10
212	Ted Drury	.10
213	Matthew Barnaby	.10
214	Denis Pederson	.10
215	John Vanbiesbrouck	.50
216	Brendan Shanahan	.60
217	Jocelyn Thibault	.25
218	Nelson Emerson	.10
219	Wayne Gretzky	2.50
220	Checklist	.10
221	*Ramzi Abid*	.75
222	*Mark Bell*	.50
223	*Mike Henrich*	.40
224	Vincent Lecavalier	2.00
225	Rico Fata	.75
226	Bryan Allen	.25
227	Daniel Tkaczuk	.10
228	*Brad Stuart*	.25
229	*Derrick Walser*	.20
230	*Jonathan Cheechoo*	.40
231	Sergei Varlamov	.40
232	*Scott Gomez*	.40
233	*Jeff Heerema*	.40
234	David Legwand	1.50
235	Manny Malhotra	.60
236	*Michael Rupp*	.40
237	Alex Tanguay	.50
238	*Mathieu Biron*	.20
239	*Bujar Amidovski*	.40
240	*Brian Finley*	.60
241	*Philippe Sauve*	.75
242	*Jiri Fischer*	.25

1998-99 Topps Autographs

Autographs are randomly seeded exclusively in hobby packs at a rate of 1:209 packs. Card fronts are stamped "Topps Certified Autograph" in gold foil.

		MT
Common Player:		20.00
Inserted 1:209 H		
A1	Jason Allison	30.00
A2	Sergei Samsonov	70.00
A3	John LeClair	90.00
A4	Mattias Ohlund	20.00
A5	Jaromir Jagr	120.00
A6	Keith Tkachuk	40.00
A7	Patrik Elias	20.00
A8	Dominik Hasek	120.00
A9	Brian Leetch	30.00

1998-99 Topps Board Members

Board Members showcase the NHL's top defensemen on a prismatic, holographic card front. Card backs have a small close-up photo and are numbered with a "B" prefix. Board Members are inserted 1:36 packs.

		MT
Complete Set (15):		50.00
Common Player:		2.50
Inserted 1:36		
B1	Chris Pronger	4.00
B2	Chris Chelios	8.00
B3	Brian Leetch	8.00
B4	Ray Bourque	8.00
B5	Mattias Ohlund	4.00
B6	Nicklas Lidstrom	8.00
B7	Sergei Zubov	5.00
B8	Scott Niedermayer	2.50
B9	Larry Murphy	2.50
B10	Sandis Ozolinsh	5.00
B11	Rob Blake	4.00
B12	Scott Stevens	2.50
B13	Derian Hatcher	2.50
B14	Kevin Hatcher	2.50
B15	Wade Redden	2.50

1998-99 Topps Ice Age 2000

This 15-card insert set focuses on the NHL's top young players. Card fronts feature a silver, holographic foil design and card backs are numbered with an "I" prefix. These were inserted 1:12 packs.

		MT
Complete Set (15):		35.00
Common Player:		1.00
Inserted 1:12		
I1	Paul Kariya	8.00
I2	Marco Sturm	1.00
I3	Jarome Iginla	1.00
I4	Denis Pederson	1.00
I5	Wade Redden	1.00
I6	Jason Allison	1.50
I7	Chris Pronger	1.50
I8	Peter Forsberg	6.00
I9	Saku Koivu	2.50
I10	Eric Lindros	8.00
I11	Sergei Samsonov	3.00
I12	Mattias Ohlund	1.00
I13	Joe Thornton	3.00
I14	Mike Johnson	1.00
I15	Nikolai Khabibulin	1.50

1998-99 Topps Local Legends

Done on a horizontal format, card fronts feature holographic foil and card backs depict the featured player's country of origin and are numbered with a "L" prefix. They were seeded 1:18 packs.

		MT
Complete Set (15):		60.00
Common Player:		1.50
Inserted 1:18		
L1	Peter Forsberg	6.00
L2	Mats Sundin	1.50
L3	Zigmund Palffy	2.00
L4	Jaromir Jagr	8.00
L5	Dominik Hasek	4.00
L6	Martin Brodeur	4.00
L7	Wayne Gretzky	12.00
L8	Patrick Roy	10.00
L9	Eric Lindros	8.00
L10	Joe Sakic	4.00
L11	Mark Messier	2.50
L12	Mike Modano	3.00
L13	Sergei Fedorov	3.00
L14	Pavel Bure	3.00
L15	Teemu Selanne	3.00

1998-99 Topps Mystery Finest

Mystery Finest were printed on a chromium stock and have a black opaque protector that must be peeled off in order to reveal the player. These have a bronze colored foil. Five parallels are also randomly seeded in packs: Silver (1:72), Gold (1:108), Bronze Refractor (1:108), Silver Refractor (1:216) and Gold Refractor (1:324).

		MT
Complete Set (20):		125.00
Common Player:		3.00
Bronze Inserted 1:36		
Silvers:		1x to 1.5x
Inserted 1:72		
Golds:		1.5x to 2x
Inserted 1:108		
Bronze Refractors:		1.5x to 2x
Inserted 1:108		
Silver Refractors:		2x to 3x
Inserted 1:216		
Gold Refractors:		3x to 4x
Inserted 1:324		
M1	Teemu Selanne	6.00
M2	Olaf Kolzig	4.00
M3	Pavel Bure	6.00
M4	Wayne Gretzky	25.00
M5	Mike Modano	6.00
M6	Jaromir Jagr	15.00
M7	Dominik Hasek	8.00
M8	Peter Forsberg	12.00
M9	Eric Lindros	15.00
M10	John LeClair	6.00
M11	Zigmund Palffy	5.00
M12	Martin Brodeur	8.00
M13	Keith Tkachuk	5.00
M14	Peter Bondra	4.00
M15	Nicklas Lidstrom	3.00
M16	Patrick Roy	20.00
M17	Chris Chelios	4.00
M18	Saku Koivu	4.00
M19	Mark Messier	5.00
M20	Joe Sakic	8.00

1998-99 Topps Reprints

This 10-card set reprints the Topps rookie for each featured player and are seeded 1:24 packs.

		MT
Complete Set (10):		40.00
Common Player:		2.00
Inserted 1:23		
1	Wayne Gretzky	12.00
2	Mark Messier	3.00
3	Ray Bourque	2.00
4	Patrick Roy	10.00
5	Grant Fuhr	2.00
6	Brett Hull	3.00
7	Gordie Howe	8.00
8	Stan Mikita	4.00
9	Bobby Hull	6.00
10	Phil Esposito	2.00

1998-99 Topps Reprints Autographs

This four-card set consists of Bobby Hull, Gordie Howe, Stan Mikita and Phil Esposito. Each card is stamped "Topps Certified Autograph" and are inserted 1:1,878 packs. The Mikita autograph is seeded 1:3,756 packs.

		MT
Complete Set (4):		750.00
Common Autograph:		150.00
Inserted 1:1,878		
Mikita inserted 1:3,756		
7	Gordie Howe	275.00
8	Stan Mikita	200.00
9	Bobby Hull	220.00
10	Phil Esposito	150.00

1998-99 Topps Season's Best

This 30-card set is broken down into five different categories: Net Minders, Sharpshooters, Puck Providers, Performers Plus and Ice Hot. Card backs are numbered with a "SB" prefix and are seeded 1:8 packs.

		MT
Complete Set (30):		50.00
Common Player:		.50
Inserted 1:8		
SB1	Dominik Hasek	4.00
SB2	Martin Brodeur	4.00
SB3	Ed Belfour	1.50
SB4	Curtis Joseph	1.50
SB5	Jeff Hackett	1.00
SB6	Tom Barrasso	1.00
SB7	Mike Johnson	.50
SB8	Sergei Samsonov	3.00
SB9	Patrik Elias	.50
SB10	Patrick Marleau	2.50
SB11	Mattias Ohlund	1.00
SB12	Marco Sturm	.50
SB13	Teemu Selanne	3.00
SB14	Peter Bondra	2.00
SB15	Pavel Bure	3.00
SB16	John LeClair	3.00
SB17	Zigmund Palffy	2.00
SB18	Keith Tkachuk	2.00
SB19	Jaromir Jagr	8.00
SB20	Wayne Gretzky	12.00
SB21	Peter Forsberg	6.00
SB22	Ron Francis	1.00
SB23	Adam Oates	1.50
SB24	Jozef Stumpel	.50
SB25	Chris Pronger	1.00
SB26	Larry Murphy	.50
SB27	Jason Allison	1.00
SB28	John LeClair	3.00
SB29	Randy McKay	.50
SB30	Dainius Zubrus	.50

1998-99 Topps Gold Label

The base set consists of 100 cards, printed on 35-point spectral-reflective rainbow stock and features gold foil stamping. Card fronts have two photos, the background photo of each card will be one of three action shots, helping to determine the card's rarity. The three action shots are as follows: Version 1: skating, Version 2: shooting (1:6 packs) and Version 3: celebration (1:12). For Goalies: Version 1: upright, Version 2: sprawling (1:6) and Version 3: mask off (1:12). The two parallels for the base set are Version 2 and Version 3. Version 1 is the base set. A one-of-one parallel for each of the three versions exists.

		MT
Complete Set (100):		100.00
Common Player:		.50
Variation 2:		2x
Inserted 1:6		
Variation 3:		3x to 4x
Inserted 1:12		
1	Brendan Shanahan	2.50
2	Mike Modano	2.00
3	Chris Chelios	1.50
4	Wayne Gretzky	10.00
5	Jaromir Jagr	6.00
6	Mark Messier	2.00
7	Teemu Selanne	2.50
8	Theoren Fleury	1.50
9	Ray Bourque	1.50
10	Martin Brodeur	3.00
11	Alexei Yashin	1.00
12	Keith Tkachuk	1.50
13	Eric Lindros	6.00
14	Owen Nolan	.50
15	Al MacInnis	1.00
16	Peter Bondra	1.00
17	Saku Koivu	1.00
18	Doug Weight	.75
19	Robert Reichel	.50
20	Sergei Fedorov	2.50
21	Peter Forsberg	5.00
22	Ron Francis	.75
23	Dimitri Khristich	.50
24	Ed Belfour	1.50
25	*Oleg Kvasha*	2.00
26	Ray Whitney	.50
27	Kenny Jonsson	.50
28	Randy McKay	.50
29	Pavol Demitra	.75
30	Pierre Turgeon	.75
31	Steve Yzerman	5.00
32	Ryan Smyth	.50
33	Tony Amonte	.75
34	Dominik Hasek	3.00
35	Jarome Iginla	.50
36	Sami Kapanen	.50
37	Patrik Elias	.50
38	Daniel Cleary	.50
39	Curtis Joseph	1.50
40	Joe Juneau	.50

41	Adam Graves	.75
42	Trevor Linden	.50
43	Olli Jokinen	.50
44	Joe Nieuwendyk	.75
45	Sergei Samsonov	2.00
46	Rico Fata	.50
47	Mark Recchi	.50
48	Rick Tocchet	.50
49	Chris Pronger	1.00
50	Jason Allison	.75
51	Paul Kariya	6.00
52	Stu Barnes	.50
53	Mats Sundin	1.50
54	Mike Richter	1.25
55	Cliff Ronning	.50
56	Keith Primeau	.75
57	Guy Hebert	.75
58	Nicklas Lidstrom	1.00
59	John Vanbiesbrouck	2.00
60	Jeff Friesen	.50
61	Vincent Lecavalier	3.00
62	Alexander Mogilny	.75
63	Olaf Kolzig	1.00
64	Doug Gilmour	.75
65	Joe Sakic	3.00
66	Mike Johnson	.50
67	Vincent Damphousse	.50
68	Eric Brewer	.50
69	Daniel Alfredsson	.50
70	Nikolai Khabibulin	1.00
71	Marco Sturm	.50
72	Marty Reasoner	.50
73	*Bill Muckalt*	2.00
74	Pavel Bure	2.50
75	Bill Guerin	.50
76	Chris Osgood	1.50
77	Patrick Roy	8.00
78	Tom Barrasso	1.00
79	Alyn McCauley	.50
80	Adam Oates	1.00
81	Joe Thornton	.75
82	Brendan Morrison	.50
83	Mike Dunham	1.00
84	Jeremy Roenick	1.50
85	Brian Leetch	1.00
86	John LeClair	2.50
87	Mattias Ohlund	.50
88	Wade Redden	.50
89	*Mark Parrish*	4.00
90	*Milan Hejduk*	2.00
91	Michael Peca	.50
92	Brett Hull	2.00
93	Manny Malhotra	.75
94	Patrick Marleau	1.00
95	Grant Fuhr	1.00
96	Rob Blake	.50
97	Damian Rhodes	1.00
98	Eric Daze	.50
99	Rod Brind'Amour	.75
100	Scott Stevens	.50

1998-99 Topps Gold Label Black

Black Label is a parallel to the 100-card base set and features black foil stamping. Three parallel Black Label versions exist for each base card: Version 1 (1:18), Version 2 (1:36) and Version 3 (1:72). A one-of-one version for each of the three versions exists.

	MT
Variation 1:	4x to 5x
Inserted 1:18	
Variation 2:	6x to 10x
Inserted 1:36	
Variation 3:	8x to 15x
Inserted 1:72	

1998-99 Topps Gold Label Red

Red Label's are a parallel to the 100-card base set and feature red foil stamping and sequential numbering. Each base card has three Red parallels: Version 1, limited to 100 numbered sets; Version 2, limited to 50 numbered sets and Version 3 limited to 25 numbered sets. A one-of-one parallel of each of the three versions exists.

	MT
Variation 1:	25x to 35x
Production 100 sets	
Variation 2:	30x to 50x
Production 50 sets	
Variation 3:	40x to 80x
Production 25 sets	

1998-99 Topps Gold Label '99 Goal Race

The 10-card set highlights the top goal scorers on a spectral-reflective rainbow stock, with gold foil stamping. These are seeded 1:18 packs. Two parallel versions are also randomly seeded: Black and Red. Blacks are distinguished by black foil stamping and are seeded 1:54 packs. Reds are distinguished by red foil stamping and are sequentially numbered to 92. A one-of-one parallel of each of the three versions exists.

	MT
Complete Set (10):	125.00
Common Player:	6.00
Inserted 1:18	
Blacks:	2x
Inserted 1:54	
Reds:	8x to 12x
GR1 Eric Lindros	25.00
GR2 John LeClair	15.00
GR3 Teemu Selanne	15.00
GR4 Paul Kariya	25.00
GR5 Jaromir Jagr	25.00
GR6 Keith Tkachuk	10.00
GR7 Theoren Fleury	6.00
GR8 Brendan Shanahan	15.00
GR9 Tony Amonte	6.00
GR10Joe Sakic	20.00

1998-99 Upper Deck

The 420-card base set is broken into two series of 210 cards. Card fronts feature a silver etched border on the left and right side, along with silver foil stamping. Card backs have a small photo, a career note and year-by-year statistics. Packs had 12-cards, with a SRP of $2.49.

	MT
Complete Set (420):	165.00
Complete Series I Set (210):	100.00
Complete Series II Set (210):	65.00
Common Player:	.10
Common (391-420):	1.50
Exclusive Stars:	80x to 140x
Yng Stars & RCs:	40x to 80x
Shortprint subsets:	8x to 12x
Production 100 sets	

1	Antti Aalto (Star Rookies)	.25
2	Cameron Mann (Star Rookies)	.25
3	*Norm Maracle* (Star Rookies)	6.00
4	Daniel Cleary (Star Rookies)	.25
5	Brendan Morrison (Star Rookies)	4.00
6	Marian Hossa (Star Rookies)	.75
7	Daniel Briere (Star Rookies)	.75
8	*Mike Crowley* (Star Rookies)	.50
9	*Darryl Laplante* (Star Rookies)	.50
10	*Sven Butenschon* (Star Rookies)	.50
11	*Yan Golubovsky* (Star Rookies)	.50
12	Olli Jokinen (Star Rookies)	3.00
13	Jean-Sebastien Giguere (Star Rookies)	.75
14	Mike Watt (Star Rookies)	.50
15	*Ryan Johnson* (Star Rookies)	.50
16	Teemu Selanne (Rookie Rewind)	5.00
17	Paul Kariya (Rookie Rewind)	10.00
18	Pavel Bure (Rookie Rewind)	5.00
19	Joe Thornton (Rookie Rewind)	1.50
20	Dominik Hasek (Rookie Rewind)	6.00
21	Bryan Berard (Rookie Rewind)	.25
22	Chris Phillips (Rookie Rewind)	.25
23	Sergei Fedorov (Rookie Rewind)	5.00
24	Sergei Samsonov (Rookie Rewind)	5.00
25	Marc Denis (Rookie Rewind)	.25
26	Patrick Marleau (Rookie Rewind)	3.00
27	Jaromir Jagr (Rookie Rewind)	10.00
28	Saku Koivu (Rookie Rewind)	2.00
29	Peter Forsberg (Rookie Rewind)	8.00
30	Mike Modano (Rookie Rewind)	5.00
31	Paul Kariya	2.00
32	Matt Cullen	.10
33	Josef Marha	.10
34	Teemu Selanne	.75
35	Pavel Trnka	.10
36	Tom Askey	.10
37	Tim Taylor	.10
38	Ray Bourque	.25
39	Sergei Samsonov	.75
40	Don Sweeney	.10
41	Jason Allison	.25
42	Steve Heinze	.10
43	Erik Rasmussen	.10
44	Dominik Hasek	1.00
45	Geoff Sanderson	.10
46	Mike Peca	.10
47	Brian Holzinger	.10
48	Vaclav Varada	.10
49	Steve Begin	.10
50	Denis Gauthier	.10
51	Derek Morris	.10
52	Valeri Bure	.10
53	Hnat Domenichelli	.10
54	German Titov	.10
55	Jarome Iginla	.10
56	Tyler Moss	.10
57	Sami Kapanen	.25
58	Trevor Kidd	.35
59	Glen Wesley	.10
60	Nelson Emerson	.10
61	Jeff O'Neill	.10
62	Bates Battaglia	.10
63	Alexei Zhamnov	.10
64	Christian LaFlamme	.10
65	Chris Chelios	.30
66	Ethan Moreau	.10
67	Eric Weinrich	.10
68	Eric Daze	.10
69	Peter Forsberg	1.50
70	Eric Messier	.10
71	Eric Lacroix	.10
72	Adam Deadmarsh	.20
73	Uwe Krupp	.10
74	Patrick Roy	2.50
75	Marc Denis	.10
76	Juha Lind	.10
77	Mike Keane	.10
78	Joe Nieuwendyk	.20
79	Darryl Sydor	.10
80	Ed Belfour	.30
81	Jamie Langenbrunner	.10
82	Petr Buzek	.10
83	Nicklas Lidstrom	.20
84	Mathieu Dandenault	.10
85	Steve Yzerman	1.50
86	Martin Lapointe	.10
87	Brendan Shanahan	.75
88	Anders Eriksson	.10
89	Tomas Holmstrom	.10
90	Doug Weight	.20
91	Janne Niinimaa	.10
92	Bill Guerin	.10
93	Kelly Buchberger	.10
94	Mike Grier	.10
95	Craig Millar	.10
96	Roman Hamrlik	.10
97	Ray Whitney	.10
98	Viktor Kozlov	.10
99	Peter Worrell	.10
100	Kevin Weekes	.10
101	Ed Jovanovski	.10
102	Bill Lindsay	.10
103	Jozef Stumpel	.10
104	Luc Robitaille	.25
105	Yanic Perreault	.10
106	Donald MacLean	.10
107	Jamie Storr	.25
108	Ian Laperriere	.10
109	*Jason Morgan*	.40
110	Vincent Damphousse	.10
111	Mark Recchi	.20
112	Vladimir Malakhov	.10
113	Dave Manson	.10
114	Jose Theodore	.30
115	Brian Savage	.10
116	Jonas Hoglund	.10
117	Krzysztof Oliwa	.10
118	Martin Brodeur	1.00
119	Patrik Elias	.20
120	Jason Arnott	.10
121	Scott Stevens	.10
122	*Sheldon Souray*	.25
123	Brian Rolston	.10
124	Trevor Linden	.20
125	Warren Luhning	.10
126	Zdeno Chara	.10
127	Bryan Berard	.20
128	Bryan Smolinski	.10
129	Jason Dawe	.10
130	Kevin Stevens	.10
131	*P.J. Stock*	.40
132	Marc Savard	.10
133	Pat LaFontaine	.20
134	Dan Cloutier	.25
135	Wayne Gretzky	3.00
136	Niklas Sundstrom	.10
137	Damian Rhodes	.30
138	Magnus Arvedson	.10
139	Alexei Yashin	.25
140	Chris Phillips	.10
141	Janne Laukkanen	.10
142	Shawn McEachern	.10
143	John LeClair	.75
144	Alexandre Daigle	.10
145	Dainius Zubrus	.10
146	Joel Otto	.10
147	Mike Sillinger	.10
148	Colin Forbes	.10
149	Chris Gratton	.10
150	Eric Desjardins	.10
151	Juha Ylonen	.10
152	Brad Isbister	.10
153	Oleg Tverdovsky	.10
154	Keith Tkachuk	.50
155	Teppo Numminen	.10
156	Cliff Ronning	.10
157	Nikolai Khabibulin	.30
158	Alexei Morozov	.10
159	Ron Francis	.25
160	Darius Kasparaitis	.10
161	Jaromir Jagr	2.00
162	Tom Barrasso	.30
163	Tuomas Gronman	.10
164	Robert Dome	.10
165	Peter Skudra	.10
166	Marcus Ragnarsson	.10
167	Mike Vernon	.30
168	Andrei Zyuzin	.10
169	Marco Sturm	.10
170	Mike Ricci	.10
171	Patrick Marleau	.75
172	Pierre Turgeon	.25
173	Pavol Demitra	.10
174	Chris Pronger	.20
175	Pascal Rheaume	.10
176	Al MacInnis	.25
177	Tony Twist	.10
178	Jim Campbell	.10
179	Mikael Renberg	.10
180	Jason Bonsignore	.10
181	*Zac Bierk*	.25
182	Alexander Selivanov	.10
183	Stephane Richer	.10
184	Sandy McCarthy	.10
185	Alyn McCauley	.10
186	Sergei Berezin	.10
187	Mike Johnson	.10
188	Wendel Clark	.20
189	Tie Domi	.10
190	Yannick Tremblay	.10
191	Jeff Ware	.10
192	Fredrik Modin	.10
193	Pavel Bure	.75
194	Todd Bertuzzi	.10
195	Mark Messier	.60
196	Bret Hedican	.10
197	Mattias Ohlund	.25
198	Garth Snow	.25
199	Adam Oates	.25
200	Peter Bondra	.50
201	Sergei Gonchar	.10
202	Jan Bulis	.10
203	Joe Juneau	.10
204	Brian Bellows	.10
205	Nolan Baumgartner	.10
206	Olaf Kolzig	.50
207	Richard Zednik	.10
208	Checklist Wayne Gretzky	1.50
209	Checklist Patrick Roy	1.00
210	Checklist Steve Yzerman	.75
211	Johan Davidsson	.10
212	Guy Hebert	.25
213	Mike Leclerc	.10
214	Steve Rucchin	.10
215	Travis Green	.10
216	Josef Marha	.10
217	Ted Donato	.10
218	Joe Thornton	.40
219	Kyle McLaren	.10
220	Peter Nordstrom	.10
221	Byron Dafoe	.40
222	Jonathan Girard	.10
223	*Antti Laaksonen*	.40
224	Jason Holland	.10
225	Miroslav Satan	.10
226	Alexei Zhitnik	.10
227	Donald Audette	.10
228	Matthew Barnaby	.10
229	Rumun Ndur	.10
230	Ken Wreggett	.25
231	Andrew Cassels	.10
232	Theoren Fleury	.25
233	Phil Housley	.10
234	*Martin St. Louis*	.40
235	Mike Rucinski	.10
236	Gary Roberts	.10
237	Keith Primeau	.25
238	Martin Gelinas	.10
239	Nolan Pratt	.10
240	Ray Sheppard	.10
241	Ron Francis	.25
242	Ty Jones	.10
243	Tony Amonte	.40
244	Chad Kilger	.10
245	Alexei Zhamnov	.10
246	*Remi Royer*	.10
247	*Milan Hejduk*	.75
248	Joe Sakic	1.00
249	Valeri Kamensky	.10
250	Sandis Ozolinsh	.20
251	Shean Donovan	.10
252	Wade Belak	.10
253	Jamie Wright	.10
254	Sergei Zubov	.10
255	Richard Matvichuk	.10
256	Mike Modano	.75
257	Pat Verbeek	.10
258	Jere Lehtinen	.10
259	Derian Hatcher	.10
260	Jason Botterill	.10
261	Igor Larionov	.10
262	Sergei Fedorov	.75
263	Chris Osgood	.40
264	Vyacheslav Kozlov	.10
265	Larry Murphy	.10
266	Darren McCarty	.20
267	Doug Brown	.10
268	Kris Draper	.10
269	Uwe Krupp	.10
270	*Fredrik Linquist*	.40
271	Dean McAmmond	.10
272	Ryan Smyth	.10
273	Boris Mironov	.10
274	Tom Poti	.10
275	Todd Marchant	.10
276	Sean Brown	.10
277	Rob Niedermayer	.10
278	Robert Svehla	.10
279	Scott Mellanby	.10
280	Radek Dvorak	.10
281	*Jaroslav Spacek*	.40
282	*Mark Parrish*	1.50
283	Ryan Johnson	.10
284	Glen Murray	.10
285	Rob Blake	.10

286 Steve Duchesne .10
287 Vladimir Tsyplakov .10
288 Stephane Fiset .25
289 Mattias Norstrom .10
290 Saku Koivu .50
291 Shayne Corson .10
292 Brad Brown .10
293 Patrice Brisebois .10
294 Terry Ryan .10
295 Jocelyn Thibault .25
296 *Miroslav Guren* .40
297 Darren Turcotte .10
298 Sebastian Bordeleau .10
299 Jan Vopat .10
300 Blair Actheynum .10
301 Andrew Brunette .10
302 Sergei Krivokrasov .10
303 *Mirian Cisar* .40
304 Patrick Cote .10
305 J.J. Daigneault .10
306 Greg Johnson .10
307 Chris Terreri .10
308 Scott Niedermayer .10
309 Vadim Sharifijanov .10
310 Petr Sykora .10
311 Sergei Brylin .10
312 Denis Pederson .10
313 Bobby Holik .10
314 *Bryan Muir* .25
315 Zigmund Palffy .50
316 Mike Watt .10
317 Tommy Salo .25
318 Kenny Jonsson .10
319 *Dimitri Nabakov* .25
320 John MacLean .10
321 Zarley Zalapski .10
322 Brian Leetch .25
323 Todd Harvey .10
324 Mike Richter .40
325 Mike Knuble .10
326 Jeff Beukeboom .10
327 Daniel Alfredsson .20
328 Vaclav Prospal .10
329 Wade Redden .10
330 Igor Kravchuk .10
331 Andreas Dackell .10
332 *Mike Maneluk* .75
333 Eric Lindros 2.00
334 Rod Brind'Amour .20
335 Colin Forbes .10
336 *Dimitri Tertyshny* .25
337 Shjon Podein .10
338 Chris Therien .10
339 Jeremy Roenick .50
340 Jyrki Lumme .10
341 Rick Tocchet .10
342 Dallas Drake .10
343 Keith Carney .10
344 Greg Adams .10
345 *Jan Hrdina* .25
346 German Titov .10
347 Stu Barnes .10
348 Kevin Hatcher .10
349 Martin Straka .10
350 *Jean-Sebastien Aubin* .75
351 Jeff Friesen .10
352 Tony Granato .10
353 *Scott Hannan* .40
354 Owen Nolan .10
355 Stephane Matteau .10
356 Bryan Marchment .10
357 Geoff Courtnall .10
358 *Brent Johnson* .25
359 Jamie Rivers .10
360 Terry Yake .10
361 Jamie McLennan .25
362 Grant Fuhr .40
363 *Michal Handzus* .40
364 Bill Ranford .25
365 John Cullen .10
366 Craig Janney .10
367 Daren Puppa .10
368 *Pavel Kubina* .25
369 Wendel Clark .10
370 Mats Sundin .50
371 Felix Potvin .40
372 *Daniil Markov* .25
373 Derek King .10
374 Steve Thomas .10
375 *Tomas Kaberle* .50
376 Alexander Mogilny .25
377 *Bill Muckalt* .10
378 Brian Noonan .10
379 Markus Naslund .10
380 Brad May .10
381 *Matt Cooke* .25
382 Calle Johansson .10
383 Dale Hunter .10
384 Jaroslav Svejkovsky .10
385 Dmitri Mironov .10
386 *Matthew Herr* .25
387 Nolan Baumgartner .10
388 Wayne Gretzky 1.00
389 Steve Yzerman .50
390 Wayne Gretzky, Steve Yzerman 1.00
391 *Brian Finley* (Program of Excellence) 8.00
392 *Maxime Ouellet* (Program of Excellence) 3.00
393 *Kurtis Foster* (Program of Excellence) 1.50
394 *Barrett Jackman* (Program of Excellence) 3.00
395 *Ross Lupaschuk* (Program of Excellence) 4.00
396 *Steven McCarthy* (Program of Excellence) 3.00
397 *Peter Reynolds* (Program of Excellence) 2.00
398 *Bart Rushmer* (Program of Excellence) 1.50
399 *Jonathon Zion* (Program of Excellence) 3.00
400 *Kris Beech* (Program of Excellence) 6.00
401 *Brandin Cote* (Program of Excellence) 2.00
402 *Scott Kelman* (Program of Excellence) 1.50
403 *Jamie Lundmark* (Program of Excellence) 4.00
404 *Derek MacKenzie* (Program of Excellence) 1.50
405 *Rory McDade* (Program of Excellence) 1.50
406 *David Morisset* (Program of Excellence) 3.00
407 *Mirko Murovic* (Program of Excellence) 3.00
408 *Taylor Pyatt* (Program of Excellence) 8.00
409 Charlie Stephens (Program of Excellence) 1.50
410 *Kyle Wanvig* (Program of Excellence) 4.00
411 *Krzystof Wieckowski* (Program of Excellence) 1.50
412 *Michael Zigomanis* (Program of Excellence) 5.00
413 Rico Fata (Calder Candidates) 3.00
414 Vincent Lecavalier (Calder Candidates) 6.00
415 Chris Drury (Calder Candidates) 2.50
416 *Oleg Kvasha* (Calder Candidates) 6.00
417 Eric Brewer (Calder Candidates) 1.50
418 *Josh Green* (Calder Candidates) 3.00
419 Marty Reasoner (Calder Candidates) 1.50
420 Manny Malhotra (Calder Candidates) 4.00

1998-99 Upper Deck Exclusives

Randomly inserted into packs, this parallel issue is sequentially numbered to 100 on the card back. The cards are distinguishable by their copper metallic foil look on the card front. A 1-of-1 parallel is also randomly seeded into packs.

	MT
Exclusive Stars:	80x to 140x
Shortprint subsets:	8x to 15x
Production 100 sets	

1998-99 Upper Deck Fantastic Finishers

This 30-card set spotlights the NHL's top goal scorers. Card fronts feature blue foil stamping and silver foil etching. Card backs have a small photo along with a career accomplishment and are numbered with a "FF" prefix. They were seeded 1:12 packs.

	MT
Complete Set (30):	75.00
Common Player:	1.00
Inserted 1:12	
FF1 Wayne Gretzky	12.00
FF2 Peter Bondra	2.00
FF3 Sergei Samsonov	3.00
FF4 Jaromir Jagr	8.00
FF5 Brendan Shanahan	3.00
FF6 Joe Sakic	4.00
FF7 Brett Hull	2.50
FF8 Paul Kariya	8.00
FF9 Keith Tkachuk	3.00
FF10 Zigmund Palffy	2.00
FF11 Eric Lindros	8.00
FF12 Mike Modano	3.00
FF13 Pavel Bure	3.00
FF14 Mats Sundin	2.00
FF15 Patrik Elias	1.00
FF16 Tony Amonte	1.00
FF17 Peter Forsberg	6.00
FF18 Alexei Yashin	1.00
FF19 Mark Recchi	1.00
FF20 Steve Yzerman	6.00
FF21 Doug Weight	1.00
FF22 Jeremy Roenick	2.00
FF23 Teemu Selanne	3.00
FF24 Jeff Friesen	1.00
FF25 John LeClair	3.00
FF26 Jason Allison	1.00
FF27 Mike Johnson	1.00
FF28 Theoren Fleury	1.50
FF29 Nicklas Lidstrom	1.50
FF30 Joe Nieuwendyk	1.00

1998-99 Upper Deck Fantastic Finishers I

This parallel is distinguishable by the platinum finish and die-cutting. They are sequentially numbered on the card front to 1,500.

	MT
Complete Set (30):	400.00
Common Player:	8.00
Production 1,500 sets	
FF1 Wayne Gretzky	60.00
FF2 Peter Bondra	12.00
FF3 Sergei Samsonov	15.00
FF4 Jaromir Jagr	40.00
FF5 Brendan Shanahan	15.00
FF6 Joe Sakic	20.00
FF7 Brett Hull	12.00
FF8 Paul Kariya	40.00
FF9 Keith Tkachuk	12.00
FF10 Zigmund Palffy	10.00
FF11 Eric Lindros	40.00
FF12 Mike Modano	15.00
FF13 Pavel Bure	15.00
FF14 Mats Sundin	12.00
FF15 Patrik Elias	8.00
FF16 Tony Amonte	8.00
FF17 Peter Forsberg	30.00
FF18 Alexei Yashin	8.00
FF19 Mark Recchi	8.00
FF20 Steve Yzerman	30.00
FF21 Doug Weight	8.00
FF22 Jeremy Roenick	12.00
FF23 Teemu Selanne	15.00
FF24 Jeff Friesen	8.00
FF25 John LeClair	20.00
FF26 Jason Allison	8.00
FF27 Mike Johnson	8.00
FF28 Theoren Fleury	8.00
FF29 Nicklas Lidstrom	10.00
FF30 Joe Nieuwendyk	8.00

1998-99 Upper Deck Fantastic Finishers II

This parallel is die-cut and is limited to 50 sequentially numbered sets. There is a tier III parallel randomly seeded limited to one set.

	MT
Common Player:	75.00
Production 50 sets	
FF1 Wayne Gretzky	600.00
FF2 Peter Bondra	120.00
FF3 Sergei Samsonov	150.00
FF4 Jaromir Jagr	350.00
FF5 Brendan Shanahan	150.00
FF6 Joe Sakic	200.00
FF7 Brett Hull	150.00
FF8 Paul Kariya	350.00
FF9 Keith Tkachuk	150.00
FF10 Zigmund Palffy	100.00
FF11 Eric Lindros	350.00
FF12 Mike Modano	150.00
FF13 Pavel Bure	150.00
FF14 Mats Sundin	120.00
FF15 Patrik Elias	75.00
FF16 Tony Amonte	75.00
FF17 Peter Forsberg	300.00
FF18 Alexei Yashin	75.00
FF19 Mark Recchi	75.00
FF20 Steve Yzerman	300.00
FF21 Doug Weight	75.00
FF22 Jeremy Roenick	120.00
FF23 Teemu Selanne	150.00
FF24 Jeff Friesen	75.00
FF25 John LeClair	150.00
FF26 Jason Allison	75.00
FF27 Mike Johnson	75.00
FF28 Theoren Fleury	90.00
FF29 Nicklas Lidstrom	90.00
FF30 Joe Nieuwendyk	75.00

1998-99 Upper Deck Frozen In Time

This 30-card set spotlights a key moment in the featured player's career and highlights the date and gives a brief recap of the moment on the card front beside the player photo. These were seeded 1:23 packs and are numbered on the card back with a "FT" prefix.

	MT
Complete Set (30):	140.00
Common Player:	2.00
Inserted 1:23	
FT1 Steve Yzerman	10.00
FT2 Peter Forsberg	12.00
FT3 Sergei Samsonov	5.00
FT4 Martin Brodeur	6.00
FT5 Theoren Fleury	3.00
FT6 Paul Kariya	12.00
FT7 Rob Blake	2.00
FT8 Jari Kurri	2.00
FT9 Eric Lindros	12.00
FT10 Dominik Hasek	6.00
FT11 Patrick Roy	15.00
FT12 Saku Koivu	4.00
FT13 Mike Modano	5.00
FT14 Alexei Morozov	2.00
FT15 Chris Osgood	4.00
FT16 Doug Gilmour	3.00
FT17 Owen Nolan	2.00
FT18 Mike Johnson	2.00
FT19 Keith Tkachuk	4.00
FT20 Adam Oates	3.00
FT21 Chris Chelios	3.00
FT22 Brendan Shanahan	5.00
FT23 Joe Sakic	6.00
FT24 Pavel Bure	5.00
FT25 Ray Bourque	3.00
FT26 Ed Belfour	3.00
FT27 John LeClair	5.00
FT28 Teemu Selanne	5.00
FT29 Jaromir Jagr	12.00
FT30 Wayne Gretzky	20.00

1998-99 Upper Deck Frozen In Time I

There are a total of three parallels: Tier I, II and III. Tier I features sequential numbering on the card front to 1,000. Tier II is limited to 25 numbered sets and Tier III is limited to one set.

	MT
Complete Set (30):	550.00
Common Player:	10.00
Production 1,000 sets	
FT1 Steve Yzerman	40.00
FT2 Peter Forsberg	40.00
FT3 Sergei Samsonov	20.00
FT4 Martin Brodeur	25.00
FT5 Theoren Fleury	10.00
FT6 Paul Kariya	50.00
FT7 Rob Blake	10.00
FT8 Jari Kurri	10.00
FT9 Eric Lindros	50.00
FT10 Dominik Hasek	25.00
FT11 Patrick Roy	60.00
FT12 Saku Koivu	12.00
FT13 Mike Modano	20.00
FT14 Alexei Morozov	10.00
FT15 Chris Osgood	12.00
FT16 Doug Gilmour	12.00
FT17 Owen Nolan	10.00
FT18 Mike Johnson	10.00
FT19 Keith Tkachuk	15.00
FT20 Adam Oates	12.00
FT21 Chris Chelios	12.00
FT22 Brendan Shanahan	20.00
FT23 Joe Sakic	25.00
FT24 Pavel Bure	20.00
FT25 Ray Bourque	12.00
FT26 Ed Belfour	12.00
FT27 John LeClair	20.00
FT28 Teemu Selanne	20.00
FT29 Jaromir Jagr	50.00
FT30 Wayne Gretzky	80.00

1998-99 Upper Deck Game Jersey Cards

Game Jersey's are randomly seeded in packs, with numbers 7-13 and 19-24 found exclusively in hobby packs at a rate of 1:288. The other Game Jerseys are seeded 1:2,500 packs. Card fronts have a swatch from a game-used jersey embedded into it.

	MT
Complete Set (24):	3500.
Common Player (1-6, 14-18):	125.00
Common Player (7-13, 19-24)	75.00
(1-6, 14-18)Inserted 1:2,500	
(7-13, 19-24)Inserted 1:288 H	
GJ1 Wayne Gretzky	700.00
GJ2 Vincent LaCavalier	200.00
GJ3 Bobby Hull	200.00
GJ4 Curtis Joseph	150.00
GJ5 Roberto Luongo	125.00
GJ6 Martin Brodeur	200.00
GJ7 Ed Belfour	125.00
GJ8 Al MacInnis	100.00
GJ9 Derian Hatcher	60.00
GJ10 Daniel Tczachuk	60.00
GJ11 Manny Malhotra	80.00
GJ12 Eric Brewer	60.00
GJ13 Alex Tanguay	100.00
GJ14 Brendan Shanahan	300.00
GJ15 Jaromir Jagr	500.00
GJ16 Chris Osgood	200.00
GJ17 Dominik Hasek	300.00
GJ18 Doug Gilmour	200.00
GJ19 Mats Sundin	200.00
GJ20 Darryl Sydor	100.00
GJ21 Chris Therien	75.00
GJ22 Darius Kasparaitis	75.00
GJ23 Alexei Zhamnov	75.00
GJ24 Joe Nieuwendyk	100.00

1998-99 Upper Deck Autographed Game Jersey Cards

Card numbers GJA1-GJA3 are randomly inserted into Series I packs and GJA4 is inserted into Series II packs. Each of the inserts have a swatch from a game-used jersey and an autograph, the total number produced is listed after the player name.

	MT
Complete Set (4):	
Common Player:	600.00
GJA1 Bobby Hull (9)	3000.
GJA2 Wayne Gretzky (99)	1800.
GJA3 Vincent LaCavalier (100)	600.00
GJA4 Wayne Gretzky (99) Dual Auto.	2000.

1998-99 Upper Deck Generation Next

Randomly inserted into series II packs, this set shows 10 of the top NHL stars featured with one of three different proteges. These were seeded 1:23 packs. The 30-card set has three parallels, which are broken down into three 10-card sections. Tier 1 (ten cards numbered to 1,000; ten cards numbered to 500 and ten cards numbered to 250; Tier 2 (ten cards numbered to 75; ten cards numbered to 25; and ten cards numbered to 10; Tier 3 (ten cards numbered to 3; ten cards numbered to 2; and ten cards numbered to 1.

	MT
Complete Set (30):	400.00
Common Player:	4.00
Inserted 1:23	
Quantum 1	
Tier 1:	1x to 1.5x
Production 1,000 sets	
Tier 2:	2x to 3x
Production 500 sets	
Tier 3:	3x to 5x
Production 250 sets	
Quantum 2	
Tier 1	8x to 20x
Production 75 sets	
Tier 2:	20x to 40x
Production 25 sets	
GN1 Wayne Gretzky, Sergei Samsonov	30.00
GN2 Wayne Gretzky, Marian Hossa	30.00
GN3 Wayne Gretzky, Vincent Lecavalier	35.00
GN4 Steve Yzerman, Brendan Morrison	15.00
GN5 Steve Yzerman, Marty Reasoner	15.00
GN6 Steve Yzerman, Manny Malhotra	15.00
GN7 Patrick Roy, Jean-Sebastien Giguere	20.00
GN8 Patrick Roy, Jose Theodore	20.00
GN9 Patrick Roy, Marc Denis	20.00
GN10Eric Lindros, Patrick Marleau	20.00
GN11Eric Lindros, Brad Isbister	20.00
GN12Eric Lindros, Joe Thornton	20.00
GN13Brendan Shanahan, Josh Green	8.00
GN14Brendan Shanahan, Ty Jones	8.00
GN15Brendan Shanahan, Mike Watt	8.00
GN16Ray Bourque, Mattias Ohlund	4.00
GN17Ray Bourque, Tom Poti	4.00
GN18Ray Borque, Eric Brewer	4.00
GN19Paul Kariya, Daniel Briere	20.00
GN20Paul Kariya, Rico Fata	20.00
GN21Paul Kariya, Chris Drury	20.00
GN22Jaromir Jagr, Robert Dome	20.00
GN23Jaromir Jagr, Richard Zednik	20.00
GN24Jaromir Jagr, Oleg Kvasha	20.00
GN25Peter Forsberg	15.00
GN26Peter Forsberg, Niklas Sundstrom	15.00
GN27Peter Forsberg, Brendan Morrison	15.00
GN28Pavel Bure, Vadim Sharifijanov	8.00
GN29Pavel Bure, Dimitri Nabakov	8.00
GN30Pavel Bure, Sergei Samsonov	10.00

1998-99 Upper Deck Lord Stanley's Heroes

This 30-card set highlights the NHL's top post-season performers and utilizes blue foil stamping and silver foil etching on the card fronts. Card backs are numbered with a "LS" prefix. These were seeded 1:6 packs.

	MT
Complete Set (30):	50.00
Common Player:	.50
Inserted 1:6	
LS1 Wayne Gretzky	8.00
LS2 Joe Sakic	3.00
LS3 Jaromir Jagr	5.00
LS4 Brendan Shanahan	2.00
LS5 Martin Brodeur	3.00
LS6 Theoren Fleury	.75
LS7 Doug Gilmour	.75
LS8 Ron Francis	.75
LS9 Sergei Fedorov	2.00
LS10Patrick Roy	6.00
LS11Mark Messier	2.00
LS12Peter Forsberg	4.00
LS13Brian Leetch	.75
LS14Steve Yzerman	4.00
LS15Sergei Samsonov	2.00
LS16Eric Lindros	5.00
LS17Paul Kariya	5.00
LS18Saku Koivu	1.50
LS19Bryan Berard	.50
LS20Chris Pronger	.50
LS21Keith Tkachuk	2.00
LS22Doug Weight	.50
LS23Ed Belfour	1.00
LS24Mats Sundin	.75
LS25John LeClair	2.00
LS26Pavel Bure	2.00
LS27Dominik Hasek	3.00
LS28Mike Modano	2.00
LS29Curtis Joseph	1.00
LS30Teemu Selanne	2.00

1998-99 Upper Deck Lord Stanley's Heroes I

This parallel set is die-cut, sequentially numbered to 2,000 on the card front and has platinum foil stamping.

	MT
Complete Set (30):	375.00
Common Player:	6.00
Production 2,000 sets	
LS1 Wayne Gretzky	50.00
LS2 Joe Sakic	15.00
LS3 Jaromir Jagr	30.00
LS4 Brendan Shanahan	12.00
LS5 Martin Brodeur	15.00
LS6 Theoren Fleury	8.00
LS7 Doug Gilmour	8.00
LS8 Ron Francis	6.00
LS9 Sergei Fedorov	12.00
LS10Patrick Roy	40.00
LS11Mark Messier	10.00
LS12Peter Forsberg	25.00
LS13Brian Leetch	8.00
LS14Steve Yzerman	25.00
LS15Sergei Samsonov	12.00
LS16Eric Lindros	30.00
LS17Paul Kariya	30.00
LS18Saku Koivu	10.00
LS19Bryan Berard	6.00
LS20Chris Pronger	6.00
LS21Keith Tkachuk	10.00
LS22Doug Weight	6.00
LS23Ed Belfour	10.00
LS24Mats Sundin	10.00
LS25John LeClair	12.00
LS26Pavel Bure	12.00
LS27Dominik Hasek	15.00
LS28Mike Modano	12.00
LS29Curtis Joseph	10.00
LS30Teemu Selanne	12.00

1998-99 Upper Deck Lord Stanley's Heroes II

This parallel is numbered to 100 on the card front. A Tier III parallel is also randomly seeded and is limited to one set.

	MT
Common Player:	50.00
Production 100 sets	
LS1 Wayne Gretzky	400.00
LS2 Joe Sakic	150.00
LS3 Jaromir Jagr	250.00
LS4 Brendan Shanahan	100.00
LS5 Martin Brodeur	150.00
LS6 Theoren Fleury	60.00
LS7 Doug Gilmour	60.00
LS8 Ron Francis	50.00
LS9 Sergei Fedorov	100.00
LS10Patrick Roy	300.00
LS11Mark Messier	80.00
LS12Peter Forsberg	200.00
LS13Brian Leetch	60.00
LS14Steve Yzerman	250.00
LS15Sergei Samsonov	100.00
LS16Eric Lindros	250.00
LS17Paul Kariya	250.00
LS18Saku Koivu	75.00
LS19Bryan Berard	50.00
LS20Chris Pronger	50.00
LS21Keith Tkachuk	80.00
LS22Doug Weight	50.00
LS23Ed Belfour	80.00
LS24Mats Sundin	80.00
LS25John LeClair	100.00
LS26Pavel Bure	100.00
LS27Dominik Hasek	150.00
LS28Mike Modano	100.00
LS29Curtis Joseph	80.00
LS30Teemu Selanne	100.00

1998-99 Upper Deck Profiles

This 30-card set focusis on the top NHL stars and features silver foil stamping. Card backs have a small photo and a brief personal profile of the player. Card backs are numbered with a "P" prefix and inserted 1:12 packs. There are three parallels randomly inserted: Tier 1, each card numbered to 1,500; Tier 2, each card numbered to 50; and Tier 3, each card numbered to one.

	MT
Complete Set (30):	150.00
Common Player:	1.50
Inserted 1:12	
Quantum 1:	1.5x to 2x
Production 1,500 sets	
Quantum 2:	15x to 25x
Production 50 sets	
P1 Marty Reasoner	1.50
P2 Brett Hull	4.00
P3 Steve Yzerman	10.00
P4 Eric Lindros	12.00
P5 Eric Brewer	1.50
P6 Martin Brodeur	6.00
P7 John Vanbiesbrouck	4.00
P8 Teemu Selanne	5.00
P9 Wayne Gretzky	20.00
P10 Jaromir Jagr	12.00
P11 Peter Forsberg	10.00
P12 Manny Malhotra	3.00
P13 Sergei Samsonov	5.00
P14 Brendan Shanahan	5.00
P15 Doug Gilmour	3.00
P16 Vincent Lecavalier	8.00
P17 Dominik Hasek	6.00
P18 Mike Modano	5.00
P19 Saku Koivu	3.00
P20 Curtis Joseph	3.00
P21 Paul Kariya	12.00
P22 Doug Weight	2.00
P23 Ray Bourque	3.00
P24 Patrick Roy	15.00
P25 John LeClair	5.00
P26 Chris Drury	2.50
P27 Theoren Fleury	2.00
P28 Mats Sundin	3.00
P29 Sergei Fedorov	5.00
P30 Rico Fata	2.50

1998-99 Upper Deck Year of the Great One

This 30-card set showcases Wayne Gretzky, with each card chronicling one of the historic dates of his career and gives his point total against that particular team over his career. Card backs are numbered with a "GO" prefix and are seeded 1:6 packs. There are also three parallels randomly inserted: Tier 1, each card is numbered to 1,999; Tier 2, each card is numbered to 99; and Tier 3, each card is numbered to 1.

	MT
Complete Set (30):	100.00
Common Gretzky:	4.00
Inserted 1:6	
Common Quantum 1:	20.00
Production 1,999 sets	
Common Quantum 2:	300.00
Production 99 sets	
GO1 Wayne Gretzky	4.00
GO2 Wayne Gretzky	4.00
GO3 Wayne Gretzky	4.00
GO4 Wayne Gretzky	4.00
GO5 Wayne Gretzky	4.00
GO6 Wayne Gretzky	4.00
GO7 Wayne Gretzky	4.00
GO8 Wayne Gretzky	4.00
GO9 Wayne Gretzky	4.00
GO10Wayne Gretzky	4.00
GO11Wayne Gretzky	4.00
GO12Wayne Gretzky	4.00
GO13Wayne Gretzky	4.00
GO14Wayne Gretzky	4.00
GO15Wayne Gretzky	4.00
GO16Wayne Gretzky	4.00
GO17Wayne Gretzky	4.00
GO18Wayne Gretzky	4.00
GO19Wayne Gretzky	4.00
GO20Wayne Gretzky	4.00
GO21Wayne Gretzky	4.00
GO22Wayne Gretzky	4.00
GO23Wayne Gretzky	4.00
GO24Wayne Gretzky	4.00
GO25Wayne Gretzky	4.00
GO26Wayne Gretzky	4.00
GO27Wayne Gretzky	4.00
GO28Wayne Gretzky	4.00
GO29Wayne Gretzky	4.00
GO30Wayne Gretzky	4.00

1998-99 Upper Deck Black Diamond

The 120-card base set features light F/X foil treatment with each card having a single black diamond in the upper left portion of the card front. Card backs have a small photo and statistics. Six-card packs had a $3.99 SRP. There are three parallels to the base set: Double, Triple and Quadruple. Doubles have red Light F/X treatment and are limited to 2,000 numbered sets. Triples have gold Light F/X treatment and limited to 1,000 numbered sets. Quadruples have green Light F/X treatment and are limited to 100 numbered sets.

	MT
Complete Set (120):	160.00
Common Player:	.25
Common Prospect (91-120):	1.00
Inserted 1:4	
Doubles:	2.5x to 5x
Prospects:	1x to 2x
Production 2,000 sets	
Triples:	5x to 10x
Prospects:	2x to 4x
Production 1,000 sets	
Quads:	40x to 70x
Prospects:	15x to 30x
Production 100 sets	
1 Paul Kariya	2.50
2 Teemu Selanne	1.00
3 Johan Davidsson	.25
4 Ray Bourque	.50
5 Sergei Samsonov	1.00
6 Jason Allison	.50
7 Joe Thornton	.50
8 Miroslav Satan	.40
9 Brian Holzinger	.25
10 Dominik Hasek	1.50
11 Rico Fata	1.50
12 Jarome Iginla	.25
13 Theoren Fleury	.40
14 Ron Francis	.40
15 Gary Roberts	.25
16 Keith Primeau	.50
17 Sami Kapanen	.40
18 Doug Gilmour	.40
19 Chris Chelios	.50
20 Tony Amonte	.40
21 Peter Forsberg	2.00
22 Patrick Roy	3.00
23 Joe Sakic	1.50
24 Chris Drury	.25
25 Brett Hull	.75
26 Ed Belfour	.50
27 Mike Modano	1.00
28 Darryl Sydor	.25
29 Sergei Fedorov	1.00
30 Steve Yzerman	2.00
31 Nicklas Lidstrom	.50
32 Chris Osgood	.75
33 Brendan Shanahan	1.00
34 Doug Weight	.50
35 Bill Guerin	.25
36 Tom Poti	.25
37 Ed Jovanovski	.25
38 *Mark Parrish*	3.00
39 Rob Niedermayer	.25
40 *Pavel Rosa*	1.00
41 Rob Blake	.25
42 Olli Jokinen	.25
43 Vincent Damphousse	.25
44 Mark Recchi	.25
45 Terry Ryan	.25
46 Saku Koivu	.50
47 Mike Dunham	.50
48 Sergei Krivokrasov	.25
49 Scott Stevens	.25
50 Martin Brodeur	1.50
51 Brendan Morrison	.25
52 Eric Brewer	.25
53 Zigmund Palffy	.75
54 Bryan Berard	.25
55 Wayne Gretzky	4.00
56 Brian Leetch	.50
57 Manny Malhotra	1.00
58 Mike Richter	.75
59 Alexei Yashin	.40
60 Wade Redden	.25
61 Daniel Alfredsson	.40
62 Eric Lindros	2.50
63 John LeClair	1.00
64 John Vanbiesbrouck	.75
65 Rod Brind'Amour	.40
66 Keith Tkachuk	.75
67 Daniel Briere	.25
68 Jeremy Roenick	.50

69	Jaromir Jagr	2.50
70	German Titov	.25
71	Alexei Morozov	.25
72	Patrick Marleau	.75
73	Andrei Zyuzin	.25
74	Mike Vernon	.50
75	Owen Nolan	.25
76	Marty Reasoner	.25
77	Al MacInnis	.50
78	Chris Pronger	.50
79	Wendel Clark	.25
80	Vincent Lecavalier	1.50
81	Craig Janney	.25
82	*Tomas Kaberle*	.25
83	Curtis Joseph	.75
84	Mats Sundin	.75
85	Mark Messier	.75
86	*Bill Muckalt*	1.50
87	Mattias Ohlund	.25
88	Peter Bondra	.75
89	Olaf Kolzig	.50
90	Richard Zednik	.25
91	Harold Druken (Prospect)	1.00
92	Roberto Luongo (Prospect)	10.00
93	Daniel Tkaczuk (Prospect)	1.00
94	Brenden Morrow (Prospect)	6.00
95	Mike Van Ryn (Prospect)	1.00
96	Brian Finley (Prospect)	10.00
97	Jani Rita (Prospect)	6.00
98	Ilkka Mikkola (Prospect)	2.00
99	Mikko Jokela (Prospect)	1.50
100	Tommi Santala (Prospect)	2.00
101	Teemu Virkkunnen (Prospect)	1.00
102	Arto Laatikainen (Prospect)	3.00
103	Kirill Safronov (Prospect)	5.00
104	Alexei Volkov (Prospect)	5.00
105	Denis Arkhipov (Prospect)	6.00
106	Alexander Zevakhin (Prospect)	1.00
107	Denis Shvidki (Prospect)	4.00
108	Maxim Afinogenov (Prospect)	6.00
109	Daniel Sedin (Prospect)	8.00
110	Henrik Sedin (Prospect)	6.00
111	Jimmie Olvestad (Prospect)	1.00
112	Mattias Weinhandl (Prospect)	1.00
113	Mathias Tjarnqvist (Prospect)	1.00
114	Jakob Johnansson (Prospect)	2.00
115	David Legwand (Prospect)	10.00
116	Barrett Heisten (Prospect)	3.00
117	Tim Connolly (Prospect)	6.00
118	Andy Hilbert (Prospect)	1.00
119	Joe Blackburn (Prospect)	4.00
120	Dave Tanabe (Prospect)	2.00

1998-99 Upper Deck Black Diamond Myriad

This set featured 30 of the NHL's best, with each card serially numbered to 1,500 sets. A rare 1-of-1 parallel is also randomly seeded in packs.

		MT
Complete Set (30):		350.00
Common Player:		4.00
Production 1,500 sets		
1	Vincent Lecavalier	15.00
2	John Vanbiesbrouck	8.00
3	Paul Kariya	25.00
4	Keith Tkachuk	8.00
5	Mike Modano	10.00
6	Dominik Hasek	15.00
7	Teemu Selanne	10.00
8	Manny Malhotra	8.00
9	Brendan Shanahan	10.00
10	Pavel Bure	10.00
11	Chris Drury	4.00
12	Curtis Joseph	8.00
13	Joe Sakic	15.00
14	Eric Lindros	25.00
15	Peter Bondra	8.00
16	Brett Hull	8.00
17	Ray Bourque	6.00
18	Jaromir Jagr	25.00
19	Steve Yzerman	20.00
20	Mark Parrish	10.00
21	Martin Brodeur	12.00
22	Saku Koivu	6.00
23	Patrick Roy	30.00
24	John LeClair	10.00
25	Doug Gilmour	6.00
26	Sergei Fedorov	10.00
27	Wayne Gretzky	40.00
28	Peter Forsberg	20.00
29	Eric Brewer	4.00
30	Sergei Samsonov	10.00

1998-99 Upper Deck Black Diamond Winning Formula

Inserted exclusively in hobby packs this insert is serially numbered to the featured players goals, or the featured goaltender's wins multiplied by 50 and are numbered on the card front.

		MT
Complete Set (30):		500.00
Common Player:		5.00
Production #'s listed H		
1	Paul Kariya (850)	50.00
2	Teemu Selanne (2,600)	12.00
3	Sergei Samsonov (1,100)	20.00
4	Dominik Hasek (1,650)	20.00
5	Vincent Lecavalier (2,200)	15.00
6	Patrick Roy (1,550)	40.00
7	Peter Forsberg (1,250)	30.00
8	Joe Sakic (1,350)	25.00
9	Ed Belfour (1,850)	8.00
10	Brendan Shanahan (1,400)	20.00
11	Steve Yzerman (1,200)	35.00
12	Chris Osgood (1,650)	8.00
13	Curtis Joseph (1,450)	8.00
14	Manny Malhotra (800)	12.00
15	Martin Brodeur (2,150)	15.00
16	Chris Drury (1,400)	6.00
17	Zigmund Palffy (2,250)	6.00
18	Wayne Gretzky (1,150)	60.00
19	Theoren Fleury (1,350)	8.00
20	Alexei Yashin (1,650)	8.00
21	Eric Lindros (1,500)	40.00
22	John LeClair (2,550)	10.00
23	Keith Tkachuk (2,000)	10.00
24	Mark Messier (1,100)	15.00
25	Jaromir Jagr (1,750)	35.00
26	Brett Hull (1,350)	12.00
27	Mats Sundin (1,650)	10.00
28	Pavel Bure (2,550)	12.00
29	Peter Bondra (2,600)	5.00
30	Mike Modano (1,050)	15.00

1998-99 Upper Deck Black Diamond Winning Formula Platinum

These are a parallel to the Winning Formula inserts and have platinum foil card fronts. These are numbered to the featured player's goals or the goaltender's wins.

		MT
Common Player:		75.00
Production #'s listed H		
1	Paul Kariya (17)	600.00
2	Teemu Selanne (52)	120.00
3	Sergei Samsonov (22)	160.00
4	Dominik Hasek (33)	220.00
5	Vincent Lecavalier (44)	100.00
6	Patrick Roy (31)	450.00
7	Peter Forsberg (25)	375.00
8	Joe Sakic (27)	250.00
9	Ed Belfour (37)	80.00
10	Brendan Shanahan (28)	175.00
11	Steve Yzerman (24)	450.00
12	Chris Osgood (33)	80.00
13	Curtis Joseph (29)	80.00
14	Manny Malhotra (16)	100.00
15	Martin Brodeur (43)	200.00
16	Chris Drury (28)	75.00
17	Zigmund Palffy (45)	100.00
18	Wayne Gretzky (23)	850.00
19	Theoren Fleury (27)	100.00
20	Alexei Yashin (33)	75.00
21	Eric Lindros (30)	375.00
22	John LeClair (51)	100.00
23	Keith Tkachuk (40)	100.00
24	Mark Messier (22)	180.00
25	Jaromir Jagr (35)	400.00
26	Brett Hull (27)	120.00
27	Mats Sundin (33)	80.00
28	Pavel Bure (51)	150.00
29	Peter Bondra (52)	75.00
30	Mike Modano (21)	200.00

1998-99 Upper Deck Black Diamond YOTGO Auto. Game Jersey

This Wayne Gretzky Game Jersey has a game-used piece of Gretzky's jersey embedded into each card along with Gretzky's autograph. 40 total cards were produced.

	MT
Complete Set (1):	
Wayne Gretzky (40)	

1998-99 Upper Deck MVP

Upper Deck MVP consists of a 220-card set, that has a white border highlighted by silver foil stamping. Card backs feature complete year-by-year statistics, a small photo and a brief career highlight. There are also three parallel insert sets randomly seeded: Silver, Gold and Super. Silvers have a silver foil facsimile signature on the card front and are seeded 1:2 packs. Golds are hobby exclusive and have a gold foil facsimile signature on the card front. These are limited to 100 serial numbered sets. Supers are hobby exclusive, have a gold foil facsimile signature on the card front and limited to 25 serial numbered sets.

		MT
Complete Set (220):		30.00
Common Player:		.15
Silvers:		2x to 4x
Inserted 1:2		
Golds:		75x to 125x
Production 100 sets H		
Supers:		200x to 350x
Production 25 sets		
1	Paul Kariya	2.00
2	Teemu Selanne	.75
3	Tomas Sandstrom	.15
4	Johan Davidsson	.15
5	Mike Crowley	.15
6	Guy Hebert	.30
7	Marty McInnis	.15
8	Steve Rucchin	.15
9	Ray Bourque	.50
10	Sergei Samsonov	.75
11	Cameron Mann	.15
12	Joe Thornton	.15
13	Jason Allison	.25
14	Byron Dafoe	.40
15	Kyle McLaren	.15
16	Dmitri Khristich	.15
17	Hal Gill	.15
18	Anson Carter	.15
19	Miroslav Satan	.25
20	Brian Holzinger	.15
21	Dominik Hasek	1.00
22	Matthew Barnaby	.15
23	Erik Rasmussen	.15
24	Geoff Sanderson	.15
25	Michal Grosek	.15
26	Michael Peca	.15
27	Rico Fata	.40
28	Derek Morris	.15
29	Phil Housley	.15
30	Valeri Bure	.15
31	Ed Ward	.15
32	Jean-Sebastien Giguere	.15
33	Jeff Shantz	.15
34	Jarome Iginla	.15
35	Ron Francis	.25
36	Trevor Kidd	.30
37	Keith Primeau	.25
38	Sami Kapanen	.25
39	Martin Gelinas	.15
40	Jeff O'Neill	.15
41	Gary Roberts	.15
42	Jocelyn Thibault	.30
43	Doug Gilmour	.25
44	Chris Chelios	.40
45	Tony Amonte	.25
46	Bob Probert	.15
47	Daniel Cleary	.15
48	Eric Daze	.15
49	Mike Maneluk	.30
50	Remi Royer	.15
51	Peter Forsberg	1.50
52	Patrick Roy	2.00
53	Joe Sakic	1.00
54	Chris Drury	.25
55	Milan Hejduk	.40
56	Greg DeVries	.15
57	Theoren Fleury	.25
58	Adam Deadmarsh	.15
59	Brett Hull	.50
60	Ed Belfour	.40
61	Mike Modano	.75
62	Darryl Sydor	.15
63	Joe Nieuwendyk	.25
64	Grant Marshall	.15
65	Sergei Zubov	.15
66	Derian Hatcher	.15
67	Jere Lehtinen	.15
68	Sergei Fedorov	.75
69	Steve Yzerman	1.50
70	Nicklas Lidstrom	.30
71	Chris Osgood	.40
72	Brendan Shanahan	.75
73	Darren McCarty	.15
74	Tomas Holmstrom	.15
75	Norm Maracle	.50
76	Doug Brown	.15
77	Doug Weight	.15
78	Janne Niinimaa	.15
79	Tom Poti	.15
80	Bill Guerin	.15
81	Mike Grier	.15
82	Ryan Smyth	.15
83	Roman Hamrlik	.15
84	Kevin Brown	.15
85	Pavel Bure	.75
86	Jaroslav Spacek	.15
87	Rob Niedermayer	.15
88	Robert Svehla	.15
89	Ray Whitney	.15
90	Peter Worrell	.15
91	*Mark Parrish*	1.00
92	*Oleg Kvasha*	.75
93	Steve Duchesne	.15
94	Rob Blake	.15
95	Olli Jokinen	.15
96	Donald Audette	.15
97	Luc Robitaille	.25
98	Josh Green	.15
99	Philippe Boucher	.15
100	Matt Johnson	.15
101	Vincent Damphousse	.15
102	Dainius Zubrus	.15
103	Terry Ryan	.15
104	Saku Koivu	.25
105	Brett Clark	.15
106	Dave Morrisette	.15
107	Eric Weinrich	.15
108	Brian Savage	.15
109	Shayne Corson	.15
110	Mike Dunham	.30
111	Greg Johnson	.15
112	Cliff Ronning	.15
113	Andrew Brunette	.15
114	Sergei Krivokrasov	.15
115	Sebastian Bordeleau	.15
116	Scott Stevens	.15
117	Martin Brodeur	.75
118	Brendan Morrison	.15
119	Patrik Elias	.15
120	Scott Niedermayer	.15
121	Bobby Holik	.15
122	Jason Arnott	.15
123	Jay Pandolfo	.15
124	Eric Brewer	.15
125	Zigmund Palffy	.40
126	Felix Potvin	.40
127	Robert Reichel	.15
128	Mike Watt	.15
129	Tommy Salo	.30
130	Kenny Jonsson	.15
131	Trevor Linden	.15
132	Wayne Gretzky	3.00
133	Brian Leetch	.25
134	Manny Malhotra	.25
135	Mike Richter	.40
136	Mike Knuble	.15
137	Niklas Sundstrom	.15
138	Todd Harvey	.15
139	Alexei Yashin	.25
140	Damian Rhodes	.30
141	Daniel Alfredsson	.15
142	Magnus Arvedson	.15
143	Shawn McEachern	.15
144	Chris Phillips	.15
145	Vaclav Prospal	.15
146	Wade Redden	.15
147	Eric Lindros	2.00
148	John LeClair	.75
149	John Vanbiesbrouck	.60
150	Keith Jones	.15
151	Colin Forbes	.15
152	Mark Recchi	.15
153	Dan McGillis	.15
154	Eric Desjardins	.15
155	Rod Brind'Amour	.25
156	Keith Tkachuk	.50
157	Daniel Briere	.15
158	Nikolai Khabibulin	.30
159	Brad Isbister	.15
160	Jeremy Roenick	.40
161	Oleg Tverdovsky	.15
162	Rick Tocchet	.15
163	Jaromir Jagr	2.00
164	Tom Barrasso	.30
165	Alexei Morozov	.15
166	Robert Dome	.15
167	Stu Barnes	.15
168	Martin Straka	.15
169	German Titov	.15
170	Patrick Marleau	.25
171	Andrei Zyuzin	.15
172	Marco Sturm	.15
173	Owen Nolan	.15
174	Jeff Friesen	.15
175	Bob Rouse	.15
176	Mike Vernon	.30
177	Mike Ricci	.15
178	Marty Reasoner	.15
179	Al MacInnis	.25
180	Chris Pronger	.25
181	Pierre Turgeon	.25
182	Michal Handzus	.15
183	Jim Campbell	.15
184	Tony Twist	.15
185	Pavol Demitra	.25
186	Daren Puppa	.25
187	Vincent Lecavalier	.75
188	Bill Ranford	.25
189	Alexandre Daigle	.15
190	Wendel Clark	.15
191	Rob Zamuner	.15
192	Chris Gratton	.15
193	Fredrik Modin	.15
194	Curtis Joseph	.40
195	Mats Sundin	.40
196	Steve Thomas	.15
197	Tomas Kaberle	.15
198	Alyn McCauley	.15
199	Mike Johnson	.15
200	Bryan Berard	.15
201	Mark Messier	.50
202	Jason Strudwick	.15
203	Mattias Ohlund	.15
204	Alexander Mogilny	.25
205	Bill Muckalt	.50
206	Ed Jovanovski	.15
207	Josh Holden	.15
208	Peter Schaefer	.15
209	Peter Bondra	.40
210	Olaf Kolzig	.30
211	Sergei Gonchar	.15
212	Adam Oates	.30
213	Brian Bellows	.15
214	Matt Herr	.15
215	Richard Zednik	.15
216	Joe Juneau	.15
217	Jaroslav Svejkovsky	.15
218	Wayne Gretzky	1.00
219	Wayne Gretzky	1.00
220	Wayne Gretzky	1.00

1998-99 Upper Deck MVP Dynamics

This 15-card set focuses on the Great One and features a holographic rainbow front, highlighted by silver foil stamping. Card backs have a small photo of Gretzky along with a note of a key moment in his career. Cards are numbered with a "D" prefix and are inserted 1:28 packs.

		MT
Complete Set (15):		125.00
Common Gretzky:		10.00
Inserted 1:28		
1	Wayne Gretzky	10.00
2	Wayne Gretzky	10.00
3	Wayne Gretzky	10.00
4	Wayne Gretzky	10.00
5	Wayne Gretzky	10.00
6	Wayne Gretzky	10.00
7	Wayne Gretzky	10.00
8	Wayne Gretzky	10.00
9	Wayne Gretzky	10.00
10	Wayne Gretzky	10.00
11	Wayne Gretzky	10.00
12	Wayne Gretzky	10.00
13	Wayne Gretzky	10.00
14	Wayne Gretzky	10.00
15	Wayne Gretzky	10.00

1998-99 Upper Deck MVP Game Used Souvenirs

This ten-card set have a piece of game-used puck embedded into the front of each card. Found exclusively in hobby packs these were seeded 1:144 packs. Two players also autographed to their respective jersey number: Steve Yzerman (19) and Vincent Lecavalier (14).

		MT
Common Player:		60.00
Inserted 1:144		
SF	Sergei Fedorov	100.00
WG	Wayne Gretzky	220.00
BH	Brett Hull	70.00
JL	John LeClair	90.00
VL	Vincent Lecavalier	75.00
VLA	Vincent Lecavalier AUTO	300.00
EL	Eric Lindros	125.00
MM	Mike Modano	75.00
PR	Patrick Roy	150.00
SS	Sergei Samsonov	75.00
SY	Steve Yzerman	125.00
SYA	Steve Yzerman AUTO	700.00

1998-99 Upper Deck MVP OT Heroes

This 15-card insert set focused on players who can save a game or decide the game in sudden death overtime. These were inserted 1:9 packs. Card backs are numbered with an "OT" prefix.

		MT
Complete Set (15):		70.00
Common Player:		2.00
Inserted 1:9		
1	Steve Yzerman	6.00
2	Patrick Roy	10.00
3	Jaromir Jagr	8.00
4	Ray Bourque	2.00
5	Wayne Gretzky	12.00
6	Sergei Samsonov	3.00
7	Dominik Hasek	5.00
8	Peter Forsberg	6.00
9	Paul Kariya	8.00
10	Eric Lindros	8.00
11	Pavel Bure	3.00
12	Keith Tkachuk	2.50
13	Brendan Shanahan	3.00
14	John LeClair	3.00
15	Joe Sakic	4.00

1998-99 Upper Deck MVP Power Game

This 15-card set is fully foiled with silver foil stamping. These were inserted 1:9 packs, with card backs numbered with a "PG" prefix.

		MT
Complete Set (15):		40.00
Common Player:		1.50
Inserted 1:9		
1	Brendan Shanahan	4.00
2	Keith Tkachuk	3.00
3	Eric Lindros	8.00
4	Mike Modano	4.00
5	Vincent Lecavalier	4.00
6	John LeClair	4.00
7	Mark Messier	3.00
8	Mats Sundin	3.00
9	Peter Forsberg	6.00
10	Jaromir Jagr	8.00
11	Keith Primeau	1.50
12	Mark Parrish	1.50
13	Patrick Marleau	2.50
14	Bill Guerin	1.50
15	Jeremy Roenick	2.50

1998-99 Upper Deck MVP ProSign

ProSign are autographed inserts found exclusively in retail packs, seeded at a rate of 1:216 packs.

		MT
Common Player:		10.00
Inserted 1:216 R		
JAr	Jason Arnott	15.00
BB	Brian Bellows	10.00
EB	Eric Brewer	15.00
CD	Chris Drury	30.00
MD	Mike Dunham	15.00
RF	Rico Fata	15.00
WG	Wayne Gretzky	350.00
JI	Jarome Iginla	15.00
MJ	Mike Johnson	20.00
VL	Vincent Lecavalier	35.00
MM	Manny Malhotra	25.00
AM	Alyn McCauley	15.00
BM	Brendan Morrison	20.00
DN	Dmitri Nabokov	20.00
RN	Rob Niedermayer	15.00
MP	Mark Parrish	25.00
ER	Erik Rasmussen	20.00
WR	Wade Redden	15.00
JT	Jose Theodore	15.00
OT	Oleg Tverdovsky	15.00
DW	Doug Weight	20.00
SY	Steve Yzerman	175.00

1998-99 Upper Deck MVP Special Forces

This 15-card set highlights players who specialize on the power play or penalty-killing lines. Card backs are numbered with a "F" prefix, they were seeded 1:14 packs.

		MT
Complete Set (15):		90.00
Common Player:		3.00
Inserted 1:14		
1	Brett Hull	3.00
2	Sergei Samsonov	4.00
3	Vincent Lecavalier	4.00
4	Dominik Hasek	6.00
5	Eric Lindros	10.00
6	Paul Kariya	10.00
7	Steve Yzerman	8.00
8	Brendan Shanahan	4.00
9	Martin Brodeur	5.00
10	Teemu Selanne	4.00
11	Jaromir Jagr	10.00
12	Wayne Gretzky	15.00
13	Patrick Roy	12.00
14	Peter Forsberg	8.00
15	Joe Sakic	5.00

1998-99 Upper Deck MVP Snipers

Snipers is a 12-card set showcasing the NHL's top sharp shooters. Card fronts are full foiled with red foil stamping. Card backs have a partial photo, career highlight note and are numbered with a "S" prefix. They were seeded 1:6 packs.

		MT
Complete Set (12):		25.00
Common Player:		1.00
Inserted 1:6		
1	Vincent Lecavalier	2.50
2	Wayne Gretzky	8.00
3	Sergei Samsonov	2.00
4	Teemu Selanne	2.00
5	Peter Forsberg	4.00
6	Paul Kariya	6.00
7	Eric Lindros	6.00
8	Pavel Bure	2.00
9	Peter Bondra	1.50
10	Joe Sakic	2.50
11	Steve Yzerman	4.00
12	Sergei Fedorov	2.00

1998-99 Upper Deck MVP YOTGO Autograph Game Jersey

This Wayne Gretzky Game Jersey has a game-used piece of Gretzky's jersey embedded into each card along with Gretzky's autograph. 40 total cards were produced.

	MT
Complete Set (1):	2,000.00
Wayne Gretzky (40)	

1998-99 UD Cubed

This 180-card base set is broken down into six 30-card subsets, each with three different technologies: Embossed, Light F/X and Rainbow Foil. Packs have three cards and had a SRP of $3.99 per pack.

		MT
Complete Set (180):		475.00
Common New Era Emb. (1-30):		.25
Inserted 1:1		
Comm. 3-Star Spot. Rainbow (31-60):		.25
Inserted 1:1		
Comm. New Era Light F/X (61-90):		.25
Inserted 1:1		
Comm. 3-Star Spot. F/X (91-120):		.40
Inserted 1:3		
Comm. New Era Rainbow (121-150):		.75
Inserted 1:5		
Comm. 3-Star Spot. Emboss (151-180):		5.00
Inserted 1:23		
1	Sergei Samsonov	1.25
2	*Ryan Johnson*	.50
3	Josef Marha	.25
4	Patrick Marleau	1.00
5	Derek Morris	.25
6	Jamie Storr	.50
7	Richard Zednik	.25
8	Alyn McCauley	.25
9	Robert Dome	.25
10	Patrik Elias	.40
11	Olli Jokinen	.40
12	Peter Skudra	.25
13	Chris Phillips	.25
14	Mattias Ohlund	.25
15	Joe Thornton	.75
16	Matt Cullen	.25
17	Bates Battaglia	.25
18	Andrei Zyuzin	.25
19	Cameron Mann	.25
20	Zdeno Chara	.25
21	Marc Savard	.25
22	Alexei Morozov	.25
23	Mike Johnson	.25
24	Vaclav Varada	.25
25	Dan Cloutier	.25
26	Brad Isbister	.25
27	Marco Sturm	.25
28	Anders Eriksson	.25
29	Jan Bulis	.25
30	Brendan Morrison	.25
31	Wayne Gretzky	5.00
32	Jaromir Jagr	3.00
33	Peter Forsberg	2.50
34	Paul Kariya	3.00
35	Brett Hull	1.00
36	Martin Brodeur	1.50
37	Eric Lindros	3.00
38	Peter Bondra	.75
39	Mike Modano	1.25
40	Theoren Fleury	.50
41	Curtis Joseph	.75
42	Sergei Fedorov	1.25
43	Saku Koivu	.75
44	Zigmund Palffy	.75
45	Ed Belfour	.75
46	Patrick Roy	4.00
47	Brendan Shanahan	1.25
48	Mats Sundin	1.00
49	Alexei Yashin	.40
50	Doug Gilmour	.40
51	Chris Osgood	.75
52	Keith Tkachuk	.75
53	Mark Messier	1.00
54	John Vanbiesbrouck	1.25
55	Ray Bourque	.75
56	John LeClair	1.25
57	Dominik Hasek	2.00
58	Teemu Selanne	1.25
59	Joe Sakic	2.00
60	Steve Yzerman	2.50
61	Sergei Samsonov	1.25
62	Ryan Johnson	.50
63	Josef Marha	.25
64	Patrick Marleau	1.00
65	Derek Morris	.25
66	Jamie Storr	.50
67	Richard Zednik	.25
68	Alyn McCauley	.25
69	Robert Dome	.25
70	Patrik Elias	.40
71	Olli Jokinen	.40
72	Peter Skudra	.25
73	Chris Phillips	.25
74	Mattias Ohlund	.25
75	Joe Thornton	.75
76	Matt Cullen	.25
77	Bates Battaglia	.25
78	Andrei Zyuzin	.25
79	Cameron Mann	.25
80	Zdeno Chara	.25
81	Marc Savard	.25
82	Alexei Morozov	.25
83	Mike Johnson	.25
84	Vaclav Varada	.25
85	Dan Cloutier	.25
86	Brad Isbister	.25
87	Marco Sturm	.25
88	Anders Eriksson	.25
89	Jan Bulis	.25
90	Brendan Morrison	.25
91	Wayne Gretzky	8.00
92	Jaromir Jagr	5.00
93	Peter Forsberg	4.00
94	Paul Kariya	5.00
95	Brett Hull	1.50
96	Martin Brodeur	3.00
97	Eric Lindros	5.00
98	Peter Bondra	1.25
99	Mike Modano	2.00
100	Theoren Fleury	.75
101	Curtis Joseph	1.25
102	Sergei Fedorov	2.00
103	Saku Koivu	1.25
104	Zigmund Palffy	1.25
105	Ed Belfour	1.50
106	Patrick Roy	6.00
107	Brendan Shanahan	2.00
108	Mats Sundin	2.00
109	Alexei Yashin	.75
110	Doug Gilmour	.75
111	Chris Osgood	1.25
112	Keith Tkachuk	1.50
113	Mark Messier	1.50
114	John Vanbiesbrouck	2.00
115	Ray Bourque	1.25
116	John LeClair	2.00
117	Dominik Hasek	3.00
118	Teemu Selanne	2.00
119	Joe Sakic	3.00
120	Steve Yzerman	4.00
121	Sergei Samsonov	3.00
122	Ryan Johnson	1.00
123	Josef Marha	.25
124	Patrick Marleau	2.00
125	Derek Morris	.50
126	Jamie Storr	1.00
127	Richard Zednik	.50
128	Alyn McCauley	.50
129	Robert Dome	.50
130	Patrik Elias	.75
131	Olli Jokinen	.75
132	Peter Skudra	.50
133	Chris Phillips	.25
134	Mattias Ohlund	.25
135	Joe Thornton	1.50
136	Matt Cullen	.75
137	Bates Battaglia	.75
138	Andrei Zyuzin	.50
139	Cameron Mann	.50
140	Zdeno Chara	.50
141	Marc Savard	.25
142	Alexei Morozov	.50
143	Mike Johnson	.75
144	Vaclav Varada	.50
145	Dan Cloutier	.75
146	Brad Isbister	.50
147	Marco Sturm	.50
148	Anders Eriksson	.50
149	Jan Bulis	.50
150	Brendan Morrison	.75
151	Wayne Gretzky	50.00
152	Jaromir Jagr	30.00
153	Peter Forsberg	25.00
154	Paul Kariya	30.00
155	Brett Hull	10.00
156	Martin Brodeur	15.00
157	Eric Lindros	30.00
158	Peter Bondra	10.00
159	Mike Modano	12.00
160	Theoren Fleury	5.00
161	Curtis Joseph	8.00
162	Sergei Fedorov	12.00
163	Saku Koivu	8.00
164	Zigmund Palffy	8.00
165	Ed Belfour	10.00
166	Patrick Roy	40.00
167	Brendan Shanahan	12.00
168	Mats Sundin	10.00
169	Alexei Yashin	5.00
170	Doug Gilmour	6.00
171	Chris Osgood	8.00
172	Keith Tkachuk	10.00
173	Mark Messier	10.00
174	John Vanbiesbrouck	12.00
175	Ray Bourque	8.00
176	John LeClair	12.00
177	Dominik Hasek	20.00
178	Teemu Selanne	12.00
179	Joe Sakic	20.00
180	Steve Yzerman	25.00

1998-99 UD Cubed Die-Cuts

This parallel set has perimeter die-cutting, with each card sequentially numbered to varying amounts depending on the technology and subset.

		MT
Common New Era Emb. (1-30):		6.00
Production 200 sets		
Comm. New Era Light F/X (61-90):		2.50
Production 1,000 sets		
Comm. 3-Star Spot. F/X (91-120):		8.00
Production 1,000 sets		
Comm. New Era Rainbow (121-150):		15.00
Production 50 sets		
Comm. 3-Star Spot. Emboss (151-180):		20.00
Production 100 sets		
1	Sergei Samsonov	30.00
2	*Ryan Johnson*	8.00
3	Josef Marha	6.00
4	Patrick Marleau	25.00
5	Derek Morris	6.00
6	Jamie Storr	10.00
7	Richard Zednik	6.00
8	Alyn McCauley	6.00
9	Robert Dome	6.00
10	Patrik Elias	8.00
11	Olli Jokinen	8.00
12	Peter Skudra	6.00
13	Chris Phillips	6.00
14	Mattias Ohlund	10.00
15	Joe Thornton	20.00
16	Matt Cullen	6.00
17	Bates Battaglia	6.00
18	Andrei Zyuzin	6.00
19	Cameron Mann	6.00
20	Zdeno Chara	6.00
21	Marc Savard	6.00
22	Alexei Morozov	8.00
23	Mike Johnson	8.00
24	Vaclav Varada	6.00
25	Dan Cloutier	10.00
26	Brad Isbister	6.00
27	Marco Sturm	6.00
28	Anders Eriksson	6.00
29	Jan Bulis	6.00
30	Brendan Morrison	10.00
61	Sergei Samsonov	15.00
62	Ryan Johnson	2.50
63	Josef Marha	2.50

64	Patrick Marleau	12.00
65	Derek Morris	2.50
66	Jamie Storr	5.00
67	Richard Zednik	2.50
68	Alyn McCauley	2.50
69	Robert Dome	2.50
70	Patrik Elias	4.00
71	Olli Jokinen	4.00
72	Peter Skudra	2.50
73	Chris Phillips	2.50
74	Mattias Ohlund	4.00
75	Joe Thornton	10.00
76	Matt Cullen	2.50
77	Bates Battaglia	2.50
78	Andrei Zyuzin	2.50
79	Cameron Mann	2.50
80	Zdeno Chara	2.50
81	Marc Savard	2.50
82	Alexei Morozov	4.00
83	Mike Johnson	4.00
84	Vaclav Varada	2.50
85	Dan Cloutier	5.00
86	Brad Isbister	2.50
87	Marco Sturm	4.00
88	Anders Eriksson	2.50
89	Jan Bulis	4.00
90	Brendan Morrison	5.00
91	Wayne Gretzky	60.00
92	Jaromir Jagr	40.00
93	Peter Forsberg	30.00
94	Paul Kariya	40.00
95	Brett Hull	10.00
96	Martin Brodeur	18.00
97	Eric Lindros	40.00
98	Peter Bondra	10.00
99	Mike Modano	15.00
100	Theoren Fleury	8.00
101	Curtis Joseph	10.00
102	Sergei Fedorov	15.00
103	Saku Koivu	10.00
104	Zigmund Palffy	10.00
105	Ed Belfour	10.00
106	Patrick Roy	45.00
107	Brendan Shanahan	15.00
108	Mats Sundin	12.00
109	Alexei Yashin	8.00
110	Doug Gilmour	8.00
111	Chris Osgood	10.00
112	Keith Tkachuk	10.00
113	Mark Messier	10.00
114	John Vanbiesbrouck	15.00
115	Ray Bourque	10.00
116	John LeClair	15.00
117	Dominik Hasek	20.00
118	Teemu Selanne	15.00
119	Joe Sakic	20.00
120	Steve Yzerman	30.00
121	Sergei Samsonov	80.00
122	Ryan Johnson	20.00
123	Josef Marha	15.00
124	Patrick Marleau	70.00
125	Derek Morris	15.00
126	Jamie Storr	30.00
127	Richard Zednik	15.00
128	Alyn McCauley	15.00
129	Robert Dome	15.00
130	Patrik Elias	20.00
131	Olli Jokinen	25.00
132	Peter Skudra	15.00
133	Chris Phillips	15.00
134	Mattias Ohlund	30.00
135	Joe Thornton	60.00
136	Matt Cullen	15.00
137	Bates Battaglia	15.00
138	Andrei Zyuzin	15.00
139	Cameron Mann	15.00
140	Zdeno Chara	15.00
141	Marc Savard	15.00
142	Alexei Morozov	20.00
143	Mike Johnson	25.00
144	Vaclav Varada	20.00
145	Dan Cloutier	30.00
146	Brad Isbister	15.00
147	Marco Sturm	15.00
148	Anders Eriksson	15.00
149	Jan Bulis	25.00
150	Brendan Morrison	30.00
151	Wayne Gretzky	250.00
152	Jaromir Jagr	150.00
153	Peter Forsberg	125.00
154	Paul Kariya	150.00
155	Brett Hull	50.00
156	Martin Brodeur	75.00
157	Eric Lindros	150.00
158	Peter Bondra	50.00
159	Mike Modano	60.00
160	Theoren Fleury	20.00
161	Curtis Joseph	40.00
162	Sergei Fedorov	60.00
163	Saku Koivu	40.00
164	Zigmund Palffy	40.00
165	Ed Belfour	40.00
166	Patrick Roy	180.00
167	Brendan Shanahan	60.00
168	Mats Sundin	50.00
169	Alexei Yashin	20.00
170	Doug Gilmour	30.00
171	Chris Osgood	50.00
172	Keith Tkachuk	50.00
173	Mark Messier	50.00
174	John Vanbiesbrouck	60.00
175	Ray Bourque	40.00
176	John LeClair	60.00
177	Dominik Hasek	80.00
178	Teemu Selanne	60.00
179	Joe Sakic	80.00
180	Steve Yzerman	125.00

1999-00 Pacific

The base set consists of 450-cards and features full bleed photos with silver foil stamping. Card backs have a photo along with year-by-year statistics. Four parallels to the base set were also randomly seeded: Copper, Gold, Ice Blue and Premiere Date. Copper's are hobby exlusive and limited to 99 serial numbered sets. Gold's are retail exclusive and limited to 199 serial numbered sets. Ice Blue's are limited to 75 serial numbered sets and Premiere Date's are limited to 47 serial numbered sets.

	MT
Complete Set (450):	35.00
Common Player:	.10
Copper:	40x to 80x
Production 99 sets	
Golds:	15x to 30x
Production 199 sets	
Ice Blues:	50x to 100x
Production 75 sets	
Premiere Date:	80x to 125x
Production 47 sets	

1	Matt Cullen	.10
2	Johan Davidsson	.10
3	Scott Ferguson	.10
4	Travis Green	.10
5	Stu Grimson	.10
6	Kevin Haller	.10
7	Guy Hebert	.25
8	Paul Kariya	2.00
9	Marty McInnis	.10
10	Jim McKenzie	.10
11	Fredrik Olausson	.10
12	Dominic Roussel	.10
13	Steve Rucchin	.10
14	Ruslan Salei	.10
15	Tomas Sandstrom	.10
16	Teemu Selanne	.75
17	Jason Allison	.25
18	P.J. Axelsson	.10
19	Shawn Bates	.10
20	Ray Bourque	.40
21	Anson Carter	.10
22	Byron Dafoe	.40
23	Hal Gill	.10
24	Steve Heinze	.10
25	Dimitri Khristich	.10
26	Cameron Mann	.10
27	Kyle McLaren	.10
28	Sergei Samsonov	.50
29	Robbie Tallas	.10
30	Joe Thornton	.25
31	Landon Wilson	.10
32	Jonathan Girard, Andre Savage	.10
33	Stu Barnes	.10
34	Martin Biron	.10
35	Curtis Brown	.10
36	Michal Grosek	.10
37	Dominik Hasek	1.00
38	Brian Holzinger	.10
39	Joe Juneau	.10
40	Jay McKee	.10
41	Michael Peca	.10
42	Erik Rasmussen	.10
43	Rob Ray	.10
44	Geoff Sanderson	.10
45	Miroslav Satan	.10
46	Darryl Shannon	.10
47	Vaclav Varada	.10
48	Dixon Ward	.10
49	Jason Woolley	.10
50	Alexei Zhitnik	.10
51	Fred Brathwaite	.10
52	Valeri Bure	.10
53	Andrew Cassels	.10
54	Rene Corbet	.10
55	J.S. Giguere	.10
56	Phil Housley	.10
57	Jarome Iginla	.10
58	Derek Morris	.10
59	Andrei Nazarov	.10
60	Jeff Shantz	.10
61	Todd Simpson	.10
62	Cory Stillman	.10
63	Jason Wiemer	.10
64	Clark Wilm	.10
65	Ken Wregget	.20
66	Rico Fata, Tyrone Garner	.10
67	Bates Battaglia	.10
68	Paul Coffey	.20
69	Kevin Dineen	.10
70	Ron Francis	.25
71	Martin Gelinas	.10
72	Arturs Irbe	.25
73	Sami Kapanen	.10
74	Trevor Kidd	.25
75	Andrei Kovalenko	.10
76	Robert Kron	.10
77	Kent Manderville	.10
78	Jeff O'Neill	.10
79	Keith Primeau	.25
80	Gary Roberts	.10
81	Ray Sheppard	.10
82	Glen Wesley	.10
83	Byron Ritchie, Craig MacDonald	.10
84	Tony Amonte	.25
85	Eric Daze	.10
86	J.P. Dumont	.10
87	Anders Eriksson	.10
88	Mark Fitzpatrick	.10
89	Doug Gilmour	.20
90	J.Y. Leroux	.10
91	Dave Manson	.10
92	Josef Marha	.10
93	Dean McAmmond	.10
94	Boris Mironov	.10
95	Ed Olczyk	.10
96	Bob Probert	.10
97	Jocelyn Thibault	.25
98	Alexei Zhamnov	.10
99	Remi Royer, Ty Jones	.10
100	Craig Billington	.10
101	Adam Deadmarsh	.10
102	Chris Drury	.25
103	Theoren Fleury	.25
104	Adam Foote	.10
105	Peter Forsberg	1.50
106	Milan Hejduk	.25
107	Dale Hunter	.10
108	Valeri Kamensky	.10
109	Sylvain Lefebvre	.10
110	Claude Lemieux	.10
111	Aaron Miller	.10
112	Jeff Odgers	.10
113	Sandis Ozolinsh	.10
114	Patrick Roy	2.50
115	Joe Sakic	1.00
116	Stephane Yelle	.10
117	Ed Belfour	.50
118	Derian Hatcher	.10
119	Benoit Hogue	.10
120	Brett Hull	.40
121	Mike Keane	.10
122	Jamie Langenbrunner	.10
123	Jere Lehtinen	.10
124	Brad Lukowich	.10
125	Grant Marshall	.10
126	Mike Modano	.75
127	Joe Nieuwendyk	.25
128	Derek Plante	.10
129	Darryl Sydor	.10
130	Roman Turek	.10
131	Pat Verbeek	.10
132	Sergei Zubov	.10
133	Jonathan Sim, Blake Sloan	.10
134	Doug Brown	.10
135	Chris Chelios	.25
136	Wendel Clark	.10
137	Kris Draper	.10
138	Sergei Fedorov	.50
139	Tomas Holmstrom	.10
140	Vyacheslav Kozlov	.10
141	Martin Lapointe	.10
142	Igor Larionov	.10
143	Nicklas Lidstrom	.25
144	Darren McCarty	.10
145	Larry Murphy	.10
146	Chris Osgood	.40
147	Bill Ranford	.20
148	Ulf Samuelsson	.10
149	Brendan Shanahan	.75
150	Aaron Ward	.10
151	Steve Yzerman	1.50
152	Josef Beranek	.10
153	Pat Falloon	.10
154	Mike Grier	.10
155	Bill Guerin	.10
156	Roman Hamrlik	.10
157	Chad Kilger	.10
158	Georges Laraque	.10
159	Todd Marchant	.10
160	Ethan Moreau	.10
161	Rem Murray	.10
162	Janne Niinimaa	.10
163	Tom Poti	.10
164	Tommy Salo	.25
165	Alexander Selivanov	.10
166	Ryan Smyth	.10
167	Doug Weight	.20
168	Steve Passmore	.10
169	Pavel Bure	.75
170	Sean Burke	.25
171	Dino Ciccarelli	.10
172	Radek Dvorak	.10
173	Viktor Kozlov	.10
174	Oleg Kvasha	.10
175	Paul Laus	.10
176	Bill Lindsay	.10
177	Kirk McLean	.25
178	Scott Mellanby	.10
179	Rob Neidermayer	.10
180	Mark Parrish	.25
181	Jaroslav Spacek	.10
182	Robert Svehla	.10
183	Ray Whitney	.10
184	Peter Worrell	.10
185	Dan Boyle, Marcus Nilson	.10
186	Donald Audette	.10
187	Rob Blake	.10
188	Russ Courtnall	.10
189	Ray Ferraro	.10
190	Stephane Fiset	.25
191	Craig Johnson	.10
192	Olli Jokinen	.10
193	Glen Murray	.10
194	Mattias Norstrom	.10
195	Sean O'Donnell	.10
196	Luc Robitaille	.25
197	Pavel Rosa	.10
198	Jamie Storr	.25
199	Jozef Stumpel	.10
200	Vladimir Tsyplakov	.10
201	Benoit Brunet	.10
202	Shayne Corson	.10
203	Jeff Hackett	.40
204	Matt Higgins	.10
205	Saku Koivu	.40
206	Vladimir Malakhov	.10
207	Patrick Poulin	.10
208	Stephane Quintal	.10
209	Martin Rucinsky	.10
210	Brian Savage	.10
211	Turner Stevenson	.10
212	Jose Theodore	.25
213	Eric Weinrich	.10
214	Sergei Zholtok	.10
215	Dainius Zubrus	.10
216	Terry Ryan, Miloslav Guren	.10
217	Drake Berehowsky	.10
218	Sebastian Bordeleau	.10
219	Bob Boughner	.10
220	Andrew Brunette	.10
221	Patrick Cote	.10
222	Mike Dunham	.40
223	Tom Fitzgerald	.10
224	Jamie Heward	.10
225	Greg Johnson	.10
226	Patric Kjellberg	.10
227	Sergei Krivokrasov	.10
228	Denny Lambert	.10
229	David Legwand	.50
230	Mark Mowers	.10
231	Cliff Ronning	.10
232	Tomas Vokoun	.10
233	Scott Walker	.10
234	Jason Arnott	.10
235	Martin Brodeur	1.00
236	Ken Daneyko	.10
237	Patrik Elias	.10
238	Bobby Holik	.10
239	John Madden	.10
240	Randy McKay	.10
241	Brendan Morrison	.10
242	Scott Niedermayer	.10
243	Lyle Odelein	.10
244	Krzysztof Oliwa	.10
245	Jay Pandolfo	.10
246	Brian Rolston	.10
247	Vadim Sharifijanov	.10
248	Petr Sykora	.10
249	Chris Terreri	.10
250	Scott Stevens	.10
251	Eric Brewer	.10
252	Zdeno Chara	.10
253	Mariusz Czerkawski	.10
254	Wade Flaherty	.10
255	Kenny Jonsson	.10
256	Claude Lapointe	.10
257	Mark Lawrence	.10
258	Trevor Linden	.10
259	Mats Lindgren	.10
260	Warren Luhning	.10
261	Zigmund Palffy	.40
262	Richard Pilon	.10
263	Felix Potvin	.25
264	Barry Richter	.10
265	Bryan Smolinski	.10
266	Mike Watt	.10
267	Dan Cloutier	.25
268	Brent Fedyk	.10
269	Adam Graves	.10
270	Todd Harvey	.10
271	Mike Knuble	.10
272	Brian Leetch	.25
273	John MacLean	.10
274	Manny Malhotra	.25
275	Rumun Ndur	.10
276	Petr Nedved	.10
277	Peter Popovic	.10
278	Mike Richter	.40
279	Marc Savard	.10
280	Mathieu Schneider	.10
281	Kevin Stevens	.10
282	Niklas Sundstrom	.10
283	Daniel Alfredsson	.10
284	Magnus Arvedson	.10
285	Radek Bonk	.10
286	Andreas Dackell	.10
287	Bruce Gardiner	.10
288	Marian Hossa	.25
289	Andreas Johansson	.10
290	Igor Kravchuk	.10
291	Shawn McEachern	.10
292	Vaclav Prospal	.10
293	Wade Redden	.10
294	Damian Rhodes	.25
295	Sami Salo	.10
296	Ron Tugnutt	.25
297	Alexei Yashin	.25
298	Jason York	.10
299	Rod Brind'Amour	.25
300	Adam Burt	.10
301	Eric Desjardins	.10
302	Ron Hextall	.25
303	Jody Hull	.10
304	Keith Jones	.10
305	Daymond Langkow	.10
306	John LeClair	.75
307	Eric Lindros	2.00
308	Sandy McCarthy	.10
309	Dan McGillis	.10
310	Mark Recchi	.10
311	Mikael Renberg	.10
312	Chris Therien	.10
313	John Vanbiesbrouck	.50
314	Valeri Zelepukin	.10
315	Greg Adams	.10
316	Keith Carney	.10
317	Bob Corkum	.10
318	Jim Cummins	.10
319	Shane Doan	.10
320	Dallas Drake	.10
321	Nikolai Khabibulin	.40
322	Jyrki Lumme	.10
323	Tappo Numminen	.10
324	Robert Reichel	.10
325	Jeremy Roenick	.40
326	Mikhail Shtalenkov	.25
327	Mike Stapleton	.10
328	Keith Tkachuk	.50
329	Rick Tocchet	.10
330	Oleg Tverdovsky	.10
331	Juha Ylonen	.10
332	Robert Esche, Scott Langkow	.10
333	Matthew Barnaby	.10
334	Tom Barrasso	.25
335	Rob Brown	.10
336	Kevin Hatcher	.10
337	Jan Hrdina	.10
338	Jaromir Jagr	2.00
339	Darius Kasparaitis	.10
340	Dan Kesa	.10
341	Alexei Kovalev	.10
342	Robert Lang	.10
343	Kip Miller	.10
344	Alexei Morozov	.10
345	Peter Skudra	.10
346	Jiri Slegr	.10
347	Martin Straka	.10
348	German Titov	.10
349	Brad Werenka	.10
350	J.S. Aubin, Brian Bonin	.10
351	Blair Atcheynum	.10
352	Lubos Bartecko	.10
353	Craig Conroy	.10
354	Geoff Courtnall	.10
355	Pavol Demitra	.25
356	Grant Fuhr	.40
357	Michal Handzus	.10
358	Al MacInnis	.30
359	Jamal Mayers	.10
360	Jamie McLennan	.25
361	Scott Pellerin	.10
362	Chris Pronger	.25
363	Pascal Rheaume	.10
364	Pierre Turgeon	.25
365	Tony Twist	.10
366	Scott Young	.10
367	Jochen Hecht, Brent Johnson	.10
368	Tyson Nash, Marty Reasoner	.10
369	Vincent Damphousse	.10
370	Jeff Friesen	.10
371	Tony Granato	.10
372	Bill Houlder	.10
373	Alexander Korolyuk	.10
374	Bryan Marchment	.10
375	Patrick Marleau	.40
376	Stephane Matteau	.10
377	Joe Murphy	.10
378	Owen Nolan	.10
379	Mike Rathje	.10
380	Mike Ricci	.10
381	Steve Shields	.25
382	Ronnie Stern	.10
383	Marco Sturm	.10
384	Mike Vernon	.25
385	Scott Hannan, Shawn Heins	.10
386	Cory Cross	.10
387	Alexandre Daigle	.10
388	Colin Forbes	.10
389	Chris Gratton	.10
390	Kevin Hodson	.25
391	Pavel Kubina	.10
392	Vincent Lecavalier	.50
393	Michael Nylander	.10
394	Stephane Richer	.10
395	Corey Schwab	.10
396	Mike Sillinger	.10
397	Petr Svoboda	.10
398	Darcy Tucker	.10
399	Rob Zamuner	.10
400	Paul Mara, Mario Larocque	.10
401	Bryan Berard	.10
402	Sergei Berezin	.10

403 Lonny Bohonos .10
404 Sylvain Cote .10
405 Tie Domi .10
406 Mike Johnson .10
407 Curtis Joseph .50
408 Tomas Kaberle .10
409 Alexander Karpovtsev .10
410 Derek King .10
411 Igor Korolev .10
412 Adam Mair .10
413 Alyn McCauley .10
414 Yanic Perreault .10
415 Steve Sullivan .10
416 Mats Sundin .50
417 Steve Thomas .10
418 Garry Valk .10
419 Adrian Aucoin .10
420 Todd Bertuzzi .10
421 Donald Brashear .10
422 Dave Gagner .10
423 Josh Holden .10
424 Ed Jovanovski .10
425 Bryan McCabe .10
426 Mark Messier .50
427 Alexander Mogilny .25
428 Bill Muckalt .10
429 Markus Naslund .10
430 Mattias Ohlund .10
431 Dave Scatchard .10
432 Peter Schaefer .10
433 Garth Snow .25
434 Kevin Weekes .10
435 Brian Bellows .10
436 James Black .10
437 Peter Bondra .40
438 Jan Bullis .10
439 Sergei Gonchar .10
440 Benoit Gratton .10
441 Calle Johansson .10
442 Ken Klee .10
443 Olaf Kolzig .40
444 Steve Konowalchuk .10
445 Andrei Nikolishin .25
446 Adam Oates .30
447 Jaroslav Svejkovsky .10
448 Rick Tabaracci .10
449 Richard Zednik .10
450 Nolan Baumgartner, Alexei Tezikov .10

1999-00 Pacific Cramer's Choice Awards

Cramer's Choice are die-cut in a trophy shape and feature silver holographic foil treatment and gold foil stamping. 299 serial numbered sets were produced.

		MT
Complete Set (10):		800.00
Common Player:		40.00
Production 299 sets		
1	Paul Kariya	125.00
2	Dominik Hasek	75.00
3	Peter Forsberg	100.00
4	Patrick Roy	150.00
5	Joe Sakic	75.00
6	Mike Modano	50.00
7	Steve Yzerman	100.00
8	Eric Lindros	100.00
9	Jaromir Jagr	125.00
10	Curtis Joseph	40.00

1999-00 Pacific Gold Crown Die-Cuts

The top portion of these inserts are die-cut into a crown shape and printed on 24-point stock with gold foil etching and stamping. They were inserted 1:25 packs.

		MT
Complete Set (36):		200.00
Common Player:		3.00
Inserted 1:25		
1	Paul Kariya	20.00
2	Teemu Selanne	8.00
3	Ray Bourque	5.00
4	Byron Dafoe	4.00
5	Dominik Hasek	10.00
6	Michael Peca	3.00
7	Chris Drury	3.00
8	Theoren Fleury	3.00
9	Peter Forsberg	15.00
10	Milan Hejduk	3.00
11	Patrick Roy	25.00
12	Joe Sakic	10.00
13	Ed Belfour	5.00
14	Brett Hull	6.00
15	Mike Modano	8.00
16	Chris Chelios	5.00
17	Brendan Shanahan	8.00
18	Steve Yzerman	15.00
19	Pavel Bure	8.00
20	David Legwand	4.00
21	Martin Brodeur	10.00
22	Felix Potvin	3.00
23	Mike Richter	4.00
24	Alexei Yashin	3.00
25	John LeClair	8.00
26	Eric Lindros	15.00
27	Mark Recchi	3.00
28	John Vanbiesbrouck	6.00
29	Jeremy Roenick	5.00
30	Keith Tkachuk	5.00
31	Jaromir Jagr	20.00
32	Vincent Lecavalier	6.00
33	Sergei Berezin	3.00
34	Curtis Joseph	5.00
35	Mats Sundin	6.00
36	Mark Messier	6.00

1999-00 Pacific Home and Away

The first 10 cards in this 20-card set are inserted exclusively in retail packs and cards 11-20 are inserted exclusively in hobby packs. Card fronts are full foiled and are inserted 2:25 packs.

		MT
Complete Set (20):		100.00
Common Player:		3.00
Inserted 2:25		
1-10 Retail, 11-20 Hobby		
1	Paul Kariya	10.00
2	Teemu Selanne	5.00
3	Dominik Hasek	6.00
4	Peter Forsberg	8.00
5	Patrick Roy	15.00
6	Mike Modano	5.00
7	Steve Yzerman	8.00
8	John LeClair	5.00
9	Eric Lindros	8.00
10	Jaromir Jagr	10.00
11	Paul Kariya	8.00
12	Teemu Selanne	4.00
13	Dominik Hasek	5.00
14	Peter Forsberg	6.00
15	Patrick Roy	10.00
16	Mike Modano	4.00
17	Steve Yzerman	6.00
18	John LeClair	4.00
19	Eric Lindros	6.00
20	Jaromir Jagr	8.00

1999-00 Pacific In the Cage Net-Fusions

This insert set spotlights the top 20 goalies in the game and have netting around a rough cutout photo of the goalie. These were seeded 1:97 packs.

		MT
Complete Set (20):		350.00
Common Player:		10.00
Inserted 1:97		
1	Guy Hebert	10.00
2	Byron Dafoe	15.00
3	Dominik Hasek	40.00
4	Arturs Irbe	10.00
5	Patrick Roy	80.00
6	Ed Belfour	25.00
7	Chris Osgood	20.00
8	Tommy Salo	10.00
9	Jeff Hackett	10.00
10	Martin Brodeur	40.00
11	Felix Potvin	15.00
12	Mike Richter	25.00
13	Ron Tugnutt	10.00
14	John Vanbiesbrouck	25.00
15	Nikolai Khabibulin	15.00
16	Tom Barrasso	10.00
17	Grant Fuhr	15.00
18	Mike Vernon	15.00
19	Curtis Joseph	20.00
20	Olaf Kolzig	10.00

1999-00 Pacific Past & Present

This 20-card set profiles 20 of the NHL's top stars pictured in both their old and current uniforms. Card fronts have a current photo with a prismatic design around the player photo. Card backs have a photo of the player in his old uniform on a felt-weave stock. They were inserted exclusively in hobby packs and seeded 1:49 packs.

		MT
Complete Set (20):		250.00
Common Player:		6.00
Inserted 1:49		
1	Paul Kariya	30.00
2	Teemu Selanne	12.00
3	Ray Bourque	8.00
4	Dominik Hasek	15.00
5	Theo Fleury	6.00
6	Peter Forsberg	25.00
7	Patrick Roy	40.00
8	Joe Sakic	15.00
9	Ed Belfour	8.00
10	Brett Hull	10.00
11	Mike Modano	12.00
12	Brendan Shanahan	12.00
13	Steve Yzerman	25.00
14	Pavel Bure	12.00
15	Martin Brodeur	15.00
16	John LeClair	12.00
17	Eric Lindros	25.00
18	John Vanbiesbrouck	10.00
19	Jaromir Jagr	30.00
20	Curtis Joseph	8.00

1999-00 Pacific Team Leaders

Each card in this 28-card set represents an NHL team. Card fronts feature holographic foil treatment around one of the featured team's top performers. Card backs have a complete team checklist from the base set. These were seeded 2:25 packs.

		MT
Complete Set (28):		60.00
Common Player:		1.00
Inserted 2:25		
1	Paul Kariya	8.00
2	Atlanta Thrashers	1.00
3	Ray Bourque	2.00
4	Dominik Hasek	4.00
5	Jarome Iginla	1.00
6	Arturs Irbe	1.00
7	Doug Gilmour	1.00
8	Patrick Roy	10.00
9	Mike Modano	3.00
10	Steve Yzerman	6.00
11	Bill Guerin	1.00
12	Pavel Bure	3.00
13	Luc Robitaille	1.00
14	Saku Koivu	1.50
15	Mike Dunham	1.50
16	Martin Brodeur	4.00
17	Zigmund Palffy	1.50
18	Mike Richter	2.00
19	Alexei Yashin	1.00
20	Eric Lindros	6.00
21	Keith Tkachuk	2.00
22	Jaromir Jagr	8.00
23	Grant Fuhr	2.00
24	Mike Vernon	1.00
25	Vincent Lecavalier	2.00
26	Curtis Joseph	1.50
27	Mark Messier	2.50
28	Peter Bondra	1.50

1999-00 Pacific Aurora

This set consists of 150 cards, in addition 50 star players are duplicated with a different background and posed photo. Each card front features a close-up photo of each player with a smaller action shot in the background and gold foil stamping. Card backs have a small photo, 1998-99 statistics and career totals. Premiere Date is the only parallel and is limited to 60 serially numbered sets.

		MT
Complete Set (150):		30.00
Common Player:		.20
Striped cards same value		
Premiere Date:		40x to 70x
Production 60 sets		
1	Guy Hebert	.40
2	Paul Kariya	2.00
3	Marty McInnis	.20
4	Steve Rucchin	.20
5	Teemu Selanne	.75
6	Andrew Brunette	.20
7	Kelly Buchberger	.20
8	Damian Rhodes	.40
9	Jason Allison	.40
10	Ray Bourque	.50
11	Anson Carter	.20
12	Byron Dafoe	.50
13	Sergei Samsonov	.60
14	Joe Thornton	.40
15	Curtis Brown	.20
16	Dominik Hasek	1.00
17	Joe Juneau	.20
18	Michael Peca	.20
19	Miroslav Satan	.20
20	Valeri Bure	.20
21	Jean-Sebastien Giguere	.20
22	Phil Housley	.20
23	Jarome Iginla	.20
24	Cory Stillman	.20
25	Ron Francis	.40
26	Arturs Irbe	.40
27	Sami Kapanen	.20
28	Keith Primeau	.40
29	Ray Sheppard	.20
30	Tony Amonte	.40
31	Jean-Pierre Dumont	.20
32	Doug Gilmour	.40
33	Jocelyn Thibault	.40
34	Alexei Zhamnov	.20
35	Adam Deadmarsh	.20
36	Chris Drury	.40
37	Theoren Fleury	.40
38	Peter Forsberg	1.50
39	Milan Hejduk	.20
40	Claude Lemieux	.20
41	Patrick Roy	2.50
42	Joe Sakic	1.00
43	Ed Belfour	.50
44	Brett Hull	.50
45	Jamie Langenbrunner	.20
46	Jere Lehtinen	.20
47	Mike Modano	.75
48	Joe Nieuwendyk	.40
49	Chris Chelios	.50
50	Sergei Fedorov	.75
51	Nicklas Lidstrom	.40
52	Darren McCarty	.20
53	Chris Osgood	.50
54	Brendan Shanahan	.75
55	Steve Yzerman	1.50
56	Bill Guerin	.20
57	Mike Grier	.20
58	Tommy Salo	.40
59	Ryan Smyth	.20
60	Doug Weight	.20
61	Pavel Bure	.75
62	Sean Burke	.40
63	Viktor Kozlov	.20
64	Rob Niedermayer	.20
65	Mark Parrish	.20
66	Ray Whitney	.20
67	Donald Audette	.20
68	Rob Blake	.20
69	Zigmund Palffy	.50
70	Luc Robitaille	.40
71	Jamie Storr	.40
72	Jozef Stumpel	.20
73	Shayne Corson	.20
74	Jeff Hackett	.40
75	Saku Koivu	.40
76	Martin Rucinsky	.20
77	Brian Savage	.20
78	Mike Dunham	.40
79	Sergei Krivokrasov	.20
80	David Legwand	.40
81	Cliff Ronning	.20
82	Scott Walker	.20
83	Jason Arnott	.20
84	Martin Brodeur	1.00
85	Patrik Elias	.20
86	Bobby Holik	.20
87	Brendan Morrison	.20
88	Petr Sykora	.20
89	Mariusz Czerkawski	.20
90	Kenny Jonsson	.20
91	Felix Potvin	.40
92	Mike Watt	.20
93	Adam Graves	.20
94	Brian Leetch	.40
95	John MacLean	.20
96	Petr Nedved	.20
97	Mike Richter	.50
98	Magnus Arvedson	.20
99	Marian Hossa	.20
100	Shawn McEachern	.20
101	Ron Tugnutt	.40
102	Alexei Yashin	.40
103	Rod Brind'Amour	.40
104	Eric Desjardins	.20
105	John LeClair	.75
106	Eric Lindros	1.50
107	Mark Recchi	.20
108	John Vanbiesbrouck	.50
109	Nikolai Khabibulin	.50
110	Teppo Numminen	.20
111	Jeremy Roenick	.50
112	Rick Tocchet	.20
113	Keith Tkachuk	.60
114	Matthew Barnaby	.20
115	Tom Barrasso	.40
116	Jaromir Jagr	2.00
117	Alexei Kovalev	.20

118	Martin Straka	.20
119	Vincent Damphousse	.20
120	Jeff Friesen	.20
121	Patrick Marleau	.20
122	Steve Shields	.40
123	Mike Vernon	.40
124	Pavol Demitra	.20
125	Grant Fuhr	.50
126	Al MacInnis	.50
127	Chris Pronger	.40
128	Pierre Turgeon	.40
129	Chris Gratton	.20
130	Kevin Hodson	.40
131	Vincent Lecavalier	.50
132	Paul Mara	.20
133	Darcy Tucker	.20
134	Sergei Berezin	.20
135	Mike Johnson	.20
136	Curtis Joseph	.50
137	Yanic Perreault	.20
138	Mats Sundin	.50
139	Steve Thomas	.20
140	Mark Messier	.60
141	Bill Muckalt	.40
142	Alexander Mogilny	.40
143	Markus Naslund	.20
144	Mattias Ohlund	.20
145	Garth Snow	.40
146	Peter Bondra	.40
147	Sergei Gonchar	.20
148	Benoit Gratton	.20
149	Olaf Kolzig	.50
150	Adam Oates	.40

1999-00 Pacific Aurora Canvas Creations

This 10-card insert set was printed on real canvas material giving it a flimsy stock and textured feel. Card fronts have gold foil stamping as well. These were seeded 1:193 packs.

		MT
Complete Set (10):		500.00
Common Player:		25.00
Inserted 1:193		
1	Paul Kariya	75.00
2	Teemu Selanne	30.00
3	Dominik Hasek	40.00
4	Peter Forsberg	60.00
5	Patrick Roy	100.00
6	Steve Yzerman	60.00
7	Pavel Bure	30.00
8	John LeClair	30.00
9	Eric Lindros	60.00
10	Jaromir Jagr	75.00

1999-00 Pacific Aurora Championship Fever

This 20-card set is fully foiled with gold etching and stamping. Card backs have a small photo and brief commentary. These were seeded 4:25 packs. Three parallel versions were also randomly seeded: Copper, Ice Blue and Silver. Coppers have copper foil stamping and etching and are serially numbered to 20. Ice Blues have blue foil stamping and etching and are serially numbered to 100. Silvers have silver foil stamping and etching and are serially numbered to 250. Martin Brodeur also signed 200 Championship Fever cards. Each autograph is stamped with "Authentic Autograph".

		MT
Complete Set (20):		50.00
Common Player:		.75
Inserted 4:25		
Copper:		50x to 80x
Production 20 sets		
Ice Blue:		15x to 25x
Production 100 sets		
Silver:		5x to 10x
Production 250 sets		
M. Broduer Auto (200):		75.00
1	Paul Kariya	6.00
2	Teemu Selanne	3.00
3	Ray Bourque	1.50
4	Dominik Hasek	4.00
5	Michael Peca	.75
6	Theoren Fleury	1.00
7	Peter Forsberg	5.00
8	Patrick Roy	8.00
9	Joe Sakic	4.00
10	Ed Belfour	1.50
11	Mike Modano	3.00
12	Brendan Shanahan	3.00
13	Steve Yzerman	5.00
14	Pavel Bure	3.00
15	Martin Brodeur	4.00
16	John LeClair	3.00
17	Eric Lindros	5.00
18	Jaromir Jagr	6.00
19	Curtis Joseph	1.50
20	Mats Sundin	1.50

1999-00 Pacific Aurora Complete Players

Two versions of each of the ten players are available with one retail exclusive and the other hobby exclusive. Card fronts have holographic silver foil treatment and are also numbered to 299.

		MT
Complete Set (10):		300.00
Common Player:		8.00
Production 299 sets		
1	Paul Kariya	50.00
2	Teemu Selanne	20.00
3	Dominik Hasek	25.00
4	Peter Forsberg	40.00
5	Patrick Roy	60.00
6	Mike Modano	20.00
7	Steve Yzerman	40.00
8	John LeClair	20.00
9	Eric Lindros	40.00
10	Jaromir Jagr	50.00

1999-00 Pacific Aurora Glove Unlimited

Glove Unlimited inserts are hobby exclusive and are perimeter diecut in the shape of a goalie catching glove. Card fronts also have gold foil etching and stamping. These goalie inserts are found on the average of 2:25 packs.

		MT
Complete Set (20):		100.00
Common Player:		4.00
Inserted 2:25		
1	Guy Hebert	4.00
2	Byron Dafoe	6.00
3	Dominik Hasek	12.00
4	Arturs Irbe	4.00
5	Jocelyn Thibault	4.00
6	Patrick Roy	25.00
7	Ed Belfour	8.00
8	Chris Osgood	8.00
9	Tommy Salo	4.00
10	Jeff Hackett	4.00
11	Martin Brodeur	12.00
12	Felix Potvin	6.00
13	Mike Richter	8.00
14	Ron Tugnutt	4.00
15	John Vanbiesbrouck	8.00
16	Nikolai Khabibulin	4.00
17	Grant Fuhr	6.00
18	Steve Shields	4.00
19	Curtis Joseph	8.00
20	Olaf Kolzig	4.00

1999-00 Pacific Aurora Styrotechs

Styrotechs feature a horizontal format, printed on a fully foiled styrene stock. Card backs have a small photo along with a career note. These were seeded 1:25 packs.

		MT
Complete Set (20):		150.00
Common Player:		3.00
Inserted 1:25		
1	Paul Kariya	20.00
2	Teemu Selanne	8.00
3	Dominik Hasek	12.00
4	Theoren Fleury	3.00
5	Peter Forsberg	15.00
6	Patrick Roy	25.00
7	Ed Belfour	5.00
8	Mike Modano	8.00
9	Brendan Shanahan	8.00
10	Steve Yzerman	15.00
11	Pavel Bure	8.00
12	Martin Brodeur	10.00
13	Alexei Yashin	3.00
14	John LeClair	8.00
15	Eric Lindros	15.00
16	Keith Tkachuk	5.00
17	Jaromir Jagr	20.00
18	Curtis Joseph	5.00
19	Mats Sundin	5.00
20	Mark Messier	6.00

1999-00 Upper Deck MVP

The 220-card set features bronze foil stamping, with a white border. Card backs have a small photo along with year-by-year statistics. There are three different parallel sets: Silver, Gold and Super. Silvers have a silver foil facsimile player signature and are seeded 1:2 packs. Golds have a gold foil facsimile player signature and are inserted in hobby packs, limited to 100 numbered sets. Supers are hobby only and have a holographic foil facsimile player signature. They are limited to 25 numbered sets.

		MT
Complete Set (220):		30.00
Common Player:		.15
Silver:		2x to 3x
Inserted 1:2		
Golds:		50x to 100x
Production 100 sets		
1	Wayne Gretzky	2.50
2	Damian Rhodes	.25
3	Jody Hull	.15
4	Paul Kariya	1.50
5	Teemu Selanne	.60
6	Guy Hebert	.30
7	Matt Cullen	.15
8	Steve Rucchin	.15
9	Oleg Tverdovsky	.15
10	Johan Davidsson	.15
11	Ray Bourque	.40
12	Sergei Samsonov	.50
13	Joe Thornton	.25
14	Anson Carter	.15
15	Jason Allison	.25
16	Kyle McLaren	.15
17	Byron Dafoe	.30
18	Shawn Bates	.15
19	Jonathan Girard	.15
20	Hal Gill	.15
21	Dominik Hasek	.75
22	Joe Juneau	.15
23	Michael Peca	.15
24	Cory Sarich	.15
25	Martin Biron	.25
26	Miroslav Satan	.25
27	Dixon Ward	.15
28	Michal Grosek	.15
29	Valeri Bure	.15
30	Phil Housley	.15
31	Derek Morris	.15
32	Jarome Iginla	.15
33	Wade Belak	.15
34	Rico Fata	.15
35	Jean-Sebastien Giguere	.15
36	Rene Corbet	.15
37	Arturs Irbe	.25
38	Keith Primeau	.25
39	Sami Kapanen	.15
40	Ron Francis	.25
41	Shane Willis	.15
42	Gary Roberts	.15
43	Bates Battaglia	.15
44	Jean-Pierre Dumont	.15
45	Ty Jones	.15
46	Tony Amonte	.25
47	Jocelyn Thibault	.25
48	Doug Gilmour	.25
49	Remi Royer	.15
50	Alexei Zhamnov	.15
51	Joe Sakic	.75
52	Peter Forsberg	1.25
53	Theoren Fleury	.25
54	Chris Drury	.25
55	Patrick Roy	2.00
56	Sandis Ozolinsh	.15
57	Adam Deadmarsh	.15
58	Milan Hejduk	.25
59	Mike Modano	.60
60	Brett Hull	.50
61	Darryl Sydor	.15
62	Ed Belfour	.40
63	Jere Lehtinen	.15
64	Jamie Langenbrunner	.15
65	Derian Hatcher	.15
66	Jon Sim	.15
67	Joe Nieuwendyk	.25
68	Sergei Fedorov	.50
69	Steve Yzerman	1.00
70	Brendan Shanahan	.60
71	Chris Osgood	.40
72	Nicklas Lidstrom	.25
73	Chris Chelios	.40
74	Igor Larionov	.15
75	Tomas Holmstrom	.15
76	Vyacheslav Kozlov	.15
77	Josef Beranek	.15
78	Bill Guerin	.15
79	Doug Weight	.25
80	Tommy Salo	.25
81	Mike Grier	.15
82	Tom Poti	.15
83	Frederik Lindquist	.15
84	Mark Parrish	.25
85	Pavel Bure	.60
86	Viktor Kozlov	.15
87	Ray Whitney	.15
88	Rob Niedermayer	.15
89	Oleg Kvasha	.25
90	Scott Mellanby	.15
91	Chris Allen	.15
92	Rob Blake	.15
93	Pavel Rosa	.15
94	Jamie Storr	.25
95	Donald Audette	.15
96	Luc Robitaille	.25
97	Jozef Stumpel	.15
98	Vladimir Tsyplakov	.15
99	Manny Legace	.15
100	Saku Koivu	.25
101	Martin Rucinsky	.15
102	Vladimir Malakhov	.15
103	Eric Weinrich	.15
104	Jeff Hackett	.25
105	Arron Asham	.15
106	Trevor Linden	.15
107	Brian Savage	.15
108	Cliff Ronning	.15
109	Sergei Krivokrasov	.15
110	David Legwand	.50
111	Kimmo Timonen	.15
112	Mark Mowers	.15
113	Mike Dunham	.40
114	Scott Stevens	.15
115	Martin Brodeur	.75
116	Patrik Elias	.15
117	Brendan Morrison	.15
118	Scott Niedermayer	.15
119	Petr Sykora	.15
120	Jason Arnott	.15
121	Vadim Sharifijanov	.15
122	John Madden	.15
123	Mariusz Czerkawski	.15
124	Felix Potvin	.25
125	Mike Watt	.15
126	Eric Brewer	.15
127	Dimitri Nabakov	.15
128	Brad Isbister	.15
129	Kenny Jonsson	.15
130	Zdeno Chara	.15
131	Wayne Gretzky	2.50
132	Brian Leetch	.30
133	Mike Richter	.40
134	Petr Nedved	.15
135	Adam Graves	.15
136	Manny Malhotra	.25
137	John MacLean	.15
138	Alexei Yashin	.25
139	Magnus Arvedsson	.15
140	Daniel Alfredsson	.25
141	Wade Redden	.15
142	Ron Tugnutt	.25
143	Sami Salo	.15
144	Marian Hossa	.25
145	Shawn McEachern	.15
146	Eric Lindros	1.25
147	Jean-Marc Pelletier	.15
148	John LeClair	.60
149	Rod Brind'Amour	.25
150	Mark Recchi	.15
151	Keith Jones	.15
152	Eric Desjardins	.15
153	Ryan Bast	.15
154	Brian Wesenberg	.15
155	John Vanbiesbrouck	.40
156	Jeremy Roenick	.40
157	Robert Reichel	.15
158	Keith Tkachuk	.40
159	Rick Tocchet	.15
160	Robert Esche	.15
161	Nikolai Khabibulin	.40
162	Daniel Briere	.15
163	Greg Adams	.15
164	Trevor Letowski	.15
165	Jaromir Jagr	1.50
166	Martin Straka	.15
167	German Titov	.15
168	Tom Barrasso	.25
169	Jan Hrdina	.15
170	Alexei Kovalev	.15
171	Mathew Barnaby	.15
172	Jean-Sebastien Aubin	.15
173	Vincent Damphousse	.15
174	Owen Nolan	.15
175	Jeff Friesen	.15
176	Patrick Marleau	.40
177	Marco Sturm	.15
178	Mike Ricci	.15
179	Gary Suter	.15
180	Scott Hannan	.15
181	Andy Sutton	.15
182	Pavol Demitra	.25
183	Al MacInnis	.40
184	Pierre Turgeon	.25
185	Grant Fuhr	.40
186	Chris Pronger	.40
187	Lubos Bartecko	.15
188	Jochen Hecht	.15

189	Michal Handzus	.15
190	Vincent Lecavalier	.50
191	Paul Mara	.15
192	Darcy Tucker	.15
193	Chris Gratton	.15
194	Pavel Kubina	.15
195	Kevin Hodson	.25
196	Mats Sundin	.40
197	Danil Markov	.15
198	Curtis Joseph	.40
199	Sergei Berezin	.15
200	Steve Thomas	.15
201	Bryan Berard	.15
202	Mike Johnson	.15
203	Tomas Kaberle	.15
204	Mark Messier	.50
205	Bill Muckalt	.15
206	Markus Naslund	.15
207	Mattias Ohlund	.15
208	Kevin Weekes	.15
209	Ed Jovanovski	.15
210	Alexander Mogilny	.25
211	Josh Holden	.15
212	Richard Zednik	.15
213	Jaroslav Svejkovsky	.15
214	Adam Oates	.40
215	Peter Bondra	.25
216	Sergei Gonchar	.15
217	Olaf Kolzig	.25
218	Jan Bulis	.15
219	Wayne Gretzky	1.00
220	Wayne Gretzky	1.00

1999-00 Upper Deck MVP Draft Report

This 10-card set highlights top rookies drafted and how the individual team fared in the draft. They are fully foiled with gold foil stamping. Card backs have a commentary on draft picks made by the respective team and are numbered with a "DR" prefix. These were seeded 1:6 packs.

		MT
Complete Set (10):		8.00
Common Player:		.75
Inserted 1:6		
1	Damian Rhodes	.75
2	Bill Muckalt	.75
3	Wayne Gretzky	4.00
4	Eric Brewer	.75
5	David Legwand	1.00
6	Peter Bondra	1.00
7	Rico Fata	.75
8	Mark Parrish	.75
9	Tom Poti	.75
10	Jeff Friesen	.75

1999-00 Upper Deck MVP Game-Used Souvenirs

These game-used inserts are found exclusively in hobby packs at a rate of 1:130. The first 14 cards in the set have a piece of game-used puck embedded into the card front, the last 14 cards have a piece of game-used stick embedded into the card front. Card backs are numbered with a "GU" prefix.

		MT
Complete Set (28):		1500.
Common Player:		15.00
Inserted 1:130		
1	Paul Kariya	75.00
2	Teemu Selanne	40.00
3	Brett Hull	30.00
4	Pavel Bure	40.00
5	Marian Hossa	15.00
6	Wayne Gretzky	150.00
7	Brendan Shanahan	40.00
8	Sergei Samsonov	25.00
9	Eric Lindros	60.00
10	Keith Tkachuk	30.00
11	Steve Yzerman	60.00
12	Jaromir Jagr	60.00
13	Alexei Yashin	15.00
14	Curtis Joseph	25.00
15	Paul Kariya	125.00
16	Teemu Selanne	60.00
17	Dominik Hasek	75.00
18	Pavel Bure	60.00
19	Peter Forsberg	100.00
20	Wayne Gretzky	200.00
21	Brendan Shanahan	60.00
22	Joe Sakic	75.00
23	Eric Lindros	100.00
24	Keith Tkachuk	50.00
25	Jeremy Roenick	40.00
26	Alexei Yashin	15.00
27	Curtis Joseph	40.00
28	Steve Yzerman	100.00

1999-00 Upper Deck MVP Game-Used Souvenirs Autographed

Wayne Gretzky and Pavel Bure each signed 25 of their Game- Used Souvenir inserts, which have a piece of game-used stick embedded into the card front. Each card is sequentially numbered to 25.

		MT
Complete Set (2):		1,300.00
1	Wayne Gretzky	1,000
2	Pavel Bure	300

1999-00 Upper Deck MVP Hands of Gold

This 10-card set focuses on players who control the puck and score often. Card fronts are full foiled with gold foil stamping. Card backs are numbered with a "H" prefix. These are seeded 1:9 packs.

		MT
Complete Set (11):		40.00
Common Player:		1.00
Inserted 1:9		
1	Wayne Gretzky	10.00
2	Brett Hull	2.00
3	Pavel Bure	2.50
4	Teemu Selanne	2.50
5	Sergei Samsonov	2.00
6	Peter Forsberg	5.00
7	Eric Lindros	5.00
8	Paul Kariya	6.00
9	Jaromir Jagr	8.00
10	Steve Yzerman	5.00
11	Mike Modano	2.50

1999-00 Upper Deck MVP Last Line

This 10-card set spotlights the top goalies in the NHL highlighted by gold foil stamping. Card backs have a small photo of the goalie, career notes and numbered with a "LL" prefix. These were seeded 1:9 packs.

		MT
Complete Set (10):		20.00
Common Player:		1.00
Inserted 1:9		
1	Dominik Hasek	4.00
2	Martin Brodeur	4.00
3	Patrick Roy	8.00
4	Byron Dafoe	2.00
5	Ed Belfour	2.00
6	Curtis Joseph	2.00
7	John Vanbiesbrouck	2.00
8	Tom Barrasso	1.00
9	Chris Osgood	2.00
10	Nikolai Khabibulin	1.50

1999-00 Upper Deck MVP Legendary One

This 10-card set salutes Wayne Gretzky and relives some of his magical moments from his first Stanley Cup championship to his 92-goal season. These were inserted 1:27 packs.

		MT
Complete Set (10):		70.00
Common Player:		8.00
Inserted 1:27		
1	Wayne Gretzky	8.00
2	Wayne Gretzky	8.00
3	Wayne Gretzky	8.00
4	Wayne Gretzky	8.00
5	Wayne Gretzky	8.00
6	Wayne Gretzky	8.00
7	Wayne Gretzky	8.00
8	Wayne Gretzky	8.00
9	Wayne Gretzky	8.00
10	Wayne Gretzky	8.00

1999-00 Upper Deck MVP Talent

This 10-card set focuses on the NHL's top players and perennial Hart Trophy candidates. Card fronts are full foiled with gold foil stamping. Card backs are numbered with a "MVP" prefix. These were seeded 1:13 packs.

		MT
Complete Set (10):		50.00
Common Player:		1.50
Inserted 1:13		
1	Wayne Gretzky	12.00
2	Paul Kariya	8.00
3	Dominik Hasek	4.00
4	Eric Lindros	6.00
5	Ray Bourque	2.00
6	Steve Yzerman	6.00
7	Patrick Roy	10.00
8	Jaromir Jagr	8.00
9	Martin Brodeur	4.00
10	Mike Modano	3.00

1999-00 Upper Deck MVP Pro Sign

This 30-card autographed set is found exclusively in retail packs at a rate of 1:144 packs.

		MT
Complete Set (30):		1100.00
Common Player:		15.00
Inserted 1:144 R		
DA	Donald Audette	15.00
RB	Ray Bourque	50.00
RBr	Rod Brind'Amour	30.00
PB	Pavel Bure	50.00
WC	Wendel Clark	25.00
MC	Matt Cullen	15.00
PD	Pavol Demitra	25.00
TD	Tie Domi	15.00
CD	Chris Drury	20.00
TF	Theoren Fleury	30.00
JF	Jeff Friesen	20.00
SG	Sergei Gonchar	20.00
WG	Wayne Gretzky	300.00
JH	Jeff Hackett	30.00
JHr	Jan Hrdina	15.00
BH	Brett Hull	50.00
JJ	Jaromir Jagr	120.00
TK	Tomas Kaberle	15.00
IL	Igor Larionov	25.00
TL	Trevor Linden	20.00
SK	Sami Kapanen	25.00
DM	Derek Morris	15.00
BM	Bill Muckalt	20.00
MP	Michael Peca	20.00
TP	Tom Poti	15.00
LR	Luc Robitaille	30.00
JR	Jeremy Roenick	35.00
JT	Joe Thornton	25.00
RT	Ron Tugnutt	20.00
SY	Steve Yzerman	150.00

1999-00 Upper Deck MVP 21st Century NHL

This 10-card set highlights young players who will become the stars of the 21st Century. Card fronts feature silver holofoil with gold foil stamping and etching. Card backs are numbered with a "21st" prefix, the insertion rate is 1:13 packs.

		MT
Complete Set (10):		25.00
Common Player:		1.00
Inserted 1:13		
1	David Legwand	1.00
2	Sergei Samsonov	2.00
3	Paul Kariya	8.00
4	Peter Forsberg	6.00
5	Vincent Lecavalier	2.00
6	Jaromir Jagr	8.00
7	Paul Mara	1.00
8	Marian Hossa	1.00
9	Pavel Bure	3.00
10	Chris Drury	1.00

1999-00 Upper Deck MVP 90s Snapshots

This 10-card set focuses on players who had the biggest impact on the game during the last decade. Card fronts are done on a horizontal format, utilizing holographic rainbow technology and enhanced by gold foil stamping. Four images of the featured player appear on the card front. Card backs have a small photo and are numbered with a "S" prefix. The insertion rate is 1:27 packs.

		MT
Complete Set (10):		75.00
Common Player:		3.00
Inserted 1:27		
1	Wayne Gretzky	20.00
2	Jaromir Jagr	12.00
3	Patrick Roy	15.00
4	Eric Lindros	10.00
5	Brendan Shanahan	5.00
6	Peter Forsberg	10.00
7	Steve Yzerman	10.00
8	Teemu Selanne	5.00
9	Dominik Hasek	6.00
10	Pavel Bure	5.00

Market Report

Young Drivers And Memorabilia Cards Drive The 1999 Market

When the green flag fell on the 1999 NASCAR Winston Cup season at the Daytona 500, nobody knew what the season would produce. Gone was the hoopla associated with NASCAR's 50th Anniversary the year before.

NASCAR's 50th Anniversary in 1998 was a shot in the arm for racing collectibles. Before that, there were nine companies producing racing trading cards, marking how popular NASCAR had become. It also filled the market with too many products, forcing collectors to pick and choose what products to collect.

That changed in 1998, when only two companies were producing racing cards. The racing card market was much the same in 1999 as it was in 1998 — with only two companies producing sets.

Between Racing Champions and Upper Deck, the two companies releasing racing cards in 1999, 13 racing card releases were scheduled. Racing Champions did release the six products they had scheduled for the year.

But by the time October rolled around, Upper Deck decided to cancel the three products they still had on the schedule — Checkered Flag, Maxximum and MVP Racing. Upper Deck stated it did not want to release racing products during the tail-end of the 1999 Winston Cup season. Company officials also stated they were unable to secure some drivers' approvals or signatures in time to be included in the releases. Ultimately they decided it would be best to hold back and launch the new 2000 sets at the start of the new year, and the new season.

This did raise some questions as to where the racing card market was heading. After all, it was a market that had nine companies producing cards only two years early. Then in 1999, of the two remaining companies, one of them was cancelling three of their releases.

As 1999 concluded, Upper Deck reassured collectors that they were not abandoning the racing card market. Instead, they had plans of releasing seven sets in 2000.

Even though 1999 racing card sales were down from 1998, the two card companies weren't alarmed. NASCAR's 50th Anniversary in 1998 helped sell more product, making it unfair to compare 1999 sales with 1998 sales. The 1999 sales wound up being closer to the 1997 sales.

Once again, Dale Earnhardt and Jeff Gordon were the main stars driving the market in 1999. Once Tony Stewart established himself as not only a rookie contender, but also a title contender, collectors started going after his cards.

After qualifying on the outside of the front row for the 1999 Daytona 500, Stewart let collectors and fans know that he was going to be a force to be reckoned with. As the season progressed, Stewart reaffirmed that there was no stopping him.

When all was said and done, Stewart had put together the finest rookie campaign in the history of NASCAR. He won three races, breaking the previous record of two held by the late Davey Allison. He also finished fourth in the final point standings, the highest ever by a rookie.

IMPACT OF YOUNG DRIVERS

Stewart was just the first young driver making an impact on the card market. In 2000, Dale Earnhardt Jr., Matt Kenseth, Dave Blaney and Scott Pruett will embark on their rookie seasons on the NASCAR Winston Cup tour. This talented group of drivers will be driving the card market for years to come.

Earnhardt Jr.'s accomplishments have been well publicized. He is the son of NASCAR legend, Dale Earnhardt. He also won the 1998 and 1999 NASCAR Busch Grand National Series championships.

Earnhardt Jr.'s main nemesis on the NASCAR Busch Grand National circuit was Kenseth. Kenseth came out of nowhere in 1998 to challenge Earnhardt Jr. for the title. Along the way he caught the eye of NASCAR driver, Mark Martin. Martin in turn, convinced car owner, Jack Rousch, to sign Kenseth to a contract.

Kenseth once again challenged

Earnhardt Jr. for the Busch title in 1999, but fell short. Now the two will battle it out for the Winston Cup Rookie of the Year award.

These two drivers created more and more interest in the card market as the year went on. Collectors could find them in numerous inserts, the most popular being the autographed versions.

RACE USED MEMORABILIA CARDS

A popular trend of 1999 was race-used memorabilia cards. This idea wasn't new in 1999, rather new items were being used on these cards.

The "Triple Gear 3 in 1" cards by Press Pass have become very popular. These cards were introduced in 1998 and returned in 1999. Each card featured a piece of race-used tire, firesuit and sheet metal. There were only 33 cards for each of the nine drivers in the set. Press Pass, Press Pass Premium and Press Pass VIP each contained 11 of the 33 cards.

The Press Pass set also included a "Skidmarks" parallel in which real pieces of tire were burned into the cards.

The Wheels High Gear release included the "Flag Chasers" insert. This insert included cards that contained Authentic pieces of seven NASCAR flags that were used during 1998 Winston Cup races.

A "Flag Chasers" insert was also included in the 1999 Wheels product.

In addition to the "Triple Gear 3-in-1" insert, Press Pass Premium included race-used firesuit cards. Press Pass VIP included race-used sheet metal cards in addition to the "Triple Gear 3-in-1" cards.

Upper Deck was also including race-used memorabilia cards in its 1999 racing products. Victory Circle included Magic Numbers card, which included actual pieces of the numbers peeled right off the side of the cars of Mark Martin, Bobby Labonte, Dale Jarrett and Rusty Wallace.

Upper Deck's Road To The Cup set included a five-card insert featuring cards that contained an authentic piece of a race-used tire from a Winston Cup car that raced in the 1999 Daytona 500.

SP Authentic, Upper Deck's final racing release of 1999, included the SP Authentics insert. This insert included redemption cards for: Jeff Gordon-autographed helmet visors, Jeff Gordon-autographed pair of racing gloves, Rusty Wallace-autographed driver suit, Rusty Wallace autographed racing helmet, and a Rusty Wallace Authentic race-used collection (1-of-1 card).

DRIVER OF THE YEAR

Sponsor:
Quality Care/Ford Credit
Hometown:
Conover, N.C.
Height:
6'2"
Weight:
205
Birthdate:
11/26/56
Car Owner:
Robert Yates
Career Highlights:
Competed in his first Winston Cup race in Martinsville (4-29-84). Won his first Winston Cup race in the Champion Spark Plug 400 at Michigan (8-18-91). Joined Robert Yates Racing in 1995, and debuted the Quality Care/Ford Credit team in 19996. Won the 1999 NASCAR Winston Cup Championship.

Dale Jarrett

CARDS TO GET: Jarrett's top cards to get include: 1999 Road To The Cup Signature (#DJ, $125), 1999 Upper Deck Victory Circle-Magic Numbers (#3, $120), 1997 Press Pass Burning Rubber (#7, $100), Press Pass Gold Signing ($175).

TOP TENS

CARD SINGLES

1.	Dale Earnhardt	1996 Press Pass Burning Rubber (#BR3)	$250
2.	Jeff Gordon	1998 Press Pass Triple Gear "3 in 1" (#STG 6)	$600
3.	D. Earnhardt/R. Petty	1998 SP Authentic Traditions (#T1)	$300
4.	Dale Earnhardt	1998 MAXX 10th Anniversary Autograph (#7)	$300
5.	Tony Stewart	1999 Press Pass VIP Used Sheet Metal (#6)	$225
6.	Dale Earnhardt	1996 Wheels Viper Diamondback Auth. (#DA2)	$175
7.	Jeff Gordon	1995 Pinnacle Zenith Z-Team (#2)	$100
8.	Jeff Gordon	1987 World Of Outlaws (#52)	$75
9.	Dale Jarrett	1999 Press Pas Signings	$75
10.	Dale Earnhardt Jr.	1999 UD Victory Circle Signature Collection	$150

REGULAR-ISSUE SETS

1.	1989 MAXX	$350/box	100-card set: $500
2.	1994 Press Pass	$35	150-card set: $18
3.	1996 Press Pass	$60	120-card set: $15
4.	1991 Traks	$30	200-card set: $24
5.	1997 SP	$75	126-card set: $125
6.	1998 MAXX 10th Anniversary	----	200-card set: $100
7.	1990 MAXX	----	200-card set: $100
8.	1994 AP Champ & Challenger	----	42-card set: $15
9.	1998 Maxximum	----	200-card set: $100
10.	1998 Wheels	$60	100-card set: $20

RACING

1998 Press Pass Stealth

This set contained 60-base cards, including 15 Teammates cards. The card fronts contained a color picture, a black and white picture and the Stealth '98 logo and the driver's name in silver foil stamping. The card backs contain a color photo and a quote about the driver's race team. The base set is paralleled by Fusion. Fusion cards featured red foil, and were inserted 1:1 pack. A bronze, silver and gold version of the #0 Jeff Gordon Champion Card was hobby exclusive. Other inserts included Press Pass Signings, Octane, Awards, Stars and Fan Talk. Press Pass Signings were part of a year long program in which random autographs were inserted in all in-season Press Pass race card products.

		MT
Complete Set (60):		30.00
Common Driver:		.30
Common Card:		.15
Fusion:		1.5x-3x
Inserted 1:1		
Wax Box:		75.00
1	Dale Earnhardt's Car	1.50
2	Dale Earnhardt's Car	1.50
3	Richard Childress	.15
4	Jeff Burton	1.00
5	Jeff Burton's Car	.50
6	Jack Roush	.15
7	Bill Elliott	1.50
8	Bill Elliott's Car	.75
9	Joe Garone	.15
10	Jeff Gordon	3.00
11	Jeff Gordon's Car	1.50
12	Ray Evernham	.15
13	Kenny Irwin	.60
14	Kenny Irwin's Car	.30
15	Robert Yates	.15
16	Dale Jarrett	1.50
17	Dale Jarrett's Car	.75
18	Todd Parrott	.15
19	Bobby Labonte	1.00
20	Bobby Labonte's Car	.50
21	Jimmy Makar	.15
22	Terry Labonte	1.50
23	Terry Labonte's Car	.75
24	Andy Graves	.15
25	Mark Martin	1.50
26	Mark Martin's Car	.75
27	Jimmy Fennig	.15
28	Ricky Rudd	.60
29	Ricky Rudd's Car	.30
30	Bill Ingle	.15
31	Rusty Wallace	1.50
32	Rusty Wallace's Car	.75
33	Robin Pemberton	.15
34	Michael Waltrip	.30
35	Michael Waltrip's Car	.15
36	Glen Wood	.15
37	Dale Earnhardt Jr.	4.00
38	Jason Keller	.30
39	Randy LaJoie	.30
40	Mark Martin	1.50
41	Mike McLaughlin	.30
42	Elliott Sadler	.30
43	Hermie Sadler	.30
44	Tony Stewart	2.00
45	Dale Jarrett TM	1.50
46	Kenny Irwin TM	.60
47	Jeff Gordon TM	3.00
48	Terry Labonte TM	1.50
49	Jeremy Mayfield TM	1.00
50	Rusty Wallace TM	1.50
51	Jeff Burton TM	1.00
52	Ted Musgrave TM	.30
53	Chad Little TM	.30
54	Johnny Benson TM	.30
55	Mark Martin TM	1.50
56	Sterling Marlin TM	.60
57	Joe Nemechek TM	.30
58	Mike Skinner TM	.60
59	Dale Earnhardt's Car TM	1.50
60	Dale Earnhardt Jr. CL	1.50
0	J Gordon Champ Gold 1:440	60.00
0	J Gordon Champ Silver 1:220	30.00
0	J Gordon Champ Bronze 1:110	20.00

1998 Press Pass Stealth Awards

This seven-card set was highlighted by the mid-season award winners in different catagories. The catagories included Most Laps Completed (1:22 packs), All Charged Up (1:68), Top Rookie (1:90), Most Money Won (1:120), Most Poles (1:200) and Most Wins (1:420). The NitroKrome process was used on all the cards.

		MT
Complete Set (7):		200.00
Common Driver:		6.00
1	Jeremy Mayfield 1:22	6.00
2	Jeff Burton 1:68	10.00
3	Kenny Irwin 1:90	12.00
4	Mark Martin 1:120	20.00
5	Jeff Gordon 1:200	60.00
6	Mark Martin 1:420	60.00
7	Jeff Gordon 1:420	100.00

1998 Press Pass Stealth Fan Talk

The cards of this nine-card set are all foil and micro-etched. The card fronts contained a picture of the driver and half of a headset along with the Stealth '98 logo. The card backs contained quotes from fans of the depicted driver. Chances of finding one of these cards was 1:10 packs. A special die-cut parallel version was also produced and inserted 1:30.

		MT
Complete Set (9):		50.00
Common Driver:		2.50
Inserted 1:10		
Die-Cut Version		1x-2x
Inserted 1:30		
1	Dale Earnhardt	12.00
2	Bill Elliott	6.00
3	Jeff Gordon	12.00
4	Dale Jarrett	6.00
5	Bobby Labonte	4.00
6	Terry Labonte	6.00
7	Mark Martin	6.00
8	Ricky Rudd	2.50
9	Rusty Wallace	6.00

1998 Press Pass Stealth Octane

Octane was a 36-card "set within a set" that featured the top 18 NASCAR Winston Cup drivers and the cars they raced. The cards were all-foil, micro-etched and inserted 1:2 packs. A special die-cut version was also produced and inserted 1:11.

		MT
Complete Set (36):		40.00
Common Driver:		.60
Inserted 1:2		
Die-Cut Version		1.25x-3x
Inserted 1:11		
1	John Andretti	1.20
2	John Andretti's Car	.60
3	Johnny Benson	.60
4	Johnny Benson's Car	.30
5	Jeff Burton	2.25
6	Jeff Burton's Car	1.00
7	Ward Burton	.60
8	Ward Burton's Car	.30
9	Dale Earnhardt's Car	3.00
10	Dale Earnhardt's Car	3.00
11	Bill Elliott	3.00
12	Bill Elliott's Car	1.50
13	Jeff Gordon	6.00
14	Jeff Gordon's Car	3.00
15	Ernie Irvan	1.25
16	Ernie Irvan's Car	.60
17	Dale Jarrett	2.25
18	Dale Jarrett's Car	1.00
19	Bobby Labonte	2.25
20	Bobby Labonte's Car	1.00
21	Terry Labonte	3.00
22	Terry Labonte's Car	1.50
23	Sterling Marlin	1.25
24	Sterling Marlin's Car	.60
25	Mark Martin	3.00
26	Mark Martin's Car	1.50
27	Jeremy Mayfield	2.25
28	Jeremy Mayfield's Car	1.00
29	Ricky Rudd	1.25
30	Ricky Rudd's Car	.60
31	Mike Skinner	1.25
32	Mike Skinner's Car	.60
33	Jimmy Spencer	.60
34	Jimmy Spencer's Car	.30
35	Rusty Wallace	3.00
36	Rusty Wallace's Car	1.50

1998 Press Pass Stealth Race-Used Gloves

This eight-card set included pieces of actual race-used gloves embedded into the cards of eight different drivers. The chances of finding one of these cards was 1:400 packs.

		MT
Complete Set (8):		1200.00
Common Driver:		100.00
Inserted 1:400		
Production 205 Sets		
1	Rusty Wallace	175.00
2	Jeff Burton	100.00
3	Terry Labonte	175.00
4	Mark Martin	175.00
5	Bobby Labonte	100.00
6	Jeff Gordon	250.00
7	Dale Jarrett	150.00
8	Dale Earnhardt	250.00

1998 Press Pass Stealth Stars

This all-foil, NitroKrome 18-card insert set featured cards of the top NASCAR drivers. Cards were inserted 1:6 packs. A special die-cut version was also produced, and inserted 1:18.

		MT
Complete Set (18):		60.00
Common Driver:		1.25
Inserted 1:6		
Die-Cut Version		1.5x-4x
Inserted 1:18		
1	Johnny Benson	1.25
2	Jeff Burton	4.50
3	Dale Earnhardt Jr.	15.00
4	Bill Elliott	6.00
5	Jeff Gordon	12.00
6	Bobby Hamilton	1.25
7	Kenny Irwin	2.50
8	Dale Jarrett	6.00
9	Bobby Labonte	4.50
10	Terry Labonte	6.00
11	Sterling Marlin	2.50
12	Mark Martin	6.00
13	Jeremy Mayfield	4.50
14	Ted Musgrave	1.25
15	Ricky Rudd	2.50
16	Jimmy Spencer	1.25
17	Rusty Wallace	6.00
18	Michael Waltrip	1.25

1998 Upper Deck Maxximum

The 100-card base set was broken into four special subsets: Iron Men, Steel Chariots, Armor Clad and Heat of Battle. Each subset contained 25 cards. All the cards featured Ionix technology on heavy stock. The card fronts contained the MAXXIMUM logo, the driver's name and picture. The card backs contained a picture of the driver on the left side, with career earnings listed on the right side. Insert sets included First Class, Battle Proven and Field Generals.

		MT
Complete Set (100):		50.00
Common Driver:		.40
Common Card:		.20
Wax Box:		90.00
1	Darrell Waltrip	.80
2	Rusty Wallace	2.00
3	Dale Earnhardt	4.00
4	Bobby Hamilton	.40
5	Terry Labonte	2.00
6	Mark Martin	2.00
7	Geoff Bodine	.40
8	Ernie Irvan	.80
9	Jeff Burton	1.50
10	Ricky Rudd	.80
11	Dale Jarrett	2.00
12	Jeremy Mayfield	1.50
13	Jerry Nadeau	.40
14	Ken Schrader	.40
15	Kyle Petty	.80
16	Chad Little	.40
17	Todd Bodine	.40
18	Bobby Labonte	1.50
19	Bill Elliott	2.00
20	Mike Skinner	.80
21	Michael Waltrip	.40
22	John Andretti	.80
23	Jimmy Spencer	.40
24	Jeff Gordon	4.00
25	Kenny Irwin	.80
26	Darrell Waltrip	.40
27	Rusty Wallace	1.00
28	Dale Earnhardt	2.00
29	Bobby Hamilton	.20
30	Terry Labonte	1.00
31	Mark Martin	1.00
32	Geoff Bodine	.20
33	Ernie Irvan	.40
34	Jeff Burton	.75
35	Ricky Rudd	.40
36	Dale Jarrett	1.00
37	Jeremy Mayfield	.75
38	Jerry Nadeau	.20
39	Ken Schrader	.20
40	Kyle Petty	.40
41	Chad Little	.20
42	Todd Bodine	.20
43	Bobby Labonte	.75
44	Bill Elliott	1.00
45	Mike Skinner	.40
46	Michael Waltrip	.20
47	John Andretti	.40
48	Jimmy Spencer	.20
49	Jeff Gordon	2.00
50	Kenny Irwin	.40
51	Darrell Waltrip	.80
52	Rusty Wallace	2.00
53	Dale Earnhardt Jr.	5.00
54	Bobby Hamilton	.40
55	Terry Labonte	2.00
56	Mark Martin	2.00
57	Geoff Bodine	.40
58	Ernie Irvan	.80
59	Jeff Burton	1.50
60	Ricky Rudd	.80
61	Dale Jarrett	2.00
62	Jeremy Mayfield	1.50
63	Jerry Nadeau	.40
64	Ken Schrader	.40
65	Kyle Petty	.80
66	Chad Little	.40
67	Todd Bodine	.40
68	Bobby Labonte	1.50
69	Bill Elliott	2.00
70	Mike Skinner	.80
71	Michael Waltrip	.40
72	John Andretti	.80
73	Jimmy Spencer	.40
74	Jeff Gordon	4.00
75	Kenny Irwin	.80
76	Darrell Waltrip	.80
77	Rusty Wallace	2.00
78	Dale Earnhardt Jr.	5.00
79	Bobby Hamilton	.40
80	Terry Labonte	2.00
81	Mark Martin	2.00
82	Geoff Bodine	.40
83	Ernie Irvan	.80
84	Jeff Burton	1.50
85	Ricky Rudd	.80

86	Dale Jarrett	2.00
87	Jeremy Mayfield	1.50
88	Jerry Nadeau	.40
89	Ken Schrader	.40
90	Kyle Petty	.80
91	Chad Little	.40
92	Todd Bodine	.40
93	Bobby Labonte	1.50
94	Bill Elliott	2.00
95	Mike Skinner	.80
96	Michael Waltrip	.40
97	John Andretti	.80
98	Jimmy Spencer	.40
99	Jeff Gordon	4.00
100	Kenny Irwin	.80

1998 Upper Deck Maxximum Battle Proven

This 15-card set featured the top drivers in NASCAR who posted more than one career Winston Cup victory. The card fronts contained a picture of the driver, the MAXXIMUM logo and the number of career wins by that driver. The card backs contained a smaller picture of the driver along with the driver's career statistics. Cards were seeded 1:4 packs.

		MT
Complete Set (15):		30.00
Common Driver:		.75
Inserted 1:4		
1	Darrell Waltrip	1.50
2	Dale Earnhardt	7.00
3	Rusty Wallace	3.50
4	Bill Elliott	3.50
5	Jeff Gordon	7.00
6	Mark Martin	3.50
7	Terry Labonte	3.50
8	Ricky Rudd	1.50
9	Geoff Bodine	.75
10	Ernie Irvan	1.50
11	Dale Jarrett	3.50
12	Kyle Petty	1.50
13	Sterling Marlin	1.50
14	Bobby Labonte	2.75
15	Jeff Burton	2.75

1998 Upper Deck Maxximum Field Generals

Field Generals was a four-tiered collection that showcased the top Winston Cup drivers. The four-tiers included One Star, Two Stars, Three Star Autographs and Four Star Autographs. Cards in the One Star tier contained Rainbow Ionix technology and were numbered to 2,000. The Two Stars tier contained die-cut cards with Rainbow Ionix technology and numbered to 1,000. The Three Star Autographs tier contained double die-cut cards with autographs, and numbered to 100. Each card in the Four Star Autographed tier was marked with a special perimeter die-cut, autographed, and numbered 1-of-1. Each tier contained 15 cards.

		MT
Complete Set (15):		70.00
Common Driver:		1.25
Listed Prices Are For One Star Cards		
Production 2,000 Sets		
Two Stars Cards		2x-4x
Production 1,000 Sets		
Three Star Autograph Cards		9x-10x
Production 100 Sets		
1	Rusty Wallace (Field Generals)	6.25
2	Jeremy Mayfield (Field Generals)	4.75
3	Jeff Gordon (Field Generals)	12.50
4	Terry Labonte (Field Generals)	6.25
5	Dale Jarrett (Field Generals)	6.25
6	Mark Martin (Field Generals)	6.25
7	Jeff Burton (Field Generals)	4.75
8	Kenny Irwin (Field Generals)	2.50
9	Darrell Waltrip (Field Generals)	2.50
10	Dale Earnhardt (Field Generals)	12.50
11	Ernie Irvan (Field Generals)	2.50
12	Bobby Labonte (Field Generals)	4.75
13	Kyle Petty (Field Generals)	2.50
14	Jimmy Spencer (Field Generals)	1.25
15	John Andretti (Field Generals)	2.50

1998 Upper Deck Maxximum First Class

This 20-card set focused on the drivers who established themselves as the most successful drivers on the current Winston Cup circuit. The cards were holographic and contained a picture of the driver. They were inserted 1:3 packs.

		MT
Complete Set (20):		30.00
Common Driver:		.75
Inserted 1:3		
1	Jeff Gordon	7.00
2	Jimmy Spencer	.75
3	John Andretti	1.50
4	Michael Waltrip	.75
5	Bill Elliott	3.50
6	Bobby Labonte	2.75
7	Kyle Petty	1.50
8	Ken Schrader	.75
9	Jeremy Mayfield	2.75
10	Dale Jarrett	3.50
11	Ricky Rudd	1.50
12	Jeff Burton	2.75
13	Ernie Irvan	1.50
14	Geoff Bodine	.75
15	Mark Martin	3.50
16	Terry Labonte	3.50
17	Bobby Hamilton	.75
18	Rusty Wallace	3.50
19	Darrell Waltrip	1.50
20	Sterling Marlin	1.50

1999 Maxx

This 90-card regular set included cards of the top Winston Cup drivers and their cars. A 30-card "Roots of Racing" subset was also included. This subset provided a retrospective of each driver's road to the top. The inserts included Racing Images, Race Tickets, Fantastic Finishes, Focus on a Champion, Focus on a Champion Gold and Racers Ink.

		MT
Complete Set (90):		25.00
Common Driver:		.20
Common Card:		.10
Wax Box:		50.00
1	Jeff Gordon	2.00
2	Jeff Gordon	1.00
3	Jeff Gordon's car	1.00
4	Jeff Burton	.75
5	Jeff Burton's car	.40
6	Jeff Burton	.75
7	Dale Jarrett	1.00
8	Dale Jarrett's car	.50
9	Dale Jarrett's car	.50
10	Ward Burton	.20
11	Ward Burton's car	.10
12	Ward Burton	.20
13	Bill Elliott	1.00
14	Bill Elliott's car	.50
15	Bill Elliott's car	.50
16	Johnny Benson	.20
17	Johnny Benson's car	.10
18	Johnny Benson	
19	Dale Earnhardt Jr.	2.00
20	Dale Earnhardt Jr.'s car	1.00
21	Dale Earnhardt Jr.'s car	1.00
22	Sterling Marlin	.40
23	Sterling Marlin's car	.20
24	Sterling Marlin	.40
25	Ken Schrader	.20
26	Ken Schrader's car	.10
27	Ken Schrader's car	.10
28	Bobby Labonte	.75
29	Bobby Labonte's car	.40
30	Bobby Labonte	.40
31	Chad Little	.20
32	Chad Little's car	.10
33	Chad Little's car	.10
34	Jeremy Mayfield	.75
35	Jeremy Mayfield's car	.40
36	Jeremy Mayfield	.75
37	Ricky Rudd	.40
38	Ricky Rudd's car	.20
39	Ricky Rudd's car	
40	John Andretti	.40
41	John Andretti's car	.20
42	John Andretti	.40
43	Rusty Wallace	1.00
44	Rusty Wallace's car	.50
45	Rusty Wallace	1.00
46	Darrell Waltrip	.40
47	Darrell Waltrip's car	.20
48	Darrell Waltrip	.40
49	Geoffrey Bodine	.20
50	Geoffrey Bodine's car	.10
51	Geoffrey Bodine's car	.10
52	Mark Martin	1.00
53	Mark Martin's car	.50
54	Mark Martin	1.00
55	Kenny Irwin	.40
56	Kenny Irwin's car	.20
57	Kenny Irwin's car	.20
58	Mike Skinner	.40
59	Mike Skinner's car	.20
60	Mike Skinner	.40
61	Kyle Petty	.40
62	Kyle Petty's car	.20
63	Kyle Petty's car	.20
64	Bobby Hamilton	.20
65	Bobby Hamilton's car	.10
66	Bobby Hamilton	.20
67	Jerry Nadeau	.20
68	Jerry Nadeau's car	.10
69	Jerry Nadeau's car	.10
70	Tony Stewart	2.00
71	Tony Stewart's car	1.00
72	Tony Stewart	2.00
73	Ernie Irvan	.40
74	Ernie Irvan's car	.20
75	Ernie Irvan's car	.20
76	Steve Park	.40
77	Steve Park's car	.20
78	Steve Park	.40
79	Kevin Lepage	.20
80	Kevin Lepage's car	.10
81	Kevin Lepage's car	.10
82	Elliott Sadler	.20
83	Elliott Sadler's car	.10
84	Elliott Sadler	.20
85	Terry Labonte	1.00
86	Terry Labonte's car	.50
87	Terry Labonte's car	.50
88	Dale Earnhardt	2.00
89	Dale Earnhardt's car	1.00
90	Jeff Gordon	1.50

1999 Maxx FANtastic Finishes

This 30-card set featured the top NASCAR drivers and their closest finishes posted during their Winston Cup careers. The front of the cards are black and gold, and featured a picture of the car driven by the depicted driver. Odds of finding one of these cards was 1:12 packs.

		MT
Complete Set (30):		125.00
Common Driver:		1.50
Inserted 1:12		
1	Jeff Gordon	15.00
2	Steve Park	3.25
3	Elliott Sadler	1.50
4	Bobby Hamilton	1.50
5	Rusty Wallace	8.00
6	Kyle Petty	3.25
7	Kenny Irwin	3.25
8	Jerry Nadeau	1.50
9	Dale Jarrett	8.00
10	Dale Earnhardt	15.00
11	Ken Schrader	1.50
12	Jeff Burton	6.00
13	Ernie Irvan	3.25
14	John Andretti	3.25
15	Dale Earnhardt Jr.	15.00
16	Bill Elliott	8.00
17	Mark Martin	8.00
18	Mike Skinner	3.25
19	Ward Burton	1.50
20	Darrell Waltrip	3.25
21	Chad Little	1.50
22	Ricky Rudd	3.25
23	Johnny Benson	1.50
24	Terry Labonte	8.00
25	Sterling Marlin	3.25
26	Kevin Lepage	1.50
27	Jeremy Mayfield	6.00
28	Tony Stewart	15.00
29	Bobby Labonte	8.00
30	Michael Waltrip	1.50

1999 Maxx Focus on a Champion

This 15-card set included cards highlighting 15 drivers who would be chasing the 1999 NASCAR Winston Cup title. Cards were inserted 1:24 packs. This set was also paralleled by Focus on a Champion Gold, which featured die-cut cards and gold Light F/X technology. These cards were inserted 1:72.

		MT
Complete Set (15):		120.00
Common Driver:		2.00
Inserted 1:24		
Gold Cards (1-15)		1x-2x
Inserted 1:72		
1	Jeff Gordon	20.00
2	Dale Earnhardt	20.00
3	Dale Earnhardt Jr.	20.00
4	Mark Martin	10.00
5	Dale Jarrett	10.00
6	Jeremy Mayfield	7.50
7	Rusty Wallace	10.00
8	Terry Labonte	10.00
9	Jeff Burton	7.50
10	Ernie Irvan	4.00
11	Bill Elliott	10.00
12	Bobby Labonte	7.50
13	Jerry Nadeau	2.00
14	Steve Park	4.00
15	Kenny Irwin	4.00

1999 Maxx Race Ticket

This 30-card scratch-off insert gave collectors the opportunity to instantly win a pair of tickets to a 1999 NASCAR Winston Cup event in either Atlanta or Charlotte. The cards were designed to resemble a race ticket. Cards were inserted 1:8 packs.

		MT
Complete Set (30):		55.00
Common Driver:		.20
Inserted 1:8		
1	Jerry Nadeau	.80
2	Jeff Burton	3.00
3	Jeremy Mayfield	3.00
4	Dale Earnhardt Jr.	8.00
5	Steve Park	1.60
6	Kenny Irwin	1.60
7	Ernie Irvan	1.60
8	Dale Jarrett	4.00
9	Kevin Lepage	.80
10	Bill Elliott	4.00
11	Bobby Hamilton	.80
12	Chad Little	.80
13	Brett Bodine	.80
14	Ken Schrader	.80
15	Ricky Rudd	1.60
16	Johnny Benson	.80
17	John Andretti	1.60
18	Tony Stewart	8.00
19	Mark Martin	8.00
20	Ward Burton	.80
21	Elliott Sadler	.80
22	Jeff Gordon	8.00
23	Kyle Petty	1.60
24	Terry Labonte	4.00
25	Sterling Marlin	1.60
26	Darrell Waltrip	1.60
27	Bobby Labonte	3.00
28	Mike Skinner	1.60
29	Michael Waltrip	.20
30	Rusty Wallace	4.00

1999 Maxx Racer's Ink

This set featured authentic autographs for five of the top drivers in NASCAR. Cards were inserted 1:670 packs.

		MT
Complete Set (5):		500.00
Common Driver:		75.00
Inserted 1:670		
DE	Dale Earnhardt Jr.	200.00
JG	Jeff Gordon	200.00
MM	Mark Martin	100.00
JM	Jeremy Mayfield	75.00
RW	Rusty Wallace	100.00

1999 Maxx Racing Images

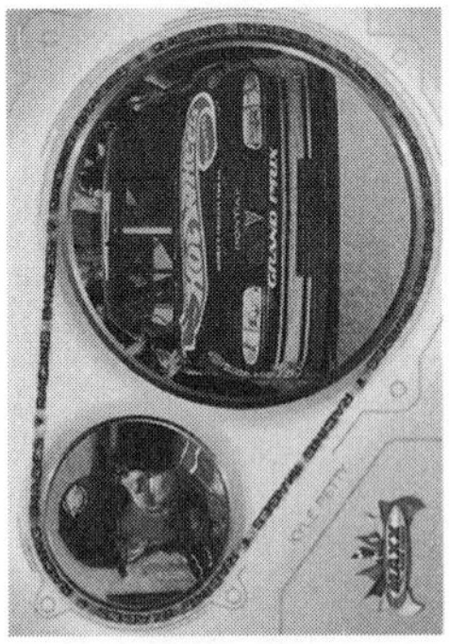

This 30-card set featured the top NASCAR drivers in their 1999 uniforms and the paint schemes of 1999 cars. The front of the card contained Light F/X technology and dual photos of the driver and the car. The back of the cards contained a picture of the car. Cards were inserted 1:3 packs.

		MT
Complete Set (30):		25.00
Common Driver:		.40
Inserted 1:3		
1	Darrell Waltrip	.80
2	Kevin Lepage	.40
3	Bobby Labonte	1.50
4	Ricky Rudd	.80
5	Jeff Burton	1.50
6	Brett Bodine	.40
7	Mike Skinner	.80
8	John Andretti	.80
9	Dale Jarrett	2.00
10	Bill Elliott	2.00
11	Ward Burton	.40
12	Terry Labonte	2.00
13	Kenny Irwin	.80
14	Ken Schrader	.40
15	Tony Stewart	4.00
16	Sterling Marlin	.80
17	Ernie Irvan	.80
18	Bobby Hamilton	.40
19	Johnny Benson	.40
20	Michael Waltrip	.40
21	Jeremy Mayfield	1.50
22	Chad Little	.40
23	Rusty Wallace	2.00
24	Jeff Gordon	4.00
25	Steve Park	.80
26	Jerry Nadeau	.40
27	Elliott Sadler	.40
28	Dale Earnhardt Jr.	4.00
29	Kyle Petty	.80
30	Mark Martin	2.00

1999 Press Pass

The card fronts featured a full-size photo with silver foil stamping. Backs have a photo along with personal information, with stats. There were eight cards per pack with 100 cards in the set. The Retro "set within a set" returned featuring past and present drivers. The Retro cards were numbered 101-136. The #0 Winston Cup Champion Card highlighted Jeff Gordon's third Winston Cup Championship. The all-foil card with special etch treatment was hobby exclusive and inserted 1:480 packs. Inserts include "Triple Gear 3 in 1," Burning Rubber, Certified Authentic Autographed Cards, Cup Chase, Pit Stop, Showman/ Chase Cars and Oil Cans. Skidmarks paralleled the complete base set with 250 of each base card individually numbered.

		MT
Complete Set (136):		30.00
Common Card:		.10
Common Driver:		.20
Wax Box:		60.00
1	Jeff Gordon	2.00
2	Mark Martin	1.00
3	Dale Jarrett	1.00
4	Rusty Wallace	1.00
5	Bobby Labonte	.75
6	Jeremy Mayfield	.75
7	Jeff Burton	.75
8	Dale Earnhardt Jr.	2.00
9	Terry Labonte	1.00
10	Ken Schrader	.20
11	John Andretti	.40
12	Ernie Irvan	.20
13	Jimmy Spencer	.20
14	Sterling Marlin	.40
15	Michael Waltrip	.20
16	Bill Elliott	1.00
17	Bobby Hamilton	.20
18	Johnny Benson	.20
19	Kenny Irwin	.40
20	Ward Burton	.20
21	Darrell Waltrip	.40
22	Joe Nemechek	.20
23	Ricky Rudd	.40
24	Mike Skinner	.40
25	Robert Pressley	.20
26	Steve Park	.40
27	Geoff Bodine	.20
28	Jeff Gordon's Car	1.00
29	Mark Martin's Car	.50
30	Dale Jarrett's Car	.50
31	Rusty Wallace's Car	.50
32	Bobby Labonte's Car	.50
33	Jeremy Mayfield's Car	.40
34	Jeff Burton's Car	.40
35	Dale Earnhardt's Car	1.00
36	Terry Labonte's Car	.50
37	Dale Earnhardt Jr.	2.25
38	Matt Kenseth	2.00
39	Mike McLaughlin	.20
40	Randy LaJoie	.20
41	Elton Sawyer	.20
42	Jason Jarrett	.20
43	Elliott Sadler	.20
44	Tim Fedewa	.20
45	Mike Dillon	.20
46	Hermie Sadler	.20
47	Glenn Allen	.20
48	Dale Jarrett	1.00
49	Mark Martin	1.00
50	Jeff Burton	.75
51	Michael Waltrip	.20
52	Ron Barfield	.20
53	Ron Hornaday	.20
54	Jack Sprague	.20
55	Joe Ruttman	.20
56	Jay Sauter	.20
57	Rich Bickle	.20
58	Dale Earnhardt Jr.	2.25
59	Elliott Sadler	.20
60	Jason Jarrett	.20
61	Tony Stewart	1.00
62	Matt Kenseth	2.00
63	Adam Petty	2.00
64	Larry McReynolds	.10
65	Jimmy Makar	.10
66	Robin Pemberton	.10
67	Todd Parrott	.10
68	Ray Everham	.20
69	Andy Graves	.10
70	Jimmy Fenig	.10
71	Paul Andrews	.10
72	Jeff Buice	.10
73	1998 Champions	2.50
74	1998 Champions	.20
75	1998 Champions	.20
76	1998 Champions	.20
77	1998 Champions	.20
78	1998 Champions	.20
79	Jeff Gordon	2.00
80	Rusty Wallace	1.00
81	Ward Burton	.20
82	Ernie Irvan	.20
83	Bobby Labonte	.75
84	Ken Schrader	.20
85	Kenny Irwin	.40
86	Bobby Hamilton	.20
87	Dale Jarrett	1.00
88	Mark Martin	1.00
89	Rick Mast	.20
90	Jeremy Mayfield	.75
91	Derrike Cope	.20
92	Elliott Sadler	.20
93	Jerry Nadeau	.20
94	Tony Stewart	1.00
95	Kevin Lepage	.20
96	Ernie Irvan	.20
97	Kenny Wallace	.20
98	Jason Jarrett	.20
99	Jeff Gordon	2.00
100	Checklist - 1999 Races	.10
101	Jeff Gordon	3.00
102	Mark Martin	1.50
103	Dale Jarrett	1.50
104	Rusty Wallace	1.50
105	Bobby Labonte	1.25
106	Jeremy Mayfield	1.25
107	Jeff Burton	1.25
108	Chad Little	.30
109	Terry Labonte	1.00
110	Ken Schrader	.30
111	John Andretti	.60
112	Ernie Irvan	.30
113	Jimmy Spencer	.30
114	Sterling Martin	.60
115	Michael Waltrip	.30
116	Bill Elliott	1.50
117	Bobby Hamilton	.30
118	Johnny Benson	.30
119	Kenny Irwin	.60
120	Ward Burton	.30
121	Darrell Waltrip	.60
122	Joe Nemechek	.30
123	Ricky Rudd	.60
124	Mike Skinner	.60
125	Robert Pressley	.30
126	Steve Park	.60
127	Geoff Bodine	.30
128	Bobby Allison	.50
129	Buddy Baker	.50
130	Ned Jarrett	.50
131	David Pearson	.50
132	Richard Petty	.75
133	Cale Yarborough	.50
134	Junior Johnson	.50
135	Benny Parsons	.50
136	Harry Gant	.50

1999 Press Pass Skidmarks Parallel

This insert paralleled the entire 100-card base set and featured real pieces of tire burned into the cards. Each card was individually numbered to 250 and was hobby exclusive. They were seeded 1:8 packs.

	MT
Skidmarks (1-100):	15x-30x
Production 175 Sets	

1999 Press Pass Autographs

This insert featured autographs of 19 Winston Cup personalities, including drivers and crew chiefs. The cards were limited to 250 of each, and individually numbered. They were seeded 1:240 packs.

		MT
Complete Set (19):		1100.00
Common Driver:		20.00
Inserted 1:240		
1	Rusty Wallace	150.00
2	Dale Earnhardt Jr.	175.00
3	Andy Graves	35.00
4	Ernie Irvan	30.00
5	Ricky Rudd	30.00
6	Michael Waltrip	20.00
7	Kenny Irwin	30.00
8	Mark Martin	100.00
9	Jeremy Mayfield	50.00
10	Dale Jarrett	75.00
11	Bill Elliott	80.00
12	Terry Labonte	80.00
13	Jack Sprague	20.00
14	Ron Hornaday	30.00
15	Tony Stewart	50.00
16	Randy LaJoie	20.00
17	Rich Bickle	20.00
18	Ray Everham	35.00
19	Jeff Gordon	250.00

1999 Press Pass Burning Rubber

This insert set contained die-cut cards featuring a piece of real race-used tire right off the cars of the best in NASCAR Winston Cup racing. They were seeded 1:480 packs.

		MT
Complete Set (9):		1000.00
Common Driver:		75.00
Inserted 1:480		
1	Terry Labonte	100.00
2	Mark Martin	100.00
3	Bobby Labonte	75.00
4	Jeff Burton	75.00
5	Dale Jarrett	100.00
6	Ricky Rudd	75.00
7	Jeff Gordon	200.00
8	Rusty Wallace	100.00
9	GM Goodwrench Service Plus	200.00

1999 Press Pass Chase Cars

This set was a duel die-cut set with laser gold foil stamping. The Chase Cars insert featured the NASCAR rides of Winston Cup drivers. The insert was retail exclusive and was inserted 1:12 packs.

		MT
Complete Set (18):		60.00
Common Driver:		1.00
Inserted 1:12 Retail		
1	Dale Jarrett	8.00
2	Bobby Labonte	6.00
3	Mark Martin	8.00
4	Jeremy Mayfield	6.00
5	Ken Schrader	1.00
6	Mike Skinner	3.00
7	GM Goodwrench	16.00
8	Jeff Burton	6.00
9	Ricky Rudd	3.00
10	Michael Waltrip	1.00
11	Jeff Gordon	16.00
12	Bill Elliott	8.00
13	Terry Labonte	8.00
14	Ernie Irvan	1.00
15	Johnny Benson	1.00
16	Sterling Marlin	3.00
17	Joe Nemechek	1.00
18	Rusty Wallace	8.00

1999 Press Pass Cup Chase

This interactive insert set featured 20 drivers, and an all-new design on foil board. Winning cards could be redeemed for a special multi-embossed, die-cut version printed on super thick 24-pt. board. The cards were seeded 1:24 packs.

		MT
Complete Set (20):		200.00
Common Driver:		3.00
Inserted 1:24		
1	John Andretti	6.00
2	Johnny Benson	3.00
3	Jeff Burton	12.00
4	Dale Earnhardt	35.00
5	Bill Elliott	16.00
6	Jeff Gordon	35.00
7	Bobby Hamilton	3.00
8	Ernie Irvan	3.00
9	Kenny Irwin	6.00
10	Dale Jarrett	16.00
11	Bobby Labonte	12.00
12	Terry Labonte	16.00
13	Sterling Marlin	6.00
14	Mark Martin	16.00
15	Jeremy Mayfield	12.00
16	Ricky Rudd	6.00
17	Ken Schrader	3.00
18	Mike Skinner	6.00
19	Rusty Wallace	16.00
20	Field Card	10.00

1999 Press Pass Oil Can

This nine-card embossed set was printed on shimmering foil board and shaped like an oil can. The front of the cards contained a picture of the driver, while the back contained a quote about the driver. They were seeded 1:18 packs.

		MT
Complete Set (9):		50.00
Common Driver:		3.00
Inserted 1:18		
1	Mark Martin	8.00
2	Jeff Burton	3.00
3	Bill Elliott	8.00
4	Dale Jarrett	8.00
5	Terry Labonte	8.00
6	Jeff Gordon	16.00
7	Bobby Labonte	3.00
8	Jeremy Mayfield	3.00
9	Rusty Wallace	8.00

1999 Press Pass Pit Stop

This 18-card set captured the best Winston Cup pit crews in action. The cards were die-cut in the shape of a stop watch with the time of the pit stop on the front. The back of the cards contained the track, date and the race that the pit stop occurred in. They were inserted 1:8 packs.

		MT
Complete Set (18):		45.00
Common Driver:		1.00
Inserted 1:8		
1	Steve Park's Car	2.00
2	Rusty Wallace's Car	6.00
3	Dale Earnhardt's Car	12.00
4	Bobby Hamilton's Car	1.00
5	Terry Labonte's Car	6.00
6	Mark Martin's Car	6.00
7	Ricky Rudd's Car	2.00
8	Jeremy Mayfield's Car	4.00
9	Johnny Benson's Car	1.00
10	Bobby Labonte's Car	4.00
11	Michael Waltrip's Car	1.00
12	Jeff Gordon's Car	12.00
13	Kenny Irwin's Car	2.00
14	Mike Skinner's Car	2.00
15	Ernie Irvan's Car	1.00
16	Dale Jarrett's Car	6.00
17	Bill Elliott's Car	6.00
18	Jeff Burton's Car	4.00

1999 Press Pass Showman

This set was a duel die-cut set with laser gold foil stamping. The Showman set featured the top NASCAR drivers, and were hobby exclusive. The cards were inserted 1:8 packs.

		MT
Complete Set (18):		120.00
Common Driver:		2.00
Inserted 1:8 Hobby		
1	Dale Jarrett	10.00
2	Bobby Labonte	8.00
3	Mark Martin	10.00
4	Jeremy Mayfield	8.00
5	Ken Schrader	2.00
6	Mike Skinner	4.00
7	Dale Earnhardt Jr.	25.00
8	Jeff Burton	8.00
9	Ricky Rudd	4.00
10	Michael Waltrip	2.00
11	Jeff Gordon	20.00
12	Bill Elliott	10.00
13	Terry Labonte	10.00
14	Ernie Irvan	2.00
15	Johnny Benson	2.00
16	Sterling Marlin	4.00
17	Joe Nemechek	2.00
18	Rusty Wallace	10.00

1999 Press Pass Triple Gear

These scarce inserts were evenly allocated across three Press Pass brands: VIP, Premium and Press Pass. A total of 33 numbered versions for each driver exist, with 11 cards for each driver seeded into each of the three products. The inserts have race-used tire, firesuit and sheet metal on each card.

		MT
Complete Set (9):		3500.00
Common Driver:		150.00
1	Terry Labonte	500.00
2	Mark Martin	500.00
3	Jeff Gordon	800.00
4	Bobby Labonte	350.00
5	Rusty Wallace	500.00
6	Dale Jarrett	450.00
7	Jeff Burton	300.00
8	Mike Skinner	150.00
9	Dale Earnhardt	800.00

1999 Press Pass #0 Champion

	MT
Complete Set (1):	60.00

1999 Press Pass Premium

The 54-card base set included all-foil micro-embossed board, and were printed on 24-point extra-thick, UV-coated stock. The Winston Cup drivers' cards were done in a horizontal format, while the car cards and Busch drivers' cards were done in a vertical format. The card back contained the race team, sponsor, car make, 1998 statistics and career statistics. The #0 1999 Daytona 500 winner card was hobby-exclusive and highlighted Jeff Gordon's second career victory at Daytona on an all-foil card with special etch. The #00 Dale Earnhardt Jr. Winston Cup card featured Earnhardt Jr. as a Winston Cup driver and was also hobby-exclusive. The inserts included Badge of Honor, Extreme Fire, Burning Desire, Steel Horses, Race-Used Firesuit Cards, Triple Gear 3 in 1, Press Pass Signings and Gold Signings. The base set and the Badge of Honor insert are paralleled by Reflectors.

		MT
Complete Set (54):		40.00
Common Driver:		.30
Wax Box:		75.00
1	John Andretti (NASCAR Winston Cup Drivers)	.60
2	Johnny Benson (NASCAR Winston Cup Drivers)	.30
3	Geoffrey Bodine (NASCAR Winston Cup Drivers)	.30
4	Jeff Burton (NASCAR Winston Cup Drivers)	1.50
5	Ward Burton (NASCAR Winston Cup Drivers)	.30
6	Dale Earnhardt (NASCAR Winston Cup Drivers)	4.00
7	Bill Elliott (NASCAR Winston Cup Drivers)	2.00
8	Jeff Gordon (NASCAR Winston Cup Drivers)	4.00
9	Bobby Hamilton (NASCAR Winston Cup Drivers)	.30
10	Ernie Irvan (NASCAR Winston Cup Drivers)	.60
11	Kenny Irwin (NASCAR Winston Cup Drivers)	.60
12	Dale Jarrett (NASCAR Winston Cup Drivers)	2.00
13	Bobby Labonte (NASCAR Winston Cup Drivers)	1.50
14	Terry Labonte (NASCAR Winston Cup Drivers)	2.00
15	Chad Little (NASCAR Winston Cup Drivers)	.30
16	Sterling Marlin (NASCAR Winston Cup Drivers)	.60
17	Mark Martin (NASCAR Winston Cup Drivers)	2.00
18	Jeremy Mayfield (NASCAR Winston Cup Drivers)	1.50
19	Joe Nemechek (NASCAR Winston Cup Drivers)	.30
20	Steve Park (NASCAR Winston Cup Drivers)	.60
21	Ricky Rudd (NASCAR Winston Cup Drivers)	.60
22	Elliott Sadler (NASCAR Winston Cup Drivers)	.30
23	Tony Stewart (NASCAR Winston Cup Drivers)	2.00
24	Mike Skinner (NASCAR Winston Cup Drivers)	.60
25	Jimmy Spencer (NASCAR Winston Cup Drivers)	.30
26	Rusty Wallace (NASCAR Winston Cup Drivers)	2.00
27	Michael Waltrip (NASCAR Winston Cup Drivers)	.30
28	Jeff Gordon's Car (NASCAR Winston Cup Machines)	2.00
29	Mark Martin's Car (NASCAR Winston Cup Machines)	1.00
30	Dale Jarrett's Car (NASCAR Winston Cup Machines)	1.00
31	Rusty Wallace's Car (NASCAR Winston Cup Machines)	1.00
32	Jeff Burton's Car (NASCAR Winston Cup Machines)	.75
33	Bobby Labonte's Car (NASCAR Winston Cup Machines)	.75
34	Jeremy Mayfield's Car (NASCAR Winston Cup Machines)	.75
35	GM Goodwrench Service Plus Dale Earnhardt's Car (NASCAR Winston Cup Machines)	2.00
36	Terry Labonte's Car (NASCAR Winston Cup Machines)	1.00
37	Mike Skinner's Car (NASCAR Winston Cup Machines)	.30
38	John Andretti's Car (NASCAR Winston Cup Machines)	.30
39	Kenny Irwin's Car (NASCAR Winston Cup Machines)	.30
40	Joe Nemechek (NASCAR Busch Grand National Drivers)	.30
41	Dale Earnhardt Jr. (NASCAR Busch Grand National Drivers)	5.00
42	Tim Fedewa (NASCAR Busch Grand National Drivers)	.30
43	Jeff Gordon (NASCAR Busch Grand National Drivers)	4.00
44	Ken Schrader (NASCAR Busch Grand National Drivers)	.30
45	Terry Labonte (NASCAR Busch Grand National Drivers)	2.00
46	Matt Kenseth (NASCAR Busch Grand National Drivers)	4.00
47	Randy LaJoie (NASCAR Busch Grand National Drivers)	.30
48	Mark Martin (NASCAR Busch Grand National Drivers)	2.00
49	Mike McLaughlin (NASCAR Busch Grand National Drivers)	.30
50	Michael Waltrip (NASCAR Busch Grand National Drivers)	.30
51	Hermie Sadler (NASCAR Busch Grand National Drivers)	.30
52	Jason Keller (NASCAR Busch Grand National Drivers)	.30
53	Todd Bodine (NASCAR Busch Grand National Drivers)	.30
54	Checklist Jason Jarrett (NASCAR Busch Grand National Drivers)	.30

1999 Press Pass Premium Badge of Honor

This 27-card set-within-a-set showcased the top NASCAR Winston Cup drivers, Dale Earnhardt Jr. and their NASCAR rides. Shaped like a badge, cards 1-18 featured a picture of the driver along with the driver's car number. Cards 19-27 featured a picture of the car driven by the named driver and the car number. They were seeded 1:2 packs.

		MT
Complete Set (27):		60.00
Common Driver:		.60
Inserted 1:2		
Reflectors:		2x-8x
Inserted 1:24		
1	Rusty Wallace	4.00
2	Dale Earnhardt Jr.	10.00
3	Michael Waltrip	.60
4	Terry Labonte	4.00
5	Mark Martin	4.00
6	Ricky Rudd	1.20
7	Jeremy Mayfield	3.00
8	Johnny Benson	.60
9	Bobby Labonte	3.00
10	Jeff Gordon	8.00
11	Kenny Irwin	1.20
12	Mike Skinner	1.20
13	Ernie Irvan	1.20
14	Dale Jarrett	4.00
15	Bill Elliott	4.00
16	Jeff Burton	3.00
17	Chad Little	.60
18	Jimmy Spencer	.60
19	Dale Earnhardt's Car	4.00
20	Terry Labonte's Car	2.00
21	Mark Martin's Car	2.00
22	Jeremy Mayfield's Car	1.50
23	Bobby Labonte's Car	1.50
24	Jeff Gordon's Car	4.00
25	Dale Jarrett's Car	2.00
26	Dale Earnhardt Jr.'s Car (#3 BGN)	5.00
27	Jeff Burton's Car	1.50

1999 Press Pass Premium Reflectors Parallel

This 81-card set paralleled the 54-card base set as well as the 27-card Badge of Honor insert set. Odds of finding a Reflector from the base set was 1:8 packs, while the odds of finding a Badge of Honor Reflector was 1:24 packs. The Reflectors were easy to identify by their mirror-like appearance and the protective Reflector Shield, which easily peeled off.

	MT
Base Card Reflectors:	2x-5x
Inserted 1:8	
Badge of Honor Reflectors:	2x-8x
Inserted 1:24	

1999 Press Pass Premium Burning Desire

This progressive insert contained nine cards of NASCAR's future stars on interlocking cards, and paired them with NASCAR's top drivers in the Extreme Fire insert. The cards had authentic race-used tire pieces burned into them. The overall insertion ratio was 1:18 packs.

		MT
	Complete Set (6):	110.00
	Common Driver:	6.00
1	Jeff Gordon - BGN 1:240	50.00
2	Dale Earnhardt Jr. 1:192	40.00
3	Jeremy Mayfield 1:144	10.00
4	Jeff Burton 1:72	6.00
5	Dale Jarrett 1:36	12.00
6	Tony Stewart 1:18	10.00

1999 Press Pass Premium Extreme Fire

This progressive insert set featured nine cards of NASCAR's top drivers on interlocking cards, and paired them with NASCAR's future stars in the Burning Desire insert. The cards contained authentic race-used tire pieces on them. The overall insertion ratio was 1:18 packs.

		MT
	Complete Set (6):	110.00
	Common Driver:	6.00
1	Jeff Gordon 1:240	50.00
2	Dale Earnhardt 1:192	40.00
3	Rusty Wallace 1:144	15.00
4	Mark Martin 1:72	12.00
5	Terry Labonte 1:36	8.00
6	Bobby Labonte 1:18	6.00

1999 Press Pass Premium Press Pass Signings

These autographs included 30 of NASCAR's top personalities. Quantities for each personality varied, with 1,478 cards of Jason Jarrett being the most. Jeff Gordon had 25 redemption cards for his autograph. Some of the autograph cards for Jeff Burton and Dale Earnhardt were used from the 1999 Press Pass product. Odds of finding a Signings in Premium was 1:48 packs.

	MT
Complete Set (30):	900.00
Common Driver:	10.00
Inserted 1:48	
Glenn Allen/1404	15.00
John Andretti/370	20.00
Buddy Baker/1500	15.00
Johnny Benson/605	15.00
Todd Bodine/497	15.00
Jeff Burton/245	50.00
Derrike Cope/500	15.00
Dale Earnhardt/75	175.00
Jeff Gordon/25	200.00
Dale Jarrett/275	75.00
Ned Jarrett/355	15.00
Jason Jarrett/1478	15.00
Jason Keller/500	15.00
Matt Kenseth/250	75.00
Randy LaJoie/705	15.00
Chad Little/500	15.00
Sterling Marlin/750	25.00
Mark Martin/125	75.00
Larry McReynolds/750	10.00
Todd Parrott/975	10.00
Robin Pemberton/750	10.00
Robert Pressley/968	15.00
Ricky Rudd/400	25.00
Hermie Sadler/500	15.00
Mike Skinner/395	25.00
Jimmy Spencer/500	15.00
Jack Sprague/750	15.00
Tony Stewart/250	90.00
Darrell Waltrip/175	30.00
Michael Waltrip/498	15.00

1999 Press Pass Premium Press Pass Gold Signings

This was a very rare set that featured autographs from NASCAR Winston Cup drivers and Busch Grand National drivers using a special metallic pen. This insert was only included in hobby packs, with an insertion ratio of 1:480 packs.

	MT
Complete Set (8):	600.00
Common Driver:	30.00
Inserted 1:480	
Dale Jarrett/50	175.00
Matt Kenseth/58	125.00
Mark Martin/50	175.00
Ricky Rudd/100	50.00
Mike Skinner/100	50.00
Jimmy Spencer/100	30.00
Tony Stewart/50	150.00
Darrell Waltrip/92	50.00

1999 Press Pass Premium Race-Used Firesuit Cards

This nine-card set featured authentic pieces of the drivers' firesuits embedded in the cards of the top drivers on the Winston Cup tour. The stated odds of finding one were 1:432 packs.

		MT
	Complete Set (9):	1200.00
	Common Driver:	60.00
	Inserted 1:432	
1	Jeff Gordon - BGN	300.00
2	Rusty Wallace	150.00
3	Dale Earnhardt	300.00
4	Bobby Labonte	100.00
5	Terry Labonte	150.00
6	Mark Martin	150.00
7	Mike Skinner	60.00
8	Dale Jarrett	150.00
9	Jeff Burton	100.00

1999 Press Pass Premium Steel Horses

This 12-card set featured the top Winston Cup drivers on all foil, multi-level embossed die-cut cards. The driver's car was featured on the front with the driver's name above the car. The approximate odds of finding one were 1:12 packs.

		MT
	Complete Set (12):	60.00
	Common Driver:	3.00
	Inserted 1:12	
1	#2 Rusty Wallace	7.50
2	#3 Dale Earnhardt	15.00
3	#31 Mike Skinner	3.00
4	#5 Terry Labonte	7.50
5	#6 Mark Martin	7.50
6	#3 (BGN) Dale Earnhardt Jr.	15.00
7	#12 Jeremy Mayfield	6.00
8	#18 Bobby Labonte	6.00
9	#24 Jeff Gordon	15.00
10	#88 Dale Jarrett	7.50
11	#94 Bill Elliott	7.50
12	#99 Jeff Burton	6.00

1999 Press Pass Premium Triple Gear 3 in 1

These scarce inserts were evenly allocated across three Press Pass brands: VIP, Premium and Press Pass. A total of 33 numbered versions for each driver exist, with 11 cards for each driver seeded into each of the three products. The inserts have all three race-used materials on them, which included tire, sheet metal and firesuit. A total of 99 cards were included in Press Pass Premium.

		MT
	Complete Set (9):	3500.00
	Common Driver:	150.00
1	Terry Labonte	500.00
2	Mark Martin	500.00
3	Jeff Gordon	800.00
4	Bobby Labonte	350.00
5	Rusty Wallace	500.00
6	Dale Jarrett	450.00
7	Jeff Burton	300.00
8	Mike Skinner	150.00
9	Dale Earnhardt	800.00

1999 Press Pass Premium 1999 Daytona 500 Winner

	MT
Complete Set (1):	60.00

1999 Press Pass VIP

The regular-sized 50-card set featured gold-foil stamping with a photo of the driver and a shadow image of the driver in the background. The back of the cards contained a photo of the driver on the upper half, with stats on the lower half of the cards. The inserts included Double Take, Rear View Mirror, Lap Leader, Out of the Box, Head Gear (foil), Head Gear (plastic), Triple Gear 3 in 1, Race Used Sheet Metal, Signed Race Used Sheet Metal, Press Pass Signings and Press Pass Gold Signings. Explosives and Laser Explosives parallel the entire 50-card base set.

		MT
	Complete Set (50):	30.00
	Common Driver:	.30
	Common Card:	.15
	Wax Box:	75.00
1	John Andretti	.60
2	Johnny Benson	.30
3	Chad Little	.30
4	Jeff Burton	1.25
5	Ward Burton	.30
6	Derrike Cope	.30
7	Dale Earnhardt	3.00
8	Jeff Gordon	3.00
9	David Green	.30
10	Bobby Hamilton	.30
11	Kenny Irwin	.60
12	Dale Jarrett	1.25
13	Bobby Labonte	1.25
14	Terry Labonte	1.50
15	Sterling Marlin	.60
16	Mark Martin	1.50
17	Jeremy Mayfield	1.25
18	Joe Nemechek	.30
19	Steve Park	.60
20	Ricky Rudd	.60
21	Elliott Sadler	.60
22	Ken Schrader	.30
23	Mike Skinner	.60
24	Jimmy Spencer	.30
25	Tony Stewart	3.00
26	Rusty Wallace	1.50
27	Michael Waltrip	.30
28	Casey Atwood	2.00
29	Dave Blaney	.75
30	Dale Earnhardt Jr.	3.00
31	Jeff Gordon	3.00
32	Jason Keller	.30
33	Matt Kenseth	2.50
34	Randy LaJoie	.30
35	Mark Martin	1.50
36	Mike McLaughlin	.30
37	Elton Sawyer	.30
38	Jimmy Spencer	.30
39	Dick Trickle	.30
40	Jeff Burton	.60
41	GM Goodwrench Svc Plus	1.50
42	Jeff Gordon	1.50
43	Dale Jarrett	.60
44	Bobby Labonte	.60
45	Terry Labonte	.75
46	Mark Martin	.75
47	Jeremy Mayfield	.60
48	Tony Stewart	1.50
49	Rusty Wallace	.75
50	Burton/Martin	.50

1999 Press Pass VIP Explosives

Each of the 50 base cards are paralleled in Explosives. The cards are etched on foil board and seeded 1:1 pack.

	MT
Explosives (X1-X50):	1x-2.5x
Inserted 1:1	

1999 Press Pass VIP Laser Explosive

The 50-card base set is paralleled by Laser Explosives. Laser Explosives were found only in hobby packs and seeded 1:19 packs. The cards are sequentially numbered on the backs to 225.

	MT
Laser Explosives (LX1-LX50):	5x-10x

Production 225 sets
Inserted 1:19 hobby only

1999 Press Pass VIP Double Take

This six-card set allowed collectors to transform their favorite drivers from black and white to color. Cards were inserted 1:29 packs.

		MT
Complete Set (6):		50.00
Common Driver:		8.00
Inserted 1:29		
1	Jeff Gordon	15.00
2	Rusty Wallace	8.00
3	Tony Stewart	15.00
4	Dale Earnhardt Jr.	15.00
5	Terry Labonte	8.00
6	Mark Martin	8.00

1999 Press Pass VIP Head Gear-Foil Card

This nine-card set featured foil-stamped, die-cut, up-close shots of drivers and their helmets. The card backs contained information about the helmet maker, the style of the helmet and the designer of the helmet. The foil cards were inserted 1:10 packs. A special plastic die-cut version paralleled this set, with those cards inserted 1:39.

		MT
Complete Set (9):		30.00
Common Driver:		3.00
Inserted 1:10		
1	Jeff Gordon	8.00
2	Rusty Wallace	4.00
3	Tony Stewart	8.00
4	Dale Earnhardt Jr.	8.00
5	Terry Labonte	4.00
6	Mark Martin	4.00
7	Bobby Labonte	3.00
8	Dale Jarrett	3.00
9	Jeff Burton	3.00

1999 Press Pass VIP Head Gear-Plastic Card

This 10-card set paralleled the foil Head Gear set. The cards were plastic. A Dale Earnhardt Jr. Winston Cup card was added to the plastic version as the tenth card. These cards were inserted 1:39 packs.

	MT
Plastic Version	1.5x-3x
Inserted 1:39	

1999 Press Pass VIP Lap Leader

This set featured nine of the top NASCAR drivers on all plastic, foil-stamped cards. The card fronts contained two pictures of the driver, while the backs contained a brief description of the lap leading accomplishment of the driver. Cards were inserted 1:20 packs.

		MT
Complete Set (9):		70.00
Common Driver:		6.00
Inserted 1:20		
1	Jeff Gordon	15.00
2	Rusty Wallace	8.00
3	Dale Earnhardt	15.00
4	Dale Earnhardt Jr.	15.00
5	Terry Labonte	8.00
6	Mark Martin	8.00
7	Bobby Labonte	6.00
8	Dale Jarrett	6.00
9	Jeff Burton	6.00

1999 Press Pass VIP Out of the Box

This 12-card set featured all-foil, gold-foil-stamped inserts of those drivers who know no limit to their ability on the track. These are found on the average of 1:9 packs.

		MT
Complete Set (12):		40.00
Common Driver:		1.00
Inserted 1:9		
1	Jeff Gordon	8.00
2	Ricky Rudd	1.75
3	GM Goodwrench Svc Plus	8.00
4	Dale Earnhardt Jr.	8.00
5	Terry Labonte	4.00
6	Mark Martin	4.00
7	Bobby Labonte	3.00
8	Dale Jarrett	3.00
9	Jeff Burton	3.00
10	Rusty Wallace	4.00
11	Tony Stewart	8.00
12	Ward Burton	1.00

1999 Press Pass VIP Press Pass Signings

These autographs included 34 of NASCAR's top personalities. Quantities for each personality varied, with 990 cards for Harry Gant being the most. Tony Stewart had the least amount of autographs included, with only 100. The autographs of Jimmy Makar, Larry McReynolds, Todd Parrott and Robin Pemberton were signed in red. Odds of finding a Press Pass Signings card in VIP was 1:60 packs.

	MT
Common Driver:	15.00
Common Card:	10.00
Inserted 1:60	
Bobby Allison/500	15.00
Brett Bodine/400	15.00
Jeff Burton/300	50.00
Ward Burton/250	15.00
Wally Dallenbach/500	15.00
Mike Dillon/250	15.00
Dale Earnhardt/200	200.00
Dale Earnhardt Jr./500	200.00
Jeff Fuller/250	15.00
Harry Gant/900	15.00
Jeff Gordon/200	200.00
David Green/400	15.00
Jeff Green/500	15.00
Bobby Hamilton/475	15.00
Kenny Irwin/250	25.00
Dale Jarrett/175	75.00
Bobby Labonte/250	50.00
Kevin LePage/300	15.00
Mark Martin/150	75.00
Mike McLaughlin/400	15.00
Joe Nemechek/300	15.00
Steve Park/750	25.00
Andy Petree/375	10.00
Ricky Rudd/150	25.00
Elliott Sadler/300	25.00
Elton Sawyer/235	15.00
Ken Schrader/575	15.00
Tony Stewart/100	90.00
Rusty Wallace/275	75.00
Darrell Waltrip/200	25.00
Jimmy Makar/500 RED	10.00
Larry McReynolds/500 RED	10.00
Todd Parrott/500 RED	10.00
Robin Pemberton/500 RED	10.00

1999 Press Pass VIP Press Pass Gold Signings

This was a very rare set that featured autographs of NASCAR Winston Cup drivers and Busch Grand National drivers using a special metallic gold pen. This insert was only included in hobby packs, with an insertion ratio of 1:398 packs.

	MT
Common Driver:	40.00
Inserted 1:398	
Ward Burton/70	40.00
Dale Earnhardt/50	300.00
Bobby Hamilton/100	40.00
Dale Jarrett/25	175.00
Matt Kenseth/40	125.00
Bobby Labonte/65	125.00
Mark Martin/25	175.00
Mike McLaughlin/100	40.00
Tony Stewart/25	200.00
Jeff Gordon/50	300.00

1999 Press Pass VIP Rear View Mirror

This six-card all-foil, die-cut insert featured a unique "rear-view" perspective of the featured NASCAR driver. The insertion ratio was 1:6 packs.

		MT
Complete Set (9):		20.00
Common Driver:		2.00
Inserted 1:6		
1	Jeff Gordon	4.50
2	Dale Jarrett	2.00
3	Dale Earnhardt	4.50
4	Dale Earnhardt Jr.	4.50
5	Jeff Burton	2.00
6	Mark Martin	2.50
7	Terry Labonte	2.50
8	Rusty Wallace	2.50
9	Tony Stewart	4.50

1999 Press Pass VIP Sheet Metal-Race Used

This set featured cards that contained real pieces of the sheet metal used on the cars of eight different NASCAR drivers. The sheet metal cards were inserted 1:364 packs.

		MT
Complete Set (8):		1000.00
Common Driver:		90.00
Inserted 1:364		
1	Rusty Wallace	115.00
2	GM Goodwrench Svc Plus	150.00
3	Jeff Gordon	225.00
4	Terry Labonte	115.00
5	Mark Martin	115.00
6	Tony Stewart	225.00
7	Dale Jarrett	90.00
8	Bobby Labonte	90.00

1999 Press Pass VIP Signed Race-Used Sheet Metal

This set featured cards that contained real pieces of the sheet metal from the cars of five NASCAR drivers, along with their autographs. Tony Stewart's first ever sheet metal card was in this set.

	MT
Complete Set (5):	700.00
Common Driver:	150.00
Dale Earnhardt/68	250.00
Bill Elliott/233	150.00
Dale Jarrett/138	150.00
Terry Labonte/158	200.00
Mark Martin/73	200.00

1999 Press Pass VIP Triple Gear 3 in 1

These scarce inserts were evenly allocated across three Press Pass brands: VIP, Premium and Press Pass. A total of 33 numbered versions for each driver exist, with 11 cards for each driver seeded into each of the three products. The inserts have all three race-used materials on it, which included tire, sheet metal and firesuit. A total of 99 cards were included in Press Pass VIP.

		MT
Complete Set (9):		3500.00
Common Driver:		150.00
1	Terry Labonte	500.00
2	Mark Martin	500.00
3	Jeff Gordon	800.00
4	Bobby Labonte	350.00
5	Rusty Wallace	500.00
6	Dale Jarrett	450.00
7	Jeff Burton	300.00
8	Mike Skinner	150.00
9	Dale Earnhardt	800.00

1999 SP Authentic

This complete 83-card set featured 31 driver cards, 30 car cards, 10 "Class Act," and 11 "Short Print" cards. The base card design contained a picture of the driver with the drivers' name and SP Authentic logo in gold foil stamping. The card backs contain a picture of the driver's car with stats from 1994 to the present. The Short Print cards are numbered to 1000. Overdrive die-cut cards parallel the regular set. Cards 1-72 are numbered to 200 each; cards 73-82 are numbered to the driver's card number; and card #83 (Dale Earnhardt Jr.) is autographed and numbered to his car number. Other inserts included SP Authentics, Sign of the Times, In the Driver's Seat, Cup Challengers and Driving Force.

		MT
Complete Set (83):		300.00
Complete Set (1-72):		45.00
Common Driver (1-72):		.30
Common Card (1-72):		.15
73-82 Print Run 1000		
83 Print Run 500		
Wax Box:		85.00
1	Jeff Gordon	3.00
2	Dale Earnhardt	3.00
3	Tony Stewart	4.00
4	Dale Jarrett	1.50
5	Bobby Labonte	1.00
6	Ken Schrader	.30
7	Jerry Nadeau	.30
8	Mike Skinner	.60
9	Kyle Petty	.60
10	Johnny Benson	.30
11	Kenny Irwin	.60
12	Ward Burton	.30
13	Kevin Lepage	.30
14	Ernie Irvan	.60
15	Jeff Burton	1.00
16	Rusty Wallace	1.50
17	Jeremy Mayfield	1.00
18	Elliott Sadler	.30
19	Bill Elliott	1.50
20	Mark Martin	1.50
21	Michael Waltrip	.30
22	Robert Pressley	.30
23	Ricky Rudd	.60
24	Geoffrey Bodine	.30
25	John Andretti	.60
26	Darrell Waltrip	.60
27	Steve Park	.60
28	Chad Little	.30
29	Bobby Hamilton	.30
30	Dale Earnhardt Jr.	3.00
31	Jason Keller	.30
32	Kenny Irwin's Car	.30
33	Geoffrey Bodine's Car	.15
34	Robert Pressley's Car	.15
35	Kevin Lepage's Car	.15
36	Tony Stewart's Car	2.00
37	Dale Earnhardt Jr.'s Car	1.50
38	Ernie Irvan's Car	.30
39	Jeff Burton's Car	.50
40	Chad Little's Car	.15
41	Rusty Wallace's Car	.75
42	Steve Park's Car	.30
43	Mike Skinner's Car	.30
44	Jeremy Mayfield's Car	.50
45	Elliott Sadler's Car	.15
46	Bill Elliott's Car	.75
47	Darrell Waltrip's Car	.30
48	John Andretti's Car	.30
49	Kyle Petty's Car	.30
50	Johnny Benson's Car	.15
51	Jeff Gordon's Car	1.50
52	Dale Jarrett's Car	.75
53	Dale Earnhardt's Car	1.50
54	Terry Labonte's Car	.75
55	Bobby Labonte's Car	.50
56	Jerry Nadeau's Car	.15
57	Ricky Rudd's Car	.30
58	Bobby Hamilton's Car	.15
59	Michael Waltrip's Car	.15
60	Ken Schrader's Car	.15
61	Mark Martin's Car	.75
62	Mark Martin	1.50
63	Darrell Waltrip	.60
64	Rusty Wallace	1.50
65	Jeff Gordon	3.00
66	Dale Earnhardt Jr.	3.00
67	Bobby Labonte	1.00
68	Jeremy Mayfield	1.00
69	Terry Labonte	1.50
70	Jeff Burton	1.00
71	Dale Jarrett	1.50
72	Dale Earnhardt Jr./ Checklist	1.50
73	Bobby Labonte	10.00
74	Ward Burton	8.00
75	Jeremy Mayfield	8.00
76	Mark Martin	12.00
77	Rusty Wallace	12.00
78	Jeff Burton	10.00
79	Dale Earnhardt	25.00
80	Dale Jarrett	10.00
81	Tony Stewart	25.00
82	Jeff Gordon	25.00
83	Dale Earnhardt Jr.	150.00

1999 SP Authentic Overdrive

Overdrive was a die-cut collection of cards that paralleled the regular set. Cards 1-72 were numbered to 200 each; cards 73-82 were numbered to the driver's card number; and card #83 (Dale Earnhardt Jr.) was autographed and numbered to his car number (3).

	MT
Overdrive (1-72)	5x-12x
Production 200 Sets	
Overdrive (73-83)	5x-25x
#'d to card number	

1999 SP Authentic Cup Challengers

This collection of 10-cards showcased the top 10 contenders for the Winston Cup title. They were inserted 1:23 packs.

		MT
Complete Set (10):		65.00
Common Driver:		1.50
Inserted 1:23		
1	Jeff Gordon	15.00
2	Dale Jarrett	6.00
3	Jeff Burton	6.00
4	Rusty Wallace	8.00
5	Mark Martin	8.00
6	Jeremy Mayfield	3.00
7	Ward Burton	6.00
8	Bobby Labonte	6.00
9	Tony Stewart	20.00
10	Elliott Sadler	1.50

1999 SP Authentic Driving Force

This 11-card set featured the 11 drivers that bring people to the races and help fill the seats. These were inserted 1:11 packs.

		MT
Complete Set (11):		45.00
Common Driver:		.75
Inserted 1:11		
1	Bobby Labonte	8.00
2	Terry Labonte	4.00
3	Jeremy Mayfield	1.50
4	Mark Martin	4.00
5	Rusty Wallace	4.00
6	Jeff Burton	3.00
7	Dale Earnhardt	8.00
8	Jeff Gordon	8.00
9	Dale Earnhardt Jr.	10.00
10	Elliott Sadler	.75
11	Tony Stewart	10.00

1999 SP Authentic In The Driver's Seat

This 10-card set contained cards of drivers who are shaping today's Winston Cup circuit. They were inserted 1:4 packs. There is no card #6, as it was never released.

		MT
Complete Set (10):		25.00
Common Driver:		2.00
Inserted 1:4		
1	Dale Earnhardt	6.00
2	Jeremy Mayfield	2.00
3	Rusty Wallace	3.00
4	Tony Stewart	6.00
5	Bobby Labonte	2.00
7	Dale Earnhardt Jr.	6.00
8	Mark Martin	3.00
9	Jeff Burton	2.00
10	Jeff Gordon	6.00

1999 SP Authentic Sign of the Times

This 26-card set featured cards displaying an authentic autograph of one of NASCAR's top drivers. Cards were inserted 1:11 packs.

		MT
Common Driver		10.00
Inserted 1:11		
JA	John Andretti	20.00
JB	Johnny Benson	10.00
GB	Geoffrey Bodine	10.00
JB	Jeff Burton	40.00
WB	Ward Burton	20.00
DE JR	Dale Earnhardt Jr.	200.00
DE	Dale Earnhardt	175.00
BE	Bill Elliott	50.00
JG	Jeff Gordon	175.00
BH	Bobby Hamilton	10.00
EI	Ernie Irvan	20.00
DJ	Dale Jarrett	40.00
BL	Bobby Labonte	40.00
TL	Terry Labonte	80.00
KL	Kevin Lepage	10.00
CL	Chad Little	10.00
SM	Sterling Marlin	20.00
MM	Mark Martin	80.00
JM	Jeremy Mayfield	30.00
JN	Jerry Nadeau	10.00
SP	Steve Park	20.00
KP	Kyle Petty	20.00
KS	Ken Schrader	10.00
MS	Mike Skinner	20.00
TS	Tony Stewart	100.00
RW	Rusty Wallace	80.00

1999 Upper Deck Road To The Cup

This 90-card regular set was comprised of 30 driver cards, 30 car cards, 15 "Fan Favorites" cards, 14 "Happy Hour" cards and one checklist card. The card fronts contain one picture with a small border, the Upper Deck logo, the driver's name and the Road to the Cup logo stamped in blue foil. The inserts include NASCAR Chronicles, A Day in the Life (with Jeff Gordon), Upper Deck Profiles, Road to the Cup, NASCAR Signature Collection, Tires of Daytona, Tires of Daytona-Autographed and Die-Cast Redemption. The Die-Cast Redemptions cards could be redeemed for one of 13 different NASCAR Winston Cup (1:43) scale model die-cast cars from Mattel. These cards were inserted 1:950 packs.

		MT
Complete Set (90):		25.00
Common Driver:		.20
Common Card:		.10
Wax Box:		60.00
1	Kenny Irwin	.40
2	Dale Jarrett	1.00
3	Terry Labonte	1.00
4	Geoff Bodine	.20
5	John Andretti	.40
6	Tony Stewart	2.00
7	Ricky Rudd	.40
8	Jeremy Mayfield	.75
9	Chad Little	.20
10	Darrell Waltrip	.40
11	Bobby Labonte	.75
12	Ken Schrader	.20
13	Sterling Marlin	.40
14	Mike Skinner	.40
15	Kevin Lepage	.20
16	Jeff Burton	.75
17	Elliott Sadler	.20
18	Mark Martin	1.00
19	Bill Elliott	1.00
20	Steve Park	.40
21	Jerry Nadeau	.20
22	Rusty Wallace	1.00
23	Bobby Hamilton	.20
24	Jeff Gordon	2.00
25	Randy LaJoie	.20
26	Dale Earnhardt	2.00
27	Ernie Irvan	.40
28	Johnny Benson	.20
29	Kyle Petty	.40
30	Dale Earnhardt Jr.	3.00
31	Jeremy Mayfield's car	.40
32	Terry Labonte's car	.50
33	John Andretti's car	.20
34	Kyle Petty's car	.20
35	Darrell Waltrip's car	.20
36	Geoff Bodine's car	.10
37	Dale Earnhardt Jr.'s car	1.50
38	Bobby Labonte's car	.40
39	Ken Schrader's car	.10
40	Johnny Benson's car	.10
41	Sterling Marlin's car	.20
42	Ernie Irvan's car	.20
43	Jeff Gordon's car	1.00
44	Mike Skinner's car	.20
45	Kevin Lepage's car	.10
46	Jeff Burton's car	.40
47	Ricky Rudd's car	.20
48	Dale Jarrett's car	.50
49	Kenny Irwin's car	.20
50	Randy LaJoie's car	.10
51	Elliott Sadler's car	.10
52	Steve Park's car	.20
53	Chad Little's car	.10
54	Jerry Nadeau's car	.10
55	Bobby Hamilton's car	.10
56	Bill Elliott's car	.50
57	Mark Martin's car	.50
58	Tony Stewart's car	1.00
59	Rusty Wallace's car	.50
60	Dale Earnhardt's car	1.00
61	Jeff Gordon	1.50
62	Terry Labonte	.75
63	Dale Jarrett	.75
64	Darrell Waltrip	.30
65	Bill Elliott	.75
66	Tony Stewart	1.50
67	Dale Earnhardt Jr.	1.50
68	Ernie Irvan	.30
69	Kyle Petty	.30
70	Bobby Labonte	.50
71	Kenny Irwin	.30
72	Jeremy Mayfield	.50
73	Ricky Rudd	.30
74	Mark Martin	.75
75	Rusty Wallace	.75
76	Jeremy Mayfield	.75
77	Jeff Gordon	2.00
78	Mark Martin	1.00
79	Kenny Irwin	.40
80	Rusty Wallace	1.00
81	Dale Jarrett	1.00
82	Bobby Labonte	.75
83	Jerry Nadeau	.20
84	Tony Stewart	2.00
85	Ernie Irvan	.40
86	Steve Park	.40
87	Kevin Lepage	.20
88	Elliott Sadler	.20
89	Terry Labonte	1.00
90	Dale Earnhardt Jr.	1.50

1999 Upper Deck Road To The Cup Day in the Life

This 10-card set featured the details of a day in the life of NASCAR star Jeff Gordon. The cards were inserted 1:6 packs.

	MT
Complete Set (10):	12.00
Common Card:	1.25
Inserted 1:6	

1999 Upper Deck Road To The Cup NASCAR Chronicles

This 20-card insert set captured the journeys taken by the top drivers on the NASCAR Winston Cup circuit. Cards were inserted 1:2 packs.

		MT
Complete Set (20):		30.00
Common Driver:		.60
Inserted 1:2		
1	Bobby Labonte	2.25
2	Jeff Gordon	6.00
3	Rusty Wallace	3.00
4	Terry Labonte	3.00
5	Kyle Petty	1.25
6	Kevin Lepage	.60
7	Jeff Burton	2.25
8	Jeremy Mayfield	2.25
9	Elliott Sadler	.60
10	Mark Martin	3.00
11	Dale Earnhardt	6.00
12	Kenny Irwin	1.25
13	Bill Elliott	3.00
14	Dale Earnhardt Jr.	7.00
15	John Andretti	1.25
16	Ricky Rudd	1.25
17	Dale Jarrett	3.00
18	Jerry Nadeau	.60
19	Tony Stewart	3.00
20	Steve Park	1.25

1999 Upper Deck Road To The Cup Road to the Cup

This 10-card set featured 10 drivers that were picked to compete for the NASCAR Winston Cup Championship in 1999. The set came in three different levels. Level one was seeded 1:12 packs. Level 2 was a die-cut parallel of the 10-card set and featured silver light F/X technology. Level 2 was inserted 1:23. Level 3 was a die-cut parallel featuring gold light F/X technology. Level 3 was inserted 1:48.

		MT
Complete Level 1 Set (10):		40.00
Common Driver:		2.50
Inserted 1:12		
Level 2:		.5x-1.5x
Inserted 1:23		
Level 3:		1x-2.5x
Inserted 1:48		
1	Jeff Gordon	12.00
2	Mark Martin	3.00
3	Rusty Wallace	6.00
4	Terry Labonte	6.00
5	Bobby Labonte	4.00
6	Jeremy Mayfield	4.00
7	Jeff Burton	4.00
8	Dale Jarrett	6.00
9	Ricky Rudd	2.50
10	Dale Earnhardt Jr.	15.00

1999 Upper Deck Road To The Cup Signature Collection

This 20-card set included authentic autographs from NASCAR's top Winston Cup drivers. Odds of finding one of these cards was 1:999 packs.

		MT
Complete Set (10):		1300.00
Common Driver:		60.00
Inserted 1:999		
JB	Jeff Burton	100.00
DE	Dale Earnhardt	300.00
DE Jr.	Dale Earnhardt Jr.	300.00
JG	Jeff Gordon	300.00
DJ	Dale Jarrett	125.00
MM	Mark Martin	150.00
SP	Steve Park	60.00
KP	Kyle Petty	60.00
TS	Tony Stewart	250.00
RW	Rusty Wallace	150.00

1999 Upper Deck Road To The Cup Tires of Daytona

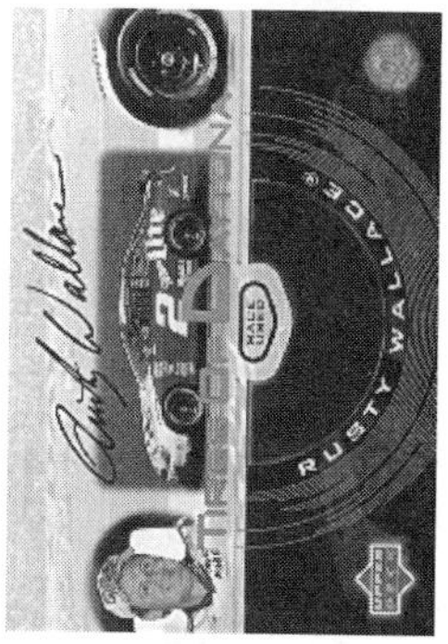

This five-card set featured cards that contained an authentic piece of a race-used tire from a Winston Cup car that actually raced at the 1999 Daytona 500. The pieces of tire came directly from Jeff Gordon, Rusty Wallace, Jeremy Mayfield, Mark Martin and Jeff Burton. Chances of finding one of the cards was 1:525 packs.

		MT
Complete Set (9):		400.00
Common Driver:		50.00
Inserted 1:525		
1	Jeff Gordon	150.00
2	Rusty Wallace	75.00
3	Jeremy Mayfield	50.00
4	Mark Martin	75.00
5	Jeff Burton	50.00

1999 Upper Deck Road To The Cup UD Profiles

This 15-card set provided an up-close look at 15 of the top drivers on the NASCAR Winston Cup tour. The insertion ratio was 1:11 packs.

		MT
Complete Set (15):		90.00
Common Driver:		1.50
Inserted 1:11		
1	Jeremy Mayfield	5.25
2	Terry Labonte	7.00
3	Dale Earnhardt	14.00
4	Jerry Nadeau	1.50
5	Dale Jarrett	7.00
6	Steve Park	2.75
7	Mark Martin	7.00
8	Bobby Labonte	5.25
9	Kenny Irwin	2.75
10	Dale Earnhardt Jr.	15.00
11	Tony Stewart	14.00
12	Elliott Sadler	1.50
13	Rusty Wallace	7.00
14	Jeff Burton	5.25
15	Jeff Gordon	14.00

1999 Upper Deck Victory Circle

The 89-card base set is comprised of 40 driver cards, 34 car cards, two distinct subsets: "NASCAR Newsstand" (10) and "Stars of Tomorrow" (4) and a checklist. The card fronts contained a picture of the driver or car with a silver border on the sides. The card backs also contained a photo along with drivers statistics.

		MT
Complete Set (89):		25.00
Common Driver:		.20
Common Card:		.10
Wax Box:		65.00
1	Dale Jarrett	1.00
2	Derrike Cope	.20
3	Jeff Gordon	2.00
4	Ricky Rudd	.25
5	Bobby Labonte	.75
6	Mark Martin	1.00
7	Jeremy Mayfield	.75
8	Terry Labonte	1.00
9	Rusty Wallace	1.00
10	Geoff Bodine	.20
11	Ward Burton	.20
12	Brett Bodine	.20
13	Jeff Green	.20
14	Dale Earnhardt Jr.	2.25
15	Jerry Nadeau	.20
16	Kenny Irwin	.40
17	Bill Elliott	1.00
18	Ernie Irvan	.40
19	Darrell Waltrip	.40
20	John Andretti	.40
21	Kyle Petty	.40
22	Steve Park	.40
23	Jeff Burton	.75
24	Ken Schrader	.20
25	Johnny Benson	.20
26	Dave Marcis	.20
27	Wally Dallenbach	.20
28	Michael Waltrip	.20
29	Bobby Hamilton	.20
30	Sterling Marlin	.40
31	Chad Little	.20
32	Dick Trickle	.20
33	Joe Nemechek	.20
34	Mike Skinner	.40
35	Kenny Wallace	.20
36	Robert Pressley	.20
37	Steve Grissom	.20
38	Kevin Lepage	.20
39	Mike Wallace	.20
40	Rick Mast	.20
41	Jeff Gordon's Car	1.00
42	Rusty Wallace's Car	.50
43	Bill Elliott's Car	.50
44	Johnny Benson's Car	.10
45	Mark Martin's Car	.50
46	Sterling Marlin's Car	.20
47	Darrell Waltrip's Car	.20
48	Jerry Nadeau's Car	.10
49	Terry Labonte's Car	.50
50	Dale Earnhardt Jr.'s Car	1.00
51	Ernie Irvan's Car	.20
52	Dale Jarrett's Car	.50
53	Jeff Green's Car	.10
54	Jeff Burton's Car	.30
55	Geoff Bodine's Car	.10
56	Chad Little's Car	.10
57	Brett Bodine's Car	.10
58	Jeremy Mayfield's Car	.30
59	Steve Park's Car	.20
60	Kenny Irwin's Car	.20
61	Derrike Cope's Car	.10
62	Kevin Lepage's Car	.10
63	Bobby Hamilton's Car	.10
64	Ken Schrader's Car	.10
65	Kyle Petty's Car	.20
66	John Andretti's Car	.20
67	Ricky Rudd's Car	.20
68	Bobby Labonte's Car	.30
69	Michael Waltrip's Car	.10
70	Joe Nemechek's Car	.10
71	Kenny Wallace's Car	.10
72	Mike Skinner's Car	.20
73	Robert Pressley's Car	.10
74	Ward Burton's Car	.10
75	Mark Martin	1.00
76	Jeff Gordon	2.00
77	Jeremy Mayfield	.75
78	Rusty Wallace	1.00
79	Mark Martin	1.00
80	Jeff Gordon	2.00
81	Rusty Wallace	1.00
82	Steve Park	.50
83	Dale Earnhardt	2.00
84	Jeff Gordon	2.00
85	Dale Earnhardt Jr.	2.25
86	Elliott Sadler	.20
87	Mike McLaughlin	.20
88	Tony Stewart	1.00
89	Rusty Wallace	.50

1999 Upper Deck Victory Circle Exclusives Parallel

This set paralleled the first 89-cards of the base set and was hobby exclusive. The card fronts contained a gold border on the sides and the Exclusives logo. Each card was sequentially numbered to 99.

	MT
Exclusives:	20x-40x
Production 99 sets	

1999 Upper Deck Victory Circle Income Statement

This 15-card set featured die-cut cards of the NASCAR drivers who received some of the largest single day payouts from the 1998 season. The cards were inserted 1:2 packs.

		MT
Complete Set (15):		25.00
Common Driver:		.50
Inserted 1:2		
1	Jeff Gordon	5.00
2	Bobby Labonte	1.75
3	Bill Elliott	2.50
4	Rusty Wallace	2.50
5	Jeff Burton	1.75
6	Kenny Irwin	1.00
7	Jeremy Mayfield	1.75
8	Dale Jarrett	2.50
9	Ken Schrader	.50
10	Mark Martin	2.50
11	Ricky Rudd	1.00
12	John Andretti	1.00
13	Ernie Irvan	1.00
14	Terry Labonte	2.50
15	Dale Earnhardt Jr.	7.00

1999 Upper Deck Victory Circle Magic Numbers

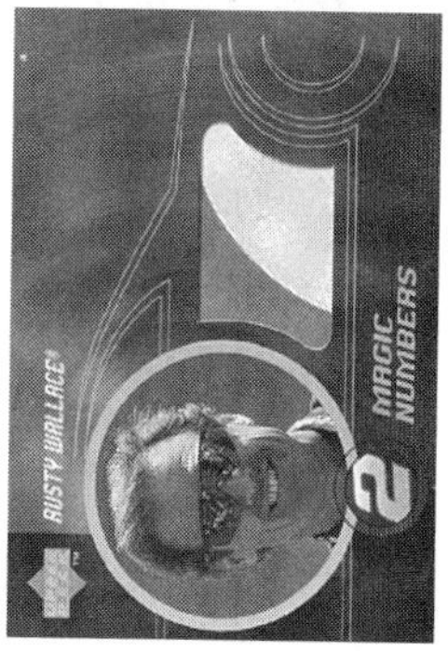

This insert featured cards that contained actual race-used numbers peeled right off the side of the cars driven by Mark Martin, Bobby Labonte, Dale Jarrett and Rusty Wallace. They were inserted 1:999 packs. There was also an autographed version in which cards were signed by the depicted driver and hand-numbered to the driver's car number.

		MT
Complete Set (4):		400.00
Common Driver:		120.00
Inserted 1:999		
1	Mark Martin	125.00
2	Bobby Labonte	120.00
3	Dale Jarrett	120.00
4	Rusty Wallace	125.00

1999 Upper Deck Victory Circle Signature Collection

This insert featured authentic signatures from 20 of NASCAR's top superstars. The cards were inserted 1:100 packs.

		MT
Complete Set (20):		1000.
Common Driver:		25.00
Inserted 1:100		
JA	John Andretti	30.00
JB	Jeff Burton	60.00
DE	Dale Earnhardt	150.00
DEj	Dale Earnhardt Jr.	150.00
JG	Jeff Gordon	150.00
EI	Ernie Irvan	25.00
KI	Kenny Irwin	30.00
DL	Dale Jarrett	75.00
BL	Bobby Labonte	60.00
TL	Terry Labonte	75.00
MM	Mark Martin	75.00
JM	Jeremy Mayfield	60.00
JN	Jerry Nadeau	25.00
SP	Steve Park	30.00
KP	Kyle Petty	30.00
RR	Ricky Rudd	30.00
ES	Elliott Sadler	25.00
RW	Rusty Wallace	75.00
DW	Darrell Waltrip	30.00
MW	Michael Waltrip	25.00

1999 Upper Deck Victory Circle Speed Zone

This set featured cards highlighting the fastest laps recorded during the 1998 NASCAR season. The card fronts included a picture of the car, with a picture of the driver on the back. They were inserted 1:2 packs.

		MT
Complete Set (15):		25.00
Common Driver:		.50
Inserted 1:2		
1	Bobby Labonte	1.75
2	Mark Martin	2.50
3	Jeff Gordon	5.00
4	Ernie Irvan	1.00
5	Bill Elliott	2.50
6	Rusty Wallace	2.50
7	Jeff Burton	1.75
8	Dale Jarrett	2.50
9	Terry Labonte	2.50
10	Dale Earnhardt Jr.	7.00
11	Steve Park	1.00
12	Jeremy Mayfield	1.75
13	John Andretti	1.00
14	Bobby Hamilton	.50
15	Ken Schrader	.50

1999 Upper Deck Victory Circle Track Masters

This 15-card insert contained die-cut cards of the top NASCAR drivers and their trademark skills that made them the ones to beat. The fronts contained a picture of the driver, while the backs contained a picture of the car. The insertion ratio was 1:11.

		MT
Complete Set (15):		80.00
Common Driver:		1.50
Inserted 1:11		
1	Jeff Gordon	15.00
2	Dale Jarrett	7.50
3	Ernie Irvan	3.00
4	Sterling Marlin	3.00
5	Rusty Wallace	7.50
6	Mark Martin	7.50
7	Jeff Burton	5.50
8	Bobby Hamilton	1.50
9	Terry Labonte	7.50
10	Jeremy Mayfield	5.50
11	Bobby Labonte	5.50
12	Bill Elliott	7.50
13	Darrell Waltrip	3.00
14	John Andretti	3.00
15	Dale Earnhardt Jr.	20.00

1999 Upper Deck Victory Circle Victory Circle

Capturing the top Winston Cup finishes of 1998, this nine-card set was inserted 1:23 packs. The cards feature Ionix technology, with the Victory Circle logo prominently displayed.

		MT
Complete Set (9):		80.00
Common Driver:		7.50
Inserted 1:23		
1	Dale Earnhardt	20.00
2	Bobby Labonte	7.50
3	Terry Labonte	10.00
4	Jeff Burton	7.50
5	Mark Martin	10.00
6	Dale Jarrett	10.00
7	Jeremy Mayfield	7.50
8	Jeff Gordon	20.00
9	Rusty Wallace	10.00

1999 Wheels

This 100-card base set featured Winston Cup drivers, Busch Grand National drivers, crew chiefs, cars, teams, Super Truck and Top Prospects cards. The card fronts contained the driver's name in silver foil stamping and the Wheels logo in the upper right corner. The card backs contained a picture of the driver, team information and career stats. Insert sets included Flag Chasers Daytona Seven, Wheels Authentic Autographs, Custom Shop PFP, Circuit Breakers, Dialed In and High Groove. Also included is the set-within-a-set, Runnin' N Gunnin'. This is a 36- card set printed in two different versions, traditional paper (1:1 pack) and foil (1:12). Golden and Solos parallel the entire base set. The Golden parallel contained a gold foil stamp and was comprised of 50 cards for each of the 100 base cards. They were hobby exclusive and inserted 1:77. The Solos parallel contained one card for each of 100 base cards, and featured a unique foil stamping. They were hobby exclusive and inserted 1:192.

		MT
Complete Set (100):		25.00
Common Driver:		.20
Common Card:		.10
Wax Box:		60.00
1	John Andretti	.40
2	Johnny Benson	.20
3	Geoffrey Bodine	.20
4	Jeff Burton	.75
5	Ward Burton	.20
6	Derrike Cope	.20
7	Kenny Wallace	.20
8	Wally Dallenbach	.20
9	Dale Earnhardt	2.00
10	Bill Elliott	1.00
11	David Green	.20
12	Jeff Gordon	2.00
13	Bobby Hamilton	.20
14	Ernie Irvan	.40
15	Kenny Irwin	.40
16	Dale Jarrett	1.00
17	Bobby Labonte	.75
18	Terry Labonte	1.00
19	Kevin Lepage	.20
20	Chad Little	.20
21	Sterling Marlin	.40
22	Mark Martin	1.00
23	Jeremy Mayfield	.75
24	Ted Musgrave	.20
25	Jerry Nadeau	.20
26	Joe Nemechek	.20
27	Steve Park	.40
28	Ricky Rudd	.40
29	Elliott Sadler	.40
30	Ken Schrader	.20
31	Mike Skinner	.40
32	Jimmy Spencer	.20
33	Tony Stewart	2.00
34	Rusty Wallace	1.00
35	Darrell Waltrip	.40
36	Michael Waltrip	.20
37	Casey Atwood	1.50
38	Todd Bodine	.20
39	Dale Earnhardt Jr.	2.50
40	Tim Fedewa	.20
41	Jeff Fuller	.20
42	Jeff Gordon	2.00
43	Jeff Green	.20
44	Dave Blaney	.40
45	Jason Keller	.20
46	Matt Kenseth	2.00
47	Randy Lajoie	.20
48	Mark Martin	1.00
49	Mike McLaughlin	.20
50	Elton Sawyer	.20
51	Jimmy Spencer	.20
52	Kevin Grubb	.20
53	Mark Green	.20
54	Glenn Allen	.20
55	Rusty Wallace's car	.50
56	Dale Earnhardt's car	1.00
57	Terry Labonte's car	.50
58	Mark Martin's car	.50
59	Bobby Labonte's car	.40
60	Jeff Gordon's car	1.00
61	Dale Jarrett's car	.50
62	Bill Elliott's car	.50
63	Jeff Burton's car	.40
64	Derrike Cope's car	.10
65	Dale Earnhardt, Jr.'s car	1.25
66	Mike Skinner's car	.20
67	Joe Nemechek's car	.10
68	Tony Stewart's car	1.00
69	Wally Dallenbach's car	.10
70	Ricky Rudd's car	.20
71	Chad Little's car	.10
72	Jeff Gordon's car	1.00
73	Robin Pemberton	.10
74	Rusty Wallace	1.00
75	Roger Penske	.10
76	Jimmy Makar	.10
77	Bobby Labonte	.75
78	Joe Gibbs	.10
79	Todd Parrott	.10
80	Dale Jarrett	1.00
81	Robert Yates	.10
82	Larry McReynolds	.10
83	Tony Furr	.10
84	Frank Stoddard	.10
85	Greg Zipadelli	.10
86	Jeff Hammond	.10
87	Sammy Johns	.10
88	Kevin Harvick	.20
89	Jay Sauter	.20
90	Jack Sprague	.20
91	Greg Biffle	.20
92	Mike Bliss	.20
93	Mike Stefanik	.20
94	Dave Blaney	.40
95	Tony Stewart	2.00
96	Dale Earnhardt Jr.	2.50
97	Elliott Saddler	.40
98	Matt Kenseth	2.00
99	Casey Atwood	2.00
100	Justin Labonte	.20

1999 Wheels Autographs

	MT
Common Card:	15.00
Common Driver:	25.00
Inserted 1:240	
Glenn Allen/300	25.00
John Andretti/100	25.00
Johnny Benson/200	25.00
Jeff Buice/250	15.00
Jeff Burton/150	40.00
Derrike Cope/295	25.00
Dale Earnhardt Jr./75 Redemption	250.00
Jeff Fuller/350	25.00
Jeff Gordon/75 Redemption	250.00
Dale Jarrett/100	80.00
Bobby Labonte/241	80.00
Terry Labonte/250	70.00
Kevin LePage/250	25.00
Chad Little/350	25.00
Mark Martin/100	125.00
Mike McLaughlin/200	25.00
Todd Parrott/500	15.00
Robert Pressley/196	25.00
Ricky Rudd/100	40.00
Kenny Schrader/199	25.00
Tony Stewart/350	125.00
9oMichael Waltrip/200	25.00

1999 Wheels Circuit Breaker

This nine-card set featured the top record-setters of NASCAR. The cards were printed on plastic and foil stamped. The card fronts included a picture of the driver, with a smaller picture of the driver's car on the lower portion of the card. The card backs included a description of the driver's accomplishments. These were seeded 1:24 packs.

		MT
Complete Set (9):		60.00
Common Driver:		4.00
Inserted 1:24		
1	Terry Labonte	10.00
2	Bobby Labonte	7.50
3	Dale Earnhardt	20.00
4	Mark Martin	10.00
5	Jeff Gordon	20.00
6	Ricky Rudd	4.00
7	Rusty Wallace	10.00
8	Dale Jarrett	10.00
9	Mark Martin (BGN)	10.00

1999 Wheels Custom Shop

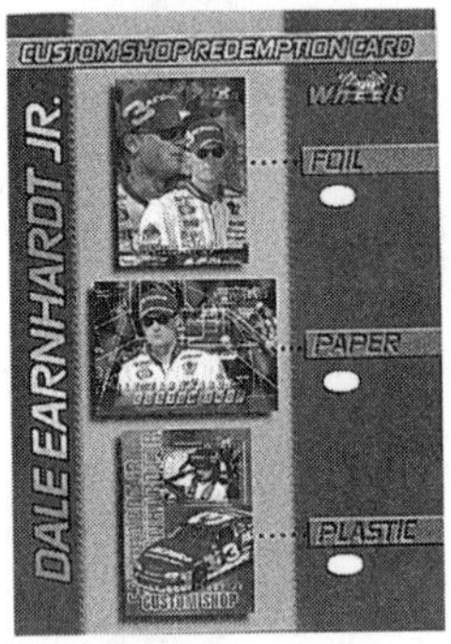

The Custom Shop redemption cards were seeded 1:192 packs and gave collectors a choice as to what material and design the card they got back would be. The material choices included plastic, foil and paper. Five different drivers were included in this insert.

		MT
Complete Set (5):		250.00
Common Driver:		50.00
Inserted 1:192		
1	Bobby Labonte	50.00
2	Jeff Gordon	75.00
3	Dale Earnhardt Jr.	75.00
4	Mark Martin	60.00
5	Rusty Wallace	60.00

1999 Wheels Dialed In

This nine-card set featured all-foil, die-cut, micro-etched cards of the top NASCAR drivers. Each card included a picture of the driver, with the top of the card rounded in the shape of a tachometer. They were seeded 1:12 packs.

	MT
Complete Set (9):	40.00
Common Driver:	3.00
Inserted 1:12	
1 Jeff Gordon	10.00
2 Rusty Wallace	5.00
3 GM Goodwrench Svc Plus	5.00
4 Dale Earnhardt Jr.	12.00
5 Terry Labonte	5.00
6 Mark Martin	5.00
7 Bobby Labonte	3.00
8 Dale Jarrett	5.00
9 Jeff Burton	3.00

1999 Wheels Flag Chasers - Daytona Seven

This progressive insert featured pieces of authentic flags used at the 1999 Daytona 500 embedded in the cards of five different drivers. The overall odds of finding a Flag Chasers card in Wheels was 1:565 packs. The checkered flag was the most difficult to find, inserted 1:6,562. The blue/yellow flag was inserted 1:5,250. The green and red flags were inserted 1:3,634, with the yellow, black, and white flags inserted 1:3,424.

	MT
Common Driver:	125.00
Black Flag Inserted 1:3,424	
White Flag Inserted 1:3,424	
Yellow Flag Inserted 1:3,424	
Green Flag Inserted 1:3,634	
Red Flag Inserted 1:3,634	
Blue-Yellow Flag Inserted 1:5,250	
Checkered Flag Inserted 1:6,562	
Black, White & Yellow Flag Prices Listed	
Green & Red Flag Cards:	.5x-1.25x
Blue-Yellow Flag Cards:	1x-1.75x
Checkered Flag Cards:	1.25x-2x
1 Jeff Gordon	200.00
2 Dale Earnhardt	200.00
3 Rusty Wallace	125.00
4 Mark Martin	150.00
5 Terry Labonte	125.00

1999 Wheels High Groove

This nine-card set featured die-cut cards of Winston Cup drivers that have excelled at different tracks on the Winston Cup circuit. The cards were cut in the general shape of the depicted track and included a picture of the driver and the car he drove. These were inserted 1:8 packs.

	MT
Complete Set (9):	30.00
Common Driver:	2.00
Inserted 1:8	
1 Bobby Labonte	3.75
2 Ernie Irvan	2.00
3 Jeff Gordon	10.00
4 Dale Earnhardt's car	5.00
5 Mark Martin	5.00
6 Rusty Wallace	5.00
7 Jeff Gordon	10.00
8 Dale Jarrett	5.00
9 Mark Martin	5.00

1999 Wheels Runnin & Gunnin

This 36-card set was die-cut, came in two versions and featured the top drivers in NASCAR. The two versions included traditional paper seeded one in every pack, and a foil version seeded 1:12 packs. The card fronts included a picture of the driver and a picture of the driver's car.

	MT
Complete Set (35):	40.00
Common Driver:	.50
Inserted 1:1	
Foil Version:	2.5x-6x
Inserted 1:12	
1 Mark Martin	3.00
2 Rusty Wallace	3.00
3 Dale Earnhardt's car	3.00
4 Terry Labonte	3.00
5 Dale Jarrett	3.00
6 Bill Elliott	3.00
7 Mike Skinner	1.25
8 Bobby Labonte	2.25
9 Jeff Gordon	6.00
10 Michael Waltrip	.50
11 Jeff Burton	2.25
12 Ernie Irvan	1.25
13 Dale Earnhardt Jr.	6.00
14 Ward Burton	.50
15 Wally Dallenbach	.50
16 Ricky Rudd	1.25
17 Jeremy Mayfield	2.25
18 Tony Stewart	6.00
19 Johnny Benson	.50
20 Geoffrey Bodine	.50
21 Derrike Cope	.50
22 Bobby Hamilton	.50
23 Matt Kenseth	4.00
24 Chad Little	.50
25 Sterling Marlin	1.25
26 David Green	.50
27 Ted Musgrave	.50
28 Joe Nemechek	.50
29 Jeff Gordon - BGN	6.00
30 Ken Schrader	.50
31 Darrell Waltrip	1.25
32 John Andretti	1.25
33 Jimmy Spencer	.50
34 Elliott Sadler	1.25
35 Kenny Irwin	1.25

1999 Wheels High Gear

This 72-card base set was stamped with a double-etch foil, printed on premium 24-point stock. The product was highlighted by the Flag Chasers, Custom Shop, Wheels Authentic Signatures, Gear Shifters, Hot Streaks, Top Tier and Man & Machine inserts. First Gear and MPH parallel the complete base set.

	MT
Complete Set (72):	25.00
Common Driver:	.20
Wax Box:	65.00
1 Jeff Gordon	2.00
2 Mark Martin	1.00
3 Dale Jarrett	1.00
4 Rusty Wallace	1.00
5 Jeff Burton	.75
6 Bobby Labonte	.75
7 Jeremy Mayfield	.75
8 Dale Earnhardt	2.00
9 Terry Labonte	1.00
10 Bobby Hamilton	.20
11 John Andretti	.40
12 Ken Schrader	.20
13 Sterling Marlin	.40
14 Jimmy Spencer	.20
15 Chad Little	.20
16 Ward Burton	.20
17 Michael Waltrip	.20
18 Bill Elliott	1.00
19 Ernie Irvan	.40
20 Johnny Benson	.20
21 Mike Skinner	.40
22 Ricky Rudd	.40
23 Robert Pressley	.20
24 Kenny Irwin	.40
25 Geoffrey Bodine	.20
26 Joe Nemechek	.20
27 Steve Park	.40
28 #2 Rusty Wallace's car	.50
29 #3 Dale Earnhardt's car	1.00
30 #5 Terry Labonte's car	.50
31 #6 Mark Martin's car	.50
32 #18 Bobby Labonte's car	.35
33 #24 Jeff Gordon's car	1.00
34 #88 Dale Jarrett's car	.50
35 #94 Bill Elliott's car	.50
36 #99 Jeff Burton's car	.35
37 Dale Earnhardt Jr.	2.00
38 Matt Kenseth	1.50
39 Mike McLaughlin	.20
40 Randy LaJoie	.20
41 Mark Martin	1.00
42 Jason Jarrett	.25
43 Michael Waltrip	.25
44 Tim Fedewa	.25
45 Tony Stewart	1.50
46 Jeff Gordon	2.00
47 Bill Elliott	1.00
48 #3 Dale Earnhardt	2.00
49 Kenny Irwin	.40
50 Mark Martin	1.00
51 Jeff Burton	.75
52 Ray Evernham	.20
53 Bobby Hamilton	.20
54 Jeff Gordon	1.00
55 Ward Burton	.20
56 Geoffrey Bodine	.25
57 Darrell Waltrip	.40
58 Jeff Gordon	2.00
59 Kenny Wallace	.20
60 Ted Musgrave	.20
61 Tony Stewart	1.50
62 Elliott Sadler	.20
63 Jerry Nadeau	.20
64 #3 Dale Earnhardt cars	1.00
65 #5 Terry Labonte cars	.50
66 #18 Bobby Labonte cars	.35
67 #28 Kenny Irwin cars	.20
68 #2 Rusty Wallace cars	.50
69 #24 Jeff Gordon cars	1.00
70 #88 Dale Jarrett cars	.50
71 #36 Ernie Irvan cars	.20
72 Checklist Jeff Gordon	1.00

1999 Wheels High Gear First Gear Parallel

This 72-card parallel set is identical to High Gear except for the holo foil and gold stamping on the card fronts. They were seeded one per pack.

	MT
First Gear:	2x
Inserted 1:1	

1999 Wheels High Gear MPH Parallel

This 72-card parallel set featured special foil stamping and are limited to 100 numbered sets. They were hobby exclusive and seeded 1:40.

	MT
MPH:	20x-40x
Production less than 125 sets	
Inserted 1:40 hobby only	

1999 Wheels High Gear Custom Shop

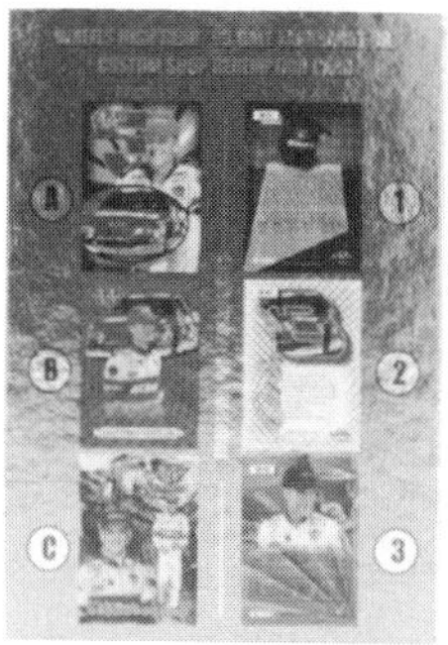

The card fronts presented a choice of three different card front designs and three different backs for the collector to choose from. The exact number of each card design for each driver version will only be decided after all collectors redeem their cards. Odds of finding a redemption card was 1:200 packs.

	MT
Complete Set (5):	300.00
Common Driver:	60.00
Inserted 1:200	
DE Dale Earnhardt	80.00
JG Jeff Gordon	80.00
MM Mark Martin	60.00
TL Terry Labonte	60.00
JR Dale Earnhardt Jr.	80.00

1999 Wheels High Gear Flag Chasers

This progressive insert featured cards that contained Authentic pieces of seven NASCAR flags waved in 1998 NASCAR Winston Cup races. Five drivers were featured in the set, with the overall insert ratio for all flags 1:400 packs. The Yellow, Black and White flags were inserted 1:2,450 packs. The Green and Red flags were inserted 1:2,600 packs. The Blue-Yellow flag was inserted 1:3,900, with the Checkered flag inserted 1:5,000.

	MT
Common Driver:	125.00
Black Flag Inserted 1:2,450	
White Flag Inserted 1:2,450	
Yellow Flag Inserted 1:2,450	
Green Flag Inserted 1:2,600	
Red Flag Inserted 1:2,600	
Blue-Yellow Inserted 1:3,900	
Checkered Flag Inserted 1:5,000	
Black, White & Yellow Flag Prices Listed	
Green & Red Flag Cards:	.5x-1.25x
Blue-Yellow Flag Cards:	1x-1.75x
Checkered Flag Cards:	1.25x-2x
1 Jeff Gordon	200.00
2 Mark Martin	150.00
3 Terry Labonte	125.00
4 Rusty Wallace	125.00
5 GM Goodwrench Service Plus Dale Earnhardt	200.00

1999 Wheels High Gear Gear Shifters

This 27-card set-within-a-set featured foil die-cut cards. The cards included a picture of the driver on the front, and a brief highlight from the 1998 season and what to expect for the 1999 season on the back. These were found 1:2 packs.

	MT
Complete Set (27):	30.00
Common Driver:	.50
Inserted 1:2	
1 Jeff Gordon	4.00
2 Mark Martin	2.00
3 Dale Jarrett	2.00
4 Rusty Wallace	2.00
5 Jeff Burton	1.50
6 Bobby Labonte	1.50
7 Jeremy Mayfield	1.50
8 Dale Earnhardt	4.00
9 Terry Labonte	2.00
10 Bobby Hamilton	.50
11 John Andretti	.80
12 Ken Schrader	.50
13 Sterling Marlin	.80
14 Jimmy Spencer	.50
15 Chad Little	.50
16 Ward Burton	.50
17 Michael Waltrip	.50
18 Bill Elliott	2.00
19 Ernie Irvan	.80

20	Johnny Benson	.50
21	Mike Skinner	.80
22	Ricky Rudd	.80
23	Darrell Waltrip	.80
24	Kenny Irwin	.80
25	Geoffrey Bodine	.50
26	Robert Pressley	.50
27	Checklist Steve Park	.50

1999 Wheels High Gear Hot Streaks

Focusing on the legendary streaks of NASCAR drivers, this six-card foil insert was seeded 1:10 packs. The card front featured a picture of the driver, while the back contained a brief description of the noted streak of that driver.

		MT
Complete Set (6):		15.00
Common Driver:		2.00
Inserted 1:10		
1	Jeff Gordon	8.00
2	Terry Labonte	4.00
3	GM Goodwrench Service Plus Dale Earnhardt	4.00
4	Ricky Rudd	2.00
5	Mark Martin	4.00
6	Dale Jarrett	4.00

1999 Wheels High Gear Machine

This 9-card retail-only insert set featured all-foil, embossed interlocking cards of the machines driven by the top drivers in NASCAR. They were seeded 1:10 packs.

		MT
Complete Set (9):		25.00
Common Driver:		1.00
Inserted 1:10 (Retail Only)		
1	DuPont Automotive Finishes #24 Jeff Gordon	8.00
2	Valvoline #6 Mark Martin	4.00
3	Quality Care #88 Dale Jarrett	4.00
4	Exide Batteries #99 Jeff Burton	3.00
5	Kellogg's Corn Flakes #5 Terry Labonte	4.00
6	Interstate Batteries #18 Bobby Labonte	3.00
7	Mobil #12 Jeremy Mayfield	3.00
8	Winston #15	1.00
9	Miller Lite #2 Rusty Wallace	4.00

1999 Wheels High Gear Man & Machine Man

This 9-card hobby-only insert set featured all-foil, embossed interlocking cards. The cards interlock with the cards in the Machine insert set. They are seeded 1:10 packs.

		MT
Complete Set (9):		30.00
Common Driver:		1.50
Inserted 1:10 (Hobby Only)		
1	Jeff Gordon	10.00
2	Mark Martin	5.00
3	Dale Jarrett	5.00
4	Jeff Burton	3.50
5	Terry Labonte	5.00
6	Bobby Labonte	3.50
7	Jeremy Mayfield	3.50
8	Jimmy Spencer	1.50
9	Rusty Wallace	5.00

1999 Wheels High Gear Top Tier

This eight-card set was a progressive insert, featuring the top eight NASCAR Winston Cup finishers from the 1998 season. Card number one was seeded 1:400 packs, number two 1:200, number three 1:100, number four 1:80, number five and six 1:40 and number seven and eight 1:20.

		MT
Complete Set (8):		100.00
Common Driver:		4.00
1	Jeff Gordon 1:400	80.00
2	Mark Martin 1:200	30.00
3	Dale Jarrett 1:100	12.00
4	Rusty Wallace 1:80	10.00
5	Jeff Burton 1:40	5.00
6	Bobby Labonte 1:40	5.00
7	Jeremy Mayfield 1:20	4.00
8	GM Goodwrench Service Plus Dale Earnhardt 1:20	5.00

1999 Wheels High Gear Wheels Authentic Signatures

This 25-card set featured autographs from the top Winston Cup drivers and Dale Earnhardt Jr. Each autographed card was individually numbered, with a maximum of 350 per driver. The cards were inserted 1:100 packs.

	MT
Complete Set (25):	1400.00
Common Driver:	20.00
Inserted 1:100	
John Andretti/350	20.00
Johnny Benson/350	20.00
Geoffrey Bodine/350	20.00
Jeff Burton/350	60.00
Ward Burton/350	20.00
Dale Earnhardt/55	300.00
Dale Earnhardt Jr./350	200.00
Bill Elliott/350	80.00
Jeff Gordon/100	300.00
Bobby Hamilton/350	20.00
Ernie Irvan/350	20.00
Dale Jarrett/350	80.00
Bobby Labonte/250	75.00
Terry Labonte/100	100.00
Chad Little/350	20.00
Sterling Marlin/350	20.00
Mark Martin/200	100.00
Jeremy Mayfield/350	40.00
Joe Nemecheck/350	20.00
Robert Pressley/350	20.00
Ricky Rudd/350	40.00
Ken Schrader/350	20.00
Mike Skinner/350	40.00
Jimmy Spencer/350	20.00
Michael Waltrip/350	20.00

FIGURINES

1999 Starting Lineup Baseball

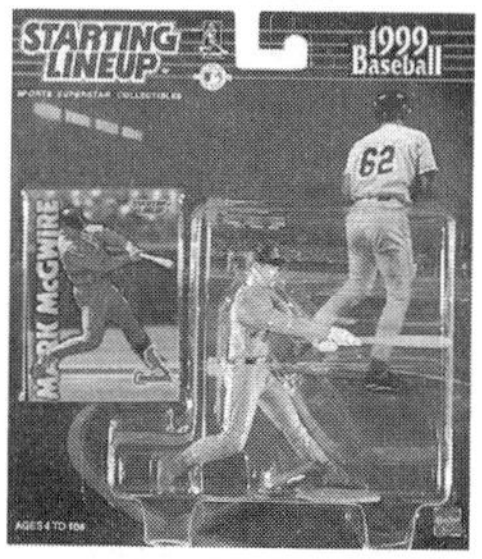

	MT
Complete Set (39):	525.00
Common Player:	12.00
Edgardo Alfonzo	12.00
Wilson Alvarez	12.00
Jeff Bagwell	15.00
Vinny Castilla	12.00
Tony Clark	12.00
Roger Clemens	12.00
David Cone	12.00
Jose Cruz Jr.	20.00
Darin Erstad	10.00
Nomar Garciaparra	15.00
Juan Gonzalez	10.00
Ken Griffey Jr.	15.00
Vladimir Guerrero	50.00
Jose Guillen	12.00
Tony Gwynn	12.00
Livan Hernandez	15.00
Derek Jeter	12.00
Randy Johnson	12.00
Chipper Jones	15.00
Travis Lee	15.00
Kenny Lofton	12.00
Mark McGwire	25.00
Pedro Martinez	25.00
Tino Martinez	12.00
Denny Neagle	12.00
Chan Ho Park	12.00
Mike Piazza	15.00
Brad Radke	12.00
Manny Ramirez	20.00
Edgar Renteria	12.00
Cal Ripken Jr.	15.00
Scott Rolen	15.00
Scott Rolen	15.00
Alex Rodriguez	15.00
Ivan Rodriguez	15.00
Sammy Sosa	20.00
Omar Vizquel	18.00
Larry Walker	15.00
Kerry Wood	20.00

1999 Starting Lineup Baseball Extended

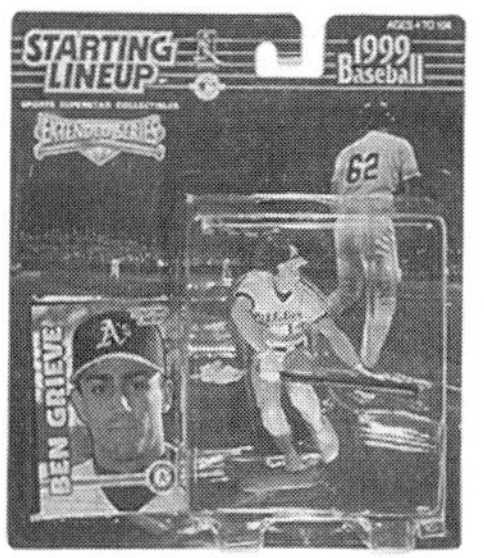

	MT
Complete Set (10):	175.00
Kevin Brown	12.00
Sean Casey	80.00
J.D. Drew	50.00
Nomar Garciaparra	15.00
Ben Grieve	20.00
Greg Maddux	12.00
Mo Vaughn	15.00
Dave Wells	10.00
Bernie Williams	15.00
Jaret Wright	15.00

1999 Starting Lineup Classic Doubles

For its 1999 Classic Doubles series, Hasbro used the theme "From the Minors to the Majors". Each 10" x 12" blister-pack contains two figures and two baseball cards; one depicting the player with his '99 major league team, and the other with one of his minor league teams. Values shown are for complete, unopened packages.

	MT
Complete Set (10):	175.00
Common Player:	10.00
Sandy Alomar	18.00
Darin Erstad	18.00
Nomar Garciaparra	20.00
Ken Griffey Jr.	25.00
Derek Jeter	20.00
Javy Lopez	18.00
Greg Maddux	18.00
Mark McGwire	25.00
Raul Mondesi	20.00
Alex Rodriguez	25.00

1999 Starting Lineup Cooperstown Collection

	MT
Complete Set (7):	80.00
Common Player:	10.00
George Brett	15.00
Pepper Davis	10.00
Bob Gibson	10.00
Juan Marichal	10.00
Nolan Ryan	15.00
Earl Weaver	15.00
Ted Williams	20.00

1999 Starting Lineup Baseball One-on-One

	MT
Complete Set (5):	100.00
Sandy Alomar, Ken Griffey Jr.	40.00
Nomar Garciaparra, Jim Edmonds	20.00
Chipper Jones, Larry Walker	18.00
Jason Kendall, Rey Ordonez	20.00
Cal Ripken Jr., Kenny Lofton	30.00

1999 Starting Lineup Baseball Stadium Stars

	MT
Complete Set (7):	160.00
Roger Clemens	30.00
Nomar Garciaparra	30.00
Derek Jeter	35.00
Chipper Jones	30.00
Kenny Lofton	25.00
Mark McGwire	40.00
Alex Rodriguez	35.00

1999 Starting Lineup Baseball 12" Figures

	MT
Complete Set (6):	150.00
Common Player:	25.00
Roger Clemens	30.00
Nomar Garciaparra	30.00
Ken Griffey Jr.	30.00
Tony Gwynn	25.00
Mark McGwire	35.00
Sammy Sosa	35.00

1999 Starting Lineup Baseball Wal-Mart Exclusives

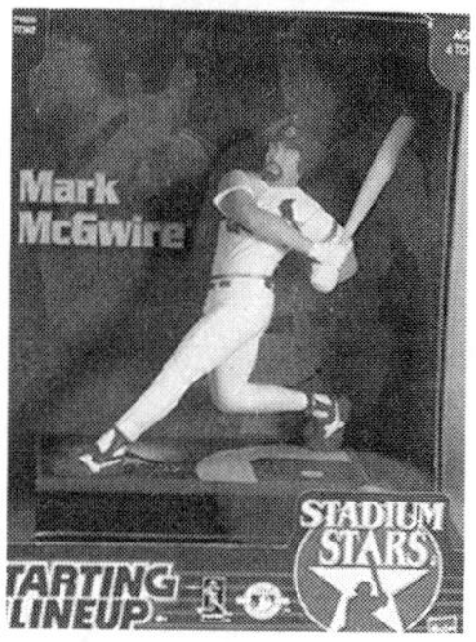

	MT
Complete Set (8):	180.00
Mark McGwire Reg.	18.00
Sammy Sosa Reg.	18.00
Mark McGwire Stad. Star	35.00
Sammy Sosa Stad. Star	35.00
Mark McGwire Sports Star	20.00
Sammy Sosa Sports Star	20.00
Mark McGwire CD, Roger Maris CD	25.00
Sammy Sosa CD, Roger Maris CD	25.00

1998 Starting Lineup Basketball FAME

	MT
Complete Set (9):	170.00
Kareem Abdul-Jabbar	10.00
Larry Bird	20.00
Patrick Ewing	10.00
Juwan Howard	10.00
Allen Iverson	15.00
Magic Johnson	15.00
Jason Kidd	100.00
Bill Russell	15.00
Sheryl Swoopes	15.00

1998 Starting Lineup Basketball 12" Figures

	MT
Complete Set (5):	80.00
Tim Duncan	20.00
Kevin Garnett	15.00
Juwan Howard	15.00
Allen Iverson	20.00
Glen Rice	15.00

1998 Starting Lineup Football Extended

The 10-figure set includes the first figures of Mike Alstott, Ryan Leaf, Peyton Manning and Charles Woodson. The figures are packaged with a full-color collectable card.

	MT
Complete Set (10):	180.00
Common Player:	10.00
Mike Alstott	20.00
Terrell Davis	25.00
Jim Harbaugh	10.00
Ryan Leaf	25.00
Peyton Manning	50.00
Curtis Martin	15.00
Steve McNair	15.00
Deion Sanders	12.00
Shannon Sharpe	15.00
Charles Woodson	25.00

1998 Starting Lineup FB Classic Doubles QB Club

Each player in this six-figure set belongs to the QB Club.

	MT
Complete Set (6):	150.00
Drew Bledsoe	30.00
John Elway	30.00
Jim Harbaugh	20.00
Dan Marino	35.00
Emmitt Smith	35.00
Steve Young	30.00

1999 Starting Lineup Football

	MT
Complete Set (36):	450.00
Common Player:	10.00
Troy Aikman	10.00
Drew Bledsoe	10.00
Mark Brunell	10.00
Chris Chandler	10.00
Wayne Chrebet	15.00
Randall Cunningham	15.00
Terrell Davis	15.00
Dermontti Dawson	10.00
Corey Dillon	12.00
Warrick Dunn	20.00
John Elway	12.00
Curtis Enis	15.00
Brett Favre	12.00
Doug Flutie	25.00
Eddie George	12.00
Napoleon Kaufman	15.00
Ryan Leaf	10.00
Dorsey Levens	15.00
Peyton Manning	15.00
Dan Marino	10.00
Curtis Martin	15.00
Randy Moss	90.00
Jake Plummer	25.00
Jerry Rice	10.00
Andre Rison	10.00
Barry Sanders	15.00
Barry Sanders Meijer's	20.00
Warren Sapp	15.00
Emmitt Smith	15.00
Jimmy Smith	12.00
Neil Smith	10.00
Robert Smith	20.00
Kordell Stewart	10.00
Eric Swann	10.00
Zach Thomas	10.00
Ricky Watters	10.00
Steve Young	10.00

1999 Starting Lineup Football Classic Doubles

	MT
Complete Set (10):	250.00
Cris Carter, Randy Moss	70.00
Jack Lambert, Jack Ham	25.00
Earl Campbell, Eddie George	20.00
Anthony Munoz, Boomer Esiason	20.00
John Elway, Terrell Davis	50.00
Mike Alstott, Warrick Dunn	20.00
Ken Stabler, Dave Casper	20.00
Archie Manning, Peyton Manning	50.00
Johnny Unitas, Rick Berry	20.00
Franco Harris, Jerome Bettis	20.00

1999 Starting Lineup Football Classic Doubles QB Club

	MT
Complete Set (5):	60.00
Troy Aikman	15.00
Terrell Davis	20.00
Brett Favre	20.00
Jake Plummer	15.00
Kordell Stewart	15.00

1999 Starting Lineup Football Gridiron Greats

	MT
Complete Set (8):	100.00
Dick Butkus	15.00
Terrell Davis	20.00
Warrick Dunn	15.00
Eddie George	15.00
Dan Marino	15.00

Curtis Martin	15.00
Barry Sanders	15.00
Kordell Stewart	15.00

1999 Starting Lineup Football 12" Figures

	MT
Complete Set (5):	100.00
Terrell Davis	25.00
Brett Favre	25.00
Barry Sanders	25.00
Kordell Stewart	25.00
Steve Young	25.00

1998 Starting Lineup Hockey Extended

	MT
Complete Set (10):	125.00
Common Player:	10.00
Peter Bondra	10.00
Theo Fleury	12.00
Grant Fuhr	16.00
Doug Gilmour	12.00
Nicolai Khabibulin	15.00
Olaf Kolzig	15.00
Trevor Kidd	16.00
Darren Puppa	15.00
Brendan Shanahan	12.00
John Vanbiesbrouck	12.00

1998 Starting Lineup Hockey Classic Doubles

	MT
Complete Set (5):	100.00
Martin Brodeur, Scott Stevens	25.00
Sergei Fedorov, Mike Vernon	25.00
Wayne Gretzky, Mark Messier	35.00
Jaromir Jagr, Tom Barrasso	25.00
Patrick Roy, John LeClair	25.00

1998 Starting Lineup Hockey One on One

	MT
Complete Set (6):	130.00
Wayne Gretzky, Pavel Bure	35.00
Eric Lindros, Andy Moog	35.00
Mark Messier, Sandis Ozolinsh	25.00
Mike Modano, Mike Vernon	25.00
Brendan Shanahan, Jeff Hackett	30.00
Keith Tkachuk, John LeClair	25.00

1998 Starting Lineup Hockey 12" Figures

	MT
Complete Set (3):	80.00
Wayne Gretzky	40.00
Mario Lemieux	30.00
Bobby Orr	30.00

1998 Starting Lineup Racing Winner's Circle

	MT
Complete Set (15):	150.00
Ward Burton	10.00
Dale Earnhardt '97 uniform	15.00
Dale Earnhardt '98 uniform	15.00
John Force	10.00
John Force Elvis	12.00
Jeff Gordon	15.00
Jeff Gordon JP	15.00
Kenny Irwin	20.00
Dale Jarrett	10.00
Bobby Labonte	10.00
Bobby Labonte sm. soldiers	15.00
Mike Skinner	10.00
Kenny Wallace	10.00
Rusty Wallace	15.00
Rusty Wallace Elvis	15.00

1999 Mattel Basketball Jams

	MT
Complete Set (21):	120.00
Common Player:	6.00
Shareef Abdur-Rahim	6.00
Vin Baker	6.00
Charles Barkley	6.00
Kobe Bryant	10.00
Kevin Garnett	6.00
Anfernee Hardaway	8.00
Tim Hardaway	6.00
Grant Hill	6.00
Allen Iverson	6.00
Michael Jordan (#1)	15.00
Michael Jordan (#2)	15.00
Shawn Kemp	6.00
Jason Kidd	6.00
Glen Rice	6.00
David Robinson	6.00
Dennis Rodman	7.00
Rodney Rogers	6.00
Steve Smith	6.00
Damon Stoudamire	6.00
Keith Van Horn	7.00
Antoine Walker	6.00

1999 Mattel Basketball Superstars

	MT
Complete Set (24):	275.00
Common Player:	8.00
Ray Allen	10.00
Vin Baker	10.00
Charles Barkley	10.00
Kobe Bryant	18.00
Tim Duncan	16.00
Kevin Garnett	12.00
Anfernee Hardaway	12.00
Grant Hill	10.00
Allan Houston	8.00
Juwan Howard	8.00
Allen Iverson	15.00
Michael Jordan (#1)	35.00
Michael Jordan (#2)	35.00
Shawn Kemp	8.00
Jason Kidd	8.00
Reggie Miller	10.00
Alonzo Mourning	10.00
Dikembe Mutombo	10.00
Scottie Pippen	10.00
Glen Rice	10.00
Dennis Rodman	12.00
John Stockton	10.00
Keith Van Horn	12.00
Antoine Walker	12.00

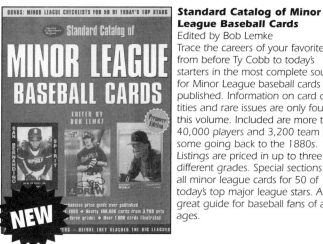

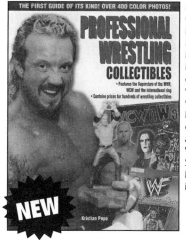

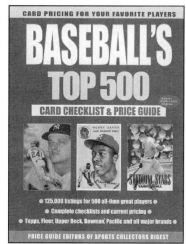

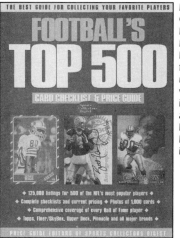

page intentionally left blank

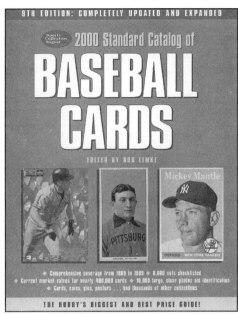

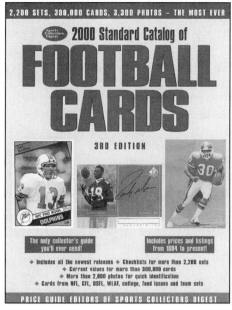

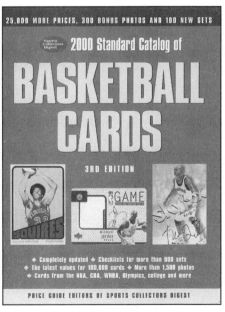

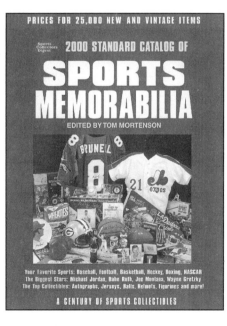

page intentionally left blank

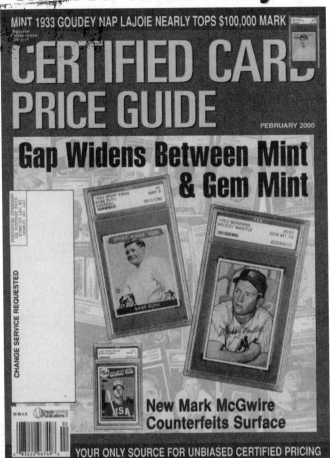